HANDBOOK OF COMMUNICATION

Contributors

Janet Alexander, *Stanford University*
Raymond A. Bauer, *Harvard University*
Leo Bogart, *American Newspaper Publishers Association*
Henry S. Breitrose, *Stanford University*
Donald T. Campbell, *Northwestern University*
Bertita E. Compton, *National Academy of Sciences*
Brenda Danet, *Hebrew University*
W. Phillips Davison, *Columbia University*
John L. Fischer, *Tulane University*
Marc A. Franklin, *Stanford Law School*
Frederick W. Frey, *Massachusetts Institute of Technology*
William E. Griffith, *Massachusetts Institute of Technology*
Allen D. Grimshaw, *Indiana University*
Randall P. Harrison, *Michigan State University*
Fred Charles Iklé, *The Rand Corporation*
Elihu Katz, *Hebrew University*
Paul Kecskemeti, *Brandeis University*
Nathan Maccoby, *Stanford University*
David G. Markle, *Stanford University*
Dwaine Marvick, *University of California, Los Angeles*
William J. McGuire, *Yale University*
Edwin B. Parker, *Stanford University*
Frank Allen Philpot, *Kaiser Broadcasting Corporation*
Ithiel de Sola Pool, *Massachusetts Institute of Technology*
William L. Rivers, *Stanford University*
Donald F. Roberts, *Stanford University*
Everett M. Rogers, *Michigan State University*
Howard Rosenthal, *Carnegie-Mellon University*
Herbert Rubenstein, *Lehigh University*
Wilbur Schramm, *Stanford University*
David O. Sears, *University of California, Los Angeles*
Fred L. Strodtbeck, *University of Chicago*
Eugene J. Webb, *Stanford University*
Richard E. Whitney, *University of California, Los Angeles*

HANDBOOK OF COMMUNICATION

EDITED BY

Ithiel de Sola Pool
Frederick W. Frey
Center for International Studies
Massachusetts Institute of Technology

Wilbur Schramm
Nathan Maccoby
Edwin B. Parker
Institute for Communication Research
Stanford University

Rand McNally College Publishing Company · Chicago

RAND McNALLY SOCIOLOGY SERIES

Edgar F. Borgatta, Advisory Editor

Handbook of Personality Theory and Research
Edgar F. Borgatta and William W. Lambert, Eds.

Handbook of Marriage and the Family
Harold T. Christensen, Ed.

Handbook of Modern Sociology
Robert E. L. Faris, Ed.

Handbook of Socialization Theory and Research
David A. Goslin, Ed.

Handbook of Organizations
James G. March, Ed.

Handbook on the Study of Social Problems
Erwin O. Smigel, Ed.

Handbook of Communication
Wilbur Schramm, Ithiel de Sola Pool,
Nathan Maccoby, Edwin B. Parker, and
Frederick W. Frey, Eds.

Printed in U.S.A. by Rand McNally & Company
Library of Congress Catalogue Card Number 72-7851

Preface

Since communication permeates every process of man's life, the study of communication is no less than one way to study society. There is no inherent limit to what could go into a handbook of communication. Indeed, the pervasiveness of communication is what makes it a useful object of study.

Each of the main social sciences may be defined in one of two ways: either as the study of a specific set of institutions or as the study of some process that occurs throughout life. Economics, for example, can be defined as the study of business firms, but most economists would reject that restriction and prefer to define it as the study of bargaining—wherever that process takes place. So, too, political science can be restrictively defined as the study of government or, more usefully, as the study of power relationships. Sociology can be called the study of those institutions remaining after business and government are taken care of by their own disciplines, or, as any sociologists would insist, the study of roles and functions throughout society. Anthropology, once thought of as the study of primitive societies, now is more likely to be called the study of all human behavior. Each social science takes all of society as its domain. It differs from its fraternal disciplines not in the objects covered but in how it describes them.

So it is with the study of communication. We could define communication as the study of the mass media and other institutions dedicated to persuasion. We choose to take a broader view. Communication is a useful concept precisely because it is one more handle whereby we can effectively study all of society. Communication is one of those relatively few fundamental and encompassing processes through which virtually any social event can be portrayed. Just as different aspects of the same physical reality can be depicted by photographing it with visible light, infrared, or X rays, so different aspects of a given social reality can be emphasized by viewing it as a bargaining process, a power hierarchy, a set of role relations, or a flow of communications. The field of communication studies has grown enormously in recent decades because its particular perspective has proved a useful one for perceiving society.

The existing literature on communication is voluminous: there are several readers containing significant selections from the journal literature as well as excerpts from books. There is also a number of textbooks both on the field as a whole and on journalism, public opinion, attitude research, and various other special topics. Nevertheless, the editors of this volume have felt that there remains a gap. Until now there has been no collection of review articles outlining the present state of research in the various parts of the discipline. We have tried to provide that here.

If the study of communication is coterminous with the study of society, then any table of contents is an arbitrary judgment about what current research is most important, and also about how our colleagues in the discipline have divided their universe. In a rapidly growing field, some of our judgments on these matters change over the years that it takes to produce a book. Moreover, in putting together such a book it is not always possible to find an author for every area the editors would like to cover. Finally, in a collection, each author's perception is his own and the various perceptions are not necessarily compatible. So gaps and conflicts there will be. We hope that the gaps will encourage others to fill them and that the conflicts of perspective will be a stimulus to their resolution.

ITHIEL DE SOLA POOL
WILBUR SCHRAMM

Contents

PART I

The Communication Process

CHAPTER 1 Communication Systems

ITHIEL DE SOLA POOL
Massachusetts Institute of Technology

Acts of communication can be described as the thread that holds any social organization together, if not the skeleton that determines its structure. If we are to describe patterns of social communication more precisely than through such vague metaphors, then a theoretical framework appropriate to the complexity is required. Systems theory appears to provide an approach that permits the complexity of social communication to be described and analyzed at a high level of abstraction, but with precision rather than vagueness. This chapter explicates a set of concepts and measures for describing communication networks, whether for comparative analysis or for mathematical modeling. The first section considers the basic characteristics of communication systems generally. The second section describes the concepts and measures appropriate for the one-to-many communication of mass media. The third describes the characteristics of interpersonal networks. The concluding section argues the potential of communication system modeling as a strategy for increasing our understanding of communication in social systems.

DEFINITION OF A COMMUNICATION SYSTEM

A *system* has been defined as any continuing entity capable of two or more states. A *communication* system is one in which the states are connections or nonconnections among objects.

Figure 1 schematically portrays a communication system among five objects, i.e., the links between them. Considered in outline, communications systems may differ along six dimensions:

1. They may differ in the number of objects in the population. This is important because as the number of units grows the number of potential links between units grows much

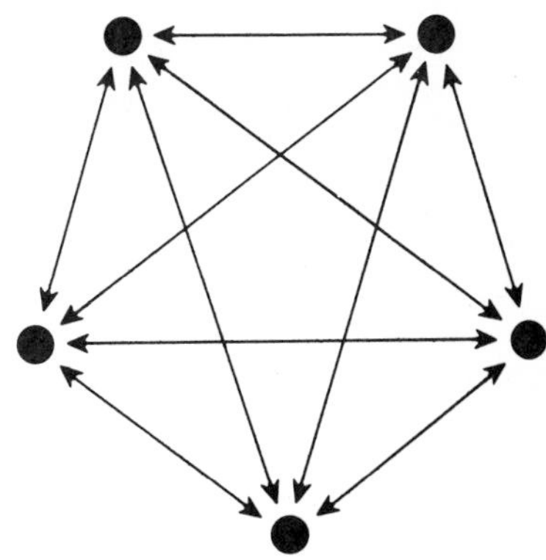

Figure 1. Schematic drawing of links among five objects.

more rapidly than just linearly with the number of units. Where n = the number of units and L = the number of potential links, the formula is

$$L = \binom{n}{2} = \frac{n!}{(n-2)!\,2!}.$$

That is why small-group behavior rapidly changes to large-group behavior as the group exceeds twenty or thirty people.

2. They may differ in the message capacity of these links. This is the subject of the mathematical theory of information which addresses itself to calculating the number of bits of information that can be transmitted through a channel, i.e., the bandwidth of the links (Shannon & Weaver, 1949).
3. They may differ in the volume of message flow through these links. Channel capacity is only a top limit. Empirical observation may measure how much information actually is transmitted through a channel.
4. They may differ in network structure. Not all possible links are necessarily used in a given structure. Structural characteristics include:
   a) Directionality. The links portrayed in Figure 1 are two-directional, but in many instances the flow goes only one way. For example, a mass media system is one-directional communication from a source to many persons.
   b) Permitted or possible links. In many systems, links are not only empirically of zero frequency but are prohibited by law or physical possibility. Structural linguistics, for example, studies what messages are grammatically allowable within a language, not which ones actually occur.
   c) Probability. A network structure can be characterized by defining the probability that any particular channel will be used. Thus a leadership study may take note of the individual to whom another individual is most likely to turn for advice.
5. They may differ in type of message carried. What flows through the links is not uniform, indistinguishable bits of information. The messages may be differentiated and characterized by either form or content. In form, they may be oral or written, in high style or low style, etc. By content, we can categorize them by the subjects with which they deal or by what they say about these subjects.
6. They may differ in triggering mechanism. At any given moment, a communication system may be in any one state along the five dimensions just listed, but at the next moment it may change. One may ask what it is that shifts it from one state of activity to another.

A complete description of a communication system is its characterization along all six of the above dimensions. Not all systems are interesting, however. One interesting type of system is a stable equilibrium; that is, a system that tends to correct itself as it deviates from its equilibrium position. Such systems are intellectually fascinating and also may be important, for they tend to survive. Other interesting systems are those that follow a fixed, predictable developmental sequence: ones that, once pushed, move in a certain direction such as growth, or modernization, or revolution. Often we are interested in a communication system insofar as it produces a certain outcome, such as attitude change, or some particular state of public opinion, such as contentment. So we may be interested in a system either because the system itself behaves in some curious and complex way or because of the outcomes it generates.

MASS COMMUNICATION SYSTEMS

Among the kinds of communication systems that are frequently distinguished, one that is of great current importance because of its outcomes is a mass communication system. By *mass communication system* we mean a linkage pattern of few transmitters to many receivers. A journalist or a broadcaster communicates to audiences of millions but, except in very limited ways, audiences do not communicate back to him. A petition is one-way communication, just as mass communication is one way, but a petition is many-to-one rather than one-to-many. In contrast to both of these is the pattern of two-way communication that prevails in conversation among face-to-face groups.

Let us first consider the abstract model of a mass communication system. Most mass communication systems have a rather strict pattern of message flow in which messages do not occur as random, independent events. Typically, in a mass communication system messages are packaged together in regularly published vehicles such as newspapers or books. A member of the audience either receives or does not receive the vehicle. Without the vehicle he cannot receive the message; with it, he has a conditional probability of being exposed to the particular message, for he does not note everything in the vehicle.

Typically, message vehicles are not disseminated as random, independent events. Usually, there is a pattern of periodical appearances of each medium. Issues of a magazine, for example, may appear weekly or monthly or quarterly; each issue of the medium carries the same name, follows a uniform format, and has a consistent editorial policy.

Typically, the initial decision by the audience member as to whether or not to expose himself is a decision about the medium, not about the message or even about the individual vehicle (Berelson, 1949; McLuhan, 1964; Ehrenberg, 1968; Wells, 1969). He may choose to subscribe or not, he may develop a viewing habit or not. If he has subscribed, he is much more likely to see any one issue of the medium and, having seen the issue, is more likely to see a particular message in it.

Media, in turn, may be grouped into media types, such as newspapers, magazines, radio stations, and TV stations. The media within a type tend to follow rather similar patterns of appearance.

These formal characteristics of a mass media system may be described by a number of well-defined parametric measures familiar to students of mass communication. Among the parameters are circulation, audience, reach, frequency, exposure, attention, recall, comprehension, persuasion, cumulation, and duplication.

Circulation is the number of copies produced of a single issue of a vehicle. For a press medium, this concept is fairly easily defined. What is usually quoted is the circulation figure averaged across issues. This is what we mean when we say, for example, that the circulation of *Izvestiya* is 7.7 million and of *Pravda*, 7.5 million. For an electronic medium, the analogy would be the number of sets tuned to a particular program—a Nielsen rating, for example.

Audience is a measurement of the number of persons seeing a particular issue. If some magazine averages three readers per copy, the audience will be three times the circulation. For an electronic medium, the audience would be the number of persons hearing or seeing the program, not the number of sets turned on.

For the print media, at least, circulation is usually a highly reliable figure, since someone knows the press run of each issue or how many copies were paid for. Circulation figures are generally available in a reference source such as *Willing's Press Guide* (Willing, 1874–), *Ayer's Directory of Newspapers and Periodicals* (Ayer & Sons, 1880–), *Comprehensive Analysis of Newspaper Circulations* (American Newspaper Markets, 1962–), *Standard Periodical Directory* (Oxbridge, 1964–), *Overseas Newspapers and Periodicals Guide Book*

(Vaughan, 1969) and *National Nielsen TV Ratings*.

Audience, on the other hand, can usually be estimated only by field surveys and with much less reliability than circulation. Such audience surveys are usually done by the media themselves and are published mostly as proprietary reports (Politz, 1950; 1953; 1956; 1964; 1965; 1966; Advertising Research Council, 1951; Life, 1958; 1965; Simmons, 1958; 1966; 1969; Sports Illustrated, 1958; Audits and Surveys, 1961a; 1961b; 1962; Bureau of Advertising, 1962; Belson, 1962; Ehrenberg & Twyman, 1967). Some of these reports are available to the public; others, like the *Nielsen Television Index*, are intended only for clients.

Reach is essentially the same concept as audience, but applied to a message rather than to an issue of a medium. An advertisement, for example, may appear in two publications. Its reach is the number of different people who saw it in at least one of those publications.

Frequency expresses the concept that a message may reach some persons more than once. The frequency figure most often quoted is the average, although one could also have a full-frequency distribution. To continue with the example of an ad in two publications: if 10 percent of the public saw it in medium A and 8 percent of the public saw it in medium B and, of these, 2 percent of the public saw it in both, then the average frequency for those who saw it at all is nine-eighths or 1.12. The full-frequency distribution is:

0	84 percent
Once	14 percent
Twice	2 percent

All of this is illustrated in Figure 2.

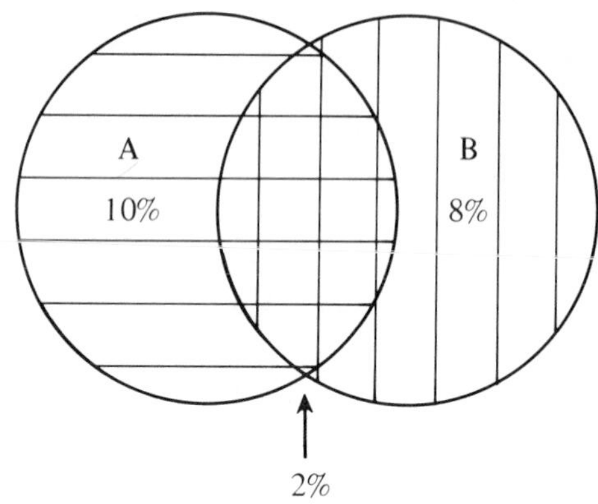

Figure 2. Frequency distribution of ad appearing in two publications, A and B.

In the previous paragraph we have been talking about exposure; i.e., the individual somehow sees the message. Having a copy of the vehicle in one's hands or having a broadcasting set turned on does not necessarily make for exposure. The probability of exposure is a complex function of the character of the source, of the message, and of the audience. If the material is salient to the member of the audience, he may pay attention. If it is not, he may pay no attention even though it is right there before him (Hobson & Henry, 1949; Nafziger, MacLean, & Engstrom, 1951; International Press Institute, 1953; C. E. Swanson, 1955; Yamanka, 1962; Pool, 1965; Troldahl, Verling, & Jones, 1965; Starch, 1966; Rees & Paisley, 1967).

No easy measure of exposure exists. Usually, the only way to know whether a person has been exposed is to ask him. If this is done on the spot, it may distort the situation; if it is done later, exposure becomes confounded with recall. As a matter of fact, most empirical studies of exposure are really studies of recall (Moran, 1951; Zielske, 1959; Appel & Blum, 1960; Ehrenberg, 1961; Greenberg & Garfinkle, 1962; Agostini, 1964; Buchanan, 1964; Ehrenberg, 1964; Ehrenberg & Twyman, 1967; Marder, 1967). The measure of recall may be one of two kinds, so-called aided and unaided recall (Lucas, 1942; 1960; Hubbard, 1954; Ferber & Wales, 1958–59; Maloney, 1961).

Unaided recall is the response to the question, "What did you see (hear)?"

Aided recall is established by presenting the material to the respondent once more and asking "Did you see that?" Each method obviously introduces a bias of measurement and in opposite directions. One question is too hard, the other too easy. At first glance, aided recall seems particularly suspect. However, market researchers and others concerned with measuring exposure have devised highly sophisticated and ingenious tricks for getting reasonably good measures; for example, offering among the aided recall stimuli ones that never appeared, thus providing a measure of the overestimate (Lucas, 1942).

Producing exposure and generating recall are seldom the main purpose that the communicator had in mind, however. He usually wants more than just to be heard. He usually wishes to secure the acceptance of some information or to produce a change in attitude. Yet often he may achieve exposure without either securing comprehension or modifying previous attitudes. One should, therefore, not interpret a measure of exposure as telling us anything about comprehension or persuasion. To measure these, one must devise different means of audience observation or interrogation. Studies of this kind are discussed in chapter 9.

Since messages come imbedded in issues of media that are periodic in their occurrence, one can measure the *cumulative* reach or frequence of some message or the cumulative audience of some medium over time. An advertising campaign, for example, repeats a message many times. It is only after a certain length of time that the message will reach the majority of the public. It reaches them with differential frequency; one can measure the number and kinds of people who are exposed to the advertisement zero, once, twice, three times, four times, etc., by any given date. Cumulation is the changing measure of such reach or frequency over time. It is generally represented by an ascending curve along a time axis, but (as with single-point measures of frequency) the full description is a distribution.

Duplication is a concept that we introduced implicitly already when we talked about an ad appearing in two media. Duplication is the extent to which the two audiences overlap.

The parameters that we have now listed in this section are ones that a simulation model of a mass communication system must take into account and represent. They characterize a mass communication system. They do not characterize the system's outputs or its effectiveness, but they do enable us to describe the system itself.

At first glance, what we have just outlined may seem to be rather a simple set of concepts. There are, however, some subtle problems that enter the modeling of a communication system and give it its intellectual interest (Kramer, 1969; Pool, 1969; Selesnick, 1970). They are designated by the now partially familiar labels "cumulation," "duplication," and "triggering."

Cumulation. As we have just finished noting, messages in the mass media are events in vehicles that appear in regular patterns over time. Broadcasts are patterned into daily or weekly programs on discrete channels. Print media appear as daily, weekly, monthly, or quarterly issues of fixed publications. The members of the audience have regular habits regarding these broadcasts or publications so that, for any one of them, message exposures are not statistically independent events. If John Doe subscribes to a pro-UN paper, then the chance of his reading repeated stories about the UN is high.

In any population, some have media habits that will expose them often, and some have habits that will expose them seldom. Consider further the difference between a scientific journal and an airdrop leaflet. Virtually all issues of a scientific journal go to subscribers; the probability of a person who sees one issue also seeing the next is perhaps 60 or 70 or 80 percent. An airdrop leaflet, on the other hand, is received quite randomly. The chances of seeing two in a row may be small. Consider the implications of this.

Consider two media, both of which reach 50 percent of the population. In two issues, a medium that always goes to exactly the same persons would reach 50 percent of the population, each such person exactly twice. The other medium with the same size audience whose distribution was completely random would have reached 75 percent of the population in two issues—50 percent of the population once, 25 percent twice. Any actual medium would have a cumulation rate falling somewhere between the two. Estimating cumulation is a problem that has been much discussed in the research literature on advertising.

There have been several models used. One of the most widely discussed and simplest is that of Agostini (1961), which makes the departure of actual repetition from chance repetition depend upon a constant, *K*. Empirical studies, however, suggest rather that *K* is a socially determined variable (Bower, 1963; Caffyn & Sagovsky, 1963; Kuhn, 1963; Marc, 1963; Engelman, 1965; Schyberger, 1965; Claycamp & McClellan, 1968). Another approach uses beta functions (Metheringham, 1964; Schreiber, 1968; 1969; Kramer, 1969). Still another approach predicates processes too complicated to permit an analytic representation by an equation, so a simulation model is used in which different types of consumers of the media are each represented as carrying out their media habits (Pool, Kramer, & Selesnick, 1966; Marc, 1968; Klensin & Nagle, 1969; Kramer, 1969; Friedman, 1970). Numerous other theoretical studies might be mentioned (Marc, 1963; Schyberger, 1963; 1965; Goodhardt, 1966; Keller, 1966; McGlathery, 1967; Simmons, 1967; C. E. Swanson, 1967) as well as empirical studies of actual audience cumulation (Politz, 1950; 1953; 1956; 1964; 1965; 1966; Life, 1958; Audits and Surveys, 1961a; 1962; Simmons, 1966; 1969; Greene & Stock, 1967).

Duplication. Cumulation is difficult to estimate, as we have just noted, because exposure to messages are not independent events but are autocorrelated over time. Duplication presents a different but analogous problem (Politz; 1953; 1966; Banks & Madansky, 1958; Agostini, 1961; Bower, 1963; Caffyn & Sagovsky, 1963; Kuhn, 1963; Kwerel, 1964; 1969; Life, 1965; Schyberger, 1965; Hofmans, 1966; Simmons, 1966; 1967; 1969; C. E. Swanson, 1967; Schreiber, 1968; Benson, 1969a; 1969b; Selesnick, 1970). Exposure to different message vehicles is also not independent. They are correlated with each other.

For example, a person who reads the *Atlantic* is more likely to read the *New Yorker* but less likely to watch "Gunsmoke" than is the average person. But is the *Atlantic* reader more or less likely to read *Harper's*? The answer is not obvious. Perhaps the *Atlantic* saturates the desire of most of its readers for elevated current commentary; or perhaps, on the contrary, the saturation factor is overridden by the similar taste to which the two magazines appeal. Whether in fact these magazines are primarily surrogates for each other or whether they share a joint demand, it is nonetheless clear that they are not statistically independent. Somehow, account must be taken of the fact that use of one medium has implications for use of the other.

Triggering. Messages reach people as a function of their basic media habits. But the messages may in turn modify these habits. If a person is exposed to the message, "Soviet troops invade Czechoslovakia," he is likely to rush to his radio set and keep it on, hearing much more news than he otherwise would have. The dramatic message acted as a trigger, setting off processes by which normal media habits get changed.

Because a mass communication system is such a highly structured thing, it lends itself well to formal modeling or to rigorous description by means of parametric measurements of the kinds we have been reviewing. To date, most systems description has been done not by academic scholars but by commerical audience researchers. The media themselves live by ratings, Audit Bureau of Circulation figures, audience studies, Starch ratings, and reach and frequency figures. Academic researchers, however, have made increasing use of such measures as they have become interested in total system descriptions, an interest arising from the growing interest in comparative international communications research. In particular, studies of the development of mass media systems in the new nations and the role of mass communications in their modernization have required comparative figures (see chapter 13). These data have been provided largely by the publications of the UN (United Nations, 1949–; UNESCO, 1964).

COMMUNICATION NETWORKS

Our discussion so far has mostly been about one-way communication processes. Examples of such one-way processes are provided by mass media systems, for mass communication is a one-to-many type of flow. The messages go from a few senders to many receivers. More accurately, that is a simplified paradigm of a mass media communication situation. In reality, of course, the senders, such as newspaper reporters and broadcasters, do pay attention to the reactions of their audience. There is feedback. If a medium runs a shocking piece it will hear about it.

Furthermore, in addition to the small amount of actual feedback, there is a great deal of imaginary anticipation of feedback. Communicators think about their audience; Zimmerman and Bauer (1956) showed that, in preparing speeches, subjects suppressed recall of facts that the prospective audience would not like to hear (cf. Rosen & Tesser, 1970). Pool and Shulman (1959) studied the fantasies of newsmen as they wrote their stories. They found that the fantasies fell into two main types: fantasies of people enjoying the story and coming to feel positively toward the communicator, and fantasies that elaborated upon the power of the writer to destroy his subject if he chose to say all he knew about him. The fantasies entertained during writing tended to be consistent within an individual even over a year's time. The pleasing fantasy tended to be found among writers of human interest material and the destructive fantasy among newsmen covering crime, politics, and scandal. The importance of such personality factors in leading people to journalism was documented in a study by Guy E. Swanson (1956) of college newsmen and college activists. The thing that distinguished these two groups of Big Men on Campus was the extent of their propensity to express themselves directly in face-to-face relations. The newsmen were more inclined to express their affect to a blank piece of paper and were apt to be milder and to be more inhibited in face-to-face situations.

Unfortunately, there have been relatively few such studies of the real and imaginary feedback process whereby the audience affects the communicator. Clearly, the reason for this is that, important as feedback may be, it is relatively muted compared to communication downstream from source to audience. That is why one-way flow models have been useful and popular.

In some communication situations, however, there is no sharp distinction to be made between communicator and audience. Communication takes place among nodes, each of which is a transceiver, that is, both a receiver and a sender. That is the situation in word-of-mouth communication among individuals.

Similar, also, is the situation in which there may be an initial source, but the receivers in turn pass the message on. The latter is the situation in which word-of-mouth communication follows upon receipt of a mass media message. Since the work of Elihu Katz and Paul Lazarsfeld (1955) on personal influence, this two-step flow of communication has been much studied, particularly because it has proved to be of great importance in producing actions such as the adoption of innovations and the making of purchase decisions and voting choices.

There is a vast literature on such personal influence processes, writings both on mass communication and on small groups. It has been well summarized elsewhere (Katz, 1957; Rogers, 1962; Katz, Levin, & Hamilton, 1963; Horvath, 1965; Kadane, Lewis, & Ramage, 1969; Rogers & Suenning, 1969; Rogers, Ascroft & Roling, 1970; Rogers & Shoemaker, 1970). It includes a substantial body of studies (originally in a quite separate tradition of rural sociology) on the adoption by farmers of new agricultural practices. All the studies reveal a common process whereby mass media provide their audience with background information directly; however, before going beyond passive receipt of that information to making a personal commitment to action, most people seek confirmation by direct face-to-face consultation with an opinion leader.

We shall not attempt here to review once more that literature on personal influence as a reinforcer of mass communication. However, for completeness, we take note here of that special kind of communication system with its own special features. We shall, in the remainder of this chapter, review some of the problems and work concerning the structure of communication in interpersonal networks. Among the interpersonal networks that have been extensively studied are small groups, contact nets, rumor, and information flows in large populations.

At the beginning of this chapter we listed some of the parameters of a communication system, such as its size, directionality, and volume of activity. We then went on to consider a few measurements such as cumulation and duplication that are important even in the very simple situation of one-way communication. Two-way interpersonal communication situations are more complex; they have additional parameters that one might wish to measure. One fairly simple set of these parameters concerns the flow of an individual message:

a) How fast does it move from node to node?
b) What proportion of the network has received it by any given time?
c) What distinguishes those communicators who receive the message from those who do not?
d) How accurate is the message transmission?
e) How effective is the message on those who receive it?

Another set of parameters describes the flow of multiple messages within the network. The volume of message flow is one such parameter and a fairly easily measured one; all sorts of content analysis and message-flow studies address themselves to that. It is much more difficult to describe the structure of the message flow, and so descriptions of structure are usually imprecise. We talk about how hierarchial a network is, how connected it is, how random or structured it is (Ando, Fisher, & Simon, 1963; Hagerstrand, 1969). Clearly, such characterizations are important, but they refer to such complex phenomena that it is often hard to give them a precise operational meaning.

The literature that has tried to use these concepts the most is that on communication in management (Simon, Smithburg, & Thompson, 1950: chaps. 10–13; Simon, 1954; March & Simon, 1958; Guetzkow, 1965). It distinguishes upward from downward communication (A. R. Cohen, 1958; Read, 1962; Barnlund & Harland, 1963) and vertical from lateral communication (Burns, 1954; Zajonc & Wolfe, 1963).Much of this literature is oriented toward improving management effectiveness. It generally concludes that, in a well-functioning organization, communication must flow both ways freely and that informal communication bypasses and parallels the formal hierarchical patterns (Barnard, 1938; Roethlisberger & Dickson, 1939; Bakke, 1950: chap. 4; Redfield, 1953; Blau, 1955: chaps. 7, 8; Leavitt, 1964; Bennis, 1966; D. Katz & Kahn, 1966: chap. 9). It stresses the value and price of feedback

(Leavitt & Mueller, 1951; Zajonc, 1962).

What a desirable structure may be depends critically on one's goals, since each type of hierarchy has both advantages and disadvantages, depending upon the complexity of the job and how heavily one weights the goals of productivity, morale, adaptability, and speed of learning (Leavitt, 1951; Guetzkow & Simon, 1955; Guetzkow & Dill, 1957; Shaw, Rothchild, & Strickland, 1957; Dubin, 1959; A. M. Cohen, Bennis, & Wolkon, 1962; Guetzkow, 1965; Carzo, 1963). Most of the rigorous work on which conclusions about desirable structures are based stems from small-group experiments in the laboratory. The conclusions may not generalize directly to the more complex situation in the field.

Analysis of small networks is more tractable than analysis of large ones because even without solving all the theoretical problems of how to describe networks in general, it is possible to fully describe a small network ad hoc. We turn, therefore, to a review of some of the concepts and measures used to describe communication networks, first in small groups and then, insofar as it has been done, in large societies.

Small Groups

In the vast literature on small-group behavior (summarized in chapter 20 of this book), one of the variables most frequently considered is the structure of the group. Perhaps the largest relevant literature is that which stems from sociometry. The early studies in this field (Moreno, 1953; Moreno & Jennings, 1960) were generally reported by means of freely drawn charts with lines connecting the various individuals in the group. Researchers who asked their subjects, for example, "From which member of the group would you seek advice?" could report the results by drawing arrows from each member to those individuals to whom he turned. Such sociometric graphs often reveal starkly the existence of "isolates" who were not chosen, and of tightly knit cliques of "stars" who were widely chosen. But the layout of such a graph, the location of its points and the distances between them, is a completely intuitive and artistic matter.

The isomorphism of a sociogram to matrix representation was quickly recognized and the power of matrix algebra was brought to bear on the analysis of small-group networks (Luce & Perry, 1949; Luce, 1950; 1952; Harary & Ross, 1957; Starbuck, 1965). With computers the nXn incidence matrices representing contacts could be manipulated with n's up to and above 100. Matrix manipulations permitted measurement of the connectedness of the graph, the mean of the lengths of chain necessary to link two persons in a communication network, and similar matters. As has been demonstrated, the same formal problems could also be dealt with by graph-theoretic approaches (Harary & Norman, 1953; Flament, 1963; Harary, Norman, & Cartwright, 1965) as well as by matrix algebra (Holland & Leinhardt, 1970).

Empirical studies have generally established fairly strong and expectable relations of sociometric mappings to communication mappings and to power mappings (French, 1956). The sociometric stars tend to receive most information, communicate most, and have most influence. That kind of result turned up in studies of interrelationships among doctors (Menzel & Katz, 1955–56; Coleman, Katz, & Menzel, 1966), in studies of community power structure, social organization in industry (Borgatta, 1954; Larsen & Hill, 1958; Jackson, 1959) and, if one is willing to extend the sociometric concept slightly, in studies of relations among nations (Rummel, 1965; 1969; Alger & Brams, 1967; Alger, 1969; Brams, 1969; Pool, 1970). Sociometric and communications patterns also regularly corresponded to the patterns of centralization or competition in leadership. The presence of a single dominant leader or of rival leaders and cliques can easily be documented by plotting the networks of consultation and influence.

Perhaps the most widely noted among

the studies of communications structures in small groups were the experiments of Alex Bavelas (1951) and his colleagues on message transmission in differently arranged task groups. Members of the groups were placed in a laboratory setting in which they could communicate only by notes, and only some of the links among individuals were allowed. Where the pattern was relatively equalitarian, with all members of the group more or less evenly in contact with other members of the group, morale was better than where some individuals formed nodes through which other individuals had to communicate with each other. Such central individuals tended to become leaders. While for some tasks and in some circumstances the output of these centralized groups might be better, the morale and commitment of the group members tended to be distinctly lower (Heise & Miller, 1951; Guetzkow & Simon, 1955; Guetzkow & Dill, 1957; Shaw, Rothchild, & Strickland, 1957; Mulder, 1960; Glanzer & Glaser, 1961; A. M. Cohen, 1962; A. M. Cohen, Bennis, & Wolkon, 1962; Carzo, 1963; Guetzkow, 1965).

Studies by Bales (1950; 1970) and others based on observation of small groups in discussion, decision, and problem-solving situations have also shown much about the structure of effective groups and the sequences in which group communication patterns change as the groups come to cohere. There is often division of labor among the leadership in a group as well as within the group as a whole. Often there is a separation between individuals who provide task-oriented leadership and those who provide social-affective leadership. Interaction analysis also frequently shows changes in the rate and content of communication as a group first comes together and gradually acquires cohesion.

The substantive findings of such small-group research and the literature on it are summarized in chapter 20. Here we wish to note only some important parameters that have been used in the characterization of groups. These include:

a) the size of the group;
b) its purpose—is it task-oriented or affective;
c) its duration—is it transitory or long-established;
d) the intensity of group interactions, i.e. the rate of flow of communications within it;
e) its homogeneity or heterogeneity in whatever makes for cohesion, such as shared attitudes, beliefs, social background, or experiences;
f) the spacial or communication arrangement of the group, as in the Bavelas experiment;
g) the character of the group's leadership, including the constitutional roles assigned to leaders, the number and division of labor among them, the way they are chosen, and the personality of the leaders;
h) the value of the group to its members—how much do they care about it;
i) its relation to other groups—is it alone, or in cooperation, or in competition with other groups.

Large Networks

The analysis of communication flows in large networks strains to the limits the mathematical methods now available (Rapoport & Horvath, 1961; Foster, Rapoport & Orwant, 1963). To a considerable degree, we lack the tools needed for modeling those complex systems.

The interesting problems to be analyzed may be differentiated into two broad types:

1. analysis of the underlying structure of possible communication linkages;
2. analysis of the message flow.

Let us illustrate the distinction.

News media throughout the world are dependent upon press services for the bulk of their foreign news. One could map the world showing for each press service the location of its bureaus, correspondents, stringers, and exchange relationships as sources for its news. One could similarly map its subscribers. Those maps would portray the underlying structure of possible communication. The scatter of dots on the maps would indicate biases in the richness of news available from and to different parts of the world. Such a map would show, for example, that a country such as Malaysia, almost a neighbor of Vietnam, gets its Vietnam news from New York and London.

We could improve the precision of the picture, however, if we could superimpose on those maps measures of the number of words per day flowing along the various links. That would be an analysis of the message flow.

Typical questions about the underlying structure concern linkages; e.g., does a path exist between points A and B? How many links, on the average, does it take to get between any two points? The mathematics appropriate to this kind of analysis has been developed largely in response to the needs of electrical engineering. An electrical network, be it a power system, a telephone system, or a computer, is a communication system. To analyze it and to optimize its efficiency require certain kinds of circuit analysis not unlike the matrix and graph-theoretic approaches noted in the discussion of small groups.

Typical questions about message flow concern the diffusion of information; e.g., how long does it take for most of the population to have heard a particular rumor? Models for analyzing such phenomena tend to be borrowed from epidemiology. A rumor is like an infection. There are those who have received it already and those who have not. Those who have not yet caught the infection at any given moment may get it from those who have. It spreads increasingly rapidly as the number of potential sources grows, but then it slows down as the number of potential receivers declines, i.e., as the untouched portion of the population gets ever smaller.

Rumor

Some of the more important studies of message flow in large populations concern the diffusion of rumor. The basic methodology of such studies is to plant rumors in a system and then to obtain reports on them as they spread. Some early studies of rumor were in closed laboratory environments. They resemble the parlor game in which the players sit in a circle and whisper a message from person to person. What comes out at the end is a gross distortion of the original message (Allport & Postman, 1947; 1958; Campbell, 1958). The apparent implication is that rumor is a grossly unreliable channel of information. However, field research seldom showed rumors to be as widespread or as wild as the laboratory studies would suggest, although there certainly are frequent cases of unfounded rumors (Caplow, 1947; Jacobson & Seashore, 1951; Davis, 1953a; 1953b; Buckner, 1965; Shibutani, 1966; Sutton & Porter, 1968). Most rumors in the field turn out to be reasonable.

One explanation for the sobriety of most rumors was identified by Festinger, Schachter, and Back (1950). They planted rumors in a married students' housing project and then traced the spread of the information they had planted. Participant observers and interviewers kept track of the message flow. The experimental rumors concerned local housing matters. What the researchers found was that the recipients of the messages, instead of passing them on at random, tended to carry them straight to appropriate members of committees of the tenant's organization. In short, rumors in a free, nonlaboratory situation tend to get passed on selectively to those individuals to whom they are specifically relevant (Davis, 1953; Zajonc & Wolfe, 1963; Sutton & Porter, 1968).

Further study has shown that the distortion process that takes place as a rumor goes from mouth to mouth is also quite different from the process in the laboratory (Campbell, 1958; Deutschmann, 1962; Buckner, 1965; Arndt, 1968). In the laboratory or parlor game we usually observe forced communication. If a person did not quite hear or understand what was told, he nonetheless has to pass on something. In life, a person repeats a report only if it makes sense to him.

That does not mean that no distortion occurs. It means that distortion, when it takes place, is usually in the direction of plausibility. A report that "the dog hit the man" would be likely to be heard or passed on as "the dog bit the man." More often than not, the "distortion" corrects errors that have crept into messages for, more often than not, what is true is what is plausible. Sometimes that is not the case, however. When the facts contradict the population's presuppositions, the report will either not be repeated or will be distorted to a more plausible but erroneous form, and so rumor will fail as a conveyor of knowledge.

The Dodd-Rapoport Studies. Perhaps the most important models of the diffusion of messages through a large population were developed from a project conducted for the U.S. Air Force by Stuart Dodd and Anatol Rapoport (Dodd, 1953; 1958; Dodd & McCurtain, 1965) concerning psychological warfare leaflet drops (DeFleur & Rainboth, 1952; DeFleur, 1956). One experiment which provided data consisted of dropping leaflets with a coffee-advertising offer from a plane over an area in the U.S.A. The free coffee created an incentive to communicate the news when received. Interviewers, who implemented the offer, then called at homes in the area and ascertained whether the housewife had heard about the offer. The design of the experiment permitted accurate recording of how many individuals had received the original leaflet and when; also determined was how many had been told about it by word of mouth and with what delay. On the basis of this data, Rapoport developed rather sophisticated mathematical models of the pattern of information flow (Rapoport, 1953; Rapoport & Horvath, 1961; Foster, Rapoport, & Orwant, 1963).

The basic pattern of message diffusion has already been roughly described as epidemiological. It produces the S shaped logistic growth curve that Dodd identifies as being so often a basic pattern of human interaction. Let us here state the relationship slightly more formally:

At any given time, the probability of an act of communicating new information from a knower of it to a member of the population who does not yet know it is directly proportional to the proportion of knowers, and inversely proportional to the proportion who have not yet heard it.

$$P = f\left[\left(\frac{k}{n}\right)\left(\frac{n-k}{n}\right)\right].$$

As K goes from 1 (the first knower) to n (the population), the probability of communication, P, is at its maximum when K is about half the population (assuming away other parameters in f). Up to that point, diffusion has been increasingly rapid. Beyond that point, it is decreasingly rapid. Thus, the spread of the message in the simplest case can be modeled as the logistic or S-shaped growth curve (see Figure 3).

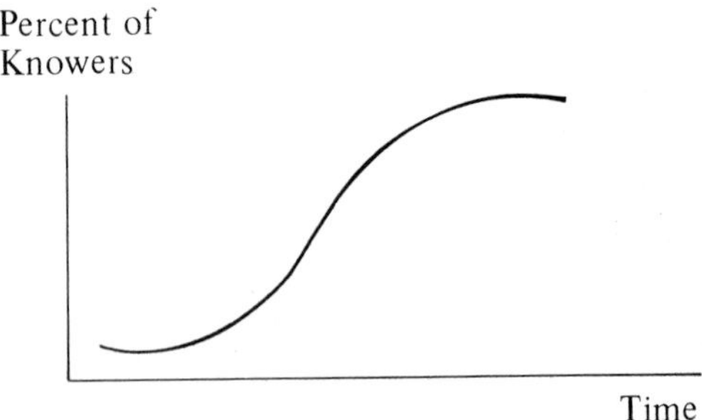

Figure 3. S-shaped logistic growth curve.

The Rapoport and similar models go far beyond this simple but basic case in taking account of time delays in communication, different population propensities, social structure, reward structures, and similar matters.

Community Integration

Karl Deutsch, and a few other scholars (Russett, 1963; Azar, 1970), have used communication flows as a measure of community integration. Many communities do not have sharp, unambiguous boundaries. Often the boundary of a system is best conceived of as a line (empirically discovered) across which interactions are relatively rare and weak compared with those within it. Thus, the boundaries of a metropolitan area or of a school of painting are somewhat arbitrary, but a well-drawn line will in each case place most interactions within the boundary. There will, of course, be some cross-boundary relations, though at a much lower rate than within the system; the cross-boundary interactions may be particularly interesting nonetheless.

The problem that Deutsch (1954; 1956; 1957; 1966; 1968) addressed is that of understanding the formation and disintegration of political communities such as nations (see also Jacob & Toscano, 1964). Deutsch's theory is that boundaries of political communities tend to form in correspondence with lines of social interaction. Thus, where boundaries developed in trade, travel, and discourse systems, such that interactions within were strong and interactions across the line were weak, national identifications tended to form with the same boundaries. Similarly, international blocs tend to form along the lines of blocs defined by trade and communication. On the other hand, nations or blocs tend to break up when schisms appear in their networks of social contacts.

Among the indicators Deutsch has used to establish the existence of a system boundary is the percent of mails within and across it, the percent of trade within and across it, the percent of travel within and across it, and the percent of scientific citations within and across it. Language areas, religious areas, and cultural areas also determine rates of interaction inside and outside; therefore they, too, affect community formation or fission.

In general, Deutsch's findings show a process whereby, as a community forms, the percentage of internal communication rises (1956). We are all conscious of the fact that technology is rapidly shrinking the world. Travel and communication across the globe become ever easier. It comes as somewhat of a surprise, therefore, to find from Deutsch's figures that in much of the world, during much of this century, the dominant phenomenon has been the creation of national institutions. This trend is indexed by such phenomena as increasing citations of national scientific journals rather than foreign ones, more rapid growth of national mails rather than international ones, and increased use of the national language in science and education. The complex and contradictory trends between growing breadth of human relations and growing integration of conflicting groups are well documented by Deutsch's type of communication analysis.

The slow processes of alliance formation and international organization by which the world is moving toward some measure of integration is increasingly being measured by such indices as exchange of emissaries, trade, or votes (Alger & Brams, 1967; Brams, 1969; Erbring, 1969; Rummel, 1969; Teune, 1970). The exchange of people (students, tourists, scholars, businessmen, immigrants) is perhaps the most studied form of communication among nations. A recent book that draws together much of the extensive literature on this subject is Kelman's (1965).

The Small-World Problem

A familiar illustration of some of the principles of contact networks is the small-world phenomenon. Who has not had the surprise of meeting a friend while traveling in a faraway place? Who has not been asked by a stranger, "Do you know so-and-so?" only to discover a mutual friend? The usual exclamation of surprise is, "It's a small world!"

The present author some years ago noted

that social scientists had barely studied this phenomenon. We did not have any estimates on how many persons a person knows and what the resulting probability is that any two people (chosen at random) have an acquaintance in common. It seemed a subject worth investigating but hard to tackle.

We started by doing a gedankenexperiment. We wanted to get a handle on the approximate size of persons' acquaintanceship universes. Using a large telephone book as a mnemonic aid, we opened the book at random and said to the subject, "Look at this page. Do you know anyone who, if he lived in this city and had a telephone, would appear on this page?" From this game it began to appear that 500 to 2,000 were plausible kinds of numbers for a man's acquaintances.

Let us think through the implications of numbers like this. Consider all pairs of adults in the United States. Between each pair there is some chain of friends, who have friends, who have friends, etc., by which they can be linked. We can be fairly sure that there is such a chain. If there were none for some pairs, it would imply that the population consists of two or more sets between which there is *no* interpersonal communication. It seems highly unlikely that there is any closed set of persons in the country who connect with each other but who have absolutely no link to the rest of the population. Note that if even one person in a linked set had one friend in the rest of the population, then immediately everyone in that set is linked to the whole. (See Figure 4.)

So, assuming that there is at least one chain linking every pair of persons in the United States, for each pair there is a shortest or minimum chain by which they could be linked. What is the longest minimum chain in the country? We surmise that it is something like six intermediaries; i.e., there is no pair of persons who cannot be linked by about six intermediaries or less. Let us assume that we have discovered this longest minimum chain. Let us further assume that it was between two hermits on opposite coasts. Each presumably knows at least a storekeeper. Each storekeeper in his list of acquaintances knows at least one person who knows his congressman, and there we are with a complete chain. With only a couple more links we could carry it to a peasant in India or to virtually anyone in the world.

The above speculation covers the extreme

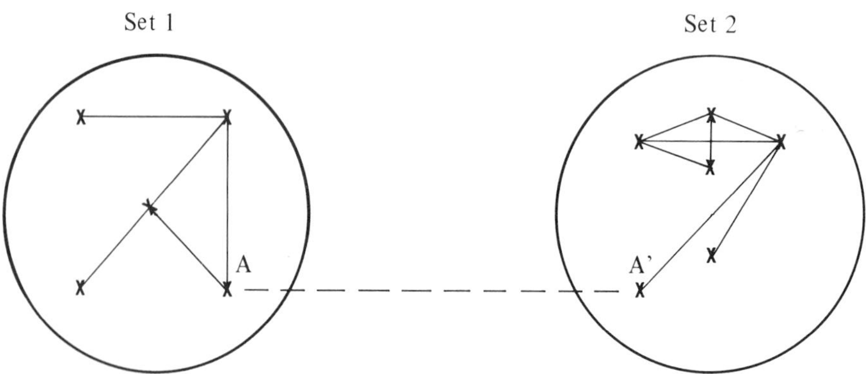

Figure 4. If link *AA′* exists, everyone in the population is linked.

case. What is the normal case? What is the probable minimum chain for a pair of persons picked at random? For the United States, we surmise that it is less than three intermediaries—probably two-point-something. Suppose each person knows 1,000 persons, then the names on the lists of friends of friends of any one person would number 1,000,000 (i.e., one thousand thousands). The lists of friends of friends of friends would number 1 billion. Since there are not 1 billion different people in America, clearly many of the same names will appear on many lists. Indeed, any one man's friends have many friends in common.

We would wish, then, some measure of the degree of ingrownness of a person's acquaintance net. That would be a very important parameter of social structure. We will discuss one such measure below; for the moment, let us simply note that even though the 1 billion names on the lists of friends of friends of friends cover many fewer different people than that, they might conceivably cover 100 million, which would mean that, on the average, two intermediaries would link any pair of Americans picked at random. Three intermediaries give us a list of a trillion names, certainly many more than are needed to blanket half the population. But perhaps 1,000 is too high an estimate of the average person's acquaintances. If we work with the figure of 500, then two intermediaries give us 125 million names, and three intermediaries give us 62.5 billion. Again we would surmise that the average minimum chain is two-point-something intermediaries.

Enough of speculation and gedanken-experiments. Having done this armchair analysis, we set out to get slightly harder data. Michael Gurevitch (1961) and the present author collected from twenty-seven persons lists by name of all the individuals with whom the subject was in contact, day by day, for 100 days each. Average number of contacts listed each day varied from 4 for the subject who was most isolated to 76 for the one who had the most contacts. The most gregarious person's contacts cumulated to 685 different acquaintances in 100 days, while the contacts of the least gregarious subject cumulated to only 72 different persons in 100 days.

The patterns of contact as measured by the type/token ratio varied greatly by kind of person. Blue-collar subjects tended to see the same persons every day. They might see many or few persons per day, but their cumulation curves rose slowly. Professional people, on the other hand, tended to see many more persons in total, but fewer times each.

As just noted, the 100-day data for each individual permitted the construction of a cumulation curve. Naturally, in the early part of the 100 days many new names were being added to the cumulative list each day. Later in the 100-day test period, fewer and fewer new names would appear each day as the man's contacts repeated themselves. In principle, this might permit an estimate, by curve extension, of a man's total set of acquaintances as accumulated over twenty, thirty, or forty years. In fact, there is difficulty making such projections because of the instability of the critical tail of the curve. Nonetheless, estimates of acquaintance volume do fall somewhere between the 200 to 4,000 range.

When the 100-day data collection was finished, we took the respondents' lists and turned them into a questionnaire. To a sample of the people who appeared on a subject's lists we sent a sample of the names on the list and asked regarding each, "Do you know that person?" This provided a measure of the degree of ingrownness of a contact net. It can be expressed, looking at Figure 5, as a count of the percent of possible triangles that are completed (cf. Holland & Leinhardt, 1970). The values ranged from 8 to 36 percent, with 12 percent being a typical figure.

With data of this kind, conceivably, a sufficiently skilled mathematical modeler could come up with methods for making more solid estimates of the kinds of system dimensions (like average length of mini-

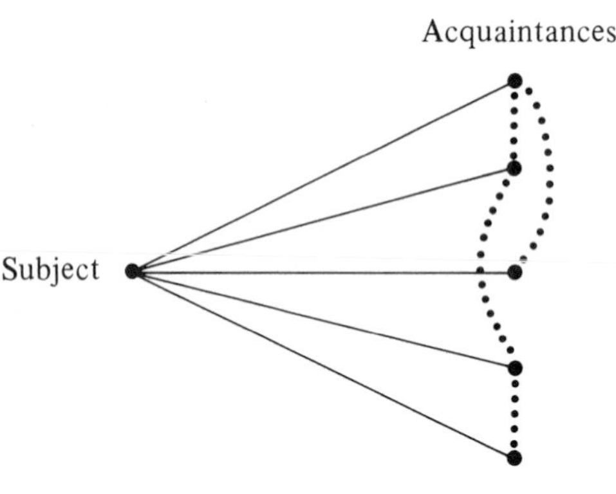

Figure 5. Measure of the degree of ingrownness of a contact net. The dotted lines connect acquaintances who know each other.

mum chain) with which we were playing in the gedankenexperiments. To date it has not been successfully done, and it is widely recognized that the mathematics of large nonrandom networks is extremely complicated (Rapoport, 1953; 1963; Rapoport & Horvath, 1961; Foster, Rapoport, & Orwant, 1963; Taylor, 1968; Holland & Leinhardt, 1970).

Recently, Travers and Milgram (1969) carried small-world research forward with some highly ingenious experiments. They set up a task not unlike the well-known chain-letter game. The subjects were given a set of postcards and told that the purpose was to reach a particular target individual in the smallest possible number of steps. However, according to the rule of the game, the cards could only be sent at each step to a person the sender already knew. The ultimate target person was a stranger in another part of the country. The subject would send one postcard report to the experimenter and forward the remaining batch of postcards to some acquaintance whom he believed would be closer to the target person. The subject would ask the receiver of the batch of cards to do the same thing in turn.

In general, Milgram's results showed that subjects reached the immediate environs of the target person with about two intermediaries. It should be pointed out that Milgram's experiment explores the skillfulness of people at finding contact chains, not whether these chains exist. The difference became most strikingly clear at the end of the postcard chains when persons in the immediate environs of the target individual (persons who clearly had short chains to him) often thrashed around unsuccessfully trying to find him. The first steps in the chain operation were more efficient because the postcard senders could aim right for the city and institution where the target person was located; without those obvious clues, however, it became hard to find the chains that existed.

CONCLUSION

While the complexities of communication-system modeling are enormous, it seems likely to have substantial payoff for social research.

The complexities are due at least partially to lack of good mathematical models and methods. None of the present methods for estimating either cumulation or duplication is altogether satisfactory. No model exists for estimating the distribution of lengths of contact-net chains. No good metric exists for describing a communication network as highly stratified, random, equalitarian, or hierarchic. Communications data permit various measurements of social structure, but we do not know what to do with the data to produce a usable statistic for any particular variable.

Nonetheless, the promise of communication-system modeling is great.

The variables dealt with are sufficiently definable and quantifiable to permit the programming of computer simulations. Computers can handle the large and complex models that result, models that, in the past, would have been mere exercises in detail because we could not have used the detail in practice.

Communications system descriptions,

because they work with definable and measurable indexes that nonetheless are highly pervasive, permit the social scientist to get a handle on such slippery concepts as social stratification, national integration, and other vague descriptions of human interaction. The structure of contact nets, for example, could provide a meaningful index of social stratification. The structure of message flows can be used to define the limits of a community.

Comparative communication system studies—comparing nations at different stages of development and comparing democratic and authoritarian communication systems—are of growing interest as new mass media systems develop around the world.

Given the various starts that have been made in computer modeling of communication systems, in defining concepts rigorously, and in providing metrics for the parameters of communication systems, there is good reason to believe that substantial progress will soon be made in communication-system modeling.

REFERENCES

Advertising Research Foundation.
1951 Continuing Study of Newspaper Reading. New York: Advertising Research Foundation.

Agostini, J. M.
1961 "How to estimate unduplicated audiences." Journal of Advertising Research 1 (No. 3): 11–14.
1962 "Analysis of magazine accumulative audience." Journal of Advertising Research 2 (No. 4): 24–27.
1964 "The case for direct questions on reading habits." Journal of Advertising Research 4 (No. 2): 28–33.

Alger, Chadwick F.
1969 "Interaction and negotiation in a committee of the United Nations general assembly," in James N. Rosenau (ed.), International Politics and Foreign Policy. New York: Free Press.

Alger, Chadwick F., and Steven J. Brams.
1967 "Patterns of representation in national capitals and intergovernmental organizations." World Politics 19: 646–663.

Allport, Gordon W., and Leo J. Postman.
1947 The Psychology of Rumor. New York: Holt, Rinehart and Winston.
1958 "The basic psychology of rumor," in Eleanor E. Maccoby, Theodore M. Newcomb, and Eugene E. Hartley (eds.), Readings in Social Psychology. Third Edition. New York: Holt, Rinehart and Winston.

American Newspaper Markets.
1962– Comprehensive Analysis of Newspaper Circulations. Northfield, Ill.: American Newspaper Markets, Inc. Annual.

Ando, Albert; Franklin Fisher; and Herbert A. Simon.
1963 Essays in the Structure of Social Science Models. Cambridge, Massachusetts: M.I.T. Press.

Appel, Valentine, and M. L. Blum.
1960 "Ad recognition and respondent set." Journal of Advertising Research 1 (No. 3): 13–21.

Arndt, Johan.
1968 "Selective processes in word of mouth." Journal of Advertising Research 8 (No. 3): 19–22.

Audits and Surveys.
1961a Look Audience Study, 1961. New York: Cowles Magazines and Broadcasting, Inc.
1961b A National Study of Newspaper Reading. New York: Audits And Surveys Company.
1962 Look Audience Study, 1962. New York: Cowles Magazines and Broadcasting, Inc.

Ayer, N. W., and Sons.
1880– Directory of Newspapers and Periodicals. Philadelphia: N. W. Ayer and Sons. Annual.

Azar, Edward.
1970 "Analysis of international events." Peace Research Reviews 4 (November): 1–113.

Bakke, E. Wight.
1950 Bonds of Organization: An Appraisal of Corporate Human Relations. New York: Harper.

Bales, Robert F.
1950 Interaction Process Analysis. Reading, Massachusetts: Addison-Wesley.

1970 Personality and Interpersonal Behavior. New York: Holt, Rinehart and Winston.

Banks, Seymour, and A. Madansky.
1958 "Estimation of multimagazine readership." Journal of Business 31:235–242.

Barnard, Chester I.
1938 Functions of the Executive. Cambridge, Massachusetts: Harvard University Press.

Barnlund, D. C., and C. Harland.
1963 "Propinquity and prestige as determinants of communication networks." Sociometry 26:467–479.

Bavelas, Alex.
1951 "Communication patterns in task-oriented groups," in H. D. Lasswell and Daniel Lerner (eds.), The Policy Sciences. Stanford, California: Stanford University Press.

Belson, W. A.
1962 Studies in Readership. London: Business Publications, Ltd.

Bennis, Warren G.
1966 Changing Organizations. New York: McGraw-Hill.

Benson, Purnell H.
1969a "Bivariate normal distribution to calculate media exposure." Journal of Advertising Research 9(No.3): 41–48.
1969b "Improvement in media-exposure prediction based upon the bivariate normal distribution." Proceedings of the American Psychological Association, 1969. Washington, D.C.: American Psychological Association.

Berelson, Bernard.
1949 "What missing the newspaper means," in Paul F. Lazarsfeld and F. N. Stanton (eds.), Communications Research, 1948–1949. New York: Harper.

Blau, Peter M.
1955 Dynamics of Bureaucracy: A Study of Interpersonal Relations in Two Government Agencies. Chicago: University of Chicago Press.

Borgatta, E. F.
1954 "Analysis of social interaction and sociometric perception." Sociometry 17:7–31.

Bower, John.
1963 "Net audiences of U.S. and Canadian magazines: Seven tests of Agostini formula." Journal of Advertising Research 3(No. 1):13–20.

Brams, Steven J.
1969 "The structure of influence relations in the international system," in James N. Rosenau (ed.), International Politics and Foreign Policy. New York: Free Press.

Buchanan, Dodds I.
1964 "How interest in the product affects recall: Print ads vs. commercials." Journal of Advertising Research 4 (No. 1):9–14.

Buckner, H. T.
1965 "A theory of rumor transmission." Public Opinion Quarterly 29:54–70.

Bureau of Advertising.
1962 Newspapers At Your Service: A Directory of Market Studies. New York: American Newspaper Publishers Association. Mimeographed.

Burns, T.
1954 "The directions of activity and communication in a departmental executive group." Human Relations 7:73–97.

Caffyn, J. M., and M. Sagovsky.
1963 "Net audiences of British newspapers: A comparison of Agostini and Sainsbury methods." Journal of Advertising Research 3(March):21–25.

Campbell, D. T.
1958 "Systematic error on the part of human links in communication systems." Information and Control 1:334–369.

Caplow, Theodore.
1947 "Rumors in war." Social Forces 25 (March):298–302.

Carzo, Rocco, Jr.
1963 "Some effects of organization structure on group effectiveness." Administrative Science Quarterly 7:393–424.

Claycamp, H. J., and C. W. McClelland.
1968 "Estimating reach and the magic of K." Journal of Advertising Research 8(No. 2):44–51.

Cohen, A. M.
1962 "Changing small-group communication networks." Administrative Science Quarterly 6:443–462.

Cohen, A. M.; W. G. Bennis; and G. H. Wolkon.

1962 "Effects of changes in communication networks on the behavior of problem-solving groups." Sociometry 25: 177–196.

Cohen, A. R.
1958 "Upward communication in experimentally created hierarchies." Human Relations 11:41–53.

Coleman, James; Elihu Katz; and Herbert Menzel.
1957 "Diffusion of an innovation among physicians." Sociometry 20:253–270.
1966 Medical Innovation: A Diffusion Study. Indianapolis: Bobbs-Merrill.

Davis, Keith.
1953a "Management communication and the grapevine." Harvard Business Review 31:43–49.
1953b "A method of studying communication patterns in organizations." Personal Psychology 16:301–312.

DeFleur, M. L.
1956 "A mass communication model of stimulus response relationships: An experiment in leaflet message diffusion." Sociometry 19:12–25.

DeFleur, M. L., and E. D. Rainboth.
1952 "Testing message diffusion in four communities: Some factors in the use of airborne leaflets as a communications medium." American Sociological Review 17:734–737.

Deutsch, Karl W.
1954 Political Community at the International Level. Garden City, New York: Doubleday.
1956 "Shifts in the balance of communication flows." Public Opinion Quarterly 20:143–160.
1957 Political Community and the North Atlantic Area. Princeton, New Jersey: Princeton University Press.
1966 Nationalism and Social Communication. Cambridge, Massachusetts: M.I.T. Press.
1968 The Analysis of International Relations. Englewood Cliffs, New Jersey: Prentice-Hall.

Deutschmann, P. J.
1962 "Viewing conversation and voting intentions," in Sidney Kraus (ed.), The Great Debates. Bloomington: Indiana University Press.

Dodd, Stuart C.
1953 "Testing message diffusion in controlled experiments." American Sociological Review 18:410–416.
1958 "Formulas for spreading opinions: A report of controlled experiments on leaflet messages in Project Revere." Public Opinion Quarterly 22:537–554.

Dodd, Stuart C., and M. McCurtain.
1965 "The logistic diffusion of information through randomly overlapped cliques." Operations Research Quarterly 16:51–63.

Dubin, Robert.
1959 "Stability of human organizations," in Mason Haire (ed.), Modern Organization Theory. New York: Wiley.

Ehrenberg, A. S. C.
1961 "How reliable is aided recall of TV viewing." Journal of Advertising Research 1 (No. 4):29–31.
1964 "A comparison of TV audience measures." Journal of Advertising Research 4(No. 4):11–16.
1968 "Factor analytic search for program types." Journal of Advertising Research 8(No. 1):55–63.

Ehrenberg, A. S. C., and W. A. Twyman.
1967 "On measuring televison audiences." Journal of Royal Statistics 130:1–59.

Engelman, Fred L.
1965 "An empirical formula for audience accumulation." Journal of Advertising Research 5(No. 2):21–28.

Erbring, Lutz.
1969 Structural Constraints in the International System. Mimeograph (unpublished).

Ferber, Robert, and H. G. Wales.
1958–59 "Advertising recall in relation to type of recall." Public Opinion Quarterly 22:529–536.

Festinger, Leon A.; Stanley S. Schachter; and Kurt W. Back.
1950 Social Pressures in Informal Groups: A Study of Human Factors in Housing. New York: Harper.

Flament, Claude.
1963 Applications of Graph Theory to Group Structure. Englewood Cliffs, New Jersey: Prentice-Hall.

Foster, C. C.; Anatol Rapoport; and C. J. Orwant.
1963 "A study of a large sociogram II." Behavioral Science 8:56–65.

French, J. R. P., Jr.
1956 "A formal theory of power." Psychological Review 63:181–194.
Friedman, Lawrence.
1970 "Constructing a media simulation model." Journal of Advertising Research 10(No. 4):33–39.
Glanzer, Murray, and Robert Glaser.
1961 "Techniques for the study of group structure and behavior." Psychological Bulletin 58:1–27.
Goodhardt, G. J.
1966 "The constant in duplicated television viewing." Nature 212:1616.
Greenberg, A., and N. Garfinkle.
1962 "Delayed recall of magazine articles." Journal of Advertising Research 2(No. 1):28–31.
Greene, J., and J. S. Stock.
1967 Advertising Reach and Frequency in Magazines. New York: Reader's Digest.
Guetzkow, Harold.
1965 "Communication in organizations." Pp. 534–573 in James G. March (ed.), Handbook of Organizations. Chicago: Rand McNally.
Guetzkow, Harold, and W. R. Dill.
1957 "Factors in the organizational development of task-oriented groups." Sociometry 20:175–204.
Guetzkow, Harold, and Herbert A. Simon.
1955 "The impact of certain communication nets upon organization and performance in task-oriented groups." Management Science 1:233–250.
Gurevitch, Michael.
1961 "The social structure of acquaintanceship networks." Ph. D. Dissertation, Massachusetts Institute of Technology.
Hagerstrand, Torsten.
1969 Innovation Diffusion as a Spatial Process. Chicago: University of Chicago Press.
Harary, Frank, and Robert Z. Norman.
1953 Graph Theory as a Mathematical Model in Social Science. Ann Arbor, Michigan: Research Center for Group Dynamics.
Harary, Frank; Robert Z. Norman; and Dorwin Cartwright.
1965 Structural Models: An Introduction to the Theory of Directed Graphs. New York: Wiley.
Harary, Frank, and Ian C. Ross.
1957 "A procedure for clique detection using the group matrix." Sociometry 20:205–215.
Heise, G. A., and George A. Miller.
1951 "Problem-solving by small groups using various communication net." Journal of Abnormal and Social Psychology 46:327–335.
Hobson, J. W., and Harry Henry.
1949 The Hulton Tables of Advertisement Attention Value. London: Hulton Press.
Hofmans, Pierre.
1966 "Measuring the cumulative net coverage of any combination of media." Journal of Marketing Research 3:269–278.
Holland, Paul, and Samuel Leinhardt.
1970 "A method for detecting structure in sociometric data." American Journal of Sociology 76:492–513.
Horvath, W.
1965 "A mathematical model of participation in small group discussions." Behaviorial Science 10:164–166.
Hubbard, A. W.
1954 "Which recall will obtain reliable information?" Journal of Marketing 18:396–398.
International Press Institute.
1953 The Flow of the News. Zurich: International Press Institute.
Jackson, J. M.
1959 "Reference group processes in a formal organization." Sociometry 22: 307–327.
Jacob, Philip E., and James P. Toscano (eds.).
1964 Integration of Political Communities. Philadelphia: Lippincott.
Jacobson, E., and S. Seashore.
1951 "Communication practices in complex organizations." Journal of Social Issues 7:28–40.
Kadane, Joseph B.; Gordon H. Lewis; and John G. Ramage.
1969 "Horvath's theory of participation in group discussions." Sociometry 32: 348–361.
Katz, Daniel, and R. L. Kahn.
1966 The Social Psychology of Organizations. New York: Wiley.
Katz, Elihu.
1957 "The two-step flow of communication: An up-to-date report on an

hypothesis." Public Opinion Quarterly 21:61–78.

Katz, Elihu, and Paul F. Lazarsfeld.
1955 Personal Influence. Glencoe, Illinois: Free Press.

Katz, Elihu; M. L. Levin; and H. Hamilton.
1963 "Traditions of research on the diffusion of innovation." American Sociological Review 28:237–252.

Keller, P.
1966 "Patterns of media-audience accumulation." Journal of Marketing 30:32–37.

Kelman, Herbert (ed.).
1965 International Behavior. New York: Holt, Rinehart and Winston.

Klensin, John C., and John D. Nagle.
1969 Mass Media Simulation Program: Users' Manual. Cambridge, Massachusetts: Center for International Studies, Massachusetts Institute of Technology.

Kramer, John.
1969 A Computer Simulation of Audience Exposure in a Mass Media System. Cambridge, Massachusetts: Center for International Studies, Massachusetts Institute of Technology.

Kuhn, W.
1963 "Net audiences of German magazines: A new formula." Journal of Advertising Research 3(No. 1):30–33.

Kwerel, Seymour M.
1964 "Estimating the unduplicated audience of a combination of media vehicles." Ph.D. Dissertation, Columbia University.
1969 "Estimating unduplicated audience exposure distribution." Journal of Advertising Research 9(No. 2):46–53.

Larsen, O. N., and R. T. Hill.
1958 "Social structure and interpersonal communication." American Journal of Sociology 63:497–505.

Leavitt, H. J.
1951 "Effects of certain communications patterns on group performance." Journal of Abnormal and Social Psychology 46:38–50.
1964 Managerial Psychology. Second Edition. Chicago: University of Chicago Press.

Leavitt, H. J., and R. A. H. Mueller.
1951 "Some effects of feedback in communication." Human Relations 4:401–410.

Life.
1958 Life Study of Consumer Expenditures. New York: Time, Inc.
1965 Media Balance. New York: Time, Inc.

Lucas, D. B.
1942 "A controlled recognition technique for measuring magazine advertising audiences." Journal of Marketing 6:133–136.
1960 "The ABC's of ARF's PARM." Journal of Marketing 25:9–20.

Luce, R. Duncan.
1950 "Connectivity and generalized cliques in sociometric group structure." Psychometrika 15:169–190.
1952 "A note on Boolean matrix theory." Proceedings of the American Mathematical Society 3:382–388.

Luce, R. Duncan, and Albert D. Perry.
1949 "A method of matrix analysis of group structure." Psychometrika 14:360–371.

McGlathery, D. G.
1967 "Claimed frequency vs. editorial interest measures of repeat magazine audiences." Journal of Advertising Research 7(No. 1):7–15.

McLuhan, Marshall.
1964 Understanding Media. New York: McGraw-Hill.

McPhee, William N.
1963 Formal Theories of Mass Behavior. New York: Free Press of Glencoe.

Maloney, J. C.
1961 "Portfolio tests—are they here to stay?" Journal of Marketing 26:32–37.

Marc, Marcel.
1963 "Net audiences of French business papers—Agostini's formula applied to special markets." Journal of Advertising Research 3(No. 1):26–29.
1968 "Combining simulation and panel data to obtain reach and frequency." Journal of Advertising Research 8(No. 2):11–16.

March, James G., and Herbert A. Simon.
1958 Organizations. New York: Wiley.

Marder, Eric.
1967 "How good is the editorial-interest method of measuring magazine audi-

ences?" Journal of Advertising Research 7(No. 1):2–6.

Menzel, Herbert, and Elihu Katz.
1955–56 "Social relations and innovation in the medical profession: The epidemiology of a new drug." Public Opinion Quarterly 19:337–352.

Metheringham, Richard A.
1964 "Measuring the net cumulative coverage of a print campaign." Journal of Advertising Research 4(No. 4):23–28.

Moran, W. T.
1951 "Measuring exposure to advertisements." Journal of Applied Psychology 35:72–77.

Moreno, Jacob L.
1953 Who Shall Survive. New York: Beacon House.

Moreno, Jacob L., and Helen H. Jennings.
1960 The Sociometry Reader. New York: Free Press of Glencoe.

Mulder, M.
1960 "Communication structure, decision structure, and group performance." Sociometry 23:1–14.

Nafziger, R. O.; M. MacLean, Jr.; and W. Engstrom.
1951 "Who reads what in newspapers?" International Journal of Opinion and Attitude Research 5:519–540.

Oxbridge.
1964– Standard Periodical Directory. New York: Oxbridge Publishing Company. Annual.

Politz, Alfred.
1950 A Study of the Accumulative Audience of Life. New York: Time, Inc.
1953 A Study of Four Media: Their Accumulative and Repeat Audiences. New York: Time, Inc.
1956 A 12-Month Study of Better Homes and Gardens Readers. Des Moines: Meredith Publishing Company.
1964 Reach and Frequency. New York: Cowles Magazines and Broadcasting, Inc.
1965 A Study of Advertising Effects in "Modern Medicine." New York: Alfred Politz Research: Politz Media Service.
1966 Audiences of Twelve Magazines. New York: Alfred Politz Research: Politz Media Service.

Pool, Ithiel de Sola.
1969 Final Report: Research Program on Problems of International Communication and Security. Cambridge, Massachusetts: Center for International Studies, Massachusetts Institute of Technology (September).
1970 The Prestige Press. Cambridge, Massachusetts: M.I.T. Press.

Pool, Ithiel de Sola, and Allan Kessler.
1965 "The Kaiser, the Tsar, and the computer: Information processing in a crisis." American Behavioral Scientist 8:31–38.

Pool, Ithiel de Sola; John Kramer; and Herbert Selesnick.
1966 "Who is listening: Evaluating audiences." Pp. 43–49 in Proceedings of the American Statistical Association, 1965 Business and Economic Statistics Section. Washington, D.C.: American Statistical Association.

Pool, Ithiel de Sola, and Irwin Shulman.
1959 "Newsmen's fantasies, audiences, and newswriting." Public Opinion Quarterly 23:145–158.

Rapoport, Anatol.
1953 "Spread of information through a population with sociostructural bias." Bulletin of Mathematical Biophysics 15:523–533, 535–543.
1963 "Mathematical models of social interaction," in R. D. Luce, R. R. Bush, and E. Galanter (eds.), Handbook of Mathematical Psychology. Volume 2. New York: Wiley.

Rapoport, Anatol, and W. J. Horvath.
1961 "A study of a large sociogram." Behavioral Science 6:279–291.

Read, W. H.
1962 "Upward communication in industrial hierarchies." Human Relations 15:3–16.

Redfield, Charles E.
1953 Communication in Management. Second Edition. Chicago: University of Chicago Press.

Rees, Matilda B., and William J. Paisley.
1967 Social and Psychological Predictors of Information Seeking and Media Use. Stanford, California: Stanford University Institute of Communication Research.

Roethlisberger, Fritz J., and W. J. Dickson.
1939 Management and the Worker. Cambridge, Massachusetts: Harvard University Press.

Rogers, Everett M.
1962 Diffusion of Innovations. New York: Free Press of Glencoe.
Rogers, Everett; Joseph R. Ascroft; and Niels G. Roling.
1970 Diffusion of Innovations in Brazil, Nigeria, and India. East Lansing: Department of Communications, Michigan State University.
Rogers, Everett, and F. Floyd Shoemaker.
1970 Communication of Innovations: A Cross Cultural Approach. New York: Free Press.
Rogers, Everett, and Lynne Suenning.
1969 Modernization Among Peasants: The Impact of Communication. New York: Holt, Rinehart and Winston.
Rosen, Sidney, and Abraham Tesser.
1970 "On reluctance to communicate undesirable information: The MUM effect." Sociometry 33:253–263.
Rummel, Rudolph J.
1965 "A social field theory of foreign conflict behavior." Papers IV, Cracow Conference, Peace Research Society.
1969 "Some empirical findings on nations and their behavior." World Politics 21:226–241.
Russett, Bruce M.
1963 Community and Contention: Britain and America in the Twentieth Century. Cambridge, Massachusetts: M.I.T. Press.
Schreiber, Robert J.
1968 "Probability assignments for the simulation of media reach and frequency." Journal of Advertising Research 8(No. 2):3–8.
1969 "The Metheringham method for media mix: An evaluation." Journal of Advertising Research 9(No. 2): 54–56.
Schyberger, B. W.
1963 "The accumulative and repeat audiences of Swedish weekly magazines." Journal of Advertising Research 3(No. 4):25–33.
1965 Methods of Readership Research. Lund, Sweden: CWK Gleerup.
Selesnick, Herbert.
1970 "Diffusion of crisis information: A computer simulation of Soviet mass media exposure during the Cuban missile crisis and the aftermath of President Kennedy's assassination." Ph.D. dissertation, Massachusetts Institute of Technology.
Shannon, Claude, and Warren Weaver.
1949 Mathematical Theory of Communication. Urbana: University of Illinois Press.
Shaw, Marvin E.; Gerard H. Rothchild; and John F. Strickland.
1957 "Decision processes in communication nets." Journal of Abnormal and Social Psychology 54:323–330.
Shibutani, Tamotsu.
1966 Improvised News: A Sociological Study of Rumor. Indianapolis: Bobbs-Merrill.
Simmons, W. R.
1958 Profile of the Millions. Second Edition. New York: New York Daily News.
1966 Mass Markets and the Media Reaching Them—1966 Magazine Reach and Frequency Reports. New York: W. R. Simmons.
1967 An Examination of Alternative Methods of Estimating Media Reach and Frequency. New York: W. R. Simmons.
1969 1969 Magazine Audience Report. New York: W. R. Simmons.
Simon, Herbert A.
1954 Centralization vs. Decentralization in Organizing the Controller's Department. New York: Controllership Foundation.
Simon, Herbert A.; Donald W. Smithburg; and Victor A. Thompson.
1950 Public Administration. New York: Knopf.
Sports Illustrated.
1958 Families Who Subscribe to Sports Illustrated. New York: Time, Inc.
Starbuck, William H.
1965 "Mathematics and organization theory." Pp. 335–386 in James G. March (ed.), Handbook of Organizations. Chicago: Rand McNally.
Starch, Daniel.
1966 Measuring Advertising Readership and Results. New York: McGraw-Hill.
Sutton, Harold, and Lyman W. Porter.
1968 "A study of the grapevine in a governmental organization." Personnel Psychology 21:223–230.

Swanson, C. E.
1955 "What they read in 130 daily newspapers." Journalism Quarterly 32: 411–421.
1967 "Frequency structure of television and magazines." Journal of Advertising Research 7(No. 2):8–14.

Swanson, Guy E.
1956 "Agitation through the press: A study of the personalities of publicists." Public Opinion Quarterly 20:441–456.

Taylor, Michael.
1968 "Toward a mathematical theory of influence and attitude change." Human Relations 21:121–139.

Teune, Henry and Sig Synnestvedt.
1970 "Measuring international alignment," in Julian R. Friedman, Christopher Bladen, and Steven Rosen, Alliances in International Politics. Boston: Allyn and Bacon.

Travers, Jeffrey, and Stanley Milgram.
1969 "An experimental study of the small world problem." Sociometry 32:425–443.

Troldahl, Verling C., and Robert L. Jones.
1965 "Predictor of newspaper advertisement readership." Journal of Advertising Research 5(No. 1):23–27.

UNESCO.
1964 World Communications: Press, Radio, Television, Film. Fourth Edition. New York: UNESCO Publications Center.

United Nations.
1949– Statistical Yearbook, 1948–. New York: United Nations. Annual.

Vaughan, H. R. (ed.).
1968 Overseas Newspapers and Periodicals Guide Book. Volume 1: Markets in Europe; Volume 2: Markets Outside Europe. London: Publishing and Distributing Company.

Wells, William D.
1969 "The rise and fall of television program types." Journal of Advertising Research 9(No. 3):21–27.

Willing.
1874– Willing's Press Guide. London: James Willing, Ltd. Annual.

Yamanka, J.
1962 "Prediction of ad readership scores." Journal of Advertising Research 2(No. 1):18–23.

Zajonc, R. B.
1962 "Effect of feedback and probability of group success on individual and group performance." Human Relations 15:149–161.

Zajonc, R. B., and D. M. Wolfe.
1963 Cognitive Consequences of a Person's Position in a Formal Organization. Technical Report No. 23. Ann Arbor: Institute of Social Research, University of Michigan.

Zielske, H. A.
1959 "The remembering and forgetting of advertising." Journal of Marketing 23:239–243.

Zimmerman, Claire, and Raymond A. Bauer.
1956 "Effect of an audience upon what is remembered." Public Opinion Quarterly 20:238–248.

CHAPTER 2 Some Problems of Meaning in Natural Languages

HERBERT RUBENSTEIN
Lehigh University

Three general topics relating to lexical semantics are treated: the nature of meaning; how the meaning of a word is to be represented; and the measurement of semantic similarity. The orientation is psychological and linguistic rather than philosophical. Thus, after a brief sketch of philosophical views of meaning, a psychological model of entries in the internal lexicon is presented. With regard to the representation of meaning, the current linguistic trend toward componential analysis is discussed and various procedures for obtaining semantic components are described. The problem of measuring the degree of similarity of meaning between words is treated both for judgmental data from scaling, sorting, and substitution as well as for data not obtained from conscious judgments.

Attempting to discuss all the various aspects of meaning in language often ends up as quixotic and unprofitable an activity as most attempts to discuss the question, "What is life?" With this caution in mind, I have focused on just a few of the many problems in natural-language semantics. (By *natural*, I mean a language like English rather than a mathematical or programming language.)

The orientation of this chapter is primarily linguistic and psycholinguistic. Thus most of the favorite problems of philosophers will be omitted. Philosophical problems are taken up in Ogden and Richards (1945), Wittgenstein (1953), Quine (1960), Ziff (1960), Austin (1965), and Katz (1966). I would especially recommend Alston's (1964) little book as an introduction to the philosopher's view of meaning in language.

Space limitations forced me to bypass certain problems although they are indeed appropriate to the psycholinguistic or linguistic view: meaning change (Ullman, 1957; 1962; Stern, 1964; Deese, 1967); grammatical meaning (Fries 1954; Ja-

---

The work on this chapter was supported by ARPA Project SD-187 while the author was a research fellow at the Center for Cognitive Studies, Harvard University; and later by NSF-GN-668 of the Center for the Information Sciences, Lehihg University.

kobson, 1959; Raun, 1959); vocabulary and world view, i.e., the Whorfian Hypothesis (Whorf, 1941; Brown & Lenneberg, 1954; Lantz & Stefflre, 1964); semantic universals (Ullman, 1966; Weinreich, 1966a). Furthermore, this chapter will consider only communal, denotative meaning of the sort found in dictionaries rather than the connotative or idiosyncratic variety often studied by investigators using the semantic differential (Osgood, Suci, & Tannenbaum 1957; Weinreich, 1958; Osgood, 1959; 1964).

Many of the above questions are treated in a very useful compendium edited by Steinberg and Jakobovits (1971).

Now that I have indicated those problems that will not be discussed, we can consider what will be discussed. Three questions will be taken up:

1. What is meant by "the meaning of an expression"?
2. How should the meaning of an expression be represented?
3. How is similarity of meaning measured?

Discussion of the first question will permit us not only to present some of the traditional views of the nature of meaning but also to introduce a cognitive view of meaning that equates the meaning of a word with the information we have stored in our long-term memory. In answering the second question, we get into the problem of semantic features, i.e., components of meaning and how these may be obtained. The third question permits a review of the considerable work already done on techniques for measuring semantic similarity.

THE MEANING OF MEANING

There is no doubt that we all have some intuitive grasp of what is meant by "the meaning of an expression," despite the difficulty that thinkers have had over the past two and a half millennia trying to find a definition. (For a sampling of different views of meaning, see Abraham, 1936.) The awareness of meaning as an independent entity is forced on us by one of the chief semantic characteristics of all natural languages; namely, *the imperfection of the relationship between form and meaning.*

In every natural language there are instances where two or more expressions have the same meaning (synonymy) or where a single expression has two or more meanings (homonymy).[1] Synonymy, although it may require an arbitrary decision on the part of the speaker about which of two equivalent expressions to use, is, by and large, a clearly useful device. It enables the speaker to respond to the question "What do you mean?" with a restatement of his original intent in other words. Homonymy, on the other hand, is a dubious economy resulting from the inherent instability of natural language.

Given the fact that we use language in the infinite variety of contexts of the real world, it is hardly surprising that we often use an expression to describe a situation which is radically different from situations that elicited the expression previously. So we have, in effect, made a homonym of the expression, since it now has two meanings. Homonymy often comes about as a result of change in the material culture. In such instances the development of the new meaning may be quite rapid, as Deese (1967) points out in the case of *compact*, meaning 'small car.' Homonymy may also result from borrowings or from a sound change that eliminates the phonemic

[1] A distinction is often made between polysemy and homonymy, depending on the degree of difference between the meanings of the expression. Polysemy refers to those instances where the connection between the meanings is readily apparent, while homonymy refers to the opposite variety of instances. Weinreich (1966b:143) defines homonyms as expressions that share no semantic features. The term *homonymy* will be used in this chapter to refer to all instances of multiple meaning regardless of the degree of difference between the meanings.

differences between two words; e.g., Old English *melu* 'flour' and *mǣl* 'repast' both became *meal*.

The use of a homonym in a sentence does not, of course, automatically make the sentence ambiguous, i.e., interpretable in more than one way. Most sentences contain homonyms, but ambiguity is eliminated by the meanings of the other words in the sentence or by the setting in which the sentence occurs. The importance of homonymy lies in its effect on the structure of the language, since the language must provide the regularities from which the user develops the rules to select the appropriate meaning. After all, we must have some way of knowing that *about* in *He sold about ten houses* means 'approximately' and not 'concerning.'

Ambiguity, however, is often used intentionally as a literary device (Empson, 1955). Ambiguity based on homonymy is also fundamental to most of our verbal humor. An interesting difference between puns and riddles, it seems to me, is that in the pun the joker wants his victim to be aware of the ambiguity (both meanings should be relevant): *The baker was well-bred but crusty and just rolling in dough*; while in the riddle the joker attempts to mislead the victim into thinking the expression is unambiguous and points him toward the inappropriate interpretation: *What has four wheels and flies*? This would not be a riddle, of course, if the question were really made unambiguous: *What has four wheels and has flies*?

Theories of Meaning

Granted that we have some intuitive grasp of what meaning is in general, how has it been more formally defined? There are two general theories of meaning, which have been developed primarily by philosophers: (1) the referential theory of meaning and (2) the ideational theory of meaning. The former is often called the theory of reference and the latter, the theory of meaning.

Referential Theory

The referential theory identifies the meaning of an expression with the object to which it refers (i.e., its referent) or holds that meaning is the *relation* between the expression and its referent. Consequently, expressions that have the same referent must have the same meaning. However, beginning with Frege in the nineteenth century, philosophers have pointed out the weakness of this view. Frege (1949) noted that *morning star* and *evening star* both refer to the planet Venus and yet have different meanings. Or, it may be pointed out that expressions such as *the boy who cut down the cherry tree and admitted it*, *the personal aide-de-camp to General Braddock during the French and Indian War*, and *the first president of the United States* all have the same referent—George Washington—but different meanings.

Proponents of referential theories may counter: True, all of these expressions refer to the person, George Washington—but at different times during his life. But is the referent really the same for all these expressions? If it is maintained that it is the same, would it also be maintained that *tadpole* and *frog* have the same referent?

Another argument against equating sameness of referent with sameness of meaning is drawn from consideration of the pronouns. The pronoun *I* has many different referents but, it is argued, has only one meaning, namely, 'the speaker.' Similarly, the adverbial pronoun *there* has many referents but only one meaning, something like 'in a place other than the one in which the utterance is made.' Furthermore, a theory of meaning must account not only for the meaning of isolated words but also for the semantic interpretation of sentences. It is difficult to see how a referential theory could yield representations of word meanings that would enable us to obtain an interpretation of even so simple a sentence as *I will go tomorrow if I can*.

Ideational Theory

The classic exposition of the ideational theory of meaning is given by the eighteenth-century English philosopher, John Locke: "The use, then, of words is to be sensible marks of ideas; and the ideas they stand for are their proper and immediate signification" (Alston, 1964:22). This view is given short shrift by Alston, who supposes that it implies that the idea of an expression must be in the speaker's consciousness—and in the listener's, too—if the communication was successful.

Alston's criticism is countered by Katz, who proposes a variety of ideational theory that "takes meanings to be representations of classes of equivalent thoughts or ideas, which thoughts and ideas are connected with linguistic constructions in the speaker's system of internalized rules" (Katz, 1966:177). Katz maintains that the ideational theory of meaning does not, in fact, require that ideas be present in the language-user's consciousness or even retrievable for introspective examination. Such ideas are unobservable in the same way that certain entities and processes about which physicists talk are unobservable. The empirical content of theories involving such unobservables, according to Katz, is ultimately established by how well such theories predict the behavior of observables. Katz's semantic theory will be discussed in some detail later in this chapter.

Psychological Theories

We now consider some psychological views of meaning: first, the behavioral theories and, then, a cognitive theory. Behavioral theories of meaning bring into consideration the response that the expression evokes in the listener. Bloomfield (1933:139, 141), one of the founders of American structural linguistics, who was strongly influenced by the behaviorist A. P. Weiss, took the meaning of an expression to consist of not only the response that it evoked in the listener but also the situational factors that prompted the speaker to utter it.

Since the same expression may evoke different responses on different occasions, the philosopher Charles Morris (1946) has proposed that meaning be equated not with the actual overt response but with the *disposition* to respond in a certain way. Charles Osgood (1966) relates meaning to the notion of the mediating response. Osgood claims that the internal response to an expression is some part of the response originally made to the referent of the expression and that this internal or mediating response is, in fact, the meaning of the expression.[2]

A more cognitive theory of meaning currently in circulation finds its basis in a particular view of the internal lexicon. Many psycholinguists today believe that the main tools of the language-user consist of an internal lexicon, which is part of the long-term memory, and rules, which enable the user to employ the information in his lexicon to understand and compose sentences. The lexicon contains not only phonemic and orthographic representations of words but also phrases and even longer units that have been "chunked" (Miller, 1956).

Together with these representations of an expression are two kinds of information:

[2] Fodor (1965) has challenged the scientific value of the concept of the mediating response. He points out that since it must be postulated that each mediating response can be part of one and only one total response (the set of responses to the stimulus object), there is a one-to-one correspondence between mediating response and total response, thus the concept of the mediating response plays no useful role. While one may take issue with the application of this kind of logical demonstration in an area where it is still unclear what the variables mean, it is difficult to see how the mediation theory or any stimulus-response theory can account for the meaning of sentences in view of our ability to compose and understand sentences we have not heard before.

a pool of perceptual information and a pool of conceptual information. The perceptual information consists of memories of percepts produced through our senses by the objects to which the expression has been applied, e.g., visual and auditory memories and, in some cases where the object involved body movement, a kinesthetic memory of what the muscular activity felt like. The conceptual pool of information might well be what Katz (1966) has described as the "lexical entry," consisting of (1) the syntactic category of the expression, (noun, verb, etc.); (2) a series of semantic markers, i.e., features of meaning such as physical, animate, natural, human, etc., that an expression shares with other expressions; (3) a semantic distinguisher, i.e., those semantic features more or less unique to the meaning of the given expression; and (4) selection restrictions, the conditions under which the expression may be used meaningfully in an utterance.

Not all words, of course, would be equally rich in both sensory and conceptual information. We would expect abstract words, for example, to be poorer in sensory information than words referring to concrete objects.

The representations of the expression, the perceptual information, and the conceptual information are all bonded together as a triad so that, starting from any one, the other two may be retrieved. If I see a chair, I may retrieve the word *chair* and as much conceptual information (artifact, furniture, etc.) about that chair or chairs in general as I choose. If I see or hear the word *cabbage*, I may retrieve visual and olfactory memories of *cabbage* as well as conceptual information (plant, growing on the ground, edible) and so on.

We may also start from the conceptual information of a definition and try to retrieve the word (Brown & McNeill,1966). Not only are the parts of such a triad bonded but, as experimental data on word association imply, bonds connect one triad with another. (A simpler, primarily associative model of the internal lexicon is given by Quillian, 1966.) An account of some of the experimental investigations of the internal lexicon is given in Rubenstein (n.d.).

The triadic theory of the internal lexicon presented here suggests, then, that *the meaning of an expression is all the information in memory that is bonded to the representation of that expression.* This is the *total* meaning of the expression.

The *communal* meaning is the portion of this total meaning that the language-user shares with the rest of his linguistic community. It is reasonable to believe that the normal language-user can distinguish the communal portion of the total from the idiosyncratic. Indeed the inability to make this distinction is often the clearest indication of psychological abnormality (see Laffal, 1965, especially chapter 6).

The triadic theory of meaning is very rich in its inclusiveness (opponents of the theory may, of course, prefer to characterize it as "unparsimonious" rather than "rich"). The bond between the representation and the pool of perceptual information takes in, it seems to me, the referential theory of meaning, while the bond between the representation and the pool of conceptual information takes in the ideational theory of meaning.

Having considered the nature of linguistic meaning—very briefly to be sure—we now turn our attention to the representation of meaning.

REPRESENTATION OF MEANING

Lexicographers have been representing the meanings of words in their dictionaries for centuries by synonyms; by phrases describing the form, composition, or function of the referent; and/or by naming the class of objects to which the referent belongs. These definitions are generally adequate for the purpose for which one resorts to a dictionary. However, it is obvious that such definitions are not in themselves useful representations for the semantic study of language.

What would constitute a useful representation of the meaning of an expression can, of course, be decided only after the goals of semantics have been set. However, it is difficult to conceive of a semantic theory that would be unconcerned with commonalities of meaning; that is, we would certainly expect that a semantic theory would require explicit representation of those features of meaning that an expression has in common with other expressions. One does not have to be a semanticist to observe that it is frequently the case that some features of the meaning of a word are shared by the meanings of many other words. For example: *man*, *boy*, *ram*, *buck*, *bull* all share the feature 'male creature' in some of their meanings at least; *boat*, *car*, *train*, *plane* share the feature 'vehicle'; *speak*, *tell*, *write*, *report* share the feature 'communication activity.'

Componential Analysis

The analysis of meaning into features is usually termed *componential analysis*. Linguists and anthropologists have done componential analysis for some years, using purely distributional rather than statistical methods. In linguistics, componential analysis has been applied to the study of grammatical meaning by Jakobson (1936), Harris (1948), and Lotz (1949) among others. Anthropologists have made even more frequent use of componential analysis in the description of kinship terminology and pronoun systems. See Wallace and Atkins (1960) for a review of the literature, and Romney and D'Andrade (1964) and E. A. Hammel (1965) for the more recent approaches.

Both the linguistic and anthropological applications of componential analysis were greatly facilitated by the fact that the objects of study formed a relatively small, closed set. The application of componential analysis to the total lexicon of a language poses far greater problems. The vast number of items to be analyzed makes systematic procedures for discovering semantic features a must.

The multiplicity of features that would result from this analysis forces us toward economy in our description. Hence, we are faced with a series of difficult questions: What is constant in the meaning of an expression? What criteria are to be used in deciding into how many features a given meaning is to be decomposed? Are the features of a particular meaning merely concatenated, i.e., joined by *and*, or are they to be related by a more elaborate syntax? Questions of this sort can be answered only if we have some notion of what we want to do with our semantic analysis. Fortunately, the general lines of a natural-language semantic theory have been worked out by Katz (1966; 1967) and his collaborators (Katz & Fodor, 1963; Katz & Postal, 1964).

Katz's Semantic Theory

The basic assumptions of the theory are these: First, the meaning of a sentence is derived from the meanings of the constituent phrases, which in turn are derived from the meanings of the words that compose them. Second, a word has a finite number of meanings, each of which is decomposable into a set of semantic features. Third, these semantic features are, for the most part, binary valued. Only their presence or absence is relevant—they do not vary in strength.

In providing a semantic interpretation of a sentence, the theory is supposed to do what the language-user is competent to do, namely, to detect the following:

1. When a sentence is anomalous, that is, has no immediately meaningful interpretation; e.g., *He smells itchy.*
2. When a sentence is ambiguous; e.g., *The sap is running.*
3. When two sentences are synonymous; e.g., *John bought the book from Mary; Mary sold the book to John.*
4. When a sentence is analytic, synthetic, or contradictory. A sentence is analytic if its truth is completely evident from the meaning of the sentence;

e.g., *Bachelors are unmarried.* A sentence is synthetic if an evaluation of its truth requires a comparison of the meaning of the sentence with empirical information; e.g., *Lincoln freed the slaves.* A sentence is contradictory if the meaning of the predicate is the negative of the meaning of the subject; e.g., *Spinsters are married.*[3]

To achieve these goals, the theory calls for a *lexicon* in which the structure of each meaning is fully described—these descriptions are called readings—and a set of *projection rules* that prescribe the way in which readings are to be combined to yield a semantic interpretation of the sentence.

Lexical Readings

The entries in the lexicon are, of course, different from the entries in ordinary dictionaries; for example:

Colorful$_1$—Adjective—(Evaluative) [Having distinctive character, vividness, or picturesqueness] ⟨(Aesthetic Object) or (Social Activity)⟩.

Ball$_1$—Noun—(Physical Object) [Having globular shape] ⟨SR⟩

A distinction is made in these lexical readings—which are not complete—between semantic features that occur in the meanings of other words and those that are peculiar to a particular meaning. The systematic features, which Katz calls *semantic markers*, are enclosed in parentheses in the readings. The nonsystematic features, shown in brackets, are called *distinguishers*.

In addition to semantic markers and distinguishers, the lexical reading contains *selection restrictions*, enclosed within angles, which give the conditions under which the given lexical reading may combine with another meaningfully. More specifically, the selection restrictions are the semantic markers present in all lexical readings with which the given lexical reading may combine. *Colorful*$_1$ 'picturesque' could not describe *ball*$_1$ 'sphere for throwing,' since this meaning of *ball* has neither the marker (Aesthetic Object) nor (Social Activity) in its reading. Consider, however, the reading for *colorful*$_2$ 'brightly colored':

Colorful$_2$—Adjective—(Color) [Abounding in contrast or variety of bright colors] ⟨(Physical Object) or (Social Activity)⟩

This reading is obviously combinable with the reading of *ball*$_1$, since the semantic marker (Physical Object) in its reading satisfies the selection restrictions of *colorful*$_2$.

Projection Rules

Projection rules vary according to the syntactic relation existing between the readings to be combined. Thus there are different rules to be applied to different relations such as modification, subject-predicate, verb-object. When an adjective modifies a noun, for example, the derived reading (the result of combining readings) is the Boolean union of the markers and distinguishers of the adjective and noun

---

[3] Abraham and Kiefer (1966), who propose a theory quite similar to Katz's, suggest some additional goals: (1) Grouping of semantically similar, but not synonymous, sentences; e.g., (*a*) *The boy is eating a delicious apple.* (*b*) *The boy is eating a good apple.* (*c*) *Yesterday Father came home late.* (*d*) *Yesterday Father came home early.* Sentence *a* should be grouped with *b*, and *c* with *d*. (2) Determining limits of deviation from syntactic and semantic well-formedness beyond which a sentence cannot be understood. (3) Semantic interpretation of a string of sentences forming a discourse. Thus semantic analysis should show that the continuity of the discourse is broken if the order of the following sentences is reversed: *Yesterday Peter saw a film he had never seen before. The film was about a famous actress.*

The semantic theory developed by Katz and Fodor has been critically examined ever since its original publication in 1963. Interesting criticisms are found in Bolinger (1965), Sparck Jones (1965), Weinreich (1966b), Bar-Hillel (1967), Wilson (1967), and Bierwisch (1969).

plus the selection restrictions of the noun alone. For example:

Colorful$_2$ ball$_1$—Noun Concrete—((Physical Object), (Color)) [[Abounding in contrast or variety of bright colors] [Having globular shape]] ⟨SR of ball$_1$⟩

With regard to projection rules for subject-predicate and verb-object relations, Katz (1967) has advanced the notion that the lexical reading of a verb consists of complex semantic markers containing dummy symbols to indicate where the readings for the subject and object are to be inserted. Thus he gives the following reading for the verb *chase* 'hurry after':

((Activity of *X*) (*Nature*: (Physical)) (Motion) (*Rate*: (Fast)) (*Character*: (Following *Y*)) (*Intention*: (Trying to catch ((*Y*) (Motion))))) ⟨SR⟩

X and *Y* indicate the positions for inserting the subject and object readings respectively. (Activity) indicates that *chase* belongs to the set of activity verbs like *eat*, *speak*, *walk* as distinguished from state verbs like *sleep*, *wait*, *suffer*, *believe* and process verbs like *grow*, *freeze*, *dress*, *dry*. (*Nature*: (Physical)) indicates that *chasing* is a physical activity as opposed, say, to *remembering*, which is a mental activity. (Motion) indicates *chasing* is an activity over distance, which the marker (*Rate*: (Fast)) indicates is carried on rapidly. (*Character*: (Following Y)) indicates *chase* includes the concept of *pursuit* as distinguished from other verbs of rapid motion like *flee*. The fact that *Y* is bracketed together with (Motion) indicates that the object of *chase* is someone or something that is in the act of moving over distance.

For two sentences to be shown to be synonymous in a particular interpretation, they would have to have the same reading. Katz (1967) has sketched out the solution for this pair of synonymous sentences:

1. John sold the book to Mary.
2. Mary bought the book from John.

He rejected the syntactic solution, i.e., to demonstrate that both sentences have the same underlying phrase marker, since this would involve arbitrary selection of one of the two sentences as the base form. Instead, he devised a single reading for both verbs that expresses the following concepts: (*a*) who owned the object at the earlier time t_1; (*b*) who owned the object at the later time t_2; (*c*) who had possession of the money at t_1; and (*d*) who had possession of the money at t_2. Thus the semantic content of both sentences is expressed by the following single reading (the italicized words would be replaced by their readings in the completed description):

((*Condition*: (Ownership of (*the book*)) of (*John*) at t_1)→(*Condition*: (Ownership of (*the book*)) of (*Mary*) at t_2)) and ((*Condition*: (Possession of sum of money) of (*Mary*) at t_1)→(*Condition*: (Possession of sum of money) of (*John*) at t_2)).

Markers and Distinguishers

Let us consider the nature of markers and distinguishers in greater detail. The semantic markers, as opposed to the distinguishers, are the elements in terms that describe the *systematic* aspects of the semantics of a language. Markers are much freer of constraints in their occurrence than are the distinguishers, which are actually dependent on the occurrence of a particular marker or set of markers.

A particular distinguisher may occur in the readings of several lexical items, for example, *red*, *reddish*, *redden*. Let us say the distinguisher is [like blood], but it will always accompany a particular marker, (color) in this case. Both the marker and the distinguisher, however, may serve as the minimal difference between readings. For a marker to be the sole source of difference between readings, the readings would, of course, have to have identical distinguishers.

The most obvious situation in which this could happen would be in the case of words that are built on the same root morpheme; e.g., the readings for *red* and *reddish* may turn out to differ only in that the latter has the marker (somewhat).

The distinguisher sometimes acts as the sole difference in the case of meanings that belong to what we recognize as the same general semantic category; that is, meanings characterized by the same set of markers. For example, (color) *red* differs from (color) *green* in the opposition of the distinguishers [like blood], [like grass]. Katz has characterized the distinguisher thus:

> Distinguishers can be regarded as providing a purely denotative distinction which plays the semantic role of separating lexical items that would otherwise be fully synonymous, such as, for instance, 'red,' 'yellow,' 'blue,' 'green,' etc. Unlike semantic markers which represent conceptual components of senses of lexical items and expressions, distinguishers mark purely perceptual distinctions among the referents of conceptually identical senses (Katz, 1967: 159).

To relate this to the triadic view of meaning described earlier, Katz's characterization of the distinguisher strongly suggests that the semantic distinguisher is a symbolic summary of the information in the pool of perceptual information that is *not* conceptualized by the semantic markers. When new semantic markers come into the language, it seems likely that they would be extracted from the distinguishers.

Semantic features (markers, distinguishers, etc.) are theoretical objects, metalinguistic terms, and we should not be too concerned about how we label them with ordinary words. For example, there is little point in arguing whether the distinguisher for *red* should be [like blood] or [like a ripe tomato]. But it is important that we use the same label in *red*, *reddish*, and *redden*; that is, we should be consistent in giving the same label to the various occurrences of the same feature.

While the notion of decomposing meaning into features seems intuitively reasonable, no universal method of accomplishing this has been devised. Approaches to the study of semantic features may be roughly classed as psychological or linguistic. These names are not particularly illuminating, but the two approaches are fairly distinguishable. In the psychological approach, the data consist of the responses of a group of subjects to some aspect of words or phrases that bears on their meaning. The data are statistically treated, e.g., factor analyzed, to obtain semantic features (see Fillenbaum & Rapoport, 1971). The linguistic approach is more of an armchair procedure, especially if the investigator acts as his own informant. In this approach the analysis is performed on the definitions or distributions of the linguistic expressions and is nonstatistical.

The difference between psychological and linguistic approaches will become clearer as we consider particular examples.

Psychological Investigation of Semantic Features

Deese (1965) had subjects associate to the word *butterfly*. He then took the eighteen most frequently occurring associates and had subjects associate to each of these. This yielded a matrix having rows and columns labeled with the same words that showed the frequency with which each word elicited each of the other words as an associate.

The analysis yielded clusters of words characterized by features that we might call 'animate' (*bees*, *fly*, *bug*, *wing*, etc.), 'animate, flight' (*wing*, *bird*, *bees*, *fly*), 'animate, relating to lepidoptera' (*bug*, *insect*, *cocoon*, *moth*, *butterfly*), 'inanimate' (*sky*, *yellow*, *spring*, etc.), 'inanimate, having to do with flowers' (*summer*, *sunshine*, *garden*, *flower*, *spring*), 'inanimate, color' (*blue*, *sky*, *yellow*, *color*). Of course the names I have given to the features here are not meant to be taken seriously, since each cluster contains so few words.

There is, perhaps, an even more basic

reason for not taking these semantic features seriously, and that is Miller's (1967: 55) criticism of word association as a tool for semantic investigation: we cannot be sure to what meaning of the stimulus the subject is associating. Were the subjects in Deese's study associating *fly* with 'a kind of insect' or with 'to move through the air'? *spring* with 'a season of the year' or 'a source of water'?

In this same paper, Miller (1967: 60–63) describes a sorting experiment and cluster analysis that may be useful for discovering semantic features. The subject is given a pack of file cards on each of which is printed a different word, along with a definition of one of its meanings and a sentence exemplifying its use in this meaning. The subject is asked to sort the cards into piles on the basis of similarity of meaning. He is allowed to form as many piles as he wants. A cluster-analysis procedure developed by S. C. Johnson (1967) is then applied to these sorting data.

Figure 1 shows the results of a cluster analysis of sorting data on forty-eight nouns. We see, for example, that forty-eight out of fifty subjects thought that *plant* and *tree* should be classed together, while forty-two subjects thought that *root* should also be classed with them. The analysis yields five independent trees, which Miller has labeled intuitively (terms in parentheses) according to what appeared to him to be the most specific semantic feature common to the words included in that tree.

In contrast to the investigations discussed above, which dealt with single words, Levelt's (1967) research dealt with phrases. His data consisted of judgments about the acceptability of adjective-noun phrases like *lazy girl* as meaningful. There were thirty adjectives (e.g., *firm*, *acute*, *sudden*, *vague*) and forty emotive nouns (e.g., *pain*, *anger*, *glee*), thus twelve-hundred phrases on which Levelt obtained judgments (from one subject in this introductory study). The following features of the phrases emerged from the factor analysis: 'pleasantness,' 'activity,' 'control,' 'overt/covert,' 'onto/from ego.' Two additional features were found which differentiate mainly among adjectives: 'future/past' and 'supra/subordinate.' Obviously, this kind of study can be extended to other phrases: verb-adverb, verb-noun subject; verb-noun object, verb-preposition-noun; etc.

Linguistic Investigation of Semantic Features

One of the basic linguistic criteria for deciding what classes of words or other language segments should be set up is similarity of distribution. That is, we say that if word *A* can occur in context *C* but word *B* cannot, then *A* and *B* have different distributions and thus may be assigned to different classes. This criterion can be used for semantic, as well as syntactic, classification.

Bierwisch (1967), investigating antonym pairs of spatial adjectives in German, used this criterion to distinguish *lang* 'long', *breit* 'wide,' *hoch* 'high,' etc., from their respective polar opposites *kurz* 'short,' *schmal* 'narrow,' *niedrig* 'low.' The former set can occur in the context "*x* times as——as," while the latter set does not normally. Thus one can say *Der Tisch ist doppelt so lang wie die Bank* 'The table is twice as long as the bench'; but the sentence **Der Tisch ist halb so kurz wie die Bank* 'The table is half as short as the bench' would be quite odd. From this distributional difference Bierwisch constructed a semantic feature of polarity.

Not every distributional difference is taken to yield a semantic feature. Bierwisch also pointed out that one can say *Der Zug ist 10 Wagen lang* 'The train is 10 cars long' and *Der Fluss ist 250 Meters breit* 'The river is 250 meters wide,' but not the corresponding sentences with *kurz* 'short' and *schmal* 'narrow.' Since it is precisely those adjectives that have the feature (+Polarity) that can occur with measure phrases, there is no reason to set up another feature corresponding to this distributional characteristic.

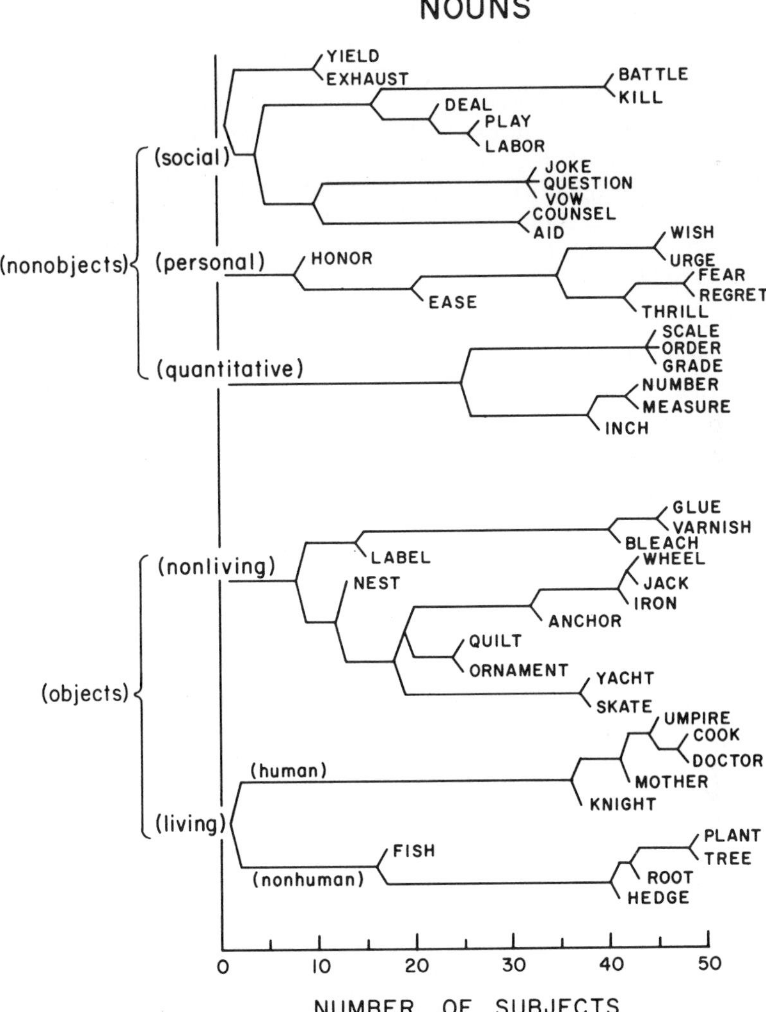

Figure 1. Results of a cluster analysis of forty-eight nouns, with suggested names for the clusters indicated in parentheses (Miller, 1967:61).

Instead of comparing the distributions of words, one can discover semantic features by comparing their definitions. One method that has been employed is to compare definitions in hyponymic order. *A* is a hyponym of *B* if the meaning of *A* is included in the meaning of *B*. Thus Lehrer (1969), in her study of the semantics of cooking terms, took *cook* 'the application of heat which produces an irreversible change in the object (food) cooked' as the most general term. The four words *boil*, *fry*, *broil*, and *bake* were taken as the immediate hyponyms of *cook*. The definition of each of these requires some addition to the definition of *cook*. The word *boil* requires the specification 'with the use of nonfat liquid'; *fry* requires 'with the use of fat'; *broil*, 'with direct heat'; *bake* 'with dry indirect heat.'

These specifications suggest three semantic features: liquid, fat, and direct heat. Lehrer then came up with the following partial readings: *boil* (+liquid), (—fat); *fry* (−liquid), (+fat); *broil* (−liquid), (−fat), (+direct); *bake* (−liquid), (−fat), (−direct). Lehrer obtained additional features by comparing the meanings of hyponyms of these four words. For example, the difference between *boil* and *simmer* is expressed by the feature, vigorous action, while the difference between *simmer* and its hyponym *stew* is expressed by the feature, long cookingtime.

Miller (1972) employed a related approach in his analysis of English verbs of motion. Miller used the notion of an incomplete definition to delimit a set of semantically similar words. An incomplete definition of a word is a phrase that may substitute for the given word but has a more general meaning. The complete definition of the word thus stands in a hyponymous relation to its incomplete definition. Given a set of words covered by the same incomplete definition, the definition may be made more specific in such a way that various subsets are obtained. If a resultant subset contains more than one word, the added specification may correspond to a recurrent semantic feature.

Starting with the generic incomplete definition 'changes position or location' represented by the verb *moves* or *travels*, Miller delimits a set of about two hundred verbs of motion. By adding specifications to this definition, he isolates a number of semantic features; for example, permissive (*releases* 'allows to move'), propellant (*kicks* 'applies force to move'), directional (*penetrates* 'moves through'), medium (*soars* 'moves through the air'), change-of-motion (*arrives* 'finishes traveling').

There obviously must be some basis on which to decide whether an aspect of meaning that one is examining should be accorded the status of a semantic feature or whether it should be considered a part or variant of some other feature. Appeal to the notion of universality, i.e., asking whether the notion in question is a feature in any other language, may ultimately be rewarding. However, this is not too profitable a procedure now, considering the primitive state of semantic investigation even of the more intensively studied languages. For the time being we must justify feature status on the basis of independent function within the language being studied.

Both of the analytic approaches discussed above are concerned with the discovery of features that do have independent functions. In the distributional approach the aim is to find features of meaning that are useful in describing the restrictions on the occurrence of words in sentences. In the hyponymic approach, on the other hand, the aim is to find features that distinguish the meanings of the words constituting the vocabulary of the language. The two approaches are not to be understood as yielding mutually exclusive sets of features. The features that serve as selection restrictions on what words may occur in a given context are drawn from the set of features distinguishing the vocabulary items. Whether all semantic features that serve to distinguish vocabulary items also serve as selection restrictions, however, still awaits a convincing answer.

Rubenstein (1965; 1968) sketched a procedure for discovering semantic features that was distributional in approach but with some special properties of its own. The procedure is based on the assumption that words that select the same member of a homonym set must share some semantic feature or features. (A homonym set is a group of words having different meanings but sounding the same, e.g., *flee* and *flea*, *yard* 'unit of measure' and 'enclosure.') This common semantic feature obviously cannot be shared by any word that selects a different member of the homonym set.

Rubenstein's homonymic procedure is illustrated below, using three of the meanings of *running*:

1. A corpus of simple sentences of the form *The X is (are) running* is generated for the meanings $running_1$ 'move rapidly on legs,' $running_2$ 'migrating in large schools,' and $running_3$ 'secreting fluid.' The sentences are divided into sets according to the meaning of *running*:

   Set 1. The man (mouse, beetle) is $running_1$.
   Set 2. The smelt (salmon, tuna) are $running_2$.
   Set 3. The sore (eye, nose) is $running_3$.

2. The potential semantic features (PSF) of the selector in each sentence (the word on whose meaning the meaning of the homonym depends) are noted:

   Set 1:
   man (physical object, natural, animate, person, male, adult, biped)
   mouse (physical object, natural, animate, animal, mammal, quadruped)
   beetle (physical object, natural, animate, animal, insect, having six legs)
   Set 2:
   smelt (physical object, natural, animate, animal, fish, Osmeridae)
   salmon (physical object, natural, animate, animal, fish, Salmonidae)
   tuna (physical object, natural, animate, animal, fish, Thunninae)
   Set 3:
   sore (physical object, natural, inanimate, moist external body part, acquired, pathological condition)
   eye (physical object, natural, inanimate, moist external body part, congenital, visual organ)
   nose (physical object, natural, inanimate, moist external body part, congenital, olfactory organ)

3. Any PSF common to selectors belonging to different sentence sets are eliminated. In our sample, this step removes the following PSFs: (physical object, natural) found in all three sets and (animate, animal) found in sets 1 and 2.
4. Any PSF not common to *all* the selectors belonging to a given set is eliminated. This restriction leaves the following semantic features to characterize the selectors:

   Set 1: (having legs)
   Set 2: (fish)
   Set 3: (moist external body part)

These features would also be included among the selection restrictions in the readings of each lexical entry of *run*. If all semantic features that should be recognized for an adequate analysis served as selection restrictions, the procedure outlined here might be sufficient; however, Katz (1967), in opposition to Weinreich (1966b), suggests there are features that never serve as selection restrictions. Presumably, these markers would play a role in the demonstration of paraphrase or analyticity, etc.

There are other techniques for discovering semantic features, however, that are not based on the study of restrictions of occurrence. One of the more promising techniques depends on the examination of analogies like *woman*: *baby*:: *mare*: *foal*:: *ewe*: *lamb*. From such an analogy we can derive the opposition *woman*, *mare*, *ewe* to *baby*, *foal*, *lamb*—i.e., (adult female) to (young offspring)—as well as the opposition *woman*, *baby* to *mare*, *foal* to *ewe*, *lamb*—i.e., (human) to (equine) to (sheep).

Whether (adult female) is to be considered one or two features depends on whether we can establish the independence of (adult) and (female). Such independence is shown by the existence of *woman* ((+adult), (+female)) as opposed to girl (+female) but with the feature (+adult) unspecified; i.e., neither (+adult) nor (−adult) is inherent in the meaning of *girl*.

Bendix (1966) describes a number of ways of using subjects to suggest and test differences in meaning about which the investigator has certain intuitions. For example, subjects are asked to paraphrase a sentence in which two semantically similar words are contrasted, *He didn't take it, he got it.* According to their responses, *take=get* + 'does something to cause getting.' Or subjects might be asked which makes more sense: *He's only given it to me and so it isn't mine* or *He's only lent it to me and so it isn't mine*; *He lost his watch but he knows where it is or and doesn't know where it is.*

We now turn to the last of our three problems: how is similarity of meaning measured?

MEASUREMENT OF SEMANTIC SIMILARITY

Of the three questions posed at the beginning of the chapter, the question of how to measure similarity of meaning between two expressions is the easiest to answer. It is clear that if a subject is asked which pair of words is closer in meaning: (*a*) *mountain - hill* or (*b*) *mountain - street*, he will reply *mountain - hill*, unless he is being completely obstructionist. There are two general approaches to the measurement of semantic similarity: the judgmental approach, in which the subject makes a conscious judgment; and the analytic approach, in which the investigator analyzes utterances that are not judgments. Let us first consider the judgmental methods, of which there are three: scaling, sorting, and substituting.

JUDGMENTAL METHODS

Scaling

A number of studies have been published in which subjects scaled the degree of similarity of meaning existing between two words (Haagen, 1949; Melton & Safier, 1951; Flavell, 1961; Rubenstein & Goodenough, 1965). People do exhibit a high degree of agreement both with each other and with themselves.

Haagen found the correlation of $r=0.92$ between two groups of subjects judging the semantic similarity of pairs of adjectives. Haagen's materials consisted of eighty sets of five adjective pairs, so designed that one adjective recurred in each of the five pairs. Subjects made their judgments of similarity of meaning on a seven-point scale on which 0.5 represented the maximum similarity and 6.5, the minimum similarity. For example: *sacred-holy*, 0.9; *sacred-hallowed*, 1.5; *sacred-divine*, 1.6; *sacred-revered*, 2.1; *sacred-taboo*, 5.6. Rubenstein and Goodenough also obtained a very high correlation between groups of subjects ($r=0.99$) and a reasonably high correlation between test and retest using the same subjects ($r=0.85$). In this experiment, subjects had to judge the similarity of meaning of sixty-five pairs of nouns on a scale from 0.00 (minimum similarity) to 4.00 (maximum similarity).

Some of the resultant similarity judgments were:

cord	smile	0.02
cushion	jewel	0.45
forest	graveyard	1.00
hill	woodland	1.48
magician	oracle	1.82
sage	wizard	2.46
brother	monk	2.74
asylum	madhouse	3.04
serf	slave	3.46
midday	noon	3.94

If one considers these pairs closely, it is apparent that two kinds of judgments are involved in some pairs and only one kind in others. In pairs where each word has only one meaning, e.g., *hill-woodland*, there is only the comparison of these two meanings. In most pairs, however, at least one of the words has more than one meaning. Judging the degree of semantic similarity in such cases involves not only a comparison of those meanings that are most alike in the two words but also consideration of the relative frequency with which the meanings of greatest similarity occur.

For example, although *brother* 'member

of a men's religious order who is not preparing for, or is not yet ready for, holy orders' is quite similar to *monk* 'one of a company of men vowed to separation from the world, etc.,' the judgment of semantic similarity between *brother* and *monk* is certainly influenced by the fact that the meaning of *brother* given above is far less common than the meaning 'male sibling,' which has little in common with the meaning of *monk*. This confusion of decision processes due to the use of homonyms is found in all the scaling studies referred to above (the same defect occurs in many kinds of word studies, especially in free-association experiments) but can be eliminated by defining and/or exemplifying the particular meaning of the homonym to be considered.

In general, the scale judgments in the studies cited are intuitively satisfying. They seem to be closely related to the number of shared semantic features, although a finding reported by Flavell (1961) seems to suggest that, in some instances, subjects may be scaling on the basis of substitutability rather than semantic similarity. Flavell's finding was that antonyms like *beggar-millionaire*, *sickness-health*, etc., which share all but one or two of their semantic features, are judged to be less similar in meaning than semantically unrelated pairs like *flower-mallet*, *hungry-round*.

Sorting

In a sorting method such as the one employed by Miller (1967), which we described earlier in this chapter, the subject is required to group those words together that he considers most alike in meaning. The sorting data allow the investigator to make a matrix, with the test words used as labels for both rows and columns. For each of the $\frac{1}{2}(N^2-N)$ possible different word pairs, where N = the number of test words, a figure is obtained representing the number of subjects who put both words into one sorting category. This figure is probably a good indicator of the degree of similarity of meaning, although it has not been tested against other measures of semantic similarity.

Substitution

Since the most obvious operational definition of a pair of synonyms would hinge on their mutual substitutability in the various contexts in which they occur, it is most natural to look to substitutability as a measure of semantic similarity. But when we say one word is substitutable for another, we must say that this substitution may be carried out without changing something—the meaning and style of the sentence, the meaning alone, the truth value, the meaningfulness, or the grammatical structure. Clearly, preserving the meaning and style imposes a much tighter condition on substitution than preserving the grammatical structure.

Eye-doctor and *ophthalmologist* are interchangeable in almost all sentences without change in meaning (other than those that refer back to the word itself: *Eye-doctor* begins with the letter *e*). Yet the substitution of the more colloquial *eye-doctors* for *ophthalmologists* in the sentence *The medical convention program was made up of papers by laryngologists, rhinologists, aurists, and ophthalmologists* would be stylistically jarring.

Because of the difficulty in defining acceptable substitution, substitutability judgments have rarely been used as an index of semantic similarity. There is, however, an unpublished study carried out by John B. Goodenough in 1964, which used some of the materials of the Rubenstein and Goodenough (1965) study. In the latter study, subjects wrote 100 sentences (2 sentences per subject) for each noun used in the sixty-five paired meaning comparisons.

Goodenough limited himself to thirty of these pairs; his selections ranged from the highly synonymous *gem-jewel*, to the semantically related *crane-rooster*, to the unrelated *cord-smile*. Serving as his own subject, Goodenough went through the

200 sentences of each pair, say, the *crane-rooster* pair, and tried substituting *rooster* for *crane* in the 100 sentences in which *crane* originally occurred and substituting *crane* for *rooster* in the 100 sentences in which *rooster* originally occurred. Obviously, there are different degrees to which one word will fit in the other's slot and, in most instances, substitution changes the meaning of the sentence.

Goodenough distinguished five kinds of substitution effects: (1) The meaning does not change: *The gem* (for *jewel*) *lay on the sidewalk unnoticed by the crowds.* (2) The meaning changes, but the sentence is still sensible and stylistically acceptable: *The bird* (for *crane*) *was huge in size, but the man handled it easily.* (3) The meaning changes, and the sentence would make sense only in some unusual context: *The crane* (for *rooster*) *is a fine animal which awakens one at sunrise.* (4) The sentence becomes nonsense: *He was a notorious gangster who disguised himself as an asylum* (for *monk*) *to avoid the police.* (5) The sentence remains meaningful but becomes false: *Going without fruit* (for *food*) *for a great length of time causes starvation.*

Goodenough accepted only the first two kinds of effects as instances of substitutability. He computed the mutual substitutability of words *A* and *B* as the mean of the proportion of sentences in which *B* could substitute for *A* and the proportion of sentences in which *A* could substitute for *B*. Plotting these mutual substitutability scores for the thirty pairs of words against their judged degrees of semantic similarity as determined by Rubenstein and Goodenough (1965) yielded a fairly linear relationship with $r = 0.88$.

Miller (1967:57–58) describes an interesting substitution procedure employed by Volney Stefflre. Stefflre had subjects write sentences for a number of words and then suggest substitutes for these words in the sentences they generated. He then constructed a matrix of all these words and contexts (a context was a sentence minus the word for which it was written) and had subjects judge in which of the total set of contexts each word could be inserted to yield a plausible sentence. He was able, then, to measure the semantic similarity between any of the words by computing the intersection-union ratio from the set of contexts in which they were acceptable, and to measure the semantic similarity between contexts by computing this ratio from the words that they accepted.

As was mentioned above, there are methods of measuring semantic similarity that are not based on the statistical analysis of judgments. Such methods infer the degree of semantic similarity between two words (1) from the similarity of the verbal contexts in which they occur, (2) from the similarity of the associations they evoke, (3) from the ease with which a response that is conditioned to one word is generalized to the other, or (4) from their thesaurus classifications.

Analytical Methods

Verbal Context

Before attempting to infer the degree of semantic similarity between two expressions from the amount of contextual similarity, one must define the context that will be considered relevant. Suppose you want to measure the similarity between the contexts in which *A* occurs and the contexts in which *B* occurs. Suppose your corpus consists of 100 sentences in which *A* occurs and 100 sentences in which *B* occurs. You could say, "By relevant context, I mean all the words in the sentence other than *A* or *B*." You might then compile a list of all the words in the *A* sentences and a list of all the words in the *B* sentences and calculate the proportion of words found in both lists. However, you might decide to include as relevant context only those words that stood in a certain positional relationship (e.g., the words directly preceding or directly following *A* or *B*) or only those words that stood in a certain syntactic or associative relationship to *A* or *B*.

Rubenstein and Goodenough (1965) tried these various ways of defining context and then measured the similarity between context sets for sixty-five pairs of nouns. Plotting similarity of context against judged similarity of meaning yielded nonlinear curves with positive slope. The results thus corroborated Harris' (1954) hypothesis: "If we consider words or morphemes *A* and *B* to be more different in meaning than *A* and *C*, then we will find that the contextual distributions of *A* and *B* are more different than the distributions of *A* and *C*." The slope obtained by Rubenstein and Goodenough was very slight, however, except for the higher values of judged similarity of meaning. The various definitions of relevant context primarily affected the slope at these higher values.

It is conceivable that similarity of verbal context might have provided a more sensitive measure of the lower and medium degrees of semantic similarity than is indicated by Rubenstein and Goodenough's results if higher orders of association—i.e., more indirect contextual similarities—had been taken into consideration. Some notion of higher orders of association might be gained from this example: Consider these four orders of association between *A* and *B* (two letters connected by a hyphen represents the occurrence of two words in the same sentence):

First	*A-B*
Second	*A-C-B*
Third	*A-C-D-B*
Fourth	*A-C-E-D-B*

First-order associations between highly synonymous words are rare, i.e., such words occur only very infrequently within the same sentence (see Lewis, Baxendale, & Bennett, 1967). Rubenstein and Goodenough only considered second-order associations, i.e., the frequency with which *A* and *C* occurred in the same sentences compared with *B* and *C*. To observe third-order relations, they would have had to study sentences in which *A* and *B* did not occur and see how many contained both a word *C*, which had occurred with *A* elsewhere, and also a word *D*, which had occurred with *B* elsewhere. For fourth-order associations, they would have had to calculate those instances when *E* occurred with *C* or *D*. A method for summing the various orders of association is described by Giuliano and Jones (1963), but no study relating such summed associative strength to synonymy has been carried out.

Association

The basic notion of association is that the degree to which two words, *A* and *B*, are semantically similar will be reflected in the number of words associated with *A* that are also associated with *B*. A number of investigators have developed measures for quantifying this overlap between two distributions of associates, and a useful summary of these measures has been compiled by Marshall and Cofer (1963).

In general, measures of overlap are various forms of the ratio of some measure of the intersection to some measure of the union of the two distributions. James Deese (1965) proposed the following measure of overlap: $S_A \cap S_B / \sqrt{N_A \cdot N_B}$, where $S_A \cap S_B$ is the number of responses that are common to the associations to word *A* and word *B*; N_A and N_B are the total number of responses made to *A* and *B*, respectively. The range of values for this metric runs from 0 to 1.

The data in Table 1, taken from a larger matrix presented by Deese, permit us to calculate the associative overlap between *moth* and each of the other words. There were fifty *S*s, each making one associative response to each stimulus. The column totals, however, came to one hundred responses each, since Deese follows Bousfield, Cohen, and Whitmarsh (1958) in assuming that each stimulus word in a free association task elicited not only the expressed response but also itself as an implicit response.

The intersection $S_A \cap S_B$ is obtained by (1) considering those instances where *A*

TABLE 1

FREQUENCIES OF ASSOCIATION

Responses	Stimulus Words						
	1. Moth	2. Inset	1. Moth ∩ 2. Insect	3. Wings	4. Fly	5. Summer	6. Butterfly
1. Moth	50	2	2	0	0	0	7
2. Insect	1	50	1	0	3	0	6
3. Wings	2	0	0	50	0	0	5
4. Fly	10	9	9	12	50	0	4
5. Summer	2	0	0	0	0	50	0
6. Butterfly	1	0	0	0	0	0	50

SOURCE: Adapted from Deese (1965:49).

and *B* have elicited the same association; (2) taking the lower frequency; (3) summing these frequencies. Thus we would calculate the intersection between *moth* and *insect* as follows: There are three associations common to both these words: *moth*, *insect*, and *fly*. The lower frequencies for each of these associations are 2, 1, and 9, respectively, so their intersection totals 12. Since $N=100$ for each stimulus, the denominator comes to $\sqrt{100 \cdot 100}=100$. Thus the associative overlap between *moth* and *insect*=0.12.

The overlap between *moth* and the other words in Table 1 is as follows: *moth-wings* =0.12, *moth-fly*=0.11, *moth-summer*= 0.02, *moth-butterfly*=0.15. If we accept associative overlap as an index of semantic similarity, these calculations quite reasonably imply that, semantically, *moth* is most similar to *butterfly*, is least similar to *summer*, and is intermediately similar to *insect*, *wings*, and *fly*.

Semantic Generalization

In the early thirties, Russian scientists observed that when they conditioned a response, e.g., salivation, to the presence of specific objects, the response was also elicited by the verbal label of the object (see Creelman, 1966). Razran in the United States carried on this research along more verbal lines.

In one study, Razran (1935) reported that the amount he salivated while subvocally pronouncing the word for 'saliva' in various languages varied as a function of his familiarity with the language. In another experiment, he found that subjects conditioned to salivate when viewing the words *style*, *urn*, *freeze*, and *surf* generalized this response more strongly to their synonyms *fashion*, *vase*, *chill*, and *wave* than to their homophones *stile*, *earn*, *frieze*, and *serf* (Razran, 1939).

Razran's findings suggest that the degree to which a conditioned response is generalized from one word to another might be a function of their semantic similarity. This was confirmed by Luria and Vinogradova (1959). These investigators found that children in whom a vascular reaction was conditioned to the word *cat* generalized this reaction to semantically related words, e.g., *kitten*, *mouse*, *animal*. Thus the degree of generalization might be used to measure degree of semantic similarity; but it has obvious weaknesses—awkwardness of the conditioning process, rapid extinction of conditioned response, and confusion of denotative and emotive factors in response to test words.

Thesaurus Information

If we had a dictionary in which each word meaning was described in terms of semantic features in the fashion of Katz's componential analysis, a comparison of the proportion of features that two entries shared would probably provide a useful index of their semantic similarity. Unfortunately, construction of such a dictionary is a matter for future research.

There is available, however, Roget's *Thesaurus* (1962), which can be used to obtain some notion of the efficiency of this approach.[4] Roget's work not only gives synonyms and antonyms for any word in which one is interested, but it also classifies each meaning of a word by hierarchically ordered dimensions—intuitively arrived at—so that, in effect, it provides a kind of componential analysis. Roget divides the English vocabulary into six main classes: abstract relations, space, matter, intellect, volition, and affections. Each of these classes is subdivided several times. Thus Roget's analysis can be thought of as yielding six independent trees, each rooted in one of his major classes.

Unfortunately, the branches do not terminate in a single meaning but in a set of semantically related words. Nevertheless, Roget's analysis seemed promising enough to Rubenstein and Goodenough to compare the overlap between the Roget trees for pairs of words with their judged degree of semantic similarity. Since most of the words in the sixty-five pairs they tested had more than one meaning and each meaning had its own Roget tree, this investigation (unpublished) provided an opportunity to get some idea of whether or not the relative frequency with which a word occurred in its various meanings had an observable effect on judgments of semantic similarity. This is the question that was asked earlier in the chapter: Is the judgment of the semantic similarity between *brother* and *monk* affected by the fact that *brother* occurs relatively infrequently with the meaning 'member of church order'?

The correlation between the Roget overlap and the judged semantic similarity was calculated two ways: with and without weighting of the Roget trees according to the relative frequency of the meanings. The resulting coefficients, the weighted $r = 0.85$ exceeding the unweighted $r = 0.79$, support the view that when subjects judged the semantic similarity between word-pairs, one or both of which was a homograph, then judgments were apparently affected by the relative frequency of the meanings of the homograph.

CONCLUSION

We have briefly considered three problem areas in semantics: the nature of meaning, the representation of meaning, and the measurement of semantic similarity. Of these, the problem of how to represent the meaning of an expression seems to me to be the most critical for the future progress of semantic research. We require dictionaries in which meanings are represented in a consistent and psychologically relevant fashion.

The requirements of consistency and psychological relevance or psychological reality are not totally independent, of course—even a trained analyst could hardly be consistent in his semantic representations if they did not correspond at least partially to his intuitions. Dictionaries with semantic representations meeting these criteria would greatly facilitate the study of semantic universals, changes in meanings, the relation between lexicon and perception, the measurement of semantic similarity, content analysis—in short, almost all aspects of the semantics of natural languages.

---

[4] Hallig and von Wartburg (1952) is useful for French semantics.

REFERENCES

Abraham, L.
1936 "What is the theory of meaning about?" The Monist 46:228–256.

Abraham, Samuel, and Ferenc Kiefer.
1966 A Theory of Structural Semantics. The Hague: Mouton.

Alston, W. P.
1964 Philosophy of Language. Englewood Cliffs, New Jersey: Prentice-Hall.

Austin, J. L.
1965 How To Do Things With Words. Edited by J. O. Urmson. New York: Oxford University Press.

Bar-Hillel, Y.
1967 "Dictionaries and meaning rules." Foundations of Language 3:409–414.

Bendix, E. H.
1966 "Componential analysis of general vocabulary: The semantic structure of a set of verbs in English, Hindi, and Japanese." International Journal of American Linguistics 32(No. 2, Part 2): Publication No. 41.

Bierwisch, Manfred.
1967 "Some semantic universals of German adjectivals." Foundations of Language 3:1–36.
1969 "On certain problems of semantic representations." Foundations of Language 5:153–183.

Bloomfield, Leonard.
1933 Language. New York: Holt.

Bolinger, Dwight.
1965 "The atomization of meaning." Language 41:555–573.

Bousfield, W. A.; B. H. Cohen; and G. A. Whitmarsh.
1958 Verbal Generalization: A Theoretical Rationale and an Experimental Technique. Technical Report No. 23. Storrs: University of Connecticut.

Brown, Roger, and E. H. Lenneberg.
1954 "A study in language and cognition." Journal of Abnormal Social Psychology 49:454–462.

Brown, Roger, and David McNeill.
1966 "The 'tip of the tongue' phenomenon." Journal of Verbal Learning and Verbal Behavior 5:325–337.

Creelman, M. B.
1966 The Experimental Investigation of Meaning. New York: Springer.

Deese, James E.
1965 The Structure of Associations in Language and Thought. Baltimore: John Hopkins University Press.
1967 "Meaning and change of meaning." American Psychologist 22:641–651.

Empson, William.
1955 Seven Types of Ambiguity. New York: Meridian (Noonday Press).

Flavell, J. H.
1961 "Meaning and meaning similarity: II. The semantic differential and co-occurrence as predictors of judged similarity in meaning." Journal of General Psychology 64:321–335.

Fillenbaum, Samuel, and Amnon Rapoport.
1971 Structures in the Subjective Lexicon. New York: Academic Press.

Fodor, J. A.
1965 "Could meaning be an r_m?" Journal of Verbal Learning and Verbal Behavior 4:73–81.

Frege, Gottlob.
1949 "On sense and nominatum." Translated by Herbert Feigl from "Über Sinn und Bedeutung." Zeitschrift für Philosophie und philosophische Kritik (1892). Pp. 85–102 in Herbert Feigl and W. S. Sellars (eds.), Readings in Philosophical Analysis. New York: Appleton-Century-Crofts.

Fries, C. C.
1954 "Meaning and linguistic analysis." Language 30:57–68.

Giuliano, V. E., and P. E. Jones.
1963 "Linear associative information retrieval." Pp. 30–46 in P. W. Howerton and D. C. Weeks (eds.), The Augmentation of Man's Intellect by Machine: Vistas in Information Handling. Volume 1. Washington, D.C.: Spartan Books.

Haagen, C. W.
1949 "Synonymity, vividness, familiarity and association value ratings of 400 pairs of common adjectives." Journal of Psychology 27:453–463.

Hallig, R., and W. von Wartburg.
1952 Begriffssystem als Grundlage für die Lexikographie. Versuch eines Ordnungsschemas. Abhandlungen der deutschen Akademie der Wissenschaften zu Berlin, Klasse für Sprachen, Literatur und Kunst, Heft 4.

Hammel, E. A. (ed.).
1965 Formal Semantic Analysis. American Anthropologist 67(No. 5, Part 2).

Harris, Z. S.
1948 "Componential analysis of the Hebrew paradigm." Language 24:87–91.
1954 "Distributional structure." Word 10:146–162.

Jakobson, Roman.
1936 "Beitrag zur allgemeinen Kasuslehre." Travaux du Cercle Linguistique de Prague 6:240–288.
1959 "Boas' view of grammatical meaning." American Anthropologist 61 (No. 5, Part 2):139–145.

Johnson, S. C.
1967 "Hierarchical clustering schemes." Psychometrika 32(No. 3):241–254.

Katz, J. J.
1966 The Philosophy of Language. New York: Harper and Row.
1967 "Recent issues in semantic theory." Foundations of Language 3(No. 2): 124–194.

Katz, J. J., and J. A. Fodor.
1963 "The structure of a semantic theory." Language 39:170–210.

Katz, J. J., and P. M. Postal.
1964 An Integrated Theory of Linguistic Descriptions. Cambridge, Massachusetts: M.I.T. Press.

Laffal, Julius.
1965 Pathological and Normal Language. New York: Atherton.

Lantz, D., and V. Stefflre.
1964 "Language and cognition revisited." Journal of Abnormal Social Psychology 69:472–481.

Lehrer, A.
1969 "Semantic cuisine." Journal of Linguistics 5:39–55.

Levelt, W. J. M.
1967 "Semantic features: A psychological model and its mathematical analysis." Urbana: University of Illinois, Center for Comparative Psycholinguistics. Mimeographed.

Lewis, P. A. W.; P. B. Baxendale; and J. L. Bennett.
1967 "Statistical discrimination of the synonymy/antonymy relationship between words." Journal of the Association for Computing Machinery 14:20–44.

Lotz, J.
1949 "The semantic analysis of the nominal bases in Hungarian." Travaux du Cercle Linguistique de Copenhague 5:185–197.

Luria, A. R., and O. S. Vinogradova.
1959 "An objective investigation of the dynamics of semantic systems." British Journal of Psychology 50: 89–105.

Marshall, G. R., and C. N. Cofer.
1963 "Associative indices as measures of word relatedness: A summary and comparison of ten methods." Journal of Verbal Learning and Verbal Behavior 1:408–421.

Melton, A. W., and D. E. Safier.
1951 "Meaningful similarity of pairs of two-syllable adjectives." Pp. 548–552 in S. S. Stevens (ed.), Handbook of Experimental Psychology. New York: Wiley.

Miller, G. A.
1956 "The magical number seven, plus or minus two: Some limits on our capacity for processing information." Psychological Review 63:81–97.
1967 "Psycholinguistic approaches to the study of communication." Pp. 22–73 in D. L. Arm (ed.), Journeys in Science. Albuquerque: University of New Mexico Press.
1972 "English verbs of motion: A case study in semantics and lexical memory." In A.W. Melton and E. Martin (eds.), Coding Processes in Human Memory. Washington, D. C.: V. H. Winston.

Morris, Charles W.
1964 Signs, Language, and Behavior. Englewood Cliffs, New Jersey: Prentice-Hall.

Ogden, C. K., and I. A. Richards.
1945 The Meaning of Meaning. Seventh Edition. New York: Harcourt Brace.

Osgood, C. E.
1959 "Semantic space revisited." Word 15:192–201.
1964 "Semantic differential technique in the comparative study of cultures." American Anthropologist 66(No. 3, Part 2):171–200.
1966 "Meaning cannot be r_m?" Journal of Verbal Learning and Verbal Behavior 5:402–407.

Osgood, C. E.; G. J. Suci; and P. H. Tannenbaum.
1957 The Measurement of Meaning. Urbana: University of Illinois Press.

Quillian, M. R.
1966 Semantic Memory. Scientific Report No. 5. Cambridge, Massachusetts: Bolt, Beranek and Newman.

Quine, W. V. O.
1960 Word and Object. Cambridge, Massachusetts: M.I.T. Press.

Raun, A.
1959 "Grammatical meaning," in Verba Docent: Juhlakirja L. Hakulinen 60 vuotispäiväksi 6.10.1959. Helsinki.

Razran, G. H. S.
1935 "Salivating and thinking in different languages." Journal of Psychology 1:145–151.
1939 "A quantitative study of meaning by a conditioned salivary technique (semantic conditioning)." Science 90:89–90.

Roget, P. M.
1962 Roget's International Thesaurus. Third Edition. New York: Thomas Y. Crowell.

Romney, K. A., and R. D'Andrade (eds.).
1964 "Cognitive aspects of English kin terms." American Anthropologist 66(No. 3, Part 2):146–170.

Rubenstein, Herbert.
1965 "Problems in automatic word disambiguation," in Harry H. Josselson (ed.), Proceedings of the Conference on Computer-related Semantic Analysis. Detroit: Wayne State University, Department of Slavic and Eastern Languages. Mimeographed.
1968 "Directions in semantic research" in A. W. Pratt, A. Hood Roberts, and K. Lewis (eds.), Seminar on Computational Linguistics. Public Health Service Publication No. 1716. Washington, D.C.: U.S. Government Printing Office.
n.d. "An overview of psycholinguistics." In T. A. Sebeok (ed.), Current Trends in Linguistics. Volume 12. New York: Humanities Press, forthcoming.

Rubenstein, Herbert, and J. B. Goodenough.
1965 "Contextual correlates of synonymy." Communications of the Association for Computing Machinery 8:627–633.

Sparck Jones, K.
1965 Semantic Markers. M.L. 181. Cambridge, England: Cambridge Language Research Unit.

Steinberg, D. D., and L. A. Jakobovits (eds.).
1971 Semantics: An Interdisciplinary Reader in Philosophy, Linguistics, and Psychology. New York: Cambridge University Press.

Stern, Gustaf.
1964 Meaning and Change of Meaning. Bloomington: Indiana University Press (reprint).

Ullman, Stephen.
1957 Principles of Semantics. New York: Barnes and Noble.
1962 Semantics, An Introduction to the Science of Meaning. Oxford, England: Blackwell.
1966 "Semantic universals." Pp. 217–262 in J. H. Greenberg (ed.), Universals of Language. Second Edition. Cambridge, Massachusetts: M.I.T. Press.

Wallace, A., and J. Atkins.
1960 "The meaning of kinship terms." American Anthropologist 62:58–80.

Weinreich, U.
1958 "Travels through semantic space." Word 14:346–366.
1966a "On the semantic structure of language." Pp. 142–216 in J. H. Greenberg (ed.), Universals of Language. Second Edition. Cambridge: M.I.T. Press.
1966b "Explorations in semantic theory." Pp. 395–520 in T. A. Sebeok (ed.), Current Trends in Linguistics. Volume III. The Hague: Mouton.

Whorf, B. L.
1941 "The relation of habitual thought and behavior to language." Pp. 75–93 in L. Spier, A. I. Hallowell, and S. S. Newman (eds.), Language, Culture, and Personality. Menasha, Wisconsin: Sapir Memorial Publication Fund.

Wilson, N. L.
1967 "Linguistical butter and philosophical parsnips." Journal of Philosophy 64:55–67.

Wittgenstein, L.
1953 Philosophical Investigations. Translation by G. E. M. Anscombe. New York: Macmillan.

Ziff, P.
1960 Semantic Analysis. Ithaca, New York: Cornell University Press.

CHAPTER 3 Sociolinguistics

ALLEN D. GRIMSHAW
Indiana University

Sociolinguistics (sometimes called the sociology of language) examines the interaction of language structure and speech performance with social interaction and social structure. This chapter examines the use of speech both as sociological data and as evidence for the several causal perspectives implied by juxtaposition of speech and other social events within social structures. Speech is used as a weapon in social conflict, as a mechanism of social control, as a vehicle for transmission of status claims, as a means of socialization, as a symbolic rallying point for group solidarity, even as a means of communication. These several functions are examined, using a variety of culture-specific and comparative lexical, phonological, and syntactic evidence. A brief postscript hints at the problematic character of speech as an obstacle in social research.

For without common language, it is hard to avoid the misfortune of Babel tower.

From a paper by a Korean graduate student, 1968.

INTRODUCTION

Ten years ago a handbook on communication would not have included a section on sociolinguistics. Fifteen years ago it is doubtful that many readers would even have heard the term. Although Hertzler sounded a call for work on the sociology of language in a pioneering paper presented at the 1952 meetings of the Midwest Sociological Society (Hertzler, 1953), sociolinguistics as an activity specifically directed to examining the interaction of language structure and social structure and the interimplications of speech behavior and social behavior has developed

I am deeply indebted to my colleagues on the Social Science Research Council Committee on Sociolinguistics, especially John J. Gumperz, Dell Hymes, and William Labov, who have given time beyond the proper demands of colleagueship in instructing a neophyte in radically new "thoughtways." I am also grateful to Irwin Deutscher for his encouragement and thoughtful skepticism and to my colleagues at Indiana University, Carl Voegelin, Wolfgang Wolck, and Owen Thomas, for professional stimulation and advice.

Some readers will note that there are few citations dating after 1967. This chapter was solicited and written in that year; the field of sociolinguistics has developed richly in the intervening period. In spite of the time gap, however, and in spite of the absence of references to some important new developments, I believe that the fundamentals of the argument and discussion in the chapter are sound. Time lag is, regretfully, a continuing hazard in the preparation of multi-authored handbooks and the problem of obsolescence will always be with us.

only since the early sixties. This is true even though sociologists have not ignored language as data. The contemporary phenomenon of "doing ethnomethodology," and the concerns central to the social psychologies of socialization and learning are all adumbrated in the work of early sociologists—Mead and Cooley, Bain and Bossard—and are continued into the present in the work of students of Park, Blumer, and Hughes.[1]

Within the last few years there has been a marked acceleration of activity and publication. The Social Science Research Council (SSRC) Committee on Sociolinguistics, established in 1963, has moved from early interests primarily in autonomous linguistics and, occasionally, in anthropological linguistics to an increasingly broad concern with the entire range of sociolinguistic phenomena.

During 1964 there were two major conferences on sociolinguistics: one, in May, was held at UCLA, with most of the participants being either linguists or anthropologists (see Bright, 1966); the other, sponsored by the SSRC Committee on Sociolinguistics, was held at Indiana University in conjunction with the Institute on Cultural Linguistics, and included several sociologists as participants. Although there were occasional problems in communication between linguists and sociologists, almost all of the participants were now clearly moving toward a focus on language structure *and* social structure (see Lieberson, ed., 1966). The SSRC committee has since sponsored two additional conferences, one in 1966 on language problems of developing nations (Fishman, Ferguson, & Das Gupta, 1968), and a second, in 1968, on pidgin and creole languages (Hymes, ed., 1971). Social scientists as well as linguists participated in both.

Sociolinguistic papers have been presented for many years at meetings of the American Anthropological Association and the American Ethnological Society; since 1966 there have been multiple sessions on sociolinguistics and related topics in ethnomethodology at the Annual Meeting of the American Sociological Association. Sociolinguistics, and the interesting new collateral activity known as "doing ethnomethodology," now seem to be as firmly established in sociology as anthropological linguistics is in anthropology. (For an interesting discussion of the "naming" of such activities as sociolinguistics, ethnolinguistics, anthropological linguistics, etc., see Hymes, 1966b; J. J. Gumperz, 1968.)

There are several standard collections of readings on sociolinguistics (see, especially, Hymes, ed., 1964; Fishman, ed., 1968; a number of symposia and collections of specially written papers (Gumperz & Hymes, 1964; 1972; Bright, 1966; Lieberson, ed., 1966); an excellent monograph focusing on microsociolinguistics (Ervin-Tripp, 1969); and a series of review articles in the *Biennial Review of Anthropology* (Lounsbury, 1959; 1961; and, especially, Bright, 1963; J. J. Gumperz, 1965; Durbin, 1968). Several other edited collections are widely cited in the sociolinguistic literature. Three of the most recent are those edited by Hymes (1971) on pidgin and creole languages; by Fishman, Ferguson, and Das Gupta (1968) on language problems of developing nations; and by Macnamara (1966) on problems of bilingualism.

Two volumes published early in the sixties—Ferguson and Gumperz's (1960) collection on linguistic diversity in South Asia and Rice's (1962) collection on the role of second languages—contain articles which have been of substantial influence in defining the field. Several of these sources

[1] Sociological readers of early drafts of this paper were quick to note the lapse of historical memory, which suggests that a concern with language is new for sociologists. It is interesting to note, however, that the several sociological commentators referred to different sets of historical forebears and to different sets of current activities as representing sociological concern with language. Historical concern there may very well have been; current interest, until very recently, has been meagre and unsystematic.

have bibliographies of considerable length and breadth; this bibliographic work has been supplemented by Pride's (1967) general overview in which he draws on citations from a number of writers in the field in order to delineate some principal problems and some critical contrasts in perspectives.

Sociolinguistic papers have only recently begun to be published in sociological journals; the bulk of such papers continue to appear primarily in linguistic, language, educational, and anthropological journals.[2] This is unfortunate, since it leaves many sociologists with the impression that *A Sociology of Language* (Hertzler, 1965) represents the extent of the potential contribution sociolinguistics can make to the two parent disciplines. That this is not so is attested to by scholars representing a wide range of sociolinguistic perspectives (Fishman, 1967b; Grimshaw, 1967; 1969b; J. J. Gumperz, 1967b; Hymes, 1967b) as well as by materials included in the remainder of this review chapter.

THEORETICAL APPROACHES

Social interaction is a reciprocal process involving communication, and most human communication requires the use of language. No two men use language in precisely the same way, and some men use language in ways obviously very different from those of other men. Thus, to state that language structure and social structure are intimately related is to reiterate a fundamental fact known to all men who participate in social interaction. It is difficult to think of a single social characteristic that is not related to differentiation in language use, although some—for example, nativity, regional provenience, class, and education—seem, at first glance, more important than others— for example, political party preference (at least between indifferent Republicans and indifferent Democrats, in some states), home ownership (but what of tax rates and crabgrass?), and marital status(although havingchildren may make a difference in some societies).[3]

There seem to be four principal perspectives on the causal relationship between social structure and language: (1) that which sees language as fundamental (or as source, cause, independent variable, or set of independent variables), a position that is at the same time congenial with interpretations of Whorf (1956; see also Fishman, 1960) and of Chomsky (1961; 1964; 1965; 1968; Chomsky & Halle, 1965); (2) that which sees social structure as determinant or as an independent variable or set of independent variables; (3) that which sees neither as prior to the other, both being seen as co-occurring and co-determining; and (4) that which sees both as determined by a third factor, whether that third factor be *Weltanschauung*, the human condition, the organization of the human mind (a position that, again, is congenial with

[2] The index of the *American Sociological Review*, Volumes 1–25, lists eight articles under the subject heading "language." It does not list the two papers on "talk" in family by Bossard (1945a; 1945b). In fact, no article on language has been listed since 1951 (see index to volumes 26–30). *Sociological Inquiry* and *Social Forces*, however, have both recently published sociolinguistics papers (Levine & Crockett, 1967; Wittermans, 1967, respectively). While there are some recent exceptions, sociolinguistics clearly has not been a flourishing specialty in sociology. There is now a new sociolinguistics journal, *Language and Society*, which began publication in 1972.

[3] While the emphasis in this chapter is on the interrelationships between linguistic and other social phenomena, it should be clear (as Labov notes in a personal communication) that there are elements of language structure that operate according to autonomously linguistic rules with no demonstratable influences on or from social structure and social interaction. This is true, for example, of the linguistic fact that certain consonants cannot follow one another serially without the intervention of vowel sounds. It is doubtful, however, whether there is any variety of social interaction that is not, in some way, conditioned by linguistic—or at least semiotic—constraints.

interpretations of Chomsky), or the intrinsic demands of an ordered universe. (This paradigm is adapted from that of Hymes, 1966a. Hymes uses the term *culture* rather than *social structure*. For present purposes, however, the meaning of the two terms is conceptually equivalent.)

Whether one starts with language or with social structure, there is evidence to support either of the first two perspectives. The fourth perspective, of whichever subvariety, would seem to be untestable, given the current and immediately prospective state of knowledge. It seems reasonable to conclude, therefore, that the first two perspectives represent incomplete examination of the evidence or unsatisfactory rigor in research design, and that findings gained from these two perspectives can probably be properly subsumed under the third perspective—that of co-determination or, as it is sometimes labeled, mutual embeddedness.[4]

Correlations between speech (as contrasted to language) and the characteristics of its users are easy to determine. Correlations between language structure and social structure are more subtle but can also be identified. As in all correlational analyses, however, the difficult problems begin when attempts are made to isolate the direction of cause and effect.

While Bright (1966: 11–15) has suggested that sociolinguistics is essentially a study of the covariation of aspects of social structure that have traditionally concerned sociologists and anthropologists and aspects of language structure that have traditionally been of interest primarily to linguists, it is questionable whether an interest in correlations alone can exhaust the explanatory richness to be found in the study of relationships between social structure and language structure. Several scholars—most noticeably J. J. Gumperz and Hymes—have taken the position that there is a far more fundamental embedding of the two structures in one another.

One purpose of this chapter is to review these two perspectives, namely, that which attempts to explain covariation in language structure and social structure from a corelational point of view, and that which looks at the two structures as being so inextricably interrelated that they require not separate but integrated study as a unitary phenomenon.

Correlational Analyses

The interrelationship between speech and other social behavior is an extremely complex one. The interrelationship between language structure and social structure may turn out to be even more complicated.

There are some instances in which the usefulness of language or speech as data is primarily as an indicator of individual social characteristics or of the characteristics of social structures. This is the case, for example, in the work of Bernstein (see references, especially, 1962b; 1964b; 1966), where class position is indicated by the use of elaborated or restricted codes (or formal or public languages). Another, more elegant, example is Labov's identification of both class position and aspiration for mobility through phonological analyses.[5]

[4] In a personal communication written in 1967, Lieberson warned against any view that sees language structure and social structure as being, in some instances, so interrelated as to be identical. Were this the case, he points out, there would be no research problem because, "if they are identical . . . there is no possibility of analyzing or decomposing them." There is, of course, the possibility that two structures can be "isomorphic" and that neither is understood. Equally likely, given the current state of liaison between sociology and linguistics, is the possibility that one structure has been "decomposed" but that students of the other discipline either do not know this or, if they do, fail to comprehend the implications for their own work.

[5] The work of Bernstein and Labov goes far beyond simple correlational analysis. Bernstein has attacked fundamental problems of learning and of social control; Labov has investigated learning and social change. Some of their work in these areas will be noted later in the chapter.

Analysis of this sort has its most obvious usefulness in helping us to locate individuals in the social structure; it does not automatically provide an explanation of why particular usages are associated with particular positions. In such instances, it can be said that language behavior *reflects* social structure. Aside from the work of social psychologists, particularly symbolic interactionists concerned with socialization and motivation, most sociologists who have used language as data have, until very recently, used it in this way.

There are other instances in which it may be said that social structure *determines* speech and/or language behavior. This has been neatly documented in studies by John Gumperz in which he has shown the intricacies of code shifting between standards and dialects that occur as social contexts and conversational topics change (see Blom & Gumperz, 1972:426ff.) Drawing on the work of Gumperz, Geertz, and others, I have indicated some of the complexities that are introduced by varying characteristics of actual participants, their audience, the location of the interaction (social as well as physical), the topic under discussion, and so forth (Grimshaw, 1966). At the level of speech communities and even nations, it can be shown that historical and structural features of societies are crucial in determining whether one or another language will become standardized, whether creoles or pidgins can move toward standardization, what are the likely outcomes of language conflict and of language planning, and so on.

While Goffman and, more recently, a growing number of ethnomethodologists have attended to situtions in which speech behavior, along with gesture and other communicative symbols, *defines* social structure, thereby constraining subsequent social interaction, this approach is, in spite of the early work of W. I. Thomas, a relatively new kind of activity in the field of sociology.

People frequently experience situations where they simply do not know what is going on and what expectations there may be for their behavior until conversation has been initiated. The topic of conversation chosen clearly is important in defining the situation. For example, the statement, "We were having an automobile discussion," was cited by Harvey Sacks in a lecture as a situation-defining comment. (See also Bossard, 1945a; 1945b.) Similarly, a new arrival at a social gathering can get many clues about patterns of interaction as he becomes aware of the topics each small group is discussing.

Sociologists have frequently neglected, however, the fact that how someone talks may be more important in defining a situation than what he talks about. Perhaps the most thoroughly documented and systematic instances of such definitions can be found in studies of pronominal usage and of honorifics. Everybody has experienced the shifting of gears that is necessary when external clues to social identity, such as dress and demeanor, are discovered to be incorrect identifiers: e.g., the high-ranking officer in a combat team, who is indistinguishable in dress and appearance from his men; the dirty college professor working in his yard who is addressed as if he were a servant; the teen-age daughter who is mistaken for her mother on the telephone.

Differences in usage are indicators here as well as in those cases where lexical and phonological selection tells us something about the location of individuals in the social structure. In this instance, however, they are indicators that are useful to participants in the interaction in defining the situation as well as to students who are collecting data.

Those few sociologists who have given any thought to the relationships between language structure and social structure have generally examined it from one of the several correlational perspectives suggested above. Each of these several perspectives interests itself in a part of what, collectively, would be an adequate and general view of the interrelation between language structure (and speech) on the one hand, and social structure (and social interaction) on the other.

Hymes (personal communication, 1967) has suggested that there is "a continuum of possible studies and interests, from the less language-involved to the more language-involved . . . from the more correlational to the more embedded." The kind of data used determines in large part where on the continuum a study will fall.

Integrative Analyses

Gumperz, Hymes, and Labov believe that representative samples of natural speech must be collected, and that with such samples of speech the researcher can move from gross identification of class correlates to apperception of situational-emotional interrelatedness (namely, embeddedness) of increasingly high degrees of predictability. Such students, who are working toward the generation of an integrated theory of sociolinguistic description, find the identification of simple co-occurrence relationships to be interesting and suggestive but, at the same time, to fall short of a goal of full utilization of sociolinguistic data. According to these scholars, there is a sense in which *the study of language is inseparable from the study of society* (Hymes, personal communication, 1967) or, as Gumperz (personal communication, 1967) phrased it, *linguistic interaction is social interaction.*

Such a view is in contrast to that of the Chomskians, who are presently interested in language structure as directly embedded in the fundamental character of the human mind in such a way as to exclude an interest in social life and social structure.[6] Chomsky believes that the structure of the mind constrains the number of possible ways in which humans may communicate and that there is, therefore, a bounded inventory of potential language behavior from which all actual languages draw.

Minimally, all human languages contain the nominative-predicative relationship. No natural language has been found that does not contain this relationship. It is equally true, of course, that no symbolic or logical system has been invented that does not contain this relationship. It would seem to be a moot question whether it is the mind of man or a fundamental logic of communication that limits certain fundamental sets of alternatives in language structure.

We do have data, however, which indicates that there are very close similarities between social structure and language structure. At the same time, while all societies seem to share certain institutions that are directed to meeting the needs of their members, it would seem that social structures vary too widely to be linked to any feature of the human psyche common to all mankind. If, because of some biological condition of man, all languages had certain fundamental characteristics in common, we should expect all social structures to also be the same (at least in equivalent "deep" social structures, which would be equivalent to the deep structure of language). We know, however, that man has met his social needs in a variety of ways

---

[6] Gumperz (personal communication, 1967) comments here: "In contrasting the sociolinguistic view with that of Chomsky you might note that the two don't necessarily conflict. They are complementary in the sense that they have different types of goals, deal with different kinds of data and use different types of field techniques. To be fair to Chomsky, you might point to his distinctions between languages and grammars. Grammars reflect competence and languages performance. All grammars are related in the sense that they share certain highly abstract rules but this is not necessarily true of languages. So far no one has attempted to draw a distinction similar to that between languages and grammars in the realm of social processes. Ethnomethodologists are making a beginning but it's not yet clear where they are going."

For a lucid and fairly nontechnical introduction to transformational grammar, the best source is probably Thomas (1965). Students with some background in linguistics and/or logic can begin directly with Chomsky (1965).

and that differences among social structures are not random.

It may be that there is no fundamental contradiction here and that, ultimately, we will learn that social structures and the ways in which they meet the needs of societal members are substantially less dissimilar than now seems to be the case. Until this has been demonstrated, however, sociologists cannot treat the differences among societies as being irrelevant nor can they treat differences in language use associated with differences in societies as being irrelevant. Moreover, it may very well be that the logic of communication does indeed limit the number of ways in which ideas can be communicated. An integrated theory of sociolinguistic description would attempt to indicate that the "selection" of one or another such alternative is neither predetermined by man's mental structure nor independent of similar "choices" that must be made in determining social structure in meeting social needs.

Uses of Language as Data

There is as yet no integrated theory of sociolinguistic description, although the scholars mentioned are working in that direction. Meanwhile, language as a source of data can be far more effectively utilized by social scientists. Adapting from Gumperz, we see that there are, again, two perspectives: the first sees language variously as an instrument in data collection or as an obstacle to data collection; the second emphasizes its use as data in a correlational examination of relationships between language structures and social structures.

The methodological or instrumental concern with language is primarily to increase the accuracy of language use in reporting aspects of social structure or individual motives or attitudes and secondarily to reduce the obfuscation and "noise" attendant upon working across languages. These are meaningful problems, and their solutions require sociolinguistic work. It should be noted, moreover, that the very difficulties attendant upon working across languages and in selecting adequate words for use in instruments indicate something about the cultures in which the student is working. If there is no way of saying "thank you" in Marathi, this says something about social structure in the area in which Marathi is spoken. (Grimshaw, 1969a).

Psycholinguistic topics are treated elsewhere in this volume; in the discussion that follows, the emphasis will be on the interaction of social structure and language structure as they mutually influence one another rather than on questions that are more generally considered to be sociopsychological, to wit, those having to do with socialization, motivation, and so on.[7] Thus, we are more interested in the consequences of bilingualism for social integration and in the development of social movements than we are with the immediate problems of interference in learning.

Broadly speaking—maybe too broadly—research on the covariation of language and social structure has focused on problems of social differentiation and social change. An interest in social and linguistic change leads one automatically to the study of languages in contact, of bilingualism, of language conflict, and of language planning (Grimshaw, 1969b). More recently, we have seen the appearance of studies that examine changes in language explicitly as a consequence of social changes. Contrasted to studies of change are studies more directly attending to relationships between language and social structure, with particular reference to social differentiation.

LANGUAGES IN CONTACT

During the early decades of the twentieth century, when millions of immigrants were coming to the United States, American sociologists had an opportunity to do

[7] For an analysis of these topics, a discussion of methods of data collection, and attention to more "micro" problems in sociolinguistics, see Ervin-Tripp (1969).

a vast amount of research on problems of language contact and its social consequences.[8] Studies of language loyalty and language maintenance, of bilingualism and multilingualism, of adoption of prestige standards—all could have been undertaken in one of the best "natural" laboratories that has ever been available.

Unfortunately, from the perspective of contemporary sociolinguists, sociologists studying the experience of these new Americans were interested almost exclusively in problems of "the assimilation of ethnic minorities." Similarly, linguists during the period were interested in historical linguistics and not in the variety of problems, particularly those related to interference, that have subsequently attracted the attention of Weinreich and other scholars.

When there was a concern with the language problems of immigrants, it was primarily a concern with language as a hindrance to assimilation, and sociologists directed their attention to such studies as that done by Thorsten Sellin (1938) for SSRC entitled *Culture Conflict and Crime*. There were a few studies of the foreign language press but, with the exception of Robert E. Park (1955), such studies were generally from a perspective that viewed the press as a hindrance to assimilation. Now that sociologists have become interested in language contact and linguists have provided students of language contact with far more sophisticated linguistic techniques, there are no longer large immigrant groups in the United States. With increasing frequency, scholars are looking elsewhere for the particular problems of bilingualism that are of interest to them.

Bilingualism

Einar Haugen (1966b; see also the other citations to Haugen), in a discussion directed largely to dialects and standards and their meaningfulness in the context of a nation, has made a distinction between the interests in language of linguists and of sociologists or sociolinguists. This distinction holds equally well for other areas of language contact. He writes:

> Our discussion has shown that there are two clearly distinct dimensions involved in the various uses of 'language' and 'dialect.' One of these is *structural*, that is, descriptive of the language itself; the other is *functional*, that is, descriptive of its social uses in communication. Since the study of linguistic structure is regarded by linguists as their central task, it remains for sociologists or, more specifically, sociolinguists, to devote themselves to the study of the functional problem (Haugen, 1966b:926).

Haugen continues by stating that the overriding consideration of those interested in structural use of language and dialect is the genetic relationship. This is in contrast to those concerned with the *functional* use of language and dialect, where the overriding consideration is the uses speakers make of the codes they master.[9] Haugen defines codification in a standard language as minimal variation in form; he defines elaboration as maximal variation in function.

The particular issues of interest in studying movement from dialects to standards, or the acceptance of one or another dialect as standard, or the creation or crystallization of new languages are: (1) selection of norm, (2) codification of form, (3) elaboration of function, and (4) acceptance by the community. Haugen states that the first two refer primarily to the form, the last

[8] Bilingualism has by no means disappeared in the United States; see Fishman (1964b; 1966a; 1966b) and the extensive corpus on ghetto dialects, especially the work of Labov cited in the references.

[9] Haugen's distinction between "structural" and "functional" is related to, but not synonymous with, other dichotomies: code structure–code use, language-speech, competence-performance. New in all these emphases is the attention not simply to a further facet of grammatical structures but to the functional problem itself—one which brings into view aspects of language and other social behavior that would otherwise be neglected.

two to the function of language. The interaction of the four, Haugen points out, form a matrix within which it is possible to discuss all the major problems of language and dialect in the life of a nation:

	Form	Function
Society	Selection	Acceptance
Language	Codification	Elaboration

This same organization is useful for discussion of most other problems of language contact, at least on the level that will be possible in this chapter.

Since its original publication in 1953, Uriel Weinreich's *Languages in Contact: Findings and Problems* (1964) has become the standard work in this area; Weinreich's premature death was a major loss to the developing field of sociolinguistics. As a linguist, Weinreich was primarily concerned with what Haugen refers to as the structural problem. However, Weinreich was among the pioneers in linguistics who became increasingly aware of what Weinreich called the psychological and sociocultural setting of language contact, and in *Languages in Contact* he specified a number of sociological questions that are of importance in language contact.

In discussing nonstructural factors, Weinreich distinguishes between those inherent in the bilingual person's relation to the languages he brings into contact—such as the generalized language facility of the individual, his relative proficiency in each language, and the manner of learning the languages—and his attitudes towards them. He continues, however, by noting that nonstructural factors are not restricted to bilinguals as individuals; rather, Weinreich notes, bilingualism is generally a group phenomenon. Thus, the size of the bilingual group and its sociocultural characteristics, the prevalence of bilinguals with different characteristics of speech, the generalized attitudes toward the languages, attitudes toward bilingualism specifically, tolerance about varying patterns of language use, and the relations between bilingual groups and the language communities are singled out as being important to the sociocultural study of bilingualism and language contact.

In a caveat to his linguistic colleagues who insisted on doing "pure" linguistics, Weinreich wrote: "The linguist who makes theories about language influence but neglects to account for the socio-cultural setting of the language contact, leaves his studies suspended, as it were, in mid air" (Weinreich, 1963:4).

The principal concerns of the linguist in examining language contact and its consequences are with a variety of types of interference: phonic, grammatical, and lexical. While these need not be discussed here, many nonlinguists will find Weinreich's examination of these types of interferences an interesting and useful introduction to some of the nonsocial aspects of linguistic studies.

Weinreich, in examining the problems of the bilingual individual, reviews psychological theories of bilingualism and discusses such characteristics as the aptitude and switching facility of the individual as well as the relative status of the languages involved for the speaker in terms of proficiency, motive use, characteristics of the situation in which learning took place, usefulness of the language in communication, and matters of emotional involvement. As Weinreich moves closer to an examination of what he has labeled sociocultural setting, he notes the importance of the speech situation itself as a source of interference for the individual speaker. If the bilingual speaker perceives one of his languages as being stigmatized, he may in certain situations shift to the other language, thus creating problems of interference. Again, situations of emotional stress may produce problems of interference, particularly when the use of one language has been associated with the management of certain social situations.

Weinreich notes that it is reasonable to expect that those sociocultural factors that determine personality traits, preferred language habits, and the structuring of speech situations will also be relevant to the control of interference. His concern is with interference.

In the process of examining possible sources of interference, Weinreich outlines the main topics of interest generally in the study of language structure and social structure. His discussion of the functions of language in bilingual groups anticipates some of the discussion in this chapter on the differentiation of language use. His discussion of parallels between group divisions and language divisions anticipates correlational studies between group and social characteristics and language and speech use. His discussion of the development and operation of language loyalty is relevant for a whole series of issues related to language conflict, language planning, and language conflict, language planning, and language maintenance. Finally, his brief discussion of the crystallization of new languages raises a series of interesting questions about the social structural features that are important in determining the acceptance or rejection of creoles, pidgins, and standards.

In addition to Weinreich's theoretical overview, there have been several other important publications in the areas of linguistic diversity and multilingualism in recent years (Ferguson & Gumperz, 1960; Rice, 1962; Macnamara, 1967a).[10] Aside from the works of Weinreich (1953; 1964) and, more recently, Hymes (1967a), few explicitly theoretical treatments of multiple code usage and diversity have been published, although there have been important theoretical considerations in the writings of Ervin-Tripp (1961), Friedrich (1962a), Mackey (1962), and Lambert (1967), for example. Ferguson (1962b; 1966), Stewart (1962a; 1962b), and Kloss (1966b) have attacked typological problems, and several authors have attempted to measure the extent of either linguistic diversity in territorial units (Greenberg, 1956; Lieberson, 1964; 1965; 1966; Hymes, 1968a) or code-switching facility and individual bilingualism (J. J. Gumperz, 1964a; 1964b; 1967a; 1968; 1969; Diebold, 1968). Other studies, such as that of Rubin (1962; 1963) on Guarani in Paraguay, have combined several of these perspectives. Banks and Textor (1963) used linguistic homogeneity as one of the raw characteristics in their cross-polity survey (see also Russett et al., 1964).

The great bulk of the psychological and social psychological literature on bilingualism (and bidialectism), however, has been devoted to two problems. The first of these is second-language learning (Ervin & Osgood, 1954; Lambert, Havelka, & Crosby, 1958; Gardner & Lambert, 1959; Center for Applied Linguistics, 1961; Ferguson, 1962a; 1962b; Lambert, Gardner, Barik, & Tunstall, 1963; Macnamara, 1966; 1967a; 1967b; Ervin-Tripp, 1967; Gaarder, 1967), a topic that has only recently received attention from sociologists (see, especially, Cicourel, 1970). The second problem, which has more obvious implications for traditional sociological concerns, involves considerations of differences in statuses of languages in problems of self-concept and in judgments of personality and status attributes (Bossard, 1954b; Pieris, 1951; Sawyer, 1959; Lambert, Hodgson, Gardner, & Fillenbaum, 1960; Anisfeld, Bogo, & Lambert, 1962; Anisfeld & Lambert, 1964; Lambert, Anisfeld, & Yeni-Komshian, 1965; Lambert, Frankel,

---

[10] Researches on bilingualism or multilingualism can be roughly dichotomized along two dimensions. The first of these distinguishes between a research focus on the individual as contrasted to one on groups or societies. The second distinguishes between situations in which there are standard languages in contact and those in which there is either a variety of dialects or both a standard language and one or more dialects. Ferguson (1964) has labeled this latter situation "diglossia." (See also Fishman, 1967a.)

& Tucker, 1966; Rona, 1966; Tucker & Lambert, 1967).

These studies have been concerned primarily with prestige factors associated with bilingualism.[11] To cite only one instance of the sociological relevance of this literature, Lambert's studies of attitudes related to language problems of bilinguals have shown that primary users of the lower-status standard language tend to denigrate the language and, in some instances, themselves; moreover, when such bilinguals listen to taped presentations (by identical speakers) in the two languages, they are likely to ascribe higher status and more positively valued personality characteristics to the "speakers" of the higher-status standard.

More specifically, sociological investigations into bilingualism or multilingualism, whether on the level of contacts between standards or on the level of diglossia, have focused on the problems of selection as presented in Haugen's matrix of language standardization. Gumperz and others working with the concept of linguistic repertoire and switching have attempted to isolate the characteristics of social setting in which one or another type of language will be used. This literature will be discussed when we examine structural constraints on language use. Such research is generally on a microsociological or group level.

Language Conflict

Contrasted to this is a larger literature that involves both social and political questions and examines such topics as language conflict, language planning, and language maintenance. These issues have to do with the displacement of languages by each other and with language dominance. Haugen (1966a) has shown the turmoil that accompanied the long struggle in Norway over the pattern of standardization to be followed in establishing a common language accepted by all citizens of that small country. In a country like India, where each of a dozen different languages is spoken by many millions of loyal adherents, the implications of dominance or subordination of one or another language has vast social and political implications.

Harrison (1960), in his thoughtful study *India: The Most Dangerous Decades*, showed how a host of political and power considerations have been superimposed on language nationalism, on concerns about the literary heritages of the many languages involved, and on simple needs for standard media of communication. After careful study of the centripetal potential and consequences of linguistic chauvinism in that troubled country, he concluded that India's experiment in democracy might well founder because of its inability to deal with its language problems. Other observers (Windmiller, 1954; Weinreich, 1957; Kelly, 1966; McCormack, 1967; Das Gupta, 1969) and subsequent events in India (viz., language rioting and governmental hesitance and inconsistency) have done little to encourage a more optimistic perspective.

Das Gupta and Gumperz (1968), however, have suggested on the basis of Indian data that language conflict is elite conflict and does not necessarily involve the interests of unmobilized populations. Moreover, language conflict—to the extent that it involves appeals for mass support—may in itself have the positive consequence of furthering the mobilization process. Das Gupta (1970) has also suggested that language associations frequently provide an institutional framework for the training of future political leaders (see also E. M. Gumperz, 1967).

In the initial chapter of his excellent and judicious study of the conflict in Norway, first between *riksmål* and *landsmål* and

[11] There is a separate and rich literature on prestige differentiation related to bidialectism (see, especially, McDavid, 1964; Labov, 1963b; 1964; 1966a; 1966b; 1966c); and also a smaller corpus of materials on the status aspects of creoles, e.g., Samarin (1966).

later between *bokmål* and *nynorsk*,[12] Einar Haugen (1966a) lists a litany of names of European nations that underwent bitter and protracted struggles over language. Those caught up in language conflicts beginning even before World War I include Norway, Greece, Belgium, Rumania, Hungary, Bulgaria, and Albania. Those nations confronted with such conflicts since World War I include Finland, Estonia, Latvia, Lithuania, Iceland, and the Irish Republic. As Haugen (1966a:7) puts it, "Each of these added its own language to the concert of Europe, or rather to its bedlam."

Some of these struggles have had to do with the search for a national identity; others have had even more profound consequences, as in the case of Turkey, where a shift of scripts generated a shift in national cultural orientation, with lasting consequences for the nation in its pattern of development. In the Norwegian case, Haugen shows how national sentiment, rural-urban schisms, political infighting, a scholarly concern for clarity in expression, and an occasional intellectual snobbery were intricately interrelated in the language struggle in Norway, beginning after the achievement of independence in 1814 and continuing up to the present.

In Norway, and in most other European countries, the language problem was debated in literary circles, the national press, and in the parliament. With the emergence of newly independent and multilingual nations in the years since World War II, struggles over language have frequently taken on more sanguinary overtones. The Indian conflict mentioned earlier, with its clash between supporters of Hindi and related Indo-European languages of the North and proponents of the languages of the South, is more public but no more bitter than other cases in Africa and in other Asian countries. Sociologists simply have not given sufficient attention to these problems of language conflict. While some aspects of language differentiation may be too subtle for the sociologist since they are observable only to the trained linguist, there are many other instances in which language serves as the most obvious clue to a whole host of other system boundaries.

Other scholars have examined the fissive and integrative impact of language loyalties in a variety of settings (Buck, 1916; Deutsch, 1942; 1953; Jakobson, 1945; Rundle, 1946; Alisjahbana, 1949; Haugen, 1952; Maza, 1957; Nugroho, 1957; R. A. Hall, 1959; Chowdhury, 1960; Taylor, 1961; Bidwell, 1962; Samarin, 1962; Sutherlin, 1962; Brosnahan, 1963; LePage, 1964; Blom & Gumperz, 1966; Rona, 1966; Kloss, 1967; Tanner, 1967; Fishman, 1968a; van den Berghe, n.d.). Almost without exception these studies deal with whole societies or major sectors of societies or even with several societies in contact. With only occasional exceptions, this literature has been neglected by social scientists interested in problems of societal integration.

Language Loyalty and Language Maintenance

Major immigration to the United States was completed shortly after the end of the first decade of the twentieth century. In 1966, with the publication of the report of the Language Resources Project under the general direction of Joshua Fishman (1966a), the study of the role of minority languages in the United States was rescued

[12] *Riksmål* 'language of the realm' was a Dano-Norwegian spoken by the educated middle classes, who were mostly city dwellers; *landsmål* 'country language' retained many of the characteristics of Old Norse and was spoken by the common, mostly rural, people; *bokmål* 'book language' is the culturally prestigious literary language derived from *riksmål*; *nynorsk* 'New Norse' is the official name for the contemporary, more standardized *landsmål*. Both *bokmål* and *nynorsk* are officially on equal footing as national languages. The ultimate goal—still a long way off—is a unified common language, sometimes referred to as *samnorsk* 'United Norwegian' (Haugen, 1957).

from a half century of neglect (see also Fishman, 1964; 1966b). *Language Loyalty in the United States* includes three types of papers:

The first section consists of papers by Fishman and his immediate associates on the actual status and distributions of immigrant languages in the United States and on the success or failure of a variety of institutions in fostering language loyalty and maintenance. There are chapters on the role of the ethnic press, of foreign-language broadcasting, of ethnic-group schools, of ethnic parishes, and of other organizational activities.

A second major section consists of studies of the language-maintenance experience of four different language communities in the United States: German-American (Kloss, 1966a), Franco-American (Le Maire, 1966), Spanish-American (Christian & Christian, 1966), and Ukrainian-American (Nahirny & Fishman, 1966).

In a third section and in a series of appendices, Fishman discusses problems of research on language maintenance and suggests both new research and direct action. He believes that language-maintenance activities can be defended not only on the basis of values associated with cultural pluralism but also because there are immediate and practical reasons for maintaining linguistic diversity in a world in which Americans are continuously and increasingly in contact with peoples speaking other languages.

Theoretical materials of interest to students of language structure and social structure are to be found in the second section. Kloss discusses a series of factors that have contributed to language maintenance. One of them, religiosocietal insulation, is sufficiently powerful that groups so endowed can resist assimilation. Such insulation is to be found only among small groups, however. Other factors, which are only analytically distinguishable from each other, include the time of immigration, the existence of language islands, affiliations with denominations fostering parochial schools, preimmigration experience with language-maintenance efforts, and the former use of a language as the *only* official tongue during the pre-Anglo-American period.

The chapter on German-Americans is particularly interesting because of a section in which Kloss, paralleling Westie's (1957) study of presupposed empirical assumptions underlying studies of racial attitudes, takes up a series of factors that are ambivalent in their affects on language maintenance. For example, he states that there are both favorable and unfavorable effects of a high (or low) level of education among immigrants—a high level of education encourages a lively intellectual life, a flourishing vernacular press, and the establishment of schools, but at the same time it also encourages occupational and, frequently, geographic mobility and rapid urbanization. Kloss finds the numerical size of a group speaking a language and the permissiveness or lack of it in the host society to have similarly ambivalent effects on language maintenance.

Christian and Christian, in their discussion of Spanish-language use in the American Southwest, emphasize cultural factors rather than the sociodemographic and organizational features discussed by Kloss. In the view of these authors, the past history of and the future prospects for the maintenance of Spanish in the Southwest can be understood only by understanding the culture of Spanish speakers and how it differs from that of the Anglos. They state:

> The nature of Hispanic culture seems to be *embedded in the language* of Spanish speakers in the Southwest. Furthermore, their culture and the language both seem to be *based upon and derived from* the reality in which they live; at the same time both language and culture seem to *create and mold* that reality (Christian & Christian, 1966:300).

In the view of the Christians, language and culture together provide the basic orientation toward the real world of persons or groups of persons, and the process of forming this orientation is circular. Their view is represented in Figure 1. They emphasize that the shift from one language to another means the shift from one culture to another and that this has implications for acceptance in the subordinated group. Unquestioned assumptions in cultures mean that the languages associated with those cultures are only partially translatable; the greater the differences in structure, the more difficulty there is in translating across the languages.

> This observation has many implications for maintenance of Spanish in the Southwest. It would explain the almost total inaccessability of the mind of the "chicano" to that of the "gringo" or "gabacho." It would suggest that the acceptance of English by the Mexican-American implies the direct and immediate submission to a foreign culture and frame of reference, as well as to a foreign language. Those who do submit are called *pochos*, bleached or faded (Christian & Christian, 1966:301).

One of the implications of this observation is the desirability of research into the use of epithet as a mechanism in the social control of those who have denied their cultural background and, perhaps, its use more generally.

In a summary chapter, Glazer (1966) reviews the factors suggested by Kloss and others as important in language maintenance and adds the factor of ideology. Glazer also discusses several countermaintenance factors. Among these factors he emphasizes mass public education and mass culture generally, the openness of American politics, and the organization of the economy with its possibilities for mobility. Most important among these countermaintenance factors, however, is the fact that many natural supports for language use are cut off in America.

The process of assimilation in the United States, with its accompanying consequences for the maintenance of immigrant languages, occasionally provoked some bitterness; however, that bitterness did not begin to compare with the prolonged acrimony that has accompanied struggles over language selection in dozens of nations throughout the world which have gained their independence in the last one and one-half centuries.

Pidgin and Creole Languages

Among the sociologically more interesting instances of language contact are those where speakers of sharply variant languages representing sharply dissimilar cultures come into contact. In numerous historical instances, these differences have been accompanied by pronounced discrepancies in power as well. Diebold (1964), in writing about incipient bilingualism, and Dozier (1951), in writing about linguistic acculturation, have examined a number of social structural variables that influence two sets of patterns resulting from such contact.

More recently, a number of sociolinguists and linguists have turned their attention to situations in which creoles and pidgins have developed (R. A. Hall, 1955; 1959; 1962; LePage & DeCamp, 1960; 1961; Stewart, 1962a; 1962b). While these

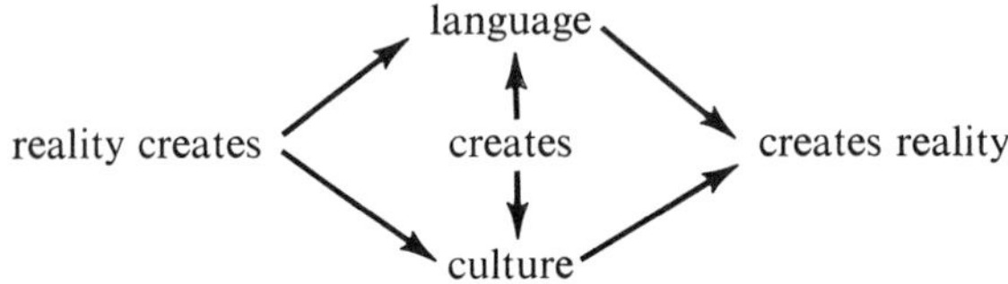

Figure 1. Relationship of language and culture in providing basic orientation toward the real world (Christian & Christian, 1966:300).

marginal patterns of communication through speech (in some instances early linguists were loath to dignify them by labeling them as languages) must have come into existence at the time of the first conquest of one group by another or of the first sustained trading contact that went beyond barter, systematic study was not started until long after linguistic traditions had been established for the European languages. The early reports of missionaries and other visitors to Haiti mentioned by Goodman (1964) in his comparative study of creole French dialects are hardly more than collections of exotica. Only in the 1930s did serious attention begin to be given to these languages and dialects, and it was only thirty years ago that Reinecke (1938) wrote his brief anticipatory article in *Social Forces*—based on an excellent and well-documented dissertation (Reinecke, 1937)—in which he noted, for the first time, some of the variety of these languages and some of the social factors that have produced them.

The publication of *Hands Off Pidgin English!* by Robert A. Hall, Jr. (1955) marked a turning point in the study of these "exotic" languages. Hall, who had been working on Melanesian Pidgin for over a decade, had been increasingly impressed by the role of the pidgins of the area not only in facilitating communication between natives and Europeans, but particularly in breaking down barriers that had been created by the multiplicity of languages in eastern New Guinea—even adjacent clusters of villages had mutually unintelligible languages.

The immediate impetus for this technically excellent yet eminently readable book was a demand by a United Nations Commission that pidgin be abolished—forthwith. The principal grounds for this demand were that pidgin was a mechanism for the permanent social subordination of natives, that it was not and could not be a language but was simply a corruption of English, and that it would not be used as a vehicle for moving its speakers into the modern period.

Hall, in responding, demonstrated that pidgin was indeed an intelligible language capable of carrying refined thought (he gives examples), that it had its own unique grammar that was not even remotely a corruption of English syntax and, most importantly, that it was playing a major role in the social and political mobilization of the populations using it. He demonstrated that processes were in motion whereby pidgins were becoming creolized and that standardization of a new language could be anticipated. He observed the parallel with the standardization of Bazar Malay into Bahasa Indonesia—in part as a consequence of a refusal of the Dutch to respond to natural language developments and needs. Any attempt to abolish pidgins, Hall indicated, might only heighten their use as a vehicle for a nationalist struggle for independence, perhaps precipitating that event before the populations in question were ready.

Although Hall has been an exception, most students of creoles have either reported on technical investigations of patterns of interference, published texts and other descriptive materials, or written historical chronologies. Only recently have scholars begun to attend to processual patterns of development that lead to the dominance of one or another speech variety in the movement toward standardization.

William Stewart (1962b) has written a pioneering article on the creoles of the Caribbean in which he has examined the functional distribution of standards and creoles and the contexts in which different speech varieties are used. He diagrams (Figure 2) the distribution in terms of two axes, public-private and formal-informal:

	FORMAL	INFORMAL
PUBLIC	Standard	Creole (Standard)
PRIVATE	Standard (Creole)	Creole

Figure 2. Functional distribution of standards and creoles (Stewart, 1962b:39).

Stewart is sensitive both to the mutual influence of language and social structures and to the value of changes in language usages in indexing social change. He writes:

For well over two centuries, Creoles and Standards have been used side by side in the Caribbean. Reflecting a traditionally rigid social structure, the relationship between Creoles and Standards has been one of a well-defined mutually exclusive social and functional distribution. As long as Caribbean society remained essentially an extension of colonial plantation social structure, little motivation existed for equalizing the linguistic opportunities for participation in local cultural and administrative affairs. More recently, however, social and technological changes have begun to penetrate the region, and this has prompted among other things the adoption of policies aimed at reducing those linguistic differences which it is felt promote social and political inequality, i.e., the contrast between literate and illiterate, and between use of the Creole and of the Standard (Stewart, 1962b:47).

It is possible that phonological and syntactic changes in creoles and pidgins can be intercorrelated with patterns of social change and that each of these types of change can be used to predict the other (Grimshaw, 1971; Mintz, 1971). It has been suggested, for example, that the appearance of new patterns in creolization and pidginization should be studied in the context of contemporary patterns of foreign relations of the particular society. It is being increasingly recognized that there is a complex interplay between the economic, political, social, and educational context of the development of special languages, and that both linguists and sociologists could profit from an examination of this interaction. Thus it should be possible to isolate probable patterns of special language development in latifundiary versus mercantile systems, in instances of colonial domination versus simple culture contact, in instances where multiple colonial spheres of domination intersect, and in instances where varying patterns of urban-rural differentiation and different kinds of demands for involvement in industrializing labor forces exist.

Linguists have generally examined patterns of creolization and pidginization in a frame of reference that emphasizes phonigrammatical and lexical interference. The social bases for support of or resistance to such interference are to be found in the social organization of the several societies themselves (including the ways in which conflict groups are bounded) and in the intrasocietal power structure (Barth, 1964; J. J. Gumperz, 1964a).

Social structure and power distribution are, in turn, influenced by macrosocietal variables. It should be at least as profitable to attempt to predict the appearance of varieties of such languages on the basis of sociohistorical analysis as on solely linguistic grounds. One might, for example, examine the character of the independence movement and of postindependence relations between the former colonial power and the new domestic government. It might be fruitful also to see the consequences of attaining independence at different historical periods, with or without the use of force, and to examine the role of transportation and communication in the nineteenth as contrasted to the twentieth century.

LANGUAGE AND SOCIETY: STRUCTURE AND BEHAVIOR

Linguists make a clear distinction between language structure (rules, competence) and language behavior (speech, performance). Sociologists, too, distinguish between social structure and social behavior or interaction, but the distinction is less clear. One reason for this lesser clarity is the fact that social structure not only includes norms (in the sense of a "syntax" for social behavior) but also incorporates the realities of differential distribution of power.

The rules for language, in the sense of competence, change very slowly. (Some linguists would substitute *grammar* for *competence* on the grounds that there are other varieties of linguistic competence and that the term *grammar* specifically bounds the phenomena to be considered.) In contrast, the consequences of conflict in a society may be to generate new structural arrangements (or at least shifts in power distribution) in very short periods of time. Thus, while relationships between language structure and social structure and between language behavior and social behavior will be found in every social situation, both micro and macro, it will frequently be difficult to identify and measure the mutual influence and codetermination of the two structures and the two types of behavior.

Several possible relationships between language structure and language behavior and between social structure and social behavior have been suggested: language behavior can *reflect* social structure; language behavior can *define or condition* social behavior (and social structure); social structure can *determine* language behavior; and *language structure and behavior can be inseparable from social structure and behavior*.

These perspectives are all correct and only analytically separable; they represent, however, some extremely subtle differences in ways of looking at the same phenomena. For example, the ways in which different speech patterns (whose users may or may not be conscious of the differences) *reflect* the users' positions in the social structure may be noticeable to an outside observer. On the other hand, the use of honorifics may *define* proper behavior and *identify* social relationships for the person entering a conversation as well as for an outside observer. A complex set of social structural variables may *determine* code selection and repertoire shifts, and the speaker may or may not be consciously aware of them. On a deeper level of analysis, there may be interrelationships between language structure and social structure in which directionality is no more discernible to the observer than to the naive speaker.

These possible relationships are by no means exhaustive of the intricate patterns that link language and social structure and behavior. Another perspective can be suggested—that which sees language usage as reflecting social structure while at the same time determining other patterns of social behavior. Others could be added, depending upon the sociological or linguistic interests of the researcher. The most important questions theoretically have to do with language definitions of social structure, with social structural definitions of language usages, and with the far more difficult issue of causality or isomorphism of language and other social phenomena. Until quite recently, however, most sociolinguistic work has been directed toward essentially correlational studies, and variation in language (particularly speech) behavior has been used to indicate social differences.

Language: A Reflection of Social Structure

The "pure" linguist is concerned with language "competence," not with language "performance." This position is best summarized in a quotation from Chomsky's *Aspects of the Theory of Syntax:*

> Linguistic theory is concerned primarily with an ideal speaker-listener in a completely homogeneous speech-community, who knows its language perfectly, and is unaffected by such *grammatically irrelevant conditions* as memory limitations, distractions, shifts of attention and interest, and errors (random or characteristic) in applying his knowledge of language in actual performance [italics added] (Chomsky, 1965:3).

Chomsky's position represents the fundamental posture of "structural" linguistics; sociologists are clearly more interested in "functional" linguistics (Hymes, 1966b; 1967a; 1967b; 1968d).[13]

[13] Hymes (1966b) uses *structural* not in the Bloomfieldian sense of structural linguistics but rather in the sociological sense of dichotomy between structure and function, as in the citation from Haugen (see p. 56).

Sociologists are committed, axiomatically, to the belief that *no* social behavior is random and that *no* social behavior is irrelevant. Speech behavior (language codes and speech behavior should be distinguished) is social behavior. Following Hymes, a distinction is made between the structural and functional positions (and the labels are unimportant). According to the structural position, concepts of speech community, speech act, fluent native speaker, and the functions of speech and of languages are taken for granted or assumed to be arbitrarily postulated. According to the functional position, these concepts and functions are considered problematic and open to investigation.

Once, in a personal conversation, J. J. Gumperz defined sociolinguistic study as "attending to those reflections of social structure which are revealed in language, particularly in speech usages, and . . . are concerned neither with motivation nor with conscious behavior."

A Speech Community

Simply defined, a speech community is a population whose members share the same set of evaluative norms with respect to language behavior. According to Labov, who has perhaps contributed most to refinements of research on the correlations between phonological and social differentiation, this community shares norms about language structure, style, and production—norms that are usually followed unconsciously but that can be made explicit. If, then, there are variations in speech usage, these variations reflect either normative variation among speech subcommunities or, possibly, the presence of underlying, covert, and competitive sets of normative values.

Continuing use in the growing research and theoretical literatures of sociolinguistics has required refinements of the concept of speech community, however, and early definitions are being replaced by others with far more complex dimensions (see, e.g., Hymes, 1967a). Hymes (personal communication) has suggested that the principal definitional problem is a choice between definitions that emphasize *shared homogenous codes* as contrasted to those that emphasize *shared norms of interpretation of use* (whatever position is taken as to numbers and repertoires of codes). He observes that *evaluative norms* may suggest either too little or too much, that it might exclude shared code (in the narrow sense of language structure) and include only norms for the handling of conversation. In some instances, language behavior could even be taken as implicitly opposed to language code.

Neither the definitional problem nor the realities of diversity can be ignored. Hymes (personal communication) specifies this in the following manner:

> Perhaps the accurate thing to say is that the sociolinguist who must face the problem of defining the speech community cannot theoretically take the easy way out of bracketing diversity, and postulating a homogeneous simplified unreal object (as Chomsky, 1965). And must take into account both diversity of codes, variety within repertoires, and the problem of shared norms for use as well as shared norms for structure of code(s) proper. . . . The problem of *types* of speech community is a very real one for comparative sociology/sociolinguistics: as to repertoires, norms of use (Haugen's functional problem), valuation of speaking as an activity. What must be rejected is the simplistic equation of language = communication = community. The three vary independently in relation to each other.

Labov (personal communication) emphasizes the fact that the sociolinguist is not solely concerned with the identification of norms. "In a word," he writes, "I agree with Homans that the object of study is not behavior, nor norms alone, but rather to account for the extent to which people deviate from those norms."

Gumperz (personal communication) underlines the ways in which actual speech be-

TABLE 1

Use of Prestige Marker /r/

Social Status of Subject	Casual Speech	Careful Speech	Reading Style	Word Lists
Upper-middle class	69%	85%	96%	100%
Middle class	00	19	24	53
Working class	00	05	14	29

Source: Labov (1964:168).

havior can reflect not shared evaluation of codes but shared norms about social relationships:

Although members of a speech community may have the same unconscious norms about speech usage, these vary or are variously interpreted depending on speakers, audiences and special situations. Speech variations, along with gestures, posture and other communicative signs serve as signals which tell speakers which social relationships are to be enacted and how norms are to be interpreted in a particular instance. . . . From the sociolinguistic point of view speech variation is an essential signaling device which provides important information about interlocutors and guides us in evaluating their messages.

In a series of careful and ingenious studies, Labov (1963a; 1963b; 1964; 1966a; 1966b; 1966c; 1968a) has demonstrated: (1) the existence of speech subcommunities that are associated with social-class strata; (2) shifts, whether conscious or not, to patterns of speech usage associated with higher strata by persons actually mobile or aspiring to mobility; and (3) marked shifts in speech patterns as contexts of speech production become more formal. In studying the prestige marker /r/, for example, Labov found the percentage distribution for three individuals from different social-class strata to vary markedly (see Table 1).

In his stratification studies, Labov has examined instances in which the variations between speech subcommunity norms were minor and noncompetitive. In more recent studies of lexical and syntactic shifts (as well as phonological variants) in urban dialects of the very poor in New York City, he has identified a situation in which there are strong social structural supports in the subcultures using those dialects that have the immediate effect of enhancing the development of a competitive and sharply differentiated speech community with an entirely different set of language norms (Labov, 1967; Labov & Robins, 1969). Teachers of children who use these dialects understand neither the normative structure of the language of the speech community nor the subculture that supports it. Nor are teachers the only ones who do not understand. Labov (personal communication) writes:

The sociolinguistic structure for a community appears to show a relatively uniform set of evaluative norms as the subjective *correlate* of a highly stratified behavior pattern. This is true in the Negro community as well as the white. Those outside the community may understand the referential content of the dialect, but have no accurate view of the social significance of the language choices made within the dialect. Thus an excellent speaker of British West Indian standard will hear no pattern at all in response to our subjective reaction tests based on Negro or white sociolinguistic variables.

Social Relationships

Labov has used quantitative methods in attempting to isolate patterns of social stratification and mobility in large populations. While his current studies on urban dialects are illuminating the quality of social relationships in ghetto populations, his stratificational studies have examined language and social behavior in the aggregate and have been less concerned with the social consequences of language differentiation than with the identification of patterns of differentiation themselves.

Roger Brown and a number of other investigators of the use of honorifics in address have attempted to move from the identification of status differences in micro social interaction to the understanding of the quality of social relationships in whole societies.

Study of situations in which there is differentiation in use of terms of address is both useful and perilous for the sociolinguist. It is useful both because the observer can quickly grasp something about the structure of the role relationship between speakers and because the speakers' perceptions of the situation in which they are interacting can influence usage choices. There is an apparent dilemma: does the observed speech behavior *reflect* social structure, or do perceptions of social structure influence speech behavior?[14]

According to Hymes (personal communication, 1967), both are going on continually: "The system in use reflects social structure and is being used to define situations at the same time, thus feeding back into the social structure." Social interaction, he suggests, can be presumed to lead social usage of speech in this ongoing system of definitions and redefinitions. Hymes concludes:

> Given the perception of the relationships, there will be a range of appropriate ways to be normal, condescending, insulting, ingratiating, etc. Not everyone in every situation will have the same choices, so that the behavior, in its possibility of alternates, will manifest both perceptions and the actual structure of the relationship.

In a series of publications (Brown & Gilman, 1960; Brown & Ford, 1961; Brown, 1965), Brown and his associates have examined the subtleties of symmetry and asymmetry in forms of interpersonal address (see also Geertz, 1960; Howell, 1967). They have demonstrated that the choice of either familiar or formal forms, and their functional equivalents of first names and last names with titles, indicate those dimensions of intimacy and solidarity, on the one hand, and of social distance and status, on the other, that characterize an interpersonal relationship. While there are exceptions, the general norm is for superiors to address inferiors and intimate equals familiarly and to address nonintimate equals formally, and for inferiors to address superiors and nonintimate equals formally and to address intimate equals familiarly. This *norm* holds in all languages that have been examined.[15]

Elaborations of this perspective have taken two directions. Friedrich (1966b) has shown, using Russian novels as sociological source materials (the translation of novels into English, with its singular "you" form removes a substantial amount of useful data from such materials), that the uses of *ty* and *vy* (roughly equivalent to *tu* and *vous*) can serve not only as indicators of status differentials and of shifting patterns of interpersonal relationships, but of extremely subtle subjective personal response as well.

Other scholars have shown the ways in which forms of address in other languages reflect even more subtle differentiations of

---

[14] Hymes (personal communication, 1967) suggests that the dilemma *is* only apparent. He distinguishes between *normal* usages across roles, statuses, and situations which, to a great extent, *reflect* social structure, and *marked* usages across different domains, again referring to roles, statuses, and situations. What may be normal usage in talking to a baby may be insulting marked usage when talking with an adult; nonetheless, this would not be a rule violation but rather the use of a rule about *the appropriate way to insult*. Marked usages, in other words, are used to *define* social relationships.

[15] Ervin-Tripp (1969) has a comprehensive discussion of this literature and develops implications not discussed in this chapter.

hierarchy and intimacy (Martin, 1964; Howell, 1965; 1967). Martin, for example, has shown that Japanese must make choices of speech level on two axes, those of reference and those of address. The axis of address—permitting choices of plain, polite, or deferential forms—reflects status differences. The axis of reference—permitting choices of humble, neutral, or exalted forms—reflects characterizations of the subject of expression.

Korean compounds the complexity by a distinction between address to ingroup or outgroup members; in the latter case, the axis of address includes polite, authoritative, and deferential forms. Selection of forms, Martin reports, is differentially determined by factors of age, sex, social position, and outgroupness. Martin feels that the importance of politeness is so great in these societies that shifts in patterns of social distance and even of intimacy and solidarity will not be automatically accompanied by a diminution in the fineness of distinctions on speech levels.

Howell (1967) has pointed out some additional subtleties of the meaning of usages within dyads. He has noted that the full exchange of forms of address must be available, that the proffered exchange of the familiar is sometimes refused, and that this refusal will be taken as an affront even when the intent of the refusal is to signify the higher status of the person proffering the usage. He has also pointed out that in situations of ambiguous status there may simply be an avoidance of the use of any terms of address. Howell offers as an example the changing patterns of race relations in the American South. An instance of equivalent ambiguity might involve relations, say, between senior graduate students and some of their senior professors.

Attention by linguists to characteristics of sender and receiver has focused largely on those attributes associated with hierarchical ordering and, to a lesser extent, with degrees of intimacy. Other variables may tend to override hierarchical considerations, however. Minard (1952), for example, has described the relationships between Negro and white miners sharing a common work situation. Shared danger and concern in crisis situations also may produce shifts in degree of familiarity and formality; shift in military address in and out of combat is a good example.

Aside from this, however, sociologists are well aware of possibilities of status inconsistencies (which may characterize social identities of either sender or receiver, or both) and of simple errors in perceiving the status of another, say, the receiver. Folk literatures are rich with cases of mistaken status identity, and these stories frequently detail the language shifts as well as the other behavior changes that occur when perceptions are corrected. The bulk of studies that have attended to conditioning factors have been done in societies where the statuses of each and every individual are known or where clues are clear and unambiguous. This is definitely not the case in urban areas of complex, industrialized, urban societies, where there are additional complexities in the meaning of *social identity* (see Grimshaw, 1966).

Uses for Research

Linguistic data on several levels can be used to identify the boundaries of significant social aggregates. Lieberson (1966) has listed a number of the uses to which language censuses can be put in studying such problems as creolization, multilingualism, and language standardization.He has further noted that linguistic developments in smaller communities will be increasingly influenced by language characteristics of the larger social units of which they are parts. He has also specified a large number of possible errors that can be introduced by the uncritical use of census materials on language.

On a more intensive level of research, dialectologists working on isoglosses have long been able to identify boundaries which frequently have social as well as linguistic significance. McDavid (1964), in his work on the postvocalic *-r* in the Piedmont, has combined highly sophisticated phonological analysis with an equally insightful perspective into the social factors environing linguistic differentiation (see also Levine & Crockett, 1966; 1967). In his work on the relationship between languages as socially defined entities and grammars as theories of languages and protolanguages as generic constructs, J. J. Gumperz (in studies done along the Mysore-Maharashtra border in India) has incidentally demonstrated the potential of linguistic analysis in identifying cultural and regional boundaries in areas of extremely complex patterns of language use, where both multilingualism and diglossia are found within individual villages (J. J. Gumperz, 1967a; see also 1961).

Limitations of space preclude the inclusion of numerous other studies that have demonstrated ways in which language usages reflect social structure and social relationships. No treatment, however, would be complete without reference to Friedrich's (1966a) innovative and convincing study of changes in kinship terminologies in Russia consequent upon major social changes in Russian society. In one of the very few genuinely diachronic researches in the sociolinguistic literature, Friedrich demonstrates how a series of cataclysmic changes in Russian society (the emancipation of the serfs, the 1917 Revolution, and two world wars) have radically transformed the social structure of Russian kinship, thereby causing a drastic diminution both in the size of the repertoire of kinship terminology and in the semantic specialization of individual terms. In the mid-nineteenth century, every Russian used easily a minimum of about sixty-five core kin terms—by 1950, the number of terms used had been reduced to about thirty.

Friedrich concludes:

> It is obviously true that the relation of the social system of behavior and principles to the several levels of languages is not by any means unidirectional in the sense that the second is an entirely dependent variable. On the contrary, as Sapir and others have argued, the semantic categories and conceptual interrelationships implicit in everyday speech to some extent precondition and in that sense determine our real decisions and our experience of life. Nevertheless, the available evidence indicates beyond cavil, I think, that the covert design and the audible stimuli of language function primarily as a conservative, stabilizing force, as a peripheral feedback system; in other words, it is change in social systems that *primarily* precedes and predetermines change in the corresponding semantic systems (Friedrich, 1966a: 159).

Social Structural Determinants of Repertoire Selection

J. J. Gumperz (1964a:151) has written:

> Social restraints on language choice . . . are also a part of social structure. They are thus susceptible to analysis in terms of generalized relational variables which apply to interaction in all human groups. The study of particular sets of grammatical systems and cultural norms in terms of these variables enables us to treat linguistic behavior as a form of social behavior, and linguistic change as a special case of social change.

The researches discussed above have generally been directed toward ways in which analysis of language usages can be used to determine the identities of speakers and persons spoken to and the relative positions of interlocutors. Characteristic *patterns of speech of individuals* have been used to locate their users in the social structure; characteristic uses of *speech in situations* have been used to identify patterned social relationships (as in the use of honorifics). The study of linguistic repertoires and of code-switching has shown that many individuals can handle more than one acceptable pattern of speech and that the pattern chosen is determined by the definition of the situation.

Gumperz introduced the concept of linguistic repertoire—defined as the totality of styles, dialects, and languages used within a socially defined community—as a unit of analysis for the cross-cultural comparison of language behavior (J. J. Gumperz, 1964a). After studying communities in India and in Norway, Gumperz concluded that social structure influenced repertoire selection on two levels. His findings have been summarized as follows:

While the choice between dialect use or the use of the standard language in each case is conditioned by such factors as the social occasion, the setting, the formal or informal roles of participants, their audiences, and the topic of conversation, in the Indian case the existence of sharply defined social barriers of caste and status has the effect of separating the repertoire into highly discrete, nonoverlapping varieties. In Norway, on the other hand, where social barriers are more fluid, the standard and the dialect are more like poles defining the end points of a continuum of linguistic variants (Grimshaw, 1967:306).

The greater importance of shifting in India reflects the greater and more rigid hierarchization of Indian society, a fundamental embedding of lingual and social structures. In both societies, however, within the specified ranges of permissibility of repertoire selection, setting and topic determine choice.

Linguists who have discussed the influence of setting on choice of speech patterns and/or dialects have done so most frequently in cases of diglossia or in other situations where there are sharp distinctions between literary and/or ritual uses and those of everyday life. Examples include the often cited study of Apache war language by Opler and Hoijer (1940) and the treatment by J. J. Gumperz (1964a) of the Indian case referred to above. Moreover, as suggested, the bulk of studies that have investigated conditioning factors have been done in societies where the statuses of conversational participants are clear and unambiguous, a situation that does not hold in most complex, industrialized, urban societies.

I have suggested elsewhere (Grimshaw, 1966) that the presence and variable characteristics of audiences may have as substantial an influence on style selection as do the topic of discussion and the actual physical setting. Using the cross-status interaction of professor and janitor as an example, I suggested that the choice of style by the actor of higher status could be considered a consequence of the interplay of variables suggested in Table 2, namely, audience characteristics and the role-taking ability of the speaker. In the absence of role-taking ability, status consciousness becomes a determining factor. Three possible responses were posited: (1) style adoption (however incorrect), (2) simplification, and (3) depersonalization.

In a further discussion of the table, I wrote:

Willingness and ability to take the role of the receiver are not, of course, randomly distributed. Shared military service experience may heighten this ability; increasing age along with increasing increments of status may be associated with a diminution of such skills. It is also possible that highly motivated and status-conscious individuals may possess the requisite skills but repress their use and permit them to atrophy. In the presence of such skills and willingness to use them, however, audience characteristics can become crucial. In the instance under discussion, suppose the janitor comes into the office while the academician is (1) alone, (2) with a senior member of the administration, (3) with a colleague of peer status, (4) with an undergraduate student, or (5) with another maintenance man. The ensuing patterns of interaction, including speech, could vary widely. Additional changes might be anticipated with the entrance of still other actors into the situation—the professor's wife, for example. Indeed in all the above situations, it might be well to assume that all the participants were male, and then to speculate on different speech styles which might emerge with the introduction of females into the situation. Before other audiences, say, the parents of students, other variations could be anticipated. Similarly, a shift from the academician's own office to another physical setting—elevator, classroom, coffee-shop, etc.—would produce other changes (Grimshaw, 1966:329–330).

TABLE 2

SPEECH PATTERN OR STYLE BY HIGH-STATUS SENDER TO LOW-STATUS RECEIVER, BY TYPE OF AUDIENCE AND ABILITY TO TAKE RECEIVER'S ROLE

Audience Characteristics	Willingness and/or Ability to Take Role of Receiver		
	Yes	No	
		Highly status conscious	Low-status consciousness
None	Style adoption	Nonpersonal communication	Simplification
Higher than sender	Lexical and grammatical simplification	Nonpersonal communication	Simplification
Same as sender	Style adoption*	Nonpersonal communication	Simplification
Lower than sender	Lexical and grammatical simplification	Nonpersonal communication	Simplification
Same as receiver	Style adoption	Nonpersonal communication	Simplification

SOURCE: Grimshaw (1966:330).
*Posits perceived role-taking on the part of audience.

I believe my concluding comment still holds:

> [What has been] suggested here is more than an additional taxonomic paradigm. If it is true that this kind of conceptual framework helps to organize and explicate linguistic behavior, and that audience is an important element in the social structure *between* language and speech, it should be equally true that sociologists could take linguistic data of the sort suggested here and use it to illuminate varieties of social structures more thoroughly. Few sociologists have ever attended to language shifts. Important and easily obtainable data are being wasted (Grimshaw, 1966:330–331).

J. J. Gumperz's (1958) paper on dialect differentiation and social stratification in North India and working papers by Bright (1968; see also Bright, 1960), McCormack (1969), and Ramanujam (1968) focus their attention on social (status) characteristics of senders in multidialectical diversity. A second focus in these papers is on the relation of intensity of communication to diffusion of linguistic phenomena (see, especially, J. J. Gumperz, 1967b). Geertz's (1960) extremely interesting and illuminating discussion of linguistic etiquette in Modjokuto underlines the importance of receiver as well as sender and notes in passing some of the elements of setting which parallel the axis of reference in Japanese discussed by Martin (1964).

Sociologists, particularly Goffman (1959; 1961; 1963; 1964), but more recently some of those doing ethnomethodology as well, have concentrated on the influence of setting on a variety of social behaviors, including language use. The most succinct review and summary of the influence of social structural factors involved in communicative events—including the interactive effects of channels, codes, settings, message-forms, topics, and events—is to be found in two articles by Hymes (1964; 1967a). In these two articles, Hymes is moving toward a general theory of descriptive sociolinguistics, and he increasingly emphasizes the isomorphic nature of the relationships between language structure and social structure.

The Case for Isomorphism

In my earlier discussion of theoretical approaches, I suggested four principal perspectives on the causal relationship between language and social structure: that which sees language as "causing" social behavior; that which sees social structure as somehow determining language; that which sees both language and social structure as determined by some third factor; and that which sees neither as prior to the other, both being seen as co-occurring and co-determining. It would seem that enough findings have been presented to demonstrate beyond reasonable argument the fact that there are causal relationships between the two sets of behavior.

At least some of the data adduced—for example, the Friedrich (1966a) study of social change and kinship terminology—seem to support the causal priority of the social structural features of the phenomena being examined. More generally, however, assessment of causal priority seems to reflect the original point of departure; the more closely a set of speech behavior and social behavior is scrutinized, the more likely the researcher will conclude that there is influence in both directions. If this is the case, then it seems probable that both of these perspectives may, in the final analysis, be subsumable under the perspective of co-determination, earlier labeled mutual embeddedness.

It is difficult to select a point of departure from which to move in an attempt to solve this problem. This difficulty has currently been exacerbated by a fundamental change in orientation of American linguistics, brought about both by the Chomskyan revolution itself and by the new perspectives of the sociolinguists, particularly Hymes. Writing of this change, Hymes states:

> In the recent past, American linguistics and anthropology seem to have emphasized invariance of structure in analysis of a single language; variation of structure as between languages; variation in the handling of use with regard to a single language (the intrusion of data dependent on special functions being handled as deviation from a norm); and invariance of use as between languages. At the present time, there seems to be coming to the fore a pattern of emphasis which is the converse of that just described. There is an emphasis on recognition of variation in the analysis of a single language; on invariance as between languages (universals of language); on invariance in the handling of speech functions in relation to a single system (language a "system of systems," or subcodes, with data dependent on special uses handled positively in terms of additional norms); and on variation as across languages. Part of this second pattern of emphasis is projected. Sociolinguistics seems to be rapidly establishing an emphasis on variation of structure in the analysis of individual languages; emphasis on variation of function across languages is the special concern of the present paper (Hymes, 1966a:115).

This shift can be seen in Table 3, which I have adapted from presentations of Hymes (1966a; 1968b; 1968d).

I noted earlier Hymes's summarization of the difference between the structural and functional perspectives as one in which concepts of speech community, speech act, fluent native speaker, and functions of speech and of language are, in the structural view, taken for granted or arbitrarily postulated and, in the functional view, taken as problematic and to be investigated. The sociolinguistic perspective assumes a considerable diversity in ways in which language and speech can be used to meet needs that are to be found within individual social structures. Needs may vary across social structures; the structure of language and speech to meet the same communicative need will not vary.

This perspective does not deny the likelihood of linguistic universals nor insist upon an uncritical linguistic relativity. If the nominative-predicative relationship is a necessity for all human communication, it

TABLE 3

CHANGES IN SOCIOLINGUISTIC ORIENTATIONS

	Descriptive (Intracultural)	Comparative (Cross-cultural)
	Presociolinguistic orientation:	
Structure	Invariance	Variation
Function	Variation	Invariance
	Postsociolinguistic orientation:	
Structure	Variation	Invariance
Function	Invariance	Variation

SOURCE: Adapted from Hymes (1966a:115).

will appear in the same structural form in all languages. The sociolinguist, however, insists that there are other types of relationships that are not common either to all language structures or to all social structures and that, in these instances, language and social structures reflect each other rather than intrinsic human psychological needs.[16]

We have reviewed research in which speech usage is seen as reflecting social structure, in which social structure is seen as determining speech usage, and in which correlations of linguistic and social structures are reported without attempting to assess causal priority. There have been no researches explicitly designed to test the hypothesis of co-determination or mutual embeddedness and only a few that can be used as evidence for the validity of that hypothesis. However, two sets of studies, each of which offers indirect evidence for this point of view, are available and will be reviewed here. The first is synchronic and deals with cross-societal differentiation of linguistic and social structures in "near" cultures—Truk and Ponape (on "near" cultures, see Smelser, 1966). The evidence here is phonological and syntactic and comes closest to meeting the demands of more traditional linguists. The second case is also synchronic and intracultural although comparative for subcultures.

Fischer's Cross-Societal Studies

In two recent reports on his cross-societal study of Truk and Ponape, Fischer (1965; 1966) has attempted to demonstrate the manner in which variations in social structure in the two societies are linked to varying patterns of phonological and syntactic differentiation (see also Garvin & Riesenbert, 1952; Goodenough, 1964). If Fischer's analysis is correct, he has shown the phonological and syntactic differences between the two related but mutually unintelligible languages to be isomorphic to differences in the social structures of the two societies. Moreover, in the phonological study he has suggested the possibility of a universal expressive value of different varieties of consonant clusters.

In the syntax study Fischer (1966) examines patterned differentiation of noun modifiers by position within the sentence. This analysis reveals that while the two languages are closely related (lexicosta-

[16] Since originally writing these lines I have looked more closely at the question of universal (extrasystemic) and categorical (intrasystemic) rules in linguistic, social, and sociolinguistic systems. See Grimshaw (1973).

tistical analysis indicates that the languages have been geographically isolated for approximately eight centuries), Ponapean noun phrases are "constructed more tightly" than those of Trukese. Fischer reports that, as a consequence of this difference, there is a greater chance in Trukese "for the listener to decide that the speaker has come to a point at which he may be interrupted, when actually the speaker intends to say more." This difference in syntax, with its accompanying consequences for speech behavior and closure in intellectual discourse, Fischer attributes to differences in the social structure of the two societies that have developed during the long years of isolation. In our view, of course, the differences in social structure have been reinforced by the differences in language structure.

Fischer characterized Ponapean social structure as being more differentiated than Trukese. There is greater variety of clearly demarcated social roles on Ponape (particularly kinship and political roles). Not only are these roles more differentiated, but individuals may change their position from one role to another through the exercise of individual initiative. Thus, Ponapean social structure is not only more hierarchical and more differentiated, but more flexible and characterized by greater social mobility. Fischer concludes that differences in syntax between Trukese and Ponapean, while moderate, are consistently and significantly in the same direction—a direction best explained in terms of *social* differences that favor a different balance between two types of thought habits, variously labeled "concrete" versus "abstract," or other such polar distinctions.

According to Fischer, there may be other variables of general thought patterns that are relevant to syntax but functionally unrelated to differential location of noun modifiers. Clues to the nature of such patterns, Fischer asserts, "may be found by careful consideration of small groups of related languages in relation to the social structure of the speech communities" (Fischer, 1966:180). In conclusion, he states what may well be a "sociolinguistic universal":

> As societies become more complex and social roles become more differentiated, the realized meaning of words in particular contexts becomes less important than the common or basic meaning. Speakers are forced to assume a greater cognitive gap between themselves and their listeners. At the same time, the basic meaning of the items of the lexicon tends to become more abstract and attenuated, since speakers have less need for words which can express much meaning in compact form to listeners who are conceived of as being much like the self; they have more need, instead, for words which can be used in many different contexts with many different listeners who are conceived of as being very different from the self and from each other. Of course, it is still necessary to speak precisely about detailed matters much of the time, but this kind of concreteness can be achieved through the combination of several words which in themselves are relatively abstract (Fischer, 1966:178).

Sociologists who have attended at all to linguistic and speech variation have, with the exception of those doing ethnomethodology and some social psychologists who have done work in semantics, generally limited their investigations to the examination of lexical inventories and to class differences in style. Analysis of syntax is beyond the competence of most sociologists; the phonological data used by Fischer (1965) in the second paper to be reviewed must seem even more esoteric.

In all languages phonetic adjustments are made at the boundaries of adjacent words during fluent speech—an example in English might be the variant handling of the terminal consonants in the two word phrases tota*l* lapse or tota*l* time, moto*r* repair or moto*r* failure. In some instances there is simple alternation of phonetic forms that are usually assigned to the same underlying consonant, quite automatic and predictable from the relations of the articulators, or one consonant is dropped entirely if followed by the same

TABLE 4
CROSS-SOCIETAL VARIATION IN SANDHI

	Truk		Ponape	
Underlying forms	Nasal stop	Stop stop	Nasal stop	Stop stop
Result of sandhi	Stop stop	Stop stop	Nasal stop	Nasal stop
Socio–linguistic differences	Less complex social structure; emphasis on flu–ency in speech.		More complex social structure; emphasis on pre–cision in speech.	

SOURCE: Based on Fischer (1965).

consonant. In other instances, however, the change is more radical, leading to a form that would be considered a different consonant if it occurred initially. (The latter changes are referred to as *sandhi*, following the usage of Sanskrit grammarians.)

Fischer has examined the different rules for consonantal sandhi in Trukese and Ponapean and associated these rules with the same differences in social structural complexity that he explicated in his syntactic study. He goes beyond the cross-societal comparison in this study, however, to suggest that changing patterns of sandhi within languages may reflect internal differentiation, and that the types of changes found within these two languages may reflect some universal expressive value of this form of phonological shift.

Fischer's findings on sandhi in Truk and Ponape are summarized in Tables 4, 5, and 6. Table 4 shows the pattern that sandhi takes in each of the two societies. In Truk, underlying forms that are characterized by double stops retain them, while nasal-stop patterns are shifted to double stops. In Ponape, a converse pattern holds, with all underlying forms ending up as nasal-stop patterns. Fischer shows that the Ponapean pattern is associated with an emphasis on precision in speech, which is consonant with and supported by the greater complexity of Ponapean society already indicated in the syntax study. In contrast, the greater emphasis on fluency and quantity in speech that is consonant with the double-stop pattern in Truk is also paralleled by a lesser complexity in that society.

Table 5, which is based on what

TABLE 5
INTRACULTURAL VARIATION IN SANDHI

Speech Situation	Consonantal Adjustments	
	Truk	Ponape
Free expression, including aggression	Double stop (normal sandhi)	Double stop (sandhi eliminated)
Restraint, gentleness, politeness	Nasal stop	Nasal stop

SOURCE: Based on Fischer (1965).

Fischer characterizes as more fragmentary evidence, shows the association of a sandhi differentiation within each of the two societies in association with different speech contexts.

In both societies free expression, including the expression of aggression, seems to be associated with the use of the double-stop pattern; more restrained, gentle, and polite speech contexts demand the use of the nasal-stop pattern. In other words, in Trukese, which generally emphasizes freedom and fluency of expression, normal sandhi is maintained in contexts of nonconstraint and the nasal-stop pattern is used in more restrained contexts. The same result is achieved in Ponapean, on the other hand, by the elimination of sandhi to produce the double-stop pattern in more relaxed speech contexts and in cases of the free expression of aggression. Thus, the phonological pattern that favors double-stops is associated in cross-societal comparison with the society that is less complex and in which fluency in speech is preferred; within both these societies the same pattern is associated with freer, more expressive interaction. Conversely, the nasal-stop pattern is associated in cross-societal comparison with the society that is more complex and in which precision in speech is preferred; within both these societies the same pattern is associated with restrained, precise, and more formal interaction. The cross-societal and intrasocietal comparisons are summarized in Table 6.

Fischer is careful to point out that there are, of course, great variations in speech situations within both cultures. The overall evidence is impressive, however, and the pattern of cross-societal and intrasocietal variation is surely consistent with Fischer's speculation that similarities in the expressive value of the two types of consonant clusters "may lead us to consider . . . whether there may not be something appropriate in these cultural meanings from the point of view of a potentially universal phonetic symbolism" (Fischer, 1965: 1500).

These examples show how detailed linguistic analysis can be combined with ethnographic information (sociological data) actually to demonstrate the "reciprocal relationship between language and human society." They also show how sociolinguistic research can lead to statements of relationships which are generalizable beyond the confines of single social structures and which, at the same time, have important methodological implications (phonology and syntax as indicators of social structural complexity *and* internal differentiation of contexts).

There have been two principal types of criticisms of Fischer's papers. The first is that his interpretation of his data is ex post facto; the second is that, in seeking reflections of social structure within the grammatical structure of a single code or speech variety, he may be guilty of naive neo-Whorfianism.

The papers *were* written after data had

TABLE 6

NASAL STOP AND DOUBLE STOP:
CROSS-SOCIETAL AND INTRASOCIETAL "FUNCTION"

	Function	
Structure	Cross-societal	Intrasocietal
Nasal stop	More complex society	Restrained, precise interaction
Double stop	Less complex	Free, expressive interaction

SOURCE: Based on Fischer (1965).

been collected; quite clearly, further studies will be needed to further document his interpretations. The kind of relationships posited are, however, singularly amenable to testing: Do Trukese take the opportunity to break in? Does the difference in noun structure function as Fischer suggests? Hymes (personal communication) notes, however:

> The basic model, of differential selection in linguistic features together with differential trends in social structure—the linguistic features being clearly such as could be motivated in interaction—seems . . . important and valid.

In the absence of contrary data, both the underlying delineation of the problem and the suggested solutions are of great heuristic value.

The answer to the charge of neo-Whorfianism, it seems to me, is to be found in Fischer's statement regarding the effect of increasing social complexity on language and thought patterns (see quotation, p. 75). The situation that he describes as being typical of increasingly complex societies with greater role differentiation is clearly one in which semantic constraints on lexical choice are correspondingly reduced as the cognitive gap between interlocutors increases. Indeed, the achievement of precision through combination of words has been observed for developing languages in less complex societies as well (see R. A. Hall, 1955; 1962).

Bernstein's Intracultural Studies

There has been one major sociological contributor to the growing corpus of the literature on sociolinguistics, the British sociologist Basil Bernstein (see the numerous citations in the reference list). It is Bernstein's fundamental view that social structure constitutes a set of intervening variables between languages, which represent the world of the possible in lexical and structural options (Bernstein, 1964b), and speech, which encapsulates the choices among the available options. This speech system, labeled by Bernstein as a linguistic code, in turn reinforces the user's selective perceptions of what is relevant in his environment. In this way, definitions of the social structure are again reinforced and again influence code selection.[17]

In actuality, however, Bernstein demonstrates that position in the social structure automatically limits the range of possible selection from the total world of lexical and structural (and phonological) options; codes or speech systems, then, are isomorphic to societal subsystems. In relatively homogeneous social systems and speech communities such as Truk and Ponape there is little intrasocietal differentiation in speech behavior because there is little or no subcultural or subsystemic variation in the social sustèm.[18] In more heterogeneous social systems, which will also be characterized by greater diversity in speech systems, particular "levels" of the social system will be associated with par-

[17] It should be noted that Bernstein's work has created considerable controversy and that both linguists and sociologists have been critical of his methods and his interpretations. This was particularly true of some of his earlier work; see, among others, John (1967). Bernstein's more recent work has been more sophisticated both linguistically and sociologically, and it has had a substantial impact on the work of scholars in both fields.

[18] This is, of course, a relative statement. There is greater stratification and differentiation generally in Ponape than in Truk; both societies, however, are characterized by lesser differentiation than is found in contemporary urban and industrialized nations. Fishman (1968b) and J. J. Gumperz (1962) both deal with the relationship between language and complexity of social systems. More generally, Gumperz (personal communication) writes, "I would say that small isolated groups tend to show a minimum of stylistic or dialect diversity. Highly stratified groups show diversity, i.e., either multidialectism or multilingualism (of the diglossia variety) and compartmentalization of language usage. More egalitarian or democratic westernized or urbanized societies may show linguistic diversity or speech variation but it tends to be of the fluid type."

ticular sectors of choice among all possible options in language.

Bernstein has used the polar concepts of what he has variously termed *elaborated codes* and *restricted codes* or *formal language* and *public language* in the elucidation of a wide range of situations and uses of language. He has attended particularly, however, to problems of learning and the process of social control.

Bernstein, in his earlier papers (1958; 1961a; 1961b; 1961c) and more recently (1972), has been interested primarily in problems of learning. He suggests that users of elaborated codes are more able to think abstractly, particularly in terms of relationships, and are therefore better able to handle materials more complex than the rote learning of the early years of school. The restricted code, while it facilitates the exchange of solidarity and permits transmission of concrete information, restricts its user from thinking conceptually, hypothetically, or speculatively about worlds and events that might exist . . . if. Its user lives in a world of addition without algebra, of historical chronology without historical causation, of melody without harmony or orchestration.[19] Consequently, restricted-code users are able to handle schoolwork during those years in which the emphasis is on rote learning (two times two is four; Look, Jane, look!), but they cannot keep up with their middle-class age peers when materials are introduced requiring understanding and articulation of relational abstract concepts.

If facility in elaborated codes enhances learning skills and provides its user with a richer conceptual world (in an almost Whorfian sense), it also brings some disadvantages. Bernstein (1972) has made the proposition that there are four principal modes of social control in the family: normative-oriented, parent-oriented, child-oriented, and status-oriented. The primary distinction is between those modes that are person-oriented and those that are status-oriented, a distinction that carries with it the occurrence of either *guilt* or *shame* as sanctions.

Social control in the restricted mode, Bernstein suggests, relies on status and authority but may provide the child with security. The elaborated mode, with its emphasis on personal characteristics and specific situations, may confuse the child although contributing to the long-range development of greater flexibility and individuality. Bernstein (1964a) has suggested that it is this difference in social control, along with the restricted-code user's relative inability to articulate meaning or individual experience verbally, that makes it so difficult for the elaborated code-using therapist to deal successfully with restricted code-using patients.[20]

The social world of the restricted-code user is constituted by membership in a small, closely knit group sharing a high sense of identification; by shared experience and mutuality of expectation; and, implicitly, by a lesser need for highly developed ability to manipulate concepts associated with problem-solving. In his earlier papers Bernstein had suggested an explicit continuum in which higher class position would be positively correlated with greater possession and use of elaborated codes. As his research has broadened, however, he has come to conclude that social subsystems with these characteristics of restricted-code users are located *throughout the society* and not just at the bottom.

Bernstein has presented no evidence, but he has suggested an examination of speech behavior of upper-class boys in English public schools might show it to be similar to that of lower- and working-class users of restricted codes. Insofar as a principal characteristic of restricted codes is the ex-

[19] Somewhat more technically, restricted coding is a pattern that emphasizes now-coding as contrasted to then-coding, with different types of hesitation pauses, with different (and more limited) lexical choices, with a simpler syntax.

[20] For another perspective on communication problems, see Grimshaw (1969–70).

change of solidarity cliches rather than relational statements, this may be true. It is likely, however, that in upper-class groups there would be a richer range of lexical choices and greater awareness of grammatical properties. Restricted codes probably exist to some extent in all relatively small, "exclusive" social systems—and this may well include certain groups of college students as well as occupational groups and working classes. Use of such codes may be determined more by the predominance of positional (status-oriented) modes of social control than by the user's command over richer or poorer lexical and syntactical inventories (see Bernstein, 1972).

It is also true that while the bulk of the interaction carried on by restricted-code users exhibits what might be called the "Marty" syndrome ("Wha d'ya wanna do tonight?" "I dunno, whad'ya wanna do?"), there is probably more concrete content and exchange of individuated experience in their communication than Bernstein had originally reported (see, e.g., Bernstein, 1964b). Bernstein recently has given greater importance to the role of nonverbal signals in transmitting content within this group.[21] Facial expressions, minor phonological shifts, changes in rhythm, tone, and loudness may all, under certain circumstances, serve as highly significant data for other restricted-code users. Although Bernstein's early work nowhere refers to Goffman, the interimplications of his discussion with Goffman's (1959) "giving impressions" and "giving off impressions" are obvious.

Bernstein's early work was generally limited to the analysis of vocabulary and grammatical usages of youth in small populations with limited characteristics (see, however, Grimshaw, 1969b). His work has been done with the spoken language, although one of his students has done analysis of a small number of cases of written work (see Lawton, 1963). Nonetheless, Bernstein's studies in an urban society present some preliminary evidence for a reflexivity of language structure and social structure in complex societies that had previously been available primarily for simpler groups.

The current state of sociolinguistic knowledge does not permit any final conclusion on the causal relationships between social structure and language structure.[22] The research evidence is scanty, and what little there is has seldom been collected for the specific purpose of isolating relationships between linguistic and social structures. While there seems to be some strength to the assertion that social factors may have precedence over autonomously linguistic factors, it also seems to be possible to demonstrate that there are processes of linguistic change which generate their own momentum through phonological or syntactical laws. The important point, however, is that the research reviewed above clearly demonstrates that the social sciences need the linguist and that his work and research can be markedly improved and simplified by attending to social structural variables.

TOWARD AN INTEGRATED THEORY OF DESCRIPTIVE SOCIOLINGUISTICS

Sociolinguistics is a hybrid discipline with a short and largely atheoretical history. Generated largely as a consequence of the "startle effect" that resulted from the rediscovery by sociologists (and some lin-

[21] There is, unfortunately, no space in this chapter to treat the growing literature on paralinguistics and proxemics. See, however, E. T. Hall (1959; 1963; 1964; 1966), Sebeok, Hayes, and Bateson (1964), Deutscher (1967; 1968), Grimshaw (1969–70).

[22] There is simply no space in this chapter to discuss all the literature bearing on this question. The interested reader should, however, examine Labov (1968c) for a rich and useful explication of three problems that must be considered: the transition, embedding, and evaluation problems.

guists) that certain linguistic events and certain social behavior seemed to be correlated, sociolinguistics developed its propositional inventory initially through statements of empirical relationships and then advanced to somewhat more ambitious theories of the "lower-middle range." The researches reviewed in this chapter have been the source of the data that have provided a direction to these preliminary, and frequently halting, steps toward a more general theory of sociolinguistics.

That an integrated theory of descriptive sociolinguistics is an attainable and reasonable goal has been demonstrated by Hymes, who in two articles has presented an outline of the form such an integrated theory must take (Hymes, 1964; 1967a). Any student who undertakes to grasp the full richness of the possibilities of the sociolinguistic enterprise must read these two articles. Hymes summarizes the need as one of "a study of speaking that seeks to determine the native system and theory of speaking; whose aim is to describe the communicative competence that enables a member of the community to know when to speak and when to remain silent, which code to use, when, where and to whom, etc." (Hymes, 1967a:13). The concepts with which such a theory must deal, he continues, are those of "speech community, speech situation, speech act, speech event, fluent speaker, native speaker, factors (or components) of speech events, functions of speech, rules of speaking, types of speech event and act" (Hymes, 1967a:15).

Three types of elements must be included in either a taxonomic or more developed relational sociolinguistic theory (Hymes, 1967a). There must be, first, a set of concepts for dealing with the characteristics of the social structure, what Hymes has labeled *the social unit of analysis*. Second, there must be a conceptual apparatus that identifies the *components of speech*. In Hymes's prototaxonomy, several of these components are closely linked to social characteristics. This is particularly the case when status characteristics of participants in a speech act are distinguished. Finally, for every instance of communication, or possible communication, there are formal *rules of speaking*. Rules of speaking are generalizations about relationships among components; for instance, code choice may be determined by status characteristics of participants in the speech act alone, by the setting in which the act occurs, or by a combination of these and other components.

The problem of generating formal rules can only be resolved by full specification of the components themselves; for example, consider code choices of a priest and a high-status and wealthy parishioner (1) in the confessional, (2) during free interaction in a golf game, and (3) in a conversation concerning bequests to the church. Much of the research reviewed above has had to do with precisely this type of specification of speech components.

The principal notions in defining the social unit of analysis are *speech community* (see Gumperz' characterization, p. 70), *speech field* (essentially the range of interactions possible given knowledge of a set or sets of codes and rules, *speech network*, (linkages actually operative within the speech field), *speech situation* (there are also situations in which communication is nonverbal; these are no less important for a full understanding of communicative interaction), *speech event* (a complete speech activity governed by rules for speech usage), and *speech act* (any subunit of a speech event).

Hymes has adopted a mnemonic device for listing the components of speech: s-p-e-a-k-i-n-g. The letters represent, serially: (1) setting or scene; (2) participants or personnel; (3) ends, both in the sense of goals and of outcomes;[23] (4) art characteristics, i.e., form and content of message;

[23] Hymes (1967a) gives an intriguing illustration of the interaction of purpose and outcomes in an example adapted from a paper by Frake (1972) on speech events among the Yakan of the Philippines.

(5) key, i.e., the manner or spirit in which the speech act is done;[24] (6) instrumentalities, i.e., the channel (oral, written, or other medium of transmission) and the linguistic code used; (7) norms of interaction and interpretation; and (8) genres, e.g., conversation, curse, professional paper, etc.

As has been noted, several of the components of speech are themselves clearly factors of social structure. This serves to underline the inextricably interrelated character of the relationships between speech and the social unit within which it occurs. Relationships between the components of speech can be generalized into formal rules of speaking. As Hymes notes, the process of the specification of these rules will demonstrate "*the inseparability of sociolinguistic analysis from the full-scale analysis of social life itself*, for it is in the analysis of social life that the requisite rules of selection for sociolinguistic features are to be found and stated" (Hymes, 1967a: 27).

A POSTSCRIPT

In the researches reviewed in this chapter, the linguistic variables that have been investigated have been phonological, grammatical, or lexical. These sociolinguistic data have been variously used in the examination of substantive empirical questions (e.g., those related to social differentiation and social change) and directed to the development of propositional statements to be incorporated into general theory about social structure and social behavior. They also have been used to test possible relationships between social structure and language structure—whether these relationships be simply correlational, whether they be causal in one or another direction, or whether they represent some more fundamental set of linkages between the two structures. They have *not* been used in an attack upon essentially methodological questions.

Hymes (1966c) has observed that some sociologists have a primarily methodological interest in the study of language while others are interested in language itself, either as data for substantive research on social structure or as a social phenomenon per se. This chapter has been directed almost solely to the second set of perspectives, language as data and as social phenomenon. The methodological questions related to language are primarily semantic rather than phonological, grammatical, or lexical (at least in the sense of simple lexical selection within codes, as the term has been used most often here). Interest in semantic problems has been growing in recent years and several treatments are available elsewhere (e.g., Phillips, 1959-60; Deutscher, 1967; Cicourel, 1964; 1969; Grimshaw, 1969a; 1969–70). For this reason, and because of limitations of space, no attempt has been made to review that literature in this chapter.

[24] Hymes (1967a:22) observes that the importance of key can be demonstrated by the fact that when content and key (or manner) are in conflict it is the manner in which the speech act is committed that carries the true significance of the message, e.g., in cases of sarcasm. He also observes that nonverbal behavior, such as facial expressions, may carry the key.

REFERENCES

Alisjahbana, Takdir.
1949 "The Indonesian language—by-product of nationalism." Pacific Affairs 22:388–392.

Anisfeld, Moshe; Norman Bogo; and W. E. Lambert.
1962 "Evaluational reactions to accented English speech." Journal of Abnormal and Social Psychology 65:223–231.

Anisfeld, Moshe, and W. E. Lambert.
1964 "Evaluational reactions of bilingual and monolingual children to spoken languages." Journal of Abnormal and Social Psychology 69:89–97.

Banks, Arthur S., and Robert B. Textor.
1963 A Cross-Polity Survey. Cambridge, Massachusetts: M.I.T. Press.

Barth, Fredrik.
1964 "Ethnic processes in the Pathan-Baluchi boundary in Indo-Iranica." Pp. 13–20 in Mélanges présenté à George Morgenstierne à l'occasion de son soixante dixième anniversaire. Wiesbaden: Otto Harassowitz.

Bernstein, Basil.
1958 "Some sociological determinants of perception." British Journal of Sociology 9:159–174.
1960 "Language and social class." British Journal of Sociology 11:271–276.
1961a "Social class and linguistic development: A theory of social learning." Pp. 288–314 in A. H. Halsey, Jean Floud, and C. A. Anderson (eds.), Education, Economy and Society. New York: Free Press of Glencoe.
1961b "Aspects of language and learning in the genesis of the social process." Journal of Child Psychology and Psychiatry 1:313–324.
1961c "Social structure, language and learning." Educational Research 3:163–176.
1962a "Linguistic codes, hesitation phenomena and intelligence." Language and Speech 5:31–46.
1962b "Social class, linguistic codes and grammatical elements." Language and Speech 5:221–233.
1964a "Social class, speech systems and psycho-therapy." British Journal of Sociology 15:54–64.
1964b "Elaborated and restricted codes: Their social origins and some consequences." American Anthropologist 66 (December, Part 2):55–69.
1966 "Elaborated and restricted codes: An outline." Sociological Inquiry 36 (Spring):254–261.
1972 "A sociolinguistic approach to socialization: With some reference to educability," in J. J. Gumperz and D. H. Hymes (eds.), Directions in Sociolinguistics. New York: Holt, Rinehart and Winston.

Bidwell, C. E.
1962 "Language, dialect, and nationality in Yugoslavia." Human Relations 15:217–225.

Blom, Jan-Petter, and John J. Gumperz.
1972 "Social meaning in linguistic structures: Code-switching in Norway." Pp. 407–434 in J. J. Gumperz and D. H. Hymes (eds.), Directions in Sociolinguistics. New York: Holt, Rinehart and Winston.

Bossard, James H. S.
1945a "Family modes of expression." American Sociological Review 10:226–237.
1945b "The bilingual as a person—linguistic identification with status." American Sociological Review 10:699–709.

Bright, William.
1960 "Linguistic change in some Indian caste dialects." International Journal of American Linguistics 26:19–26.
1963 "Language." Pp. 1–29 in B. J. Siegel (ed.), Biennial Review of Anthropology, 1963. Stanford, California: Stanford University Press.
1966 "Introduction: Dimensions of sociolinguistics." Pp. 11–15 in William Bright (ed.), Sociolinguistics: Proceedings of the UCLA Sociolinguistics Conference, 1964. The Hague: Mouton.
1968 "Social dialect and semantic structure in South Asia." Pp. 455–460 in M. Singer and B. S. Cohn (eds.), Structure and Change in Indian Society. Chicago: Aldine.

Bright, William (ed.).
1966 Sociolinguistics: Proceedings of the UCLA Sociolinguistics Conference, 1964. The Hague: Mouton.

Brosnahan, L. F.
1963 "Some historical cases of language imposition." Pp. 7–24 in J. F. Spencer (ed.), Language in Africa. London: Cambridge University Press.

Brown, Roger W.
1965 Social Psychology. New York: Free Press.

Brown, Roger W., and Marguerite Ford.
1961 "Address in American English." Journal of Abnormal and Social Psychology 62:375–385.

Brown, Roger W., and Albert Gilman.
1960 "The pronouns of power and solidarity." Pp. 253–276 in T. A. Sebeok (ed.), Style in Language. New York: Wiley.

Buck, C. D.
1916 "Language and the sentiment of

nationality." American Political Science Review 10:44–69.

Center for Applied Linguistics.
1961 Second Language Learning as a Factor in National Development in Asia, Africa, and Latin America. Washington, D.C.: Center for Applied Linguistics.

Chomsky, Noam.
1961 "Some methodological remarks on generative grammar." Word 17:219–239.
1964 Current Issues in Linguistic Theory. The Hague: Mouton.
1965 Aspects of the Theory of Syntax. Cambridge, Massachusetts: M.I.T. Press.
1968 Syntactic Structures. The Hague: Mouton.

Chomsky, Noam, and Morris Halle.
1965 "Some controversial questions in phonological theory." Journal of Linguistics 1:97–138.

Chowdhury, Munier.
1960 "The language problem in East Pakistan." International Journal of American Linguistics 26(No. 3, Part III):64–78.

Christian, Jane M., and C. C. Christian, Jr.
1966 "Spanish language and culture in the Southwest." Pp. 280–317 in J. A. Fishman (ed.), Language Loyalty in the United States. The Hague: Mouton.

Cicourel, Aaron V.
1964 Method and Measurement in Sociology. New York: Free Press of Glencoe.
1969 "Generative semantics and the structure of social interaction." Pp. 173–202 in International Day of Sociolinguistics. Rome: Luigi Sturzo Istituto.
1970 "The acquisition of social structure: Towards a developmental sociology of language and meaning." Pp. 136–168 in Jack D. Douglas (ed.), Understanding Everyday Life: Toward the Reconstruction of Sociological Knowledge. Chicago: Aldine.

Das Gupta, Jyotirindra.
1969 "Official language: Problems and policies in South Asia." Pp. 578–596 in T. A. Sebeok (ed.), Current Trends in Linguistics. Volume 5. The Hague: Mouton, forthcoming.
1970 Language Conflict and National Development: Group Politics and National Language Policy in India. Berkeley: University of California Press.

Das Gupta, Jyotirindra, and John J. Gumperz.
1968 "Language communication and control in North India." Pp. 157–166 in Joshua A. Fishman, Charles A. Ferguson, and Jyotirindra Das Gupta (eds.), Language Problems of Developing Nations. New York: Wiley.

Deutsch, K. W.
1942 "The trend of European nationalism —the linguistic aspect." American Political Science Review 36:533–541.
1953 Nationalism and Social Communication: An Inquiry into the Foundations of Nationality. New York: Wiley.

Deutscher, Irwin.
1967 "Notes on language and human conduct: Some problems of comparability in cross-cultural and interpersonal contexts." Syracuse: Maxwell Graduate School of Social Sciences and the Youth Development Center, Syracuse University (unpublished).
1968 "Asking questions cross-culturally: Some problems of linguistic comparability." Pp. 318–341 in Howard Becker et al., Institutions and the Person. Chicago: Aldine.

Diebold, A. Richard, Jr.
1964 "Incipient bilingualism." Pp. 495–510 in D. H. Hymes (ed.), Language in Culture and Society. New York: Harper and Row.
1968 "Code-switching in Greek-English bilingual speech," in Richard J. O'Brien (comp.), Georgetown University Round Table Selected Papers on Linguistics, 1961-1965. Washington, D.C.: Georgetown University Press. Originally presented at the 13th Round Table Meeting on Linguistics and Language Study (1962).

Dozier, Edward P.
1951 "Resistance to acculturation and assimilation in an Indian pueblo." American Anthropologist 53:55–56.

Durbin, Marshall.
1968 "Language," in B. J. Siegel (ed.), Biennial Review of Anthropology, 1967. Stanford, California: Stanford University Press.

Ervin-Tripp, Susan M.
1961 "Semantic shift in bilingualism." American Journal of Psychology 74:233–241.
1967 "An Issei learns English." Journal of Social Issues 23:78–90.
1969 "Sociolinguistics," in Leonard Berkowitz (ed.), Advances in Experimental Social Psychology. Volume 4. New York: Academic Press.

Ervin, Susan M., and Charles E. Osgood.
1954 "Second language learning and bilingualism." Journal of Abnormal and Social Psychology 49 (October, Part 2):139–146.

Ferguson, Charles A.
1962a "Background to second language problems." Pp. 1–7 in F. A. Rice (ed.), Study of the Role of Second Languages in Asia, Africa, and Latin America. Washington, D.C.: Center for Applied Linguistics.
1962b "The language factor in national development." Pp. 8–14 in F. A. Rice (ed.), Study of the Role of Second Languages in Asia, Africa, and Latin America. Washington, D.C.: Center for Applied Linguistics.
1964 "Diglossia." Pp. 429–439 in D. H. Hymes (ed.), Language in Culture and Society. New York: Harper and Row.
1966 "National sociolinguistic profile formulas." Pp. 309–324 in William Bright (ed.), Sociolinguistics: Proceedings of the UCLA Sociolinguistics Conference, 1964. The Hague: Mouton.

Ferguson, C. A., and J. J. Gumperz (eds.).
1960 Linguistic Diversity in South Asia: Studies in Regional, Social and Functional Variation. International Journal of American Linguistics 26(No. 3, Part III):1–118.

Fischer, John L.
1965 "The stylistic significance of consonantal sandhi in Trukese and Ponapean." American Anthropology 67: 1495–1502.
1966 "Syntax and social structure: Truk and Ponape." Pp. 168–187 in William Bright (ed.), Sociolinguistics: Proceedings of the UCLA Sociolinguistics Conference, 1964. The Hague: Mouton.

Fishman, Joshua A.
1960 "A systematization of the Whorfian hypothesis." Behavioral Science 4: 323–339.
1964 "Language maintenance and language shift as a field of inquiry." Linguistics 9:32–70.
1966a Language Loyalty in the United States. The Hague: Mouton.
1966b "Language maintenance and language shift: The American immigrant case." Sociologus n.s. 16:19–39.
1967a "Bilingualism with and without diglossia; Diglossia with and without bilingualism." Journal of Social Issues 23:29–38.
1967b "Basic issues in the sociology of language: A review of Joyce O. Hertzler's Sociology of Language." Language 43:586–604.
1968a "Nationality-nationalism and nation-nationism." Pp. 39–52 in J. A. Fishman, C. A. Ferguson, and J. Das Gupta (eds.), Language Problems of Developing Nations. New York: Wiley.
1968b "Varieties of ethnicity and varieties of language consciousness," in R. J. O'Brien (comp.), Georgetown University Round Table Selected Papers on Linguistics, 1961–1965. Washington, D.C.: Georgetown University Press. Originally presented at the 16th Round Table Meeting on Linguistics and Language Study (1965).

Fishman, Joshua A. (ed.).
1968 Readings in the Sociology of Language. The Hague: Mouton.

Fishman, Joshua A.; Charles A. Ferguson; and Jyotirindra Das Gupta (eds.).
1968 Language Problems of Developing Nations. New York: Wiley.

Frake, Charles O.
1972 "Struck by speech: The Yakan concept of litigation." Pp. 106–129 in J. J. Gumperz and D. H. Hymes (eds.), Directions in Sociolinguistics. New York: Holt, Rinehart and Winston.

Friedrich, Paul.
1962 "Language and politics in India." Daedalus 91 (Summer): 543–559.
1966a "The linguistic reflex of social change: From Tsarist to Soviet Russian kinship." Sociological Inquiry 36: (Spring): 31–57.
1966b "Structural implications of Russian pronominal usage." Pp. 214–259 in William Bright (ed.), Sociolinguistics: Proceedings of the UCLA Sociolinguistics Conference, 1964. The Hague: Mouton.

Gaarder, A. Bruce.
1967 "Organization of the bilingual school." Journal of Social Issues 23: 110–120.

Gardner, R. C., and Wallace E. Lambert.
1959 "Motivational variables in second-language acquisition." Canadian Journal of Psychology 13:266–272.

Garvin, Paul L., and S. H. Riesenbert.
1952 "Respect behavior on Ponape: An ethnolinguistic study." American Anthropologist 54:201–220.

Geertz, Clifford.
1960 The Religion of Java. New York: Free Press of Glencoe.

Glazer, Nathan.
1966 "The process and problems of language-maintenance: An integrative review." Pp. 358–368 in J. A. Fishman (ed.), Language Loyalty in the United States. The Hague: Mouton.

Goffman, Erving.
1959 The Presentation of Self in Everyday Life. Garden City, New York: Doubleday.
1961 Encounters: Two Studies in the Sociology of Interaction. Indianapolis: Bobbs-Merrill.
1963 Behavior in Public Places. New York: Free Press of Glencoe.
1964 "The neglected situation." American Anthropologist 66 (December, Part 2): 133–136.

Goodenough, Ward H.
1964 "Property and language on Truk: Some methodological considerations." Pp. 185–188 in D. H. Hymes (ed.), Language in Culture and Society. New York: Harper and Row.

Goodman, Morris F.
1964 A Comparative Study of Creole French Dialects. The Hague: Mouton.

Greenberg, Joseph H.
1956 "The measurement of linguistic diversity." Language 32:109–115.

Grimshaw, Allen D.
1966 "Directions for research in sociolinguistics: Suggestions of a nonlinguist sociologist." Sociological Inquiry 36 (Spring): 319–332.
1967 "A review of Joyce O. Hertzler, A Sociology of Language." Harvard Educational Review 37:302–308.
1969a "Language as obstacle and as data in sociological research." Items 23:17–21.
1969b "Sociolinguistics and the sociologist." American Sociologist 4:312–321.
1969–70 "Some problematic aspects of communication in cross-racial research in the United States.' Sociological Focus 3 (Winter): 67–85.
1971 "Some social sources and some social functions of Pidgin and Creole languages," in D. H. Hymes (ed.), Creolization and Pidginization of Languages. London: Cambridge University Press.
1973 "Rules in linguistic, social, and sociolinguistic systems and possibilities for a unified theory," in Georgetown University Monograph Series on Languages and Linguistics, No. 25. Washington, D. C.: Georgetown University Press. Originally presented at the 23rd Round Table Meeting on Linguistics and Language Study (1972).

Gumperz, Ellen M.
1967 "Growth of regional consciousness in Maharashtra." Paper presented to the Interdisciplinary Graduate Seminar on South Asian Studies, University of California at Berkeley, October (unpublished).

Gumperz, John J.
1958 "Dialect differences and social stratification in a North Indian village." American Anthropologist 60:668–681.
1961 "Speech variation and the study of Indian civilization." American Anthropologist 63:976–988.
1962 "Types of linguistic communities." Anthropological Linguistics 4:28–40.
1964a "Linguistic and social interaction in two communities." American An-

thropologist 66 (December, Part 2): 137–153.
1964b "Hindi-Punjabi code switching in Delhi," in Proceedings, IX International Congress of Linguists. The Hague: Mouton.
1965 "Language," in B. J. Siegel (ed.), Biennial Review of Anthropology, 1965. Stanford, California: Stanford University Press.
1967a "On the linguistic markers of bilingual communication." Journal of Social Issues 23:48–57.
1967b "Language and communication." Annals of the American Academy of Political and Social Science 373: 219–231.
1968 "Linguistic repertoires, grammars, and second language instruction," in R. J. O'Brien (comp.), Georgetown University Round Table Selected Papers on Linguistics, 1961–1965. Washington, D. C.: Georgetown University Press. Originally presented at the 16th Round Table Meeting on Linguistics and Language Study (1965).
1969 "Measurement of bilingualism in social groups," in L. G. Kelly (ed.), The Description and Measurement of Bilingualism. Toronto: University of Toronto Press.

Gumperz, John J., and Dell H. Hymes (eds.).
1964 The Ethnography of Communication. American Anthropologist 66 (December, Part 2): 1–186.
1972 Directions in Sociolinguistics. New York: Holt, Rinehart and Winston.

Hall, Edward T.
1959 The Silent Language. Garden City, New York: Doubleday.
1963 "A system for the notation of proxemic behavior." American Anthropologist 65: 1003–1026.
1964 "Adumbration as a feature of intercultural communication." American Anthropologist 66 (December, Part 2): 154–163.
1966 The Hidden Dimension. Garden City, New York: Doubleday.

Hall, R. A., Jr.
1955 Hands Off Pidgin English! Sydney: Pacific Publications.
1959 "Colonial policy and Melanesian." American Linguistics 1:22–27.
1962 "The life cycle of pidgin languages." Lingua 11:151–156.

Harrison, S. S.
1960 India: The Most Dangerous Decades. Princeton, New Jersey: Princeton University Press.

Haugen, Einar.
1946 Bilingualism in the Americas: A Bibliography and Research Guide. University, Alabama: American Dialect Society.
1952 "The struggle over Norwegian," in Norwegian-American Studies, XVII. Northfield, Minnesota: Norwegian–American Historical Association.
1953 The Norwegian Language in America. 2 volumes. Philadelphia: University of Pennsylvania Press.
1954 "Some pleasures and problems of bilingual research." International Journal of American Linguistics 20:116–122.
1957 Beginning Norwegian. Third Edition, Revised. New York: Appleton-Century-Crofts.
1965 "Construction and reconstruction in language planning: Ivar Aasen's grammar." Word 21:188–207.
1966a Language Conflict and Language Planning: The Case of Modern Norwegian. Cambridge, Massachusetts: Harvard University Press.
1966b "Semicommunication: The language gap in Scandinavia." Sociological Inquiry 36(Spring): 280–297.
1966c "Dialect, language, nation." American Anthropologist 68:922–935.
1966d "Linguistics and language planning." Pp. 50–71 in William Bright (ed.), Sociolinguistics: Proceedings of the UCLA Sociolinguistics Conference, 1964. The Hague: Mouton.
1968 "Schizoglossia and the linguistic norm," in R. J. O'Brien (comp.), Georgetown University Round Table Selected Papers on Linguistics 1961–1965. Washington, D.C.: Georgetown University Press. Originally presented at the 13th Round Table Meeting on Linguistics and Language Study (1962).

Hertzler, Joyce O.
1953 "Toward a sociology of language." Social Forces 32:109–119.

1965 A Sociology of Language. New York: Random House.

Howell, Richard W.

1965 "Linguistic status markers in Korean." The Kroeber Anthropological Society Papers 55:91–97.

1967 "Linguistic choice as an index to social change." Ph.D. dissertation. Berkeley: University of California (unpublished).

Hymes, Dell H.

1964 "Introduction: Toward ethnographies of communication." American Anthropologist 66 (December, Part 2): 1–34.

1966a "Two types of linguistic relativity (with examples from Amerindian ethnography)," in William Bright (ed.), Sociolinguistics: Proceedings of the UCLA Sociolinguistics Conference, 1964. The Hague: Mouton.

1966b "On 'anthropological linguistics' and congeners." American Anthropologist 68:143–153.

1966c "Teaching and training in sociolinguistics." Paper prepared for SSRC Committee on Sociolinguistics (unpublished).

1967a "Models of the interaction of languages and social setting." Journal of Social Issues 23:8–28.

1967b "The anthropology of communication," in F. E. Dance (ed.), Human Communication Theory. New York: Holt, Rinehart and Winston.

1968a "Linguistic problems in defining the concept of 'tribe.'" Pp. 23–48 in June Helm (ed.), Essays on the Problem of Tribe. Seattle: University of Washington Press.

1968b "Linguistics." Pp. 351–386 in David L. Sills (ed.), International Encyclopedia of the Social Sciences. Volume 9. New York: Macmillan.

1968c "Why linguistics needs the sociologist." Social Research 34:632–647.

1968d "On communicative competence." Paper presented at Conference on Mechanisms of Language Development, London, May.

Hymes, Dell H. (ed.).

1964 Language in Culture and Society: A Reader in Linguistics and Anthropology. New York: Harper and Row.

1971 Creolization and Pidginization of Languages. London: Cambridge University Press.

Jakobson, Roman.

1945 "The beginnings of national self-determination in Europe." Review of Politics 7:29–42.

John, Vera P.

1967 Communicative Competence of Low-Income Children: Assumptions and Programs. A report to the Language Development Study Group of the Ford Foundation, March 30.

Kelley, Gerald.

1966 "The status of Hindi as a lingua franca," in William Bright (ed.), Sociolinguistics: Proceedings of the UCLA Sociolinguistics Conference, 1964. The Hague: Mouton.

Kloss, Heinz.

1966a "German-American language maintenance efforts." Pp. 206–252 in J. A. Fishman (ed.), Language Loyalty in the United States. The Hague: Mouton.

1966b "Types of multilingual communities: A discussion of ten variables." Sociological Inquiry 36(Spring):135–145.

1967 "Bilingualism and nationalism." Journal of Social Issues 23:39–47.

Labov, William.

1963a "The social motivation of a sound change." Word 19:273–309.

1963b "Phonological indices of stratification." Paper presented at the annual meeting of the American Anthropological Association, San Francisco, November 22 (unpublished).

1964 "Phonological correlates of social stratification." American Anthropologist 66 (December, Part 2):164–176.

1966a The Social Stratification of English in New York City. Washington, D.C.: Center for Applied Linguistics.

1966b "The effect of social mobility on linguistic behavior." Sociological Inquiry 36(Spring):186–203.

1966c "Hypercorrection by the lower middle class as a factor in linguistic change." Pp. 84–113 in William Bright (ed.), Sociolinguistics: Proceedings of the UCLA Sociolinguistics Conference, 1964. The Hague: Mouton.

1967 "Some sources of reading problems

for Negro speakers of non-standard English." Pp. 140-167 in New Directions in Elementary English. Urbana, Illinois: National Council of Teachers of English.

1968a "Reflections of social processes in linguistic structures." Pp. 240–251 in J. A. Fishman (ed.), Readings in the Sociology of Language. The Hague: Mouton.

1968b "The non-standard vernacular of the Negro community: Some practical suggestions." Pp. 4–7 in Position Paper from Language Education for the Disadvantaged. Report No. 3 of the NDEA National Institute for Advanced Study in Teaching Disadvantaged Youth (June).

1968c "On the mechanism of linguistic change," in R. J. O'Brien (comp.), Georgetown University Round Table Selected Papers on Linguistics, 1961–1965. Washington, D.C.: Georgetown University Press. Originally presented at the 16th Round Table Meeting on Linguistics and Language Study (1965).

Labov, William, and C. Robins.

1969 "A note on the relations of reading failure to peer-group status in urban ghettos." Teachers College Record 70(Fall):396–405.

Lambert, Wallace E.

1967 "A social psychology of bilingualism." Journal of Social Issues 23: 91–109.

Lambert, Wallace E.; Moshe Anisfeld; and G. Yeni-Komshian.

1965 "Evaluational reactions of Jewish and Arab adolescents to dialect and language variations." Journal of Personality and Social Psychology 2:84–90.

Lambert, Wallace E.; H. Frankel; and G. R. Tucker.

1966 "Judging personality through speech: A French-Canadian example." Journal of Communication 16:305–321.

Lambert, Wallace E.; R. C. Gardner; H. C. Barik; and K. Tunstall.

1963 "Attitudinal and cognitive aspects of intensive study of a second language." Journal of Abnormal and Social Psychology 66:358–368.

Lambert, Wallace E.; J. Havelka; and C. Crosby.

1958 "The influence of language acquisition contexts on bilingualism." Journal of Abnormal and Social Psychology 56:239–244.

Lambert, Wallace E.; R. C. Hodgson; R. C. Gardner; and Samuel Fillenbaum.

1960 "Evaluational reactions to spoken languages." Journal of Abnormal and Social Psychology 60:44–51.

Lawton, Denis.

1963 "Social class language differences in language development: A study of some samples of written work." Language and Speech 6:120–143.

LeMaire, Herve-B.

1966 "Franco-American efforts on behalf of the French language in New England." Pp. 251–279 in J. A. Fishman (ed.), Language Loyalty in the United States. The Hague: Mouton.

LePage, R. B.

1964 The National Language Question: Linguistic Problems of Newly Independent States. New York: Oxford University Press.

LePage, R. B., and David DeCamp.

1960 Creole Language Studies. Volume 1: Jamaican Creole. New York: St. Martin's Press.

1961 Creole Language Studies. Volume 2. London: Macmillan.

Levine, Lewis, and Harry J. Crockett, Jr.

1966 "Speech variation in a Piedmont community: Post-vocalic 'r,'" Sociological Inquiry 36 (Spring): 204–226.

1967 "Friends' influences on speech." Sociological Inquiry 37(Fall):109–128.

Lieberson, Stanley.

1964 "An extension of Greenberg's linguistic diversity measures." Language 40:526–531.

1965 "Bilingualism in Montreal: A demographic analysis." American Journal of Sociology 71:10–25.

1966 "Language questions in censuses." Sociological Inquiry 36(Spring): 262–279.

Lieberson, Stanley (ed,).

1966 Explorations in Sociolinguistics. Sociological Inquiry 36(Spring): 131–332. Republished as Publication 44, Indiana University Research Center in Anthropology, Folklore, and Linguistics (1967).

Lounsbury, Floyd G.
1959 "Language." Pp. 185–209 in B. J. Siegel (ed.), Biennial Review of Anthropology, 1959. Stanford, California: Stanford University Press.
1961 "Language." Pp. 279–322 in B. J. Siegel (ed.), Biennial Review of Anthropology, 1961. Stanford, California: Stanford University Press.

McCormack, William C.
1967 "Language identity: An introduction to India's languages problems." Pp. 435–465 in J. W. Elder (ed.), Chapters in Indian Civilization. Volume II: British and Modern Period. Madison: University of Wisconsin Department of Indian Studies.
1968 "Occupation and residence in relation to Dharwar dialects." Pp. 475–486 in Milton Singer and B. S. Cohn (eds.), Structure and Change in Indian Society. Chicago: Aldine.

McDavid, Raven I., Jr.
1964 "Postvocalic -r in South Carolina: A social analysis." Pp. 473–482 in D. H. Hymes (ed.), Language in Culture and Society: A Reader in Linguistics and Anthropology. New York: Harper and Row.

Mackey, William F.
1962 "The description of bilingualism." Canadian Journal of Linguistics 7:51–85.

Macnamara, John.
1966 Bilingualism in Primary Education. Edinburgh: Edinburgh University Press.
1967a "The bilingual's linguistic performance—a psychological over-view." Journal of Social Issues 23(April): 58–77.
1967b "The effects of instruction in a weaker language." Journal of Social Issues 23(April):121–135.

Macnamara, John (ed.).
1966 Problems of Bilingualism. Journal of Social Issues 23(April):1–135.

Martin, Samuel.
1964 "Speech levels in Japan and Korea." Pp. 407–415 in D. H. Hymes (ed.), Language in Culture and Society: A Reader in Linguistics and Anthropology. New York: Harper and Row.

Maza, H.
1957 "Language differences and political integration." Modern Language Journal 41:365–372.

Minard, R. D.
1952 "Race relationships in the Pocahontas coal field." Journal of Social Issues 8:29–44.

Mintz, Sidney.
1971 "Comments on the socio-historical background to pidginization and creolization," in D. H. Hymes (ed.), Creolization and Pidginization of Languages. London: Cambridge University Press.

Nahirny, Vladimir C., and Joshua A. Fishman.
1966 "Ukrainian language maintenance efforts in the United States." Pp. 318–357 in J. A. Fishman (ed.), Language Loyalty in the United States. The Hague: Mouton.

Nugroho, R.
1957 "The origins and development of Bahasa Indonesia." Publications of the Modern Language Association of America 72:23–28.

Opler, Morris E., and Harry Hoijer.
1940 "The raid and warpath language of the Chiricahua Apache." American Anthropologist 42:617–634.

Park, Robert E.
1955 Collected Papers. Volume 3: Society. Edited by E. C. Hughes et al. Glencoe, Illinois: Free Press.

Phillips, Herbert P.
1959–60 "Problems of translation and meaning in field work." Human Organization 18(Winter):184–192.

Pieris, R.
1951 "Bilinguality and cultural marginality." British Journal of Sociology 2:238–339.

Pride, J. B.
1967 "A guide to the study of language in culture and society" (unpublished paper).

Ramanujam, A. K.
1968 "The structure of variation: A study of caste dialects." Pp. 461–474 in Milton Singer and B. S. Cohn (eds.). Structure and Change in Indian Society. Chicago: Aldine.

Reinecke, John E.
1937 "Marginal languages." Ph.D. dissertation. New Haven: Yale University (unpublished).
1938 "Trade jargons and creole dialects as

marginal languages." Social Forces 17:107–118.

Rice, Frank A. (ed.).
1962 Study of the Role of Second Languages in Asia, Africa, and Latin America. Washington, D.C.: Center for Applied Linguistics.

Rona, Jose Pedro.
1966 "The social and cultural status of Guarani in Paraguay." Pp. 277–298 in William Bright (ed.), Sociolinguistics: Proceedings of the UCLA Sociolinguistics Conference, 1964. The Hague: Mouton.

Rubin, Joan.
1962 "Bilingualism in Paraguay." Anthropological Linguistics 4:52–58.
1963 "Stability and change in a bilingual Paraguayan community." Paper presented at the annual meeting of the American Anthropological Association, San Francisco, November 21.

Rundle, Stanley.
1946 Language as a Social and Political Factor in Europe. London: Faber and Faber.

Russett, Bruce M., et al.
1964 World Handbook of Political and Social Indicators. New Haven: Yale University Press.

Samarin, William J.
1962 "Lingua francas, with special reference to Africa." Pp. 54–64 in F. A. Rice (ed.), Study of the Role of Second Languages in Asia, Africa, and Latin America. Washington, D.C.: Center for Applied Linguistics.
1966 "Self-annulling prestige factors among speakers of a Creole Language." Pp. 188–213 in William Bright (ed.), Sociolinguistics: Proceedings of the UCLA Sociolinguistics Conference, 1964. The Hague: Mouton.

Sawyer, J. B.
1959 "Aloofness from Spanish influence in Texas English." Word 15:270–281.

Sebeok, Thomas A.; Alfred S. Hayes; and Mary C. Bateson (eds.).
1964 Approaches to Semiotics: Transactions of the Indiana University Conference on Paralinguistics and Kinesics. The Hague: Mouton.

Sellin, Thorsten.
1938 Culture Conflict and Crime. New York: Social Science Research Council.

Smelser, Neil J.
1966 "The methodology of comparative analysis" (unpublished paper).

Stewart, William A.
1962a "An outline of linguistic typology for describing multi-lingualism." Pp. 15–25 in F. A. Rice (ed.), Study of the Role of Second Languages in Asia, Africa, and Latin America. Washington, D.C.: Center for Applied Linguistics.
1962b "Creole languages in the Caribbean." Pp. 34–53 in F. A. Rice (ed.), Study of the Role of Second Languages in Asia, Africa, and Latin America. Washington, D.C.: Center for Applied Linguistics.

Sutherlin, Ruth E.
1962 "Language situation in East Africa." Pp. 65–78 in F. A. Rice (ed.), Study of the Role of Second Languages in Asia, Africa, and Latin America. Washington, D.C.: Center for Applied Linguistics.

Tanner, N.
1967 "Speech and society among the Indonesian elite, a case study of a multilingual community." Anthropological Linguistics 9:15–40.

Taylor, Douglas.
1961 "New languages for old in the West Indies." Comparative Studies in Sociology and History 3:277–288.

Thomas, Owen P.
1965 Transformational Grammar and the Teacher of English. New York: Holt, Rinehart and Winston.

Tucker, G. Richard, and Wallace E. Lambert.
1967 "White and Negro listeners' reactions to various American-English dialects." Speech given at McGill University. Tape-recorded.

van den Berghe, Pierre L.
n.d. "Language and 'nationalism' in South Africa" (unpublished paper).

Weinreich, Uriel.
1953 "Functional aspects of Indian bilingualism." Word 13:203–233.
1957 "The troubles of Hindi." Paper presented at the annual meeting of the American Anthropological Association, Chicago, December.
1963 Languages in Contact: Findings and

Problems. The Hague: Mouton.
Westie, Frank R.
1957 "Toward closer relations between theory and research: A procedure and an example." American Sociological Review 22:149–154.
Whorf, Benjamin L.
1956 Language, Thought and Reality. Selected Writings of Benjamin Lee Whorf. Edited by J. B. Carroll. New York: Wiley.
Windmiller, Marshall.
1954 "Linguistic regionalism in India." Pacific Affairs 27:291–318.
Wittermans, Elizabeth P.
1967 "Indonesian terms of address in a situation of rapid social change." Social Forces 46:48–51.

CHAPTER 4 Nonverbal Communication

RANDALL P. HARRISON
Michigan State University

Nonverbal communication refers to gestures, postures, facial expressions, symbolic clothing, and similar phenomena. The study of nonverbal communication has been one of the liveliest fields in the last few years, with much novel research under way. The present chapter classifies the major directions of effort and reviews the literature available on each.

The term *nonverbal communication* has been applied to a broad range of phenomena: everything from facial expression and gesture to fashion and status symbol, from dance and drama to music and mime, from flow of affect to flow of traffic, from the territoriality of animals to the protocol of diplomats, from extrasensory perception to analog computers, from the rhetoric of violence to the rhetoric of topless dancers (e.g., Bosmajian, 1971).

This review focuses on emerging theory and empirical data. It concentrates on definable communication systems that use explicable nonverbal signs with observable semantic, syntactic, and pragmatic consequences. It omits the more esoteric and less researched areas such as ESP, potential communication with intergalactic intelligences, perfumery, etc. Special emphasis is given to theoretic trends and the integration of diverse traditions into a communication perspective.

Several recent reviews have summarized additional studies in the general area of nonverbal communication (Duncan, 1969; Barker & Collins, 1970) and in specific related areas: the face (Frijda, 1969; Vine, 1970; Izard, 1971; Ekman, Friesen, & Ellsworth, 1972); small-group ecology (Sommer, 1967; 1969; Collins & Ravens, 1969); social interaction (Argyle, 1969; Marlowe & Gergen, 1969); interaction analysis (Jaffe, 1968; Matarazzo, Wiens, Matarazzo & Saslow, 1968; Weick, 1969); person and social perception (Cline, 1964; Tagiuri, 1969; Tajfel, 1969); extralinguistic phenomena (Crystal & Quirk, 1964; Mahl & Schulze, 1964); and esthetics (Pratt, 1961; Child, 1969; 1972). In addition, recent popular books have given overviews of the area (Fast, 1970; Poiret, 1970; Nierenberg & Calero, 1971), and introductory texts have begun to provide integrated summaries (Eisenberg & Smith, 1971; Mehrabian, 1971b; Hinde, 1972; M. L. Knapp, 1972; Mehrabian, 1972b; Harrison, 1973). Finally, annotated bibliographies are beginning to appear (e.g., Davis, 1972), and recent book-length contributions have been received and evaluated (e.g., Harrison, Cohen, Crouch, Genova, & Steinberg, 1972).

BASIC DISTINCTIONS

Nonverbal communication is frequently framed in terms of paralanguage and kinesics (Osgood & Sebeok, 1954; Sebeok, Hayes, & Bateson, 1964) plus other articulated areas such as proxemics (Hall, 1959; 1966). For a more exhaustive classification of nonverbal signs, four broad categories can be used:

a) performance codes, where nonverbal signs emanate from bodily actions, such as facial expressions, eye movements, gestures, body posture, tactile contact, and olfaction; a special subcategory of performance codes encompasses paralinguistic phenomena, such as voice quality, speech nonfluencies, sighs, yawns, laughter, grunts, etc.;

b) artifactual codes, where nonverbal signs emerge in the manipulation of dress, cosmetics, furnishings, art objects, status symbols, architecture, etc.;

c) mediational codes, where nonverbal signs arise from selections, arrangements, and inventions within the media; e.g., an editor can crop a photograph in various ways, he can choose black-and-white or color, he can select a photo or a drawing; similarly, the filmmaker can select close-up or long shot, he can add music or sound effects, he can rearrange his shots into a new syntax;

d) contextual codes, where nonverbal signs arise in the use of time and space, through the temporal and spatial location of communication systems, and in the arrangement of communicators and their artifacts.

While these categories encompass a broad spectrum, the use of the construct "sign" implies that not all nonverbal stimuli and behavior have communication value.

Focusing on nonverbal signs, we can make several immediate distinctions in terms of (*a*) modality, (*b*) code, and (*c*) function. While linguistic communication is restricted to the vocal-auditory channel in speech and the visual channel in writing, nonverbal signs occur in additional modalities: e.g., taste, touch, smell. Within a given modality, several different nonverbal codes may operate. Similarly, a nonverbal sign may cross modalities (e.g., a handshake may involve vision and pressure as well as a thermal dimension).

While linguistic codes appear quite similar in complexity and evolution as we move from language to language, nonverbal codes range from the very simple to the very complex and from the high analogic, easily learned to the noniconic, formally learned. Finally, nonverbal signs seem to function at three different levels in the operation of communication systems:

1. Nonverbal signs define, condition, and constrain the system; e.g., time, place, and arrangement may provide cues for the participants as to who is in the system, what the pattern of interaction will be, and what is appropriate and inappropriate communication content.
2. Nonverbal signs help regulate the system, cueing hierarchy and priority among communicators, signaling the flow of interaction, providing metacommunication and feedback.
3. Nonverbal signs communicate content, sometimes more efficiently than linguistic signs but usually in complementary redundancy to the verbal flow.

HISTORICAL PERSPECTIVES

The phrase "nonverbal communication" has gained currency in the literature during the past two decades (e.g., Ruesch & Kees, 1956). However, the underlying phenomenon has deep intellectual roots—in classical philosophy, in the study of expressive behavior, in experimental esthetics, semiotic (i.e., "the science of signs"), linguistics, person perception, animal behavior, etc.

Expressive behavior caught the attention of several Greek philosophers, the most influential being Aristotle, whose analyses were recorded in *Physiognomia, Historia Animalium, De Anima,* and *Parva Naturalia.* From classical times until the nineteenth century, intermittent studies were made of the human face. In 1586, for instance, Porta published a tome called *De Humana Physiognomia* and, in 1774, Lavater published his *Fragments Physiognomoniques.* Few of these pre-1800 studies are remembered today, but with the nineteenth century came a chain of research, launched by Duchenne, Bell, Darwin, Wundt, James, and Piderit. Some of the issues, theories, and methodologies framed by those scholars remain part of the research scene today.

Early Studies

Duchenne (1862) published a study of facial muscles in which he used mild electrical stimulation to produce the appearance of emotional expressions on the paralyzed face of an old man. Sir Charles Bell (1865) published his investigation of facial expression about the same time, and both Duchenne and Bell influenced Charles Darwin (1965), who published *The Expression of the Emotions in Man and Animals* in 1872. Darwin is of interest not only because of his theory of evolution; some of his ideas about emotional response are shaping research more than a century later (P. H. Knapp, 1963; Ekman, 1973).

Darwin, for instance, argued that facial expressions are innate, thus suggesting certain nonverbal universals. While this view prevailed among European psychologists, the American tradition tended to follow Sherman (1927a; 1927b) and Landis (1924; 1929), arguing that expressions were socially learned habits. This issue was still being explored at the 1971 Nebraska Symposium on Motivation (Ekman, 1972).

While Darwin's observations were launching a century of research, Wundt and particularly James were laying a foundation of theory that has also stimulated succeeding theorists and experimenters. Similarly, current methodology can trace its lineage to the nineteenth century. Duchenne, for instance, took photographs of his subject's electrically stimulated expressions, and these photos were used by Darwin in his study of facial expressions. Meanwhile, the German anatomist Piderit (1867) created a detailed set of line drawings of the human head that were arranged so that parts of the face could be interchanged at will. These drawings were used in the studies of Boring and Titchener (1923), and the technique is still being employed today.

Pre-World War II

In the 1930s, expressive behavior was studied by Blake (1933), Allport and Vernon (1933), and Critchley (1939), while Woodworth (1938) and Schlosberg (1941) were launching the search for dimensions in facial affects. Meanwhile, the anthropological-linguistic foundations for nonverbal study were being set by Boas, Sapir, Bloomfield, and Efron.

Of special note is Efron's (1941) classic, *Gesture and Environment,* long out of print but now being reissued. Like Sapir, Efron was a student of Boas. And Boas, during the thirties, was concerned with countering the Nazi theories of a master race. He encouraged Efron to study the gestural communication of immigrant Jews and Italians in New York's Lower East Side.

Efron introduced several constructs which have recently been picked up and amplified by Ekman & Friesen (1969b). He first distinguished *emblems,* which are gestures that replace words and are encoded arbitrarily and with intent (e.g., the hand signals of a baseball catcher or coach). Next, he identified several types of gestures that are used in conjunction with speech: (*a*) *batons,* movements that accent a particular word or phrase; (*b*) *ideographs,* movements that trace the flow of an idea; (*c*) *deictic* gestures, movements that point to available referents; (*d*) *spatial* gestures, movements that portray relationships in space; and (*e*) *kinetographs,* movements that depict a bodily action.

Using motion pictures of interaction, plus an artist's line drawings of specific gestures, Efron isolated distinctive patterns for the two groups; Jewish immigrants used more batons and ideographs while the Italians employed more kinetographs. Efron further traced the attrition of these gestural patterns among offspring with looser ties to traditional custom. Unfortunately, with the advent of war, Efron returned to his native Argentina and his research lead fell dormant in the U.S. for almost three decades.

Post-World War II

Building on the linguistic tradition in anthropology, Birdwhistell (1952) advanced an alternate scheme for analyzing body communication. Stimulated by Sapir (1921; 1931), Bloomfield (1933), Bateson and Mead (1942), and particularly Trager and Smith (1957), Birdwhistell attempted to frame a comprehensive coding scheme for body motion, just as the linguist had done for spoken language.

Where the linguist identified a *phone,* a minimal sound, Birdwhistell proposed the *kine,* a minimal movement. Where the linguist isolated a *phoneme,* a group of interchangeable sounds, Birdwhistell sought the *kineme,* a set of interchangeable movements. Where the linguist looked for the meaningful *morpheme*, Birdwhistell searched for the *kinemorph*, a range of movement that would be meaningful in the context of larger patterns. Beyond this level of *microkinesics* was to be "social kinesics," now more frequently called *macrokinesics,* where the *act,* a meaningful pattern in one body area, or an *action,* a pattern involving more than one area, would be related to larger communication frames.

Mining the same anthropological tradition, Hall extended the linguistic analogy beyond body movement to all the "primary message systems" of culture (Hall & Trager, 1953; Hall, 1959; 1966). Where the linguist spoke of phonemes, morphemes, and syntax, Hall proposed comparable constructs of *isolates, sets,* and *patterns.* Hall's particular focus was space, an area he elaborated as *proxemics.*[1] In his analysis of American communication systems, he distinguished four distinct zones for interaction: intimate, personal, social, and public. With a shift in distance, Hall noted, different patterns of nonverbal signs become available in kinesthetic, thermal, olfactory, visual, and oral-aural modalities.

Goffman, an early student of Birdwhistell, moved away from the linguistic tradition to provide a sociological perspective in his first work (Goffman, 1959) and in a series of contributions since (Goffman, 1961a; 1961b; 1963a; 1963b; 1967; 1969; 1971. While Goffman has focused on the presentation of self and the collaborative efforts of participants in social interaction, his writings have drawn increased attention to the role of nonverbal signals in the formation, operation, and maintenance of communication systems.

Ruesch (1955; Ruesch & Bateson, 1951; Ruesch & Kees, 1956) provides an example of psychotherapy's growing interest in nonverbal communication during the 1950s. Nonverbal symbols, of course, had been part of the psychiatrist's tool kit since the days of Freud and Jung. But increasingly, clinicians were becoming aware of the nonverbal interaction taking place in therapy and of the importance of the patient's nonverbal encounters in the outside social world. Ruesch argued that the distinction between analogic and digital coding was

[1] Hall defined proxemics as "the study of how man unconsciously structures microspace—the distance between men in the conduct of daily transactions, the organization of space in his houses and buildings, and ultimately the layout of his towns" (Hall, 1963:1003).

vital for the therapist to grasp. In calling for attention to nonverbal communication, he proposed a categorization of nonverbal signs into three "languages": (*a*) sign language, where nonverbal symbols replaced words, numbers, and punctuation; (*b*) action language, where behaviors not intended as communication actually do have informational value to a perceiver; and (*c*) object language, the intentional and unintentional display of objects, including the body and its clothing.

The experimental psychologists of the 1950s might best be represented by Osgood, Suci, and Tannenbaum (1957). While *The Measurement of Meaning* did not have its primary focus in nonverbal communication, Osgood later extended his dimensional theory to nonverbal signs (Osgood, 1959) and particularly to the face (Osgood, 1966). Meanwhile, the semantic differential provided a tool for measuring responses to nonverbal signs and for comparing verbal and nonverbal stimuli on a common metric. Within the book, research is reported on art objects, color,. music, and film. And since 1957, a vast range of stimuli has been explored (Snider & Osgood, 1969; Darnell, 1970).

This sampling of book-length contributions from a decade reflects the state of research at midcentury: (*a*) a growing number of scholars, from a range of disciplines, was becoming aware of, and interested in, nonverbal communication; (*b*) much of what was known was anecdotal, based on insightful observation, but with little attempt to systematically record or replicate; (*c*) theory was primitive, the most comprehensive paradigm being an extension of the linguistic model; (*d*) potential major issues were not as yet being framed into testable hypotheses; and (*e*) methodology, and particularly technology, limited the range of nonverbal phenomena being studied. Finally, it might be noted that the face, a nonverbal sign system which had received a century of scientific investigation, remained an area pocked with unresolved questions (Bruner & Tagiuri, 1954; Tagiuri & Petrullo, 1958).

TRENDS IN THEORY

In broad strokes, the current trends in nonverbal communication can still be drawn along disciplinary lines. Anthropology and psychology were the strongest early forces in the field. While their encounter in language led to psycholinguistics, there is not as yet a "psychokinesics." Psychotherapists have a strong pragmatic interest in the field, and they have spread their research orientations across the anthropological-psychological spectrum. Similarly, researchers in speech, education, and mass communication have been eclectic, with a leaning toward psychological constructs. Meanwhile, sociologists and social psychologists have slipped into the field without the dramatic clash of paradigms seen between psychology and anthropology. Finally, in this decade a major new encounter is shaping up as behavioral scientists become increasingly aware of work in ethology.

While labeling traditions is useful for orientation, the tagging of specific researchers is increasingly dangerous; nonverbal research is populated with interdisciplinary scholars. Birdwhistell (1970), of course, is the most obvious standard-bearer for the anthropological-linguistic tradition. Meanwhile, the psychological tradition is perhaps best typified by Ekman (1972). Both have worked in psychotherapy, Birdwhistell as a member of an interdisciplinary research team and Ekman as a clinician before moving into research.

In contrasting Birdwhistell and Ekman, differences become apparent in focus, theory, and methodology. First, they disagree in their definitions of communication. Birdwhistell (1968a; 1968b), for instance, objects to the term *nonverbal communication*. He likens this to noncardiac physiology, arguing that the communicative process is a behavioral flow, occasionally employing words, rather than a string of verbal stimuli sometimes embellished with actions. He similarly would object to the emphasis given nonverbal sign, arguing instead for attention to pattern and a rejection of any stimulus-response focus.

Ekman, meanwhile, uses intentionality as a defining criterion for communication (Ekman & Friesen, 1969b). Nonverbal acts are communicative if performed with the intent of providing a message to another interactant. Acts may be informative in that they provide reliable information to an observer. They may be interactive in that they have a clear effect on the decoder. But neither of these categories would be communicative if done without conscious intent. Interestingly, the decoding of intended meaning is not a defining characteristic; i.e., the receiver may misinterpret the intended message, or not realize that a message was sent, but still be engaged in communication.

These definitions underscore a basic difference in focus between the kinesicist and the psychologist. The latter is interested in the behavior of the individual, and he assumes that important discoveries can be made by taking the individual as a self-contained unit. The psychologist is as interested in linking nonverbal behavior to psychological variables, such as emotion or personality, as he is in exploring interpersonal consequences. He finds idiosyncratic behavior, which may have meaning to only one observer (e.g., a therapist), as fascinating as behavior that has broadly shared meaning.

Meanwhile, the tradition in linguistics is to focus on culturally patterned behavior. The kinesicist would like to screen out the idiosyncratic and emerge with the structure of behavior shared by all members of a given cultural group. Similarly, the interest is on communicative or interactive consequences of behavior; the same act may relate to personality or emotion, but that is of peripheral interest.

This difference in focus leads to divergent research strategies. The psychologist is happy to study the individual in relative isolation; the kinesicist insists the individual must be studied in social context, the crucial phenomenon being the interrelationship of behaviors among interactants. The kinesicist attempts to embrace all the behavior in an interaction, later dropping the unimportant; the psychologist moves in the opposite direction, first isolating the most promising behavior, adding others as he must.

Traditionally, the linguist saw no need for quantification—the important phenomena were either absent or present—and this orientation has been carried over into kinesics. Birdwhistell eschews statistics, and his long-time colleague, Scheflen (1966), stoutly defends the nonstatistical approach. Ekman, meanwhile, would argue that an area of scientific investigation can remain nonquantitative only so long as (*a*) it is unimportant, and/or (*b*) only one investigator is involved. Since neither is true any longer for nonverbal research, issues will be increasingly adjudicated by quantitative methods. Modern linguistics is, of course, increasingly quantitative and, given the sophisticated statistical methods which might be useful to the kinesicist, nonquantification may become a fading earmark of kinesic research.

Theoretical Approaches

Birdwhistell

Birdwhistell's (1970) collection provides a glimpse of his struggle to extend the linguistic model to body motion. In its strongest form, the kinesic hypothesis suggests that the nonverbal body code is parallel to language structure: (*a*) elemental units can be isolated, (*b*) these elements combine into larger wholes, (*c*) this total system is learned and used by members of a common culture and, hence, (*d*) the linguistic methods appropriate to language study can be applied to body movement.

Birdwhistell (1970: 82) himself points to some of the difficulties in the linguistic-kinesic analogy. The informant technique, for instance, which is so fundamental to descriptive linguistics, is difficult to use in kinesic research. This in itself seems to indicate that the "kineme" is not as robust a phenomenon as the phoneme.

A more telling criticism is outlined by Dittmann (1971). In brief, Dittmann argues that a growing body of research indicates the untenability of the basic kinesic assumption; a demonstrably large area of body behavior, while communicative in one way or another, does not share the underlying structure of a spoken language.

Birdwhistell's greatest success appears to be in those areas where body motion is most closely tied to the verbal stream, e.g., in kinesic stress, juncture, and with various kinesic markers. He is currently examining markers of interruption and continuation in conversation.

Ekman and Friesen

Whereas Birdwhistell started with a strong theoretic model which he has modified in the light of research, Ekman and his associates began with an empirical bias and only recently started formalizing theory to guide future research (Ekman & Friesen, 1968; 1969b). Examining the origin, usage, and coding of nonverbal behaviors, Ekman and Friesen distinguished five key classes: (1) *emblems,* intentional communicative signs that have widely shared meanings, the most direct counterpart of verbal symbols; (2) *illustrators,* actions that accompany verbal behavior and perform the functions suggested earlier by Efron; (3) *regulators,* actions that help manage the flow of conversation; (4) *affect displays,* behaviors that reveal or portray feelings; and (5) *adaptors,* behaviors that began as useful manipulations of the self, objects, or others but that may now have additional informative value.

In each category, Ekman and Friesen list ongoing research. Whereas their early research focused largely on the problem of facial-affect display, they are now engaged in a broad range of communication problems. As one example, they are exploring the role of illustrators, adaptors, and affect displays during deception attempts (Ekman & Friesen, 1969a).

Mehrabian

In contrast to Birdwhistell and Ekman, Mehrabian (1970a; 1971b; 1972a; 1972b) has proposed a dimensional theory for the exploration of nonverbal communication. In brief, he suggests that the dimensions found by Osgood, Suci, and Tannenbaum (1957) for verbal symbols may have a counterpart for nonverbal behavior. While verbal signs can be located in a semantic space defined by evaluation, potency, and activity, nonverbal behaviors reveal a communicator's stance on liking, potency, and responsiveness. Proximity, for instance, may signal liking, but this is one of a set of verbal and nonverbal signs that may communicate that message.

The dimensional approach is advanced by Mehrabian in part because it permits the study of inconsistencies between verbal and nonverbal signs. On the basis of his research, for instance, he argues that facial expression and paralinguistic factors outweigh verbal content (Mehrabian, 1970d; 1971b; Mehrabian & Wiener, 1967). He has studied the role of nonverbal cues in a series of studies (Mehrabian, 1967; 1968a; 1968b; 1968c; 1969a; 1969b; 1970a; 1970b; 1970c; 1971a; 1971c; 1972a; Mehrabian & Ferris, 1967; Mehrabian & Friar, 1969; Mehrabian & Williams, 1969). Wiener, who worked with Mehrabian on paralinguistic phenomena, recently framed a theoretical stance that sharpens the distinction between nonverbal *behavior* and nonverbal *communication* (Wiener, DeVoe, Rubinow, & Geller, 1972). For the latter, Wiener and his associates emphasize goal-directed encoding.

Other Positions

Scheflen, following the lead of Birdwhistell, has articulated the macrokinesic level; he suggests, for instance, that nonverbal regulators mark off "points," "positions," and "presentations"—succeedingly larger units in total interaction (Scheflen, 1963; 1964; 1965a; 1965b; 1966; 1967; 1972). Like many researchers in therapy and family communication, Scheflen links his approach to general systems theory (Watzlawick, Beavin, & Jackson, 1967; Gray, Duhl & Rizzo, 1969). Von Cranach (1970) has similarly proposed that sociopsychological research in nonverbal interaction would profit from systems considerations. Meanwhile, in theorizing on the communication of emotion, Dittmann (1972) has employed an extension of information theory.

Recently, ethological studies have had a growing impact on nonverbal studies, creating what Argyle (1969) called the "new look" in social interaction research. Borrowing methods used in the study of animal social behavior, researchers have emerged with an area called "human ethology" or "interaction ethology" (Sebeok, 1968; Sherzer, 1971; Blurton-Jones, 1972).

Writers in several other areas have stimulated interest in nonverbal communication; e.g., McLuhan (1964) in mass media, Schutz (1967) in encounter groups, and Perls (1969; Perls, Hefferline, & Goodman, 1951) in gestalt therapy. For the most part, these writings have not led to directly testable hypotheses, but they may have an indirect effect on empirical research.

Research

While empirical research has surged in all areas of nonverbal communication, facial research seems worthy of special note for several reasons: (*a*) the face has the longest history of empirical study given any nonverbal sign system; (*b*) as a complex and central sign system, the face may reflect the problems and potential of other, less-explored areas; (*c*) it is a domain where differing theories and methodologies can be compared directly; and (*d*) the last decade has seen some major questions move toward definitive answers.

The Face

Researchers of the face can be dichotomized, first, into those who give the face separate attention and those who study the face only as part of a larger system. Birdwhistell, for instance, does not believe meaningful statements can be made about the face when it is isolated from other bodily acts. Among those who focus on the face, a dichotomy can be drawn between those who are primarily interested in emotion and those who are interested in other factors, e.g., the face as a regulator (Vine, 1970). Finally, among those who study facial affect, a distinction can be made between those who take a "dimensional" approach (Frijda, 1969) and those who take a "category" approach (Boucher, 1969; Ekman, 1972).

Of theoretic interest, facial affect has become a key testing ground for the generality of the kinesic hypothesis. Birdwhistell (1952) has taken the stance that he will assume all body movement is learned and communicational until it is proven otherwise. He has specifically stated that he does not believe there are universals in facial expression (Birdwhistell, 1970: 9), a position also espoused by LaBarre (1947; 1964). If there are pancultural universals, it of course means that at least one aspect of facial display is not learned like language; kinesic analysis based on linguistic assumptions would not therefore be appropriate in that area.

On the basis of cross-cultural research, including work with primitive people who have had minimal exposure to Westerners or the mass media, Ekman (1972; Ekman, Sorenson, & Friesen, 1969; Ekman & Friesen, 1971) now argues that there is clear evidence for at least a basic set of universal affect displays. Working with the category approach suggested by Tomkins (1962; 1963; Tomkins & McCarter, 1964), Ekman and his associates find high cross-cultural agreement in the recognition of surprise, fear, anger, disgust, sadness, and happiness. In short, Ekman argues that there are certain facial configurations which, when displayed, mean either that the individual is experiencing a specific emotion or that he is portraying that affect for observers.

Ekman recognizes that cultural differences will influence what will elicit a specific emotion and the extent to which an emotion will be suppressed or displayed openly. These cultural "display rules" he sees as a strong overlay, but they cannot completely erase the primary affects. Birdwhistell seems to argue for the overriding importance of cultural patterning, even in the area of smiles (Birdwhistell, 1970: chap. 5).

A second test of the kinesic approach comes from the isolation of cues in emotion studies. Birdwhistell (1970: 99) states that he has isolated thirty-two kinemes in the face and head area. He lists four brow kinemes (lifted brow, lowered brow, knit brow, and single-brow movement), four eye positions (overopen, slit, closed, and squeezed), four nose kinemes (wrinkled-nose, compressed nostrils, bilateral nostril flare, and unilateral nostril flare or closure) and, finally, seven mouth kinemes (compressed lips, protruded lips, retracted lips, apically withdrawn lips, snarl, lax open mouth, and overopen mouth).

The adequacy of this list would seem to be challenged by other observers, e.g., Kendon (Argyle, 1969: 123), Grant (1969), and Brannigan and Humphries (1972). Kendon, for instance, lists sixteen mouth positions, and Brannigan and Humphries articulate thirty-nine mouth behaviors. While these researchers have not called their units "kinemes," several behaviors seem to meet the requirements for a kineme, although they appear to have been omitted from the Birdwhistell observations.

Birdwhistell, of course, has proposed his set as "American kinemes," and he could argue that observations made by Kendon, Brannigan, Humphries, and Grant on the British should generate a different list of kinemes. Brannigan, Humphries, and Grant, however, are working in an ethological tradition; they have made their observations, for example, on young nursery-school children and they advance their findings as potentially panhuman.

A more direct test comes in the area of emotion, where specific facial cues have been isolated and presented to observers for decoding. Harrison (1964), for instance, presented drawings of faces, including some cues not mentioned by Birdwhistell, and obtained reliable interpretations from American decoders. Using the same stimuli with some additions, Cuceloglu (1967) obtained similar results in a cross-cultural study, and corresponding results have been found by other researchers (Thayer & Schiff, 1969).

While schematic drawings may oversimplify crucial cues, research with still photos and videotaped motion now provides additional evidence. The Facial Affect Scoring Technique (FAST), developed by Ekman, Friesen, and Tomkins (1971; Ekman & Friesen, n.d.), isolates one or more configurations in each of three areas—the brow, eyes, and lower face—for most of the major affects; e.g., there are distinctive brow positions for surprise, fear, sadness, disgust, and anger. None of these appears to be represented in Birdwhistell's list of kinemes.

The isolation of specific affect cues appears to be a major breakthrough in research on the face. In their critical survey of the facial literature, Ekman, Friesen, and Ellsworth (1972) note that a key methodological problem was the lack of "pure" affect stimuli. Frequently, the stimuli presented to judges were "blends," containing cues of more than one affect, and the obtained results were inevitably ambiguous.

Given the affect categories isolated in FAST, previous stimuli can be reexamined (Ekman, Freisen, & Tomkins, 1971), facial behavior can be analyzed from videotape recordings (Ekman & Friesen, 1971), and new stimuli can be produced. Ekman and Friesen, for instance, have developed a Brief Affect Recognition Test (BART) in which pure affect photographs are presented tachistoscopically. Research indicates that individuals differ in general ability to decode affects, and a given individual may block on a specific affect. This ability to decode micromomentary cues may, of course, relate to a range of communication phenomena (Greenbaum, 1956; Haggard & Isaacs, 1966; Shannon, 1971). Currently, Ekman and Harrison are developing a Drawn Affect Recognition Test (DART) in which the same affect is presented with variations in sex and race.

While the application of FAST is still expensive and time consuming, the availability of tests such as BART opens the door to studies using judges in which the researcher can use BART to screen out unreliable judges or to gauge the performances of his judges against those of other experimenters. Perhaps equally important, the emerging findings on the recognition of facial affect give new hope for the validity of studies using judges, whether a screening such as BART is used or not.

The following is an example of a finding from a study in which affect was judged: Young boys who were judged to look happy and aroused while watching television violence engaged in significantly more post-viewing aggression (Ekman, Liebert, Friesen, Harrison, Zlatchin, Malmstrom, and Baron, 1972). The unobtrusive recording of communication contexts presents a range of research possibilities. Similarly, once affect data is clearly identified and extracted, research can proceed on other uses of facial expression in interaction.

Other Areas of Research

Whereas a decade ago empirical research was largely restricted to the face or paralinguistic phenomena, now most areas of nonverbal behavior can boast at least some experimental work (Harrison & Knapp, 1972).

Extralinguistic phenomena—Several systems have been proposed for classifying extralinguistic phenomena (Newman, 1939; Sanford, 1942; Sebeok, Walker, & Greenberg, 1954; Pittenger & Smith, 1957; Pittenger, 1958; Sapir, 1958; Trager, 1958). In the Trager approach, paralanguage has two principal dimensions: (*a*) vocalizations—i.e., vocal noises such as laughing, crying, and groaning; vocal variations in intensity and pitch; and vocal segregates such as "uh-huh"—and (*b*) voice qualities such as resonance, range of pitch, and articulation control.

Mahl and Schulze (1964) present a major review of research in the area and also spotlight a difference in approach similar to the one discussed earlier in kinesics. Mahl and Schulze preferred the term *extralinguistic* to *paralinguistic*. Meanwhile, linguists at the Indiana University interdisciplinary conference on paralinguistics and kinesics argued for *paralanguage*, defending Trager's conceptualization against a more psychological construal that would give greater emphasis to the expression of emotion, personality traits, psychopathology, etc. (Mahl & Schulze, 1964:109).

In recent studies, Addington (1968) found that judges attributed distinct personality characteristics to speakers on the basis of paralinguistic cues, and Nerbonne (1967) found that speakers could make precise discriminations of sex, race, age, education, and regional origin on the basis of vocal cues. The effect of paralinguistic cues on experimental bias has been studied by Rosenthal (1966). And Dittmann (1972b) has been exploring verbal and nonverbal "listener responses."

Eye behavior—Gaze and eye contact have received major research attention, and eye behavior is emerging as a paramount regulator of interaction. Direction and amount of eye contact relates to speaker-switching, status differences, sex, and attitudes (Exline, 1963; Gibson & Pick, 1963; Lambert & Lambert, 1964; Argyle & Dean, 1965; Exline, Gray, & Schuette, 1965; Exline & Winters, 1965; Hess, 1965; Hess,

Seltzer, & Shlien, 1965; Efran & Broughton, 1966; Hutt & Ounsted, 1966; Exline & Messick, 1967; Kendon, 1967; Simms, 1967; Stass & Willis, 1967; Argyle, Lalljee, & Cook, 1968; Efran, 1968; Ellsworth & Carlsmith, 1968; Kleck, 1968; Strongman & Champness, 1968; Barlow, 1969; Exline, Thibaut, Hickey, & Gumpert, 1970; Woodmansee, 1970; Ellsworth & Ludwig, 1972; Exline, 1972).

Head nods—Similarly, head nods play a key role in regulating interaction according to research by Dittmann (1962), Dittmann and Llewellyn (1968), Rosenfeld (1966; 1967; 1972), and Gunnell and Rosenfeld (1971).

Body posture and orientation—Attitude, status, cultural differences, and interaction variables have been linked to posture and body orientation (Hewes, 1957; Mahl, Danet, & Norton, 1959; Dittmann, 1962; 1972; Reece & Whitman, 1962; Ekman, 1964; 1965a; 1965b; Scheflen, 1964; 1965b; Dittmann, Parloff, & Boomer, 1965; Lamb, 1965; Rosenberg & Langer, 1965; Charney, 1966; Ekman & Friesen, 1967; Mehrabian, 1967; 1968a; 1968b; 1969a; Wachtel, 1967; Mahl, 1968).

Spacing—Interpersonal distance and the arrangement of communicators in space has similarly been related to status, cultural expectations, attitude, and communication flow (Steinzor, 1950; Bass & Klubeck, 1952; Gullahorn, 1952; Byrne & Buehler, 1955; Hearn, 1957; Carpenter, 1958; Hall, 1959; 1963; 1966; Byrne, 1961; Strodtbeck & Hook, 1961; Winick & Holt, 1961; Calhoun, 1962; Hazard, 1962; Howells & Becker, 1962; Hare & Bales, 1963; Horowitz, 1965; Little, 1965; 1968; Rosenfeld, 1965; Triandis, Davis, & Takezawa, 1965; Campbell, Kruskal, & Wallace, 1966; Felipe & Sommer, 1966; Hutt & Vaizey, 1966; Watson & Graves, 1966; Willis, 1966; Altman & Haythorn, 1967; Lott & Sommer, 1967; Lyman & Scott, 1967; Priest & Sawyer, 1967; Russo, 1967; Sommer, 1967; 1969; Barker, 1968; Forston & Larson, 1968; Mehrabian, 1968a; 1968b; Jones, 1969; Albert & Dabbs, 1970; Jourard & Friedman, 1970; Watson, 1970; 1972).

Gestures—Hand movements have been increasingly differentiated by function (Freedman & Hoffman, 1967; Ekman & Friesen, 1969) and have been related to the communication of specific content (Saitz & Cervenka, 1962; Stokoe, Casterline, & Cronberg, 1965) as well as to such phenomenon as leakage in deception (Ekman & Friesen, 1969a). Other gestural studies include Hayes (1957), Michael and Willis (1968), Rosenfeld (1966), and Sainesbury (1955), Stokoe (1972), and Cohen and Harrison (n.d.).

Touch—Tactile communication has been reviewed by Frank (1957) and explored in the interpersonal context by Jourard (1966), Jourard and Rubin (1968), and Agulera (1967). Meanwhile, a complete tactile code system has been proposed by Geldard (1968). And Montagu (1971) has summarized a vast range of empirical and anecdotal data.

Artifacts—The consequences of artifactual manipulations, e.g., with clothing, furnishings, and architecture, have been examined by Festinger (1951), Maslow and Mintz (1956), Ellis and Keedy (1960), and Wheeler (1967).

Media—At least a start has been made on analyzing mediatory codes by Harrison (1964) and by Worth (e.g., Worth & Adair, 1972). Harrison calls his analysis of the pictorial code *pictics*, while Worth labels his work on film *vidistics*.

Future Trends

In contrast to the scene at midcentury, nonverbal communication appears today to be an area moving into scientific maturity, with a shift from anecdote to empirical research, a move from loose models to articulated theory, and a swing from casual observation to sophisticated methodologies. Looking to the future, it is easy to anticipate better theoretic formulations, a diffusion of research methodology and technology, a quickening pace of empirical research, and an increased application of findings to pragmatic communication problems.

To date, theory in the area has been largely borrowed, partly because of the general state of communication theory, partly because available communication theory had a strong verbal focus. Increasingly, communication theories subsume nonverbal signs (Krippendorff, 1969; 1970), and theories with a nonverbal focus seem increasingly likely.

In particular, the inflow of ethological theory and methodology is likely to stimulate a reexamination of paradigms. In the fall of 1970, for instance, Sebeok and Goffman organized a working conference in Amsterdam attended by behavioral scientists and ethologists from Europe and the U.S. (Sherzer, 1971). Sebeok, a key catalyst in the emergence of psycholinguistics (Osgood & Sebeok, 1964) and in the articulation of semiotics (Sebeok, Hayes, & Bateson, 1964; Sebeok, 1972), appears to be playing a similar role in the merger of human communication and ethology.

On the research front, the availability of recording technology, such as quality half-inch videotape, means that an increasing number of researchers will be able to do in-depth research on nonverbal phenomena. In what was a classic demonstration of kinesic and linguistic analysis—examining a conversation between Gregory Bateson, a mother, and her child (Birdwhistell, 1970)—the visual record was quite poor, since the motion picture camera had to be reloaded every ten minutes, and the single camera zoomed in and out on the various participants. With the advent of low-cost video equipment, the use of multiple cameras and continuous recording has become common. Similarly, sophisticated videotape-computer installations may become more common (Ekman, 1969).

Matching the advances in technology, new methodologies have been proposed for examining interaction which involves verbal and nonverbal bands (Harrison, 1969; Weick, 1969; Frahm, 1970), and several theoretically based observational systems are beginning to tackle the difficult problem of units of analysis (Argyle, 1969: 123; Duncan, 1969; Grant, 1969; Birdwhistell, 1970; Ekman, Friesen, & Tomkins, 1971; Brannigan & Humphries, 1972).

Finally, research is likely to increase on the application of findings to communication problems in therapy, medicine, education, and a variety of related areas. In an early study, Jecker, Maccoby, Breitrose, and Rose (1964) examined teachers' abilities to interpret students' nonverbal cues. Since then an increasing body of research has explored the possibility of improving nonverbal communication skills (Galloway, 1966; M. L. Knapp, 1972; Mehrabian, 1972b; Harrison, 1973).

REFERENCES

Addington, D. W.
1968 "The relationship of selected vocal characteristics to personality perception." Speech Monographs 35: 492–503.

Agulera, D. C.
1967 "Relationships between physical contact and verbal interaction between nurses and patients." Journal of Psychiatric Nursing 5:5–21.

Albert, Stuart, and J. M. Dabbs, Jr.
1970 "Physical distance and persuasion." Journal of Personality and Social Psychology 15:265–270.

Allport, Gordon W., and P. E. Vernon.
1933 Studies in Expressive Movement. New York: Macmillan.

Altman, Irwin, and W. W. Haythorn.
1967 "The ecology of isolated groups." Behavioral Science 12:169–182.

Argyle, Michael.
1969 Social Interaction. New York: Atherton.

Argyle, Michael, and Janet Dean.
1965 "Eye contact, distance and affiliation." Sociometry 28:289–304.

Argyle, Michael, M. Lalljee, and M. Cook.
1968 "The effects of visibility on interaction in a dyad." Human Relations 21(February):3–17.

Barker, L. L., and N. B. Collins.
1970 "Nonverbal and kinesic research." Pp. 343–372 in Philip Emmert and

W. D. Brooks (eds.), Methods of Research in Communication. Boston: Houghton Mifflin.

Barker, Roger G.
1968 Ecological Psychiatry. Stanford, California: Stanford University Press.

Barlow, J. D.
1969 "Pupillary size as an index of preference in political candidates." Perceptual and Motor Skills 28:587–590.

Bass, B. M., and Stanley Klubeck.
1952 "Effects of seating arrangement on leaderless group discussions." Journal of Abnormal and Social Psychology 47(July):724–727.

Bateson, Gregory, and Margaret Mead.
1942 Balinese Character: A Photographic Analysis. New York: New York Academy of Sciences.

Bell, Charles.
1865 Anatomy and Philosophy of Expression. Fifth Edition. London: H. B. Bohn.

Birdwhistell, Ray L.
1952 Introduction to Kinesics. Louisville: University of Kentucky Press. (Now available in microfilm only. Ann Arbor, Michigan: University Microfilms.)
1968a "Communication." Pp. 24–29 in D. L. Sills (ed.), International Encyclopedia of the Social Sciences. Volume 3. New York: Macmillan.
1968b "Kinesics." Pp. 379–385 in D. L. Sills (ed.), International Encyclopedia of the Social Sciences. Volume 8. New York: Macmillan.
1970 Kinesics and Context. Philadelphia: University of Pennsylvania Press.

Blake, W. H.
1933 A Preliminary Study of the Interpretation of Bodily Expression. New York: Teachers College, Columbia University.

Bloomfield, Leonard.
1933 An Introduction to the Study of Language. New York: Henry Holt.

Blurton-Jones, N. (ed.).
1972 Ethological Studies of Infant Behavior. London: Cambridge University Press.

Boring, E. G., and E. B. Titchener.
1923 "A model for the demonstration of facial expression." American Journal of Psychology 34:471–485.

Bosmajian, Haig (ed.).
1971 The Rhetoric of Nonverbal Communication. Glenview, Illinois: Scott, Foresman.

Boucher, J. D.
1969 "Facial displays of fear, sadness and pain." Perceptual and Motor Skills 28:239–242.

Brannigan, C. R., and D. A. Humphries.
1972 "Human non-verbal behavior: A means of communication," in N. Blurton-Jones (ed.), Ethological Studies of Infant Behavior. London: Cambridge University Press.

Bruner, J. S., and Renato Tagiuri.
1954 "The perception of people." Pp. 634–654 in Gardner Lindzey (ed.), The Handbook of Social Psychology. Volume 2. Reading, Massachusetts: Addington-Wesley.

Byrne, Donn.
1961 "The influence of propinquity and opportunities for interaction on classroom relationships." Human Relations 14 (No. 1):63–69.

Byrne, Donn, and J. A. Buehler.
1955 "A note on the influence of propinquity upon acquaintanceships." Journal of Abnormal and Social Psychology 51:147–148.

Calhoun, J. B.
1962 "Population density and social pathology." Scientific American 206 (February):139–148.

Campbell, D. T.; W. H. Kruskal; and W. P. Wallace.
1966 "Seating aggregation as an index of attitude." Sociometry 29:1–15.

Carpenter, C. R.
1958 "Territoriality: A review of concepts and problems," in Anne Roe and G. G. Simpson (eds.), Behavior and Evolution. New Haven: Yale University Press.

Charney, E. J.
1966 "Postural configurations in psychotherapy." Psychosomatic Medicine 28:305–315.

Child, I. L.
1969 "Esthetics." Pp. 853–916 in Gardner Lindzey and Elliot Aronson (eds.), Handbook of Social Psychology. Volume 3. Second Edition. Reading, Massachusetts: Addison-Wesley.

1972 "Aesthetics." Annual Review of Psychology 23:669–694.

Cline, V. B.
1964 "Interpersonal perception." Pp. 221–284 in Brendan A. Maher (ed.), Progress in Experimental Personality Research. Volume 1. New York: Academic Press.

Cohen, Akiba A., and Randall P. Harrison.
n.d. "Intentionality in the use of hand illustrators in face-to-face communication situations." Journal of Personality and Social Psychology, forthcoming.

Collins, B. E., and B. H. Raven.
1969 "Group structure: Attraction, coalitions, communication, and power." Pp. 102–204 in Gardner Lindzey and Elliot Aronson (eds.), Handbook of Social Psychology. Volume 4. Second Edition. Reading, Massachusetts: Addison-Wesley.

Critchley, Macdonald.
1939 The Language of Gesture. London: Arnold.

Crystal, David, and Randolph Quirk.
1964 Systems of Prosodic and Paralinguistic Features in English. (Janua Liguarum, Series Minor, No. 39.) The Hague: Mouton.

Cuceloglu, D. M.
1967 "A cross-cultural study of communication via facial expressions." Ph.D. Dissertation, University of Illinois. Ann Arbor, Michigan: University Microfilms No. 68–8046.

Darnell, D. K.
1970 "Semantic differentiation." Pp. 181–196 in Philip Emmert and W. D. Brooks (eds.), Methods of Research in Communication. Boston: Houghton Mifflin.

Darwin, Charles.
1965 The Expression of the Emotions in Man and Animals. Chicago: University of Chicago Press (reissue). First published in 1872.

Davis, Martha.
1972 Understanding Body Movement: An Annotated Bibliography. New York: Arno Press.

Dittmann, A. T.
1962 "The relationship between body movements and moods in interviews." Journal of Consulting Psychology 26:480.
1971 "Review of R. L. Birdwhistell, 'Kinesics and Context.'" Psychiatry 34:334–342.
1972a Interpersonal Messages of Emotion. New York: Springer.
1972b "Developmental factors in conversational behavior." Journal of Communication 22 (No. 4):404–423.

Dittmann, A. T., and L. G. Llewellyn.
1967 "The phonemic clause as a unit of speech decoding." Journal of Personality and Social Psychology 6: 341–349.

Dittmann, A. T., M. B. Parloff, and D. S. Boomer.
1965 "Facial and bodily expression: A study of receptivity of emotional cues." Psychiatry 28:239–244.

Duchenne, G. B. A.
1862 Mechanisme de la physiognomie humaine. Paris: Bailliere et fils.

Duncan, Starkey.
1969 "Nonverbal communication." Psychological Bulletin 72:118–137.

Efran, J. S.
1968 "Looking for approval: Effects on visual behavior of approbation from persons differing in importance." Journal of Personality and Social Psychology 10:21–25.

Efran, J. S., and Andrew Broughton.
1966 "Effect of expectancies for social approval on visual behavior." Journal of Personality and Social Psychology 4:103–107.

Efron, David.
1941 Gesture and Environment. New York: Columbia University Press. (Republished as Gesture, Race, and Culture. The Hague: Mouton, 1972).

Eisenberg, A. M., and R. R. Smith.
1971 Nonverbal Communication. Indianapolis: Bobbs-Merrill.

Ekman, Paul.
1964 "Body position, facial expression, and verbal behavior during interviews." Journal of Abnormal and Social Psychology. 68:295–301.
1965a "Communication through nonverbal behavior: A source of information about an interpersonal relationship." Pp. 390–442 in S. S. Tomkins and C. E. Izard (eds.), Affect, Cognition and Personality. New York: Springer.
1965b "Differential communication of affect by head and body cues." Journal

of Personality and Social Psychology 2:726–735.
1969 "VID-R and SCAN: Tools and methods for the automated analysis of visual records," in G. Gerbner, O. R. Holsti, K. Krippendorff, W. J. Paisley, and P. J. Stone (eds.), The Analysis of Communication Content. New York: Wiley.
1972 "Universals and cultural differences in facial expression of emotion," in James K. Cole (ed.), Nebraska Symposium on Motivation, 1971. Volume 19. Lincoln: University of Nebraska Press.
1973 "Darwin and cross-cultural studies of facial expression," in Paul Ekman (ed.), Darwin and Facial Expression: A Century of Research in Review. New York: Academic Press, forthcoming.

Ekman, Paul (ed.).
1973 Darwin and Facial Expression. New York: Academic Press, forthcoming.

Ekman, Paul, and W. V. Friesen.
1967 "Head and body cues in the judgment of emotion: A reformulation." Perception and Motor Skills 24:711–724.
1968 "Nonverbal behavior in psychotherapy research." Pp. 179–216 in John M. Shlien (ed.), Research in Psychotherapy. Volume 3. Washington, D. C.: American Psychological Association.
1969a "Nonverbal leakage and clues to deception." Psychiatry 32:88–106.
1969b "The repertoire of nonverbal behavior: Categories, origins, usage, and coding." Semiotica 1:49–98.
1971 "Constants across cultures in the face and emotion." Journal of Personality and Social Psychology 17: 124–129.
1972 "Hand movements." Journal of Communication 22 (No. 4):353–374.
n.d. Unmasking the Face (in preparation).

Ekman, Paul; W. V. Friesen; and P. C. Ellsworth.
1972 Emotion in the Human Face. New York: Pergamon Press.

Ekman, Paul: W. V. Friesen; and S. S. Tomkins.
1971 "Facial affect scoring technique: A first validity study." Semiotica 3: 37–58.

Ekman, Paul; R. M. Liebert; W. V. Friesen; R. P. Harrison; C. Zlatchin; E. Malmstrom; and R. A. Baron.
1972 "Facial expressions of emotion while watching televised violence as predictors of subsequent aggression." Pp. 22–58 in G. A. Comstock, E. A. Rubinstein, and J. P. Murray (eds.), Television and Social Behavior, Reports and Papers. Volume V: Television's Effects: Further Explorations. Rockville, Maryland: National Institute of Mental Health.

Ekman, Paul; E. R. Sorenson; and W. V. Friesen.
1969 "Pan-cultural elements in facial displays of emotion." Science 164: 86–88.

Ellis, R. A., and T. C. Keedy.
1960 "Three dimensions of status: A study of academic prestige." Pacific Sociological Review 3:23–28.

Ellsworth, P. C., and J. M. Carlsmith.
1968 "Effects of eye contact and verbal content on affective response to a dyadic interaction." Journal of Personality and Social Psychology 10: 15–20.

Ellsworth, P. C., and L. M. Ludwig.
1972 "Visual behavior in social interaction." Journal of Communication 22 (No. 4): 375–403.

Exline, Ralph.
1963 "Explorations in the process of person perception: Visual interaction in relation to competition, sex, and need for affiliation." Journal of Personality 31:1–20.
1972 "Visual interaction: The glances of power and preference," in James K. Cole (ed.), Nebraska Symposium on Motivation, 1971. Volume 19. Lincoln: University of Nebraska Press.

Exline, Ralph; D. Gray; and D. Schuette.
1965 "Visual behavior in a dyad as affected by interview content and sex of respondent." Journal of Personality and Social Psychology 1:201–209.

Exline, Ralph, and David Messick.
1967 "The effects of dependency and social reinforcement upon visual behavior during an interview." British Journal of Social and Clinical Psychology 6:256–266.

Exline, Ralph; J. W. Thibaut; C. B. Hickey; and Peter Gumpert.
1970 "Visual interaction in relation to Machiavellianism and an unethical act." Pp. 53–75 in Richard Christie and Florence L. Geis et al., Studies in Machiavellianism. New York: Academic Press.

Exline, Ralph, and Lewis Winters.
1965 "Affective relations and mutual glances in dyads," in S. S. Tomkins and C. E. Izard (eds.), Affect, Cognition and Personality. New York: Springer.

Fast, Julius.
1970 Body Language. New York: M. Evans.

Felipe, N. J., and Robert Sommer.
1966 "Invasions of personal space." Social Problems 14(Fall):206–214.

Festinger, Leon.
1951 "Architecture and group membership." Journal of Social Issues 1: 152–163.

Forston, R. F., and C. U. Larson.
1968 "The dynamics of space: An experimental study in proxemic behavior among Latin Americans and North Americans." Journal of Communication 18:109–116.

Frahm, J. H.
1970 "Verbal-nonverbal interaction analysis: Exploring a new methodology for quantifying dyadic communication systems." Ph. D. Dissertation, Michigan State University. Ann Arbor, Michigan: University Microfilms No. 71-2069.

Frank, L. K.
1957 "Tactile communication." Genetic Psychology Monographs 56:123–155.

Freedman, Norbert, and S. P. Hoffman.
1967 "Kinetic behavior in altered clinical states: Approach to objective analysis of motor behavior during clinical interviews." Perceptual and Motor Skills 24:527–539.

Frijda, N. H.
1969 "Recognition of emotion." Pp. 167–224 in Leonard Berkowitz (ed.), Advances in Experimental Social Psychology. Volume 4. New York: Academic Press.

Galloway, Charles M.
1966 "Teacher nonverbal communication." Educational Leadership. 24 (October):55–63.

Geldard, F. A.
1968 "Body English." Psychology Today 2(December):42–47.

Gibson, J. J., and A. D. Pick.
1963 "Perception of another person's looking behavior." American Journal of Psychology 76:386–394.

Goffman, Erving.
1959 The Presentation of Self in Everyday Life. Garden City, New York: Doubleday.
1961a Asylums. Garden City, New York: Doubleday.
1961b Encounters. Indianapolis: Bobbs-Merrill.
1963a Behavior in Public Places. New York: Free Press of Glencoe.
1963b Stigma. Englewood Cliffs, New Jersey: Prentice-Hall.
1967 Interaction Ritual. Garden City, New York: Doubleday.
1969 Strategic Interaction. Philadelphia: University of Pennsylvania Press.
1971 Relations in Public. New York: Basic Books.

Grant, E. C.
1969 "Human facial expression." Man 4 (No. 4):525–536.

Gray, William; F. J. Duhl; and N. D. Rizzo (eds.).
1969 General Systems Theory and Psychiatry. Boston: Little, Brown.

Greenbaum, M.
1956 "Manifest anxiety and tachistoscopic recognition of facial photographs." Perceptual and Motor Skills 6:245–248.

Gullahorn, John T.
1952 "Distance and friendship as factors in the gross interaction matrix." Sociometry 15:123–134.

Gunnell, Pamela, and H. M. Rosenfeld.
1971 "Distribution of nonverbal responses in a conversational regulation task." Paper presented at the meeting of the Western Psychological Association, San Francisco, April.

Haggard, E. A., and K. S. Isaacs.
1966 "Micromomentary facial expressions as indicators of ego mechanisms in psychotherapy." Pp. 154–165 in L. A. Gottschalk and A. H. Auerbach (eds.), Methods of Research in Psy-

chotherapy. New York: Appleton-Century-Crofts.

Hall, E. T.
1959 The Silent Language. Garden City, New York: Doubleday.
1963 "A system for the notation of proxemic behavior." American Anthropologist 65(No. 5): 1003–1026.
1966 The Hidden Dimension. Garden City, New York: Doubleday.

Hall, E. T., and G. L. Trager.
1953 The Analysis of Culture. Washington, D.C.: American Council of Learned Societies.

Hare, A. Paul, and Robert F. Bales.
1963 "Seating position and small group interaction." Sociometry 26:480–486.

Harrison, R. P.
1964 "Pictic analysis: Toward a vocabulary and syntax for the pictorial code; with research on facial expression." Ph.D. Dissertation, Michigan State University. Ann Arbor, Michigan: University Microfilms No. 65-6079.
1969 "Verbal-nonverbal interaction analysis: The substructure of an interview." Paper presented to the Association for Education in Journalism, Berkeley, California, August.
1973 An Introduction to Nonverbal Communication. Englewood Cliffs, New Jersey: Prentice-Hall, forthcoming.

Harrison, R. P., and M. L. Knapp.
1972 "Toward an understanding of nonverbal communication systems." Journal of Communication 22 (No. 4): 339–352.

Harrison, R. P.; A. A. Cohen; W. Crouch; B. K. L. Genova; and M. Steinberg.
1972 "The nonverbal communication literature." Journal of Communication 22 (No. 4): 460–476.

Hayes, F. C.
1957 "Gestures: A working bibliography." Southern Folklore Quarterly 21: 218–317.

Hazard, J. N.
1962 "Furniture arrangement as a symbol of judicial roles." ETC 19:181–188.

Hearn, Gordon.
1957 "Leadership and the spatial factor in small groups." Journal of Abnormal and Social Psychology 54: 269–272.

Hess, E. H.
1965 "Attitude and pupil size." Scientific American 212 (April): 46–54.

Hess, E. H.; A. L. Seltzer; and J. M. Shlien.
1965 "Pupil response of hetero- and homosexual males to pictures of men and women: A pilot study." Journal of Abnormal Psychology 70:165–168.

Hewes, G. T.
1957 "The anthropology of posture." Scientific American 196(February): 123–132.

Hinde, R. A. (ed.).
1972 Non-Verbal Communication. London: Cambridge University Press.

Horowitz, M. J.
1965 "Human spatial behavior." American Journal of Psychotherapy 19: 20–28.

Howells, L. T., and S. W. Becker.
1962 "Seating arrangement and leadership emergence." Journal of Abnormal and Social Psychology 64:148–150.

Hutt, Corinne, and Christopher Ounsted.
1966 "The biological significance of gaze aversion with particular reference to the syndrome of infantile autism." Behavioral Science 11:346–356.

Hutt, Corinne, and M. J. Vaizey.
1966 "Differential effects of group density on social behavior." Nature 209: 1371–1372.

Izard, C. E.
1971 The Face of Emotion. New York: Appleton-Century-Crofts.

Jaffe, Joseph
1968 "Computer assessment of dyadic interaction rules from chronographic data," in John M. Shlien (ed.), Research in Psychotherapy. Volume 3. Washington, D.C.: American Psychological Association.

Jecker, Jon; Nathan Maccoby; H. S. Breitrose; and E. D. Rose.
1964 "Teacher accuracy in assessing cognitive visual feedback from students." Journal of Applied Psychology 48: 393–397.

Jones, Stanley.
1969 "Nonverbal communication in the streets: A comparative proxemics analysis of dyadic interaction in selected subcultures of New York City." Paper presented at the con-

vention of the Speech Association of America, New York City, December.

Jourard, S. M.
1966 "An exploratory study of body-accessibility." British Journal of Social and Clinical Psychology 5:221–231.

Jourard, S. M., and Robert Friedman.
1970 "Experimenter-subject 'distance' and self disclosure." Journal of Personality and Social Psychology 15:278–282.

Jourard, S. M., and J. E. Rubin.
1968 "Self-disclosure and touching: A study of two modes of interpersonal encounter and their inter-relation." Journal of Humanistic Psychology 8:39–48.

Kendon, Adam.
1967 "Some functions of gaze-direction in social interaction." Acta Psychologica 26:22–63.

Kleck, R. E.
1968 "Physical stigma and nonverbal cues emitted in face-to-face interaction." Human Relations 21:19–28.

Knapp, M. L.
1972 Nonverbal Communication in Human Interaction. New York: Holt Rinehart and Winston.

Knapp, P. H. (ed.).
1963 Expression of the Emotions in Man. New York: International Universities Press.

Krippendorff, Klaus.
1969 "Values, modes and domains of inquiry into communication." Journal of Communication 19:105–133.
1970 "On generating data in communication research." Journal of Communication 20:241–269.

LaBarre, Weston.
1947 "Cultural basis of emotions and gestures." Journal of Personality 16:49–68.
1964 "Paralinguistics, kinesics, and cultural anthropology." Pp. 191–220 in T. A. Sebeok, A. S. Hayes, and M. C. Bateson (eds.), Approaches to Semiotics. The Hague: Mouton.

Lamb, Warren.
1965 Posture and Gesture. London: Duckworth.

Lambert, W. W., and W. E. Lambert.
1964 Social Psychology. Englewood Cliffs, New Jersey: Prentice-Hall.

Landis, Carney.
1924 "Studies of emotional reactions. II. General behavior and facial expression." Journal of Comparative Psychology 4:447–509.
1929 "The interpretation of facial expression in emotion." Journal of Genetic Psychology 2:59–72.

Lipman, Aaron.
1968 "Building design and social interaction." The Architect's Journal 147:23–30.

Little, K. B.
1965 "Personal space." Journal of Experimental Social Psychology 1:237–247.
1968 "Cultural variations in social schemata." Journal of Personality and Social Psychology 10:1–7.

Lott, D. V., and Robert Sommer.
1967 "Seating arrangements and status." Journal of Personality and Social Psychology 7:90–94.

Lyman, S. M., and M. B. Scott.
1967 "Territoriality: A neglected sociological dimension." Social Problems 15:236–249.

McLuhan, Marshall.
1964 Understanding Media. New York: McGraw-Hill.

Mahl, G. F.
1968 "Gestures and body movements in interviews," in John M. Shlien (ed.), Research in Psychotherapy. Volume 3. Washington, D.C.: American Psychological Association.

Mahl, G. F.; B. N. Danet; and N. Norton.
1959 "Reflection of major personality characteristics in gestures and body movements." American Psychologist 7:357.

Mahl, G. F., and G. Schulze.
1964 "Psychological research in the extralinguistic area." Pp. 51–124 in T. A. Sebeok, A. S. Hayes, and M. C. Bateson (eds.), Approaches to Semiotics. The Hague: Mouton.

Marlowe, David, and K. J. Gergen.
1969 "Personality and social interaction." Pp. 590–665 in Gardner Lindzey and Elliot Aronson (eds.), The Handbook of Social Psychology. Volume 3. Second Edition. Reading, Massachusetts: Addison-Wesley.

Maslow, A. H., and N. L. Mintz.
1956 "Effects of esthetic surroundings: I.

Initial effects of three esthetic conditions upon perceiving 'energy' and 'well-being' in faces." Journal of Psychology 41:247–254.

Matarazzo, J. D.; A. N. Wiens; R. G. Matarazzo; and G. Saslow.

1968 "Speech and silence behavior in clinical psychotherapy and its laboratory correlates," in John M. Shlien (ed.), Research in Psychotherapy. Volume 3. Washington, D.C.: American Psychological Association.

Mehrabian, Albert.

1967 "Orientation behaviors and nonverbal attitude communication." Journal of Communication 17:324–332.

1968a "Inference of attitudes from the posture, orientation, and distance of a communicator." Journal of Consulting and Clinical Psychology 32:296–308.

1968b "Relationship of attitude to seated posture, orientation, and distance." Journal of Personality and Social Psychology 10:26–30.

1968c "Communication without words." Psychology Today 2 (September): 52–55.

1969a "Significance of posture and position in the communication of attitude and status relationships." Psychological Bulletin. 71:359–372.

1969b "Some referents and measures of nonverbal behavior." Behavior Research Methods and Instrumentation 1:203–207.

1970a "A semantic space for nonverbal behavior." Journal of Consulting and Clinical Psychology 35:248–257.

1970b Tactics of Social Influence. Englewood Cliffs, New Jersey: Prentice-Hall

1970c "The development and validation of measures of affiliative tendency and sensitivity to rejection." Educational and Psychological Measurement 30: 417–428.

1970d "When are feelings communicated inconsistently?" Journal of Experimental Research in Personality 4: 198–212.

1971a "Nonverbal betrayal of feeling." Journal of Experimental Research in Personality 5:64–73.

1971b Silent Messages. Belmont, California: Wadsworth.

1971c "Verbal and nonverbal interaction of strangers in a waiting situation." Journal of Experimental Research in Personality 5:127–138.

1972a "Nonverbal communication," in James K. Cole (ed.), Nebraska Symposium on Motivation, 1971. Volume 19. Lincoln: University of Nebraska Press.

1972b Nonverbal Communication. Chicago: Aldine-Atherton.

Mehrabian, Albert, and S. R. Ferris.

1967 "Inference of attitudes from nonverbal communication in two channels." Journal of Consulting Psychology 31:248–252.

Mehrabian, Albert, and J. T. Friar.

1969 "Encoding of attitude by a seated communicator via posture and position cues." Journal of Consulting and Clinical Psychology 33:330–336.

Mehrabian, Albert, and Morton Wiener.

1967 "Decoding of inconsistent communications." Journal of Personality and Social Psychology 6:109–114.

Mehrabian, Albert, and M. Williams.

1969 "Nonverbal concomitants of intended and perceived persuasiveness." Journal of Personality and Social Psychology 13:37–58.

Michael, Geraldine, and F. N. Willis, Jr.

1968 "The development of gestures as a function of social class, education, and sex." Psychological Record 18:515–519.

Montagu, Ashley.

1971 Touching: The Human Significance of the Skin. New York: Columbia University Press.

Nerbonne, G. P.

1967 "The identification of speaker characteristics on the basis of aural cues." Ph.D. Dissertation, Michigan State University. Ann Arbor, Michigan: University Microfilms No. 68-4196.

Newman, Stanley S.

1939 "Personal symbolism in language patterns." Psychiatry 2:177–184.

Nierenberg, Gerard I., and Henry H. Calero.

1971 How To Read a Person Like a Book. New York: Hawthorne Books.

Osgood, C. E.

1959 "The cross-cultural generality of vis-

ual-verbal synesthetic tendencies." Behavioral Science 5:146–169.
1966 "Dimensionality of the semantic space for communication via facial expression." Scandinavian Journal of Psychology 7:1–30.

Osgood, C. E., and T. A. Sebeok (eds.).
1954 Psycholinguistics: A Survey of Theory and Research Problems. Baltimore: Waverly Press.

Osgood, C. E.; G. J. Suci; and P. H. Tannenbaum.
1957 The Measurement of Meaning. Urbana: University of Illinois Press.

Perls, F. S.
1969 Gestalt Therapy Verbatim. Lafayette, California: Real People Press.

Perls, F. S.; R. F. Hefferline; and Paul Goodman.
1951 Gestalt Therapy. New York: Julian Press.

Piderit, Theodor.
1867 Wissenschaftliches System, die Mimik und Physiognomik. Detmold, Germany: Meyers.

Pittenger, R. E.
1958 "Linguistic analysis of tone of voice in communication of affect." Psychiatric Research Reports 8:41–54.

Pittenger, R. E., and H. L. Smith.
1957 "A basis for some contributions of linguistics to psychiatry." Psychiatry 20:61–78.

Poiret, Maude.
1970 Body Talk. New York: Universal-Award.

Pratt, C. C.
1961 "Aesthetics." Annual Review of Psychology 12:71–92.

Priest, R. F., and Jack Sawyer.
1967 "Proximity and peership: Bases of balance in interpersonal attraction." American Journal of Sociology 72: 633–649.

Reece, M. M., and R. N. Whitman.
1962 "Expressive movements, warmth, and verbal reinforcement." Journal of Abnormal and Social Psychology 64:234–236.

Rosenberg, B. G., and J. Langer.
1965 "A study of postural-gestural communication." Journal of Personality and Social Psychology 2:593–597.

Rosenfeld, H. M.
1965 "Effect of approval-seeking induction on interpersonal proximity." Psychological Reports 17:120–122.
1966 "Instrumental affiliative functions of facial and gestural expressions." Journal of Personality and Social Psychology 4:65–82.
1967 "Nonverbal reciprocation of approval: An experimental analysis." Journal of Experimental Social Psychology 3:102–111.
1972 "The experimental analysis of interpersonal influence processes." Journal of Communication 22 (No. 4): 424–442.

Rosenthal, Robert.
1966 Experimenter Effects in Behavioral Research. New York: Appleton-Century-Crofts.

Ruesch, Jurgen.
1955 "Nonverbal language and therapy." Psychiatry 18:323–330.

Ruesch, Jurgen, and Gregory Bateson.
1951 Communication: The Social Matrix of Psychiatry. New York: Norton.

Ruesch, Jurgen, and Weldon Kees.
1956 Nonverbal Communication: Notes on the Visual Perception of Human Relations. Berkeley: University of California Press.

Russo, N. J.
1967 "Connotation of seating arrangement." Cornell Journal of Social Relations 2:37–44.

Sainesbury, P. A.
1954 "A method of recording spontaneous movements by time-sampling motion pictures." Journal of Mental Science 100:742–748.

Saitz, R. L., and E. Cervenka.
1962 Colombian and North American Gestures, A Contrastive Inventory. Bogotá: Centro Colombo American. (Being republished as Handbook of Gesture: Colombia and the United States. The Hague: Mouton, forthcoming.)

Sanford, F. H.
1942 "Speech and personality: A comparative case study." Character and Personality 10:169–198.

Sapir, E. A.
1921 Language: An Introduction to the Study of Speech. New York: Harcourt, Brace.
1931 "Communication." Pp. 78–81 in En-

cyclopedia of the Social Sciences. Volume 4. New York: Macmillan.
1958 "Speech as a personality trait." Pp. 533–543 in D. G. Mandelbaum (ed.), Language, Culture, and Personality. Berkeley: University of California Press.

Scheflen, A. E.
1963 "Communication and regulation in psychotherapy." Psychiatry 26:126–136.
1964 "The significance of posture in communication systems." Psychiatry 27: 316–331.
1965a "Quasi-courtship behavior in psychotherapy." Psychiatry 28:245–257.
1965b Stream and Structure of Communicational Behavior. Commonwealth of Pennsylvania: EPPI, Behavioral Studies Monograph No. 1.
1966 "Natural history method in psychotherapy: Communicational research," in L. A. Gottschalk and A. H. Auerbach (eds.), Methods of Research in Psychotherapy. New York: Appleton-Century-Crofts.
1967 "On the structuring of human communication." American Behavioral Scientist 10 (No. 8):8–12.
1972 Body Language and the Social Order: Communication as Behavioral Control. Englewood Cliffs, New Jersey: Prentice-Hall.

Schlosberg, H. A.
1941 "A scale for the judgment of facial expressions." Journal of Experimental Psychology 29:497–510.

Schutz, W. C.
1967 Joy: Expanding Human Awareness. New York: Grove Press.

Sebeok, T. A.
1972 Semiotics: A Survey of the State of the Arts. The Hague: Mouton, forthcoming.

Sebeok, T. A. (ed.).
1968 Animal Communication. Bloomington: Indiana University Press.

Sebeok, T. A.; A. S. Hayes; and M. C. Bateson (eds.).
1964 Approaches to Semiotics. The Hague: Mouton.

Sebeok, T. A.; D. E. Walker; and J. H. Greenberg.
1954 "Non-linguistic organization," in C. E. Osgood and T. A. Sebeok eds.), Psycholinguistics: A Survey of Theory and Research Problems. Baltimore: Waverly Press.

Shannon, Anna.
1971 "Facial expression of emotion: Recognition patterns in schizophrenics and depressives." Proceedings: 1971 ANA Research Conference. New York: American Nurses' Association.

Sherman, Mandel.
1927a "The differentiation of emotional responses in infants: I. Judgments of emotional responses from motion picture views and from actual observations." Journal of Comparative Psychology 7:265–284.
1927b "The differentiation of emotional responses in infants: II. The ability of observers to judge the emotional characteristics of the crying of infants and of the voice of the adult." Journal of Comparative Psychology 7:335–352.

Sherzer, Joel.
1971 "Conference on interaction ethology." Language Sciences (No. 14): 19–21.

Simms, T. M.
1967 "Pupillary response of male and female subjects to pupillary difference in male and female picture stimuli." Perception and Psychophysics 2:553–555.

Snider, J. G., and C. E. Osgood (eds.).
1969 Semantic Differential Technique. Chicago: Aldine.

Sommer, Robert.
1967 "Small group ecology." Psychological Bulletin 67:145–152.
1969 Personal Space. Englewood Cliffs, New Jersey: Prentice-Hall.

Stass, J. W., and F. N. Willis, Jr.
1967 "Eye contact, pupil dilation, and personal preference." Psychonomic Science 7:375–376.

Steinzor, Bernard.
1950 "The spatial factor in face-to-face discussion groups." Journal of Abnormal and Social Psychology 45: 552–555.

Stokoe, W. C.
1972 Semiotics and Human Sign Language The Hague: Mouton.

Stokoe, W. C.; D. C. Casterline; and C. G. Cronberg.
1965 A Dictionary of American Sign Language on Linguistic Principles. Washington, D.C.: Gallaudet College Press.

Strodtbeck, F. L., and L. H. Hook.
1961 "The social dimensions of a twelve-man jury table." Sociometry 24:397–415.

Strongman, K. T., and B. G. Champness.
1968 "Dominance hierarchies and conflict in eye contact." Acta Psychologica 28:376–386.

Tagiuri, Renato.
1969 "Person perception." Pp. 395–449 in Gardner Lindzey and Elliot Aronson (eds.), The Handbook of Social Psychology. Volume 3. Second Edition. Reading, Massachusetts: Addison-Wesley.

Tagiuri, Renato, and Luigi Petrullo.
1958 Person Perception and Interpersonal Behavior. Stanford, California: Stanford University Press.

Tajfel, H.
1969 "Social and cultural factors in perception." Pp. 315–394 in Gardner Lindzey and Elliot Aronson (eds.), The Handbook of Social Psychology. Volume 3. Second Edition. Reading, Massachusetts: Addison-Wesley.

Thayer, Stephen, and William Schiff.
1969 "Stimulus factors in observer judgment of social interaction: Facial-expression and motion pattern." American Journal of Psychology 82:73–85.

Tomkins, S. S.
1962 Affect, Imagery, Consciousness. Volume 1: The Positive Affects. New York: Springer.
1963 Affect, Imagery, Consciousness. Volume 2: The Negative Affects. New York: Springer.

Tomkins, S. S., and R. McCarter.
1964 "What and where are the primary affects? Some evidence for a theory." Perceptual and Motor Skills 18: 119–158.

Trager, G. L.
1958 "Paralanguage: A first approximation." Studies in Linguistics 13:1–12.

Trager, G. L., and H. L. Smith, Jr.
1957 An Outline of English Structure. Washington, D.C.: American Council of Learned Societies.

Triandis, H. G.; E. Davis; and Shin-Ichi Takezawa.
1965 "Some determinants of social distance among American, German, and Japanese students." Journal of Personality and Social Psychology 2: 540–551.

Vine, I.
1970 "Communication by facial-visual signals: A review and analysis of their role in face-to-face encounters," in J. H. Crook (ed.), Social Behavior in Birds and Mammals: Essays on the Social Ethology of Animal and Man. New York: Academic Press.

Von Cranach, Mario.
1970 "Some considerations in the study of communication." Munich: Max Planck Institute (unpublished).

Wachtel, P. L.
1967 "An approach to the study of body language in psychotherapy." Psychotherapy: Theory, Research, and Practice 4(No. 3):97–100.

Watson, O. M.
1970 Proxemic Behavior: A Cross-cultural Study. The Hague: Mouton.
1972 "Conflicts and directions in proxemic research." Journal of Communication 22 (No. 4): 443–459.

Watson, O. M., and T. D. Graves.
1966 "Quantitative research in proxemic behavior." American Anthropologist 68:971–985.

Watzlawick, Paul; J. H. Beavin; and D. D. Jackson.
1967 Pragmatics of Human Communication. New York: Norton.

Weick, K. E.
1969 "Systematic observational methods." Pp. 357–451 in Gardner Lindzey and Elliot Aronson (eds.), The Handbook of Social Psychology. Volume 2. Second Edition. Reading, Massachusetts: Addison-Wesley.

Wheeler, Ladd.
1967 Behavioral Research for Architectural Planning and Design. Terre Haute, Indiana: Ewing Miller Associates.

Wiener, Morton; Shannon DeVoe; Stuart Rubinow; and Jesse Geller.
1972 "Nonverbal behavior and nonverbal

communication." Psychological Review 79:185–214.

Willis, F. N., Jr.
1966 "Initial speaking distance as a function of the speaker's relationship." Psychonomic Science 5:221–222.

Winick, Charles, and Herbert Holt.
1961 "Seating positions as a non-verbal communication in group analysis." Psychiatry 24:171–182.

Woodmansee, J. J.
1970 "The pupil response as a measure of social attitudes." Pp. 514–533 in G. F. Summers (ed.), Attitude Measurement. Chicago: Rand McNally.

Woodworth, R. S.
1938 Experimental Psychology. New York: Henry Holt.

Worth, Sol, and John Adair.
1972 Through Navajo Eyes: An Exploration in Film Communication and Anthropology. Bloomington: Indiana University Press.

CHAPTER 5 Channels and Audiences

WILBUR SCHRAMM
Stanford University

This chapter analyzes the different channels for delivering communication, traces the developing concepts of audience behavior at the receiving end of these channels, then summarizes much of what is known about the size and nature of mass media audiences. In course, it takes up the question, Why is the audience there? and summarizes some of the chief conclusions concerning selective attention and perception, the motivations of mass media audiences, and the differential capabilities and effects of the media, including the ideas of men like Innis and McLuhan.

Channel is a word borrowed from telecommunication and applied to a number of different aspects of the communication process. One may talk, for example, of *sensory* channels, of *interpersonal* channels, or of *mass media* channels. In this chapter, the word *channels* will be used broadly to refer to the ways the signs in a message are made available to a receiver.

Audience is a word borrowed from the performing arts and public speaking, and is used to describe receivers or potential receivers of messages. These receivers may be of any number, and they may be engaged in a variety of behaviors; they may be related in a variety of ways to the sender, and they may make a variety of uses of the message. Here *audience* will be used simply to mean receivers of messages; however, we shall devote much of our attention to the receivers who have been most studied—the audiences of the mass media.

THE NATURE OF CHANNELS

One of the reasons for treating channels and audiences together is that we have come increasingly to posit an active and selective, rather than a passive, audience. Consequently, the analogy derived from electronic or hydraulic channels has proved less and less adequate to describe the relationship between senders and receivers of human communication.

Different kinds of channels are involved in the communication process, and different kinds of signals pass through them—e.g., light and sound waves through the atmosphere, and electrical impulses over neural pathways. But no one signal passes from cortex to cortex. The image of human communication that seems to be emerging is one of a relationship between two or more active persons, entered into with the aid of shared signs.

Whereas the relationship between a power source and the filament of a light bulb might be described adequately in terms of a connecting channel to a passive receiver, the relationship between sender and receiver has proved to be immensely more complex. To describe it, communication scholars have had to take into account the motivations and activity of two parties, and to specify a number of elements in the communication situation in addition to channels.

Deutschmann (1957) suggested a simple classification for communication situations, to which we have added examples of each type (see Table 1).

Other people have complicated this classification. The size of the assembled group obviously makes a difference: a two-person group, a group small enough for a living room, a group that requires a public hall or other meeting place. Clinical sociologists have argued that "context is content," which has a McLuhan-like ring but means essentially that the social setting and the shared or differing goals of the participants help to determine the nature of the communication relationship. In other words, it makes sense to assume that the different relationships of, say, two lovers under a moon, or a potential client to a salesman with his foot in the door, or a student to his teacher, or a father to his son, or a demagogue to an aroused audience will make some difference in the way communication occurs. The agreed-upon goals have some effect upon the relationship: for example, the goals of a discussion group versus those of a football team versus those of the crowd that gathered in Yankee Stadium to participate in the Papal Mass. As Blumer (1946) has pointed out, the situation for communication in a mob, or an acting crowd, is different from that in a work group or a play group.

It has also been said that the constrictions of the sign system itself are essential elements in the relationship. Thus Innis (1950; 1951) and McLuhan (1962; 1964) have concerned themselves with the determinism of printed signs. And critics have often pointed out, for example, that the relationship of a painter and someone viewing the painter's work is considerably different from the relationship of the maker of a road sign and the viewer of a road sign.

The simplifying insights are not yet at hand to explain this very complicated situation by which persons share a symbolic message and usually arrive at some degree of commonality of understanding. Theory in both the behavioral and the natural sciences typically moves ahead in an accordionlike pattern through alternating simplifications and complications. At the moment we can say that the idea of "channel" to describe the relationship of sender to receiver has proved too simple, and a principal trend of the last twenty years has been to complicate it by introducing new elements and new concepts.

TABLE 1

COMMUNICATION SITUATIONS

Private			Public	
Face-to-face	Interposed	Face-to-face	Interposed	
(two people converse at dinner)	(two people converse on telephone)	(Public meeting)	Assembled	Nonassembled
			(Movie theater audience)	(Viewing television at home)

"NAIVE PSYCHOLOGY" OF CHANNELS

In the absence of more general theoretical insights, researchers have typically worked on parts of the relationship—selective attention or perception, sensory-channel capacity, or learning through audio-visual presentation as opposed to audio presentation or printed media, to take a few examples. We shall have more to say about some of their results.

Some of the most useful generalizations in the area were made twenty-five or more years ago, and were based not so much on new research as on the kind of approach that Heider and his contemporaries called "naive psychology." This is not at all a pejorative term. It refers to insightful and stimulating observations that were only partly, if at all, supported by existing research but that contributed to useful understanding and to future research. We refer to books like *The Psychology of Radio* (Cantril & Allport, 1935) and *Radio and the Printed Page* (Lazarsfeld, 1940), and to the historic paper by Lazarsfeld and Merton (1948), "Mass Communication, Public Taste, and Organized Social Action," writings of a kind too infrequently seen in communication scholarship today.

Approaches of this kind have offered a kind of commonsense basis for at least partially classifying delivery systems. For example:

1. *The senses affected*—Face-to-face communication makes it possible to stimulate all the senses, if necessary and desirable. When anything is interposed in communication, some restriction is put on the use of the senses. Thus television and sound movies reach the eye and the ear (although McLuhan says, without evidence, that television affects the tactile sense also). Radio and the telephone reach only the ear, and print only the eye (although we must not underestimate the tactile pleasure of handling a beautifully made book). This line of classification calls for study of the handling of information in different sensory apparatus.

2. *The opportunity for feedback*—In a face-to-face situation the opportunity for quick exchange of information is maximal. As the face-to-face group grows larger, attention is diffused and a smaller proportion of the available feedback is used by any given person. When anything is interposed, the feedback is attenuated. For example, a telephone restricts not the speed but the amount of feedback because it is limited to one kind of sensory input. A *photo*-telephone would supposedly provide more feedback. Interposing a mass medium restricts both the speed and the amount of feedback, and the impersonality of media organization discourages it. When feedback to mass media is regarded as very important—as, for example, in teaching by television—devices such as pretesting, studio audiences, and reports from the classroom are introduced to approximate as closely as possible the face-to-face situation. This line of classification calls for research on how feedback is used and how communication can best be conducted when feedback is less than efficient.

3. *The amount of receiver control*—In face-to-face communication, a person can ask questions, help steer the conversation, and exert some control over the pace of it. A person reading print can set his own pace, pause to think over a point, repeat a passage, or reread the whole book or article if he thinks it necessary or desirable to do so. A listener to radio, or a viewer of films or television has no such control. To be sure, he can turn off the receiver, leave the theater, or allow his attention to wander, but he cannot control the pace or cause the flow of information to repeat or pause while he thinks. This is one of the reasons why television advertising has drawn more complaint than newspaper advertising, and why printed texts have proved so effective for individual study.

Traditionally, people have believed that sender control makes for more effective persuasion, receiver control for more effective learning. During the last decades, technology has moved to satisfy both—to provide more efficient circulation of information from a central point (e.g., via satellites) and to provide more control to the receiver (e.g., by recording devices and computerized methods of individualizing instruction). The problem is how to combine these two advantages.

4. *The type of message-coding*—In face-to-face communication, a high proportion of all the available information is nonverbal. This is only slightly less true of television and sound movies, still less true of radio and silent movies, and least true of print. Therefore, the silent language of culture, the language of gesture and emphasis and body movement, is more readily codable in some delivery systems than in others.

A high proportion of printed communication is coded in orthographic signs compared to a very low proportion of television and movies, while almost no painting, sculpture, music, or dance is coded orthographically. Thus, it is possible in printed media to abstract easily; in the audiovisual media, to concretize. This leads to a series of questions still not fully answered about the effects of different sign systems on individuals and societies, and the most effective combinations of sign types for given purposes.

5. *The multiplicative power*—Face-to-face communication can only be multiplied with great effort. Mass media, on the other hand, have an enormous ability to multiply a message and make it available in many places. They can overcome distance and time and, in developing regions, the audiovisual media can also overleap the barriers of illiteracy. Therefore, the advantages of this multiplicative power must be weighed against the advantages of the feedback provided by face-to-face communication.

A considerable amount of attention has been given in recent years to combinations of the two, in an effort to salvage some of the best of each: for example, the radio rural forum in which face-to-face groups meet together to hear and discuss broadcasts made especially for them, and the combination of television teaching with related, face-to-face activities in the classroom. Attention has also been given to the ways in which face-to-face communication is itself extended, either by very large meetings or by interpersonal networks. For example, when one hundred thousand people come together at a sports event or a political rally, the crowd effects are themselves an element of great importance in the communication. When a message is spread person-to-person, the networks may be spectacularly effective, as they were when the news that "Gandhi-ji is dead!" spread by word of mouth throughout India. Such messages may be distorted, however, as the students of rumor have discovered (see, for example, G. W. Allport & Postman, 1945; Festinger & Thibaut, 1951).

6. *The power of message preservation*—Face-to-face communication is evanescent. So, without recording machines, are the electronic media. It is difficult, therefore, for a person to relive a moving experience or enjoy a television program again, except in memory. The printed media have a great advantage in being able to preserve facts, ideas, pictures. Not until a way was found to record meaningful visual symbols was it possible to preserve human records, except on monuments or in the memories of old men and women. The importance of libraries, archives, and encyclopedias testifies to the significance of this function today. Now that the glut of information is so great, new retrieval systems are needed to supplement the storage of information; now that the audiovisual media are so important in our lives, new storage and retrieval mechanisms are needed for them also.

These are a few of the qualities of distributive systems that seem to be self-evident. But it must be admitted that the implications of these qualities are not always so clear as they might seem, nor is it always easy to test the implications by research.

SELECTIVE ATTENTION AND PERCEPTION

Regardless of how the signs are made available, no communication will take place except as a receiver selects from the signs available to him, processes the resulting stimuli, and translates them into something cognitive or behavioral. Much of the theorizing and research in this part of the communication process has been organized around two sets of behaviors usually called selective attention and selective perception.[1]

Any individual has available to him many more cues than he can possibly accept. It is necessary, therefore, for him to give his attention selectively. What he selects is not a random sample of what is available. The question is, What determines how he draws the sample?

Over fifteen years ago this author suggested a rule-of-thumb approach to this question which he called a "fraction of selection":

$$\frac{\text{expectation of reward}}{\text{effort required}}.$$

This fraction of selection was designed to help determine the probability of any particular communication being selected. When one tries to translate this into specific terms, however, the situation looks far less simple than the fraction would make it seem.

Freedman and Sears (1965) have reviewed the literature on selective exposure, seeking to answer the question, What do we know about the motivation that leads an individual to expose himself to one set of communication stimuli rather than another? With this excellent summary of selective exposure readily available, it will not be necessary to go over the same ground here.

They conclude that there is good evidence, mainly from field studies, that exposure to communication really is selective, and that regularities within the pattern suggest a tendency for people to expose themselves to information with which they agree rather than to informaton with which they do not.

> Republican rallies are mainly attended by Republicans, Baptist services are attended mainly by Baptists, the readers of the *New Republic* are mostly liberals and those of the *National Review* mostly conservatives. AMA journals are read primarily by doctors, and APA journals primarily by psychologists. The audiences for most mass communications are disproportionately made up of those with initial sympathy for the viewpoints expressed . . . (Freedman & Sears, 1965:61).

They point out, however, that none of this indicates a general psychological tendency to prefer supportive information. As a review of their examples indicates, there may be many other reasons—useful information, friendships, social roles and customs, for example—that help to explain such selective exposure.

Examining the laboratory studies bearing on the proposition that individuals seek information in agreement with their opinions, Freedman and Sears found five studies that seemed to support it, five that showed the opposite tendency, and seven that appeared inconclusive. They also tested against the literature the proposition that subjects under high dissonance will show a greater preference than those under low dissonance for supportive over nonsupportive information. This proposition was supported by only one study out of nine.

After some discussion of alternative reasons for exposure, they concluded as follows:

1. People are, in fact, exposed to disproportionate amounts of supportive

[1] The scholarly literature on attention and perception is too large to treat in detail here. The Freedman and Sears (1965) article has no counterpart in the field of selective perception. A helpful nontechnical introduction can be found in Berelson and Steiner (1964:100ff., 529ff.), and in Berlo (1960). More technical treatments are in Osgood (1953), F. H. Allport (1955), and Broadbent (1958).

information, although this is not an overwhelming nor completely ubiquitous phenomenon.
2. Laboratory evidence does not support the hypothesis that people prefer to be exposed to supportive as opposed to nonsupportive information.
3. The evidence does not support the hypothesis that the greater the magnitude of cognitive dissonance the greater will be the relative preference for exposure to supportive as opposed to nonsupportive information.
4. Although a variety of other factors such as confidence and familiarity may limit the conditions under which selective exposure occurs, at the present time there is not sufficient evidence to support any hypothesis concerning the effect of these factors on selectivity.
5. It is suggested that research in this area turn away from questions dealing primarily with the selective exposure hypothesis, and focus more on the questions of what factors chiefly determine voluntary exposure to information and how people resist persuasive messages with which they have been confronted (Freedman & Sears, 1965:94–95).

These results suggest that selective exposure is due to a complex set of causes, some of which may be operative at one time, some at another, and any of which in any particular case may be more powerful than the tendency to try to reinforce one's own opinions. What might some of these causes be?

1. *The availability of the stimulus*—How easily at hand is it? Advertisers know that more people look at large ads than at small ones, and political candidates know that if they saturate a broadcasting station with spot announcements most listeners will attend to at least one of them. Similarly, it is easier to see an audiovisual program on one's television screen than in the movie theater, although there may be other compelling reasons for going to the movies; and one is more likely to read a magazine if it is beside one's easy chair than if one has to go out and buy it.

2. *The contrast with its background*—Does the stimulus stand out from the field around it? How big is it? How loud? How much in contrast to the colors or patterns around it? All of us have had our attention jerked to a sudden contrast or change in our environment: a swift movement in a calm forest, a baby's wail in the night, a few seconds of silence in the midst of a rock-and-roll party, a falling star against the sky, a spot of orange against the blue of the sea. We find our attention drawn to large headlines and, if we are parents, we know that we must raise our voices if we want our children to "pay attention" while they are playing.

3. *The set of the receiver*—A person comes to any communication supermarket prepared by previous experiences to look for certain things. A fisherman is set to look for fish rather than wildflowers beside the stream. A student goes to class prepared to look for different cues than he seeks in the cafeteria.

4. *Estimated usefulness of the stimuli*—At any given time, a subject may be seeking information that he needs for a particular purpose—to pass a test, to decide whether to take along an umbrella, to find a quotation for a talk he has to give, or merely to be informed about a topic that he is likely to have to talk about. Some sources will prove over time to have utility for certain kinds of information, some for others, and thus an individual tends to develop habits and patterns of information seeking. A student who has been in class long enough knows pretty well what he must pay attention to, and how much attention. When a physician looks at a patient he looks for certain signs of illness or of well-being. When a commuter settles down into his seat with a familiar newspaper, he is set to look at certain parts of that paper and probably in a certain order. Most of us, as Stephenson (1967) cogently points out, are likely to learn that the act of reading or viewing or listening is pleasant in itself—other things being equal—and to develop habits of satisfying this pleasure, such as reading the newspaper at breakfast

or turning on the television, without much regard for the program, to relieve a boring evening.

5. *Education and social status of the receiver*—Finally, some qualities within the experience of any individual help to determine his communication behavior. Chief among these are education and social class. Freedman and Sears (1965: 80–81) review some of this evidence and note that there is perhaps no other correlation with information-seeking that is so strongly supported in the literature. For example, more education goes with more frequent choice of television news, information, and public affairs shows (for one national study supporting this, see Steiner, 1963: 168–170). Both social class and education relate to preference for print over television and to the use of educational television (see Schneider & Lysgaard, 1953; Schramm, Lyle, & Parker, 1961; Schramm, Lyle, & Pool, 1963). Education, especially, seems to be a function both of reading skill and of an appetite for information built up by acquiring a wider knowledge (see Wade & Schramm, 1969).

Obviously, there is a great deal more to be found out before the reasons for patterns of selective exposure are made completely clear.

The situation is much the same with selective perception and selective recall, except that data are somewhat harder to obtain. After a person has directed his attention to some set of stimuli, he organizes them according to his experience with coding data, his estimate of probable need for them, and the other information he has already stored. We really know surprisingly little about this coding process, but it is what we call selective perception—meaning that some elements in the available information are emphasized more than others, some are rejected entirely, and some or all are reinterpreted to fit into the frame of reference of the receiver. Over time the selective processes are further intensified as selectiveness in recall eliminates that which contradicts the receiver's predispositions (Hovland, Lumsdaine, & Sheffield, 1949) or his needs (Zimmerman & Bauer, 1956).

The need to organize information received is a deep human characteristic. If we see a pattern of dots on a television screen, we make figure and ground of it. If we look at an ink blot, we are likely to see in it a picture or story that tells more about us than about the ink blot. When we meet another person, we need to classify and code him in relation to the categories and classes of persons we have developed out of our experience. When we are confronted with an idea, we are likely to code it according to our established system rather than looking at it fresh. If our codes are few and rigid, both persons and ideas may be forced into rigid stereotypes—Communist, imperialist, leftist, rightist, hippie, or the like.

It is clear, then, that we are compelled to perceive any new information in terms of our frame of reference, meaning our funded and organized store of experience. If we hear the word *dog*, we can interpret it only in terms of the kinds of dog we have known. If we meet information for which we have no referable experience, it bothers us, and we seek closure, either by pretending it never happened, by reinterpreting it until it becomes comfortable, or by seeking new information to put it in its niche.

As we select against a background of our needs, we perceive personal characteristics, relevant group relationships, values, and beliefs. We interpret cues, once they are selected, to fit as comfortably and usefully as possible. This has been many times documented, and it is necessary here only to mention the Mr. Biggott study (Kendall & Wolf, 1949), in which prejudiced people completely missed the point of antiprejudice cartoons by interpreting them in such a way as to support prejudiced viewpoints; and the Asch (1958) studies, in which group influences led to the misperceptions of physical phenomena that were objectively verifiable.

Hsia (1968), Travers (1964), and others

have emphasized the significance of the fact that the central nervous system can apparently handle only a small part of the information that the sense receptors and the peripheral nervous system are capable of receiving. The human capacity to process sensory information has been measured in various ways and with various results,[2] but it is clearly much less than the amount of information available to the channel. Jacobson (1950; 1951a; 1951b) estimates that the input channel can handle only 1 percent of the information that can be taken in by the ear. Therefore, some mechanism of selection has to exist beyond selective exposure. It is reasonable to think that when the combined input from the two senses exceeds the amount of information the central system can handle, the conditions of interference are set up; and unfortunately this means that interference between channels may occur at any rate of presentation except a very slow one.

Broadbent (1958) has interpreted some of the selective process and interference phenomena in terms of a one-channel model for human information processing, and Feigenbaum and Simon (1961) also have suggested a simulated model that includes a single channel as a limit on the ability to process information. Travers (1964), following closely on Broadbent's model, has suggested that many of the results of learning experiments on single versus multiple channels can be interpreted if it is posited that the human system for utilizing information "has the properties" of a single channel.

It is important to speak of "properties" in this case, because the neural channels from the sense receptors are clearly separate. Travers' modification of Broadbent's model provides for a series of "compressions" of information, first by the sense organs and the peripheral nervous system, then by recoding and categorizing the input.[3] Then he assumes a short-term memory (maximum of two or three seconds) which can store information from one channel while the other channel is discharging through some gatekeeping and organizing mechanism.

Individual differences enter into the relative ability to learn from different channels, as May (1965) points out. A Soviet psychologist, Nebylitsyn (1961), found very low correlation between individuals' rankings for auditory acuity and visual sensitivity. Asher (1961) found that students who were visually dominant learned Spanish vocabulary with fewer errors when the stimulus words were presented visually and the response words were spoken than when the stimuli were presented aurally and the response words were spoken; he found the opposite to be true of those students who were aurally dominant.

Thus the learning effectiveness of different channels and combinations of channels seems to depend even more on how the channels are used, and for whom, than on the channels themselves. There is no particular magic in multimedia presentation per se. Hartman gives some advice to movie and television producers about using audiovisual media. If the conditions for interference are present, he warns, multiple channels

> may actually produce inferior learning because attention is divided and optimal learning is not possible in any of the channels . . . Pictorial illustrations in many cases may distract rather than illustrate. Attention-getting devices are of value only if they neither distract from learning which is already taking place nor continue in competition with the material

[2] Jacobson (1951a) estimated the maximum input from reading at 50 bits/sec. Pierce and Karlin (1957) estimated 43 bits/sec. for reading, and 78 bits/sec. for receiving music. Travers and Bosco (1967) estimated the possible reading input at 79 bits/sec.

[3] George A. Miller (1956) says that this process of recoding sensory information, in particular linguistic recoding, is "the very lifeblood of the thought process" and deserves much more explicit attention than it has received.

to which they are supposed to direct attention. The tradition in the television message is to place the majority of the information in the verbal audio channel and to attract attention and illustrate it in the pictorial. Too often the picture is not properly related to the sound and a real barrier to effective communication is created by a tendency to focus attention on the picture when the message to be learned has been coded in the sound track (Hartman, 1961:41).

McLUHAN AND SOCIAL-CHANNEL EFFECTS

An argument impossible to disprove is that studies of learning from different media channels are necessarily incomplete measures of learning, and that in particular what is learned from pictorial material is much more than any of the tests measures (for one thing because the tests are made by print-oriented scholars). One writer who would so argue is Marshall McLuhan (1962; 1964). Like his mentor, Innis (1950; 1951), McLuhan interprets the history of the modern West as "the history of a bias of communication and a monopoly of knowledge founded on print." The quotation is from an extraordinary paper by Carey (1967); because of McLuhan's somewhat oracular style of writing, it is often more satisfactory to quote his interpreters than his own statements.

Innis and McLuhan are technological determinists, concentrating on the influence of communication, and especially the influence of the printed media. The growth of communication through print, Innis argues, has killed the oral tradition, replaced the temporal organization of Western society with a spatial organization, transformed religion, shifted the locus of authority from church to state, brought about a relativity of values, and encouraged rampant nationalism. McLuhan is in accord with this but, as Carey points out, his approach is psychological rather than institutional, and is not unlike the Sapir-Whorf hypothesis that the language a person uses influences his view of the world and the nature of his thought (cf. Whorf, 1956). McLuhan extends the idea of "language" to media. His central idea, as Carey (1967:18) says, is that

Media of communication . . . are vast social metaphors that not only transmit information but determine what is knowledge; that not only orient us to the world but tell us what kind of world exists; that not only excite and delight our senses but, by altering the ratio of sensory equipment that we use, actually change our character.

McLuhan (1962, 1964) is not the first to claim that "the things on which words were written down count more than the words themselves," but his way of saying it is the one most often quoted: "The medium is the message."

McLuhan's chief contribution to the understanding of communication channels is his analysis of the supposed effect of print which, he contends, imposes a "particular logic on the organization of visual experience." It leads us to break down reality into discrete units, logically and causally related, perceived linearly, abstracted from the wholeness and disorder and multisensory quality of life. It "privatizes" man, encouraging withdrawal and individual study rather than communal activities. It "detribalizes" man, removes him, as Carey says, from the need to participate in a tightly knit oral culture. Finally, it encourages nationalism by standardizing the vernacular and making possible the growth of large political institutions.

For both McLuhan and Innis, the growth of print seems disastrous. McLuhan, however, looks beyond the age of print (which he considers dead) to a new age of television. Television, he believes, will restore the balance of the senses, "retribalize" man, lead him back to the communal experiences of an oral culture, encourage talking rather than reading, involvement and participation rather than withdrawal, action rather than meditation. It is this vision of the effect of television—

conceived at a time when many other persons are deploring the effects of television's materialism and violence—that more than anything else has been responsible for McLuhan's recent vogue.

RESEARCH ON MEDIA AS SOCIAL CHANNELS

These propositions, exciting as they are, do not readily lend themselves to testing. Moreover, McLuhan holds that testing is illegitimate because, among other reasons, modern research has a bias toward print. But so far as social research on the media can be summed up (e.g., in Berelson, Lazarsfeld, & McPhee, 1954; Katz & Lazarsfeld, 1955; Klapper, 1960; DeFleur, 1966; and the like), the findings seem to suggest that effects are more likely to arise from variability within media than from variability between media.[4]

Here, for example, are some of the generalizations it seems justifiable to make with respect to the effectiveness of the media as social channels:

1. Media have the power to focus attention, and thus to direct much of the interpersonal discussion within society. One of the first scholars to develop this point was Lasswell (1948). All the media seem to have this power. An exposé in print is as likely to focus attention as an event on radio or television.
2. Media have the power to confer status, as Lazarsfeld and Merton (1948) pointed out. Men like James Reston and Walter Lippmann have acquired special status from their writing in print, just as Edward R. Murrow and H. V. Kaltenborn acquired it from radio, and Walter Cronkite and David Brinkley from television.
3. The best evidence available indicates that face-to-face persuasion is more effective than persuasion on the audiovisual media, and that it is more effective than persuasion in print. But as Klapper (1960: 109) points out, "Some topics . . . may be susceptible of better presentation by visual rather than oral means, or by print rather than by film, while for other topics no such differences exist. The relative persuasive power of the several media is thus, in real-life situations, likely to vary from one topic to another."
4. A combination of face-to-face and media communication is likely to be more effective than either alone. But this seems to be true of all media, as can be shown from the effects of the radio rural forum in countries like India, the great books discussion groups in the United States, the combination of television teaching with classroom teaching in use in many countries.
5. A great part of any social effect of any medium depends on the audience at any given time. Indeed, one of the most solid findings in this area was expressed by Waples in 1940: "What reading does to people is not nearly so important as what people do to reading" (cited by Berelson & Steiner, 1964:529), and reiterated by Schramm, Lyle, and Parker (1961: 2):

> What televison is bringing to children . . . is not essentially different from what radio and movies brought them; but what children bring to television is infinitely varied . . . When we talk about the effect of television on children, we are really talking about how children use television.

Most of the variables (treated throughout this volume) that have been shown by research to be related to the social effects of the mass media channels are content or audience variables: prestige or perceived trustworthiness of the source, nature of the appeals, repetition, practice, order of presentation, age, ability, attitudes, motivations of the audience, salience of group

[4] Research on the media as social institutions, and the effects of the media, are treated elsewhere in this volume.

relationships, and so forth. This is not to say that there are no media effects apart from content and audience; indeed, there is good reason to think that there are such effects, whether or not they are as powerful as McLuhan suggests. But there is at least as good reason to think that there are powerful effects arising from the content, and especially from the interaction of content characteristics with audience characteristics. The message is more than the medium.

RELATION OF CHANNELS TO AUDIENCES

At this point we must take note of one of the clearest trends in communication research during the last several decades: the changing concept of audience.

From World War I to the 1950s, the dominant concept of the mass media audience was what propagandists and some advertisers called the "target" audience. In the early years of this period it was really thought of as a passive, relatively defenseless target which, if it could be hit by ideas from the mass media, could be knocked over. This is why World War I propaganda, and later Communist and Nazi propaganda, were so frightening to many people. The concept of a highly vulnerable audience was also responsible for the origin of many of our early propaganda studies, and for the development of the basic techniques of content analysis by Harold Lasswell and others (Lasswell, 1927; Lasswell & Blumenstock, 1939).

Along with this concept of the audience went a concept of communication as the transferring of something—ideas, feelings, knowledge, motivations—from one mind to another. A well-known encyclopedia, published by a major university in this country, defined communication as "the transfer of thoughts." This viewpoint has sometimes been called the *bullet theory* of communication: a propagandist could shoot the magic bullet of communication into a viewer or a listener, just as an electric circuit could deliver electrons to a filament and make the bulb light up.

Very soon, however, scholars began to modify this picture of the magic bullet and the passive target. The audience, when observed closely, often refused to fall over and play dead when hit by the bullet. Sometimes the bullet seemed not to penetrate at all; at other times the audience actually seemed to enjoy being hit, and suffered no change at all. (This was what happened, for example, when the Mr. Biggott cartoons were so completely misinterpreted.)

In trying to explain the failures of the bullet theory, sociologists and advertisers developed a new explanation that we might call the *category theory* of communication. It was necessary for advertisers and media heads to find a simple way of classifying audiences so that their responses to communication—the content they chose and the goods they wanted to buy—could more easily be predicted. With the development of survey research, it was quickly discovered that college-educated people had different media tastes from those of grade-school educated people, young people from old, men from women, Easterners from Midwesterners, rich from poor, and so forth. As the research went deeper, it was found that people who held certain clusters of attitudes, or certain beliefs, would react differently from others. These people could conveniently be described in categories, and it could be demonstrated that a given kind of media content (such as educational television) was likely to draw more response from the highly educated category, while another kind of media content was more likely to attract women than men (e.g., the soap operas, which were so readily available during daytime viewing hours), and still another kind to appeal to teen-agers (e.g., popular music).

Paul Lazarsfeld assumed much of the leadership for the development of audience research and the establishment of useful audience categories (e.g., Lazarsfeld, 1948). As he, his colleagues, and students examined audiences more closely they found that people in the audience belonged to groups, and that these people would not only discuss the content of the mass media in their groups but would also think of a "reference group" and test some of the content of the media against the norms of that group.

In other words, an audience was not a passive, but an extraordinarily active thing. This finding led to the study of the personal influence in groups compared with the influence of media content. Several voting studies indicated the importance of personal influence (Lazarsfeld & Merton, 1948; Berelson, Lazarsfeld, & McPhee, 1954), and several field studies identified "opinion leaders," persons whose advice was sought by others in the audience and who often passed on the content of mass media (sometimes modified by the leaders) to their followers. Katz and Lazarsfeld (1955) summed up this line of research in *Personal Influence*, in which they generally devalued the idea that mass media had great power over their audiences and substituted the concept that personal influence was responsible for most of the social control within media audiences.

If the rediscovery of the importance of personal influence was largely brought about by sociologists, psychologists were largely responsible for a parallel examination of personality, ability, and message variables in the effects of communication. Hovland, Janis, and others found that the I.Q. of a receiver, his motivations at a given time, and the responses he had learned were more specific than categories in predicting the effect of communication, and that these factors reacted specifically with message characteristics like source, appeals, and form of content (Hovland, Lumsdaine, & Sheffield, 1949; Hovland, Janis, & Kelley, 1953; Hovland, 1957; Janis et al., 1959).

Klapper summed up his interpretation of the effects of the mass media, in part, as follows:

1. Mass communication ordinarily does not serve as a necessary and sufficient cause of audience effects, but rather functions among and through a nexus of mediating factors and influences.
2. These mediating factors are such that they typically render mass communication a contributory agent, but not the sole cause, in a process of reinforcing the existing conditions.... Regardless of whether the effect in question be social or individual, the media are more likely to reinforce than to change.
3. On such occasions as mass communication does function in the service of change, . . . either:
   a) The mediating factors will be found to be inoperative and the effect of the media direct; or
   b) the mediating factors that normally favor reinforcement will be found to be themselves impelling toward change.
4. There are certain residual situations in which mass communication seems to produce direct effect, or directly and of itself to serve certain psycho-physical functions.
5. The efficacy of mass communication, either as a contributory agent or as an agent of direct effect, is affected by various aspects of the media and communication themselves or of the communication situation . . . (Klapper, 1960:8).

Even before Klapper wrote that summary, the bullet theory was, so to speak, shot full of holes. The media were no longer felt to be irresistible, nor was the audience any longer conceived of as passive. About this time the Zimmerman-Bauer (1956) experiment demonstrated that audiences not only refuse to be sitting ducks but they clearly seek and remember the media experiences they think will be useful. In a later paper Bauer (1964) wrote of the *Obstinate Audience* that refused to act like a target (see also chapter 6 in this volume). By the time two major studies of the effect of television on children and a major survey of general television-viewing habits had demonstrated that the audience is every bit as active in the communication situation as the senders of messages, it became apparent that communication theory had come 180 degrees from the idea of a target audience to that of an active audience.

Given an audience fully as active as the communicator, and recognizing that cognitive and semantic studies have discredited the idea that anything is really transferred between sender and audience, then we must ask whether the concept of channel is still very important to understanding the communication process. Rather than thinking of an unbroken channel from sender to receiver, through which passes a message, we might think of a different kind of relationship made up of related acts rather than of transfer. We might think, for example, of (*a*) two equal partners acting within a certain situation and a certain relationship to each other, one of whom (*b*) performs a communication act that results in (*c*) making public a set of signs available to any receiver who is able and willing to attend to them; the other partner then (*d*) performs a communication act that results in (*e*) attending or not attending, rejecting or accepting, and, if the latter, recoding his impression of the signs for storage or other use.

This would be the simplest communication situation. It would correspond less to a thought or an idea passing from cortex to cortex, or a mass medium shooting magic machine-gun bullets of propaganda into an audience, than to such a homely scene as a wife putting before her husband the dinner she has cooked, or a baker putting into his display case the pastries he wants to sell. The husband may or may not eat; any given passerby may or may not buy. And if either eats, he may or may not eat all of it, and he may or may not like it. But it takes two acts to complete the transaction.

The Question of Why the Audience Is There

Most of the explanations advanced to explain why people read or view or listen (beyond the work on selective attention already mentioned) have the disadvantage of being either overly general or overly specific. That is to say, they either propose a model that applies to many kinds of behavior besides communication or they list a number of reasons that seem to apply to different readers, different content, and different situations.

One of the former was the so-called fraction of selection (Schramm, 1954) mentioned earlier in this chapter:

$$\frac{\text{expectation of reward}}{\text{effort required}}.$$

This, of course, has face validity, and it may help to organize more specific data. For instance, there is considerable work yet to do on the kinds and degrees of reward people expect from mass media and on what they are willing to "pay" (not necessarily in money) for these rewards. We know, for example, that a teen-ager is typically more willing to pay for the social rewards of going to a movie theater, whereas his parents are likely to evaluate the rewards less highly and the effort more highly and to stay home with television. Some research just completed in Japan compares the evaluations given by a very large sample of people, fifteen to sixty-nine years of age, of certain qualities in different media as sources of entertainment (Fujiwara, 1969). How those sampled compared movies and television is shown in Table 2.

So far as rewards go, this table balances privacy against the pleasure of watching with the family. The judgments of entertainment rewards go to movies by more than 2 to 1. But the great difference is the relative handiness or convenience of the two media: stay at home or go downtown. Here television wins by a large margin. And it is not surprising that four times as many people reported they used television as movies for satisfying the need to relax and be entertained. In other words, the denominator of the fraction of selection bulked very large in this choice. But it must be pointed out that the fraction of selection

TABLE 2

REASONS GIVEN BY JAPANESE AUDIENCES FOR LIKING MOVIES AND TELEVISION

Qualities of Medium	Percent Responding Favorably	
	Movies	TV
Handy	14	70
Conveniently usable	8	22
Can enjoy quietly	9	5
Can enjoy privately	36	13
Rich in variety	18	7
Charm absent in others	19	5
Whole family can enjoy	9	44

would apply equally well to most voluntary behavior, including deciding whether to sign up for a certain class and whether to dine at Maxim's.

Another approach is Stephenson's (1967) "play theory." It makes a great deal of sense to think of reading a newspaper as a skilled act, the mere performance of which provides pleasure, like riding a bicycle or surfing. Yet one wonders whether this is all the reason for reading a newspaper or viewing television, and whether it applies specifically enough to communication behavior.

Berelson (1949) set the pattern for an interesting kind of study, repeated several times since, by interviewing a sample of people during a newspaper strike on what parts of the newspaper they missed. He came up with a long spectrum of rewards, ranging from the most rational—keeping up with the world, use as a tool of daily living, etc.—to some that could hardly be articulated—a feeling that reading is a "good thing to do," and a compulsiveness about the need to perform each morning the ritual of reading the paper.

One other approach used by several investigators has been to try to distinguish, at a deeper level than demography, the kinds of audiences who typically choose one kind of material rather than another. For example, people who hold delayed gratification norms (save up today to be ready for tomorrow) are much more likely than people who believe in immediate gratification to read about social and political problems, to view noncommercial television, and so forth (Schramm & White, 1949; Schneider & Lysgaard, 1953; Geiger & Sokol, 1959; Schramm, Lyle, & Pool, 1963).

At this stage, therefore, it is necessary to focus on interactions between different kinds of content and different kinds of values, abilities, and needs. The search goes on for organizing ideas.

THE YOUNG AUDIENCE

We are going to limit this description of the mass media audience almost wholly to the United States, not only because that is where most of the data are available, but also because to introduce even fragmentary data from elsewhere would make the chapter impossibly long.

The mass media are part of the environment of American children almost from the beginning of life. The electronic media are dominant until the child learns to read, after which his use of the printed media increases rapidly, as Table 3 indicates.

It is probable that television is even more dominant today in the first years of media use than it was in 1958 when these survey data were obtained. For example, a 1968 study in Japan (Tada, 1969) found that television had achieved the same level of saturation (91 percent) among Tokyo children at age four as among San Francisco

TABLE 3

CUMULATIVE PERCENTAGE OF CHILDREN WHO HAVE BEGUN TO USE GIVEN MEDIA BY A GIVEN AGE, SAN FRANCISCO, 1958
($N = 754$)

Age	TV	Radio	Maga-zines	Comic Books	Movies	Books		Newspapers	
						Read to Them	They Read	Read to Them	They Read
2	14	11	3	1	0	38	0	0	0
3	37	20	11	6	8	58	0	0	0
4	65	27	20	17	21	72	2	4	0
5	82	40	33	35	39	74	9	9	0
6	91	47	41	50	60	75	40	12	9
7	94	53	53	61	70	75	73	12	44
8	95	62	59	68	76	75	86	12	59

SOURCE: Schramm, Lyle, and Parker (1961:218).

children, ten years earlier, at age six. But the general pattern today must be much the same as it was then.

A child's use of the media in his second ten years of life reflects the development of new skills, the broadening of knowledge and interests, the demands and uncertainties of new social roles, and the gradual maturing of tastes toward adult patterns. During a child's early years the mass media available at home and the media tastes of the family are the greatest influence on his own media use. As he grows older, school and peer groups begin to be influential.

At first the child's media choices are almost wholly for entertainment. He seeks the comics in the newspaper, the light entertainment programs on television and, a little later, popular music on the radio. As he experiments with teen-age roles, social communication activities (such as going to the movies or the library) become more attractive. The influence of school is felt both in his choice of material and in restrictions upon his time. He actually makes less use than before of the media: he has more homework to do and more social activities to fill his time. He reads fewer comics, more about hobbies. The newspaper becomes more important to him. He reads more public affairs news, and some children discover the editorials. As younger children turn toward slapstick and fantasy, so do teen-agers begin to seek out the advice columns.

The general pattern of teen-age media use is shown in Table 4.

THE ADULT AUDIENCE

Two of the mass media, television and newspapers, are used by nearly every adult. Television is in more than 90 percent of American homes, and newspapers are read by more than 85 percent of American adults. Magazines reach approximately two-thirds of the adult population; somewhat less than half of American adults seem to attend movies with any regularity; and apparently only 25 to 35 percent read as much as one book a month. Radio has changed its role since the advent of television; now it seems to attract on the average about half the listening time per person that it used to get before television, and about half as much time per person as television does now. But radio is still feeling its way, and we must wait a little while before we can fit it realistically into current patterns of media use.

A number of studies have shown that an adult's newspaper reading rises to a peak during his forties and tapers off during his later years, perhaps because of eye changes.

TABLE 4

USE OF DIFFERENT MEDIA BY CHILDREN AND YOUNG PEOPLE IN THE FOURTH THROUGH THE TWELFTH GRADES, SAN FRANCISCO, 1958–1959

Medium	Grade				
	4 (N = 263)	6 (N = 262)	8 (N = 219)	10 (N = 201)	12 (N = 232)
Television (median hours per day)	2.2	2.5	3.2	2.9	2.4
Radio (median hours per day)	1.1	1.3	1.4	2.0	1.9
Movies (median number in last month)		1.4	1.8	1.4	1.2
Newspapers (percent who read every day)			47.6	55.3	66.2
Books (median number per month, nonschool use)	1.8	2.1	1.6	1.0	0.9
Magazines (median number read per month)			4.1	3.9	2.8
Comic books (median number read per month)	1.8	2.4	3.9	2.2	0.8*

SOURCE: Data compiled from Schramm, Lyle, and Parker (1961:219–266).

* There is some reason to think that comic book reading for the fourth, sixth, and eighth grades is underestimated because the measuring instrument did not provide for any entry above nine books per month, thus undermeasuring some very heavy readers. Higher figures were obtained by the same study in Colorado and British Columbia small towns. Baxter's Des Moines study (1960) estimates an average of two to four comic books a month for pupils in the fifth through eleventh grades. For comparable figures on television use, see the Baxter study and also Merrill's (1961) study in Lansing, Michigan. Nielsen's 1965 estimates are a bit higher than the ones in the table: 3 hours 29 minutes per day for children six to eleven, 3:14 hours for boys and 2:52 hours for girls in their teens. All studies of teen-age media use show a decrease in media time after the middle teens.

Several other studies corroborate this finding that from the late teens to the forties there is a substantial increase in time spent on the newspaper (see Schramm & White, 1949). Television use is somewhat greater in the years before thirty-five than in middle age, but peaks again in the years after fifty. Table 5 illustrates these patterns.

As a rule, magazine and book reading decline somewhat throughout adult life. Table 6 is taken from a fairly old survey that was made before television was widely available, when radio played much the same role in people's lives that television plays today. There are no really satisfactory figures on these audiences available from recent published studies; the many commercial audience surveys are not generally available to the public.

There is corroborative evidence that the use of magazines, books, and movies declines with age, however. For example, a *Newsweek* survey of five national magazines showed that the audiences of *Life*, *Time*, *Saturday Evening Post*, *Newsweek*, and *U.S. News and World Report* all declined slowly but steadily, beginning in the midteens and continuing through age sixty-five (Advertising Research Foundation, 1962). A *Saturday Evening Post* survey by Politz (1947: 4) found the audience of that magazine decreasing steadily with age, from 16.8 percent of teen-agers to 10.8 percent of people over fifty-five.

TABLE 5

TEEN-AGE AND ADULT USE OF TELEVISION AND NEWSPAPERS, BY AGE

	Teens		*20–35*	*35–49*		*50 and over*
Mean daily television M	3:14		3:00	2:58		3:58
viewing time[a] F	2:52		4:08	3:53		4:49
	15–16	*17–19*	*20–29*	*30–49*		*50 and over*
Read newspaper within last six days (Canada)[b]	72%	78%	80%	82% (N = 3,222)		82%
	15–17	*18–20*	*21–29*	*30–39*	*40–54*	*55 and over*
Read daily newspaper in U.S.[c]	69.4%	74.2%	74.9%	81.9% (N = 2,449)	83.0%	77.8%
	10–19	*20–29*	*30–39*	*40–49*	*50–59*	*60 and over*
Proportion of news read in daily newspaper[d]	9.3%	18.3%	21.8%	21.2%	21.4%	19.4%[e]

[a] Data compiled from Nielsen report, January, 1965.
[b] Data compiled from Canadian Daily Newspaper Publishers Association (1962:11).
[c] Data compiled from Newsprint Information Committee (1961:17, 31).
[d] Data compiled from Schramm and White (1949:156).
[e] The Westley and Severin (1964) study of nonreaders is in accord with this pattern.

All library figures support the idea that borrowers of books from libraries are predominantly young people. Indeed, the Survey Research Center survey of 1948 concluded that only 7 percent of people over twenty-one used libraries (see Berelson, 1949:199 ff. for a review of these book and library studies).

Finally, the National Opinion Research Council survey done in 1947 (reported in Lazarsfeld & Kendall, 1948:11) found that the proportion of persons in different age groups who saw *no* movies rose from 19 percent of those twenty-one to twenty-nine years of age to 73 percent of persons over sixty.

Persons over sixty continue to be active users of the mass media, especially television, and the media seem to play an important part in the years after retirement,

TABLE 6

PROPORTION OF DIFFERENT AGE GROUPS WHO USED EACH MEDIUM "YESTERDAY" (U.S. NATIONAL SURVEY, 1946; N = 4,000)

Medium	Age Groups *15–19*	*20–29*	*30–39*	*40–49*	*50–59*	*60 and over*
Newspaper	84%	85%	84%	87%	86%	83%
Radio	77	74	71	74	77	75
Magazines	51	44	38	36	35	35
Books	34	27	19	17	16	18
Movies	27	16	11	8	9	6

SOURCE: Link and Hopf (1946:116).

apparently serving in part to counteract the sense of loneliness and disengagement that comes when people are no longer with their work groups and many of their friends. The figures on the media activity of older people cited by Riley (1969) are truly impressive.

Even more significant than the changing *amount* of use of the mass media with advancing age is the changing *nature* of use. As people come to value wisdom more than physical prowess, their tastes in mass media also change. This can be illustrated from Steiner's 1963 report on the proportion of information programs selected by television viewers of different ages (see Table 7).

A parallel increase with age in the reading of public affairs news in newspapers was found by Schramm and White (1949: 156–158). The same study found that the reading of comics declined markedly, beginning some time in the teen years, and sports reading decreased after the thirties, as did the reading of crime and disaster news. Lazarsfeld and Kendall (1948: 136), using a national NORC survey, found that preference for news broadcasts, discussions of public issues, classical music, and religious programs increased with age, whereas comedy, popular and dance music, mystery programs, and sports became less popular. And Handel (1950) reported similarly changing patterns of story preferences on the part of moviegoers of different ages (see Table 8).

Some General Patterns

As people grow older, then, they increasingly prefer serious and informative content. That seems to be one basic trend in the way audiences cluster around mass media channels. Another such trend, many times documented (e.g., Link & Hopf, 1946: 114; Lazarsfeld & Kendall, 1948: 134; Berelson, 1949: 26; Schramm & White, 1949: 150 ff.; Steiner, 1963: 177; Schramm, Lyle, & Pool, 1963: 66; etc.), is that selection of serious and informative material rises with education. Use of print media increases, use of television decreases with education. When allowance is made for available free time (inasmuch as highly educated people are typically busy with nonmedia activities), then education appears to be positively related also to use of television and the other audiovisual media (Samuelson, Carter, & Ruggels, 1963); but when time is precious, highly educated people tend to seek their informational material in print rather than elsewhere.

The most promising way to explain these

TABLE 7

Proportion of Television Viewers Who Select Information Programs Over Entertainment Programs, by Age Group (National Survey, 1960; N = 2,427)

Age Group	Select Information Programs	Avg. Number Information Programs Per Viewer Per Week
Under 25 years	20%	5.2
25–34 years	33	8.9
35–44 years	31	8.8
45–54 years	35	11.2
55–64 years	44	16.4
65 years and over	48	22.4

Source: Data compiled from Steiner (1963: 178, chart).

TABLE 8

CHANGING LIKES AND DISLIKES FOR DIFFERENT TYPES OF MOTION PICTURE STORIES, BY AGE (1942 SURVEY IN 45 CITIES AND TOWNS; N = 2,000)

	Types of Stories			
Age Group	Slapstick	Mystery, Horror	History, Biography	Serious Drama
12–16 years				
Like	4.0%	8.5%	3.8%	5.1%
Dislike	4.4	7.6	8.7	6.4
17–29 years				
Like	2.4	5.4	5.8	10.3
Dislike	10.8	8.3	7.3	3.9
30–44 years				
Like	2.9	4.5	6.3	10.8
Dislike	11.0	10.4	4.5	2.9
45 years and over				
Like	1.1	5.3	7.1	12.2
Dislike	12.6	11.3	3.7	5.3

SOURCE: Handel (1950:125).

audience trends is in terms of the enlargement of the "life space," as Lewin called it. The more one's life space is enlarged, the more possibilities one has to interest himself in the mass media. Both in-school and out-of-school experiences enlarge the life space, but the most intensive and organized accumulation of experiences takes place in the school years, which is also the time when one develops the skill of reading. Therefore, it is not surprising that education is strongly related to use of the media, especially the printed media.

As a person's life space is further enlarged by experience after the school years and as his responsibilities become heavier and time begins to pinch, it is to be expected that serious interests would direct him to a higher proportion of serious media content. In school, however, an individual has learned ways to learn, and his interests have been shaped toward what to learn. So, as people with more highly developed reading skills and with a school experience that prepares them to read about science and social problems grow older and develop increasing interest in the policies and problems surrounding them, they naturally turn toward the printed media for their informational material (especially toward the newspaper, which is the most easily available of the printed media) and toward the serious parts of the audiovisual media. Such people, for example, form the bulk of the audience of public television.

This is not to imply any rejection of the audiovisual media for entertainment or for events or special reports. But the heavy use of television throughout life can be explained largely in terms of its power to furnish entertainment, only secondarily by its informational services. The strong and increasing use of the newspaper throughout the life cycle can be explained by its success in meeting the need that increases with age and experience for serious information, and in a form that persons with highly developed reading skills consider most convenient.

Clearly, there are other elements in the general patterns of mass media audiences. One of these is the changing role patterns that people are called upon to play throughout life; these patterns are clearly reflected in the selections made from the mass media channels. Still another is the declining vitality of human beings with age. A third is the procession of events and personalities through the media themselves. Certainly more Americans found themselves going to the mass media to learn about coronary thrombosis when President Eisenhower had his heart attack, to learn about presidential history and constitutional law when President Kennedy was killed, and to learn about astronautics and Newtonian mechanics at the time of the moon shots than would have done so had those spectacular events not occurred.

Thus, a program rating, a readership percentage, or the head count of a movie audience is not such a simple figure as it seems when one looks at the complex skein of causes that determine what audiences will gather around what channels at what time.

REFERENCES

Allport, F. H.
1955 Theories of Perseption and the Concept of Structure. New York: Wiley.

Allport, Gordon W., and L. J. Postman.
1945 "The basic psychology of rumor." Transactions of the New York Academy of Science (second series) 8:61–81.

Asher, J. J.
1961 Sensory Interrelationships in the Automated Teaching of Foreign Languages. Washington, D.C.: U.S. Office of Education.

Bauer, R. A.
1964 "The obstinate audience." American Psychologist 19 (No. 5):319–328.

Baxter, W. S.
1960 "The mass media and young people." Journal of Broadcasting 5: 49–58.

Berelson, Bernard.
1949 The Library's Public. New York: Columbia University Press.

Berelson, Bernard; P. F. Lazarsfeld; and W. N. McPhee.
1954 Voting: A Study of Opinion Formation in a Presidential Campaign. Chicago: University of Chicago Press.

Berelson, Bernard, and G. A. Steiner.
1964 Human Behavior: An Inventory of Research Findings. New York: Harcourt, Brace and World.

Berlo, David K.
1960 The Process of Communication. New York: Holt, Rinehart and Winston.

Blumer, Herbert.
1946 "The crowd, the public, and the mass," in Alfred McClung Lee, Jr. (ed.), New Outline of the Principles of Sociology. New York: Barnes and Noble.

Broadbent, D. E.
1958 Perception and Communication. New York: Pergamon Press.

Canadian Daily Newspaper Publishers Association.
1963 Report of a Study on the Daily Newspaper in Canada and Its Reading Publics (September-October, 1962). Toronto: Canadian Daily Newspaper Publishers Association.

Cantril, Hadley, and Gordon W. Allport.
1935 The Psychology of Radio. New York: Harper.

Carey, J. W.
1967 "Harold Adams Innis and Marshall McLuhan." The Antioch Review 27 (No. 1):5–39.

DeFleur, M. L.
1966 Theories of Mass Communication. New York: McKay.

Deutschmann, P. J.
1957 "The sign-situation classification of human communication." Journal of Communication 7 (No. 2):63–73.

Feigenbaum, E. A., and H. A. Simon.
1961 "Brief notes on the EPAM theory of verbal learning." Pp. 333–335 in C. N. Cofer and Barbara S. Musgrave (eds.), Verbal Behavior and Verbal Learning. New York: McGraw-Hill.

Festinger, Leon, and John W. Thibaut.
1951 "Interpersonal communication in small groups." Journal of Abnormal and Social Psychology 46:92–99.

Freedman, J. L., and D. O. Sears.
1965 "Selective exposure." Pp. 58–97 in Leonard Berkowitz (ed.), Advances in Experimental Social Psychology. Volume 2. New York: Academic Press.

Fujiwara, N.
1969 "Televiewing of Japanese people." Studies of Broadcasting 7:55–104.

Geiger, Kent, and Robert Sokol.
1959 "Social norms in television-watch-

ing." American Journal of Sociology 65(September):174–181.

Handel, Leo A.
1950 Hollywood Looks at Its Audience: A Report of Film Audience Research. Urbana: University of Illinois Press.

Hartman, F. R.
1961 "Single and multiple channel communication: A review of research and a proposed model." AV Communication Review 9 (No. 6):235–262.

Hovland, Carl I. (ed.).
1957 The Order of Presentation in Persuasion. New Haven: Yale University Press.

Hovland, Carl I.; I. L. Janis; and H. H. Kelley.
1953 Communication and Persuasion. New Haven: Yale University Press.

Hovland, Carl I.; A. A. Lumsdaine; and F. D. Sheffield.
1949 Experiments on Mass Communication. Princeton: Princeton University Press.

Hsia, H. J.
1968 "On channel effectiveness." AV Communication Review 16 (No. 3): 245–267.

Innis, H. A.
1950 Empire and Communications. London: Oxford University Press.
1951 The Bias of Communication. Toronto: University of Toronto Press.

Jacobson, Homer.
1950 "The information capacity of the human ear." Science 112:143–144.
1951a "The information capacity of the human eye." Science 113:292–293.
1951b "Information and the human ear." Journal of the Acoustical Society of America 23:463–471.

Katz, Elihu, and P. F. Lazarsfeld.
1955 Personal Influence: The Part Played by People in the Flow of Mass Communications. Glencoe, Illinois: Free Press.

Kendall, P. L., and K. M. Wolf.
1949 "Deviant case analysis in the Mr. Biggott study." Pp. 152–179 in P. F. Lazarsfeld and F. N. Stanton (eds.), Communication Research, 1948–49. New York: Harper and Row.

Klapper, J. T.
1960 The Effects of Mass Communication. New York: Free Press of Glencoe.

Lasswell, H. D.
1927 Propaganda Technique in the World War. New York: Knopf.
1948 "The structure and function of communications," in Lyman Bryson (ed.), The Communication of Ideas. New York: Harper.

Lasswell, H. D., and Dorothy Blumenstock.
1939 World Revolutionary Propaganda: A Chicago Study. Chicago: University of Chicago Press.

Lazarsfeld, P. F.
1940 Radio and the Printed Page. New York: Duell, Sloan and Pearce.
1948 Radio Listening in America. New York: Prentice-Hall.

Lazarsfeld, P. F., and P. L. Kendall.
1948 "The communication behavior of the average American." Pp. 1–17 in Radio Listening in America: Report on a Survey Conducted by the National Opinion Research Center of the University of Chicago. New York: Prentice-Hall.

Lazarsfeld, P. F., and R. K. Merton.
1948 "Mass communication, popular taste, and organized social action," in Lyman Bryson (ed.), The Communication of Ideas. New York: Harper.

Lewin, K.
1953 "Studies in group decision," in Dorwin Cartwright and A. F. Zander (eds.), Group Dynamics. Evanston, Illinois: Row Peterson.

Link, H. C., and H. A. Hopf.
1946 People and Books. New York: Book Industry Committee, Book Manufacturers' Institute.

McLuhan, Marshall.
1962 The Gutenberg Galaxy. Toronto: University of Toronto Press.
1964 Understanding Media. New York: McGraw-Hill.

May, M. A., and A. A. Lumsdaine.
1958 Learning from Films. New Haven: Yale University Press.

Merrill, I. R.
1961 "Broadcast viewing and listening by children." Public Opinion Quarterly 25(No. 2):263–276.

Miller, G. A.
1956 "The magical number seven, plus or minus two: Some limits on our capacity for processing information." Psychological Review 63:81–97.

Nebylitsyn, V. D.
1961 "Individual differences in the strength and sensitivity of both visual and auditory analysers." Pp. 52–74 in Neil O'Connor (ed.), Recent Soviet Psychology. Translation by Ruth Kisch [and others]. New York: Liveright.

Newsprint Information Committee.
1961 A National Study of Newspaper Reading—March, April, 1961. Prepared for Newsprint Information Committee. New York: Audits and Surveys Company.

Osgood, C. E.
1953 Experimental Psychology. New York: Oxford University Press.

Pierce, J. R., and J. E. Karlin.
1957 "Reading rates and the information rate of a human channel." Bell System Technical Journal 36:497–516.

Politz, Alfred.
1947 The Readers of the Saturday Evening Post. Prepared by Alfred Politz Research, Inc. Philadelphia: Curtis Publishing Company.

Riley, Matilda W.
1969 Aging and Society. Volume 2. New York: Russell Sage.

Samuelson, M.; R. F. Carter; and W. L. Ruggels.
1963 "Education, available time, and use of mass media." Journalism Quarterly 40(No. 4):491–496.

Schneider, Louis, and Sverre Lysgaard.
1953 "Deferred gratification pattern." American Sociological Review 18(April):142–149.

Schramm, Wilbur.
1954 "How communication works." Pp. 3–26 in Wilbur Schramm (ed.), The Process and Effects of Mass Communication. Urbana: University of Illinois Press.

Schramm, Wilbur; Jack Lyle; and E. B. Parker
1961 Television in the Lives of Our Children. Stanford, California: Stanford University Press.

Schramm, Wilbur; Jack Lyle; and Ithiel deS. Pool.
1963 The People Look at Educational Television. Stanford, California: Stanford University Press.

Schramm, Wilbur, and D. M. White.
1949 "Age, education, economic status: Factors in newspaper reading." Journalism Quarterly 29(No. 2): 149–159.

Steiner, G. A.
1963 The People Look at Television. New York: Knopf.

Stephenson, W. P.
1967 The Play Theory of Mass Communication. Chicago: University of Chicago Press.

Tada, T.
1969 "Image-cognition: A developmental approach." Studies of Broadcasting 8:105–174.

Travers, R. M. W.
1964 "The transmission of information to human receivers." AV Communication Review 12:373–385.

Travers, R. M. W., and J. J. Bosco.
1967 "Direct measures of the human information channel capacity." Pp. 273–274 in Proceedings of the 75th Annual Convention [Washington, D.C., September 1–5]. Washington, D.C.: American Psychological Association.

Wade, Serena, and Wilbur Schramm.
1969 "Mass media as sources of public affairs, science, and health knowledge." Public Opinion Quarterly 33: 197–209.

Waples, Douglas; Bernard Berelson; and F. R. Bradshaw.
1940 What Reading Does to People. Chicago: University of Chicago Press.

Westley, B. H., and W. J. Severin.
1964 "A profile of the daily newspaper nonreader." Journalism Quarterly 41(No. 1):45–50.

Whorf, B. L.
1956 Language, Thought, and Reality. Edited by J. B. Carroll. New York: Wiley.

Zimmerman, Claire, and R. A. Bauer.
1956 "The effect of an audience upon what is remembered." Public Opinion Quarterly 20:238–248.

ADDITIONAL READINGS

Arnheim, Rudolf. "What Do the Eyes Contribute?" AV Communication Review 10 (1962, No. 5):10–21.

Asch, S. E. "Effects of Group Pressure on the Modification and Distortion of Judgments."

In Readings in Social Psychology, edited by Eleanor Maccoby et al. 3rd ed. New York: Holt, Rinehart and Winston, 1958.

Bailyn, Lotte. "Mass Media and Children: A Study of Exposure Habits and Cognitive Effects." Psychological Monographs 71 (1959):1–48.

Baker, E. J., and Alluisi, E. A. "Information Handling Aspect of Visual and Auditory Form Perception." Journal of Engineering Psychology 1(1962):159–179.

Barrow, L. C., and Westley, B. H. "Comparative Teaching Effectiveness of Radio and Television." AV Communication Review 7 (1959, No. 1):14–23.

Bauer, R. A., and Bauer, Alice H. "America, Mass Society, and Mass Media." Journal of Social Issues 16(1960):3–66.

Bourisseau, W. S.; Davis, O. L., Jr.; and Yamamoto, Kaoru. "Sense-impression Responses to Differing Pictorial and Verbal Stimuli." AV Communication Review 13 (1965, No. 3):249–258.

Brandt, H. F. "The Psychology of Seeing Motion Pictures." In Film and Education, edited by E. M. Godfrey. New York: Philosophical Library, 1948.

Bruner, J. S., and Tagiuri, Renato. "The Perception of People." In Handbook of Social Psychology, edited by Gardner Lindzey, Vol. 2, pp. 634–654. Reading, Mass.: Addison-Wesley, 1954.

Cartwright, Dorwin, and Haray, Frank. "Structural Balance: A Generalization of Heider's Theory." Psychological Review 63 (1956):277–293.

Carver, M. E. "Listening Versus Reading." In The Psychology of Radio, by Hadley Cantril and Gordon W. Allport, pp. 158–180. New York: Peter Smith, 1941 (reprint of 1935 edition).

Cheatam, P. G. A Comparison of the Visual and Auditory Senses as Possible Channels for Communication. U.S. Air Force Technical Report 5919(PB-110278). Washington, D.C.: Air Materiel Command, 1950.

Cherry, Colin. On Human Communication. New York: Wiley, 1957.

Coffin, T. E. "Television's Effects on Leisure Time Activities." Journal of Applied Psychology 32(1948):550–558.

Corey, S. M. "Learning from Lectures Versus Learning from Reading." Journal of Educational Psychology 25(1934):459–470.

Davitz, J. R. The Communication of Emotional Meaning. New York: McGraw-Hill, 1964.

Day, W. F., and Beach, B. R. A Survey of the Research Literature Comparing the Visual and Auditory Presentation of Information. U.S. Air Force Technical Report 5921 (PB-102410). Charlottesville: University of Virginia, 1950.

Dember, William N. Psychology of Perception. New York: Holt, 1960.

Deutschmann, P. J.; Barrow, L. C., Jr.; and McMillan, A. "The Efficiency of Different Modes of Communication." AV Communication Review 10(1962, No. 3):176–178.

DuBois, C. "What is the Difference Between a Reader and a Viewer?" M/S 3(1959, No. 9):53–58.

Elliott, F. R. "Memory for Visual, Auditory and Visual-auditory Material." Archives of Psychology 29(1936):199.

Festinger, Leon. A Theory of Cognitive Dissonance. New York: Harper, 1957.

Gagné, R. M. The Conditions of Learning. New York: Holt, Rinehart and Winston, 1965.

Gibson, J. J. "A Theory of Pictorial Perception." AV Communication Review 2(1954, No. 1):3–23.

Goldstein, Harry. Reading and Listening Comprehension at Various Controlled Rates (Contributions to Education No. 821). New York: Teachers College, Columbia University, 1940.

Gropper, G. L. A Behavioral Analysis of the Role of Visuals in Instruction (Studies in Televised Instruction). National Defense Education Act, Title 7, Project No. 637. Pittsburgh: Metropolitan Pittsburgh Television Stations and the American Institute for Research in the Behavioral Sciences, 1963.

———. "Why Is a Picture Worth a Thousand Words?" AV Communication Review 11 (July-August, 1963):75–95.

Hall, E. T. The Silent Language. Garden City, N.Y.: Doubleday, 1959.

Harrison, R. P. "Pictic Analysis: Toward a Vocabulary and Syntax for the Pictorial Code; With Research on Facial Communication." Ph.D. Dissertation, Michigan State University, 1964. (University Microfilms No. 65-6079, Ann Arbor, Michigan.)

Hartman, F. R. "Investigations of Recognition Learning Under Multiple Channel Presentation and Testing Conditions." AV

Communication Review 9(1961, No. 1): 24–43.

Harwood, K. A. "Listenability and Readability." Speech Monographs 22 (1955):49–52.

Heider, Fritz. The Psychology of Interpersonal Relations. New York: Wiley, 1958.

Henneman, R. H. "Vision and Audition as Sensory Channels for Communication." Quarterly Journal of Speech 38(1952):161–166.

———, and Long, E. R. "A Comparison of the Visual and Auditory Senses as Channels for Data Presentation." WADC Technical Report 41(1954):54–363.

Himmelweit, Hilde T.; Oppenheim, A. N.; and Vince, Pamela. Television and the Child. New York: Oxford University Press, 1958.

Hsia, H. J. "Effects of Redundancy and Noise in Two-channel Information Processing." Ph.D. Dissertation, University of Wisconsin, 1967.

———. "The Information Processing Capacity of Modality and Channel Performance." AV Communication Review 19(1971, No. 1):51–75.

Janis, Irving L., et al. Personality and Persuasibility. New Haven, Conn.: Yale University Press, 1959.

Kay, B. R. "Intra-individual Differences in Sensory Channel Preference." Journal of Applied Psychology 42(1958):166–167.

Klapper, J. T. "The Comparative Effects of Mass Media." In The Effects of Mass Media, edited by J. T. Klapper. New York: Columbia University Bureau of Applied Social Research, 1949.

Klemmer, E. T. "Time Sharing Between Frequency Coded Auditory and Visual Channels." Journal of Experimental Psychology 55(1958):229–235.

Kopstein, F. F., and Roshal, S. M. "Learning Foreign Vocabulary from Pictures Versus Words." Paper presented at the annual meeting of the American Psychological Association, September, 1954. Abstracted in The American Psychologist 9(1954):407–408.

Lumsdaine, A. A. "The Effectiveness of Pictures Versus Printed Words in Learning Simple Verbal Associations." Ph.D. Dissertation, Stanford University, 1949.

———. "Cue and Response Functions of Pictures and Words." In Learning from Films, by M. A. May and A. A. Lumsdaine, pp. 123–149. New Haven, Conn.: Yale University Press.

———. "Instruments and Media of Instruction." In Handbook of Research on Teaching, edited by N. L. Gage, pp. 583–682. Chicago: Rand McNally, 1963.

McBeath, R. J. A Comparative Study on the Effectiveness of the Filmstrip, Sound Filmstrip, and Filmograph for Teaching Facts and Concepts. No. 7-04-102-00. Washington, D.C.: Office of Education, Department of Health, Education and Welfare, 1961.

McCormick, E. J. Human Engineering. New York: McGraw-Hill, 1957.

May, M. A. Word-picture Relationships in Audio-visual Presentation. Report to the U.S. Office of Education (July). Washington, D.C.: Office of Education, Department of Health, Education and Welfare, 1965.

Miller, J. G. "The Individual as an Information Processing System." In Information Storage and Neural Control, edited by W. S. Fields and Walter Abbott, pp. 301–328. Springfield, Ill.: Charles C Thomas, 1963.

Miller, N., et al. Graphic Communication and the Crisis in Education. Washington, D.C.: National Education Association, Department of Audio-Visual Instruction, 1957. (Published as Vol. 5, No. 3, of AV Communication Review.)

Morris, C. W. Signs, Language, and Behavior. New York: Prentice-Hall, 1946.

Nelson, H. E., and Moll, K. R. Comparison of the Audio and Video Elements of Instructional Films. Technical Report SDC 269-7-18, Instructional Film Research Program. University Park: Pennsylvania State University, 1950.

Parker, E. C.; Barry, D. W.; and Smythe, D. W. Television-Radio Audience and Religion. New York: Harper, 1955.

Pierce, J. R. Symbols, Signals and Noise: The Nature and Process of Communication. New York: Harper and Row, 1961.

Rohracher, H. Kleine Characterkunde. Vienna: Urban and Schwarzenberg, 1961.

Schramm, Wilbur, and Carter, R. F. "Effectiveness of a Political Telethon." Public Opinion Quarterly 23 (1959):121–126.

Seldes, Gilbert V. The Great Audience. New York: Viking Press, 1950.

Star, Shirley A., and Hughes, Helen MacGill. "Report on an Educational Campaign: The Cincinnati Plan for the United Nations."

American Journal of Sociology 55 (1950): 389–400.

Stickell, D. W. "A Critical Review of the Methodology and Results of Research Comparing Televised and Face-to-face Instruction." Ph.D. Dissertation, Pennsylvania State University, 1963. Cited by L. P. Greenhill in Improvement of Teaching by Television, edited by B. L. Griffith and D. W. MacLennan et al., pp. 17–21. Columbia, Mo.: University of Missouri Press, 1964.

Swanson, C. E. "What They Read in 130 Daily Newspapers." Journalism Quarterly 32(1955):411–421.

Travers, R. M. W., et al. Research and Theory Related to Audiovisual Information Transmission. Salt Lake City: University of Utah Bureau of Educational Research, 1964.

Westley, B. H., and Barrow, L. C., Jr. Exploring the News: A Comparative Study of the Teaching Effectiveness of Radio and Television. Research Bulletin No. 12. Madison University of Wisconsin Television Laboratory.

CHAPTER 6 The Audience

RAYMOND A. BAUER
Harvard University

As the preceding chapter demonstrates, our ideas of what a mass media audience is and does have changed markedly in recent decades. The author of this chapter is the scholar who first wrote about the "obstinate audience," and whose research and analysis played a key part in finally demolishing the idea of the audience as passive. Here he presents a model of the audience that is far from the passive and atomistic audiences conceived of thirty years ago, and he analyzes the studies that lead to that model.

The audience is, of course, the whole point of communication. The traditional Laswellian formulation of the communication process reads: "Who says what in which channel *to whom* with what effect" (italics added) (Lasswell, 1948:37). Yet the audience has been given a rather grudging role in communication writing and communication research. For a long time it was regarded in a peculiarly passive way. It was "the object of influence" that was counted and described in order to establish the numbers and types of people who were affected. The fact and nature of influence was taken for granted.

Over time it became obvious that not everybody potentially exposed to a communication paid attention to it, that some people perceived it differently from others, that they remembered it differently, that they reacted to it differently, and that they reacted to it not as isolated individuals but as members of social groups. A few investigators discovered that the audience even had an influence on the communicator by virtue of the way in which his expectations of the nature and response of his audience caused him to organize and process information before transmitting it.

THE CHANGING CONCEPT OF AUDIENCE ROLE

The modern history of communication research and communication theory can be written to a great extent in terms of the enlarged role of the audience as a factor mediating the effects, if any, of communication. Communication research of thirty years ago was generally known as "propaganda analysis" (cf. Doob, 1935). The major effort of "propaganda analysts" was to expose the mechanisms whereby propagandists achieve their influence over people, and to study the structure of the various media to show how the means of exerting influence were coming progressively into the hands of a smaller and smaller clique of rich men who used them to maintain the existing social order.

Another concern was audience measurement. Audience measures were made of newspaper and magazine readership, and the sample survey was developed to a great extent to obtain measures of radio listening. The purpose of these measures, however, was to set advertising rates. There was scarcely any concern with the consequences of exposure to these media (a typical textbook of the period was Albig, 1939).

A few attempts at measuring the effects of communications were made in the 1930s. Probably most notable were the studies of the correlation of movie viewing with socially undesirable behavior (e.g., Blumer, 1933; Blumer & Houser, 1933). These studies failed to have much effect on the image of the communication process because it was assumed that where a correlation existed, it was the result of the effect of the movies on behavior rather than the possibility that juveniles who behaved in an undesirable way might prefer certain types of movies; i.e., the effect was taken for granted, not investigated.

Substantial attention began to be paid to the audience in the early 1940s as two things became apparent: (1) The audience plays an active role in deciding what it will pay attention to; and (2) different people react to the same communication in different ways (for a more extended treatment, see Bauer & Bauer, 1960). Later in the 1940s the notion that citizens of a "mass society" react to communications as "social atoms" began to be displaced by an increasing awareness of the fact that people react to communications as members of social groups (see Freidsen, 1953). Furthermore, as the limitations of formal communications were realized, attention was turned to the role played by informal communication.

With the coining of the notion of a two-step process in communication in which "opinion leaders" use the information they get from the mass media to influence other people, the audience became in turn a potential communicator (Katz, 1957). Furthermore, once attention was paid to informal, person-to-person communication, then the part of feedback from the audience in the person-to-person situation became apparent and, implicitly, the audience was again accorded a slightly more active role.

In this recounting we can see a series of steps in which the audience is accorded an increasingly more active role. The built-in logic of the sequence that has been depicted can be extended another step. If feedback takes place and the communicator responds to it so as to correct any errors that may have resulted from his original communication, then it is only reasonable to assume that a communicator would try in advance to imagine what the audience would be like and how it was likely to react to the messages he sent. Therefore, to the extent that he wanted to produce a given effect he would couch what he had to say in terms relevant to that particular audience. In other words, *the audience would have influenced what he said before the audience ever heard or read what he had to say*. If this logic is accepted, then in some sense the direction of "influence" is moot. It is just as proper to say that the audience influences the communicator as to say that the communicator influences the audience. The process of influence works in both directions.

This notion of a transactional model of communication as a process of mutual two-way influence had a brief flurry in the mid-1950s when some of us demonstrated that the prospect of communicating to an audience of specified characteristics could affect the way people handle incoming information. Specifically, we demonstrated that a "communicator" exposed to new information with the thought that he or she was going to have to write a speech for an audience (which had previously been described to him or her) could not recall, one week later, as much material that was opposed to that audience's point of view as he or she could material that favored the audience's view. Furthermore, students of journalism, whom we had expected to be more "audience-sensitive," were more selective in remembering material that their potential audience might favor than were persons directly involved in the issue—for example, students in teachers' colleges, involved with the subject of teachers' pay (Zimmerman & Bauer, 1956; replicated by Schramm & Danielson, 1958). This demonstration that an imagined audience could leave a lasting impact on a prospective communicator even though he never communicated to that audience is the furthest empirical extension of a transactional model of which I am aware.

While lip service is often given to the proposition that the communication process is a transactional one in which communicator and audience play equally active roles, this notion has little effective impact on the organized research or systematic writing that is done. One might expect this transactional model to be most reflected in writing on the theater, particularly in the light of the oft-expressed mystique of the relationship of the actor to the audience. In point of fact, it is difficult to find much if any in the way of even systematic speculation about the nature of this relationship.

A moderate amount of research in the spring of 1967 uncovered examples such as the following:

> . . . think of the audience not only as a passive witness of the dramatic spectacle, but as an active and creative participant. Periods of greatness in dramatic art have always reflected an awakening of social consciousness (Downs, 1953:23).

There were several other references that, like this one, deal with the audience in anecdotal perspective.

> . . . audience reaction will not be the same night after night. These variations in audience reaction affect the actor in the same way that stubbing his toe on an unexpected stone affects a pedestrian. It is disconcerting when a joke which has hitherto got a big laugh fails to do so and also disconcerting when this is followed by laughter over a joke which has not gone down too well previously. Most jarring of all, of course, are the occasions when there are a few giggles during a play which is not a comedy (Lane, 1960:83).

This comes closer to the recognition of a transaction but of course is far from being systematic. A fairly recent book by Baumol and Bowen (1966) includes a description of characteristics of the theater audience. That is, these audiences are composed largely of well-educated, well-to-do, white-collared professionals. This is a systematic, but very different, view of the audience than this chapter is concerned with (see, especially, Baumol & Bowen, 1966:71–98).

With diligence one could piece together a considerable number of such examples in which the communication process is seen as a two-way transaction. But this diligence would create a false image of the way in which the audience is ordinarily treated in communication research and writing. The flow of influence is still treated predominantly as a linear one from the communicator to the audience, with the "result" being some change in the audience in line with some intention of the communicator. The audience is seen as exercising a mediating role in which it can stop, deflect, or modify the intent of the communicator. But for practical purposes, the model is almost always one based on a concern with the intent of the communicator. It is to this view of the audience as mediator that we now turn.

THE AUDIENCE AS MEDIATOR

Selective attention, selective perception, selective retention, selective recall—these are the key concepts associated with the mediating role of the audience. It has been regularly observed that people will pay selective attention to the messages that are offered to them. By and large, they pay attention to messages with which they agree. For example, in political campaigns they are likely to read newspaper articles concerning the candidate they already prefer (Lazarsfeld, Berelson, & Gaudet, 1948:

37). People will read advertisements for products they already use (Ehrlich, Guttman, Schonbach, & Mills, 1957). On the whole, the mechanism of selective attention poses a formidable obstacle for the communicator who wants to get attention for some point of view or topic that the audience is not already convinced it is interested in.

Two or more people exposed to the same physical stimulus are seldom if ever in an identical relationship to it. It is a moot point whether people perceive things differently or whether physically identical things mean different things to different people. For instance, to an experienced ball player, a baseball flying in his direction is a thing to be caught; to a little old lady, it is a thing to be ducked. In any event, it has long been demonstrated that different people do not pull the same meaning out of a given message. For example, when highly prejudiced people were shown a cartoon of "Mr. Biggott," a character depicted as expressing extreme anti-Semitic views, some of these highly prejudiced people thought the purpose of the cartoon was to reassure them that other people shared their views (Cooper & Jahoda, 1947).

The distinctions between *perception*, *retention*, and *recall* are rather hard to keep clear since both perception and retention ordinarily have to be measured in terms of what a person can recall at a later period. When recall (or reaction) is recorded virtually immediately after exposure to a stimulus, we can usually assume that retention (memory) is not a factor. And if, as in the example cited above, we can assume that people are telling us what they actually think they are seeing rather than biasing their response to influence us in some way or other, we can then assume we are dealing with perception.

Despite these difficulties of keeping the three concepts neatly distinguished from each other, the evidence is that all three can be found to operate at one time or another—with the times not being infrequent.

A simple example would be that of being introduced to a stranger. A person might or might not physically *perceive* the sounds of the name as it is being communicated to him. If it were a particularly unfamiliar name, say, Milodragovich, he might attempt repetitions of it to get the pronunciation right (immediate recall) and yet find that five minutes later he cannot remember it. That would be perception without retention. Given that a person has heard the name, he might *retain* it so that he could only recognize it when transmitted to him again, or he might *retain* it (or memorize it) so that he could later *recall* that name and transmit it to someone else.

LIKES AND DISLIKES OF THE AUDIENCE

The general knowledge that the likes and dislikes of the audience affect the ways in which it reacts to communications has produced a considerable amount of practical concern and activity.

Even in an early era when communication effects were not the object of much study, measures were made of the likes and dislikes of movie and radio audiences with the view of attracting large audiences to the entertainment offered. This practice continues today and is, of course, extended to all the media that depend on attracting to themselves a voluntary audience.

Marketing research deals with many topics, not the least of which are the feelings of people about actual or potential products, the activities with which such products are associated, and the things which might be said about those products. The reason behind these concerns is the desire to offer to the potential consumer a product and message that not only will gain his attention but hopefully will persuade him to buy it.

The same logic that applies to marketing research holds for research on people's political and social attitudes, for purposes either of setting policy or for selling some policy or person to the public.

To the extent that the above activities are directed at designing a "product" (television show, physical product, or political program) to please the person in the "market," we might regard the consumer of these products and services as the "communicator" telling the researcher what he wants, in which case the researcher and his client may be regarded as "audiences." However, information gathered from such actual or prospective "consumers" is more usually thought of as furnishing the researcher and his client with the means for influencing the consumer.

Some more formal propositions have emerged that bear on the importance of the likes and dislikes of the audience in the communication process. They bear mainly on the agreement or disagreement of the audience with the position advocated by the communicator. Under ordinary circumstances there is a certain critical "distance" between the position of the communicator and that of the audience beyond which attempts to persuade will backfire. If the position advocated by the communicator is regarded as too extreme, the members of the audience will perceive him as biased, immoderate, and so on. The communicator will accomplish less than if he advocated a less extreme position (Hovland, 1959).

It has also been found that if the audience disagrees with the position advocated by the communicator, the communicator will be more successful if he uses a "two-sided" communication, i.e., a communication that acknowledges the existence of arguments opposed to the position of the communicator which he then attempts to counter rather than simply to present only the "positive" side of the argument (Hovland, Lumsdaine, & Sheffield, 1949: chap. 8).

These and other propositions bearing on the role of the likes and dislikes of the audience are quite well established in communication literature. Their acceptance has been quite complete since approximately World War II.

THE AUDIENCE AS INFORMATION PROCESSOR

People differ in their preferences for types of information and in their characteristic ways of handling information. Probably the most generally recognized relevant personal characteristic is education and/or intelligence. Better educated, and presumably more intelligent, people prefer print media more than do lesser educated people. Better educated people retain more of the information transmitted in a communication, but they are not necessarily easier (or as easy) to shift from one attitudinal position to another. Better educated people also prefer more complex and sophisticated arguments.

As information processing takes place over time, the dimension of time in and of itself may prove important, since the audience's information processing may proceed unevenly over the issues associated with the effects of communication. The most notable example of this is the so-called sleeper effect. While the sleeper effect has several manifestations, its most general form involves the atrophy of source-effect over time. The member of the audience forgets where he heard an argument even though he remembers the argument itself and/or accepts and retains its conclusion. The fact that the forgetting of the source of an argument proceeds more rapidly than the forgetting of the argument or its conclusions means that the argument and its conclusions tend to be accepted in their own terms after the passage of some time. Forgetting the source can also make the members of the audience very vulnerable to counter propaganda, since they no longer know why they believe some of the opinions that they hold (Hilibrand, 1964).

There are some additional attributes of people that affect their information processing habits and that have been found relevant to understanding the effects of communication. One of these is "need cognitition," an attitude toward wanting to know that is close to the old-fashioned notion of curiosity. Need cognition would appear to be an identifiable variable that affects the probability of an individual's paying attention to a communication independently of his interest in the substance of that communication (Berkowitz & Cottingham, 1960).

Related to but somewhat different from need cognition is personal cognitive style. Kelman and Cohler (1959) have posited two different styles, which they have labeled "clarifiers" and "simplifiers." The clarifying cognitive style involves a willingness to entertain information that is in conflict with one's existing beliefs. The simplifying person is more inclined to stereotypy. Cox (1967) found that persons with these two contrasting cognitive styles were about equally likely to be persuaded, as demonstrated in an experiment using a "stooge" to advocate a change of position. However, there was more halo effect to the attitudes of the "simplifiers." If they favored one position, they were more likely than the "clarifiers" to favor all aspects of it; if they shifted positions, they were more likely to shift all their associated beliefs.

Cunningham (1963) cites a considerable body of research findings that suggest there are consistent differences between men and women in their information processing habits. Women seem to ingest, store, and reproduce information with less distortion than do men.

THE AUDIENCE AS DEFENDER OF ITS EGO

One of the purposive acts that has been attributed to the audience has been the defense of its ego.

Ego-defense may be treated as one of the mediating mechanisms referred to above, but it is singled out here because of the semipurposive nature of the concept. One can find scattered about the communication literature of the past few decades many instances in which some mechanism of ego-defense—denial, suppression, repression, projection, etc.—is invoked as an explanation for the reaction of people to communications, usually instances in which the individual refused to be persuaded (Berelson, 1948: 183–184).

In the past decade, one particular form of psychic self-defense has had great popularity. It is based on what Nathan and Eleanor Maccoby (1961) call "homeostatic theory." This broad notion of homeostasis is dominated by theories from the psychology of cognition—Heider's balance theory, Festinger's dissonance theory, Osgood and Tannenbaum's congruity theory, and Newcomb's strain for symmetry. Despite differences in these theoretical positions, they all see individuals as deliberately seeking out information either to reinforce shaken convictions or to consolidate those recently acquired. As such, they depict the audience as being reasonably deliberate in its use of information; they also give us an understanding of why and for what reasons *some* communications are attended to.

THE AUDIENCE AS PLEASER OF OTHERS

A second purposive activity that has been attributed to the audience is that of ingratiating itself with others by agreeing with what they say. This seems to be the dominant proposition that lies behind a long-standing body of research literature on persuasibility. In large measure this work has been concerned with the relationship between a person's disposition to adopt a position advocated by the communicator and that person's personality attributes. The most common personality measure employed is that of "generalized self-confidence," which, as used in most experiments, seems to be a measure of self-professed disposition toward being socially compliant. While there are complications in this body of data, the most pervasive finding has been that persons low in generalized self-confidence are more persuasible than persons higher in generalized self-confidence (Bauer, 1964).

As I shall indicate below, the generality

of this finding has been challenged by a series of recent experiments. However, as suggested elsewhere (Bauer, 1967), this may be because persons in these recent experiments have been concerned with solving a different order of problem.

Many personality variables have been introduced to explain differences in the reactions of audiences. Here we are concerned solely with the motive to please others by compliance.

THE AUDIENCE AS PROBLEM SOLVER

In formal writings on communication the audience is seldom treated explicitly as a group of people solving problems. Yet once the issue has been raised, it is obviously sensible to think of some fraction of consumers as deliberately seeking information from advertising, of some fraction of voters as gathering facts and analyzing arguments to reach a political position, and so on. In an article written in the mid-1960s (Bauer, 1964), I contended that our view of the communication process was sadly distorted because of our very limited concern with the purposive activities of the members of the audience in seeking out and using information. Lest the reader think that I have been discussing such purposive activities in the preceding sections on selection, attention, etc., I point out that the general tendency of work dealing with such phenomena has been to treat them from the point of view of the communicator without systematic consideration of the objectives of the audience.

Nevertheless, there is scattered about a considerable number of individual pieces of writing that treat the audience as a group of problem solvers. One recent reader on communications (Dexter & White, 1964) has been organized around this point of view, generally called the "functional" approach to communication.

Writings in the functional tradition approach the audience's use of communication through the broad range of functions that those communications may serve for the user. In one of the more diligent and entertaining excursions into functional analysis of use of the media, Katz and Foulkes (1962) consider the question of the use of mass media for escape. They point out that if man is to cope adequately with his environment, he must occasionally retreat to gather strength. He may sleep or he may indulge in some form of re-creation, which may be active participation in sport or passive attendance to movies and TV. Hence, escape per se is not a bad, but a necessary, thing. Evaluation of any given individual's use of the mass media would involve an incredibly complex estimate of his alternatives for recreation, his capacity to do without escape, and so on—an impossible task under any circumstance. However, the functional approach offers at least a framework within which to begin to understand why individuals use communications as they do.

In the preceding section I mentioned that recent experiments on the relationship of persuasibility of people to generalized self-confidence had shown patterns of response different from those that had been found in the past. A number of researchers have found that, under some circumstances, people who are *high* on self-confidence as well as people who are *very low* on self-confidence are difficult to persuade, while people of medium self-confidence are the most easy to persuade. My own analysis is that the situations confronted in these experiments are ones where people try to solve cognitive problems rather than decide whether or not to ingratiate themselves by agreeing with someone (Bauer, 1967). Under these conditions, a person very low in generalized self-confidence might freeze at the prospect of deciding whether to resist or accept advice from another party. Such a person might become very resistant to being persuaded and behave very much like a person high in self-confidence, who also resists persuasion but for a different reason—he has no reason to believe that another party would have superior competence to himself.

The above reasoning might sound like gratuitous rationalizing. However, it leads to a specific prediction—namely, that when members of the audience are primarily concerned with whether to be ingratiating, we should expect a linear relationship between persuasibility and self-confidence, with people lower in self-confidence being the easiest to persuade. However, when the members of an audience are engaged in cognitive problem solving, we should anticipate the sort of curvilinear relationship that recent investigators have found. A doctoral thesis completed late in 1966 is consistent with this distinction, although it does not support it decisively (Wilding, 1967).

A systematic approach to members of the audience as problem solvers is far from achieved, yet it seems to be an approach that is gathering strength. It promises to bring into balance the prevailing one-sided picture of initiative in the communication process—a picture that presents the initiative as lying almost wholly in the hands of the communicator.

THE AUDIENCE AS MEMBER OF A GROUP

Early treatments of the audience in the communication process, particularly in the mass communication process, literally referred to the members of the audience as social "atoms," as isolated individuals who reacted to communications as though they had no social ties (for a discussion of this point of view, see Freidson, 1953). Suffice it to say that in recent decades this view has been thoroughly replaced by one which places great emphasis on group membership as a factor that conditions response to communication.[1]

We are fortunate in that John and Matilda Riley (1959) have given us an unusually fine systematic view of the relationship between communication and social organization. Findings indicate that people who regard their group memberships most seriously are most likely to resist an attack on the beliefs associated with that group. In fact, those people who have the most serious regard for a group membership may have a counterreaction, and the communication may boomerang or have an opposite effect from that intended.

Much propaganda directed at getting people to defect from groups to which they belong is probably effective only after they have decided to defect for other reasons. Shils and Janowitz (1948) found that members of the Wehrmacht paid attention to Allied propaganda in World War II only after unit morale had disintegrated.

Many studies indicate that people use reference groups as a guide for what to expect and how to react to the messages directed at them (Sherif, 1935; Asch, 1940; Kelley & Volkart, 1952). The social structure of the groups to which people belong determines the lines along which communication, both formal and informal, will flow.

People live, buy, work, vote, and play as members of groups. They communicate as members of groups, and they receive and react to communications as members of groups. Any conception of audience that does not recognize its group nature will be badly misleading.

THE AUDIENCE AS A SYSTEM

If people communicate as members of groups and they receive and react as mem-

[1] The reader may wonder how such a patently nonsensical idea gained currency. It can be explained largely in terms of the notion that the new industrial society had destroyed all the traditional patterns of association that characterized the previous society. It was thought that group memberships and patterns of interpersonal association would have no role in modern society. This hypothetical view of things to come was imposed on the world in the face of substantial evidence to the contrary. For a survey of the development of attitudes toward primary groups in Western society, see Shils (1951).

bers of groups, then any one communication cannot be seen as having an impact on a single individual but must be seen as a start of a chain of events or as an input into a complex system. As I have indicated, the notion of a two-step flow was built around the idea that one of the functions of the mass media is to activate its readers and listeners to become communicators in their own right. This is, of course, but the first link in the chain of potential subsequent events. What will happen is a function of the structure and the state of the social system of which the first recipient of a message is a member. Whatever the nature of the communication, its impact will be only in part, and perhaps in small part, a function of its own content and form.

At times, only the general subject matter of a message may be important; the actual content—whether it favors or opposes a given issue—may be irrelevant. For example, an editorial on location of a new highway may be equally effective in arousing both supporters and opponents of the highway, regardless of which side of the argument the editorial presents. Its main function may be simply to alert both sides to the existence of the issue. The result may, of course, be more favorable to the side opposing the stand of the editorial *if* the opposing forces alerted by the editorial are able to muster a stronger effort than are the supporters. In such instances—probably rare, but certainly not unknown—the outcome can be said to be more a function of the state of the system than of the content of the communication. *Any* communication that would alert both sides to the issue might produce substantially the same outcome.

We may note in passing that all of the above might be said in principle about a communication directed to an individual. When we look at social groups, as social scientists have often commented, we are able to observe processes of communication, argument, negotiation, obstruction, compromise, etc., that obviously take place in a less observable form inside the skulls of people. We know full well that there are people who will say what is on the top of their minds regardless of what the most recent message to them was. One way or another, they will convert what was said to them and use it as a pretext for saying what they wanted to say. And then, there are other persons who must ponder so deep and long over the import of some of the things they hear that the resulting impact of the communication is vastly out of proportion to the message that triggered the ensuing process.

The notion that a communication or message is an input into an ongoing system is not especially new in principle.[2] The systematic exploitation of this point of view is limited, but specific—namely, in the computer simulation of the impact of communication on processes in social systems.

Such simulation models incorporate the theoretical principles of social communication (e.g., effective attention, perception, and so on), the probability of the various relevant phenomena (attitudes toward issues, educational levels of various groups, etc.), and the relevant elements of social structure. On the basis of such a model one can calculate the probable eventual outcome of a given message or of a message campaign.

The reader for whom the idea of computer simulation is threatening can find a simple version of what is entailed in an article entitled "Mating Behavioral Science and Simulation" (Bauer & Buzzell, 1964). Those who can benefit from an example of what a full-scale model looks like are referred to the treatment of a simulated fluoridation controversy by Abelson and Bernstein (1963).

[2] This formulation was developed by Pool, Dexter, and myself in *American Business and Public Policy* (Bauer, Pool, & Dexter, 1963). Our first draft statement was made some time in the mid-1950s and was the stimulus to Pool's own work on simulation of complex systems.

SUMMARY

One of the most significant trends in the development of our view of communication has been the shift in the role accorded the audience. This shift ranged from a view of the audience as a grouping of passive objects to be influenced and counted—with the influence being taken for granted—to that of a complex system containing its own dynamics which is activated in an unpredictable direction by the input of a communication. The earlier view saw the audience as an individual who was an isolated social atom designed to respond in the direction suggested. The newer view sees the audience as a complex individual with complex group affiliations, or it sees the audience itself as a complex group.

Reactions, in turn, are also seen as complex. Given that people, for one reason or another, pay attention to a particular communication, there is no reason to believe that the message will have the particular effect intended by the communicator. The mind of the recipient, beyond exercising the option of paying or not paying attention, acts as a filter effecting selective perception, selective retention, and selective recall; and the recipient may selectively reject or reinterpret opinions deviating too strongly from his existing viewpoint.

Far from being passive, people actively seek out information for such diverse purposes as reinforcing or consolidating their existing opinions, preserving or strengthening their self-image, ingratiating themselves with other persons, or even for the solving of cognitive problems. Viewed from the position of the functional tradition of communication research, any one of these goals may be viewed as a problem to be solved. The bias of the behavioral sciences, ironically, has been to concentrate selectively on those goals that do *not* involve the rational solving of problems. This bias appears to be an offsetting compensation for the prevailing position that pursuance of ego and social goals is somehow "irrational." However, it has generally left the communication researcher unequipped to handle the more traditionally "rational" behavior.

In addition to being an active individual with a complex set of goals, the member of the audience is also a member of a complex set of groups that condition his response to a given communication. The more salient his membership in a given group, the more this membership will affect his reactions. In fact, attacks on beliefs held by a group of which he is a member may result in the communicator being discredited and the belief being held more firmly than previously. In less extreme situations, the group will act as a reference group, reinterpreting, dampening, or amplifying the original message.

The so-called two-step flow of communication actually sees the audience as a second-stage communicator. This view can be embraced in the more encompassing notion that the audience itself is a system with its own dynamics such that a communication input into that system cannot in principle produce a determinate output. That output is as much a function of the state of the system as it is of the content and form of the communication.

An even broader view of the communication process sees it as a transaction in which the communicator is influenced by the audience as truly as the audience is influenced by the communicator.

There is concrete evidence in support of the latter two broad views. They are not, however, much developed.

REFERENCES

Abelson, Robert P., and Alex Bernstein.
1963 "A computer simulation model of community referendum controversies." Public Opinion Quarterly 27 (Spring):93–122.

Albig, J. William.
1939 Public Opinion. New York: McGraw-Hill.

Asch, S. E.
1940 "Studies in the principles of judgments and attitudes: II. Determina-

tion of judgments by group and ego standards." Journal of Social Psychology 12:433–465.

Bauer, R. A.
1964 "The obstinate audience." American Psychologist 19(May):319–328.
1967 "Source effect and persuasibility: A new look." Pp. 559–578 in Donald F. Cox (ed.), Risk Taking and Information Handling in Consumer Behavior. Boston: Harvard University Division of Research.

Bauer, R. A., and Alice H. Bauer.
1960 "America, mass society and mass media." Journal of Social Issues 16 (No. 3):3–66.

Bauer, R. A., and R. D. Buzzell.
1964 "Mating behavioral science and simulation." Harvard Business Review 42(September-October):116–124.

Bauer, R. A.; I. deS. Pool; and L. A. Dexter.
1963 American Business and Public Policy. New York: Atherton Press.

Baumol, W. J., and W. G. Bowen.
1966 Performing Arts: The Economic Dilemma. New York: Twentieth Century Fund.

Berelson, Bernard.
1948 "Communications and public opinion." Pp. 167–185 in Wilbur Schramm (ed.), Communications in Modern Society. Urbana: University of Illinois Press.

Berkowitz, Leonard, and D. R. Cottingham.
1960 "The interest value and relevance of fear-arousing communications." Journal of Abnormal and Social Psychology 60:37–43.

Blumer, Herbert.
1933 Movies and Conduct. New York: Macmillan.

Blumer, Herbert, and P. M. Houser.
1933 Movies, Delinquency, and Crime. New York: Macmillan.

Cooper, Eunice, and Marie Jahoda.
1947 "The evasion of propaganda: How prejudiced people respond to anti-prejudiced propaganda." Journal of Psychology 23:15–25.

Cox, Donald F.
1967 Risk Taking and Information Handling in Consumer Behavior. Boston: Harvard University Division of Research.

Cunningham, Scott.
1963 "Sex differences in critical evaluation" (unpublished mimeographed paper).

Dexter, L. A., and D. M. White.
1964 People, Society and Mass Communications. New York: Free Press of Glencoe.

Doob, L. W.
1935 Propaganda; Its Psychology and Technique. New York: Holt.

Downs, Harold.
1953 The Critic in the Theater. New York: Pitman.

Ehrlich, Danuta; Isaiah Guttman; Peter Schonbach; and Judson Mills.
1957 "Post-decision exposure to relevant information." Journal of Abnormal and Social Psychology 54:98–102.

Festinger, Leon.
1957 The Theory of Cognitive Dissonance. Evanston, Illinois: Row, Peterson.

Freidson, Eliot.
1953 "Communications research and the concept of the mass." American Sociological Review 18(June):313–317.

Hilibrand, Murray.
1964 "Source credibility and the persuasive process." Ph.D. Dissertation, Harvard Business School (unpublished).

Hovland, Carl I.
1959 "Reconciling conflicting results derived from experimental and survey studies of attitude change." American Psychologist 14:8–17.

Hovland, Carl I.; Arthur A. Lumsdaine; and Fred Sheffield.
1949 Experiments in Mass Communications. Princeton: Princeton University Press.

Katz, Elihu.
1957 "The two-step flow of communication; an up-to-date report on a hypothesis." Public Opinion Quarterly 21(Spring):61–78.

Katz, Elihu, and David Foulkes.
1962 "On the use of the mass media for 'escape.'" Public Opinion Quarterly 26(Fall):377–388.

Kelley, H. H., and E. H. Volkart.
1952 "The resistance to change of group-anchored attitudes." American Sociological Review 17:453–465.

Kelman, Herbert, and Jonas Cohler.
1959 "Reactions to persuasive communication as a function of cognitive needs and styles." Paper presented at the meetings of the Eastern Psychological Association, Atlantic City, April 3.

Lane, Yoti.
1960 The Psychology of the Actor. New York: Day.

Lasswell, H. D.
1948 "The structure and function of communication in society." Pp. 37–51 in Lyman Bryson (ed.), Communication of Ideas. New York: Harper.

Lazarsfeld, P. F.; Bernard Berelson; and Hazel Gaudet.
1948 The People's Choice. Second Edition. New York: Columbia University Press.

Maccoby, Nathan, and Eleanor E. Maccoby.
1961 "Homeostatic theory in attitude change." Public Opinion Quarterly 25(Winter): 538–545.

Riley, J. W., and Matilda W. Riley.
1959 "Mass communication and the social system." Pp. 537–578 in Robert K. Merton et al. (eds.), Sociology Today. New York: Basic Books.

Schramm, Wilbur, and Wayne Danielson.
1958 "Anticipated audiences as determinants of recall." Journal of Abnormal and Social Psychology 56:282–283.

Sherif, Muzafer.
1935 "A study of some social factors in perception." Archives of Psychology 187:1–60.

Shils, E. A.
1951 "The study of the primary group." Pp. 44–69 in Daniel Lerner and H. D. Lasswell (eds.), Policy Sciences; Recent Developments in Scope and Method. Stanford: Stanford University Press.

Shils, E. A., and Morris Janowitz.
1948 "Cohesion and disintegration in the Wehrmacht in World War II." Public Opinion Quarterly 12 (Summer): 280–315.

Wilding, John.
1967 "Experimental approach to problem solving and psycho-social aspects of the communication process, with an investigation of product evaluation dimension, purchase cycle and advertising preference." Ph. D. Dissertation, Harvard Business School.

Zimmerman, Claire, and R. A. Bauer.
1956 "The effects of an audience on what was remembered." Public Opinion Quarterly 20 (Spring): 238–248.

CHAPTER 7 Communication and Learning

NATHAN MACCOBY and DAVID G. MARKLE
Stanford University

One of the often cited functions of the mass media is to instruct. Effective use of mass communication for instruction requires as much or more understanding of the process of learning as it does of the media. This chapter briefly reviews theories of learning and methods of research on human learning and provides an extensive review of what is known about learning from media. Much of what is learned from media is incidental learning in that the explicit purpose of the communicator was not to teach the specific information learned. Not a great deal can be said about this process other than that it occurs. This may simply reflect the fact that we use the label "incidental learning" for processes not well understood and reclassify a process as "intentional" when it is better understood. The better understood aspects of learning information concepts, skills, and attitudes from mass media (including teaching machines) are discussed at greater length.

Communications can serve a variety of functions. They may entertain, inform, instruct, or persuade. The newest and most often used medium of communication, television, in the eyes of most observers of the current scene, devotes far too much of its time to entertainment and far less than it should to information, instruction, and persuasion. In this discussion, we shall devote our attention to these allegedly underemphasized functions of the mass media in general. Most especially, we shall devote the discussion primarily to communication and learning. The role of mass media in learning as against that of face-to-face communication will be the primary focus of attention.

Theory and experiment in learning have had more attention by psychologists than any other aspect of behavior; yet it is generally agreed that very little has been done to translate this voluminous body of work into a viable theory of instruction. There are, to be sure, some recent exceptions to this statement that we will discuss below. We know a very great deal about the nature and conditions of learning, but we have very little well-established knowledge about teaching. For example, we still do not know how to teach people to read. True, a great deal of professional attention has been devoted to the teaching of reading; there is much folklore on the subject; and there are many individual instructors who have the knack of teaching reading. However, we still lack a systematic theory of reading instruction that can be used as a basis for prescribing techniques for the successful teaching of reading skills.

In this chapter we shall first review briefly some theories of learning. In later sections we shall discuss a number of areas of investigation in which there is an intersection of learning theory and human communication: learning from the mass media, incidental learning, the design of instructional systems, and the learning of attitudes.

LEARNING THEORIES

Let us first review some of the major formulations of learning theory. These may be classified either as stimulus-response theories or as cognitive theories. The former had a great run from E. L. Thorndike's day at the turn of the century until after World War II. They still pervade the thinking of most research psychologists—no matter what their special field of endeavor might be. Some fundamental ideas coming out of stimulus-response theory, such as conditioning and reinforcement, pervade everybody's thinking about learning and behavior. However, it is also evident that all psychologists employing learning principles have been influenced to some degree by the emergence and development of cognitive theory.

It is commonplace for psychologists of the strongest stimulus-response stripe to concern themselves with problems of organization of learned behavior just as cognitive theorists use some notions of association and reinforcement in their thinking. Does this mean that there are no longer major differences in the theoretical approaches to learning?

Quite the contrary is true. There has been a marked proliferation of learning paradigms and models. What has taken place is that the great movement to devise and carry out crucial experiments designed to show Hull (1943) right and Guthrie (1952) wrong, or Tolman (1932) right and Hull, Skinner (1953), and Guthrie wrong have long ceased to fill the pages of psychology journals. Rather, the problems that researchers tackle and the ways in which they approach their tasks are heavily influenced by their intellectual ancestry. Thus, at least until quite recently, it was not too difficult from reading a journal article to identify the theoretical orientation of the writer or at least to identify whether his background was in some form of stimulus-response psychology or in cognitive theory.

It should be pointed out that within each of these two major approaches to learning theory there are many differences. To psychologists and to a new and growing body of instructional technologists these differences are all important.

Perhaps the most numerous and most devoted workers are Skinnerians, who in one form or another stress the importance of shaping behavior through operant conditioning—providing reinforcement when behavior is close to that which is wanted and withholding reinforcement when it is not. This is often done according to theoretically prescribed schedules of reinforcement. But also very much with us are neo-Hullians, who rely on N. E. Miller and John Dollard's (1941) drive-cue-response reward paradigm, and neo-Guthrians, who begin with the principle of simple contiguity—that stimuli accompanying a response tend on their reoccurrence to evoke that response.

Cognitive theory has spawned group participation, problem solving, and highly permissive, unstructured environments for learning. Brain functioning rather than muscular responses are emphasized as being important. Understanding rather than practice, insight rather than reward, cognitive structures rather than habits are all stressed by those who apply cognitive theory to the instructional process.

Köhler (1925; 1959) emphasized the role of perception rather than of learning. Changes took place not as a result of reinforced practice but because of structural reorganization. For Tolman (1932), behavior had to be looked at in molar rather than in molecular units, and goals could be attained by apprehending signs or paths and purposefully following them. One interesting development has been the attempt by Sheffield to develop cognitive and organizational principles and translate these into stimulus-response theory—that is, a stimulus-response formulation that later generates organizational and cognitive principles. We will return later to a fuller discussion of this approach.

RESEARCH METHODS

Methods for investigating the role of communication in learning range from the laboratory to a variety of field settings. Laboratory work with many species of animals has been employed to investigate theoretical variables in the learning process, usually with the discovery of human learning principles the ultimate objective. The proverbial white rat, cats, pigeons, and even cockroaches as well as subhuman primates and other species have served as subjects of psychological investigation of such variables as the role of reward or reinforcement in the acquisition and retention of learned behavior, or some theory of forgetting.

For example, the interference theory of forgetting states that nothing is really forgotten, but old stimulus-response connections are broken by the substitution of new ones that are incompatible with the old ones. Thus, if a bell that had previously become a cue associated with food is now accompanied only by the presentation of a female in heat to the appropriate male animal, the connection of the bell with food will be "forgotten." Or is forgetting really a "decay" phenomenon—a function of time?

Investigation of the "decay" phenomenon was frequently blocked by the fact that complex organisms such as people are highly engaged in activity during the "decay" intervals, and such activity might well involve new learning that is incompatible with the old. Jenkins and Dallenbach (1924) long ago demonstrated that for human beings there was much less loss of learning after an interval of sleep than after a similar period of waking activity. Even in sleep, however, interfering cognitions may promote forgetting. As Shakespeare observes in *Hamlet*, "To sleep: perchance to dream: ay, there's the rub."

Minami and Dallenbach (1946) reported an experiment in which a cockroach was placed in a dark and damp place where it remained virtually without movement for a good many hours. The cockroach was then taught to avoid a corner of the cage through the use of electric shock whenever it went there. After twenty-four hours in which considerable activity was generated in the cockroach by having it walk a treadmill in a dry and lighted cage, substantial "forgetting" took place as measured by the Ebbinghaus savings method. That is, many new training trials with the shock were needed to produce reavoidance of the corner. After immobilization in the dark, damp passageway, however, very little loss of learning occurred.

While the "decay" theory of forgetting seems not to work in the cockroach, it may still be a factor among more complex organisms. Nevertheless, the Minami and Dallenbach experiment does illustrate how experiments, even if among relatively simple organisms, can help throw some light on the psychology of human learning and retention.

RESEARCH WITH HUMANS

Of course, studies conducted with human beings have more direct and immediate relevance to the practical problems of teaching and learning in people. An enormous amount of research in the field of human learning has been accumulating for almost a century. The German psychologist, Hermann Ebbinghaus, employing only himself as a laboratory subject, conducted hundreds of experiments which enabled him to discover a great many facts about learning (Ebbinghaus, 1964). The results of these experiments have stood up remarkably well in replications with many more cases.

While some of the early work on human learning dealt with extending to man some of the conditioning principles found in animal studies, most of the human work has been in the general area of verbal learning. Problems of meaningfulness, proactive and retroactive interference, organization and distribution of practice, transfer of training, and the role of knowledge of results and of active participation in the learning process are among some of the principal problems extensively investigated. Motor learning—the acquisition and retention of motor skills—has also occupied considerable attention of researchers. More recently, nonverbal communication and learning of nonverbal skills has become the focus of several researchers' investigations (Ekman, Friesen, Ellsworth, 1972).

For example, Maccoby, Jecker, Breitrose, and Rose (1964) carried out a series of studies in classrooms, the main object of which was to develop principles for teaching teachers how to "read" nonverbal behavior of pupils for their degree of understanding of what was being explained to them. Preprogrammed lessons were taught by teachers, and comprehension by pupils was immediately tested for. Close-up movie films of individual pupils were later played back to teachers, who were asked to judge whether or not the pupil being filmed understood what was being explained to him. Test data provided criterion measures against which these judgments could be compared. Training in the content analysis of such filmed nonverbal behavior resulted in modest but significant improvements in teachers' abilities to make correct judgments. However, the authors, after considerable subsequent exploration, have never been able to identify the cues that formed the basis for these improved guesses.

Perhaps the most novel direction taken by students of learning has been the most recent one. Learning and memory have been approached from the standpoint of information intake and processing. Basic distinctions have been discovered between short-term and long-term memory, including different storage mechanisms for each. Information has to be processed or coded after being apprehended if the material learned is to be remembered for a long period of time.

The fact that these two processes are quite distinct is perhaps most dramatically illustrated by a recent study of football players with head injuries. Immediately after injuries that rendered them temporarily unconscious, players were able to recall in detail the events immediately preceding their injuries, including the number of the play called on which the injury occurred. Later, however, the period preceding the injury was blacked out and they could recall nothing about it. The coding and storage processes for longer term memory and the immediate recall processes are evidently quite distinct.

Perhaps the clearest statement of the current status of this approach to learning is that of Estes (1970:28):

> Although, inevitably, some investigators continue to have reservations, it seems fair to say that the majority of investigators of human learning at the present time are operating on the assumption that at least for human beings, and perhaps for all the higher organisms, learning is primarily a matter of storing in memory information concerning relationships between events which have occurred contiguously in past experience, and that one aspect of this learning has to do with the relationships between stimulus-response sequences and rewarding or punishing outcomes. The primary function of rewards and punishments is not to control learning directly but rather to enter into the learning process as important classes of events about which information must be stored in order that the learner can later modify his choices among alternative actions in the light of past experience.

Finally, the role of motivation in learning and in forgetting has been occupying considerable attention by investigators. The role of motivation has been studied over the range of learning variables from animal conditioning to the management of learning in instructional settings; it varies greatly in importance in different theories. In Guthrian theory, for example, motivation is important only in order to achieve an adequate level of responding. In attempts to formulate theories of instruction, on the other hand, it plays an extremely important role.

LEARNING FROM COMMUNICATIONS

In discussing learning in the context of communication, we can distinguish between learning in face-to-face settings and learning that takes place in mediated situations. Face-to-face settings involve communication of any intrapersonal sort, also interpersonal communication and communication in small and large groups. Mediated communication refers to communications via some medium so that no face-to- face setting is involved. Generally, reproduced sound, print, or visual information is transmitted through mediated communication. In such situations, only one-way message sending is generally feasible, at least on an immediate basis. This obstacle is a serious one for the use of mass communication techniques in instruction, and below we will discuss some of the means that have been devised for minimizing this difficulty.

The question then becomes, How do people learn from the mass media? While perhaps not entirely impossible, it is difficult to provide rewards or reinforcements via the media. It could be presumed that commercial messages frequently employ a reward of some sort when they state that if the product or service is bought, the purchaser will gain some desired end, such as sex, fame, or fortune. Estes is suggesting, however, that such reward does not work directly but only leads to the anticipation of such outcomes, and then that these assumptions modify choices the learner makes among possible courses of action based on past experience.

One suspects, however, that the use of such rewards for teaching information and skills via the media has limited utility. While use of anticipatory rewards may be of some aid in increasing the motivation of the learner (and even this utility may be limited), surely this cannot be the most satisfactory way to teach school subjects.

More important ingredients that are typically, if not inherently, missing from media teaching are active practice and feedback to the learner of the results of such practice. These are important features of programmed instruction. A problem is presented to the learner; he attempts to solve it; and he is immediately informed whether his attempted solution is correct.

Mass media are group-paced; therefore, it is harder to present this pattern of practice and feedback as flexibly as can be done with individualized modes of instruction. Let us explore this problem a bit. Although it is not commonly done, there are a number of ways to incorporate practice and feedback into mass media instruction. A direct parallel to an individualized approach is to present at a fixed pace essentially the same pattern of questioning and feedback that would otherwise be presented individually. As long as the response time for any single answer is short and the variance of the response time is small, it is possible to provide answer pauses that will be satisfactory for most students. To do this well, materials must be developed empirically with deliberate attention to timing. The more heterogeneous the population, the more difficult it is to develop a presentation with timing satisfactory to most students.

A second approach is to make explicit plans for practice to follow immediately after presentations on mass media. Problems can be presented by the mass media, by supplementary media such as print, by teachers, or by combinations of these. Utilization programs in which live classroom instruction is coordinated with televised instruction on a large scale have been undertaken (Comstock & Maccoby, 1966), and printed questions and teacher-led practice have been integrated with film presentations (Markle, 1967).

A third approach is to present stimuli that encourage covert practice. Learners can think about the problems instead of practicing talking or writing. Research has established that for some topics covert practice can be as effective as overt practice if students actually engage in it. Covert practice is particularly effective when knowledge of the results is made available (Michael & Maccoby, 1961).

In some cases, it would not seem to be necessary to provide explicit feedback on performance and thus be forced to schedule pauses in the instruction. Instead, instruction can be designed so that students know they are right when they respond, or so they can develop methods of evaluating their own responses. There are few disciplines, after all, in which someone can become truly competent without developing ways to evaluate his own performance. A most obvious example is in algebra instruction. If the problem calls for solving for an unknown, the learner can practice solving the equation and can tell whether or not he has solved it correctly by substituting the value he obtains in the original equation.

A special example of student-provided feedback is illustrated in an experiment by Gibson, Gibson, Pick, and Osser (1962). They had subjects go through a deck of cards with the task being to identify which ones were like the standard. They deliberately did not inform the subjects whether or not their answers were correct. Nevertheless, the subjects improved their performance in successive tries. Evidently, they were able to improve by forming new codes of card-squiggle categories that enabled them to identify more cards correctly on successive trials.

The extent to which programs can be constructed so that learners can tell for themselves when they are making progress is the extent to which active practice can be taken advantage of in the mass media teaching-learning setting, without provision of deliberate pauses and feedback, and without external utilization programs. Further research along these lines is much needed.

INCIDENTAL LEARNING

One of the more interesting aspects of learning via communication is the learning that takes place unintentionally or incidentally. We tend to think of learning principally in a tutorial or didactic sense. Actually, most learning takes place in a more informal manner. Not all the learning that does take place is of the formal task accomplishment variety. Actually, little of it is. Most of it is not characterized as learning; in fact, it is not noticed at all. Psychologists who study learning generally refer to this process as incidental learning—that is, learning that is not planned or designed for.

It may well be that the amount of incidental learning that takes place in the communication situation is far greater than the amount of direct or formal learning. Such is the case not only in ordinary face-to-face interactions but also for mass-mediated exposure. We learn when we read newspapers or magazines, when we watch television or films, or when we listen to the radio just as surely as when we read textbooks or journal articles or listen to lectures. And we learn not only information, such as what happened and who were the participants, but also attitudes and opinions. Furthermore, the attitudes and opinions we learn are often not formally specified or planned for; the learner may not know that he has acquired these attitudes, nor may he be able to specify what they are.

If learning is regarded as modification of behavior due to practice, behavior is almost constantly undergoing such change. Every time we perceive any input, even a familiar one, the perception takes place in a different setting, even if that difference is limited to internal bodily states. Generally speaking, a great deal of what we learn we do not characterize as learning since it is neither desired, nor intended, nor sought. One explanation of why highly anxious people learn less of what is formally taught them than do people at a lower level of anxiety is precisely of this sort. It seems that highly anxious people learn much that is irrelevant to the task, such as worries, and these incidentally learned things often interfere with rather than facilitate the learning of the desired behavior (Mandler & Sarason, 1952).

Actually, incidental learning can be deliberately employed by a skillful instructor to teach a recalcitrant student. As Alexander Pope judiciously observed, "They must be taught as if you taught them not, and things unknown proposed as things forgot."

SPECIFYING OBJECTIVES

The most important first step in the instructional process is specifying objectives. What is to be learned? Describing this precisely gives rise to serious problems. The theoretical predelictions of those planning the instruction influence the specification of the criterion task in a fundamental way.

Skinnerians, for example, are most likely to specify a set of responses that constitute an accomplishment, such as answering certain questions with the "right" answers, since this kind of behavior can be shaped through strategic problem setting and skillful schedules of reinforcement. Those who apply Skinnerian methods to the instructional situation are not concerned merely with teaching simple things. Practitioners employing Skinnerian methods have taken on the teaching of quite complicated knowledges and skills.

If selective reinforcement is to be applied in shaping behavior, however, the desired behavior has to be codable as being correct or incorrect. We should note that a reinforcement approach can be applied to situations in which a broad range of behavior is "right," if the reinforcement apparatus and task definition are sophisticated enough to handle it, or if students themselves are taught to evaluate their own behavior.

Guthrians would undoubtedly concentrate on the responses themselves rather than on the outcomes of these responses. In other words, the Guthrian would ask, What behavior actually occurs under given conditions regardless of whether or not the behavior is "correct"?

Of course, the Guthrian would seek, by revising his instruction, to produce "correct" behavior, as would the Skinnerian, even though his theoretical orientation leads him to focus on stimulus-response connections rather than on reinforcement contingencies (Skinner, 1969). Much of the recent work in instructional technology received its initial impetus from Skinnerian theorizing. It is interesting to note, however, that much current work can be interpreted more parsimoniously in Guthrian terms, especially in view of the controversy that surrounds the reinforcement issue. If confirmation is often not a reinforcer, the instructional programmer is primarily manipulating stimulus-response pairings, not reinforcement contingencies.

Piagetians would be likely to adopt a more cognitive approach and specify those tasks that are judged to be at the right level of conceptualization for the age and developmental stage of the learner.

Reflecting a cognitive viewpoint, Ausubel (1965) suggests that efficient learning requires the acquisition of adequate cognitive structure, and he stresses means of achieving this rather than lower level behaviors of the student. A different side of cognitive activity is presented by Bruner and his associates (Bruner, Goodnow, & Austin, 1956). Affective states that accompany thinking are thought to be important motivators. Thus an instructional objective might, from this viewpoint, include such affective states as "cognitive frustration" and "insight."

A third line of reasoning on such an approach has been postulated by G. A. Miller, Galanter, and Pribram (1960). They introduce the notion of a *plan*, which is intended to bridge the theoretical gap between cognition and action. Following their line of attack, instructional objectives should map, in some way, the structure which underlies behavior.

Applied group dynamicists might be concerned more with group process and participation and would be more likely to select as task outcomes skills in interpersonal perception in group settings. Obviously, if instructional objectives are not comparable, neither are measures of the effectiveness of varying instructional programs based on differing theories of instruction comparable.

We mentioned above the attempt by Sheffield to employ stimulus-response theory to the learning of complex materials. He begins with the idea that cognitive theorists are basically correct in their concern with perceptual and organizational matters in understanding how learning takes place. However, Sheffield feels that the cognitive theorists have not progressed sufficiently beyond making some global statements. That is, saying that stimuli are perceived as organized wholes may be true but, as such, does not offer a theory of learning. Sheffield applies and extends Guthrie's contiguity theory to the perception and learning of organized patterns of behavior.

In an analysis of learning complex manual assembly tasks, such as the assembly of the pieces making up a complex component of an airplane, Sheffield applies the principles of cross-conditioning and reintegration to the learning of percepts as responses. Using these principles, he and his colleagues show how subassemblies are learned and how these are integrated into larger order assemblies (Sheffield, 1961).

These theoretical formulations led to a series of experiments by Sheffield, Maccoby, and their colleagues (cf. Lumsdaine, 1961). In these experiments the concept of the demonstration-assimilation span was invented to describe the smallest segments of demonstration and practice. A *D-A span* was defined as the largest segment of a sequential task that could be practiced or performed correctly after one viewing of a demonstration. In group-learning settings, the *D-A span* was characterized as the longest sequence that could be practiced correctly by at least 75 percent of the audience after a single viewing of a demonstration.

The next larger unit of demonstration and practice was labeled a *natural* unit. This rather non-stimulus-response-like nomenclature was operationally defined for a manual-assembly task as the largest subassembly characterized by common context cues that were uniquely present for that subassembly. A wheel subassembly on an automobile would be such a natural unit since the wheel is present for all parts of the wheel but could be left out of other subassembly tasks. Thus, natural units could be tested unambiguously as the parts of each unit that were assembled together into a single substructure different from that of other units. Finally, the entire assembly could be treated as a whole unit. In this way, one could organize demonstration and practice-learning sessions in various ways.

The experimenters used film for demonstration, actual parts for the learner's practice in motor tasks, and words or drawings in paper and pencil, or oral tasks. Combinations of different-sized demonstration practice units were varied in order to discover the most effective principles of learning from film. It was found, for example, that whole rather than smaller units of demonstration and practice had certain advantages, perhaps best described by the phrase "seeing the forest instead of just the trees," as well as certain disadvantages that derived from not adequately grasping the individual trees.

The best of both worlds could be achieved by a selected combination of different sized demonstration-practice units in each learning session. For example, the following method was employed: Learners went through the task the first time with small units (say, D-A spans), the next time with larger units (say, natural units), and the third time through the entire assembly task was demonstrated with no interruption for practice. At the end of the filmed demonstration, the learners practiced the entire task.

This procedure is thus one way of patterning the advantages of each sized demonstration-practice unit. This method was labeled *transition* since it involved moving from smaller to more inclusive larger demonstration-practice units on successive trials. And it worked. Perhaps it would have worked even better if the intermediate sized demonstration-practice units had been engineered more nearly to fit the conception of natural units. Now we need work on further theoretical developments on how best to organize and present for demonstration and practice more highly conceptual material for optimal learning.

Some workers have approached this problem from a logical standpoint, attempting to analyze conceptual subject matter in terms of its structure. Gagné (1965), for example, has described some content areas in hierarchical terms, building from lower order elements such as facts or concepts up to higher order principles. To date, however, it has been difficult for practitioners to apply such analysis directly to the design of instruction. It seems that even excellent logical analyses of content do not have unequivocal behavioral implications. Thus many specifications of objectives can result from a single logical analysis—some fruitful and some not. The problem becomes even more difficult if we consider objectives like insight. It is not clear how the practitioner operationalizes the sort of insight that Köhler describes in *The Mentality of the Apes* as "the appearance of a complete solution with reference to the whole layout of the field" (G. A. Miller et al., 1960:10).

One way to treat these difficulties may be to analyze short-term instructional objectives as testable hypotheses rather than as rationally determined "givens." In this formulation, one can hypothesize that the instruction that produces certain tangible evidence of short-term learning will have a desired influence on long-term or less tangible objectives. An important reason to link easily observable behavior with more remote goals is that methods are available for producing results of the "closer in" variety, whereas "further out" objectives often can be treated only in a speculative manner.

Empirical methods for developing instruction and research in education have not always been coordinated to the best advantage. A general approach to hypothesis testing of objectives requires coordination of the two, since hypotheses about the value of short-term observable objectives cannot be tested unless instruction is developed that will in fact produce the desired performance.

Within this framework, Sheffield's extension of S-R theory to perceptual responses relates to problems of specifying objectives. We have essentially a construct validation problem, in which different observable criterion behaviors can be used to evaluate whether analysis in terms of unobservable mediating S-R connections makes sense or is worthwhile.

On a more molar basis we can describe some of the problems and findings in learning from mass media.

INFORMATION GAIN

Schramm and Wade (1967) have summarized information available as of 1967 on public dependence on the media for information in the United States. They limited their study to public affairs, science, and health knowledge; their report summarizes survey studies of respondents' reports on what medium of communications they depend upon for information in these areas. Obviously, carefully controlled field experiments designed specifically to test just how much and what kinds of information are acquired through each source would provide more solid knowledge in this area. Unfortunately, data of this sort were not available. Funkhouser and Maccoby (1971) have since reported some data on stylistic variables in the communication of science information but, as of this writing, no such data are available on learning from the mass media. We still must depend on interview survey data in which respondents report to interviewers what source they use for what kinds of information.

Schramm and Wade indicate that in the area of public affairs great changes have been taking place in the extent to which particular media of communication are used. For example, during presidential election campaigns the dependence on television rose from being not too different from radio and magazines in 1952 to a reliance on TV in 1964 that clearly overshadowed the other two media. Radio and magazine use fell correspondingly during this period. Surprisingly, however, the use of newspapers as the major source of information on campaigns remained quite constant.

With the exception of age—there seems to be very little difference among varying age groups in their dependence on the media—very substantial differences in media use occur among different groups. As might be expected, highly educated, white males in the highest occupation groups making the most income are more likely to report using the newspaper most for public affairs information. Poorly educated, nonwhite females and low-income farm and blue-collar workers report using television the most.

It would seem that, for very large segments of the voting population, an increasingly higher proportion of the electorate may come to use newspapers more. This would be a highly encouraging development, since newspapers report the news in much greater depth than television does or is likely to do even if the amount of time on television devoted to news continues to increase. Unfortunately, the data reported by Wade and Schramm do not promise such a trend. Even with the substantial increase in the mean number of years of schooling in the U.S. population during the twelve-year period covered, the percentage of the population citing newspapers as their major news source during election campaigns remains approximately the same. Perhaps increasing education is just offsetting the otherwise increasing dependence on television.

LEARNING OF ATTITUDES

Thus far we have been discussing communication and learning in terms of learning information, concepts, and skills. One can also talk about the learning of attitudes. Without getting into a lengthy discussion of the nature of attitudes, let us for the purposes of exposition adopt Gordon Allport's definition. For Allport (1935) "an attitude is a mental and neural state of readiness, organized through experience, exerting a directive or dynamic influence upon the individual's response to all objects and situations with which it is related." If indeed attitudes do exercise a directive influence on great classes of events, attitudes should become the great organizing and predictive concept in social behavior. It no longer becomes necessary to treat every bit of behavior as unique, and great varieties of behavior can be regarded as interchangeable. The concept of attitude is to social behavior what the discovery of "learning how to learn" is for learning theory.

While students of the field have suggested a sizable number of theoretical approaches to attitude change (cf. Insko, 1967; Kiesler, Collins & Miller, 1969; McGuire, 1969), we suggest that these really boil down to two basic approaches: consistency theory and learning theory (Maccoby & Maccoby, 1961). The earlier work in attitude change, done primarily by Hovland and his associates, first in the Research Branch of the Information and Education Division of the War Department during World War II and subsequently at Yale, derived its theoretical focus from learning theory—particularly from the Hullian or neo-Hullian reinforcement variety (Hovland, Lumsdaine & Sheffield, 1949).

More recently, a variety of consistency-theory approaches to attitude change have occupied center stage. Beginning with Heider (1946), and followed by Newcomb (1953), Cartwright and Harary (1956), Osgood and Tannenbaum (1957), and brought to full flower by Festinger (1957; 1964) and his students and followers, consistency theory has been a prolific source of hypotheses for experiments in attitude change. (See Jones & Gerard, 1967, for an excellent critical summary of the contributions of Festinger's cognitive dissonance theory to conformity and persuasion.) The principal point of attack of these consistency theories, particularly of dissonance theory, has been on the motivational components of the persuasive process; they focus on what it is that motivates a person to change his attitude.

Given that motivation exists, however, why is it that some attitudes are learned and adopted while other persuasive communications frequently fail to persuade, even under conditions of generally high motivation? True, dissonance theory does point out that there are means of reducing dissonance other than by changing one's attitude, and dissonance theory, applied in this way, has contributed brilliantly to explaining some apparent anomalies in experimental findings. But such theories pay little attention to learning factors in attitude change. Even when dissonance leads to attitude change as the means of reducing the motivation of dissonance, the attitude that is changed cannot be specified. It may well be that, given motivation to change, the particular pattern of behavior resulting from the impact of a persuasive communication can best be tackled via learning theory (Maccoby & Maccoby, 1961).

The recent development of theories and techniques for automating instruction has made available a relatively stable context in which to investigate human learning. Automated instruction provides reproducible learning situations comparatively free of the variability of human teachers. Responses of the individual students can be monitored systematically throughout the learning process, and it is possible to control variations in instructional methods. Increased availability of media resources has further increased hopes for progress in instructional technology and theory.

Many studies have been conducted on new techniques and media. Some have attempted to use a specific instructional setting to investigate broader theoretical issues; others have been oriented to more immediate technological concerns with the specific materials used in the research. Expectations for rapid advances that were voiced in the early 1960s have not been met, however.

One who turns to the research literature or to reviews of it will not find clear guidance in how to design instruction. There are "no-difference" studies and apparently conflicting results on virtually every point of interest. Many no-difference findings can be ascribed to methodological problems, and many apparent conflicts can be seen to be the result of differences in experimental procedures, materials, or the values of related variables. In the few cases in which a specific treatment pattern has been replicated across different content areas and programming styles, most findings have not been consistent (e.g., Hamilton & Porteus, 1965). The one consistent finding is that able students do better.

To further complicate matters, technological studies that can legitimately be used for practical decision-making purposes have sometimes been presented as generalizable scientific studies. Comparing "conventional" instruction with an innovative treatment may answer the practical question of whether to adopt the new treatment but says little or nothing about that form of innovation in general (Lumsdaine, 1963a; 1963b).

In response to these difficulties with

research, Chu and Schramm (1967) suggest that too much emphasis has been placed on formal research as a means to learn about instructional design, and too little emphasis has been placed on empirical development. Empirical development or *formative evaluation*, as it has more recently been named, involves trying out an early draft of a lesson on a few students, revising it on the basis of their performance data, retrying it, revising again, and continuing with this iterative process until a satisfactory performance criterion is reached.

This is not at all like formal classroom evaluation studies, in which essentially completed materials are administered to large groups. Although large-group evaluation studies provide information on the degree to which lessons meet their objectives, they do not provide the detailed data needed for sound empirical development. See Hovland, Lumsdaine, and Sheffield (1949:26) for an early discussion of this issue, and Markle (1967) for documentation of the procedures used in developing an instructional system under explicit constraints of instructional effectiveness and instructional time. Maccoby, Jecker, and Breitrose (1969) recently carried out a project in which classroom film was being prepared in such a manner.

The distinction between empirical development procedures and empirical evaluation studies has often been ignored in practice, with most attention being given to the evaluation study. One reason for this appears to be the glamor or status of the large-N, formal "experiment," as contrasted with the unimpressive developmental tryout. The developmental tryout is not a formal experiment, does not provide scientific information, and is contaminated with reactive measures and experimenter effects. A second reason is the lack of well-established criteria for documenting and evaluating developmental procedures. "The lesson was tried out on N students" can mean many different things.

A third reason that disproportionate attention has been given to evaluation studies is general disbelief that one can obtain consistent, reliable information from three or four students—information that is more valuable than summary data from fifty students for solving many problems that arise while materials are being developed. The differences between the decision problems that face the developer and those that face the evaluator are clear enough when they are faced as decision problems, but the traditions surrounding classroom research have obscured the issue. As a result, many lessons have been developed with inappropriate empirical procedures or no empirical procedures at all, and thus fail to realize the promise of the "new instructional technology" regardless of their superficial appearance.

Further, and more to the point of this chapter, weaknesses of lessons that have not been developed "adequately" obscure the effects of variables that are manipulated in experimental studies. In this regard, we should note that the effects of inadequate developmental procedures are not limited to failure of materials to teach. Incorrect procedures can also produce excessively redundant materials, trivial response requests, and other undesired features that will obscure the effects of variables of interest. See, for example, Holland (1965) and May (1966) for a discussion of how this difficulty has had unfortunate effects on research on the designs of instruction.

As discussed earlier, it has been difficult for researchers to identify instructional variables that will stand the test of replication. We would like to suggest that many of the variables that have been investigated are at least one step removed from the proper object of investigation. It is as though a chemist were manipulating the distance from a Bunsen-burner flame or the size of the flame when he meant to be investigating the effect of different amounts of heat on a reaction. The chemist needs a measure of heat; analogously, the investigator of human learning needs measures of the effects of his manipulated "variables" on the conditions of learning so that he can then relate the conditions of learning to learning itself.

For example, in investigating the effects of feedback or "knowledge of results" on learning, one needs an independent measure of whether the feedback manipulation is in fact providing information that is not available in a no-feedback condition. Similarly, in investigations of whether or not preinstruction directions influence learning, one needs to know if actually following the preinstruction directions has an effect on learning. This cannot be evaluated without an independent measure of whether the directions were followed.

This analysis is easy to apply when observations of the consequences of an independent variable can be made separately from observations of the dependent learning variable. In the case of prepresentation instructions which involve observable procedures, we can observe whether subjects follow instructions. However, some mediating links are hypothetical constructs; they cannot be observed so easily. For example, in investigating how overt response requests control related covert responses, we need independent measures of covert responding. That is, we need measures to support inferences about processes that are not normally observable. Intervention techniques used informally in empirical development of instruction and used formally in recent attitude-change research should be useful here (Maccoby & Roberts, 1971). Response-time data is a promising tool for making inferences about behavior that is not observable in conventional response records (Brooks, 1967).

VARIABLES OF INTEREST

If we examine instructional variables in terms of the mediating processes that intervene between the initial manipulation and learning, it is easier to see why research results are so inconsistent. Explicit consideration of mediating processes enables us to consider investigations at a minimum of two levels, where frequent practice has been to operate at a single, confounded level. The two levels are (1) an "engineering" level, in which interest lies in determining which combinations of externally manipulable variables will control the mediators necessary for learning; and (2) a learning-theory level, at which relationships between mediators and learning are investigated.

Reinforcement and Feedback

A popular research question has been, Does reinforcement contribute to learning? Rules for instructional programming given by Skinner (1960; 1965) and his followers naturally included the need for reinforcement, since this is a focal concept in Skinnerian theory. Skinner argued that telling a student his answer is correct will increase the probability that he will make that same answer under similar stimulus conditions in the future. Placed in a system in which students usually make correct answers, we have a persuasive idea. Only in outlandish circumstances would the converse hold.

Now suppose we ask, Does reinforcement contribute to learning? It is possible to compare experimentally a program that provides the information that each correct answer is correct with an alternate version of the very same program that lacks that feature. Suppose in our experiment that the program meets other requirements of the Skinnerian system, e.g., frequent questions, with few student errors. What does it mean if we cannot demonstrate that the "reinforced" version is superior to the other? Many have concluded from such studies that *reinforcement* in general is unnecessary. But we can say only that we have been unable to demonstrate a need for the stimuli that are present in one program and absent in the other.

Let us assume for purposes of argument that our experiment was sensitive enough to detect differences of a meaningful size. We nevertheless cannot distinguish between rejecting a theoretical position about the need for reinforcement and rejecting our explication of "reinforcement" in this situation.

It is not our purpose to defend or attack reinforcement as an issue here. The argument applies as well to other theory structures. Let us look at a parallel treatment of the same example experiment in terms of feedback or knowledge of results. If we assert initially that feedback should aid learning and then are unable to demonstrate that it does, we still have no way of deciding whether the difficulty lies in our theory or in our explication. If comparing treatments that do and do not deliberately provide feedback does not yield consistent results, it would be useful to ask how we can make a lesson that *withholds* feedback while holding constant other elements of our problem.

In most meaningful instruction, students can give themselves feedback some of the time, from context, sequence, etc. Students' responses themselves are feedback sources. Can we eliminate unplanned feedback while maintaining other desired elements of the system? Viewed in this light, our feedback versus no-feedback study is better characterized as: one form of providing what we hypothesize to be feedback plus other possible forms of feedback versus other possible forms of feedback minus our hypothetical form of feedback. Such a study has many technological elements. It is most useful for deciding whether to go to extra expense to provide a given pattern of feedback in a specific program under study. If *no extra* expense is involved in providing a given pattern, it would be hard to cost-justify a technological study for this purpose in the first place.

Let us extend this argument. Whenever a series of no-difference studies suggests that a variable of apparent importance is not important, ask if other things that are available to the student can function in the same way as that variable. Then ask if it is possible to design a contrasting treatment with all such effects withdrawn. In some instances it would also be worthwhile to ask whether we would seriously consider using that treatment for practical instructional purposes.

Another approach is to ask when it is most catastrophic not to provide formal feedback. A tentative answer is that feedback is most critical when other elements of the communication network are below par or when there is a lot of uncertainty in the system, such as when we are dealing with especially difficult material or working with relatively slow learners.

With regard to feedback, we conclude, in spite of disagreement in experimental findings, that knowing *in some way* whether you are successful or proceeding correctly is important to learning.

When working on trivially easy materials, students will sometimes use feedback to reassure themselves that there is no trickery involved. We can call this "content irrelevant" or "process" feedback. Once accustomed to the game, students often ignore the feedback completely. With moderately difficult materials, observers note wide variation in feedback use, ranging from none to consistent and persistent (Geis, Jacobs, Spencer, & Nielsen, 1970). This can be termed "content relevant information" feedback, and it may depend on learner characteristics and instructional characteristics.

As response complexity increases and chances for there to be a "single right answer" decrease, information feedback appears to become more important. When materials are excessively difficult, students often become dependent on feedback, and must sometimes use it as initial instruction. In that case *feedback* is a misnomer. Unanswerable questions or problems that are followed by "feedback" then serve as preinstruction preparatory questions. In explaining the function of feedback in one study, Michael and Maccoby (1961) argue that a delay of a couple of seconds following the presentation of feedback provided the occasion for further covert practice of the correct response.

Thus, in different situations formal provision of feedback may function, alone or in some combination, as (1) initial instruction, (2) an occasion for covert practice, (3) process feedback, and (4) information feedback. Variations in the context, form, and timing of feedback will vary the likelihood that it will serve these different functions.

Practice

All instructional programming systems that have a learning-theory basis or an empirical orientation place strong emphasis on the response component of instruction. The question of feedback would not occur without this orientation. Just as with research on feedback, findings from research on "active responding" are not as unanimously favorable as early theorizing would lead one to expect. Moreover, a developer's decision problem about the extent to which he should include response requests is not as simple as the one regarding feedback. He can usually decide to include formal feedback, even though it may not contribute to learning for all students in all situations, because it is unlikely to have a negative effect and it costs little to include. Occasions for practice, on the other hand, are difficult to design, awkward to include in some presentation systems, and often increase the length of time instruction takes.

Frequent requests for overt responses make it possible for a developer to use fine-grained empirical development procedures. One would expect lessons in which response requests are included as important components to be improved by empirical procedures that are directed toward achieving correct responses. Of course, empirical procedures will be to no avail if the response requests are not functionally related to the learning task. No amount of careful work devoted to increasing the probability of correct responses to functionless tasks can be expected to pay off. Lessons that do not contain response requests cannot be developed directly in a fine-grained empirical way. They may be derived from lessons that initially contained frequent response requests, or they may be developed according to procedures that make less use of student responses. Thus research that compares lessons that do and do not contain response requests may involve different possible combinations of empirical development and response requests, depending on the procedures used to produce the lessons.

Let us assume that the lessons teach reasonably well regardless of whether or not they have been empirically developed, and consider the different possible instructional functions of response requests, apart from developmental functions. Briefly, they are (1) no function (irrelevant, representing behavior already in repertoire, etc.), (2) communication of objectives, (3) direction of attention, (4) overall inducement of attention, (5) control of covert practice, and (6) provision for practice that needs to be overt.

As this overlapping list suggests, we should not be surprised that research on overt practice has found apparently inconsistent results. Lumsdaine and May (1965) have tallied the results of experiments on overt responding in printed programs, and they were unable to identify specific conditions in which overt responding was demonstrably superior.

Holland (1965) has noted some conditions under which overt responding should not be expected to provide a measurable benefit, most of which involve program-design flaws such as requests for trivial responses. Applying the mediational analysis developed in the earlier section on feedback, we can conclude that many functions of overt-response requests can be served by other lesson-design features. The more these functions are shared among such features, the less a single feature will appear to contribute.

Further, the demand characteristics of experiments are especially likely to have some of the same functions as response requests. Thus it appears necessary to be cautious in applying to practical situations no-effect conclusions about "active practice" that are found in experimental situations. The only cases in which such confounding cannot be expected to wash out the effects of response requests are those in which (1) motor responses need practice, (2) nonmotor reponses of some complexity must be learned *de novo*, (3) complex chains of responses are being taught in which earlier parts of the response are stimuli for later parts, and (4) other techniques do not control attention adequately. We would expect (4) to be important with students who do not have "standard" reading and study skills.

In view of the beneficial influence that provisions for overt student responses have on designers of instruction, it appears reasonable to develop instruction initially with deliberate provisions for overt responding. Once the materials are functioning well, one may then consider eliminating some overt response requests, converting them to parallel presentational materials, or making the response component less time-consuming. Large time savings with no decrement in criterion performance can be achieved by such means (Markle, 1967), but the validity of the changes must be verified empirically.

STEP SIZE

The requirement for "small steps" that was included in a number of programmed-instruction systems has been interpreted variously as number of words between response requests, length of time between response requests, complexity of response requested, and difficulty level. Questions of step size have been asked in terms of stimulus dimensions and response dimensions of a lesson. Clearly, *step size* is the name for more than one variable (Lumsdaine, 1960). Whichever variable is intended, that variable can have or interact with the mediating functions that are associated with response requests and stimulus organization.

Some designers of instruction have adopted empirical means of determining step size. The basic method is to start developmental work with what appear to be excessively large steps, then use data on student performance to determine where and how to break these down into smaller units. The operational principles applied here are (1) a small step is the largest step students can take successfully, and (2) feedback about student performance that is useful to the designer is basically negative: that is, right answers do not reveal malfunctions such as excessively small steps, but wrong answers do reveal excessively large steps. The concepts of D-A span and natural units discussed earlier in this chapter can provide a systematic basis for such an empirical approach.

PACE

Pacing is also the name given to several different variables. Two clear-cut aspects of it are (1) the pace of the materials as they proceed through the subject-matter domain, and (2) the pace of the student as he works through the materials.

The pace of the materials is similar to the concept of step size, although one can talk of pace in this sense whether or not response requests or explicit steps are present in the materials. We may also wish to include in the category of "materials pace" external constraints which operate on the materials without student mediation. Examples of these are speed of narration on a tape or in a film, and mechanical delays between elements of presentation.

The pace of the student, or rate at which he works, is another matter. The student's pace is dependent, to some extent, on the pace of the materials. For example, if the pace of the materials is too fast for the student, his pace may be zero. Many other combinations are possible.

Early theoretical discussions of programmed instruction made much of the virtues of student pacing, suggesting that the student who works individually can choose a beneficial working speed. While it is true that individualization of instruction gives students control over how long they will spend looking at a given page or display, it is misleading to think of the student as being in complete control. The pacing of the materials limits the possibilities open to the student, even in the most flexible instructional system.

Further, most administrators of individualized instruction have found that some students adopt inappropriate rates of working. External contingencies, such as events that follow completion of a lesson, often determine how quickly students work. Peer pressure often can be seen to slow down a fast worker or speed up a slow worker to the point where he makes many errors. Even lacking such obvious controlling factors, it is clear that many students do not know how to choose a reasonable working pace, and they must be taught how to before self-pacing can be expected to work. Margolius and Sheffield (1961) found that good learners elected pacing intervals similar to those found to be most effective in previous research.

Given all these qualifications, it should not be surprising that self-pacing, in all its variety, has not been proven to be unequivocally superior. If we think more in terms of suitable pacing, the question becomes easier to deal with. Empirical development can take care of a major part of the suitability of the pace of the materials. Then what remains is a combination of factors relating to student ability and motivation, and administrative factors. Administrative factors often encourage an imposition of pace even on individualized lessons in order to coordinate the grouped student activities. Pace must often be imposed when student time is an accountable cost. Pace is sometimes imposed to good advantage when students choose unsuitable paces for themselves. When considerations like these do not require the imposition of external controls of pace, which themselves should be empirically tested, then student control of pace is likely to work.

Choice of Medium

In a chapter on communication and learning it seems appropriate to discuss the deliberate use of communication media in instruction. Some workers have sought clear-cut guidelines on how to choose media of instruction to match instructional objectives (Briggs, Campeau, Gagné, & May, 1967), but it seems that only the most obvious generalizations can be made. For example, pictures are useful for showing students what something looks like. Print media are generally inappropriate for nonreaders. Audio tape is useful for letting students hear their own verbal performance. Other statements like this can be made, but most are useful from an "engineering" point of view and have little theoretical interest.

Even if it were possible to make more precise matchings of media with types of objectives, the heterogeneity of objective types within any single lesson would lead to frequent medium changes or frequent compromises.

As with other variables we have discussed, it appears that learning effects of medium choice are easily overridden by the quality of the developmental effort. Empirical development of the simplest media can be expected to be superior to poor development and implementation of the most expensive media (Chu & Schramm, 1967). In practice, it turns out that factors associated with the costs and administration of a course have a large bearing on medium choice. If it is necessary to distribute a course to many administration sites very inexpensively, a developer is unlikely to consider film. If, on the other hand, the students are unlikely to finish a reading assignment but will watch a film to the end, film is a natural choice. If national distribution to home viewers is needed, then TV is needed. For a discussion of how television might be used to implement literacy training, see Hamilton, Markle, and Maccoby (1970).

Throughout this discussion we have

emphasized the role of empirical development and cautioned against reifying single "variables" that have multiple overlapping functions. *Medium* is a prime example of this problem, since it is even one step further removed from many fundamental instructional variables. That is, essentially the same instructional sequence can be presented via different media without changing the values of many of the variables we have discussed.

A final comment on problems associated with medium choice is an extension of a finding reported by Hovland et al. (1949). They found that a crude film of a storyboard was as effective a teaching device as the final professional-looking version of the film. Current practice that reflects this finding is to develop crude, inexpensive materials empirically before making final choices of media or investing in polished versions (Markle, 1965; 1967; Maccoby, Jecker, & Breitrose, 1969).

A lesson that actually teaches may seem too slowly paced or insufficiently embellished to a medium specialist who does not base his decisions on student-performance data. Great care must be exercised in the final production stages of courses that are presented in complex media to ensure that medium considerations do not interfere with instructional values.

In sum, it must be said that our understanding of teaching and learning of motor skills, verbal and nonverbal information and concepts, and the role of communication in this process is still far from being fully understood. Moreover, our understanding of the communication processes involved in the acquisition, retention, and resistance to persuasion is as yet really primitive. Hopefully, however, we are at least beginning to make some definite progress in our learning about the roles communication and learning play in persuasion.

REFERENCES

Allport, Gordon W.
1935 "Attitudes." Pp. 798–844 in C. M. Murchison (ed.), Handbook of Social Psychology. Worcester, Massachusetts: Clark University Press.

Ausbel, D. P.
1965 "Cognitive structure and facilitation of verbal learning." Pp. 103–115 in R. C. Anderson and D. P. Ausbel (eds.), Readings in the Psychology of Cognition. New York: Holt, Rinehart and Winston.

Briggs, L. J.; P. L. Campeau; R. N. Gagné; and M. A. May.
1967 "Instructional media: A procedure for the design of multi-media instruction, a critical review of research, and suggestions for future research." Monograph No. 2. Palo Alto, California: American Institutes for Research.

Brooks, L. O.
1967 "Note on revising instructional programs." Psychology Reports 20:117–118.

Bruner, J. S.; J. J. Goodnow; and G. A. Austin.
1956 A Study of Thinking. New York: Wiley.

Cartwright, Dorwin, and Frank Harary.
1956 "Structural balance: A generalization of Heider's theory." Psychological Review 63:277–293.

Chu, G. C., and Wilbur Schramm.
1967 Learning from Television: What the Research Says. Stanford, California: Institute for Communication Research.

Comstock, G. A , and Nathan Maccoby.
1966 The Peace Corps ETV Project in Colombia—Two Years of Research. Reports 1–10 plus Introduction and Summary. Stanford, California: Institute for Communication Research.

Ebbinghaus, Hermann.
1964 Memory. Translation by Henry A. Ruger and Clara R. Bussenius (reissue). New York: Dover Publications. First published as Über das Gedächtnis (Leipzig, 1885).

Ekman, Paul; W. V. Friesen; and Phoebi C. Ellsworth.
1972 Emotion in the Human Face. New York: Pergamon Press.

Estes, W. K.
1970 "Reward in human learning: Theoretical issues and strategic choice

points." Pp. 16–36 in Robert Glaser (ed.), The Nature of Reinforcement, Part I. Pittsburgh: University of Pittsburgh Learning Research and Development Center.

Festinger, Leon.
1957 A Theory of Cognitive Dissonance. New York: Harper.

Festinger, Leon, et al.
1964 Conflict, Decision, and Dissonance. Stanford, California: Stanford University Press.

Funkhouser, G. R., and Nathan Maccoby.
1971 "Communicating specialized information to a lay audience." Journal of Communication 21:58–71.

Gagné, R. N.
1965 The Conditions of Learning. New York: Holt, Rinehart and Winston.

Geis, George L.; William Jacobs; Dwight Spencer; and Susan Nielsen.
1970 "The role of the printed answer in programmed instruction." NSPI Journal 9 (July):8–18.

Gibson, E. J.; J. J. Gibson; A. D. Pick; and Harry Osser.
1962 "A developmental study of the discrimination of letter-like forms." Journal of Comparative and Physiological Psychology 55:901.

Guthrie, E. R.
1952 The Psychology of Learning. Revised Edition. New York: Harper.

Hamilton, N. R.; D. G. Markle; and Nathan Maccoby.
1970 The Role of Television in Literacy Programs. Stanford, California: Institute for Communication Research.

Hamilton, N. R., and B. D. Porteus.
1965 Increasing Long-term Retention of Knowledge. Experiment 2. Final Report: U.S. Office of Education, Title 7, Grant #7-48-7670-204. Palo Alto, California: American Institute for Research.

Heider, Fritz.
1946 "Attitudes and cognitive organizations." Journal of Psychology 21: 107–112.

Holland, J. G.
1965 "Research on programming variables." Pp 66–117 in Robert Glaser (ed.),Teaching Machines and Programmed Learning: II. Data and Directions. Washington, D. C.: National Education Association Department of Audiovisual Instruction.

Hovland, C. I.; A. A. Lumsdaine; and F. D. Sheffield.
1949 Experiments on Mass Communication. Princeton: Princeton University Press.

Hull, C. J.
1943 Principles of Behavior. New York: Appleton-Century-Crofts.

Insko, C. A.
1967 Theories of Attitude Change. New York: Appleton-Century-Crofts.

Jenkins, J. G., and K. M. Dallenbach.
1924 "Oblivescence during sleep and waking." American Journal of Psychology 35:605–612.

Jones, E. E., and H. B. Gerard.
1967 Foundations of Social Psychology. New York: Wiley.

Kiesler, C. A.; B. E. Collins; and N. E. Miller.
1969 Attitude Change: A Critical Analysis of Theoretical Approaches. New York: Wiley.

Köhler, Wolfgang.
1925 The Mentality of the Apes. Translation by E. Winter. New York: Harcourt, Brace and World.
1959 Gestalt Psychology. New York: Liveright.

Lumsdaine, A. A.
1960 "Automated learning." Pp. 517–539 in A. A. Lumsdaine and Robert Glaser (eds.), Teaching Machines and Programmed Learning: A Source Book. Washington, D. C.: National Education Association.
1963a "Instruments and media of instruction." Pp. 583–682 in N. L. Gage (ed.), Handbook of Research on Teaching. Chicago: Rand McNally.
1963b "Some problems in assessing instructional programs," in R. T. Filep (ed.), Prospectives in Programming. New York: Macmillan.

Lumsdaine, A. A. (ed.).
1961 Student Response in Programmed Instruction: A Symposium. Publication 943. Washington, D. C.: National Academy of Sciences, National Research Council.

Lumsdaine, A. A., and M. A. May.
1965 "Mass communication and educational media," in Paul R. Farnsworth, Olga W. McNemar, and Quinn

McNemar (eds.), Annual Review of Psychology. Volume 16. Palo Alto, California: Annual Reviews, Inc.

Maccoby, Nathan; Jon Jecker; and H. S. Breitrose.
1969 Criteria for the Production and Selection of Film for the Classroom: A Preliminary Study. Stanford, California: Institute for Communication Research.

Maccoby, Nathan; Jon Jecker; H. S. Breitrose; and E. D. Rose.
1964 Sound Film Recordings in Improving Classroom Communications. Experimental Studies in Classroom Communication. Stanford, California: Institute for Communication Research.

Maccoby, Nathan, and Eleanor E. Maccoby.
1961 "Homeostatic theory in attitude change." Public Opinion Quarterly 25(Winter):538–545.

Maccoby, Nathan, and D. F. Roberts.
1971 "Cognitive processes in persuasion." Paper presented at the American Marketing Association's Attitude Research Conference, St. Thomas, Virgin Islands, November.

McGuire, William.
1969 "The nature of attitudes and attitude change." Pp. 136–314 in Gardner Lindzey and Elliot Aronson (eds.), Handbook of Social Psychology. Volume 3. Second Edition. Reading, Massachusetts: Addison-Wesley.

Mandler, George, and S. G. Sarason.
1952 "A study of anxiety and language." Journal of Abnormal and Social Psychology 47:166–173.

Margolius, G. J., and F. D. Sheffield.
1961 "Optimum methods of combining practice with filmed demonstration in teaching complex response sequences: Serial learning of a mechanical-assembly task." Pp. 33–53 in A. A. Lumsdaine (ed.), Student Response in Programmed Instruction: A Symposium. Publication No. 943. Washington, D. C.: National Academy of Sciences, National Research Council.

Markle, D. G.
1965 "Empirical film development." National Society for Programmed Instruction Journal 4(No. 6):9–11.
1967 The Development of the Bell System First Aid and Personal Safety Course. Final Report, AIR-E-81-4/67-FR. Palo Alto, California: American Institutes for Research.
1968 "Controlling behavior changers' behavior." AV Communication Review 16 (Summer):188–203.

May, M. A.
1966 The Role of Student Response in Learning from the New Educational Media. Bethesda, Maryland: ERIC Document Reproduction Service, ED 010 389.

Michael, D. N., and Nathan Maccoby.
1961 "Factors influencing the effects of student participation on verbal learning from films: Motivating versus practice effects, 'feedback,' and overt versus covert responding." Pp. 271–293 in A. A. Lumsdaine (ed.), Student Response in Programmed Instruction: A Symposium. Publication 943. Washington, D. C.: National Academy of Sciences, National Research Council.

Miller, G. A.; Eugene Galanter; and K. H. Pribram.
1960 Plans and the Structure of Behavior. New York: Holt, Rinehart and Winston.

Miller, N. E., and John Dollard.
1941 Social Learning and Imitation. New Haven: Yale University Press.

Minami, Hiroshi, and K. M. Dallenbach.
1946 "The effect of activity upon learning and retention in the cockroach." American Journal of Psychology 59 (January):1–58.

Newcomb, T. M.
1953 "An approach to the study of communication acts." Psychology Review 60:393–404.

Osgood, C. E.; G. J. Suci; and P. H. Tannenbaum.
1957 The Measurement of Meaning. Urbana: University of Illinois Press.

Schramm, Wilbur, and Serena Wade.
1967 Knowledge and the Public Mind. Final Report to U.S. Office of Education, Contract No. 4-6-001981-1981. Stanford, California: Institute for Communication Research, Stanford University.

Sheffield, F. D.
1961 "Theoretical consideration in the learning of complex sequential tasks from demonstration and practice." Pp. 13–32 in A. A. Lumsdaine (ed.), Student Response in Programmed Instruction: A Symposium. Washington, D.C.: National Academy of Sciences, National Research Council.

Skinner, B. F.
1953 Science and Human Behavior. New York: Macmillan.
1960 "Teaching machines." Pp. 137–158 in A. A. Lumsdaine and Robert Glaser (eds.), Teaching Machines and Programmed Learning: A Source Book. Washington, D. C.: National Education Association.
1965 "Reflections on a decade of teaching machines." Pp. 5–20 in Robert Glaser (ed.), Teaching Machines and Programmed Learning, II: Data and Directions. Washington, D.C.: NEA Department of Audio-visual Instruction.
1969 Contingencies of Reinforcement: A Theoretical Analysis. New York: Appleton-Century-Crofts.

Tolman, E. C.
1932 Purposive Behavior in Animals and Men. New York: Appleton-Century.

CHAPTER **8**

Communication and Children: A Developmental Approach

DONALD F. ROBERTS
Stanford University

By the age of three, with the benefit of little direct instruction, children accomplish the remarkable feat of learning a language. Between the ages of three and sixteen they spend approximately as much time looking at television as they spend in school. This chapter traces the development of children's use of communication and their learning of communication skills, and it considers much of the child-development literature that contributes to the understanding of this process. Finally, it explores the effects of communication on children, especially the evidence on the effect of violence in the mass media.

Childhood is a period of information seeking during which the child learns what to expect from the world and what the world expects from him. The years between infancy and adulthood witness the formation and elaboration of a conception of reality, both physical and social, within which the child, and later the adult, will function. Roger Brown (1965: 193) notes:

> Human infants do not possess culture at birth; they do not have a conception of the world, a language, or a morality. All of these things must be acquired by them and the process of acquisition is called socialization.

Brown might well have added that man is unique in that a large proportion of this socialization proceeds through the *social* mediation of information.

It is clear that children derive information about their world from many sources, both social and nonsocial. Direct experience with the environment provides a good deal of information about the child's immediate reality. Through direct experience he learns that some objects are hard and some soft, some rough and some smooth, some hot and some cold. But one need only observe the interaction of parent and child for a short time to see that information from other persons plays a major role, even in instances where direct experience is possible. It is the rare parent who would allow his child to experience the heat of a stove by touching rather than steer him away from such danger by explaining, warning, forbidding.

The sheer fact of human ability to engage

in symbolic communication greatly accounts for our heavy reliance on socially mediated information. Jones and Gerard (1967) point out that human language is uniquely suited to facilitate the child's definition of the world in which he lives. It enables rich and precise communications about various states of the world—communications in which the signs can be varied to assist the child's understanding.

Even more important, symbolic communication extends the scope of human reality far beyond immediate experience. The world that the child must come to define contains abstract conceptions such as morality and justice; it extends backward into history and forward into the future; it crosses oceans and cultures; it touches upon gods and devils. The distinctive thing about such a reality, about the information necessary to define it, is that "it can be mediated *only* by other persons, whether directly or indirectly through the pages of a book or the channels of a television set" (Jones & Gerard, 1967: 127).

The present chapter, then, defines communication at its broadest—as simply the social mediation of information. We approach children's communication behavior from a dual perspective, viewing it both as a process facilitating socialization and as a product of that socialization. Although children's mass media behavior will be emphasized, we assume that such behavior cannot be understood in isolation from intrapersonal development or from the context of interpersonal communication in which the child develops. Hence, brief consideration will be given to children's communication behavior at the intrapersonal and interpersonal levels, looking at such topics as value acquisition, cognitive development, language development, and imitation before examining their use of and response to the mass media.

Our attempt is to examine how children come to participate in and respond to a system characterized by the social transmission of information. How do they learn to produce and respond to communications? What are the conditions that affect which communications they will receive and act upon or how a particular communication will be interpreted? What are the implications for children of a world where the mass media are almost inescapable, where by the time the average child has graduated from high school he has spent more time in front of a television set than in the classroom? These are a few of the questions we attempt to engage.

COMMUNICATION AND SOCIALIZATION

Gerbner (1967:41) characterizes man's ability to engage in "symbolic representation and re-creation of aspects of the human condition" as the critical "humanizing" element in the transformation of hominoid into *Homo sapiens*. In a sense, we witness aspects of such a transformation each time we concern ourselves with communication and children. To a large extent, it is through learning to use and respond to socially mediated signs and symbols that the infant, possessing no culture at birth, becomes a socialized, "humanized" adult.

Socialization refers to the child's taking on the "way of life of his family and of the larger social groups in which he must relate and perform adequately in order to ultimately qualify for full adult status" (Clausen, 1966:4). It is the process of acquisition of the rules and norms that comprise the various systems of the child's culture (e.g., language, religion, political philosophy, morality, etc.).

We noted above that communication may be conceived of as both a process facilitating socialization and as a product of that socialization. As process, communication functions to help define for the child the "way of life" he must internalize, to mediate information about the cultural systems he must adopt—or adapt. As product, the child's communication behavior reflects the definition of the world he has gained through socialization. Clausen and Williams (163:63) write that through socialization children learn "to communicate effectively with others (to interpret their behavior with some accuracy)." Socialization affects the child's selection of the others to whom he will communicate, from whom he will receive communications, and how he will respond to such communications. In short, at the same time the social mediation of information plays a central role in defining reality for the child, his conception of reality at a given time influences how he uses and how he responds to such socially mediated information.

This is not to say that the norms and rules which comprise the various systems of a culture all are explicitly communicated to children by adults, or that socialization is simply the communication, from one generation to the next, of an unchanging view of the world. Quite the contrary, the system of rules and norms that a child, or for that matter an adult, holds at any one time results from the interaction between learning and inference from explicit communications, implicit communications (e.g. observed behavior) and, of course, direct experience. Moreover, what is communicated either explicitly or implicitly is a function of ongoing events at any point in time, and what is learned or inferred is a function of each child's idiosyncratic experience, needs, and capabilities. Hence, the cultural system adopted by the child "need not, in the end, simply reproduce the rules that prevail in his society. The outcome can be unique and is sometimes revolutionary" (Brown, 1965:195).

That the outcomes of socialization are infrequently revolutionary derives primarily from the *almost* monopolistic control over information exercised by the young child's primary group. Jones and Gerard (1967) conceive of childhood in terms of two major dependency conditions: effect dependence and information dependence. Effect dependence refers to adult control of the outcomes of children's behavior, to the child's dependence on parents for the stimuli that maintain life and serve as rewards and punishments. Information dependence characterizes the young child's dependence on others, particularly parents, for information about his world, dependency in terms of both the amount and the nature of information made available to him.

Given that a large proportion of the information necessary for the child to define "reality" must be socially mediated, parental monopoly of the communications to which the child is exposed during the early years can be expected to exert a conserving influence on the cultural patterns adopted. If we assume that parents define reality to their children in terms of the rules and norms prevailing in society, and that few competing definitions are available, then children should accept the prevailing rules and norms.

Several other factors act to increase the potency of such an information monopoly and the maintenance of cultural patterns. First, information dependence operates within the context of effect dependence. Parents can facilitate learning of whatever information they choose to communicate by controlling tangible rewards and punishments. Moreover, through association with such primary reinforcers as food and warmth, parents themselves eventually take on reinforcing properties.

> Among other things, the mother who dispenses primary reinforcements may herself acquire the properties of a secondary reinforcer, so that her very presence or absence can become "effects" on which the child is dependent (Jones & Gerard, 1967: 86).

In addition, information mediated by parents reaches the child when, struggling toward a conception of the world in which he must function and lacking a backlog of experience, he is most open to new information.

Piaget (1952), in his discussion of assimilation and accommodation, argues that the child's conception of reality at any given time influences his processing of new information (see also Flavell, 1963). Interpretation of information received at a later time will to some degree be a function of how the child has organized information received at an earlier time. Parentally mediated information, then, provides not only the initial definitions of social reality but also the frame of reference within which later information will be interpreted.

Clearly parental control of a large part of the information reaching the child mitigates against a revolutionary outcome of socialization. Nevertheless, the outcomes *are* usually unique. Children do form conceptions of reality different from their parents. The most obvious source of such differences lies in the fact that the two generations face different worlds.

> Under conditions of rapid social and technological change, many parental interests, attitudes, and role behaviors that were serviceable at an earlier period may have little functional value for members of the younger generation (Bandura, 1969: 248).

In other words, survival may depend on a new conception of reality.

Even in periods when change is not rapid, the child's view of reality will differ from that of his parents. The parental information monopoly is never absolute, becoming less so as the child grows older and encounters information sources outside his immediate family. Some of the child's conception of the world derives from direct experience over which parents have only partial control. Even very young children encounter adults other than their parents. Older children establish relationships with peer groups and teachers, relationships that imply communication. As the sources of socially mediated information increase, so, too, does the probability that the child will encounter new and different interpretations of reality. Furthermore, social relationships established outside the primary group also become reinforcing, thus heightening the impact of information derived from these new sources.

For the twentieth-century child in a society such as ours, the picture is even more complex. The mass media, especially the pictorial media to which he has early access, enable him to experience vicariously the world far beyond his own backyard. Through the media he may confront systems of norms and rules very different from those espoused not only by his family, but even by his local community. He is exposed to information in far greater quantities and of far greater variety than that available at first hand.

As the child encounters new information from new sources, he also experiences discrepancies in how these sources interpret "reality." He learns to discriminate among sources and to evaluate the relevance and credibility of both the sources and their information. Although new information is partially assimilated in terms of the child's current conception of reality, which in large part initially derives from his parents' conception, that conception of reality is also accommodated to the new information (cf. Piaget, 1952; Flavell, 1963). Hence, parental definitions of the rules and norms will be modified; in some instances they may even be rejected. Indeed, Bandura goes so far as to state:

> Although a family can provide general prescriptions for conduct, parental models cannot possibly serve as primary sources of the elaborate skills and modes of behavior required at different stages of social development. Complex cultural patterns of behavior are, in large part, transmitted and regulated at a social-systems level (Bandura, 1969:255).

To summarize, the way a child defines and approaches his world is to a large extent a function of the information communicated to that child. To the extent that parents "get there firstest with the mostest," the child's conception of reality should reflect that of his parents, presumably a conception based on the rules and norms prevailing in their society. However, to the extent that there is a proliferation of information sources available to the child, to the extent that these sources mediate different information, and to the extent that there is a different world about which to mediate information—to this extent the probability of changes in the outcomes of socialization is increased.

DEVELOPMENTAL APPROACH

The preceding discussion of communication's role in socialization indicates the importance of viewing children's communication behavior from a developmental perspective. Childhood and adolescence are periods of rapid change. As children grow older their interests, needs, skills, experience, capabilities, and capacities all change. That which is novel to the young child may not be so to his older counterpart; the grade-school child may ignore information that the teen-ager actively seeks; the child who has learned to read has access to communications which remain a mystery to the preschool child. In short, age-related differences in communication behavior occur not only in terms of the proliferation of information sources that come with increasing age, but also in terms of what children of different ages bring to the communication situation.

While a number of ontogenetic changes might affect communication behavior, three areas seem particularly important to the present discussion in that they have direct implications for understanding the relationship between children and the mass media. The first two, research on cognitive development and on the acquisition and development of languages provide insights on children's changing capacities to deal with symbolic information. Both the child's capacities for comprehending language and for cognitively processing new information influence what he may take from the media. The third line of research, observational learning, pertains directly to what children might learn from the media. Although few developmental studies have been reported, Hartup and Coates (1970) recently noted numerous reasons for expecting age differences in observational learning. The next few pages, then, contain brief discussions of how developmental changes in these three areas might affect children's communication behavior.

Cognitive Development

We have already mentioned that children interpret and organize new information in terms of their existing frame of reference. In one sense, the frame of reference can be conceived in simple quantitative terms. The older the child, the more information about his world he can be expected to have been exposed to and to have stored. Assuming that new information is interpreted in the context of previous experience, older children should respond differently than younger children to the same communication because they have more reference points influencing their perception and interpretation of the communication.

Equally important as the differences in the amount of information children of various ages have stored, however, are *qualitative* differences in how they process that information, in how they *structure* their definition of reality. In other words, the child's cognitive capabilities, his available strategies for relating new information to old, affect how he deals with any socially mediated information. Although space constraints preclude a full discussion of the various approaches to cognitive development, a brief description of how changing cognitive capabilities can affect children's responses to communications is necessary.

Cognitive structures are defined as "the organizational properties of intelligence" (Flavell, 1963:10), and the cognitive processing of information as "any representational act which is an integral part of an organized network of acts" (Flavell,1963: 166). For new information (object, event, concept) to be cognized, then, it must be represented in relation to some organized network of related acts or concepts.

At the risk of oversimplification, cognitive processing can be described as the relating of new information to an already existing cognitive structure that is composed of interrelated concepts and that determines the kinds of possible relational operations that can be made. Many developmental psychologists agree that there is an ontogenetic pattern to the development of children's cognitive operations, certain cognitive capacities being necessary predecessors to others (Piaget, 1952; Flavell, 1963; Wallach, 1963; Bruner, 1964; Bruner, Olver, & Greenfield, 1966). Hence, there are discriminable stages or periods of cognitive development, each stage (approximately located by age) characterized by differences in how children relate new information to their cognitive structures.

Piaget and Bruner, two leading figures in the study of cognitive development, posit three major stages through which the child's intelligence passes (Piaget, 1952; Bruner, 1964; Bruner et al., 1966). During the first stage (Piaget's sensorimotor period and Bruner's enactive period), which lasts until approximately the age of eighteen months, the child's dominant relational operation is active. He touches, grasps, shakes—engaging in direct experimentation with objects around him, finally developing the concept of object as constant and as distinct from self, a concept necessary to the development of the cognitive operations performed during the second stage.

The second stage (Piaget's concrete-operational period and Bruner's ikonic period) extends approximately from eighteen months to eleven or twelve years. Actually, this stage breaks into two periods. During the first half (Piaget's preoperational—until about age seven), the child develops the capacity to engage in symbolic representation of concrete objects, discovering that certain objects or events can stand for others. During the latter half of the second stage, he develops the capacity to perform certain basic logical operations on these concrete representations; e.g., his thought comes to manifest such logical operations as reversibility and conservation. In short, this period witnesses the unfolding of many of the cognitive capacities necessary for adult thought—the ability to represent, to symbolize, to combine and recombine various *concrete* cognitions. During this period, however, the child's cognitive operations are still limited to the making of those relationships that lead to the "organized cognition of concrete objects and events *per se*" (Flavell, 1963:205).

It is only during the third stage (Piaget's period of formal operations and Bruner's symbolic period) that children become capable of engaging in propositional thinking, of moving from the real to the possible, from the concrete to the abstract. Formal operations enable consideration not only of relationships among concrete elements, but of hypothetical relationships, relationships that *might* exist.

To summarize, during the first stage the child deals with differentiating between self and concrete object; during the second he engages in symbolic representation and in making relationships among concrete elements; during the third stage he becomes capable of considering relationships among abstractions and relationships among relationships themselves.

It should be noted that such stage theories of cognitive development have been attacked on the grounds that the approach underemphasizes the influence on thought of cultural and experiential factors (see, for example, Bandura & Walters, 1963). Zigler and Child (1969), however, argue that such attacks miss the point. The stages of cognitive growth are defined in terms of their formal, structural properties, properties that determine "the upper limits of what can be learned" and "the particular process which mediates learning itself" (Zigler & Child, 1969:457). Experience afforded by the environment, however, determines the content of what is learned. Hence, children at the same level of cognitive development may manifest very different behavior.

Bruner's model of the course of cognitive development provides a good example of such an interactionist approach

(Bruner et al., 1966). He conceives of the major stages of cognitive growth in terms of the child's changing capacity to *represent* his experience of the world. While the mode of representation (enactive, ikonic, or symbolic) available to the child defines the kinds of logical operations that can be performed, "the ways of acting, imaging, and symbolizing that 'exist' in his culture" (Bruner et al., 1966:321), and the nature of the life the individual leads within his culture define how he uses the available modes. Such an approach makes clear why Bruner (1964) argues that cognitive development cannot be considered independently of language development, the topic of our next section.

This too brief and oversimplified description of the general model of cognitive development has important implications for children's communication behavior. Socially mediated information can be conceived as being composed of events or elements that the child must relate to his cognitive structure. Thus, his capacity at a given age to perform certain cognitive operations will clearly influence how he deals with any communication. For example, it is reasonable to assume that an adult would have more success communicating to a young child how to tie a shoe or build a house of blocks (concrete acts) than communicating to him a clear conception of a term such as *justice* or *government* (abstract, relational concepts). The child in the concrete or ikonic stage simply does not have the relational capacity necessary for adult understanding of such concepts.

However, this does not mean that the child will ignore all information pertaining to abstracts if it is made available to him. Rather, he may simply construe such information in terms of his own cognitive capabilities. Studies of political socialization (Greenstein, 1965; Hess & Torney, 1967) provide excellent illustrations of how young children conceptualize abstract systems and relationships in concrete terms. For example, Hess and Torney write that the "conceptualization of government is tied to personal figures for young children, then to institutions, and finally to political processes for older children" (Hess & Torney, 1967:33), clearly a progression from concrete to formal modes of understanding. In short, what the child takes from a given communication will be some function of his cognitive capacity to deal with new information, and this generalization should be as valid for mass-mediated communications as it is for interpersonal messages.

Language Development

The acquisition and development of language skills also bear on children's communication behavior, both as a symbol system affecting cognitive processes and as a medium of information exchange. Like cognitive development, language development demands an interactionist approach. The available evidence indicates that language learning probably depends both on biological bases and on environmental influences. (For comprehensive reviews of research on children's language development, see McCarthy, 1954; Ervin-Tripp & Miller, 1963; Ervin-Tripp, 1966; G. A. Miller & McNeill, 1969.)

Children progress from diffuse babbling, to the babbling of recognizable consonant and vowel sounds, to the production of words and then two-word sentences, to the construction of simple grammatical sentences by the end of the third year (Carroll, 1961). This is a remarkable feat considering that young children receive little direct language instruction and that linguists have yet to develop a theory of language structure that can generate the almost infinite possible constructions of which natural language is capable, even though children of all language communities learn to comprehend and produce such constructions.

Children face the task of inducing structure from the language corpus that they encounter. The process appears to be one of discovering rules that enable recognition and production of acceptable language constructions. The rules, however, are not those of traditional grammars. Rather, they seem to characterize some kind of generative grammar—a structure which appears to underlie all natural languages (cf. Bruner et al., 1966) and which enables production of an infinite set of novel constructions. Although linguists have yet to specify a set of rules for inferring the structure from observable features in strings of a language corpus (cf. Fodor, Jenkins, & Saporta, 1967), there is evidence supporting developmental induction of such a latent structure.

Brown (1965) contends that children's overgeneralizations of traditional grammatical rules indicate the working out of the latent structure of language. Relative to adult speech, samples of child language manifest numerous "irregularities" of usage. To the extent that such irregularities are systematic, and to the extent that they manifest developmental changes in the direction of "correct" usage (i.e., successive approximations of permissible, adult speech), they may be conceived of as evidence for induction of language structure. Thus, data demonstrating systematic overgeneralization of inflectional forms and developmentally progressive discrimination of the various inflections (Berko, 1958; W. Miller & Ervin-Tripp, 1964; Brown, 1965) point to the induction of structure at the morphological level. Similarly, data indicating the existence of "pivot grammars" (Braine, 1963; Brown & Fraser, 1963; W. Miller & Ervin-Tripp, 1964), systematic irregularities in these grammars, and progressive differentiation of grammatical subclasses and privileges of occurrence provide evidence for the induction process at a syntactical level (Brown & Fraser, 1963; Brown, 1965).

Such induction implies an extremely complex process. Given that children exposed to different language samples rapidly come to induce structure, and that they generate constructions never before encountered, it is difficult to believe that traditional learning theories can completely explain the process of acquisition. Chomsky (1959) and G. E. Miller, Galanter, and Pribram (1960) have convincingly attacked operant conditioning models of language acquisition; Lenneberg (1962) has shown that practice is not necessary for language comprehension; and there are several studies which, taken together, indicate that simple imitation cannot account for language learning (Fraser, Bellugi, & Brown, 1963; Ervin-Tripp, 1964; Cazden, 1965). In short, there is probably some critical biological basis for language acquisition (see, especially, Lenneberg, 1967).

Nevertheless, biology alone is not enough. The communication environment is also critical. Ervin-Tripp and Slobin (1966:438) write: "As yet, the link between the biologically given and the forms of experience necessary to convert potential into language has not been described." The forms of experience necessary certainly include learning opportunities, and these opportunities are inherent in the child's communication environment. Communication environment refers both to the child's speech community—the language to which he is exposed and is expected to reproduce—and to the nonverbal environment—the social and physical contexts that provide the referents and norms of communication.

One of the more straightforward means of examining the effects of environment on language development is to compare groups of children from different environments. Studies of subcultural differences, particularly socioeconomic class differences, in child language are reviewed by McCarthy (1954), Cazden (1966), and G.A. Miller and McNeill (1969).[1]

Referring to socioeconomic class comparisons, Cazden finds that on all measures of language development, "in all the studies, children of upper socioeconomic status, however defined, are more advanced than those of lower socioeconomic

[1] On sociolinguistics in general, see chapter 3 of this volume.

status" (Cazden, 1966:191). Measures have ranged from amount of phonetic production (Irwin, 1960), to measures of grammatical development (Cazden, 1965), to comparisons of concrete versus abstract modes of expression (Bernstein, 1962). Since "there is no evidence that heredity factors are segregated by socioeconomic levels" (Davis, 1948:64), we must look for features of the environment that are located by socioeconomic class and that may lead to language differences.

Socioeconomic class differences in such features as amount and nature of adult-child verbal interaction; amount of noise; parental attitudes toward speech, curiosity, and modes of discipline; and differing group consciousnesses have been documented and pointed to as influencing children's language development. The crucial role of parent-child verbal interaction is indicated in Brown's (1958) description of "the original word game." Several investigators have noted the paucity of adult stimulation available to the child in lower-class families (Milner, 1951; Deutsch, 1962; John, 1963), and at least two experiments which manipulated the amount of verbal stimulation demonstrated the importance of parental verbal stimulation to child language development (Irwin, 1960; Cazden, 1965).

It has also been shown that middle-class parents value curiosity more than do lower-class parents (Sears, Maccoby, & Levin, 1957; Kohn, 1959a; 1959b); that they are more likely than lower-class parents to encourage questions and independent investigation, to entertain questioning of demands, and to ask the child to respond and use language at more than a concrete level (Kohn, 1959a; 1959b); and that working-class parents are more likely to employ physical punishment while middle-class parents rely on verbal reasoning and appeals to guilt (Bronfenbrenner, 1958). A number of investigators contend that such differences in value and behavior norms influence the child's sensitivity to and use of language.

Bernstein (1960; 1961; 1964) argues that differing subcultural sensitivities to a way of organizing and responding to experience give rise to differing linguistic codes and modes of speech, and that mode of expression is a matter of learning, particularly the early learning of speech forms that create and reinforce different dimensions of significance in the user. Bossard (1945; Bossard & Boll, 1960) contends that the child learns a language determined by the culture in which he is reared, and Brown (1962:285) writes that the "process of first language learning is also the process of cognitive socialization."

There is growing evidence, then, that various features of the communication environment affect the development of children's language skills. Still lacking, however, is adequate specification of the operating variables and explication of the cause-effect sequence that such variables are thought to engender. Nevertheless, it is clear that the child's language development and the environmental factors that affect that development will influence how he responds to any social communication.

Observational Learning

There is a good deal of evidence that observation of social models accounts for much of the information communicated to children. Eleanor Maccoby (1959) forcefully contends that children's observation of adult role behaviors plays an important part in socialization. Bandura and Walters (1963) review a number of anthropological studies of children's imitative learning of a wide variety of behavior, and go on to argue that questions of efficiency, survival, and sheer complexity of the behavior children must learn to perform all point to the importance of observational learning in social training. Moreover, a wide range of behaviors has been experimentally demonstrated to be susceptible to modeling influences, including aggression, altruism, problem solving, moral judgments, self-rewarding behavior, speech, resistance to temptation, and so forth (for reviews, see Bandura & Walters, 1963; Flanders, 1968; Hartup & Coates, 1969).

Such learning is particularly important when considering children and the mass media, since media provide an enormous number of models and behaviors from which children might learn. Bandura and Walters (1963) write that, given the large amount of time children spend with the media, pictorially mediated models such as those presented via television exert strong influence on children's social behavior and may make parents relatively less influential as role models, a contention similar to our earlier point concerning the effect of multiple information sources. We will consider research on children's observational learning specifically from the media later. The purpose of this section is to provide a brief sketch of the principles of observational learning and to indicate some of the variables that have been demonstrated to affect such learning.

Observational learning refers to any learning proceeding from vicarious experience—from observation of the behavior of some model, either live or symbolic. Such process constructs as imitation, role-taking, social learning, and identification may all be included under this rubric. Each uses similar behavioral indicators of learning: "the occurrence of matching behavior as a function of exposure to modeling cues" (Bandura, 1969:218). Matching behavior may represent either the acquisition of new responses or the inhibition or disinhibition of responses already in the observer's repertory. In the latter case, observational learning pertains not so much to the acquisition of new behavior as to the learning of conditions under which existing responses should or should not be performed.

Even though matching behavior is the usual measure of observational learning, a distinction between *acquisition* and *performance* is necessary. While matching behavior indicates learning has occurred, failure to perform matching behavior need not mean that acquisition has not occurred (cf. Bandura & Walters, 1963; Bandura, 1965b). Children may learn a new behavior but fail to perform it until the proper eliciting conditions are present. Bandura (1965a) demonstrated that children who originally failed to imitate behavior they observed later displayed this behavior when sufficient incentives were provided, and Maccoby (1959) contends that adult role behaviors observationally acquired by young children may not be performed until the child reaches adulthood.

Bandura (1969) describes four basic mechanisms mediating observational learning: attention processes, retention processes, motoric reproduction processes, and incentive or motivational processes. Each of these may be affected by individual capacities of the observer, by factors in both the observation and performance contexts, and by factors in the modeling stimuli.

For example, complexity of modeling behavior; discriminability of cues within modeling stimuli; and presentation of incentives within modeling stimuli, such as contingent reinforcement delivered to the model and observed by the child (Bandura, 1965b), various social properties of the model—e.g., age, sex, social status (cf. Bandura, 1969)—and perceived utility of the modeled behavior, may all affect the child's ability and incentive to attend to, store, and perform the observed events. By the same token, conditions in both the observation and performance contexts, such as presence or absence of distraction, instructions to attend and learn, opportunity for overt or covert rehearsal, incentives to attend, store, rehearse, and perform, also affect imitative learning.

Finally, individual needs and capacities of the observer, and their interaction with stimulus and contextual factors, are important determinants of the rate and level of observational learning. Motivation derives not only from stimulus and contextual incentives, but also from the child's own needs, which are a function of his history and his present state. Individual capacities to attend to, recognize, and differentiate features of the model's responses affect observational learning at the level of sensory registration. Availability of necessary motoric responses within the observer's response repertory affects both learning and performance. Since recent evidence indicates that learning and retention are affected by symbolic encoding of observed behavior (Bandura, Grusec, & Menlove, 1966; Coates & Hartup, 1969), ability to engage in such encoding and later to use symbolic representations as guides to overt performance also influences observational learning (cf. Bandura, 1969).

The influence of such individual capacities indicates that observational learning should also be approached from a developmental perspective. To the extent that abilities and needs change with age, so should the learning and performance they mediate. However, little research on developmental differences in imitative learning exists. Hartup and Coates (1970) found only nine studies in the literature on imitation that looked directly at age differences. Taken together, these studies indicate no age differences in performance of simple model behaviors observed without explicit instructions to imitate, but increases with age in performance of complex behaviors observed under explicit instructions to imitate. In addition, Leifer (1966) found that with increasing age children imitated more of a series of complex play behaviors even without explicit instructions to imitate. At minimum, then, there is direct evidence for an interaction between age of the child and complexity of the modeled behavior that may be performed.

Evidence from several other lines of inquiry provides reason to expect older children to learn more of any modeled performance. For example, research on both cognitive development and language development reviewed in preceding sections leads to predictions that older children will be better able than younger children to represent, remember, and rehearse complex modeled behavior.

Studies of the development of verbal mediation (Flavell, Beach, & Chinsky, 1966; Marsh & Sherman, 1966; Flavell, 1970), indicating that occurrence and efficiency of verbal encoding in a learning situation are positively related to age, dovetail nicely with experiments showing that subjects' relevant verbalizations enhance observational learning (Bandura, Grusec, & Menlove, 1966; Coates & Hartup, 1969), and also point to possible developmental differences. Moreover, there is evidence for age-related differences in attention to symbolically mediated complex behavior. Roberts (1968) found that young children were more likely than older children to attend to a speaker rather than the content of his speech in an audiovisual presentation, while older children attended more to the content, and several studies have shown that focusing on "essential" information in an entertainment film increases with age (Hale, Miller, & Stevenson, 1968; Collins, 1970).

The acquisition/performance distinction must also be considered developmentally. Although older children may observationally acquire more of a complex behavior, they may be less likely to perform what they have learned. Several factors might account for such a learning-performance interaction.

First, as argued earlier, the older the child the more alternative behaviors from which to choose he may be expected to have in his response repertory. Hence, when encountering a situation similar to that in which the modeled behavior occurred, the *young* child may be faced with a choice of performing what he observed, doing nothing, or improvising a new response and dealing with the attendant uncertainty inherent in such a course of action. The older child's choice, on the other hand, need not be between matching behavior or uncertainty; because of greater experience, he may have a number of alternative responses from which to select.

Second, to the extent that socialization is cumulative (Clausen, 1966) and implies increasing awareness of social sanctions for or against certain behaviors, and to the extent that older children are better able than their younger counterparts to discriminate among cues, we might expect them to be more sensitive to the presence or absence of contingency cues in both the modeling stimuli and in any later context. While both older and younger children may observationally acquire new behaviors, for the young child simply the opportunity to try out an observed, novel behavior might be elicitor enough. Older children should be more apt to note relatively subtle cues controlling behavior, and more attuned to responding to such cues. We might also expect older children to be more under the control of sanctions learned elsewhere in the socialization process, internalized cues which appear neither in the modeling stimuli nor in the performance context but which may be operative in the symbolic associations the child makes.

Finally, to the extent that learning and performance of modeled behavior are a function of available motor responses in the observer's repertory (Bandura, 1969), age changes in motor development should also lead to age differences in performance. In this case, older children will have the advantage.

To summarize, a wide variety of behaviors has been shown to derive from observation of the behavior of models. Such learning, and its later performance, is a function of attentional, retentional, motoric, and motivational processes, all of which may be affected by various factors in the modeling stimuli, the observation and performance context, and by individual capacities. Evidence from several lines of research provides reason to expect age differences in observational learning and performance. Although, for the most part, empirical testing of developmental differences in imitative learning remains to be done (cf. Hartup & Coates, 1970), awareness of the possibility of age-related differences should aid understanding of children's communication behavior, particularly in terms of what various children might learn from the mass media.

Other Variables

The foregoing by no means exhausts the variables that may affect children's communication behavior. Such factors as sex-role identification, intelligence, creativity, need for achievement, dependency, and numerous other personality characteristics may all influence how the child interacts with others and with the mass media. While space precludes full consideration of the potential effects of each of these variables, some will be touched upon in the following discussion of children's media behavior. For the present, suffice it to say that what anyone, child or adult, brings to and takes from a communication situation is a function of any number of factors which determine each person's needs and capabilities, needs and capabilities that differ from one person to the next and that may undergo change within any individual from one time to the next.

The present chapter takes a developmental approach to communication because it is during childhood that changes in both needs and capabilities are most magnified. Less than twenty years witness the transition from the almost totally dependent state of infancy to the active, problem-solving posture of early adulthood. If we accept that socially mediated information guides, if not engenders, much of this transition, then cognizance of age-related changes in factors affecting communication behavior is central to any understanding of communication and children, whether our concern is with how children learn to express themselves to parents and peers or with what effect numerous hours in front of the television screen will have.

CHILDREN AND THE MASS MEDIA

The opening sections of this chapter argue that childhood is a period characterized by the seeking and processing of information in order to form some definition of the world, that a large part of the information needed for such a definition is socially mediated, that as the number of information sources increases the parameters of that definition are subject to change, and that what a child takes from any communication situation will be a function of at least his individual needs and capabilities, which are to some extent locatable by age.

Clearly, then, in our society the mass media appear to have a *potential* for playing an influential role in the lives of our children. The mass communication media are pervasive, accessible, and attended to by children of all ages. They make available information in amounts and varieties well beyond what the child might be expected to obtain from primary groups. In short, they provide a window on a much larger world than children of past centuries had available to them.

To note the mass media's potential for influencing children, however, is not to demonstrate that they do, in fact, have an effect or what the effect might be. Certainly many of us have observed what appear to be effects of mass media on children. The rapid diffusion of teen-age fads, the grade-school child's knowledge of rocketry and space exploration, the preschooler's humming of a television jingle—all seem logically attributable to the media. However, the mass media are simply one facet of a larger informational system. It is possible that much of our hypothetical child's knowledge of rocketry was gained in school, or that the television jingle was learned not from television but from a parent or playmate who learned it from television.

The separating out of such variables is one of the more difficult tasks confronting researchers. Moreover, the media do not function in precisely the same way as an interpersonal information source. The opportunities for feedback, for tailoring messages to individual needs, for providing direct reinforcement for attention, comprehension, and/or acceptance are radically different for the media than for parent or peer. Hence, it is dangerous to generalize directly from children's interpersonal communication behavior to their mass media behavior.

Nevertheless, as Schramm (1971) has recently pointed out, the similarities between the processes of mass and interpersonal communication are, on the whole, far greater than the differences. Fundamentally, the mass media may be viewed as "message multipliers," channels which increase the number, distance, and speed of messages sent and the size of audience reached.

While the relationship between sender and receiver is not a duplicate of the interpersonal relationship, a message transmitted by the media faces many of the same hurdles as a message from father to son or teacher to student. Both must gain attention, interpretation, acceptance, and some disposition. And just as there are individual differences in how children respond to communication from parents, teachers, or peers, so are there differences in how they use and are affected by the mass media.

Children are not totally at the mercy of the media; they are not sponges soaking up everything beamed at them. *They* decide if, when, and to what they will attend; *they* interpret, accept, and dispose. Given the diversity among children in needs, capabilities, personalities, and situations, we cannot ask the straightforward question, "What are the effects of the mass media on children?" Rather, with children as with adults, we must echo Berelson (1948) and ask, "Which media, under which conditions, lead to which effects, among which children?"

The picture emerging from the research is one of an active child, bringing to the media the sum of his experiences, abilities, and needs, taking from the media what he can and will. Moreover, because childhood is a period of such rapid change it has become clear that how a child uses the media today is probably very different from how he will use it next year. In other words, only a "motion picture" of his development will suffice.

PATTERNS OF MEDIA USE

To understand how various children might be affected by the mass communication media, it is necessary to determine their individual patterns of media use. How much do they use which media? What content do they select? Such use patterns are best described in terms of variables like age, I.Q., sex, family socioeconomic status, and so on. The following pages review data describing children's media use and attempt to examine some of the factors which appear to operate as determinants of the various patterns of media use located by the above variables.

Amount of Children's Mass Media Use

There is little question that the mass media consume a substantial proportion of children's time. Schramm, Lyle, and Parker (1961), in their detailed study of the media usage of North American children, found that between the ages of three and sixteen years the average child devotes over one-sixth of his waking hours to television, more time than he spends in school. Moreover, children give additional time to the other media—comics, radio, newspapers, movies, books, and magazines. All media combined accounted for over 40 percent of the leisure time of children between the ages of five and eight years; among twelve-year-olds this figure rose to over 50 percent.

While such averages are convenient summary statistics, it must be kept in mind that the "average" child is a rare animal. More important than figures representing children in general is the wide range of differences in media use among children. For example, in one sample of sixth-grade boys, television-viewing time ranged from less than fifteen minutes to more than four hours per weekday (Schramm et al., 1961).

Television, because of its early accessibility, is one of the first media used. Indeed, reports of playpens placed in front of a television set so that infants can watch the screen are not uncommon (cf. Schramm et al., 1961; Maccoby, 1964). Schramm and his colleagues (1961) report that, typically, televiewing starts at about age two, consumes forty-five minutes per weekday by age three, and has increased to over two hours per day among five-year-olds. Through the early grade-school years, viewing increases gradually to about two and one-half hours per weekday, then manifests a sharp rise to a little over three hours, the peak occurring between the fifth and eighth grades. The teen years produce a gradual drop until, at about age seventeen, viewing time levels off to between two and two and one-half hours per weekday.

Although various studies have reported total volume of viewing at different ages to be both lower (Himmelweit, Oppenheim, & Vince, 1958) and higher (Greenberg & Dominick, 1968; 1969) than the data reported by the Schramm group, and while televiewing among children probably has become even more dominant than it was at the end of the fifties (e.g., the A. C. Nielsen reports for the past several years estimate viewing time of children two to five years old at over three and one-half hours daily), the general pattern reported here appears to be valid.[2]

---

[2] Comparisons among the many studies of children's media use are often hindered by differences in how use is estimated (e.g., does the parent or child report the data? are the data based on free or aided recall? supervised or unsupervised diaries? general estimates?) and by differences in how data are reported (e.g., daily vs. weekly? if weekly, a five- or seven-day week?). Schramm, Lyle, and Parker (1961: app. III) provide an excellent discussion of the problem of estimating viewing time. While changes in the total amount of use of any one medium may have occurred in the decade since the Schramm group conducted its study, the fact that their conclusions were based on eleven separate studies, that they employed four different techniques for estimating viewing time, and that the figures they report lie in the middle of these several estimates lends validity to the general patterns of media use they describe.

Children are also exposed very early to books, often before televiewing begins, not as print media per se but rather as sources of stories read to them by parents. Such story reading appears to increase steadily until the early school years, when it drops off sharply as the child begins to read for himself. Pictures provide young children with another entrée to the print media. Most children are introduced to the newspaper via the comic pages, and it is not unusual to see a very young child poring over the pictures in general magazines.

Pictures are certainly the basis of the comic book's attraction for young children. Comic book reading starts among preschoolers, increases through the grade-school years to a median of about four books per month at the eighth grade (based on a sample of San Francisco children in 1959), then swiftly declines to near zero again by the end of high school. Again, however, we are talking about general patterns. Among various samples of children who had television available to them, Schramm and his colleagues (1961) found the median number of comic books read monthly ranged from 1.4 (the low for girls) to 8.5 (the high for boys).

Use of print media as print, of course, depends on the child's developing ability to read. On the whole, print media use increases steadily during the school years, but there are differences in the patterns of use of books, magazines, and newspapers. In a sample of San Francisco children, book reading (books read outside of school) increased steadily until the end of grade school, then dropped off to a median of just under one book per month by the end of high school (Schramm et al., 1961). The drop is not unusual when one considers that as the child grows older he reads more books directly pertinent to classwork.

Magazine reading follows a similar pattern except that the decrease occurs a bit later. The newspaper is generally the last medium the child engages. Only at around age seven does any substantial amount of newspaper reading appear. From this point on, however, newspaper use increases. By the tenth grade well over 50 percent of children surveyed indicate *daily* newspaper reading, a figure that continues to increase through the remainder of the high school years (Schramm et al., 1961; Greenberg & Dominick, 1968).

Finally, movie and radio use, while by no means rare among young children, increases abruptly during the early teens. In the Stanford studies, Schramm and his colleagues (1961) point out that the motion picture theater, itself, serves an important social function for teen-agers. And radio, because it can be listened to while engaging in other activities and because of its heavy emphasis on popular music, has become an important part of adolescent culture. The Stanford group found teen-agers devoting more time to radio than to any other medium except television, but practically every respondent indicated he habitually did something else while listening.

Further differences in media use occur within these age patterns. Several studies have demonstrated that among teen-agers televiewing varies inversely with I.Q. and print use varies positively (Himmelweit et al., 1958; Schramm et al., 1961). Indeed, Himmelweit states that intelligence is the single most important background factor predicting television viewing among British children (Himmelweit et al., 1958:12), and Schramm writes that between the tenth and thirteenth year the more intelligent children tend to disappear from the ranks of heavy viewers (Schramm et al., 1961:34).

The exception to these patterns exists in the Stanford group's finding that in grade school the brighter children tend to be heavy users of television. They explain that this group "seemed to do more of everything—viewing, reading, radio, and so forth" (Schramm et al., 1961:34). They also found that teen-agers of lower mental ability remain heavy comic book readers while their higher I.Q. counterparts usually cease reading them altogether. Also among teen-agers Wade (1966; 1971) discovered a negative relationship between creativity and use of pictorial media, and no relationship between creativity and use of print media.

Although the British study demonstrated only small relationships between family socioeconomic status (SES) and television viewing (Himmelweit et al., 1958), studies conducted in North America have consistently found that children of lower SES families use pictorial media more and print media less than do children of middle and upper SES families (cf. Bailyn, 1959; Schramm et al., 1961; Greenberg & Dominick, 1968; 1969). These relationships replicate whether socioeconomic level is operationalized on the basis of family income, education of parents, or some index of occupational prestige.

Schramm and colleagues (1961) also note that media use in general, and print use in particular, tend to occur earlier among the children of better educated parents, and that low parental level of education and low socioeconomic status tend to locate high use of comic books. Finally, the Michigan State studies (Greenberg & Dominick, 1968; 1969) revealed more use of television, record players, and movies among black children and more newspaper reading among white children, regardless of socioeconomic level. It should be noted, however, that televiewing was high for both racial groups.

Content Preferences

Schramm, Lyle, and Parker (1961) distinguish between two general kinds of media fare—reality content and entertainment or fantasy content. The former constantly refers the user to the real world, working chiefly through realistic materials, stressing facts and information, inviting alertness, activity, and cognition. The latter invites the user to take leave of real-world problems, appealing to emotion, stressing fantasy and often escape.

While both types of fare may serve either informational or entertainment purposes, content and media that stress information (e.g., news and public affairs programming; hard news as opposed to features; print media as opposed to television, movies, or radio) may usually be classified as reality oriented; content and media that stress entertainment (e.g., Westerns, situation comedy, and variety programming; the audiovisual as opposed to print media) may usually be classified as fantasy oriented. With this rather broad distinction in mind, the same variables that locate amount of media use are also useful for describing differences and changes in media-content preferences.

Usually the first media content children encounter may be classified as fantasy material. Their early experience with books as sources of stories read to them, the first television shows, the comic book world—all these stress entertainment. Orientation toward reality content follows the onset of reading capability and the development of a broader interest in the world as the child grows older.

In short, several changes in content orientation occur with age. As he grows older, the child devotes more time to the print media and, within any one medium, he devotes more time to reality content (although this does not necessarily mean that he devotes less time to audiovisual or fantasy content). A clear substitution does occur in terms of content aimed at children versus content aimed at adults. Over time, adult content almost completely replaces children's content.

The Stanford group (Schramm et al., 1961) found that the first television programs to become children's favorites are what the broadcasters call "children's programs"—animated cartoons, puppets, animal stories, children's adventure stories, and so forth. By the time the child is settled in school, however, these programs have given way to children's variety shows, adventure, science fiction, and Westerns, soon to be followed by more adult-type programs such as situation comedies, crime programs, and popular music variety shows. Children learn very early to watch adult programs.[3]

In one sample of first graders, 40 percent of their televiewing was devoted to adult shows; by the sixth grade it was 79 percent (Schramm et al., 1961). A similar early swing to adult programming was also found among English children (Abrams, 1956; Himmelweit et al., 1958). Finally, serious viewing of news and public affairs programs occurs late in the high school years (Schramm et al., 1961), a pattern that is congruent with changes in children's newspaper-reading interests.

The age-related move away from children's programming manifested in televiewing is mirrored by the sharp drop in comic book use noted in the preceding section. Comic book content is generally aimed at a youth audience; hence comic books may simply be outgrown.[4] Age changes in preferences for various types of comic books support this line of reasoning; children's preferences move from "funny animal," to "fantastic adventure," to "true/classics" type comics as they grow older (Wolf & Fiske, 1949).

Generally radio can be characterized as a music medium for children, becoming particularly important around the early teen years. Some listening to radio news is reported by teen-agers (Schramm et al., 1961), but this may well result from the fact that most stations broadcast short news spots at least every hour and the teenager simply does not switch the dial.

Finally, the predominance of reality content that characterizes the newspaper may account for children's late orientation toward the press. Within the newspapers, the comic section is usually the first content children use. As they grow older and begin to recognize newspaper content that meets their developing interests, these materials engage their attention. For example, in the late grade-school years, boys read some sports and girls some columns; by the eighth grade, children make use of a good deal of the paper.

Clarke (1968a) had a sample of ninth-grade boys rate the probability that they would read a number of stories on the basis of story leads. Stories dealing with science, "speed and violence," sports, and "teen news" all received high ratings; the mean probability for reading public affairs news, however, was between "not likely to read" and "extremely sure not to read." A later study (Clarke, 1968b) provides a picture of age changes in newspaper content preference. In a sample of ninth- and twelfth-grade children containing both boys and girls, interest in public affairs news manifested a clear increase with age, while interest in "teen news" manifested a decrease. In short, with newspapers as with other media, the child's preference for and/or use of various types of content is closely connected to age-related needs and interests.

As with amount of viewing, large differences in content preferences exist within age patterns. Schramm and his colleagues (1961) note that sex differences appear as early as first grade, boys liking adventure programs, girls liking popular music.

> The pattern continues throughout most of the school years—the girls preferring programs built around romance (popular music) or the family role (situation comedy), the boys preferring "masculine" programs of excitement and adventure (Schramm et al., 1961:45).

[3] One of the difficulties with this type of classification lies in distinguishing where children's programming stops and adult programming begins. While the two ends of the continuum are not difficult to categorize (e.g., cartoons versus public affairs), much of the entertainment programming that dominates television draws large audiences among both children and adults. It is left to the reader to decide whether, in fact, children are watching adult programs or vice versa.

[4] This is not to argue that the comic book audience is composed exclusively of children. Recent years have witnessed a comic book fad among college students. Lyle (1969) points out that the military uses comic books for instructional purposes and several publishers of "true-confession" type fare aim at a more adult audience.

Similar sex differences appear in other media for which data are available. Among teen-agers, Clarke (1968b) found girls interested in newspaper stories dealing with fashion and grooming, homemaking, and teen news, while boys chose science, sports, and stories dealing with cars and hot rodding.[5] Similar patterns appear in book and magazine choices; and boys are more likely to listen to radio news than are girls, while girls are more avid listeners of radio music (Schramm et al., 1961).

The Stanford study (Schramm et al., 1961) found that children with higher I.Q.'s tend to try all media earlier, that they move toward reality content earlier, and that by the teen years they use reality content much more than do children of lower intelligence. Schramm and associates found that almost twice as large a percentage of brighter eighth graders than of their less bright counterparts both watched television coverage of the 1958 elections and indicated greater enjoyment of such programming. Children with higher intelligence also appear to be more selective in their media content tastes.

Similar trends are located by family socioeconomic status and by amount of parents' education. Children from middle-class families or whose parents have more than a high school education are more likely to choose reality content and to use the print media than are working-class children or children whose parents have high school educations or less (the latter groups devoting more time to fantasy-type material). The Schramm group (1961) also found that, in addition to starting to use all media earlier, children of better educated parents are more likely to start with children's material in all the media.

[5] Another interesting fact revealed in Clarke's (1968b) data is that among boys in both the ninth and twelfth grades, much more interest was expressed in science than in sports stories—perhaps a sign of the times.

Determinants of Media Use

As we have already indicated, to some extent the preceding patterns of media use may be explained in terms of ability, interests, and available time. The demands of school, both academic and social, cut into the teen-ager's televiewing time. As the child learns to read, he may subtract from time spent with pictorial media but increase time spent with print media. Older children and brighter children begin to find greater challenge, and greater reward, in print and in reality content. The creative child is more likely to spend time on a wide variety of nonmedia activities, pursuing interests less active children might not consider. The decrease in the amount of time higher SES children spend with the media, particularly pictorial media, may be a function of the numerous alternative opportunities and activities available to them but not to their lower SES counterparts.

These patterns are typical, not absolute, however. Brighter children, children of middle-class families, and children of highly educated parents are frequently found in the ranks of heavy users of pictorial media, of fantasy content. Conversely, many of their opposites may be heavy users of the print media or active seekers of reality content.

Two general sets of determining elements seem to be operating here. The first pertains to family socialization patterns, which includes both the media-behavior model set by parents and siblings and the value systems explicitly and implicitly communicated to children. The second, by no means independent of the first, pertains to individual personal and social problems of any given child.

Both the Stanford and British studies (Himmelweit et al., 1958; Schramm et al., 1961) found that the media behavior of children correlates highly with that of parents. A pattern of light or heavy television viewing, light or heavy print use, will usually go through a family. Hence, many of the differences in children's media use described above may be partially explained by the principles of observational learning discussed earlier (cf. Bandura & Walters, 1963; Bandura, 1969). Children's media behavior categorized on the basis of variables such as socioeconomic status or education often matches patterns of parental media behavior relative to the same variables (cf. Geiger & Sokol, 1959; Samuelson, Carter, & Ruggels, 1963; Greenberg & Dervin, 1967a; 1967b; 1968). The fact that children born into larger families, where older siblings may act as models, tend to begin televiewing earlier and to move from children's to adult fare earlier provides further support for such a modeling hypothesis (cf. Schramm et al., 1961), as does the finding that as a son's identification with his father increases so, too, do father-son similarities in some measures of reading behavior (Clarke, 1969).

However, Clarke (1969) also reports results that do not support the modeling hypothesis; more recent data reported by Chaffee, McLeod, and Atkin (1971) also indicate that such an observational learning explanation of patterns of media use may not be as powerful as once thought, at least in terms of adolescent media use. Although they consistently find positive correlations between adolescent and parental behavior on various measures of mass media use, they also note that the magnitude of the correlations is rather low. These researchers present several intriguing interpretations of their data in terms of "negative modeling" and in terms of family communication structure, which will be touched on later.

Parental media behavior may also be a reflection of a general value orientation communicated to children during socialization which may affect children's media use. In the earlier discussion of language development we noted several differences in socialization values and techniques that are located by socioeconomic class and that might be expected to engender different types of media behavior (e.g., the value of curiosity might encourage middle-class children to seek reality information).

In addition, there is good evidence that middle-class people espouse norms of work, activity, self-improvement, and planning. Working-class people, on the other hand, manifest less of a drive for upward mobility and self-improvement, and prefer to enjoy life for the moment (Schneider & Lysgaard, 1953). Values like these appear to be operative in media behavior in Schramm's (1949) finding that people with more education or who are higher on the occupational scale were more apt to read newspaper stories dealing with realistic materials than the more escapist content selected by people with less education or lower on the occupational scale.

These values also appear in data indicating that the activity of television watching is more highly regarded by working-class than by middle-class respondents (Geiger & Sokol, 1959; Steiner, 1963). In other words, children *learn* to use the media, and what they learn is generally the parental norm, communicated to them via both precept and example.

The Stanford group provides extended analysis of media behavior relative to social class (Schramm et al., 1961: esp. chap. 7), which offers good evidence that the norms described above are located by socioeconomic class, that children do learn and respond to them, and that they are strongly related to media use. More interesting, however, is their evidence that many children from lower-class families subscribe to middle-class norms and vice versa. Hence, it should not be surprising that some working-class children are avid seekers after reality content or that the child of highly educated parents falls into the ranks of heavy television viewers. They may simply be responding to socialization patterns which, though atypical for their demographic group, are what they are taught.

Given the above norms, the kinds of interpersonal relations the child experiences within the family may also influence his media behavior. That is, while two families might both value norms of work and self-improvement, one might also stress harmonious social relationships at the expense of a kind of concept orientation that would stress the expression of the child's own ideas and the challenging of others' beliefs, while the other might encourage exploration and controversy in an environment comparatively free of social restraints.

McLeod, Chaffee, and their students at Wisconsin (Chaffee, McLeod, & Wackman, 1966; McLeod, Chaffee, & Eswara, 1966; McLeod, Chaffee, & Wackman, 1967; Chaffee, McLeod, & Atkin, 1971) have been conducting research along this line. They found that teen-agers from families that stress the pursuit and communication of ideas while placing relatively less emphasis on the maintenance of harmonious interpersonal relations tend more often to use the media for information, reading more newspapers, watching more public affairs television, but spending less time with television in general. Moreover, controls for socioeconomic level fail to wash out these relationships (see, especially, McLeod, Chaffee, & Wackman, 1967).

Finally, interpersonal problems, be they with family or peers, strongly affect media behavior. When frustrations get too high, when anxiety or insecurity passes some critical point, the media, particularly those stressing fantasy, offer a readily available escape. Numerous studies indicate it is an avenue often taken.

In a study of fifth and sixth graders, Bailyn (1959) found that children who worried about acceptance and success in their peer group *and* who rated high on a test of "rebellious independence" tended to spend more time on "aggressive hero" type television content. Himmelweit and her colleagues discovered that "the insecure child, in particular the child who had difficulties in making friends with other children," and the child who felt rejected by his peer group were more likely to be heavy viewers of television and go to movies more often (Himmelweit et al., 1958: 388). Wolf and Fiske (1949) report that insecure, poorly adjusted children were more likely to be comic-book "fans," and Riley and Riley (1951) report a preference for television programs characterized by violence, action, and aggression among children with few friends, children frustrated in their desires to belong to a peer group.

"Parent problems" produce similar results. Eleanor Maccoby (1954) found that middle-class children who experience more family conflict, who encounter many parental restrictions and are not warmly treated, tend to spend more time with television than do other children of the same age. This relationship did not obtain for lower-class children, however, probably because turning to television does not enable them to escape from parents, who are likely to be heavy viewers themselves.

Schramm and his colleagues (1961) operationalized parent-child conflict in terms of the child's perception that his parents' aspirations for him were higher than his own. Such conflict was shown to be fairly widespread and to be related to a variety of media behaviors. The greater the conflict the more television the child viewed, the more radio he heard, the more movies he saw, and the fewer magazines and books he read. Moreover, when parent and peer conflict were combined, these patterns became even more pronounced. Finally, they found that children who scored highest on an index of antisocial aggressive tendencies were more likely to be those who indicated high levels of interpersonal conflict, hence more likely to be those using the fantasy media.

There is good evidence, then, that under some conditions children with personal or social problems search for escape in the mass media, obtaining vicariously some of the satisfaction not afforded by their real-life situation.

To summarize, children's mass media behavior—which media they use, how much they use them, which content they prefer—is a function of individual needs and capabilities *and* of the environment, both physical and social, in which they develop. Environmental factors influence which media are available in what degree, provide norms of media use, and affect a good number of the child's needs and interests. Individual factors mediate what the child can and will do with the media within the context of his environment. In short, while the media may play an important role in the process of socialization, the child's mass media behavior is, to a large extent, a product of socialization.

Effects of Mass Media on Children

Several difficulties arise in any discussion of research on the effects of mass media on children. First, almost no studies of long-term effects exist. This, in spite of the fact that it may be the long-term effects about which we should be most concerned.

Second, although we have continually argued that age changes are critical in children's media behavior, no longitudinal studies exist. The cross-sectional data reported thus far and in the following pages enable us to look at age-related differences, but not at age-related change.

Third, it is impossible in most industrialized countries, and fast becoming impossible in the developing nations, to make comparisons between groups of children who differ only on the basis of media availability. Those few children who do not have access to a television set or to a newspaper usually differ from media users on a number of other variables, rendering comparisons almost meaningless. While, at least for television, we are fortunate in having a few studies based on before-after and/or television–no television comparisons (e.g., Himmelweit et al., 1958; Schramm et al., 1961; Furu, 1962), it must be remembered that when those studies were conducted the novelty of the new medium may have affected the results. We are now faced with a generation of children for whom television is no more unusual than the family car.

Finally, most of the research on media effects pertains to the pictorial media. Parents, politicians, and educators call for investigations (scholarly and congressional) of the effects on children of movies, of comics, of television, but seldom of the press. Given that the largest proportion of children's media use is directed toward these media, however, this state of affairs is not unreasonable.

The term *effects* covers a broad range of consequences. Effects may be direct (as when the child takes something from the media) or indirect (as when time spent with the media precludes time spent on other activities). They may be immediate (e.g., emotional arousal or gratification of needs during or closely following exposure) or long-term (e.g., facts, behaviors, or attitudes learned from the media and operative long after exposure).

A recurrent theme throughout this chapter has been that any communication effect results from the interaction between what the child brings to the communication situation and what the communication situation offers to the child. Hence, while there can be little question that the mass media offer powerful symbolic experiences, it is an unusual instance where the media can be demonstrated to be the *sole* cause of any specific effect.

Although experimental research demonstrates that, all other things being equal, the media can strongly influence children, in real life all other things are seldom equal. The child lives in a world full of symbolic experiences, replete with potential causes of potential effects. Even though the mass media bulk large in the lives of our children, it must be remembered that the media are just one part of the larger social system. Their impact should not be approached in terms of all-or-nothing propositions. Rather, they are better viewed as sources of *contributory* effects. With this caution in mind, we turn to the research on effects of the mass media on children.

Reallocation of Time

Just as media use depends to a large extent on available time, so time spent with the media may, in and of itself, lead to a variety of effects—reducing the amount of time spent on other activities, possibly affecting such things as schoolwork and bedtime.

In general, the amount of time spent with the media varies inversely with the attractiveness of competing activities. While at least one early study indicated that television cut into the time children spent in play and household tasks (Maccoby, 1951), research conducted in the late fifties found that the media seldom take children away from such structured activities as organized team sports, school activities, household duties, and so forth (Himmelweit et al., 1958; Schramm et al., 1961).

Now, with a generation of children who have always known television, it is probably safe to say that, given a choice between engaging in some kind of activity with school or playmates or watching television, most children will choose the former. The bulk of the time given to the media comes from those periods when no structured activities are scheduled, when the opportunities for play are limited. The casual play hours, the long afternoons when "there is nothing to do," provide the media with their audiences. This generalization receives support from the Schramm group's (1961) finding that televiewing increases in the winter and in those areas of the country where inclement weather is most likely. It is also supported by findings that indicate that time given to television generally is taken from time previously devoted to other fantasy media such as comic books, movies, and radio (cf. Maccoby, 1951; Himmelweit et al., 1958; Furu, 1962).

Television has led to a slight delay in children's bedtimes, somewhere between fifteen and twenty-five minutes per night (Himmelweit et al., 1958; Schramm et al., 1961; Furu, 1962). Again, this is an average; some children do not change bedtimes at all, some retire as much as an hour later. Loss of sleep may be less than the change in bedtime indicates, however. Many parents report that even though children may stay up a bit later with television, when they do go to bed they are more likely to go right to sleep rather than to read. There is also evidence that those who stay up latest with television are those least able to afford it—children of lower intelligence, or from homes where parental control is lax, or where school performance is less important (cf. Schramm et al., 1961).

Yet, in general, television appears to have had little effect on school performance. No relationship between amount of televiewing and amount of time spent on homework was found either in the United States (Maccoby, 1951) or in England (Himmelweit et al., 1958). Neither was there any relationship between amount of viewing time and school performance when intelligence was taken into account (cf. Himmelweit et al., 1958). At least in the Western countries, then, it appears that the child who selects television instead of homework would probably engage in some other fantasy pastime were television not available.

The evidence is not unanimous, however. Furu (1962) studied a group of Japanese students before and after television was available in their community, post-television measurement including children both with and without television in the home. Compared to controls (matched on school grade, sex, and intelligence), children with television in the home spent less time on homework; and boys, particularly in school grades five to seven, manifested a loss in reading ability. On the other hand, girls with television showed gains in science achievement scores.

Such results point to the danger of making gross generalizations about the effects of the media. Children from different cultures probably bring different experiences and expectations to the media, use them for different things, take different things from them. Moreover, media in other cultures may offer different things to children.

Emotional Responses

One facet of the Payne Fund studies of the 1930s (cf. Charters, 1933) concerned children's emotional responses to movies. Dysinger and Ruckmick (1933) collected physiological measures of children's emotional responses (heart and breathing rate, galvanic skin response) during exposure to a film. They found that changes in responses followed the screen action, and that different children reacted differently. For example, girls were more responsive to romantic scenes, while boys tended to manifest more arousal during scenes of high adventure and aggression—a pattern consistent with earlier described content preferences.

Under certain conditions, media content may frighten children. Ritual violence such as the Western shoot-out is generally accepted, even by young children, as a convention and seldom evokes fear. However, less conventional fare is not so easily discounted. The threat of harm to a character with whom the child has closely identified, particularly when the threat is of an unusual nature (e.g., the more direct, less conventional threat of a knife at the hero's throat), often arouses fear. Similarly, content that reminds children of their own often unexpressed fears—fears of darkness, loneliness, and the unknown—can evoke powerful emotions. The more involved a child is in a program with fearful content, the more he can imagine himself in a similar situation, the higher the probability that he will experience fright.

It follows that both age and experience will affect the kind and degree of emotional response a child makes to the media. The more real the images presented by the media seem to the child, the more likely he is to become emotionally aroused. The young child, who has not yet developed the "adult discount" that enables him to distinguish clearly between reality and fantasy, is more likely to be frightened by stressful scenes. He is not yet certain that "things will come out all right." Studies have indicated that, among children, perceived reality of a program is inversely related to age (cf. Halloran, 1969) and to socioeconomic class (Greenberg & Dominick, 1968). It also seems plausible that children of higher intelligence, those who turn to reality content earlier, would also develop adult discount earlier.

There is some evidence in the literature that heavy use of the pictorial media is related to anxiety about the world. Himmelweit and her associates (1958) found that adolescent girls with television in the home were more likely to express worries about the future, about growing up and marrying, than were their counterparts without television. Generally, these were girls who tended to view a good number of daytime serials. Emery and Martin (1957) showed boys a Western film that broke the conventional pattern—the hero was, for a time, allied with the forces of evil; the outcome, while moral, was depicted as the result of chance rather than the power of good. Projective tests administered after exposure indicated an increase in the viewers' feelings of being surrounded by a hostile environment.

Finally, concern has been expressed that too much stimulation from the pictorial media may have a desensitization effect, blunting the child's sensibilities, creating unreal expectations of real life. Given the lack of long-term studies, there is no good evidence on either side of this speculation. However, children may build defenses against such overstimulation from television. Thompson (1959) exposed teen-agers to several crime dramas. Photographs taken of the viewers during exposure indicated considerable buildup of tension, but projective tests completed after exposure revealed an increase in depressive effect. Thompson reports that children who were frequent viewers of such media content manifested a lower degree of emotional responsiveness on both prefilm and postfilm protocols than did children who viewed less frequently, and he wonders whether the frequent crime-viewer might not become insensitive to the suffering of others in real life.

Most children, then, no matter what their age or interests, are likely to find some media content that will excite them, that will arouse some emotion at some time. The question for which there is no clear answer, however, is just what the long-term effects of such arousal might be.

Learning

Formal learning—There is little question that children can and do learn from the media. Print media, of course, form a major part of the backbone of their school experience, and the audiovisual media are fast making their presence known in the classroom. Indeed, under the right conditions children in the classroom can learn as efficiently from television as from conventional methods.

Chu and Schramm (1967) reviewed 421 comparisons between conventional and television teaching and found that 12 percent favored conventional methods, 15 percent favored television, and 73 percent showed no significant differences. Moreover, in strictly controlled studies, where the same teacher presented the same material to randomly assigned children either via television or face-to-face, no significant differences in learning occurred. However, the authors go on to point out that the success of *instructional* television depends on "simplicity of presentation, clear organization of material, motivation of the learners, knowledge of results, practice—things that are by no means unique to television" (Chu & Schramm, 1967:60). To the extent that program content meets the standards of good pedagogical organization, and to the extent that it is presented in a "learning context," televised instruction is successful.

Clearly most of the *mass* media to which children expose themselves, and the conditions under which exposure occurs, do not meet these criteria. Typically, the mass media do not program to teach. They are not concerned with motivating learners, or with providing opportunity for practice, or with highlighting cues. Moreover, the child does not usually approach the media, particularly the pictorial media, expecting to be taught. While children will admit that television teaches them about the world in which they live (Greenberg & Dominick, 1968; 1969) and that information garnered from pictorial media sometimes helps them with schoolwork by providing topics and material for themes (Schramm et al., 1961), these are nevertheless seen as incidental dividends.

Overt attempts by the pictorial media to be "educational" often irritate children; they frequently class educational television as square, something adults have decided is good for them (Schramm et al., 1961). In other words, a distinction between the functions of reality and fantasy media occurs quite early—print media is accepted as justifiably educational; television, radio, movies, and comics are categorized as primarily entertainment media. For example, Wilson and Shaffer (1965) hoped to put the attraction of comic books to work by using them for educational purposes. They offered third graders a choice of learning about how fish swim by reading from a typed page, a textbook, or a comic book. Contrary to expectations, children chose the comic book least of all, explaining that they preferred comics for entertainment. For "authentic" information, they chose textbooks.

Incidental learning—Still, learning from the mass media does occur. Given the amount of time children spend with the media and the degree to which they are capable of becoming involved with media presentations, it would be surprising if they didn't learn, in spite of the fact that information is not actively sought. Such acquisition and storing of facts, attitudes, and behaviors without actively seeking them is termed *incidental learning* (cf. Schramm et al., 1961).

One of the early hopes for television was that it would be instrumental in helping raise a better informed generation, where being better informed implied knowledge of objects and events in the real world. Television, it was pointed out, was capable of providing concrete representations of events as they happened.

There seems little reason to doubt that the generation now approaching adulthood is better informed about such things as foreign affairs, science, social problems, and so forth than were their parents and grandparents. However, as Schramm and his colleagues (1961) point out, it is not at all certain that television can be credited with much of the improvement. Changes in school curricula and teaching methods, the increasing affluence of our society which has engendered both more education and more travel, and changes in social norms which encourage more frank and full discussion all tend to raise the level of sophistication of our children. Moreover, while the potential for bringing the "real world" into our living rooms exists and is exercised, the fact remains that entertainment content comprises the largest proportion of programming, and that entertainment content is what children are most likely to view.

Hence, it is not surprising that Schramm, Lyle, and Parker (1961) found heavy television viewers more able than light viewers to name singers and band leaders, while light viewers performed better at naming writers and statesmen. As pointed out in our earlier discussion of media-use patterns, in all probability the light television viewers were more likely to be heavier print users, and the print media are more likely to provide such information.

If, then, our criterion for learning is the acquisition of information beyond the entertainment industry, we should expect the high users of reality media and reality content to be better informed than those who use the pictorial media more. Children of high intelligence, children who espouse middle-class norms, children whose parents are among the better educated should all perform better on tests of such knowledge. On the other hand, children of high intelligence who are heavy users of pictorial media might be expected to be less well informed about the "real" world than comparable children who view less because they probably expose themselves to the fantasy media at the expense of the print media. And yet, there are also instances where television might aid *some* children in becoming better informed. The child of low intelligence who views television a great deal may be slightly better informed because of incidental exposure to reality information he would not otherwise encounter in movies or comic books (cf. Schramm et al., 1961).

A similar interaction between the skills of the child and what the media offer is manifested in the Schramm group's finding that, when compared with children living in a town with no television, children in the highest and lowest intelligence groups who had television available to them went to school with about a one-year advantage in vocabulary. The implication is that children in the lowest intelligence group gained from exposure to a language corpus they might not otherwise have encountered, while children in the highest intelligence group were simply better equipped to make use of the increased vocabulary television offered. It should also be noted that by the sixth grade, the vocabulary advantage of television over nontelevision children was gone, both incidental and formal learning from the other media working to cancel out the difference (Schramm et al., 1961).

The preceding is not meant to imply that most of what is learned from the pictorial media is trivial. What we have labeled fantasy content contains a great deal of information which may be important to and learned by the child. The drama, the situation comedy, the quiz show—all present roles, behaviors, attitudes, norms containing information about what to expect from and how to behave in the social world.[6] In many ways, such information is no less "authentic" than information contained in the print media or presented in the classroom.

Perhaps the most impressive finding in the research on children and the mass media is the enormous amount of learning that appears to take place, even at early ages. Holaday and Stoddard (1933) tested several thousand children, ranging in age from eight years old to the midteens, using seventeen different motion pictures, asking questions about both the central action of the film and the setting in which the action took place. They found that a child of eight could remember three out of every five facts that an attentive adult could recall, when tested on selected items, after viewing a motion picture; by the midteens, children remembered nine out of ten adult-recalled facts. Moreover, on a retest conducted three months later, the average recall was 90 percent of what had been cited on the initial test.

Peterson and Thurstone (1933) reported similar results with regard to the learning of attitudes. They demonstrated that a single showing of a movie such as "All Quiet on the Western Front" or "Birth of a Nation" to children ranging from the fourth-grade to senior high school age produced significant changes in attitudes on issues as varied as capital punishment, war, the Chinese, the Negro. Many of the changes persisted as long as nineteen months after the film was seen. Moreover, the effect of such films on children's attitudes was shown to be cumulative, exposure to several films on the same general topic leading to more attitude change than a single film.

More recently, Siegel (1958) exposed naive second graders to a series of "radio dramas" dealing with taxi drivers. Half of the children heard episodes in which the driver dealt with a problem "aggressively"; the other half heard episodes in which problems were solved "constructively." A story-completion test revealed that the children's role expectations of real taxi drivers paralleled the role portrayals in the dramatic episodes. Bandura and his colleagues (Bandura, Ross, & Ross, 1963a; 1963b; Bandura, 1965b) have demonstrated that preschool children are capable of learning novel verbal and motor behaviors from a single viewing of a film, and Hicks (1965) found that film-mediated behavior may be remembered and imitated by five-year-olds as long as six months after exposure.

Factors affecting learning—The preceding examples should suffice to demonstrate the large amount of learning from the media that can take place. Given such learning, the more interesting questions pertain to factors that influence learning. Many of these were touched upon in our earlier discussions of socialization, cognitive and language development, and observational learning, each of which bears upon what the child brings to, hence how he interacts with, media presentations.

A number of studies indicate that cues inherent in the content of a given film or program may mediate attention and learning. In general, the more the characters, the action, the information contained in a program mesh with the child's own motivational system, the more likely he is to learn from the program. For example, Maccoby and Wilson (1957) found that seventh graders identified with film characters of the same sex and with characters representing the social class to which the child aspired. In both cases, identification

[6] Whether or not the picture of the world presented by the entertainment media is, in fact, a valid representation of attitudes, norms, and behaviors in the real world is a separate question left to the reader's judgment. Although a number of critics argue that the television world is populated by stereotyped characters engaged in stereotyped actions, the fact remains that there are similarities between the picture on the screen and what the child observes in the real world. Moreover, there is little reason to expect young children to perceive stereotypes as such.

mediated more learning about that character and his or her actions. They also found that boys remembered aggressive content better and girls romantic content better, but only when performed by the same-sexed character. In other words, in this experiment sex-appropriate behavior was learned to the extent that it was performed by a sex-appropriate model.

Rosekrans (1967) also found that perceived similarity of a model increased observational learning. Several investigators have argued that the more realistic a child perceives a given film to be, the more likely he is to learn from that presentation (cf. Berkowitz, 1962a; Schramm, 1969), and that the more useful the child perceives a given act to be, the more likely he is to learn it. As pointed out in the discussion of observational learning, vicarious reinforcement (i.e., observation of reward or punishment delivered to a filmed model contingent on some act performed by the model) has been demonstrated to affect both learning and performance (Bandura, Ross, & Ross, 1963b; Rosekrans, 1967), and Hicks (1968) has shown that when children observed film-mediated behavior in the presence of an adult who either praised or condemned the action, imitation of that action was affected.

In summary, studies of observational learning have indicated that children will learn behaviors from a film as a function of characteristics of the model, degree of involvement with the model or the action, contingent reinforcement or punishment delivered to the model, perceived utility of the behavior observed, and novelty of the behavior observed (cf. Flanders, 1968; Bandura, 1969; Schramm, 1969).

Clearly, age-related differences in degree of socialization, cognitive development, needs, interests, and so forth should influence how children perceive and respond to such cues. A number of investigations have shown that amount of learning from a given media presentation is positively related to age (Holaday & Stoddard, 1933; Roberts, 1968; Halloran, 1969; Collins, 1970; Leifer et al., 1971). This relationship is not as straightforward as it might first seem, however; it is not simply that as children get older they are more able to process more information. Several studies of children's learning from dramatic films have demonstrated that sixth- and seventh-grade children are *better able* than adults to remember material that is incidental to the main story action.

Hale, Miller, and Stevenson (1968) and Collins (1970) showed dramatic films to children who did not expect to be tested on what they viewed. Tests immediately following exposure dealt with material unessential to the narrative sense of the presentation, incidentals such as the dress of the characters, furnishings in the rooms portrayed, names of minor characters and so on. Both studies demonstrated a significant curvilinear trend, the learning of such details increasing until about the age of twelve or thirteen years, then decreasing. Collins also tested his subjects' learning of information essential to the action and found a linear increase with age.

These data indicate that not only does the processing of more information increase with age, but the ability to *focus* on essential information and to *ignore* nonessential information is also a function of age.

> In other words, pre-adolescent children tend to take in increasingly more environmental information with age, without regard for the relative value of the different information inputs, while older children tend to attend selectively to the many information inputs that confront them (Collins, 1970: 1140).

The development of selective attention, then, can be viewed as an age-related process of learning to learn, and can affect how the child responds to cues in a media presentation (or for that matter, whether certain cues are even perceived). There is evidence that although younger children learn selected behaviors from media-like presentations, they may often fail to note various dramatic and contextual cues that indicate under what conditions such behaviors are applicable and/or acceptable. Himmelweit and her colleagues (1958) report that younger children are more likely to attend to and remember scenes of high action, emotion, and conflict than events surrounding such action, and Dysinger and Ruckmick write that

> the younger the child, the more he appreciated and emotionally responded to the separate items in the film, and the less he appreciated or even assimilated... the moral or ultimate outcome of the picture (Dysinger & Ruckmick, 1933:116).

Leifer and her students (1971) directly tested developmental differences in perception and comprehension of certain cues inherent in a complex behavioral sequence and found that, with increasing age, children better remembered the sequence of events in an entertainment film and better understood the feelings and motivations of the characters. The four-year-olds in this study understood very little of the characters' feelings or motivations. In other words, the more complex or more subtle cues—those that provide the larger social context within which specific acts are portrayed (e.g., motives, justifications, complex cause-and-effect relationships)—appear to affect learning only as the child grows older.

Effects on Aggressive Behavior

One of the more frequently researched areas of learning from the mass media deals with aggressive behavior (for reviews, see Berkowitz, 1962a; 1962b; Maccoby, 1964; Baker & Ball, 1969; Schramm, 1969; Goranson, 1970).[7] Indeed questions about the relationship between the large amount of televised violence[8] and violent behavior in children have provided much of the impetus for the study of children and the mass media. Television- or film-mediated violence may affect children in at least three ways: by teaching techniques of aggressive behavior; by inhibiting or disinhibiting previously learned aggressive behaviors; by increasing or decreasing hostile wishes (cf. Berkowitz, 1962a; 1962b).

There is evidence that children are equally likely to learn modeled aggressive behaviors whether they observe a live or a film-mediated model (Bandura, Ross, & Ross, 1963a). Several studies that have not made live model versus film model comparisons have nevertheless demonstrated that children learn a significant number of specific aggressive behaviors from a film model (Bandura, Ross, & Ross, 1963b; Hicks, 1965; Rosekrans, 1967).

---

[7] Since this chapter was written, a large program of research on television and social behavior, with particular emphasis on the effects of TV on children's agressive behavior, has been carried out under the auspices of the Office of the Surgeon General. The program produced a total of sixty research reports and papers covering such topics as television content, patterns of television use, and the effect on children of observing television-mediated violence. The research provided a good deal of new information and filled some of the gaps in our knowledge. For the most part, however, the new data tend to support most of the generalizations made in the following pages.

For a somewhat controversial summary report of this program of research, see *Television and Growing Up: The Impact of Televised Violence* (National Institute of Mental Health, 1972). Individual research reports and papers are available under the general title, *Television and Social Behavior* (Comstock & Rubinstein, 1972a; 1972b; Comstock, Rubinstein, & Murray, 1972; Murray, Rubinstein, & Comstock, 1972; Rubinstein, Comstock, & Murray, 1972). In addition, the research program also produced a valuable bibliography of prior research on this topic: *Television and Social Behavior: An Annotated Bibliography of Research Focusing on Television's Impact on Children* (Atkin, Murray, & Nayman, 1971).

[8] Gerbner and his colleagues (1969) analyzed the content of a week of prime-time network television for both 1967 and 1968 and found that some violence prevailed in eight out of every ten plays. The casualty count for the two weeks was "at least 790" injured and dead. For additional analyses of media content, see Baker and Ball (1969).

Each of these studies also showed that children who observed film-mediated violence later manifested more nonimitative aggressive behavior than children who observed either no film or a nonviolent film. In addition, Mussen and Rutherford (1961) found that first graders who viewed an aggressive cartoon manifested more desire to pop a balloon than did children who observed a nonaggressive cartoon (a measure of aggression that is open to question), and Lovass (1961) found that nursery-school children who observed an aggressive cartoon were more likely than their controls to choose an aggressive over a nonaggressive toy.

In a more realistic vein, several studies (Walters & Llewellyn Thomas, 1963; Hartman, 1969) exposed adolescents to either violent or nonviolent films, after which they were placed in a situation in which they thought they were actually administering shocks to another person. In both cases, subjects who had viewed the more aggressive films gave much longer "shocks" than did their controls. Hence, it seems that film-mediated violence may not only teach specific aggressive behaviors, but may generalize to a class of aggressive behaviors.

Moreover, relative to other kinds of film-mediated behavior, aggressive behavior appears to have a high probability of being learned. To some extent this may be because portrayals of aggression tend to fulfill many of the conditions that increase incidental learning. For example, media violence occurs in contexts of emotion, action, and conflict, contexts that increase younger children's attention. Media violence is often committed by characters with whom children identify. When the hero triumphs through aggressive behavior, that behavior is often portrayed as inherently effective and rewarded.

In addition, at least one experiment indicates that the tendency for children to imitate violence is strong in and of itself. Bandura and Huston (1961) found that while preschool children were generally more likely to imitate a live model with whom they had earlier had a rewarding experience, the model's aggressive behavior was imitated *regardless* of any earlier relationship between the child and the model. Finally, Bandura (1965a) demonstrated that children learned the violent behaviors of a model even though the model was punished for his actions. Nursery-school children who observed a punished model failed to imitate his behavior during the initial measurement situation, but were perfectly capable of performing this behavior when sufficient incentives were made available. Apparently they simultaneously learned the behavior *and* became sensitized to sanctions that inhibited performance of what was learned.

The Bandura experiment points to the crucial distinction made earlier between learning and performance. On the one hand, most children probably have available to them a wide range of aggressive responses independent of the specific acts portrayed in the media. On the other hand, given that North American society socializes in such a way as to bring about early inhibition and attenuation of aggressive responses (Whiting & Child, 1953), performance of learned aggressive behavior is likely to be inhibited. Hence, the critical information contained in a media presentation of violence pertains not so much to ways of performing aggression as to conditions under which aggression may be performed.

Several cues within media portrayals of violence have been shown to affect the probability that children will later perform aggressively, cues that tend to increase or decrease the salience of sanctions against such behavior. Children performed less imitative and nonimitative aggressive behavior after viewing an aggressive model who was punished for his behavior (Bandura, Ross, & Ross, 1963b; Bandura, 1965a). Moreover, a model who was neither rewarded nor punished was imitated more than a model who was punished and no less than a model who was rewarded

(Bandura, 1965a). Brodbeck (1955) also reported a study in which levels of aggression in children rose markedly after they had seen a cartoon story in which the villain was not punished.

These latter two findings indicate that disconfirmation of expected consequences (i.e., most children are socialized to expect that aggression will be punished) increases the probability that observed aggression will elicit performance. This is not to say that children do not recognize "wrong" acts. Hope Klapper (1969) reported that nine- and ten-year-olds were very capable of pointing out when television characters engaged in morally wrong behaviors (although often they were not sure why an act was wrong). However, perception that an act may be morally unacceptable does not guarantee inhibition of that act, particularly if the villain is rewarded or goes unpunished.

Bandura, Ross, and Ross (1963b) found that children negatively evaluated an aggressive model but still imitated his behavior if he was *successful.* Zajonc (1954) showed that children between the ages of ten and fourteen consistently expressed a preference for a successful character regardless of whether he was portrayed as power oriented or affiliation oriented. In short, there is good evidence that negative consequences to an aggressor will decrease, and positive or neutral consequences will increase, the performance of observed aggression, and that behavior that "works" is perceived as an implication of positive consequences.

Aggressive behaviors are also more likely to be performed after viewing violence that is perceived as "justified." Berkowitz and Rawlings (1963) found that when the victim of a filmed prize fight was pictured as a scoundrel who deserved the beating, aggressive feelings among adolescents and young adults increased. Albert (1957) demonstrated that more aggression followed observation of a film in which the "good guy" won than a film in which the villain was successful or one in which neither was victorious. Such results lead one to ask whether prosocial violence—e.g., the sheriff beating up the villain—is the best means of portraying the message that crime does not pay. How often does the young child feel that his aggressive behavior is *not* justified?

Finally, we have considered the preceding studies in terms of the learning and inhibition-disinhibition of *behavior*, regardless of how exposure to media violence might affect hostile feelings. A number of investigations, however, have aimed at assessing whether observation of violence increases or decreases aggressive feelings, which in turn, of course, may mediate increases or decreases in aggressive behavior.

Feshbach (1955; 1956; 1961; 1969; Feshbach & Singer, 1971) has argued that there are conditions under which observation of violence may *decrease* hostility. This "catharsis" hypothesis derives from the psychoanalytic concept (which echoes Aristotle) that if an individual can express some of his aggression—let off steam, so to speak — the pressure to behave aggressively is reduced. If one gets the same result vicariously, by watching a violent program, that he might get by enacting aggressive behavior, then the effect of media violence might be socially beneficial. Feshbach demonstrated that, among adults who were angered before viewing violent films, aggressive feelings as measured by stories written about a TAT (thematic apperception test) picture (Feshbach, 1955) and by a word association test (Feshbach, 1961) decreased. However, the same experimental design administered to children failed to show differences in aggressive feelings (Feshbach, 1956).

These results led Feshbach to hypothesize that perhaps among adults, who are more completely socialized against aggression, the viewing of violence led to the arousal of aggression anxiety (i.e., guilt or anxiety over showing aggressive feelings), hence inhibition of such expression, hence the apparent decrement in hostility. Children, on the other hand, are not so well socialized, hence they might not inhibit their aggressive feelings (see also Berkowitz, 1962a).

Several other studies have failed to show reduction in aggression or hostility following exposure to film-mediated violence. Siegel (1956) found that nursery-school children who viewed a violent cartoon displayed slightly, but not significantly, *more* aggressive behavior in a natural play situation than did children who saw a neutral cartoon. Emery and Martin (1957) found no decrease in aggressiveness on paper-and-pencil measures among children who viewed a violent Western film.

Several investigators have tested the hypothesis that subjects angered before viewing violence would manifest "catharsis." The Hartman (1969) study cited earlier found that juvenile delinquents who were angered before exposure responded more punitively (gave longer shocks) than those who were not angered, and that the more punitive the film, the more punitive the response. Experiments by Berkowitz and his colleagues (Berkowitz, Corwin, & Heironomous, 1963; Berkowitz & Rawlings, 1963) aimed at assessing the effect on college students of "justified" violence also compared angered versus nonangered subjects. In neither study was there any decrement in aggressive feelings, and justifying the violence *increased* aggressive feelings, particularly among those who had been angered.

At least one study with children, however, found evidence supporting the catharsis hypothesis. Feshbach and Singer (1971; see also Feshbach, 1969) conducted a field experiment, using several hundred boys ranging in age from ten to seventeen years, in three private residential schools and four boys' homes. Boys in each school and institution were assigned to either an "aggressive" or "nonaggressive" television diet for a period of six weeks, with a variety of personality and attitude scales administered before and after the experiment, and behavior ratings by supervisors completed before, during, and after.

Feshbach and Singer's data indicate that viewing violent programs led to no overall increment in aggressive behavior. More intriguing, however, is their finding that boys from the children's homes (mainly lower-SES children) produced significantly higher preexposure aggression scores, and that within this group of children, over time, those exposed to an aggressive television diet manifested a decrease in aggressive behavior while those exposed to the nonaggressive diet manifested an increase in aggressive behavior. In other words, at least for lower-class children, the Feshbach and Singer data tend to support the catharsis hypothesis.

Given that the Feshbach and Singer findings run counter to most of the studies that have attempted to test the catharsis hypothesis, the study clearly demands both consideration and replication—consideration because, although anomalous, the results manifest striking consistency across a variety of measures of aggression and types of analysis; replication because they are anomalous, and because several methodological weaknesses open the results to question.[9]

Dangers in Generalizing Experimental Findings

From the preceding it seems that the bulk of experimental evidence overwhelmingly supports the position that observation of media-portrayed violence increases the probability that children will behave aggressively. However, we must exercise caution in generalizing laboratory findings

[9] An exchange of criticism and rebuttal dealing generally with the catharsis hypothesis and specifically with the Feshbach and Singer (1971) study has begun to appear in the literature. The discussion is characterized in four papers appearing in *Television and Social Behavior*, volume V: *Television's Effects: Further Explorations* (Comstock, Rubinstein, & Murray, 1972). Another critique of the catharsis research is to be found in Goranson (1969).

to children *in vivo*. It has been pointed out that both the experimental stimuli and the postexposure measurement situations in most experiments create very different conditions than those under which children usually view and respond to media portrayals (cf. J. T. Klapper, 1968).

Many of the experiments cited above used films that were short, that focused on the behaviors to be learned, and that portrayed novel, attention-getting behaviors the child could easily reproduce in the testing situation. Often the films manifest little character development, richness of setting, or display of behaviors and roles that are found in "real" television programs. Hence, we may argue that actual television films or video tapes might provide additional information or present information in a context such that the probability of aggressive behavior following from exposure is attenuated.

There is, however, reason to believe that stimulus aspects of television or movie violence might also be more likely to encourage aggression in an observer. Many studies of imitation or disinhibition expose children to stimuli in which the consequences of a given behavior closely follow performance of that behavior, and to sequences in which relevant cues are emphasized. Hence, discriminability of response contingencies is probably increased. Television drama, however, may not be quite so explicit. Reward or punishment for an act performed early in a program often does not occur until near the end of the program. The message that crime does not pay or that virtue is rewarded frequently occurs at the climax of the drama, long after the criminal or violent act has been performed. Thus, particularly for young children, we may ask if cues such as the consequences of or justification for an act are even associated with that act (cf. Leifer et al., 1971).

A more cogent threat to the external validity of experiments on aggression pertains to the testing situations employed in most studies. The evidence reviewed above indicates that when sanctions against aggression are made salient, the probability of aggressing is decreased. Most laboratory experiments, however, carefully create measurement situations that remove or make ambiguous the normally operative sanctions against aggression so that differences in learning (and/or disinhibition) can be observed.

It can be argued, however, that under most circumstances in children's lives, sanctions are operative. For example, those few studies that attempted to observe aggression, following viewing, in a naturalistic setting found no significant increase in amount of aggressive behavior (e.g., Siegel, 1956; Feshbach, 1969). In other words, socialization against aggression begins very early in the child's life, and the preexisting aggressive habits and sanctions he brings with him to the media exercise strong influence on the probability of aggression in a "real" context. This probably helps to explain why the plethora of violence in the media does not lead to more aggression in real life.

Still, there are real-life situations in which sanctions against aggression may not be so apparent, or in which aggression in some attenuated form is sanctioned, or in which socialization has been ineffective. Moreover, it has been argued that the more realistic the filmed violence (i.e., the greater the perceived association between observed violence and a situation in which the child might later find himself), the more likely real sanctions will be perceived as nonoperative (cf. Berkowitz, 1962b). In the same vein, Feshbach (1969) casts his catharsis hypothesis in terms of "fantasy aggression," noting that perception of aggressive behavior as real will lead to very different results, possibly increasing the probability of disinhibition of aggression or arousal of hostility.

Again, the importance of age variables is clear. The younger the child, the less internalized sanctions against aggression will be; and the younger the child, the less he has developed adult discount—i.e., the more likely he is to perceive "fantasy aggression" as "realistic aggression." Both conditions tend to increase the probability that aggression may be imitated or disinhibited. Further, it can be argued that the sheer amount of violence portrayed in the media either desensitizes young children to the consequences of violence, or carries with it the message that a frequent, and often successful, means of dealing with a conflict situation is to resort to violence. Indeed, Gerbner (1969) points out that this is a world view provided by the media.

Finally, in terms of social implications, we might ask if it is even necessary to demonstrate that differential exposure to film- or television-mediated violence leads to statistically significant differences in the performance of violence across *groups* of children. Exposure to a heavy diet of media violence may have little effect on the aggressive behavior of most children; it may even tend to reduce levels of hostility among a small subset of viewers. Still, there may remain a subset of children, however large or small in numbers, who might be adversely affected. Berkowitz writes:

> While it may be that television, movies, and comic books will excite anti-social conduct from only a relatively small number of people, we can also say the heavy dosage of violence in the media heightens the probability that someone in the audience will behave aggressively in a later situation (Berkowitz, 1962b: 134).

UNANSWERED QUESTIONS

The preceding pages have sacrificed detailed analysis of various studies in favor of providing some sense of the scope of research relevant to children's communication behavior. Our coverage has not been comprehensive, particularly in terms of intrapersonal and interpersonal factors affecting communication behavior. Nevertheless, it should be clear that the social system in which children develop can be characterized as a communication system, that neither interpersonal communication behavior nor mass communication behavior can be understood in isolation from the other, that communication behavior must be approached as both a process and a product of socialization, and that age-related changes in a number of variables strongly influence children's communication behavior.

The past two decades have witnessed a proliferation of research directly relevant to children and the mass media. There can be little doubt that the media play an important role in the child's developing conception of reality. Children devote time to the media; they are aroused by media presentations; they learn facts, attitudes, and behaviors from the media.

Still, there remain large gaps in our knowledge. We lack data on specific social effects of such learning in natural settings. Nor can we point with confidence to specific long-term effects of media exposure. We do not know if children who grow up on a diet of television violence become desensitized to violence in real life. We cannot say how much of the sophistication of today's youth derives from the mass media as opposed to changes in education or to increased affluence. We do not know how much of the world view presented by the media becomes the world view of the developing child.

We can say, in answer to a concern voiced some years ago, that television does not appear to have produced a passive generation. On the other hand, we cannot attribute the political activism of today's youth solely (if at all) to the mass media. In short, we have not yet solved the problem of separating out the effects of the media from the effects of other information inputs in the system.

There remain, however, numerous questions with important social implications that may be at least partially answered either in the laboratory or in the field, using the methodology available to us today. For example, we do not have much information on the extent to which different children perceive the world of the mass media as a valid representation of the real world. To the extent that it is perceived as valid, we may ask whether children note discrepancies between the lives they lead and the ones portrayed by the media, and what effects perception of such discrepancies might engender. Does the "good life" so often presented in television programs and commercials anger the ghetto child? or frustrate him? or motivate him?

In the same vein, we need to investigate rather than speculate about the development of adult discount. How is it learned? When does it develop? How does the distinction between reality and fantasy content differ from the distinction between realism and lack thereof within a given dramatic program? And more important, exactly how do such distinctions affect both learning and performance?

We have already noted the lack of developmental studies of observational learning, an area of obvious importance. There is evidence that very young children perceive movies or television programs in terms of isolated incidents while young adults seem to perceive a dramatic whole. We should begin to trace the course of this transition and specify the implications for learning and performance through the course of its development.

We need to know if and when the more subtle social cues portrayed by the media, cues such as motivations, justifications, and long-term consequences for a wide variety of acts, are perceived by children and what effect they might have. We should begin to investigate the effect of varying time spans between modeled behaviors and contingency cues. Now that the basic principles of observational learning have been formulated, it is time to expose children to real television shows (commercials included) under conditions as similar as possible to those in which they normally view, and to develop techniques for measuring changes in response hierarchies rather than limiting ourselves to creating sanctionless measurement situations.

Research along the lines of that initiated by the Wisconsin group (see, for example, Chaffee, McLeod, & Atkin, 1971) should be extended. There is much more to learn about the interaction between interpersonal communication and the child's mass-media behavior. There are indications that parental expectations influence how the child uses the media. We might also ask whether what the child does with the media influences parental expectations.

Returning to a point made in the opening pages of this chapter, the simple fact of a proliferation of information sources may have a profound influence on how children approach their world. The opportunity to compare interpretations, to become aware of alternatives other than those offered by any single source, to see that different people think and do different things at different times implies the possibility of development of a much more complex and flexible conception of the world than was available to earlier generations—or the possibility of an information overload which might lead to "tuning out," to avoidance of new information. We need to conduct research in this area.

Finally, it is time to take a long, hard look at what the media present. On the one hand, the evidence indicates that the child is the active participant in the child-media relationship, that what he takes from television, newspapers, or the movies is a function of what he brings to them. However, it is also obvious that to the extent mass-mediated communications are used as sources of information, the definition of the world the child develops will also be a function of the picture presented by the media.

Earlier we quoted Bandura's contention that in a society experiencing technological and social change as rapidly as ours, communications at the social-systems level may provide children with more functional information than can parents. Interests, attitudes, and behaviors developed before Little Rock, before "the pill," before environmental pollution, computers, and thirty-hour workweeks may lack validity for today's children. They have little recourse but to turn to society's institutions, to the schools and the mass media, for much of the information they need. And clearly, much of this information may be obtained from the media.

There is, however, another world presented by television, by the press, by motion pictures. It appears to be a world in which a large proportion of problems are solved through violence; in which crime, though punished, is highly prevalent; in which fathers often bumble. It is a world of white-collar occupations, three-bedroom homes, and quarter-hourly messages that "to consume is to be happy." We may well be concerned over how much of this type of information children incorporate into their own picture of the world.

Twenty years ago Wilbur Schramm described television as

> a great and shiny cafeteria from which children select what they want at the moment.... The very nature of television makes for a minimum of variety in the cafeteria; the nature of human beings makes for great variety on the side of the children (Schramm et al., 1961:1–2).

Continuing the metaphor, we are all aware that young children prefer dessert to vegetables, that health is a function of diet and diet a function of what is available, and that an exclusive diet of cafeteria food may well lack necessary nutritional value. In short, although the child is the active party in the cafeteria, there is still cause for concern over the menu.

REFERENCES

Abrams, Mark.
1956 "Child audiences for television in Great Britain." Journalism Quarterly 33:35–41.

Albert, Robert S.
1957 "The role of the mass media and the effects of aggressive film content upon children's aggressive responses and identification choices." Genetic Psychology Monographs 55:221–285.

Atkin, Charles K.; John P. Murray; and Oguz B. Nayman (eds.).
1971 Television and Social Behavior: An Annotated Bibliography of Research Focusing on Television's Impact on Children. Washington, D.C.: U.S. Government Printing Office.

Bailyn, Lotte.
1959 "Mass media and children: A study of exposure habits and cognitive effects." Psychological Monographs 73:1–48.

Baker, Robert K., and Sandra J. Ball.
1969 Violence and the Media. Washington, D.C.: U.S. Government Printing Office.

Bandura, Albert.
1965a "Influence of models reinforcement contingencies on the acquisition of imitative responses." Journal of Personality and Social Psychology 1:589–595.
1965b "Vicarious processes: A case of no-trial learning." Pp. 1–55 in Leonard Berkowitz (ed.), Advances in Experimental Social Psychology. Volume 2. New York: Academic Press.
1969 "Social-learning theory of identificatory processes." Pp. 213–262 in D. A. Goslin (ed.), Handbook of Socialization Theory and Research. Chicago: Rand McNally.

Bandura, Albert; Joan E. Grusec; and Frances L. Menlove.
1966 "Observational learning as a function of symbolization and incentive set." Child Development 37:499–506.

Bandura, Albert, and Aletha C. Huston.
1961 "Identification as a process of incidental learning." Journal of Abnormal and Social Psychology 63:311–318.

Bandura, Albert; Dorothea Ross; and Sheila A. Ross.
1963a "Imitation of film-mediated aggressive models." Journal of Abnormal and Social Psychology 66:3–11.
1963b "Vicarious reinforcement and imita-

tive learning." Journal of Abnormal and Social Psychology 67:601–607.

Bandura, Albert, and Richard H. Walters.
1963 Social Learning and Personality Development. New York: Holt, Rinehart and Winston.

Berelson, Bernard.
1948 "Communication and public opinion." Pp. 156–166 in Wilbur Schramm (ed.), Communications in Modern Society. Urbana: University of Illinois Press.

Berko, Jean.
1958 "The child's learning of English morphology." Word 14:150–177.

Berkowitz, Leonard.
1962a Aggression: A Social-psychological Model. New York: McGraw-Hill.
1962b "Violence in the mass media." Pp. 107–137 in Paris-Stanford Studies in Communication. Paris: Institut Français de Presse, University of Paris; Stanford, California: Institute for Communication Research, Stanford University.

Berkowitz, Leonard; Ronald G. Corwin; and Mark Heironomous.
1963 "Film violence and subsequent aggressive tendencies." Public Opinion Quarterly 27(Summer):217–229.

Berkowitz, Leonard, and Edna Rawlings.
1963 "Effects of film violence on inhibitions against subsequent aggression." Journal of Abnormal and Social Psychology 66:405–412.

Bernstein, Basil.
1960 "Language and social class." British Journal of Sociology 11:271–276.
1961 "Social class and linguistic development: A theory of social learning." Pp. 288–314 in A. H. Halsey, Jean Floud, and C. A. Anderson (eds.), Education, Economy and Society. New York: Free Press of Glencoe.
1962 "Social class, linguistic codes and grammatical elements." Language and Speech 5:221–240.
1964 "Elaborated and restricted codes: Their social origins and some consequences." American Anthropologist 66(December, Part 2):55–69.

Bossard, J. H. S.
1945 "Family modes of expression." American Sociological Review 10: 226–237.

Bossard, J. H. S., and Eleanor S. Boll.
1960 The Sociology of Child Development. New York: Harper.

Braine, Martin D. S.
1963 "The ontogeny of English phrase structure: The first phrase." Language 39:1–13.

Brodbeck, Arthur J.
1955 "The mass media as a socializing agency." Paper presented at the annual meeting of the American Psychological Association, San Francisco, September.

Bronfenbrenner, Urie.
1958 "Socialization and social class through time and space." Pp. 400–425 in Eleanor E. Maccoby, T. M. Newcomb, and E. L. Hartley (eds.), Readings in Social Psychology. New York: Holt.

Brown, Roger W.
1958 Words and Things. New York: Free Press of Glencoe.
1962 "Language and categories." Pp. 247–312 in J. S. Bruner, Jacqueline J. Goodnow, and G. A. Austin, A Study of Thinking. New York: Wiley.
1965 Social Psychology. New York: Free Press.

Brown, Roger W., and Collin Fraser.
1963 "The acquisition of syntax." Pp. 158–197 in C. N. Cofer and Barbara S. Musgrave (eds.), Verbal Behavior and Learning. New York: McGraw-Hill.

Bruner, Jerome S.
1964 "The course of cognitive growth." American Psychologist 19:1–16.

Bruner, Jerome S.; Rose R. Olver; and Patricia M. Greenfield.
1966 Studies in Cognitive Growth. New York: Wiley.

Carroll, John B.
1961 "Language acquisition, bilingualism, and language change." Pp. 331–345 in Sol Saporta (ed.), Psycholinguistics: A Book of Readings. New York: Holt, Rinehart and Winston.

Cazden, Courtney B.
1965 "Environmental assistance to the child's acquisition of grammar." Ph.D. Dissertation, Harvard University (unpublished).
1966 "Subcultural differences in child language: An inter-disciplinary re-

view." Merrill-Palmer Quarterly 12: 185–219.

Chaffee, Steven H.; Jack M. McLeod; and Charles K. Atkin.
1971 "Parental influences on adolescent media use." American Behavioral Scientist 14:323–340.

Chaffee, Steven H.; Jack M. McLeod; and Daniel B. Wackman.
1966 "Family communication and political socialization." Paper presented at meetings of the Association for Education in Journalism, Iowa City, Iowa, August.

Charters, Werrett W.
1933 Motion Pictures and Youth: A Summary. New York: Macmillan.

Chomsky, Noam.
1959 "A review of 'Verbal Behavior' by B. F. Skinner." Language 35:26–58.

Chu, Godwin C., and Wilbur Schramm.
1967 Learning from Television: What the Research Says. Washington, D.C.: National Association of Educational Broadcasters.

Clarke, Peter.
1968a "Does teen news attract boys to newspapers?" Journalism Quarterly 45:7–13.
1968b "Reading interests and use of the print media by teenagers." Report to the American Newspaper Publishers Association Foundation (mimeo).
1969 "Identification with father and father-son similarities in reading behavior." Seattle: University of Washington Communication Research Center (mimeo).

Clausen, John A.
1966 "Family structure, socialization, and personality." Pp. 1–53 in Lois W. Hoffman and Martin L. Hoffman (eds.), Review of Child Development Research. Volume 2. New York: Russell Sage.

Clausen, John A., and Judith R. Williams.
1963 "Sociological correlates of child behavior." Pp. 62–107 in H. W. Stevenson (ed.), Child Psychology, Part I. Chicago: National Society for the Study of Education.

Coates, Brian, and William W. Hartup.
1969 "Age and verbalization in observational learning." Developmental Psychology 1:556–562.

Collins, W. Andrew.
1970 "Learning of media content: A developmental study." Child Development 41:1133–1142.

Comstock, George A., and Eli A. Rubenstein (eds.).
1972a Television and Social Behavior; Reports and Papers, Volume I: Media Content and Control. Washington, D.C.: U.S. Government Printing Office.
1972b Television and Social Behavior; Reports and Papers, Volume III: Television and Adolescent Aggressiveness. Washington, D.C.: U.S. Government Printing Office.

Comstock, George A.; Eli A. Rubinstein; and John P. Murray (eds.).
1972 Television and Social Behavior; Reports and Papers, Volume V: Television's Effects: Further Explorations. Washington, D.C.: U.S. Government Printing Office.

Davis, Allison.
1948 Social-Class Influences Upon Learning. Cambridge: Harvard University Press.

Deutsch, Morton.
1962 "The disadvantaged child and the learning process." Pp. 162–179 in H. A. Passow (ed.), Education in Depressed Areas. New York: Teachers College.

Dysinger, W. S., and C. A. Ruckmick.
1933 Emotional Responses of Children to the Motion Picture Situation. New York: Macmillan.

Emery, F. E., and David Martin.
1957 Psychological Effects of the Western Film: A Study in Television Viewing. Melbourne: University of Melbourne Department of Audio-Visual Aids.

Ervin-Tripp, Susan M.
1964 "Imitation and structural change in children's language." Pp. 163–190 in E. H. Lenneberg (ed.), New Directions in the Study of Language. Cambridge, Massachusetts: M.I.T. Press.
1966 "Language development." Pp. 55–105 in Lois W. Hoffman and Martin L. Hoffman (eds.), Review of Child Development Research. Volume 2. New York: Russell Sage.

Ervin-Tripp, Susan M., and W. R. Miller.
1963 "Language development." Pp. 108–

143 in Harold W. Stevenson (ed.), Child Psychology, Part I. Chicago: National Society for the Study of Education.

Ervin-Tripp, Susan M., and Dan I. Slobin.
1966 "Psycholinguistics." Pp. 435–474 in P. R. Farnsworth, Olga McNemar, and Quinn McNemar (eds.), Annual Review of Psychology. Volume 17. Palo Alto, California: Annual Reviews, Inc.

Feshbach, Seymour.
1955 "The drive-reducing function of fantasy behavior." Journal of Abnormal and Social Psychology 50:3–11.
1956 "The catharsis hypothesis and some consequences of interaction with aggressive and neutral play objects." Journal of Personality 24:449–462.
1961 "The stimulating vs. cathartic effects of a vicarious aggressive experience." Journal of Abnormal and Social Psychology 63:381–385.
1969 "The catharsis effect: Research and another view." Pp. 461–472 in Robert K. Baker and Sandra J. Ball, Violence and the Media. Washington, D.C.: U.S. Government Printing Office.

Feshbach, Seymour, and Robert D. Singer.
1971 Television and Aggression. San Francisco: Jossey-Bass.

Flanders, James P.
1968 "A review of research on imitative behavior." Psychological Bulletin 69:316–337.

Flavell, John H.
1963 The Developmental Psychology of Jean Piaget. Princeton, New Jersey: Van Nostrand.
1970 "Developmental studies of mediated memory." Pp. 181–211 in Lewis P. Lipsitt and C. C. Spiker (eds.), Advances in Child Development and Behavior. Volume 5. New York: Academic Press.

Flavell, John H.; David R. Beach; and Jack M. Chinsky.
1966 "Spontaneous verbal rehearsal in a memory task as a function of age." Child Development 37:283–299.

Fodor, Jerry A.; James J. Jenkins; and Sol Saporta.
1967 "Psycholinguistics and communication theory." Pp. 160–201 in Frank E. X. Dance (ed.), Human Communication Theory: Original Essays. New York: Holt, Rinehart and Winston.

Fraser, Collin; Ursula Bellugi; and Roger W. Brown.
1963 "Control of grammar in imitation, comprehension, and production." Journal of Verbal Learning and Verbal Behavior 2:121–135.

Furu, Takeo.
1962 Television and Children's Life. Tokyo: Radio and Television Cultural Research Institute, Japan Broadcasting Corporation.

Geiger, Kent, and Robert Sokol.
1959 "Social norms in television-watching." American Journal of Sociology 65(September):174–181.

Gerbner, George.
1967 "Mass media and human communication theory." Pp. 40–60 in Frank E. X. Dance (ed.), Human Communication Theory: Original Essays. New York: Holt, Rinehart and Winston.
1969 "The case for cultural indicators, with violence in the mass media as a point in case." Paper presented at the meetings of the American Political Science Association, New York City, September.

Gerbner, George; Marten Brouwer; Cedric C. Clark; and Klaus Krippendorff.
1969 Dimensions of Violence in Television Drama. Philadelphia: University of Pennsylvania, The Annenberg School of Communications (mimeo).

Goranson, Richard E.
1970 "Media violence and aggressive behavior: A review of experimental research." Pp. 1–31 in Leonard Berkowitz (ed.), Advances in Experimental Social Psychology. Volume 5. New York: Academic Press.

Greenberg, Bradley S., and Brenda Dervin.
1967a "Communication and related behaviors of a sample of low-income urban adults compared with a general population sample." Communication Among the Urban Poor, Report No. 1. East Lansing: Michigan State University Department of Communication (mimeo).
1967b "Communication and related behaviors of a sample of urban adults in three low-income areas." Communi-

cation Among the Urban Poor, Report No. 2. East Lansing: Michigan State University Department of Communication (mimeo).
1968 "Communication and related behavior of low-income white and Negro adults." Communication Among the Urban Poor, Report No. 3. East Lansing: Michigan State University Department of Communication (mimeo).

Greenberg, Bradley S.; and J. R. Dominick.
1968 "Television usage, attitudes and functions for low-income and middle-class teen-agers." Communication Among the Urban Poor, Report No. 4. East Lansing: Michigan State University Department of Communication, November (mimeo).
1969 "Television behavior among disadvantaged children." Communication Among the Urban Poor, Report No. 9. East Lansing: Michigan State University Department of Communication (mimeo).

Greenstein, Fred I.
1965 Children and Politics. New Haven: Yale University Press.

Hale, Gordon A.; Leon K. Miller; and Harold W. Stevenson.
1968 "Incidental learning of film content: A developmental study." Child Development 39:69–78.

Halloran, James D. (ed.).
1969 Findings and Cognition on the Television Perception of Children and Young People Based on the Prize-winning Programmes of Prix Jeunesse 1966: Patrick and Putrik and Clown Ferdl. Munich: Internationales Zentralinstitut für das Jugend und Bildungsfernsehen.

Hartman, Donald P.
1969 "Influence of symbolically modeled instrumental aggression and pain cues on aggressive behavior." Journal of Personality and Social Psychology 11:280–286.

Hartup, William W., and Brian Coates.
1970 "The role of imitation in childhood socialization." Pp. 109–142 in Ronald A. Hoppe, G. Alexander Milton, and Edward C. Simmel (eds.), Early Experiences and the Processes of Socialization. New York: Academic Press.

Hess, Robert D., and Judith V. Torney.
1967 The Development of Political Attitudes in Children. Chicago: Aldine.

Hicks, David J.
1965 "Imitation and retention of film-mediated aggressive peer and adult models." Journal of Personality and Social Psychology 2:97–100.
1968 "Effects of co-observer's sanctions and adult presence on imitative aggression." Child Development 39: 303–309.

Himmelweit, Hilde T.; A. N. Oppenheim; and Pamela Vince.
1958 Television and the Child. London: Oxford University Press.

Holaday, P. W., and G. D. Stoddard.
1933 Getting Ideas from the Movies. New York: Macmillan.

Irwin, O. C.
1960 "Infant speech: The effect of systematic reading of stories." Journal of Speech and Hearing Research 3: 187–190.

John, Vera P.
1963 "The intellectual development of slum children." American Journal of Orthopsychiatry 33:813–822.

Jones, Edward E., and Harold B. Gerard.
1967 Foundations of Social Psychology. New York: Wiley.

Klapper, Hope L.
1969 "'Did anyone do anything that would be wrong for you to do?': Children's perceptions and moral evaluations of television programs." Paper presented at the meetings of the American Association of Public Opinion Research, Lake George, New York, May.

Klapper, Joseph T.
1968 "The effects of mass-media-depicted violence: A review of research findings." Paper presented at the meetings of the American Orthopsychiatric Association, Chicago, March.

Kohn, M. L.
1959a "Social class and parental values." American Journal of Sociology 64: 337–351.
1959b "Social class and the exercise of parental authority." American Sociological Review 24:352–366.

Leifer, Aimée D.
1966 "The relationship between cognitive awareness in selected areas and differential imitation of a same-sex model." Master's Thesis, Stanford University (unpublished).

Leifer, Aimée D.; W. Andrew Collins; Barbara M. Gross; H. P. Taylor; Lew Andrews; and Elizabeth Blackmer.
1971 "Developmental aspects of variables relevant to observational learning." Child Development 42:1509–1516.

Lenneberg, Eric H.
1962 "Understanding language without ability to speak: A case report." Journal of Abnormal and Social Psychology 65:419–425.
1967 Biological Foundations of Language. New York: Wiley.

Lovaas, O. Ivar.
1961 "Effect of exposure to symbolic aggression on aggressive behavior." Child Development 32:37–44.

Lyle, Jack.
1969 "Contemporary functions of the mass media." Pp. 187–216 in R. K. Baker and Sandra J. Ball, Violence and the Media. Washington, D.C.: U.S. Government Printing Office.

McCarthy, Dorthea.
1954 "Language development in children." Pp. 492–630 in Leonard Carmichael (ed.), Manual of Child Development. Second Edition. New York: Wiley.

Maccoby, Eleanor E.
1951 "Television: Its impact on school children." Public Opinion Quarterly 15(Fall):421–444.
1954 "Why do children watch television?" Public Opinion Quarterly 18(Fall): 239–244.
1959 "Role-taking in childhood and its consequences for social learning." Child Development 30:239–252.
1964 "Effects of the mass media." Pp. 323–348 in Martin L. Hoffman and Lois W. Hoffman (eds.), Review of Child Development Research. Volume 1. New York: Russell Sage.

Maccoby, Eleanor E., and W. C. Wilson.
1957 "Identification and observational learning from films." Journal of Abnormal and Social Psychology 55: 76–87.

McLeod, Jack M.; Steven H. Chaffee; and H. S. Eswara.
1966 "Family communication patterns and communication research." Paper presented at the meetings of the Association for Education in Journalism, Iowa City, Iowa, August.

McLeod, Jack M.; Steven H. Chaffee; and Daniel B. Wackman.
1967 "Family communication: An updated report." Paper read at the meetings of the Association for Education in Journalism, Boulder, Colorado, August.

Marsh, George, and Marian Sherman.
1966 "Verbal mediation of transposition as a function of age level." Journal of Experimental Child Psychology 4: 90–98.

Miller, George A.; Eugene Galanter; and K. H. Pribram.
1960 Plans and the Structure of Behavior. New York: Holt, Rinehart and Winston.

Miller, George A., and David McNeill.
1969 "Psycholinguistics." Pp. 666–794 in Gardner Lindzey and Elliot Aronson (eds.), Handbook of Social Psychology. Volume 3. Second Edition. Reading, Massachusetts: Addison-Wesley.

Miller, Wick, and Susan Ervin-Tripp.
1964 "The development of grammar in child language," in Ursula Bellugi and Roger W. Brown (eds.), The Acquisition of Language. Lafayette, Indiana: Child Development Publications of the Society for Research in Child Development, Purdue University.

Milner, Esther.
1951 "A study of the relationship between reading readiness in grade-one school children and patterns of parent-child interaction." Child Development 22:95–112.

Murray, John P.; Eli A. Rubenstein; and George A. Comstock (eds.).
1972 Television and Social Behavior; Reports and Papers, Volume II: Television and Social Learning. Washington, D.C.: U.S. Government Printing Office.

Mussen, Paul H., and Eldred Rutherford.
1961 "Effects of aggressive cartoons on

children's aggressive play." Journal of Abnormal and Social Psychology 62:461–464.

National Institute of Mental Health.
1972 Television and Growing Up: The Impact of Televised Violence, a Report to the Surgeon General of Public Health Service from Surgeon General's Scientific Advisory Committee on Television and Social Behavior. Washington, D.C.: U.S. Government Printing Office.

Peterson, Ruth C., and L. L. Thurstone.
1933 Motion Pictures and the Social Attitudes of Children. New York: Macmillan.

Piaget, Jean.
1952 The Origins of Intelligence in Children. New York: International Universities Press.

Riley, Matilda W., and John W. Riley, Jr.
1951 "A sociological approach to communication research." Public Opinion Quarterly 15:444–460.

Roberts, Donald F.
1968 "A developmental study of opinion change: Source orientation versus content orientation at three age levels." Ph.D. Dissertation, Stanford University (unpublished).

Rosekrans, Mary A.
1967 "Imitation in children as a function of perceived similarity to a social model and vicarious reinforcement." Journal of Personality and Social Psychology 7:307–315.

Rubinstein, Eli A.; George A. Comstock; and John P. Murray (eds.).
1972 Television and Social Behavior; Reports and Papers, Volume IV: Television in Day-to-Day Life: Patterns of Use. Washington, D.C.: U.S. Government Printing Office.

Samuelson, Merrill; Richard F. Carter; and Lee Ruggels.
1963 "Education, available time, and use of mass media." Journalism Quarterly 40:491–496.

Schneider, Louis, and Sverre Lysgaard.
1953 "The deferred gratification pattern: A preliminary study." American Sociological Review 18:142–149.

Schramm, Wilbur.
1949 "The nature of news." Journalism Quarterly 26:259–269.
1969 Motion Pictures and Real-life Violence: What the Research Says. A working paper for the Motion Picture Association of America. Stanford, California: Institute for Communication Research (mimeo).
1971 "The nature of communications between humans." Pp. 3–53 in Wilbur Schramm and D. F. Roberts (eds.), The Process and Effects of Mass Communication. Revised Edition. Urbana: University of Illinois Press.

Schramm, Wilbur; Jack Lyle; and Edwin B. Parker.
1961 Television in the Lives of Our Children. Stanford, California: Stanford University Press.

Sears, Robert R.; Eleanor E. Maccoby; and Harry Levin.
1957 Patterns of Child Rearing. Evanston, Illinois: Row, Peterson.

Siegel, Alberta E.
1956 "Film-mediated fantasy aggression and strength of aggressive drive." Child Development 27:365–378.
1958 "The influence of violence in the mass media upon children's role expectations." Child Development 29:35–56.

Steiner, Gary A.
1963 The People Look at Television. New York: Knopf.

Thompson, R. J.
1959 Television Crime Drama. Melbourne: University of Melbourne Department of Audio-Visual Aids.

Wade, Serena.
1966 "An exploration into the media behavior of the creative adolescent." Ph.D. Dissertation, Stanford University (unpublished).
1971 "Adolescents, creativity, and media." American Behavioral Scientist 14: 341–351.

Wallach, Michael A.
1963 "Research on children's thinking." Pp. 236–276 in H. W. Stevenson (ed.), Child Psychology, Part I. Chicago: National Society for the Study of Education.

Walters, Richard H., and Edward Llewellyn Thomas.
1963 "Enhancement of punitiveness by visual and audio-visual displays."

Canadian Journal of Psychology 17: 244–255.

Whiting, John W. M., and Irvin L. Child.
1953 Child Training and Personality. New Haven: Yale University Press.

Wilson, R. C., and E. J. Shaffer.
1965 "Reading comics to learn." Elementary School Journal 66:81–82.

Wolf, Katherine M., and Marjorie Fiske.
1949 "The children talk about comics." Pp. 3–50 in P. F. Lazarsfeld and F. N. Stanton (eds.), Communications Research: 1948–49. New York: Harper.

Zajonc, Robert B.
1954 "Some effects of the 'space' serials." Public Opinion Quarterly 18(Winter): 367–374.

Zigler, Edward, and Irvin L. Child.
1969 "Socialization." Pp. 450–589 in Gardner Lindzey and Elliot Aronson (eds.), Handbook of Social Psychology. Volume 3. Second Edition. Reading, Massachusetts: Addison-Wesley.

CHAPTER 9 Persuasion, Resistance, and Attitude Change

WILLIAM J. McGUIRE
Yale University

After a brief listing of some nonverbal determinants of attitudes, the author devotes the remainder of the discussion to verbal-communication effects on attitudes. Following an explication of the concept of attitude, the communication-persuasion process is analyzed into five communication aspects: namely, source, message, channel, receiver, and destination; and into six stages in the process of persuasion: presentation, attention, comprehension, yielding, retention, and action.

Five theoretical approaches that have been used to account for attitude change are discussed: learning, categorizing, perceptual, consistency, functional, and information-processing. The information-processing paradigm is especially suited to the discussion of persuasion in the context of communication.

Persuasion, or changing people's attitudes and behavior through the spoken and written word, constitutes one of the more interesting uses of communication. The present chapter reviews the conceptual and theoretical analyses of the persuasion process and the body of empirically tested generalizations that we can now make about it.

We shall first discuss some determinants of attitudes other than verbal communications. Our preoccupation in this chapter with verbal determinants is put into better perspective by at least mentioning the determinants other than the written and spoken word.

DETERMINANTS OF ATTITUDES

While the present chapter will focus on the spoken and written word as determinants of attitudes and behavior, it should be recognized that our belief systems derive from a number of factors other than these verbal communications from other people. For one thing, verbalizations do not constitute the only persuasive communications we receive from other people, so a word should be said about the role of nonverbal communication in the persuasion process.

Still further removed are determinants of whatever type outside the communication process. We have in mind here genetic factors, other physiological influences, direct experience with the object or belief (instead of simply communications regarding it), and the total institutions through which the person's whole environment serves to mold his beliefs and actions. We shall touch briefly on each of these other five areas of determinants before focusing on verbal communications.

Nonverbal Communication

There has been a recent revival of laboratory research on nonverbal communication. While this work is descriptive and exploratory rather than guided by general theoretical formulations, it has increased considerably our appreciation of the extent to and modes by which people transmit and receive feelings and even specific content via nonverbal communications, including nonlinguistic vocalizations, gestures and postures, eye contact and facial expressions, and the use of space. A number of extensive and convenient reviews of aspects of this work are already available (Mehrabian, 1969; see also chapter 4 of this volume), so we shall not consider this work in any detail.

The aspect of the work that bears most directly on the present discussion is how the nonverbal communication of a transmitter affects the positivity of the recipient's attitudes to him and to his message. There is a considerable literature suggesting that the person's attitude is affected most favorably when the communicator stands closer to the recipient, engages in more eye contact with him, etc. However, when the full range of such variables is investigated, it may turn out that the overall relationship is nonmonotonic, with an intermediate level in these variables producing the most positive attitudes. The work of Mehrabian and his students (e.g., Mehrabian & Williams, 1969) has particularly focused on how posture, movement, facial expression, and nonlinguistic aspects of verbalization affect both perceived and intended persuasiveness.

Genetic Determinants

During the second quarter of this century, American behavioral science was dominated by an environmentalistic ideology, and it became almost a truism in persuasion research that attitudes develop through experience. For example, in a classic debate during the 1940s between a personalistic and a behavioristic theorist regarding the nature of attitudes, one of the few points on which they agreed was that our attitudes are acquired through experience rather than being inborn (Doob, 1947; Chein, 1948).

Earlier in the century there had been conjectures, such as the racial unconscious notion of Jung and Freud, that some of our basic attitudinal content might be transmitted genetically. From an environmentalistic viewpoint, such notions seemed implausible and almost self-contradictory, arousing philosophical difficulties associated with innate ideas and the synthetic *a priori*. At most, the notion seemed tolerable as a somewhat unfortunate metaphor, or Platonic myth, in a period when it had generally been taken for granted that the individual is born with a *tabula rasa* as far as attitudinal content is concerned. On the other hand, Campbell (1959) called attention to Spencer's notion that there might be synthetic *a priori* content ontogenetically innate although phylogenetically acquired which made the notion of inborn attitudinal content somewhat more plausible without providing any positive evidence in its support.

While genetic transmission of specific attitudinal content remains in doubt, it does seem that general attitudinal tendencies have an innate component. The distinction involved here becomes clearer if we regard the individual's attitude as a positive or negative response tendency directed toward a class of objects.

For example, outgroup hostility (which is probably the most studied of all attitudes) can be characterized as a tendency to make hostile responses toward members of racial, religious, or occupational groups different from one's own. The general tendency involved here, a proneness to aggressive acts, seems to be influenced by genetic factors if we can generalize across species (Scott & Fuller, 1965). Hence, outgroup hostility may have a genetic component in that hereditary factors seem to affect one's general level of hostility, although it is improbable that the specific target group is written into the genetic code of the prejudiced person.

Other Physiological Determinants

Since people are organisms, it can be assumed that any attitude or attitude change has a bodily representation, but the primitive state of neuroscience allows us to discuss the physiological manipulation of attitudes only in terms of gross conditions, such as the person's internal environment. A wide variety of drugs, most obviously alcohol, can alter the attitudinal and behavioral states of the individual, though it is difficult to predict just how these agents will manifest themselves in a given individual. Other consciousness-altering treatment, such as lobotomy, food deprivation, or hyperventilation, can likewise alter the person's mood and attitudinal state. These alterations might be in the intensity domain, or even in particular content, targets, and behavior.

Somewhat more conjectural are the attitudinal effects of sensory and social deprivation, and of certain disease conditions and their aftereffects (such as tuberculosis, encephalitis, etc.). The aging process itself is thought by some to alter the individual's attitudinal state. For example, it is believed by some that interest in politics and generally altruistic attitudes tend to flourish during the adolescent period, and that the individual's attitudes become more conservative with age. However, empirical data are by no means clear on these points (Hyman, 1959; Greenstein, 1965).

Direct Experience with the Object

We in the communication areas sometimes lose sight of the possibility that an individual's attitude is determined not only by communications from other people about the attitude object, but also through his direct experience with that object. On the other hand, the believer himself probably makes the opposite error of assuming that his attitudes are determined more by direct experience than is actually the case. We shall not try here to apportion the determination of our attitudes between direct contact and indirect communication; but especially since this chapter focuses almost exclusively on indirect determination through social communications, we should mention in passing at least that direct experience with the object does in numerous cases affect the individual's attitude to that object.

Both salient single incidents and more prosaic accumulated experience may have lasting attitudinal effects. Traumatic or otherwise deeply significant single experiences are often reported in the religious biographies of the "twice born" (James, 1970) as having completely altered the person's religious orientation and belief. Direct experience with the attitude object probably acts less sensationally but more frequently as a determinant when it takes the form of more mundane experience which continues for a prolonged period.

This phenomenon has been studied most frequently with regard to how intergroup contact, such as racial integration, affects prejudice. While there is good evidence to believe that racial hostility does not derive solely from the individual's experience with individuals of the disliked group, an issue of extreme social importance is the way in which socially engineered or legally compelled removal of segregation barriers will affect the mutual liking of the individuals involved.

Some theoretical formulations (Homans, 1950) and many social engineers assume that under most conditions interpersonal contact will tend to result in enhanced liking. Empirical research suggests, rather, that contact can increase or decrease interpersonal liking, depending on numerous conditions of the contact such as ideological similarity, status equality, duration and mutual goal facilitation. A fine and readily available review of this important research has been prepared by Harding, Proshansky, Kutner, and Chein (1969).

Total Institutions

To some extent the individual's attitude toward objects is determined not by his personal experiences with the object nor by specific communications from others about those objects, but rather by the conditions of the total environment in which he lives. The psychoanalytic school, for example, argues that the person's ideological outlook is almost totally formed in early childhood by one such total institution, his early family environment.

Environments constitute such total socializing institutions to the extent that they completely determine the stimuli to which the individual is exposed, the response options that are made available to him, and rewards that are scheduled on the basis of his behavior in these situations. The family situation in which the young child is reared is a pervasive example of such a total institution. Less universal but more notorious are the total institutions in which some individuals find themselves in later life. We have in mind here such environments as the army in wartime (to a lesser extent even domestic military service in peacetime), prisons, and mental hospitals. It seems likely that the individual's attitudes are to a large extent molded by such a total institution which controls his stimulation, his response opportunities, and the rewards he receives.

All of the factors considered in this section probably do affect the individual's attitudes. We merely mention them here, rather than attempting to do them justice, in order to put into better perspective the fact that, henceforth, in concentrating only on persuasive communication we shall be neglecting other determinants of attitude and behavior.

CONCEPTUALIZATIONS OF THE COMMUNICATION-PERSUASION PROCESS

The theoretical and empirical advances that have been made in our understanding of the communication-persuasion process can be more efficiently reviewed if some clarifications of the conceptions used in this area are first made. We shall first review the meanings of *attitude*. Subsequent sections will analyze *communications* (the independent-variable side of the attitude-change process) into five classes of components, and *being persuaded* (the dependent-variable side of the process) into six behavioral steps. We shall then describe the matrix of persuasive communication that is generated by these dependent and independent variable analyses. A brief synopsis of six general theories of the persuasion process will be presented, and then the scope of the empirical review to be discussed here will be outlined.

The Logical Status of Attitude

Definition

The term *attitude* seems to play its most useful role in our thinking when it is taken to refer to an intervening variable that mediates between generalized reception and response tendencies. On the reception side, it involves a tendency to group a whole class of stimulus situations into a single conceptual category; on the response side, it refers to the tendency to respond to this set of stimuli with a characteristic class of responses. Alternative formulations of this sort are discussed in more detail by McGuire (1969a).

Such a mediating concept simplifies our depiction of a person's behavior when we observe him behaving in a fairly consistent way in a definable set of stimulus situations. Aside from being a hypothesized mediational state, *attitude* has surplus meaning in that it can be directly measured in terms of the self-report of the individual as to how he feels about the stimuli in question and his behavioral intentions toward them. While this conceptualization of attitudes is only definitional, it does suggest two ways in which attitude change or persuasion can occur; namely, by inducing the person to reconceptualize the stimuli so that he categorizes specific instances differently, or by changing his response tendencies to the given class of stimuli.

Distinctions

This informal definition does not attempt to distinguish between attitudes and related terms such as *opinions*, *beliefs*, *values*, etc. Many distinctions have been made among these terms and maintained vehemently by one or another theorist, although hardly any of these distinctions has received universal acceptance.

For example, some would distinguish *values* by saying it is a more general construct than attitudes, while others would distinguish it by saying that the person's attitude toward an object is the sum of his perceptions of how conducive that object is to the attainment of his values. Some would say that opinions are narrower beliefs than attitudes; others would distinguish them by saying that attitudes refer to beliefs about matters of taste, and opinions to beliefs about matters of fact, etc.

Many students of the area take considerable pleasure in developing a precise vocabulary of this sort. We shall not discuss these terminology questions further, however, since the alternative glossaries have been conveniently reviewed elsewhere (McGuire, 1969a).

Aspects of Attitudes

There has been a long tradition of distinguishing among three aspects of attitudes, usually called cognitive, affective, and connative. The cognitive aspect refers to the intellectual content of the attitude such as might be measured by a checklist of traits to ascertain the person's stereotype of an ethnic group. The affective aspect refers to the emotional, evaluative component of the attitude, which could be measured by a rank ordering of various ethnic groups with respect to liking. The connative aspect involves the behavioral intentions in the attitude, frequently measured by a Bogardus-type social distance scale.

Since these three components usually covary very closely, the analysis, though of respectable age, is of questionable utility in a domain already cluttered with distinctions that do not make a difference. Katz (1960) has provided a useful discussion of some of the complexities in this tripartite analysis.

Components of Persuasive Communications

Teachers of communication have provided various analyses of the components involved in the process. Usually these components are put in the form of a set of questions such as those a good reporter is supposed to answer in describing a newsworthy incident: who? what? where? when? how? Perhaps the most elaborate analysis is Doob's (1961) discussion of twelve components, organized in a quartet of triads, involved in any communication situation.

The analysis most widely used by students of persuasion is a five-component analysis that goes back to Lasswell's (1948) interrogative formulation of the communication process as involving who says what to whom, via what medium, and with what effect. Translating these notions to a language of communication engineering, the five components become *source*, *message*, *channel*, *receiver*, and *destination*. We shall devote a major section of this chapter to each of these five components, reviewing in each section the persuasive impact of a variety of the independent variables involved in that aspect of communication.

Behavioral Steps in Persuasion

Just as it is convenient to analyze the communication side of the communication-persuasion process into separate classes of independent variables, it correspondingly makes the dependent-variable side more manageable if we single out the successive behavioral steps that constitute being persuaded. A convenient and commonsensical analysis divides the process into six states: being presented with the communication, attending to it, comprehending its content, yielding to it, retaining this new position, and acting on the basis of it.

Presentation

While being presented with the persuasive communication is a logically necessary first step, it is obviously not sufficient to guarantee effectiveness. And yet some students of the communication process do focus on this earliest of steps—for example, scholars and practitioners who carry out content analysis of what is presented on the various mass media.

Presupposing that what is presented is ipso facto effective is implied by the practice of ad agencies' billing their clients a percentage of the money they spend for media time and space, and also by attempts to determine whether TV entertainment programs are influencing viewers to violent behavior by doing a content analysis of the number of violent incidents presented over the various channels at various hours. (A finding that a high level of violent incidents is being presented would certainly be of interest, and enlightening in other respects as well, but without a consideration of the next five steps in the persuasion process, it would provide extremely weak evidence that the depictions were indeed inciting to violence.)

Attention

Given that the communication is presented to the receiver, the second question arises of whether the receiver pays attention to it. Common sense suggests that in order to be influenced by something the person must have attended to it (although believers in subception and the efficacy of subliminal presentation might feel that there are marginal cases in which the person can be persuaded by communications of which he was not aware).

The reasonable assumption that people will tend to be more influenced by communications of which they are aware than by those of which they are not aware has given rise to such procedures as advertisement recognition tests as a means of appraising the persuasive efficacy of a campaign. But this intermediate process is still rather far from payoff behavior in the persuasion process, so that while it provides a criterion that may be better than nothing, it remains a noisy criterion of communication effectiveness.

Comprehension

Message comprehension constitutes the third step in the persuasion process in the sense that, given the person's attention to the message, he is more likely to be influenced by it if he understands its content, particularly the conclusion being urged and the warrants put forth in support of that conclusion. It would seem obvious that the more the person comprehends a persuasive message the more he should tend to be influenced by it. Despite this obviousness, a large number of experiments have failed to supply adequate support for such a relationship (see Watts & McGuire, 1964; McGuire, 1968b).

It is possible that laboratory research has been investigating comprehension of the wrong aspects of the communication. Like the man who lost his wallet in the middle of the block but looked for it under the corner lamppost because the light was better there, laboratory researchers have usually tried to get a good quantitative measure of comprehension by giving a recall test which measures details and subtleties of the message rather than simply the conclusion and basic arguments.

It may be that attention to and comprehension of these details are not important (or are even counterproductive) to the comprehension of the main point of the message rather than being positively correlated with it. Along these lines, Janis and Terwilliger (1962) have suggested that fear-arousing communications do not affect the amount of message that is comprehended so much as they affect what part of the message is comprehended. For example, as a public health message becomes more anxiety-arousing by increasing stress on the dangers, the person comprehends better and better the nature of the threat, but at the expense of a poorer comprehension of the means being urged to avoid that threat.

Yielding

A fourth step in the persuasion process involves the extent to which the person yields to what is comprehended. Yielding is typically measured by administering to the person a self-report opinionnaire immediately after the communication and calculating his verbal agreement with the position being urged in the message (as compared with the level of agreement shown by a control, no-communication group or by the person himself prior to receipt of the communication). This step is so crucial in the persuasion process that laymen, and even some students of the topic, tend to identify the persuasion process with it. That is to say, in thinking about how a certain communication variable will affect its persuasive impact, we tend to oversimplify the process by thinking only of how this variable will affect the person's yielding.

Such an oversimplification can be misleading because variables that are positively related to yielding might well be negatively related to other steps in the persuasion process. For example, a subtle, disguised message might seem more conducive to yielding than would an obvious, blatant one; on the other hand, the latter might be more efficacious in achieving adequate message comprehension. Hence, blatant persuasive attempts might be more or less influential than subtle ones, depending upon whether message comprehension or yielding constitutes the major barrier to effectiveness in the given situation, a complexity often overlooked when one identifies being persuaded with yielding.

Retention

If one is interested in persuasive impact that lasts over any extended period of time, a fifth step must be considered, namely, retention of the immediate impact. A limitation of most laboratory research on attitude change is that it measures effect by means of an opinionnaire administered immediately after receipt of the persuasive communication. Insofar as retention is affected by the communication variables being studied, it is hazardous to generalize from such laboratory research to field situations where the attitudinal or behavioral change is of interest only some time after the message.

For example, if a variable in a TV commercial is shown to have a certain impact on intention to buy as immediately measured in a laboratory situation, this fifth step calls our attention to the necessity of investigating whether it will have a like effect at some subsequent occasion when the viewer is in a supermarket with the opportunity to act on such an intention. Lehmann (1970), for instance, in research on getting mothers in the maternity ward to return a month after their release for a postpartum examination, found that the type of message that was most effective with a given type of patient tended to reverse, depending on whether effectiveness was measured in terms of immediate intention to return or actually showing up for the examination one month later.

Overt Behavior

The final step in the persuasion process is actually carrying out the urged behavior. Through the fourth and fifth steps of yielding and retention, we were measuring immediate or delayed attitudinal impact, as measured by an appropriate opinionnaire. Such a verbal report is the criterion usually employed (for the sake of convenience) in laboratory, theory-testing research. But the communicator in the extralaboratory world feels somewhat uncomfortable with these verbal indices of message effectiveness. If he is trying to market a product or a political candidate, or is engaged in a public health campaign to urge people to obtain a cancer checkup or to stop smoking, or a public service campaign urging interracial brotherhood or contributions to medical research, then the communicator wants to design a campaign that not only gets the person to say he will do these things but actually gets him to do them.

Ultimately, the practical payoff of the communication campaign and the efficacy of the separate variables in the communication situation must be assessed in terms of their impact on this sixth payoff variable of actual behavior. It might, therefore, seem surprising that so much of the applied and theoretical research has assessed the communication variables only as far as the earlier steps.

As regards the theoretical work, it tends to be more convenient and equally as interesting theoretically to test the relationships of the independent variables to these earlier steps as to the later ones. As regards the applied research, it is much more efficient to assess the campaign in terms of these earlier steps, which are assumed to estimate adequately the effects on later ones; hence, it becomes a cost-effectiveness question whether the tradeoff between the greater economy of assessment only through the earlier steps is worth the diminution in validity as we focus on the earlier rather than the payoff steps.

Communication-Persuasion Matrix

An Organizing Framework

In the previous sections we singled out five classes of communication factors as our independent variables and six behavioral steps in being persuaded as the dependent variables. The two sets can be arrayed into a columns-versus-rows matrix (see Figure 1) to form a convenient framework

	Source	Message	Channel	Receiver	Destination
Presentation					
Attention					
Comprehension					
Yielding					
Retention					
Overt behavior					

Figure 1. Matrix of persuasive communication showing five classes of communication factors (independent variables) as column headings and six behavioral steps (dependent variables) as row headings.

for understanding the communication-persuasion process, organizing our knowledge about it, applying what is known to concrete situations, and identifying gaps in our knowledge.

In this matrix, the independent variables that would serve as the column headings include the five aspects of communication mentioned earlier, namely, source, message, channel, receiver, and destination. The dependent variables that would constitute the row headings would be behavioral steps in persuasion just reviewed, namely, presentation, attention, comprehension, yielding, retention, and overt behavior. When for theoretical or practical reasons we want to estimate the persuasive efficacy of a campaign or hypothesize the relation to persuasion impact of some communication variable, then we can analyze the communication aspects of the situation into the various column headings (and the subcolumn headings that we will consider subsequently in this chapter), and estimate how each of these communication aspects will affect each of the behavioral steps shown row by row. Such a column-by-row analysis makes the question more manageable and also calls our attention to aspects that might otherwise be overlooked.

Or if our specific task is not the critical one of evaluating an existing communication campaign but rather the creative one of designing a persuasive campaign, then once again this matrix analysis is useful. The column and subcolumn headings suggest to us the available options in designing the communication situation, and the six rows involving the behavioral steps provide a checklist for estimating the requirements and efficacy of these communication components, singly and in combination, as we build them up.

Situational-Weighting Considerations

Insightful use of this communication-persuasion matrix will reveal unexpected complexities in designing an effective persuasive campaign or in hypothesizing the persuasive impact of some particular communication variable. While complexities are distasteful to some, this situation can be looked at with enthusiasm rather than resignation, since a device that teases out unexpected complexities offers a royal road to valid creative insights. While the simpler representations offer commonsense rules of thumb, the more adequate depiction that reveals new complexities suggests also nonobvious principles, the discovery of which gives creative pleasure to the researcher and provides unexpected utility to the user.

One pervasive complexity revealed by this matrix analysis is that a communication factor that is conducive to persuasion via one of the behavioral steps (for example, comprehension) tends to be detrimental to it via another step (such as yielding). We have such a situation in the case of "fear appeals," where pointing out more vividly the dangers of noncompliance might increase yielding but decrease comprehension and retention of the relevant message content (McGuire, 1972). It also occurs with certain personality characteristics, like self-esteem, which are conducive to attitude change through increased attention and comprehension but are detrimental via increased yielding (McGuire, 1968b).

Another example is the effect of time passage on the persuasive impact of propaganda from a suspect source (Hovland & Weiss, 1951). In such situations where the communication variable is related to persuasive impact in opposite directions via two or more of the mediating steps, it can be shown (McGuire, 1968a) that under a wide range of conditions the overall relationship between that communication variable and persuasive impact will be nonmonotonic in the form of an inverted U. That is, there will be maximum persuasive impact at some intermediate level of the variable.

Knowing this general shape of the relationship is useful, but once the student of persuasion becomes facile in utilizing it, he begins to demand to know more about the precise parameters of the relationship. For example, at precisely what point does the inflection point that indicates the level of the communication variable at which maximum persuasion occurs fall? The present state of the art of scaling psychological variables does not allow an absolute answer to this question. However, one can with some analytic skill answer the question relativistically; that is, one can compare the level at which the maximum impact occurs in one situation with that in other situations. For example, if we learn empirically in a particular public health campaign the level of fear arousal that is optimal for getting the public to take adequate health measures in a given situation, we can then with some interpretative skill state in other situations whether a higher or lower level of fear arousal will be most efficacious. In general, one analyzes the situation to take into account how much of the variance in attitude-change impact will derive from each of the six mediating steps discussed above. Some examples of this procedure are found in McGuire (1972).

Thus, the use of this communication-persuasion matrix leads us to make complex hypotheses involving nonmonotonic relationships and higher order interactions. Such difficulties are not for those who demand their analyses neat, with rectilinear main effects. But those who know Sarnoff's law—to describe a pretzel-shaped reality one must have a pretzel-shaped theory—will recognize that to demand simplicity condemns one to an inadequate theory.

Persuasion and Education

The discussion of how the contribution of the various mediators to the ultimate persuasive impact varies from situation to situation throws some light on a distinction that should be considered before we proceed further. The distinction to which we refer can be denoted by a variety of polar terms, for example, information versus propaganda, knowledge versus belief, education versus persuasion. There is a value judgment connoted by these terms, the first member of each pair being positively evaluated and the second having a certain pejorative or, at best, neutral implication. It seems appropriate that we should mention at least briefly some of the distinctions between education and persuasion in the hopes of clarifying (although hardly resolving) the nature of the moral issues involved, and the extent to which communication factors relate differentially to educating and to persuasive impact.

Education and persuasion (or information and propaganda, and similar pairs of terms) clearly have something in common: both typically employ communications from one source to change the views of a target receiver. One distinction that is sometimes made is that education aims only at changing the person's beliefs (or "cognitions") while persuasion aims also at changing his feelings and dispositions to action. Others might deny the possibility of changing the one without the other but would perhaps recognize that there is a gradation in the extent to which a belief change necessarily involves a change in feeling or action. Another distinction in terms of target is to say that education aims at changing factual or verifiable beliefs while persuasion aims at changing beliefs about matters of taste or on unverifiable issues.

Still other distinctions are based on the source's motives. The term *education* may be reserved for situations in which the source is disinterested in the topic and does not stand to gain by the target's acceptance of the communication, and *persuasion* for situations where the source is prejudiced and stands to profit from the success of his communication. Or, we may use *persuasion* when the source has an intent to deceive and *education* where he has no such intent. Other distinctions would use still a different criterion having to do with one's judgment of the content of the communication. For example, it might be held that we are dealing with education when the person conveys correct information or uses only rational arguments, while we are dealing with persuasion when he uses incorrect or uncertain information and emotional arguments.

In teasing out and listing the above distinctions, we have been deliberately stressing the formulations that depict education as a benign process and persuasion as a rather unsavory one in order to make explicit some of the bases for such a value judgment. Perhaps in recent years the moral distinction has become less certain to many commentators for the melancholy reason that they are less inclined to see education as benign.

Without trying to resolve any of the basic issues involved, we must point out that most of these distinctions are conceptually orthogonal to one another. For example, one can urge either the true or the false (or what one regards as true or as false) by means of either rational or emotional arguments, for one's own gain or not, etc. Furthermore, on any one of these dimensions it should be recognized that there are many gradations between the two poles where a given communication might fall. It might be emotionally cathartic but intellectually stifling to visualize two polar-opposite types of communication, one involving disinterested sources communicating true information by use of rational arguments and the other involving prejudiced sources communicating untruths by means of emotional appeals.

Turning from cathartic but obscuring distinctions based on value judgments, we feel that the analysis of the matrix of persuasive communication discussed above suggests a distinction between *education* and *persuasion* that does justice to common usage and also differentiates in terms of generalizability of empirically determined relationships. *Education* is applied to situations in which most of the variance in ultimate impact of the communication is mediated by the attention and comprehension factors, while *persuasion* is used to refer to communication in which ultimate impact is determined mostly by the yielding mediator. To a lesser extent the final two steps in the behavioral chain can also be associated with the two labels in that, to the extent that the retention step is involved, we are dealing more with education, and to the extent that behavioral action is involved, we are dealing with persuasion. These last two steps are less tied in with the distinction than are the previous three, however.

Let us give some polar examples. On the one hand, a classroom lecture on the basic principles of thermodynamics by a physics instructor can be considered education in that the instructor's impact is primarily mediated by the audience's attention and comprehension of what he is saying, since in such a situation the audience would be inclined to accept pretty much all of what they understood. On the other hand, an advertising campaign based on repetition of a slogan would epitomize a persuasion situation, since nearly anyone approaching the normal-ability level can attend to and comprehend the brief repetitious message adequately; therefore, the extent to which a person is affected by the communication depends almost completely upon the extent to which he yields to it. Such a distinction becomes useful in that we can predict the relationship of some communication variable to impact in an educational as opposed to a persuasion situation by contrasting how that communication variable affects attention and comprehension with how it affects yielding.

General Theoretical Orientations

Because the topic of persuasion has attracted many researchers with diverse backgrounds and purposes, it is inevitable that a variety of theoretical orientations have guided the past and current work. This theoretical diversity obtains not simply for alternative hypotheses regarding specific relationships but even for basic theoretical points of departure. Our discussion so far, while for the most part definitional and noncontroversial, has been guided to some extent by one of the alternative theoretical orientations, namely, what we call the *information-processing paradigm.* We shall describe briefly this and four additional theoretical orientations, since they provide a useful framework for appreciating the significance of the empirical results that we shall be reviewing in the remainder of the chapter.

The Learning Paradigm

Some theorists, particularly psychologists who have interested themselves in the social-influence process after first being learning theorists, have treated persuasion largely as a learning process. Included here would be psychologists who range in time from Clark Hull, who in the 1930s described how suggestion obeyed the laws of learning, to the contemporary verbal conditioners who demonstrate that attitudes can be conditioned toward classes of stimuli by the usual laws of contiguity and reinforcement (Greenwald, Brock, & Ostrom, 1968).

It is particularly appropriate to mention this learning orientation immediately after a discussion of the similarities and differences between persuasion and education. The gist of this orientation is to predict that any communication variable will be related to attitude change as it is related to learning. Any communication factor that enhanced learning would tend to enhance attitude change.

Since the dependent-variable analysis discussed above indicates that attention, comprehension, and retention should all be positively related to ultimate persuasive impact, one can make considerable progress with this learning approach. However, this viewpoint tends to ignore the more dynamic mediating step of yielding, and the important role it plays in the persuasion process. If it is indeed valid that communication variables related in one direction to intellectual mediators such as comprehension tend to be related in the opposite direction to yielding, then we can expect that the learning approach will have to be supplemented by broader analyses that take into account the yielding mediator.

The Categorizing Paradigm

An alternative conceptualization of the persuasion process views man as a categorizer who enters into any communication situation with a set of preconceived categories (or "schema" or "stereotypes") and files away the information in the message as best he can among these categories (only to a very small extent changing his categorizing system). How he will respond to the attitude object will depend on where he fits the information into his preconceptions and what habitual responses he makes to these cognitive categories.

Proponents of this general orientation include social-judgment theorists such as Muzafer and Carolyn Sherif and those with a perceptual approach such as Asch. Unlike the learning theorists, who view attitude change as a matter of conditioning a new evaluative response to an old stimulus, these theorists view persuasion as involving a shifting of the person's perception of what stimulus he is evaluating.

On a general level, the two approaches seem different enough in that the learning approach stresses the response side and the categorizing approach the reception side of the process. But the differences are hard to operationalize in terms of contrasting predictions. Some experimenters who have grappled with the distinction have tried to ascertain to what extent persuasion involves reception processes as opposed to response processes, but the heuristic potential in the suggestive contrast between the two theories has not yet been exploited by the empirical researchers.

The Conflict-Resolving Paradigm

A third view of the persuasion process sees the person receiving the communication as a harassed honest broker, trying to find a reasonable resolution among many conflicting demands. He feels his attitude toward the object must take into account his own information, his self-interest, the demands of other people, and this new communication. In the end, he adjusts his attitude to keep from getting too far out of line with any one of these demands. The theorists have a rich body of suggestions regarding how the information is synthesized and how the different demands are weighted in one situation compared with another.

Many formulations fall within this consistency or integration approach, including Osgood's and Tannenbaum's (1968) congruity theory, Festinger's (1957) dissonance theory, McGuire's (1960) consistency theory, and Anderson's (1971) information-integration position. These approaches have been particularly popular during the past ten years, although presently the interest seems to be shifting slightly from a gross search for the critical variables involved to investigations of the microprocesses involved in the information integration.

The Functional Paradigm

A fourth conceptualization of the persuasion process views the person as confronting the communication with a less intellectual stance than assumed by the approaches we have been discussing so far. These functional theorists stress that man has many needs which his attitudes must gratify and for whose satisfaction persuasive communications can be used. These needs include intellectual ones, such as having one's attitude conform to one's information about the object, but it also includes nonrational components, such as needing to maintain one's self-esteem, the respect of one's loved ones, and repression of one's inadmissible drives.

Research drawing inspiration from this approach includes the work on the authoritarian personality by Adorno and his associates (1950) and the work by Katz (1960) and his students on an ego-defensive conceptualization of attitude change. Typical here is the idea that a person's attitude toward a racial minority might reflect, not his information about that group, but rather his needs to keep repressed his own unconscious problems about dealing with authority that derive from his early childhood experiences with his parents.

To the extent that such a conceptualization is valid, communications can best reduce prejudice not so much by providing new information about the targets of those attitudes but rather by enabling the individual to deal in other ways with his underlying personality problems. The functional approach offers a number of insights of a type often ignored by the other theories, but to date it has been somewhat neglected and its success has been rather indifferent where it has been used.

The Information-Processing Paradigm

The general approach to attitude-change research that guided our earlier discussion of the communication-persuasion matrix constitutes a fifth general orientation. It is not diametrically opposed to any of the other four any more than they are intrinsically contradictory to one another. This approach attempts to tease out exhaustively the logically necessary steps between being presented with a persuasive communication and ultimate compliance with its directives. It further analyzes as exhaustively as possible the components of the communication and considers how each of them will affect each of the behavioral steps into which the persuasion process has been analyzed.

This eclectic information-processing approach, which attempts to delineate the total system involved in a persuasion situation, underlies much of the work of the Yale group from Hovland, Janis, and Kelley (1953) to McGuire (1969a). It draws upon insights provided by the other approaches as well as new insights that arise from its own analysis. However, it neglects some of the suggestive aspects provided by the other approaches (such as the ego-defensive and the expressive values in attitudes which are emphasized by the functional theories), although this neglect may be an accident of the personality of the theorists rather than deriving from something intrinsic to the theory itself.

Since the information-processing approach underlies much of the discussion in this chapter, the reader should keep in mind that, while it is an extremely inclusive approach, it has tended to neglect certain insights offered by other approaches.

Scope of the Present Review

There is a very extensive literature on how variable after variable in a communication situation affects attitude change. Fairly thorough recent reviews are readily available (for example, Kiesler, Collins & Miller, 1969; McGuire, 1969a). Since our discussion must be highly compressed, it is essential that it be structured and selective. Structure is here provided by the matrix of persuasive communication presented in the previous section.

The basis for selectivity is more difficult and less obvious, so we should be explicit regarding our selective strategy. If we selected for discussion only those communication variables that contribute most to persuasive impact, we would be dealing with important variables but possibly ones so obvious that they hardly need mentioning. It could be argued, however, that the variables that are most pervasive are those that are least likely to be perceived, as epitomized in the expression that the fish will be the last to discover the ocean. Therefore, a detailed listing of even the obvious factors would serve as a useful checklist to assure that important variables will not be overlooked. At the opposite extreme, we might discuss only the subtle variable whose effects are unexpected, but these might play only a minor role in most situations.

Our selective strategy here will be to preserve some sense of proportion by mentioning the more powerful and obvious variables in the communication situation and pointing out their typical impacts on the various steps in the persuasion process; in addition, we shall avoid both oversimplification and belaboring the obvious by discussing the special circumstances in which the commonsense relationships are reversed. To cover the whole range of independent variables, we shall select examples from each of the five classes of communication variables, namely, source, message, channel, receiver, and destination.

SOURCE VARIABLES IN PERSUASION

In discussing how the source of the communication affects persuasive impact, we will focus on variables having to do with the perceived source of the communication, since differences in persuasive tactics among actual sources involve idiosyncratic considerations that do not yield very usable generalizations. The usually studied source variables can be grouped into three general subclasses on the basis of the target person's motivation for accepting the position being urged (Kelman, 1961).

One such motivational basis is the person's desire to be correct on a given issue; thus the source gains persuasive valence to the extent that he is credible (for example, is perceived as being expert and objective on the issue). A second motivation is the target person's desire to identify with or otherwise form an emotionally satisfying relationship with the source; so the source has impact insofar as he is attractive (for example, perceived by the target person as being similar to himself or likable). Or, third, the person may yield because he is anxious about the source's ability to reward or punish him; the source has such power insofar as he is perceived actually to control the receiver's reward and punishment, has concern about compliance, and can ascertain whether the target person has complied.

Since space is limited and the research on this third source—the power factor—has been less interesting than the work on the first two, we shall not pursue it here. Only the first two—source credibility and source attractiveness—will be discussed.

Source Credibility

The source's believability reflects the extent to which his message is perceived by the recipient as being correct and in accord with empirical evidence. Hence, it depends on the recipient's perception of the source as knowing what is correct and being motivated to communicate what he knows—or, more briefly, his perceived expertise and objectivity.

Perceived Expertise

In accord with commonsense expectation, it has generally been found that a message has greater persuasive impact to the extent that the source is perceived as expert, whether this expertise is specific to the issue or of a more general nature such as derives from appearing better educated or of a higher social status or professional occupation (Aronson & Golden, 1962). Moreover, others tend to pick up these general expertise cues even when the cues are fairly subtle; for example, jurors tend to be more influenced by their members whose occupations are on a higher socioeconomic class level (Strodtbeck, James, & Hawkins, 1958).

There is evidence (Hovland, Janis, & Kelley, 1953; Anderson, 1966) that these source-credibility factors affect attitude change via the yielding mediator rather than the attention and comprehension steps. While the source-credibility effect tends to show up in ultimate change, the source variables tend not to be manifested in detectable differences in the extent of learning of the message contents, at least not in a rectilinear way—although there is some suggestion that messages from unknown sources may be better learned than messages from sources known to be high or low in credibility (Bauer, 1965; McGuire, 1969a).

A qualification of the commonsense, positive relation between expertise and persuasive impact is the possibility that there might be such a thing as too much perceived expertise. For example, children tend to be influenced more by children somewhat older than themselves than by their age peers, but they are less influenced by those considerably older than by those a few years older (Stukát, 1958). Likewise, the "pratfall" experiments (Aronson, Willerman & Floyd, 1966; Helmreich, Aronson, & LeFan, 1970) suggest that a highly prestigious person actually becomes more attractive if he shows some human failing (which in a less prestigious person would cause his being rejected altogether).

These findings that a source who is a little bit superior to the recipient makes more of an impact than sources who are not superior at all or who are a great deal superior are in accord with social comparison theory (Festinger, 1954; Latané, 1966). This nonmonotonic relation between the source's expertise and his persuasive impact is also predicted by teasing out two alternate effects of source expertise: a tendency for people to be influenced by those who know more than themselves and a tendency to be influenced by those who are similar to themselves, with the usual proviso of everything else being equal. However, since most people do not perceive themselves as being expert on the usual communication topics, these two processes tend to go in opposite directions, with the more expert source gaining from his being perceived as having a greater fund of knowledge but losing from being perceived as very different from the recipient.

As mentioned in the previous section, when we have a situation where an independent variable (here, source expertise) and a dependent variable (such as persuasive impact) are related through the mediation of two underlying factors that go in opposite directions, then the overall relation between dependent and independent variables will tend to be nonmonotonic, with the maximum persuasive impact occurring at some intermediate level on the independent variable.

Perceived Objectivity at the Source

For maximum believability, the source must be perceived as not only knowing the truth but being objective enough to be motivated to tell it as he sees it. In keeping with this commonsense expectation, there is a considerable empirical literature demonstrating that sources are more persuasive when they are perceived as being disinterested, that is, not standing to profit from the recipient's agreement (Hovland & Mandell, 1952); when they are perceived in advance as having some intention other than to persuade the audience (Freedman & Sears, 1965); or when they are perceived as not even knowing that they are being overheard (Walster & Festinger, 1962). All of these sets of results support the widely held assumption that "white" propaganda is more effective than "black" propaganda, or that favorable material introduced as "news" by a public relations expert is more influential than advertisements clearly labeled as such.

But while there is support for the commonsense notion that communications sometimes gain in impact if their persuasive intent is disguised, there are a number of circumstances under which precisely the opposite can occur. For example, where the recipient wishes to ingratiate himself with a powerful person (Jones, 1964) or with a beautiful woman (Mills & Aronson, 1965), then such a source is more effective to the extent that the persuasive intent is obvious. Also, to the extent that the audience or the subject is responding to the "demand character" (Orne, 1969), then the more blatant attempt to persuade will be more influential.

McGuire (1969b) has described a wide variety of circumstances under which blatant attempts to persuade are more effective in producing opinion change than are disguised communications. In general, the commonsense belief that disguised communications are more persuasive focuses unduly on the mediational step of yielding; when one considers also that adequate comprehension of the message is also necessary if it is to have a persuasive impact, then one sees that a clear and blatant attempt to persuade gains somewhat in impact, since the prior warning of the purpose of the communication provides the recipient with an intellectual set that allows him to better understand its contents.

Source Attractiveness

A source has valence for producing attitude change through the attraction mechanism insofar as the recipient perceives the source in a way that would make sharing an opinion with him gratifying. For example, the source might be so liked or admired that the recipient would receive gratification from identifying with him through shared beliefs. Or the source might be perceived as so familiar or so similar to the recipient that the latter would assume identity of interests that would motivate him to take the same position as advocated by the source. Here again we shall review the validity and the limitations of such commonsense expectations about source valence.

Likableness of the Source

The balance theories that have been so influential in the attitude-change area during the past ten years (Abelson et al., 1968) have as one of their underlying assumptions the principle that people tend to agree with those whom they like. According to Heider's (1946; 1958) classical formulation, if one person likes another and he learns that that other person likes or dislikes a certain object, he himself will tend to like or dislike that object. There is a fairly extensive literature showing that people tend to agree with those whom they like, although the causal direction of the relation is often ambiguous.

Perhaps even more interesting are the exceptional conditions in which people are most influenced by those whom they dislike. One well-known case is the dissonance theory formulation (Brehm & Cohen, 1962; Zimbardo et al., 1965) that people require some justification for their behavior. If, at the urging of a source, a person complies in some counterattitudinal behavior, then he is most likely to change his opinion toward that urged to the extent that he dislikes the source. Behind this formulation is the dissonance theory notion that our behavior must seem justified to us. Hence, if we carry out the orders of a likable person, we can say we did it because we liked him without changing our opinions to justify the behavior; but if we complied even though we disliked the man who ordered it, then there is more pressure to justify or explain the behavior by changing our attitude so that we can attribute our behavior to our own attitude. There is some evidence, for example, that military personnel who are ordered to eat disliked foods change their attitude in a direction favorable to the food to the extent that the order is given by a disliked person (Smith, 1961), even when one controls for the amount of compliance (Zimbardo et al., 1965).

Another such reversal is suggested by the finding that people are more influenced by praise from a stranger than from a friend. For example, children's behavior is more influenced if they are praised by a stranger than if the praise comes from a familiar person or a parent (Gewirtz & Baer, 1958). Aronson and Linder (1965) suggest that this finding is peculiar to praise and can be interpreted in terms of a gain-loss notion, such that praise from one's mother is ineffective because it is expected, while praise from a stranger has more impact because it is a gain over what one would routinely expect.

Source Similarity

A relationship that has been frequently demonstrated by Byrne (1969) and his students is that the recipient likes a source to the extent that he perceives the source as being similar to himself. Ideological similarity, particularly, is even more important than demographic similarity (Rokeach, 1960; Stein, Hardyck, & Smith, 1965). It appears that there is a strong tendency for people to like others to the extent that they perceive the others as sharing their beliefs and, by extension, it would seem a very effective source tactic to use Burke's (1962) "strategy of identification," whereby the source shows the recipient that their interests are similar.

One possible limitation on this obvious relationship has already been adverted to when we discussed source expertise. Most people are not expert on the topic of communication usually studied; hence, for the source to be seen as similar to the receiver, his perceived expertise must suffer somewhat. As we mentioned earlier, the resultant of these two opposed tendencies would be for a nonmonotonic relationship, such that a person would be most influenced by those slightly superior to himself but not too much superior. To paraphrase Groucho Marx's comment that he would not want to belong to a club that would let a person like him in, the average person usually may not care to listen to a source who knows no more about the topic than he himself does.

MESSAGE VARIABLES IN PERSUASION

More laboratory research on persuasion has probably been done on message factors than on any other class of communication variables. Here we can only indicate the range of this research and select for fuller discussion a few variables of particular interest. We shall deal with three classes of message variables in turn, namely, message content, inclusions and omissions in the message, and the organization of the inclusions.

Content Variables

A heterogeneous class of variables is included under message content, some of them questions of style, such as emphatic presentation or use of metaphor or humor, although most research has been on the type of motivational appeal used in the message. We shall discuss briefly some of the work on style and on appeals.

Stylistic Variables

A fair amount of research has been done on speaking skill as it relates to persuasive impact. The general indication is that such infelicities as faulty grammar, poor organization, and pauses indicative of nonfluency are accurately perceived by the audience and produce a poorer rating of the speaker. They do not, however, reduce the persuasive impact of the speech (Addington, 1965), although Bettinghaus (1961) reports a case in which rated delivery effectiveness does relate to the attitude-change impact.

Researchers in the speech area who have studied whether dynamic versus subdued style of delivery has any differential effect have generally found that the differential impact tends to be rather slight, although there is some suggestion that the use of metaphorical as opposed to literal expressions may enhance persuasive impact (Bowers, 1964; Bowers & Osborn, 1966). The use of humor in speech has received some theoretical discussion but little empirical research, which is surprising in view of the widespread tendency to begin a talk with humor and interlard it with humorous comments wherever possible. It might well be that humor enhances attention to the speech but deters comprehension, while facilitating yielding by putting the recipient in a more accepting mood. However, these conjectures remain to be investigated empirically.

Appeals

At least since Aristotle's monographs on *Rhetoric* there has been an interest in the type of appeal made in persuasive messages. His tripartite analysis of ethos, pathos, and logos, on the basis of whether the appeal is to the hearer's moral principles, his emotions, or his intellect, underlies much of the work. There has been a body of research on the use of emotional versus rational appeals, of appeals to self-interest versus appeals to justice, and the like, but the definitions of such independent variables tend to be so idiosyncratic to the conditions of each study that generalizations are difficult. The state of the art is such that typologies are useful in suggesting the alternative options that are available for message appeals even though we are unable at this point to judge their relative effectiveness in various communication situations.

The functional theorists (whose general approach will be discussed later in the chapter) have illuminated the appeals question through their analysis that a person's attitude toward an object is a composite of his perception of how the object facilitates attainment of various goals and how highly he evaluates those goals. Research remains to be done on appeals based on different goals; however, Carlson (1956) found that attitudes can be changed more effectively by communications aimed at perceived instrumentality to goals already held than by changing the attractiveness of goals to which the object is already perceived as being instrumental. Other functional theorists have found that, in the long run at least, attitudes can be changed by manipulating the underlying motivation that is served by the attitude (Katz, 1960).

A great deal of attitude-change research

has investigated how the level of threat used in a persuasive message affects its impact. There are readily available general theoretical treatments of this fear-appeals variable (Janis, 1967). Its application to advertising (McGuire, n.d.) and to public health (Leventhal, 1970) have also been studied. As empirical work has continued, it has revealed increasingly the complexities in this variable's mode of operation. Higher fear arousal should increase yielding by showing that noncompliance will have dire consequences. For example, to the extent that the dangers of cancer or of cigarette smoking are stressed in the communication, the more effective it should be in inducing the person to get an examination for cancer or to cease smoking. On the other hand, fear arousal might be detrimental to other steps in persuasion, such as comprehension and retention. For example, high levels of fear arousal might make the hearer so anxious that his comprehension of the recommendations would be interfered with or he would repress the whole topic.

Discovering that a variable operates complexly is discouraging because it indicates the answer will not be a simple one, but is encouraging because complexities can serve as creative tools for generating hypotheses about interaction effects. Some progress has been made along these lines, but it must be admitted that complexity appears to develop upon complexity. For example, the two-factor analysis (McGuire, 1968b) suggests that there is a nonmonotonic relationship such that some intermediate level of anxiety is more efficacious for persuasion than no anxiety arousal or very high anxiety arousal. It further predicts that the level of anxiety arousal that is most efficacious goes down as message complexity increases and as the person's chronic anxiety level goes up. Partial support for such a contention was found by Millman (1968), but Lehmann (1970) and Leventhal (1970) suggest that there is a still higher order interaction with the person's self-esteem.

Inclusions and Omissions

Research has been done on the persuasive effectiveness of including certain materials within the message versus leaving them out. For example, is it better to ignore opposition arguments or to refute them? Should one draw the conclusion explicitly for the reader or leave it to him to draw? Should one make the point only once or repeat it again and again? We shall review briefly the results on each of these three questions.

Treatment of Opposition Arguments

Ever since research coming out of World War II (Hovland, Lumsdaine, & Sheffield, 1949) showed that neither ignoring opposition arguments nor explicitly refuting them has greater efficacy under all conditions, more refined questions have been asked about the conditions under which one or the other tactic is the more efficacious. In general, it seems that mentioning and refuting the opposition arguments is better than ignoring them when the audience is initially hostile to one's view or is highly intelligent. Apparently, one should also refute rather than ignore the opposition arguments when the audience would be expected to know of them in any case. Also, refuting the opposition arguments is more efficacious than ignoring them when we are dealing not with the direct persuasive impact of the communication but rather with the extent to which it confers resistance to subsequent countercommunications (Lumsdaine & Janis, 1953; McGuire, 1964).

Implicit Versus Explicit Conclusions

Is it more effective to draw the conclusion explicitly within the communication or leave it to the receiver to draw for himself? The former strategy should enhance message clarity and assure that the point will be adequately comprehended. However, leaving the conclusion unstated but so obvious that it can be drawn by the receiver himself should augment yielding; that is, by giving the receiver the opportunity for active participation, he comes to regard the conclusion as his own rather than something externally imposed by the source.

This latter mechanism was considered more effective by earlier workers whose thinking was influenced by learning research, which indicated that active participation is more efficacious than passive reading for adding material permanently to the person's cognitive repertory, and by the psychotherapeutic assumption that the patient is more influenced by nondirective therapy that requires him to participate actively in drawing the conclusion regarding the nature of his problems. It has been shown in persuasive communication, however, that drawing the conclusion explicitly within the message is more efficacious than leaving it for the audience to draw (Hovland & Mandel, 1952; McGuire, 1964). If the belief that nondirective therapy is more efficacious than directive is valid, then the results of participation seem to be reversed for persuasive-communication situations compared with therapeutic ones. Perhaps the recipient of persuasive communications tends to be much less motivated to draw the communicator's conclusion than is the patient taking part in psychotherapy.

Repetition of the Persuasive Message

That repetition adds to persuasive impact has been demonstrated in research ranging from the Peterson and Thurstone (1933) field study, which demonstrated that several commercial films that do not produce a detectable effect singly do so in combination, to the rather abstract laboratory studies on verbal conditioning that showed that compliance increases with repetition (Staats, 1968). The effectiveness of repetitive advertising in newspapers was subjected to an unusually thorough study by Stewart (1964).

In general, the most impressive finding of the research on repetition in attitude change is not that repetition has some effect but that it has so little. An increase in impact usually appears for one or two repetitions but quickly reaches an asymptote beyond which further repetitions have little effect. It may be that with a captive audience comprehension is quickly maximized by the first several repetitions, so there is nothing more to be learned through further repetition. However, when one considers the initial step in the chain of behaviors leading to persuasion, namely, being presented with the message in the first place, then repetition may well be efficacious up to a high level when one has a changing audience. In this case, while the effect of repetition on a given listener soon reaches its asymptote, repetitions at different times expose successive samples of listeners to the message.

Organization of Message Content

Given that several elements are to be included within the persuasive message, the question inevitably arises as to how they are to be ordered. For example, we noted the efficacy of including a mentioned repetition of the opposition argument and the explicit mention of the conclusion. In terms of the inclusions discussed in the previous section, if we are going to refute the opposition arguments, should they be refuted before or after we present our own arguments; and if we are to draw the conclusion explicitly, should it be presented at the outset or at the end of the message?

Research has been done on these and other ordering questions (such as whether, when one has a number of arguments that vary in strength, one should use the strongest arguments first or save them for last, or whether one should begin or end with the most desirable part of one's message). But we shall confine our discussion to two illustrative organizational variables, namely, ordering the material with respect to desirability and the primacy-recency question.

Ordering Contents for Desirability

Frequently a communicator has to deal with a number of topics within the single message, advocating a certain position on each; for example, when he is reviewing a year's varied activities, or proposing a multifaceted program. Questions arise as to how these topics should be ordered with respect to a number of variables, one of which is the relative desirabilities of the positions that he is urging on the several issues.

McGuire (1957) has shown that there is greater total agreement over the whole range of issues if the desirable ones come first. With this sequence, the early contents reward and habituate the person for attending to the contents, while the undesirable-desirable sequence tends to punish paying attention at the outset, so that by the time the desirable content is presented the audience may no longer be attending.

It has been suggested that when the stands differ in the extent to which they agree with the audience's initial positions, it is analogously more efficacious to present the agreeable stands first followed by the disagreeable ones, rather than using a disagreeable-agreeable order. However, empirical work remains to be done on this question of ordering the topics with respect to the initial agreeableness of the stands taken, and there is some reason to question the analogy. The agreeable-disagreeable order may provide initial practice to the audience in agreeing with the speaker, but the critical question is whether that initial practice is rewarding or punishing. If the audience is agreeing with desirable positions, they are getting rewarded and the habit of paying attention is strengthened; but if they are agreeing with undesirable realities, then their agreement responses are being punished and should tend to extinguish.

The Primacy-Recency Question

The most heavily researched order variable has to do with the question of which side, the first or the last, has the advantage in a debate between advocates of opposite positions. There is some reason for expecting a "law of primacy" such that if a given presentation comes before the opposition it is more efficacious than if it is presented after. In learning the message contents, there tends to be a primacy effect in that the earlier part of a list of items tends to be better learned than the later part (although the full serial-position curve indicates that the overall relationship between the order of presentation and amount of learning is U-shaped, with the material just past the middle being the poorest learned). Also, there tends to be a "set" effect: that is, one's initial impression tends to cause an assimilation error in how one perceives subsequent information.

On the other hand, there is a reason to expect a "law of recency" such that the last material, still fresh in the person's mind through its recency, should be most effective. Regarding the retention step in the persuasion process, the second side has the advantage since recall of the message contents tends to decline progressively with the passage of time. Also, linear-operator models (Rosenberg, 1968), which assume that the amount of change produced is a monotonic-increasing function of the amount of change urged, yield the prediction that the second side will be more effective in the yielding step also.

In view of this diametrically opposed set of considerations, it is not surprising that the two earliest studies in the area came up with opposite indications: Lund (1925) reported a primacy effect while Cromwell (1950) reported, if anything, a recency effect. Subsequent research (Hovland et al., 1957) furnishes ample evidence that either effect can occur, depending on other aspects of the communication situation.

One of the most promising notions is Miller and Campbell's (1959) hypothesis that timing is the critical factor: When there is a considerable interval between the presentation of the first and second sides, a recency effect should tend to occur, while an interval between the presentation of the second side and the ultimate measure of persuasive impact should tend to produce a primacy effect. There has been some empirical support for this theoretical derivation, although the picture is not as clear as one would like (Wilson & Miller, 1968).

This primacy-recency question, while it has not been neglected, should probably be receiving more experimental attention than it has because it is rich in both theoretical implications and practical significance. It is a crucial question in any kind of formal or informal debate and also in American trial procedures, where the prosecution case is always presented to the jury first (on the principle that a man is innocent until proven guilty), so that the prosecution gains by the "law of primacy" and loses by the "law of recency." Under what conditions these considerations are important and how and whether they should be equalized are points that should be given consideration once the empirical basis for the discussion is adequate.

CHANNEL FACTORS

We started out with a neo-Lasswellian analysis of the communication processes, a matter of "who says what, via what channel, to whom and with what effect," or, as we rephrased the interrogatives: source, message, channel, receiver, destination. The previous two sections were devoted to source variables and to message variables; here we appropriately turn to channel variables. Since a number of chapters in this handbook are either explicitly or implicitly devoted to an analysis of the separate media or channels, we shall abridge our comments to leave room for a discussion of persuasive impacts of communications aspects not so fully covered in other chapters.

We shall simply mention some of the questions that have received research attention in connection with channel factors in persuasion. Most basic is the question of the relative roles in determining attitudes of direct experience with the object compared with indirect contact via communication about it. Where the attitude does derive from communication about the object, there are questions of the sensory modality of presentation. To what extent is pictorial presentation better or worse than verbal accounts in eliciting attention, comprehension, yielding, and the other steps in the persuasion process? And given verbal presentation, is the written or the spoken word more effective?

All of these questions have important practical implications and so have received some empirical research (see McGuire, 1969a; Weiss, 1969); however, they tend to be somewhat sparse in theoretical interest and so have been somewhat neglected. Since there seems currently to be a swing back to emphasis on practical rather than theoretical relevance, there will probably be a resurgence of research on these channel factors.

RECEIVER VARIABLES IN PERSUASION

The class of communication variables to which we turn here includes those having to do with characteristics of the person at whom the communication is directed. What kinds of people tend to be more persuasible and in what state is a given individual most persuasible? Traditional variables studied here include how personal characteristics of the receiver correlate with persuasibility, how persuasive impact is affected by the extent to which the recipient is initially opposed to the position being advocated, and the extent to which the receiver actively participates in the communication process.

Here, again, the amount of research is vast and has been reviewed elsewhere (McGuire, 1968a; 1969a), so we shall select only a couple of receiver variables on which research has been particularly revealing. We shall discuss personality correlates of persuasibility and the effect of discrepancy between the receiver's initial opposition and the position urged in the message.

Individual Differences

Many individual-difference correlates of persuasibility have been investigated, including demographic characteristics, ability levels, and personality traits. We shall not attempt to summarize here all of the findings but merely mention some of the more significant ones, and then discuss some underlying principles to explain these obtained relationships.

Demographic Characteristics

The two most frequently investigated demographic characteristics are age and sex. There appears to be a rapid rise in persuasibility from infancy to the age of five or six, presumably reflecting greater motivation and ability for attention and comprehension of persuasive messages. After the age of six there might be a slight decline until adolescence, at which time the curve levels off until senility once again causes a decline through lessened exposure, attention, and comprehension. Parametric studies have actually not been done along the entire age range under a given set of conditions, but the above generalization can be made by piecing together the results of separate studies.

Where a difference in persuasibility is found between the sexes, women tend to be more persuasible than men. A second-order sex difference is the finding, reported in several studies, that personality characteristics are more predictive of persuasibility in men than in women (Hovland & Janis, 1959; McGuire, 1968a). Some research has been done on the relationship to persuasibility of such demographic characteristics as race, socioeconomic class, and religion without any sizable relationships being uncovered. Even where they are found, demographic relationships to persuasibility lend themselves to many interpretations.

Ability Factors

The two ability factors that have been most studied in relation to persuasibility are intelligence and mental health. Various indices of intelligence (such as chronological age, mental age, and years of schooling) have been investigated for their relation to persuasibility, usually with the expectation that the more intelligent the person is, the more resistant to persuasion he will be. While such a negative relationship between intelligence and persuasibility has sometimes been reported, there are perhaps as many studies in which a positive correlation has been found.

It has been suggested that the reason for these mixed and sometimes surprising results is that intelligence makes a person more susceptible to persuasion through the increased attention and comprehension it allows, while it reduces persuasibility via increased resistance to yielding (McGuire, 1968a). As a result, one can expect an overall nonmonotonic relationship of the inverted-U family such that people of moderate intelligence are more persuasible than persons of extremely high or low intelligence, with the level of intelligence at which maximum persuasibility occurs going up as the complexity of the communication situation increases.

The same mediating processes have to be considered in understanding how mental health is related to persuasibility. While the mentally ill tend to have low self-confidence and therefore are prone to yielding, mental illness is also characterized by a withdrawal tendency that interferes with attention to and comprehension of persuasive messages, thus affording protection from social influence. Schizophrenics, for example, are notoriously resistant to social influence even in the obvious repetitive form of suggestion or hypnosis. Their withdrawal symptoms seem to protect the severely mentally ill from persuasion through poor reception even more than their low self-image makes them vulnerable to yielding.

Personality Characteristics

Personality characteristics have been studied as correlates of persuasibility even more than demographic or ability factors. The vast body of results on how such variables as self-esteem and anxiety relate to susceptibility to social influence constitute a very confusing picture. The most comprehensive theory that has attempted both to account for these varied results and to provide a creative tool for new predictions is that developed by McGuire (1968a; 1968b), which derives hypotheses (such as the one that most personality characteristics will have an inverted-U-shaped relationship to persuasibility) from five general assumptions that we shall consider in the next section.

Underlying Principles

McGuire's (1968a) theory of personality-persuasibility relationships is based on five postulates, some of which were mentioned earlier. First, it is assumed that the receiver's personality characteristics, like other aspects of the communication situation, affect attitude and behavioral change via each of the six mediators discussed above (see Fig. 1, page 223). Hence, if we are dealing with a variable such as self-esteem, we have to consider its likely relationship to attention and comprehension and not just to yielding, as is sometimes done.

The second principle involves a "compensation" tendency such that a personality variable that makes a person more susceptible via some of the mediating steps tends to protect him via others. For example, anxiety tends to make the person more persuasion prone through increased yielding but less susceptible through depressed attention and comprehension. Discussion of the empirical and theoretical justifications of such an assumption can be found elsewhere (McGuire, 1968a).

The third "situational-weighting" principle states that the relationship of a given personality variable to persuasibility will depend on how widely the different mediating steps can vary in the given situation. For example, if a persuasive communication is extremely simple and repetitious (as in hypnotic induction), then the normal range of the population will show very little variation in attention and comprehension since everyone will totally comprehend the message; hence, the personality characteristic will be related to persuasive impact via other mediators such as yielding. On the other hand, when the communication is fairly complex, so that there will be a considerable range of attention and comprehension to what it says, then the personality variable's relationship to these reception steps will loom large in determining its persuasive impact.

A fourth postulate of the theory is that most chronic personality traits are embedded in a syndrome of other personality characteristics that facilitate the individual's coping with the opportunities and weaknesses afforded by that trait. For example, the highly anxious person, because he would tend to lack resistance to social influence, will tend to learn social withdrawal tendencies so that he will avoid exposure to influence attempts. This assumption that chronic personality traits become embedded in compensatory tendencies means that the relationship of a chronic variable (such as a person's persisting level of self-esteem) will tend to relate to persuasibility in ways rather different from his acute level on this trait due to some momentary factor (such as an experimental manipulation of his success or failure). For this reason, certain systematic differences will be expected on how a given personality variable will relate to persuasibility, depending on whether we are talking about its chronic or acute level.

The final principle that must be kept in mind is that these personality characteristics interact with other aspects of the communication situation in deciding impact on persuasibility. We have already seen that the recipient's intelligence interacts with refuting versus ignoring the opposition arguments in determining persuasion impact, and that sex moderates the relationship between personality characteristics and persuasibility (the relationship being more sizable in males than females). Putting together these five principles has allowed "saving the appearances" of or accounting for a sizable portion of the complex findings in this area. It has also led to the prediction of new relationships, although with a rather modest ratio of empirical confirmation (McGuire, 1968a; 1968b; Lehmann, 1970; Zellner, 1970).

Source-Receiver Discrepancy

A different type of receiver variable is the extent to which the receiver is initially opposed to the position being urged in the message. From the source's point of view, the problem is to determine how far to urge the recipient to change in order to produce maximum change. If only a slight change is advocated, then even complete success would produce only a slight change; on the other hand, if a vast change is advocated, the recipient may reject the whole communication as absurd. The question of the most efficacious discrepancy size can be understood in terms of the underlying processes that we have been discussing in this chapter.

Selective Perception

Many communication theorists have argued that people love redundancy and like to expose themselves to arguments with which they already agree and try to avoid information discrepant with their initial impressions. In his early review of the communication field, Klapper (1949) stated that a selective-exposure, selective-avoidance tendency was the most basic process established by research on the effects of the mass media. A closer look at the evidence suggests that the selective-avoidance tendency is the most excessive extrapolation beyond the data so far offered by communication theorists.

In retrospect, it is somewhat surprising that so many communication theorists could have imagined that people would have survived on this earth for a period that even the most conservative estimates put at greater than six-thousand years if they operated on this redundancy principle, strenuously avoiding any disconfirmation of their beliefs and any opportunity to learn anything new or to correct their mistakes. While there may be a selective-avoidance tendency, there seems to be an equal or greater opposite tendency to seek out surprising and discrepant information (McGuire, 1968c; Mills, 1968; Sears, 1968).

Discrepancy and Attitude Change

Muzafer Sherif and Hovland (1961), and Carolyn Sherif, Muzafer Sherif, and Nebergall (1965) have developed an assimilation-contrast theory that postulates that people include within their latitude of acceptance a range of opinions on any one issue; this acceptance band is surrounded on either side by a borderline indecisive zone beyond which extends regions of rejection. As the individual becomes more involved in the issue, these rejection regions tend to grow into the indifference zones.

In general, when a persuasive message falls within the latitude of acceptance, there tends to be an assimilation error; that is, the recipient perceives the message as closer to his own position than it actually is and he tends also to move his position toward it. When the communication supports a position that falls in his latitudes of rejection, then a contrast effect occurs; the receiver perceives the message as lying farther away from his own position than it actually is and may move his own position still farther so that the message will have a boomerang effect on his opinion.

There is some evidence from laboratory and field that supports this social judgment approach, although the evidence on contrast effects is indecisive.

In general, over fairly wide ranges of discrepancy, the obtained change is a positive function of the amount of change advocated (Fisher & Lubin, 1958; Whittaker, 1964; Singer, 1965). However, the proportionate change tends to go down with discrepancy; that is, the more change urged in the communication, the greater the change obtained, although the obtained change becomes a progressively smaller percentage of the urged change. There may be turndown at extremely wide discrepancies (Fisher & Lubin, 1958; Bergin, 1962), at least under certain conditions such as low-credibility sources; however, the extent to which amount of persuasion goes up with more extreme claims is more impressive than the occasional finding that beyond a certain point extremely discrepant changes tend to be counterproductive.

DESTINATION VARIABLES IN PERSUASION

Destination variables have to do with the specific target at which the message is directed, including the type of issue (for example, whether it deals with a political issue, a health practice, a purchasing decision, or whatever), and the kind of response urged (for example, whether the communication is designed to generate consciousness of a product, a favorable attitude toward it, or actual purchase). As two illustrative destination variables, we shall review the research on temporal factors in attitude change, particularly long-term versus short-term effects, and research on inducing resistance to persuasion as opposed to producing attitude change. We select these two variables because they have been most thoroughly researched among the destination factors, and because the findings have both practical implications and general theoretical relevance.

Temporal Effects of Persuasive Communications

Insofar as the retention step is an important one in persuasion, there would be a steady decay of the induced attitude change as time passed after receipt of the communication. There is empirical evidence for such decay; also, the peculiarity has emerged that under many circumstances persuasive communications have a delayed-action effect. We shall discuss briefly the circumstances of both the temporal decay and the delayed-action effects.

Temporal Decay of Induced Attitude Change

One of the earliest studies on the persistence of induced persuasion is the Peterson and Thurstone (1933) study of the permanence of the ideological change produced by commercial films. They found a tremendous range of results—from no persistence to complete persistence after the passage of months. Subsequent research, summarized briefly by Watts and McGuire (1964), has yielded equally varied results.

If one were forced to make a single generalization to summarize the results, one could (with fear and trembling) conclude that there is a negatively accelerated decay curve for induced opinion change similar to the shape of the retention curve for recall of message contents. The onset of this decay curve would probably be some time after the message was presented, however, with an initial increase in impact (somewhat analogous to the reminiscence phenomenon in learning) for a short time after presentation of the message. The decay portion of this curve could take the form of any of a wide family of curves, and the parameters would vary with the conditions of the communication situation. As illustrative of the variety, the half-life of this negatively accelerated decay curve (that is, how long it takes for half of the initially induced change to decay) was found by Hall (1938) to be about six months, while under the conditions of the Watts-McGuire (1964) experiment it was somewhat under six weeks, and in the McGuire (1957) study it was about one week.

This variation in the rate of decay with circumstances is to be expected: if the persistence of attitude-change impact depends on retention of the convincing material in the message, then characteristics that affect the rate of forgetting would also affect the decay of persuasive impact. One would expect, for example, more rapid decay of impact in less intelligent receivers, with more complicated messages, and with the presentation of confusing materials in the interim.

This analysis is based on the assumption that retention of message content is essential for persistence of induced attitude change. However, the obtained relationship even between initial learning of message contents and initial persuasive impact tends to be surprisingly small. McGuire (1957) found a corelation of +0.53 and Janis and Rife (1959) found one of +0.21 between immediate recall and immediate attitude change, but many studies have found trivial or even, under certain conditions, negative relationships (Miller & Campbell, 1959). Even were it necessary initially to comprehend the message content to be persuaded by it, once the change is induced it might become functionally autonomous of continued retention of message content. Like the throw switch in an electric circuit, some pressure is needed to switch it on; then it stays on until counterpressure is exerted, throwing it back again. Watts and McGuire (1964) found evidence for functional autonomy of recall of some aspects of the communication, although more typically the decay of attitude change paralleled that of forgetting of the contents.

Delayed-Action Effects

The most interesting finding regarding time passage in attitude change is that under a striking variety of conditions a persuasive communication tends to produce delayed-action effects; that is, more persuasion is shown some time after receipt of the communication than immediately after. This phenomenon was first reported in the World War II research of Hovland, Lumsdaine, and Sheffield (1949), who suggested a variety of circumstances that might produce such delayed-action effects. Subsequent work by Hovland and Weiss (1951) demonstrated the discounting-cue case, where the message has a delayed-action effect if initially presented with some cue that leads the receiver to discount it (for example, if it is initially attributed to a suspect source, or is labeled as propaganda or as untrue).

Delayed-action effects have also been shown with complex and qualified communications, particularly in some types of receivers (Cohen, 1957; Stotland, Katz, & Patchen, 1959; McGuire, 1960; Papageorgis, 1963). In general, a delayed-action effect is likely where a "sinking-in" period is needed or where the recipient must overlook some questionable element initially perceived in the communication before its full persuasive impact can be felt.

Immunization Against Persuasion

While most persuasion research has focused on how attitude change can be enhanced, a few researchers have studied how people can be pretreated to make them resistant to persuasion (McGuire, 1964; Kiesler, 1971). Immunization against persuasion is not the reverse of persuasion, wherein characteristics that make a communication more persuasive are reversed to reduce its persuasive impact. Rather, immunization deals with positive pretreatments that can make the person more resistant to a given persuasive communication of whatever strength. We shall discuss briefly in this section five types of approaches made to this problem of producing resistance to persuasion.

The Commitment Approach

One general approach to inducing resistance to persuasion is to commit the person in some manner to his initial view before he is exposed to the persuasive communication. One effective technique is to have the person publicly express his belief prior to exposure. Even a private decision, where the individual reviews his belief in his own mind without expressing it publicly, is effective in conferring resistance (Bennett-Pelz, 1955).

A more serious kind of commitment is to have the person act publicly on the basis of his belief. There is some evidence that the more active the person's rehearsal of his belief and the less pressure put upon him to elicit this rehearsal, the stronger will be the committing effect and the greater the resistance to countercommunications. A fuller discussion of the commitment approach can be found in Kiesler (1971).

Anchoring Approach

Another class of immunization techniques involves linking the belief to other aspects of the person's cognitive domain. For example, his belief can be linked in advance to the ideologies of admired others, either by telling him of their endorsement or by making an already known endorsement more salient in the receiver's mind. The anchoring tactic has also been used in linking the belief to the person's accepted values, showing that it is conducive to states of affairs that he likes (Carlson, 1956; Nelson, 1968; Holt, 1970). Another type of linkage is to tie the given belief into other beliefs in the person's ideology so that it is brought home to him that any change on the given belief would require other cognitive adjustments as well (McGuire, 1960).

Conditioned Avoidance

A third line of approach, which is perhaps less attractive than the others, involves enhancing human inclinations to avoid unpleasant and disconcerting news. While the extent of such selective-avoidance tendencies is perhaps exaggerated (as we mentioned above), such tendencies do exist and can be enhanced by arousing the individual's anxiety about the topic so that he avoids discussion of it, or by reinforcing his tendencies to distort what he hears or repress what he learns. It has been observed that such selectivity and distortion are common ways of resisting persuasion campaigns (Cooper & Jahoda, 1947; Cooper & Dinerman, 1951).

Personality Change

Changing the person's general motivational orientation, either permanently or at the moment countercommunications are presented to him, represents another way of inducing resistance to persuasion. For example, insofar as general hostility makes the person resistant to persuasion (Janis & Rife, 1959), the person can be made more resistant by exposing him to insults, hostile models, and the like prior to receipt of the persuasive communication. However, it seems that being in a more aggressive mood makes the individual less susceptible to benign communications but more open to hostile ones (Weiss & Fine, 1956).

Alternatively, one might raise the person's self-esteem by giving him success experiences, since there are a number of experiments suggesting that people are more resistant to persuasion when their self-esteem is raised (Mausner, 1954; Samelson, 1957). However, as we have noted, it is an intermediate level of self-esteem that makes the person most susceptible; to develop resistance the person should be given either very high or very low self-esteem.

Inoculation Approach

On the basis of the biological analogy of producing resistance to disease by pre-exposing an organism to attenuated doses of the attacking material, McGuire (1964) did a series of studies on producing resistance to persuasion by first exposing the individual to weakened forms of the subsequent attack. This research concentrated on cultural truisms, which were accepted at extreme levels of conviction by most of the members of the target population. These beliefs proved extremely vulnerable to persuasive attacks, as one would expect for such overprotected beliefs, just as one would expect an organism that had been raised in a germ-free environment to be extremely vulnerable when suddenly exposed to attacking viruses against which it has had no opportunity to build up resistance.

It was found that preexposing the person to a weakened form of the attacking arguments produced more resistance to subsequent strong attacks than did providing him with arguments in support of his own belief. As with biological inoculation, it was found that a certain time was needed to build up resistance after the preexposure, and other parallels were likewise found between biological and ideological immunization. The preexposure tended to develop resistance, not only against the attacking arguments to which the individual was preexposed but also against other arguments attacking the same belief.

In general, while less research has been done on producing resistance to persuasion than on techniques for increasing persuasion, the work that has been done is by no means negligible and has been at least as interesting in terms of theoretical relevance as the work on persuasion. Moreover, it has obvious social importance as a corrective measure against the current prevalence of social-influence attempts.

EVALUATION

During the past fifteen years the topic of persuasive communication has been the major focus of research in social psychology, as well as a popular topic in a number of other disciplines. By a conservative estimate, 5 percent of the approximately nineteen thousand books and articles abstracted yearly in *Psychological Abstracts* deals with persuasive communication. That is, close to one thousand studies are published each year on this topic. In the preceding sections we have sampled the results of this research in terms of illustrative findings ranging over the whole scope of topics studied. In this final section we shall make some general evaluations of the strengths and weaknesses of this past research as well as try to put it in the historical perspective of past accomplishments and future trends.

Strengths of Current Work

Among the strong points of the present research are its investigation of a wide range of independent variables, its attempts to describe rather fully the conditions of verbalized attitude change, its penchant for turning up somewhat paradoxical, nonobvious findings. Each of these trends deserves a somewhat fuller statement.

Wide Scope of Independent Variables

As the previous sections demonstrate, almost every aspect of communication has been investigated, analyzing a variety of the independent variables it involves. In general, the independent variables have been selected for their relevance to one or other of the theoretical orientations mentioned at the outset of this chapter, and then studied singly (or occasionally in two- and three-way interactions) by means of laboratory manipulations. Within the limits of this methodological paradigm, an attractively wide net has been cast to cover independent variables in the persuasive communication situation.

Insights into Verbalized Attitude Change

Earlier in this chapter the total persuasion process was analyzed into a series of steps, beginning with presentation of the communication through attention, comprehension, yielding, retention, and on to some ultimate target behavior. During the past fifteen years the vast majority of attitude-change studies have tapped the process through the yielding step by means of an immediately postcommunication measure of verbalized attitude change. Delayed effects and gross behavioral effects have been neglected, as have direct measures, steps of attention, etc. However, as far as verbalized attitude change is concerned, the vast amount of research in recent years has considerably clarified our understanding and raised our questions to a much more sophisticated level than was the case, say, in the years immediately following the second world war.

The neglect of gross behavioral change has been deplored by most observers interested in practical applications, since one worries about generalizing results in terms of verbalized attitude change to effects on later gross behavior. From the theoretical point of view, however, the verbalized attitude-change effects are themselves quite interesting, and restricting studies to this stage of the process has been quite efficient in allowing research on a broad range of independent variables with the funds available.

Zest for the Nonobvious

The past decade or so of research has been characterized by a preoccupation with subtle and unexpected effects rather than detailed investigations that would refine and clarify straightforward effects or plot their parametric characteristics. For example, those interested in source effects have not devoted themselves so much to teasing out the many components of source valence that contribute to a positive relationship between source attractiveness and attitude change; rather, attention has been given to finding a variety of circumstances in which the paradoxical occurs, such as circumstances in which negatively valenced sources are more effective than positive in producing attitude change. Again, those interested in temporal factors such as the persistence of induced attitude change have tended to neglect the parametric shape of the decay curve and the conditions which affect its parameters, and have instead concentrated on discovering paradoxical delayed-action effects such as those discussed above.

This zest for the nonobvious has produced a variety of intriguing if somewhat evasive and idiosyncratic results. It symptomatizes the high value that social psychology researchers have put in recent years on originality and the manifestation of creative thinking. Indeed, the paradoxical has been pursued so ostentatiously as to betoken a failure of nerve (a number of researchers seem to feel that their creativity is sufficiently in doubt that they must manifest it in rather flamboyant forms, otherwise their subtleties may not be perceived).

Some Needed Correctives of the Recent Work

The recent years have been such swinging ones in the persuasive-communication area because workers in this field found a good thing and moved productively with the tide. The dominant methodological paradigm has been a provocative and powerful one, and within its scope the work has been very productive. Inevitably, the very utility of the paradigm has resulted in the slighting of questions that could not be easily formulated within it.

We shall review here a number of limitations in the present work and mention some of the correctives needed. Among these are an escape from the laboratory situation to naturalistic communication settings in which numerous factors covary. Also needed is an extension of the dependent variable from preoccupations with verbalized attitude change to steps earlier and later in the persuasion process. Finally, there could be a redirection of effort from some relatively overinvestigated independent variables to some neglected ones.

Redirection from Laboratory to Field

During the past fifteen years the great majority of good researchers have concentrated on laboratory work in which a very few independent variables are manipulated while other factors are held constant. As a result, the work has tended to concentrate on independent variables that laboratory researchers are interested in and able to manipulate. They have tended to neglect such questions as what variables in the communication situation tend actually to vary in the natural world, how these covary together, and what effects they have in complex constellations. We feel that there is a healthy trend back to naturalistic research that will be facilitated by a number of recent methodological advances (McGuire, 1967; 1969c).

Broadening Scope of Dependent Variables

The recent exclusive focusing on immediate verbalized attitude change has provided us with a good understanding of that part of the persuasion process, but has resulted in the neglect of other steps. For example, past research has been rather deficient in the measuring of prior steps in the process (such as attention and comprehension of the contents), with a resulting loss of a more analytic knowledge of the processes involved. This failure to obtain direct measures of the earlier steps is especially regrettable because, when these mediating processes have been measured, the results have often been quite puzzling. Future researchers will be very unwise to neglect getting direct measures of the postulated mediating steps in the persuasion process.

Even more obvious a neglect to both outsiders and insiders in the field is the current failure of most researchers to pursue the persuasion process beyond verbalized attitude change to the ultimate payoff variable, which is usually some delayed gross behavior such as purchasing, voting, getting a medical checkup, or whatever. It should be understood that pursuit of the process to this last stage is not without cost. The greater expense of measuring these payoff variables will curtail the number of studies that can be done and the number of independent variables that can be investigated. Still, the past disproportionate emphasis on verbal attitude change probably makes these costs worth paying. When future researchers obtain direct measures of earlier and later steps, besides looking at how each step relates to the independent variables, they should analyze more thoroughly the interrelations among the steps themselves.

New Types of Questions

While past research has been commendably broad and inclusive in the range of independent variables studied, it is inevitable that some types of variables have been overstudied compared with others; any assessment would suggest some compensating reemphasis in future work. For example, theory-oriented researchers, who have done so much of the good work in this area, have overemphasized source variables at the expense of channel variables. Since channel variables have been neglected and are of practical importance, it seems that a redirection of interest in this class of variables would be timely and probably uncover some interesting theoretical aspects that have been overlooked.

Also, even those variables that have been rather heavily investigated recently need to be investigated in ways that have been neglected. As we mentioned, the exercise of creativity to demonstrate the paradoxical might better be directed to plotting the shape of functional relationships, isolating factors that affect the several parameters, and refining the components of gross commonsensical formulations.

The Current Work in Historical Perspective

The current flourishing of research on persuasive communication has probably reached its zenith. The topic has always been an interesting one but, as with most scholarly preoccupations, there have been waxings and wanings of interest in it. There was a strong interest in attitude research during the 1920s and early 1930s, when social psychology began to flourish within both psychology and sociology. During that earlier period of concentrated activity there was great interest in attitude measurement, scaling, and public opinion, characterized by descriptive advances and the discovery of static relationships.

From the mid-1930s to the mid-1950s, this vein of attitude research appeared to be spent, and the more creative workers in the field concentrated on the study of group processes. But beginning with the 1950s, attitudes again became the major interest of social psychologists, with the concentration now being on the more dynamic processes of attitude change and the communication factors that produced them. Elsewhere (McGuire, 1969a) we have tried to tease out some of the historical factors underlying these fluctuations of interest.

Such yins and yangs of interest are both inevitable and healthy, however disconcerting they may be to researchers who try to follow the trends in choosing research topics. As new foci of interest arise, the more perspicacious and energetic trend-spotters hasten to them and exploit their heuristic potential. When the topic is mined out, it is allowed to lie fallow for a while, and the new people flock elsewhere. When after a time interest in a given topic re-emerges, new workers are able to give it a fresh look and bring new insights to bear upon it.

At the moment it appears that research on persuasive communication is flourishing, and it is our feeling that the high point has now been reached and in the next decade we will see this topic decline in the proportion of research that it invites. However, so basic a topic as persuasive communication will continue to get a sizable amount of research attention even if it is no longer number one. Even if during the next fifteen years it is overshadowed by other research topics, such as social conflict or nonverbal communication or group processes, a healthy level of research will need to be carried out on persuasive communication. Then, somewhere around 1985, its hour will come again when some exciting leads develop out of the undercurrent of work and provide insights that will attract a new generation of enthusiastic researchers.

REFERENCES

Abelson, Robert P.; Elliot Aronson; William J. McGuire; Theodore M. Newcomb; Milton J. Rosenberg; and Percy H. Tannenbaum (eds.).
1968 Theories of Cognitive Consistency. Chicago: Rand McNally.

Addington, D. W.
1965 "Effect of mispronunciations on general speaking effectiveness." Speech Monographs 32:159–163.

Adorno, T. W.; Else Frenkel-Brunswik; D. J. Levinson; and R. N. Sanford.
1950 The Authoritarian Personality. New York: Harper.

Anderson, Lynn R.
1966 "Discrediting sources as a means of belief defense of cultural truisms." American Psychologist 21:708.

Anderson, Norman H.
1971 "Integration theory and attitude change." Psychological Review 78:171–206.

Aronson, Elliot, and B. W. Golden.
1962 "The effect of relevant and irrelevant aspects of communicator credibility on attitude change." Journal of Personality 30:135–146.

Aronson, Elliot, and Darwyn Linder.
1965 "Gain and loss of esteem as determinants of interpersonal attraction." Journal of Experimental Social Psychology 1:156–171.

Aronson, Elliot; B. Willerman; and Joanne Floyd.
1966 "Effect of a pratfall on increasing interpersonal attraction." Psychonomic Science 4:227–228.

Bauer, Raymond A.
1965 "A revised model of source effect." Presidential address of the Division

of Consumer Psychology, American Psychological Association, presented at the annual meeting of the American Psychological Association, Chicago, September 3–7.

Bennett-Pelz, Edith.
1955 "Discussion, decision, commitment and consensus in 'group decisions.'" Human Relations 8:251–274.

Bergin, A. E.
1962 "Effects of dissonant persuasive communications on changes in a self-referring attitude." Journal of Personality 30:423–438.

Bettinghaus, E. P.
1961 "Operation of congruity in an oral communication setting." Speech Monographs 28:131–142.

Bowers, John W.
1964 "Some correlates of language intensity." Quarterly Journal of Speech 50:415–420.

Bowers, John W., and M. M. Osborn.
1966 "Attitudinal effects of selected types of concluding metaphors in persuasive speech." Speech Monographs 33:147–155.

Brehm, Jack W., and A. R. Cohen.
1962 Explorations in Cognitive Dissonance. New York: Wiley.

Burke, Kenneth.
1962 A Grammar of Motives; and A Rhetoric of Motives. 2 volumes. New York: Meredian Books.

Byrne, Donn.
1969 "Attitudes and attractions," in Leonard Berkowitz (ed.), Advances in Experimental Psychology. Volume 4. New York: Academic Press.

Campbell, Donald T.
1959 "Methodological suggestions for comparative psychology of knowledge processes." Inquiry 2:152–182.

Carlson, E. R.
1956 "Attitude change through modification of attitude structure." Journal of Abnormal and Social Psychology 52:256–261.

Chein, Isidor.
1948 "Behavior theory and the behavior of attitudes." Psychological Review 55:175–188.

Cohen, Arthur R.
1957 "Need for cognition and order of communication as determinants of opinion change." Pp. 79–114 in Carl I. Hovland et al. (eds.), Order of Presentation in Persuasion. New Haven: Yale University Press.

Cooper, Eunice, and Helen Dinerman.
1951 "Analysis of the film 'Don't Be A Sucker': A study of communication." Public Opinion Quarterly 15:243–264.

Cooper, Eunice, and Marie Jahoda.
1947 "The evasion of propaganda." Journal of Psychology 23:15–25.

Cromwell, H.
1950 "The relative effect of audience attitude on the first versus the second argumentative speech of a series." Speech Monographs 17:105–122.

Doob, Leonard W.
1947 "The behavior of attitudes." Psychological Review 54:135–156.
1961 Communication in Africa. New Haven: Yale University Press.

Festinger, Leon.
1954 "A theory of social comparison processes." Human Relations 7:117–140.
1957 A Theory of Cognitive Dissonance. Evanston, Illinois: Row, Peterson.

Fisher, Seymour, and Ardie Lubin.
1958 "Distance as a determinant of influence in a two-person serial interaction situation." Journal of Abnormal and Social Psychology 56:230–238.

Freedman, Jonathan L., and David O. Sears.
1965 "Warning, distraction and resistance to influence." Journal of Personality and Social Psychology 1:262–266.

Gewirtz, J. L., and D. M. Baer.
1958 "Deprivation and satiation of social reinforcers as a drive condition." Journal of Abnormal and Social Psychology 57:165–172.

Greenstein, Fred I.
1965 Children and Politics. New Haven: Yale University Press.

Greenwald, Anthony G.; Timothy C. Brock; and Thomas M. Ostrom (eds.).
1968 Psychological Foundations of Attitudes. New York: Academic Press.

Hall, Wallace.
1938 "The effect of defined social stimulus material upon the stability of attitudes toward labor unions, capital

punishment, social insurance and Negroes." Pp. 7–19 in H. H. Remmers (ed.), Further Studies in Attitudes. Series 3. (Studies in Higher Education No. 34.) Lafayette, Indiana: Purdue University, Division of Educational Reference.

Harding, J.; Harold M. Proshansky; Bernard Kutner; and Isidor Chein.
1969 "Prejudice and ethnic relations." Pp. 1–76 in Gardner Lindzey and Elliot Aronson (eds.), Handbook of Social Psychology. Volume 5. Second Edition. Reading, Massachusetts: Addison-Wesley.

Heider, Fritz.
1946 "Attitudes and cognitive organization." Journal of Psychology 21:107–112.
1958 The Psychology of Interpersonal Relations. New York: Wiley.

Helmreich, Robert; Elliot Aronson; and J. LeFan.
1970 "To err is humanizing—sometimes." Journal of Personality and Social Psychology 16:259–264.

Holt, L. E.
1970 "Resistance to persuasion on explicit beliefs as a function of commitment to, and desirability of, logically related beliefs." Journal of Personality and Social Psychology 16:583–591.

Homans, George C.
1950 The Human Group. New York: Harcourt, Brace.

Hovland, Carl I.; Irving L. Janis; and H. H. Kelley.
1953 Communication and Persuasion. New Haven: Yale University Press.

Hovland, Carl I.; A. A. Lumsdaine; and F. D. Sheffield.
1949 Experiments on Mass Communications. Princeton: Princeton University Press.

Hovland, Carl I., and Wallace Mandell.
1952 "An experimental comparison of conclusion-drawing by the communicator and by the audience." Journal of Abnormal and Social Psychology 47:581–588.

Hovland, Carl I., and Walter Weiss.
1951 "The influence of source credibility on communication effectiveness." Public Opinion Quarterly 15:635–650.

Hovland, Carl I., and Irving L. Janis (eds.).
1959 Personality and Persuasibility. New Haven: Yale University Press.

Hovland, Carl I., et al. (eds.).
1957 Order of Presentation in Persuasion. New Haven: Yale University Press.

Hyman, H. H.
1959 Political Socialization. New York: Free Press of Glencoe.

James, William.
1970 Varieties of Religious Experience. New York: Random House, Modern Library. First published in 1902.

Janis, Irving L.
1967 "Effects of fear arousal on attitude change: Recent developments in theory and experimental research." Pp. 166–224 in Leonard Berkowitz (ed.), Advances in Experimental Social Psychology. New York: Academic Press.

Janis, Irving L., and David Rife.
1959 "Persuasibility and emotional disorder." Pp. 121–137 in Carl I. Hovland and Irving L. Janis (eds.), Personality and Persuasibility. New Haven: Yale University Press.

Janis, Irving L., and Robert F. Terwilliger.
1962 An experimental study of psychological resistances to fear-arousing communications." Journal of Abnormal and Social Psychology 65:403–410.

Jones, E. E.
1964 Ingratiation: A Social Psychological Analysis. New York: Appleton-Century-Crofts.

Katz, Daniel.
1960 "The functional approach to the study of attitudes." Public Opinion Quarterly 24:163–204.

Kelman, H. C.
1961 "Processes of opinion change." Public Opinion Quarterly 25:57–78.

Kiesler, C. A.
1971 The Psychology of Commitment. New York: Academic Press.

Kiesler, C. A.; B. E. Collins; and Norman Miller.
1969 Attitude Change. New York: Wiley.

Klapper, J. T.
1949 The Effects of the Mass Media. New York: Columbia University Bureau of Applied Social Research.

Lasswell, Harold D.
1948 "The structure and function of communication in society." Pp. 37–51 in Lyman Bryson (ed.), Communication of Ideas. New York: Harper.

Latané, Bibb (ed.).
1966 Studies in Social Comparison. Journal of Experimental Social Psychology Monograph Supplement.

Lehmann, Stanley.
1970 "Personality and compliance: A study of anxiety and self-esteem in opinion and behavior change." Journal of Personality and Social Psychology 15:76–86.

Leventhal, Howard.
1970 "Findings and theory in the study of fear communications," in Leonard Berkowitz (ed.), Advances in Experimental Social Psychology. Volume 5. New York: Academic Press.

Lumsdaine, A. A., and Irving L. Janis.
1953 "Resistance to 'counterpropaganda' produced by one-sided and two-sided 'propaganda' presentations." Public Opinion Quarterly 17:311–318.

Lund, F. H.
1925 "The psychology of belief, IV. The law of primacy in persuasion." Journal of Abnormal and Social Psychology 20:183–191.

McGuire, William J.
1957 "Order of presentation as a factor in 'conditioning' persuasiveness." Pp. 78–114 in Carl I. Hovland et al. (eds.), Order of Presentation in Persuasion. New Haven: Yale University Press.
1960 "A syllogistic analysis of cognitive relationships." Pp. 65–111 in Milton J. Rosenberg and Carl I. Hovland (eds.), Attitude Organization and Attitude Change. New Haven: Yale University Press.
1964 "Inducing resistance to persuasion." Pp. 191–229 in Leonard Berkowitz (ed.), Advances in Experimental Social Psychology. Volume 1. New York: Academic Press.
1967 "Some impending reorientations in social psychology." Journal of Experimental Social Psychology 3: 124–139.
1968a "Personality and susceptibility to social influence." Pp. 1130–1187 in E. F. Borgatta and W. W. Lambert (eds.), Handbook of Personality Theory and Research. Chicago: Rand McNally.
1968b "Personality and attitude change: An information-processing theory." Pp. 171–196 in Anthony G. Greenwald et al. (eds.), Psychological Foundations of Attitudes. New York: Academic Press.
1968c "Selective exposure: A summing up." Pp. 797–800 in Robert P. Abelson et al. (eds.), Theories of Cognitive Consistency. Chicago: Rand McNally.
1969a "Nature of attitudes and attitude change." Pp. 136–314 in Gardner Lindzey and Elliot Aronson (eds.), Handbook of Social Psychology. Volume 3. Second Edition. Reading, Massachusetts: Addison-Wesley.
1969b "Suspiciousness of experimenter's intent as an artifact in social research." Pp. 13–57 in Robert Rosenthal and R. L. Rosnow (eds.), Artifacts in Behavioral Research. New York: Academic Press.
1969c "Theory-oriented research in natural settings." Pp. 21–51 in Muzafer Sherif and Carolyn W. Sherif (eds.), Interdisciplinary Relationships in the Social Sciences. Chicago: Aldine.
1972 "Attitude change: The information-processing paradigm." Pp. 108–141 in C. G. McClintock (ed.), Experimental Social Psychology. New York: Holt, Rinehart and Winston.
n.d. "An information-processing model of advertising effectiveness," in H. L. Davis and A. J. Silk (eds.), Behavioral and Management Sciences in Marketing. New York: Ronald Press (forthcoming).

Mausner, Bernard.
1954 "The effect of prior reinforcement on the interaction of observed pairs." Journal of Abnormal and Social Psychology 49:65–68.

Mehrabian, Albert.
1969 "Significance of posture and position in the communication of attitude and status relationships." Psychological Bulletin 71:359–372.

Mehrabian, Albert, and Martin Williams.
1969 "Nonverbal concomitants of perceived and intended persuasiveness." Journal of Personality and Social Psychology 13:37–58.

Miller, Norman, and D. T. Campbell.
1959 "Recency and primacy in persuasion as a function of the timing of speeches and measurement." Journal of Abnormal and Social Psychology 59:1–9.

Millman, Susan.
1968 "Anxiety, comprehension and susceptibility to social influence." Journal of Personality and Social Psychology 9:251–256.

Mills, Judson.
1968 "Interest in supporting and discrepant information." Pp. 771–776 in Robert P. Abelson et al. (eds.), Theories of Cognitive Consistency. Chicago: Rand McNally.

Mills, Judson, and Elliot Aronson.
1965 "Opinion change as a function of communicator's attractiveness and desire to influence." Journal of Personality and Social Psychology 1: 173–177.

Nelson, C. E.
1968 "Anchoring to accepted values as a technique for immunizing beliefs against persuasion." Journal of Personality and Social Psychology 9: 329–334.

Orne, M. T.
1969 "Demand characteristics and the concept of quasi-control." Pp. 143–179 in Robert Rosenthal and R. L. Rosnow (eds.), Artifacts in Behavioral Research. New York: Academic Press.

Papageorgis, Demetrios.
1963 "Bartlett effect and the persistence of induced opinion change." Journal of Abnormal and Social Psychology 67: 61–67.

Peterson, Ruth C., and L. L. Thurstone.
1933 The Effect of Motion Pictures on the Social Attitudes of High School Children. Chicago: University of Chicago Press.

Rokeach, Milton.
1960 The Open and Closed Mind. New York: Basic Books.

Rosenberg, Seymour.
1968 "Mathematical models of social behavior." Pp. 179–244 in Gardner Lindzey and Elliot Aronson (eds.), Handbook of Social Psychology. Volume 1. Second Edition. Reading, Massachusetts: Addison-Wesley.

Samelson, Franz.
1957 "Conforming behavior under two conditions of conflict in the cognitive field." Journal of Abnormal and Social Psychology 55:181–187.

Scott, J. P., and J. L. Fuller.
1965 Social Behavior of the Dog. Chicago: University of Chicago Press.

Sears, D. O.
1968 "The paradox of de facto selective exposure without preferences for supportive information." Pp. 777–787 in Robert P. Abelson et al. (eds.), Theories of Cognitive Consistency. Chicago: Rand McNally.

Sherif, Carolyn W.; Muzafer Sherif; and R. E. Nebergall.
1965 Attitude and Attitude Change. Philadelphia: Saunders.

Sherif, Muzafer, and Carl I. Hovland.
1961 Social Judgment. New Haven: Yale University Press.

Singer, Alice.
1965 "Anchor effects on mean judgments and latitudes of acceptance under varying conditions of involvement and discrepancy." Ph.D. Dissertation, Columbia University (unpublished).

Smith, E. E.
1961 "The power of dissonance techniques to change attitudes." Public Opinion Quarterly 25:626–639.

Staats, A. W.
1968 "Principles of the attitude-reinforcer-discriminative system." Pp. 33–66 in Anthony G. Greenwald et al. (eds.), Psychological Foundations of Attitudes. New York: Academic Press.

Stein, D. D.; J. A. Hardyck; and M. B. Smith.
1965 "Race and belief: An open and shut case." Journal of Personality and Social Psychology 1:281–289.

Stewart, John Bell.
1964 Repetitive Advertising in Newspapers: A Study in Two New Products. Boston: Harvard University Division of Research.

Stotland, Ezra; Daniel Katz; and Martin Patchen.
1959 "The reduction of prejudice through the arousal of self-insight." Journal of Personality 27:507–531.

Strodtbeck, Fred L.; R. M. James; and C. Hawkins.
1958 "Social status in jury deliberations." Pp. 379–388 in Eleanor E. Maccoby et al. (eds.), Reading in Social Psychology. Third Edition. New York: Holt.

Stukát, Karl–Gustav.
1958 Suggestibility: A Factorial and Experimental Study. Stockholm: Almqvist and Wiksell.

Tannenbaum, Percy H.
1968 "The congruity principle: Retrospective reflections and recent research." Pp. 52–72 in Robert R. Abelson et al. (eds.), Theories of Cognitive Consistency. Chicago: Rand McNally.

Walster, Elaine C., and Leon Festinger.
1962 "The effectiveness of 'overheard' persuasive communications." Journal of Abnormal and Social Psychology 65:395–402.

Watts, William A., and William J. McGuire.
1964 "Persistence of induced opinion change and retention of inducing message content." Journal of Abnormal and Social Psychology 68: 233–241.

Weiss, Walter.
1969 "Effects of the mass media of communications." Pp. 77–195 in Gardner Lindzey and Elliot Aronson (eds.), Handbook of Social Psychology. Volume 5. Second Edition. Reading, Massachusetts: Addison-Wesley.

Weiss, Walter, and B. J. Fine.
1956 "The effect of induced aggressiveness on opinion change." Journal of Abnormal and Social Psychology 52: 109–114.

Whittaker, J. O.
1964 "Parameters of social influence in the autokinetic situation." Sociometry 27:88–95.

Wilson, Warner, and Howard Miller.
1968 "Repetition, order of presentation and timing of arguments and measures as determinants of opinion change." Journal of Personality and Social Psychology 9:184–188.

Zellner, Miriam.
1970 "Self-esteem, reception, and influencibility." Journal of Personality and Social Psychology 15:87–94.

Zimbardo, P. G.; Matisyohu Weisenberg; Ira Firestone; and Burton Levy.
1965 "Communicator effectiveness in producing public conformity and private attitude change." Journal of Personality 33:233–255.

CHAPTER 10 Political Persuasion

DAVID O. SEARS and RICHARD E. WHITNEY
University of California, Los Angeles

For many people, the very conception of a democratic political system rests fundamentally upon processes of political persuasion. Topics such as the effects of political propaganda, the nature of various publics, the impact of the mass media, the role of political socialization, and the attitudinal functions of partisanship thus assume crucial importance. These topics constitute the focus of this chapter. The authors also explore, among other things, recent findings regarding selectivity in exposure and perception, the positivity and agreement biases, the importance of source trustworthiness, and the opinion processes underlying major electoral changes. In conclusion, the authors note a potentially serious challenge to the American political system posed by established communication practices.

Between the world wars, social scientists became intensely interested in the persuasive effects of political propaganda as practiced with such startling success by such demagogues as Mussolini, Hitler, Goebbels, Huey Long, and Father Coughlin, among others. The great popularity of radio, and the consequent availability of enormous mass audiences for propaganda, provided much concern about the future of democracy. With such seductive totalitarian leadership, and such an eminently seducible citizenry, how could democracy survive?

Preparation of this chapter was partially supported by a National Science Foundation grant to David O. Sears. The authors wish to thank David E. Kanouse for numerous helpful suggestions and Sura Boxerman for secretarial assistance.

Early propaganda analysts shared four distinctive orientations:

1. Their work was motivated largely by their social-action concerns, particularly by their fears for the longevity of democracy in the face of growing totalitarianism.
2. Their major goal was the pragmatic one of reducing the impact of demagogic propaganda by giving individual citizens greater insight into the mechanisms by which propaganda has persuasive impact. According to Doob (1935:5), "The recognition and understanding of a phenomenon enables an individual to free himself to a certain extent from the forces that the phenomenon represents."
3. In their analysis of propagandistic effect, they assumed a wholly gullible

and captive audience. In *The Fine Art of Propaganda: A Study of Father Coughlin's Speeches* (Institute for Propaganda Analysis, 1939), the gullibility of Coughlin's modern radio audience is contrasted with the earlier skepticism of men sitting around the cracker barrel in the crossroads store, fabled in American mythology. In mass radio propaganda, not even a heckler existed to stand in for the skeptical give-and-take imagined in cracker-barrel discussions. And it was assumed that almost everyone would be listening.

4. Psychological explanations for persuasion focused almost exclusively upon the propagandist's tricks of the trade. That is, the major independent variables were thought to reside in communication content. The assumption was that propaganda could be made almost irresistible with sufficiently clever use of propagandistic gimmicks in the content of the communication. For example, Coughlin's effectiveness was attributed to his use of seven specific tricks, designated as "name-calling," "glittering generality," "transfer," "testimonial," "plain folks," "card stacking," and "bandwagon." This early view, then, pictured political propaganda as having great persuasive impact, primarily because of wily tricks of the trade performed upon gullible audiences who were entirely captive and unable to defend themselves.

During the 1940s, this view was challenged by research coming from three quite different sources. One was the radio research conducted by Lazarsfeld, Stanton, and colleagues at Columbia's Office of Radio Research, culminating in the prototypical voting study, *The People's Choice* (Lazarsfeld, Berelson, & Gaudet, 1948). They found relatively little direct media impact upon voting choices.

Systematic empirical laboratory research on persuasive communications also challenged this overestimate of propaganda's effect. Even by 1937, Murphy, Murphy, and Newcomb's early text had cited dozens of experimental studies of attitude change. The major impact, though, came from the work of Carl I. Hovland and his colleagues during World War II in the "information and education" division of the army, particularly upon the persuasive effectiveness of orientation films. Their carefully documented conclusions (see Hovland, Lumsdaine, & Sheffield, 1949; Hovland, 1954) were that the films produced large increases in factual information and modest amounts of opinion change on points specifically covered. More general attitude changes toward the war, the enemy, and our allies were rare, and there was apparently little effect on motivation to serve as a soldier, although all of these were intended by the films' designers. These early experiments did help to define the conditions under which opinion change might occur but, more important, they failed to find evidence for the kind of massive and general opinion change feared by the earlier propaganda analysts.

Finally, Kurt Lewin and his colleagues, conducting experiments in a variety of different realms, emphasized the greater effectiveness of democratic consensus and small-group decision-making, as opposed to authoritarian leadership. Studies of authoritarian and democratic leadership with children, of worker participation in decision-making and resistance to change in industry, of group decision and changes in food habits during World War II—all led to the conclusion that authoritarian leadership was considerably less effective than democratic decision-making for producing long-standing behavioral or attitudinal changes (Cartwright & Zander, 1968).

Thus, research from several sources counterbalanced the earlier fears of the propaganda analysts, down playing the effectiveness of political propaganda. Moreover, the research served to divert attention from the "tricks of the trade" to other social psychological variables in the persuasion situation. More often, they pointed to the self-selection of audiences, their initial resistance to change, the credibility of the source, and the participation of the influencees as variables determining the success of persuasive attempts.

Today the researcher does not speak of a wholly gullible captive audience but of an "obstinate audience" (Bauer, 1964), and he concludes that face-to-face contacts are considerably more influential than mass communications (McGuire, 1969). Propaganda is rarely seen as directly influential, its influence being occasional and indirect, perhaps mediated interpersonally through the "two-step flow of communication" (E. Katz, 1957).[1]

We have four main goals in this chapter: (1) to describe the effects of political propaganda in more detail; (2) to present a simple social psychological model of persuasive effect; (3) to begin to define the conditions under which mass communications contribute to political change; and (4) to focus attention upon new cognitive dimensions. As well as looking at partisanship and consistency biases, we wish also to introduce research findings on positivity and agreement biases in political evaluation, and to begin to explore their ramifications in American political life.

EFFECTS OF POLITICAL PROPAGANDA

Studies of political propaganda conducted over relatively short time spans have typically found rather little persuasive effect (Hovland, 1959; Klapper, 1960). A few examples will illustrate. Schramm and Carter (1959) studied effects of a twenty-hour telethon conducted by Senator William Knowland two days before his defeat in the California gubernatorial election of 1958. Out of 563 respondents, 2 voters had been influenced positively and 1 negatively. From an exhaustive review of more than thirty studies of the Kennedy-Nixon debates of 1960, Elihu Katz and J. J. Feldman (1962: 208) concluded that the debates "resulted primarily in a strengthening of commitment to one's own party and candidate."

Even longer-term propaganda campaigns have seemed to have little effect. The impact of the 1940 presidential campaign in Erie County, Ohio, was carefully studied (Lazarsfeld et al., 1948); few voters had changed their candidate preferences, and even fewer could be found whose changes could be traced directly to mass media propaganda. Similarly slight persuasive effects were found by Hyman and Sheatsley (1958) and by Star and Hughes (1950) in their studies of extended propaganda campaigns favoring the admission of Jewish immigrants to Palestine, and supporting the United Nations. These cases are typical: the measurable persuasive impact of a short-term propaganda campaign or single media program is usually unimpressive.

Rather, the major effect is a reinforcement of preexisting attitudes. This point is graphically illustrated by the Kennedy-Nixon debates in 1960. An enormous audience watched with great anticipation the first confrontation on television of the two major parties' presidential candidates. Journalists widely agreed that the debates were a decisive victory in Kennedy's successful campaign for the presidency. Surveys, however, indicated relatively slight persuasive impact of the debates.

Table 1 shows perceptions of "who won" the first debate, which was generally thought to be the most decisive of the four. The major effect was that partisans thought their own candidate won the debate. Some

[1] However, Katz's two-step flow effect may reflect more of a relay and reinforcing function than any causal influence (Deutschmann & Danielson, 1960; Tannenbaum & Greenberg, 1968: 368). Troldahl (1966) experimentally tested Katz's hypothesized effect by planting and tracing messages in a monthly newspaper. He found that opinion leaders did not change their views at all and the little attitude change occurring in the general public could be attributed to direct media exposure.

pro-Kennedy persuasive effect is discernible: Kennedy had some advantage among previously undecided voters, and lost fewer of his own partisans than did Nixon. Nevertheless, the dominant effect was reinforcement of preexisting opinions.

TABLE 1

RESULTS OF FIRST 1960 TELEVISED DEBATE

Predebate Preference	*Who did "better job" in the debate?* Kennedy	No Choice	Nixon
Kennedy	71%	26%	3%
Undecided	26	62	12
Nixon	17	38	45

Klapper's (1960) review of mass communication effects is the most comprehensive available, and emphasizes that major attitude changes are rare. He concludes that they occur primarily when the individual has a weak initial opinion (such as on new issues) or when other influences bolster the media's pressure toward change. This emphasis upon reinforcement, rather than conversion, is now a part of the conventional social science wisdom about voting behavior: the media change very few votes (cf. Berelson & Steiner, 1964; Rossi, 1966).

While this conclusion is supported by much research, and must be considered the most general single principle about media effects, there are numerous and important exceptions to it. Before looking at them in more detail, let us consider the psychological dynamics by which reinforcement (rather than major attitude change) turns out to be the dominant effect of mass communication.

A SIMPLE INFLUENCE MODEL

Any persuasion situation consists at root of a source (O) communicating with his target (P) about some attitude object (X). A variety of rather simple cognitive theories has been applied to this basic situation (cf. Osgood & Tannenbaum, 1955; Festinger, 1957; Heider, 1958; Abelson et al., 1968; Zajonc, 1968a). They have mainly been concerned with the cognitive links between P, O, and X as they are represented symbolically within the target's (P's) cognition. For the most part these theories represent the links as being either positive or negative. A considerable amount of research has documented widespread preferences for certain combinations of links. Three of these preferences, or *cognitive biases*, form the basis for much of the remainder of this chapter, and thus should be introduced here.

The most widely studied has been the *consistency* bias. Consistency holds when P agrees about X with a liked O, or disagrees with a disliked O. Much research has documented a general strain toward these two states rather than toward their inconsistent opposites: disagreeing with a liked source or agreeing with a disliked one.

The *positivity* bias has received considerable attention in the social psychology literature in recent years. Except for an earlier preliminary discussion (Sears, 1969a), it has not been extended to political situations until now. We devote considerable attention to it below. The positivity bias consists of the tendency toward positive rather than negative relations among P, O, and X, particularly, as will be seen, a bias toward positive feelings between P and O. And finally, the *agreement* bias is simply the tendency to agree more often than disagree with O about the various X's they communicate about, quite independent of whether P likes O or not.

EXPOSURE PROBLEMS

A further useful distinction in research on persuasion is between the *reception* and the *acceptance* of information. For example, Hovland and Janis (1959) and McGuire (1969) have distinguished attention to and comprehension of a persuasive communication, on the one hand, from acceptance of or yielding to its conclusion, on the other. The failure of a persuasive communication may result either from failure to reach the target individual in substantially accurate form because the receiver did not attend to it or failed to comprehend it, or from his rejection of it, even though he understood it perfectly well.

We wish to contend that most failures of political propaganda result from (1) low interest in public affairs and, consequently, low rates of exposure to any communications about them, and (2) defensive processes operating at the acceptance stage. Resistances or defensive processes operating at the reception stage (i.e., in exposure, attention, or comprehension) are comparatively unimportant.

Absolute Exposure

The level of exposure to any given political communication tends to be quite low. The problem for most political propagandists is not that they fail to reach their enemies but that they fail to reach anybody at all. For instance, single programs, with rare exceptions, draw small audiences, as illustrated by the Knowland telethon. This twenty-hour extravaganza, a fantastic effort at the last minute of the campaign, reached a relatively small number of people; only 11.5 percent had watched any part of it at all (Schramm & Carter, 1959). G. A. Steiner (1963) has presented data on exposure to mass media news programs and other public affairs programs that indicate the same point; the audiences tend to be very small.

Very rarely will such a program reach a large audience. The Kennedy-Nixon debates were one such case; at least 55 percent of the adult population heard or watched each one, no doubt due partly to the fact that all the networks presented them, leaving few viewing alternatives. Similarly, the average adult watched the media coverage of President Kennedy's assassination more than eight hours per day for four days (Sheatsley & Feldman, 1965) but, again, all the networks covered it, and most sports events were cancelled, places of employment were closed, and so on. But these events are rare.

Even if we consider prolonged propaganda campaigns, widespread exposure is uncommon. To be sure, exposure to some part of a presidential campaign is typically widespread but to any part of lesser election campaigns, quite rare. In the campaign of 1958, Miller and Stokes (1966) found that only 24 percent of a nationwide sample had heard or read *anything* about both congressional candidates in their district. Forty-six percent had heard or read *nothing* about *either* candidate (as might be expected, the nonincumbents had the hardest time reaching anyone—only 29 percent had heard or read anything about them). Converse (1962) notes the abandonment of an attempted content analysis of media references to these congressional candidates, because media references were so rare. With most political contests, then, the problem is both an indifferent public and a lack of media attention. But the outcome is the same: low absolute levels of exposure.

Informational Level

The low level of exposure to political propaganda results in relatively little political information in the general public. The approximate parameters of public information in America have been presented elsewhere (Sears, 1969a); here let us briefly retrace that discussion.

At one extreme are the chronic "know-nothings" identified by Hyman and Sheatsley (1954:36): "In almost every instance where the polls have tested public information, at least 20 percent of the population have revealed complete ignorance." To be sure, the major party presidential candidates are commonly known to well over 90 percent of the public, as are overwhelming public events such as the assassination of President Kennedy—e.g., 99.8 percent of a national sample had heard of it five hours afterwards (Sheatsley & Feldman, 1965). Aside from such rare exceptions, however, the know-nothings are almost completely out of the mainstream of information flow, unfamiliar with any but the few most visible public figures, and with almost all public issues.

Still, the know-nothings represent a minority. How knowledgeable is the "average" voter? A good thumbnail estimate is that, in general, 50 to 80 percent of the population will have heard of the most salient public figure in any given arena: for example, the best-known union leader, congressional leader, general, and so on. And they will be aware of the two or three issues that dominate any given political campaign. For example, they had heard of the Taft-Hartley Law (72 percent) in 1948, the House Committee on Un-American Activities (64 percent) in 1949, or Medicare (81 percent) or the Peace Corps (71 percent) in 1962, but not the Bricker Amendment (19 percent) in 1953, or the Hoover Commission Reports (28 percent) in 1949 (Sears, 1969a).

Finally, the "attentive public," a fraction that varies between 10 and 30 percent, is typically familiar with most of the issues and public figures that persist in the media for any length of time. In 1956, when Lyndon Johnson was majority leader of the Senate, 32 percent had heard of him; 34 percent had heard of Adlai Stevenson before he was nominated in 1952 (Sears, 1969a). We must caution ourselves that it is this more limited fraction of the public that comes to the minds of informed observers when they think of the effects of the media on political attitudes.

Candidate Visibility

While over 90 percent of the public is familiar with each major party candidate in a presidential campaign, candidates for other offices are typically visible to only a minority. Representative statistics are 35 percent accurately naming both their senators, 38 percent their congressman, and 57 percent naming one of their two senators (Erskine, 1963), as well as the 24 percent cited earlier that had heard or read something about both congressional candidates vying for their votes (Miller & Stokes, 1966).

Salience

Obviously politics are not very salient to most people. They are much more preoccupied with their private lives. For example, Cantril (1965) found that only 2 percent mentioned political matters, and 10 percent international affairs, in giving their "fondest hopes." Sixty-five percent mentioned personal economic matters, and 48 percent personal health. Similarly, their "worst fears" focused on political matters and international affairs (mostly the avoidance of war and the maintenance of peace) for 5 percent and 24 percent, respectively; much more common, again, were personal economic matters (46 percent) and personal health (56 percent). Therefore, the flow of political information to the average citizen is sure to be slight, regardless of his attempts to defend against persuasion, because public affairs are so remote from his day-to-day life.

Obviously there are important exceptions to this, when important personal needs become closely intertwined with political policy. For example, basic survival and social needs sometimes have political effects (Davies, 1963); personal economic welfare often does (Hennessey, 1965), sometimes for the majority, as in the Depression or, more commonly, for particular interest groups, such as the farmers (Campbell, Converse, Miller, & Stokes, 1960). An oppressive caste system affects the lower caste persons intimately (Sears, 1969b; Sears & McConahay, 1973), and universal military service policies can have particularly acute effects when combined with an unpopular war. However, it must be emphasized that these have in the past been the exceptions, rather than the rule, of American political life. For the most part the average citizen has not seen politics as affecting his personal life very directly.

Selectivity in Information Reception

Still, it has been widely assumed that political persuasion is impeded in an important way by defensive selection of information at the reception stage. The first obstacle is thought to be selective exposure. This, in the political arena, has two meanings. One, *de facto selectivity*, refers to the tendency for voluntary audiences to mass communications to be biased in the direction of unusual initial agreement with the communicator. The second is *motivated selectivity*, which presumes that people deliberately seek supportive information and avoid nonsupportive information.

De facto selectivity does seem to occur rather generally, but the effect is seldom overwhelmingly strong, particularly in the mass media (see Sears & Freedman, 1967; E. Katz, 1968, for reviews of the evidence on de facto selectivity). Face-to-face political meetings may elicit more de facto selectivity than communications in newspapers, magazines, TV, and radio because they attract fewer people and hence probably only the most involved partisans.

There is little evidence that motivated selectivity is an important obstacle to persuasion, despite many efforts to demonstrate it or to specify the conditions under which it occurs—e.g., with greater cognitive dissonance, or little confidence in initial opinions (Festinger, 1957; 1964). A large number of experimental studies have met with little success and are reviewed in detail elsewhere (Freedman & Sears, 1965; Sears & Abeles, 1969). The existence of de facto selectivity without motivated selectivity is perhaps best explained as a result of the unusual availability of supportive information in the average individual's natural environment (Sears, 1968).

Additionally, motivated selectivity has often been hypothesized at the attention, perception, learning, or retention stages of information reception and storage (cf. Klapper, 1960). Here again the evidence has not indicated much selectivity. It appears that there is little tendency to perceive or to learn more readily information supporting one's opinions than information contradicting them (Greenwald & Sakumura, 1967; Brigham & Cook, 1969; Sears & Abeles, 1969). Selectivity of attention within a communication has been obtained in two recent experiments by Brock and his colleagues, although not uniformly across all issues used (Brock & Balloun, 1967; Brock & Fromkin, 1968).

From this it appears that motivated selectivity in *information reception* is not a particularly important impediment to political persuasion. However, the naturalistic correlation of audiences with their preferred viewpoints does present an obstacle in the sense that audiences do normally underrepresent the optimal targets for persuasion—those initially opposed or undecided. And selective attention, perhaps the main exception to this rule, probably does facilitate resistance of discrepant communications when the individual is exposed to them, and reinforcement of prior opinions when exposed to supportive information.

Resistance Problems

Partisan evaluation of information (or *selective interpretation*, as it is sometimes called) is, on the other hand, a powerful obstacle to persuasion: people evaluate incoming stimuli on the basis of their prior predispositions. Partisans' evaluations of the Kennedy-Nixon debate, shown in Table 1, illustrate the point; all saw the same debate but each evaluated his own favorite as the winner. Similarly, the Knowland telethon was evaluated in terms of prior preferences: 27 percent of the Republican viewers, and only 6 percent of the Democrats, said they were impressed by the program's quality. On the other hand, 45 percent of the Democratic viewers and 13.5 percent of the Republican viewers were impressed by "nothing" (Schramm & Carter, 1959).

New political figures, like mass communications, are evaluated in terms of the voters' predispositions. Here the clearest illustrations are the entries of previously well-known but nonpolitical men, such as Generals Eisenhower and De Gaulle, into partisan politics. When each declared his party allegience, public evaluations swiftly polarized along partisan lines (Converse & Dupeux, 1966). Normally, support for well-known political figures is highly correlated with party preference: for instance, the strong Republican support for, and Democratic opposition to, Father Coughlin and Senator Joseph McCarthy (Lipset, 1963).

Whether partisan evaluation divides people into supporters versus opponents, or strong versus mild supporters, or strong versus mild opponents obviously depends in some degree upon the objective characteristics of the communication, or of the political figure. Some may be so clearly of high quality and excellent reputation, or so clearly abysmal, that most viewers on each side would be agreed on an evaluation. We will consider such cases in more detail below in discussing positivity biases. But even in these cases one is almost certain to find strong partisan differences in evaluation.

Involvement and Forewarning

What determines the degree of selective interpretation? That is, what determines the magnitude of impact that prior predispositions have upon an individual's evaluation of incoming information? Here let us emphasize two of the most powerful such variables.

The individual's "involvement" in his initial attitude has served as a general rubric for summarizing many factors that affect the partisanship of information evaluation. The greater the involvement, the greater the selectivity in interpretation. The term *involvement* has proved to be discouragingly general, encompassing perhaps too wide a range of psychological phenomena, but since it is so important we will overlook some of its vagueness in the service of staking out an important set of variables.[2] The most balanced treatment of it is Kiesler, Collins, and Miller's (1969).

Among the variables contributing to greater involvement are (1) greater cognitive support for one's opinion, whether derived from greater information or knowledge about the issue (N. H. Anderson, 1965) or from more experience in defending the opinion from counterattack (McGuire, 1969); (2) greater social support for one's opinion (Festinger, 1957) or other benefits of anchorage in group norms (Hovland, Janis, & Kelley, 1953; Campbell et al., 1960; Klapper, 1960); and (3) greater commitment of time, money, or ego (Aronson, 1968) or prior expression of a public position with which one has to maintain consistency (Deutsch & Gerard, 1955; Hovland, Campbell, & Brock, 1957). While there are ambiguities and exceptions in some cases, by and large each of these variables contributes to greater involvement in the subject's initial position and thus to greater resistance to change of his attitude and to more partisan evaluation of new information relevant to it.

A second variable affecting the selectivity of interpretation is forewarning. Forewarnings about the nature of the incoming information seem mainly to exaggerate the normal response to them. They increase the individual's resistance to change when he is highly involved in his initial attitude (Freedman & Sears, 1965), and facilitate change when he is not (Apsler & Sears, 1968). Forewarnings apparently motivate people to gather their cognitive resources before actually being exposed to the

[2] Involvement in the individual's initial attitude must also be distinguished from *response involvement* (Zimbardo, 1960; Freedman, 1964). We are not concerned here with the level of the individual's involvement in the situation or with the importance of the consequences he perceives to follow his making a response. These variables too are important in analyzing public opinion and voting (Campbell et al., 1960), but in this context we are concerned only with the individual's involvement in his initial attitude.

communication in question (McGuire & Papageorgis, 1962).

Moreover, there is evidence that forewarnings inspire anticipatory attitude change in the directions just noted. Sears, Freedman, and O'Connor (1964) noted that debates such as those between Kennedy and Nixon generally tend to polarize the opinions of committed partisans, and to convert the uncommitted. Some of this effect is no doubt due to evaluations of the debate as it is viewed. However, they also obtained experimental evidence that *anticipation* of a debate produced partisan polarization among subjects publicly committed to their position. In contrast, it moderated the opinions of those only privately committed, presumably in preparation for receiving information that might be decisive in making up their minds.

Communicator Credibility

A third major variable determining reactions to new information is communicator credibility. As defined originally by Hovland, Janis, and Kelley (1953), this concerned both the communicator's expertness and his trustworthiness. From subsequent research, expertness appears to be considerably more important than trustworthiness in determining attitude change (McGuire, 1969).

One aspect of trustworthiness that is important, however, is the incongruence of the source's position with his own ideology or personal interest. For example, Mills and Jellison (1967) found that a speech was more influential, and its communicator regarded as more sincere and impartial, when it was presented as having originally been delivered to an audience whose interest it opposed (rather than an audience whose interest it supported). Walster, Aronson, and Abrahams (1966) found that criminals and prosecutors alike were more credible and more persuasive when advocating positions counter to their interests. And Koeske and Crano (1968) found that statements by General Westmoreland and Stokely Carmichael were regarded as much more credible when incongruent with their known positions on Vietnam and the racial crisis than when congruent with them.

Communicator Discrepancy

A fourth powerful variable is the discrepancy between the initial position of the subject and that taken by the communication. In general, the greater the discrepancy, the greater the attitude change, but only up to a point. At some degree of discrepancy, attitude change falls off (i.e., there is an inverted-U relationship between communication discrepancy and attitude change, with the maximum amount of attitude change occurring at moderate degrees of discrepancy). The empirical and theoretical question, then, is at what point it typically happens. A second question concerns the process or mechanism by which influence is resisted at high degrees of discrepancy.

Two major determinants of the point of maximum effect of discrepancy are involvement and credibility. The less the subject's involvement in his initial position, or the greater the communicator's credibility, the more discrepant will be the position that can effectively be advocated (Aronson, Turner, & Carlsmith, 1963; Freedman, 1964; Bochner & Insko, 1966; Sears & Abeles, 1969). Apparently people are more receptive to serious contradiction when they have little social support or are only privately committed to their prior position, etc., or when it comes from an expert.

Social-judgment theory suggests a useful method for distinguishing positions that can be argued effectively from those that cannot (cf. Sherif & Hovland, 1961). Every individual's attitude is seen as consisting of (1) a particular position that he most favors, (2) a range of other acceptable positions (latitude of acceptance), and (3) range of unacceptable positions (the latitude of rejection). Often there is also a no-man's-land between the two latitudes.

The main hypothesis is that discrepancy is positively related to attitude change within the latitude of acceptance, but negatively related to change within the latitude of rejection. This itself has not been adequately tested (Sears & Abeles, 1969), but influence does appear to be substantially greater within the latitude of acceptance than within the latitude of rejection (Atkins, Deaux, & Bieri, 1967). Considering political situations, most people seem to be positively influenced by leaders and reference groups they classify as being within the latitude of acceptance, but negatively influenced by those in the latitude of rejection (Sears, 1965).

Mechanisms of Resistance

The most common view (deriving most directly from cognitive-dissonance theory) is that various mechanisms are typically used to resist persuasion, and that they are more or less functionally equivalent. Those cited most often, besides attitude change, are source derogation, distortion of the source's position, dissociation, and the gaining of social support.

The main weakness of this view has been inadequate empirical support. In the numerous studies that have been conducted on discrepancy, attitude change has indeed generally increased with greater discrepancy up to a point, and then diminished. According to dissonance theory, some other mode of dissonance reduction should have replaced attitude change at that point. However, there is little evidence that this in fact did happen in these experiments.

Something that *is* clear is that the communication itself becomes increasingly disparaged with greater discrepancy (Hovland, Harvey, & Sherif, 1957; Bochner & Insko, 1966). And in many cases the source of information also receives the same treatment. At high discrepancy, then, the effective block to further influence may be a blanket rejection of the communication, once it advocates what appear to be ridiculous positions. Sometimes this also involves discrediting the source of information. In either case, apparently, people are willing to settle for a response that is no more complicated or detailed than a simple blanket rejection whenever something begins to disagree too sharply with their own position. The viewers of the Kennedy-Nixon debates, and Democrats watching the Knowland telethon, apparently responded in just this way and, accordingly, avoided having to change their minds.

A second consistency theory, developed specifically for mass communication effects such as those under consideration here, is congruity theory (Osgood & Tannenbaum, 1955). It focuses especially on attitude change and source derogation, which it regards as reciprocal effects. That is, to the extent that an individual changes his opinion, he will not derogate the source, but to the extent that he resists changing his opinion, he will derogate the source instead. There is an impressive amount of empirical evidence for congruity theory (Tannenbaum, 1967). In political situations, certainly, a most common response to discrepant information is source derogation, along with blanket rejection.

To summarize:

1. Most people do not acquire a very large proportion of the political information available to them in their normal environments. Nevertheless, they seem to sample more or less randomly from what is available; there is little evidence of widespread motivated selective exposure, selective learning, or selective perception. In short, they appear to receive just about what is in their environment, although their rate of receptivity is not very great.
2. They do *evaluate* incoming information extremely selectively. The key variables in determining their evaluations are communication discrepancy, communicator credibility, and their involvement in their initial attitudes. People are particularly adept at avoiding acceptance of information that is

discrepant from strongly held prior attitudes.

3. Consequently, mass communications lead to resistance, rather than substantial opinion change, when they advocate a discrepant position *and* the target individual is strongly attached to his initial position. Reinforcement of prior attitudes should occur with messages of low discrepancy presented by high credibility sources. Other combinations of involvement, credibility, and discrepancy should, however, lead to much more promising opportunities for persuasion.

POLITICAL PERSUASION

If we translate these general social psychological variables into their most common political manifestations, what additional insights do we get about *political* persuasion, and particularly into the political occasions for each of these three types of communication effects? Let us consider the dimensions of involvement in an initial attitude, and source credibility, in turn, focusing upon the overcoming of resistance to change rather than upon solving the "exposure problem."

Predispositions versus Nonattitudes

Certain attitude objects obviously evoke attitudes with all the earmarks of high involvement. Many even seem to do so on an enduring, long-term basis. Yet on the whole, most Americans are uninvolved in their political attitudes, at least when compared with the standard set by political activists (although not, perhaps, when compared with citizens of other nations, according to Almond and Verba, 1963). Indeed, one writer (Converse, 1970) has gone so far as to label many responses to attitude questions as "nonattitudes," on the grounds that they merely represent momentary and transitory dispositions to respond in one way or another, quickly replaced by another, equally ephemeral, disposition. Let us consider this contrast in more detail.

One might pose a number of criteria by which long-standing attitudinal dispositions could be contrasted with transitory and ephemeral preferences: (1) earlier acquisition in life; (2) greater stability; (3) greater internal consistency; and (4) greater ability to control opinion formation on other issues. As research has accumulated, it has begun to appear that most attitudes fitting these criteria refer either to groups or to persons. In contemporary America, the most salient among these are, perhaps, those attitudes referring to political party, to racial issues, to nation, and to some particularly well-known political personalities. Let us here merely suggest some of the evidence for this contention (see Sears, 1969a, for a more detailed treatment).

There is now convincing evidence of the early acquisition of racial attitudes (Proshansky, 1966), nationalism (Hess & Torney, 1967), and political partisanship (Greenstein, 1965; Hess & Torney, 1967). Whether or not children acquire these in anything like their adult form is not so clear; rather, they seem to be simple affects or commitments, with little informational content. Still, most children do not acquire attitudes on other political and social matters until later (Sigel, 1968), and these early preferences show a certain stability, consistency, and ability to determine other opinions (Hess & Torney, 1967; Sears, 1969a).

It seems clear, moreover, that early familial influence is more marked on the child's racial attitudes and party identification than in a whole host of other areas, partly because the parents' racial and partisan attitudes are a good deal clearer to the child than any of their other political and social attitudes (Niemi, 1967). The same holds for parents' presidential preferences; these probably are the political and social attitudes most clearly communicated by parents to their children. By these several standards, then, it appears that attitudes referring to political party, race, nation, and some public personalities are acquired earlier than are other social and political attitudes.[3]

These attitudes appear also to be more stable, over both long and short terms. Panel studies have demonstrated short-term stability most convincingly. For example, Converse (1964) has shown that racial attitudes and party identification are more stable over two- or four-year periods than are any of a variety of other political attitudes tested. The stability of presidential preferences through a campaign is well-known (Lazarsfeld et al., 1948; Benham, 1965).

Longer term stability is more of an unknown, since longitudinal studies of attitudes have been conducted only on a few rather specialized, and usually highly politicized, samples (cf. Bloom, 1964; Newcomb, Koenig, Flacks, & Warwick, 1967). Retrospective reports can yield some information, and relatively few respondents do report having changed parties (Campbell et al., 1960).

Another imperfect, but somewhat edifying, test of stability is to look at persons subjected to major environmental changes, especially changes from one attitudinally homogeneous environment to another. For example, social and geographical mobility may not influence party or racial attitudes as much as is usually thought (Campbell et al., 1960; Barber, 1965; Sears, 1969a). Marriage may have substantial effects, and thus be an exception in this respect, but the change of environment marriage involves is considerably more proximate and immediate, and the affective ties more complex, than is the case for most other environmental changes—and even so, the data on its effects are not yet very clear (Sears, 1969a).

Systematic tests of the relative internal consistency or controlling power of various kinds of attitudes have been less common. What indications there are indicate that by both criteria, the predispositions we have spoken of tend to be more coherent and powerful (Converse, 1964; Sears, 1969a).

By these several tests, then, group-related predispositions seem to be acquired rather early in life, with heavy affective loading and little informational content, and to be maintained with considerable persistence. Most important for our purposes, these core predispositions represent organizing influences on the individual's other attitudes. When one is invoked, other attitudes tend to fall into line. A prominent leader of the individual's own political party tends to be believed more than does a leader of the opposition. When nonracial matters get mixed up with race, they tend to be evaluated consistent with racial attitudes. Indeed, it now seems likely that many political attitudes reflect little more than the evaluation of new information consistent with basic predispositions to which the individual is highly committed, especially party and race.

Other, nonpolitical, residues of socialization also can form a basis for political evaluation. Recent disputes about styles of clothing, obscenity, hallucinogenic drugs, and comportment toward authority have illustrated their political potential, as liberals have learned to their sorrow. Such matters may not become a question of partisan dispute very often, but the socialization of most Americans to a common set of conventions and norms provides a basis for highly resistant attitudes that are

[3] Why groups and persons as stimuli should attract such stable and consistent attitudes is not clear. Perhaps sometimes they simply conveniently symbolize shared interests for the individual voter (cf. Key, 1955), becoming a tradition passed from generation to generation, because they are repeatedly evoked in election campaigns. A second possibility is that they are unusually simple as cues and, hence, consistently evoke a standard response. A complex political issue, on the other hand, may evoke a variety of different responses when it arises in different forms in public life. This would seem to be a good area for additional research.

every bit as powerful as group-related predispositions.

And adults' private interests—economic, self-preservation, or otherwise—sometimes become politically relevant. It is likely that the evaluation of incoming information is fully as selective when protecting one's economic interests as when protecting one's racial views. Sometimes one's private interests are pitted against group-related predispositions. Americans do appear to have some enthusiasm for military adventures, so long as they are glamorous, successful, short, and cheap. The mild military adventurism of postwar American foreign policy has rested on some fairly solid nationalistic popular support. But Americans have likewise shown little patience for war as casualties and expenses mount; with perhaps the sole exception of World War II, every American war has met with great domestic division and hostility. The desire for a return to "normalcy" has soon manifested itself in the protracted and seemingly inconclusive wars of the twentieth century. Americans do not seem to be "stayers," once their own lives become affected, although they are strong early nationalistic sprinters (Mueller, 1971).

On these matters involving stable predispositions and other residues of socialization, or those occasions when private interests become politically relevant, one could safely predict massive resistance to persuasion attempts. Even if one can penetrate the exposure barrier, little attitude change can be expected from high-discrepancy messages on matters of great involvement and commitment.

Aside from these, however, most people are not highly involved in their attitudes on most issues. When asked by pollsters, some people say they have no opinion while other people express opinions that Converse (1970) describes as "non-attitudes," since with time they turn out to be transitory and meaningless, following a pattern that looks statistically like random movement over time. In fact, he has estimated that as few as 20 percent of the public have genuine and stable attitudes on the ordinary policy issue.

There are other indicators of the general lack of involvement in political-policy attitudes. They tend to be quite unstable over time (Converse, 1964). Most policy attitudes are only weakly intercorrelated within individuals, even when activists see positions on them as ideologically closely related. And most people do not organize their political thinking around any abstract ideology; Campbell and associates (1960) estimated that during the 1950s only 11.5 percent of the general public held some version of the common liberal or conservative ideologies about domestic economic ideology. More recent studies using more lenient criteria still come up with no more than a third of a national sample as ideologues (Field & Anderson, 1970).

Thus policy attitudes are rarely invested with much involvement.

The clear implication is that political persuasion is easy and perhaps even very common on these policy matters; indeed, what Converse describes statistically as random movement may in fact be simply the oscillation that occurs as a consequence of persuasion back and forth with every new piece of information input. Obviously there is no such thing as pure randomness; what is involved in "random movement" is hyperresponsiveness to incidental and transitory stimulation. Presumably, then, concerted propaganda campaigns on them meet relatively little resistance in the public as a whole; the problem is one of exposure rather than of resistance. This is not to minimize the depth of the problem, of course; as seen earlier, the exposure problem is so serious as to be insurmountable on most issues most of the time.

Political Communicators

At first glance, political communicators would seem to operate in quite a disadvantageous context. Most notably, their obvious partisanship should depress their persuasiveness by minimizing their credibility. Furthermore, their biases are usually known in advance, and some experiments indicate that resistance to discrepant information is increased with advance warning of the position to be advocated, or when a biased communicator has clear persuasive intent (Allyn & Festinger, 1961; McGuire and Papageorgis, 1962; Walster & Festinger, 1962). Indeed, the voter's defenses and resistances should be at a maximum, since the political campaign seems almost to be the ideal case of overt persuasive intent by obviously biased and partisan communicators. Finally, there is the popular belief that voters generally "vote against" a candidate rather than "vote for" the person they indeed vote for. This would suggest again rather low credibility for most political candidates.

Things are not as simple as they seem, however. In the first place, this may underestimate the credibility of political candidates. Political roles have high prestige in America, as in other nations (Inkeles & Rossi, 1956; Hodge, Siegel, & Rossi, 1964). Ratings of federal appointees, congressmen, and top-level civil servants were all highly positive in a variety of samples, including the general public, according to a large-scale study by Jennings, Cummings, and Kilpatrick (1966).

Second, oppositional voting is probably considerably less common than this would indicate. Lane (1965) reports that fewer than one-fourth of the public "votes against" the disfavored presidential candidate rather than "votes for" his opponent. This skewness toward positive evaluations of political persons, or the *positivity bias*, will be considered in considerable detail below because of its important implications for the success of efforts at political persuasion. Here it is enough to note its two main consequences: (1) political sources have, on the average, generally high credibility, and (2) the positivity bias is sufficiently strong that in America even the best-known members of the opposition political party are typically regarded as positive sources, and command positive influence (Sears, 1965; 1969a).

Finally, it is not even so clear that "untrustworthy" sources generally operate at a disadvantage in persuasion situations, whether political or not. McGuire's (1969) copious review of the attitude change literature suggests that trustworthiness is not a particularly important determinant of communicator effects, particularly by contrast to variables such as expertness and attractiveness.

Even overt intent to persuade or forewarnings of the position to be advocated, once thought to inhibit attitude change, have been shown actually to promote it under some circumstances. Subjects tend to change their attitudes more when forewarned or when an overt attempt is made to persuade them when they find the source attractive (Mills & Aronson, 1965) or when the subject is comparatively uninvolved in his initial view (Apsler & Sears, 1968). If indeed the positivity bias means that most political sources are regarded as attractive, the overtly partisan nature of much political propaganda may actually facilitate attitude change, rather than inhibit it. Thus, as far as communicator attributes are concerned, it is easy to underestimate the advantages that a political propagandist works under.

Finally, there is the very important case of the credibility of the president in making foreign policy. The loss of credibility under President Johnson (the so-called credibility gap) was so widely noted partly because in the postwar period the president has been viewed so generally as a highly credible source on foreign policy. In fact, there is substantial evidence that during that period, the more information a citizen had about foreign policy, the more likely he was to support the president's position (Rosi, 1965; Rogers, Stuhler, & Koenig, 1967; Sears, 1969a; etc.). Foreign policy issues fit what Gamson and Modigliani (1966) call the "mainstream model"; i.e., increases in information simply tended to bring the individual around to a mainstream position.

Since in foreign policy this most often meant converting the individual to the president's position, whatever it currently was and however unstable *it* was, this was a case in which the extraordinary credibility of the president produced continuing attitude change among informed persons.[4]

The Reinforcement Conclusion Revisited

The conclusion that communications mainly reinforce preexisting attitudes is obviously incomplete. However, it does seem to fit presidential campaigns (in which little change from any source occurs),[5] and they have been most widely studied. And Converse (1962) has reported that information exposure was negatively related to change among those exposed to the campaign in the mass media.

So little persuasion occurs in presidential campaigns because resistance to change is high, due principally to high involvement. Moreover, circumventing the exposure problem actively reinforces prior preferences, partly because de facto selectivity insures that information reaches its supporters more often than it reaches its opponents, thereby reinforcing rather than converting. Moreover, partisan interpretation rules in evaluating new information.

Presidential campaigns have this effect principally because of the relevance of long-standing, organizing, partisan predispositions. This is just one case of a general rule: whenever these predispositions are relevant, additional information can be expected mainly to reinforce the individual's prior attitudes and to bring them into immovable harmony with his predispositions. Obviously, elections differ greatly in the salience of group-related predispositions to the voting choice. For example, partisan elections elicit more stable voting than nonpartisan or primary elections (Abelson, 1968). Elections in which race is salient tend, over the course of the campaign, to align the voter's attitudes with his basic racial dispositions (Becker & Heaton, 1967; Wolfinger & Greenstein, 1968; Sears & Kinder, 1971). Very stable attitudes should also be characteristic regarding candidates toward whom the voters have long-standing attitudes, e.g., incumbents.

The same outcome—implementation of preexisting opinions—has also been hypothesized for individuals who receive little or no information about an election campaign but who have durable predispositions (Converse, 1962). These are especially common in lesser elections, such as congressional or local races, in which one can therefore expect party-line voting in partisan elections, or unusual popularity of the incumbent when there is no party label. Where salient, other group labels may prove to be useful indicators for the voter, such as ethnicity or race, and these function much the same as incumbency or party affiliation in determining the vote.

In short, given strong predispositions, both voters with no current information and those with high information tend not to change very much. In the latter case, de facto selectivity and partisan interpretation prevent change; in the former, the absence of any new information insures that the individual will implement his standing predisposition.

Maximum change in presidential elections occurs, according to Converse (1962), among those with modest amounts of information who also happen to have relatively weak preexisting opinions. In fact, if one looks at the *switchers* in presidential elections, their partisanship and informa-

---

4 This may also be a special case of the general principle that Americans are strongly attached to the major institutions of their government and to the individuals within it. This will be discussed below in greater detail (see also Prothro & Grigg, 1960; McClosky, 1964; Greenstein, 1965; Hess & Torney, 1967).

5 Panel studies in 1940, 1960, and 1964 measured 8 percent, 7 percent, and 10 percent, respectively, of the voters changing during the campaign (see Lazarsfeld, Berelson, & Gaudet, 1948; Benham, 1965).

tion level are both usually low (Sears, 1969a).

Change is more common in other political situations, most generally when such predispositions are weak or nonexistent; then overcoming the exposure problem should lead to more attitude change. In some of these, strong predispositions are not relevant, such as in nonpartisan elections, elections with no ethnic or racial cues, or in primary elections in which party differences are not varied. Similarly, communications about new and unfamiliar candidates, or during the precampaign or early campaign phases, should be particularly influential. Klapper (1960) observes more generally that mass communications are quite effective on new issues. And of course "nonattitudes" are very susceptible to change, even if it is only momentary and unsustained attitude change (see McGuire, 1969, for a provocative discussion of the conditions under which change is maintained or dissipates over time).

Finally, it might be added that activation of latent preferences and other minor changes does occur even under the least optimal conditions for substantial conversion. For example, although the Kennedy-Nixon debates changed relatively few votes, they did lead many people to feel somewhat more favorable toward Kennedy and somewhat less favorable toward Nixon. Similarly, the debates aided many vacillating Democrats to crystallize their preference for the Democratic candidate. These are important and substantial changes, even though not as glamorous as converting a strong Nixon supporter into a strong Kennedy supporter.[6]

ELECTORAL CHANGE

On the basis of this analysis, major electoral changes would seem to be rare. Insofar as partisan predispositions remain constant, familiar incumbents remain in office, and issues remain constant. Thus the two most apparent preconditions for electoral change would seem to be (1) change in political predispositions, or in their relevance, and (2) turnover of the objects of political evaluation, such as the arrival of new candidates, or the raising of new issues.

Realignment and Resocialization

Research has focused on two ways in which political predispositions change: in terms of the political realignment of large social groups (Key, 1955), and in terms of the political resocialization of individuals (Langton, 1967; Newcomb et al., 1967). In the first place, fundamental realignments tend to occur very rarely. More common are "deviating elections," in which established older voters temporarily defect from their habitual party identification (Campbell et al., 1960). When realignment does occur, it results primarily from changes in the political allegiances of a new cohort of voters just entering the electorate rather than from changes in allegiances of established older voters (Wolfinger, 1965; Sears, 1969a). It seems unlikely at the moment that party identification changes very much at the individual level through the life span.

The role of political persuasion is not minimized by assuming that realignment occurs more as a result of intergenerational

[6] There are other ways in which the media may indirectly influence political behavior. Further research is needed on (*a*) the effects of broadcasting early election returns on both voter turnout and voting decisions, although what little research there is indicates minimal effects (Lang & Lang, 1968); (*b*) similarly, the effects of public opinion polls and estimates of crowd size at political rallies on the voter's perceptions of candidate popularity (e.g., Rucker, 1960); (*c*) the persuasive effects of "entertainment" programs that contain political messages or deal with political issues, such as TV programs or movies: e.g., Phillips, Hansen, & Carlson's (1965) study of dramatic productions and attitude change; (*d*) the ability of candidates to enhance their TV image (cf. Wyckoff, 1968); (*e*) the effects of news coverage of riots and demonstrations on actual riot activity or on the voter's idea of the extent of rioting.

discontinuity than individual attitude change, however. Rather, it focuses on persuasion of a particular age group, those entering adulthood and the electorate. Substantial political changes can be and are produced among those in late adolescence and early adulthood, especially those in contact with progressive intellectual and media sources (Middleton & Putney, 1964; Newcomb et al., 1967).

Major political events, such as the Great Depression or the war in Vietnam, also have especially powerful political consequences upon the young (Campbell et al., 1960; Sears, 1969a). Resocialization experiences in school and college, whether caused by peers or teachers (Langton, 1967; Newcomb et al., 1967) or outside of school in other settings, such as integration of the military (Stouffer, Suchman, DeVinney, Star, & Williams, 1949), also have been shown to have major effects. Most of these effects can be attributed to the lower involvement in political predispositions, and less marked de facto selectivity, typical of this age level. However, this potentially exciting area of research (i.e., life-cycle effects) has not been adequately explored to date.

Predispositions may also change rather sharply in their relevance to political decisions. Social class appears to have diminished in importance since the days of the New Deal (Campbell et al., 1960), whereas race has become much more important throughout the nation (Wolfinger & Greenstein, 1968; Sears & Kinder, 1971). The Democratic New Deal coalition based upon an alliance between labor, minority groups, and the South appears currently to be fragmenting due to the increased tendency for the white working class to vote its conservative racial attitudes rather than its more liberal economic attitudes, and for Southern whites to vote more on the basis of race than party (Converse, Clausen, & Miller, 1965; Riley, Sears, & Pettigrew, 1969). Again it should be emphasized that this in itself is a major source of electoral realignment, and is quite rare.

Image Politics

A much more common contributor to electoral change than attitude change toward a familiar object is what Stokes (1966a) has called "object turnover," in which one political object is replaced with another. Stokes particularly emphasizes the turnover of candidates, presuming substantial stability of attitudes toward specific political figures.[7] In fact, relatively little is known about the stability of attitudes toward public persons, but Stokes's aggregate data on presidential voting, as well as data on individual candidate preferences (Lazarsfeld et al., 1948; Benham, 1965, etc.) tend to sustain his contention. On the other hand, ratings of presidents' performances have consistently shown systematic and substantial declines over their tenures in office (Dahl, 1967). Still, Stokes's argument seems extremely plausible, and it suggests primary attention to the formation of the "images" of new candidates to account for major electoral changes.

Content of Images

It seems clear that the affective or evaluative component accounts for much of the variance in the content of images or impressions of other people (Osgood, 1962). This is demonstrated most graphically in the importance that adjectives such as *warm* have in determining the likability of another person (Kelley, 1950). Osgood and his colleagues (1957) also emphasize the activity and potency dimensions in meaning, and it is a reasonable hypothesis that these same dimensions also play a key role in the determination of interpersonal impressions.

[7] One can go even further. Sears and Freedman (1967) found that simply advertising some arguments as novel and unfamiliar increased their persuasiveness, even when exactly the same arguments were given to all subjects. Perhaps unfamiliar political persons have some extra attractiveness for that reason alone.

Other discussions of person perception (cf. Tagiuri, 1969) have emphasized other dimensions of interpersonal perception, but there is little enough that has been done of a systematic nature in describing political figures' images. The few attempts (cf. McGrath & McGrath, 1962; Converse & Dupeux, 1966; L. R. Anderson & Bass, 1967) have been rudimentary and have emphasized little besides a basic affective disposition. Of course this may account for so much of the variance that little else need be said; but the research done so far has not adequately tested this notion.

Origins of Images

A discussion of the origins of images most profitably begins with the determinants of liking or interpersonal attraction in general. Here a most powerful variable is agreement with the stimulus person on matters of opinion. Osgood and Tannenbaum's (1955; Tannenbaum, 1967) congruity theory views attraction to another person as a function of agreement on attitude issues, with the most influential issues being those that are most intensely evaluated. Byrne (1969) also has documented the contribution of simple belief similarity to interpersonal attraction. The more sophisticated versions of the "race and belief" experiments treat attaction as a function of similarity on many important dimensions, particularly attitudinal and racial (Sears & Abeles, 1969).

Party identification, racial attitudes, and other simple predispositions are extremely important in determining attitudes on other political issues, as indicated earlier, and determination of impressions of political figures is merely a special case of this general principle. It is likely that by far the most important determinants of impressions of political figures is party identification (Converse & Dupeux, 1966), followed by other group dimensions such as ethnicity and race.

Above and beyond the contribution of these simple predispositions, however, are substantial variations in attraction to public figures. A Democratic voter may like some Democratic candidates much more than others. What accounts for these variations? Stokes (1966b) has pursued further attitudinal similarities between voter and candidate by distinguishing between *valence* and *position* issues as determinants of candidate images.

Valence Issues

The valence issue is one that has only one good side; e.g., corruption, support for motherhood, and patriotism. The only question is whether the candidate will be labeled with the good or the bad side of it, since there is no disagreement about which is good and which is bad. The conditions under which a given public figure becomes associated with one or the other side of a valence issue are as yet very poorly understood, and this should be an important subject for research. It is one of the great obsessions of campaign managers, but so far there has been little systematic theoretical or empirical headway on the problem.

Position Issues

Position issues, on the other hand, are those on which viable and popular alternatives exist. It has often been thought that the voter evaluates a candidate as a function of their agreement on the pressing and compelling issues of the day. Key (1966) made the most exhaustive effort to document this proposition empirically with, however, indifferent success (Sears, 1969a). Moreover, much research done by others (Lazarsfeld et al., 1948; Campbell et al., 1960; and others) has deprecated the role of issues in determining candidate evaluation. A virtual avalanche of more recent studies has, however, grown out of the conviction that issues are very important (see Kessel, 1972, for a good bibliography).

According to our view expressed above,

position issues should be most likely to play a role in candidate evaluation when they invoke some long-standing predisposition held by the individual voter. A clear, forthright stand on the racial issue, some association of the candidate with the voter's own economic standing, or some invocation of patriotism should produce marked changes in candidate evaluations. The Democrats' successful labeling of Barry Goldwater as opposed to social security and in favor of nuclear war is a clear example, as is Goldwater's successful pursuit of "the Southern strategy" by his failure to support civil rights strongly (Benham, 1965; Converse et al., 1965).

Tannenbaum (1967) has conducted a number of experiments that suggest image change can most effectively be induced by first changing attitudes toward a position with which the political figure is associated. In fact, a direct attack on a source (U.S. Public Health Service) by a news agency (Associated Press) was ineffective in eliciting negative attitude change towards the source. In this series, direct attacks were effective only once: when a (presumably highly respected) faculty committee dismissed a professor for unethical conduct.

This raises the more general question of the impact upon images of circumstances beyond the political leader's control. For example, it is not clear under what conditions a national crisis helps or hurts a particular candidate. The example of Hoover, whose reputation was broken by the onset of the depression, and the example of Lyndon Johnson, who apparently was broken by Vietnam, contrasts with the experience of Eisenhower and Kennedy, both of whom seem to have been helped by minor national disasters such as the U-2 incident and the Bay of Pigs fiasco (Katz & Piret, 1964).

Other Determinants of Attractiveness

There are, of course, numerous other variables that contribute to the attractiveness of one individual to another. Some simple physical proximity, for example, is a surprisingly powerful variable (Festinger, Schachter, & Back, 1950; Newcomb, 1961). The "friends and neighbors effect" is perhaps the political analogue (Key, 1949; Miller & Stokes, 1966). Familiarity tends to increase attractiveness also, as will be discussed in greater detail below (Greenwald & Sakumura, 1967; Zajonc, 1968b). However, much work remains to be done.

POSITIVITY BIASES IN POLITICAL EVALUATION

A second major cognitive bias is toward positive evaluations. Its political importance in evaluating political persons has already been suggested in connection with the credibility of political communicators, and by the centrality of candidate images in promoting electoral change. In this section we wish to consider the extent to which this bias is characteristic of political evaluation in the American public, present some possible explanations for it, and then consider how positivity biases affect the formation and change of impressions of other people.

Prevalence of Positivity Biases

Adult Americans tend more often to be positive than negative in evaluating people in general, and political figures in particular. The empirical data are quite compelling on this point; ratings of stimulus persons elicited in laboratory and field studies are consistently positive, whether the person being described is known (Deutsch & Solomon, 1959; Gerard, 1961; Price, Harburg, & Newcomb, 1966) or unknown (Zajonc & Burnstein, 1965a; 1965b; Podell & Amster, 1966; Feather & Armstrong, 1967; Feather & Jeffries, 1967). Bruner and Tagiuri (1954) review the earlier work on person perception showing this tendency to give positive evaluations (the "leniency effect"). Finding that subjects were unwilling to rate a low credibility source negatively, Greenberg and Miller (1966:136) suggest that: "In the absence of personal experience with the source, audiences may respond to sources in a somewhat positive manner."

Political figures also receive typically positive evaluations, whether they are known to their respondent or not. Adams (1960; 1962) tested the credibility and persuasive power of a variety of news sources and found a general tendency for unnamed sources (e.g., "a government official") to be evaluated positively and to have a positive effect on opinion change.

Gallup's ratings of presidential performance have, over a considerable length of time, tended much more often to be positive than negative (Dahl, 1967). Even members of the opposition party tend to rate presidential performance positively (Lane, 1965), just as Republicans rated Adlai Stevenson's performance in the United Nations positively, despite his partisan history (Hero, 1966). Presidential candidates in general have been rated positively, with the notable exceptions of Stevenson in 1956 and Goldwater in 1964 (Stokes, 1966a). In fact, it is surprising to informed pollsters when any major candidate is rated negatively overall (Becker & Heaton, 1967).

Even seemingly obvious instances of disaffection and cynicism, when viewed more closely, reveal positivity (Levin, 1960). The extent of this bias toward positivity is suggested in the ratings of political leaders by UCLA students (Sears, 1965). The average student rated almost all leaders in his own party positively, and about half the opposition leaders as well. Newcomb and his associates (1967:24) report a comparable finding with Bennington students.

Evaluations of political groups tend also to be positive much more often than not. The political parties are generally positively rated (although not as sharply as political leaders), since respondents are generally more favorable to their own party than they are negative toward the opposition (Campbell, Gurin, & Miller, 1954; Almond & Verba, 1963; Sears, 1965; 1969a; Campbell, 1966). On balance, then, the population is positive toward each (assuming that partisans of each side are roughly equally numerous).

Civil rights groups and black leaders of all persuasions have been evaluated overwhelmingly positively by Negroes in a wide variety of studies (Marx, 1967; Campbell & Schuman, 1968; Sears, 1969b; and others). In almost all cases Negroes have evaluated negatively only the most extreme black nationalists. This holds even in those communities that are just recovering from the effects of major riots, and even among persons arrested during riots, whom one would think would have every reason for being disaffected and antagonistic toward almost everything (Sears, 1969b).

These examples of asymmetry in ratings of people and groups are strong indications of a positivity bias: a tendency to expect and prefer positive rather than negative stimuli in one's perceptions and a tendency to emit positive responses more often than negative. For example, people prefer positive to negative information on unfamiliar topics (Freedman & Sears, 1965), and there have been numerous demonstrations of bias toward positive interpersonal relations, in terms of pleasantness ratings (Morrisette, 1958; Feather & Armstrong, 1967; Feather & Jeffries, 1967; Rodrigues, 1967), expectations about changed attitudes or changed relations (DeSoto & Keuthe, 1959, Burnstein, 1967), and ease of learning (Zajonc & Burnstein, 1965a; 1965b; Zajonc & Sherman, 1967). Presumably this is an indication of the same general disposition to prefer, to learn, and to expect more positive relations than negative relations.[8]

[8] Related findings that go beyond the scope of this chapter include reports by Bradburn and Caplovitz (1965), Cantril (1965), and Brink and Harris (1966) that reveal strong biases toward positive affects expressed about the future, and positive rather than negative affects about oneself.

Demographic Correlates

How general is this positivity bias; to what extent is it characteristic of persons with a wide variety of backgrounds? So far the data here are less complete, but they reveal some important differences. As indicated above, blacks, as well as whites, show it. However, college-educated persons are vastly more likely than less-educated respondents to express negative evaluations of presidential and vice-presidential candidates, and of the two major parties (Sears & Riley, 1969).

Almond and Verba (1963) report more positivity in the United States than in the other Western democracies they tested. Citizens of England, Germany, Italy, and Mexico were much more likely to say negative things about members of political parties other than the one they belong to, and much less likely to be happy about their child marrying someone of the opposite party, than were Americans. These data, although only fragmentary, suggest that there may be something unique to Americans about positivity, although Whitney and Sears (1969) found that Chinese students in Hong Kong give quite positive ratings of most American, British, and Chinese sources. In any case, positivity biases represent a phenomenon found throughout American political life.

Explanations

Let us suggest three alternative explanations for positivity biases: (*a*) the individual's informational environment is predominantly positive, therefore positive stimuli and responses are more available; (*b*) the positivity bias is a habitual response tendency, resulting from prior experiences in which the individual's positive responses were rewarded and negative responses punished; (*c*) the immediate incentives in most situations encourage positive responses and attention to positive stimuli. Available research is not yet adequate to test these explanations; our intention here is simply to explore some new territory, rather than to describe any final answers.

Informational Environment

The first of these explanations has the advantage of simplicity because if most people live in a positive informational world, then even random information sampling would produce predominantly positive input. This in turn should produce predominantly positive attitudes since most contemporary opinion-acquisition models presume either an additive or an averaging process (cf. N. H. Anderson, 1965).

Both Thorndike and Lorge (1944) and Johnson, Thomson, and Frincke (1960) have shown that words with positive meaning occur more frequently than words with negative meaning. Moreover, Lindauer's (1968) content analysis of eighteen standard reference books, short stories, plays, and poetry quotations revealed that 73 percent of the literary references to emotion were pleasant.[9]

As a subset of general linguistic tendencies, we would expect political propaganda also to be mainly positive. While the data are skimpy, content analyses of campaign propaganda indicate generally positive content (Lane, 1959; Ellsworth, 1965), although the end of a campaign may see increasingly negative propaganda (Lazarsfeld et al., 1948; Ellsworth, 1965). There is some evidence that newspaper headlines are more often positive than negative. Winship and Allport (1943) found a three-to-one ratio of optimistic to pessimistic headlines in twelve big-city newspapers over a three-month period during World War II.

[9] Psychologists, perversely, appear to prefer the study of negative emotions. Carlson (1966) found that 69 percent of the references to emotion in 172 introductory psychology texts were of a negative nature (fear, anxiety, hate, etc.), and Lindauer (1968) found that 78 percent of a sample of emotion references in *Psychological Abstracts* were negative.

These studies of mass communications do not necessarily adequately represent the content of informal interpersonal communication about public affairs. We do not know whether it is generally positive or generally negative, whether or not it is a representative sample of people's opinions, whether it is skewed in one direction or another. Additional research would be useful here.

There are two other reasons why the normal process of opinion acquisition ought to skew people's attitudes toward the positive. The exposure preferences of naive subjects tend to favor positive information, although with greater information levels they tend to become more negative (Freedman & Sears, 1965; Sears, 1966; Johnson, 1967). Secondly, familiarity has been shown to promote favorability: Zajonc (1968b) has found that merely increasing the exposure to a stimulus results in increasingly favorable evaluations. This is also implied in studies of friendship (Newcomb, 1961) and of opinion formation (Greenwald & Sakumura, 1967). There could be some indigenous process by which favorability inevitably emerges from familiarity. Harrison (1968) replicated Zajonc's (1968b) findings and presented evidence that increasing familiarity with a stimulus is accompanied by decreased response competition (i.e., response to the target stimulus) and hence less unpleasant affect.

Habitual Tendencies

Alternatively, people may begin early in life to develop habitually positive response tendencies because socialization experiences reward positive response rather than negative. These response tendencies may then persist through life. For example, Feather and Armstrong (1967) suggest that the positivity bias results from past experiences in which positive interpersonal relations have been associated with goal attainment, while negative relations have been associated with failure and unpleasant experiences.

Without here attempting to deal with the full range of children's socialization, some specifically political learning experiences early in childhood can be mentioned. For example, teachers in early grade school try to emphasize positive things about the nation, deliberately refraining from presenting any critiques until junior high school (Hess & Torney, 1967). And a variety of studies have indicated that young children have unusually positive political attitudes: e.g., their benevolent images of political authority (Greenstein, 1965; Hess & Torney, 1967; though Jaros, Hirsch, & Fleron, 1968, present one set of regional exceptions to this); the absence of expressed negative affects about the victory of an opposition presidential candidate (Hess & Torney, 1967); or the highly positive affect young children express toward people of other nationalities, even when they feel highly dissimilar from those peoples (Lambert & Klineberg, 1967). As children grow older, their attitudes become less single-mindedly positive in each of these respects, but in the early stages of political socialization it appears that peer contacts, as well as curricular content, emphasize the positive.

Situational Incentives

A third explanation of the positivity bias is that immediate social reinforcements may often be contingent upon positive overt responses by the individual. For example, Jones (1964) has discussed "ingratiatory" behavior, in which the individual obtains social rewards (such as approval) through praise and flattery. Some careful analysis of the home interview as a social situation might reveal such pressures toward positive responding, thus partially accounting for the positivity bias.

Positivity in Impression Formation and Change

The individual's evaluation of the communicator is an important factor in determining his response to persuasive communications: positively evaluated communicators are more likely to elicit acceptance of the communication. In this section we will consider the role of positivity in determining (*a*) how the individual forms evaluative impressions of communicators, and (*b*) the respective ease of developing and changing positive impressions as opposed to negative ones.

Forming Impressions

Do people accept positive information about others more readily than they accept negative information? At first glance, it would seem that the general preference for positive affects would encourage the formation of positive attitudes towards new people and discourage negative impressions. And, indeed, given a choice, they discount negative information more readily than positive information (N. H. Anderson & Jacobson, 1965).

The preference for positive affects does not necessarily mean that positive information is more useful in forming impressions of others, however. Positive information about a person is ambiguous: it may be an accurate description of him, or it may be invalid, simply reflecting a social norm favoring polite positive descriptions of other people (Briscoe, Woodyard, & Shaw, 1967). As a result, positive information is of limited usefulness in forming first impressions.

Negative information, on the other hand, should be much less ambiguous. As attribution theorists have argued (Jones & Davis, 1965), the noncommonness or unique nature of an event or bit of information aids the attribution process: i.e., unique information is more useful in forming an impression about a specific individual. Negative information should generally be more informative than positive information simply because, given a positive social norm, negative information is more likely to be unique.

The greater pleasantness of positive experiences yields a second reason why negative information would be more informative in many situations. Whenever negative information is useful in helping the individual avoid negative experiences and unpleasant outcomes, he should be particularly attentive to it.

A reasonable general hypothesis is that people prefer hearing about the positive aspects of the stimulus person being described when the situation implies minimal personal consequences for the individual, such as in Anderson & Jacobson's (1965) relatively uninvolving laboratory experiment. However, with increasing implications for his own personal experiences, the individual should become increasingly attentive to negative information: better to be safe than sorry. For example, negative information about a candidate for high political office would be especially important to the voter when he is preoccupied with avoiding negative consequences (such as war or economic reversals) that might personally affect him.

The attribution of responsibility is another area in which positivity-based impressions are important. Like evaluations in general, it depends upon the individual's attitudinal predispositions. Thus a Democrat is much less willing to attribute blame for a negative outcome to a Democratic candidate than to a Republican. Similarly, blacks have been much more loath than whites to blame black rioters (Campbell & Schuman, 1968; Sears & Tomlinson, 1968). And Kingdon (1967) found that successful candidates "congratulated" the voters upon their informedness, while the unsuccessful candidates attributed defeat to factors beyond their control, and to a foolish electorate. Even so, a positivity bias intrudes into causal attributions. For example, Lane (1962) reports that his interviewees were reluctant to place personal blame upon political leaders for things that go wrong. And presumably this affects which causal explanations voters will accept for political events.

Changing Impressions

We noted earlier that positive descriptions of a person are more ambiguous than are negative ones, since it is unclear whether the stimulus person is truly a "good" person or whether he (or whoever describes him) is distorting in order to present himself in a positive light.

In the political world, especially in campaigns, the obvious desires of the candidate to please the voters should act to make his positive behavior especially ambiguous, and any negative behavior especially revealing. Hence, in forming impressions of new candidates a "wait and see" attitude should prevail for positive first impressions; however, initial missteps which elicit negative reactions produce impressions that the voter feels more certain about. Hence these negative first impressions should be less susceptible to change than the positive ones.

There is in fact some impressive evidence that negative first impressions are more stable. Pastore (1960) found that disliked people are seen as having personalities that are less susceptible to change than are those of positively evaluated persons. Similarly, experimental data from several studies indicate that negative first impressions are indeed more resistant to change than are positive first impressions (Freedman & Steinbruner, 1964; Leventhal & Singer, 1964; Briscoe, Woodyard, & Shaw, 1967) although Bossart and DiVesta (1966) found no such differences.

Granting that negative first impressions are difficult to change, under what conditions can initially unfavorable evaluations be overcome? Several laboratory studies suggest that negative first impressions are susceptible to change provided the perceiver maintains some sort of psychological contact with the stimulus person. *Initially* hostile stimulus persons (who are thus, presumably, initially disliked) can elicit quite favorable evaluations of themselves if they change their behavior and become more friendly to the subject (Berkowitz, 1960; Aronson & Linder, 1965; Sigall & Aronson, 1967).

This can be accomplished, of course, only if some sort of contact or interpersonal interaction is maintained. Sustained contact may be difficult to accomplish in many political campaigns, of course, since political candidates often have trouble achieving exposure. To the extent, however, that the candidate attains some degree of exposure, increasing familiarity through mere exposure may result in more positive evaluations of him (Zajonc, 1968b). Thus simple exposure of a candidate to publicity should enhance his attractiveness and help overcome initially negative impressions.

This suggests that the common practice of plastering billboards, walls, and bumpers with posters and other advertisements accomplishes more than merely making the candidate's name more familiar—it should also increase attraction to him. To what extent this familiarity-liking phenomenon is overriden by additional (negative) information about the person or issue is still unclear. It seems likely that the familiarity-liking effect is strongest in the earlier stages of contact with the stimuli. In later stages, other variables may interfere, such as boredom and satiation.

CONFLICT AND INTERPERSONAL AGREEMENT

The third source of cognitive bias critical to the persuasion process is the agreement bias: the preference for interpersonal agreement, and the overestimation of the extent of agreement between oneself and positively valued others.

Both Byrne (1969) and Newcomb (1961) have shown that attitudinal agreement is associated with attraction; some indirect evidence that disagreement is disturbing is provided by I. D. Steiner's (1966) review of several studies showing that disagreement with attractive others is physiologically arousing. However, the agreement bias involves more than just a preference for agreement from positively valued others.

In addition, it includes (*a*) greater *assumed* agreement with attractive others than is objectively the case, as Levinger and Breedlove (1966) found for the political attitudes of married couples; (*b*) preference for agreement from *disliked* others, as indicated by Price, Harburg, and Newcomb's (1966) study of reported peer relations and further implied in several similar laboratory investigations of the pleasantness of perceived social relations (Gerard & Fleischer, 1967; Rodrigues, 1967; Zajonc, 1968a; Whitney, 1971). It is this latter aspect of the agreement bias that distinguishes it most clearly from the consistency bias: with respect to disliked (or negatively rated) others, consistency would be achieved through disagreement which is, of course, contrary to the agreement bias.

That agreement from even disliked others is frequently rated as pleasant rules out cognitive-consistency pressures as the sole explanation for the agreement bias. The implication is that even disliked or inexpert people are right much of the time—more often than liked or expert people are wrong. Thus one possibility is that agreement with almost any human being validates one's views of the world, hence enhancing one's self-esteem.

Like the positivity bias, the agreement bias may result from early socialization experiences. Many writers have pointed especially to the schools in this connection. In the political realm, Hess and Torney (1967) have suggested that grade-school teachers may instill unfavorable attitudes toward political conflict; furthermore, Jennings and Zeigler (n.d.) indicate classroom expression of conflict on controversial matters is suppressed most by the most normative teachers; that is, by teachers with most longevity, by education majors, by those in small towns, and by those in the South and Midwest. In other words, teachers in the heartland of America are the ones who are most concerned about not exposing children to conflict in any form.

In another study it was found that community leaders apparently favored teaching "politics as the resolution of group conflict" only in upper-status communities (Litt, 1963). Teachers are apparently most cautious about teaching political conflict during the period when partisan loyalties are developing, i.e., just before adolescence (Hess & Torney, 1967). It would be interesting to develop more systematic evidence documenting the educational system's teaching children an abhorrence for conflict, a situation obviously placing an almost traumatic limitation upon presentation of the realities of political life.

The degree of relationship between children's rejection of conflict within the political system and their attitudes about ordinary interpersonal conflict and disagreement is an important subject for further research.

Distaste for Political Conflict

This distaste for conflict and disagreement is clearly evident in the political attitudes of adult Americans. For example, Dennis (1966) has presented data indicating that party competitiveness is desired only at an abstract level. Most adults feel that political parties confuse people, that they hurt the country, and that they should not disagree as often as they do. Moreover, it is clear that basic civil liberties, such as freedom of speech, are also supported much more in the abstract than in concrete application (Stouffer, 1955; Prothro & Grigg, 1960). Both support for party competitiveness and endorsement of civil liberties are greater among the young and well educated. Perhaps tolerance for conflict or deviation in general is greater among the young and well educated.

What Lane (1962) has called the "fear of partisanship" also manifests itself in many ways. He observed that the existence of conflict leads most Americans to feel there is something to be said for both sides, so they search for the middle ground. One example is the experiments with American students which indicate that even the most partisan individuals are likely to take a position between the two parties when they disagree (Sears, 1965). They try to strike a middle ground. This kind of behavior follows from our earlier assumption, discussed previously in connection with positivity biases, that Americans think both sides have merit and should be evaluated positively.

This fear of partisanship is normally expressed in terms of a "rational independent norm." According to this norm, the ideal citizen is (1) candidate oriented, (2) independent of fixed party loyalties, and (3) free of influence—he "makes up his own mind" about politics. (Lane wryly notes that, according to this view, most political opinions must be parthenogenic.)

Each of these tendencies may be observed among young children. Hess and Torney (1967) document the internal consistency of these beliefs in preadolescents by showing that "Independents" are more likely to see "voting" as the symbol of government (they call this the "personal-clout illusion"), to vote for the candidate rather than the party, to feel that party membership is not very important and to feel that the parties don't differ very much. This norm implies a distaste for long-standing and permanent partisan commitments that are often divisive and conflictual; these children prefer to be in a position where they can shift around to avoid conflicts. Lane (1962) notes one of the costs of the "rational independent norm": doubt and confusion are rife in Americans' political thinking. Partisanship would be (and indeed often is) a great clarifier, but the positivity and agreement biases work against it.

THREE BIASES WORKING IN CONCERT

Some data on opinion formation reveal just how penetrating the positivity and agreement biases are. Using a hypothetical bill before Congress, Sears (1965) presented each party's position separately to 228 UCLA undergraduates during a period from April 1963 to December 1964. The positivity bias would encourage subjects to agree somewhat with each of the two parties' positions regardless of the subject's own party identification, and this is in fact what happened. The findings showed that 56 percent of these students were positively influenced by both parties (positivity effect), 24 percent were positively influenced by their own party and negatively influenced by the opposition (simple partisanship effect), and only 1 percent were negatively influenced by their own party (negativity effect). Thus, twice as many subjects followed the positivity bias as obeyed a simple partisan or consistency principle.

The dominance of the positivity and agreement biases is even more apparent from trials in which *both* parties' positions were presented simultaneously. In these trials, 87 percent of the subjects were influenced positively by both parties (positivity and agreement effects) and only 5 percent were positively influenced by their own party and negatively by the opposition (partisan effect). That is, almost all the subjects adopted a position somewhere between the two parties' positions when they disagreed; almost none was stimulated by the conflict to endorse his own party's position even more strongly. When these experiments were repeated in late 1969, the same effects obtained.

Our emphasis in the last section of this chapter upon positivity and agreement biases should not be taken to mitigate the significance of political partisanship, or of more general tendencies towards cognitive consistency, as presented earlier. Almost to a man, these students were more influenced by their own party than by the opposition, and usually by significant amounts. Indeed, our impression is that the consistency bias, in the form of group partisanship, is the dominant force in political evaluation. But positivity and agreement biases, by themselves, are theoretically independent of the consistency bias. Because partisanship has received so much attention in the past, and the positivity and agreement biases so little, we wished to give them special emphasis here.

We have not discussed yet a further cognitive bias, *personalizing*. The tendency to use candidate or personal variables in opinion formation rather than long-standing partisan dispositions should follow from the positivity bias and the "fear of partisanship" noted above. That is, if people are generally rated more positively than negatively, and if there is a general preference for positive evaluations, then it is understandable why there would be a reluctance to use cues that involve divisive, conflictful, partisan evaluations (and, consequently, negative affects) and a greater desire to use the pollyannaish world of positive candidate images.

Origins of Partisanship

It does seem that positivity and agreement appear earlier, developmentally, than does partisanship. Hess and Torney (1967) have shown that children have generally positive attitudes until they begin to develop partisan political affects, at about age ten or so. At this point their attitudes toward a variety of political objects (e.g., their reactions to elections, their evaluations of the job each party is doing, and so on) become consistent with their partisan dispositions. Similarly, Lambert and Klineberg (1967) find that affects toward different nationality groups become consistent with felt similarity toward these groups only after about age ten. Since generalized positivity seems to precede consistency, partisan attitudes are generally based on acquiring positive information about preferred objects, not on acquiring dislikes and antagonisms about nonpreferred objects.

Political Implications

Both the positivity and agreement biases should promote satisfactory interpersonal relations and some degree of political consensus. For example, the positivity bias should facilitate the ease of succession in competitive party systems, since both the favored and the opposition side are positively evaluated. That is, the opposition should receive the compliance of the electorate more readily if all along it has been evaluated as an acceptable alternative. There are even some data that indicate a positivity norm is invoked after presidential elections; partisan polarization is reduced, and both winning and losing presidential candidates are more positively evaluated (see Sears, 1969a).

The positive evaluations of both parties should also increase the lability of electoral outcomes, since the opposition is so often seen as an acceptable alternative rather than as an unacceptable alternative. Consequently, the average voter sees defection to the opposition as legitimate and acceptable. Presumably in a system that embodied a more strict partisanship, with the favored party being positively evaluated and the opposition being negatively evaluated, defection would be less acceptable as an alternative, regardless of the relative merits of the candidates or of the implications of campaign issues.

An additional implication of the positive evaluations of both parties is that agreement between representatives of each party is usually interpreted as indicating that everything is all right (Dahl, 1961). It is true that many of the politically alienated (e.g., black militants and the New Left) interpret agreement between representatives of opposing factions as evidence that the individual citizen has been sold out, and they view both major parties as representing a power establishment that does not have their interests in mind. Nevertheless, apparently the dominant pattern in America, as Dahl says, is for interparty agreement to mean everything is all right, and for disagreement to lead to the public's adopting a position somewhere in between the contending factions, as Lane predicted.

One rather foreboding implication of biases for agreement and positivity, however, is that important social problems and failures to solve them may be swept under the rug. Whereas the bulk of the present chapter has focused on persuasion of the electorate by those vying for political office, consider for a moment the attempts by voters to persuade officeholders. In the political unrest of the past several years, there have been recurrent attacks on the lack of responsiveness of American society to its social blemishes. Thus the positivity and agreement biases may be major obstacles to social change via persuasion of the elite by vocal minorities.

One must raise the question whether or not societies best protect themselves by insisting on a greater number of positive relations and descriptions within the society and by psychologically suppressing or forgetting negative relations and events. Allegedly, if there is a consistent pressure away from negative relations toward positive relations, presumably there will be less conflict within the society and the society will be more stable and longer lived. When such pressures to avoid conflict and unpleasantness lead public officials and the majority of the electorate to ignore the needs and desires of various minorities, however, the situation can become volatile, as indicated by the riots and violent demonstrations during the last decade. The bulk of the white electorate, moreover, has been generally disapproving of such overt expressions of disaffection by a minority (Erskine, 1967), and the next few years may provide the testing ground for the viability of a positivistic, conflict-avoidance ideology in an era with so many undeniable conflicts. A society with such strong norms for positive evaluation and for agreement with others may be poorly equipped for dealing directly with internal social strains.

It may be that childhood socialization that includes the teaching of conflict and its resolution in the political realm might help overcome some of the difficulties now being encountered. Teaching this view ought to be in the interest of the Establishment, since it is likely to make a child a conventional, even if more sophisticated, political participant. Yet our children are trained to be ambivalent about the mechanisms for channeling and regulating conflict, such as "politicians" and the two-party system (Sears, 1969a). Evidently there is some fear that acceptance of conflict will impair attachment to the overall system, perhaps by substituting loyalty to narrower interests; however, highly partisan children are currently just as attached to the system as Independents or otherwise uncommitted children (Hess & Torney, 1967).

The existence of such widespread positivity and agreement biases in political evaluation has brought with it, historically, a relatively docile and compliant electorate. The longevity of the American democracy is surely a tribute to, among other things, these norms and the advantages of conflict minimization. However, if past data are any guide, an increasingly educated electorate is likely to be both less uniformly positive and less inclined unquestioningly to accept government policies.

Traditionally, conflict has been dealt with in America by delegating its resolution to representatives in one or another elite, with the presumption that their agreement will be accepted by the public. The question in our mind is whether or not this convention has generated a false sense of security in elites, both in terms of their ability to control minority groups and to control the white, less-affluent majority. These groups now seem less inclined to trust the privileged elite and more inclined to criticize and disagree. Thus the success and stability of the American political system in the next few years may hinge upon its ability to blend its predispositions towards positive descriptions and agreement, with a willingness to acknowledge and deal with its social ills.

REFERENCES

Abelson, Robert P.
1968 "Computers, polls, and public opinion—some puzzles and paradoxes." Trans-action 5:20–27.

Abelson, Robert P.; Elliot Aronson; William J. McGuire; Theodore M. Newcomb; Milton J. Rosenberg; and Percy H. Tannenbaum (eds.).
1968 Theories of Cognitive Consistency: A Sourcebook. Chicago: Rand McNally.

Adams, J. B.
1960 "Effects of reference groups and status in opinion change." Journalism Quarterly 37:408–412.
1962 "Relative credibility of 20 unnamed news sources." Journalism Quarterly 39:79–82.

Allyn, Jane, and Leon Festinger.
1961 "The effectiveness of unanticipated persuasive communications." Journal of Abnormal and Social Psychology 62:35–40.

Almond, Gabriel A., and Sidney Verba.
1963 The Civic Culture. Princeton, New Jersey: Princeton University Press.

Anderson, Lynn R., and Alan R. Bass.
1967 "Some effects of victory or defeat upon perception of political candidates." Journal of Social Psychology 73:227–240.

Anderson, Norman H.
1965 "Averaging vs. adding as a stimulus-combination rule in impression formation." Journal of Experimental Psychology 70:394–400.

Anderson, Norman H., and Ann Jacobson.
1965 "Effect of stimulus inconsistency and discounting instructions in personality impression formation." Journal of Personality and Social Psychology 2:531–539.

Apsler, Robert, and David O. Sears.
1968 "Warning, personal involvement, and attitude change." Journal of Personality and Social Psychology 9:162–166.

Aronson, Elliot.
1968 "Dissonance theory: Progress and problems." Pp. 5–27 in Robert P. Abelson et al. (eds.), Theories of Cognitive Consistency: A Sourcebook. Chicago: Rand McNally.

Aronson, Elliot, and Darwyn Linder.
1965 "Gain and loss of self-esteem as determinants of interpersonal attractiveness." Journal of Experimental Social Psychology 1:156–172.

Aronson, Elliot; J. A. Turner; and J. M. Carlsmith.
1963 "Communicator credibility and communication discrepancy as determinants of opinion change." Journal of Abnormal and Social Psychology 67:31–36.

Atkins, Alvin L.; Kay K. Deaux; and James Bieri.
1967 "Latitude of acceptance and attitude change: Empirical evidence for a reformulation." Journal of Personality and Social Psychology 6:47–54.

Barber, James A., Jr.
1965 "Social mobility and political behavior." Ph.D. Dissertation, Stanford University (unpublished).

Bauer, Raymond A.
1964 "The obstinate audience: The influence process from the point of view of social communication." American Psychologist 19:319–328.

Becker, John F., and E. E. Heaton, Jr.
1967 "The election of Senator Edward W. Brooke." Public Opinion Quarterly 31:346–358.

Benham, Thomas W.
1965 "Polling for a presidential candidate: Some observations on the 1964 campaign." Public Opinion Quarterly 29:185–199.

Berelson, Bernard, and Gary A. Steiner.
1964 Human Behavior. New York: Harcourt, Brace and World.

Berkowitz, Leonard.
1960 "Repeated frustrations and expectations in hostility arousal." Journal of Abnormal and Social Psychology 60:422–429.

Bloom, Benjamin S.
1964 Stability and Change in Human Characteristics. New York: Wiley.

Bochner, Stephen, and Chester A. Insko.
1966 "Communicator discrepancy, source credibility, and opinion change." Journal of Personality and Social Psychology 4:614–621.

Bossart, Philip C., and F. J. DiVesta.
1966 "Effects of context, frequency, and order of presentation of evaluative assertions on impression formation." Journal of Personality and Social Psychology 4:538–544.

Bradburn, Norman M., and David Caplovitz.
1965 Reports on Happiness. Chicago: Aldine.

Brigham, John C., and S. W. Cook.
1969 "The influence of attitudes on the recall of controversial material: A failure to confirm." Journal of Experimental Social Psychology 5:240–243.

Brink, William, and Louis Harris.
1967 Black and White. New York: Simon and Schuster.

Briscoe, M. E.; H. D. Woodyard; and M. E. Shaw.
1967 "Personality impression change as a function of the favorableness of first impressions." Journal of Personality 35:343–357.

Brock, Timothy C., and J. L. Balloun.
1967 "Behavioral receptivity to dissonant information." Journal of Personality and Social Psychology 6:413–428.

Brock, Timothy C., and H. L. Fromkin.
1968 "Cognitive tuning set and behavioral receptivity to discrepant information." Journal of Personality 36:108–125.

Bruner, Jerome S., and Renato Tagiuri.
1954 "The perception of people." Pp. 601–633 in Gardner Lindzey (ed.), Handbook of Social Psychology. Volume 2. Reading, Massachusetts: Addison-Wesley.

Burnstein, Eugene.
1967 "Sources of cognitive bias in the representation of simple social structures: Balance, minimal change, positivity, reciprocity, and the respondent's own attitude." Journal of Personality and Social Psychology 7:36–48.

Byrne, Donn.
1969 "Attitudes and attraction." Pp. 36–90 in Leonard Berkowitz (ed.), Advances in Experimental Social Psychology. Volume 4. New York: Academic Press.

Campbell, Angus.
1966 "Interpreting the presidential victory." Pp. 256–281 in M.C. Cummings, Jr. (ed.), The National Election of 1964. Washington, D. C.: Brookings Institution.

Campbell, Angus; Philip E. Converse; Warren E. Miller; and Donald E. Stokes.
1960 The American Voter. New York: Wiley.

Campbell, Angus; Gerald Gurin; and Warren E. Miller.
1954 The Voter Decides. Evanston, Illinois: Row, Peterson.

Campbell, Angus, and Howard Schuman.
1968 "Racial attitudes in fifteen American cities." Pp. 1–67 in Supplemental Studies for the National Advisory Commission on Civil Disorders. Washington, D. C.: U. S. Government Printing Office.

Cantril, Hadley.
1965 The Pattern of Human Concerns. New Brunswick, New Jersey: Rutgers University Press.

Carlson, Earl R.
1966 "The affective tone of psychology." Journal of General Psychology 75: 65–78.

Cartwright, Dorwin, and Alvin F. Zander.
1968 "Origins of group dynamics." Pp. 3–21 in Dorwin Cartwright and Alvin F. Zander (eds.), Group Dynamics: Research and Theory. Third Edition. New York: Harper and Row.

Converse, Philip E.
1962 "Information flow and the stability of partisan attitudes." Public Opinion Quarterly 26:578–599.
1970 "Attitudes and non-attitudes: Continuation of a dialogue." Pp. 168–189 in Edward R. Tufte (ed.), The Quantitative Analysis of Social Problems. Reading, Massachusetts: Addison-Wesley.
1964 "The nature of belief systems in mass publics." Pp. 206–261 in D. E. Apter (ed.), Ideology and Discontent. New York: Free Press of Glencoe.

Converse, Philip E.; A. R. Clausen; and Warren E. Miller.
1965 "Electoral myth and reality: The 1964 election." American Political Science Review 49:321–336.

Converse, Philip E., and Georges Dupeux.
1966 "De Gaulle and Eisenhower: The public image of the victorious general." Pp. 292–345 in Angus Campbell et al. (eds.), Elections and the Political Order. New York: Wiley.

Dahl, Robert A.
1961 Who Governs? Democracy and Power in an American City. New Haven, Connecticut: Yale University Press.
1967 Pluralist Democracy in the United States: Conflict and Consent. Chicago: Rand McNally.

Davies, James C.
1963 Human Nature in Politics: The Dynamics of Political Behavior. New York: Wiley.

Dennis, Jack.
1966 "Support for the party system by the mass public." American Political Science Review 60:600–615.

DeSoto, C. B., and J. L. Keuthe.
1959 "Subjective probabilities of interpersonal relationships." Journal of Abnormal and Social Psychology 59:290–294.

Deutsch, Morton, and H. B. Gerard.
1955 "A study of normative and informational social influences upon individual judgment." Journal of Abnormal and Social Psychology 51:629–636.

Deutsch, Morton, and Leonard Solomon.
1959 "Reactions to evaluations by others as influenced by self evaluations." Sociometry 22:93–112.

Deutschmann, Paul J., and Wayne Danielson.
1960 "Diffusion of knowledge of a major news story." Journalism Quarterly 37:345–355.

Doob, Leonard W.
1935 Propaganda, Its Psychology and Technique. New York: Holt.

Ellsworth, J. W.
1965 "Rationality and campaigning: A content analysis of the 1960 presidential campaign debates." Western Political Quarterly 18:794–802.

Erskine, Hazel Gaudet.
1963 "The polls: Textbook knowledge." Public Opinion Quarterly 27:133–141.
1967 "The polls: Demonstrations and race riots." Public Opinion Quarterly 31:655–677.

Feather, Norman T., and D. J. Armstrong.
1967 "Effects of variations in source attitude, receiver attitude, and communication stand on reactions to source and content of communications." Journal of Personality 35:435–455.

Feather, Norman T., and D. G. Jeffries.
1967 "Balancing and extremity effects in reactions of receiver to source and content of communications." Journal of Personality 35:194–213.

Festinger, Leon.
1957 A Theory of Cognitive Dissonance. Evanston, Illinois: Row, Peterson.
1964 Conflict, Decision, and Dissonance. Stanford, California: Stanford University Press.

Festinger, Leon; Stanley Schachter; and Kurt Back.
1950 Social Pressures in Informal Groups: A Study of a Housing Project. New York: Harper.

Field, John O., and R. E. Anderson.
1970 "Ideology in the public's conceptualization of the 1964 election." Pp. 329–346 in E. C. Dreyer and W. A. Rosenbaum (eds.), Political Opinion and Behavior: Essays and Studies. Second Edition. Belmont, California: Wadsworth.

Freedman, Jonathan L.
1964 "Involvement, discrepancy, and change." Journal of Abnormal and Social Psychology 69:290–295.

Freedman, J. L., and D. O. Sears.
1965 "Selective exposure." Pp. 58–97 in Leonard Berkowitz (ed.), Advances in Experimental Social Psychology. Volume 2. New York: Academic Press.

Freedman, J. L., and J. D. Steinbruner.
1964 "Perceived choice and resistance to persuasion." Journal of Abnormal and Social Psychology 68:678–681.

Gamson, William A., and Andre Modigliani.
1966 "Knowledge and foreign-policy opinions: Some models for consideration." Public Opinion Quarterly 30:187–199.

Gerard, Harold B.
1961 "Disagreement with others, their credibility, and experienced stress." Journal of Abnormal and Social Psychology 62:559–564.

Gerard, H. B., and Linda Fleischer.
1967 "Recall and pleasantness of balanced and unbalanced cognitive structures." Journal of Personality and Social Psychology 7:332–337.

Greenberg, Bradley S., and G. R. Miller.
1966 "The effects of low credible sources on message acceptance." Speech Monographs 33:127–136.

Greenstein, Fred I.
1965 Children and Politics. New Haven, Connecticut: Yale University Press.

Greenwald, Anthony G., and J. S. Sakumura.
1967 "Attitude and selective learning: Where are the phenomena of yesteryear?" Journal of Personality and Social Psychology 7:387–397.

Harrison, Albert A.
1968 "Response competition, frequency, exploratory behavior, and liking." Journal of Personality and Social Psychology 9:363–368.

Heider, Fritz.
1958 Psychology of Interpersonal Relations. New York: Wiley.

Hennessey, Bernard C.
1965 Public Opinion. Belmont, California: Wadsworth.

Hero, A. O., Jr.
1966 "The American public and the U.N., 1954–1966." Journal of Conflict Resolutions 10:436–475.

Hess, Robert D., and J. V. Torney.
1967 The Development of Political Attitudes in Children. Chicago: Aldine.

Hodge, R. W.; P. M. Siegel; and P. H. Rossi.
1964 "Occupation prestige in the United States, 1925–1963." American Journal of Sociology 70:286–302.

Hovland, Carl I.
1954 "Effects of the mass media of communication." Pp. 1062–1103 in Gardner Lindzey (ed.), Handbook of Social Psychology. Volume 2. Reading, Massachusetts: Addison-Wesley.
1959 "Reconciling conflicting results derived from experimental and survey studies of attitude change." American Psychologist 14:8–17.

Hovland, Carl I.; E. H. Campbell; and Timothy C. Brock.
1957 "The effects of 'commitment' on opinion change following communication." Pp. 23–32 in Carl I. Hovland, Wallace Mandell, E. H. Campbell, T. C. Brock, A. S. Luchins, A. R. Cohen, W. J. McGuire, I. L. Janis, R. L. Feierabend, and N. H. Anderson, The Order of Presentation in Persuasion. New Haven, Connecticut: Yale University Press.

Hovland, Carl I.; O. J. Harvey; and Muzafer Sherif.
1957 "Assimilation and contrast effects in reactions to communication and attitude change." Journal of Abnormal and Social Psychology 55:244–252.

Hovland, Carl I., and I. L. Janis.
1959 "Summary and implications for further research." Pp. 225–254 in Carl I. Hovland and I. L. Janis (eds.), Personality and Persuasibility. New Haven, Connecticut: Yale University Press.

Hovland, Carl I.; I. L. Janis; and H. H. Kelley.
1953 Communication and Persuasion. New Haven: Yale University Press.

Hovland, Carl I.; A. A. Lumsdaine; and F. D. Sheffield.
1949 Experiments on Mass Communication. Princeton, New Jersey: Princeton University Press.

Hyman, H. H., and P. B. Sheatsley.
1954 "The current status of American public opinion." Pp. 33–48 in Daniel Katz, Dorwin Cartwright, S. Eldersveld, and A. M. Lee (eds.), Public Opinion and Propaganda. New York: Holt, Rinehart and Winston.
1958 "Some reasons why information campaigns fail." Pp. 164–173 in Eleanor E. Maccoby, T. M. Newcomb, and E. L. Hartley (eds.), Readings in Social Psychology. New York: Holt.

Inkeles, Alex, and P. H. Rossi.
1956 "National comparisons of occupational prestige." American Journal of Sociology 61:329–339.

Institute for Propaganda Analysis.
1939 The Fine Art of Propaganda: A Study of Father Coughlin's Speeches. New York: Harcourt and Brace.

Jaros, Dean; Herbert Hirsch; and Frederic J. Fleron, Jr.
1968 "The malevolent leader: Political socialization in an American subculture." American Political Science Review 62:564–575.

Jennings, M. Kent; M. C. Cummings, Jr.; and F. P. Kilpatrick.
1966 "Trusted leaders: Perceptions of

appointed federal officials." Public Opinion Quarterly 30:368–384.

Jennings, M. Kent, and H. L. Zeigler.
n.d. "Political expressivism among high school teachers: The intersection of community and occupational values." Unpublished paper.

Johnson, Paula B.
1967 "Exposure preference." Senior honors thesis, Psychology Department, University of California, Los Angeles (unpublished).

Johnson, Paula B.; David O. Sears; and John B. McConahay.
1971 "Black invisibility, the press, and the Los Angeles riot." American Journal of Sociology 76:698–721.

Johnson, Ronald C.; C. W. Thomson; and Gerald Frincke.
1960 "Word values, word frequency, and visual duration thresholds." Psychological Review 67:332–342.

Jones, Edward E.
1964 Ingratiation: A Social Psychological Analysis. New York: Appleton-Century-Crofts.

Jones, E. E., and Keith E. Davis.
1965 "From acts to dispositions: The attribution process in person perception." Pp. 220–266 in Leonard Berkowitz (ed.), Advances in Experimental Social Psychology. New York: Academic Press.

Katz, Elihu.
1957 "The two-step flow of communication: An up-to-date report on an hypothesis." Public Opinion Quarterly 21:69–78.
1968 "On reopening the question of selectivity in exposure to mass communication." Pp. 788–796 in Robert P. Abelson et al. (eds.), Theories of Cognitive Consistency: A Sourcebook. Chicago: Rand McNally.

Katz, Elihu, and J. J. Feldman.
1962 "The debates in the light of research: A survey of surveys." Pp. 173–223 in Sidney Kraus (ed.), The Great Debates. Bloomington: Indiana University Press.

Katz, F. E., and F. V. Piret.
1964 "Circuitous participation in politics." American Journal of Sociology 69: 367–373.

Kelley, Harold H.
1950 "The warm-cold variable in first impressions of people." Journal of Personality 18:431–439.

Kessel, John H.
1972 "Comment: The issues in issue voting." American Political Science Review 66:459–465.

Key, V. O., Jr.
1949 Southern Politics in State and Nation. New York: Vintage Books.
1955 "A theory of critical elections." Journal of Politics 17:3–18.
1966 The Responsible Electorate. Cambridge: Harvard University Press.

Kiesler, Charles A.; Barry E. Collins; and Norman Miller.
1969 Attitude Change: A Critical Analysis of Theoretical Approaches. New York: Wiley.

Kingdon, John W.
1967 "Politicians' beliefs about voters." American Political Science Review 61:137–145.

Klapper, Joseph T.
1960 The Effects of Mass Communications. New York: Free Press of Glencoe.

Koeske, Gary F., and W. D. Crano.
1968 "The effect of congruous source-statement combinations upon the judged credibility of a communication." Journal of Experimental Social Psychology 4:384–399.

Lambert, Wallace E., and Otto Klineberg.
1967 Children's View of Foreign Peoples. New York: Appleton-Century-Crofts.

Lane, Robert E.
1959 Political Life: Why People Get Involved in Politics. Glencoe, Illinois: Free Press.
1962 Political Ideology: Why the American Common Man Believes What He Does. New York: Free Press of Glencoe.
1965 "The politics of consensus in an age of affluence." American Political Science Review 59:874–895.

Lang, Kurt, and G. E. Lang.
1968 Politics and Television. Chicago: Quadrangle Books.

Langton, Kenneth P.
1967 "Peer group and school and the political socialization process."

American Political Science Review 61:751–758.

Lazarsfeld, Paul F.; Bernard Berelson; and Hazel Gaudet.
1948 The People's Choice. Second Edition. New York: Columbia University Press.

Leventhal, Howard, and D. L. Singer.
1964 "Cognitive complexity, impression formation and impression change." Journal of Personality 32:210–226.

Levin, M. B.
1960 The Alienated Voter: Politics in Boston. New York: Holt, Rinehart and Winston.

Levinger, George, and James L. Breedlove.
1966 "Interpersonal attraction and agreement: A study of marriage partners." Journal of Personality and Social Psychology 3:367–372.

Lindauer, M. S.
1968 "Pleasant and unpleasant emotions in literature: A comparison with the affective tone of psychology." Journal of Psychology 70:55–67.

Lipset, Seymour M.
1963 "Three decades of the radical right: Coughlinites, McCarthyites, and Birchers—1962." Pp. 313–378 in Daniel Bell (ed.), The Radical Right. Garden City, New York: Doubleday.

Litt, Edgar.
1963 "Civic education, community norms, and political indoctrination." American Sociological Review 28:69–75.

McClosky, Herbert.
1964 "Consensus and ideology in American politics." American Political Science Review 58:361–382.

McGrath, Joseph E., and M. F. McGrath.
1962 "Effects of partisanship on perceptions of political figures." Public Opinion Quarterly 26:236–248.

McGuire, William J.
1969 "The nature of attitudes and attitude change." Pp. 136–314 in Gardner Lindzey and Elliot Aronson (eds.), The Handbook of Social Psychology. Volume 3. Second Edition. Reading, Massachusetts: Addison-Wesley.

McGuire, William J., and Demetrios Papageorgis.
1962 "Effectiveness of forewarning in developing resistance to persuasion." Public Opinion Quarterly 26:24–34.

Marx, G. T.
1967 Protest and Prejudice: A Study of Belief in the Black Community. New York: Harper and Row.

Middleton, Russell, and Snell Putney.
1964 "Influences on the political beliefs of American college students: A study of self-appraisals." Il Politico 29: 484–492.

Miller, Warren E., and D. E. Stokes.
1966 "Constituency influence in Congress." Pp. 351–372 in Angus Campbell et al. (eds.), Elections and the Political Order. New York: Wiley.

Mills, Judson, and Elliot Aronson.
1965 "Opinion change as a function of the communicator's attractiveness and desire to influence." Journal of Personality and Social Psychology 1:173–177.

Mills, Judson, and J. M. Jellison.
1967 "Effect on opinion change of how desirable the communication is to the audience the communicator addressed." Journal of Personality and Social Psychology 6:98–101.

Morrissette, J. O.
1958 "An experimental study of the theory of structural balance." Human Relations 11:239–254.

Mueller, John E.
1971 "Trends in popular support for the wars in Korea and Vietnam." American Political Science Review 65:358–375.

Murphy, Gardner; Lois B. Murphy; and Theodore M. Newcomb.
1937 Experimental Social Psychology. Revised Edition. New York: Harper.

Newcomb, Theodore M.
1961 The Acquaintance Process. New York: Holt, Rinehart and Winston.

Newcomb, T. M.; K. E. Koenig; R. Flacks; and D. P. Warwick.
1967 Persistence and Change: Bennington College and Its Students After 25 Years. New York: Wiley.

Niemi, R. G.
1967 "A methodological study of political socialization in the family." Ph.D. Dissertation, University of Michigan (unpublished).

Osgood, Charles E.
1962 "Studies on the generality of affective meaning systems." American Psychologist 17:10–28.

Osgood, C. E.; G. J. Suci; and Percy H. Tannenbaum.
1957 The Measurement of Meaning. Urbana: University of Illinois Press.

Osgood, C. E., and P. H. Tannenbaum.
1955 "The principle of congruity and the prediction of attitude change." Psychological Review 62:42–55.

Pastore, Nicholas.
1960 "Attributed characteristics of liked and disliked persons." Journal of Social Psychology 52:157–163.

Phillips, G. M.; B. K. Hansen; and D. L. Carlson.
1965 "A preliminary experiment in measuring attitude shifts as a result of viewing a dramatic production." Speech Monographs 32:209–213.

Podell, Jerome E., and Harriet Amster.
1966 "Evaluative concept of a person as a function of the number of stimulus traits." Journal of Personality and Social Psychology 4:333–335.

Price, Kendall O.; Ernest Harburg; and T. M. Newcomb.
1966 "Psychological balance in situations of negative interpersonal attitudes." Journal of Personality and Social Psychology 3:265–270.

Proshansky, Harold M.
1966 "The development of intergroup attitudes." Pp. 311–371 in Lois W. Hoffman and Martin L. Hoffman (eds.), Review of Child Development Research. Volume 2. New York: Russell Sage.

Prothro, J. W., and C. W. Grigg.
1960 "Fundamental principles of democracy: Bases of agreement and disagreement." Journal of Politics 22:276–294.

Rodrigues, Aroldo.
1967 "Effects of balance, positivity, and agreement in triadic social relations." Journal of Personality and Social Psychology 5:472–476.

Rogers, William C.; Barbara Stuhler; and Donald Koenig.
1967 "A comparison of informed and general public opinion on U.S. foreign policy." Public Opinion Quarterly 31:242–252.

Rosi, Engene J.
1965 "Mass and attentive opinion on nuclear weapons tests and fallout, 1954–1963." Public Opinion Quarterly 29:280–297.

Rossi, Peter H.
1966 "Trends in voting behavior research: 1933–1963." Pp. 67–78 in E. C. Dreyer and W. A. Rosenbaum (eds.), Political Opinion and Electoral Behavior. Belmont, California: Wadsworth.

Rucker, B. W.
1960 "News services' crowd reporting in the 1956 presidential campaign." Journalism Quarterly 37:195–198.

Schramm, Wilbur, and R. F. Carter.
1959 "Effectiveness of a political telethon." Public Opinion Quarterly 23:121–126.

Sears, David O.
1965 "Effects of the assassination of President Kennedy on political partisanship." Pp. 305–326 in B. S. Greenberg and E. B. Parker (eds.), The Kennedy Assassination and the American Public. Stanford California: Stanford University Press.
1966 "Opinion formation and information preferences in an adversary situation." Journal of Experimental Social Psychology 2:130–142.
1968 "The paradox of de facto selective exposure without preferences for supportive information." Pp. 777–796 in Robert P. Abelson et al. (eds.), Theories of Cognitive Consistency: A Sourcebook. Chicago: Rand McNally.
1969a "Political behavior." Pp. 315–458 in Gardner Lindzey and Elliot Aronson (eds.), Handbook of Social Psychology. Volume 5. Second Edition. Reading, Massachusetts: Addison-Wesley.
1969b "Black attitudes toward the political system in the aftermath of the Watts insurrection." Midwest Journal of Political Science 13:515–544.

Sears, David O., and Ronald P. Abeles.
1969 "Attitudes and opinions." Annual Review of Psychology 20:253–288.

Sears, David O., and Jonathan L. Freedman.
1967 "Selective exposure to information: A critical review." Public Opinion Quarterly 31:194–213.

Sears, David O.; Jonathan L. Freedman; and Edward F. O'Connor, Jr.
1964 "The effects of anticipated debate and commitment on the polarization of audience opinion." Public Opinion Quarterly 28:615–627.

Sears, David O., and Donald R. Kinder.
1971 "Racial tensions and voting in Los Angeles." Pp. 51–88 in Werner Z. Hirsch (ed.), Los Angeles: Viability and Prospects for Metropolitan Leadership. New York: Praeger.

Sears, David O., and John B. McConahay.
1973 The Politics of Violence. Boston: Houghton-Mifflin.

Sears, David O., and Robert T. Riley.
1969 "Positivity biases in evaluations of political candidates." Los Angeles: University of California, Los Angeles (unpublished).

Sears, David O., and T. M. Tomlinson.
1968 "Riot ideology in Los Angeles: A study of Negro attitudes." Social Science Quarterly 49:485–503.

Sheatsley, Paul B., and J. J. Feldman.
1965 "A national survey of public reactions and behavior." Pp. 149–177 in B. S. Greenberg and E. B. Parker (eds.), The Kennedy Assassination and the American Public. Stanford, California: Stanford University Press.

Sherif, Muzafer, and Carl I. Hovland.
1961 Social Judgment. New Haven, Connecticut: Yale University Press.

Sigall, Harold, and Elliot Aronson.
1967 "Opinion change and the gain-loss model of interpersonal attraction." Journal of Experimental Social Psychology 3:178–188.

Sigel, Roberta S.
1968 "Image of a president: Some insights into the political views of school children." American Political Science Review 62:216–226.

Star, Shirley A., and Helen M. Hughes.
1950 "Report of an educational campaign: The Cincinnati plan for the United Nations." American Journal of Sociology 55:389–400.

Steiner, Gary A.
1963 The People Look at Television. New York: Knopf.

Steiner, Ivan D.
1966 "Personality and the resolution of interpersonal disagreements." Pp. 195–239 in B. A. Maher (ed.), Progress in Experimental Personality Research. Volume 3. New York: Academic Press.

Stokes, Donald E.
1966a "Some dynamic elements of contests for the presidency." American Political Science Review 60:19–28.
1966b "Party loyalty and the likelihood of deviating elections." Pp. 125–135 in Angus Campbell et al. (eds.), Elections and the Political Order. New York: Wiley.

Stouffer, Samuel A.
1955 Communism, Conformity, and Civil Liberties. New York: Doubleday.

Stouffer, S. A.; E. A. Suchman; L. C. DeVinney; S. A. Star; and R. M. Williams, Jr.
1949 The American Soldier: Adjustment During Army Life. Volume 1. Princeton, New Jersey: Princeton University Press.

Tagiuri, Renato.
1969 "Person perception." Pp. 359–449 in Gardner Lindzey and Elliot Aronson (eds.), Handbook of Social Psychology. Volume 3. Second Edition. Reading, Massachusetts: Addison-Wesley.

Tannenbaum, Percy H.
1967 "The congruity principle revisited: Studies in the reduction, induction, and generalization of persuasion." Pp. 272–320 in Leonard Berkowitz (ed.), Advances in Experimental Social Psychology. Volume 3. New York: Academic Press.

Tannenbaum, P. H., and B. S. Greenberg.
1968 "Mass communication." Annual Review of Psychology 19:351–386.

Thorndike, E. L., and Irving Lorge.
1944 Teachers' Workbook of 30,000 Words. New York: Teachers College, Columbia University.

Troldahl, V. C.
1966 "A field test of a modified two-step flow of communication model."

Public Opinion Quarterly 30:609–623.

Walster, Elaine C.; Elliot Aronson; and D. Abrahams.
1966 "On increasing the persuasiveness of a low prestige communicator." Journal of Experimental Social Psychology 2:325–342.

Walster, Elaine C., and Leon Festinger.
1962 "The effectiveness of 'overheard' persuasive communications." Journal of Abnormal and Social Psychology 65:395–402.

Whitney, Richard E.
1971 "Agreement and positivity in pleasantness ratings of balanced and unbalanced social situations: A cross-cultural study." Journal of Personality and Social Psychology 17:11–14.

Whitney, Richard E., and David O. Sears.
1969 "Political evaluations and influence among Hong Kong Chinese students." Los Angeles: University of California, Los Angeles (unpublished).

Winship, E. C., and Gordon W. Allport.
1943 "Do rosy headlines sell newspapers?" Public Opinion Quarterly 7:205–209.

Wolfinger, Raymond E.
1965 "The development and persistence of ethnic voting." American Political Science Review 59:896–908.

Wolfinger, Raymond E., and F. I. Greenstein.
1968 "The repeal of fair housing in California: An analysis of referendum voting." American Political Science Review 62:753–769.

Wyckoff, Gene.
1968 The Image Candidates: American Politics in the Age of Television. New York: Macmillan.

Zajonc, Robert B.
1968a "Cognitive theories in social psychology." Pp. 320–411 in Gardner Lindzey and Elliot Aronson (eds.), Handbook of Social Psychology. Volume 1. Second Edition. Reading, Massachusetts: Addison-Wesley.
1968b "Attitudinal effects of mere exposure." Journal of Personality and Social Psychology Monograph Supplement 9 (June, Part 2):1–27.

Zajonc, Robert B., and Eugene Burnstein.
1965a "The learning of balanced and unbalanced social structures." Journal of Personality 33:153–163.
1965b "Structural balance, reciprocity, and positivity as sources of cognitive bias." Journal of Personality 33:570–583.

Zajonc, Robert B., and S. J. Sherman.
1967 "Structural balance and the induction of relations." Journal of Personality 35:635–650.

Zimbardo, Philip G.
1960 "Involvement and communication discrepancy as determinants of opinion conformity." Journal of Abnormal and Social Psychology 60:86–94.

CHAPTER 11 Mass Media and Interpersonal Communication

EVERETT M. ROGERS
Michigan State University

Dr. Rogers has himself conducted much of the recent field research on diffusion of innovations that has been a rich source of new ideas about the relationship between mass media and interpersonal communication. In this chapter he reviews and analyzes much of the literature on this relationship and considers such hypotheses as the two-step flow and its latter-day variants. He concludes that mass and personal channels have different but potentially complementary roles, and sketches out what these roles appear to be.

The purpose of this chapter is to discuss the interfaces of two different types of communication channels: mass media and interpersonal. Following a synthesis of the roles of these two channel types in the mass communication process, we review (1) the various models of mass communication flow, (2) the nature of opinion leadership, (3) factors influencing interpersonal relays in the mass communication process, and (4) methods of combining mass media and interpersonal channels. The chapter closes with a focus on future research directions and needed methodological advances.

One theme of the present essay is that *interpersonal and mass media channels have different and potentially complementary roles in creating various communication effects.* Our evidence for this point comes from research on the diffusion of innovations, political and consumer behavior, and the modernization of traditional peoples in less developed nations.

COMMUNICATION CHANNELS

Communication *channels* are the means through which a source(s) conveys a message to a receiver(s). Channels can be thought of as the paths or the vehicles that carry messages from an originating point to a destination.

Grossly categorizing communication channels as either interpersonal or mass media provides an initial focus for analyzing channel effects in the communication process. Word-of-mouth communication

This chapter was written with Dr. Rodolfo N. Salcedo, Assistant Professor, Office of Agricultural Communications, University of Illinois. It profits directly from Rogers with Svenning (1969) and Rogers with Shoemaker (1971).

TABLE 1

CHARACTERISTICS OF COMMUNICATION CHANNELS

Characteristics	Interpersonal Channels	Mass Media Channels
1. Message flow	tends to be two-way	tends to be one-way
2. Communication context	face-to-face	interposed
3. Amount of feedback readily available	high	low
4. Ability to overcome selective processes (primarily selective exposure)	high	low
5. Speed to large audiences	relatively slow	relatively rapid
6. Possible effect	attitude formation and change	knowledge change

that occurs in face-to-face interaction between two or more individuals is classified as *interpersonal.* The channel in the interpersonal situation becomes the individual through whom the message is flowing.[1] *Mass media* channels are all those means of transmitting messages that involve a mechanism to reach a wide and often noncontiguous audience. Newspapers, magazines, film, radio, and television are all channels that permit a source to reach a large and often widely dispersed audience.

Some of the important distinguishing characteristics of interpersonal and mass media channels are shown in Table 1.

The choice of a communication channel depends largely on the purposes or goals of the source. Research findings indicate that the *mass media can effectively change cognitions (that is, increase knowledge), but interpersonal communication is more likely to be effective when attitude change is the goal of the source* (Rogers, 1962).[2] Messages transmitted over the mass media are *alone* unlikely to effect *substantial* changes in strongly held attitudes or overt behavior.[3] Such changes often require that individuals expose themselves to messages that are dissonant with previously held attitudes or beliefs. Messages that reinforce prevailing attitudes and beliefs are more likely to get through, while

[1] In the interpersonal communication situation, the source and channel can be the same individual. However, it is also possible for the source to choose an interpersonal channel other than himself through which he transmits his message. For example, a change agent (source) wants to communicate to a peasant village, so he seeks a village opinion leader to carry his message to the other villagers; the opinion leader becomes the channel (interpersonal). He is not the originator of the message but is merely the means used by the change agent to transmit a given message. If the change agent were to carry the message to the villagers himself, the source and channel become the same.

[2] However, Frey (1966) points out that, when asked what prompted the adoption of a new idea, respondents are more likely to recall a recent conversation with a neighbor than a radio program heard several months before.

[3] An exception to this statement is messages dealing with new products in more developed countries. Analyses of advertising campaigns seem to indicate that mass media can be effective in persuading individuals to try new products. When the individual feels a strong awareness of need for a change, the impetus of the mass media message may be enough to motivate the overt act of trying the new product. Where a need for change must be created, however, the mass media are not potent enough to secure attitude and behavior change.

conflicting messages are filtered through the individual's mental screens of selective exposure, perception, and retention.[4] Selective mechanisms operate in both the interpersonal and mass media communication situations, but they are likely to be more important in the mass media context. A person can change to a different radio station, switch television channels, or put down a magazine with far greater ease than he can "turn off" another human being.

So, the most appropriate channel should be selected in terms of the goals of the source and the content of the message if it is to effect a given set of receivers. Often the goal of the source can best be served by the combination of various mass media and interpersonal channels. This is particularly true when the goal of the source involves reaching a mass audience with messages advocating change.

MODELS OF MASS COMMUNICATION FLOWS

To better understand such a mass communication process, we shall now examine several models of mass communication flows, roughly in the temporal sequence of their introduction in communication research.

Hypodermic Needle Model

The hypodermic needle model, essentially a one-step flow model, postulated that the mass media had direct, immediate, and powerful effects on a mass audience. The direct and immediate effects attributed to the mass media bore a close parallel to the stimulus-response notions current in psychological research in the 1930s and 1940s. Based on the S-R notion, the hypodermic needle model came prior to the recognition by communication researchers of the many intervening variables operating between the initial communication stimulus (source) and the ultimate response by a mass audience (receivers). Thus the mass media were pictured as a giant hypodermic needle, pecking and plunging at a passive audience. According to Katz:

> The model in the minds of early researchers seems to have consisted of: (1) the all-powerful media, able to impress ideas on defenseless minds; and (2) the atomized mass audience, connected to the mass media but not to each other (Katz, 1963:80).

The hypodermic needle model also drew support from notions concerning the development in the United States during this era of a *mass society*, which was seen as consisting of a mass audience of standardized and atomized individuals bound only loosely by interpersonal relations. Observers noted a trend to homogeneity in dress, speech patterns, and values that seemed to result from mass media exposure and mass production and to point toward a mass culture. Conceived of as an all-powerful influence on human behavior, the mass media were pictured as sending forth messages to atomized masses waiting to receive them, with nothing intervening (Katz & Lazarsfeld, 1955: 16). Evidence of the great manipulative power of the mass media came from such historical events as: (1) the role of U.S. newspapers in arousing positive public opinion toward the Spanish-American War with such shibboleths as "Remember the Maine"; (2) the apparent power of Goebbels' propaganda machine in World War II; and (3) fear of Madison Avenue's influence on consumer and voting behavior.

Eventually the more sophisticated research methods that came to be utilized

---

[4] *Selective exposure* is the tendency to attend to communication messages that are consistent with one's existing attitudes and beliefs. *Selective perception* is the tendency to interpret communication messages in terms of one's existing attitudes and beliefs. *Selective retention* is the tendency to remember messages that are consistent with one's existing attitudes and beliefs.

in communication inquiry cast considerable doubt on the hypodermic needle model. It was based primarily on intuitive theorizing about historical events and was too simple, too mechanistic, too gross to account accurately for mass media effects.

Two-Step Flow Model

The decisive discarding of the hypodermic needle model resulted serendipitously from a classic study of the 1940 presidential election (Lazarsfeld et al., 1944).[5] This inquiry was designed with the hypodermic needle model in mind, and it aimed at analyzing the role of mass media in clinching political decisions. As Lazarsfeld and Menzel admit:

> This study went to great lengths to determine how the mass media brought about such changes. To our surprise, we found the effect to be rather small... People appeared to be much more influenced in their political decisions by face-to-face contact with other people... than by the mass media directly (Lazarsfeld & Menzel, 1963:96).

While the evidence indicated that almost no voting choices were directly influenced by the mass media, the data did seem to indicate "... that ideas often flow from radio and print to opinion leaders and from these to the less active sections of the population" (Lazarsfeld et al., 1944:151). The first step, from sources to opinion leaders, is merely a transfer of information while the second step, from opinion leaders to their followers, also involves the spread of influence. Because the conceptualization was not part of the original design, this so-called two-step flow hypothesis was not really well-documented by the data. Later investigations tested the two-step flow model in a great variety of communications situations and found, generally, that this model provided a usable conceptual framework for examining mass communication phenomena.[6]

The two-step flow model helped focus attention upon the role of mass media–interpersonal interfaces. Instead of assuming, as did the hypodermic needle model, that the masses were a large body of disconnected individuals hooked up to the media but not to each other, the two-step flow model views the masses as interacting individuals. It put people back into mass communication. An individual exposed to a new idea either through mass media or interpersonal channels may then engage in communication exchanges about the message with his peers. In most mass communication flows (whatever one takes as his point of reference in the process), there is likely to be a flow of messages from a source, via mass media channels, to a receiver who in turn reacts to the message and/or passes it on to those individuals with whom he interacts (Rogers, 1962:313).

Communication research of the last twenty-five years has profited greatly from use of the two-step flow model; at the same time this research has also demonstrated several shortcomings inherent in the model. Basically, the model does not tell us enough. Research on the dif-

[5] A parallel rejection of the hypodermic needle model occurred in another research tradition at about the same time. Researchers investigating the diffusion of agricultural innovations rejected the notion of all-powerful mass media because "the rural sociologists never assumed, as students of mass communications had, that their respondents did not talk to each other" (Katz, 1960).

[6] This model served as a basis for a series of investigations conducted by communication researchers in Columbia University's Bureau of Applied Social Research: the Rovere study of opinion leadership in a suburban community (Merton, 1949); the Decatur study of consumer decisions (Katz & Lazarsfeld, 1955); the Elmira study of election behavior (Berelson et al., 1954); and the medical drug diffusion study (Coleman et al., 1966). These studies utilized the two-step flow model in their design, and amplified our understanding of mass communication flows and of opinion leadership.

fusion of innovations brought many of these shortcomings to the fore because these investigations necessarily include *time* as a variable, which the original 1940 study did not.[7] Six limitations of the two-step flow model are:

1. The two-step model implied that active individuals in information seeking were opinion leaders and that the remainder of the mass audience was passive.[8] The activity of the opinion leaders was thought to provide the main thrust to initiate the communication flow. A more accurate reflection of reality would probably be a model that indicates that opinion leaders can be either active or passive, that they seek receivers and are actively sought by them, and that opinion leaders often play *both* active and passive roles in most communication situations (Troldahl et al., 1965; Rogers with Svenning, 1969: 222).
2. The view that the mass communication process is essentially two-stepped limits analysis of the process. The mass communication process may involve more or less than two steps. In some instances, there may be only one step; that is, the mass media may have direct impact on a receiver. In other instances, the impetus of the mass media may lead to a multi-staged communication process. By focusing only on the two-step aspects of the process, research that mirrors reality is severely limited (see Menzel & Katz, 1955).
3. The two-step flow model implies a reliance by opinion leaders on mass media channels, and most past research on the two-step flow assumed the primacy of mass media channels for opinion leaders. But, recently, there are some indications that opinion leaders obtain messages from channels other than mass media. For village leaders in less developed countries, where little or no mass media are available, channels like personal trips to cities, conversations with change agents, etc., can be the initiating force (Rogers with Svenning, 1969). The specific channels utilized by opinion leaders depend on such considerations as the nature of the message, its origin, and the social location of the opinion leaders in the social structure. Opinion leaders utilize channels that are *most relevant* for initiating the mass communication flow, but these are not mass media in all cases.
4. The original 1940 inquiry did not take into consideration the different channel behavior by receivers on the basis of their time of knowing about a new idea. Diffusion research shows that relatively earlier knowers (and adopters) of innovations utilize mass media channels much more than later knowers (and adopters). So the opinion leaders may simply be the earlier knowers of new ideas, and their dependence upon mass media channels may be a function of their early knowing rather than of their opinion leadership per se. Earlier knowers must necessarily depend on mass media channels because, at the time of their awareness of new ideas, few of their peers in the system are yet knowledgeable about the innovation. Hence interpersonal channels could hardly function as very important

[7] Diffusion inquiries are further helpful in analyzing the flow of communication messages because they deal primarily with innovations. It is relatively easier to isolate the effects of messages whose main theme is a new idea because respondent recall is facilitated. New ideas seem to leave deeper scratches on men's minds than do more routine messages.

[8] The two-step flow notion was proposed at a period when the conception of a passive audience was widely accepted in communication research (Bauer, 1963).

creators of knowledge for the earlier knowers.

5. Different communication channels function at different stages in the receiver's innovation-decision process. The original two-step flow model did not recognize the role of different communication channels at the varying stages of innovation-decision (van den Ban, 1966). Diffusion studies indicate that individuals pass (*a*) from awareness-*knowledge* of an innovation, (*b*) to *persuasion* of a favorable or unfavorable attitude toward the innovation, (*c*) to *decision* to adopt or reject, and (*d*) to *confirmation* of this decision (Rogers with Shoemaker, 1971). Mass media channels are primarily knowledge creators, while interpersonal channels are more important at persuading; that is, at forming and changing attitudes.[9] This notion was masked in the original statement of the two-step model because the time sequence involved in decision-making was explicitly ignored. Such channel differences at the knowledge-versus-persuasion stage exist for *both* opinion leaders and followers. Thus it is not only the opinion leaders who use mass media channels, as the original statement of the two-step flow model seemed to suggest.
6. An audience dichotomy of opinion leaders versus followers was implied by the two-step flow model (Katz, 1957). We know that, in fact, opinion leadership is a continuous variable and should be conceptualized (even though it cannot always be measured) as such. Further, many "nonleaders" are not followers of the leaders, at least in any direct sense.[10]

The overall criticism of the two-step flow model, as originally postulated, is mainly that *it does not tell us enough.* The flow of communication in a mass audience is far more complicated than two steps. What is known about the mass communication process is too detailed to be expressed in one sentence. Nevertheless, two intellectual benefits from the two-step flow hypothesis are evident in communication research: (1) a focus upon opinion leadership in mass communication flows, and (2) several revisions of the two-step flow, such as the one-step and multi-step flow.

One-Step Flow Model

The one-step flow model states that mass media channels communicate directly to the mass audience, without the message passing through opinion leaders, but that the message does not reach all receivers equally nor does it have the same effect on each (Troldahl, 1966). The one-step flow model probably results from a refinement of the hypodermic needle model discussed earlier. But the one-step model recognizes: (1) the media are not all-powerful; (2) the screening aspects of selective exposure, perception, and retention affect message impact; and (3) differing effects occur for various members of the receiving audience. Further, it allows for direct effects of communication emanating from mass media channels.

The one-step flow model most accurately

[9] Troldahl (1966) proposes on the basis of balance theory that followers who are exposed to mass media messages that are inconsistent with their predispositions will initiate interpersonal communication with opinion leaders to reduce their dissonance. Troldahl found tentative support for his hypothesis.

[10] In order to identify the followers from the nonfollowers among the category of nonleaders, researchers should use leader-follower sociometric *dyads* as units of analysis rather than *individuals*, as has generally been the case in past inquiry on opinion leadership. All nonleaders are not followers of opinion leaders, as Troldahl at al. (1965) have demonstrated.

describes the flow of messages to a mass audience when the saliency of the message is extremely high or perhaps very low.[11] For news events of medium saliency, awareness-knowledge of the ideas is created almost entirely by the mass media, indicating a one-step flow. This notion is supported by Deutschmann and Danielson's (1960) conclusion from a study of the diffusion of six news events: "Initial mass media information on important events goes directly to people on the whole and is not relayed to any great extent."

Multi-Step Flow Model

This model incorporates all of the others previously discussed. The multi-step flow model is based on a sequential relaying function that seems to occur in most communication situations. It does not call for any particular number of steps, nor does it specify that the message must emanate from a source via mass media channels. This model suggests that there are a variable number of relays in the communication flow from a source to a large audience. Some members will obtain the message directly through channels from the source, while others may be several times removed from the message's origin. The exact number of steps in this process depends on the intent of the source, the availability of mass media and the extent of their exposure, the nature of the message, and its salience to the receiving audience.

Today, most communication researchers place credence in the multi-step conceptualization of the mass communication process and at least intuitively subscribe to it, as evidenced in their research designs. Perhaps the multi-step model permits a more accurate analysis of the mass communication process because it allows the researcher to account for different variables in different communication situations. The multi-step model is the least specific or restrictive of the models we have considered.

OPINION LEADERSHIP IN THE MASS COMMUNICATION PROCESS

Recognition that certain members of a mass audience are especially influential in shaping the opinions and decisions of their peers—and the identification of these individuals as "opinion leaders"—was one of the most significant contributions made by Lazarsfeld et al. (1944) in their study of voting behavior in Erie County, Ohio, in the presidential election of 1940.[12]

Opinion leadership is the ability to influence informally other individuals' attitudes or overt behavior in a desired way with relative frequency. Leadership is exerted in both formal and informal situations; our interest is in the informal type of opinion leadership existing outside of formally prescribed role relationships. Patterns of opinion leadership in a system may be almost invisible unless an observer is looking carefully for them:

> What we shall call opinion leadership, if we may call it leadership at all, is leadership at its simplest: it is casually exercised, sometimes unwitting and unbeknown ... it is the almost

---

[11] Greenberg (1964) argues that the amount of interpersonal relaying that occurs in the case of news-event diffusion is greatest when the event is of medium saliency. When a news event is either of very low or very high saliency (for example, a routine local government decision versus President Kennedy's assassination), mass media channels are of greatest importance.

[12] Coinage of the term *opinion leader* helped to some extent to overcome the wide-ranging list of synonyms used to describe opinion leadership. Past writings utilized such terms as *influentials*, *tastemakers*, *sparkplugs*, *influencers*, etc. The standardization of concepts and measures related to opinion leadership is still in process but was spurred by the study of Lazarsfeld and his colleagues.

invisible, certainly inconspicous, form of leadership at the person-to-person level of ordinary, intimate, informal, everyday contact (Katz & Lazarsfeld, 1955:138).

Opinion leadership is awarded by followers and, therefore, may be unrecognized even by the leaders so designated.[13]

Opinion leaders are, by definition, the *source* of information or opinion, and their followers are *receivers*.[14] Some opinion leaders initiate the communication flow by seeking receivers for their messages (opinion-giving). Other opinion leaders are sought by their followers (opinion-seeking). In both instances, the opinion leader is the source of information. This notion recognizes that both opinion leaders and followers are capable of active and/or passive roles.[15]

Because opinion leadership results from the attitudes and perceptions of the receivers, opinion leaders can act, in turn, as followers of other opinion leaders. Wright and Cantor (1967) reported that 68 percent of opinion leaders for foreign affairs sought information from other leaders. Troldahl et al. (1965) found opinion leaders to be generally active in both providing and obtaining messages related to a given topic; this can be interpreted as evidence of a multi-step flow.

Measuring Opinion Leadership

Three main methods of measuring opinion leadership have been utilized in communication research: (1) sociometric, (2) informants' ratings, and (3) self-designating techniques. The sociometric method consists of asking respondents whom they sought (or, hypothetically, *might* seek) for information or advice about a given topic, such as a technological innovation, news event, or public issue. Opinion leaders are those members of a system who receive the greatest number of sociometric choices.[16] Undoubtedly the sociometric technique is the most valid measure of opinion leadership because it is measured through the followers.

An alternative is to select judges or key informants who are especially knowledgeable about the patterns of influence in a system. For example, in a Latin American village, the priest may be able to identify the local influentials. These judges are asked to identify the opinion leaders for a given topic or topics.

The self-designating technique asks respondents to indicate the tendency for others to regard them as influential. A typical self-designating question is: "Do you think people come to you for information or advice more often than to others?" Instead of asking respondents, "Who is your leader?" as in the case of the sociometric method, the respondents are asked, "Are you a leader?" The self-designating method is especially appropriate when interrogating a random sample of respondents in a system, a sampling design that often precludes use of sociometric methods.

Two or three types of opinion leadership operations have been utilized with the same respondents, and positive correlations among the three measures have been obtained, although these relationships are less than perfect (Abelson & Rugg, 1958; Rogers & Burdge, 1962; Sollie, 1966;

[13] While opinion leadership can be unwitting and unbeknownst, research studies indicate that most opinion leaders are aware of their influential powers.

[14] For convenience, nonleaders have been lumped into the category of "followers" although, in a strict sense, nonleaders may not all be followers (see footnote 10).

[15] The basic notion of the two dimensions of message exchange (source-receiver and initiator-noninitiator) comes from Sicinski (1963) and Wright and Cantor (1967).

[16] When sociometric opinion leadership is measured across several systems, these choices must be standardized to correct for differences in the number of members in each system.

Rogers with Svenning, 1969:224–225). This finding suggests that the choice of any one of the three methods can be based on convenience; all three are about equally valid.

Characteristics of Opinion Leaders

Several studies have sought to differentiate the opinion leaders from the other members of a defined social system (Rogers and Burdge, 1962; van den Ban, 1966; Troldahl, 1966; Yadav, 1967; Rogers with Svenning, 1969:227–229; Sen, 1969). A comparative analysis of opinion leaders and followers finds opinion leaders generally characterized by (1) more formal education, (2) higher social status and wealth, (3) greater innovativeness in the adoption of new ideas, (4) more mass media exposure, (5) greater empathic ability, (6) more social participation, and (7) more cosmopoliteness. Although opinion leaders are distinguishable from other members of the social system, the differences are usually small in magnitude.

Leaders lead not so much because they possess certain unique traits or characteristics—in fact, most researches show that leaders are very much like the followers with whom they interact—but rather because they are easily *accessible* to their followers, more *competent* (but not *too* much so) than their followers, and in general *conform* to the norms of the system (Katz, 1957).

Homans (1961) stated that leaders obtain their position of influence by rendering valuable and rare services to their system. Leader conformity to norms is a valuable service to the system in that the leader provides a living model of the norms for his followers. "A man of high status [that is, leadership] will conform to the most valued norms of his group as a minimum condition of maintaining his status" (Homans, 1961:339).

How can opinion leaders conform to system norms and also lead in the adoption of new ideas? *When the system's norms favor change, opinion leaders are more innovative; but when the norms are traditional, opinion leaders are not especially innovative.*[17] In traditional systems, the opinion leaders are usually separate individuals from the innovators (the first to adopt new ideas); the innovators are perceived with suspicion and often with disrespect by the members of traditional systems. For instance, in a study of Colombian peasants, Rogers with Svenning (1969: 230–231) found that opinion leaders in the relatively more modern villages were more innovative than their followers; but in the traditional villages, the opinion leaders were only slightly more innovative than their followers, and they were older and less cosmopolite.

Yadav (1967) provides support for this proposition in his analysis of a modern and a traditional village in India, as do Herzog et al. (1968) in Brazil. From the Brazilian study, the authors conclude:

> In the most traditional communities, neither the leaders nor their followers are innovative and, as a result, the community remains traditional. In the most modern communities, community norms favor innovativeness and both the leaders and followers are innovative. In the middle range communities, where modernization is just getting under way, divisions occur and the community opinion leaders lead the way toward modernization by trying new ideas before the other farmers in the community (Herzog et al., 1968:72).[18]

Because the rate of change in the traditional villages was very slow, there was little need for the opinion leaders to

[17] Obviously, opinion leaders can either favor or oppose change although, as Klapper (1960:35) notes, opposition has been little studied. In one of the few such analyses, Arndt (1968) concluded: "Those receiving favorable word-of-mouth communications [from opinion leaders] were three times as likely to buy the new product as were those receiving unfavorable word-of-mouth."

[18] A similar finding in India was reported by Sen (1969). The original study on norms, opinion leadership, and innovativeness is by Marsh and Coleman (1954).

be oriented outside their social systems because few ideas were entering the villages from external sources. "It is the opinion leader's function to bring the group into touch with this relevant part of its environment through whatever media are appropriate" (Katz, 1957). When external sources are not important, as in traditional villages, there is less need for opinion leaders to be cosmopolites.

This conclusion is consistent with Lazarsfeld and Menzel's hypothesis:

> New kinds of opinion leaders seem to come to the fore as traditional folk communities make the transition to the modern industrial world. When this happens, the community's traditional elders tend to lose much of their pre-eminence to individuals whose position allows them to act as the pipeline to the great world outside (Lazarsfeld & Menzel, 1963:100).

So the cosmopolite opinion leader in a peasant village has an important function as a gatekeeper, as DeFleur (1962:262) proposed and Stycos (1952) found.

Monomorphic and Polymorphic Opinion Leadership

As opinion leadership came under greater study, researchers began to wonder if opinion leadership was universal; that is, was there one set of all-purpose opinion leaders in a system or were there different opinion leaders for each issue? Merton (1949) used the term *polymorphism* to indicate the degree to which an individual acts as an opinion leader for a variety of topics. Its opposite, *monomorphism*, was used to indicate the tendency for an individual to act as an opinion leader for only one topic. The degree of polymorphic opinion leadership in a given social system seems to vary with such factors as the diversity of the topics (on which opinion leadership is measured), the type of system norms (modern or traditional), and so forth.

From their analysis of opinion leadership among housewives in Decatur, Illinois, for four different topics, Katz and Lazarsfeld (1955:334) concluded that "the hypothesis of a generalized leader receives little support in this study. There is no overlap in any of the pairs of activities. Each arena, it seems, has a corps of leaders of its own." Their data seem less conclusive, however, since they found that about one-third of the opinion leaders exerted their influence in more than one of the four areas (fashions, movies, public affairs, consumer products).

Marcus and Bauer (1964) reanalyzed the Katz and Lazarsfeld data by computing the expected probability that any given leader would be polymorphic and comparing this with the proportion of leaders that actually demonstrated polymorphism. Marcus and Bauer's recalculations showed that the actual frequency of polymorphic opinion leadership was greater than chance alone could account for. So they concluded, contrary to Katz and Lazarsfeld, that there was some degree of polymorphism among the Decatur housewives. These different conclusions drawn from the same data point to the difficulty in constructing a standardized measure of polymorphism that is not open to subjective interpretation.[19]

System norms are thought to effect the degree of polymorphism among opinion leaders in a social system. When the norms of a system are more modern, opinion leadership is expected to be more monomorphic although the evidence is not completely clear-cut on this hypothesis.[20]

---

[19] Silk (1966) found a generally low degree of polymorphism among Los Angeles residents for new dental products and services, although this conclusion may have partially resulted from the narrow range of topics he studied. Palmore (1967:319) similarly reports little polymorphism for family planning opinion leaders on nonfamily planning issues in Chicago.

[20] Rogers with Svenning (1969:227) found that opinion leadership in more modern Colombian villages was no more monomorphic than in the traditional villages. This may have been the result

As the technological base of a system becomes more complex, a division of labor and specialization of roles results, which in turn leads to different sets of opinion leaders for different issues. In more traditional systems, there is less role differentiation on the basis of occupation, etc. The leaders in such systems are more likely to serve as opinion leaders for all issues in the system. This point is illustrated by Lerner's interview with the chief of a Turkish village who, when asked on what topics he was influential, replied: "About all that you or I could imagine, even about their [the villagers'] wives and how to handle them, and how to cure their sick cow" (Lerner, 1958:26).

FACTORS INFLUENCING INTERPERSONAL RELAYS

The importance of the interpersonal relaying process in mass communication was mentioned in our previous discussion of the multi-step flow model. Understanding the nature of communication flows through interpersonal channels can be enhanced by an examination of the concepts of (1) homophily-heterophily, and (2) empathy. The nature of *who* relays to *whom* is brought out in communication research dealing with similarities and dissimilarities between source and receiver.

Homophily-Heterophily

One of the most obvious and fundamental principles of human communication is that the transfer of ideas most frequently occurs between a source and a receiver who have certain similarities. *Homophily* is the word that has been devised to describe the degree to which pairs of individuals who interact are similar in certain attributes, like beliefs, values, education, social status, etc.[21] *Heterophily*, the mirror opposite of homophily, is defined as the degree to which pairs of individuals who interact are different in certain attributes. In a free-choice situation, when a source can interact with any one of a number of different receivers, there is a strong tendency for him to select a receiver who is most like himself. Homans (1950:184) noted that "the more nearly equal in social rank a number of men are, the more frequently they will interact with one another."

While a conceptual label—homophily—has been assigned to this phenomenon only in recent years by Lazarsfeld and Merton (1964:23), the existence of homophilic behavior was noted more than half a century ago by the French sociologist, Gabriel Tarde. "Social relations, I repeat, are much closer between individuals who resemble each other in occupation and education" (Tarde, 1903:64).

Why does homophily occur? Similar individuals are likely to belong to the same groups, live near each other, and be attracted by the same interests. This physical and social propinquity leads to homophily. Further, *more effective communication occurs when source and receiver are homophilous.*[22] When the source(s) and receiver(s) share common meanings, attitudes, and language, communication between them is likely to be more effective. The commonality between individuals makes it more likely for them to communicate and, in turn, more likely for that communication to be meaningful. Most individuals enjoy the comfort of

of a rather restricted range in the degree of modernization of the village norms. On the other hand, other investigations (Yadav, 1967; Attah, 1968; Sengupta, 1968; Sen, 1969) seem to support the notion of greater monomorphism of opinion leadership in more modern villages.

[21] The term *homophily* is derived from the Greek word *homoios* ("alike" or "equal"). Thus, homophily literally means affiliation or communication with a similar person.

[22] Support for this proposition comes from numerous small-group laboratory studies, which show that heterophilous communication leads to message distortion, one type of ineffective communication (Barnlund & Harland, 1963).

interacting with others who are quite similar in social status, education, beliefs, etc. Interaction with those quite different from ourselves involves more effort to make communication effective. Heterophilic interaction is likely to cause cognitive dissonance because the receiver is exposed to messages that may be inconsistent with his existing beliefs, an uncomfortable psychological state.

Homophily and effective communication nurture each other. The more communication between members of a dyad, the more likely they are to become homophilous; the more homophilous they are, the more likely they are to communicate effectively. According to Lazarsfeld and Merton (1964:34), homophily may be either the *result* of interaction or the basis of *choice* of those with whom one interacts. One conclusion of the 1940 presidential election study was that "the changes in vote intention increase group homogeneity. . . . The majority of voters who change at all change in the direction of the prevailing vote of their social group" (Lazarsfeld et al., 1944:139).

Individuals who break the homophily boundary and attempt to communicate with others quite different from themselves are beset with the frustrations of ineffective communication. For example, the middle-class teacher in the ghetto classroom and the change agent diffusing innovations to peasants in developing countries meet problems caused by attempting to communicate with receivers much different from themselves. Differences in technical competence, social status, attitudes, and beliefs all contribute to heterophily in language and meaning, thereby leading to messages that go unheeded.

One of the distinctive problems in the communication of *new ideas* is that the source's competence with the innovations is itself a basis of heterophily. Such heterophily often leads to ineffective communication between change agents and clients and contributes to the failure of many diffusion campaigns. One result of the high degree of heterophily in diffusion is that *change agents tend to interact most intensively with clients who are relatively most like the change agents in innovativeness, social status, and beliefs.*[23] However, these more homophilous clients need the efforts of the change agent less than do the more laggardly and lower-status clients.

Further, there is some research evidence that the more "successful" change agents are those who are most like their average client. For instance, the Allahabad Agricultural Institute (1957) in India found that village-level change agents with only an elementary education were more effective in reaching villagers (who were mostly illiterate) than were change agents with a high school or university education.

Perhaps one reason why change agents concentrate their efforts on opinion leaders is to "halve" the heterophily gap between themselves and their average clients. But if the opinion leaders are *too* much more innovative than the average clients, the heterophily (and accompanying ineffective communication) that formerly existed between the change agents and their clients now exists between the leaders and their fellow clients. This is why innovators are poor opinion leaders in traditional systems; they are *too* elite and change-oriented. Such persons serve as unrealistic models for the average client, and they know it.[24] Sometimes change agents

[23] Support for this point comes from an analysis of completed research on the diffusion of innovations, which provides overwhelming evidence that clients with a relatively high degree of change-agent contact have higher social status, more education, and greater innovativeness than does the average client (Rogers with Svenning, 1969:179).

[24] Perhaps there is a "tolerable" degree of heterophily between a source-receiver pair in which the source is enough different from the receiver to be perceived as competent but not so much different as to lack comparison as a role model. It is possible that this tolerable range of heterophily may provide "energy" to the com-

identify appropriate and potentially effective opinion leaders among their clients, but they concentrate their change efforts too much on the leaders, who soon become innovators and, hence, lose their following (Hardin, 1951; Rogers with Svenning, 1969:219–220). These former leaders became too heterophilous with their former followers for effective communication to occur.

Homophily can act as a barrier to the rapid flow of innovations within a system. New ideas usually enter through higher-status and more innovative members of the system. When a high degree of homophily is present, these elite individuals interact mainly with each other and few of the innovations "trickle-down" to nonelites. Rogers with Svenning (1969: 237–238) found that more traditional Colombian villages were characterized by a greater degree of homophily in interpersonal diffusion. Only when the norms of a village became more modern did diffusion become more heterophilous. And this breakdown of homophilous diffusion patterns acted to make the system even more modern by facilitating the trickling-down of innovative messages within the village.[25]

Empathy: Bridging the Heterophily Gap

Most heterophilous communication is ineffective, as we have shown. Yet *some* ghetto teachers do get through to their pupils; some change agents reach their peasant clients very effectively. Why? One reason is the empathic ability of the source.

Empathy is the ability of an individual to project himself into the role of another. When either the source or the receiver or both (in an heterophilous situation) is able to empathize with the other, effective communication is more likely to take place. If it is possible to see how the other individual in the situation is feeling and to share these feelings, it is then possible to better suit the message to the receivers. When a source has high empathy with a heterophilous receiver, source and receiver are really homophilous in a sociopsychological sense. This point suggests that our earlier proposition about heterophily and ineffective communication now needs modification: *Heterophilous communication is less effective than homophilous communication unless the source has a high degree of empathy with the receiver.*

Perhaps there is an ideal level of source empathy with receivers. For instance, it is possible that a change agent could become so empathic with his clients that he would no longer wish to change them. In such an extreme case, he would perceive his planned change program only through his clients' eyes; that is, unfavorably. Although such an instance is probably rare, one is reminded of the anthropological observer among the Pueblo Indians who abandoned his discipline and joined the tribe.

Receivers, of course, have some degree of empathy with sources. Gans (1962) found that most social workers in a Boston slum had relatively low empathy with their clients, whereas the ghetto residents were able to take the role of the change agents with greater ease. This provided the clients with a manipulative advantage; they understood the social workers' objectives and strategies and acted accordingly. One result was that the change agents' programs were largely unsuccessful in changing clients' behavior.

---

munication exchange, hence facilitating effective communication. While there is no research to date designed to determine whether such tolerable heterophily exists, the notion is suggested by Lionberger's (1959) data, and is discussed by Rogers and Bhomik (1971).

[25] Bose (1967) found a very high degree of homophily among the residents of an Indian village on the basis of caste ranking, education, and farm size. In nearby Calcutta, however, caste was unimportant in structuring interaction patterns, but income was very important. So the exact attributes on which homophily occurs seem to vary with the nature of the system.

So we have seen that heterophily is an important barrier to effective communication but that it may be overcome by source-receiver empathy.

COMBINING MASS MEDIA AND INTERPERSONAL CHANNELS

There are certain tasks that the mass media can do, and others that they cannot do. While Schramm (1964:126–144) was referring specifically to modernization tasks in this statement, this conclusion would seem generally applicable to any mass communication situation. When the task is to reach large numbers and to affect them in a substantial way, the combination of mass media and interpersonal communication channels is the most effective means of (1) reaching people with new ideas, and (2) persuading them to utilize these innovations.

Media forums developed originally in Canada among farm families, and later spread to Japan and such developing nations as India, Nigeria, Ghana, Malawi, Costa Rica, and Brazil. *Media forums* are organized, small groups of individuals who meet regularly to receive a mass media program and discuss the contents of this program. The mass media linked to the forum may be a radio, as in India and the radiophonics schools of Latin America; print fare, as is usually the case in Communist Chinese study groups; or television, as in the Italian *Telescuola* or in India.

TYPES OF MEDIA FORUMS

Radio Forums

Undoubtedly the largest, most thoroughly researched media-forum program today is India's, representing "a degree of experience with the radio rural forum unequalled in the world" (Schramm et al., 1967:107). Radio forums help make farmers aware of agricultural and health innovations and encourage them to try these new ideas. Regularly scheduled radio programs beamed at meetings of forum members gathered in homes or public places to hear the broadcast serve as impetus for the group discussion that follows. As a rule the forums provide regular feedback reports of decisions and questions of clarification to the broadcaster. Using the same format, but exchanging the radio for television, UNESCO has sponsored experimental television-watching groups in France and Italy.

Mass Media "Schools"

Media schools attempt to provide a basic education, including literacy training, for people living in remote rural areas. The Italian *Telescuola* and the *radiophonics* programs in Latin America are examples of such schools, as is Brazil's Cruzada ABC, which uses print materials. The radiophonic broadcasters intersperse "lessons" with news, agricultural programs, religious training, and music. Each school group is led by a trained monitor who helps the students learn and encourages them to listen regularly.

Chinese Study Groups

The Chinese Communist Party has employed magazine and newspaper discussion groups as a means of indoctrination and learning among their party cadres and recruits for fifty years. Approximately 60 percent of the adult Chinese population regularly participates in study groups where print material is read and discussed (Hiniker, 1968). Strict control of discussion is maintained by the cadre leader, who forces each member to take a position on each issue and voice his opinion to the group. Study groups are considered essential elements in the special communication campaigns launched to achieve such varied goals as fly-killing, river-swimming, anti-spitting, family planning, farm production, and the learning of ideology.

In all of these various types of media forums currently in operation, some form of mass media communication is combined with the impact of interpersonal communication in small groups. The group seems to be an important element in moving the individuals toward greater acceptance of the messages being transmitted through the mass media. The media forums are used primarily in less developed countries, principally to introduce new ideas to vast audiences.

Effects of Media Forums

Although there are important country-to-country and program-to-program differences in the types of media-forum systems we have just reviewed, they possess certain common elements. All utilize a mass medium (radio, television, or print) to carry the major load of disseminating messages about technical innovations to the discussion forums. All feature small-sized groups, which are exposed to the mass media channel and whose members then participate in discussion of the message. All of the media-forum programs *seem* to be generally effective in creating knowledge, forming and changing attitudes, and in catalyzing behavioral change. But adequate scientific evidence of these media-forum effects is rare; one exception is Neurath's (1960; 1962) field experiment with Indian radio forums.

Neurath designed his field experiment so that comparisons could be made in knowledge increase among peasants who lived in three types of villages: (1) those in which radio forums were established; (2) those in which radios were already present, but no forums were organized; and (3) those with neither a radio nor a forum (used as control villages). Forum villages had much greater gain in knowledge of innovations than did the control villages.[26] In fact, the non-forum villages with a radio showed only slight gains in knowledge level; this emphasized that *the effects of mass media communication channels among peasants in less developed countries are greater when these media are coupled with interpersonal communication channels in media forums.*[27]

Why do individuals learn more when they are members of media forums? Following are some of the reasons:

1. Interest in attendance and participation is encouraged by group presure and social expectations.
2. Attitude change appears to be more readily achieved when individuals are in groups. Further, group decisions are more likely to be accepted by the individual if he participates in making the decision, as usually occurs in the media forums.
3. The "novelty effect" of new channels and the subsequent high credibility that may be attached to these media (both electronic and interpersonal) may account for some of the success of these media forums.
4. Feedback to the broadcaster from forums is comparatively immediate.

FUTURE RESEARCH

In this chapter we have shown some of the main research findings dealing with mass media and interpersonal communication channels. In the process, certain gaps in our knowledge are highlighted; we shall deal with five in this section. The first three (field experiments, relational analysis, and homophily measurement) are largely methodological, while the last two (opinion leadership and media forums) are mainly substantive.

[26] To measure knowledge, each respondent was queried both before and after the twenty forum broadcasts about six topics that were included in the broadcast programs.

[27] Further evidence for this generalization is provided by Menefee and Menefee (1967), who found that in Indian villages the effect on political knowledge of a weekly community newspaper was much greater when the newspaper was read and discussed in forums.

Field Experiments on Channels

An important improvement in research designs on communication flows in the 1960s was the field experiment. In this approach, a message is released ("planted") through certain individuals in a mass audience, and its flows are traced sociometricly over time. The audience members are then interrogated about their channel behavior relative to the message. The field experiment allows the researcher to combine some of the advantages of the survey (e.g., the ability to generalize one's results to a larger population) with some of the advantages of the experiment (e.g., control over unwanted variables). The before and after measurements of the effects of a given channel are taken by surveys, and the experiment is conducted in the field rather than the laboratory. The main advantage of the field experiment is that it provides evidence of the time-order of one's variables; that is, one can determine whether a change in variable *X* leads to a change in variable *Y*.

Several such field experiments have been completed recently in less developed countries that deal with the effects of radio forums, literacy classes, and opinion-leader training on knowledge, attitude, and adoption of innovations (Neurath, 1960; 1962; Spector et al., 1963; Menefee & Menefee, 1967; Hursh et al., 1968; Stanfield et al., 1968; Roy et al., 1969). The general picture that emerges from these studies is that mass media channels can have considerable effects in diffusing technological ideas in health, family planning, and agriculture—especially when these mass media are combined with interpersonal channels in media forums.

We should capitalize on the results of correlational studies and move forward in a series of carefully designed and conducted field experiments on the effects of various types of prototypic communication channels. The time-order of various communication variables and their "effects" could thus be determined, both in less developed and more developed countries.[28]

Relational Analysis

Historically, most communication research has focused on individuals as units of analysis, largely ignoring the importance of *communication relationships* as units of analysis. Pointing to the need for relational analysis, Coleman (1958) asserted that survey research approaches were, in part, responsible for the focus on the individual. "Samples were random, never including (except by accident) two persons who were friends, interviews were with one individual as an atomistic entity, and responses were coded onto separate IBM cards, one for each person." The net result: "aggregate psychology" (Coleman, 1958).

This methodological cul-de-sac often focused content interests in communication research improperly on intrapersonal *characteristics* of sources or receivers, leaving the interactive *process* of communication flows from a source to a receiver largely neglected. We see this point illustrated in the voluminous research completed on the diffusion of innovations. The field began in the late 1930s, when social scientists were asked by extension services to study the diffusion of agricultural research results to farmers; surveys of the receivers focused upon the individual as the unit of analysis.[29] Now, forty years and 1,800 publications later, we know a great deal about the individual

[28] Field experiments have been completed in the U.S. on the nature of the multi-step flow by Troldahl (1966) and Arndt (1967; 1968).

[29] Perhaps diffusion research also illustrates another implicit "bias" in much communication research: it is usually sponsored by the source, conducted by scientists who gather data from the receivers for the eventual utilization by the source in order to bring about desired behavioral outcomes on the part of the receivers. Thus, diffusion researchers seem unwittingly to side

characteristics of farmers, physicians, and teachers who are relatively earlier or later to adopt new ideas, etc.; but we know precious little about the communication relationships involved in innovation diffusion. (A content analysis of 1,084 empirical diffusion studies in the Michigan State University Diffusion Documents Center shows only 136—or 2 percent—utilized a dyadic approach, the most common type of relational analysis.) A similar point can be made in the case of persuasion research, studies of media institution gatekeepers, etc.

We have erroneously assumed that if individuals are the units of *response*, they must also be the units of *analysis*. A few recent communication researchers have demonstrated that even when the individual provides the response data (as perhaps must ultimately be the case in the social sciences), the dyadic communication relationship, the communication chain or network, or a sociometricly determined communication clique within a larger system can be the unit of analysis.

Most of the research findings contained in this chapter resulted from monadic analysis and sought primarily to explain one main kind of dependent variable—communication effects which, according to DeFleur (1965), are the dependent variable in almost all communication research. Among the specific effects studied were (1) knowledge change, (2) attitude formation or change, and (3) overt behavioral change. In the past, communication research has dealt with how to optimize various combinations of source variables, message variables, channel variables, and receiver variables in order to produce desired effects. But we can often pursue these research objectives (that is, emphasize the explanation of communication effects) more efficiently with various types of relational analysis. Moreover, this approach can help shift our research concentration from an overemphasis on effects to a probe of the *process* of communication.

Even with the use of survey methods, which are often essential for gathering large-scale amounts of data as a basis for generalization, various techniques of conceptualization, measurement, data gathering, and data analysis can be utilized to provide a focus upon communication relationships rather than on individuals. We mainly lack appropriate concepts (like homophily-heterophily, for instance) to guide our analysis of dyadic or other types of relational data, and these new concepts must be created. The measurement devices usually must include some type of sociometric question. The data-gathering techniques consist of sampling intact groups (or subsystems) or pairs of individuals, as with so-called "snowball sampling." The data-analysis methods amount to using the dyad, the chain or network, or the subsystem as the unit of analysis.

Network or clique identification and analysis can be facilitated by computer matrix multiplication procedures (Festinger, 1949; Hubbell, 1965). This approach consists of reducing sociometric data about interpersonal communication to a who-to-whom matrix in which the source individuals are located on one dimension of the matrix and the receivers on the other. The matrix is squared, cubed, etc., usually by computer techniques. Cliques and networks soon become apparent within the total matrix of interpersonal relationships (see Sen, 1969).

So one of our methodological suggestions for future inquiry is to *utilize relational analysis as a means of probing the nature of communication flows*. This approach should prove especially valuable in determining the actual number of interpersonal relays in the serial transmission of a message through an audience. Certainly the number of such who-to-

---

with the change agents, not the client; persuasion investigators with the persuaders, not the audience; modernization scholars with the development planners, not the peasant.

whom dyadic exchanges, as well as their nature, are priority targets in future research studies on multi-step flow of communication.

Measuring Homophily

We have argued that it is important to know the degree of homophily-heterophily in communication flows. But we need to improve our measures of homophily at both the dyadic and the system level. The measures presently used by communication researchers for continuous variables are (1) the Pearsonian zero-order correlation at the dyadic level, and (2) indicants derived from computer matrix multiplication procedures at the system level (Ho, 1969). For dichotomous variables, some version of Coleman's (1958) index may be utilized (Signorile & O'Shea, 1965).

Perhaps with improved operations of homophily, and the resulting greater precision in correlates of this variable, we can gain a clearer picture of the role of homophily in communication flows. For example, most communication research to date in peasant villages suggests that there is a rather low degree of homophily (in such variables as social status, literacy, mass media exposure, etc.) in the interpersonal diffusion of innovations. However, this finding may simply be an artifact of inadequate measurement of homophily.

Opinion Leadership

Most past research on opinion leadership has simplisticly concentrated on comparing all opinion leaders with all nonleaders in an audience. We feel that further research on such aggregated categories is of little value. Instead, communication researchers should seek answers to the following questions:

1. To what extent and on what variables—social status, mass media exposure, etc.—does homophily-heterophily operate in the flow of communication?

2. What are the gatekeeping and liaison functions of opinion leaders? In other words, what role do opinion leaders play in controlling the flow of messages and in providing links between two or more cliques within the system?

3. What variables affect the *concentration* of opinion leadership in a system? We expect that change is facilitated in a system where opinion leadership is concentrated in the hands of a relatively few rather than diffused throughout the population. We need, therefore, to determine the nature of social systems in which opinion leadership is concentrated and in which it is dispersed. Such measurements are possible using some device such as the Gini ratio, which expresses the degree of possession of any specific characteristic by members of a social system (see Whiting et al., 1967).

4. Practically no research attention has been paid to the possible influence of opinion leaders in discouraging change (Klapper, 1960:35). On the basis of communication research, change agents are often advised to concentrate their attention upon opinion leaders in their audience if they wish to speed up the diffusion process. This strategy assumes that opinion leaders can be persuaded to support change. Perhaps an equally important approach for change agents in diffusion campaigns is to identify, and hopefully neutralize, those opinion leaders in a system who actively oppose change. We need to find out.

Media Forums

Much more needs to be known about how best to combine mass media and interpersonal channels in media forums. Specifically, we need to know:

1. Were the knowledge gains found by Neurath (1960; 1962) in the India radio forums mostly a function of the short-term novelty effect of the forums or can they be realistically reproduced in a variety of cultural locales?

2. Do attitude change and adoption of innovations accompany the knowledge gains that occur in media forums? The tentative evidence at hand suggests the answer is yes, but more definitive answers can only come from field experiments that run over a number of years.

3. How important is *feedback* from the forums to the mass media institutions that produce the messages in leading to more effective communication systems?

4. What is the relationship of various *message strategies* in the mass media to their differential effects?

REFERENCES

Abelson, Herbert I., and W. Donald Rugg.
1958 "Self-designated influentiality and activity." Public Opinion Quarterly 22:566–567.

Allahabad Agricultural Institute.
1957 Extension Education. Allahabad, India: Allahabad Agricultural Institute Report.

Arndt, Johan.
1967 "Role of product-related conversations in the diffusion of a new product." Journal of Marketing Research 6:291–295.
1968 "A test of the two-step flow in diffusion of a new product." Journalism Quarterly 45:457–465.

Attah, Effiong Ben.
1968 "An analysis of polymorphic opinion leadership in eastern Nigerian communities." Master's Thesis, Michigan State University.

Barnlund, Dean C., and Carroll Harland.
1963 "Propinquity and prestige as determinants of communication networks." Sociometry 26:467–479.

Bauer, Raymond A.
1963 "The initiative of the audience." Journal of Advertising Research 3 (No. 1):2–7.

Berelson, Bernard R., et al.
1954 Voting. Chicago: University of Chicago Press.

Bose, Santi Priya.
1967 "Social interaction in an Indian village." Sociologia Ruralis 7:156–175.

Coleman, James S.
1958 "Relational analysis: The study of social organizations with survey methods." Human Organization 16:28–36.

Coleman, James S., et al.
1966 Medical Innovation: A Diffusion Study. Indianapolis: Bobbs-Merrill.

DeFleur, Melvin L.
1962 "The emergence and functioning of opinion leadership: Some conditions of informal influence transmission," in Norman F. Washburne (ed.), Decisions, Values and Groups. New York: Pergamon Press.
1965 Theories of Mass Communication. New York: McKay.

Deutschmann, Paul J., and Wayne A. Danielson.
1960 "Diffusion of knowledge of the major news story." Journalism Quarterly 37:345–355.

Festinger, Leon.
1949 "Analysis of sociograms using matrix algebra." Human Relations 2:153–158.

Frey, Frederick W.
1966 The Mass Media and Rural Development in Turkey. Cambridge: Massachusetts Institute of Technology, Center for International Studies. Rural Development Research Report 3.

Gans, Herbert J.
1962 The Urban Villagers: Group and Class in the Life of Italian-Americans. New York: Free Press of Glencoe.

Greenberg, Bradley S.
1964 "Person-to-person communication in the diffusion of news events." Journalism Quarterly 41:490–494.

Hardin, Charles M.
1951 "'Natural leaders' and the administration of soil conservation programs." Rural Sociology 16:279–281.

Herzog, William A., et al.
1968 Patterns of Diffusion in Rural Brazil. East Lansing: Michigan State University, Department of Communication. Diffusion of Innovations Research Report 10.

Hiniker, Paul.
1968 "The mass media and study groups in communist China," in David K. Berlo (ed.), Mass Communication and the Development of Nations.

East Lansing: Michigan State University, International Communication Institute.

Ho, Steve.
1969 "An analysis of homophily in Brazilian communities." Master's Thesis, Michigan State University.

Homans, George C.
1950 The Human Group. New York: Harcourt, Brace and World.
1961 Social Behavior: Its Elementary Forms. London: Routledge.

Hubbell, Charles H.
1965 "An input-output approach to clique identification." Sociometry 28:377–399.

Hursh, Gerald D., et al.
1968 Field Experiments on Communication in Eastern Nigeria. East Lansing: Michigan State University, Department of Communication. Diffusion of Innovations Research Report 14.

Katz, Elihu.
1957 "The two-step flow of communication: An up-to-date report on an hypothesis." Public Opinion Quarterly 21:61–78.
1960 "Communication research and the image of society: Convergence of two traditions." American Journal of Sociology 65:435–440.
1963 "The diffusion of new ideas and practices," in Wilbur Schramm (ed.), The Science of Human Communication. New York: Basic Books.

Katz, Elihu, and Paul F. Lazarsfeld.
1955 Personal Influence. Glencoe, Illinois: Free Press.

Klapper, Joseph T.
1960 The Effects of Mass Communication. New York: Free Press of Glencoe.

Lazarsfeld, Paul F., and Herbert Menzel.
1963 "Mass media and personal influence," in Wilbur Schramm (ed.), The Science of Human Communication. New York: Basic Books.

Lazarsfeld, Paul F., and Robert K. Merton.
1964 "Friendship as a social process: A substantive and methodological analysis," in Monroe Berger et al. (eds.), Freedom and Control in Modern Society. New York: Octogon.

Lazarsfeld, Paul F., et al.
1944 The People's Choice. New York: Duell, Sloan and Pearce.

Lerner, Daniel.
1958 The Passing of Traditional Society: Modernizing the Middle East. New York: Free Press of Glencoe.

Lionberger, Herbert F.
1959 "Community prestige and the choice of sources of farm information." Public Opinion Quarterly 23:110–118.

Marcus, Alan S., and Raymond A. Bauer.
1964 "Yes: There are generalized opinion leaders." Public Opinion Quarterly 28:628–632.

Marsh, C. Paul, and A. Lee Coleman.
1954 "Farmers' practice-adoption rates in relation to adoption rates of 'leaders.'" Rural Sociology 19:180–181.

Menefee, Selden, and Audrey Menefee.
1967 "A country weekly proves itself in India." Journalism Quarterly 44:114–117.

Menzel, Herbert, and Elihu Katz.
1955 "Social relations and innovation in the medical profession: The epidemiology of a new drug." Public Opinion Quarterly 19:337–352.

Merton, Robert K.
1949 "Patterns of influence: A study of interpersonal influence and communication behavior in a local community." Pp. 180–219 in Paul F. Lazarsfeld and Frank N. Stanton (eds.), Communication Research, 1948–49. New York: Harper.

Neurath, Paul M.
1960 Radio Farm Forums in India. Delhi: Government of India Press.
1962 "Radio farm forums as a tool of change in Indian villages." Economic Development and Cultural Change 10:275–283.

Palmore, James.
1967 "The Chicago snowball: A study of the flow and diffusion of family planning information," in Donald J. Bogue (ed.), Sociological Contributions to Family Planning Research. Chicago: University of Chicago, Community and Family Study Center.

Rogers, Everett M.
1962 Diffusion of Innovations. New York: Free Press of Glencoe.

Rogers, Everett M., and Philip K. Bhomik.
1971 "Homophily-heterophily: Relational

concepts for communication research." Public Opinion Quarterly 34:523–538.

Rogers, Everett M., and Rabel J. Burdge.
1962 Community Norms, Opinion Leadership, and Innovativeness Among Truck Growers. Wooster, Ohio: Ohio Agricultural Experiment Station Research Bulletin 912.

Rogers, Everett M., with F. Floyd Shoemaker.
1971 Communication of Innovations: A Cross-Cultural Approach. New York: Free Press.

Rogers, Everett M., with Lynne Svenning.
1969 Modernization Among Peasants: The Impact of Communication. New York: Holt, Rinehart and Winston.

Roy, Prodipto, et al.
1969 Communication and Rural Development: A Field Experiment in Costa Rica and India. Paris: UNESCO.

Schramm, Wilbur.
1964 Mass Media and National Development. Stanford, California: Stanford University Press.

Schramm, Wilbur, et al.
1967 The New Media: Memo to Educational Planners. Paris: UNESCO.

Sen, Lalit K.
1969 Opinion Leadership in India: A Study of Interpersonal Communication in Eight Villages. East Lansing: Michigan State University, Department of Communication. Diffusion of Innovations Research Report 22.

Sengupta, T.
1968 "Opinion leaders in rural communities." Man in India 48:159–166.

Sicinski, Andrzej.
1963 "A two-step flow of communication: Verification of an hypothesis in Poland." Polish Sociological Bulletin 1:33–40.

Signorile, Vito, and Robert M. O'Shea.
1965 "A test of the significance for the homophily index." American Journal of Sociology 70:467–470.

Silk, Alvin J.
1966 "Overlap among self-designated opinion leaders: A study of selected dental products and services." Journal of Marketing Research 3:255–259.

Sollie, Carlton R.
1966 "A comparison of reputational techniques for identifying community leaders." Rural Sociology 31:301–309.

Spector, Paul, et al.
1963 Communication and Modernization in Community Development: An Experiment. Washington, D.C.: Institute for International Services.

Stanfield, J. David, et al.
1968 Field Experiments on Communication in Brazil. East Lansing: Michigan State University, Department of Communication. Diffusion of Innovations Research Report 13.

Stycos, J. Mayone.
1952 "Patterns of communication in a rural Greek village." Public Opinion Quarterly 16:59–70.

Tarde, Gabriel.
1903 The Laws of Imitation. Translation by Elsie C. Parsons. New York: Holt.

Troldahl, Verling C.
1966 "A field test of a modified 'two-step flow of communication' model." Public Opinion Quarterly 30:609–623.

Troldahl, Verling C., et al.
1965 "Public affairs information-seeking from institutionalized sources." Journalism Quarterly 42:403–412.

van den Ban, A. W.
1966 "A revision of the two-step flow of communication hypothesis." Gazette: International Journal for Mass Communication Studies 12:109–111.

Whiting, Gordon C., et al.
1967 Innovation in Brazil: Success and Failure of Agricultural Programs in 76 Minas Gerais Communities. East Lansing: Michigan State University, Department of Communication. Diffusion of Innovations Research Report 7.

Wright, Charles R., and Muriel Cantor.
1967 "The opinion seeker and avoider: Steps beyond the opinion leader concept." Pacific Sociological Review 10:33–43.

Yadav, Dharam P.
1967 "A comparative analysis of communication structure and innovation diffusion in two Indian villages." Ph.D. Dissertation, Michigan State University.

PART II Communication Settings

CHAPTER 12 Communication in Primitive Systems

J. L. FISCHER
Tulane University

First, there is a careful setting down of the criteria characterizing a primitive society, such as small size, relative homogeneity, technological inefficiency, and a greater dependence on oral rather than written communications. The mechanisms of communication (speech being the principal one) result in dependence on memory and folklore for historical record. The dense, compact structure of primitive societies has important effects on the communication patterns within such cultures. Gesture, contrary to popular notions, is relatively less important in primitive societies, partly because there is less need for nonverbal communication within relatively homogeneous societies whose contact with neighboring cultures, while present, is limited. There is, however, some such contact and even some intermarriage. In general, primitive societies are relatively self-sufficient economically, which tends to reduce the need and opportunity for intercultural relations.

DEFINITION OF PRIMITIVE

Let the reader be warned, if he is not already aware, that the word *primitive* in the title of this chapter is controversial.[1] *Nonliterate* or perhaps *small* might offend fewer people, but these terms are less informative. Therefore primitive is retained.

The greatest objections to the scientific use of the term *primitive* are aroused when it is applied to contemporary or recent small, isolated societies with simple subsistence technologies. Such societies, it has often been argued, should not be called primitive because they are contemporaneous with large societies that are generally regarded as "civilized." These small societies have had just as long a time to develop as the large societies; they have not remained static all this time but may simply have developed some other aspect of their culture in place of technology—perhaps they have developed religion or marriage rules, for instance.

An opposing view, which argues in favor of calling these small, isolated, contemporary societies primitive depends on a functional interpretation of society and culture, in which many sociocultural features are interrelated and in which the

[1] For a presentation of the case against *primitive*, see Tax and Mednick (1960).

subsistence technology in conjunction with the environment imposes certain crucial limitations on the size of the society and the development of other aspects of culture. In this view (which I share), given a relatively inefficient, time-consuming subsistence technology, the size of the community is limited, there are few if any persons with full-time occupational specialties, and the development of nonsubsistence aspects of culture is therefore relatively limited. While changes in such cultures do occur, they are likely to be random historical accidents without cumulative effect, or they may sometimes be progressively more specialized adjustments to features of the local environment. Moreover, the assumption made by some critics of the use of the term *primitive* that "all cultures change at an approximately equal rate" does not seem at all plausible from a functional point of view.

Part of the objection to the use of the term *primitive* is that it is unclear whether it is intended to apply to culture or to biology. In the past some have argued that the primitive societies were culturally simple because their population was biologically primitive and hereditarily incapable of full participation in a civilized or advanced culture. Physical anthropologists have studied various fossil men and protomen, and there is little question that if one goes far enough back in geological time one comes to small-brained ancestors who were mentally inferior by virtue of heredity. Some discussion of what little we are able to infer about the culture and communications system of biologically primitive (ancient fossil) man follows below. I would simply note here that while physical anthropologists have by no means unraveled the origin and function of the various hereditary differences between different contemporary human populations, it is the overwhelming consensus of most professional anthropologists who have studied the matter that the average individual capacity for culture in all contemporary populations is very similar.

The capacity for culture is essentially a capacity for learning an arbitrary, traditional way of life through social communication, and for changing this way of life when environmental or social circumstances require. No human society can be said to practice a natural instinctive way of life in the sense that a troop of monkeys or a pack of lions could be said to. Moreover, all known human societies seem to have had enough contact with some other societies so that there would have been repeated opportunities for the genetic bases for the capacity for culture to be introduced into the group and to be increased in frequency by natural selection. To be sure, the degree of contact between societies in the past has evidently not been enough to prevent the development of various hereditary physical differences between geographical populations which are presumably responses to local environmental factors.

This geographical variation in many hereditary features is not inconsistent with the assumption of an effective uniformity in capacity for culture in contemporary human populations, however. This is because the capacity for culture has been a universally useful and essential feature of mankind everywhere for hundreds of thousands of years, while the hereditary somatic features in which geographical populations differ appear to be specialized adaptions to local environments not affecting biological capacity for culture, or to be in some cases perhaps random variations irrelevant to the capacity for culture arising in small populations which became ancestral to larger populations. Thus it seems to be a sound working assumption that the range and distribution of the hereditary capacity for culture is about the same in all major geographical populations.

It follows, then, that in speaking of

some contemporary, recent, and even historical societies as primitive the reference is to their social organization and culture, not to the biological qualities of the members. From the point of view of the individual, probably any culture is about equally complex to the individual living in it and practicing it. To put it another way, the average amount of cultural information in the brain of the hunter is about the same as that in the brain of the resident of New York City. The difference in amount of cultural information between the two societies involves the size of the societies, degree of specialization of roles, and means for storing information outside of the brains of members.

Obviously, *primitive* and *civilized* are relative terms which assume that the temporal succession of changes in human culture has direction in broad perspective, at least in some important structural and functional aspects. Civilized societies and cultures, as contrasted with primitive, show larger territories, greater population size and density, a more effective basic subsistence technology, a greater store of culture information (in part due to writing and other records external to the individual human memory), greater occupational differentiation, etc. Human sociocultural evolution still has a great potential distance ahead of it. Hopefully we will be regarded as rather primitive by our descendants a few millennia hence. But this should not interfere with our evaluation of contemporary and recent cultures in terms of their formal similarity to those in the forefront of panhuman cultural change on the one hand or to simple ancestral cultures known only archeologically on the other.

Since cultures are complex and we are dealing with a continuous scale of development, it is not very useful to discuss at length just where the line between primitive and civilized should be drawn. In this chapter I will stick close to the primitive end of the continuum of observed cultures. For a further discussion of the ranking of cultures on an evolutionary scale, see White (1959) and Sahlins and Service (1960).

Information on the cultures and societies of human ancestors preceding modern *Homo sapiens* is scanty. It is inferred that, like a number of species of existing great apes and monkeys, our protohuman ancestors lived in small bands with a clear hierarchical structure; that the immature members tended to watch closely those of higher rank and imitate their reactions and behavior, while those of higher rank tended to protect their inferiors against threats from inside or outside the band. In these respects the behavior of the Japanese macaques as reported by Japanese primatologists since World War II is highly suggestive.[2] Such groups exhibit what may be termed a shared "protoculture" that is communicated more by the observation of knowledgeable members than by intentional messages.

Many physical anthropologists recognize three biological evolutionary stages of "man" preceding fully modern man: the australopithecine, the pithecanthropine, and the Neandertal (cf. Brace & Montagu, 1965). It is agreed that even the australopithecines, who lived as much as two million years ago or more, were ground-dwelling and walked erect. They are thought to have subsisted on small game as well as on roots, seeds, and fruits. Some suppose that the greater importance of hunting among these creatures, compared with the great apes and other primates, provided a selective advantage to individuals who were able to communicate with each other enough to cooperate more effectively in surrounding game and to teach others how to make and use tools and weapons of some sort.

While the australopithecines obviously

---

[2] For a summary of this work see the articles by Frisch (1959) and Imanishi (1960).

had some kind of protoculture or tradition, it is uncertain whether this involved true language. The view used to be popular that tools were impossible without language, but this argument has now been effectively shattered by observations of tool use among the great apes without language. The most spectacular of such evidence is perhaps Jane Goodall's (1963) report of the use of "termite fishing poles" by wild chimpanzees. Many australopithecine tools seem to be little more complicated than those of a chimpanzee.

The next stage, the pithecanthropines, are named after the former generic name of Java man, *Pithecanthropus*. This and related forms, including Peking man (formerly called *Sinanthropus*) are now generally grouped in a single species of the genus *Homo*, *H. erectus*. Some have even proposed that these forms be regarded as a subspecies of modern man, *H. sapiens erectus*. While the average brain size was smaller than any population of modern man, there is an overlap in range. These creatures also differed from modern man in having a more rugged skull and skeleton, more rugged, in fact, than their predecessors, the australopithecines.

The pithecanthropines are known to have hunted large as well as small game. The hunting of large game probably required more effective communication and more effective hunting weapons than were possessed by the australopithecines. The weapons also made it possible for these people to hunt each other. It is widely agreed that the skulls found in caves near Peking imply a regular ritual cannibalism. The increased skeletal ruggedness of *H. erectus* may have evolved as a result of widespread close combat between club-wielding men. The Peking men clearly used fire. Both this and the ritual cannibalism suggest to me that *H. erectus* had language.

H. erectus was followed in the fossil record by *H. neandertalensis*, which includes the earlier forms of the European cavemen. These Neandertal men are regarded by some as a subspecies of *H. sapiens* but as a separate, though closely related, species by others. Even the most extreme forms have brains of fully modern size or a little better. The principal difference from modern men is in a greater ruggedness of bones, although usually not as extreme as *H. erectus*. There is clear evidence of intentional burials, which implies some kind of belief about an afterlife. This would clearly seem to require language to develop. The inventory of tool types is more varied and the manufacture more refined.

Even through the Neandertal stage, human cultural remains are characterized by a relative conservatism of tool types. The so-called hand-axes were used over the inhabited areas of Africa, Europe, and West Asia with little change for hundreds of thousands of years, although other types of crude stone tools appear to have been found in East and Southeast Asia at this time. This uniformity of tool types may have been maintained in part by contact between wandering hunting bands following the migrations of large game animals. However, such contact has not prevented considerable local cultural and linguistic differentiation among long-established populations of hunters and gatherers in recent times, such as among the natives of Australia. Anthropologists argue about how much of the pre-*sapiens* cultural conservatism can be explained biologically, i.e., by an inferior hereditary capacity for culture, but this is probably an important part of the explanation, at least for the earlier periods.

MECHANICS OF COMMUNICATION

The most important means of communication in all human societies, including the most primitive technologically, is oral language. The languages of existing primitive societies that have been well studied have all proved to be approximately equal in structural complexity and subtlety to languages of civilized societies, although the semantic areas covered thoroughly by the vocabulary differ from one language to the next. The members of a hunting society, for instance, will obviously have a large vocabulary connected with behavior of prey, with the places where prey are found, with things that indicate the probable presence of prey, with things that may be easily mistaken for prey or signs of prey, etc., but will have no words for various modern mechanical inventions.

Since primitive societies lack most of the modern extensions of language, such as writing and long-distance transmission, the role of face-to-face speech in communication is probably greater in primitive than in civilized societies. In any event, the dependence on face-to-face speech is connected with limitations on the storage and transmission of social information.

Other media of communication exist even in primitive societies, however. In all human societies, as in societies of many kinds of animals, communication by nonverbal gesture is of some importance. The principal type of information communicated by gesture is interpersonal attitudes. Interpersonal attitudes are, in fact, often communicated more effectively by gesture and posture and by gestural aspects of speech such as loudness and intonation than they are by the literal content of the words and sentences. Much of this communication of attitudes is preconscious and sometimes contrary to conscious intention. In terms of sheer quantity and variety of detailed information, gestures communicate less than language, but in social decision-making the information provided by gestures can be quite important.

Gestures are also used to communicate some of the same kinds of information transmitted by speech. Gestures of pointing at objects appear to be universal, although some people point some or all of the time with the lips or nose instead of the hand or fingers. Gestures are also used occasionally to coordinate action in noisy work or battle situations or in situations where silence is important. Gestural communication as a language substitute apparently develops spontaneously with deaf mutes, although usually this is much more limited than ordinary speech. A full gestural language for deaf mutes appears to have developed only in Europe in the last few centuries.

The North American Plains Indians and some other midwestern groups have in recent times possessed an elaborate gesture language capable of transmitting a wide variety of information between tribes speaking mutually unintelligible natural languages (cf. Mooney, 1910). Such a fully developed "sign language" has not been reported from other primitive areas, and there is some reason to believe that the North American Indian sign language was developed after the arrival of Europeans from a French sign language for the deaf used by Catholic missionaries (cf. Stokoe, 1966).

There is a popular impression that primitive men rely more on gestures than do civilized men, on the false supposition that their languages are very simple. No doubt cultures vary in their use and variety of supplemental gestures in conversation. However, insofar as it is possible to gain an impression from solid ethnographic work, there is the suggestion that, contrary to popular notions, gestures are less important in ordinary conversation within the primitive community than they are in civilized conversation.

There are theoretical reasons for expecting this to be true. In general, people are more likely to resort to supplemental gestures when they are having difficulty communicating with each other. The extreme case is when the parties speak mutually unintelligible languages. This, of course, can be the situation when primitive men of two different speech communities meet, but it is also the situation in which the casual civilized explorer communicates with primitive men.

It would seem that less extreme obstructions to effective linguistic communication should have the same effect in increasing dependence on gestural communication. These might include situations where people are using second languages rather than their native language, where people are speaking markedly different dialects of the same language, and even where they are talking about specialized subject matter where they do not know the detailed vocabulary, or are talking with strangers with whose linguistic habits they are not well acquainted. The last two situations are not so common within primitive communities but are quite ordinary in civilized societies.

Various kinds of recreational and religious activities are found in all human societies, and these have communicative aspects. Both verbal and nonverbal communication is involved. Dancing could be considered a form of gestural communication that is found practically universally. Primitive dances occur both for recreation and for serious religious purposes.

While primitive ritual dances often have reference to an important myth or tradition, the symbolism of the dance is generally not complex enough to constitute a "sign language" in which new messages can be easily stated. A dance or a ritual would not communicate a detailed myth independently of a preceding oral account, although it might celebrate and help recall such an account. Ritual representations of myth, as well as the myths themselves, are often subject to multiple interpretations, as Fernandez (1965) has shown, although this does not necessarily destroy their effectiveness.

Myths and traditions may also be referred to by graphic and plastic art, whether reasonably realistic representations or simple geometric designs. In most primitive societies the art forms do not represent the entire myth in detail but simply show one or two selected important scenes, actors, or objects involved in the myth. Occasionally one comes across a fairly detailed series of pictures that represents a whole series of scenes (e.g., the pictures painted on the men's clubhouses in Palau, Caroline Islands, or the pre-Columbian Aztec manuscripts), but this much detail is rare and, even in these cases, the pictures are not entirely self-explanatory. In general, graphic and plastic art in primitive societies is limited to simple representations of well-known traditional narratives and is not used much for current events.

Some graphic and plastic art has the additional feature of asserting the owner's social status, e.g., the famous "totem poles" of the Indians of the Northwest Coast.[3] Architecture may serve a similar function, as where a chief or a rich man has a specially large or ornate dwelling. Dress, personal ornament, body painting, tattooing, etc., also are often used to assert group or family membership or individual rank, and thus have a communicative aspect.

The physical environment itself acquires much communicative significance for primitive people. Hunting peoples, especially, are sharp observers of the evidence of the activity of other humans, who thus in a sense communicate involuntarily with later passersby. Moreover, the landscape itself becomes impregnated with cultural information about its products and about the human events, real and imagined, that took place at various points. Many primitive peoples have a system of natural omens, in which selected events in the natural environment are regarded as indications of supernatural favor or disfavor or answers to questions about uncertain matters.

In a sense, the artifacts of a society constitute a way of storing information about the technology. Once one has learned to make or use an artifact properly, the

[3] Many anthropologists would say that the Northwest Coast Indians lacked true totems.

very sight of the artifact at a later time tends to recall its manufacture or use. If one has forgotten how to make a special kind of basket, for instance, an examination of such a basket will help remind one. The fact that the form of an artifact tends to suggest its manufacture and use also enables archeologists to reconstruct much about extinct cultures from their material remains. It is partly because of the mnemonic value of environment and artifacts that most people are much better informants about their culture when in home surroundings than when in a strange place.

Nevertheless, the amount of information that can be stored external to the brain in primitive societies is much less than can be stored in societies with an adequate writing system. To some extent members of primitive societies compensate for the relative lack of external storage by greater reliance on their memories, especially in youth and young adulthood. Phenomenal feats of memorization of traditional literature and other cultural materials are sometimes reported from primitive societies. There are suggestions also that more acute visual memory (eidetic imagery) is also characteristic of primitive societies. Some of the materials remembered are culturally stereotyped and have added redundancy for ease in memorization (e.g., metrical chants and songs), but there can be little question that many primitive peoples can memorize much better than civilized people.

EFFECT OF PRIMITIVE SOCIAL STRUCTURE ON COMMUNICATION

Primitive social structure, compared with civilized, is less differentiated and at the same time denser or more compact. The typical primitive society is composed of a number of households, each of which is largely self-sufficient for its own subsistence and each of which has available roughly the same technology and resources. The households in a single community or society are allied with each other by ties of intermarriage and by interests of common defense and territory. In the most primitive societies—especially some hunting and gathering societies—there is little difference between one household and another; even where there is someone holding a position of nominal authority and prestige, such as band chief, his actual power to give orders to other members of the community will probably be slight and his standard of living will be little different from anyone else's.

Primitive social structure is denser than civilized social structure since the primitive community and society are small, even infinitesimal, compared with modern nations. In hunting and gathering societies many bands (communities) contain about fifty to one hundred people of all ages; even in primitive agricultural societies a population of a few hundred or a couple of thousand people is rather common. In the smaller communities this means that each member of the community is likely to know every other member personally. Even in somewhat more populous primitive societies where all members cannot know each other, the number and variety of personal contacts are likely to be much smaller than in civilizations. In effect, in primitive societies the members tend to meet with strangers infrequently; even when they do, the stranger is likely to turn out to be a member of their own society who shares a similar local culture.

We shall have more to say about contacts between primitive societies, but let us note here that while communication within a single community is typically dense, there is likely to be little regular contact with people of other communities. This homogeneity, compactness, and isolation of primitive societies permit the members to share fully a basic cultural tradition and to be aware that they share it. In communication between normal adults there is a richness of shared background information which permits a high degree of ellipsis in ordinary conversation without sacrificing precision or subtlety.

At the same time, the homogeneity, compactness, and isolation of primitive societies must not be exaggerated. All human societies show major differentiation by sex and age, at least. Moreover, the organization into households and the different marital ties between households (through movement of members of one household into another at marriage) insure both that there will usually be closer communication among members of a household than between members of the household and outsiders, and that outsiders will tend to be classified according to genealogical (kin) relations.

For human culture to persist in any society, it is essential that cultural information be passed on from older to younger people. As in any society, much of this information is passed on within the household, from parents, elder siblings, grandparents, etc., to children, especially to children of the same sex as the older person. These same lines of cultural transmission tend to coincide with lines of authority and gradients of prestige in the community: senior close relatives generally control the labor of their juniors insofar as labor is not purely individualistic, and the seniors are also entitled to receive signs of deference from the juniors.

In many primitive societies, most notably in parts of Africa and aboriginal Australia, a formalized age-grading system exists. Usually the age-grading system is more marked for men than for women. The transition from one age grade to another is often marked by a group initiation ceremony, which is held periodically.

The most elaborate ceremony is usually held some time around puberty, marking the transition from child to man. In general, each older age grade has more prestige and authority and is considered to have more information than the preceding age grade, although in some systems there is an age grade for retired elders who are supposed to take little part in community affairs. Special functions may be assigned primarily to one age grade: thus in some parts of East Africa the initiated youths had the function of guarding the herds of cattle, while the young men of marriagable age formed the bulk of the armed forces, and middle-aged men and elders governed the community in council.

The age-grade system often provides a kind of schedule for imparting cultural information, and the transition ceremonies may be a dramatic occasion for some of this teaching. Typically at the puberty initiation ceremony, for instance, the initiated boys not only acquire new status in the society but also learn certain myths and rituals that are kept secret from women and children. This progressive transmission of esoteric religious information has been very well described for the Aranda of Central Australia by the younger Strehlow (1947).

While these transition ceremonies confer additional prestige on those who undergo them, they are at the same time occasions for reaffirming the social superiority of the seniors. Those who are being initiated into the next higher rank must often undergo various physical punishment, bodily mutilations, and other indignities at the hands of their seniors. After completion of the ceremony, the initiates receive new privileges in the community at large, e.g., the right to marry, or to eat certain special foods reserved for adults, or to wear certain insignia; often, however, they never achieve full equality with their seniors except through the death of the latter.

To a considerable extent age grading provides a hierarchical structure *within* face-to-face groups such as households, work or ritual groups. However, age grading also can serve as the basis for dividing the society into separate functioning groups. The young unmarried people in some primitive societies leave their households and go live in a special dwelling, either during their transition ceremonies or for several years until they get married and form a household of their own.

This tendency for a separation of generations is especially marked in parts of East Africa. Perhaps the most extreme development of this trend has been reported by Monica Wilson (1951) for the Nyakyusa of Malawi and Tanzania. The Nyakyusa had age-grade villages, so that young couples typically lived in a village apart from those of either of their parents. As the inhabitants of a village grew old, the village would decline in population and eventually disappear.

The tendency to form more or less exclusive age groups for some purposes is probably universal. One might think that this would interfere with the transmission of culture between generations, and to some extent it may, especially when it is as extreme as the Nyakyusa case. However, transmission of culture from older to younger can also occur within an age grade, which usually spans several years' difference in age. While a teacher who is slightly older than his pupil may have less social prestige than an older person and may not know too much more than his pupil, this same slightly older teacher will be a very plausible model for his pupil. Moreover, the little extra information he does possess is likely to be just what his pupil is looking for, since the two will share more current interests than would a teacher and pupil with a marked age difference.

In the above discussion the transmission of cultural information has been emphasized; that is, information about customs, beliefs, traditional history, etc. There is also information about current events that does not become a permanent part of the lore of the community but is necessary to share for limited periods in the course of daily life: information about who has done what, who is sick, who has been successful in hunting or fishing, who has quarreled with whom, etc. Ethnographic reporting on the diffusion of information about current events is not so clear. Possibly this is because the channels of diffusion are less patterned than the channels of transmission of cultural information. It would seem that often information about current events would be transmitted from junior to senior, especially from young adults to older adults, since the juniors would be more physically active and mobile.

Individual differences by wealth form a principle of hierarchy, especially for males, in some primitive societies. This is more characteristic of primitive agricultural (horticultural) societies than of hunting and gathering societies, since the way of life of the latter usually discourages the accumulation of wealth. Often the wealth of a man does not carry on to his heirs or sons, since it is dissipated in periodic feasts and in funeral ceremonies. In such societies the use of wealth for conspicuous consumption as described by Veblen has been carried to extremes. Many of the societies in New Guinea and parts of Melanesia exemplify this sort of wealth competition (see, e.g., Oliver, 1955). A man who is able to accumulate and disburse much wealth (often consisting of food, personal ornaments, and ritual objects) becomes a de facto leader of his community or a part of it.

Genuine class differences, in which wealth or some other mark of high status tends to persist from one generation to the next and in which people tend to associate with and marry others of roughly equal prestige and power, are found in a number of moderately primitive communities, but rarely in hunting and gathering societies. Where such differences develop, sometimes on the basis of conquest, they can become rather rigid since a man's status is marked at birth and is clear at all times to other members of the community.

The tendency to form more or less exclusive groups by sex for some purposes is probably as universal as the tendency to form such groups by age. In all societies there are some subsistence tasks as well as other less critical activities that are considered to be the normal province of one or the other sex; all male or all female groups form around these tasks if cooperation is required. Such groups talk more with each other than with outsiders and share more information about their tasks; they are also likely to share more information of other sorts passed along in gossip and incidental conversation.

Primitive societies vary considerably in the degree to which men and women tend to form exclusive groups in work and leisure. It is the male role that shows the greater variation cross-culturally. Two activities that tend to be exclusively male when found are the hunting of large game animals and warfare. Where either of these is prominent, the men are likely to have frequent occasions to form exclusive groups and to draw away from the women much of the time. In such societies the men may develop special elaborate ceremonies that are reserved exclusively for men (often involved in part with transition between the male age grades as previously discussed).

In various parts of the tropics (especially Africa, South America, New Guinea, Australia), there was traditionally a death penalty for women who were discovered to have seen accidentally or intentionally certain male ceremonies. Male anthropologists have sometimes speculated that some woman anthropologist should investigate female ceremonies in the same tribes, which might prove equally complex. Where this has been done, however, it has turned out that while the women may have their exclusive ceremonies and ritual knowledge, these are not as elaborate as the men's. On a little reflection, this is hardly surprising since women's work tends to be in child care and routine gathering and preparation of foods, and cannot be as easily interrupted for ceremonies as the men's work can.

Some observers have occasionally noted differences between men's and women's speech that could be called stylistic or dialectal. Probably there are in all languages some vocabulary items which both sexes understand but which tend to be used more by one sex than the other, e.g., certain common obscene words in English. However, in a couple of primitive languages, regular phonetic transformations have been reported, so that men typically pronounce certain words one way and women another. This difference in men's and women's speech was described by Sapir (1949) for Yana, an Indian language in northern California, and by Mary Haas (1944) for Koasati, a southeastern U.S. American Indian language. Interestingly, Haas reports that when men were telling stories in which they quoted a female character they would assume the female pronunciation for the quotation (and vice versa).

It is clear, then, that these differences in pronunciation could not be explained solely on the grounds that the two sexes were isolated in daily life and did not get a chance to become thoroughly familiar with the speech of the other sex. We may think of these sex differences in speech as symbols of sex identity in the same sense that dress in our own society is such a symbol. They are probably differences that are stimulated especially when men and women are in interaction and wish to emphasize their special roles.

We have already mentioned the organization of primitive societies into households or families, which constitute more or less exclusive groups tending to share common information about current events as well as the culture. We must also consider larger kinds of kin groups such as unilineal descent groups (variously called *clans*, *lineages*, etc., by anthropologists) and other groups of kin formed with reference to living individuals or to deceased ancestors.[4]

---

[4] For a review of methods of forming kin groups, see the section on "The Biological Network" in Bohannan (1963).

Each of these kinds of groups may have occasions when the members communicate among themselves and, therefore, come to share some kind of information. However, as anthropologists have noted, the only type of descent group that can be both exclusive and exhaustive, so that any member of the society belongs to one and only one, is a unilineal group in which membership is assigned consistently through only one parent, whether this be the father (patrilineal) or the mother (matrilineal)—or possibly some prescribed alternation between the two—but never both. It is in societies with unilineal descent groups (patrilineages or matrilineages) that kin groups larger than the family tend to develop characteristic separate subcultures and elaborate ways of symbolizing their identity.

The existence of these larger kin groups tends to be related to particular forms of household and community. Patrilineages typically, though not inevitably, are found in societies with patrilocal extended families; that is, where a man's married sons continue to live with their father as married adults, either in the same household or in a nearby household in the same community. This results in a core of related men who know each other well, and a "fringe" of unrelated women whom they have married and brought to live with them. In matrilineal societies the picture is typically similar with the sexes reversed. Murdock (1949) has proposed that where unilineal descent is not currently associated with the appropriate household or extended-family pattern, one may suspect that the system is undergoing change and that at an earlier period the association was probably found.

It can be seen that the development of family subcultures will be influenced by the type of family and household found in the society. In a patrilineal, patrilocal society, where related adult men form a tight, cooperating group and their wives come in from outside, the parts of the culture carried by males are likely to be more specialized by family but locally consistent, while the parts of the culture carried by females will be more broadly diffused but locally more subject to variation. In a matrilineal, matrilocal society, the reverse would be expected. Using this reasoning some archeologists have proposed that it should be possible to infer residence and even descent patterns of extinct people by looking at the relative variability of artifacts which were made by men and women (cf. Deetz, 1965).

The exchange of women implied in family exogamy has been treated as a form of communication by some anthropologists, most notably by the French anthropologist Lévi-Strauss (1949). It is clear that in many primitive societies men are quite explicit about exchanging their daughters or sisters for wives for themselves, and that marriage is not a simple matter of two individuals falling in love. A variety of exchange systems is possible. Some of these systems lead to stable relationships between descent groups, so that a desirable marriage partner for any particular man already has a certain kinship relation to him, e.g., a "cross-cousin" (father's sister's child or mother's brother's child). At the same time there are always some close relatives who are forbidden as spouses, at least for the ordinary member of the society.

These systems of larger kinship groups and marital exchange often involve special communicative relationships between various types of kin. A "mother-in-law taboo" is found in many primitive societies, for instance. In such a society a man's contact with his wife's mother may be severely restricted. Perhaps he is not allowed to talk about light subjects in her presence, or perhaps he may not talk with her at all, or even look at her directly. Such a relationship would be termed a *respect relationship* or, in the extreme case, an *avoidance relationship*.

Certain other relatives may be "joking relatives" with whom one engages in jokes and horseplay. In societies with cross-cousin marriage (where the children of a man marry the children of his sister), the cross-cousin of opposite sex may be in this relationship. Any of these relationships can distort and limit the information that can be shared by certain individuals in the society, although if need be they can communicate with each other indirectly through a third party.

In many primitive societies there are also a number of special roles whose occupants have special functions in the communicative system of the society. In some primitive agricultural societies one finds a few occupational specializations, usually part-time. A simple example might be the canoe and house carpenters of ancient Samoa. These specialists typically have trade secrets which are passed on only to selected apprentices. Often these apprentices are limited to kinsmen, although in Samoa it appears that any youth really interested in becoming a carpenter could get started in training by having himself adopted into a master carpenter's family. In some primitive cultures, the making of certain personal ornaments and ritual objects is a specialization involving restricted information.

Some system of exchange of goods between households or family groups is probably universal in primitive societies, even though the households approach self-sufficiency as far as ordinary subsistence goes. As students of primitive economics have noted, the systems of exchange of material goods and services in primitive cultures are subject to many limitations not found in civilized societies. The variety of objects that may be traded is often quite limited. Also, objects subject to trade tend to be paired or grouped; that is, for any particular kind of object only a very limited number of other objects may be given in return. In many parts of the Pacific islands, for instance, people who catch fish may "trade" this fish for vegetable food produced by other families, but the fishermen would not think of asking for shell necklaces for their fish, nor would anyone think of making such an offer.

In some primitive societies the individuals who engage in trade are again quite limited. A man does not offer the goods he wishes to trade on the open market to the highest bidder but has a particular trading partner with whom he must conduct his transactions. Malinowski's (1922) description of the *kula* system in the Trobriand Islands and vicinity is illustrative of this, with the further restriction that each partner had a prescribed type of object to give the other: for each pair of trading partners one partner was always obligated to give shell armbands and the other always to give shell necklaces, although each would also have another partner with whom the roles were reversed.

While the ostensible function of the trading partnerships may be to exchange certain ritual or ornamental objects, meetings between trade partners may also be the occasion for trading more utilitarian objects as well as exchanging news and cultural tradition. Individuals in trade partner relationships thus act as intermediaries for information from outside the community. They may also act as ambassadors who reduce hostility and often prevent the outbreak of fighting between independent communities.

Many primitive societies have at least a nominal chief. The powers of these chiefs vary considerably from one society to the next, but usually they are not very strong. The chief is often regarded as a person who is generally recognized to be experienced and gifted in speaking, and his most important function may be to propose group action, to lead discussion, and eventually to state the consensus when it becomes clear that one has been reached. The chief may also arbitrate disputes when the parties cannot settle them by themselves. In most primitive societies the chief is not a full-time specialist but spends most of his time in subsistence pursuits like everyone else. Even in such a relatively complex and populous society as pre-Christian Hawaii it is said that King Kamehameha spent some of his time in taro gardening, although he could certainly have been fed by tribute if he had insisted.

A few other specialized political roles are found in some primitive societies. The role of war leader is sometimes distinct from that of chief, as was the case among some of the American Indians of the Great Plains.

Some primitive societies have a role which could be described as mediator or judge, e.g., some of the mountain tribes in northern Luzon as described by Barton (1949). In northern Luzon these are men who are wealthy and powerful in their own right and who are appealed to by parties in a dispute to serve as arbitrators. These men listen to the arguments of both sides and eventually propose a settlement, or repeated settlements, until both parties agree to accept the settlement or agree to continue their feud. The arbitrator does not have any recognized right to force a decision on the disputants, however.

In Polynesia the role of "talking chief" is often developed. The talking chief is a sort of executive and public relations officer for the high chief or sacred chief, who is often taboo in Polynesia and can have only limited contact with his subjects. Decisions of the high chief are thus announced and explained to the people by the talking chief. Because of his greater contact with the people the talking chief may know more about many problems than the high chief and be more in a position to make decisions. One of the functions of the talking chief in some Polynesian societies is to serve as a repository of political tradition. In Samoa, for instance, it is the talking chiefs, especially, who are supposed to memorize the genealogies that legitimate the positions of the high chiefs, as well as memorize other traditions of the history of the communities and their interrelations (cf. Keesing & Keesing, 1956).

Traditional history and the mythology of the origin of the descent group, the community, and society are often controlled by part-time specialists in primitive societies. Usually these are old people who have been instructed by earlier experts. Actually, the general outlines of the traditional history are usually widely known, but the function of these specialists in tradition is to narrate an approved version on public occasions and to be able to correct erroneous variants as they arise.

Specialists in tradition and myth often make much of their unique secret knowledge which they and their pupils alone know. Often this secret knowledge consists largely of proper names or esoteric terms for things already generally known, although sometimes the esoteric version of a myth is quite different from the commonly accepted one. This may be because the esoteric version has recently changed. Since the esoteric version is held by a few persons, it can be changed rather easily—for example, when an expert dies before passing on all his knowledge and his successor needs to fill out gaps by a trance or dream. The popular version cannot be so easily changed.

Similar attitudes of exclusiveness often attach to traditional narratives told for entertainment and other types of artistic and recreational performance. Even though other people may know a particular folktale perfectly well, there may be certain narrators who are considered to own the tale and have a recognized right to public performance. Even where property rights in tales are not recognized, skill in narration usually is; thus, in effect, a minority of leisure-time specialists perform most tale narrations in the community. Similar considerations apply for other forms of expressive culture, such as song, dance, and so forth.

Various kinds of part-time medical-magical specialists are common in primitive society. Such persons usually regard their practices as based on valuable esoteric knowledge, and they receive some kind of payment for treating or diagnosing a patient's illness or otherwise helping him.

The division between magical and religious specialists in primitive societies is arbitary and has been made variously by different investigators according to the criteria that seemed most useful in analyzing the particular society they were studying. Some of the commonly used distinctions are (1) religious activity is for socially approved purposes while magic is socially indifferent or antisocial; (2) religion is conducted publicly while magic is conducted privately; (3) religion has no definite empirical goal while magic does; (4) religion involves an attitude of supplication of a superior power while magic involves coercion. Whether or not we wish to distinguish religion and magic along any of these lines, various primitive cultures have activities that can be differentiated by one or another of these variables, and often have different specialists to perform these. Regardless of the distinction, any specialist dealing with the supernatural is likely to be treated with special respect and often with fear as well.

This brief review should make it clear that even small primitive societies do not lack considerable differentiation of communicative roles. At the same time the differentiation of primitive societies must not be exaggerated. As noted above, primitive specialists generally work at their specialty only part-time. Moreover, most primitive societies do not have all the kinds of specialists mentioned. In general, the smaller the society and the simpler its technology, the less differentiated it will be.

Anthropologists have speculated about the relationship between the size of the society and the stability of its culture. Obviously, in a small society with relatively little role differentiation, the total cultural inventory must be small. Because of the small number of members, it would seem that the chance would be great that information (including not just items of personal history but also cultural items) would be lost from one generation to the next due to the loss of knowledgeable older members before they had passed on their complete store of culture. The lost items would then have to be replaced by new inventions or by borrowing from neighboring cultures.

On the other hand, it has been argued that because the society is small there are few people to propose innovations in it and fewer occasions for contacts with outsiders, and innovations that do arise can be easily forgotten and suppressed. Elbert's (1953) comparative study of Polynesian basic vocabulary seems to indicate that the latter argument carries more weight, at least for common words considered as items of culture. Elbert found evidence suggesting that the basic vocabularies of some of the smaller and more isolated islands in Polynesia showed greater stability than did the vocabularies of the larger islands for the same concepts.

Possibly it might be useful to distinguish between *core* items of culture (those that are transmitted from generation to generation with much redundance) and *fringe* items (those that are transmitted with little redundance). It may be that small societies favor increased stability of transmission of the core items and decreased stability of fringe items. An extension of Elbert's study of Polynesian basic vocabulary to some fringe vocabulary might be an interesting way of approaching this question.

PURPOSES AND FUNCTIONS OF PRIMITIVE COMMUNICATION

We may analyze the effects of human communication on a receiver as cognitive, affective, or conative in varying degrees. A message of any length usually has a complex mixture of these effects: some parts may transmit information about the world without evoking much specific immediate emotional response or overt action (cognitive effect); others may produce an emotional or evaluative response without adding much new information or evoking any definite action (affective); still others may evoke a definite action without much intense emotional response and little increase in information (conative).

Anthropologists do not agree on the differences in balance between civilized and primitive societies in the relative emphasis each places on these general effects of communication. However, the writings of some investigators suggest that affective communication plays a greater role in the life of primitive peoples, while cognitive communication plays a greater role in the life of civilized peoples, at least those in a secure economic and political position.

The French philosopher-anthropologist Lévy-Bruhl (1922) once proposed a distinction between logical and prelogical thought, which he associated with civilized and primitive cultures, respectively. He was much attacked for this and later admitted that the difference between civilized and primitive peoples was one of proportion of the two kinds of thought rather than of absolute difference (Leenhardt, 1949). Lévy-Bruhl did not, however, completely retract his basic position, contrary to statements in some critiques of his work.

Lévy-Bruhl's "logical thought" corresponds rather well to "thought about cognitive messages," while his "prelogical thought" corresponds somewhat less well to "thought about affective messages" in terms of the classification presented above. The problem of correspondence arises from Lévy-Bruhl's characteristically French interest in logic and reason and his relative lack of interest in emotion. He was perhaps most interested in affective messages when they involve cognitive assumptions and distortions due to wishful thinking, i.e., the kind of thinking involved in ritual which is inadequately tested empirically.

However we may wish to classify the functions of messages, it does seem to be a fair generalization that the average primitive generates and is exposed to a greater proportion of messages of primarily emotional significance than is the average member of civilized society. The fascination of primitives with physiology—blood, birth, sex, excretion, death—of which Kroeber (1948) wrote is a manifestation of this. This fascination is emotional rather than cognitive, and sometimes results in some curious distortions of obvious physiological facts, e.g., the myth of the Chagga of East Africa that adult initiated men did not need to defecate (Raum, 1940:318–319). The men, of course, were perfectly aware that this was a fiction but the women were supposed to believe it, and the men went to great lengths to avoid being detected. The point to note is not that this assertion was false but that the men felt an emotional need to assert it.

This example should also make clear that the greater predominance of affective messages among primitives is not a matter of more simple and spontaneous expression of emotion. Rather, it is a matter of greater participation of primitives in magical and religious ritual, which expresses and relieves unpleasant emotion and is often elaborate and prescribed in detail. Some authors have claimed that primitive ritual is typically devoid of emotion and is performed automatically (e.g., Lévi-Strauss, 1963). While this may be true in some instances, it seems unlikely that the ritual, which generally lacks direct practical value, would persist indefinitely in a culture unless it had some expressive value. Moreover, the emotion in back of ritual is anxiety. The performers of a ritual may attempt to gain some peace of mind by simply denying the anxiety while at the same time trying to relieve it by the ritual.

Some magical and religious rites raise the question of the value of classifying messages by their effect on the receiver, since these may be performed in isolation and addressed to supernatural beings whose existence cannot be verified scientifically. In ordinary communication the sender assumes that he can evaluate the effect of his message on the hearer, and there is usually a coincidence between the sender's intention and the effect on the hearer, thus making a classification from either point of view similar.

In ritual communication addressed to nonexistent and nonresponsive beings, it is more useful to classify the messages from the point of view of the sender. More specifically, it is useful to classify these messages on the basis of their psychological function (affective) rather than on the overt intent of the sender, which is most often to persuade a supernatural being to do something for him. (Incidentally, while civilized people often laugh at the naiveté of primitive peoples in addressing nonexistent spirits, primitive ritual sometimes exhibits striking structural and functional similarities to much modern commercial advertising and political propaganda, where the main audience is not the ostensible addressee but rather the group that is sending the message, and where the main effect is to instill confidence in one's own partisans rather than to convert customers or supporters of one's political opponents.)

Of course, the primitive who practices magic does not accept that he receives no personal response to his communication. In the simplest case, he waits for the requested event to be decided and attributes the favorable or unfavorable result to the corresponding intent of the supernatural power addressed.

A more elaborate method of obtaining responses is through divination: a question with clear alternative answers is posed to the supernatural and some process is started with two or more random possible outcomes that are set in advance to correspond to the alternative answers. The outcome of the random process is then considered an answer to the question. Throwing dice to decide whether or not to do something would be an example if one considered that a supernatural being determined which faces of the dice came up. Divination is frequently used when there is no good empirical reason for preferring either alternative, but when either alternative is reasonably plausible. In this situation it is reasonably rewarding.

In some cases the sender of the message does not recognize that he is really in some sense the sender, and he attributes the source of a message arising from himself to a supernatural being. Common examples of this in primitive society are the treatment of dreams as prophetic or directive, the alleged possession of mediums by the ghosts of the deceased, and the alleged possession of shamans by familiar spirits of animals or other supernaturals.

In psychological terms it may be useful to consider such messages as coming from the unconscious part of the sender's personality to his conscious part. These messages from the unconscious are then often relayed further to normal human receivers. These allegedly supernatural communications can be a device for transmitting socially sensitive messages, which would be resented if produced directly and consciously by the human sender and which the sender for this reason would be likely to repress in the psychoanalytic sense, or certainly to suppress if consciously aware of them. No doubt it is partly for this reason that such messages from the unconscious are often phrased ambiguously and may require further discussion and interpretation after they have been received before any action can be taken: since the content is likely to be delicate, it must be broken gradually to the receivers.

Messages may also be classified according to whether their effects are long or short range. Messages with long-range effects form part of the process of education or enculturation. These are the messages that are not quickly forgotten and that are recognized to have applicability to more than one momentary situation. Other messages may be intended to have only short-range effects. Either long- or short-range messages may have cognitive, affective, or conative effects.

It has been observed that in some primitive cultures there are few messages with intentional long-range effects from the sender's point of view. The people of Atimelang on the Indonesian island of Alor as described by Cora DuBois (1944) are an example of this. DuBois speaks of enculturation there as characterized by "absorptive learning" without overt instruction. Of course, even here there often may be long-range intent on the part of the learner, if not of the teacher or model. Boys in Atimelang may learn about native finance in part by conscious attempts to observe the activities of their elders, even though the elders largely ignore them.

Certain kinds of subsistence activities may lead to an emphasis on foresight and long-range views even in otherwise primitive societies. This emphasis may be reflected in child care and personality generally. Barry, Child, and Bacon (1959) made a comparative study that suggested that foresight tends to be developed where the main subsistence dependence is on animal husbandry or on agriculture of a sort requiring an annual harvest, rationing of the crop over a nonproductive period, and saving of seed for the next year. Both these types of subsistence are more characteristic of civilizations than of primitive societies, although not exclusively so.

Another occasion in some primitive societies that may give rise to intentional long-range messages (intentional enculturation or education) is when two societies with contrasting cultures are in fairly intimate contact and the members of each consciously wish to preserve their own traditions. In this situation there may be conscious attempts to inculcate those aspects of the cultures that contrast the two societies, and to inhibit the alien culture where it differs from one's own.

More commonly, however, the point made by Margaret Mead (1943) is valid, that even where more or less formal cultural instruction is given in primitive societies by senior members, this is likely to be at the request of the juniors. The seniors may give up the desired information only with reluctance and for a price. Mead contrasts this with the modern attitude of children undergoing compulsory education, or (she might have added) the consumer subjected to commercial advertising or the citizen subjected to political propaganda.

Another occasion for intentional cultural instruction in primitive societies is the work situation, where teacher and learner share a common interest in accomplishing a cooperative task connected with daily living. When necessary, the teacher will instruct the learner on points that he needs to know to participate in the work. The long-range intent here is usually secondary to the immediate aim of accomplishing the task at hand, but a long-range effect is likely to be achieved.

To some extent, long-range messages (enculturation) can be generalizations which the learner makes for himself from many short-range messages that he receives in the course of his daily activities. This relative lack of explicit generalization and instruction in primitive societies tends to be reflected in a lesser ability to deal with abstract concepts, which has been shown by most administrations of personality tests in primitive societies.

This emphasis on the enculturative functions of communication may give the impression that communication in primitive cultures is mostly conservative. Probably this is true in any organized society that retains its identity, although our attention is likely to be more attracted by the use of communication to spread innovations or "news." When cultural innovations do become established in primitive society, they must be passed on in the same communicative network with older cultural items if they are not simply to vanish.

On the whole, the general attitude toward cultural innovation is unfavorable in most primitive societies. The existing store of culture is valued as a proven way of life adapted to the special environmental circumstances of the group, and it is likely that the most obvious possible innovations have been tested before, found wanting, and been discarded and forgotten. Moreover, one's participation in the customary routine of the culture serves as a badge of membership in a cooperative community and a pledge of allegiance to that community. To propose or accept an innovation may symbolize rejection of one's community.

There are exceptions to this general attitude toward innovation. In ecological crises (e.g., when the society moves or is driven into a new environment or where environment itself changes greatly), major changes in the ancestral culture may be necessary and adaptive. Primitive societies that are defeated in war may lose confidence in their old culture even if they retain their independence. It is especially at such times of crisis that people are ready to listen to alleged supernatural messages transmitted by mediums, shamans, prophets, etc. (cf. Wallace, 1956).

We have mentioned the possibility of innovation through communicative error, where the sender is unsuccessful in transmitting his full cultural message and the receiver, so to speak, must fabricate a substitute for the missing information. Within a single culture this is especially likely to occur with esoteric fringe elements that are relatively unimportant and of little consequence. For instance, in field work in Ponape, Caroline Islands, it appeared to me that most of the traditional astronomical lore had been lost by about 1940, although the language and most of the rest of the culture had been preserved. Astronomy was used by the old Ponapeans mainly for interisland navigation, but navigation was of little importance to the Ponapeans since they lived on the largest island for hundreds of miles around. The number of astronomical experts was therefore small, and when they failed to pass on their lore it rapidly disappeared.

Simple practical innovations with obvious utility in reducing labor and increasing its efficiency are often accepted rather quickly once they are introduced into a primitive culture. Of course, it is just such innovations that tend to be rare in primitive cultures, and perhaps in any culture. In historically observed instances, innovations of this sort have usually been introduced through contact with civilizations rather than from other primitive cultures, e.g., metal tools and factory-made cloth replacing stone and shell tools and skin or handwoven fiber clothing.

In sheer quantity, short-range messages dealing with problems of daily living are more numerous than enculturative messages. These short-range messages are often essential for cooperation in work and mutual defense. It should be remembered, however, that communication can be divisive as well when it is used by men as a tool to assert their special interests and to try to gain control over others. There has been no convincing report of a society, primitive or civilized, that is without division into opposed interest groups. Sometimes when one of these groups (lineage, community, clique) gains special power, it may try to rewrite custom to its own advantage. More often, it will simply displace an earlier special-interest group without attempting any basic cultural reform. Individuals as well as groups have their special interests in all societies and try to advance these usually by persuasion in preference to brute force.

There are limitations on the use of verbal and other communication to advance special interests. The special interest is advanced most effectively if the other party can be convinced that it is in accord with the interest of the broader community in which both parties are included and that it is also in accord with customary precedent. At the same time the other party has a special interest in denying these conditions. Moreover, the special interests of individuals or subgroups often do not meet these conditions from the view of an objective third party. In these circumstances, the only peaceful solution is for both parties to compromise and abide by customary precedent.

Occasionally, of course, there is no peaceful solution and the community splits or ejects one party. This process helps keep primitive societies small in size. It could be argued that difficulties in effective communication between special-interest groups within a relatively undifferentiated primitive community are sufficient to insure that the community must split when it becomes too numerous.

INTERSOCIETAL COMMUNICATION

Strictly speaking, the notion that the typical primitive society is a self-contained communications system is a fiction. A society is a system in which internal communication is generally denser than external communication, but external communication exists in practically all primitive societies, if only intermittently. The nearest approach to a completely self-contained primitive society is perhaps the Polar Eskimo of northwestern Greenland (cf. Holtved, 1951). These people when discovered believed themselves to be the only people on earth except for some supernaturals who were thought to live on the Greenland icecap. Nevertheless, they had evidently not been separated too long from other Eskimo groups, since their dialect was still mutually intelligible with other Eastern Eskimo dialects.

The populations of some of the more remote islands in the farther parts of the Pacific showed a similar isolation. The people of Easter Island in eastern Polynesia lacked ocean-going canoes when first discovered by Europeans. They did, however, have traditions of coming from another inhabited island (cf. Métraux, 1957). In some of the other remote Polynesian islands that lacked sea-going canoes at the time of discovery, the people still had occasional contact with outsiders who came ashore as castaways after accidents at sea.

More typically, even the simplest societies at the hunting and gathering subsistence level would be in periodic contact with other basically similar neighboring societies. If the two societies spoke different languages there would usually be a number of bilinguals in both societies. A certain amount of intermarriage would be common, even between members of societies that engaged in warfare from time to time. As a result of the intermarriage, ties of kinship might be possible to trace with any member of a neighboring society.

Often where actual genealogical ties could not be traced, there would be conventions of relationship between lineages in different societies which would serve to provide a basis for treating a stranger as a kinsman. It has been said that the natives of Australia, who before discovery were exclusively dependent on hunting and gathering for subsistence, generally assumed before contact that it would be possible to define an alien stranger as some kind of relative after discussion; if they could not do so, which was rare, they would be likely to kill him.

Given ties of kinship between two neighboring primitive societies, this would provide a basis for visits between relatives and for mutual participation in each other's major ceremonies. In the desert regions of Australia and in other primitive areas, major ceremonies were often restricted to periods of special abundance which could support a larger than usual concentration of population. The gathering of people of different tribes for a ceremony would thus have the advantage of sharing an otherwise unusable abundance of food, for which a return would be made by the visitors on a later occasion.

Kinship and friendship ties between neighboring societies would also provide a basis for aid to a group that was the victim of some unexpected natural disaster such as a flood, a drought, or decline in game and wild food products due to disease.

While primitive societies are generally self-sufficient for basic subsistence needs, a certain amount of trade involving a limited number of items generally occurs between societies as well as between different communities of the same society. As mentioned earlier, the goods involved are often ornamental or ritual in significance. Archaeological evidence for trade of ornamental shells and material for especially good stone tools goes back to the Paleolithic period. Often these objects are found hundreds of miles from their source, although presumably as the result of a series of successive trades.

Usually trade is accomplished by face-to-face contact involving speech, although occasional instances of what has been called the "silent trade" have been reported. In this, one trading party brings goods to a certain place and leaves them there; the second party then brings goods it wishes to trade for these and leaves them. The first party then returns and, if satisfied, takes away the goods left by the second party, who then comes again and claims the goods left by the first. This is not, however, the usual method of primitive trade, and is probably one which has been devised especially where the parties are of unequal strength and the weaker party is afraid of direct contact with the stronger. It may in fact be more characteristic of primitive peoples in contact with civilization than among themselves.

In some areas the institution of trading partners, discussed earlier, applies to relations between members of different societies as well as to members of different communities within the same society. Most of these trading relationships offer some opportunity for the exchange of other information beyond that involved in the exchange of goods. One of the functions of the trading relations and other intersocietal relationships, sometimes consciously recognized, may be to introduce some novelty into life. Within a small face-to-face community life can become rather dull. The environment and its exploitation provide some novelty, but the society itself may not provide much. Occasional visitors may therefore be welcomed in primitive society if they are not threatening.

The welcome extended to alien visitors in primitive society probably bears a fairly clear inverse relationship to the frequency of outside contact and the general population density in the region. In areas of fairly high population density, there is a serious danger that one's own society could be totally destroyed in a fight with a neighboring group living only a few miles away, e.g., in the areas inhabited by primitive agriculturalists in the New Guinea Highlands (cf. Berndt, 1962) or in the mountains of northern Luzon (cf. Barton, 1949). Moreover, since the neighbors are near enough to be in regular contact, they are not thought of as such an entertaining novelty as would be a visitor to an isolated Pacific island or to a band of aborigines in the middle of the Australian desert.

It is perhaps this inverse relation between population density and receptivity to aliens that accounts for the finding of M. S. Edmonson (1961), who studied diffusion rates of certain archaeological traits dated by radio-carbon. Edmonson found that, regardless of environment, there appears to be a rather constant primitive diffusion rate of cultural traits of about 1.15 miles per year, taken over long distances and periods, where long water voyages are not involved. In other words, primitive societies in frequent contact with aliens are less likely to accept culture traits from these contacts than are those in infrequent contact.

This points to another aspect of communication between primitive societies that has been illuminated in the work of Gregory Bateson and Claude Lévi-Strauss, among others, namely, that the process which Bateson (1936) called *schismogenesis* operates with special force between neighboring independent societies in close contact. In other words, the societies, in trying to point up their special identity and avoid confusion with their neighbors, emphasize and come to exaggerate those features of their culture that distinguish them from neighboring cultures. The "transformations" of myth and ritual discussed by Lévi-Strauss (e.g., 1958; 1962) often appear to have this motivation. Linguistic and dialectal differentiation are also often used by people as symbols of identity, although not solely produced for the purpose.

Of course, there are limits to this process of differentiation which are imposed by practical considerations. It is easier for expressive culture (religion, art, recreation) to become differentiated in this way than it is for the practical aspects of culture directly involved in daily subsistence. It is not to be expected, for instance, that a society would abandon agriculture for hunting just to be different from its agricultural neighbors, although if different ecological niches made both ways of subsistence possible in the same region it is likely that the societies would seize on their means of subsistence as symbols of their separateness.

SUMMARY

By a primitive communication system we mean the communication system of a culturally primitive society. Some of the important characteristics of such societies are their small size, relative homogeneity, technological inefficiency in subsistence, greater reliance on oral communication, and absence of writing. The persistence of primitive systems until recent times in some parts of the world may be explained by geographical, ecological, and historical factors. It appears unlikely that hereditary racial differences are causally related to the position of modern or recent cultures on the evolutionary scale, although at some point in the past the nervous systems of our ancestors were undoubtedly inadequate to participate in existing cultures even of the most primitive sort remaining.

All known human societies have elaborate and subtle languages, and speech is the most important form of communication. The absence of writing places greater emphasis on speech and memory. Gesture, ritual, and other activities may be regarded as supplementary forms of communication; they are much less precise than speech, however, and the message content tends to emphasize emotions and interpersonal attitudes.

While primitive social structure is more homogeneous than that of large civilized societies, important differentiation exists in all human societies which affects the lines of communication and message content within the society. Important differentiation by sex, age, and kin group is universal. Differentiation by wealth is also widespread, even in rather primitive societies, although usually minimal in the most primitive. Occupational differentiation is also found, although the occupations are usually part-time.

Compared with civilized communication, primitive communication may have somewhat greater emphasis on affective messages and less on strictly cognitive messages. In primitive communication systems there are more messages addressed to beings for whose existence there is no scientific evidence, and there is a greater tendency to interpret natural events and mental activity in trance or dream states as messages from supernatural powers. Less effort is devoted by the senior members of the society to formal enculturation of the junior members but, conversely, the junior members may show more initiative in seeking out cultural information.

The typical primitive society is in contact with several neighboring societies and a certain amount of intermarriage and trade usually occurs. At the same time, intermittent hostilities are likely to break out between many primitive communities. Even where overt fighting is absent, a strong sense of community identity usually characterizes these communities so that communication between them often consists of an asserting of cultural difference, or even a development of difference where none previously existed. This, with the economic self-sufficiency of the communities, tends to reduce the amount of intersocietal communication among primitive communities.

REFERENCES

Barry, Herbert, III; I. L. Child; and Margaret K. Bacon.
1959 "Relation of child training to subsistence economy." American Anthropologist 61:51–63.

Barton, R. F.
1949 The Kalingas, Their Institutions and Custom Law. Chicago: University of Chicago Press.

Bateson, Gregory.
1936 Naven. Cambridge, England: The University Press.

Berndt, R. N.
1962 Excess and Restraint. Chicago: University of Chicago Press.

Bohannan, Paul J.
1963 Social Anthropology. New York: Holt, Rinehart and Winston.

Brace, C. Loring, and M. F. A. Montagu.
1965 Man's Evolution: An Introduction to Physical Anthropology. New York: Macmillan.

Deetz, James.
1965 The Dynamics of Stylistic Change in Arikara Ceramics. Urbana: University ofIllinois Press.

DuBois, Cora A.
1944 The People of Alor: A Socio-Psychological Study of an East Indian Island. Minneapolis: University of Minnesota Press.

Edmonson, Munro S.
1961 "The Neolithic diffusion rate." Current Anthropology 2:71–102.

Elbert, Samuel H.
1953 "Internal relationships of Polynesian languages and dialects." Southwestern Journal of Anthropology 9:147–173.

Fernandez, James W.
1965 "Symbolic consensus in a Fang reformative cult." American Anthropologist 67:902–929.

Frisch, J. E.
1959 "Research on primate behavior in Japan." American Anthropologist 61:584–596.

Goodall, Jane.
1963 "My life among wild chimpanzees." National Geographic 124 (August):272–308.

Haas, Mary R.
1944 "Men's and women's speech in Koasati." Language 20:142–149.

Holtved, Erik.
1951 The Polar Eskimos, Language and Folklore. Copenhagen: Reitzel.

Imanishi, Kinji.
1960 "Social organization of subhuman primates in their natural habitat." Current Anthropology 1:393–407.

Keesing, Felix M., and Marie M. Keesing.
1956 Elite Communication in Samoa: A Study in Leadership. Stanford, California: Stanford University Press.

Kroeber, Alfred Lewis.
1948 Anthropology. New York: Harcourt, Brace.

Leenhardt, Maurice (ed.).
1949 Les Carnets de Lucien Lévy-Bruhl. Paris: Presses Universitaires de France.

Lévi-Strauss, Claude.
1949 Les Structures Élémentaires de la Parenté. Paris: Presses Universitaires de France.
1958 Anthropologie Structurale. Paris: Plon.
1962 La Pensée sauvage. Paris: Plon.
1963 Totemism. Boston: Beacon Press.

Lévy-Bruhl, Lucien.
1922 La Mentalité Primitive. Paris: Librairie Félix Alcan.

Malinowski, Bronislaw.
1922 Argonants of the Southwestern Pacific. New York: Dutton.

Mead, Margaret.
1943 "Our educational emphases in primitive perspective." American Journal of Sociology 48:633–639. (Also pp. 309–320 in G. D. Spindler, ed., Education and Culture: Anthropological Approaches. New York: Holt, Rinehart and Winston, 1963.)

Métraux, Alfred.
1957 Easter Island: A Stone-Age Civilization of the Pacific. London: Andre Deutsch.

Mooney, James.
1910 "Sign Language." Pp. 567–568 in F. W. Hodge (ed.), Handbook of American Indians North of Mexico. Part 2. (Smithsonian Institution Bureau of American Ethnology Bulletin No. 30.) Washington, D.C.: U.S. Government Printing Office.

Murdock, George P.
1949 Social Structure. New York: Macmillan.

Oliver, D. L.
1955 A Solomon Island Society. Cambridge: Harvard University Press.

Raum, Otto.
1940 Chaga Childhood: A description of Indigenous Education in an East African Tribe. London: Oxford University Press.

Sahlins, M. D., and E. R. Service (eds.).
1960 Evolution and Culture. Ann Arbor: University of Michigan Press.

Sapir, Edward.
1949 Selected Writings in Language, Culture and Personality. Edited by David G. Mandelbaum. Berkeley: University of California Press.

Stokoe, William C., Jr.
1966 "Linguistic description of sign languages." Pp. 243–250 in F. P. Dinneen (ed.), Problems in Semantics, History of Linguistics, Linguistics and English. Washington, D.C.: Georgetown University Press. Originally presented at the 17th Round Table Meeting on Linguistics and Language Study (1966).

Strehlow, T. G. H.
1947 Aranda Traditions. Melbourne: Melbourne University Press.

Tax, Sol, and Lois Mednick.
1960 "'Primitive' peoples." Current Anthropology 1:441–445.

Wallace, Anthony F. C.
1956 "Revitalization movements." American Anthropologist 58:264–281.

White, Leslie A.
1959 Evolution of Culture: The Development of Civilization to the Fall of Rome. New York: McGraw-Hill.

Wilson, Monica H.
1951 Good Company: A Study of Nyakyusa Age-Villages. London: Oxford University Press.

ADDITIONAL READINGS

Bright, William O., ed. *Sociolinguistics: Proceedings of the UCLA Sociolinguistics Conference*. The Hague: Mouton, 1966.

Devereux, George. "Mohave Indian Verbal and Motor Profanity." In *Psychoanalysis and the Social Sciences*, edited by Geza Roheim, pp. 99–127. New York: International Universities Press, 1951.

Dozier, Edward P. "Cultural Matrix of Singing and Chanting in Tewa Pueblos." *International Journal of American Linguistics* 24 (1958):268–272.

Durkheim, Émile. *The Elementary Forms of the Religious Life*. New York: Macmillan, 1915.

Fischer, John L. "The Sociopsychological Analysis of Folktales." *Current Anthropology* 4 (1963):235–295.

Greenberg, Joseph H. "Language and Evolution." In *Evolution and Anthropology: A Centennial Appraisal*, edited by Betty Meggars, pp. 61–75. Washington, D.C.: Anthropological Society of Washington, 1959.

Gumperz, John J. "The Measurement of Bilingualism in Social Groups." In *The Description and Measurement of Bilingualism*, edited by L. G. Kelly, Toronto: University of Toronto Press, 1969.

Gumperz, John J., and Hymes, Dell H., eds. The Ethnography of Communication. *American Anthropologist* 66 (December 1964, pt. 2).

Haas, Mary R. "Bilingualism." In *Results of the Conference of Anthropologists and Linguists*, by Claude Lévi-Strauss, Roman Jakobson, C. F. Voegelin, and Thomas A. Sebeok, pp. 42–44. Bloomington: Indiana University Publications in Anthropology and Linguistics; Memoir No. 8, 1953.

Hall, Edward T. "Adumbration as a Feature of Intercultural Communication." *American Anthropologist* 66 (December 1964, pt. 2): 154–163.

Hammel, Eugene, ed. Formal Semantic Analysis. *American Anthropologist* 67 (October 1965, pt. 2).

Helm, June, ed. *Essays on the Verbal and Visual Arts. Proceedings of the 1966 Annual Spring Meeting, American Ethnological Society.* Seattle: University of Washington Press, 1967.

Hill, A. A. "A Note on Primitive Languages." *International Journal of American Linguistics* 18 (1952): 172–177.

Hymes, Dell H. "Lexicostatistics So Far." *Current Anthropology* 1 (1960): 3–44.

———. "Functions of Speech: An Evolutionary Approach." In *Anthropology and Education*, edited by Frederick C. Gruber, pp. 55–83. Philadelphia: University of Pennsylvania Press, 1961.

———. "The Ethnography of Speaking." In *Anthropology and Human Behavior*, edited by Thomas Gladwin and William C. Sturtevant, pp. 13–53. Washington, D.C.: Anthropological Society of Washington.

———. *Language in Culture and Society*. New York: Harper & Row.

Jacobs, Melville. *Patterns in Cultural Anthropology*. Homewood, Ill.: Dorsey Press.

Kluckhohn, Clyde. "Notes on Some Anthropological Aspects of Communication." *American Anthropologist* 63 (1961): 895–909, with comment by A. L. Kroeber, 63: 910–912.

Lee, Dorothy. *Freedom and Culture*. New York: Spectrum Books, 1959.

Lomax, Alan. "Folk Song Style." *American Anthropologist* 61 (1959): 927–954.

Malinowski, Bronislaw. "The Problem of Meaning in Primitive Languages." In *The Meaning of Meaning*, by C. K. Ogden and I. A. Richards, pp. 451–510. London: Kegan Paul, 1923. (Also in Bronislaw Malinowski, *Magic, Science and Religion and Other Essays*, pp. 451–510. Glencoe, Ill.: Free Press, 1948.)

———. *Coral Gardens and Their Magic. A Study of the Methods of Tilling the Soil and of Agricultural Rites in the Trobriand Islands.* Vol. II, *The Language of Magic and Gardening*. New York: American Book Company, 1935.

Milner, G. B. "The Samoan Vocabulary of Respect." *Journal of the Royal Anthropological Institute* 91 (1961): 296–317.

Munn, Nancy D. "Walbiri Graphic Signs: An Analysis." *American Anthropologist* 64 (1962): 972–984.

Sapir, Edward. *Language*. New York: Harcourt, Brace, 1921.

———. "Communication." In *Encyclopedia of the Social Sciences*, vol. 4, edited by E. R. A. Seligman, pp. 78–80. New York: Macmillan.

Silverman, Julian. "Shamans and Acute Schizophrenia." *American Anthropologist* 69 (1967): 21–31.

Smith, Alfred G., ed. *Communication and Culture: Readings in the Codes of Human Interaction.* New York: Holt, Rinehart and Winston, 1966.

Stern, Theodore. "Drum and Whistle Languages: An Analysis of Speech Surrogates." *American Anthropologist* 59 (1957): 487–506.

Trager, George I., and Hall, Edward T., Jr. "Culture and Communication: A Model and an Analysis." *Explorations* 3 (1954): 157–249.

Turner, Victor. *The Forest of Symbols: Aspects of Ndembu Ritual.* Leiden: Brill, 1967.

CHAPTER 13 Communication and Development

FREDERICK W. FREY
Massachusetts Institute of Technology

Most of this book deals with societies flooded by information via print, radio, and TV. It deals largely with societies that have already gone through the mass media revolution of the past two centuries. But two-thirds of the world's population are only now experiencing that revolution. They live in underdeveloped countries where illiteracy is widespread. For millions, tradition conveyed by word of mouth has been the dominant message. That, however, is changing rapidly, paced by the transistor revolution. In this chapter, the author reviews the extent of diffusion of modern communications and then examines the relation of the mass media revolution to the process of development in its various aspects. Development and mass media growth go together, but in which direction does the causal relation run? Does the growth of a mass media system generate development, and in what respects? A large literature exists on these points, but it presents sharply opposed theses which this chapter reviews.

Of all the technological changes which have been sweeping through the traditional societies of the underdeveloped world in the last decade. . . the most fundamental and pervasive in their effects on human society have been the changes in communications (Max F. Millikan, 1967).

INTRODUCTION

The importance of the topic "Communication and Development" is rather obvious. Most nations on earth bear the "underdeveloped" label. Even more significantly, the so-called developing societies contain more than two-thirds of the world's population, with four-thirds of the world's afflictions and problems—or so it seemed before pollution, drugs, and violence. Other exercises in parading numbers could be even more intimidating, but perhaps it is sufficient to point out that since World War II all but one of the major violent conflicts involving the great powers of the world have erupted in these transitional societies. And, although there has been marked progress in a few developing societies and some progress in virtually all, there seems little basis for confidence that

Most of this chapter was written while the author was a Fellow at the Center for Advanced Study in the Behavioral Sciences, Stanford, California. He wishes to express his deep gratitude to the center and its staff for their help and support.

the main problems of modernization are now on the verge of being solved, or that the gap between the "have" and "have not (never had)" nations is being clearly reduced.[1]

The drama from a communications perspective is hardly less. A well-heralded "communications revolution" has struck many portions of the globe. Modern man lives in a "high information society" that has entered the Exponential Age. Rather than informational starvation, his key problem seems to be how to organize, digest, and control the surfeit of messages surrounding him. Yet in many countries he does not have to travel far to encounter still a cultivator who is at the other end of the continuum, mired in a village that has been passed by. Between the two extremes live most of the world's inhabitants.

Focus

Communication is one of the most pervasive of social relationships; development or modernization is one of the most complex of social changes. Hence, to attempt even a moderately complete discussion of their intersection is premature and probably an act of hubris. However, it may be useful nonetheless, for it can reveal relative degrees of sophistication and ignorance in our current understanding of these matters. It may indicate types of problems whose solutions are pending and the areas most critically demanding work.

The present discussion involves some large exclusions. We shall say little or nothing about international and foreign affairs, about the Communist developing countries, about primitive or preliterate societies, or about the impact of new communications technology such as satellites on developing societies. Most of these matters, however, are covered elsewhere in this volume. We shall also neglect many linguistic aspects of communication in developing societies—topics such as diglossia, the adequacy of native languages for modern needs, bilingualism, and the like. In other words, the focus will be more sociopolitical than psycholinguistic, although an essay from the latter vantage would be extremely valuable. Nor will the myriad economic aspects of communication in developing societies be explored in any depth. The central emphasis will be on the role of communication in the developmental process.

Historical and Observational Background

It is useful to appreciate the outstanding social phenomena that have led recent analysts to think so frequently in terms of development, modernization, growth, and evolution. Beginning in the eighteenth century in northwestern Europe, a number of conspicuous, unprecedented, and seemingly highly interrelated changes have swept across the world. They commenced most notably in Great Britain, spread southward throughout much of Western Europe, gathered momentum in the nineteenth century while moving eastward to Russia and Japan and to areas on other continents settled chiefly by European migrants. There the same pattern apparently was repeated, with the lands settled by northern Europeans (the United States, Canada, Australia, etc.) changing first, and only later in the lands (mainly in Latin America) settled by migrants from other European countries, which themselves developed later.

In the twentieth century, and especially since World War II, initial signs of similar trends—and conscious plans to produce them—have spread to many parts of Asia and, to a lesser extent, Africa. By the end of the third quarter of the twentieth

[1] "Of all our assumptions concerning economic development, the most characteristically American is that economic development cannot fail.... Yet, taking into account the obstacles in their way, the likelihood is very great that for the majority of nations now attempting the long climb the outcome in our time will be defeat" (Heilbroner, 1963:27).

century—or roughly two hundred years after their visible start—the change processes to be described had clearly spread to all parts of the globe and to nearly half the world's population (Easterlin, 1968).

The economic aspects of change have been most vivid. Their central feature has been a rapid and sustained rise in real output per capita. For example, the average rate of growth in gross national product per capita each decade from 1700 to 1780 in England and Wales was approximately 2 percent. From 1780 to 1841 this growth rate jumped dramatically to more than 13 percent per decade and has never been less than that since. (It is, however, theoretically quite important to observe that within the pronounced secular trend there is significant variability in shorter run rates for particular nations and regions. Inferences based on periods as short as a decade or two may therefore be quite hazardous.)

In Italy the corresponding growth rate was approximately zero as late as the period 1841–1881; however, from that point to 1913 it leaped to 9 percent, and from then on it has averaged over 17 percent per decade. In the United States, the average rate of growth of real product per capita for the 122 years from 1839 to 1961 was over 17 percent per decade (Easterlin, 1968; Kuznets, 1968). Thus, striking and previously unknown rates of growth in the economies of many nations have now been sustained for periods as long as two centuries.

This precipitous rise in real output per capita has been but the leading characteristic in a series of economic changes; and these economic transformations are, in turn, but the most visible and measurable aspects of a series of societal alterations. In the economic realm, also notable are the marked increases in mechanization, high energy inputs, and the shift toward a mineral-based economy rather than one based on agricultural and forest products. The scale of production has been enormously enlarged, attended by mass markets, monetization of the economy, and burgeoning commercial-industrial organization. There has been an abrupt decline in the percentage of the labor force engaged in agriculture and other primary sectors, and a corresponding rise in the percentage engaged in industrial, secondary, and tertiary sectors.

The technological sophistication of productive processes has increased remarkably along with the amount of capital investment per worker. New patterns in the composition of the national product have emerged. There is appreciably less self-employment, and extraordinarily more occupational specialization and differentiation. Production, employment, and markets are more concentrated in their location, so that rising urbanization is a leading characteristic of the overall process.

As we shall see, transportation and communication facilities have also expanded greatly. Moreover, foreign trade, international contacts, and cross-cultural communications are many times their previous magnitudes per capita. Literacy is almost universal in the most advanced societies, and formal educational attainment has climbed steadily. Mass media have developed and internal communications have proliferated with awesome speed. The death rate has plunged as infant mortality and epidemic-type diseases have been impressively reduced, with the result that a momentous rise in the world's population has occurred.

Along with these more quantifiable changes there seem to have been less measurable but no less important changes in social structures and human beliefs, values and expectations (see, e.g., Smelser, 1966; Hoselitz, 1968). The role of government, particularly central government, has expanded critically. The "middle class" has moved to a position of cultural and structural preeminence in many societies. Nationalism, secularism, individualism, desires for participation, egalitarianism, cosmopolitanism, and other such orientations are perceived to have expanded mightily. One can say that most of the population in societies affected by these profound changes "has experienced in the last one hundred years a greater advance in material well-being and a more sweeping change in way of life than occurred in any previous century of human history" (Easterlin, 1968:395). Some even contend that these changes constitute the visible surfacing of a "universal pattern of modernity," the third of the "great revolutionary transformations of mankind," the first two being the emergence of human beings from primate life and the advance from primitive to civilized societies beginning about 5,000 B.C. (Black, 1966a; 1966b).

The Idea of "Development"

It has proven most tempting to regard these dramatic societal changes as a single, ordered, global syndrome. They are commonly perceived as a unified process featuring necessary clustering and sequence.

Such interpretations are obviously supported by some aspects of the historical data. If they can be substantiated, they have great significance for policy and theory. Rigorous conceptualization of the supposedly central process involved has, however, been far from easy. Several popular candidates have won adherents: *development*, *modernization*, *industrialization*, *Westernization*, *growth*, and *sociocultural evolution*. Most of these, though useful notions for different purposes, seem inappropriate for the phenomena of interest here, being either too broad (*growth*), too narrow (*industrialization*), or dubiously parochial (*Westernization*).[2]

The most popular of these conceptions which purport to represent the basic historical trends of the past two centuries have been *modernization* and *development*. Sometimes these two terms are used synonymously. On occasion (e.g., Rogers, 1969), *development* is used to refer to processes at the level of the social system while *modernization* refers to related processes at the level of the human individual. Most often, however, if the terms are distinguished at all, *development* is applied to the economy while *modernization* refers to noneconomic sectors or is used more inclusively to comprehend all analogous or concomitant processes in the society as a whole (e.g., Smelser, 1966; Lerner, 1969).

At present, the meaning of *development* and *modernization*, within this orientation, is highly ambiguous. It varies critically from one analysis to another and even within the confines of a single study. Thus research on communication and development suffers from the vagueness and conflict which surround the latter term. *Development* and *modernization* have certainly been convenient impressionistic umbrellas for loosely covering the immense changes involved in moving from a traditional to an advanced contemporary society. But effective empirical theory requires greater conceptual clarity and consensus for these core notions than has yet been manifested.

Problems of Conceptualization

The main problems confronting conceptualization of development and modernization are the following:

1. *Descriptive versus Normative Status.* One of the most important difficulties with *development* and *modernization* stems from their uncertain status as relatively objective scientific terms. They are "halo" words with strong normative overtones, much like the word *progress.* Despite sporadic efforts at restraint, they tend to entangle descriptive and evaluative elements that ought to be kept separate. One can, of course, stipulate a purely descriptive definition. But then it must be entirely legitimate to say, "Yes, I understand what you mean by development and it is *bad.* I am against development!" Riggs (1964), for example, explicitly allows for "negative development," but such a notion and such careful

[2] See Black (1966b).

descriptive usage are awkward for most people and hard to maintain. Indeed, the descriptive-evaluative ambiguity of these terms seems covertly attractive. It permits one to adopt a stance of value neutrality in scientific analyses, allowing one to define things as he will, and yet to gain support for subsequent policy recommendations by subtly switching to an implicit evaluative usage (Bay, 1965). Lewontin's (1968:206) warning is always useful: "The shibboleths of progressivism are the superiority of man in the cosmos, industrial man in the world economy, and liberal democratic man in world society."

2. *Determinism and the Duration of Change.* A related issue concerns the inevitability and perpetuity of developmental trends or sequences. For some, the process of development or modernization is at least tacitly inexorable and endless. Rather than being merely an observed, specific, historical trend of uncertain duration, it is part of the "tide of events," the "march of history," and a process which, once begun, knows no termination. As Marx proclaimed, the advanced nations of the world reveal their future to the less advanced. Even many of the subprocesses of development are commonly regarded as irreversible. Retreat from literacy to illiteracy, industrialization to agrarianism, the mass media to an oral tradition, etc., is nowhere observed and is deemed somehow contrary to the fundamental processes of history.

Such contentions or assumptions appear quite shaky, however. As Washburn and Lancaster (1968:216) have commented about biology, "There are no laws in the usual scientific sense determining the course of evolution. In biological history there are no ultimate goals, inevitable trends, or vitalistic explanations. . . . There is no biological momentum that carries past trends into the future." The presumed internal dynamic that makes modernization a self-enhancing, ever-continuing process has never been convincingly explained and, indeed, runs into profound problems.

One basic consideration is that the necessity behind any given developmental sequence must be a logicotheoretic necessity. It cannot be purely empirical. Since most putative developmental sequences are at present essentially empirical, few make any cogent claim to necessity. Moreover, the kind of necessity involved would deal with the ordering of stages, the patterning of moves, and would not stipulate the absolute necessity of any given amount of movement per se for any specific unit. Even under the most plausible developmental schemata (e.g., cognitive development), no unit has to move to a certain position. All permit fixation, even regression under trauma. At best one can support the conditional that if a unit does actually move to a certain position, then this and that stage will have to be passed and any subsequent advances will be through a known sequence. At the societal level, however, even this degree of necessity will probably be pared down to at best a stochastic tree structure, giving (within certain confidence limits) the probability of movement from a given position to various other positions, though we are far from even this capacity at present (cf., e.g., Nordlinger, 1968).

3. *The Dimensions and Directionality of Development.* One of the most conspicuous difficulties in the conceptualization of development involves characterization of the underlying continuum of change. Development, under any conception, refers to a process of change. Change in what? Moreover, neither random nor cyclical change is intended, but rather a *trend*—change that is repetitive and cumulative. Cumulative in what direction? There has been little precise consensus on these basic issues.

The units that are conceived as developing or modernizing run from social systems, societies, nations, and cultures, through the economy and the polity (to say nothing of administrative, legal, military, agricultural, and other systems) to the level of the individual personality. A truly integrated and profound picture of development would indeed have to give a coordinated portrayal of the process at each of these levels. Presently, however, most authors simply pick one of these systems and essentially ignore the others.

More confounding is the plethora of suggestions for characterizing the underlying dimension or dimensions of developmental change. As noted, most analysts have favored conceptualization of development in terms of a single fundamental continuum. Thus we find the "Great Dichotomies" (S. P. Huntington, 1971) of tradition vs. modernity, underdeveloped vs. developed, non-Western vs. Western, agrarian vs. industrial, poor vs. rich, old vs. new, folk vs. urban, community vs. association, status vs. contract, sacred vs. secular, mechanical vs. organic, subsistence vs. market, etc., each stressing a different though intuitively important dimension. The beckoning endpoint of such change is variously seen as higher per capita income, greater control over the environment, increased efficiency, approximation to contemporary Western standards, greater national prestige, heightened adaptability, increased differentiation and complexity, and a number of more specific traits. Similarly, the mechanisms of change, where specified, run a wide gamut from technology, knowledge, and complex organization, through capital formation, high energy sources, and mechanical tools, to specialization, mobility, participation, communication, and so on.

In the present state of our knowledge, it seems patently impossible to synthesize or reduce all these notions to a single generally acceptable formulation. Scholars have perceived different things, placed different emphases, and considered different aspects of these historic phenomena. Of course, it is frequently alleged that these disparate notions can be organized into a single, basic syndrome, with one or a few characteristics constituting the main lever of change and the others following systematically upon its activation. Such reductionist approaches have focused upon differentiation, capability, adaptation, institutionalization, integration, participation, interdependence, information, complexity, mobilization, and similar notions. But, up to now, it seems fair to say that either the crucial reductionist notion itself has grave conceptual problems or else the empirical assertion of its universal application has been unsubstantiated or proven false.

A less important but still significant criticism involving the directionality problem refers to the specification of the termini of the underlying continuum of change. One end of that continuum is frequently conceived rather clearly, but the other is often much weaker in conception, being virtually a residual category (see Miner, 1952; Rostow, 1967; S. P. Huntington, 1971). Examples of such unfortunate conceptual dumping may be the "traditional" pole of the traditional-modern continuum, the "civil" end of the civil-military dimension, and even the "underdeveloped" side of the underdeveloped-developed polarity. Huntington (1971) also points out the tendency toward a "zero-sum" conception of these developmental relationships. As one aspect (e.g., modernity) increases, the other (e.g., tradition) is thought ipso facto to decrease correspondingly. However, such a conception, based on simplistic polarized approaches, may grossly misconstrue the true relationships among the variables. For example, even in a modern society, major elements of tradition may be essential.

Finally, in this connection, one finds among the common criticisms of *development* and *modernization* the contention that they are overly global terms which "may thus foster a misleading sense of coherence and compatibility among other processes and obscure crucial questions from discussion" (S. P. Huntington, 1971: 304). How much clustering there is among the various indicators of social change described earlier is plainly an empirical question that should not be begged by definition. Existing data, as we shall see, suggest that societal systems may be much more loosely organized—may have much more subsystem autonomy in many respects—than many notions of development and modernization would allow.

4. *Stages of Development.* Many—perhaps most—of the writers on development have seen the process as fruitfully divided into discrete "stages" or "phases." In one sense, this is predicated on the assumption that development is not a smooth, continuous movement but instead displays important intrinsic discontinuities.

The various stage descriptions and categories that have been proposed are too diverse and numerous to enumerate here. Best known is probably Rostow's (1960) five-stage sequence for economic development: traditional society, establishment of the preconditions for take-off, take-off into self-sustained growth, the drive to maturity, and the age of high mass consumption. Stages of religious development (e.g., Bellah, 1964), legal development (e.g., Schwartz & Miller, 1964), political development (e.g., Frey, 1965; Organski, 1965; Black, 1966b), and other forms of development have frequently been suggested.

Several conspicuous problems plague such stage-analytic formulations. First, the stages themselves need to be qualitatively different and clearly formulated. They should also be logically related, so that each subsequent stage in some sense emerges from, comprehends, and transcends prior stages. If the stage notion is to have much intellectual power at all, the sequencing should be regarded as necessary, invariant, and irreversible without trauma or other special conditions. The logic of the staging derives from a conception of underlying functions or processes being performed in every stage, but in different ways, through different structures, and with different degrees of sophistication.

Each stage represents an equilibrium for the units at that level. Hence, that equilibrium must be described and, more importantly, the *mechanisms of transition* that impel or induce a unit to leave that equilibrium and move to another stage must be specified.

Most stage-analytic models of development and modernization have been so weak and flaccid in most of these fundamental respects that they explain or predict nothing at all. Stage delineation is not an end in itself. Moreover, we know that even when the appropriate intrinsic discontinuities which warrant stage analysis are present, such analysis understates cross-stage similarities (something Piaget, for example, tries to avoid with his notion of *decalages*). Thus, a fairly strong stage conception would seem necessary to justify its use; weak conceptions may be far more dangerous than helpful. In developmental studies, the stage models offered up to now seem lamentably weak, not only because of the inadequacies of the data, but also because of lack of sophistication concerning the problems and the logic of such an approach.

Orientation

Smelser (1966:111–112) has conjectured that "a developing nation, if it could be depicted graphically, would resemble a large, awkward animal lumbering forward by moving each of its parts, sometimes in partial coordination and sometimes in opposition to each other." How accurate this image is for developing societies is debatable, but it seems a fairly accurate representation of scholarly activity in search of "development." Judging from a few recent works (e.g., Frey, 1965:408; 1970a; Milne, 1969; Binder et al., 1971; S. P. Huntington, 1971), however, there may be a budding consensus on major pitfalls in the developmental analysis of societies and even on the rudiments of a preferred strategy for avoiding them.

If development is to be viewed as an extremely coherent, tightly knit pattern of changes, one should at least work up to that notion carefully and empirically. It ought not to be assumed. It seems more fruitful to specify a number of major dimensions of social change and ascertain their trends and interrelations. If these cluster in demonstrable fashion and requisite degree, and if they manifest regular and plausible sequencing, then they will support and indeed help define a concept of development or modernization. Until then, such notions can be kept on the back burners of our minds as intriguing possibilities. It is probably useful to have some such terms for popular discussion or as an umbrella for a large set of vaguely and loosely related facts and conjectures. But in more careful discourse it might be helpful to restrict ourselves to specific types of social trends, not assuming global clustering until it is plainly demonstrated.

WORLD PATTERNS OF GENERAL AND COMMUNICATIONS DEVELOPMENT

It is useful at this point to examine some relevant data on development and communications around the world, even if they are fairly gross, in order to obtain an initial glimpse of the substantive domain under investigation. Such is the purpose of this section. We shall first inspect some maps and tables that portray the distribution of several main indicators of development among nations of the world. Then we shall focus in more detail on national, regional, and global measures of communication, including data tracing the changes over the past two decades.

General Development

An intuitive feeling for certain aspects of the change processes at issue is gained from playing what might be called the "color me underdeveloped" game. There are three main elements: maps of the world, shading devices (vertical and diagonal lines of various weights), and data. Several leading indicators of development are selected. Data are assembled for these indicators from each nation of the world. On the basis of these data, the countries are divided into six classes for each indicator, the classes reflecting how much or little of each indicator the nations in the class individually possess. The higher the country's relative standing on the indicator, the lighter its shading (naturally). The lower its standing, the darker its shading. (For an explanation of this predictable choice, see Isaacs, 1958.)

The indicators chosen for this exercise date from the middle or late 1950s, but the overall patterns have not changed appreciably since then. These indicators are: gross national product per capita in U.S. dollars, gross energy consumption in megawatt-hours per capita, percentage of the active population in agricultural occupations (more is darker here), percentage of adults literate, daily newspaper circulation per 1,000 population, pieces of international mail per 1,000 population, motor vehicles per 1,000 population, and million ton-kilometers of railway freight per 100,000 population.[3] This seems a reasonable selection of developmental indicators for our purpose, with a deliberate bias toward transportation and communication after the most common economic measures are included. Many other indicators might have been selected to display the same general patterns.

Let us consider the worldwide patterning of the developmental classes for each of these indicators. The relevant maps are presented in Appendix A and should be consulted. The first (Figure A.1) displays levels of gross national product per capita among the world's nations. Even at a glance it seems clear that, at least geographically, the darker areas denoting lower levels of GNP per capita are not randomly distributed about the globe. On the contrary, they clearly tend to cluster in a band on both sides of the equator. There is also a tendency, obviously, for them to lie in the continents or subcontinents of that region, viz., Latin America, Africa, and South Asia. While not ready to support Ellsworth Huntington's (1915; 1945) theories presenting a climatic explanation for national development, one can see from the map how

---

[3] All of these data and maps for each of them can be found in the excellent collection prepared by Ginsburg (1961).

Huntington might have been led to his hypotheses.

Another of Ginsburg's maps shows worldwide energy consumption per capita (Figure A.2). Although the Soviet Union, the countries of southern Europe, and the oil- and coffee-producing nations of northern Latin America have slipped a little compared to their GNP position, the overall pattern is still strikingly the same. Leafing through the other maps reinforces this initial general impression, which is graphically depicted in Figure 1. That map displays a composite index of technological development, based on factor analysis, that includes many socioeconomic and communication variables of the type being discussed. On the whole, the nations that have the lowest levels of development—economic, educational, transportational, and communicational—tend to cluster in what Schramm (1964) has well called a "band of scarcity" that girdles the globe about the equator.

One other point should be made concerning such maps. An implication from the geographical clustering is that all the variables employed are significantly correlated at this national level of aggregation. That in turn, of course, implies that communication and transportation levels are significantly related to economic levels. More specific expression of some of these relationships is presented in Table 1. The data are from roughly the same time period, 1957–1959, and pertain to all *underdeveloped* countries in Africa, Latin America, the Middle East, and Southeast Asia with a population of at least one half million (UNESCO, 1961:17). The United Nations defines an "underdeveloped" country, for statistical purposes, as one with less than three hundred dollars per capita income.

Even within the subgroup of underdeveloped nations, the positive association among these main developmental variables stands out. In other words, these data crudely suggest that the pattern that distinguishes the developed nations from the underdeveloped also internally distinguishes the more advanced from the less advanced within the underdeveloped group. However, we must note even now that these are correlation coefficients which, of course, should be squared to get an indication of the variance "explained" by any designated variable that is presumed independent. When that is done it is evident that in most cases there is an appreciable amount of residual variance. One might also add that a correlational display of associations among highly aggregated *levels* (as opposed to *rates*) of development such as this probably puts the best face possible on the case for a coherent general developmental process.

The upshot of such a preliminary overview of data on national levels of develop-

TABLE 1

CORRELATION MATRIX OF INDICATORS REFLECTING SOCIOECONOMIC DEVELOPMENT AND COMMUNICATIONS DEVELOPMENT

	Newsprint Consumption Per Capita	Daily Newspaper Circ. Per 100 Pop.	Radio Receivers Per 100	Cinema Seats Per 100
Income per capita	0.83	0.83	0.86	0.86
Literacy[a]	0.82	0.79	0.72	0.68
Urbanization[b]	0.69	0.75	0.71	0.86
Industrialization[c]	0.68	0.51	0.78	0.86

[a] Literacy is the percentage of the adult population able to read and write.
[b] Urbanization is the percentage of the population in localities of 2,000 or more.
[c] Industrialization is the percentage of gainfully employed males outside agriculture.

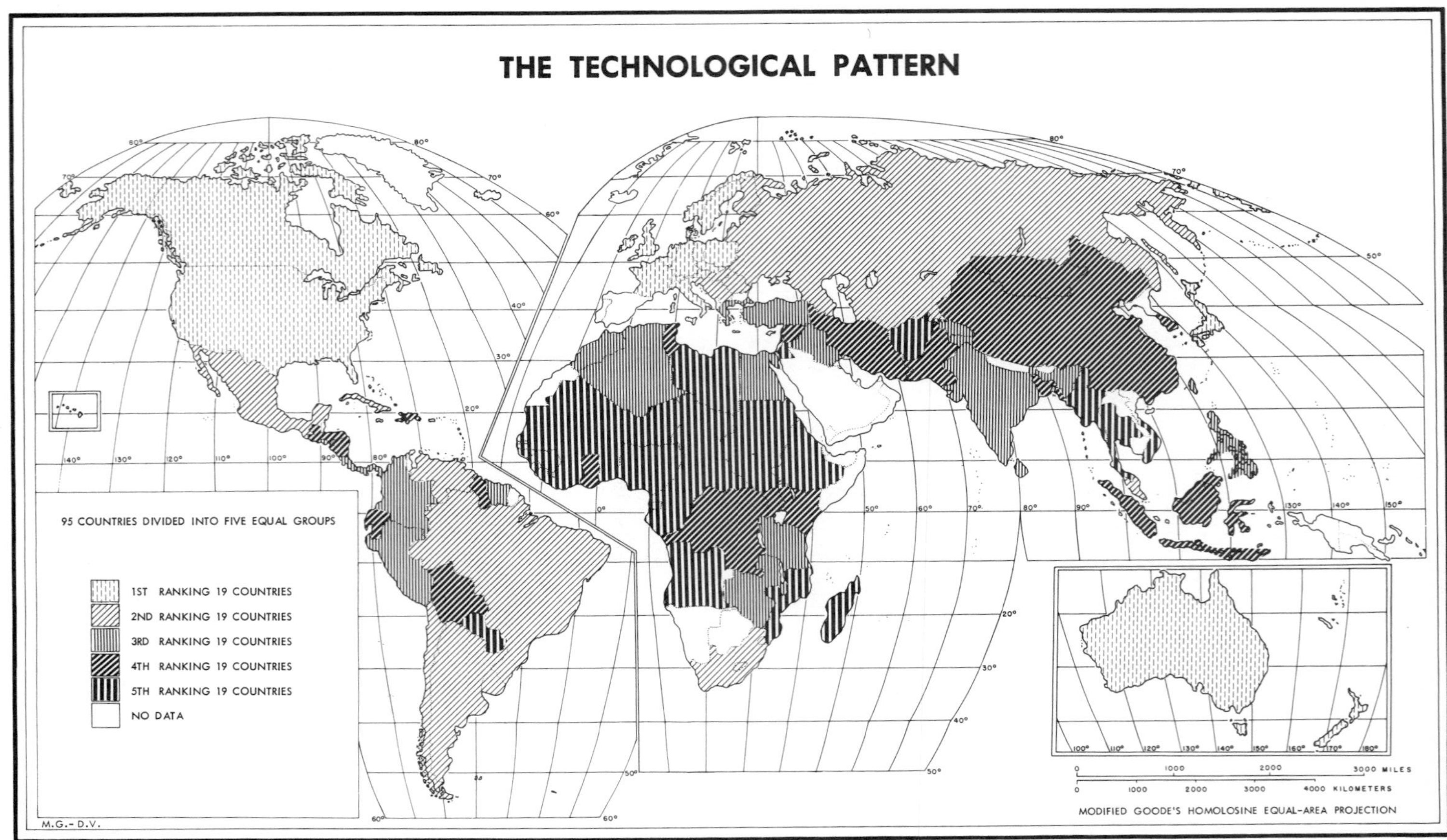

Figure 1. Worldwide levels of technological development based on a composite index (from Ginsburg, 1961:111, fig. 1).

ment is to spotlight several general features of interest. First, even a cursory inspection of such data reveals *great variation among national units* in virtually all indicators. Let us simply take one basic indicator as an illustration—total energy consumption per capita (in million metric tons of coal equivalent). And let us look at regions of the world rather than nations, which should balance out some of the most egregious disparities. Nonetheless, the relevant data for 1968 indicate great variations (Table 2).

TABLE 2

ENERGY CONSUMPTION PER CAPITA, BY REGION (1968)

Region	
World consumption	1,733
Africa	294
North America	10,155
Central America	1,033
South America	654
Asian Middle East	575
Asia (rest)	406
Oceania	3,866
Europe (except Eastern)	3,309
Centrally planned economies	1,553

SOURCE: United Nations, *Statistical Yearbook* (1969: 1140–1143).

Such statistics often understate development in subsistence economies, but on the other hand, national rather than regional comparisons could readily unearth numerous cases where the differences in level per capita between the most and least developed countries were roughly two orders of magnitude. The variations are impressive by any calculation.

The second general feature that stands out is that, at this level, there is apparently an *appreciable degree of clustering* or interrelatedness among the main variables. We shall inspect this phenomenon in much more detail in a subsequent section, but it is clear that this is what has led analysts to notions of a single developmental process.

Although judgment becomes more difficult when we examine measures of economic *growth*, certainly the general impression obtained from a similar survey is that the relative rates of growth per capita of the various regions, for example, do not portend any rapid reduction of the observed disparities. The variations in national levels would appear to be relatively *durable* in the sense that they do not show great change over a few decades, and the relative rates of growth per capita in most indicators are not conspicuously different, especially when compared with the differences in starting points and the growth rates needed to remove the major discrepancies.

To illustrate this with but one simple measure again, let us look at changes from 1950 to 1970 (the span for most of our communication data and the period for which fairly good statistics are available) in gross domestic product per capita for major world regions. These growth rates are expressed in index numbers. The first uses 1950 as the base of 100 and expresses the 1970 level in those terms, thus covering two decades; the second lets 1960 be the base and covers one decade (Table 3).

In these data we see significant world growth whose *relative* rate may have declined somewhat in the last decade compared to the preceding one. Unfortunately, data from Africa are not available, but

TABLE 3

1970 INDEX NUMBERS, GROSS DOMESTIC PRODUCT PER CAPITA

	World	Africa	North America	South America	Asia	Europe	Oceania	USSR
1950 = 100	190	...	155	145	215	220	130	320
1960 = 100	135	...	135	120	145	140	130	155

SOURCE: United Nations *Statistical Yearbook* (1969: xxiii).

other information suggests that the rates of growth there are significantly below world rates, probably somewhat higher than South America, but not much. Thus, in the underdeveloped world, the Asian nations seem to have made the most progress, but even there it has not been more than Europe or the USSR and, in the past decade, not much more than North America.[4] Both Africa and South America, on the other hand, seem generally to have been unable to make more relative progress than the developed regions and may, in fact, have been losing ground slightly.

Other, more ample, data qualify this picture but do not seem to alter the general observation that the discrepancies in economic development among nations are not being conspicuously or rapidly reduced, even though the absolute situation in the world is probably significantly improved. Hence, it remains meaningful to distinguish a group of relatively underdeveloped nations for special examination. Membership in this group has not altered very markedly in the past several decades.

Communications Development

Now let us look more specifically at the picture with regard to communications. The patterns of communication development for newspaper circulation, international mail, and literacy for the late 1950s are displayed in Figures A.4, A.5, and A.6 of Appendix A. With the exception of international mail flow per 1,000 population, these patterns conform closely to the general developmental model.

Appendix B provides data on a number of communication indicators for most of the significant nations of the world at selected intervals from about 1950 to 1970. Inspection of those data will reveal two main features: (1) the sharp rise in leading communication indicators, such as radio, television, and telephones, for most nations of the world, and (2) the continuation of glaring discrepancies among nations in the levels of communications development. A general indication of the world situation in 1969 is provided by regional comparisons shown in Table 4.

The absolute number of newspaper dailies around the world seems not to vary as strongly with economic development as the other variables. The contrast with newspaper circulation suggests that there are many rather insignificant dailies in existence, and also that a smaller share of the population of the underdeveloped regions is reached by the press. The remaining variables are adjusted for population and essentially present a picture of pronounced disparities in levels of mass communications that parallel the variations in economic and general development. The range of the variations is from about one to two orders of magnitude. Africa and South Asia have the lowest access to these mass media, followed by South America, Oceania, and the USSR, Europe, and North America. Within this pattern there are also some distinctive regional characteristics that will be discussed in more detail later.

It is interesting to compare these mass media data with minimal standards suggested by the United Nations (UNESCO, 1961:16). These urged that every country should provide at least the following media facilities per 1,000 population: 100 copies of daily newspapers, 50 radio receivers, 20 cinema seats, and 20 television receivers. The percentage of our selection of seventy-five to eighty nations for which data were available that failed to meet each of the minimal UN standards, both in 1960 and 1969, is given in Table 5.

The true percentages are probably somewhat higher than these, since the least developed nations are much more likely to have missing data. However, the trends and the gross picture seem roughly accurate. They show that significant improvement toward meeting these minimal absolute standards has been made. World coverage by radio seems appreciably better by these

[4] Also, much of this progress is attributable to a single nation—Japan.

TABLE 4

SELECTED COMMUNICATION INDICATORS FOR THE WORLD AND MAIN REGIONS, 1969

Indicators	World	Africa	North America	South America	East Asia[a]	South Asia	Europe[b]	Oceania	USSR
Number of dailies	7,680	210	1,880	1,085	360	1,600	1,800	114	630
Newspaper circulation[c]	130	11	299	65	341	16	259	296	321
Newsprint consumption (kg. per capita)	7.1	0.6	42.0	3.6	11.4	0.6	12.2	26.5	3.8
Other printing paper (kg. per capita)	8.7	0.9	47.3	2.9	12.0	0.6	19.3	12.6	4.2
Radio receivers[c]	232	45	1,339	167	192	33	280	190	375
TV receivers[c]	89	3	397	54	138	2	188	175	128
Cinema seats[c]	28	5	44	29	19	7	58	55	89

SOURCE: UNESCO, *Statistical Yearbook* (1969; 1970).

[a] Primarily Japan.

[b] Excluding USSR.

[c] Per 1,000 population.

TABLE 5

PERCENTAGE OF NATIONS BELOW UN STANDARDS

Media Facilities Per 1,000 Population	1960	1969
Newspaper circulation (< 100)	62 %	49 %
Radio receivers (< 50)	39	15
Television receivers (< 20)	60	42
Cinema seats (< 20)	n.d.	48

arbitrary norms than coverage via the other media, which hover at essentially equal levels. Yet despite clear progress, for three of the four media nearly half the nations of our selection are still below these very minimal standards even today.

Growth of Specific Media

Thus far we have been inspecting communications development at a very aggregated level. It is also important to peer more closely at national patterns for specific media, and to do this through time. The charts of Appendix B furnish the vehicle for such a perspective. They show for the selected countries the rates of growth over approximately the last two decades (1950–1970) in (1) three major mass media — daily newspaper circulation, radio receivers, and television receivers — (2) three indicators of domestic communication — mail, telephones, and telegrams — and (3) foreign mail.

Theoretic assumptions lie behind even such simple graphic presentations as these. The charts employ a logarithmic scale, which essentially signifies that we think any given absolute amount of change is more difficult at lower levels of development than at higher levels — in other words, that going from 1 to 10 radios per capita is harder than going from 91 to 100, and that the latter is harder than going from 991 to 1,000. It is, of course, possible to argue the contrary, but such is the assumption behind the graphs.

We should also warn that while each graph is based on several data points, data are not presented for every year. Hence, the lines are somewhat smoother than a more detailed plotting would yield. If the precise figure for any nation is desired (or if a nation not depicted on the graphs is of interest), the tables in the UN and UNESCO yearbooks should be consulted.

Daily Newspaper Circulation. The first graph (Figure B.1) of Appendix B deals with daily newspaper circulation per 1,000 population. Two quick impressions stand out. The first is again the range of variation among the countries of the world, from those whose newspaper circulation is but 2 or 3 copies per 1,000 to those with over 500 copies. To live in one part of the world rather than another is, in general, to have an extremely different degree of access to this medium. And, of course, if we put in an even finer lens and contrast peasant farmers in Pakistan, say, with intellectuals in New York, London, or Tokyo, one could uncover more enormous differences. But the great variation is clear enough even here.

At the same time it appears that the range of national variation for this medium may be decreasing. It seems that at the upper levels of the scale the main characteristic is relative stability over the two decades, perhaps even some tendency for decline in very advanced countries such as the United Kingdom, United States, France, etc. Sweden and Japan have replaced the United Kingdom at the top of the group, and Germany and the USSR have supplanted the United States in fourth position. Nevertheless, the overall situation among the more advanced countries suggests that newspaper circulation is a well-stabilized phenomenon.

At the other end of the metric, however, there are signs of growth, especially for the decade of the 1950s. At the very lowest levels the transition has been made from virtually no press at all to a significant degree of newspaper circulation even though the level is still well below minimal UN standards. One can also discern some rather drastic fluctuations, including clear regressions, among certain nations. These would seem to reflect such things as wars and civil unrest (Algeria, Indonesia), changing governmental policies vis-à-vis the press, foreign-exchange problems, and simply bad data.

Radio Receivers. Compared with the graph of newspaper circulation, the outstanding feature of Figure B.2, which shows the number of radio receivers, is its dynamic aspect. Stability is not the overall image here. The underdeveloped countries in particular appear to have made very notable progress, even relatively. Uganda, for example, moved in the course of two decades from less than one radio per 1,000 persons to more than sixty. Ghana moved from three to eighty. Such changes are truly impressive and imply rather momentous alterations in the life-styles of people and the functioning of institutions in the developing nation.

One of the most interesting aspects of this graph emerges when data for the United States (and, most recently, Canada) are compared with those from some of the European countries, particularly Sweden, France, and the United Kingdom. In the latter nations, the growth of radio seems to have leveled off over the past two decades—unlike television, as we shall see. One reason might be the competition from television. In the United States, on the other hand, and perhaps in Canada (recently), Germany, or the USSR, the rise of television is not associated with any leveling off of the growth in radios. One obvious suggestion is that, at least in the United States, there has been an adjustment in the way radios are used—a switch to employing radios as an auxiliary to other activities and as a portable accessory to be taken where its competitors cannot be carried. In any event, the continued climb in the number of radio receivers in the United States to a point where there are 1.5 radios for each person in the country is quite remarkable.

A final facet of interest in Figure B.2 involves the minor changes made in the ordering of the countries. Some of the developing nations, especially in Latin America, along with Communist nations, intrude into the club of affluent societies at the top of the scale, and even less advanced developing societies are to be found in the middle reaches of the ladder. Indeed, the general reduction in the range of differences is striking.

Television Receivers. If we label the picture for radio receivers "dynamic," we are left with no word for television. The graph in Figure B.3 is a dramatic representation of a major world innovation captured in its early stages of diffusion. Change is everywhere, although more in some places than in others.

Several different basic national patterns can be detected. At one end of the continuum, as usual, is the United States, exhibiting less overall change than most other nations. For this innovation as for many others, the United States was (in the terminology of diffusion) an "early adopter" or, more accurately perhaps, an "innovator" (i.e., among the first 5 percent of adopters). Along with Canada, the United Kingdom and, more recently, Sweden, Germany, and Japan, the U.S.'s distribution of television receivers has seemingly stabilized, and will remain at roughly the same level until new patterns of usage develop (e.g., more truly portable television sets, television in every room, etc.) or a new competitive medium arises.

At the other end of the scale are countries like Turkey, Pakistan, India, and Ghana where, until very recently, there was no television except possibly on the most miniscule experimental level. But, under very strong cultural pressures, even these nations are being forced to change; when they do, it is usually with great rapidity.

One of the most interesting aspects of Figure B.3 is its depiction of what happens when major "modern" nations decide to adopt an innovation. Consider Germany, Sweden, and Japan, for example. Their curves skyrocket from the bottom of the page to the top. In the course of about five years such nations can move from virtually no television to one set for every ten persons, and in another ten years can essentially provide a set for every family. Hence, in fifteen years a major communications and cultural innovation can jump from near nonexistence to near complete household coverage in these highly developed societies.

One would think that perhaps this rapid innovative capacity would be confined to the more affluent nations, and such may be the case. However, there are some instances of comparably rapid adoption in the underdeveloped world—Peru, for example, or Taiwan or Tunisia. Closer inspection, however, suggests, although very tentatively, the hypothesis that the adoption of an innovation like television may "peak out" much sooner in these underdeveloped countries. It may be that it is economically harder to sustain the change at the higher levels since the masses lack purchasing power comparable to that wielded by mass elements in developed societies. It may also be that elites control the decisional processes with regard to communication so thoroughly that mass demand for the medium is reduced (e.g., purely elite-oriented programs) or that the medium is essentially restricted to urban elite use by deliberate choice (i.e., transmitters to reach rural masses are not established). Whatever the reasons, there are signs of what one might call a "premature stabilization of distribution" in television receivers at what seem essentially elite levels in many underdeveloped societies.

Domestic Mail. We now turn from the mass media, strictly construed, to indicators of internal communication—in this first instance, to domestic mail. Figure B.4 shows the number of items of domestic mail per capita for the two decades of interest. The picture here is more like that for newspaper circulation than for radios or television, leading to a possibly important distinction concerning "old" versus "new" media of communication. In general, the impression is one of overall stability defined to include regular and gentle growth. A few countries, such as Israel, Taiwan, and Japan, have experienced a rather appreciable rise in domestic mail per capita, but the increase is slight and without abrupt movements.One unfortunate aspect of this figure is that a number of developing countries did not offer data on this indicator until about 1965.

Telephones. In contrast to the other two indicators of domestic communication, the picture with regard to change in the number of telephones per capita is one of notable growth (see Figure B.5). Again the pattern is more like that for, say, radio and other relatively "new" media than for other indicators in that growth seems to be across the board in developed and underdeveloped countries alike. The range of variation among nations consequently does not seem to be dwindling, although the "floor" effects at the bottom of the scale may mask an underlying tendency in this direction. A few of the underdeveloped nations such as Korea and Taiwan have made striking progress, moving from one to three telephones per 1,000 people to about twenty in sixteen years.

In certain respects one should probably expect different implications from given amounts of growth in domestic communications and in the mass media. With domestic communications the emphasis is on lateral or horizontal linkages among elements of the population (reciprocal relations), while the mass media involve more of a unilateral, asymetric, elite-mass relationship. A telephone is useful only if the person one wishes to call also has a telephone. A very small telephone exchange has limited utility.

This is less true for radio. Thus, one would expect that the deployment of telephones available to a nation would be much more bunched and concentrated than the deployment of radios now that transistors have eliminated the need for electric lines. Hence, a given gross measure of instruments (telephones or radios) per population unit can mean very different things in the two cases. Be that as it may, the telephone, along with radio and television, is among the fastest growing media of communication in the world.

Domestic Telegrams. In Figure B.6 we encounter the most deviant of all the graphs. Lest it be thought that almost all movement is upward, that growth is ubiquitous, we here witness a very instructive case of general decline in a medium of communication. The trend is particularly prominent among the most developed countries. Domestic use of telegrams in the United States, for example, has plummeted from one and one-half telegrams per person in 1948 to only one telegram for every three persons in 1969. It would seem that both domestic mail and, more significantly, the telephone are supplanting the telegraph, just as the airplane and automobile are supplanting another "old" indicator of development, the railroad.

Actually, this is one of the most intriguing of all the graphs because one can discern a number of possibly prototypical "stage" patterns in it. The first is the aforementioned decline of a previously advanced medium. But if we look carefully at the figure we can see other patterns as well. For instance, our lens seems to have caught some nations in midstream. Israel, Japan, and Lebanon, all very dynamic nations emerging from underdeveloped to developed status, start off with still rising curves, level off, then decline like the older, developed nations. At the same time it is possible to find several nations whose curves display a steady rise rather than decline in domestic telegrams per capita. Hungary, Bulgaria, the USSR, and probably Yugoslavia are examples. It is quite significant, we shall argue, that these are Communist or formerly Communist-bloc nations, for these may have a somewhat different communications style from other nations.

Foreign Mail. The final graph (Figure B.7) exhibits the number of items per capita of foreign mail for selected nations. This provides an initial look at international communications. Not surprisingly, perhaps, the clear trend is upward, as for domestic mail, with a general tendency to preserve the overall range of national variation or reduce it very slightly. The order of national positions along this metric is, however, somewhat anomalous. There clearly seem to be certain nations that "specialize" in international communications, such as Switzerland, Lebanon, and some of the smaller European countries. There are also others—Israel and Ireland for example—whose external ties with another country, such as the United States or Great Britain, are so significant that an inordinate volume of international communication occurs. The graph also displays more aberrations, more jumping around, than most of the others for reasons not readily understood.

Not all the communications data found in the UN and UNESCO yearbooks have been graphically displayed. For instance, the growth in consumption of printing paper other than newsprint is a revealing indicator of communications development, but since it correlated so strongly with the others it was not graphed, although the data are presented in Table C.1 of Appendix C. Tables C.2 and C.3 of the same set offer other data on external communications that are of interest. Karl Deutsch (1964: 79–80) suggests the provocative hypotheses that: (1) "advanced countries tend to send out more mail than they receive," and (2) since 1913 the world is getting "more nationally minded and less internationally preoccupied" in the sense that the ratio of domestic to foreign mail has been rising. Deutsch cites data from fifty countries for 1880–1913 and from 1913 on to establish this point.

Table C.2 ranks the nations for which data are available in terms of their 1969 ratio of foreign mail sent to foreign mail received. There is some positive correlation between these ratios and the usual measures of development, but there are numerous exceptions. On a ranking scale of from 1 to 100, Turkey, for example, ranks 5th, Nigeria 9th, Taiwan 17th, and Zambia 18th, while Sweden is 67th, Finland 83rd, and the United States 79th. Similarly, the data in Table C.3 show little increase over the past twenty years in the ratios of domestic to foreign mail. It is possible, however, that a longer time perspective is necessary for these changes to become manifest.

World and Regional Patterns

The main available data on growth in the mass media for the past two decades, in the world as a whole and in two underdeveloped regions—Africa and Latin America—are sketched in Figure 2. Scanning the world patterns first, we see that the most rapidly rising mass medium has been television, with radio close behind. In terms of absolute coverage, radio reaches more people than any other medium, with newspapers second, television third, and cinema fourth, although variations in numbers of people using each radio, newspaper, television set, and cinema seat may make such comparisons extremely gross. Over the world as a whole, however, there is about one radio for every five persons, one daily newspaper for every eight persons, one television set for every eleven persons, and one cinema seat for every thirty-six people. The world averages are well above the minimal UN standards, but the intense clustering of media in the more advanced nations makes the overall average a rather meaningless statistic for many purposes.

At the world level, two other points are significant. One is the apparent start of a decline in the cinema, if the very slight drop in seats per 1,000 is any kind of harbinger (see Table C.4 in Appendix C). Television seems mainly responsible for the drop, although this generalization does not take into account the reorientation of the film industry toward production for television. In some respects all that has happened is a change in film-viewing locale, from a theater to the home. But in other respects, such changes may be extremely important.

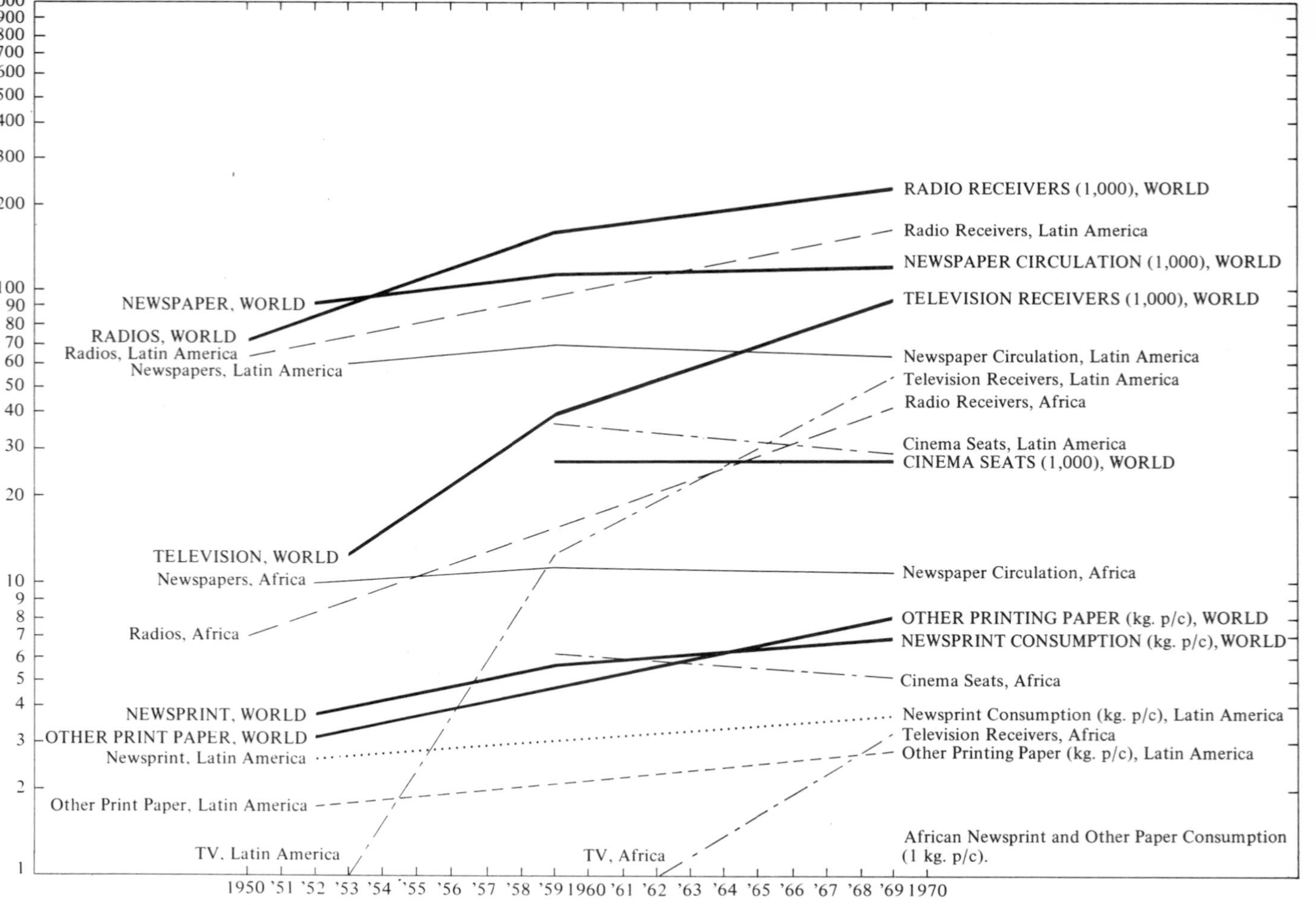

Figure 2. Trends in Mass Media Growth for the World, Africa, and Latin America, ca. 1950-1970.

The second point is that, as with some economic indicators, the rate of mass media change appears to have been greater in the 1950s than in the 1960s. Except for two items—other printing paper and cinema (where the earlier data are lacking)—the remaining curves all had steeper slopes in the earlier decade.

Examining the two underdeveloped regions we see that their curves are always below the world averages (except for the number of cinema seats in Latin America), thus portraying their underdeveloped status, and that Latin America is always ahead of Africa. In general, however, the disparity between the figures for the underdeveloped regions and the world averages has remained fairly constant. In Africa the gap for radios and possibly for television receivers has narrowed, but the gap for newspapers, newsprint and other printing paper, and cinema seats has widened slightly.

Latin America has closed the gap appreciably for television receivers, while the gap for radios widened during the fifties then narrowed somewhat during the sixties, but not enough to regain the proximity of 1950. The disparity in newspaper circulation and the consumption of newsprint and other printing paper has increased. The original Latin American superiority in the number of cinema seats compared with the world average has largely disappeared. Hence, within the general context of extension of the mass media, the relative gaps between the rest of the world and these two underdeveloped regions have not on the whole been conspicuously reduced. On the contrary, more often than not they have increased slightly.

Mass Media and Domestic Communications. The various indicators of communications development that we have employed so far can be grouped into three main sets: mass media, domestic communications, and external communications. Let us consider the first two of these a priori groupings a little more carefully. In Table C.5 of Appendix C, each of the selected nations is given a rank from 1 to 100 that reflects its relative development of a given communications medium compared with the other nations for which data were available. In other words, any entry in the columns of that table should be put over 100 to yield the relative ranking. Thus, Afghanistan occupied the equivalent of the 98th rank out of 100 in the availability of other printing paper. (Data were available for only 65 nations, and Afghanistan was 64th).[5]

In the last two columns of Table C.5 two composite ranks are given, one for the mass media and one for domestic communications excluding telegrams. The situation with regard to the volume of domestic telegrams seemed so different that it confounded the simple weighting scheme employed, which was to average the adjusted (1–100) ranks for each nation for each medium in the group and then to rank the average ranks on a 1–100 scale. In Figure 3 the rankings for each medium are displayed graphically for a selection of "modern" and of "developing" nations.

Figure 3 clearly demonstrates that the modern nations are always quite distinct from the developing nations in rank for every medium except telegrams. There are no overlaps, except for telegrams. There, however, the switching in position is quite striking.

Among the modern nations, the tendency to cluster in the very highest ranks is most pronounced for four variables: other printing paper, television receivers, domestic mail, and telephones. Among the developing nations the tendency to have relative ranks that are especially low is found for television and for telephones.

In Figure 4 the same procedure is applied to selected European Communist nations, for these are often thought to

---

[5] Ranks in different ranges were converted to ranks in range 1 to 100, using the formula $R_i = (R_i - 1)(99/N - 1) + 1$.

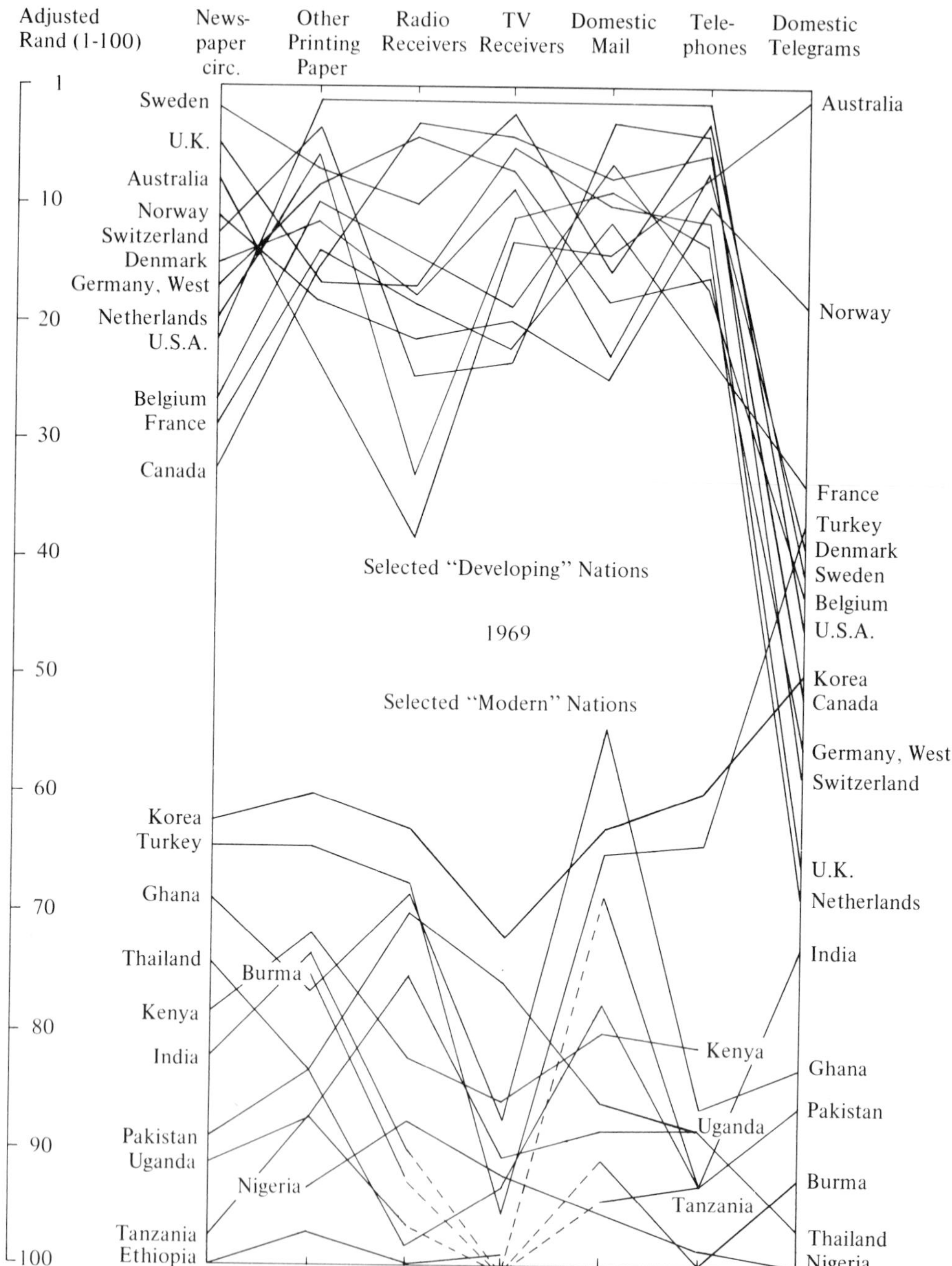

Figure 3. International rankings of selected "modern" and "developing" nations for mass media and domestic communication indicators, 1969.

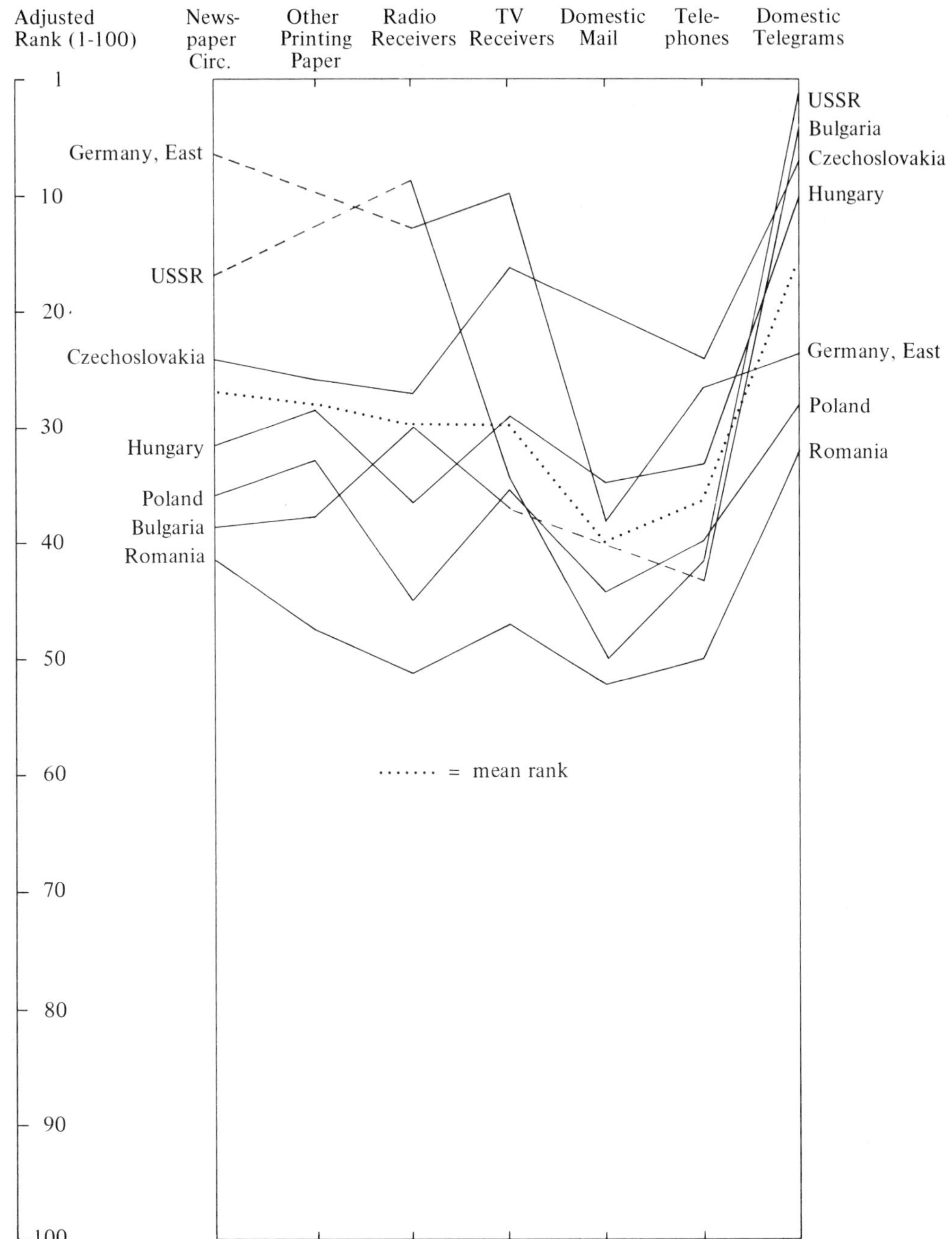

Figure 4. International rankings of selected European Communist nations for mass media and domestic communication indicators, 1969.

employ distinctive policies in the communications realm (see, e.g., Pool, 1963; Fagen, 1964a; 1964b). In general we see that the European Communist nations rank in an intermediate position for most media—below the highly developed countries of Western Europe and North America but well above the underdeveloped societies. Although the judgment is highly tentative, there is some indication that these European Communist nations exhibit relatively higher development with respect to the mass media than they exhibit for domestic communication, except domestic telegrams, where they rank extremely high and reverse the prevailing world trends. The gross outline of this pattern is sketched by the broken line of the mean rank of all seven Communist nations for each medium. That average rank is fairly constant for the four mass media at about 30th on a scale of 100. It falls to about 40th for the two main indicators of domestic communication and then shoots up sharply to 15th for domestic telegrams.

One obvious hypothesis to explain this difference, if it is a difference, is to assume that these nations wish to emphasize social control in their communications policy. Thus, they prefer asymetric and centralized media and discourage as much as possible lateral or horizontal communication among their citizens. They emphasize the mass media and deemphasize domestic communication by mail and telephone, but not by telegraph since that channel is much more easily monitored and controlled. Indeed, most of the personal messages sent over this channel in these nations seem to be limited to canned sets of communications, much like the lists of preworded greetings used by Western Union. In any event, these very crude data lend at least initial support to such an hypothesis.

In order to obtain a more sophisticated check on hypotheses that predict that certain kinds of nations would place differential stress on either the mass media or domestic communications, a special analysis of the raw data on media access was run. Because of manifest substitution effects among some of the variables (e.g., television and cinema, telephones and telegrams), a multiple regression approach was used rather than the usual unidimensional scaling tactics or factor analysis.[6] Each of our media variables was appropriately transformed and regressed against three criterion variables, also appropriately transformed. Supposed to reflect general development, these criterion variables were gross national product per capita, physicians per capita, and hospital beds per capita. Similar basic patterns were obtained for all three criterion variables, except that the Communist countries appeared to be much more developed in health terms than in general economic terms. For this reason and because it was the most common measure of development, further analysis concentrated on GNP per capita as the criterion variable.

---

[6] The factor analytic model assumes that there is an underlying trait that is reflected, although with some error, in the observable variables. The concept of an aggregate communication variable that we adopted does not resemble this model. A more useful approach, we felt, was to conceive of the accumulation of different mechanisms of communication of a particular type (mass media or domestic communications) into a variable that reflected the total communication of that type. Such a conception along "productive" lines seemed more useful than the "reflective" one implied by factor analysis. The weights appropriate for the productive conception should emerge from the relationships between the variables to be aggregated and other criterion variables rather than through the internal relations among the variables themselves. In fact, as was true for the variables where substitution effects were found, when the variables are complementary, even negative internal relations might be expected even though the reasonable aggregate would still have positive weights for each of the variables. (I am indebted to David Wiley for much assistance, advice, and even financial support for this analysis; to Perry Gluckman for statistical and computational help; and to Ann Rice for data collection and processing.)

To alleviate missing data problems, subsequent regression analysis was used to consolidate the original five mass media indicators into three—radio, cinema, and an index formed from newspaper circulation, consumption of other printing paper, and television, which prior analysis had shown to bear very similar relations to GNP per capita. Thus, from this type of multiple regression analysis weights were assigned to three resultant mass media variables (radio, cinema, and a composite print-television index) and to three domestic communications variables (domestic mail, telephones, and domestic telegrams) in terms of their regressions on GNP per capita.

Using these weights we then plotted each nation's scores for the composite indices of mass media and domestic communications development. That scatter plot is displayed in Figure 5.

In general, this analysis reveals the overall tendency toward balance in the communications development of most countries. The linearity and clustering about the diagonal shown in the chart reflect the rather clear correlation between a nation's relative development of its mass media and its domestic communications. Some interesting regional and political emphases do, nonetheless, emerge.

Six of the seven Communist nations, for example, are below the diagonal, indicating relatively greater development of mass media than of domestic communications. Except for West Germany, most of the Western European nations are approximately on or plainly above the diagonal, indicating relatively greater development of domestic communications than of mass media. Political and cultural explanations for these patterns come readily to mind. A less expected finding is the tendency for the Mediterranean countries to be above the diagonal. Eight of the ten countries in that area are relatively more advanced in domestic communications than in the mass media. Only the U.A.R., which has explicitly pursued a heavy media propaganda policy, and Lebanon deviate from this pattern.

On the whole, the sub-Saharan African nations for which data are available tend to have a relative mass media emphasis, while no clear pattern emerges for Asia or Latin America. Among Latin American countries the comparatively highly developed mass media position of Uruguay and Argentina is notable, although they fall back to a middle position in domestic communications. Also notable are the relative positions of the U.S.A. and Canada, which are so highly developed in their mass media that they occupy outlying positions, especially the United States. Finally, the developed versus developing nation distinction is clearly etched in these data. The developing nations are rather tightly bunched in the lower left sector of the chart, while the more developed nations spread upwards and to the right.

Exposure to the Mass Media

Thus far we have explored the general availability of various media of communication around the world, concentrating particularly on the contrasts and similarities between developed and underdeveloped nations. The obviously necessary next step is to move from consideration of *access* to consideration of actual *exposure*. That the radio is accessible, for example, does not mean it is used. In another section we will penetrate even further into our topic by considering the *impact* of communications as well as access and exposure to them. A topological representation of this crude model is shown in Figure 6.

We have no data to permit comparable exploration of varying amounts of exposure to domestic communications, and of course we have yet to deal with direct, face-to-face interactions. But there are scattered studies that yield some insight into exposure variations within relatively constant degrees of access to the mass media, although on deeper analysis the concept of access turns out to be rather

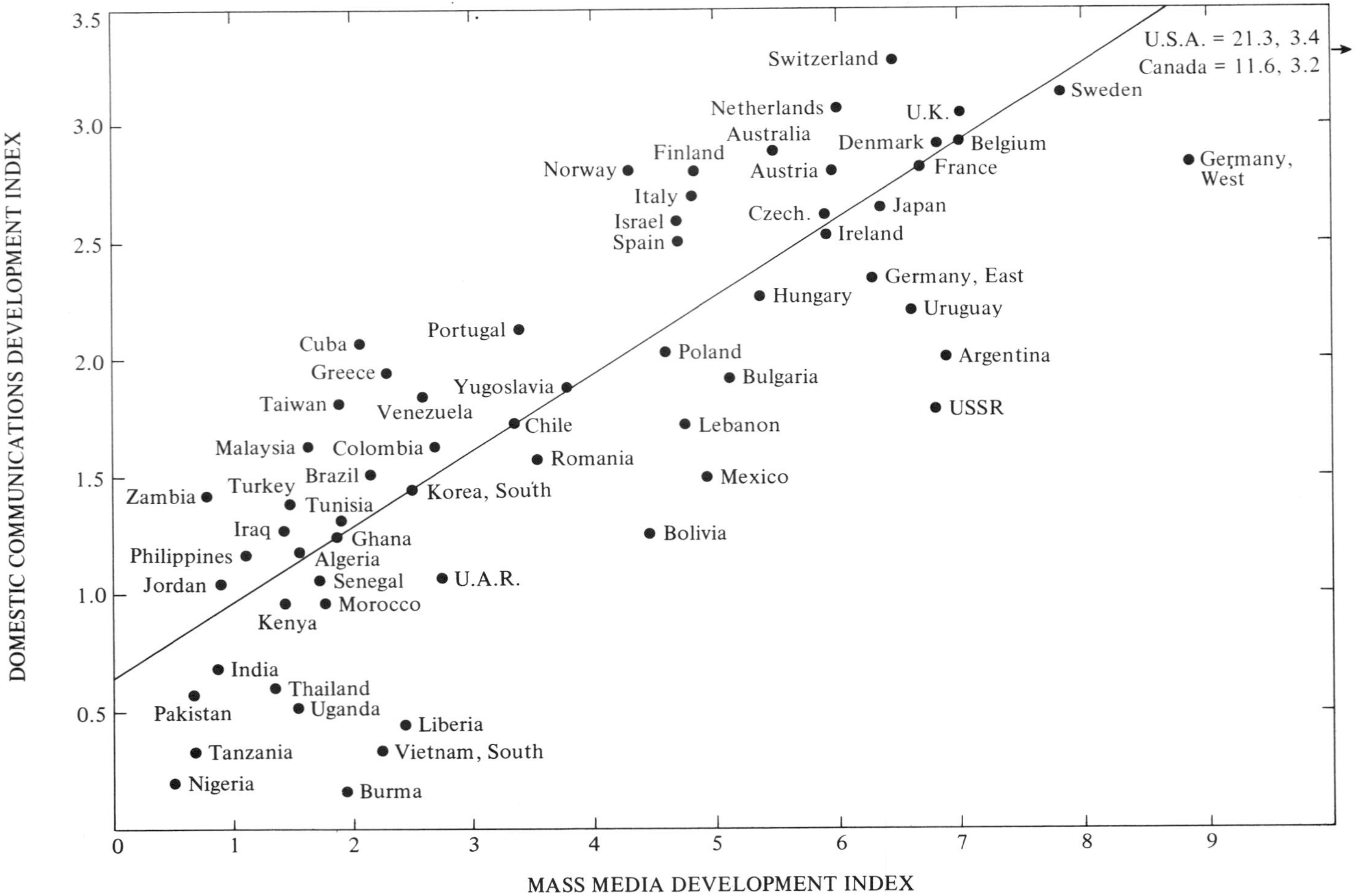

Figure 5. Comparative development of the mass media and domestic communications for selected nations, ca. 1969.

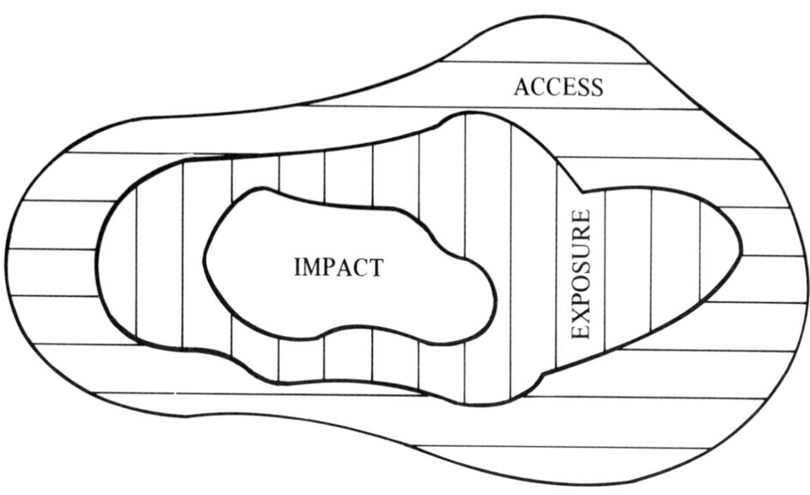

Figure 6. Topological model of communication phenomena (from Frey, 1966:101-102).

complicated. Our overall gestalt of communication differences between developed and underdeveloped countries will be improved by contemplation of this evidence.

First of all, this keener look reemphasizes that the national averages in access to communications mask pronounced *intra*-national variability. In Turkey, for instance. although there were between forty-five and fifty copies of daily newspapers and fifty-four radio receivers per 1,000 people around 1962–1963, 20 percent of the peasants lived in a village to which a newspaper "never" came, and nearly half lived in a village where a newspaper appeared less than once a week. Twelve percent lived in a village that had no radios at all, and about two-thirds lived in a village that had less than ten radios (for over 400 people, on the average).

Regional variations made these differences even more acute. For instance, in one of the more developed regions of Turkey (the Aegean region), 87 percent of the peasants lived in village that received newspapers at least weekly; in one of the less developed regions (the southeastern region) the corresponding figure was but 22 percent. In the Aegean region, 84 percent of the villagers lived in a community with five or more radios, while in the southeastern region the comparable figure was but 10 percent. Thus we see that access to the mass media may have flagrant internal variations within the developing society, not only in terms of region, but also community size, proximity to large cities, transportational isolation, etc. (Frey, 1966).

Although such internal variations are found in all societies, with rural areas generally less integrated into the mass communications structure than urban, these internal variations seem significantly more pronounced in the underdeveloped world. McNelly (1966), for example, presents data that well reveal the great range in media use typical of most underdeveloped societies, where the elite urban intellectuals may be as exposed and informed as anyone in the world while some peasant villagers have no awareness of the mass media at all (see Table 6).

It also seems that exposure is regularly less than the limits set by access (if there is any access at all), and that it is conspicuously linked with an entire set of environ-

TABLE 6

PERCENTAGE WHO USED THE MASS MEDIA "YESTERDAY" IN THE U.S. AND LATIN AMERICA

	Adults in Six Midwest U.S. Cities[a]	Argentina Urban Adults[b]	Argentina Rural Adults[b]	Brazil Urban Primary Education[b]	Brazil Urban No Education[b]	San Jose High Status Men[c]	Latin American Professionals and Technicians[d]	Costa Rica University Students[e]
Newspapers	92%	65%	40%	35%	6%	95%	95%	97%
Magazines	40	30	20	12	2	59	45	37
Books	17	19	10	8	1	56	71	39
Radio	58	59	61	56	47	45	76	74
Television	70	32	1	16	8	39	51	29
Movies	–	6	5	5	3	14	12	15
(N)	(700)	(2,000)	(300)	(1,033)	(357)	(66)	(214)	(280)

SOURCE: McNelly (1966:349, Table 1).

[a] Inland Daily Press-Midwest Universities Research Committee, *Images of Six Inland Daily Newspapers: A Summary Report of the Attitudes of Six Communities Towards Their Newspapers*. East Lansing: Michigan State University (May 1964).

[b] U.S. Information Service, *The General Pattern of Exposure to Mass Media in Seven Latin American Countries*. Washington, D.C., November 1961.

[c] John T. McNelly and Paul J. Deutschmann, "Media Use and Socioeconomic Status in a Latin American Capital," *Gazette* 9 (1963):1–15.

[d] Paul J. Deutschmann, John T. McNelly, and Huber Ellingsworth, "Mass Media Use by Sub-Elites in 11 Latin American Countries," *Journalism Quarterly* 39 (Autumn 1961):460–472.

[e] John T. McNelly and Eugenio Fonseca, "Media Use and Political Interest at the University of Costa Rica," *Journalism Quarterly* 41 (Spring 1964):225–231.

mental and personal characteristics. There are no good data on the first point, but the Turkish peasant study again offers some relevant though crude information. An impression of the situation can be gained from the fact that although only 20 percent of the Turkish villagers lived in a community to which a newspaper never came, 52 percent indicated that they never read a newspaper. Conversely, although 53 percent lived in a village to which newspapers came at least weekly, only 20 percent read a newspaper with at least that frequency. Thus there appears to be, at least in the rural areas of this developing society, considerable slippage between access and exposure, although access itself is limited enough to start. Moreover, the attrition between access and exposure is largely regular and predictable, clearly affecting some types of persons more than others.[7]

In rural Turkey, mass media exposure is relatively greatly enhanced for males and for literates, no matter what other conditions are controlled. Men and women, and literates and illiterates, even though they may reside in the same village and possibly in the same family, live to a considerable extent in different communication worlds.

In Turkey literacy was found to be slightly more important for mass media exposure than was sex, although both were independently powerful. Actually this was true for newspaper and radio exposure but not for cinema exposure, for which religious and moral factors constrain female participation, and for which travel outside the village is necessary and much less available to women.

The following statistics may convey some rough idea of the magnitude of these differences: among Turkish peasants, 70 percent of the men had attended a cinema as opposed to 19 percent of the women. Fifty percent of the male literates read a newspaper at least weekly in contrast to 15 percent of the male illiterates.[8] And 53 percent of the female literates (a very small and somewhat exotic category, indeed) listened to the radio at least weekly as opposed to 27 percent of the female illiterates. These differences narrow when obvious controls for access are introduced, but they remain substantial at all times.

Sex and literacy, then, are the prime personal determinants among Turkish peasants of variations in mass media exposure beyond those determined by access. Other factors are also significant to a lesser degree. Even after controlling for sex and literacy, it was found that education (years of schooling) and economic status are both positively and independently related to media exposure. Age is similarly associated, although in some cases the curve bends down again after old age is reached. Young people (sixteen to nineteen years of age) among these peasants use the media differently from their elders, being less likely to read newspapers even though more literate, and being less interested in

[7] It would be useful to have access-exposure ratios calculated for many nations and groups, although such calculations are not possible with most available data sets. An interesting effort in this direction is the Exposure/Facilities Ratio calculated by Hiniker (1968: Table 1). He used survey data to estimate the percentage and absolute number of persons exposed to the newspaper and the radio. The absolute number of such exposed persons was then divided by the total number of newspapers or radios available during the time period. The resulting ratios for four nations were, for newspapers: U.S., 1.6/1; USSR, 1.8/1; Turkey, 3.9/1; and Communist China, 7.8/1; for radios: U.S., 1/2; USSR, 2/1; Turkey, 6.5/1; and Communist China, 30.2/1. In short, each item of mass media production seems to get much greater use in the less developed societies, thus acting to reduce somewhat the influence of the enormous differences in media availability that have been previously described. See also Mosel (1963:206–207) for a report of the same phenomenon in Thailand.

[8] The 15 percent of illiterates exposed to the newspaper at least once a week may seem strange but in Turkey as in many other developing societies there is an appreciable amount of informal public reading of the newspaper in the coffeehouse, teahouse, or someone's home by a literate villager to the illiterates.

news on radio. This is probably a reflection of their social role in the community: not yet possessing much adult status or power, they find such information less valuable. On the other hand, villagers with elite roles, such as the headman, are disproportionately likely to use the media, especially for news. Interestingly, these data suggest that literacy accelerates the process of transition from child to adult status (Frey, 1966; 1968).

If one can extrapolate cross-sectional differences as a tentative clue to trends, it appears that one of the probable consequences of modernization and urbanization is a marked reduction in these sex and literacy distinctions. In Turkey, for example, such distinctions are progressively less as one moves from village to town to city to metropolis (Stycos, 1965).

There are few studies presenting detailed data on the communications behavior of peasants in underdeveloped societies. Rogers (1969:97), for example, says that his search of the literature revealed only four, and only six investigations of the media exposure of urbanites in underdeveloped nations. A few more may exist. However, the important point is that, although few, these studies show strong agreement in findings. The general picture is remarkably uniform across a number of nations. The factors associated with different degrees of mass media exposure in rural Turkey prevail among most peasant populations with only minor differences (Lerner, 1958; Fink, 1959; Deutschmann & Fals Borda, 1962; Deutschmann, 1963; Mosel, 1963; Marco Surveys, 1965; Stycos, 1965; Frey, 1966; Rogers, 1968; 1969; Keith, Yadav, & Ascroft, 1968).

In fact, one of the most salient findings is that mass media exposure tends to assume the form of a unidimensional scale (Rogers 1969:103). As a rule radio reaches the largest audience and television the smallest, although the order of particular media may vary slightly across cultures. But the main observation concerns what has been called the "centripetal effect"; that is, exposure to any one mass medium implies a higher probability of exposure to any other. The peasants who are reached by radio are more likely to be exposed also to the newspaper, the cinema, and so on. In one respect, this may be quite welcome, for it opens the possibility of message reinforcement over different channels. However, the centripetal effect also implies that people *not* reached by one medium are *not* likely to be reached by another. Thus, the rural areas of most developing societies may contain significant "pockets of unreachables," and the cultural bifurcation of the society may be exacerbated as the rest of the nation increases its communication contacts and bypasses these isolates (Frey, 1966:182; Rogers, 1969:103).

In assessing mass media exposure in developed and underdeveloped societies it would be extremely useful to have data on the relative amounts of time allocated to the media in addition to the usual information about whether there is exposure at all. Unfortunately, such data are not presently available, although with further development of international research on time budgets this information may become available fairly soon for urban sectors. In rural sectors the researcher confronts the severe problem of the peasant's poor time perceptions and accounting notions.

Data from more modern societies can be used to flesh out the bony statistical data presented earlier. Robinson and Converse (1972:37), for instance, assessed the growth of television in these terms:

> If one were asked to imagine the way in which daily life in the United States has changed most dramatically since the 1930's, the introduction of television after the Second World War would seem an obvious choice. And indeed, our 1965–66 data show that, by that period, television viewing was occupying a figure approaching two hours a day, averaged over seven days a week, for the urban national sample. This figure is the more impressive when it is recognized as something on the order of one-third to one-half of all leisure or discretionary time available to the adult population.

This describes the change wrought by the introduction of television into an already nearly media-saturated society. One can imagine the impact of the initial introduction of such media into underdeveloped societies, especially their rural sectors, where there is extremely little or no prior media development.

Nor do these conditions seem to be peculiar to the United States. Robinson and Converse cite data from the Multinational Time-Budget Research Project in nine European countries, including five Communist-bloc nations, Yugoslavia, France, Belgium, and West Germany. In each country more than one hour per day, seven days per week, was spent on the mass media (radio, television, and reading), with television usually obtaining the lion's share of time (Robinson & Converse, 1972:30–31, table 1).[9]

Mass Media Ownership and Content

Our overview of communications in underdeveloped as contrasted to developed societies cannot conclude without some mention of two important features—the ownership and content of the media. Schramm (1964:256) has summarized the general situation regarding mass media ownership:

> ... the most typical pattern of media ownership in developing countries is a mixed one. Most often the radio is owned by the government and the press by private industry, whereas some of the films are made by government and others made or imported privately. Most of the related services and powers—education, adult education and other development information programs, telecommunications, import restrictions and tariffs on newsprint and other mass media equipment and supplies—are in government hands.

Around 1960, the main types of domestic radio broadcasting systems in 174 countries were categorized as follows: government control or public corporation, 122; private enterprise, 25; both government and private enterprise, 27. The comparable figures for the 70 nations with television were: government control or public corporation, 35; private enterprise, 26; both government and private enterprise, 9 (UNESCO, 1963:6, 20). Thus television seems to be somewhat more in the hands of private enterprise than radio. Even some of these distinctions need further interpretation, however. For example, although much of the press is not government controlled and so is classed as private enterprise, in many underdeveloped countries a number of the leading newspapers are arms of political parties.

There seems to be no major difference between the developed and underdeveloped worlds in terms of mass media ownership. There are, however, distinct regional and cultural differences that cut across the developed-underdeveloped cleavage. The nations of the Western Hemisphere, in both North and South America, are significantly less likely to have radio broadcasting mainly in the hands of the government. Only one-third of the North American countries do so and one-seventh of the South American. In every other region of the world at least three-fourths of the countries place radio broadcasting primarily in government hands (i.e., not classed as either mainly private or mixed). The same pattern generally holds for television broadcasting, save that the governmental predominance is relatively reduced in all regions except Europe, where twenty-one of twenty-five countries (including the

[9] These data also are a caveat against easy inferences from availability to exposure. The growth of television cut most sharply into the amount of time spent on radio, but this has not been as strongly reflected in data on the number of radio sets available. It seems that in many countries people are buying more radios but listening to them less, although there is always the possibility that radio listening itself has become such an auxiliary activity that it is strongly underestimated in the reporting. Unlike television (for all but teen-agers), radio listening is something one does as an adjunct to a more primary activity—"a medium to do other things by."

USSR) put television directly under state control.

Detailed and comparative information regarding content is even harder to assemble. Some data classifying radio broadcasts into three categories—news, music, and other types of programs—and then giving the percentage of total broadcast time devoted to each are available for a "typical week" around 1960. Grouped by continents, the average percentages are shown in Table 7.

These are extremely gross data, so one is reluctant to attend to any but very strong patterns. In general, the overall radio programming at this level does not seem to vary greatly by continents. And since some of the continents (Africa, Asia, and South America) are nearly coterminous with the underdeveloped areas, it seems that the developed and underdeveloped countries are not sharply different in their general radio content. Latin America (only four countries) and Asia seem slightly low on news, but Africa is relatively high in that respect. Otherwise, there are no striking differences at this very gross level, but better comparative content analyses of the mass media are sorely needed.

More impressionistically, it is usually thought that the mass media in developing nations are urban, elite-oriented, and nationalistic in focus (for the press, see Sommerlad, 1966). Otherwise, there is great variety that confounds easy generalization. Not surprisingly, the mass media of underdeveloped societies seem to concentrate just as heavily on the great powers as do the mass media of developed nations (Schramm, 1964:60). This is not simply because the five major world news services are in the hands of four major nations—the U.S.A. (2), Britain, France, and the USSR. It would be expected on the basis of importance and the power realities around the world.

Nonetheless, the news coverage between the developed and underdeveloped worlds is disturbingly thin on both sides. Once beyond the primary reporting of signal events, the secondary and tertiary coverage, factual and interpretive, falls off grievously (Frey, 1962; Schramm, 1964:64–65). Many chronic misunderstandings are partly attributable to these deficiencies, it would seem. McNelly (1966) suggests that there is a strong prodevelopmental thrust to the media in Latin America, and Markham (1961) shows that Latin American newspapers carry a higher proportion of foreign

TABLE 7

RADIO PROGRAMMING FOR "TYPICAL WEEK"

Continent	No. of Countries	Percentage of Total Broadcast Time		
		News	Music	Other
Africa	23	21.5 %	43.5 %	30.8 %
North America	10	16.8	50.0	31.3[a]
South America	4	11.3	48.0	40.8
Asia	16	11.5	50.7	37.6
Europe	23	14.5	54.6	32.3
Oceania	8	15.4	46.6	37.4

SOURCE: Data from UNESCO (1963:69–71).
NOTE: Percentages may not add up to 100 because of averaging. These are author's calculations from the indicated source.
[a] Excluding U.S.A.

news than do U.S. newspapers. To make more than these few very general observations, however, would require a research base that is almost entirely lacking at present.

COMMUNICATION AND THEORIES OF DEVELOPMENT

We have surveyed the historical and contemporaneous conditions that provoke developmental thinking about societal change, and sketched the current world situation and recent trends regarding the major media for which data are available. In this section we shall examine efforts to put all these pieces together into theories of the developmental process, concerning ourselves particularly with their communications aspects.

There are many different theories purporting to explain societal development. They variously invoke as *primum mobile*: race, climate, religion, national character, capital formation, environmental challenge, elites, child-rearing, status deprivation, and so on. Naturally, we cannot treat all theories of development that have been proffered in one form or another, so we shall concentrate on representatives or distillations of leading types in four main areas: economic, psychological, political, and communications.

In the first three areas we shall devote particular attention to the role envisioned for communication. Under the general rubric of communication theories of development we shall discuss two main approaches. The first is the "diffusionist" approach, ranging from the anthropological diffusionists to Hagerstrand and the contemporary rural sociologists. The second is difficult to label, but it involves essentially a more social psychological than social structural approach to the role of communication in development. It focuses on the significance of communication for modernization at the individual level. There is nothing incompatible about the last two approaches; on the contrary, they are supplementary and should be conjoined.

Economic Theories of Development

With few exceptions, most theories of economic development have been generated in the tradition of economic growth theory, i.e., the economic change process in advanced societies (Hirschman, 1958: 29–47; Ranis, 1968:415). The starting point for these theories of economic development is the distinction of basic factors of production—the familiar triad of land, labor, and capital. The classicists, however, regarded land as fixed and labor (population) as a function of real wages with little independent variation. Hence the dominant dynamic factor in the scheme was capital, and capital formation was the key to economic growth. Marx, too, envisioned the same three factors of production but paid much more attention to technology.

Schumpeter altered the notion of technological development to include more qualitative consideration of markets and supply sources and the climate for economic change, but he is even better known for his stress on the importance of the entrepreneur. Economic growth was seen as dependent upon the appearance of such gifted entrepreneurs and assumed a sporadic, discontinuous character.

In the post-Keynesian era, economists backed off from some of the impressionistic formulations of previous thinkers and concentrated on more rigorous analysis of a limited set of relationships. The influential Harrod-Domar model of economic growth, for example, considers the total output of the economy as a function of the available capital stock, the capital-output ratio (assumed constant), and the propensity to save (Harrod, 1939; Domar, 1957).

Since the late 1940s, much of the analysis of economic growth has consisted of complicating additions to the basic Harrod-Domar model to make it more realistic.

Thus, a labor factor has been added and changes in the quality of the labor force have been considered; the capital-output ratio has been made variable; the distribution of income in the society enters some models along with the wage rate, profit rate, etc.; and, finally, technological change has been reintroduced as a basic factor. Suggestions of the importance of "human capital" and organizational arrangements are increasingly noted. Econometric analyses that indicated that only about 15 to 20 percent of the growth in per capita output in the United States in recent years could be attributed to increases in the stock of capital and that about 80 to 85 percent had to be attributed to the residual "technological change" gave a strong impetus to attempts to peer beneath that "semantic umbrella" (Solow, 1957; see also Hagen, 1962a:49; Spengler, 1963:207; Ranis, 1968:413).[10]

Economic theories more specifically related to underdeveloped societies stemmed from the tradition just described. Since models of rapid growth existed in the industrial world and were not quickly copied, it was assumed that the problem consisted of "barriers," "obstacles," or "missing components" that prevented such rational response. The main barrier contemplated in leading theories was, not surprisingly, lack of capital.

Much thinking on these matters has implicitly employed a "trap" model, which perceives the problem as one of breaking out of the circular, self-reinforcing bind of underdevelopment. The usual remedy prescribed has been an external infusion of capital or technical assistance or both to provide the initial pump-priming resource surplus and technological know-how for escape. The underdeveloped economy is also generally conceived as displaying extreme "dualism," i.e., two highly differentiated economic sectors, one relatively advanced and the other resolutely traditional. The problem is to mobilize the labor surplus found in the rural, traditional sector and transfer it to the progressive sector. In fact, the entire process of development can be conceived as that of transforming the two sectors of the typical underdeveloped economy into one sector that employs the usual economic market calculus.

The Role of Communications

Economic thinking has displayed very little direct concern with or interest in communication. True, at the start of their discussions many economists insert a paragraph or two giving lip service to the importance of values, the human factor, environing social institutions, and so on, "but virtually without exception, the economists who make such acknowledgements in passing then proceed to present economic theories of growth as though they were the full and sufficient explanations"(Hagen, 1962a:37, n. 2).[11] Although there are outstanding individual exceptions to this generalization, it most definitely applies to communications, which is often seemingly regarded as but an adjunct to transportation—the rear half of that horse, in fact. When a broader perspective on development is adopted by economists, their focus is commonly on values, political structure, and demography and is very rarely explicitly devoted to communications.

Close scrutiny, nevertheless, reveals that there are many facets of economic theories of development in which communication plays a crucial, if latent, role. For example,

[10] Also quite interesting in this connection is Kuznets' (1968:36) finding that "in all countries for which we have long records, capital formation proportions either do not rise at all or cease to rise after a while, although the upward trend in per capita income continues."

[11] See also Hirschman (1958: chap. 1) and Kuznets (1968:120–122). De Schweinitz (1965:3) even goes so far as to say that "economics is concerned with market phenomena in nationally integrated economies. Where these do not exist, its analytical techniques are nonoperative."

the price system can be viewed as a highly specialized and vitally important communications system which ideally provides economic decision-makers at all levels with information essential to rational calculation and planning. As Spengler (1963:211) observes (almost in the vernacular of communications research), the price system "also functions as a servo-mechanism in that it enables decision-makers to modify their courses of action whenever prices relevant for them undergo sufficient change."

One of the paramount problems for developing societies is that such a communication system is lacking or at least inadequate, not merely in the gathering and dissemination of information but also perhaps in the encoding, decoding, and interpreting abilities of significant actors.[12] Part of the process of economic development is the creation and improvement of this fundamental communications system. It would be most interesting to analyze the price systems of various economies from the perspective of theories of communication, much as Shils (1956) did for the governmental security classification system, as well as to apply certain aspects of economic and price theory to communications systems. Useful insights for both domains might well emerge. For example, an insufficiently studied aspect of communications is the cost to various actors of certain types of communication, including the costs in and of time (cf. Becker, 1965). Such an analysis might do much to explain the behavior of peasants and merchants which often seems arbitrary, perverse, or simply ignorant.

The importance of entrepreneurship for development has been vigorously flagged in economic theories as has, even more generally, the important role of developmentally minded elites. Unfortunately, economic theories are far from strong in suggesting what accounts for the postulated surge of entrepreneurial talent. Nor are they very strong in describing the crucial mechanics that link the initially small, developmentally minded elite to the rest of society and determine its gradual expansion into a dominant group, as must happen with development. Communication would certainly play a major part in theories adequate to the explanation of either of these phenomena.

Most stage-analytic theories of economic development such as those of Rostow (1960), Adelman and Morris (1967), or even Sombart or List, postulate an early stage of traditional, agricultural, or tribal organization with a preponderant non-market sector whose penetration by market-oriented forces is essential to the developmental process. The breakdown of the established preindustrial order is a key transition. Sociocultural factors, especially communication, would seem absolutely critical to this procees. Profound analysis of this transition, however, requires a greater ability than has yet been demonstrated in the field of communications research itself to conceive of and obtain reliable data on pre–mass media communications.

Many economic theories of development list institutional requisites for growth such as an effective legal system, postal system, adminstrative system, etc. In the Rostowian analysis, for instance, the third condition for "take off" is the controversial stipulation of "the existence or quick emergence of a political, social and institutional framework which exploits the impulses to expansion in the modern sector and the potential external economy effects of the take-off and gives to growth an on-going character" (Rostow, 1960: 38). Obviously, there are strong communication aspects to all these institutions; some of them are even direct and formal institutions of communication. But their treatment is one of the least successful aspects of the analysis.

[12] There has been a good deal of debate in economics and anthropology about the second part of this proposition, much of it revolving about how price responsive peasants and other actors are (see, e.g., Balogh, 1961; Schultz, 1964; Dean, 1966; Geertz, 1968:108–116; Cancian, 1972:121–124).

Kuznets' (1960:28) complaint that he did not know from the discussion "what 'a political, social and institutional framework which exploits the impulses to expansion in the modern sector, etc.' is; or how to identify such a framework except by hindsight and conjecture . . ." must be regarded as a reasonable reaction. And Rostow is more politically sensitive and familiar with the significance of communications than are many theorists of economic growth.

Economic theories of development usually emphasize the importance of organization and economies of scale. Organization itself has a communication aspect at its very core, as Barnard (1938), Simon (1957), Guetzkow (1965), and many others have insisted. Similarly, economic theories sometimes strongly stress the education of the labor force and the investment in "human capital" (see, e.g., Schultz, 1961; 1964; Harbison & Myers, 1964). Much valuable work has been done on the costs of this effort and some on the evaluation of its benefits, but the investigation of the communication aspects of the process is generally relegated to other disciplines.

Finally, the role of scientific knowledge and technology has been recognized in economic theorizing about growth and development. On the whole, however, the factors behind the marked expansion in the stock of human knowledge and the mechanisms by which it gets disseminated to important economic actors have been regarded as extraneous or given, and beyond the appropriate ken of rigorous economic theory except for some work at the level of the firm. Hence, despite obviously enticing observations by other scholars, such as Price's (1961:95) suggestion that it was the seventeenth-century establishment and subsequent exponential growth of the scientific journal and the learned paper that constituted "the vital process that made science assume a strongly cumulative character," economists have not been induced to deep consideration of the role of communication in economic development.

Psychological Theories of Development

In the psychological realm, although many writers assert that modernization or development basically involves change in people, the attempts at general theorizing are very few. Thus, we shall concentrate on the two most influential and comprehensive attempts to construct a psychologically oriented theory of development—Hagen's *On the Theory of Social Change* (1962b) and McClelland's *The Achieving Society* (1961). At the same time, of course, one should note the existence of several extremely valuable but more narrowly focused psychological studies of modernization such as Mannoni's *Prospero and Caliban* (1956), Le Vine's *Dreams and Deeds* (1966), or Fromm and Maccoby's *Social Character in a Mexican Village* (1970).

Both Hagen and McClelland commence by pointing out telling inadequacies in the existing theories of development. There are too many obvious exceptions to the climatic theories: Toynbee's "challenge" hypothesis is conceptually circular or else unoperational; Weber's Protestantism theory is empirically inadequate (development has been led by numerous other groups), too particularistic, and too superficial, although perhaps on the right track; the "diffusionists" explain the spread of development once it starts but not how it starts in the first place. The economic explanations that stress overcoming barriers of inadequate capital, scale, technological skill, entrepreneurship, etc., are also faulty. They are either (1) misinterpretations (in the sense that deeper inspection shows the factors that are supposedly missing not to be absent after all under suitable conditions, or else it shows them to be nonessential) or (2) superficial (in the sense that the basic and largely unaddressed problem is *why* the inadequacy and how to remedy it, not its mere existence). Hagen's critique of the prevailing economic explanations of development and McClelland's of the historical and sociological explanations are penetrating and on the whole quite effective. The need for more satisfying explanations is established.

Hagen's constructive argument begins with a characterization of the traditional social system—the predevelopmental base point. Its quintessential features are its unchanging, undeveloping character, its hierarchical social structure, its custom-bound culture, its ascriptive status system with a severe elite-mass gap, its oligarchic yet low-capability power structure, and its unproductive economy. Some fluctuations appear in these systems, but underneath these limited, superficial, and at best cyclical movements the fundamental patterns persist. Particular innovations occur; *sustained* change does not.

One of Hagen's major assertions is that social structure is basically a function of personality. He implies that certain modal types of personalities are essential to and result in certain key types of social systems. Thus, traditional society is based upon the traditional personality, and innovative society is based upon the innovative or creative personality. To move from one type of social system to the other initially requires an extensive alteration in personality types.

The typical personality in traditional society is authoritarian, displaying rigidity and resistance to innovation, low achievement motivation, scant inclination to perceive the world as orderly and manipulable, self-centeredness, and fundamentally low self-esteem. Two other attitudinal characteristics of traditional societies are of particular importance. One is a pervasive sense of powerlessness vis-à-vis the main forces that are seen to shape one's life. The second is the intense need of the elite to feel different from nonelite elements, which generally manifests itself in an aversion to manual labor.

For development to occur, something must happen on a fairly extensive scale to change these personalities, and this must presumably be done through a fundamental change in the home environment. How can this happen? Hagen sees the answer in a chain of events occurring over several generations that is produced by the "withdrawal of status respect" from a previously valued group. In other words, the triggering phenomenon is a change in the society such that a significant group, usually with or near elite status and fully accepting the traditional outlook, slips unmistakably in the prestige accorded it by other groups, especially elite groups. Hagen does not consider at length *why* this should occur but does suggest two main historical reasons: (1) the displacement of indigenous elites by European elites who show contempt for all or some of the indigenous groups, and (2) the "corrosion" by "the events of history" of the attitudes held by indigenous elites toward some group. Contact with the West has been by far the most common cause of this status decline in either of its forms.

Whatever its origins, the withdrawal of status respect from a group causes severe conflict and tension for its members. The group values the other groups in society and the traditional ways that are all it knows, but at the same time it also must regard itself as worthy. The dissonance and anxiety thus produced are enormous.

Hagen then traces the consequences of this conflict in such groups through several generations. The course is from anxiety, frustration, and increased rage, through retreatism, the erosion of values, and the repression of needs, to a variety of more stable reactions, including reformism of two kinds, ritualism and innovativeness or creativity. Thus, a significant percentage —although far from all or even most—of the group that experiences a withdrawal of status respect should manifest, several generations later, the innovative personality that is essential for social change.

This innovativeness still may or may not be channeled into economic growth and societal development. The last determinants that direct such potential into one outlet or another are the structure of valued and effective activities in the society, the scale of markets and the size of the savings flow, the state of knowledge at the time, and the shape of social blockages to mobility. The innovative members of the fallen group will, in short, gravitate to the route where "the opportunity seems best to exercise one's talents, prove one's worth to oneself, and gain social recognition" (Hagen, 1962b:241). Obversely, the flow will be away from blocked channels. In many traditional societies the blocked channels historically have been landholding, religion, top political and military positions, etc.; the most open avenue promising power and recognition has been in business and the economy.

Once the fallen group contains a critical number of innovative personalities and finds an outlet in economic activities, there is still the problem of whether and how this enclave comes to influence the society as a whole and reorient it toward modernization. Hagen does not develop this aspect of the process as fully as other aspects largely because he feels that many of the ideas suggested in prevailing theories of development, which are really theories of diffusion, now become relevant. He is at pains, however, to warn that the fallen group cannot be an alien group if modernization is to result. Alien groups are too insecure to invest in the less liquid assets crucial to development and, more importantly, they occupy too peripheral a power and communication position in the traditional structure and are too suspect to be able to take the lead in modernization and have others imitate them.

Hagen also comments on Lerner's model of development, which envisions a sequence of urbanization, literacy, mass media, and increased participation. The gist of his response is that Lerner's data suggest that the initial stimulus is an unexplained increase in "empathy," a critical but somewhat enigmatic variable for Lerner. Such a *personality* change would be produced by the process Hagen describes. Finally, nationalism and alterations in the religious ethic are similarly regarded as useful in the spread of the developmental impetus but not a cause of its original formation. In Hagen's (1962b:258) words:

> To sum up: increase in the scale of the society, the appearance of cities, literacy, and modern communications media, and the appearance of nationalism are all steps in the transition to economic growth, once it has begun, rather than starting points or causes. This is probably also true of change in religious ethic. . . .

McClelland submits a psychologically oriented theory of development—again economically defined—that is similar to Hagen's in certain basics, but different in style and focus. Like Hagen, he stresses the primary significance of personality and socialization, but he is less concerned to give a complete causal picture than to demonstrate the importance of certain factors; he is more concerned with cross-societal empirical evidence and less with illustrative cases.

McClelland was particularly intrigued by Weber's thesis relating religion (Protestantism) and the rise of capitalism. McClelland feels that it was not simply Protestant ideology that was so congenial to economic development, but rather the fact that Protestantism promoted the need for achievement among its devotees, and this in turn fostered entrepreneurship and development. The main theme of McClelland's work is that changes in the need for achievement are strongly, critically, and causally related to changes in the economic development of societies.

The need for achievement (shortened to need achievement, *n* achievement, or *n*/Ach) refers to an individual's motivation to establish for himself and then to meet demanding standards of excellence. It denotes his desire to do well, to find and surmount challenges, to be tested, to strive, and to succeed. After much research, it was found that need achievement could be satisfactorily measured by Thematic Apperception Tests in which the respondent constructs stories to fit ambiguous pictures. The imagery used in these stories is then content analyzed for various themes, including achievement. Inference to group *n*/Ach levels could be made from similar content analyses of the most popular children's readers and folk literature and even from analyses of artifacts such as Greek vases.

Why might one think there was a relationship between need achievement and economic development? Work on achievement motivation in the United States had suggested that high *n* achievement leads a person to better performance if the task is construed as challenging; that is, if it furnishes a sense of accomplishment. There is also some evidence that boys with high *n* achievement differed from others, both in the United States and in Germany, in favoring business and entrepreneurial occupations. It therefore seemed plausible to hypothesize that need achievement is a significant factor in economic development because (1) the entrepreneurial element is crucial to developmental success and (2) need achievement might well be crucial to entrepreneurial accomplishment.

This hypothesis, especially the second part, was tested and examined in several ways, particularly three: (1) group measures of *n* achievement over time and cross-sectionally were correlated with measures of overall rates of economic development; (2) individual measures of *n* achievement were correlated with occupational interests and various types of performance; and (3) the motives and behaviors of actual entrepreneurs were compared with the qualities displayed by persons demonstrating high *n* achievement.

On the relationship between the need achievement level of the society (as inferred from the literature prepared for its children and other sources) and economic development, McClelland found supportive correlations from both the cross-sectional and longitudinal analyses. Such findings held separately, *mutatis mutandis*, for preliterate cultures and contemporary nations as well as for recent and long past eras. Cross-sectionally, the societies high in economic performance tended to be those high in *n*/Ach, and vice versa. Longitudinally, a high level of achievement motivation was shown to precede economic growth (by roughly thirty to fifty years), and a lower level of achievement motivation to presage economic decline. This was true in ancient Greece, in pre-Incan Peru, in Spain from about 1400 to 1700, in England from Tudor times to the Industrial Revolution (three separate cycles), and in the United States from 1810 to 1950.

According to McClelland, the entrepreneurial role places a premium on moderate risk-taking if it involves skill, not chance; decisiveness; energy; individual responsibility; knowledge of the results of decisions (concrete feedback); anticipation of future possibilities; and organizational skills. Extensive analysis indicated that high need achievement was positively associated with all but the last of these characteristics, which was not investigated. The high need achievers were not totally more energetic but were so only when the task was one that counted for personal achievement and in which their personal efforts were perceived to make a difference in the outcome. Routine tasks, sure things, or forlorn ventures would not engage their energies.

In general, business was a preferred career for high *n*/Ach boys who were also from lower-middle-class status.

> Thus if the *n* Achievement level in a society rises, it should not affect all occupations equally, but business occupations more since they tend to recruit particularly boys with high *n* Achievement from the more numerous middle and lower classes, at least in many countries that have already developed (McClelland, 1961:253).

The third test was to examine the existing groups of entrepreneurs in various societies to ascertain if they indeed displayed higher need achievement than reasonable comparison groups. Contrasting business executives and male university graduates in the United States and contrasting "managers" (entrepreneurs) with a comparison group of "professionals" (of similar status and responsibility) in four countries (U.S., Italy, Turkey, and Poland) generally revealed that the entrepreneurs did have higher *n*/Ach levels, except for Turkey.

McClelland does not regard need achievement as the sole determinant of economic development nor even as the only psychological determinant. Two other needs—*n* affiliation and *n* power—were examined with less intensity. Selected values and cognitions asserted to be significant for development, such as universalism, self-esteem, and other-directedness, were also studied.

Need affiliation is perceived as an important variable affecting population growth and thus affecting economic development. Need power is not seen as directly affecting economic development but as influencing the choice of means through which that goal is pursued. It is also hypothesized on the basis of country classifications that the combination of high *n* power with low *n* affiliation tends to characterize authoritarian and totalitarian political systems.

In analyzing certain values considered crucial to social change, it was found that economically advanced countries appear to stress hard work more than do less economically advanced countries. Advanced countries give more emphasis to nature as a force to be reckoned with and as a pressure for cooperative action among men although they were not inordinately committed to optimism about man's ability to subdue nature. "In societies which subsequently develop rapidly economically, the force which holds society together has shifted from tradition, particularly impersonal institutional tradition, to public opinion which helps define changing and functionally specific interpersonal relationships" (McClelland, 1961:192). The developed societies are oriented psychologically toward a "generalized other," which is vital to market morality, flexibility, and social cohesiveness during the developmental process.

The sources of need achievement are seen to lie in familial socialization. The parents of sons with high *n* achievement set higher standards for them (but are not too demanding), encourage independence, self-reliance, and early mastery of appropriate activities. They respond emotionally, especially positively, to their son's performance, and the father in particular is not authoritarian. It is *not* the case that parents with very high *n* achievement are likely to rear offspring with the same characteristic, since they tend to place too high demands and too much pressure on their children, producing dependence and caution rather than self-reliance and confidence.

In analyzing what produces change in child-rearing practices, especially change in mastery training and independence, McClelland points out several basic well-springs of change. One is war, which may have a significant effect by removing authoritarian fathers from the scene. Another is mass ideological conversion. The Protestant revolution is an example, and so might be Soviet or Chinese communism. Foreign educational influences might also be considered a watered-down version of the same phenomenon.

Finally, and this is quite important for McClelland's argument in more ways than one, affluence and success itself can alter child-rearing practices so as to affect need achievement. In this case, however, the effect is to reduce *n*/Ach. McClelland cites ancient Greece as a dramatic example. As their empire became more wealthy and powerful, affluent Greeks increasingly turned over their child-rearing responsibilities to slaves, who naturally did not inculcate the same achievement motivation that the parents had received. McClelland contends that, perhaps in fitting justice, the slaves unwittingly undermined the motivational basis behind Greek accomplishments. The decline of the empire set in when the slave-reared generation reached positions of decision-making.

This final point, along with the earlier observation that parents with very high need achievement are unlikely to produce offspring with similar *n*/Ach levels, may cast some doubt on the adequacy of McClelland's explanation of the relationship between economic development and need achievement, at least in this respect. McClelland's hypotheses are well suited to the explanation of *cyclical* phenomena—the rise and fall of societies and the oscillations of economic growth curves. However, most developmental theorists have assumed or stated that the modernization during the past two centuries is a unique and continuing process—that growth is now the essential characteristic of modern societies. McClelland's theory is much less well suited to this type of phenomenon.

The Role of Communications

Since both Hagen and McClelland give an interactional psychological explanation of development, almost everything they say can be construed to have a communications aspect. Both writers urge the fundamental significance of *personality* for the nature of the social system. It is interesting to ask how types of personality and types of communications systems might be linked. Is there any necessary or even empirically common personality basis for distinctive kinds of communication systems, e.g., for the four types distinguished by Siebert, Peterson, and Schramm (1956)? Is there, for instance, an open and communicative personality corresponding to an open and communicative society, and a closed and secretive personality corresponding to a closed and secretive society? In short, do different communication systems and their distinctive roles demand certain types of personalities, or at least certain limits in the range of acceptable personalities? Many suggestions relevant to this issue lie strewn about in communications research and development studies, but no systematic treatment is available.

One of the relevant strengths of Hagen's discussions for understanding communication and development is the emphasis placed upon deeper analysis of the *effects* of communication. This concern is manifested in two ways. One is the attention paid to the internal processing of communication once the basic message is received—the process of *intrapsychic, within-the-self communication*. Hagen also suggests that while the psychic costs of modernization may be formidable, they may to some extent be *manageable through the communication system*. But in any event, his analysis brings out the developmental significance of the internal processing of messages once they are received by important actors.

The second insight accentuated by both Hagen and McClelland concerns the generational reverberations induced by certain developmentally relevant communications. Hagen, particularly, maps in some detail a plausible sequence of intergenerational effects arising from the original communication of a decline in prestige that some groups in the society have unmistakably conveyed to another group. We are thus led to consider the developmental impact of a particular message not merely upon the original audience but also, through them, on subsequent audiences several times removed. Hagen and McClelland both give an important place to communication within the family, especially to its stylistic side effects on motivations regarded as crucial for developmental activity. *Familial socialization* is a key element in their developmental theories and communication is obviously one of the vital aspects of this socialization process, yet empirical inquiries from the underdeveloped nations that delve into these topics are rare indeed.

Both writers regard the developing

nation's *contact with the West* as a crucial feature of the developmental process. Stimulating analyses of selected developmental aspects of cross-cultural communications exist in Hall (1959; 1966), Pye (1962), Arensberg and Niehoff (1964), and many other works, but no comprehensive analysis of a developing nation's overall pattern of contacts with the West, through time, has yet been made. There is a clear need for more than one such work and then for a multinational summary leading to theoretical generalization.

Hagen and McClelland touch upon several other matters of interest for communication. Hagen suggests, for example, that the increase in *scale of the society* that comes with modernization reduces parochialism, which in turn furthers modernization. Behind this suggestion is the assumption that acquaintance with more than one community in particular, and diversity of communication in general, is conducive to mental flexibility and conversely that homogeneity of communication and restriction to a single community is conducive to rigidity.

McClelland similarly tosses out the idea that certain types of *feedback* are of key importance to entrepreneurs, who assess their interest in various activities partly in terms of the perceived opportunity for such concrete feedback. Both analysts also seem to assign great importance to consideration of the *power positions and communication positions held by the actors strongly inclined toward modernization.* Commenting on the success of a course in achievement motivation held for businessmen in Kakinada, India, for example, McClelland asks us to "note how a small shift in attitude toward doing a better job had a tremendous impact locally, *when it occurred in a man in a position to make an important decision*" (McClelland, 1966:33; emphasis added). In both theories, the modernizing group that possesses the appropriate personalities must still accomplish two things: (1) it must first have sufficient *internal communication* for self-recognition, cohesiveness, and protection of its threatened members, and (2) it must extend its influence through *external communication* to significant portions of the rest of the society in order to spread its modernizing message. Neither author probes deeply into either of these processes, although Hagen does offer the comments on the disabilities of alien groups that were stated.

On balance, however, perhaps the most original and provocative analysis relating directly to communication lies in McClelland's comments on *the importance of public opinion for development.* He claims that in economic development the force holding society together shifts from an institutionalized tradition to a public opinion that can accommodate changing and functionally specific interpersonal relationships. In other words, rigid and prescribed ways of relating to others give way to flexible patterns adapted to specific needs. The society thus becomes more open and effective because individuals can enter into relationships with others for specific purposes and yet participate confidently because these relationships are now generally controlled by the opinions and wishes of the "others" (McClelland, 1961:192).

Many developmentally important relationships are not possible under traditional mores since no ethic and no standards applicable to the new functionally specific and universalistic situations are available. Prescriptive institutional authority has broken down and is not appropriate anyway. But in successful development it apparently is functionally supplanted by an ethic involving the "generalized other"—by new conceptions of consensus on how things should be done. Thus, how an individual treats the stranger in the bus queue, what his obligations are regarding taxes, how he goes about switching his job, and when and why he disciplines his children are all matters on which new social norms are being established that are more appropriate for a developing society.

In McClelland's view, these new norms—this more generalized and yet more specific ethic, these new sources of authority—are most importantly presented in the mass media. The new outlook is tacitly absorbed from dramatizations in books, magazines, and newspapers, on the radio, and in films. It is also picked up at political party meetings, sports clubs, and through conversations while working. In essence, therefore, the communications system is the main instrument for producing the "other-directedness" vital to the new system of social control that holds the society together during its wrenching transformation. And it would seem that the comparative rates with which the old, institutional, traditional controls are abandoned and the new, media-engendered controls installed become critical for the prospects of relatively rapid but peaceful change.

Political Theories of Development

Economic and psychological theories of development tend to define the underlying directionality of change in similar terms. Both operationally conceive of development as an increase in gross national product per capita or some near equivalent, although the psychological approaches more often regard this measure as a token of deeper trends. When we consider political studies of development, however, we lose such consensus. Except for symmetry, the title of this subsection is better phrased as "Theories of Political Development" in order to indicate that the underlying directionality and phenomena of interest have shifted. The economic and psychological theories on the one hand and the political theories on the other do not purport to explain the same things.

Students of political development have defined their focus in many ways—indeed, too many. Frey (1963a), for instance, listed four fundamentally variant conceptions and discussed a basic logical difference between economic and political notions of development, while Pye (1966) listed no less than ten conceptualizations of political development, only two of which refer primarily to the political changes attending economic development. The remaining conceptions are all at least denotatively independent of economic development. They include such objectives as democracy, stability, mobilization and power, administrative and legal institutions of a certain character, and so on.

Many writers on political development see communication as an extremely important aspect of the process. It has been variously styled the "nerves," "blood," or "skeleton" of the political system—metaphors that reveal the significance attributed, although also the divergence of perceived function. The most useful insights can be grouped under five main rubrics, reflecting aspects of the political developmental process regarded as most affected by communication.

The first rubric involves provision of *information* for more effective instrumental decision-making, since increased rationality is considered a basic feature of political development. The second involves communication as it affects *power and control.* Here the focus is dual: communication for *integration* necessitated by the differentiation, specialization, and heightened collective aspirations attendant on development, and communication for *responsiveness* by power holders to nonelite elements necessitated by the demand for "participation" that often accompanies development. The third rubric involves consideration of the *individual psychic consequences* of modernization that can be presumed to have at least latent political significance. The fourth rubric refers more explicitly and analytically to *the change process itself*, dealing with thresholds, sequences, and similar aspects of communication and development. Finally, the fifth rubric relates rather generally to *interunit and interlevel problems* of communication for political development such as unit/environment, domestic/foreign, and macro/micro exchanges.

Information for Developmental Decision-Making

A "modern" society and polity are seen as requiring much more information than a "traditional" society and polity. As previously stated, one main reason for this is that decision-making is more rational in the modern polity. Ends-means calculations are regularly, deeply, and explicitly made and the growth of scientific understanding provides more elaborate theoretical indications of what types of information are necessary for various kinds of decisions. Not only is more and better information needed, but that information must be transmitted to the more specialized actors making the decision for which it is relevant. Since information does not necessarily arise at the locus of decision-making, a communication system adequate to distributing it to the critical control points must develop.

Students of political development, both in the United States and elsewhere, have emphasized and given graphic illustrations of these informational aspects of modernization. In Mandelbaum's analysis of *Boss Tweed's New York*, for example, the essential argument, accompanied by a vivid tableau of life in that developing city during the 1860s and 1870s, is that:

> The problems of New York a century ago were no less complex than those of a twentieth century metropolis of comparable size. Its communications network could not, however, link the several parts of the city together. The techniques of the era for gathering and analyzing information could not cope with the complexity of its problems. As a result, difficult issues took on a forced simplicity, in spite of themselves and at great cost. Rigid social stereotypes were perpetuated and political decisions were forced into the marketplace (Mandelbaum, 1965: vi).

In the marketplace, everything had its price, including politicians; social costs were ignored, and grievous problems were unrecognized or unmet. The communications structure of the system was simply inadequate to a more rational and effective political process.[13]

Holt and Turner (1966) raise similar considerations in reaching almost an opposite judgment regarding appropriate governmental policy in the traditional stage of development. Essentially their argument urges that the communications structure of such a society is so inadequate that a centralized decisional system is less efficient for allocating and managing resources than a decentralized system, prior to "take-off." The decentralized decision-maker is likely to have much more detailed information, much quicker feedback, and fortuitously more limited alternatives.

Mandelbaum and Holt and Turner give quite similar pictures of the relationship between communications and political decision-making in the early stages of development, although New York in 1970 may not be regarded as a "traditional" community. In any case, the crucial point at present is that *the nature of the communications system is seen to set clear constraints on the character of the political system and on the prospects for its development.*

The degree of national planning suitable for development at various stages is a matter of dispute. In general, however, the incidence of planning increases with development, and this planning critically involves planning for communication itself as well as communication for planning (see, e.g., Schramm, 1963). This in turn means that the increased informational requirements of modernization involve more *information about communication.* Pool (1963) noted that developing nations must decide: (1) how much to invest in communications, (2) what roles to assign

[13] A most interesting discussion and analysis of the problem of complexity and its decisional consequences is Alexander (1964); see also Brunner and Brewer (1971). Inadequate communication between government and immigrants also entered into Merton's (1957) explanation of bossism.

to the public and private sectors, (3) how much freedom or control is appropriate for various media, and (4) how high a cultural level to use for media output. Political decisions of this sort logically depend on explicit or implicit theory regarding the role of communication in political and economic development.

Development in any form not only requires improved distribution of information for more rational decision-making but it also involves for all sectors of the population the learning of new *skills*, ranging from literacy to nuclear physics (Schramm, 1963; 1967; Inkeles, 1966a). Parallel to the informational needs regarding communication itself, the catalog of new skills implied by modernization conspicuously includes *new communication skills*. Pye (1963:28–29) provides one basic political example. He suggests that the communication role of leaders in traditional societies stressed the ability to interpret and elaborate very spotty and limited information. The leaders of modern societies, on the contrary, must have great skill at sifting and winnowing awesome amounts of information. Part of the communication component of political development consists in learning—and teaching—new communication skills of this type.

A final illustrative point regarding the informational requirements of political development involves the very *language* employed. Passin (1963), Fishman, Ferguson, and Das Gupta (1968), and others have noted that a significant obstacle to the necessary communication for political development may inhere in the language of the traditional culture. Both in vocabulary and in logical structure it may be inadequate or cumbersome for expressing important developmental ideas (e.g., see Needham, 1954, on China).

Communication and Control: Integration and Responsiveness

The more the parts, the more the specialization, and the more the interdependence, the greater the need for communication to bind the various elements together. Hence, the improvement of integrative and coordinative communication is seen as a crucial part of political development.

The integrative aspects of communication, as they relate to political development, have been inspected in many forms and fashions. In their summary of the literature, Jacob and Teune (1964) discussed ten factors adduced by various analysts as exerting integrative influence: (1) geographical proximity, (2) homogeneity, (3) transactions or interactions among persons or groups, (4) knowledge of each other, (5) shared functional interests, (6) the "character" or "motive" pattern of a group, (7) the structural frame or system of power and decision-making, (8) the sovereignty-dependency status of the community, (9) governmental effectiveness, and (10) previous integrative experiences. The communication aspect of most of these factors is obvious. As Deutsch (1953) had previously noted, interaction, complementarity of interests, and structural involvement were generally seen to promote integration. From a communications perspective, the relevant insights in this area can be assembled under two main categories—orientations and structure. Certain outlooks and motivations are seen as conducive to developmental integration, and certain structural changes and problems also pervade the entire process.

Orientations. The list of orientations that some theorist or other has thought crucial for political development is long indeed. However, a much smaller set of orientations appears over and over again in the leading analyses. The role envisioned for communication can be adequately displayed through examining several of these, namely, national identification, legitimacy, trust, and finally the more comprehensive matter of consensus.

It is widely thought that perhaps the first step in the arduous process of political development is the formation of a strong sense of *national identity and identification* (see, e.g., Rustow, 1967; Nordlinger, 1968). The Italian patriot Mazzini referred to a people's "demand to exist and have a name"—a feeling that Geertz (1963:108) suggests is "fired by a humiliating sense of exclusion from the important centers of power in world society." Moreover, he notes, ". . . all but the most unenlightened members of [fragmented societies] are at least dimly aware—and their leaders are acutely aware—that the possibilities for social reform and material progress they so intensely desire . . . rest . . . on their being enclosed in a reasonably large, independent, powerful, well-ordered polity" (Geertz, 1963:109).

Many political analysts have further reasoned that "unless those individuals who are physically and legally members of a political system (that is, who live within its boundaries and are subject to its laws) are also psychologically members of that system (that is, feel themselves to be members) orderly patterns of change are unlikely" (Verba, 1965:529). There is, however, some uncertainty about this type of hypothesis (Emerson, 1962; Wilson, 1963: 85). For one thing, analysts also recognize a pathological side to national identification and our present inability to explain convincingly the appearance of one face rather than the other (Frey, 1968). Nationalism often seems more conducive to the fight for independence than for the constructive efforts that must follow (Deutsch, 1953:166). Also, very little empirical research specifically details the *assumed* link between national identification and a greater tendency to sacrifice for the nation, pay taxes, serve in the armed forces, refrain from violence, etc.; such connections may or may not in fact exist.

There is considerable evidence from various societies of a strong association between extramural communication, especially mass media exposure, and heightened national identification, at least for major sectors of developing societies such as the peasantry (Elder, 1964; 1966; Frey, 1968). More comprehensive aggregate analyses of nationalism as a consequence of communication have been furnished by Deutsch (1953; 1969). Hence, considerable confidence in the importance of extended communication for nationalism does seem warranted, although the significance of nationalism for political development remains complicated and only partly understood (see, e.g., Silvert, 1963; Cottam, 1964; Doob, 1964; Deutsch, 1969; and the bibliography by Deutsch & Merritt, 1970).

Along with national identification, the other main orientation of concern for analysts of political development has probably been *legitimacy* (e.g., Binder, 1962; Bendix, 1964; Apter, 1965). This is understandable in terms of the relationship between legitimacy and authority. Authority has been defined in various ways, but most conceptions ultimately regard it as the legitimate power of one role over another.

Authority is viewed by many as the defining characteristic of the political system, which is seen to involve the authoritative allocation of values for a society (Easton, 1953). As a type of power, authority has special qualities that are of major developmental significance. It has high initial establishment costs (i.e., inculcating the fundamental ideas of legitimacy is expensive) but very low usage costs thereafter compared with other types of power such as force or bargaining. It is a type of power that works well under conditions of poor communication where compliance observability is low. If the proper orientational groundwork for legitimacy has been laid, the influencer in an authoritative relationship can rely on the influencee's compliance regardless of the influencer's ability to monitor the performance. These qualities of authority make it an especially attractive type of power for all polities and particularly for developing societies (cf. Friedrich, 1958; Easton, 1965; Frey, 1971).

Although the relationship between legitimacy and political development is probably clearer than the relationship between national identification and development, we are in the opposite position regarding its relationship to communication. Fundamental ideas of legitimacy are thought to be inculcated early in the life cycle through the main institutions of socialization—the family, the school, the peer group, the church, and perhaps the mass media. Much of the learning may be latent, picked up from such clues as the status system, the packaging in which more obvious media content is wrapped, and the actual behavior rather than the preachments of role models (Hyman, 1959; 1963; LeVine, 1960; 1965; Hess & Torney, 1967; Easton & Dennis, 1969; Greenstein, 1969). However, the specific mechanisms through which this occurs and many other aspects of legitimacy, particularly the less formal, have not been thoroughly studied anywhere, least of all in developing societies. (Relevant bibliography on socialization in the developing world is found in Dennis, 1967; Frey et al., 1969; and Cohn, 1971.)

Developing societies encounter severe difficulties in maintaining critical structures of authority during the modernization process. Intrafamilial communication often breaks down, the authority of the family erodes, and other traditional institutions are similarly shaken. Hence, because of communication difficulties and other problems, this vital type of power may be less available to the political system just when it is most needed. The consequences range from loss of independence to anarchy, stagnation, erratic and anguished growth, or charismatic interventions and authoritarian take-overs of both a tutelary and exploitative sort.

A third orientation that has been emphasized in studies of political development is *trust* (Pye, 1962; 1963; 1965). "The presence of diffuse distrust seems to impede seriously the creation of the kinds of public organizations essential for national development" (Pye, 1965:22). Family fails to cooperate with family for community purposes, ethnic groups refuse to accept the electoral victory of another ethnic coalition because they suspect its intentions, and bureaucrats and politicians cannot work together effectively because each doubts the other's good faith. Such conditions have been reported many times in many areas, developed and underdeveloped (Lewis, 1951; Luethy, 1955; Banfield, 1958; Lopreato, 1962; Pye, 1962; Crozier, 1964; Foster, 1965; LaPalombara, 1965; LeVine, 1965; Zonis, 1971).

Trust and communication are dually related: trust or distrust is itself usually a product of communication, and the basic effect of distrust is to make communication less effective and more costly. More credible and diverse communication sources and greater redundancy are thereby required to convince actors of important information, if it can be done at all. Moreover, the governmental centralization of the mass media adopted for economy and control may be counterproductive in this respect. As Mosel (1963:203) observed in Thailand, "government control of all radio, the low credibility of newspapers, and the fact that the government public relations office is the sole source of official news on domestic affairs means that there is always a need to know the 'inside story.'" Under conditions of high cynicism and distrust, the modernizing messages of the mass media may be abnormally distorted by the traditional face-to-face communications network (see, e.g., Binder, 1965, for similar comments on Egypt).

As usual there is another side to the matter, however. Pye (1965:22) avers that "an equal obstacle to development . . . is the widespread existence of an uncritical and childlike trust in the rulers and in all forms of higher authority." In this area also we do not yet have any effective theory explaining precisely what the desirable degree of trust or distrust is, what its causes are, and for what roles and topics it is most crucial.

In a broader view, the orientational aspects of integration and responsiveness in the developmental process are often seen as part of the problem of *consensus*. Reduced to barest essentials, the matter can be put as follows: Development ultimately involves reliably concerting the behaviors of many previously isolated or uncoordinated elements of the traditional society. Only thus can national systems of education, political organization, defense, taxation, welfare, communication, industry, etc., be established and maintained. Such regular and predictable behavioral coordination occurs in one of two basic ways—either through power or through consensus. The greater the spontaneous consensus, the less the need to use power for coordination. The democratic approach to political development is commonly regarded as implying an emphasis on consensus rather than power wherever feasible (Jacob & Teune, 1964:35–36).

Deeper analysis always reveals a profound interaction between power and consensus since power, particularly in the form of socialization, is used to help establish consensus and since actors often psychologically adjust their wishes to their perceived power positions. On the other hand, consensus regarding the legitimate distribution and usages of power and the appropriate social and individual goals (including the goal of gaining power) basically affects how power is employed in the society.

Structures. Political development fundamentally implies change in the power structure of the society as well as changes in the orientations of its members. The structural changes can generally be regarded as movement either toward greater ability to coordinate behaviors (capacity, integration) or toward greater sharing of power (equality, responsiveness), although striking an appropriate balance between the two is the prime problem of politics.

The basic obstacle confronting many developing societies on the integrative side is a paucity of structural links, both in communication and in power. The overall "connectivity" of the society is so low as to preclude concerted action. Many crucial elements are unconnected with other elements. In fact, the paramount structural difference between developed and underdeveloped societies is not in the distribution (concentration or dispersion) of existing power, communications, and other links, but rather in the overall *amount*, density, or connectedness of links (Frey, 1963a: 303; 1965: chap. 13; 1970; S. P. Huntington, 1966; 1968b: 140–147).[14] Hence, one of the first concerns of political development is to tie the thousands of isolated villages and groups together into a connected whole—to transform the traditional "sack of potatoes," as Marx characterized rural France, into a single organic entity (see Fagen, 1966: chaps. 6, 7).

Many developing societies have adopted the most economical short-run strategy for creating new structural links, which is a hierarchical linking of elements. An effort is made to connect all critical actors and subsystems together through a single node. Sometimes that node is the party, sometimes the government (particularly the bureaucracy), sometimes the military, and even sometimes a single charismatic leader and his cronies. Whatever the specific manifestation, there is a plausible economy lying behind the strategy of unilateral and hierarchical political development in addition to the ideological and motivational appeal it may have for traditional personalities.

It is important to recognize that communication is very much a two-edged sword. Its integrative capabilities, for example, can be used for national coordination and development, but they can also be used by traditional opposition to close ranks against development. In a similar vein we should note the importance of communication for many uses of power, not just for power wielded in support of societal

[14] Technically, the *amount* of power or communication (defined as the ratio of actual links to potential links, given certain assumptions about transitivity and chain length) is not the same as the *connectivity* (defined as the distance in links between average or extreme members), but the relationship between the two is strong enough so that we shall not pursue the distinction here.

integration and development. Generally speaking, "knowledge is power," and knowledge about power is especially likely to enhance power. For this reason, the main actors in domestic as well as international competitions for power devote much attention and many resources to "the intelligence function"—gathering information regarding the power structure and the other actors in their arena (see, e.g., Wilensky, 1967). One of the problems of political development is that this function at comprehensive levels is frequently novel and badly performed. Miscalculations, which might be eliminated by better communications, abound.

Finally, at this general level, we must consider the *institutions* of communication as well as the processes. In particular, we must take cognizance of the "fourth branch of government" function that is commonly assigned to communications institutions, especially the mass media (Cater, 1959). "An autonomous communication system 'regulates the regulators' and thereby preserves the autonomies and freedoms of the democratic polity," as Almond (1960:47) puts it. The mass media function as an integral part of the governing mechanism, checking and controlling the main branches of formal government and parties by giving publicity to their operations, supplementing official communication, and providing essential information to diverse actors—especially to those outside government but also to those within.

Intraelite Communication. As a society changes, the elite comes under pressure to admit rising social groups or their representatives to its ranks. These new entrants are usually unfamiliar with the communication habits of the elite and frequently posses a style of their own that is repugnant to the former elite. Misunderstandings ensue and much of the old ease of communication possible in narrower social confines is lost, to the frustation of all concerned and often with a real drop in political effectiveness as well as tranquility. This happened, for instance, in the British Parliament when Clydeside Labour M.P.'s first invaded the House of Commons. Weathering such storms is often extremely difficult for fragile developing polities.

The opposite problem is commonly seen in the bureaucracy. There internal communication at least among the highest administrative class is likely to be excellent. Top officials often have attended the same schools and have in any event absorbed the heady elite atmosphere bequeathed by their colonial or imperial predecessors. But excellence of internal communication is purchased at the price of severe insulation. The bureaucracy may function well by its own elitist standards but be an active obstacle to national development in an expanding political system (Braibanti, 1966). Thus, in virtually all sectors of the political elite in developing societies, a delicate accommodation between change and communication must be attempted. Too rapid change may render communication impossible; too intimate communication may lead to cliquishness and isolation from the rest of society.

Shils has stressed the importance of an elite balance wheel for political development—a "vital center" that is progressive, moderate, and resistant to the fly-by-night adventurism and emotional extremism that plague rapidly changing societies. "The formation of this sober, task-oriented, professionally responsible stratum of the population is, perhaps, the most important precondition of the political development of the new states" (Shils, 1963:69). Communication patterns have much to do with the emergence of such a core elite group, not always favorably. The press of developing societies, though often nationalistic and promodernization, tends to be inflammatory, irresponsible, partisan, and oppositional. Part of this is the legacy of colonialism and imperialism, which has meant that "as the transitional states emerge into independence . . . they have an oppositional, partisan press which finds it difficult to transform itself into the kind of responsible, nonpartisan press that the new situation requires" (Passin, 1963: 102). Moreover, the mass media constitute excellent bases for political operations (Coleman, 1960:350; Pool, 1963:239ff.). Hence, the mass media themselves become objects of political conflict and embroiled in partisan dispute. Their polarization aggravates the polarization of political elites so often found in developing societies. Political competition thus tends to extremes with consequent loss of developmental opportunities.

Obviously, this is the negative "ideal-typical" picture and many developing societies do not completely conform to it, but it is surprising how few modifications have to be made to obtain a reasonably good fit in numerous developing nations.

A final structural point on the elite side is the problem of communications overload. Factors previously mentioned, such as the prevalence of distrust and the unilateral-hierarchical linkage preference, tend to produce great centralization of decision-making. Top leaders try to keep all the reins in their own hands, including all aggregation of information. The result frequently is a communications overload at the top, with consequent increase in error, reaction time, and stress (Meier, 1962: 68–83, 171).

Intramass Communication. Ultimately, development must imply a marked and novel increase in lateral or horizontal communication within the mass sector. The probable outcome of this will be, at least at first, to heighten mass consciousness, to reinforce mass tastes and mass resistance to elite cultural and political hegemony, and to improve mass organizational capacities. At least such has been common speculation by classic writers such as DeTocqueville and Ortega y Gasset.

We are speaking now, however, of relatively advanced stages of political development currently entered by only a few truly "mass societies" of the world. The transition to this degree of mass influence is always a conflictful and disturbing adjustment for the elite. Their reactions largely decide the degree of developmental turmoil to be faced. But such change seems nevertheless to be a highly probable consequence of increased communication and development.

Elite-Mass Communication. Most analytic attention regarding the relationship between communication and political development has been given to elite-mass and mass-elite interaction. The reason is that elite-mass bifurcation of the society is seen as perhaps the crucial problem for development, and the incorporation of the mass sector, especially the rural or peasant contingent, into active social, political, and economic participation is viewed as perhaps the final hurdle in the contemporary developmental process.

Mass media in many developing societies are elite-oriented and, on the surface, ineffective with villagers, many of whom are extremely divergent from the elite groups and frequently divergent from each other. The elite have much more influence than the masses and the communication system is much more attuned to pick up feedback from them, so the media become primarily elite instruments and entertainment. The very choice of language and cultural level is one conspicuous example. When the decision is made between sophisticated unintelligibility for the masses and understandable "vulgarity" for elites, as Pool (1963:244–245) has described, the outcome is usually the former. The problem may be compounded (or reduced) by the fact that mass sectors may be responding as much to the latent, packaging effects of the media as to the direct content (Hyman, 1963). But in any event, the great heterogeneity of transitional societies plus elite unfamiliarity with and even strong distaste for reciprocal interaction with the masses makes appropriate developmental communication difficult.

The same type of communication problem affects governance and administration. Frey (1971) suggests that there exist in most developing societies at least three diverse "administrative cultures" based on communication. Under modern conditions of excellent communication, what in organization theory is called "feedback" control can be employed. Agents in the field can readily inform the key decision-makers of critical or unusual situations and receive appropriate instructions. Similarly, the central planners can readily monitor the agents' activities and guide them when they feel it necessary (March & Simon, 1958:160 ff.).

At the other extreme, according to Frey, is the system of "venal control." This is the most traditional system and is employed under conditions of very poor communication. The rulers realize that they cannot easily monitor or supply quick decisional guidelines to their distant agents, so they try to make it in the venal self-interest of the agent to do at least some of what the rulers want done. They let the agent keep part of the taxes he collects if he also will send part to the rulers (tax-farming). They let him exercise authority and judicial power if he will to some extent protect the interests of the regime. They let him conscript soldiers if he will supply the central power with a stipulated number of troops, and so on. In return, the central authorities lend the agent a certain degree of legitimacy and agree to support him against other claimants to power in the region should that be necessary.

This venal control system is obviously limited in what it can accomplish. Moreover, the greater the distance from the center and the poorer the communications, the lower the proportionate remissions of taxes and troops and the higher the probability of the agent's declaring himself independent.

In some traditional societies an intermediate control system developed which Frey calls the "programmed control system" and which in organization theory is sometimes called "control by plan." It assumes the same poor communication as the venal system but attempts to get around this by indoctrinating the central authority's field representatives, usually very early and very heavily, with values of loyalty and service to the regime. If such values are thoroughly inculcated, then the agents will behave appropriately even when communication with the center is very poor. This was the function of the mandarin system in traditional China, the Palace School and *devşirme* system of the Ottoman Empire, and also of the "public" school system of the British Empire (see, e.g., Wilkinson, 1964). The problem with the programmed control system, however, was first of all rigidity (when the regime line changed it was difficult to *re*program all the agents) and, second, corruption (it was hard to maintain the élan and dedication of the critical schools and the favored agents).

Frey sees these three administrative control systems as characteristically pursuing different goals. The venal system pursues exploitative goals, the programmed system regulatory goals, the feedback system welfare or developmental goals. Actually, every system, traditional or modern, is a mix of the three tendencies, but one or another emphasis tends to predominate.

One of the most egregious problems for developing societies is that policy-makers desirous of affecting the entire nation have to work in all three control cultures at once. At the level of the central cabinet, state-planning organization, and similar units, the prevailing system is that of feedback control. If an agent remains at the center but moves to certain ministries such as Justice or Interior, he enters the realm of programmed control. When he moves out to the more remote towns and villages, he finds himself in a system of venal control where powerful families and local leaders still continue to operate on an exploitative basis. Hence it is extremely difficult to steer nationwide policies effectively through these three different cultures.

Students of communication and political development have frequently flagged the crucial importance of the intermediaries between elite and mass elements (Pye, 1958; Wriggins, 1966). These crucial mediators, especially those more remotely located in the mass sector, are strongly affected by communications, particularly the mass media. One danger for such actors is that they feel isolated, embedded as they are in a traditional environment. They may therefore succumb to local pressure and be captured by their clientele, sundering the elite-mass link and abandoning their coordinative function. The administrator or field representative who has "gone native" or, alternatively, withdrawn into apathy, is a common phenomenon. The mass media, however, constitute a crucial counterweight to such tendencies. They provide vital psychic and moral reinforcement for agents of modernization far distant from the modern sector. As classic experimental work in social psychology suggests, only a limited amount of support may be necessary to keep a "deviant" or innovator going in a hostile setting. But some support is essential if he is to maintain his external reference group. This necessary minimum of support to prevent capitulation is what the village radio or the belated newspaper often provides.[15]

Mass-Elite Communication. The opposite side of the communications coin—the *mass-elite linkage*—is no less significant than the elite-mass connection for developing societies. For one thing, the elite, often colossally ignorant of mass mores although naively confident of the contrary, urgently needs feedback from the masses to carry out its integrative objectives. For another, as political development proceeds, considerations of equality and participation loom larger and some mass elements become an increasingly potent force in the nation. And, for a third, in many areas such as agriculture, valuable generalizable solutions to developmental problems are discovered at various points in the mass sector.

Probably the most notorious aspect of mass-elite communications that pertains to political development is the political arousal of the masses that is said to occur. Great danger is foreseen if demand-arousing communication grows more rapidly than demand-satisfying economic development and demand-channeling political institutions (Lerner, 1963; 1967; S. P. Huntington, 1968). The dread result is the well-known "revolution of rising expectations," revised by Lerner to the "revolution of rising frustrations."

In Lerner's formula, the critical consideration is the "Want/Get Ratio." If this is very unfavorable, dissatisfaction and frustration result and presumably political action follows. If this political action is unrestrained and exceeds the system's institutional capacity for handling it peacefully and legitimately, political instability occurs, with negative effects on all forms of development. Samuel P. Huntington (1968:55) has formulated the

[15] The problem of administrative control and elite-mass intermediaries is also manifested in what can be called the "bureaucratic transmission belt." Like the old rumor game, it is often striking how decisions taken at high levels in developing societies either fail to emerge or emerge looking almost unrecognizable at the grass-roots level. The same happens to reverse flows of information. It seems highly probable that these breakdowns in administrative influence and communication chains are far from random. They occur regularly and predictably at certain critical points along the line. One such point is where there are severe status gaps between nodes. Another is where the reference groups of the articulating agents are extremely different. Another occurs when there are extreme differences in social background between the connecting agents. For an empirical investigation of one end of this transmission belt employing such hypotheses, see Frey and Roos (1967) and Roos and Roos (1972).

basic progression into three equations:

$$\frac{\text{Social mobilization}}{\text{Economic development}} = \text{Social frustration} \quad (1)$$

$$\frac{\text{Social frustration}}{\text{Mobility opportunities}} = \text{Political participation} \quad (2)$$

$$\frac{\text{Political participation}}{\text{Political institutionalization}} = \text{Political instability} \quad (3)$$

For Lerner, Huntington, and others (e.g., Deutsch, 1961), communication in general and the mass media in particular are important tools of social mobilization. From this perspective they may appear quite threatening because they acquaint the poor, who constitute the vast majority of the population of most developing nations, with all kinds of desirable things that they do not have, and also because they stimulate a sense of relative as well as absolute deprivation.

It is interesting to juxtapose this interpretation with two other issues involving communication and development. One is the superficially competing views of the media as "stimulant" or "narcotic" (Schramm, 1963:53–54). Against the arousal image of the media must be placed the sedation image. Here the media are seen as providing people an escape from reality. Through the media the masses can retreat into fantasy or a more successful vicarious existence. Rather than being stimulated and then frustrated by the media, the masses are seen to be lethargized and diverted from more constructive activities.

The other issue relates to the perceived effectiveness of the mass media. As Pool (1963:237–238) suggests, the policy-makers of non-Communist societies seem to display a prevailing "disillusionment" with the media as a developmental instrument. The media are thought to be ineffective for changing actions or behavior. Thus, like social science in general, the mass media in developing societies are cast into a "damned-if-you-do and damned-if-you-don't" role. They are at the same time seen to be disastrously effective and disappointingly ineffective. However, as Pool points out, although these images are quite compatible and even plausible at a certain level, they are superficial and tell only part of the story. Indeed, we should add that they are highly misleading in several respects.

The expressions "revolution of rising expectations" and "revolution of rising frustrations" seem more speculation than fact. It is difficult to survey political life in the developing world and find much support for these images from the behavior of *mass* elements. Rogers (1969:23) records that peasants have played a significant though far from leading role in at least four major revolutions: the Mexican revolution of 1910, the Russian revolution of 1917, the Chinese Communist revolution, and the Cuban revolution under Fidel Castro. A few other instances may be found after careful search, and the tactic of insurgency has made peasant support a much more prominent political factor. Nonetheless, this is not a large haul from a volatile half-century. The cases of peasant uprising from dissatisfaction and frustration in the developing world are very few and far between. As Weiner (1966:207) comments, "though we speak metaphorically of the revolution of rising expectations and of the great upheavals stirring Asia, Africa, and Latin America, in fact the number of people actively in politics still remains quite small" (cf. Pye, 1963:150). Moreover, just as we were wrong about the political volatility of rural-urban migrants squatting in the cities, so there is evidence that the suggested mass political volatility engendered by the communications media is probably wrong (Frey, 1966:185; Nelson, 1969). What "revolution of rising expectations/frustrations" exists is much more an elite phenomenon than a mass phenomenon and can by no means be clearly attributed to expanded communications. Given the conditions, the masses in developing societies have been remarkably quiescent.

More generally, the entire matter of the developmental impact of the mass media on mass political behavior becomes quite complex as one examines the relevant literature. Even some presumably established truths come into doubt. For example, it is accepted that the media directly produce awareness but not adoption, information but not action, etc. Yet this conclusion is based primarily on studies from advanced Western societies, and the evidence from the developing world is presently mixed (Spector et al., 1963; Chu, 1966; Frey & Roos, 1967; Rogers, 1969:110). There is, however, much evidence that organizational support, for example, allied with media exposure can be relatively successful in altering behavior (Nicol et al., 1954; Louis & Rovan, 1955; Dumazadier, 1956; Cassirer, 1959; Mathur & Neurath, 1959; etc.).

Another ill-founded basis for disillusionment with the influence of the media in developing nations is that they presumably cannot effect much attitudinal change. This, too, may be a highly parochial observation based primarily on Western experience, for attitude *formation* may be more at issue than attitude change (Frey, 1966:196–197). It is a mistake to apply ready inferences from a media-saturated society to one where the media are entering people's horizons for the first time. Moreover, the supposedly negative features of communication in developing societies can actually be advantages in some important contexts. Take the narcotic or sedation effect, for example. This effect may take the edge off frustration and reduce the number of demands the political system has to process (see Braibanti, 1966:167). The strategy of Ataturk is instructive in this respect. Rather than lamenting the communications bifurcation of Turkish society, he accepted and exploited it. It provided him with a useful halfway house in the task of modernization. He could concentrate his limited resources on elite modernization and effectively ignore the dormant and isolated peasantry. After elite modernization had been clinched, then full effort could be focused on the peasantry.

The days when the leadership could successfully ignore the peasantry and concentrate upon the elite may, however, be over. Through international communication, world culture impinges upon the developing society, frequently shaping or reducing its options. The exploitation of communication gaps to equate aspirations with resources may also exacerbate the eventual problems of peasant assimilation if the leadership waits too long—as may have happened in Turkey. But to determine how long is too long requires better theory than we possess at present.

One of our most plausible and relevant conjectures has been made by Schramm (1964; 1967). After reviewing the role and uses of communication for development, he notes the half-hearted, mincing, narrow and stingy approach to communication planning employed in most societies. The policy-makers of most developing societies have made little effort to use communication as a tool for social change. Rather they have simply drifted or reacted tardily and feebly to the communications revolution that swirls about them. In India and Turkey, two leading and fairly representative emerging nations, less than one-half of 1 percent of investment outlays from the early five-year plans were committed to communication (Pool, 1963:231; Frey, 1966:201).

As a result, an important opportunity for economic and political development may have been neglected. There is considerable evidence for significant economies and advantages of scale in developmental communication. The use of multiple channels, diversely reinforced messages, subtle and pervasive content, continuous transmission, and so on seem necessary to create the encompassing "climate for development" that may be so effective. Integrating the mass media more closely with the educational system, transportational planning, informal communications network, mass organizations, and other institutions of the developing society pays extra dividends. But it also requires imaginative appreciation of a more ambitious communication strategy and a planning capacity that has yet to be demonstrated in any developing society.

Psychic Consequences of Development

There are many factors favoring charismatic authority in developing societies, not the least of which is the famed "solvent" quality of charisma. It is perhaps the best type of authority for dissolving the old order (traditional or rational) and paving the way for the new. But another basis for charisma is a feeling of deep insecurity in the face of unfamiliar experiences. Charismatic relationships occur when people feel profoundly threatened by something novel, something almost impossible for them to diagnose and for which there is no established solution. Under such conditions, experience provides no guide to where to look for leadership. People are therefore inclined to latch onto any sign of a "gift of grace"—any miraculous escape, incredible success, inexplicable potency. From this viewpoint, it is no accident that charismatic leaders are so common in developing societies.

One of the political consequences of increased communication may be to increase these charismatic tendencies at first, as individuals initially apprehend the eddies of change that surround them. Then, however, communication should decrease charismatic propensities, as information reduces the novelty of change if not the threat. In essence, this expectation is based on the hypothesis that the inclination toward charismatic followership has a curvilinear relationship with information and communication. It rises as change impinges on the traditional individual through increased communication and then, after a threshold, declines as he becomes increasingly sophisticated.

Another frequently mentioned and politically significant psychic consequence of development that basically involves communication is "atomization"—the loss of ties and contacts with community, friends, and family. Modern man is often depicted as an alienated "loner," divorced from close human bonds by the pace of his life, the enormity and impersonality of his institutions, and the seductiveness of his mass media. Amidst more effective and elaborate opportunities for communication than ever before he finds it difficult to communicate closely with anyone. He sits alone and mute, with television on and telephone at hand, interacting only with the "generalized other."

This theme has been worked and reworked in academia and media. The Age of Anxiety still lurks behind the Age of Aquarius. Despite the initially graphic image, however, the suggestion is vague and the facts are uncertain. At best we can say that if atomization is a major psychic consequence of modernization, then its roots and remedies probably lie in alterations in communication.

In general, the entire realm of the psychic products of development and their relation to communication and to political change is largely unexplored territory. Speculation about stress, anxiety, charisma, atomization, insecurity, identity, personal instability, anomie, etc., on the one hand, and about a sense of mastery, excitement, gratification, optimism, purpose, efficacy, self-fulfillment, etc., on the other, has been almost a vogue. But relevant, systematic, and convincing empirical research is quite scarce. Consequently, we are much richer in metaphor than in tested theory.

The Change Process

One of the greatest problems of communication and political development is adjusting to the very changes that have been set in motion. A continuous process of adaptation is necessary. The problem is complicated, partly because of the powerful human and institutional tendency toward short-run perspectives and effort—the ubiquitous urge to conceive the job as terminable, after which one can sit back and rest.

Even more awkward is the fact that the feedback process itself needs to change with change, and that information about the adequacy of information is required. Second-order insight and activity of such a nature seems enormously difficult for men and social systems. In all kinds of developmental situations, therefore, one can discern critical lags. Parents do not adjust to the changes they have wrought in their children, teachers do not adapt to their changing students, and developing societies characteristically do not allow for the effects of their development. A quick and conspicuous example of the last is the tardiness in recognizing and accommodating newly qualified elite groups.

We referred previously to the kinds of change in communication that analysts feel must attend stages of economic or social development. Similar considerations apply to political development. Pye, for instance, argues that when countries are at a very early stage of political development, appropriate communications policy would direct all instruments of communication toward supporting the legitimacy of the government and its administrative structures which will be essential for further social change.

> In those countries with a small modernized elite the weight of communications policies should be on the side of protecting the freedom of these leaders and strengthening their influences throughout the society. At later stages of development the elite may have expanded and the prime problem of communications becomes that of mobilizing increasingly larger segments of the mass of the people. At this phase . . . the time is ripe for broad appeals and for the repetition of theses basic to civic education. At still later stages in the transitional process the problems of communications tend to center more on facilitating adjustments among different emerging interests and on the need for providing the population with effective channels for communicating its views to the elite.
>
> Clearly the communications policies appropriate at one stage of development may be either irrelevant, or, more likely, directly damaging if applied at other stages (Pye, 1963:229–130).

In sum, what all polities and societies need, and developing societies more than others, is institutional and structural *flexibility*—the capacity to adjust their patterns of power, communication, and status to changed internal or external conditions.

One of the thorniest developmental problems for policy-makers and theoreticians alike is the fact that so many change processes seem to be threshold phenomena. Literacy may be one example of such a variable. Marginal investments seem to have little payoff until about 40 percent literacy is reached, at which point marked changes occur in related variables. After that there may again be no appreciable marginal return until about 90 percent literacy is reached (Bowman & Anderson, 1962). Quite obviously these thresholds may relate to elite literacy and mass literacy. But to the policy-maker deciding investments and to the theorist with too short a time perspective, most incremental investments in literacy seem ineffective.

Superficially it appears that communication variables would be especially likely to display these threshold effects. Such an assumption lies behind the "climate of opinion" notion, which urges that the psychic and behavioral significance of a belief or attitude depends fundamentally on the holder's perception of how many others around him also hold that view.

A related difficulty suggested by many writers—and one that can serve as a final illustration of the trials of dynamic analysis—is the problem of balance in development. Whether one accepts the theory of balanced or unbalanced development, the "big push" or the coordinated nudge, one cannot avoid consideration of the interdependence of the economic, political, communication, and other aspects of modernization. Newspaper delivery requires transportation facilities. Radio and television require electronic materials and skills. In many countries, newsprint must be imported and such imports require government-issued licenses. Mail delivery requires large-scale organization, and so on. Many suggest that if an essential area falls too far behind, the developmental pattern gets warped.

In sum, then, theorizing and planning for development involves explicit attention to change processes per se at a very difficult second-order level. The society needs to handle the changes produced by change, to have communication about communication, feedback about feedback, and so forth. The planner is concerned about thresholds, critical sizes, timing, sequencing, floor and ceiling effects, syndromes and balances, contexts and climates, saturation and isolation. The level of understanding thus required may be an entire notch in difficulty beyond that commonly required for more standard analyses—and a notch beyond existing sophistication.

Intersystem and Interlevel Problems

The external world of nations impinges mightily on the developing society. Indeed, as Pye (1963:3) has observed, in many respects "it was the pressure of communications which brought about the downfall of traditional societies"—mainly communications from the more modern, great-power nations.

It is frequently suggested that any developing nation's particular path depends substantially upon the nature of its "contacts with the West." The original impetus to change usually comes from this source (Frey, 1965). Which Western nation is chosen as a role model for a given activity seems of major importance. A popular example is the British versus the French presence in colonial Africa (see, e.g., Herskovits, 1962; Banks & Textor, 1963).

More specifically, the internal characteristics of institutions in the developing societies are greatly influenced by international communications. The great sway of the French-styled lycée and the British-styled "public school" in the politics and education of many developing societies is an illustration, together with the conflict within ministries among those who have been trained in one Western style as opposed to another or to an indigenous style. The military provide an equally basic illustration. There are many reasons for the prominence of the military in developing polities. Not least among these is the fact that these nations disproportionately encountered the "cutting edge" of Western civilization—its military prowess. Thus, the national emphasis on military strength, the relations of other institutions to the military, and the quality and goals of the military itself have all been profoundly shaped by Western, great-power contact.

Several basic developmental hazards have been seen to inhere in these international communications relations. For example, Pye (1958:342) has called attention to the problems that can arise if part of the society has been altered by development and is mainly attuned to world culture and external referents while the rest remain extremely parochial and oblivious of these factors: "For all their differences, the Confucian scholar and the Chinese peasant belonged to one world. The same cannot be said of the Westernized intellectual and the contemporary Asian peasant."

Despite the importance of international communications for the process of development, no systematic, comparative, and comprehensive analysis of these relationships exists. It would be most useful even to have a good descriptive inventory of the external communication contacts of a single developing society over time to place alongside its domestic developmental chronicle. But these constitute further additions to our list of necessary future work, and at the present time we possess mainly shrewd but limited and rather vague insights.

Communication Theories of Development

In the economic and psychological theories of development, communication played a rather latent and general role, albeit an important one if the theories are scrutinized deeply. We shall now consider communication theories of development, i.e., theories that put communication at the heart of an explanation of modernization.

On the whole, the development being explained is that found in the economic and psychological theories, viz., increasing gross national product per capita. In some cases, however, another conception of development is employed, such as increased electoral participation or certain kinds of attitudinal change, so that the explicandum is altered.

The global process of modernization or development has, as mentioned previously, two fundamental aspects. One can be called "invention"—the original generation of the change process under examination; the other can be called "diffusion" or "innovation"—the process by which the invention is spread, copied, and disseminated. The communication theories of development can be fruitfully displayed under these two headings.

Theories of Diffusion

While the diffusion theories may at first seem less interesting because they do not include the invention process, reflection may alter this judgment. One can argue that it matters little how the industrial system was invented. It may very well have been a unique historical accident. But whatever the reason, the crucial developmental process in the world for the past century has been diffusion. None of the so-called underdeveloped or developing societies need worry about inventing the industrial or postindustrial system. Instead, the problem is how to explain their differential rates of adoption of available changes and, from a policy perspective, to know how to accelerate the laggards. We shall focus on three related types of theories: (1) anthropological theories of cultural diffusion, (2) sociological theories on the diffusion of innovations, and (3) geographical or spatial models of diffusion developed primarily by Torsten Hagerstrand.

Anthropological Theories of Cultural Diffusion. A compelling concern of cultural anthropology and archeology has been to explain change in cultures or civilizations (to use the more archaic and ethnocentric term). As recently as the turn of the century, the dominant outlook was that of the cultural evolutionists, who essentially posited independent, natural, lawful, individual development of each major culture.

To the "diffusionists" who emerged from 1890 on, this seemed highly implausible. On the contrary, the evidence indicated to them that "as far as most cultures are concerned, there can be little doubt that the elements that have been borrowed predominate over those that have originated from within" (Herskovits, 1969:499). Moreover, if one specifically considers modernization or development, one finds that "acculturation between Euroamerican and native peoples in the nineteenth and twentieth centuries is no more than a special instance of a process that is as old as man himself" (Herskovits, 1969:534). Thus, at least for some leading anthropologists, there is a specific claim that theories of modernization or development are in fact theories of cultural diffusion.

The early diffusionists developed little explicit theory of the diffusion or acculturation process, being engaged instead, like most protagonists, in exposing the error of their opponents (the evolutionists) by showing that an enormous, even preponderant, amount of cultural borrowing did occur. More recent writers, however, have made a more conscientious effort to deal with "the 'why' of cultural dynamics" and to make their key hypotheses more explicit.

The main determinants of diffusion have

been seen by most diffusionists as *contact* (communication) and *orientation*. Without some contact, of course, there is no diffusion. It is not accidental that the most isolated peoples of the world "have remained the most primitive known in modern times" (Heine-Geldern, 1968:173). Beyond this extreme, however, various aspects of contact must be considered. The following hypotheses relating contact and diffusion, other things being controlled, have obtained support:

1. "If diffusion is to occur, contact must be long enough to get the new response tried out and rewarded" (Miller & Dollard, 1941:264).
2. "Short or inadequate contact seems likely to favor imperfect transmission of a trait" (Miller & Dollard, 1941: 264). This suggests a diffusion-developmental phenomenon analogous to incomplete socialization in the teaching-learning realm.
3. The longer and presumably more frequent and intense the contact, the greater the diffusion. This seems implicit in such statements as "when two societies are in long-continued contact... sooner or later the entire culture of each will be made available to the other" (Linton, 1936:337).
4. Although the *valence* (in Lewinian terms) of the contact will affect the diffusion, diffusion can nonetheless occur from any type of contact, not merely from friendly interaction (Herskovits, 1969:531).
5. Contacts are almost always reciprocal in the sense that cultural diffusion flows in both directions. Although we are ethnocentrically prone to conceive the flow as unilateral, advanced Western nations, for example, have been strongly influenced by the less advanced, non-Western nations from the days of discovery to the present. Much of our food, dress, and even philosophy has diffused from less developed to more developed cultures (Herskovits, 1969: 482, 532).
6. Weak or resistant links in the chain of intercultural communication may interrupt the process. "A group which is reluctant to take over a new trait interposes a bar between the origin point of that trait and more remote groups which might be quite willing to accept it given the opportunity" (Linton, 1936:331). One thus needs to note the influence of what might be called *buffer groups*.

Much more attention has been devoted to the orientational aspects of cultural diffusion. In this realm, the diffusionists have independently suggested many principles that correspond quite closely to theories of attitudinal change in social psychology. For instance, they are emphatic in stressing the *selectivity* present in all cultural diffusion. In Malinowski's (1927:41) words, "Whenever one culture 'borrows' from another, it always transforms and readapts the object or custom borrowed."

The diffusionists have also used implicit notions of cognitive structure, consistency, and centrality in emphasizing the *compatibility* of the innovation with the established customs, habits, and orientations of the recipients. In this connection, they have suggested the useful distinction between competing habits and incompatible habits. The former are cultural habits that are reasonably effective in satisfying the drive that the innovation also satisfies; hence they retard or prevent diffusion. The latter are habits that are directly repugnant to the innovation and so inhibit diffusion. If power figures, for instance, obtain part of their influence from the institution of ancestor worship, they may resist Christianity despite the modern gifts and medical aid that attend it (Miller & Dollard, 1941: 257–258).

Among the characteristics of source and message that markedly affected diffusion are the "agents" involved. If the main intercultural contacts were through males in a hunting context, then one could predict certain inclusions and exclusions in the content of mutual influence. Contacts involving traders, missionaries, economists, officials, or military men likewise have their biases: each type "can transmit no more of his culture than he himself knows" (Linton, 1936:336). Moreover, the *prestige* of the source was discovered to be significant. The higher the prestige, the greater the diffusion. Wanting to be like the donor is a critical aspect of diffusion in many instances. Some diffusionists found it useful to distinguish two types of prestige—that of the culture represented by the agent and that of the agent himself (his status).

The power relations between cultures and between agent and recipient have also been noted as significant, again without much elaboration. It has been suggested, however, that *dominance* probably inhibits diffusion more than it helps (Herskovits, 1969:534). Finally, it is suggested that general *similarity* in a wide range of habits between donor and recipient facilitates the diffusion of all practices between them.

The content of the message or invention was also stressed by the diffusionists. In this domain they attached particular significance to such features as its *complexity*, *communicability*, and *utility*, in addition to its compatibility and other characteristics already mentioned. They noted that "while elements of culture may be diffused alone they are more likely to travel in groups of elements which are functionally related" (Linton, 1936:332). In fact, it was common to observe that recipients often did not grasp the dynamic or logic of their borrowing. Almost opposite to the idea of incomplete diffusion is that of inexorable diffusion—the notion that borrowing one element of a functionally related package sets up strong pressures toward borrowing or developing the others.

The diffusionists also hinted at some interesting psychic processes of the recipient. Kroeber employed the idea of "stimulus diffusion," for example, referring to a situation where a concrete practice encounters resistance but the more general pattern it reflects does not. A culture might desire writing but not the particular form held up by the diffuser, or it might be impressed by animal husbandry but not the particular animals husbanded. Europeans were impressed with Chinese porcelain but not with its cost, so they were led to invent the process for themselves—an unlikely occurrence if they had not known the Chinese model.

Many developing societies today explicitly yearn for a similar process regarding industrialization and economic development. Somehow they would like to borrow the underlying pattern but cast it into a form more congenial to their culture. Unfortunately, this attractive idea often turns out to be naive because they wishfully misread the pattern of economic development or their own culture and ignore stubborn incompatibilities and adjustments.

Inventions adopted by other cultures may have *catalytic* qualities for the recipients. They are not, as Boas noted, merely mechanical additions to the existing culture; rather they stimulate processes of internal development that may far transcend the original innovation. An example is the adoption of printing or firearms in Europe. If this is true, of course, the policymaker and theoretician would dearly love to locate specific seminal practices that would stimulate self-sustaining growth.

Cultural anthropologists probably more than any other analysts also called attention to the phenomenon of *resistance* to change. For example, African peoples such as the Masai of Kenya and Tanganyika, the Pakot from the same general area, and the Bakongo of Congo and Angola have been cited as groups extremely resistant to change while other peoples, such as the Ibo of Nigeria, are extremely flexible, adaptable, and responsive. This resistance is due in part to the difficulty of the habitat. A very marginal existence in a very demanding environment, such as that of the Nuer in Africa, the Paiute in Utah and Nevada, the Eskimos, or the Australian aborigines, makes it perilous to experiment or take any risks at all, and the culture reflects this situation.

The wide differences in acceptance of change by various cultures are not solely attributable to the hostility of the environment, however. Some anthropologists feel that in certain instances resistance has become customary and was originally provoked by bad experiences with earlier copying. In other cultures this resistance has even become institutionalized in contra-acculturative movements (Herskovits, 1969:531). The American Indian ghost dance, some aspects of the African labor movement, and the Gandhian cottage industry movement in India are mentioned as examples.

Sometimes resitance to change is regarded as the normal cultural and human reaction, with heightened acceptance of change being the anomalous characteristic that calls for special explanation. When an explanation for a culture's being relatively change-prone is attempted, it usually is in terms of opportunity for more varied and rapid interchange with other cultures (see, e.g., Heine-Geldern, 1968:172).

A few writers consider stages and sequences in the diffusion process, usually suggesting three stages such as exposure, establishment, dissemination; or presentation, acceptance, and integration. These should be compared with the five-stage sequence of the sociologists discussed in the next subsection. The distinctions of awareness, early adoption ("innovation"), and full or substantial adoption are found in all discussions.

The anthropological diffusionists commented at length on the sporadic and irregular qualities of diffusion, suggesting that any acceptable explanation would have to account for these characteristics (Linton, 1936:331; Kroeber, 1944:838–840). Implicit in some treatments are again the notions of context, critical sizes, and bandwagon effects. They argued the significance of reassurance for adopters from the mere numbers of other adopters, along with the negative effects of the "wrong" group's being an early adopter. Finally, they also were quite sensitive to dissonance-like effects from recognized prior behavior.

Altogether, then, we see that among the "diffusionists" from cultural anthropology —beginning with Boas and Ratzel after the turn of the century and Graebner in 1911, through Wissler, Dixon, and Kroeber in the 1920s, Linton, Lowie, and others in the 1930s, and Herskovits and many others in the 1940s (not all of whom were "diffusionists," strictly speaking)—there emerged a treatment of cultural interchange that anticipated or developed independently many of the notions also stressed by later analysts in other disciplines, including communication research. (More recent anthropological work of a similar nature is summarized in Foster, 1962; Niehoff & Anderson, 1964; and Arensberg & Niehoff, 1971).

Sociological Studies of the Diffusion of Innovations. Meanwhile, back on the farm, rural sociologists were also becoming interested in the diffusion of innovations and were developing their own theories about the process, while their nonrural brethren focused on the spread of new drugs among physicians, new tastes among audiences, and attempts to mold political opinions. This research has been well summarized elsewhere (Lionberger, 1960; Rogers, 1962; Katz, 1968) and is also treated at various other places in this volume, so merely the highlights will be presented here.

The starting point for most of the hundreds of rural sociological studies of diffusion has been the collection of reports on when various specific agricultural practices and devices were actually adopted by farmers living in small, well-defined communities. Such data display a remarkably consistent pattern in many kinds of societies and for many kinds of innovations. When graphically depicted, plotting the cumulative number or percentage of adoptions against time, they form the classic S curve. This is to say that the rate of adoption starts off slowly, increases fairly rapidly, then slacks off again asymptotically as ceiling effects occur. Looked at another way, when the absolute (noncumulative) number of people who adopted within each distinct time period is plotted, the resulting curve is approximately normal or bell-shaped. Few people adopt very early, few very late, and most fall in the middle.

Using the basic statistical measures of the mean and standard deviation, this approximately normal distribution can be divided into various adopter categories. The earliest $2\frac{1}{2}$ percent of adopters (i.e., those more than two standard deviations in the earlier direction from the mean length of time for adoption) are labeled "innovaters"; they are simply the very first people to adopt the specific practice under investigation. The next $13\frac{1}{2}$ percent (those between two and one standard deviations earlier than the mean) are called the "early adopters"; the 34 percent between one standard deviation early and the mean are called the "early majority." The counterpart 34 percent on the other side of the mean are called the "late majority"; and the final 16 percent (symmetrical to the "innovators" and "early adopters") are called the "laggards."

One main thrust of diffusion research in sociology has been to identify the characteristics, if any, that distinguish each of these adopter groups from the others. Earlier adopters differ from later adopters in personal characteristics, communications behavior, and social structural position. In personal differences, earlier adopters are usually younger, of higher social status, better off financially, engaged in more specialized operations, and better able to handle abstractions than are later adopters. Peasant innovators in particular are characterized by greater literacy, mass media exposure, empathy, social status, achievement motivation, occupational and education aspirations, "cosmopoliteness," farm size, and contact with extension agents. These characteristics tend to increase or decrease consistently as one moves across the adopter range (Rogers, 1962:172–192; 1969:296–299).

In terms of communication behavior, the earlier adopters are distinguished by their greater use of the mass media, by their use of more communication channels, and by their *relatively* reduced use of direct interpersonal channels. Innovators and early adopters are more cosmopolitan and are more likely to be opinion leaders than are later adopters.

Most of these findings seem to apply in the developing world as well as the developed world with one major exception. In Rogers' study of several relatively modern and relatively traditional Colombian villages, he found that the innovators were opinion leaders in the more modern villages; in the more traditional communities, where the innovators were very much more modern than their fellow villagers, they were accorded relatively little opinion leadership. In general, many diffusion studies suggest a picture of the underlying power-communication process that shows the innovator as an individual with comparatively strong communication links to more modern sectors outside his community. He may or may not have a conspicuously large opinion leadership domain himself, but in the more progressive community the innovators are either powerful themselves or at least linked to early adopters who are disproportionately influential in the community.

The distance in modernity of the innovator from the remainder of the community, especially from persons with power, appears to be a crucial factor. If he is not very distant at all, his influence and communication contacts may be quite good, but his capacity for moving the community in a developmental direction is slight. On the other hand, if he is notably more modern than his powerful neighbors in the community, he may have a great potential for developmental guidance but be so far out as to lose his power and communication links.

In Turkey's villages, for example, Frey

and Roos (1967) found that the village headman exemplified the former case: he was in an excellent structural position in the village, but he was so little different from the rest of the villagers, even though he was usually slightly more modern, that he could exert no real influence for development. The county prefect, on the other hand, was in the opposite position—so much different from the villagers that his ability to communicate with them and lead them was negligible.

The other main thrust of the diffusion studies of rural sociologists has been to confirm and elaborate the psychological stages of the overall adoption decision for the individual decision-maker (Lionberger, 1960; Rogers, 1962). Five such stages are usually conceived: awareness, interest, evaluation, trial, and acceptance. Furthermore, different communication channels and sources are primarily associated with various stages. The most basic finding is that the mass media are reported as influential mainly in the awareness stage. After that, interpersonal communication with close associates seems to be the predominant factor in the adoption of these discrete innovations.

The main contribution of the nonrural sociologists also working on the diffusion of innovations and opinions has been the stress on interpersonal networks of communication (Lazarsfeld, Berelson & Gaudet, 1944; Katz & Lazarsfeld, 1955; Coleman, Katz, & Menzel, 1957; Klapper, 1960). It was initially found that mass communications were quite ineffective in inducing attitudinal change, which was actually rather rare. When such change did occur, it was apparently most often the result of direct interpersonal contacts with trusted others. In general, a two-step flow of communication and influence was posited—from the media to opinion leaders and from opinion leaders to the masses via personal interaction.

More recently, the model has been perceived to be an oversimplification and various corrections have been offered (Van den Ban, 1964; Troldahl, 1966; Arndt, 1968; Katz, 1968:178–180; Lin, 1969; Rogers, 1969:221–222). These include allowance for direct media effects as well as for mediated effects, for lateral communication among mass elements, for greater complementarity between mass media and interpersonal communication, for more reciprocity in the leader-follower relationship, for multiple steps rather than two, and so on. Actually, the two-step flow model "as applied to the diffusion of information, best fits developing areas," according to Katz (1968:181).

Various reasons have been suggested for the greater effectiveness of direct interpersonal communication as opposed to the mass media, including its two-way flow, flexibility, immediate reward or punishment, and use of more proximate and trustworthy sources. It is also pointed out, however, that the interpersonal network tends to be predominantly conservative in most settings and so a doubtful instrument for development if left alone. Looked at from either end of the chain—the mass media or personal communication—it seems there is marked advantage in coordinating the two systems rather than trying to use either unsupported by the other.

Until recently, almost all investigations of innovation diffusion focused on very specific practices adopted over rather short time spans or on media and political campaigns. Whether the essential model developed will apply to larger, more long-run, and more complex innovations in other areas of life remains to be seen. The research has also concentrated heavily on individuals in relatively small communities or closed systems. This has been a sage strategy to get a leg up on the problem without being swamped or intimidated by extremely large and complicated social systems. However, one feels that as an explanation of development or modernization, the approach is much too piecemeal. There would seem to be a veritable gulf between the diffusion of 2-4D fertilizer or knowledge of the United Nations and the modernization of a society. How the small pieces fit together into the societal picture may be the most challenging problem of all.

Spatial Models of Diffusion. Probably the most careful, sophisticated, and imaginative attempt to reduce and focus the plethora of diffusion research has been made by Torsten Hagerstrand (1965; 1967; 1968). As a geographer, Hagerstrand became interested in the spatial aspect of diffusion and undertook a detailed inspection. He concentrated on a semirural area and on a number of different innovations for which good data over time were available. Among these innovations were the control of bovine tuberculosis, soil mapping, an agricultural subsidy, postal-checking service, automobile ownership, and telephone subscription. The empirical approach employed can be likened to time-lapse photography of, say, the unfolding of a flower, with one frame being taken every day. Hagerstrand, through maps and historical data, could watch how an innovation suffused over an area—how it flowed or failed to flow from one part of the region to another.

The spread of most innovations that Hagerstrand inspected featured a rather slow start, more rapid acceleration, and then a tailing-off, as one would have predicted from the S curves of prior research. However, the spatial picture added other dimensions. The innovations tended to spread concentrically. A fairly clear boundary between the zone of adoption and the unreached zone existed in most cases. And the outward spread was accompanied by an intensification or increase in the density of adoptions at the core.

Hagerstrand argued that the various adopter characteristics that had been stressed up to then by rural sociologists did not seem to explain this type of pattern. His analyses showed a marked neighborhood or proximity effect—a clustering that was not paralleled by personal or economic characteristics. Hagerstrand, moreover, took his task to be not that of unearthing more factors bearing some statistically significant relationship to adoption but rather of finding a few more basic and powerful explanatory variables. He posed the problem of finding the simplest "model" that could be developed to generate an innovational sequence with the same characteristics he had found empirically. In response, using Monte Carlo simulation techniques in a pioneering way, he constructed three important models that were increasingly similar to his data yet retained their strong parsimony and displayed profound insight and ingenuity.

Model 1 involved the following basic assumptions: (1) that there existed an innovation of exogenous origin; (2) that awareness of this innovation was necessary for acceptance; (3) that all actors in the system were so aware; (4) that all adoption decisions were individually autonomous; and (5) that, therefore, the course of the growth curve need not be considered. He set up a theoretic space of 81 cells (9×9), intended to correspond to a 25 km.^{2} geographic area. He peopled this space evenly with thirty simulated persons per cell. The process in Model 1 was simply randomly to allocate 1 through 200 acceptances cumulatively to this population. Model 1 might be called a simple random diffusion model. It afforded an opportunity to ask whether the observed pattern could have occurred by chance of this type.

Perhaps surprisingly for some, the answer was in part affirmative. The random process did generate some characteristic agglomeration or clustering, and Hagerstrand notes how common and easy it would be to suggest various "reasons" why these patterns had to be, even though they were quite random. As a matter of fact, either a completely egalitarian pattern with no clustering or a completely hierarchial pattern with complete agglomeration would be the rarity, and some degree of agglomeration is the likely chance pattern.

On the other hand, Model 1 did not match the empirical data well in important respects. In the late stages of the diffusion process it managed a fairly good fit, but in the early stages it was quite dissimilar, being far too evenly distributed. It did not show the sharp boundaries, secondary agglomerations, and simultaneous central condensation of the real data. The model needed adjustment if it were to do better. Two basic types of adjustment were thought fruitful: (1) a receptiveness-resistance variable or (2) a variable allowing for uneven information or awareness. In the end, both adjustments were made.

In Model 2, Hagerstrand developed a more truly communication-oriented simulation. As a foundation, he drew a distinction between "public" and "private" information. Public information seems to involve an actor's communicating to a majority of the other actors in his group without an intermediary's altering the content. Private information occurs when an actor communicates to one other actor (Hagerstrand, 1967:138–139). More loosely, private information tends to connote direct, dyadic, face-to-face communication, and it becomes the focus for Hagerstrand's analysis. Indeed, Hagerstrand (1965:263) has said that "dissemination through private or group conversation easily outbalances other means of communication. Even today we are very neolithic in that respect..."

Model 2 employs the following assumptions: (1) only one person is initially aware of the exogenous innovation; (2) awareness means adoption; (3) awareness is forwarded by private (not public) communication; (4) decisions are not autonomous; and (5) private communication occurs with a constant time interval. In operation, Model 2 also assumed that awareness is always communicated and produces awareness. Hence, the model started with the communication from the one initially informed person to a person in his "private information field" and proceeded similarly from there, in steps, with one dyadic communication from each aware person at each step.

Model 2, in two versions, provided an improved fit with the data, correcting many of the faults of Model 1. It showed the appropriate clustering or "neighborhood effects"; it revealed the importance (in a stochastic sense) of the "initial scatter"; and more importantly it displayed a "blockage effect" whereby those who commence the diffusion process are soon limited to ineffective contacts, since the density of adopters at the core is so great there is no one left to convert. In such a process lies the reason for the asymptotic tail-off of the S curve as near saturation is reached.

Model 2 also manifested some unrealistic characteristics. The empirical data displayed a slower start for the diffusion process than the model, and the center in the model needed to approach saturation more rapidly vis-à-vis outward expansion.

Model 3, also in two versions, made the final change in this direction incorporating a receptivity-resistance variable. Hagerstrand reasoned that although he did not know the actual distribution of resistance, he was willing to make certain plausible assumptions about its shape and range. He felt that it should be normally distributed. He also was willing to assume that the range was half an order of magnitude. Using these assumptions and his Monte Carlo techniques he randomly assigned resistances to his simulated population. Model 3, thus constructed, yielded the best fit of all to the empirical data.

Several important relationships were suggested between resistance and the spatial distribution of diffusion. For example, it seemed that the higher the resistance in an area, the greater the spatial concentration of diffusion. Or, the lower the resistance, the shorter the introductory phase of the diffusion process. These are quite plausible hypotheses once they are stated, but they are less easily arrived at without the assistance of the model. Overall, it is impressive how a limited, almost purely communications model of this type can accord so well with observed patterns of innovation diffusion and can be so suggestive for developmental analysis in general.

General Communication Theories of Development

The diffusion theories attempt to model or explain the spread of social changes once these are invented. As noted, they do this primarily in terms of two types of variables: communication contacts and psychological orientations. Sometimes selected economic and community characteristics are also introduced, although these are often psychologically mediated. The main emphasis, however, has been on communication networks and individual attitudes.

There also exist a few more general communication theories of development that purport to probe even more deeply into the role of communication in modernization. This is done through explaining current communication contacts as a function of previous contacts and through explaining the psychological orientations relevant to both diffusion and invention as a function of communication. The more general communication theories of development address various aspects of these fundamental relationships.

Lerner's Theory. Probably the most influential theory of this type has been proposed by Daniel Lerner (1957; 1958). There is a provocative communications core to the theory plus a penumbra of other theoretical suggestions that are related but less clearly elaborated. At the core, the theory describes the process of modernization in terms of four variables: urbanization, literacy, mass media exposure, and "participation." The first three variables have standard meanings, but the fourth, "participation," is somewhat elusive. Lerner (1958:71) employs the "traditional-transitional-modern" continuum, regarding modernization as "the transition to a participant society." "Participation" is described to include political participation (voting, making personal decisions on public issues), economic participation (increased per capita income, market activity), communication participation (expressing opinions, attending to the media), psychological participation (empathy, psychic mobility), etc. In general, it appears to be assumed that these various forms of "participation" all cohere—i.e., are strongly and positively linked—and that all figure similarly in the essential modernization process.

Lerner's fundamental thesis is expressed in two key passages of *The Passing of Traditional Society*. The first, more brief and simple exposition states that "everywhere . . . increasing urbanization has tended to raise literacy; rising literacy has tended to increase media exposure; increasing media exposure has 'gone with' wider economic participation (per capita income) and political participation (voting)" (Lerner, 1958:46). Expressed this way, the hypothesis takes the following simple schematic form:

$$U \rightarrow L \rightarrow M \rightarrow P.$$

Later in the book, this suggestion is complicated somewhat. Urbanization still causes increased literacy which, in turn, increases mass media exposure, but this mass media exposure feeds back to increase literacy in what Lerner (1958:60) styles "a supply-and-demand reciprocal in the communication market . . ." Hence, the more complicated core hypothesis can be schematically represented as follows:

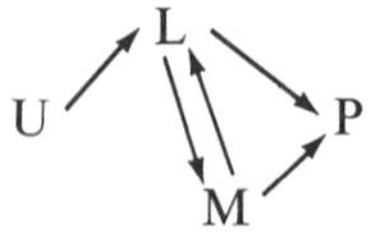

L
U P
M

(Empirical evidence from aggregate data for and against these relationships will be discussed in the following section.)

These basic hypotheses are qualified somewhat in Lerner's fuller discussion. The shift of population from rural to urban settings triggers the "take-off" toward widespread participation only after about

10 percent urbanization. The strong influence of urbanization on literacy then continues until an upper threshold of about 25 percent urbanization is reached, after which urbanization again plays no determinant role. Similar threshold characteristics are envisioned for literacy as well, although they are less precisely stated. One can interpret Lerner (1958:62), however, to have designated the two thresholds of about 40 percent literate and nearly complete literacy that other research (e.g., Bowman & Anderson, 1962) has found developmentally significant.

Lerner's characterization of the predominant public communication systems of the ideal-typical traditional and modern societies is shown in Table 8.

The direction of social change in this respect has always been from the oral system to the media system, never the reverse, according to Lerner, although the degree of change is correlated with changes in other key sectors of society. Especially important are the political change from a "designative" to an electoral polity, from an illiterate to a literate culture, and from a rural to an urban socioeconomic system; the specifics of these interactions are not given, however.

Once people have learned from their rural-urban mobility and from their literacy and mass media exposure to handle the new experiences thereby presented, "they now seek satisfactions which integrate these skills" (Lerner, 1958:62). To satisfy new desires for improvement, novelty, diversity, and challenge, they require empathy, which in turn transforms their life-styles and their reactions to new communication experiences.

One of the great attractions of Lerner's analysis compared with most developmental theories is that he operates at both the macroanalytic and microanalytic levels. Parallel to his description of what occurs at the societal level in modernization is an analysis of what modernization means at the individual level. The modern participant society is seen to require modern participant human beings. A characterological change is necessary for modernization, not merely institutional changes superimposed on unaltered individuals.

The modern man who creates modern society is seen as most distinctively different in mental flexibility and involvement with his environment, especially his social environment. He has a "mobile personality" distinguished by a high capacity for accommodating change, by a high degree of empathy (the ability to envision oneself in another's role), and by a tendency to have opinions on many public matters that are unheeded by traditional folk. He also tends to be future oriented and to have augmented desires coupled with the belief that something can be done to realize many of his aspirations. In all these respects he has the antithesis of the "constrictive personality" of traditional man.

Despite the refreshing attention to both

TABLE 8

TYPES OF PUBLIC COMMUNICATION SYSTEMS PREDOMINATING IN IDEAL-TYPICAL SOCIETIES

Communication Aspect	Traditional (Oral) System	Modern (Media) System
Channel	Personal (face-to-face)	Broadcast (mediated)
Audience	Primary (groups)	Heterogeneous (mass)
Content	Prescriptive (rules)	Descriptive (news)
Source	Hierarchical (status)	Professional (skill)

SOURCE: Lerner (1958:55).

microanalytic and macroanalytic levels, it is rather difficult to put all the pieces together and establish a comprehensive communications interpretation of development at both the societal and individual levels. The role of empathy in the developmental process perceived by Lerner provides an important example of this problem. In the macroanalytic formulation it appears that empathy is a form of "participation" produced by prior developments in urbanization, literacy, and the mass media—the key antecedent variables. An empathic populace is the final hallmark of modernity. Thus, Lerner (1958:50) states that "it is a major hypothesis that high empathic capacity is the predominant personal style only in modern society, which is distinctively industrial, urban, literate and participant." On the other hand, his survey data from the Near East produced the typology for individual modernization shown in Table 9.

Thus we see that apparently the initial and "easiest" step in the process of individual modernization is the acquisition of the requisite degree of empathy. The macro and micro pictures are reversed. Empathy seems to come *before* urbanization, literacy, and media exposure at the individual level, whereas in the more aggregated analysis it seems to be the *result* of those factors.

Actually, Lerner's analytic gaze is wider than even the ambitious core model suggests. In various parts of his discussions he sketches additional features of the developmental process and the role of communication therein. Of particular interest is his attempt to peer beyond the immediately triggering urbanization variable and suggest factors that stimulate its initial growth. Two main comments are offered. One maintains that urbanization cannot be regarded merely as a certain density of population. Urbanization and density have quite different effects. Urbanization critically increases literacy whereas density, unless counteracted, usually is an "antiliteracy force." Moreover, at the societal level, urbanization is negatively related to the "man-land ratio" (Lerner, 1958:66). Rather, urbanization, through some unelaborated qualities of its own and not mere density of population, is the intervening variable that transforms density from a negative to a positive factor relative to literacy and modernity (Lerner, 1958:66).

The second intriguing comment urges that the modernization process, sweepingly conceived, commenced with the increased physical mobility that occurred in the West many generations ago when "ordinary men found themselves unbound from their native soil and relatively free to move" (Lerner, 1958:47). This physical mobility, presumably resulting from the demise of serfdom and the discovery of new worlds, engendered social and psychic mobility, according to Lerner. Gradually, institutions more appropriate to these processes developed and a system of social values "that embraced change as normal" was produced.

TABLE 9

A Typology for Individual Modernization

Personality Type	Literate	Urban	Exposed to Media	Empathic	Opinion Range
Modern	+	+	+	+	1
Transitional A	—	+	+	+	2
Transitional B	—	—	+	+	3
Transitional C	—	—	—	+	4
Traditional	—	—	—	—	5

Source: Lerner (1958:71).

Both the additional comments contrasting urbanization and mere density of population and those linking physical mobility with psychic mobility should be noted because they implicitly reveal an important and even more general conception underlying Lerner's work.

Variations on Lerner's Theme. Subsequent research into the relationship between communication and development has been profoundly influenced by Lerner's perspective. One reaction has been to refine and elaborate various aspects of the theory (e.g., Rogers, 1969). Another has been to formalize and check the suggested core interrelationships against aggregate data (Alker, 1966; McCrone & Cnudde, 1967; these are discussed in the next section). Finally, Frey (1966; 1971) has endeavored to generalize the Lerner model still further and to eliminate some of the internal inconsistencies mentioned above, especially at the microlevel.

Frey's (1963b) efforts originated with a national sample survey of the Turkish peasantry. This large scale study suggested that literacy and mass media exposure were indeed the relatively powerful factors for individual modernization that Lerner had maintained (Frey, 1966). Physical mobility also was associated with attitudinal modernity, though weakly if literacy and media exposure were controlled. Other research in the same society indicated that urban residence exerted a similar influence, while more detailed analysis through the peasant data of specific media revealed that newspaper, radio, and cinema exposure almost always worked in the same attitudinal direction.

An inventory of similar studies in other societies generally corroborated these findings. Altogether, the evidence showed that clear, independent, and relatively strong associations existed between certain social background variables such as literacy, mass media exposure, education, physical mobility, occupational change, and urban residence on the one hand, and indicators of attitudinal modernity, knowledge, empathy, tolerance of deviant behavior, innovativeness, etc. on the other.[16]

Pondering such evidence, Frey was led to the obvious question: What if anything do these variables have in common that would produce such effects? What if anything do the effects have in common? Considering Lerner's core model and particularly its subsequent emendations, the question might be more specifically put: What do physical mobility, urbanization, literacy, and media exposure have in common that would produce empathy and psychic mobility? On analysis, certain plausible answers to these queries seem to form an integrated communication theory of at least one crucial aspect of the developmental process.

Frey's (1971) essential hypothesis synthesizes the numerous variables of previous analyses into two very general and abstract factors: *exposure to change* and *cognitive flexibility.* What urbanization, literacy, mass media exposure, physical mobility, education, and such variables have in common from a developmental perspective is that they tend to constitute exposure to change for the individual. What empathy, innovativeness, tolerance of deviant behavior, open-mindedness, attitudinal modernity, and even knowledge to some degree have in common is that they are manifestations of cognitive flexibility. While this is not all there is to development by any means, the functional relationship

[16] This research also assuaged some, although certainly not all, of the doubts about the measurement of empathy. Lerner's evidence at the individual level relied heavily on peasant "don't know" responses (sometimes quite graphic) to questions asking them to project to another role, such as president of the republic or the head of the state radio. The problem here is that such questions may merely tap lack of *knowledge* of that role rather than lack of *empathy.* In the Turkish peasant study, questions for which knowledge could be presumed to be a negligible factor were also asked, and the "don't know" group for these items again emerged as meaningfully different from other comparable respondents.

of these two factors lies at the heart of the process of individual modernization.

Although the details are somewhat different, in principle cognitive flexibility seems to refer to the same capacities that Lerner had in mind with his concept of psychic mobility. Empathy is just one aspect of cognitive flexibility, which includes the capacity for learning new practices, adjusting to new situations, abandoning old ideas, etc., as well as projecting oneself into the role of another. Measuring cognitive flexibility requires one to assess the facility with which different individuals perform a given amount of cognitive structural alteration, although technically it becomes extremely subtle since the amount of alteration required by any specific change depends for each individual on his existing cognitive structure.

Exposure to change refers to the amount of subjectively perceptible change per some time unit that occurs in the individual's environment. Environments differ sharply in this respect. Generally, the most salient characteristic of traditional villages is their *static* quality. Were Julius Caesar or Hammurabi to visit the more backward Near Eastern villages today, for example, he would find things quite familiar. While the changes of the individual life cycle of course occur universally (and even these are minimal in traditional villages compared with more modern cultures), the environing culture and community have largely remained the same over the millennia. Very little exposure to change occurs for the typical adult peasant in such an environment. By contrast, however, the urban professional in a modern society is almost inundated by change in his environment, and Julius Caesar or Hammurabi would be bowled over by the difference between the world he knew and the modern world. In fact, one now has to go back but three generations to be certain of obtaining a resurrected ancestor who would find today's world filled with astounding change. Change is the essence of modern life, and modern man is constantly confronted by it. The exposure-to-change variable refers to this type of continuum.

The fundamental relationship between the two variables is depicted in Figure 7. The basic contention is that there exists a reciprocal relationship between cognitive flexibility and exposure to change.

Frey (1971:265–272) has mapped the critical features of this relationship. There is a lower threshold, called the *impingement point*, below which change occurs in the environment so rarely and irregularly that it produces no significant psychic reaction. Rather, the change simply appears unexpectedly and adventitiously, more an act of the gods or fates than an expected and manageable aspect of the environment. This is generally the case in extremely traditional villages, whose peasants are psychologically unprepared for change and tend to find it quite repugnant, individually and culturally.

When change (i.e., a qualitatively different experience) does begin to appear frequently and markedly enough to produce a psychic reaction, as in the initial stages of development, the acceptance of change is extremely low. It is the dilemma of development that the resistance to change is strongest just when the forces pressing for change are likely to be weakest. One would therefore expect the oft-noted "vicious circle" aspect of development.

With increased exposure to change, the individual seems to make the psychic adjustments necessary to take change more in stride. He becomes more agile in cognitive restructuring, learns to anticipate and predict change, and develops a repertory of strategies for dealing with it. He even comes to find emotional gratification and challenge in its variety, and would balk at any return to a static environment. Sending cognitively flexible people back to the villages is regarded by them as near penal servitude in most developing societies. Incidentally, one of the prominent developmental functions of the mass media is to provide a window to the larger and more stimulating external world for such

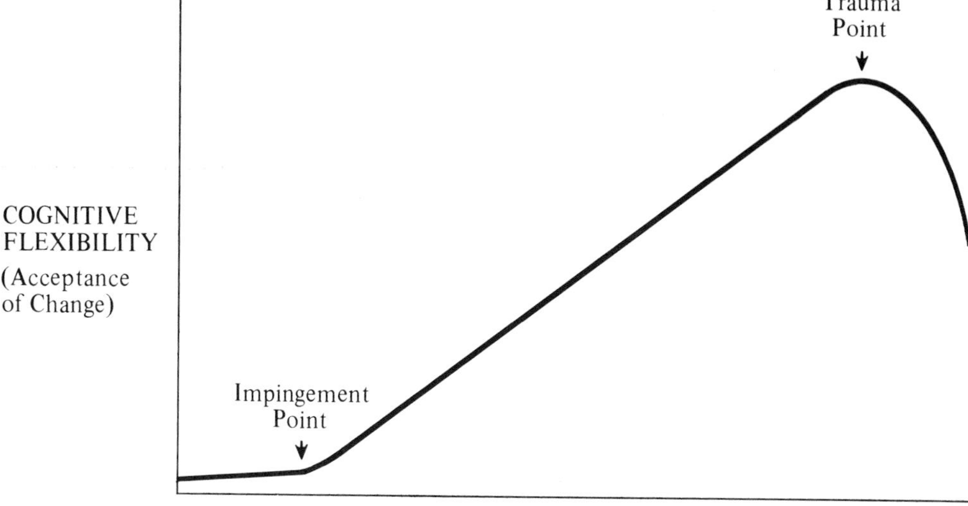

Figure 7. Hypothesized relationship between cognitive flexibility and exposure to change.

village-bound developmental agents (see, e.g., Makal, 1954; Fraenkel, 1959).

There seems to be also an upper threshold in the relationship between exposure to change and cognitive flexibility. Beyond this point change floods in on the individual faster than he can handle it and the acceptance of added increments of change drops precipitously. We call this the *trauma point*.

The best analogy for understanding these relationships is to regard the mind as a muscle. It needs exercise to develop. With only minimal exercise it languishes and finds any exertion beyond its narrow normal limits quite unpleasant. Work that others may accomplish relatively easily requires inordinate effort. With regular and varied exercise, however, its capacities increase. Nonetheless, at any given moment those capacities have limits; if the muscle is overtaxed and subjected to too great a strain it will collapse and be injured, thus reducing its capacities below their immediate pretrauma level.

From this perspective, the objective of modernization is to raise the trauma level of the individual or system—to expand the system's capacities for handling change or to increase cognitive flexibility in the case of the individual. This is done by creating an environment that challenges the individual, that moves him very near the trauma threshold but not over it. It is done by subjecting the individual to increased exposure to change, without swamping him.

Communication advances development when, in addition to furnishing information, it provides appropriate exposure to change. Hence, the communications that an individual receives must be examined developmentally, not from the viewpoint of their number or absolute content but from the viewpoint of the amount of change that they bring to the particular audience involved.

Such an hypothesis explains the exceptions as well as the basic tendencies in the mass communication data. The mass media, for instance, are not always associated with development. As noted, they may be either a narcotic or a stimulant, depending on the factors mentioned above. The media may disseminate the most jejune and hackneyed fare (by sophisticated standards) and still be a strong source of individual development in a culture that has not encountered these messages before. On the other hand, quite sophisticated messages may have little or no developmental impact in a media-saturated society that has heard them many times.

Similarly, the city may promote individual modernization for the villager who partakes of its diversity and difference but may have scant impact on the "urban villager" who settles into a tight enclave not basically different from his original community. The factory may be a stimulating modernization school for inexperienced villagers but a deadening rut for the man who has spent twenty years on the assembly line (Inkeles, 1966b; 1969). Finally, in all these cases exposure to change may result in an actual worsening of developmental prospects if the trauma point is passed and the individual is confronted with more change than he can handle.

One should note that this basic hypothesis jibes with work in very diverse areas and makes sense out of scraps of evidence or relatively unintegrated suggestions from various quarters. For example, it accords well with recent work on class differences in cognitive development, where perhaps the main finding has been that middle-class families furnish a more stimulating environment—but not overly stimulating—for their infants and toddlers (Pines, 1969). It accords well with such facts as the clustering of geniuses in time and space, the sporadic characteristics of development, and the urban-cosmopolitan base of most great civilizations. It seems no accident that cultural advances have occurred primarily in cities with heterogeneous and interacting populations and in other "crossroads" situations. Even originally "it was the opportunity for relatively rapid interchange of inventions and ideas between a number of local cultures that made possible the birth of the oldest civilizations in the Near East" (Heine-Geldern, 1968:172).

The nature of the crucial differences between urbanization and density would also seem to be suggested by this hypothesis. These differences are two. First, urbanization is much more likely than is mere density to produce increased communication among people (because of proximity and collective goals); second, it is also more likely to produce communication among heterogeneous people—people who are different enough to expose each other to change, but not so different as to preclude communication.

In general, this basic communication model of development suggests that modernization can be fruitfully analyzed as a special kind of learning experience. Indeed, the cognitive flexibility/exposure-to-change curve is very similar to S-shaped learning curves, and the exposure-to-change hypothesis provides an explanation of observed occupational variations in the age of eventual decline in learning capacities. Other writers (Simon, 1957b:261–278; Hirschman, 1958:47–49) have noted the promise of such an approach to development, but its implications have never been very fully worked out. Frey, unfortunately, does not provide detailed empirical support for his hypothesis, since it only emerged after the original data collection.

The two highly abstract variables are very difficult to measure, moreover, because they are not completely independent of one another in the sense that greater cognitive flexibility is presumably associated with an increased tendency to perceive change in any given environment. Also to be taken into account are such important factors as the valence of the changes—i.e., whether they are seen as good or bad by the individual. Finally, the distinction between an orientation toward change per se and the specific qualities of each particular change must be demonstrated. Hence, although the cognitive flexibility/exposure-to-change hypothesis seems powerful and promising, much more thought and evidence are required before it becomes other than an interesting hypothesis.

ANALYSES OF NATIONAL-LEVEL DATA

After World War II there occurred a great growth in analyses of national-level data on various aspects of the developmental process. With the achievement of independence by many former colonies and territories, the number of "nations" in the world available for analysis increased severalfold. Simultaneously, national record-keeping around the world improved, aided by the United Nations. Internationally comparable statistics on gross national product, population, health, literacy, mass media facilities, energy production, transportation, education, urbanization, agriculture, and the like became conspicuously available for the first time. Moreover, scholars interested in the relationship between these economic and social indicators, on one hand, and the political features of nations, on the other, added judgmental ratings of national political systems to the overall picture (Almond & Coleman, 1960; Banks & Textor, 1963). Hence, an essentially new corpus of developmentally relevant data on national units emerged, along with heightened social scientific skills at multivariate analysis of such materials.

Communication and General or Socioeconomic Development

A number of correlational and factor analytic studies of development have been performed with national-level data. Some of the earliest of these dealt with the role of urbanization and literacy (Davis & Golden, 1954; Golden, 1955). Others attempted more general cluster or factor search and discriminant analysis designed to ascertain whether there is an empirical basis for reducing the great variety of variables relevant to modernization into a much smaller set of basic dimensions or even into a single dimension (Berry, 1961; Schnore, 1961; Deutschmann & McNelly, 1964; Russett et al., 1964; Simpson, 1964; Adelman & Morris, 1965; 1967; 1968a; 1968b; Eitzen, 1967; Sawyer, 1967; Russet, 1968). These studies covered sets of nations from all over the world ranging in number from about seventy to ninety-five, as well as separate analyses for twenty Latin American countries and for forty-seven and seventy-four non-Communist developing societies. The number of variables considered ranged from three to over two hundred. The earliest studies employed data from around 1950 while the latest have used data from the early 1960s.

From these correlational and factor analytic studies of national data on general or socioeconomic development one can precipitate the following tentative conclusions relevant to communications and development.

1. National development, by almost any conception, involves the interaction of numerous economic, social (including communication), and political elements. Even when development is defined purely economically, the social elements are quite significant. On the other hand, the situation regarding the political elements is less clear. There is evidence that political participation may be significantly related to economic and social development only at certain stages in the developmental process. Political factors seem sometimes closely associated with and sometimes independent of the socioeconomic developmental process. Hence, political development, defined in terms of expanded participation, may not be guaranteed by socioeconomic or communications development and may instead require distinct and special efforts (Adelman, 1971).

2. Mass media exposure, literacy, and several other communication measures are correlated significantly with most indicators of socioeconomic development. Fairly typical levels of association are displayed in Table 10 taken from Russett et al. (1964).

TABLE 10

CORRELATIONS OF MASS MEDIA EXPOSURE, DOMESTIC MAIL, AND LITERACY WITH SELECTED INDICATORS OF SOCIOECONOMIC DEVELOPMENT, CA. 1955–1960

Communication Variable	GNP/pc[a]	Urban.[b]	Violent Deaths[c]	People per MD[d]	Labor Force in Agric.[e]
Daily newspaper circulation (per 1,000)	0.80	0.69	−0.35	−0.89	−0.81
Radios (per 1,000)	0.85	0.68	−0.38	−0.89	−0.76
Television sets (per 1,000)	0.75	0.54	−0.28	−0.73	−0.75
Cinema attendance per capita	0.65	0.62	−0.25	−0.79	−0.60
Percent literate (15 years and over)	0.80	0.66	−0.37	−0.83	−0.76
Domestic mail per capita	0.89	0.65	−0.55	−0.83	−0.80
Average annual increase radios (per 1,000)	0.63	0.37	−0.26	−0.53	−0.50

SOURCE: Data from Russett et al. (1964: Part B, 261–292).

[a] Gross national product per capita, 1957, U.S. dollars.

[b] Percentage of population in cities of over 20,000 inhabitants.

[c] Deaths from domestic violence per million population, 1950–1962.

[d] Inhabitants per physician.

[e] Percentage of labor force employed in agriculture.

3. Factor analyses of cross-sectional economic, social, and political indicators of development commonly reveal a paramount first factor that includes variables reflecting: level of economic development, communication (mass media exposure, mail, and literacy), transportation, urbanization, industrialization, and welfare (health, housing, etc.). Although some evidence supports a single factor interpretation of development, there is probably more evidence that, along with a predominant first factor, additional orthogonal factors relating to size, type of political system, and perhaps stability versus tension are meaningfully related to national development.

4. Within the socioeconomic factor, communication variables usually occupy a role that superficially seems second in importance only to economic development. At the same time, it is not yet clear whether these communication variables are simply derivative concomitants of more dynamic economic variables with which they are highly correlated or whether they are significant contributors in their own right to socioeconomic development. Sometimes the statistical signs appear to suggest that mass communication is a kind of consumer good produced by development but not strongly causing development (thus similar, essentially, to some of the welfare indicators such as physicians per capita). At other times the statistical signs appear to suggest that mass communication is an important factor of production in its own right, making an essential contribution to development. Existing national-level analyses are not yet adequate to decide among these interpretations or, more probably, to assign some intermediate significance to the role of communication in development.

5. One important consequence of available national-level analyses is that distinctions within the total set of all nations have been shown to be crucial. Several studies, for example, have made compelling use of multinational regions such as Latin America, the Near and Far East, sub-Saharan Africa, and so on. Several studies have also shown the relevance of subgrouping nations into different levels of development, usually three or five. Although it may be

quite dubious to label level categorizations as dynamic "stages" of development, these studies do indicate that one must check the applicability of any models of the developmental process within such subgroupings.

6. Several investigations demonstrate the discrepancy that apparently exists between long-run and short-run findings and, more particularly, between explanations of levels of development and rates of growth. The existing national-level analyses that have explored long-run versus short-run effects give us clear reason not to be content with inferences to developmental processes based solely on long-run investigations of levels of development.

7. The precise role of communication in development, i.e., how communication variables relate causally to other developmental variables, is unclear from these analyses. Some evidence suggests an inextricably enmeshed cluster of variables including communication. Other evidence suggests a possibly crucial causal role for communication, while still other data imply a relatively peripheral, derivative, or insignificant role. Furthermore, the key relationships may change during various stages of the developmental process. Correlational and factor-analytic investigations alone seem inadequate for probing further into the within-factor causal patterns that may exist. On the other hand, it must be regarded as striking that general, economic, and social analyses of this nature have so frequently, if not always, discovered a clear communication component in the developmental syndrome despite the limitations of the indicators employed.

Communication and Political Development

A number of researchers have examined national data in order to comprehend political development, its causes and concomitants. Some of these studies present interesting data relating either to the role of communication in the process of political development or to the effect of political development on communication (Shannon, 1957; 1958; 1959; 1962; Lipset, 1959; Almond & Coleman, 1960; Deutsch, 1961; Cutright, 1963; 1968; Marsh & Parish, 1965; Neubauer, 1967; 1968; Duff & McCamant, 1968; Adelman, 1971).

Unfortunately, it is difficult to extract many clear conclusions concerning the relationships between communication and political development from the literature using national-level data to explore political change. One of the obvious reasons for this uncertainty is the elusiveness of the very concept of political development. Although defined in various ways in the theoretical treatments of modernization, political development, in most statistical analyses, has been operationally equated with increased political participation. This may seem to make the research problem somewhat more manageable (at uncalculated theoretical cost), but such a tactic has not helped much since effective conceptualization and measurement of political participation has proven almost as difficult as that of political development. Nonetheless, a few tentative findings and trends in interpretation are discernible.

1. The early view of political development as strongly related to socioeconomic development—indeed, as part of a highly interdependent single developmental syndrome—has been seriously called into question.
2. While absolute and relative *levels* of socioeconomic development (including communication) are strongly correlated with measures of political participation, *rates* of economic growth and measures of political participation are not significantly correlated among developing nations.
3. There may be an upper threshold of political participation beyond which even *levels* of socioeconomic development (including communication) and political participation are no longer significantly related.
4. Factors other than level of socio-

economic development (including communication), such as region or culture area, also seem to be related to levels of political participation. This is manifested in Lipset's data that show "unstable democracies and dictatorships" in Europe at higher levels of "wealth" than the "stable democracies" of Latin America (cf. Cutright, 1963:254). Similarly, in Coleman's (1960:540) data "authoritarian" systems in Latin America generally show higher socioeconomic development, including communications, than the "semicompetitive" and often the "competitive" systems of Africa and Asia.

5. There are usually weak but statistically significant correlations between many indicators of socioeconomic development (including communication) and self-government among the political entities of the world.
6. Mass communication does not seem to be correlated with the strength of Communist and non-Communist leftist political movements.
7. No clear relationship between mass communication and sociopolitical tension or instability has yet been established using national-level data, although studies such as Adelman (1971) provided opportunity for such findings to emerge.
8. The status of mass communication, either in general or for each of its component elements, as demand-arousing or demand-satisfying (or both) has been queried, but no convincing answer has yet been found in national-level data.

National-Level Analyses of Communication Variables

Thus far we have examined analyses of national-level data that have focused primarily on socioeconomic, political, or general development. Although communication variables figured significantly in each analysis, they were not the central concern. Now we shall turn to analyses of national-level data that focus primarily and directly on communication factors in development (Lerner, 1957; 1958; Nixon, 1960; Greenberg, 1961; UNESCO, 1961; Gillmor, 1962; Fagen, 1964a; 1964b; Farace & Donohew, 1965; Nixon, 1965; Farace, 1966; Schramm & Ruggels, 1967; Taylor, 1969; Banks, 1970).

The aggregative studies that focused primarily on communication factors in development largely reinforce and elaborate the findings obtained from similar studies with general, socioeconomic, or political foci. Starting from an initial impression of the strong interdependence of various levels of development, even to the extent of conceiving the developmental process as a unidemensional phenomenon, there has been an increasing recognition of the complexities and variations occurring within gross patterns of association. The major findings can be summarized as follows.

Levels of Development

Levels of literacy, mass media availability, gross national product or income per capita, industrialization, urbanization, electoral participation, etc., among the nations of the world are all positively and significantly correlated. Inspection of the correlations between other variables and specific media variables reveals that national levels of newspaper and radio availability can be well predicted by very limited "core" subsets of other developmental variables.

Newspaper circulation levels per 1,000 persons correlate most strongly with literacy and national income. Approximately 86 percent of the intercountry variance in these levels can be accounted for by four indicators—literacy, national income per capita, secondary school enrollment ratio, and population increase. For radio receivers per 1,000, approximately 84 percent of the intercountry variance can be accounted for by two variables—national income per capita and literacy. On the other hand, although cinema availability is most strongly associated with urbanization, industrialization, and per capita income and less strongly associated with literacy, no core set of variables accounts for a high proportion of its intercountry variance. The pattern of television availability seems generally like that of cinema availability, though slightly less associated with urbanization and more with industrialization, but data to permit full comparison were not available for most of these investigations.

Important regional variations exist despite some of the high global correlations. For example, urbanization lags behind other variables in Latin America, literacy behind others in the Near East, and GNP per capita and urbanization lag behind in Asia. Inspection of the regional data suggests the interesting hypothesis that the lagging element among these three main variables (literacy, GNP per capita, and urbanization) is usually the best predictor of mass media availability (newspaper and radio).

Press freedom around the world correlates positively and significantly with GNP per capita, literacy, newspaper circulation, and most other indicators of social, economic, and political development. The higher the level of socioeconomic and political development, the greater the likelihood of freedom of the press.

Several suggestions have been made regarding the presence of critical thresholds and ceiling effects in communication development. Fagen presented some evidence for the idea that newspaper and radio growth become more difficult after a certain "ceiling" level has been reached. Lerner maintained that the relationship between urbanization and literacy (and perhaps that between literacy and other aspects of development, especially media availability) were threshold phenomena. Thus, below 10 percent and above 25 percent urbanization, any change in urbanization had little effect on literacy, while between those levels a significant and critical relationship was hypothesized to exist.

Schramm and Ruggels' data, however, indicated that the lower threshold must be moved lower still (probably to about one-third of the Lerner level) or else abandoned while the ralationship with the critical range of 10 to 25 percent seemed much weaker than hypothesized. They did find, nonetheless, that, as Lerner suggested, literacy was a better predictor of media availability than any of the main economic variables for the group of developing nations past the 25 to 30 percent urbanization threshold.

Rates of Development

When *rates* of growth in communication and other variables were examined along with data on *levels* of development, discrepancies were uncovered that prompted adjustments in fundamental models of the modernization process and the place of communication therein. The long-run and short-run pictures did not seem fully compatible, at least superficially. The short-run changes necessary to produce the long-run associations seemed not to work in expected directions.

For example, *level* of newspaper circulation, as noted, is strongly associated with per capita income and literacy. But, on a world-wide scale, *growth* in newspaper circulation apparently bears no significant relation to levels of socioeconomic development, to rates of growth in other developmental indicators including income and literacy, or even to growth in another medium, radio, whose level of development is highly related to level of newspaper development. For the subgroup of developing societies alone, growth in newspaper circulation is significantly but weakly related to some of these indicators, namely, GNP and literacy. Radio growth, on the other hand, *is* significantly correlated among all nations with per capita GNP and literacy levels and also with level of newspaper circulation. Growth in newspaper circulation appears to be a rather erratic process with numerous reversibilities (net declines), perhaps similar to many aspects of political development, while radio growth seems less volatile, similar to many aspects of socioeconomic development.

The regime's stance toward the use of the mass media as a developmental instrument seems an important factor in shaping media development. Media growth appears disproportionately rapid in those societies, such as "modernizing autocracies" and Communist countries, which have made mass media an explicit and emphasized tool of state-stimulated development.

There is very little indication that communications development is associated with political instability, defined either in terms of violence or in terms of the incidence of regime changes, violent or not. In fact, explicit attempts to explore these relationships through national-level data basically emerge with evidence of no association at all among these phenomena. Any argument to the contrary must now confront this body of evidence.

In short, one can argue with some confidence, based on reported research, *against* claims of calamitous consequences from communications growth, although, undoubtedly, more profound comparative examination of specific subsets of nations displaying extremely rapid and/or unbalanced communications growth would be welcome. On the other side, however, equally confident assertions of mass communication as a prime tool *for* increasing democratic performance cannot yet be clearly supported by the existing literature. Mass communications do not seem to be the bad actor that some have pictured them to be, but it remains to be demonstrated that they can play the hero role that others project for them.

Causal-Path and Time-Series Analyses of Developmental Models

A major drawback to the cross-sectional analyses of national-level data that we have been inspecting is that little insight is obtained into possible *causal* relationships among associated variables of importance. Sophisticated application of standard multivariate techniques can fairly effectively rule out certain variables on the basis of a gross lack of associations with other variables deemed crucial to the developmental process. But if, as happens, a sizeable cluster of interrelated variables emerges from the cross-sectional analysis, most standard techniques are insufficient to disentangle further these relationships and assess causal orderings within the cluster of interdependencies.

Some additional insight can be obtained even from cross-sectional data, however, through various forms of causal modeling and path analysis. These techniques essentially involve examination of the fit between patterns of empirical association among variables and theoretically based expectations regarding associations among the same variables. Two published attempts (Alker, 1966; McCrone & Cnudde, 1967) have been made to apply causal modeling of cross-sectional associations to national-level data related to Lerner's model of the role of communications in development.

Lerner's Model

As previously noted, although there are some ambiguities in the verbal statements expressing the putative relationships between urbanization (U), literacy (L), mass media exposure (M), and electoral—or other—participation (P), at least two basic models of Lerner's hypotheses can be formulated. Both are oversimplified, the first appreciably so. They are schematically represented in Figure 8.[17]

[17] Variables such as population density and empathy also enter some discussions of these models, but they have been eliminated here because they were dropped in the analyses to be examined and because it is not altogether clear exactly how they figure in the models. These models, of course, relate to national-level data and are not necessarily

Model A

U→L→M→P

Model B

L
U P
M

Figure 8. Schematic representation of Lerner's basic models of the modernization process. (Data for Model A from Lerner, 1958:46; for Model B from Lerner, 1958:60–62.)

In Model A, urbanization increases literacy, literacy then increases mass media exposure, which in turn increases participation. Model B says that urbanization increases literacy, literacy increases mass media exposure, which in turn feeds back to increase literacy further, and both literacy and mass media exposure increase participation.[18] Note that in both models there is no direct link between urbanization and participation. These two variables are connected only through the intervening variables of literacy and mass media exposure and so, if the models are valid, this correlation in the empirical data can be expected to be solely a function of the relationships through the intervening variables.

Alker's Analysis

In the course of a more comprehensive treatment of causal inference in political analysis, Alker (1966) published the first hierarchically modeled examination of Lerner's hypotheses, using data from Russett et al. (1964) and Banks & Textor (1963). Alker examined three models related to Lerner's hypotheses. For simplicity's sake, all of them were hierarchical, ignoring the reciprocity specified by Lerner for the connection between literacy and mass media exposure. These three models and the associated correlation coefficients are presented in Figure 9.

If Model 1 holds, it can be predicted that the following correlational relationships should obtain: UP=(UL) (LM) (MP); UM=(UL) (LM); and LP=(LM) (MP). The numerical values actually found for these relationships were as follows: 0.42 vs. 0.12; 0.41 vs. 0.41; and 0.66 vs. 0.24. Hence, the fit is not very good and Model 1 can be rejected as rather clearly repugnant to the available data.

Similar types of predictions were made for the other two models, yielding fits of 0.42 vs. 0.46 for Model 2, and 0.41 vs. 0.41 and 0.42 vs. 0.46 for Model 3. Thus, both of these models bear a sufficiently close relationship to the empirical data to preclude their elimination. Any further choice among the two models must be based on external criteria such as simplicity or plausibility.

McCrone and Cnudde's Models

At the same time that Alker was using causal modeling to explore the Lerner hypotheses, McCrone and Cnudde (1967) were attempting the same thing. They, however, employed Cutright's data on four variables from seventy-six nations. The four variables were t-scores for urbanization (U), education (E), communication

---

coincident with the model of individual modernization sketched by Lerner.

[18] The *direct* link between literacy and participation is not clearly indicated in Lerner's exposition, even at those points where the model is most explicitly described. My impression is that it is implied by the total discussion. Alker (1966) apparently agrees; however, McCrone and Cnudde (1967) and Winham (1970) interpret Lerner to intend a direct link only between media exposure and participation and none between literacy and participation. The matter might be of little moment if both versions were empirically tested. Unfortunately, only one has been examined in most studies.

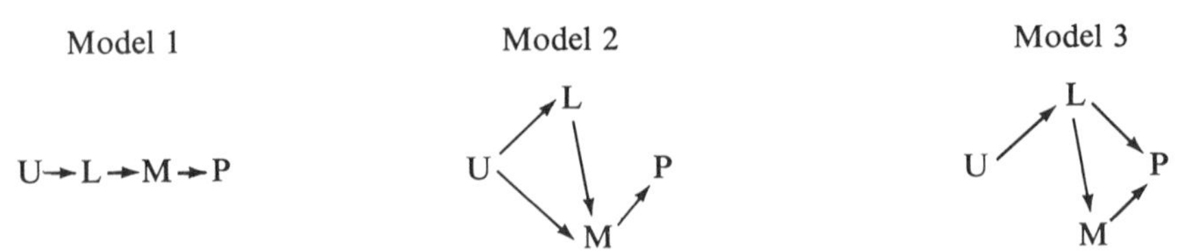

Correlations: UL = 0.70; UM = 0.41; UP = 0.42; LM = 0.58; LP = 0.66; MP = 0.42

Figure 9. Models related to Alker's examination of the Lerner hypotheses. (Adapted from Alker, 1966:21–22, fig. 1.)

(C), and institutional political democracy (D).

Making certain common assumptions for causal modeling (e.g., linearity, additivity, no reciprocity), and also assuming that urbanization is an independent variable and democracy the dependent variable, the authors examined several possible causal connections among the four variables. These are portrayed in Figure 10, which furnishes a basic schema together with the six alternative models investigated and a diagram giving path coefficients for the chosen model.

The prediction equations based on Cutright's data showed, first of all, that models involving a direct linkage between urbanization and communication should be rejected in favor of models showing urbanization linked directly only to education and then through education to communication. Hence, of the first three models (A, B, C), A and B were discarded in favor of C.

The next set of three models (D, E, F), therefore, starts from this premise. Here the relevant correlation coefficients support the inference that education is related to democracy indirectly through its effect on communication. Model D is therefore abandoned. Finally, there is the question of a direct relationship between urbanization and democracy in addition to the indirect one through education and communication. In this case the associations among the variables indicate that the better model

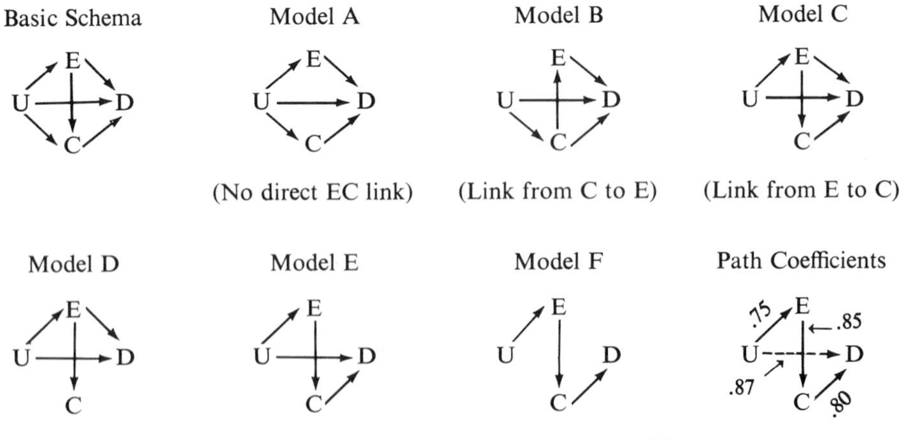

Figure 10. Causal models for McCrone and Cnudde's examination of the Lerner hypothesis. (Adapted from McCrone & Cnudde, 1967:75–77.)

is E rather than F; there seems to be some direct association between urbanization and democracy in addition to the established indirect association. (No test is reported for a model of the DEF type, but which contains both ED and CD links—in short, for Model C.)

Since the correlation coefficients employed in causal modeling only measure the degree of association between variables rather than the amount of change in the dependent variable associated with standardized changes in the independent variable, path analysis was also used to explore these relationships. The resultant path coefficients for the two paths permitted by Model E are given in Figure 10 (lower right). These indicate that the overwhelmingly important causal connection is the indirect one from U to E to C to D. Hence, McCrone & Cnudde (1967:78) feel that the overall analysis indicates a "... remarkable correspondence between this empirically derived causal model of democratic political development and the original causal model postulated ..." by Lerner (McCrone & Cnudde, 1967:78). At the same time, they also point out that the causal relationships specified in the model accepted are far from perfect, leaving a significant portion of the variance unexplained, perhaps to be handled by other variables.

Time-Series Analyses

Almost all analyses of national-level data on development and communication have been cross-sectional, including the causal modeling and path analyses just described. As noted earlier, the paramount problem with the cross-sectional approach is its assumption that cross-sectional patterns reveal longitudinal processes. A second problem with cross-sectional analyses involves the conceptual comparability of the very units of analysis themselves—namely, nations. For many purposes, it seems dubious to lump together as equal in a statistical analysis all units that have been "sovereign for at least two years and have over one-half million population," as the UN, for example, often does. This equates the United States, USSR, U.K., China, and India with Togo, Burundi, Malawi, Sarawak, and Singapore. A third and obvious problem of cross-sectional analysis is the difficulty in securing accurate data for many variables from such a wildly heterogeneous collection of units. Any close inspection of the data on literacy, mass communications, GNP, etc., for many nations discloses considerable basis for anxiety.

Time-series analysis has much to offer from these perspectives. It is "an inherently time-oriented" method particularly well suited for studying a historic process like development. Unlike cross-sectional analysis even at its best, time-series analysis provides data directly relevant to causal sequences and also to the *amount* of time lag that occurs between cause and effect, which may be a crucial consideration for both theory and developmental planning. Concentrating on those developed and developing countries for which reasonably good data are available, this technique also permits much more use of ancillary data sources that are not available on a global basis. Even the problem of comparability in judgmental ratings is presumably eased.

On the other hand, the big drawback to national time-series analysis is the problem of generalization. Cross-sectional analysis at least superficially deals with the universe of all existing nations and supports generalization to that group. Time-series analysis usually deals with one or just a few nations and clearly raises uncertainty as to generalization. Hence, a reasonable position would not argue for abandoning or neglecting cross-sectional approaches, but rather for much greater use of time-series analysis and a self-conscious link between these two approaches (Burrowes, 1970). Time-series analyses of relevance to understanding communication and development have been published by Bowman and Anderson (1962; 1963), Schramm and

Ruggels (1967), Cutright and Wiley (1969–1970), Banks (1970), and Winham (1970).

The main substantive findings from both the causal modeling and time-series analyses are the following. Three studies set out explicitly to test the Lerner model relating urbanization, literacy (or education), mass media exposure (or mass communications), and participation (or political democracy). Two of these used causal modeling (Alker, and McCrone and Cnudde) and one used time-series analysis (Winham). A gross comparison of their findings can be obtained from Table 11.

The rather sad tale depicted in Table 11 is that it is currently difficult to be very confident about any causal priorities among the variables in the Lerner model. If we give greater emphasis to Alker's analysis of "other data" than to his own, then the causal influence of mass media exposure or mass communication on political participation may be the one unanimously supported link. But the overall picture reveals numerous discrepancies. These might be attributed to the two different testing techniques employed—causal modeling and time-series analysis. However, the two causal-modeling investigations disagree among themselves on three of the six relationships. One might also attribute the disagreement to different data bases and somewhat divergent conceptualization of variables. However, the McCrone and Cnudde and the Winham studies employed data and concepts that were quite comparable and they still disagree in at least half their findings. On the whole, it appears that further research is required to unravel causal priorities among these—and, one hopes, other—important developmental variables.

The most salient findings not related to the Lerner model that emerge from the causal-type analyses examined are these:

1. According to Bowman and Anderson, GNP per capita is more probably a cause of primary-level educational development than the latter is a cause of changes in GNP per capita.

2. According to Schramm and Ruggels, urbanization and GNP per capita are each more likely to be causes of rising literacy in developing societies than the latter is to be a cause of either of them. These authors also found no clear causal priorities in any of the following relations (presumed independent variable given first): urbanization/

TABLE 11

COMPARISON OF CAUSAL-MODELING AND TIME-SERIES TESTS OF THE LERNER MODEL

Causal Linkage	Lerner	Causal Modeling		Time-Series
		Alker	McC. & C.	Winham
Urbanization → Literacy	Yes	Yes	Yes	No (or reciprocal)
Urbanization → Media exposure	No	No	No	Yes, but *reversed*
Urbanization → Participation	No	No	Yes, weak	Yes, 20-year lag
Literacy → Media exposure	Yes	Yes	Yes	Yes, but *reversed* or reciprocal
Literacy → Participation	? (Yes)	Yes	No	Yes
Media exposure → Participation	Yes	No[a]	Yes	Yes

NOTE: The entries are affirmative if the analysis supported the existence of a direct causal linkage between the two designated variables and negative if not. Although possible reciprocal relationships are only noted for the time-series analysis (because Winham specifically referred to them), they may also exist in the other cases but were excluded from consideration by hierarchical assumptions.

[a] When Alker used other data than those employed in his original analysis, this link may have become affirmative (and the L → P link may have disappeared).

newspaper circulation, urbanization/radio receivers, literacy/newspaper circulation, GNP/radio receivers, and GNP/newspaper circulation.

3. According to Cutright and Wiley, changes in political representation are unlikely when literacy is low or when socioeconomic security is high. When literacy is high and security is low, increasing literacy acts to increase political representation over what it would otherwise have been, predicted on the basis of the country's level of economic development (measured by energy consumption per capita) and social development (measured by literacy). If political representation is greater than predicted by the economic and social indicators, then it will tend to decline. But increased literacy will exert a "maintenance effect," reducing the amount of that decline. If political representation is less than predicted by the economic and social indicators, it will tend to rise. Here increased literacy will exert a "mobilization effect," accelerating the rise in political representation.

4. According to Banks, political democracy (representativeness) is a cause of modernization (increased mass communication and transport) rather than the reverse.

A Computerized Simulation

Finally, although not time-series analysis in the ordinary sense, an interesting and related attempt to construct an empirically defensible causal model of the developmental process using historical national-level data was presented by Domingo (1968).[19] It essentially involves creation of a computerized simulation of historical data on modernization variables for several selected nations (Turkey, Venezuela, Guiana, India, the Philippines, and the United Arab Republic). The variables chosen, employing an adaptation of the Lerner model, were GNP per capita, urbanization, literacy, per capita newsprint consumption, and per capita radio receivers.

The time period covered was 1935–1965. Starting with the adapted Lerner hypotheses and the time-series data on the five variables, an effort was made to work out a series of equations coordinating the two so that a Lerner-type theory having a good fit to actual historical data from six disparate countries would be created. Time-lagged correlations among variables, threshold and ceiling or floor effects, nonlinearities, reciprocal relationships, etc., were all considered in the process of accommodating Lerner's model to fairly reliable national-level data over thirty years. The equations were fitted for a single nation first, and then after a satisfactory fit was obtained, that model was applied to a second nation, adjusted, rechecked with the first, applied to a third nation, and so on. Every successive modification had to be tried in all cases already fitted. If such fitting cannot be accomplished, the basic model must be changed.

The initial theoretical model adapted from Lerner took GNP per capita as the single exogenous variable. Urbanization was then assumed to be an increasing function of GNP per capita, with an adjustment for a ceiling effect. Literacy was also taken to be an increasing function of GNP per capita, and it, too, responded to a ceiling effect that was itself a function of urbanization. Newspaper consumption was an increasing function of GNP per capita and literacy, without adjustments, while radio receivers per capita were taken to be an increasing function of GNP per capita and to have a ceiling of 280 per 1,000.

The "findings" from the simulation process are not easy to summarize because they involve a good deal of variation from country to country in the influence of each variable. In fact, the dual observations (1) that it was possible to fit a modified Lerner

[19] The interesting and more elaborate simulation by Brunner and Brewer (1971) for Turkey and the Philippines will not be considered here because communication variables enter so slightly into the model.

model to historical data from six different developing societies, and (2) that the relative strengths of each component variable shifted from country to country (and even over time for the radio variable) must be regarded as the main substantive significance of the effort.

Conclusion

On the whole, it is evident that we have merely scratched the surface in our efforts to use national-level data in fathoming the role of communication in development. Our capacities now are such that a major, truly sophisticated and theoretically informed analysis of national-level data is eminently in order. Both multination, multivariable time-series analysis for countries with appropriate data sets and more comprehensive cross-sectional analysis and causal modeling can and should be done as definitively as possible. A significant synthesis based on a new research effort seems possible and sorely needed at this point in our investigations.

REFERENCES

Adelman, Irma.
1971 Final Report: Part I: Summary, Conclusions, and Recommendations; Part II: A Conceptualization and Analysis of Political Participation in Underdeveloped Countries; Part III: An Anatomy of Patterns of Income Distribution in Developing Nations. Washington, D.C.: United States Agency for International Development, Grant AID/csd-2236 (February 12).

Adelman, Irma, and Cynthia T. Morris.
1965 "A factor analysis of the interrelationship between social and political variables and per capita gross national product." Quarterly Journal of Economics 79(November):555–578.
1967 Society, Politics, and Economic Development: A Quantitative Approach. Baltimore: The Johns Hopkins Press.
1968a "Performance criteria for evaluating economic development potential: An operational approach." Quarterly Journal of Economics 82(May): 260–280.
1968b "An econometric model of socio-economic and political change in underdeveloped countries." American Economic Review 58(December, Pt. 1):1184–1218.

Alexander, Christopher W.
1964 Notes on the Synthesis of Form. Cambridge, Massachusetts: Harvard University Press.

Alker, Hayward R., Jr.
1966 "Causal inference and political analysis." Pp. 7–43 in Joseph Bernd (ed.), Mathematical Applications in Political Science. Dallas: Southern Methodist University Press.

Almond, Gabriel A.
1960 "Introduction: A functional approach to comparative politics." Pp. 3–64 in Gabriel A. Almond and James S. Coleman (eds.), The Politics of the Developing Areas. Princeton, New Jersey: Princeton University Press.

Almond, Gabriel A., and James S. Coleman (eds.).
1960 The Politics of the Developing Areas. Princeton, New Jersey: Princeton University Press.

Apter, David E.
1965 The Politics of Modernization. Chicago: University of Chicago Press.

Arensberg, Conrad M., and Arthur H. Niehoff.
1971 Introducing Social Change. Second Edition. Chicago: Aldine.

Arndt, Johan.
1968 "A test of the two-step flow in diffusion of a new product." Journalism Quarterly 45(Autumn): 457–465.

Balogh, Thomas.
1961 "Economic policy and the price system." Economic Bulletin for Latin America 6(March):41–53.

Banfield, Edward C.
1958 The Moral Basis of a Backward Society. Glencoe, Illiniois: Free Press.

Banks, Arthur S.
1970 "Modernization and political change:

The Latin American and Amer-European nations." Comparative Political Studies 2(January): 405-418.

Banks, Arthur S., and Robert Textor.
1963 A Cross-Polity Survey. Cambridge, Massachusetts: M.I.T. Press.

Barnard, Chester I.
1938 The Functions of the Executive. Cambridge, Massachusetts: Harvard University Press.

Bay, Christian.
1965 "Politics and pseudopolitics: A critical evaluation of some behavioral literature." American Political Science Review 59 (March): 39–51.

Becker, Gary S.
1965 "A theory of the allocation of time." Economic Journal 75(September): 493–517.

Bellah, Robert N.
1964 "Religious evolution." American Sociological Review 29 (June): 358–374.

Bendix, Reinhard.
1964 Nation-Building and Citizenship. New York: Wiley.

Berry, Brian J. L.
1961 "Basic patterns of economic development." Pp. 113–119 in Norton Ginsburg, Atlas of Economic Development. Chicago: University of Chicago Press.

Binder, Leonard.
1962 Iran: Political Development in a Changing Society. Berkeley: University of California Press.
1965 "Egypt: The integrative revolution." Pp. 396–449 in Lucian W. Pye and Sidney Verba (eds.), Political Culture and Political Development. Princeton, New Jersey: Princeton University Press.

Binder, Leonard, et al.
1971 Crises and Sequences in Political Development. Princeton, New Jersey: Princeton University Press.

Black, Cyril E.
1966a "Change as a condition of modern life." Pp. 17–27 in Myron Weiner (ed.), Modernization: The Dynamics of Growth. New York: Basic Books.
1966b The Dynamics of Modernization. New York: Harper and Row.

Bowman, Mary Jean, and C. A. Anderson.
1962 "The role of education in development." Pp. 153–180 in Robert E. Asher et al., Development of the Emerging Countries. Washington, D. C.: Brookings Institution.
1963 "Concerning the role of education in development." Pp. 247–279 in Clifford Geertz (ed.), Old Societies and New States. New York: Free Press.

Braibanti, Ralph.
1966 "Administrative modernization." Pp. 166–180 in Myron Weiner (ed.), Modernization: The Dynamics of Growth. New York: Basic Books.

Brunner, Ronald D., and Garry D. Brewer.
1971 Organized Complexity: Empirical Theories of Political Development. New York: Free Press.

Burrowes, Robert.
1970 "Multiple time-series analysis of nation-level data." Comparative Political Studies 2(Jaunary): 465-480.

Cancian, Frank.
1972 Change and Uncertainty in a Peasant Economy. Stanford, California: Stanford University Press.

Cassirer, Henry R.
1959 "Audience participation, new style." Public Opinion Quarterly 23 (Winter): 529–536.

Cater, Douglass.
1959 The Fourth Branch of Government. Boston: Houghton Mifflin.

Chu, Goodwin C.
1966 "When television comes to a traditional village." Paper presented at the Pacific Chapter of the American Association for Public Opinion (unpublished).

Cohn, Andrew H.
1971 "Political socialization: A holistic approach." Hacettepe Bulletin of Social Sciences and Humanities 3(June): 1–33.

Coleman, James S.
1960 "Conclusion: The political systems of the developing areas." Pp. 532-576 in Gabriel A. Almond and James S. Coleman (eds.), The Politics of the Developing Areas. Princeton, New Jersey: Princeton University Press.

Coleman, James S.; Elihu Katz; and Herbert Menzel.
1957 "The diffusion of an innovation among physicians." Sociometry 20(December):253–270.
Cottam, Richard W.
1964 Nationalism in Iran. Pittsburgh: University of Pittsburgh Press.
Crozier, Michel.
1964 The Bureaucratic Phenomenon. Chicago: University of Chicago Press.
Cutright, Phillips.
1963 "National political development: Measurement and analysis." American Sociological Review 28(April): 253–264.
1968 "Letter to the editor." American Political Science Review 62(June): 578–581.
Cutright, Phillips, and James A. Wiley.
1969–70 "Modernization and political representation: 1927–1966." Studies in Comparative International Development (Monograph Series) 5(No. 2):23–41.
Davis, Kingsley, and Hilda Hertz Golden.
1954 "Urbanization and the development of pre-industrial areas." Economic Development and Cultural Change 3(October):6–24.
Dean, Edwin.
1966 Supply Responses of African Farmers. New York: Humanities Press.
Dennis, Jack.
1967 A Survey and Bibliography of Contemporary Research on Political Learning and Socialization. (Occasional Paper No. 8.) Madison: Center for Cognitive Learning, University of Wisconsin.
de Schweinitz, Karl, Jr.
1965 "Economics and the underdeveloped economies." American Behavioral Scientist 9(September):3–5.
Deutsch, Karl W.
1953 Nationalism and Social Communication. New York: Wiley.
1961 "Social mobilization and political development." American Political Science Review 55(September): 493–514.
1964 "Transaction flows as indicators of political cohesion." Pp. 75–97 in Philip Jacob and James V. Toscano (eds.), The Integration of Political Communities. Philadelphia: Lippincott.
1969 Nationalism and Its Alternatives. New York: Knopf.
Deutsch, Karl W., and Richard L. Merritt.
1970 Nationalism and National Development. Cambridge, Massachusetts: M.I.T. Press.
Deutschmann, Paul J.
1963 "The mass media in an underdeveloped village." Journalism Quarterly 40(Winter):27–35.
Deutschmann, Paul J., and Orlando Fals Borda.
1962 Communication and Adoption Patterns in an Andean Village. San Jose, Costa Rica: Programa Interamericano de Información Popular and Facultad de Sociología, Universidad Nacional de Colombia.
Deutschmann, Paul J., and John T. McNelly.
1964 "A factor analysis of characteristics of Latin American countries." American Behavioral Scientist 8 (September):25–29.
Domar, Evsey.
1957 Essays on the Theory of Economic Growth. New York: Oxford University Press.
Domingo, Carlos.
1968 Building Dynamic Models from Historical Data, Cambridge: Center for International Studies, Massachusetts Institute of Technology (August).
Doob, Leonard W.
1964 Patriotism and Nationalism: Their Psychological Foundations. New Haven, Connecticut: Yale University Press.
Duff, Ernest A., and John F. McCamant.
1968 "Measuring social and political requirements for system stability in Latin America." American Political Science Review 62(December): 1125–1143.
Dumazadier, Joffre.
1956 Television and Rural Adult Education. Paris: UNESCO.
Easterlin, Richard A.
1968 "Economic growth: I. Overview." Pp. 395–408 in David L. Sills (ed.), International Encyclopedia of the

Social Sciences. Volume 4. New York: Macmillan.

Easton, David.
1953 The Political System. New York: Knopf.
1965 A Systems Analysis of Political Life. New York: Wiley.

Easton, David, and Jack Dennis.
1969 Children in the Political System. New York: McGraw-Hill.

Eitzen, D. Stanley.
1967 "The use of Banks and Textor's 'Cross-Polity Survey' for the ranking of nations." Social and Economic Studies 16(September):326–329.

Elder, Joseph W.
1964 "National loyalties in a newly independent nation." Pp. 77–92 in David Apter (ed.), Ideology and Discontent. New York: Free Press of Glencoe.

Emerson, Rupert.
1962 From Empire to Nation. Boston: Beacon Press.

Fagen, Richard R.
1964a "Mass media growth: A comparison of communist and other countries." Journalism Quarterly 41(Autumn): 563–567, 572.
1964b "Relation of communication growth to national political systems in the less developed countries." Journalism Quarterly 41(Winter):87–94.
1966 Politics and Communication. Boston: Little, Brown.

Farace, R. Vincent.
1966 "A study of mass communication and national development." Journalism Quarterly 43(Summer): 305–313.
1968 "Mass communication and national development: Some insights from aggregate analysis." Pp. V-1 to V-19 in David K. Berlo (ed.), Mass Communication and the Development of Nations. East Lansing: International Communication Institute, Michigan State University.

Farace, R. Vincent, and Lewis Donohew.
1965 "Mass communication in national social systems: A study of 43 variables in 115 countries." Journalism Quarterly 42 (Spring):253–261.

Fink, Raymond.
1959 "Political awareness in Laos." Sample survey conducted by the United States Information Agency.

Fishman, Joshua A.; Charles A. Ferguson; and Jyotirindra Das Gupta (eds.).
1968 Language Problems of Developing Nations. New York: Wiley.

Foster, George M.
1962 Traditional Cultures and the Impact of Technological Change. New York: Harper.
1965 "Peasant society and the image of limited good." American Anthropologist 67(April):293–315.

Fraenkel, Peter.
1959 Wayaleshi. London: Weidenfeld and Nicolson.

Frey, Frederick W.
1962 "The coverage of the Near East in the U.S. mass media" (mimeograph).
1963a "Political development, power, and communications in Turkey." Pp. 298–326 in Lucian Pye (ed.), Communications and Political Development. Princeton, New Jersey: Princeton University Press.
1963b "Surveying peasant attitudes in Turkey." Public Opinion Quarterly 27(Fall):335–355.
1965 The Turkish Political Elite. Cambridge, Massachusetts: M.I.T. Press.
1966 The Mass Media and Rural Development in Turkey. Report No. 3, Rural Development Research Project. Cambridge, Massachusetts: Center for International Studies, Massachusetts Institute of Technology.
1968 "Socialization to national identification among Turkish peasants." Journal of Politics 30(August): 934–965.
1970 "Political development and political participation: 'Lost in the Horse Latitudes'?" (mimeograph). Keynote Address prepared for the MUCIA conference on Requirements and Consequences of Political Participation for Development Policies, Chicago, December 5–6 (unpublished).
1971 "Developmental aspects of administration." Pp. 219–272 in Paul J. Leagans and Charles P. Loomis (eds.), Behavioral Change in Agri-

culture. Ithaca, New York: Cornell University Press.

Frey, Frederick W., and Leslie L. Roos.
1967 Social Structure and Community Development in Rural Turkey: Village and Elite Leadership Relations. Report No. 10, Rural Development Research Project. Cambridge: Center for International Studies, Massachusetts Institute of Technology.

Frey, Frederick W., et al. (eds.).
1969 Survey Research on Comparative Social Change: A Bibliography. Cambridge, Massachusetts: M.I.T. Press.

Friedrich, Carl J. (ed.).
1958 Authority. Nomos, 1. Cambridge, Massachusetts: Harvard University Press.

Fromm, Erich, and Michael Maccoby.
1970 Social Character in a Mexican Village. Englewood Cliffs, New Jersey: Prentice-Hall.

Geertz, Clifford.
1963 "The integrative revolution: Primordial sentiments and civil politics in the new states." Pp. 105–157 in Clifford Geertz (ed.), Old Societies and New States. New York: Free Press of Glencoe.
1968 Agricultural Involution. New York: Twentieth Century Fund.

Geertz, Clifford (ed.).
1963 Old Societies and New States. New York: Free Press of Glencoe.

Gillmor, Donald M.
1962 "Freedom in press systems and the religious variable." Journalism Quarterly 39(Winter):15–26.

Ginsburg, Norton.
1961 Atlas of Economic Development. Chicago: University of Chicago Press.

Golden, Hilda Hertz.
1955 "Literacy and social change in underdeveloped countries." Rural Sociology 20(March):1–7. Also in Lyle W. Shannon (ed.), Underdeveloped Areas. New York: Harper, 1957.

Greenberg, Bradley S.
1961 "Additional data on variables related to press freedom." Journalism Quarterly 38(Winter):76–78.

Greenstein, Fred I.
1969 Personality and Politics. Chicago: Markham.

Guetzkow, Harold.
1965 "Communications in organizations." Pp. 534–573 in James G. March (ed.), Handbook of Organizations. Chicago: Rand McNally.

Hagen, Everett E.
1962a "A framework for analyzing economic and political change." Pp. 1–38 in Robert E. Asher et al., Development of the Emerging Countries. Washington, D.C.: Brookings Institution.
1962b On the Theory of Social Change. Homewood, Illinois: Dorsey Press.

Hagerstrand, Torsten.
1965 "Quantitative techniques for analysis of the spread of information and technology." Pp. 244–280 in C. Arnold Anderson and Mary Jean Bowman (eds.), Education and Economic Development. Chicago: Aldine.
1967 Innovation Diffusion as a Spatial Process. Chicago: University of Chicago Press.
1968 "Diffusion: II. The diffusion of innovations." Pp. 174–178 in David L. Sills (ed.), International Encyclopedia of the Social Sciences. Volume 4. New York: Macmillan.

Hall, Edward T.
1959 The Silent Language. New York: Premier Books.
1966 The Hidden Dimension. Garden City, New York: Doubleday.

Harbison, Frederick, and Charles A. Myers.
1964 Education, Manpower and Economic Growth. New York: McGraw-Hill.

Harrod, Roy F.
1939 "An essay in dynamic theory." Economic Journal 49(March):14–33.

Heilbroner, Robert L.
1963 The Great Ascent. New York: Harper and Row.

Heine-Geldern, Robert.
1968 "Diffusion: I. Cultural diffusion." Pp. 169–173 in David L. Sills (ed.), International Encyclopedia of the Social Sciences. Volume 4. New York: Macmillan.

Herskovits, Melville J.
1962 The Human Factor in Changing Africa. New York: Knopf.
1969 Man and His Works. New York: Knopf.

Hess, Robert D., and Judith Torney.
1967 Development of Political Attitudes. Chicago: Aldine.

Hiniker, Paul J.
1968 "The mass media and study groups in communist China." Pp. VI-1 to VI-24 in David Berlo (ed.), Mass Communication and the Development of Nations. East Lansing: Michigan State University.

Hirschman, Albert O.
1958 The Strategy of Economic Development. New Haven, Connecticut: Yale University Press.

Holt, Robert T., and John E. Turner.
1966 The Political Basis of Economic Development. Princeton, New Jersey: Van Nostrand.

Hoselitz, Bert F.
1968 "Economic growth: IV. Noneconomic aspects." Pp. 422–429 in David L. Sills (ed.), International Encyclopedia of the Social Sciences. Volume 4. New York: Macmillan.

Huntington, Ellsworth.
1915 Civilization and Climate. New Haven, Connecticut: Yale University Press.
1945 Mainsprings of Civilization. New York: Wiley.

Huntington, Samuel P.
1966 "The political modernization of traditional monarchies." Daedalus 95(Summer):763–788.
1968 Political Order in Changing Societies. New Haven, Connecticut: Yale University Press.
1971 "The change to change: Modernization, development, and politics." Comparative Politics 3(April):283–322.

Hyman, Herbert H.
1959 Political Socialization. Glencoe, Illinois: Free Press.
1963 "Mass media and political socialization: The role of patterns of communication." Pp. 128–148 in Lucian W. Pye (ed.), Communications and Political Development. Princeton, New Jersey: Princeton University Press.

Inkeles, Alex.
1966a "Social structure and the socialization of competence." Harvard Educational Review 36(Summer): 265–293.
1966b "The modernization of man." Pp. 138–150 in Myron Weiner (ed.), Modernization: The Dynamics of Growth. New York: Basic Books.
1969 "Making men modern: On the causes and consequences of individual change in six developing countries." American Journal of Sociology 75(September):208–225.

Isaacs, Harold.
1958 Scratches on Our Minds. New York: John Day.

Jacob, Philip E., and Henry Teune.
1964 "The integrative process: Guidelines for analysis of the bases of political community." Pp. 1–45 in Philip E. Jacob and James V. Toscano (eds.), The Integration of Political Communities. Philadelphia: Lippincott.

Jacob, Philip E., and James V. Toscano (eds.).
1964 The Integration of Political Communities. Philadelphia: Lippincott.

Katz, Elihu.
1968 "Diffusion: III. Interpersonal influence." Pp. 178-184 in David L. Sills (ed.), International Encyclopedia of the Social Sciences. Volume 4. New York: Macmillan.

Katz, Elihu, and Paul F. Lazarsfeld.
1955 Personal Influence. Glencoe, Illinois: Free Press.

Keith, Robert F.; Dharam P. Yadav; and Joseph R. Ascroft.
1968 "Mass media exposure and modernization among villagers in three developing countries: Towards cross-national generalizations." Pp. IV-1 to IV-18 in David K. Berlo (ed.), Mass Communication and the Development of Nations. East Lansing: Michigan State University.

Klapper, Joseph T.
1960 The Effects of Mass Communication. New York: Free Press of Glencoe.

Kroeber, A. L.
1944 Configurations of Culture Growth.

Berkeley: University of California Press.

Kuznets, Simon.
1960 "Notes on the take-off." Paper presented at the International Economic Association Conference, Konstanz, West Germany. Reprinted in Gerald M. Meier (ed.), Leading Issues in Development Economics. New York: Oxford University Press, 1964.
1968 Toward A Theory of Economic Growth. New York: Norton.

LaPalombara, Joseph.
1965 "Italy: Fragmentation, isolation and alienation." Pp. 282–329 in Lucian W. Pye and Sidney Verba (eds.), Political Culture and Political Development. Princeton, New Jersey: Princeton University Press.

Lazarsfeld, Paul F.; Bernard Berelson; and Hazel Gaudet.
1944 The People's Choice. New York: Columbia University Press.

Lerner, Daniel.
1957 "Communication systems and social systems: A statistical exploration in history and policy." Behavioral Science 2(October):266–275.
1958 The Passing of Traditional Society. Glencoe, Illinois: Free Press.
1963 "Toward a communication theory of modernization." Pp. 327–350 in Lucian W. Pye (ed.), Communications and Political Development. Princeton, New Jersey: Princeton University Press.
1967 "Communication and the prospects of innovative development." Pp. 305–317 in Daniel Lerner and Wilbur Schramm (eds.), Communication and Change in the Developing Countries. Honolulu: East-West Center Press.
1969 "Managing communications for modernization: A developmental construct," in Arnold Rogow (ed.), Politics, Personality, and Social Science in the Twentieth Century. Chicago: University of Chicago Press.

LeVine, Robert A.
1960 "The internalization of political values in stateless societies." Human Organization 19(Summer):51–58. Reprinted in Robert C. Hunt (ed.), Personalities and Cultures. Garden City, New York: Natural History Press, 1967, pp. 185–203.
1965 "Socialization, social structure, and intersocietal images." Pp. 45–49 in Herbert C. Kelman (ed.), International Behavior. New York: Holt, Rinehart and Winston.
1966 Dreams and Deeds: Achievement Motivation in Nigeria. Chicago: University of Chicago Press.

Lewis, Oscar.
1951 Life in a Mexican Village: Tepoztlan Re-Studied. Urbana: University of Illinois Press.

Lewontin, R. C.
1968 "Evolution: I. The concept of evolution." Pp. 202–210 in David L. Sills (ed.), International Encyclopedia of the Social Sciences. Volume 5. New York: Macmillan.

Lin, Nan.
1969 "Information flow, influence flow and the decision-making process—testing a new conceptualization of the communication flow." Unpublished revision of a paper presented at the 1969 meeting of the American Association for Education in Journalism, Berkeley, California.

Linton, Ralph.
1936 The Study of Man. New York: Appleton-Century-Crofts.

Lionberger, Herbert F.
1960 Adoption of New Ideas and Practices. Ames: Iowa State University Press.

Lipset, Seymour Martin.
1959 "Some social requisites of democracy: Economic development and political legitimacy." American Political Science Review 53(March): 69–105.

Lopreato, Joseph.
1962 "Interpersonal relations in peasant society: The peasant's view." Human Organization 21(Spring):21–24.

Louis, Roger, and Joseph Rovan.
1955 Television and Tele-Clubs in Rural Communities: An Experiment in France. Paris: UNESCO.

Luethy, Herbert.
1955 France Against Herself. New York: Praeger.

McClelland, David C.
1961 The Achieving Society. Princeton, New Jersey: Van Nostrand.
1966 "The impulse to modernization." Pp. 28–39 in Myron Weiner (ed.), Modernization: The Dynamics of Growth. New York: Basic Books.

McCrone, Donald J., and Charles F. Cnudde.
1967 "Toward a communications theory of democratic political development: A causal model." American Political Science Review 61(March):72–79.

McNelly, John T.
1966 "Mass communication and the climate for modernization in Latin America." Journal of Inter-American Studies 8(July):345–357.

Makal, Mahmut.
1954 A Village in Anatolia. Translation by Sir Wyndham Deedes. London: Vallentine, Mitchell.

Malinowski, Bronislaw.
1927 "The life of culture." Pp. 26–46 in Grafton E. Smith et al., Culture: The Diffusion Controversy. London: Routledge.

Mandelbaum, Seymour J.
1965 Boss Tweed's New York. New York: Wiley.

Mannoni, Otare.
1956 Prospero and Caliban: The Psychology of Colonization. New York: Praeger.

March, James G., and Herbert A. Simon.
1958 Organizations. New York: Wiley.

Marco Surveys Ltd.
1965 A Baseline Survey of Factors Affecting Agricultural Development in Three Areas of Kenya. Nairobi: Ministry of Labour and Social Services, Government of Kenya.

Markham, James W.
1961 "Foreign news in the United States and South American press." Public Opinion Quarterly 25(Summer): 249–262.

Marsh, Robert M., and William L. Parish.
1965 "Modernization and communism: A re-test of Lipset's hypothesis." American Sociological Review 30(December):934–942.

Mathur, J. C., and Paul Neurath.
1959 An Indian Experiment in Farm Radio Forums. Paris: UNESCO.

Meier, Richard L.
1962 A Communications Theory of Urban Growth. Cambridge, Massachusetts: M.I.T. Press.

Merton, Robert K.
1957 Social Theory and Social Structure. Glencoe, Illinois: Free Press.

Miller, Neal E., and John Dollard.
1941 Social Learning and Imitation. New Haven, Connecticut: Yale University Press, 1941.

Millikan, Max F.
1967 "The most fundamental technological change." Pp. 3–4 in Daniel Lerner and Wilbur Schramm (eds.), Communication and Change in Developing Countries. Honolulu: East-West Center Press.

Milne, R. S.
1969 "Differentiation and administrative development." Journal of Comparative Administration 1(August): 213–233.

Miner, Horace.
1952 "The folk-urban continuum." American Sociological Review 17(October):529–537.

Mosel, James N.
1963 "Communication patterns and political socialization in traditional Thailand." Pp. 184–228 in Lucian W. Pye (ed.), Communications and Political Development, Princeton, New Jersey: Princeton University Press.

Needham, Joseph.
1954 Science and Civilization in China. Volume 1. London: Cambridge University Press.

Nelson, Joan M.
1969 Migrants, Urban Poverty, and Instability in Developing Nations. Occasional Papers in International Affairs, No. 22. Cambridge: Harvard University, Center for International Affairs.

Neubauer, Deane E.
1967 "Some conditions of democracy." American Political Science Review 61(December):1002–1009.
1968 "Letter to the editor." American Political Science Review 62(June): 581.

Nicol, John, et al.
1954 Canada's Farm Radio Forum. Paris: UNESCO.

Niehoff, Arthur H., and Charnel J. Anderson.
1964 "The process of cross-cultural innovation." International Development Review 6(June):5–11.

Nixon, Raymond B.
1960 "Some factors related to freedom in national press systems." Journalism Quarterly 37(Winter):13–28.
1965 "Freedom in the world's press: A fresh appraisal with data." Journalism Quarterly 42(Winter):3–14, 118–119.

Nordlinger, Eric A.
1968 "Political development: Time sequences and rates of change." World Politics 20(April):494–520.

Organski, A. F. K.
1965 The Stages of Political Development. New York: Knopf.

Passin, Herbert.
1963 "Writer and journalist in the transitional society." Pp. 82–123 in Lucian W. Pye (ed.), Communications and Political Development. Princeton, New Jersey: Princeton University Press.

Pines, Maya.
1969 "Why some children get A's and others get C's." New York Times Magazine, July 6.

Pool, Ithiel de Sola.
1963 "The mass media and politics in the modernization process." Pp. 234–253 in Lucian W. Pye (ed.), Communications and Political Development. Princeton, New Jersey: Princeton University Press.

Price, Derek J. de Solla.
1961 Science Since Babylon. New Haven, Connecticut: Yale University Press.

Pye, Lucian W.
1958 "Administrators, agitators, and brokers." Public Opinion Quarterly 22(Fall):342–348.
1962 Politics, Personality, and Nation Building. New Haven, Connecticut: Yale University Press.
1965 "Introduction: Political culture and political development." Pp. 3-26 in Lucian W. Pye and Sidney Verba (eds.), Political Culture and Political Development. Princeton, New Jersey: Princeton University Press.
1966 Aspects of Political Development. Boston: Little, Brown.

Pye, Lucian W. (ed.).
1963 Communications and Political Development. Princeton, New Jersey: Princeton University Press.

Ranis, Gustav.
1968 "Economic growth: II. Theory." Pp. 408–417 in David L. Sills (ed.), International Encyclopedia of the Social Sciences. Volume 4. New York: Macmillan.

Riggs, Fred W.
1964 Administration in Developing Countries. Boston: Houghton Mifflin.

Robinson, John P., and Philip E. Converse.
1972 "Social change reflected in the use of time," in Angus Campbell and Philip E. Converse (eds.), The Human Meaning of Social Change. New York: Russell Sage.

Rogers, Everett M.
1962 Diffusion of Innovations. New York: Free Press of Glencoe.
1968 "Mass media exposure and modernization among Colombian peasants." Pp. III-1 to III-19 in David K. Berlo (ed.), Mass Communication and the Development of Nations. East Lansing: Michigan State University.
1969 Modernization Among Peasants: The Impact of Communication. New York: Holt, Rinehart and Winston.

Roos, Leslie L., Jr., and Noralou P. Roos.
1971 Managers of Modernization. Cambridge, Massachusetts: Harvard University Press.

Rostow, Walt W.
1960 The Stages of Economic Growth. London: Cambridge University Press.

Russett, Bruce M.
1968 "Delineating international regions." Pp. 317–352 in J. David Singer (ed.), Quantitative International Politics: Insights and Evidence. New York: Free Press.

Russett, Bruce M., et al.
1964 World Handbook of Political and Social Indicators. New Haven, Connecticut: Yale University Press.

Rustow, Dankwart A.
1967 A World of Nations. Washington, D.C.: Brookings Institution.

Sawyer, Jack.
1967 "Dimensions of nations: Size, wealth,

and politics." American Journal of Sociology 73(September): 145–172.

Schnore, Leo F.
1961 "The statistical measurement of urbanization and economic development." Land Economics 37(August): 229–245.

Schramm, Wilbur.
1963 "Communication development and the development process." Pp. 30–57 in Lucian W. Pye (ed.), Communications and Political Development. Princeton, New Jersey: Princeton University Press.
1964 Mass Media and National Development. Stanford, California: Stanford University Press.
1967 "Communication and change." Pp. 5–32 in Daniel Lerner and Wilbur Schramm (eds.), Communication and Change in the Developing Countries. Honolulu: East-West Center Press.

Schramm, Wilbur, and W. Lee Ruggels.
1967 "How mass media systems grow." Pp. 57–75 in Daniel Lerner and Wilbur Schramm (eds.), Communication and Change in the Developing Countries. Honolulu: East-West Center Press.

Schultz, Theodore W.
1961 "Investment in human capital." American Economic Review 51(March): 1–17.
1964 Transforming Traditional Agriculture. New Haven, Connecticut: Yale University Press.

Schwartz, Richard, and James C. Miller.
1964 "Legal evolution and societal complexity." American Journal of Sociology 70 (September): 159–169.

Shannon, Lyle W.
1958 "Is level of development related to capacity for self-government?" American Journal of Economics and Sociology 17(July): 367–381.
1959 "Socio-economic development and political status." Social Problems 7(Fall): 157–169.
1962 "Socio-economic development and demographic variables as predictors of political change." Sociological Quarterly 3(January): 27–43.

Shannon, Lyle W. (ed.).
1957 Underdeveloped Areas. New York: Harper.

Shils, Edward A.
1956 The Torment of Secrecy. Glencoe, Illinois: Free Press.
1963 "Demagogues and cadres in the political development of the new states." Pp. 64–77 in Lucian W. Pye (ed.), Communications and Political Development. Princeton, New Jersey: Princeton University Press.

Siebert, Fred; Theodore Peterson; and Wilbur Schramm.
1956 Four Theories of the Press. Urbana: University of Illinois Press.

Silvert, Kalman H. (ed.).
1963 Expectant Peoples: Nationalism and Development. New York: Random House.

Simon, Herbert A.
1957a Administrative Behavior. Second Edition. New York: Macmillan.
1957b Models of Man. New York: Wiley.

Simpson, Dick.
1964 "The congruence of the political, social and economic aspects of development." International Development Review 6(June): 21–25.

Smelser, Neil J.
1966 "The modernization of social relations." Pp. 110–121 in Myron Weiner (ed.), Modernization: The Dynamics of Growth. New York: Basic Books.

Solow, Robert M.
1957 "Technical change and the aggregate production function." Review of Economics and Statistics 39(August): 312–320.

Sommerlad, E. Lloyd.
1966 The Press in Developing Countries. Sydney: Sydney University Press.

Spector, Paul, et al.
1963 Communication and Motivation in Community Development: An Experiment. Washington, D.C.: Institute for International Services.

Spengler, Joseph J.
1963 "Bureaucracy and economic development." Pp. 199–232 in Joseph LaPalombara (ed.), Bureaucracy and Political Development. Princeton, New Jersey: Princeton University Press.

Stycos, J. Mayone.
1965 "The potential role of Turkish village opinion leaders in a program of

family planning." Public Opinion Quarterly 29(Spring):120–130.

Taylor, Charles Lewis.
1969 "Communications development and political stability." Comparative Political Studies 1(January):557–563.

Troldahl, Verling C.
1966 "A field test of a modified two-step flow of communication model." Public Opinion Quarterly 30(Winter):609–623.

UNESCO.
1961 Mass Media in the Developing Countries. Reports and Papers on Mass Communication No. 33. Paris: UNESCO.
1962– Statistical Yearbook. Paris: UNESCO. Annual.
1963 Statistics on Radio and Television, 1950–1960. Paris: UNESCO.

United Nations.
1948– Demographic Yearbook. New York: United Nations. Annual.
1948– Statistical Yearbook. New York: United Nations. Annual.

Van Den Ban, A. W.
1964 "A revision of the two-step flow of communications hypothesis." Gazette 10 (No. 3):237–249.

Verba, Sidney.
1965 "Comparative political culture." Pp. 512–560 in Lucian W. Pye and Sidney Verba (eds.), Political Culture and Political Development. Princeton, New Jersey: Princeton University Press.

Washburn, Sherwood L., and Jane B. Lancaster.
1968 "Evolution: III. Human evolution." Pp. 215–221 in David L. Sills (ed.), International Encyclopedia of the Social Sciences. Volume 5. New York: Macmillan.

Weiner, Myron.
1966 "Political participation and political development." Pp. 205–217 in Myron Weiner (ed.), Modernization: The Dynamics of Growth. New York: Basic Books.

Wilensky, Harold L.
1967 Organizational Intelligence. New York: Basic Books.

Wilkinson, Rupert.
1964 Gentlemanly Power; British Leadership and the Public School Tradition. New York: Oxford University Press.

Wilson, David.
1963 "Nation building and revolutionary war." Pp. 84–94 in Karl W. Deutsch and William J. Foltz (eds.), Nation Building. New York: Atherton.

Winham, Gilbert R.
1970 "Political development and Lerner's theory: Further test of a causal model." American Political Science Review 64(September):810–818.

Wriggins, Harold.
1966 "National integration." Pp. 181–191 in Myron Weiner (ed.), Modernization: The Dynamics of Growth. New York: Basic Books.

Zonis, Marvin.
1971 The Political Elite of Iran. Princeton, New Jersey: Princeton University Press.

ADDITIONAL READINGS

Abegglen, James C. "Personality Factors in Social Mobility: A Study of Occupationally Mobile Businessmen." *Genetic Psychology Monographs* 58(1958):101–159.

Adelman, Irma. *Theories of Economic Growth and Development*. Stanford, Calif.: Stanford University Press, 1961.

Almond, Gabriel A. "Political Development: Analytical and Normative Perspectives." *Comparative Political Studies* 1(January, 1969):447–469.

Anderson, C. Arnold. "The Modernization of Education." In *Modernization: The Dynamics of Growth*, edited by Myron Weiner, pp. 68–80. New York: Basic Books, 1966.

Axelrad, Sidney. "Infant Care and Personality Reconsidered: Rejoinder to Orlansky." In *The Psychoanalytic Study of Society*, edited by Warner Muensterberger and Sidney Axelrad, pp. 75–132. New York: International Universities Press, 1962.

Bastian, Jarvis. "Communication, Animal: I. Social and Psychological Analysis." In *International Encyclopedia of the Social Sciences*, edited by David L. Sills, Vol. 3, pp. 29–33. New York: Macmillan, 1968.

Bauer, Peter T., and Yamey, Basil S. *The Economics of Underdeveloped Countries*. Chicago: University of Chicago Press, 1957.

Bettinghaus, Erwin P. "Communication Models." In *Research, Principles, and Practices in Visual Communication*, edited by John Ball and Francis Byrnes. East Lansing, Mich.: National Project in Agricultural Communications, Michigan State University, 1960.

Birdwhistell, Ray L. "Communication." In *International Encyclopedia of the Social Sciences*, edited by David L. Sills, Vol. 3, pp. 24–29. New York: Macmillan, 1968.

Bock, Walter J., and von Wahlert, Gerd. "Two Evolutionary Theories—A Discussion." *British Journal for the Philosophy of Science* 14(August, 1963):140–146.

Bwy, Douglas P. "Correlates of Political Instability in Latin America: Over-Time Comparisons from Brazil, Cuba, The Dominican Republic, and Panama." Unpublished paper presented to the Annual Meeting of the American Political Science Association, 1968.

———. "Political Instability in Latin America: The Cross-Cultural Test of a Causal Model." *Latin American Research Review* 3(Spring, 1968):17–66.

Caplow, Theodore, and Finsterbusch, Kurt. "Development Rank: A New Method of Rating National Development." Unpublished paper, Bureau of Applied Social Research, Columbia University, 1964.

Carter, Roy E., Jr., and Sepulveda, Orlando. "Some Patterns of Mass Media Use in Santiago de Chile." *Journalism Quarterly* 41(Spring, 1964):216–224.

Cattell, Raymond B. "The Dimensions of Culture Patterns by Factorization of National Characters." *Journal of Abnormal and Social Psychology* 44(October, 1949):443–469.

———. "The Principal Culture Patterns Discoverable in the Syntal Dimensions of Existing Nations." *Journal of Social Psychology* 32(August, 1950):215–253.

———, et al. "An Attempt at More Refined Definition of the Cultural Dimensions of Syntality in Modern Nations." *American Sociological Review* 17(August, 1952):408–421.

Cherry, Colin. "The Communication of Information (An Historical Review)." *American Scientist* 40(October, 1952):640–663.

———. *On Human Communication*. New York: Wiley, 1957.

Coleman, James S. "Modernization: II. Political Aspects." In *International Encyclopedia of the Social Sciences*, edited by David L. Sills, Vol. 10, pp. 395–402. New York: Macmillan.

Deane, Phyllis. "The Long-Term Trends in World Economic Growth." Reprinted in part in *Leading Issues in Development Economics*, edited by Gerald M. Meier, pp. 5–11. New York: Oxford University Press, 1964.

Deutsch, Karl W., and Foltz, William J., eds. *Nation Building*. New York: Atherton, 1963.

Deutschmann, Paul J.; Ellingworth, Hubert; and McNelly, John T. *Communication and Social Change in Latin America*. New York: Praeger, 1968.

Dobzhansky, Theodosius. *Mankind Evolving*. New Haven, Conn.: Yale University Press, 1962.

Doob, Leonard W. *Communication in Africa: A Search for Boundaries*. New Haven, Conn.: Yale University Press, 1961.

Eisenstadt, S. N. "Communication Systems and Social Structure: An Exploratory Comparative Study." *Public Opinion Quarterly* 19(Summer, 1955):153–167.

———. "Social Change, Differentiation and Evolution." *American Sociological Review* 29(June, 1964):375–386.

———. "Evolution: V. Social Evolution. In *International Encyclopedia of the Social Sciences*, edited by David L. Sills, Vol. 5, pp. 228–234. New York: Macmillan.

Elder, Joseph W. "Socialization to National Identification: Indian Students." Unpublished paper presented at the Annual Meeting of the American Political Science Association, New York City, 1966.

Elkind, David, and Flavell, John H. *Studies in Cognitive Development*. New York: Oxford University Press, 1969.

Festinger, Leon A. *A Theory of Cognitive Dissonance*. Evanston, Ill.: Row, Peterson, 1957.

Finsterbusch, Kurt, and Caplow, Theodore. "A Matrix of Modernization." Unpublished paper presented at the Annual Meeting of the American Sociological Association, 1964.

Flanigan, William, and Fogelman, Edwin. "Patterns of Democratic Development: An Historical Quantitative Analysis." Unpublished paper presented to the Annual Meeting of the American Political Science Association, 1968.

Flavell, John H. *The Developmental Psychology of Jean Piaget*. Princeton, N.J.: Van Nostrand, 1963.

Forbes, Hugh Donald, and Tufte, Edward R. "A Note of Caution in Causal Modelling." *American Political Science Review* 62(December, 1968):1258–1264.

Frey, Frederick W. "Political Science, Education, and National Development." In *The Social Sciences and the Comparative Study of Educational Systems*, edited by Joseph Fischer, pp. 349–408. Scranton, Pa.: International Textbook, 1970.

Gerschenkron, Alexander. *Economic Development in Historical Perspective*. Cambridge, Mass.: Harvard University Press, 1962.

Gregg, Phillip M., and Banks, Arthur S. "Dimensions of Political Systems: Factor Analysis of a Cross-Polity Survey." *American Political Science Review* 59(September, 1965):602–614.

Grossholtz, Thelma Jean, and Hendrickson, Richard. "A Selected Bibliography." In *Communications and Political Development*, edited by Lucian W. Pye, pp. 351–368. Princeton, N.J.: Princeton University Press, 1963.

Hagen, Everett E. "How Economic Growth Begins: A General Theory Applied to Japan." *Public Opinion Quarterly* 22(Fall, 1958):373–390.

Hansen, Donald A., and Parsons, J. Herschel. *Mass Communication: A Research Bibliography*. Santa Barbara, Calif.: Glendessary Press, 1968.

Hoselitz, Bert F. "Theories of Stages of Economic Growth." In *Theories of Economic Growth*, edited by Bert F. Hoselitz, pp. 193–238. Glencoe, Ill.: Free Press, 1960.

Hurwicz, Leonid. "Conditions for Economic Efficiency of Centralized and Decentralized Structures." In *Value and Plan*, edited by Gregory Grossman, pp. 162–175. Berkeley: University of California Press, 1960.

———. "Optimality and Informational Efficiency in Resource Allocation Processes." In *Mathematical Models in the Soctal Sciences*, edited by Kenneth Arrow et al., pp. 27–46. Stanford, Calif.: Stanford University Press, 1960.

Hymes, Dell. "Linguistic Aspects of Comparative Political Research." In *The Methodology of Comparative Research*, edited by Robert T. Holt and John Turner, pp. 295–341. New York: Free Press, 1970.

Johnson, Wendell. "The Communication Process and General Semantic Principles." In *Mass Communications: A Book of Readings*, edited by Wilbur Schramm, pp. 301–315. Urbana: University of Illinois Press, 1960.

Kahl, Joseph A. *The Measurement of Modernism*. Austin: University of Texas Press, 1968.

Kohlberg, Lawrence. "Stage and Sequence: The Cognitive-Developmental Approach to Socialization." In *Handbook of Socialization Theory and Research*, edited by David A. Goslin, pp. 347–480. Chicago: Rand McNally, 1969.

Langer, Jonas. *Theories of Development*. New York: Holt, Rinehart and Winston, 1969.

LaPalombara, Joseph, ed. *Bureaucracy and Political Development*. Princeton, N.J.: Princeton University Press, 1963.

Lasswell, Harold D. "The Structure and Function of Communication in Society." In *The Communication of Ideas*, edited by Lyman Bryson, New York: Harper and Row, 1948.

Lerner, Daniel, and Schramm, Wilbur, eds. *Communication and Change in Developing Countries*. Honolulu: East-West Center Press, 1967.

Levy, Marion J., Jr. "Contrasting Factors in the Modernization of China and Japan." In *Economic Growth: Brazil, India, Japan*, edited by Simon S. Kuznets et al., pp. 496–536. Durham, N.C.: Duke University Press, 1955.

Lewis, W. Arthur. *The Theory of Economic Growth*. London: George Allen and Unwin, 1955.

Mayr, Ernst. "The Nature of the Darwinian Revolution." *Sciences* 176(June, 1972): 981–989.

Meier, Gerald M., ed. *Leading Issues in Development Economics*. New York: Oxford University Press, 1964.

Moore, Wilbert E. *Social Change*. Englewood Cliffs, N.J.: Prentice-Hall, 1963.

———. "Social Change." In *International Encyclopedia of the Social Sciences*, edited by David L. Sills, Vol. 14, pp. 365–375. New York: Macmillan, 1968.

Morris, Charles W. "Foundations of the Theory of Signs." In *International Encyclopedia of Unified Science*, edited by Otto Neurath, Rudolf Carnap, and Charles Morris, Vol. 1, pp. 77–139. Chicago: University of Chicago Press, 1938.

———. *Signs, Language and Behavior*. New York: Prentice-Hall, 1940.

Mowlana, Hamid. "Toward a Theory of Communication Systems: A Developmental Approach." Paper presented to the Association for Education in Journalism, Washington, D.C., August, 1970.

Myren, Delbert T. *Bibliography: Communications in Agricultural Development.* Mexico; n.p., 1965.

Newman, John B. "A Rationale for a Definition of Communication." *Journal of Communication* 10(1960):115–124. Reprinted in *Communication and Culture*, edited by Alfred G. Smith, pp. 55–63. New York: Holt, Rinehart and Winston, 1966.

Nurkse, Ragnar. *Problems of Capital Formation in Underdeveloped Countries.* New York: Oxford University Press, 1953.

Olsen, M. E. "National Development: Social, Economic, and Political." Unpublished paper, Indiana University, 1967.

Parsons, Talcott. "Evolutionary Universals in Society." *American Sociological Review* 29(June, 1964):339–357.

Piaget, Jean. "Developmental Psychology: II. A Theory of Development." In *International Encyclopedia of the Social Sciences*, edited by David L. Sills, Vol. 4, New York: Macmillan, 1968.

Pool, Ithiel de Sola. "Communication, Political: I. Introduction." In *International Encyclopedia of the Social Sciences*, edited by David L. Sills, Vol. 3, pp. 90–96. New York: Macmillan, 1968.

———. "The Role of Communication in the Process of Modernization and Technological Change." In *Industrialization and Society*, edited by Bert F. Hoselitz and Wilbert E. Moore, pp. 279–295. The Hague: Mouton, 1963.

Popper, Karl R. *The Poverty of Historicism.* New York: Basic Books, 1960.

Pye, Lucian W. "Communication Patterns and the Problems of Representative Government in Non-Western Societies." *Public Opinion Quarterly* 20(Spring, 1956): 249–257.

———, and Verba, Sidney, eds. *Political Culture and Political Development.* Princeton, N.J.: Princeton University Press, 1965.

Report on Communication and A.I.D. Washington, D.C.: Department of State, Agency for International Development, December, 1964.

Retzlaff, Ralph H. "The Use of Aggregate Data in Comparative Political Analysis." *Journal of Politics* 27(November, 1965): 797–817.

Rogers, Everett M. "A Communication Research Approach to the Diffusion of Innovations." In *Diffusion Research Needs*, chap. 4, pp. 27–30. North Central Regional Research Bulletin 186. Columbia, Mo.: University of Missouri Agricultural Experiment Station, 1968.

Rosenstein-Rodan, Paul N. "Notes on the Theory of the 'Big Push.'" In *Economic Development for Latin America*, edited by H. S. Ellis and H. C. Wallich, chap. 3. New York: St. Martin's Press, 1963. Also in *Readings in Economic Development*, edited by Theodore Morgan et al., pp. 143–150. Belmont, Calif: Wadsworth, 1963.

Roy, Prodipto; Waisanen, Frederick B.; and Rogers, Everett M. *The Impact of Communication on Rural Development.* Paris: UNESCO, 1969.

Sahlins, Marshall D., and Service, Elman R., eds. *Evolution and Culture.* Ann Arbor: University of Michigan Press, 1960.

Schramm, Wilbur, ed. *Mass Communications: A Book of Readings.* Urbana: University of Illinois Press, 1960.

Sebeok, Thomas A. "Communication, Animal: II. Communication Models and Signalling Behavior." In *International Encyclopedia of the Social Sciences*, edited by David L. Sills, Vol. 3, pp. 33–40. New York: Macmillan, 1968.

Service, Elman R. "Evolution: IV. Cultural Evolution." In *International Encyclopedia of the Social Sciences*, edited by David L. Sills, Vol. 5, New York: Macmillan, 1969.

Shils, Edward. "Intellectuals, Public Opinion and Economic Development." *World Politics* 10(January, 1958):232–255.

———. "The Intellectuals in the Political Development of the New States." *World Politics* 12(April, 1960):329–368.

———. "On the Comparative Study of the New States." In *Old Societies and New States*, edited by Clifford Geertz, pp. 1–26. New York: Free Press of Glencoe, 1963.

Simpson, George G. *The Meaning of Evolution.* New Haven, Conn.: Yale University Press, 1950.

———. "The Study of Evolution: Methods and Present Status of Theory." In *Behavior and Evolution*, edited by Anne Roe and George G. Simpson. New Haven, Conn.: Yale University Press, 1958.

———. *This View of Life: The World of an Evolutionist*. New York: Harcourt, Brace and World, 1964.

Smith, Alfred G., ed. *Communication and Culture*. New York: Holt, Rinehart and Winston, 1966.

Smith, David H., and Inkeles, Alex. "The OM Scale: A Comparative Socio-Psychological Measure of Individual Modernity." *Sociometry* 29(December, 1966):353–377.

Spengler, Joseph J. "Economic Factors in the Development of Densely Settled Areas." *Proceedings of the American Philosophical Society* 95(February, 1951):20–53.

Stevens, S. S. "Introduction: A Definition of Communication." *Journal of the Acoustical Society of America* 22(November, 1950): 689–690.

Steward, Julian H. *Theory of Culture Change*. Urbana: University of Illinois Press, 1955.

Udy, Stanley. "Dynamic Inferences from Static Data." *American Journal of Sociology* 70(March, 1965):625–628.

UNESCO. *Rural Television in Japan*. Paris: United Nations Educational, Scientific and Cultural Organization, 1960.

Weaver, Warren. "The Mathematics of Communication." *Scientific American* 181(July, 1949):11–15.

Weiner, Myron, ed. *Modernization: The Dynamics of Growth*. New York: Basic Books.

Westley, Bruce H., and MacLean, Malcolm S. "A Conceptual Model for Communications Research." *Journalism Quarterly* 34(Winter, 1957):31–38.

Wharton, Clifton R. "Modernizing Subsistence Agriculture." In *Modernization: The Dynamics of Growth*, edited by Myron Weiner, pp. 258–269. New York: Basic Books, 1966.

APPENDIX A Graphic Depictions of Developmental Indicators for Selected Nations, ca. 1960

The eight maps in Appendix A are reprinted from *Atlas of Economic Development* by Norton Ginsburg (Chicago: University of Chicago Press, 1961), by permission of the author and the publisher.

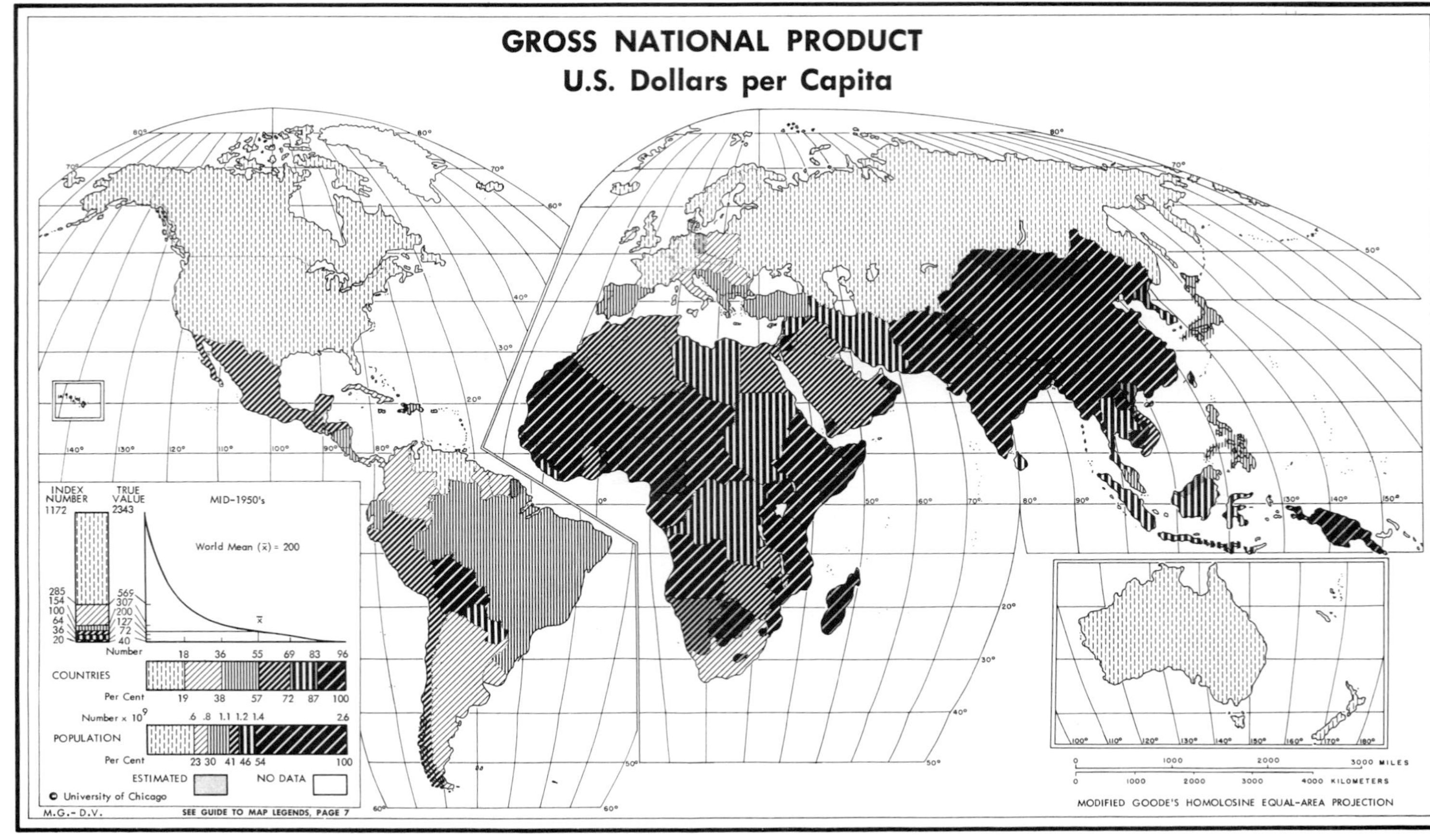

Figure A.1. Gross national product per capita in U.S. dollars (from Ginsburg, 1961:19, map 3).

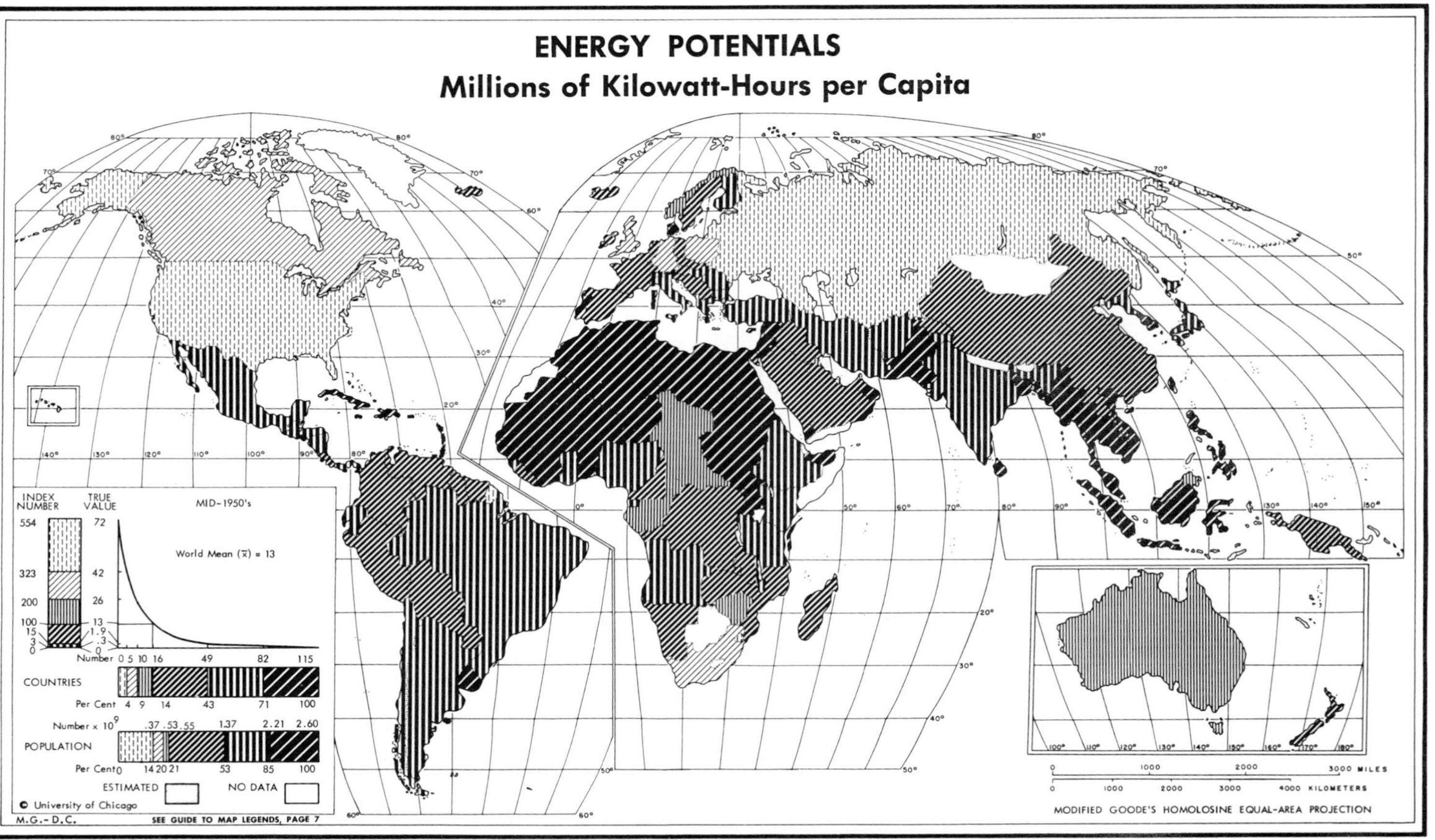

Figure A.2. Gross energy consumption in megawatt-hours per capita (from Ginsburg, 1961:59, map 23).

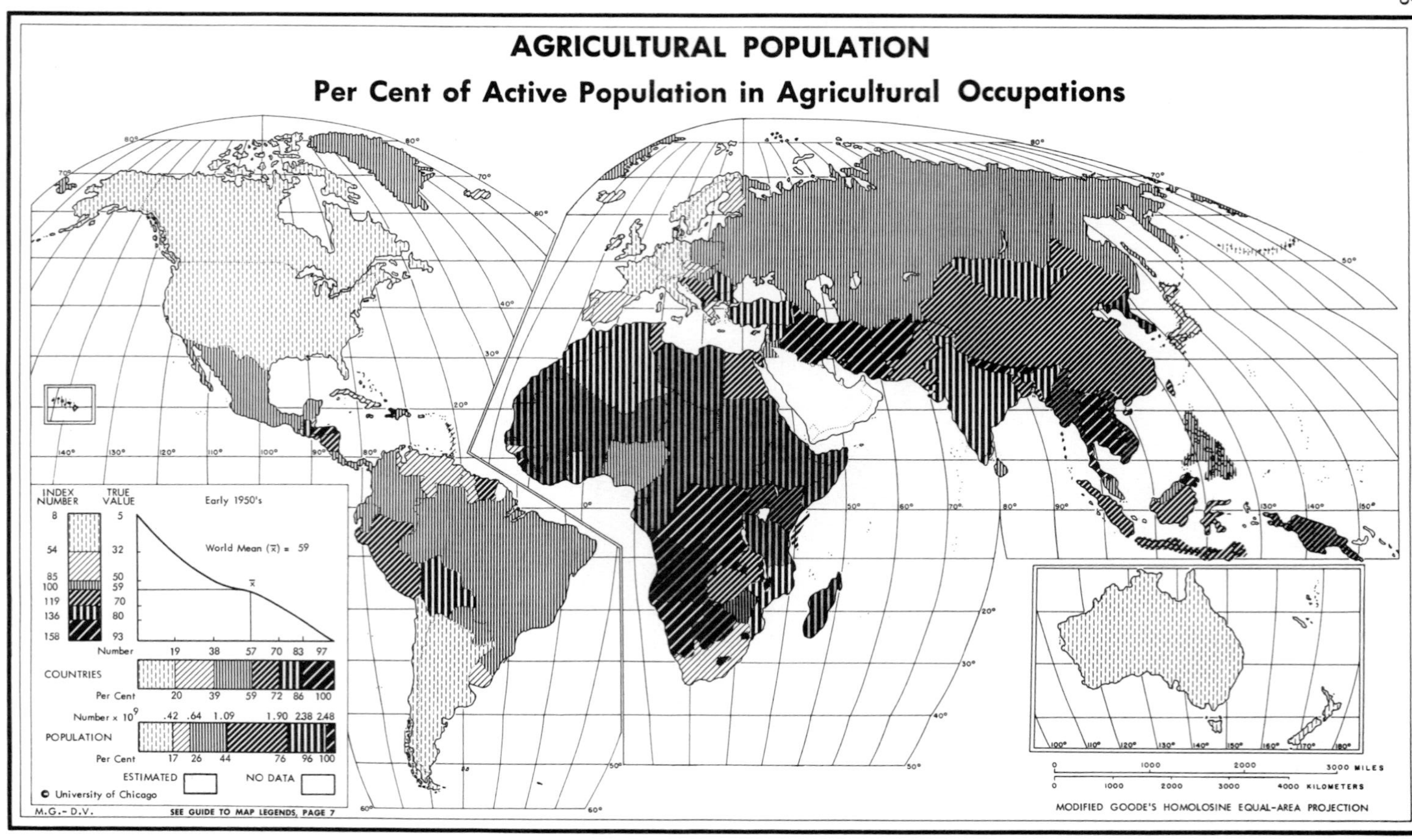

Figure A.3. Percentage of the active population in agricultural occupations (from Ginsburg, 1961:33, map 10).

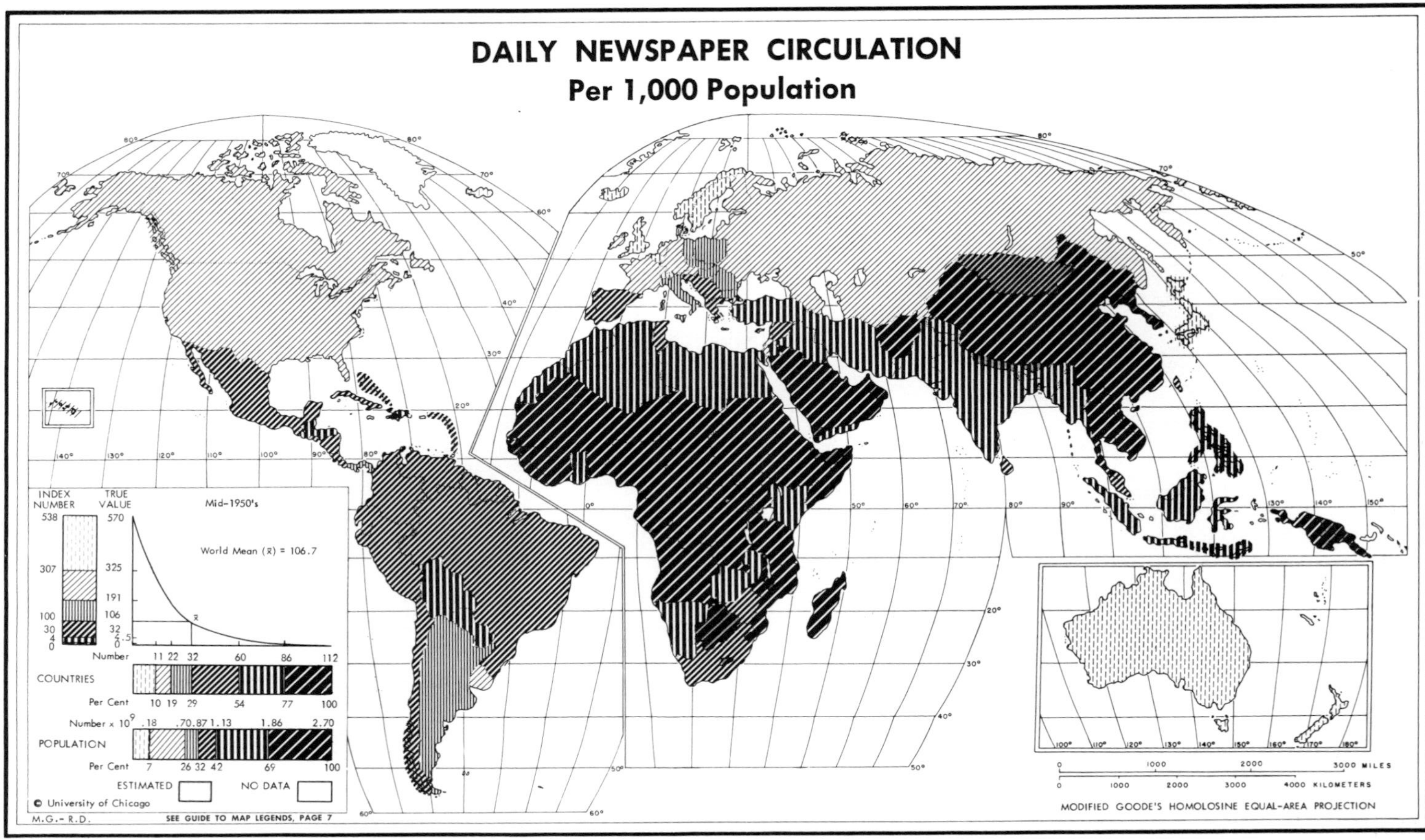

Figure A.4. Percentage of adults who are literate (from Ginsburg, 1961:39, map 13).

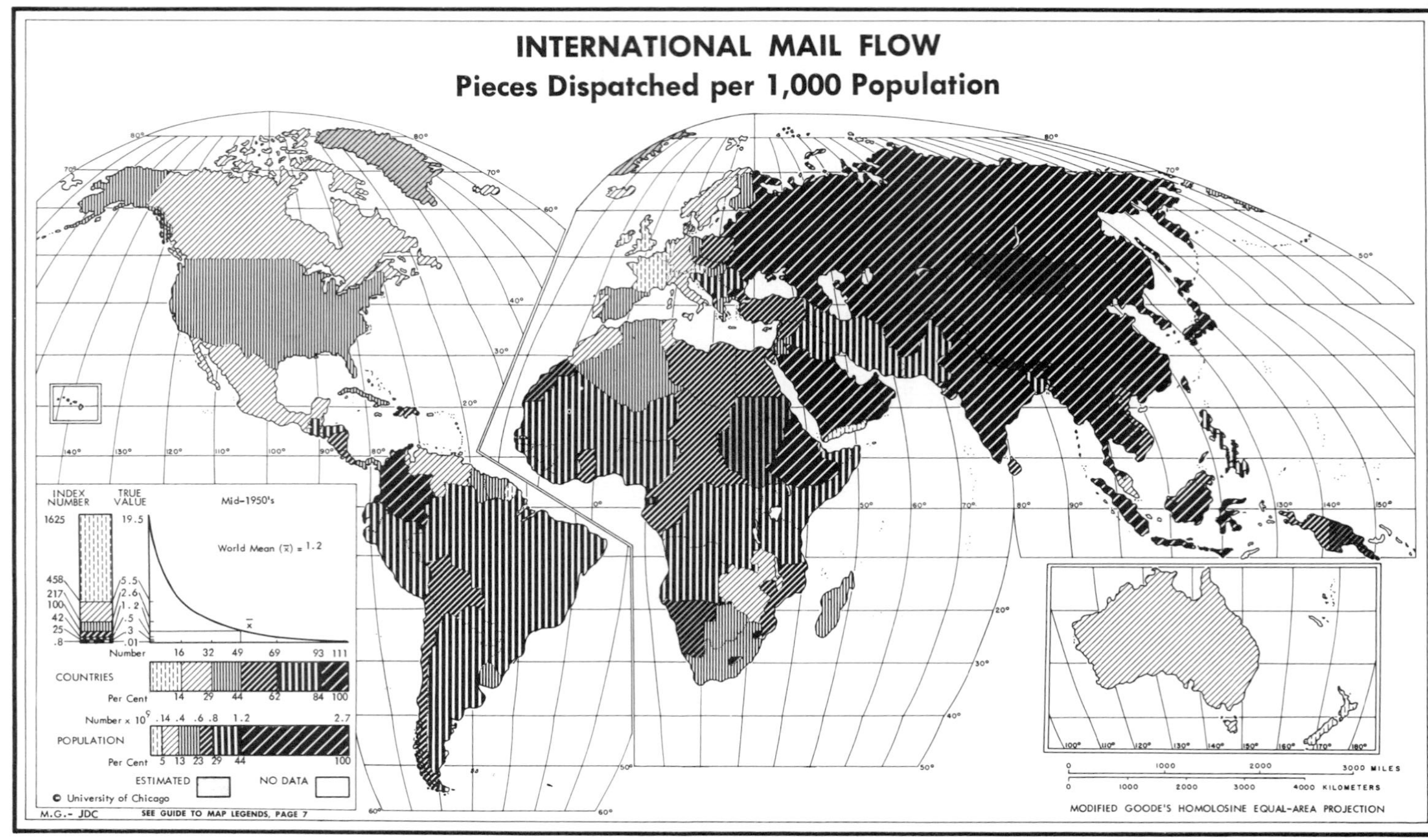

Figure A.5. Daily newspaper circulation per 1,000 population (from Ginsburg, 1961:41, map 14).

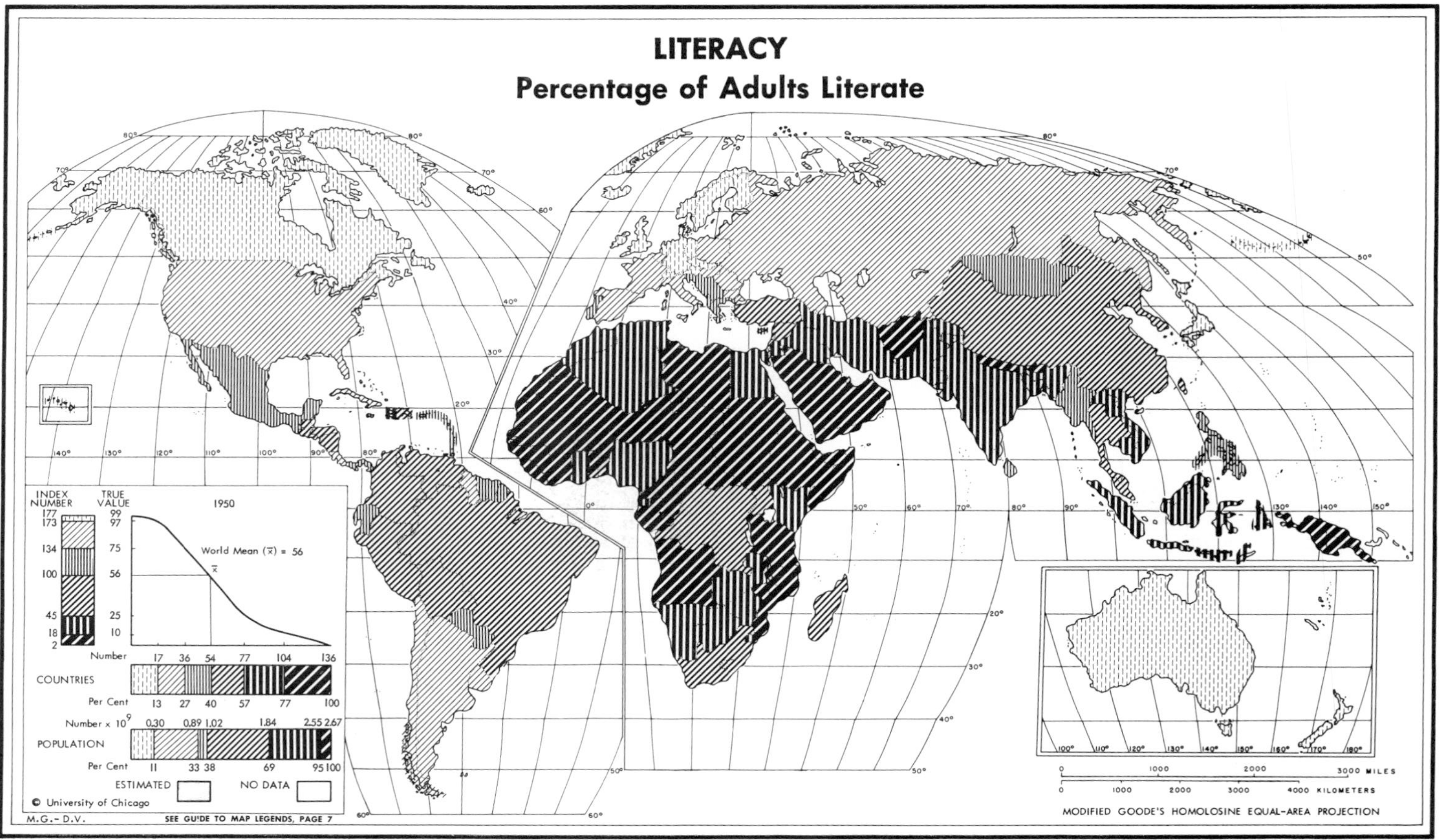

Figure A.6. Pieces of international mail per 1,000 population (from Ginsburg, 1961:101, map 44).

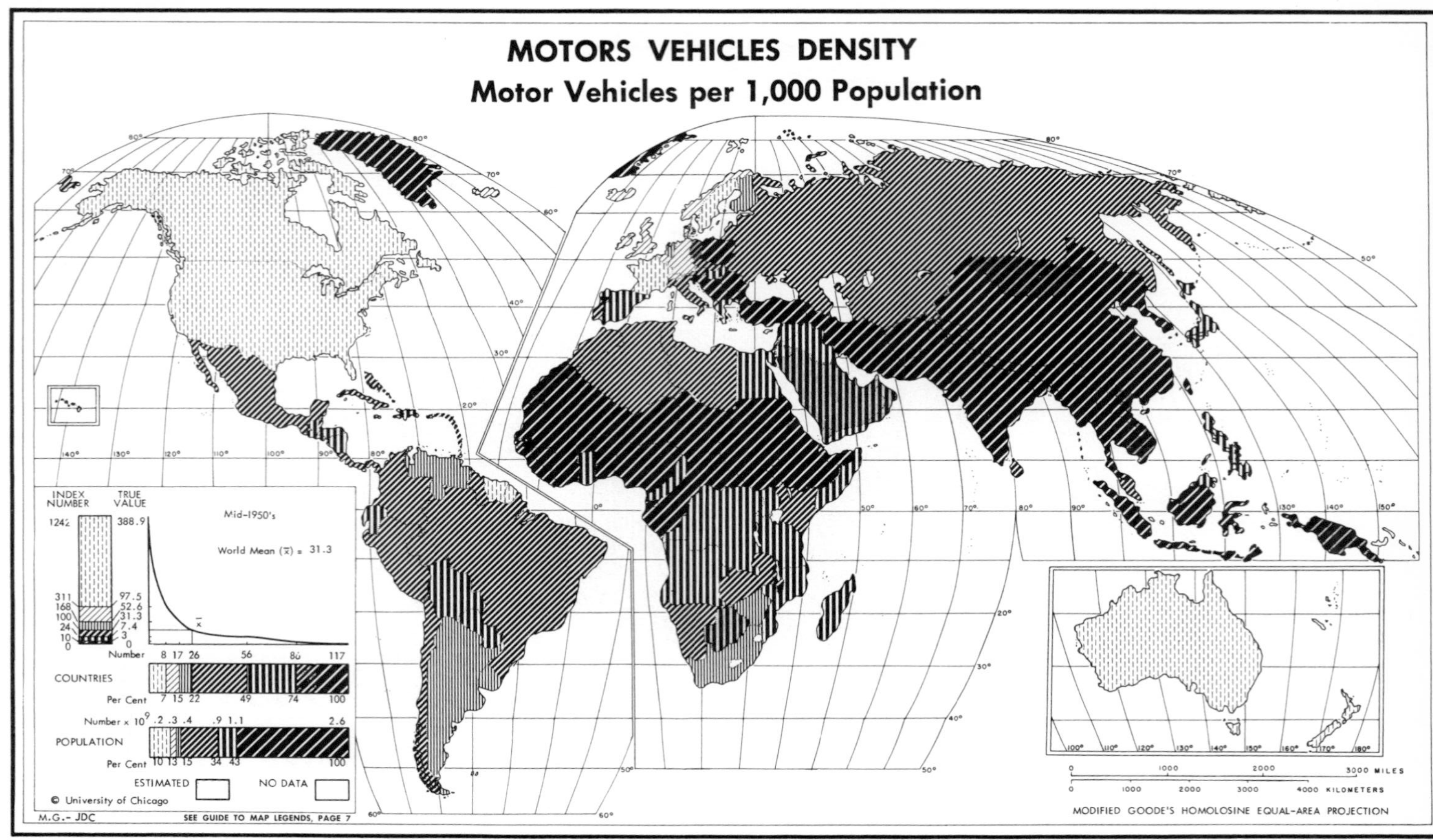

Figure A.7. Motor vehicles per 1,000 population (from Ginsburg, 1961:75, map 31).

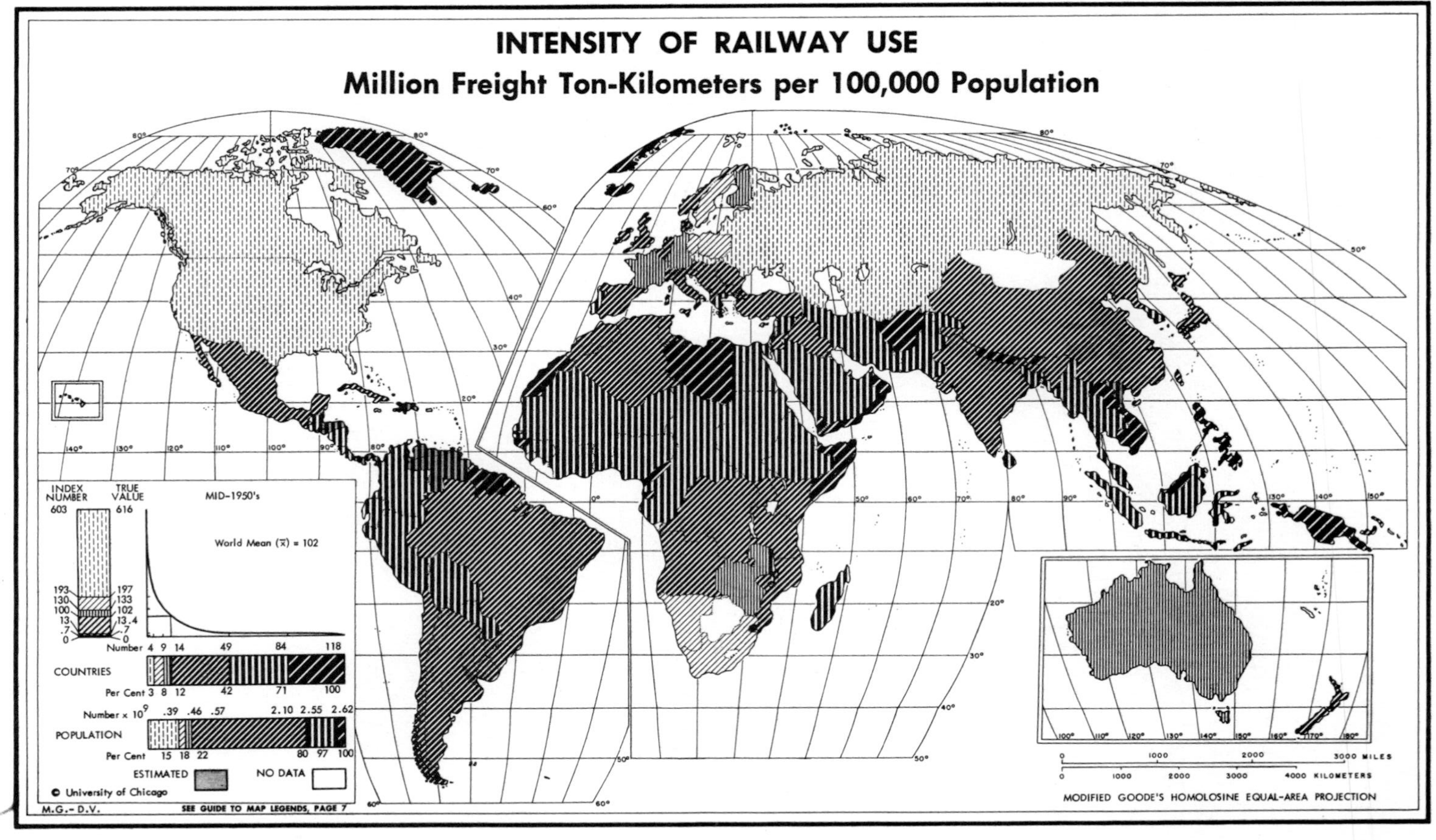

Figure A.8. Million ton-kilometers of railway freight per 100,000 population (from Ginsburg, 1961:69, map 28).

APPENDIX B The Growth of Specific National Communications, ca. 1950-1970

The charts in Appendix B employ a logarithmic scale denoting growth on the vertical ruling and an arithmetic scale denoting time on the horizontal ruling.

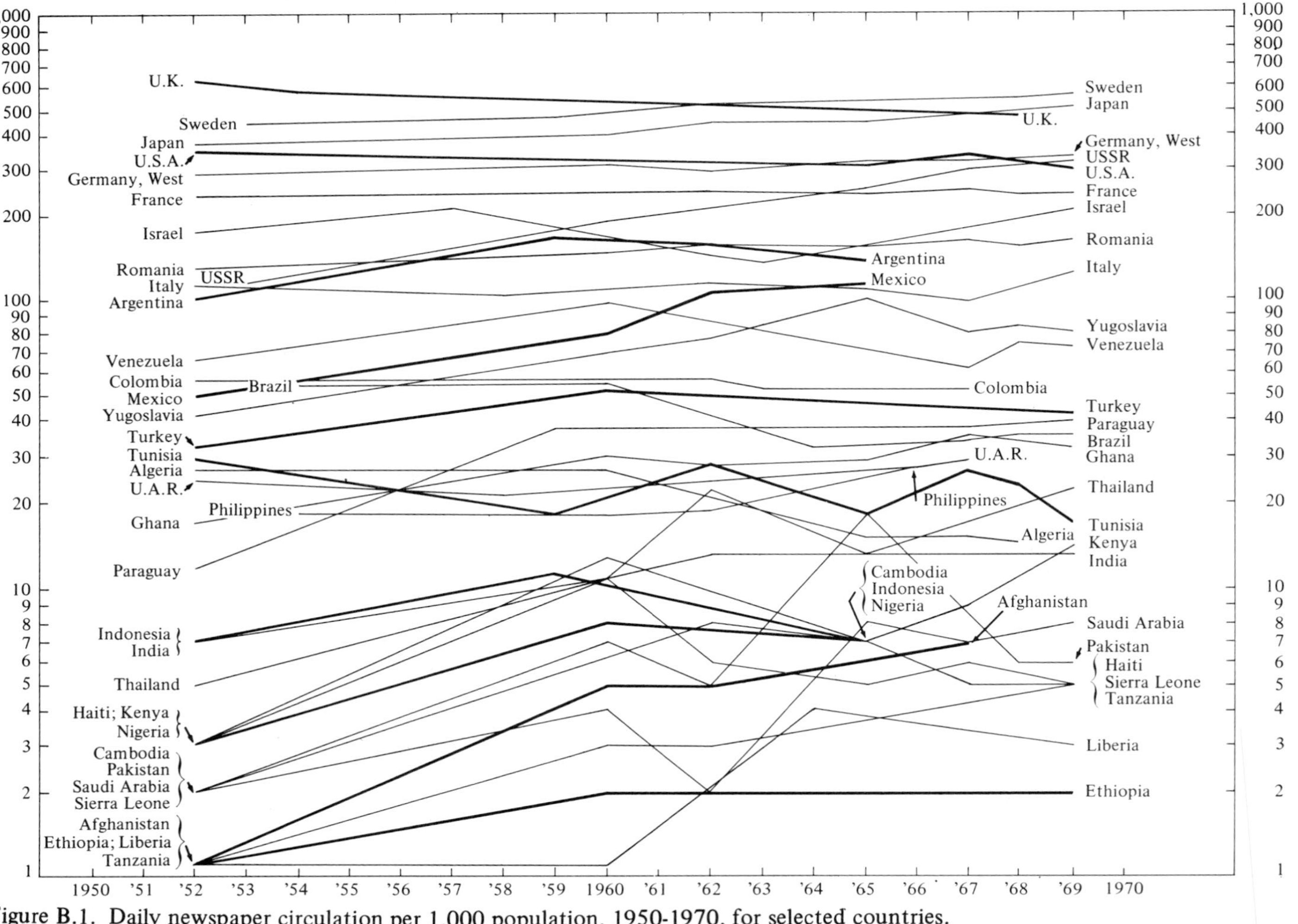

Figure B.1. Daily newspaper circulation per 1,000 population, 1950-1970, for selected countries.

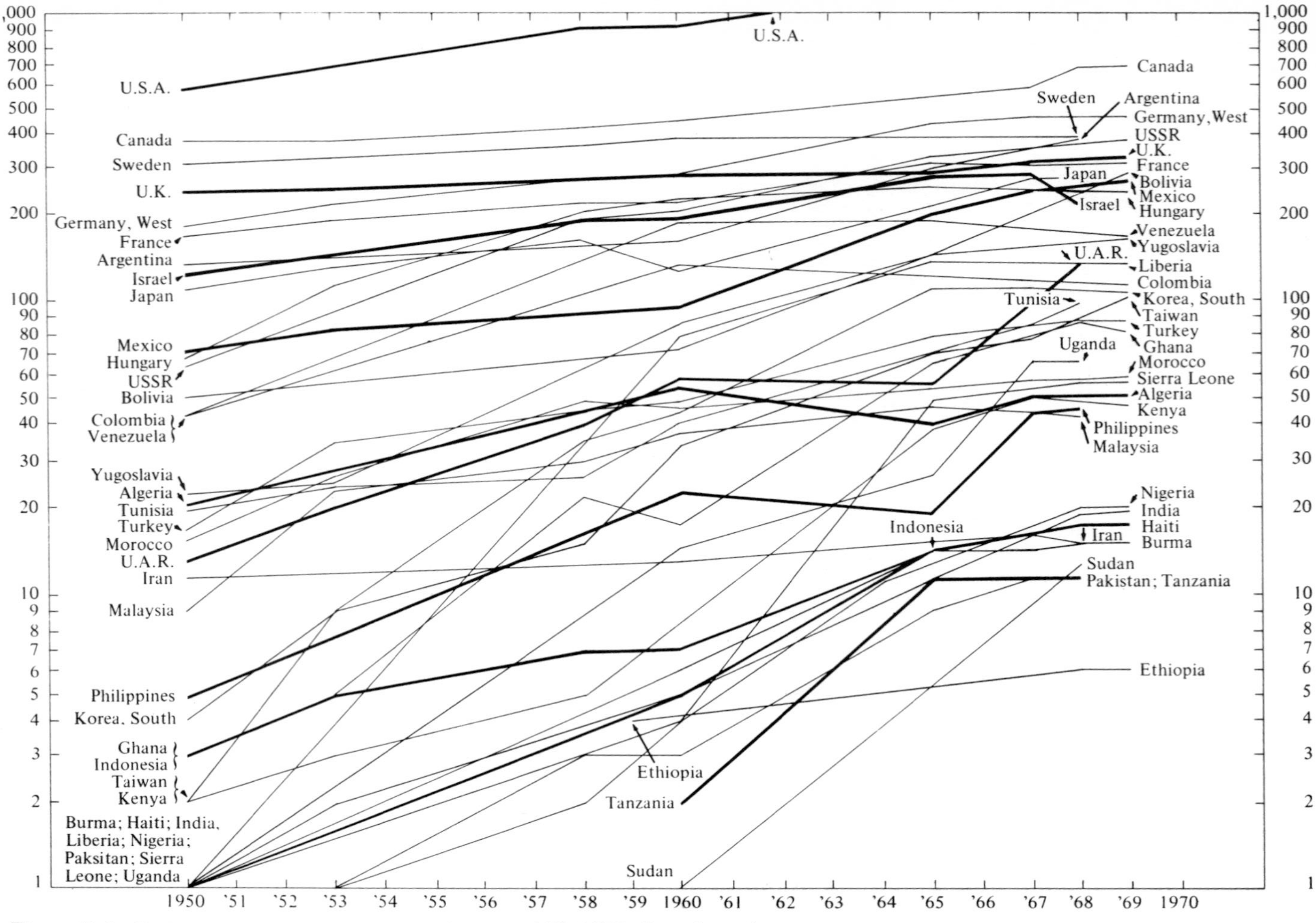

Figure B.2. Radio receivers per 1,000 population, 1950-1970, for selected countries.

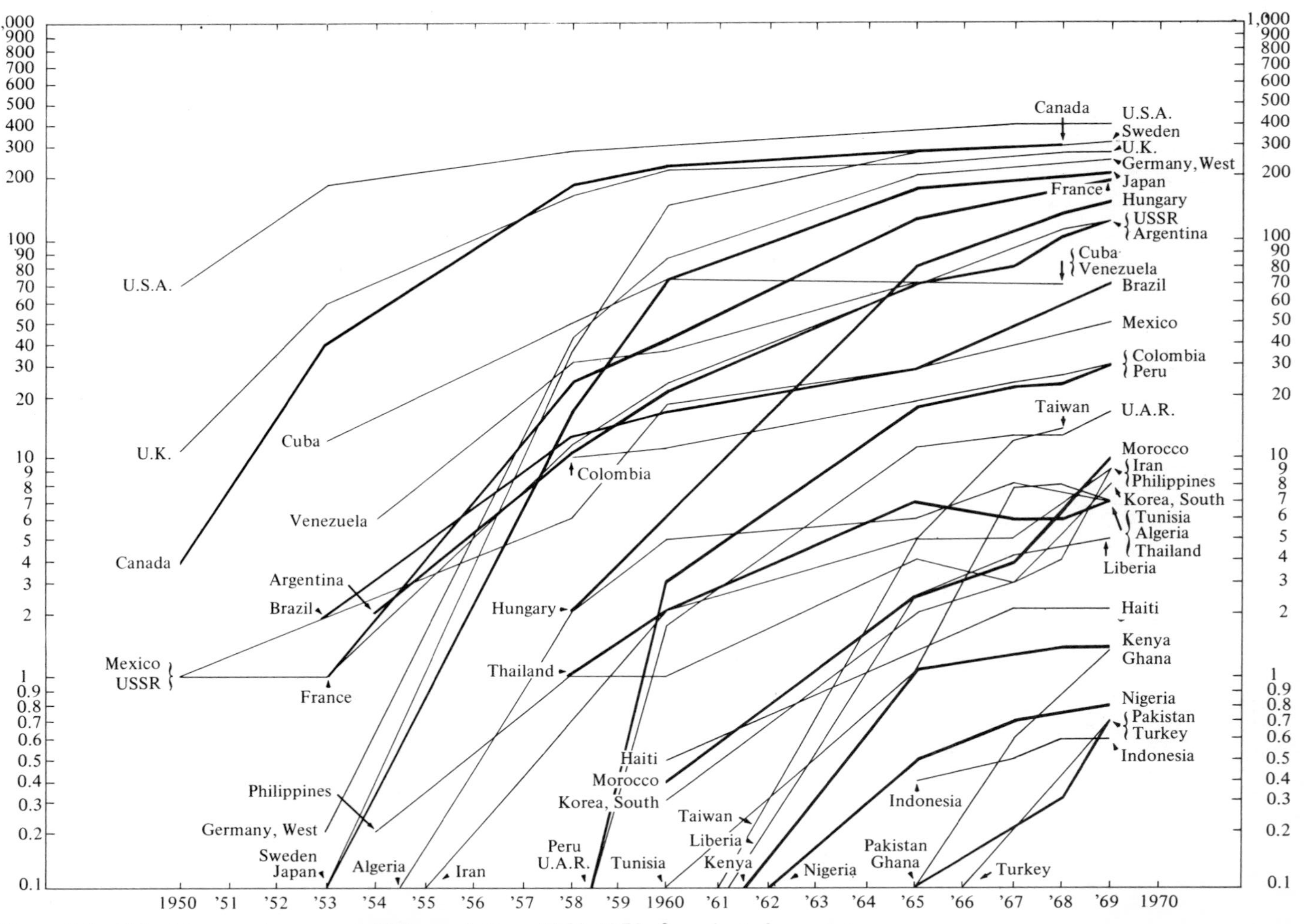

Figure B.3. Television receivers per 1,000 population, 1950-1970, for selected countries.

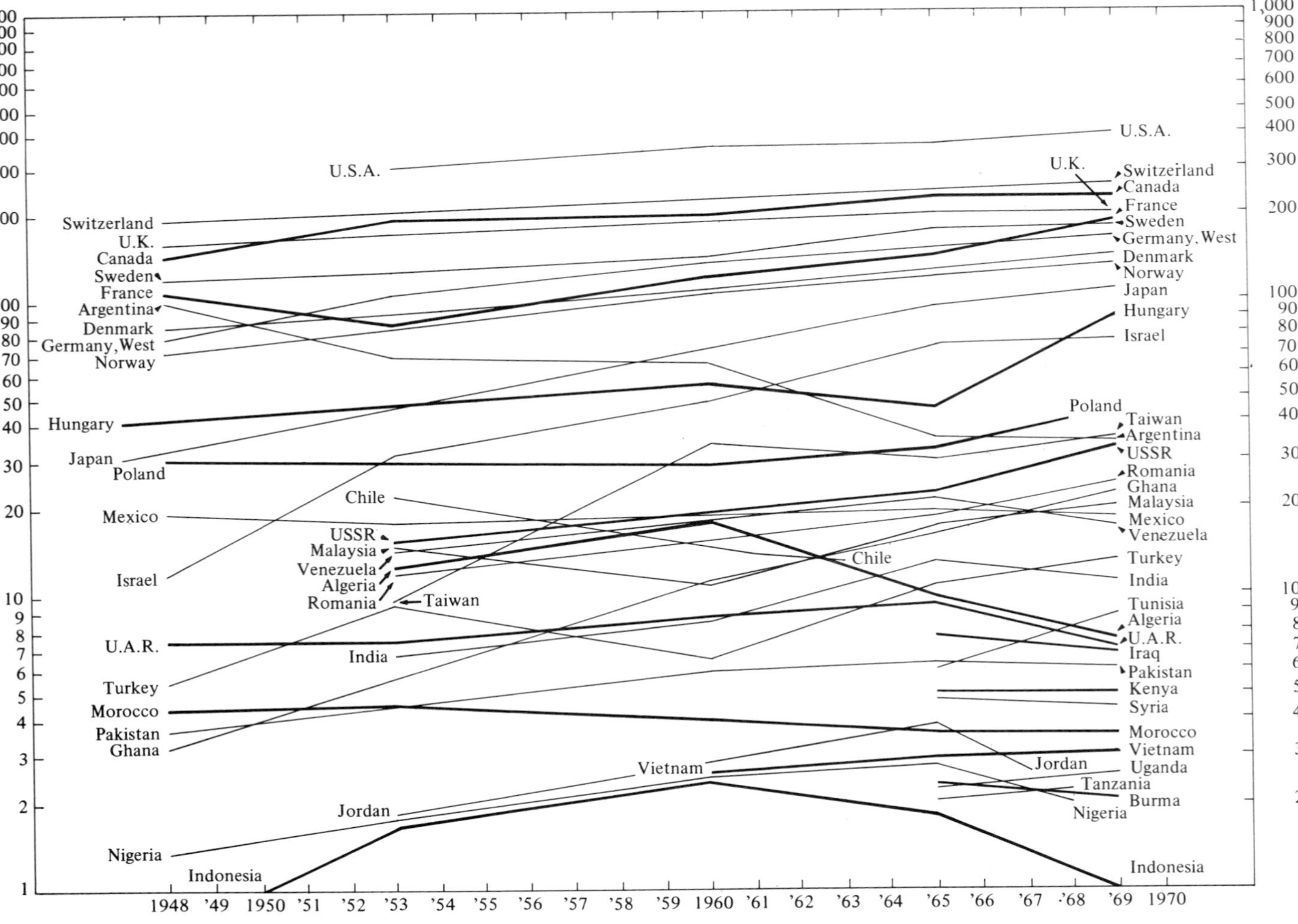

Figure B.4. Items per capita of domestic mail, 1948-1970, for selected countries.

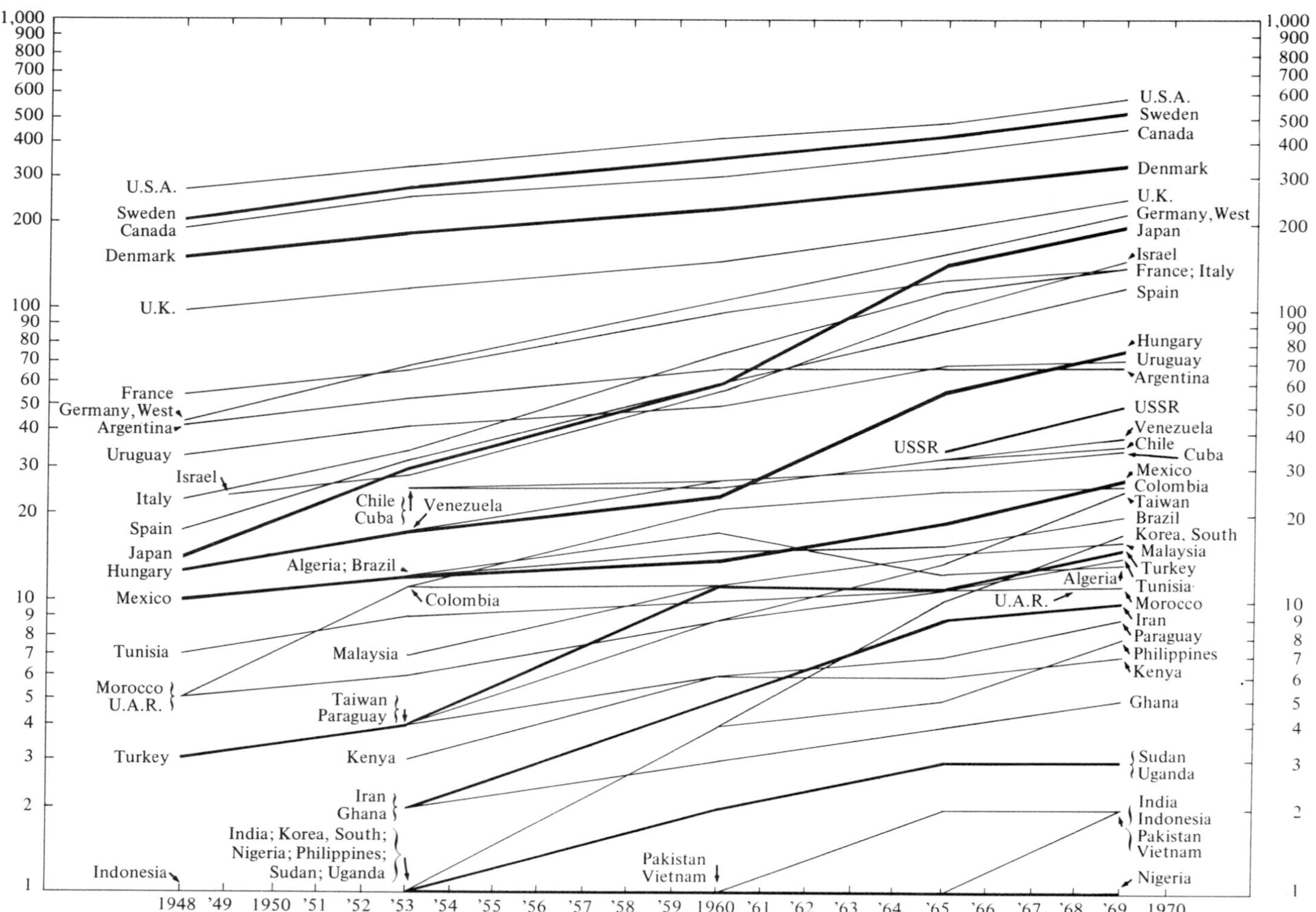

Figure B.5. Telephones per 1,000 population, 1948-1970, for selected countries.

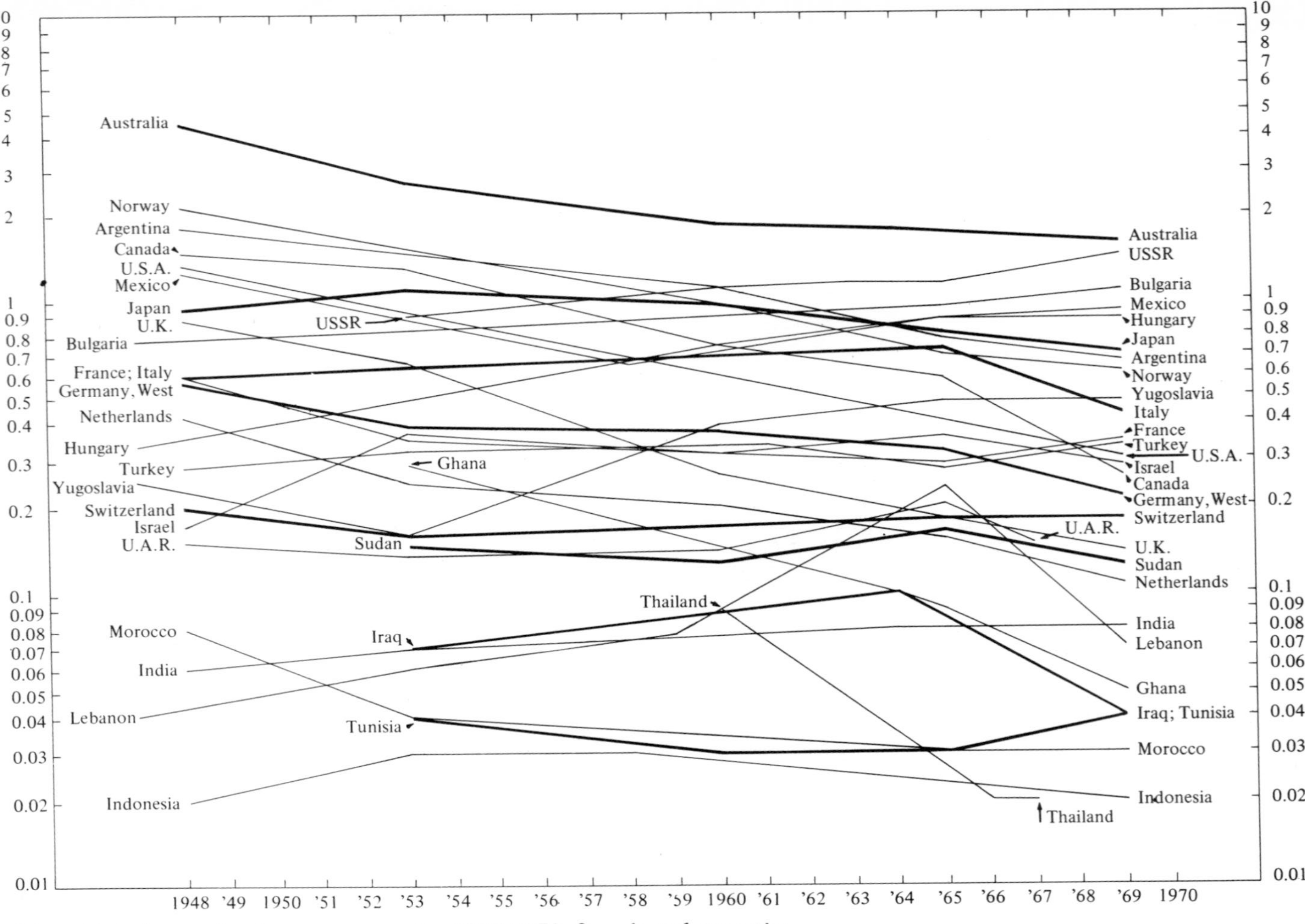

Figure B.6. Domestic telegrams per capita, 1948-1970, for selected countries.

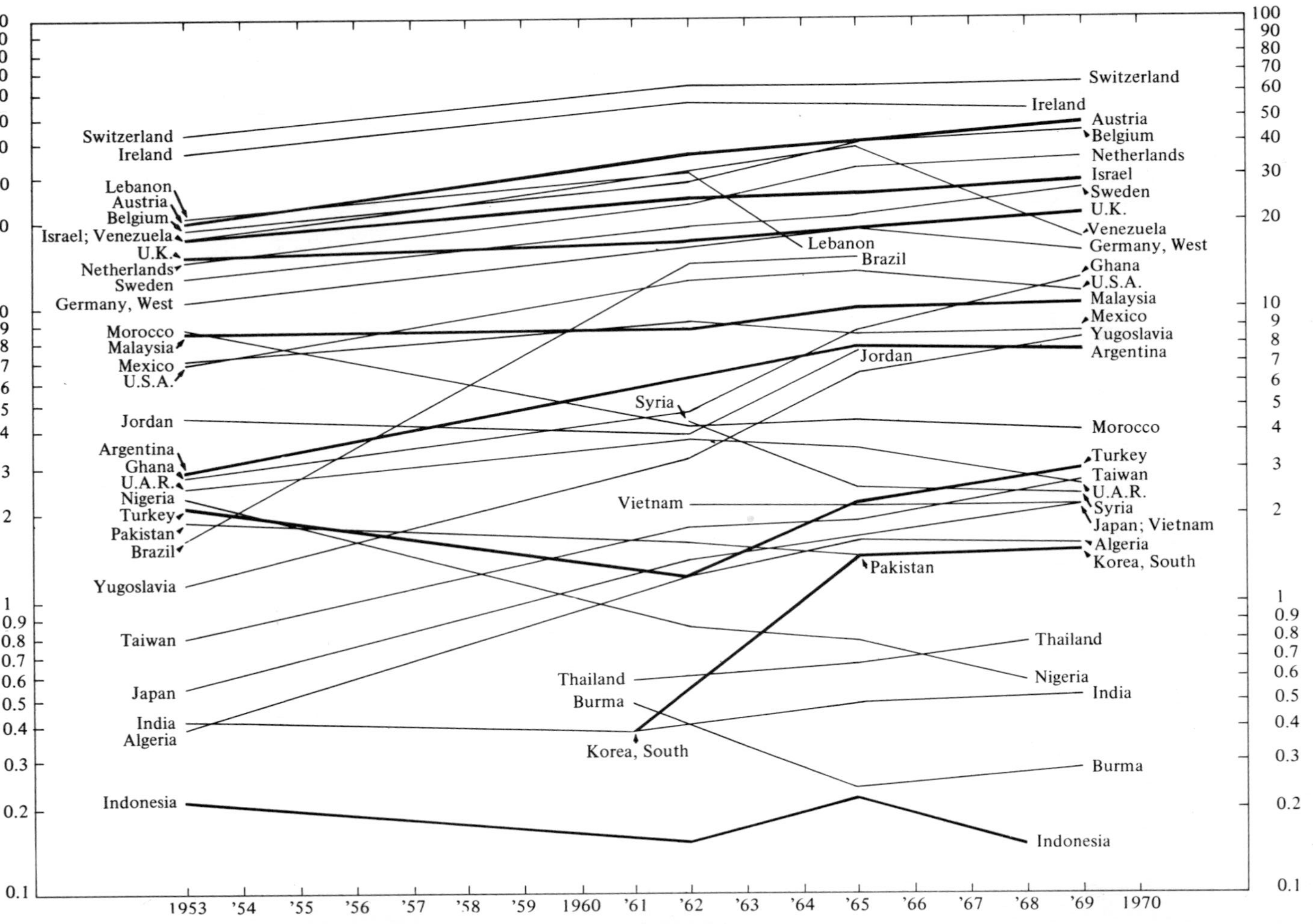

Figure B.7. Items per capita of foreign mail, 1953-1969, for selected countries.

APPENDIX C Communications Data for Selected Nations, ca. 1948-1970

TABLE C.1

CONSUMPTION OF PRINTING PAPER OTHER THAN NEWSPRINT
(Kilogram per capita)

Country	1960	1965	1967	1969
Afghanistan	–	0.02	0.03	0.05[c]
Algeria	2.6	0.7	0.9	–
Argentina	3.0	5.0	4.2	4.6[c]
Australia	11.7	12.3	15.2	17.1
Austria	9.4	16.3	13.8	15.3
Belgium	15.8	23.6	22.8	31.1
Bolivia	–	0.4	0.4	0.4[c]
Brazil	2.3	1.9	2.3	2.6[c]
Bulgaria	2.8	3.9	4.8	5.1
Burma	0.2	–	0.2	0.7
Cambodia	0.1	–	0.3	0.4[c]
Canada	17.6	22.3	24.5	28.1
Chile	2.9	3.2	4.0	4.8
China, Mainland	–	–	–	–
China, Taiwan	3.6	3.4	3.8	5.1
Colombia	1.9	–	1.8	1.9[c]
Cuba	1.9	2.9	2.8	3.0[c]
Czechoslovakia	4.9	5.6	9.6	10.3
Denmark	16.2	20.2	26.9	28.7
Ethiopia	–	0.04	0.1	0.1[c]
Finland	14.9	18.0	30.5	40.7
France	15.5	19.5	22.2	28.7
Germany, Dem. Rep.	9.0	10.4	–	–
Germany, Fed. Rep.	16.1	27.1	26.9	33.5
Ghana	0.2	0.6	1.0	0.6
Greece	3.3	4.4	3.9	4.5
Haiti	0.02[a]	0.04	0.04	0.04
Hungary	4.2	6.5	7.8	8.4
India	0.5	0.7	0.7	0.7
Indonesia	0.4	–	–	–
Iran	0.6	1.1	–	–
Iraq	1.1	0.7	0.9	1.0[c]
Ireland	3.7	5.2	4.9	5.6[c]
Israel	6.0	7.4	9.0	12.1
Italy	7.2	11.2	15.3	19.3
Japan	9.3	11.3	14.3	17.7
Jordan	1.2	0.9	0.5	–
Kenya	0.8	0.6	0.7	0.7[c]
Korea, Rep.	0.7	1.0	1.3	1.5
Lebanon	–	–	–	–
Liberia	0.05	0.3	–	–
Malaysia	1.0	1.4	1.3	1.9[c]
Mexico	1.0	3.4	3.9	4.0
Morocco	0.9	–	0.6	0.6[c]
Netherlands	18.5	29.2	29.3	34.9
Nigeria	0.1	0.1	0.1	0.2
Norway	19.6	22.4	24.1	22.2

TABLE C.1 *(Continued)*

Country	1960	1965	1967	1969
Pakistan	0.2	0.4	0.4	0.4[c]
Paraguay	0.2	0.2	0.3	0.2
Peru	0.8[a]	1.1	1.3	1.4[c]
Philippines	1.0[a]	1.1	–	–
Poland	4.8	4.9	6.1	6.7
Portugal	1.8	3.0	3.2	4.3
Puerto Rico	–	–	–	–
Romania	2.7	2.9	3.9	4.1[c]
Saudi Arabia	0.1	0.5	0.7	0.8[c]
Senegal	1.3	0.7	–	0.7
Sierra Leone	0.04	0.09	0.1	0.1
South Africa	3.2[a]	6.4	6.7	6.7[c]
Spain	3.4	5.4	6.8	8.2[c]
Sudan	0.1	0.2	0.2	0.3
Sweden	22.7	25.8	27.9	33.6
Switzerland	25.2	37.8	41.2	41.7[c]
Syria	0.3	0.7	1.4	1.3
Tanzania	0.1	0.2	0.2	0.3[c]
Thailand	0.6	–	0.4	0.4[c]
Tunisia	2.5	0.3	0.5	–
Turkey	–	0.8	1.1	1.3
Uganda	0.1	0.2	0.3	0.3
U.S.S.R.	3.1	3.7	4.2	–
U.A.R.	1.6	1.2	1.4	1.3[c]
U.K.	18.0	19.6	21.2	24.1
U.S.A.	25.1	33.4	44.6	49.4
Uruguay	4.8	3.4	3.3	4.0
Venezuela	3.0	3.1	3.6	3.6[c]
Vietnam, Rep.	–	1.0	1.0	–
Yugoslavia	3.0	5.3	5.0	5.7
Zambia	–	0.7	0.7	0.4[c]

SOURCE: UNESCO, *Statistical Yearbook* (1961; 1966; 1968; 1970).

[a] 1959

[b] 1966

[c] 1968

TABLE C.2

1969 Communication Rankings of Selected Nations Based on Various and Domestic Mail Ratios

(adjusted to 1–100)

Selected Nations	Domestic/Foreign Mail Ratio	Foreign Mail Sent/ Received Ratio	Foreign Mail (per capita)
Afghanistan	–	–	–
Algeria	50	50	84
Argentina	48	88	55
Australia	24	63	15
Austria	55	34	7
Belgium	44	48	9
Bolivia	–	–	–
Brazil	–	–	–
Bulgaria	–	–	–
Burma	18	75	97
Cambodia	100	100	75
Canada	–	–	–
Chile	–	–	–
China, Mainland	–	–	–
China, Taiwan	7	17	71
Colombia	–	–	–
Cuba	–	–	–
Czechoslovakia	–	–	–
Denmark	40	44	17
Ethiopia	–	–	–
Finland	38	83	26
France	67	24	32
Germany, Dem. Rep.	88	26	3
Germany, Fed. Rep.	11	36	34
Ghana (Gold Coast)	77	86	40
Greece	–	–	–
Haiti	–	–	–
Hungary	20	3	43
India	5	90	96
Indonesia	32	94	100
Iran	–	–	–
Iraq	86	98	59
Ireland	75	40	5
Israel	61	20	13
Italy	28	65	36
Japan	1	42	83
Jordan	–	–	–
Kenya	81	32	65
Korea, Rep.	9	84	86
Lebanon	–	–	–
Liberia	98	73	67
Malaysia	73	57	46
Mexico	65	61	51
Morocco	94	71	61
Netherlands	34	1	11

TABLE C.2 (*Continued*)

Selected Nations	Domestic/Foreign Mail Ratio	Foreign Mail Sent/ Received Ratio	Foreign Mail (per capita)
Nigeria	57	9	94
Norway	36	53	20
Pakistan	–	–	–
Paraguay	–	–	–
Peru	–	–	–
Philippines	–	–	–
Poland	13	11	63
Portugal	63	28	24
Puerto Rico	–	–	–
Romania	15	15	79
Saudi Arabia	96	69	57
Senegal	–	–	–
Sierra Leone	–	–	–
South Africa	22	51	50
Spain	42	22	28
Sudan	–	–	–
Sweden	26	67	18
Switzerland	51	7	1
Syria	71	92	77
Tanzania	79	55	88
Thailand	53	81	92

SOURCE: UNESCO, *Statistical Yearbook* (1970).

TABLE C.3

Domestic to Foreign Mail and Foreign Mail Received to Sent Ratios, 1953–1969

Country	Domestic/Foreign Mail Ratio				Foreign Mail Received/Sent Ratio			
	1953	1962	1965	1969	1953	1962	1965	1969
Afghanistan	–	–	–	–	–	–	–	–
Algeria	34.79	–	6.04	4.38	1.04	–	1.07	1.22
Argentina	23.54	19.20	4.51	4.45	4.99	5.44	1.69	1.89
Australia	10.43	7.51	7.13	7.37	2.08	1.08	1.48	1.33
Austria	4.20	3.05	2.81	3.64	0.93	1.01	0.97	1.01
Belgium	11.56	8.15	5.85	5.20	0.88	0.85	1.02	1.22
Bolivia	–	–	–	–	–	–	–	–
Brazil	22.22	3.74	0.88	–	1.24	1.51	0.39	–
Bulgaria	–	–	–	–	–	–	–	–
Burma	–	1.34	10.53	8.64	–	3.99	2.55	1.51
Cambodia	–	–	–	0.12[a]	–	–	–	4.13[a]
Canada	–	–	–	–	–	–	–	–
Chile	–	–	–	–	–	–	–	–
China, Mainland	–	–	–	–	–	–	–	–
China, Taiwan	12.15	18.09	16.11	12.94	1.50	1.45	1.26	0.86
Colombia	–	–	–	–	–	–	–	–
Cuba	–	–	–	–	–	–	–	–
Czechoslovakia	–	–	–	–	–	–	–	–
Denmark	7.35	6.45	6.34	5.58	1.13	1.13	1.14	1.21
Ethiopia	–	–	–	–	–	–	–	–
Finland	5.32	5.57	5.72	6.08	2.65	2.33	1.69	1.79
France	–	–	9.26	2.01[a]	–	–	0.83	0.94[a]
Germany, Dem. Rep.	–	9.14	8.30	1.01	–	0.32	0.38	0.99
Germany, Fed. Rep.	10.43	9.92	8.20	10.97	0.95	0.69	0.60	1.08
Ghana (Gold Coast)	2.05	2.49	1.69	1.69	1.49	2.28	1.27	1.84
Greece	–	–	–	–	–	–	–	–
Haiti	–	–	–	–	–	–	–	–
Hungary	–	5.98	4.56	8.22	–	1.30	0.92	0.73
India	17.15	22.88	26.56	22.09	1.37	1.37	1.40	2.03
Indonesia	8.09	13.91	8.39	6.27[a]	2.08	1.37	1.61	2.81[a]
Iran	–	–	–	–	–	–	–	–
Iraq	–	–	0.55	1.14	–	–	0.62	3.95
Ireland	2.09	1.66	1.71	1.90[a]	0.98	1.39	1.31	1.11[a]
Israel	1.89	2.47	2.71	2.66	1.45	1.27	1.11	0.91
Italy	11.16	8.09	7.03	6.49	1.03	0.91	1.08	1.35
Japan	81.44	64.17	58.72	49.92	1.23	1.18	1.15	1.14
Jordan	0.41	1.01	0.48	–	1.99	1.22	1.17	–
Kenya	–	–	1.82	1.40	–	–	0.89	1.01
Korea, Rep.	–	21.59	12.77	11.00	–	0.56	1.44	1.82
Lebanon	0.22	0.27	0.31[b]	–	1.56	1.77	1.41[b]	–
Liberia	–	–	0.21	0.25	–	–	1.93	1.48
Malaysia (West)	1.87	1.65	1.74	1.93	1.36	1.22	1.23	1.30
Mexico	2.42	2.33	2.16	2.15	1.03	1.14	1.28	1.33
Morocco	0.55	0.88	0.78	0.87	1.46	1.34	1.72	1.48
Netherlands	10.16	7.25	6.16	6.22	0.88	0.72	0.53	0.60
Nigeria	0.79	3.31	3.48	3.44[a]	3.84	1.33	1.44	0.81[a]

TABLE C.3 (*Continued*)

Country	Domestic/Foreign Mail Ratio				Foreign Mail Received/Sent Ratio			
	1953	1962	1965	1969	1953	1962	1965	1969
Norway	6.66	5.97	5.35	6.21	1.23	1.30	1.18	1.23
Pakistan	2.49	4.07	4.69	–	3.09	3.10	2.26	–
Paraguay	–	0.42[c]	0.65[b]	–	–	2.79[c]	3.27[b]	–
Peru	–	–	–	–	–	–	–	–
Philippines	–	–	–	–	–	–	–	–
Poland	–	11.87	10.75	10.37[a]	–	0.66	0.63	0.82[a]
Puerto Rico	–	–	–	–	–	–	–	–
Romania	–	–	10.30	10.22	–	–	0.76	0.86
Saudi Arabia	–	–	0.75	0.73	–	–	1.64	1.41
Senegal	–	–	–	–	–	–	–	–
Sierra Leone	–	–	–	–	–	–	–	–
South Africa	–	6.46	5.00	7.97	–	1.43	1.70	1.22
Spain	9.08	5.06	4.25	5.55	1.30	1.03	1.08	0.93
Sudan	–	–	–	–	–	–	–	–
Sweden	9.52	8.45	8.49	7.24	1.60	1.28	1.33	1.41
Switzerland	5.03	4.46	3.94	4.04	0.87	0.81	0.81	0.81
Syria	–	1.09	1.87	1.94	–	2.47	1.65	2.61
Tanzania (Tanganyika)	–	–	1.23	1.51	–	–	1.37	1.27
Thailand	–	2.76	3.55	3.68[a]	–	2.66	1.83	1.74[a]
Tunisia	–	–	1.03	0.91	–	–	1.02	1.57
Turkey	4.17	7.59	4.95	4.93	1.77	0.78	1.00	0.80
Uganda	–	–	1.99	1.96	–	–	1.20	1.00
U.S.S.R.	–	–	–	–	–	–	–	–
U.A.R. (Egypt)	3.04	2.57	2.69	2.76	1.58	1.34	1.26	1.21
U.K.	11.74	11.08	10.72	9.39	0.66	0.78	0.78	0.84
U.S.A.	43.28	29.08	26.47	36.11	1.40	3.48	3.62	1.71
Uruguay	–	–	–	–	–	–	–	–
Venezuela	0.91	–	0.55	1.00[a]	3.83	–	2.95	3.66[a]
Viet Nam, Rep.	0.80	1.41	1.39	1.36	1.69	1.38	1.28	1.30
Yugoslavia	10.44	15.73	8.16	6.45	0.85	1.29	0.97	1.11
Zambia	–	–	0.95	1.28	–	–	1.57	0.90

SOURCE: UNESCO, *Statistical Yearbook* (various years).

[a] 1968

[b] 1964

[c] 1961

TABLE C.4

CINEMA UTILIZATION

Country	Seats (per 1,000) ca. 1969	Attendance (per capita) ca. 1960	ca. 1969
Afghanistan	0.6[a]	–	0.4[a]
Algeria	13.0[b]	2.6	2.3[b]
Argentina	38.0	7.9	4.0
Australia	38.0	21.3	3.0
Austria	43.0	14.2	7.0
Belgium	42.0	8.8	3.0
Bolivia	18.0[h]	–	0.9[h]
Brazil	22.0[j]	4.5	3.0
Bulgaria	78.0	14.8	13.0
Burma	14.0[k]	5.5	8.0[k]
Cambodia	4.5[j]	–	3.0[j]
Canada	32.0[j]	6.5	5.0[j]
Chile	28.0[k]	3.8	7.0[k]
China, Mainland	–	2.2	6.0
China, Taiwan	56.0[j]	6.8	66.0[j]*
Colombia	22.0[k]	4.8	5.0[k]
Cuba	48.0[f]	7.2	7.0[f]
Czechoslovakia	71.0	12.9	8.0
Denmark	28.0	9.6	5.0
Ethiopia	–	–	–
Finland	22.0	6.3	2.0
France	49.0[j]	7.1	4.0
Germany, Dem. Rep.	20.0[k]	13.8	6.0[k]
Germany, Fed. Rep.	–	9.2	3.0
Ghana (Gold Coast)	6.0	1.6	2.0
Greece	42.0[f]	6.3	16.0[k]
Haiti	2.9[h]	–	0.3[h]
Hungary	60.0	13.5	8.0
India	7.0	3.6	4.0
Indonesia	6.0[p]	3.0[p]	–
Iran	9.0	2.5	0.6
Iraq	8.0[a]	–	1.3[a]
Ireland	52.0[f]	13.5[f]	–
Israel	63.0	18.5	17.0
Italy	–	15.1	10.0
Japan	15.0	9.2	3.0
Jordan	10.0[a]	3.2	3.0[a]
Kenya	1.4[g]	0.5	0.8[g]
Korea Rep. (South)	14.0	4.3	6.0
Lebanon	33.0[k]	22.5	14.0[a]
Liberia	6.7[i]	0.6	0.8[i]
Malaysia (West); Malaya, Federation	23.0	8.9	9.4
Mexico	22.0[k]	10.4	7.0[k]
Morocco	7.6[j]	1.5	1.3[j]
Netherlands	19.0[i]	4.4	3.0[i]
Nigeria	–	0.1	–

TABLE C.4 (*Continued*)

Country	Seats (per 1,000) ca. 1969	Attendance (per capita) ca. 1960	ca. 1969
Norway	44.0[i]	9.4	4.0[i]
Pakistan	3.0[k]	1.0	3.0[k]
Paraguay	–	–	–
Peru	30.0[f]	6.6	–
Philippines	–	0.6	–
Poland	19.0	6.2	4.0
Portugal	29.0[k]	2.9	3.0[k]
Puerto Rico	–	–	3.0[g]
Romania	11.0	8.8	10.0
Saudi Arabia	–	–	–
Senegal	10.0[a]	–	1.5[a]
Sierra Leone	2.2	–	0.05
South Africa	–	–	–
Spain	134.0	12.2	12.0
Sudan	2.8[k]	1.4	–
Sweden	–	6.6	4.0
Switzerland	35.0	7.3	5.0
Syria	10.0[j]	2.1	–
Tanzania (Tanganyika)	–	0.5	–
Thailand	4.0[h]	–	–
Tunisia	9.0[k]	1.5	1.6[k]
Turkey	–	1.1[e]	–
Uganda	2.1[a]	0.3	0.3[a]
U.S.S.R.	–	17.7	19.0
U.A.R. (Egypt)	4.7[k]	2.6	1.9[k]
U.K.	28.0	9.6	4.0
U.S.A.	35.0[j]	11.8	7.0[j]
Uruguay	71.0	9.1	6.0
Venezuela	54.0	9.2	4.0
Vietnam, Rep. (South)	4.0[j]	1.4	1.4[j]
Yugoslavia	25.0	7.0	4.0
Zambia	2.4[f]	–	–

SOURCE: UNESCO, *Statistical Yearbook* (various years).

[a] 1946 [i] 1966
[b] 1947 [j] 1967
[c] 1949 [k] 1968
[d] 1958 [m] 1948
[e] 1959 [n] 1953
[f] 1961 [p] 1957
[g] 1963 [q] 1965
[h] 1964 * provisional or estimated data

TABLE C.5

1969 COMMUNICATION RANKINGS OF SELECTED NATIONS

(adjusted to 1–100)

Selected Nations	MASS MEDIA				DOMESTIC COMMUNICATIONS			COMPOSITE	
	Newspaper Circulation (per 1,000)	Radio Receivers (per 1,000)	Television Receivers (per 1,000)	Other Printing Paper (kg.p/c)	Domestic Mail (p/c)	Telephones (per 1,000)	Domestic Telegrams (p/c)	Mass Media	Domestic Communications (excl. tlgrm)
Afghanistan	—	—	—	98	—	—	—	—	—
Algeria	81	81	76	—	73	70	78	79	72
Argentina	—	6	32	43	48	37	15	27	43
Australia	8	39	13	23	14	8	1	21	11
Austria	25	27	25	24	17	20	42	25	19
Belgium	27	15	19	10	5	17	44	18	11
Bolivia	70	25	—	83	—	78	—	59	—
Brazil	67	76	44	55	—	56	55	61	—
Bulgaria	39	30	36	38	—	43	5	36	—
Burma	—	93	—	75	91	100	93	—	96
Cambodia	72	49	76	83	—	—	—	70	—
Canada	34	3	4	15	6	5	53	14	6
Chile	50	54	50	41	—	45	23	49	—
China, Mainland	—	—	—	—	—	—	—	—	—
China, Taiwan	—	64	62	40	46	54	—	55	50
Colombia	—	61	53	57	—	53	14	57	—
Cuba	—	—	45	54	—	47	—	—	—
Czechoslovakia	24	28	17	27	21	25	6	24	23
Denmark	15	18	8	12	23	7	39	14	15
Ethiopia	100	100	99	97	—	—	—	99	—
Finland	10	12	16	4	26	14	60	11	20
France	29	19	22	13	12	23	35	21	18
Germany, Dem. Rep.	6	13	10	—	39	27	24	10	33
Germany, Fed. Rep.	17	14	7	9	19	15	57	10	17
Ghana (Gold Coast)	69	69	88	77	55	86	82	76	72
Greece	51	60	68	44	51	30	17	56	41

TABLE C.5 *(Continued)*

Selected Nations	Mass Media				Domestic Communications			Composite	
	Newspaper Circulation (per 1,000)	Radio Receivers (per 1,000)	Television Receivers (per 1,000)	Other Printing Paper (kg.p/c)	Domestic Mail (p/c)	Telephones (per 1,000)	Domestic Telegrams (p/c)	Mass Media	Domestic Communications (excl. tlgrm)
Haiti	93	91	84	100	—	—	—	92	—
Hungary	32	36	29	29	35	33	10	32	34
India	83	90	—	74	68	94	73	82	81
Indonesia	—	—	97	—	98	94	96	—	96
Iran	—	—	69	—	—	76	—	—	—
Iraq	—	87	56	68	77	70	87	70	74
Ireland	31	22	31	37	32	31	62	30	32
Israel	36	37	—	26	37	21	51	33	29
Italy	44	43	26	20	28	24	33	33	26
Japan	3	33	14	21	30	18	12	19	24
Jordan	84	—	65	—	93	67	—	—	80
Kenya	79	82	87	72	80	81	—	80	81
Korea Rep.	62	63	72	60	64	60	50	64	62
Lebanon	—	40	38	—	69	38	77	—	54
Liberia	98	58	81	—	100	84	—	79	92
Malaysia	55	84	63	58	57	61	84	65	59
Mexico	—	31	48	49	60	51	8	43	56
Morocco	—	78	66	78	84	74	95	74	79
Netherlands	20	34	11	6	8	12	69	—	10
Nigeria	—	88	93	94	96	99	100	92	98
Norway	11	21	20	18	24	10	19	18	17
Pakistan	90	99	94	83	78	94	86	92	86
Paraguay	67	—	76	92	—	77	71	78	—
Peru	60	57	54	61	—	64	—	58	—
Philippines	—	84	70	—	—	80	—	—	—
Poland	37	45	35	33	44	40	28	38	42
Portugal	—	52	51	46	42	35	48	50	39
Puerto Rico	48	—	—	—	—	—	—	—	—
Romania	41	51	47	47	53	50	32	47	52
Saudi Arabia	88	—	—	69	—	83	75	—	—

TABLE C.5 *(Continued)*

Selected Nations	Mass Media				Domestic Communications			Composite	
	Newspaper Circulation (per 1,000)	Radio Receivers (per 1,000)	Television Receivers (per 1,000)	Other Printing Paper (kg.p/c)	Domestic Mail (p/c)	Telephones (per 1,000)	Domestic Telegrams (p/c)	Mass Media	Domestic Communications (excl. tlgrm)
Senegal	95	72	100	71	—	—	—	85	—
Sierra Leone	76	79	90	95	—	—	—	85	—
South Africa	—	—	—	32	—	—	—	—	—
Spain	46	42	28	30	33	28	21	37	31
Sudan	—	96	85	89	—	89	68	90	—
Sweden	1	10	2	7	15	3	41	5	9
Switzerland	13	24	23	3	3	4	59	16	4
Syria	—	—	57	64	82	57	91	—	70
Tanzania	97	97	—	89	95	94	—	94	95
Thailand	74	70	76	83	87	89	98	76	88
Tunesia	77	66	76	—	71	66	89	73	69
Turkey	64	67	96	64	66	63	37	73	65
Uganda	91	75	91	89	89	89	—	87	89
USSR	18	9	34	—	50	41	3	20	46
U.A.R. (Egypt)	—	55	60	64	75	73	64	60	74
U.K.	4	16	5	16	10	11	66	10	11
U.S.A.	22	1	1	1	1	1	46	6	1
Uruguay	43	7	39	51	—	34	26	35	—
Venezuela	57	45	42	52	62	44	—	49	53
Vietnam, Rep.	58	72	59	—	86	94	80	63	90
Yugoslavia	53	47	41	35	41	48	30	44	45
Zambia	86	94	82	83	59	71	—	86	65

SOURCE: UNESCO, *Statistical Yearbook* (1969).

CHAPTER 14 Communication in Totalitarian Societies

ITHIEL DE SOLA POOL
Massachusetts Institute of Technology

Mass persuasion undergoes perhaps its greatest test in modern totalitarian states. This chapter looks at two such states, the Soviet Union and Maoist China, where tightly controlled mass communication and mass organization are designed to mold public opinion and mobilize the people behind the goals of the regime. To demonstrate how deeply concerned totalitarian regimes are over public opinion, the author describes how these two states have gone about trying to affect public opinion. In this process China follows where the USSR was thirty years earlier when it, too, was attempting to industrialize a peasant society and was forced to depend upon labor-intensive methods because of the shortage of mass media. In the 1930s, the USSR was trying to produce "the new Soviet man"; in the late 1960s Mao tried to lead his people to purge themselves of old errors by studying the little red book. The author feels that the essential difference in the methods adopted by the two regimes at comparable periods is not so much in procedures as in intensity: "Seldom in human history, and never in as primitive a society as China's, has as much agitation reached so many people with as high an intensity as in the Mao experiment." The author sums up the available evidence on how people in the two countries have responded to that kind of communication.

In the past half century a score or so of totalitarian regimes have attempted to transform large disjointed nations into cohesive pseudo primary communities by the use of propaganda and mass organization. The dream of every totalitarian movement has been to make the whole nation into a loyal devoted family dedicated to the ideals of the leader or party (Friedrich & Brzezinski, 1956; Friedrich, 1964; Aron, 1969). Although totalitarian dictatorships have used much terror to repress the so-called enemies of the people, they have relied, at least equally, upon mass persuasion to try to win the enthusiasm and willing cooperation of the bulk of the population.

A dictatorship, of course, never succeeds in fully eliminating differences of opinion. In any dictatorship one can find private views both in support of and in opposition to the regime. But what significance do these private views have in a dictatorship? Do they make any difference against the steamroller of a police state?

In Chapter 25 (on the role of public opinion in democratic systems), a question is raised of how far one may legitimately speak of public opinion in a totalitarian society and what role it may play there. It is an oversimplification to say that because a totalitarian regime rides roughshod over the opinions of dissenters, public opinion and communications have no influence upon it. It is equally oversimple to assume that totalitarian regimes do succeed in mobilizing their people into a community of purpose by their massive infusions of propaganda and by rigorous social controls. What can we say about the character of public opinion and communication in totalitarian societies?

1. Totalitarian regimes are highly conscious of public opinion and make major efforts to affect it.
2. The controlled communications put out by totalitarian regimes—designed more for effects than for truthfulness—tend to become highly formalized and stilted.
3. Eventually the public becomes sated with such propaganda material and grows inattentive, apathetic, and apolitical.
4. Despite that, the public has a hunger for trustworthy and credible information.
5. In seeking the facts, the public learns to read between the lines. It becomes accustomed to interpreting clues to the truth that are buried in the unreliable information available to them.
6. The kind of unity and cohesion created by totalitarian methods is fragile. Whenever the structure of controls breaks down, the apparent unanimity collapses quickly.

We consider these six points at greater length.

OPINION CONSCIOUSNESS

Throughout history there have been regimes caring little for public opinion. Feudal monarchs and classical emperors were satisfied to maintain a loose bargain with their subjects at the grass roots, by which tribute was paid to the court but the provinces and villages were largely left to run themselves (Wittfogel, 1957; Eisenstadt, 1963). A Vietnamese proverb expresses this relationship: The Emperor's writ stops at the village gate.

Modern authoritarian (nontotalitarian) dictatorships like that of czarist Russia or the Spanish monarchy in the 1920s also remained largely indifferent to public opinion. They claimed authority on some other basis than popular support, and cared little what the people thought. They made little effort to mobilize support among the people. In czarist Russia, as in modern democracies, the head of state, the czar, opened the annual session of parliament, the Duma, with a state address. However, his speeches generally lasted but three or four minutes. He simply proclaimed it to be his beneficent will that the members of the Duma should act for the public welfare. Unlike the British monarch's Speech from the Throne, or the American president's State of the Union message, or the reports of the presidium to the Supreme Soviet, the czar made no attempt to use the occasion as a sounding board for national policies nor for the mobilization of public opinion behind them (Pool, 1970a).

There are few such authoritarian regimes remaining in the modern world. Some are to be found among the princely and monarchic desert states of Arabia; however, even there the authoritarian monarchy in Yemen was successfully challenged by rebels from a more participant (although no more democratic) political movement. Recent authoritarian regimes are discoverable in such places as Bhutan, Sikkim, and Nepal. But aside from such atypical cases, modern dictatorships, just as modern democracies, seek the political mobilization of at least a major segment of the population. Totalitarian regimes seek not only to rule over but also to mobilize the entire population. A traditional military junta may be willing to rest its power upon a well-armed, politically motivated army with perhaps some support from middle-class strata. The aspirations of totalitarian regimes, on the other hand, have been to have every citizen organized as a cheering, active member of a party-controlled organization.

We can attribute to Lenin the formulation of the totalitarian approach to politics. He did not think he was the inventor of it, for in his mind he was implementing efficiently and on a national scale an approach to mass-mobilization that had been emerging throughout the nineteenth century.

In France, Great Britain, and Germany, since the 1830s small plebeian radical groups who styled themselves Socialist, Communist, Anarchist, or Democratic (for in those days that was a radical label, too) dreamed of transforming society into a utopia in which human relations would be governed by consensus rather than by competition and conflict. Some of those groups sought to implement their ideals in small communes where they lived and worked. Others, more in the tradition of the French Revolution, looked to achieving their ideals by national revolutions. Many of these groups, being small, chiliastic, and highly ideological, absorbed the full energies of their members in lives wholly devoted to their cause.

Out of these movements of protest there developed in the latter half of the century the mass, labor-based Social Democratic parties of Europe, each with their newspapers, social, cultural, athletic, and educational associations, and a membership party with unprecedented discipline (Rosenberg, 1939). The members paid dues and belonged to local branches that met regularly. They elected delegates to congresses at which binding resolutions were adopted. The parties often claimed the right to compel their members in parliament to vote in accordance with those resolutions. The German Social Democratic party, or at least a distorted image of it, as well as the earlier small putschist revolutionary groups, were part of the legacy that shaped Lenin's image of a disciplined party.

Another source of Lenin's thinking about parties was a misreading of the facts concerning American political machines. In the United States, as in Europe, the late nineteenth century saw the rise of unprecedentedly disciplined party organizations (Ostrogorski, 1902; Weber, 1958). The city machines mobilized immigrant and slum followers by providing social services, jobs, and small payments to the citizens in return for voting as they were told. With a voting block in his pocket, the party boss could then shake down businessmen seeking franchises, licenses, and other forms of protection (Steffens, 1931; Gosnell, 1937). Not only Lenin but also Max Weber, M. Ostrogorski, and other turn-of-the-century students of democratic politics saw in the American party machine, as well as in the corresponding developments in England and the Continent, a new shape of democratic politics in which the masses were mobilized into highly disciplined parties.

Lenin's doctrine of democratic centralism carried this image of party organization to the limit. Under that doctrine, issues might be discussed until settled by party authorities, after which all party members were bound by discipline to support the official position; decisions of higher bodies held categorically over lower ones.

The party in his image was not, however, a body encompassing all of the supporting masses. The masses would be organized in mass organizations, such as labor unions. The party was to be a tightly knit, small organization of professional revolutionists who, however they might earn their living, made conquest of power their primary, full-time occupation. It was on this conception of the party that the Russian Social Democratic party split into two factions, the Bolsheviks and the Mensheviks. The vote on which they divided at the 1903 convention concerned the definition of a party member.

While Lenin's approach to party organization was dictatorial and elitist, it was also an approach that emphasized the need to organize the masses as a whole. The totalitarian party was not to be an elite in isolation, but an elite devoted to the organization, coordination, and mobilization of the masses (Lenin, 1929b). The standard Bolshevik phrase was a party with "roots in the masses" (Selznick, 1952).

The Bolsheviks, once in power, unhesitatingly imprisoned and executed those who opposed them. In their writings they quite openly defended the use of terror (Lenin, 1929a; Trotsky, 1961). By the time Stalin's purges were finished, literally millions had died and tens of millions had been repressed. At the cost of five million lives, the individual peasant farmers were forced into collective farms (Brzezinski, 1956; Conquest, 1968).

At the same time, the Bolsheviks sought for the first time in Russia to bring the large majority of the population into the processes of politics. Under strict control of the Party, they organized councils throughout the country known by the Russian word *Soviets*, councils of workers, of peasants, of soldiers, which constituted the structure of the first government of the revolutionary regime. At places of work everywhere, and generally weekly, the workers would be assembled for briefings, to discuss problems, to be propagandized, and frequently to vote resolutions or criticisms. The Party, of course, maintained its power through factions in all such mass organizations.

The dramatic success of Lenin's new style of political organization in taking over power in a great nation, and also in creating a powerful international movement, produced both alarm and imitation in rival political camps. The organization of the Kuo Min Tang, for example, was modeled consciously and in detail on the Bolshevik party. The most important imitation, however, was by that new totalitarian movement of the right that we have come to know as fascism. Mussolini, who organized the Italian fascist takeover in 1921, had been a leader in the Italian Socialist movement; when he split with it, he copied the Bolshevik organization. In Germany, too, there was a series of imitations of which the most important was Hitler's National Socialist movement.

Nazism, fascism, communism, and indeed all totalitarian movements have thus differed from classical authoritarianism in that they have sought to impose their dictatorial authority by means of the controlled mobilization of the masses. Public opinion, propaganda, and mass communication were always of central concern to them.

The interest of totalitarian regimes in influencing public opinion is manifested by their large investment of resources and energy in the instruments of communication. The proportion of the gross national product devoted by totalitarian countries to literacy, newspaper publication, radio and television expansion is, in general, substantially higher than the proportion spent by nontotalitarian countries which are at the same level of GNP per capita.

The concern of totalitarian leaders with winning mass support has been voluble and explicit. Lenin (1929a; 1929b), Hitler (1939), Mao Tse-tung (1965) and Ché Guevara (1968; 1969a; 1969b) have all written profusely and sometimes insightfully about the art of propaganda—about how to win, organize, and dupe the masses.

Totalitarian rulers have spent fortunes in incessant campaigns and monster rallies marked by lengthy expositions of doctrines. Never has as much been spent to produce public demonstrations of support as by the totalitarian movements of the twentieth century.

We should not confuse attention to public opinion with a willingness to be guided by it. Neither Lenin with his doctrine of party leadership nor Hitler with his Führerprinzip held to the democratic notion that public opinion should determine policy. Consciousness of the importance of public opinion may be either consciousness of the importance of controlling it or of obeying its mandates. It is in the former respect that totalitarian regimes have shown a sharp sensitivity to public opinion. They have recognized that, in the modern world, public opinion is a critical matter for the functioning of their societies and have therefore made massive efforts to control it (Harper, 1929; Inkeles, 1958; Yu, 1964; 1970; Bramsted, 1965; Hiniker, 1966; Markham, 1967; Liu, 1971; G. Hollander, 1972).

Indeed, one of the more interesting and widely studied aspects of totalitarian education and propaganda is the attempt to change human nature by massive exhortation. In the Soviet Union the goal is formulated as the creation of the "new Soviet man" (Bauer, 1952). He is a paragon of discipline, punctuality, obedience, and party spirit, but also of initiative and energy on behalf of party goals (Mead, 1951; Gorer, 1962; Higher Party School . . . of CPSU, 1963; P. Hollander, 1966; Bronfenbrenner, 1970). In China similar efforts have been carried to unprecedented extremes, to which we shall return below.

CONTENT OF TOTALITARIAN COMMUNICATIONS

Lenin, Hitler, Mao, and Ché Guevara were skillful propagandists and significant writers on the art of propaganda, yet the communications systems that they created have produced mainly boredom.

What makes totalitarian propaganda so boring is the excessive rigidity with which it is controlled. The totalitarian propagandists have themselves become adherents of the myth of propaganda, the myth that people are easily manipulated. They have, therefore, been alarmed at the prospects that their people might hear undesirable things instead of their own messages. As a result, throughout the totalitarian world the censor has triumphed over the propagandist (George, 1959; Morozov, 1966; Siniavskii, 1966; Friedberg, 1968; Reve, 1969; Hopkins, 1970; Pospielovsky, 1970).

In the Khrushchev period, a major effort was made in the USSR to replace the harsh controls of the Stalin era with the softer controls of mass persuasion. The regime's investment in agitprop activities was greatly increased (G. Hollander, 1972). Under Adzhubei, Khrushchev's son-in-law and the editor of *Izvestia*, the media were livened up and human interest material added. When Khrushchev fell, Adzhubei was the first to go. In Brezhnev's Russia in the 1960s, the openings to fresh breezes in the arts and mass media were gradually sealed again. The censor won out once more.

For such self-conscious propagandists, the prime consideration in controlling communications is not whether statements are true or false but what consequences they are likely to have. For Marxists this instrumental approach came naturally. They could quote Marx to the effect that ideas are mere rationalizations of class rule, growing out of the particular stage of development of the forces of production.

This materialist conception of history suggested that one assess ideas, detached from any emotional bias of concern for truth and preoccupied instead only with the social scientific question of their pragmatic significance as an element of ideology (Marx, 1848; Engels, n.d.). This scientistic approach has provided the impetus for important advances in the sociology of knowledge by Marxists and non-Marxists alike. It has also permitted Marx's Communist followers to approach political doctrines as class rationalizations to be judged empirically by their consequences, rather than by some norm of truth-value.

The Marxist propensity to view words as ideological superstructure is evidenced in Lenin's doctrine on the proper relation of agitation to organization (Lenin, 1929b; Selznick, 1952; Leites, 1953). Since the basic strategy of Communist politics is to root the party cadres among the organized masses, verbal output is assessed by its effect in producing such organization. The Communist movement places very little emphasis on the power of its literature to persuade directly, and very great emphasis on formulating demands that will get people to organize under Communist leadership. Resolutions and demands are the occasion for holding mass meetings rather than the meetings being for the purpose of putting out statements.

Some Communists, such as Daniel de Leon in the United States, objected to Lenin's tactic of centering agitation on immediate demands for which people could be organized. He argued that that tactic misled people into believing that by organized action they could win improvements in conditions under capitalism. As a Communist, de Leon argued that this was false. The existing evil system could produce no progress; it had to be destroyed. The only way to achieve improvements, he believed, was by revolution.

Lenin replied in a 1920 pamphlet entitled *Left Wing Communism, An Infantile Disorder* (Lenin, 1940). In this he agreed that immediate demands misrepresented the Communists' view since only Communist revolution could achieve the realization of the demands. However, Lenin argued for putting forward unrealizable demands because workers were not ready to listen to preachment of Communist revolution. The only way to organize them was on behalf of immediate demands. To Lenin the important thing was not the veracity or demagogic character of the slogans, but the struggle itself. In 1901 he had proposed to establish a legal newspaper in czarist Russia even though it could not print what he considered to be the truth, because he saw in a newspaper the backbone of a political machine with reporters traveling around collecting information and with distributors traveling around delivering messages (Lenin, 1929a).

In this view that the propaganda was nothing and the movement was all, Lenin was an accurate disciple of Marx. Marx refused to spell out any goals of his own to be imposed on the proletarian movement. He steadily refused to describe what a Socialist society would be like (Marx, 1954). To him the real thing was not some ideal goal, but the movement itself. His demands were whatever grew out of the movement. Perhaps the most extreme illustration of the Marxist-Leninist approach to truth, as an expedient on behalf of the interests of a class, was one which would have horrified Marx and Lenin themselves; namely, the confessions in the Stalin-era show trials. Old Bolsheviks were persuaded to confess to absurd charges of treason and to heinous crimes on the basis that by so doing they would help protect the Soviet state against its enemies (Koestler, 1941; Leites & Bernaut, 1954).

Of course, it is easy for those of us in the democratic and liberal tradition to note the lack of concern for truth among totalitarians, and to note their frequent use of the technique of the big lie. It is such a gratifying observation that it is easy for us to slip into it as a propagandistic assertion. Fairness, however, compels us to note that a greater concern for the consequences of statements than for their correspondence to some criterion of objective truth has characterized not only modern totalitarians, but most human societies. The democratic liberal tradition is the unusual one in this respect, not the totalitarian one.

Very few societies have been willing to tolerate persons' saying shocking, dangerous, immoral, or subversive things just because they were true, or at least because someone thought them true. In this respect there are interesting parallels between Communist and preindustrial communication systems. Both are more concerned with the social functions of statements than with their literal meaning. In preindustrial societies honorifics, taboos, propriety, and ritual are more important controls over what is said than is any formal criterion of logic or empirical observation (Keesing & Keesing, 1956). That is true, too, in authoritarian and totalitarian states. It is only in that small sector of the world that has inherited both the Judeo-Christian tradition of prophetic outspokenness and the Greek tradition of philosophy that science and truth-testing have acquired special value.

In any case, one characteristic of totalitarian societies (even if not of theirs alone) is that they have been carefully censored against "wrong" ideas. It is interesting to note what the Soviet authorities tell their journalists about truth in reporting. The Party laid down seven guidelines for editors of which the first is *partiinost* ("party-mindedness") and the fourth *pravdivost* ("truthfulness") (G. Hollander, 1968; 1972). But truthfulness, the journalism student is told, is not to be confused with mere empirical factuality. A distinction is made between factual and essential truth. It would be mere factuality to report that a Wall Street businessman did a kind act if he did so; his essence is his "imperialist" or "exploitative" role that would be obscured by reporting a generous act. Recently, however, in an exchange in *Zhurnalist* (February, 1967, pp. 22–25), a reporter who had been chided for writing "just any truth" instead of the "political truth" was reassured that there is no such thing as "political truth" (G. Hollander, 1968). If that notion were extended generally to what has previously been called essential truth and were accepted, it would be a most important change in Soviet journalism.

At times, particularly during the Stalin years, Soviet fear that dangerous thoughts might creep into publication assumed almost unbelievable proportions. During the great purges, prevention of typographical errors became a fetish for fear that some politically tendentious pun or innuendo might be smuggled in as a typo. A typesetter or the responsible editor might be sent to Siberia for a typographical error.

Similarly, there has been extreme control over mimeograph machines. The Bolsheviks knew from their own experience as revolutionaries how much could be done with portable reproducing devices. Hence, each major institution in the Soviet Union has had a central mimeographing office so that machines would not be available in each office. A serial number is precut into each stencil; when a stencil is given out, a card is filled out listing the receiver and the stencil number. The cards are filed with the police.

The effect of these controls has been to reduce many of the advantages of mimeographing over regular printing. Speed and economy in informal reproduction comes from using office staff that is already on the payroll. If one has to send something to a central mimeographing office, get on its queues, and pay its charges, then it is often just as efficient to use a letterpress. In ironical consequence, much material that might otherwise appear only in the relatively private channel of informal circulation is placed in regular publication, where it is more conspicuous.

The end result of the entire system of controls is a highly rigid, formalized, and bureaucratic flow of communication. The output is reviewed closely to see that it contains the appropriate formulas (Yakobson & Lasswell, 1949). Every published statement must adhere to rigid conventions both of format and content. The whole art of Kremlinology, described in the next chapter by William Griffith, rests upon the fact that certain verbal formulas are so strictly required that it is easy to spot changes in them when they occur. Of course, all political movements rely to a substantial degree on the popularization of set formulas such as slogans and catchwords. All content analysis of political propaganda rests upon the existence of such repetitive patterns (Lasswell, 1939; Lasswell et al., 1945; George, 1959; Pool, 1970a).

But there are marked differences of degree between the creative rhetoric of even revolutionary totalitarian propaganda before power is achieved and the stilted formalism into which it lapses afterwards. Rigidity is a disease to which totalitarian propagandists succumb when they no longer need to compete verbally against threats to their power. Occasionally, totalitarian regimes have fallen prey to internal conflict giving rise to brief periods of revival of lively mass media. In Czechoslovakia during the summer of 1968, censorship was virtually unenforced and the press and radio led a liberalizing movement. When the Russians replied by invasion, the media personnel, operating as an underground, provided the country's leadership in resistance (Radio Liberty Committee, 1968; Tatu, 1968; Remington, 1969; Schwartz, 1969; Tigrid, 1969: 142; Wechsberg, 1969; Zeman, 1969).

Shortly before that, the Czech government had acquired a number of mobile transmitters ostensibly for defense purposes in case of a German invasion; these kept broadcasting for a week despite the invasion. Similarly, in the period of dominance of the Red Guards during the Cultural Revolution in China, the established media system largely broke down. Red Guard groups started bringing out one-sheet newspapers, attacking their particular enemies. Under those conditions of near civil war, a measure of freedom of the press returned, although it did not serve to reopen China to real news of the world, for the wall bulletins and two-page papers were primarily factional propaganda tracts (Commerce Department, 1967; Union Research Institute, 1968; Liu, 1969; 1971; Yu, 1970). They contained virtually no news except of party disputes or deviations of supposedly bad people. They had no access to wire services or even to effective radio broadcasts from abroad oriented to the needs of the Chinese audience. (During the Czech resistance, Radio Free Europe and similar sources provided that input for the domestic Czech media.) In any case, these were passing moments of media vitality. They were soon followed by a return to the rigid, dull formulae of a media system afraid above all of deviation.

DEPOLITIZATION

The passage from revolutionary exhiliration to ossified routines, which we have just described, has been experienced by every totalitarian regime. Excitement and a spirit of hope mark a revolution. It promises reform of past evils and it sweeps strata into politics who never before expected their voices to be heard. A certain amount of disillusionment is bound to follow. Many revolutionary aims turn out to be impractical. (The early Bolsheviks thought they were building a classless society in which the workers would run the factories and in which bureaucratic authority would give way to mere bookkeeping that anyone could do.) Abuses with deep cultural roots begin to reappear. Prejudice and ignorance do not vanish. A new elite begins to impose its control. So every revolution has its Thermidore and eats its own best young.

Though not every revolution swings all the way to a brutal totalitarianism, some do. A few revolutions, as in Mexico and the United States, while they disappoint their most radical prophets, leave behind a heritage of moderate reform and a substantial measure of popular political life. But where the end is totalitarianism, the political enthusiasm of the start gives way to dreary apathy of a rigid dictatorship. Regimes that try to get 99 percent support in mass plebiscites and that expect everyone to attend weekly meetings and mass rallies end up depoliticizing them instead. When regimes impose daily propaganda in large doses, people stop listening.

That does not happen immediately. One can generally find evidence of voluntary participation and enthusiasm during the first few years of a totalitarian regime. It can, for a while, call on its people to work overtime, cut sugar cane, or march behind banners (Townsend, 1967). The charm runs out in the face of incessant demands and the unending din of only slightly credible propaganda. Newspapers are filled with long and tedious speeches and resolutions; loudspeakers in public places blare endlessly. Along with oversaturation comes fear of the terror that is used against those who make political mistakes. Before long, the general popular reaction is to play the role of the little man who does nothing and has no interest in the dangerous world of politics.

Thus totalitarianism fails in its effort to create a community of loyal and enthusiastic citizens (Kecskemeti, 1950; Hiniker, 1966; Powell, 1967). People begin to find excuses to avoid attending meetings. They stop reading propaganda. What they do hear goes in one ear and out the other. They turn inward into their private world and away from politics (Inkeles & Bauer, 1959; Nowak, 1962; Higher Party School . . . of CPSU, 1963; Kassof, 1965; Pool, 1966).

NEWS HUNGER

But privatization and depolitization are only one aspect of what happens under a totalitarian regime. While people turn away from the incessant propaganda din, they nonetheless desire to know what is really going on in the world. As they lose confidence in official media of whose dishonesty they are conscious, they develop hunger for accurate, reliable news and information. Rumor, clandestine publications, and foreign radio listening become important sources of news, competing with the official media.

In general, if people have even minimal confidence in their ordinary mass media, they do not strive to supplement them with esoteric sources. In democratic countries, although people may gripe about their media, they are not sufficiently dissatisfied or motivated to seek alternatives. In the United States, for example, the amount of listening to shortwave broadcasts from abroad is miniscule (Smith, 1969–70). Subscriptions to foreign journals or magazines are so rare as to be insignificant (Bauer, Pool, & Dexter, 1963: 163–164). For most people, word-of-mouth rumor is not a serious source of information on national politics. Where it is, it reflects a massive lack of confidence in the national media, which is exactly what is to be found in totalitarian regimes.

Examples that illustrate the alienation of the citizens from the media are many. Later we shall examine use of the media in the Soviet Union. At this point let us draw examples from elsewhere. Viet Cong officers show a marked preference for BBC as a news source. They do not trust radio Hanoi or Radio Liberation for they know that these do not tell the truth. They do not trust Radio Saigon or the Voice of America for they represent the enemy. BBC is seen as a neutral, objective source. Where the Viet Cong controls, they attempt to prevent listening to Radio Saigon or VOA. Typically, they seize radios of three-time violators. However, division-level officers are allowed to listen to whatever they wish, and regimental-level commanders and political officers likewise. BBC becomes the accepted source for such higher echelons.

From Eastern Europe there is evidence of massive listening to Western broadcasts (Durham, 1965a; 1965b; Karemyaye, 1967; Selesnick, 1970). Numerous unpublished surveys have been conducted both by Western broadcasters and by Eastern European broadcast organizations. The general findings show that most people in the East do listen to foreign broadcasts, usually every few days. In Czechoslovakia during the short period of free press and broadcasting, the amount of listening to sources like Radio Free Europe dropped off sharply because credible domestic sources existed. With the reimposition of censorship, foreign listening picked up again. Foreign radio listening is a second choice for use when credible domestic sources are lacking.

Where shortwave radio is not available, or for information on local matters which foreign broadcasters cannot cover, rumor is likely to be the chief supplement to the controlled media (Whaley, Schueller, & Scott, 1961). The fullest study of rumor in a totalitarian system was done by Harvard's Russian Research Center using Soviet displaced persons at the end of World War II (Rossi & Bauer, 1952; Bauer & Gleicher, 1953; Inkeles & Bauer, 1959). Rumor emerged prominently in their reported sources of information during the prewar years. Ninety-five percent of the professionals said that rumor was a more *reliable* source for them than official sources. As shown in Table 1, the evaluation of the reliability of the rumors that they get goes

TABLE 1
IMPORTANCE AND RELIABILITY OF RUMOR AS SOURCE OF NEWS IN THE SOVIET UNION

	Word of Mouth Most Important Source	Rumor More Reliable Than Official Media
Professional	32%	95%
Employee	22	85
Worker	41	71
Peasant	73	56

SOURCE: Bauer and Gleicher (1953:302, 307).

down as the status of the person in the society goes down; even among peasants, however, more than half thought rumors more reliable than official sources.

While rumor might be reliable, it is not as voluminous a source as the media. Rumor was therefore listed less often than the media as the most *important* source by all except peasants. Nonetheless, a third of the professionals mentioned rumor as their main source. Among the peasants, less fully reached by the mass media thirty years ago than now, almost three-quarters listed rumor as their main source.[1] These results are plausible. The peasants got whatever they could from friends and neighbors, unreliable as they knew it was. The professionals relied less exclusively on rumor, but the things they heard by word of mouth tended to come from high, and therefore relatively reliable, sources.

Inkeles, Bauer, and their colleagues also addressed themselves to the question of how freely people dare to talk to each other in a dictatorship. What is shown by the experience of Stalin's Russia and Hitler's Germany, two dictatorships as severe as any ever known, is that even under the most extreme circumstances people tend to establish contact with at least one or two close friends whom they can trust and to whom they can talk with some measure of understanding. Perhaps there is a circularity of cause and effect in that observation.

It is probably impossible to retain an independent view where even that minimum support of dissent or questioning does not exist. Information and attitudes not supported by at least one friend would probably disappear from consciousness. Thus the finding that a person shared with at least one close friend whatever residual independence he felt would still be confirmed by overt replies even though there had been transient and therefore forgotten situations where a person could express his views to no one. In any case, the pattern found empirically is that almost everyone in a dictatorship has at least one confidant, seldom more than a very few, but that is enough to create a rumor network that can cover a country rapidly. Major news events that the media try to suppress do get around the country in a very few days even under such a limited network (Inkeles & Bauer, 1959).

Among the fastest moving messages are jokes. They are relatively safe to repeat. Even dictators have generally felt that they could not punish people who could claim that "it was only a joke."

READING BETWEEN THE LINES

When communication is dangerous, people find subtle ways to get tabooed messages circulated. Jokes are one such device. There are others. The strict dogmatic requirements of conformity result in Aesopian communication, the topic of the next chapter.

A complex modern society cannot work without spreading a vast amount of information among a large number of persons. People need policy guidance to do their jobs toward national goals in myriad scattered towns and factories. People need hard facts about what is going badly, as well as about what is going well. An Aesopian communication system spreads that

[1] Findings of increased reach of media into the countryside seem to have eliminated that rural-urban difference since then (G. Hollander, 1967; 1972; Rogers, 1968).

information without violating the taboos against open statements on sensitive topics. The information gets around at least to the people who know how to read the code between the lines.

Kremlinologists are such people although they are not the ones to whom the messages are addressed. We know relatively little about how well people within a totalitarian system actually do know how to read the clues. How skillful are they and what proportion of the population knows how to play the game? Clearly the top leaders do, but what about the rest of the population?

Dr. Rosemarie Rogers (1968) conducted an experiment designed to explore that matter. She found a number of subjects who had recently lived in the Soviet Union, but who were now abroad. They included persons of various educational and status levels. She gave each subject a pencil and a copy of *Pravda* or *Izvestia* covered with transparent plastic. She asked them to read, pencil in hand, pointing to where they were reading, and to mark important passages. They were to read the paper the way they would have read it back home. She could thus evaluate what they read, what they skipped, what cues they used for skipping, and what superficially innocuous passages were deemed important.

Her general conclusion was that educated professional people and Party members read like Kremlinologists, skimming a good deal and picking out key clues. Uneducated people, on the other hand, did not have the reading skill to do this. If they chose to read an item at all, they tended to go word for word through the filler as well as through important material. Clearly some degree of differential communication is achieved by Aesopian communication, and that is its purpose. It serves to send messages to the insiders in the know without being informative to the ordinary reader.

Such a system, of course, conveys much misinformation also. A couple of illustrative examples may make the point. In 1938 the controlled Nazi press was loaded with stories about alleged Czech atrocities against members of the German minority in Czechoslovakia. This was a propaganda preparation for the German demand for Czech territory. At the Munich conference of Hitler, Mussolini, Daladier, and Chamberlain, it was agreed that Germany should be given the Sudetenland claimed by Hitler.

Interviews with Germans after the end of World War II revealed that some had not believed the stories in the Nazi press about the Munich conference. To them it seemed beyond credibility that the heads of state of France and England could grant Hitler a piece of Czech territory. It was not theirs to grant. On the other hand, they had no doubt that the Czech atrocities against Germans living in the Sudetenland had occurred—which they had not. They knew that the Czechs disliked their German minority and that tensions were high. The German newspaper readers, therefore, had no reason to doubt the reported atrocities. In short, they disbelieved that which was true because it was implausible, and believed that which was false because it was plausible.

A similar reversal appeared in an interview with a Soviet defector in 1964. He was a young former prison guard and Komsomol secretary who, despite having grown up with no foreign contact except a few broadcasts heard six years before, was secretly dissident from the regime. His media access was to wired radio and TV in the club of the barracks where he lived. He was too young to remember the war. All that he knew about the Nazis was that the Soviet media kept attacking the powerful Nazis who, they claimed, were in command in West Germany. This young man decided that if the Soviet regime disliked the Nazis so much, they must be good. He succeeded in escaping to West Germany, where he went to join the Nazis whom he thought to be in control there. It was only when he got there that he discovered how inaccurate was the mental picture of contemporary Germany that he had concocted by reading between the lines of the Soviet media.

Recognition of the alarming phenomenon by which even those who oppose the regime have their minds captured and their view of the world shaped when there is total control of information was what led many free-world writers in the latter years of the Stalin regime to fearfully anticipate a 1984 of brainwashed, automated men. Orwell (1949), Koestler (1941), Milosz (1953), and many other writers expected the younger generations, wholly educated under totalitarian control, to yield to a value system and world view utterly at odds with Western civilization. Now, in retrospect, we see that they were too pessimistic.

Reading between the lines, while not foolproof, often works very well. The two anecdotal cases noted above represented situations where foreign sources were simply not available. Shortwave radios were much scarcer in the 1930s and were not available in the Soviet guard barracks. In general, it does not take much corrective information to make censored media interpretable. It would have taken only one foreign broadcast confirming the existence of the Munich Agreement to permit a more accurate reinterpretation of the daily Nazi press. It would have taken only one solid denial of the claim that Nazis were playing a major role in contemporary West Germany to permit a more accurate reinterpretation of the daily Soviet foreign news. In general, it is not equal time that is needed but merely the occasional planting of a corrective by rumor or radio to permit the audience to free itself from the prison of a self-contained system of distortions.

For that reason, among others, it is wrong to assume that rumor is a grossly distorted news source. Laboratory experiments, modeled on the game of passing a message from person to person around a room, always show that the end message is very different from the message that started out (Allport & Postman, 1947). That, however, is a forced communication situation. Experiments have also shown that in free, real-life situations people do not pass on rumors unless they make sense to them. The result is that the rumors, as they are relayed, are generally corrected for plausibility and are delivered to target persons who can use and understand them (Festinger, Schachter, & Back, 1950; Buckner, 1965).

One can neither assume full knowledge nor total ignorance on the part of the audience in a totalitarian society. It is a strange mixture that depends critically upon their motivation to learn, their perceptual biases, and what few corrective messages break through the barriers.

THE COLLAPSE OF COHESION

An assumption one should not make about the Soviet or other totalitarian audience is that it believes it is being told the truth. Distrust of the media is general. If people are nonetheless often misled, it is because they have no rudder by which to guide themselves through the maze of what they know to be distortions.

The lack of genuine trust in the political system becomes apparent whenever a totalitarian system breaks down. In every instance so far, when the power of compulsion is broken, a totalitarian regime proves very fragile indeed. It was hard to find a believing Nazi the day after Germany lost the war, and not just because it was healthier not to have been one, although that was certainly true. But it was also true that most people's behavior under the dictatorship was one of passive conformity rather than internalized faith. There were some true believers, but a lot more unquestioning followers.

Likewise, in Hungary in 1956 when an anti-Communist revolution temporarily succeeded, until the Russian tanks arrived it was hard to find anyone who had been a believing Communist previously (Kecskemeti, 1961). There were plenty of persons who had been a part of the Communist regime, but few who turned out to have believed in it. The same thing happened in

Czechoslovakia in 1968. Public opinion polls from that year document how few genuine Communist conservatives there were in that country (Pool, 1970). Censorship creates an illusion of unanimity that is not there. Furthermore, the very intensity of controls creates an environment in which the controls are not internalized.

COMMUNICATIONS REVOLUTION: SOVIET STYLE

So far we have been describing the totalitarian communication system as an ideal type. In the real world, however, pure totalitarianism seldom lasts long. How much of that model applies to post-Stalinist Russia and how much applies to any country with a modern communication system is a question that may legitimately be raised. The explosive growth of mass communications has revolutionized the environment in which totalitarian movements operate and has undermined some of their organizational assumptions.

During the past two decades, perhaps the most underanalyzed change in Soviet life has been the development and growth of mass communications and, particularly, of the capacity of Soviet citizens to receive shortwave broadcasts. This aspect of Soviet development has been neglected by most specialists. Scholars have explained Soviet developments by national character, history, or economics—indeed by virtually every conceivable factor—but have largely missed the variable that we here analyze, the diffusion of knowledge from the West.

Three main groups of theories are widely used to interpret trends and developments in the USSR (Bell, 1960; Inkeles, 1966). First, there are those theories that attempt to explain Soviet developments in terms of indigenous characteristics of the system or culture. These particularistic theories fall into two subclasses. There is the theory that Soviet development is the expression of the character of eternal Russia, and there is the theory that explains Soviet development by the Bolshevik tradition. Historians may argue whether the regime is more czarist or more Leninist, but in either version those theories propose that the Russian future is very largely conditioned by that nation's past. Those theories we may call the Russian or Soviet uniqueness theories.

A second set of theories may be called the stages-of-growth theories. These interpret Soviet events as reflecting general patterns of social development. They explain Soviet characteristics as expressions of the country's level of technological maturity. Those theories again fall into two groups: those that explain Soviet events as manifestations of an underdeveloped society, and those that explain Soviet events as manifestations of an industrializing society. The former see the arbitrary characteristics of the Soviet regime as expressing the primitive condition of that country. They note the similarities between Soviet bureaucratic practices and those of imperial regimes in peasant countries everywhere. As a corollary they may predict a softening of the regime with industrial progress and modernization. The industrial-society theories place more emphasis on the emerging industrial economy and less on peasant Russia. They visualize the Soviet Union as a typical industrializing society, going through the pains of rapid capital accumulation and the disciplining of a peasant labor force, using different slogans but with many brutal characteristics common to urban Europe in the nineteenth century.

A third set of theories has received far less attention; these are the communication theories. They explain Soviet developments by the diffusion of ideas from abroad. The communication theories recognize that at each stage of its history, Russia faced unique problems set by its particular geography, institutions, and historical heritage; these theories maintain, however, that the particular response was largely shaped by imitation of current thought in more advanced countries. Communism was a mimicking of German social democracy. The Five-Year-Plans were modeled on

Western planning methods. Soviet strategy today copies U.S. deterrence practices.

Communication theories of development, like the industrial-society theory, may suggest convergence between trends in the Soviet Union and in the West, but the explanation of the mechanism of convergence (and therefore of the outcome of it) is different. Communication theories do not argue that similar stages of technological or industrial evolution lead to similar developments. Rather they argue that a society, whatever its stage of development, if faced with a problem is likely to copy the solution from a more advanced country rather than to invent a new solution; that is, countries other than the most advanced are likely to tackle a problem in the way that other countries did when they coped with the problem earlier.

If such a communications theory is valid, then the way in which the first countries cope with a problem has great impact on the world, for it shapes the ways in which other societies will deal with it. It does not follow that the results will be the same, for similar remedies applied in different circumstances may produce different results. Khrushchev planted corn in Siberia, but it does not necessarily grow. Establishing profit criteria in industry does not necessarily work in the absence of a capital market. Nonetheless, there is a strong tendency to follow paths that have been laid out by experience. The established solution seems the most practicable one. To the extent that this mechanism explains Soviet evolution, we should be interested in the way and the extent to which information about the outside world diffuses into the USSR.

The Soviet Union is an imitative society (Pool, 1966). It is hard to think of major social innovations that have come out of Bolshevism since the invention of the Leninist type of Party in the first decade of this century. Unfortunately that has been a most effective social innovation. Another major practice that might be called an innovation is collectivization of agriculture, which has been an economic contretemps.

Most of the devices that the Party proclaims as its ideas are procedures that have been proved to work elsewhere first. Soviet socialism is an adaptation in the service of the controlling Party organization of planning techniques, police techniques, industrial techniques, educational techniques, communication techniques, etc., that were already well known in countries that modernized earlier. Whether it be jazz, or consumer-goods markets, or cybernetics, or deterrence strategy, or concrete sociological research, or scientific management, every major idea that becomes a heated intellectual issue in Soviet circles is a cosmopolitan idea that some or many Soviet thinkers wish to adopt. Before World War II, the Soviet regime tried to hinder this imitative process by ruthless means. Printed matter from abroad was virtually unobtainable by most of the population. Shortwave radios were accessible to only 2 percent. To be seen talking to a foreigner was dangerous. In the past twenty years, however, that iron curtain has fallen before a communications revolution.

Today, with the permeability of the Soviet frontier, and particularly with the voice of international radio loud and clear, one may assert that there is no major trend in international thought that does not reach the Soviet Union and become an issue there, too. Clearly that is true in science; it is equally true in jazz and art. The fashions of the Left Bank become issues, if not fashions, in Moscow also.

Such a communications theory of Soviet development is not necessarily a theory of convergence. The theory of convergence says that we are both moving to be more like each other—we more like them as well as they more like us. But a theory predicated on imitation asserts only one direction in the process of influence. There are forces pushing the Soviet Union toward modernized Western models, but at the same time the already modernized countries are changing in autonomous ways. That fact makes it quite indeterminate whether at any future time our countries will be more alike or more different than they are today.

In a greyhound race the dogs chase a "rabbit," but they do not necessarily get any closer to it. In this sense *chase* may be a better metaphor than *convergence*. A chase may generate tensions, conflict, yet need not necessarily lead the Soviets in any immediate future to what is often called liberalization. Western liberal political practices do exert an attractive force on Soviet thinkers, but at the same time a police regime is likely to see conditions of chase as demanding tightening up of controls to achieve progress. Nonetheless, it is clear that what we in the modernized world do, what we think, what we develop that succeeds has a profound impact on the direction of Soviet development. This is increasingly so since the communications revolution has penetrated the iron curtain.

The communications revolution in the USSR is only now being documented by social researchers in the West. Some major studies of Soviet public opinion and communication using interviews with displaced persons were conducted by the Harvard Russian Research Center after World War II. The studies of Inkeles and Bauer, therefore, refer basically to communication patterns of the 1930s (Inkeles, 1958; Bauer & Gleicher, 1953; Inkeles & Bauer, 1959). Since then there have been a number of studies of Soviet international propaganda (Barghoorn, 1960; 1964; Clews, 1964; Dasbach, 1966). Also UNESCO, in its worldwide compilation of information about mass media, has included data on the Communist countries (UNESCO, 1963–1964; United Nations, 1949–). There have been studies of the intellectuals and the arts in post-Stalin Russia (Blake & Hayward, 1962; Hayward & Labedz, 1963; Hayward & Crowley, 1964; Johnson, 1965; Siniavskii, 1966; Reve, 1969; Pospielovsky, 1970). There is an interesting study of Party schools (Mickiewicz, 1967).

New comprehensive studies of the internal Soviet communication system are just now appearing. Most of the material in our treatment here derives from a project on Communist communication systems and Soviet sociology that has been conducted at the Center for International Studies at M.I.T., and which has included two major studies of the recent Soviet communication developments, one by Dr. Gayle Durham Hollander (Durham, 1965b; 1965c; 1966; Hollander, 1967; 1968; 1972) and one by Dr. Rosemarie Rogers (1967; 1968; 1969). The data for these studies arise largely from reading the voluminous professional, administrative, and reportorial publications in the Soviet Union concerning their mass media and propaganda activities. A great and growing mass of statistics and analysis is published there.

One of the best sources is the sociological research being conducted in the Soviet Union. From the middle 1920s until about 1960, there was virtually no sociological research in the Soviet Union. Sociology itself became a bad word. A priori tracts on dialectical materialism replaced the empirical study of real phenomena. Starting in the 1950s this situation changed (Weinberg, 1964; G. Fischer, 1964; 1967; P. Hollander, 1965; 1969; Parsons, 1965; Simirenko, 1967; 1969; Ahlberg, 1968; Berger, 1969; Dunn, 1969; D. E. Powell & Shoup, 1969; Katz, 1971).

One of the first areas of sociology allowed to be revived was the study of leisure time through time budgets (Prudenskiy, 1961; Beliaev et al., 1962; Gazette, 1962; Goncharenko, 1963; Orientation Center of Publishers and Distributors, 1965; Petrosyan, 1965; Durham, 1966; Szalai, 1966; Artemov et al., 1967; Grushin, 1967). There were several reasons for the acceptability of this type of research. For one thing, it was an area in which the Soviets led and did not need to feel that they were copying American sociology. In the 1920s excellent time-budget studies were being done in the Soviet Union while only later were some imitations begun in the West. Furthermore, the instigators of this type of research argued that it could save the USSR millions of man and woman hours by identifying socially unproductive uses of time, such as home cooking or waiting in line. Time-budget studies could be presented as an efficiency device. For our purposes, the important fact about these studies of leisure time was that they provided information on the use of mass media.

Other relevant areas in which Soviet sociology has developed, although slowly and less adequately, are market research, audience research, community studies, youth culture, and public opinion surveying (Uledov, 1963; Bukhalov & Yakuba, 1968; Rubin, 1968; Ikonnikova & Lisovsky, 1969). A major "Middletown" type community study is under way in Taganrog, with much emphasis on flows of information and influence within the town (Grushin et al., 1969; Levikov, 1970). By now many media have done surveys of their audiences.[2] While the samples used are often imperfect, nevertheless the studies can be of considerable interest. Dr. Rosemarie Rogers (1967) examined this literature closely and discovered surprising congruence between the published Soviet surveys on media behavior and the results obtained through a survey of 108 former Soviet residents in the West.

There are extensive data published by the Soviets themselves on such things as number of radio sets, TV sets, and loudspeakers; number of newspapers and magazines published and their distribution by type and region; number of libraries and library books, lectures, cultural centers, etc. One of the characteristics of the highly centralized Soviet regime is that many things on which we keep no statistics receive elaborate documentation there.

For example, in this country myriad speeches are given at churches, clubs, schools, and associations by thousands of private individuals who would not think of reporting their talks to anyone. In the Soviet Union all such lecturing activity is organized in one of a relatively few ways by formal institutions which keep records of their activities. There are oral agitators, all part of an organized structure, who must report and are counted; there are universities of culture; and there is *Znaniye*, a society that provides most public speakers. This society was reported to have arranged over 15 million lectures in 1967 for a total audience of 800 million (G. Hollander, 1972).

It would be an illusion to believe that our knowledge of Soviet mass media behavior is complete or precise. Nonetheless, one should not underestimate the information available. In this area, as in all areas of Soviet study, the job is partially one of detective work.

Nonetheless, mass communication is one aspect of a society that no society can hide. If it chooses to talk to its people, it is talking to the whole world, too. The basic picture of the recent communication revolution in the Soviet Union is beyond concealment.

Today information from the outside world is there for Soviet citizens to learn. Instead of only 2 percent of the Soviet people having the physical possibility of hearing foreign radio broadcasts as was the case when Stalin ruled the Soviet Union, today one-half of the population has that chance. How much of what is available they choose to absorb and believe

---

[2] For *Izvestia*, see *Izvestia* for July 11, 1968, and July 12, 1968; *Nedelya*, No. 11, 1967; *Zhurnalist*, No. 2, 1968, pp. 23–25.

For *Pravda*, see Gerasimov (1967); Yevladov (1969); V. Z. Kogan and Tapilina (1970).

For *Trud*, see *Zhurnalist*, No. 7, 1968, pp. 46–48.

For *Red Star*, see *Krasnaya Zvezda*, December 27, 1969.

For *Literaturnaya gazeta*, see Soviet Sociological Association (1969); Center for Study of Media, University of Novosibirsk (1970); Shlyapentokh (1970).

For *raion* ("district") press, see Partenov (1968); *Zhurnalist*, No. 6, 1970, pp. 42–45.

For radio, see Yaroshenko (1966).

For television, see Firsov (1967; 1968; 1971); L. Kogan (1969); Khmara (1971).

is another matter, depending upon many subtle psychological and ideological variables. However, the information is there; that fact is one of the most important changes between the character of life in the complete straightjacket of Stalin's Russia and the character of life in the uneasy and shifting Soviet society of today.

The Soviet Union is no longer a fully closed society. It is no longer impenetrable to information. The regime can no longer assume that it can effectively keep from its people the facts of what is going on in an international crisis or military situation. That development has many consequences. One of these consequences, but only one, is the creation of a powerful pressure toward liberalization. Another consequence is the creation of pressure towards anti-bourgeois propaganda and increased anti-liberal repression in order to resist the liberalizing influence of communications. In the West, a widely accepted myth perceives the Soviet Union as somehow ordained to move towards liberalization. Every so often the trial of a protestor or the flight of someone like Svetlana Alliluyeva or Anatole Kuznetsov reminds us that this is not so. World communications create a pressure toward liberalization, but the reaction to that pressure can be either change or repression.

There are other factors besides foreign information that also create pressure to open up Soviet society. There is the general erosion of ideological faith through which every revolution passes as it learns by experience that its new truths include chimeras and that old truths had some merit. There is the fact that Stalin was clinically paranoid while his successors have only normal quotas of illusion and fanaticism. There is the fact that no regime could permanently survive the unabated fear in which men lived in the 1930s and the constant extermination of the cream of the nation. There is also the growth of a new generation which rebels against the pieties of the old.

All of these things are taking place, and all of them would in any case have tended to moderate the militant terror of 1935–1938 into a tired old tyranny. But if the winds of free thought did not penetrate into the Soviet Union, the abatement of the revolution would have been both slower and less liberal in orientation. Most of the things of a positive character that are happening in the Soviet Union today are explainable only in terms of foreign influence, for which the most important single channel is radio.

There never was a time when the Bolshevik attempt to control the information that reached Soviet citizens was fully successful. There were always dissidents who kept alive in the privacy of their own heads or within their families, political or national or religious faiths that the regime proscribed (Powell, 1967; for Eastern Europe, cf. Kecskemeti, 1961; Radio Free Europe, 1969a; Pool, 1970b).

There were also always islands of freedom in prison. Men to whom arrest and imprisonment had already happened, who had already written off rewards in this life, who knew that their neighbors were also enemies of the regime could sometimes talk more freely to each other than could people still trying to make their way up the treadmill.

Tarsis (1965) in his novel *Ward 7* has described such an island of free thought: a psychiatric ward to which dissidents were sent so that the regime could avoid being accused of making them political prisoners. Ward 7 was a place where men of deviant views could say whatever they wished under the protective eye of the psychiatric orderlies, for they had been officially ruled insane for what they believed.

In Stalin's Russia there was always the rumor net to which we referred before and that covered the country. It played a vital role in preventing the successful imposition of a permanently closed society (Bauer & Gleicher, 1953; Inkeles & Bauer, 1959; Kassof, 1965; for Eastern Europe, cf. Nowak, 1962; Higher Party School . . . of CPSU, 1963).

Another evidence of the incompleteness of totalitarian control is that Soviet youth is unquiet. The rebellious and liberal spirit sometimes found among Soviet youth is often attributed to the psychology of adolescence and the inevitable conflict of generations. That is too simple. Generational conflict can take many forms. It was not foreordained that Soviet youth would like rock music or that Soviet artists would paint abstractions. These are not the only forms that protest can take. The style of rebellion of the flappers and their companions in the 1920s was not the same as the style of today's adolescents. Rebellion against tradition in the intellectual milieu of the *philosophes* was not the same as that in Greenwich Village and Leningrad today.

Why are the forms of rebellious individuality so similar in Russia and in the West today? Clearly not by coincidence nor by any inevitable laws of industrial society, but because of communication. There is now enough communication to make us part of a single civilization, to keep us influencing each other, to assure that any Western idea circulates in the Soviet Union, too. The pessimistic expectation that totalitarianism could develop an accepted heinous civilization of its own by 1984 or any other year has been defeated primarily by the forces of communication and, above all, by international radio.

That is a central point that we wish to make. What is the evidence?

First, let us look at the facts of the spread of listening capability. Unfortunately, we do not have good figures on shortwave receivers in the Soviet Union. Soviet figures on radios in general are somewhat unreliable. It is important to distinguish between wave sets (ordinary radios as we conceive them) and wired loudspeakers. It is also important to distinguish private sets from communication sets. These distinctions are not always clear in Soviet statistics. Furthermore, one must consider what proportion of sets is in working order, a serious matter in a country where service remains a major problem.

Most important, however, the Soviets do not tell us what proportion of sets can receive shortwave. Most of the non-transistor sets do, because the Soviets themselves use some shortwave broadcasting domestically to cover the vast spaces of their land. Soviet domestic broadcasts go as low as the 25 meter band. The sets widely available on the market go no lower than that. That is low enough for international reception, however, although the best reception is of still shorter waves. It is common Soviet practice for citizens to purchase radios with wavelength bands down to 25 meters and rewind the condensor to make it capable of receiving shorter waves. That fact alone is testimony to how much Soviet citizens value foreign broadcasts. That is also attested to by other purchase behavior. Radios that can receive shortwave are most heavily in demand. The few models of transistor sets that can receive shortwave, the Spidola and the Transistor-10, disappear from stores almost before they hit the counter.

In 1940 there were about one million radio sets in the Soviet Union. By 1952 there were about 5.8 million. By 1967 there were 42 million (Pool, 1971: 32). If we simply assume that two-thirds of the sets could receive foreign shortwave broadcasts and that a set is available to all members of a family, then as a very rough approximation we can say that about one person in fifty-seven could listen to a foreign broadcast (if he dared to) in 1940, one in thirteen in 1952, and one in two today. This is a highly significant change, for it alters drastically (1) the richness of foreign information available and, therefore, also alters (2) the role of rumor and (3) the role and behavior of the domestic media. Let us review these three points.

We have said that the accessibility of foreign broadcasts to something like half the Russians (and that means to a large majority of urban, educated, white-collar Russians) increases the richness of foreign information available. Mere availability, however, would be of no interest if the available broadcasts were not used. After all, only 2 percent of American adults listen to foreign broadcasts in a month (Smith, 1969–70). All the evidence, however, is that the Russian listener eagerly uses his shortwave bands. Evidence comes from the readiness with which Soviet citizens can tell you where on the dial to pick up foreign news broadcasts. They obviously have had experience.

Other evidence comes from conversations and interviews. In unsystematic ways one constantly hears Soviet citizens these days referring to foreign radio listening. Of the 108 former Soviet residents interviewed in the study referred to above, eighty had owned shortwave sets, substantially more than one would find in a true cross-section sample. Of these, seventy-seven reported that they listened once or twice a week or more, and the majority listened three to five times a week to foreign broadcasts. The modal amount of time spent was from one-half to one and one-half hours of listening per day (Rogers, 1967).

More significant than their own tastes (for this is a very unrepresentative sample) is what they tell us based on their relation to other Soviet citizens. Of these shortwave listeners whom were interviewed, thirty-four said they felt free in recent years to mention their foreign source of news in conversations while thirty-one said it was tacitly understood but not mentioned. Only thirteen said they listened to foreign radio alone; the majority mentioned listening with friends as well as family, a testimony not only to their own interest in international broadcasts but also to their perception of the acceptability to others of knowledge that they were listening.

Those respondents, although a diverse group with little in common besides alienation from the regime, would be an illegitimate sample for assaying matters such as attitudes toward communism. Also, those people probably participated in the Soviet media less than Soviet citizens of similar status for, as we know from the Inkeles-Bauer studies (1959), the more effectively socialized a Soviet citizen, the more he uses the mass media; the more alienated he is, the less he uses them. Furthermore, only forty-three respondents were Great Russians. With due caution, however, we can draw some further conclusions from those interviews, for extensive audience research has shown that the differences in gross media habits associated with differences in attitudes are relatively small.

The examples that could be offered to document this assertion are numerous. For example, in the United States people who like higher level cultural content in their television programming watch TV as it actually is somewhat less than the mass audience, but the difference is perhaps twenty minutes a day out of nearly three hours (Schramm, Lyle, & Pool, 1963). Or, to cite a more directly revelant example, Inkeles and Bauer (1959) found that with class held constant, the percentage of heavy users of Soviet radio among pro-Soviet respondents was only about 10 percentage points higher than among the most anti-Soviet respondents. They found no difference in foreign radio listening between these groups, again with class held constant. In those prewar years, 14 percent of the intelligentsia claimed to be frequent listeners and only 1 percent of ordinary workers and collective farmers. Social status sharply affected media habits, but attitudes affected them only a little. So we may look at our atypical but diverse group of ex-Soviet respondents and still get some partially representative information about facts on such matters as use of radio or TV, or what people do for recreation.

Even wide access to news does not necessarily overcome distortion and misunderstanding in the information flow between countries or cultures. After all, the understanding by the American citizen of life in Russia is poor indeed, even though no censorship bars knowledge from him. The obstacle to the American's knowledge is the nonfunctionality of the information to him. He misunderstands because he has little motivation to learn about Soviet affairs.

On the Soviet side, the development of worldwide media have in one respect made the situation similar to that in the West, although in other respects it is quite different. The growth of access to foreign news sources with their rich picture of reality means that, as in the West, the only absolute barrier to full and accurate information is the psychological one. No longer do the devices of a police state successfully keep the Soviet citizen in the dark. What he learns or fails to learn is now primarily determined by the filters of what is functional to him.

For five years, from June 1963 to August 1968, the Soviets even stopped jamming almost all foreign broadcasts. That period marked the height of liberalization in various fields, a liberalization from which there has now been a major retreat. Jamming was resumed to obscure news of the invasion of Czechoslovakia and has been maintained since. However, even under jamming, news can be received with effort, although it requires close attention and careful tuning by the listener. For a few years, however, any radio owner wanting world news could get it without significant effort. Now once more he must fiddle with the dial and listen closely, but he can get the news.

For the Soviet citizen who craves information about the outside world, international radio is but one, although the most important one, among a number of media that maintain the channels of contact with Western civilization. There are exhibits, dramatic performances, TV kinescopes, and other items that are part of cultural-exchange programs. Personal contact with visitors from abroad has also been increasing as has travel abroad by Soviet citizens. The number of Russians traveling abroad has passed one million per year (although the overwhelming majority travel to noncapitalist countries). Travelers to the Soviet Union now run to about 1.6 million tourists and business, cultural, educational, scientific, and marine personnel (United Nations, 1969).

The 108 interview respondents, being persons oriented toward going abroad and many knowing foreign languages, had contact with foreigners much more than do most Soviet citizens. Yet only half of the respondents had had such contacts as often as twice a year during the period just before leaving the Soviet Union. Only a few individuals have many such contacts. For a few writers, scientists, and high officials, direct foreign contact is a major source of information. Such privileged persons may often be domestic communicators also, as well as important men in their own right. As persons well informed about, and possibly well disposed toward, the West, they can be influential forces for liberalization of the society. They are also gatekeepers through whom information flows to the average Soviet citizen, who himself rarely sees foreigners.

The printed word from abroad is available only sparsely, although more so now than before Stalin's death. Two-thirds of our respondents, despite their exceptional motivation to read foreign materials and their frequent knowledge of foreign language, had never read a book published abroad. Almost half had never even had access to a foreign magazine or journal. But to put the same matter another way, a third of our peculiar respondents were regular readers of some foreign journal, thereby demonstrating that such people do exist in the Soviet Union.

A motivated Soviet citizen can also receive considerable international information from the domestic Soviet media. The Soviet media have had to respond to an increasingly competitive environment. During the Stalin era an unfavorable development abroad might be smothered in silence. Generally, the Soviet media system waited a day or two until *Pravda* could first be told by the Party secretariat how to treat an unfortunate event, and thus indicate to the other media how to treat it. That is no longer possible. As officially stated in 1960, and reiterated in 1963:

> The central radio stations in Moscow must first of all assure timely broadcasts of important political information, effective commentary on domestic and foreign events and the organization of various artistic programs. Because radio should give the population the important news before the newspapers do, *TASS* has been instructed to transmit news immediately to central and local radio stations (*Par-tiynaya Zhizn*, No. 4, February, 1960:26).

> Radio should communicate to the population all important news earlier than do the newspapers (Boglovskiy & L'vov 1963).

The Soviet radio has had to change drastically in response to the increasing fact of foreign competition. Soviet newscasters now have to report the world news as it occurs, for if they wait they will be scooped by shortwave broadcasts with an interpretation other than the Soviet one. There is, of course, for the Soviet media as for all media systems a wide discretion in emphasis. Schramm (1959) illustrated that dramatically by reproducing front pages from fourteen countries for a day when the Hungarian and Suez invasions were happening simultaneously; the relative attention to the two wars reflected quite different worlds. Any content analysis of Communist-block coverage of major news will show massive displacements of emphasis (Barghoorn, 1950; Blücher, 1959; Reisky-Dubnic, 1961; Kempers, 1968). But absolute embargos on mentioning bad news is now the exception (Jones, 1966; Robinson, 1970) for silence encourages the public to listen to foreign radio.

For the Soviet elite there is, as there has always been, substantial coverage of foreign news sources in classified monitoring reports (Whaley, 1964; 1969). They are of differing degrees of completeness, according to the receiver's rank. Every day *Tass* sends virtually the entire nonlocal, political contents of the *New York Times* to the Soviet Union (Kruglak, 1962). Translations of entire Western books get produced in editions not for sale to the general public (Whaley, 1962). Daily monitor reports can be read by authorized persons (besides those who get them personally) in numerous government offices and research institutes. The classified foreign news reports issued daily by *TASS*, the so-called Red Tass, run to about two hundred pages a day (Whaley, 1964). Somewhat expurgated, less sensitive editions are fairly widely available to students, intellectuals, professionals, and higher level bureaucrats.

Intriguing information on one such limited circulation, but wide coverage news-reporting device in the Communist system comes from an East European country. We know that the system is a direct copy of one in the Soviet Union. There is a special telephone system with sets available to the top elite in the country (two hundred in the Soviet Union). Each set has a key which one must have to use the phone. Just as in the United States one can dial certain numbers for the correct time or the weather report, so the users of the key telephone system can dial a special number and listen to a tape recording of the unexpurgated world news for elite ears only.

For a wider audience the Soviets have also started regular open publication of magazines that specialize in reprinting foreign materials. There is *Inostrannaya Literatura* ("Foreign Literature") and *Za Rubezhom* ("Abroad"). The latter is the great success story of the Soviet magazine world. This weekly, started in 1960, had reached a circulation of 500,000 by September 1966. In earlier years of paper shortages, rationed magazine subscriptions, and absence of foreign or domestic competition, such a press run for alien material would have been forbidden. But the Soviet Union today proudly claims that it can meet the demand for all magazines and that it now sells subscriptions to general magazines to all comers. *Za Rubezhom* has been allowed to meet the spontaneous and phenomenal demand. The interested Soviet citizen can now read Walter Lippmann or the editorials from *Le Monde* in a legitimate and extensive, even if highly selective, Soviet source.

To put these special publications about foreign affairs in context, we should note that the circulations of *Pravda* and *Izvestia* have both been over 7 million, and that newspaper circulation in the Soviet Union added up to 126 million in 1968 (G. Hollander, 1967; 1972; Rogers, 1968). That figure for newspapers includes weeklies. The UNESCO figure for newspapers issued at least four days a week for 1967 is 69.6 million. Circulation of print media grew rapidly as the USSR overcame its paper shortage during the 1950s and early 1960s. In 1952, according to UNESCO (1969), circulation of newspapers per 1,000 inhabitants amounted to 109; in 1960, 172; in 1967, 295, which may be compared with 342 per 1,000 in the U.S.A. in 1952 and 309 in 1967. Quantitative saturation of the newspaper market has effectively been reached, with a per capita circulation that is by now higher than that in the U.S.A.

It is perhaps belaboring the obvious to stress that among educated Russians there is a deep and active craving to learn about what goes on in the outside world. They strive to satisfy their curiosity by every safe means available. A most telling and surprising indication of how far Russians do in fact model themselves on the secretly admired West came in a recent Soviet market-research poll. The poll dealt with tastes and fashions in what people bought. About one-third of the respondents said that they got their ideas from fashions in the West. In contrast to the situation in the U.S.A., all surveys show that the foreign news is among the most widely read and most prized part of the paper (Sicinski, 1966; Rubin & Kolesnikov, 1968; Ikonnikova & Lisovsky, 1969; Hungarian Radio and Television Mass Communication Research Center, 1970).

The change in access to foreign information that we have been describing is taking place in the context of a still wider, though not deeper, change in the Soviet communication system, namely, the growth of domestic mass media. Just as in a still broader economic context the Soviet Union is changing from an underdeveloped into an industrialized nation so, too, is its communication system changing from a word-of-mouth system into a mass media system.

Twenty-five years ago, when there were only about a million radios, an extreme paper shortage kept newspaper circulation down, and there was no television. Wired radio—the poor countries' approximation of an electronic media system—existed (Sorenson & Meyer, 1955), as it does in Communist China today (Liu, 1964a; 1964b), but counted only about 2 million loudspeakers. In 1967 there were over 22 million TV sets in addition to 41 million radios, about 39 million wired speakers, and enough paper so that only twenty-one of our 108 former Soviet respondents indicated that they would have subscribed to more Soviet magazines if they could have.

We know too little about the psychological differences between living in a mass media system of communication and a pre-mass media system, but there are differences. In the literature on communication and development (discussed in Chapter 13), we find assertions that the mass media widen empathic capacity (i.e., enabling people to understand ways of life and roles that they have not experienced first hand), homogenize society, create a mass society, or debase culture. Some of these changes can be seen in the Soviet Union. Russification, decay of folk culture, amalgamation of rural and urban ways of life, adoption of middle-class ways and modern values, and increased consumer orientation may have other causes besides media growth, but the development of modern mass media reinforces such tendencies.

The Soviet press writes about some of these related trends in ways that sometimes sound much like parallel discussions in this country. There are Soviet pedagogues, for example, who worry that TV watching is impinging on reading. One recalls the frequent post-Sputnik observation that the Russians are a nation of book readers. The taxi driver with a classic in hand is a favorite idol of visiting journalists. It must be recognized that, in part, this book-reading habit simply reflected the aridity and also to some degree the unavailability of mass media entertainment. Magazines, newspapers, radio, and TV were scarce, and what was available was ponderous, political, and dull—dull to the point of driving the audience away.

How completely many Soviet citizens disengage themselves from the Soviet version of the "vast wasteland" is dramatically illustrated in an interview with a man who had been a miner in the far north in 1957. We asked him how he first heard of Sputnik. One night, he said, he was walking home from the mine with a friend when the friend exclaimed, "Look at that drunken star!" They debated what it might be and bet three bottles of vodka. Not until three days later could the bet be settled. That was so even though Soviet media for those three days were saturated with paeans about the great triumph of the socialist fatherland. It is true that the miners were too remote to have current newspapers, but radio was there. These miners cared so little to listen to the Soviet radio, however, and those of their colleagues who listened cared so little to talk about what the regime was proclaiming, that even Sputnik did not become known to these two men for three days.

Such alienation is not average, but neither is it rare. Tolstoy, Sholokhov, Puskhin, and Chekhov are the authors who show up in first places in surveys of favorite authors (G. Hollander; 1972). Classic authors represent at least an escape from the sodden dullness of party resolutions, letters of self-criticisms, or odes to agricultural production.

Rejection of the dull Soviet mass media is a characteristic citizen reaction. Dullness and repetition in programming are also prime subjects for Soviet discussions of radio and television. To cite a newspaper article entitled "Television: 7% Fun":

> Your working day begins. You set off for work, recalling on the way what entertained you yesterday: nothing, it turns out, even though you spent the entire evening at the television set... You learned how automobile tops are manufactured, they demonstrate how smoking injures your health, you even learned a few words of English. "No matter," you think, "they've probably been saving the entertainment for tonight."
>
> Hope still lives in the viewer. Let's not allow it to die (*Sovietskaya Kultura*, September 9, 1965:3).

The mass media revolution that is in process in Soviet society consists of not only the increased availability of magazine subscriptions, tape recorders, transistor sets, and TV, but also a major effort to lighten their content. In Khrushchev's day, when this effort was at its height, his son-in-law Adzhubei introduced "Family Circle," a feature section, into *Izvestia* along with much exhortation of journalists for better writing and a more human touch. Soap opera was introduced on the air; it was political insofar as it attempted in a low-keyed way to convey proper socialist morality regarding such matters as waiting in queues, alcohol consumption, participation in civic activities, etc., but no more moralistic in its terms than is Western soap opera. We know that "The Family Szabo" has been the most popular program on Hungarian radio and that an equivalent program is the most popular on Polish radio. We may well suspect that "In Our Circle," the serial program dealing with the daily life of the Kuznetsov family, has had a similar status on Soviet television. Soviet radio, in its competition for an audience, has introduced a fourth program, "Mayak" (or "Beacon"), which, following much of the formula of current Western radio, features a continuous pattern of light music and news. On TV the hit programs, the ones that people look for, are the French and Italian movies that Soviet

TV sometimes shows. Thirty-four of the 108 respondents mentioned foreign films as their favorite kind of film (Pool, 1971).

With such changes under way, and particularly with the growth of TV, participation in mass media is growing and older reading habits and social habits are changing. A particularly interesting testimony to changing habits may be found in a Leningrad time-budget study (Beliaev et al., 1962). The study distinguished, among various categories of use of leisure time, three that are of particular interest to us: television and radio, reading of political and social material, and reading of belles lettres.

In one of the cross-tabulations, respondents were classified by age. Comparing the young and the old, those between the ages of eighteen and thirty spent 11 percent of their free time on TV and radio compared with 14 percent for those aged thirty-one to forty and 19 percent for those forty-one years or over. The reading of belles lettres was common to all age groups: people from eighteen to thirty years of age spent 10 percent of their free time on this type of literature, those from thirty-one to forty spent 9.5 percent, and those over forty, 8.5 percent. Time spent on social and political material, however, presents a striking contrast: only 2.5 percent of the free time of eighteen- to thirty-year-olds was spent on social and political literature compared with 6 percent for those thirty-one to forty and 10 percent for those over fifty.

The youth can no longer be enticed to read dull propaganda. To reach them, the regime has had to accept and offer jazz, French movies, women's magazines, and other such material. Currently there is also substantial discussion of the development of increased advertising (O'Keefe, 1967; Pool, 1971:41).

As popularized material has become available, and as effective mass media have become a major means of coordinating social action and organizing life, a subtle but important consequence has been the decline of the agitprop system. When Inkeles (1958) wrote his classic book on *Public Opinion in Soviet Russia*, the most characteristic feature of the Soviet communication system was the use of oral agitators. Two million agitators, getting their guidelines from *Bloknot Agitatora*, bored the rest of their fellow countrymen at regular, sometimes daily, meetings at all sorts of places of work.

None of that has changed in any dramatic way, but a distinct erosion has set in. The meetings are less frequent. Their content is more often the normal administrative content of an office meeting and less often political agitation. All this has happened despite frantic campaigns from time to time in recent years to raise the level of propaganda activity as an offset to the decline of police controls. In 108 interviews, the following distributions of attendance at meetings was found: 14 respondents attended one to three times a month, 2 attended five to ten times a month, 1 attended practically daily, 22 rarely attended, and 31 generally attended no meetings at all (Pool, 1971).

The organizational network can, of course, still be mobilized at important moments. One total mobilization occurred in 1956 after Khrushchev's de-Stalinization speech at the Twentieth Congress of the Communist Party of the Soviet Union, which was diffused not by publication but at meetings of Party members all over the country. After the invasion of Czechoslovakia, the Soviet explanation was given everywhere in meetings.

All interview respondents mentioned meetings as one source (although not the main source) of information, especially in crises or during other periods of noteworthy news. They were asked about major events that occurred while they were still in the Soviet Union. Table 2 indicates the events they discussed in the interview and whether or not they attended any meetings at the time about each event. Clearly mobilization via agitational meeting still plays some role in Soviet crises communication.

TABLE 2

CRISIS MEETINGS ATTENDED BY INTERVIEW RESPONDENTS

Year	Event	Number of Respondents Reporting on Event	Number Who Attended a Meeting	Total Number of Meetings Attended
1956	Twentieth Congress CPSU de-Stalinization speech	2	1	1
1956	Hungarian revolution	3	1	1
1957	Sputnik launching	9	6	15+
1960	U-2 incident	11	10	15+
1961	Berlin wall	11	2	2
1962	Cuban missile crisis	28	14	18
1963	Death of Kennedy	30	3	3
1964	Khrushchev's ouster	25	7	17
1965	Vietnam	11	5	15

Only a small role in personal guidance was played by the local, on-the-spot Party official (cf. also Ikonnikova & Lisovsky, 1969). It is still true that the Party machine, with its secretary in every organization, is the ruling body. Vigilantes called *druzhinniki* are recruited, largely from the ranks of the Komsomol, to control the personal morals, alcoholism, or rowdyism of their neighbors. The Society for Dissemination of Political and Scientific Knowledge (*Znaniye*) does organize a vast number of lectures which are attended by an average of over 2 million persons per day. However, as in the West, the political machine has been eroded by the regime's direct use of the mass media to reach the public. Just as the Chautauqua circuit has given way to the Nielsen "top ten" so, too, in the Soviet Union, the growth of the mass media is modifying the forms of social control and reducing the function of the face-to-face political machine.

The trend is not completely linear by any means. Khrushchev tried to replace the totally coercive methods of Stalin by much greater reliance on persuasion. His era was marked by the greatest emphasis in Soviet history on political agitation and propaganda, increase and popularization of the mass media, some liberalization in the arts and, concurrently, a shake-up of the Party organization, which might well have undermined it. Khrushchev's successors, in rejecting his "harebrained" schemes, have tightened up Party organization, clamped down on the artists and writers and, consequently, lost ground in the effectiveness of their propaganda. But they cannot turn the clock back on the growth of the mass media, although they may try. Thus pressure toward a more Khrushchevian policy will remain.

In the Soviet Union, as wherever it takes place, modernization substitutes mass media influence for certain forms of traditional control and for indoctrination within the family and other primary groups. While modernization loosens the grip of these primary institutions, it does not destroy them. It also impels the growth of various forms of civic, commercial, and social organizations. At the same time, the media take over some of the functions of these very organizations.

It is this double-barreled process that has been taking place in the USSR. On the one hand, as the Soviet Union becomes a more complex industrial society, the number and variety of organizations needed to carry out its myriad economic, social, and scientific programs grow. On the other hand, as the mass media becomes increasingly important as mobilizing, homogenizing, and value-setting institutions, many of the functions previously performed by the most primary and personally controlling organizations, particularly the family and the local Party organizations, are taken over by the media.

In a non-Communist developing society, pluralism is the most natural outcome of reliance on a mixture of mass media and organization. A complex society that mobilizes itself partly by the noncoercive but unindividualized means of mass media persuasion on the one hand, and partly by a myriad of specialized organizations on the other, tends most naturally toward a pluralistic pattern of partial and overlapping loyalties and affiliations. This pattern is in sharp contrast to the kind of premodern society that socializes and controls each person within a single all-embracing primary group, be it family, caste, clan, guild, or Party cell.

The Soviet conception of organization of society, via an encompassing structure of activities arranged at the place of work under the full direction of the local Party organization, was appropriate for mobilizing an underdeveloped country without an effective mass media system. It is an incubus in the complex society of today. A tightly knit hierarchical organizational structure is eroded to the degree that there are effective mass media.

The Soviet leadership would like to mobilize in a centrally planned way all of the same forms of initiative and action in production, in leisure, in education, and in science that are mobilized in this country by corporations, voluntary associations, foundations, institutions, and mass media. In our society we do this by a remarkable process of loose coordination. Neither law nor party resolution specifies that virtually all corporations have an essentially similar structure of top and middle management, headquarters office and branches, accounting, legal, and sales departments, etc. No law or party resolution specifies that all voluntary organizations use Robert's Rules of Order. One could go on indefinitely pointing to ways in which convention loosely but effectively coordinates an incredibly large organizational structure in a free society.

The Soviet leadership wants to mobilize an equally large structure but without accepting the risks of spontaneity, i.e., the danger of loss of control. They wish to mobilize social action through a bureaucratic structure reaching down to the lowest level, all controlled by Party fiat. No issue in Soviet life will be more important in the coming years than the struggle over the role of the Party. The conservatives will continue to insist on effective control via Party organization, even at the inevitable cost of inefficiency and backwardness. The liberalizers will seek new modes of organization.

The struggle will center to some degree on the role and character of the mass media. Liberalizers will seek to make better use of the mass media. The issue may be joined in many other forms also. It may be joined on the matter of style of language. Along with their other consequences, revolutions always produce vast changes in language. The Russian Revolution was no exception (Rzhevskii, 1951; Fesenko & Fesenko, 1955; Vakar, 1956a; 1956b; Pool, 1970b).[3] Totalitarianism, in turn, results in extreme rigidity of usage (Kris & Speier, 1944; Lasswell, 1949; George, 1959; G. Hollander, 1967; Pool, 1970a). The effort to free up styles of expression has considerable political significance. So, too, does the effort to have the press report airplane accidents, crimes, natural catastrophes, and other human-interest matters that the Soviet press does not now normally cover, but in which the public is interested.

The rise of audience and opinion research in the Soviet Union and Eastern Europe since Stalin's death is one strong influence toward humanizing and popularizing the media. The first polls in Russia were organized by the paper *Komsomolskya Pravda* (Rogers, 1967; for Eastern Europe, cf.

[3] Cf. Serruys (1962) on China, and Radio Free Europe (1969a) on Eastern Europe.

Sicinski, 1963a; 1963b; 1966; 1967; Duma, 1965; Kiss, 1967; Shippee, 1969; Pool, 1970b; Radio Free Europe, 1970a; 1970b). Ambitious editors wanted to know what their public wanted; once that became known, however, it was harder to refuse it to the public. That embarrassing consequence makes opinion research vulnerable in totalitarian countries. The main Polish and Czech survey organizations have both been penalized and shaken up for the independence of their results (Sicinski, 1967; Pool, 1970b).

If the official media do not respond to audience interests, one possible outcome is the emergence of an underground press. One of the most significant Soviet developments of the last few years is the emergence of *samizdat*—typewritten copies of stories, essays, and poems that cannot be published legally. Devoted partisans of *samizdat* type as many carbon copies as a typewriter will make, destroy the original because it could pinpoint the typewriter, and pass the copies to friends. A copy is kept only overnight and then passed on. Thousands of copies circulate this way among the intellectuals; the average Russian never sees any, however, for that would take hundreds of thousands of copies. Nonetheless, it is a mystery why the police have not chosen to, or not succeeded in, seriously hampering this new form of protest (Siniavskii, 1966; Reve, 1969; Pospielovsky, 1970; Reddaway, 1970; 1972; Katz, 1972).

If the official mass media are to become lively and appealing, they must increasingly escape Party control and in so doing they will also tend to undermine Party control. To the extent that the mass media are, on the contrary, held to the limited role of loudspeakers for Party policies and resolutions, their potential for effectively mobilizing society is partially sacrificed. The debaters may not be fully aware of it, but the debate over the mass media is also a debate over the Party.

It is in the light of these issues about domestic Soviet media that the importance of international media must be evaluated. Foreign radio and other foreign media have a profound influence on the course of Soviet development over and above their influence as direct sources of ideas. As competitors for the audience, they force the Soviet media to become more candid, more lively, more varied. (In that respect, incidentally, foreign media succeed precisely as they lose their audience; their objective is to produce change, not to win ratings.) To the extent that the domestic media change in order to compete, the role of the Party is also changed and diminished. To the extent that the media become vital, the Party loses its monopoly on the management of life and on many of its most valued functions.

Such general trends in the direction of Soviet society may be temporarily reversed in moments of crisis. During the Czech invasion, jamming of foreign broadcasts was suddenly resumed after five years virtually without it. That fact demonstrated how much importance the Kremlin attached to public reactions, for the jamming transmitters had to be diverted from their dual functions as part of the defense communication system. By such behavior the Soviets show that they are concerned enough with internal political reactions to adapt crisis plans to take these reactions into consideration.

A critical question is how far the Soviet leadership have it in their power quickly or selectively to close down the access of the Soviet population to particular facts in a world crisis. Their ability or inability to do so appears to be a serious factor in their crisis tactics. In recent crises the availability of information to the Soviet population has compelled the Soviet leadership to adapt their behavior in significant ways for the purpose of reassuring their public.

Before 1960 it was, as we have noted, standard practice for the Soviet media in any crisis situation to try to suppress knowledge of the difficulties by silence for at least two or three days until an adequate explanation could be presented by *Pravda*. Today the Soviet media follow that practice rarely and only with great difficulty. But they did respond that way to the Czech invasion. The Soviet media failed to inform the public of the Czech reaction and simply dropped the issue of the supposed Czech invitation to the Soviet troops when no Quisling came forth. By all reports, silence failed to keep knowledge from the Soviet public. More recently, in the case of the Chinese border incidents, the USSR has clearly alternated between vitriolic condemnation of the Chinese and restraint designed to avoid alarming a concerned public and to limit such behavior as hoarding. The regime has not been able to keep world news reports of these events quiet. What remains unrevealed to the attentive citizen today is substantially the same for the Soviet and the world audience.

We intend no implication that the *major* decisions of Soviet military policy are conditioned by anxiety about public opinion. The Kremlin is willing and able to take actions that entail great political costs. But recognition that the decisive facts in Soviet crisis behavior are not in the realm of public-information policy is not to assert that such considerations are of no importance. Soviet crisis behavior has shown a distinct attempt to ride both horses—seeking to control and moderate domestic public reactions as if the regime genuinely feared what public reactions might do, while at the same time initiating whatever military measures they felt impelled to undertake. The awareness of this dual character of Soviet crisis behavior suggests that it is important to recognize that there are things that can be done to reach the Soviet public with messages that will not be dismissed lightly by the regime, and that will place a significant burden on patterns of aggressive action.

To assess the reach of world news to the Soviet public we examine the output of a computer simulation of information flow in the Soviet Union during crisis.

Herbert Selesnick (1970) applied the simulation model to the flow of messages in the Soviet Union during the Cuban missile crisis, October 23–26, 1962. A content analysis provided information about media coverage of seven themes. The simulation applied audience figures to the scenario of appearance of the themes to arrive at estimates of reach and frequency. The seven themes were:

1. U.S. naval quarantine of Cuba
2. Reports of pro-Soviet or anti-U.S. reactions
3. Reports of pro-U.S. or anti-Soviet reactions
4. Soviet allegations of U.S. hostility toward Cuba
5. Soviet agreement to remove their missiles from Cuba
6. U.S. threats directed against the Soviets
7. Soviet threats directed against the U.S.

Of these seven themes, the most interesting in some ways are themes 2 and 3, reports of pro-Soviet and pro-American reactions.

The main bald facts—for example, the U.S. naval quarantine—were so important that every news medium covered them and most people learned about them almost immediately. However, the more subtle matters of pro-Soviet or pro-American interpretations of the events lent themselves to more selective handling by the news media.

Nonetheless, by the third day of the crisis, the bulk of the Soviet population of all ages and educational levels apparently had an awareness not only of pro-Soviet views expressed around the world but also of the pro-American ones. This is demonstrated in Figure 1, which shows the simulation estimates of the spread of exposure to themes 2 and 3.

Selesnick estimates that the young and the educated were reached most. By the second day of the crisis, virtually all people with ten years or more of education had been reached by pro-American messages as well as by pro-Soviet ones. Indeed, young, educated people typically had apparently seen or heard over ten items dealing with pro-American views. On the other

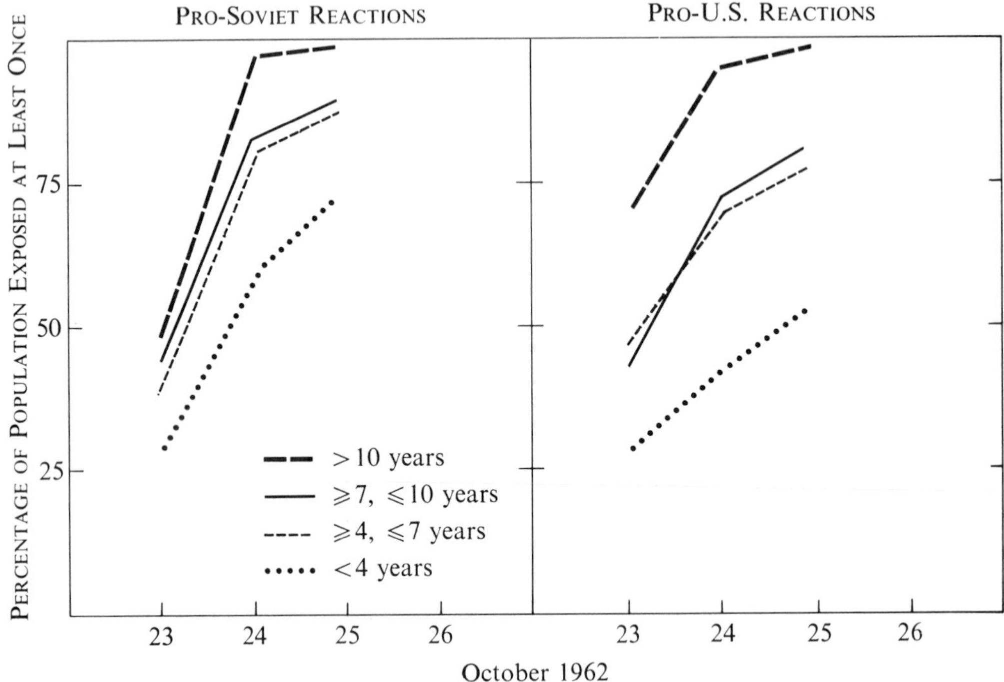

Figure 1. Simulation estimates of reach and frequency of media exposure to pro-Soviet and pro-U.S. reactions during Cuban missile crisis, by education.

hand, even by the third day, old uneducated persons typically had heard only one such message and less than half had heard such a message at all.

Foreign radio is the key to the estimates obtained (see Figure 2). Domestic radio was the prime source of spot news from which the Russians could learn about the crisis at all. Newspapers were initially less important in this particular crisis because the timing was such that the papers missed the first day. Thus domestic radio was the main initial news source. But without foreign radio, only about one-fourth of the population would have received the information of pro-American responses on the first day. That assumes, of course, that without the competition of foreign radio the Soviet media would have carried as much news about pro-American reactions as they did. Even on that unrealistic assumption, the crucial role of foreign radio for non-Party-line news seems clear.

It should be noted also that the biggest difference between social groups in media use is in the use of foreign radio. Over half the young are estimated to have heard the story of the quarantine over foreign radio as against only about one-fifth of the old. Domestic radio reaches all social groups and reaches them fast. Newspapers reach the most literate, so their audience is somewhat selective. TV reaches the middle-aged more than the young because in crowded Soviet housing the young are out of the house more. But foreign radio is decidedly of more importance for the well educated, who are an increasing proportion of the young. Selesnick estimates the frequency of news of the quarantine received from foreign radio by persons with over ten years of education at eight times that re-

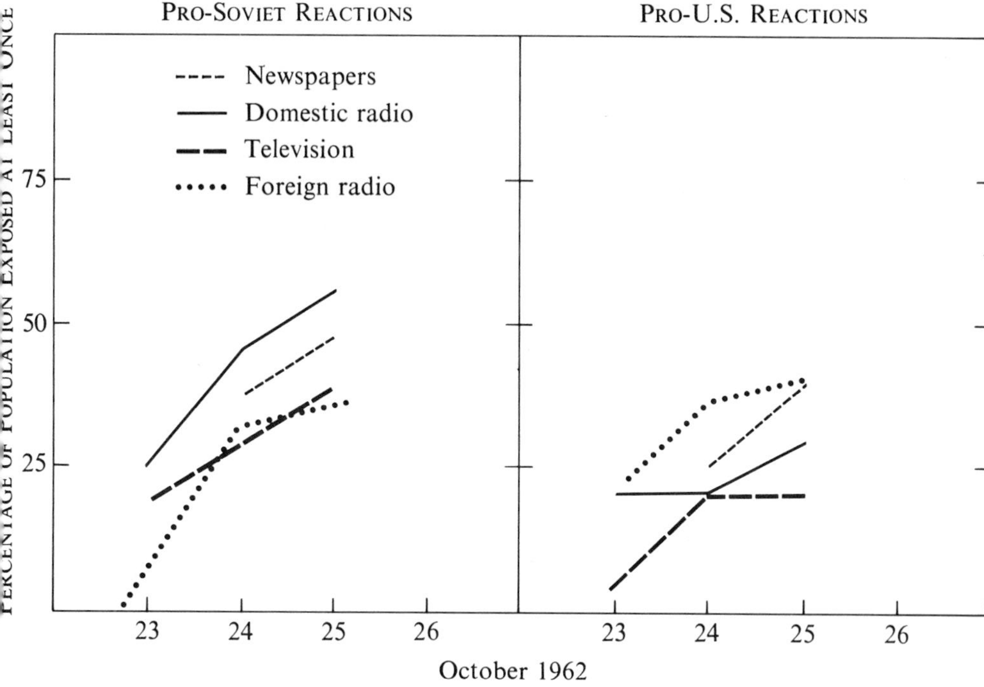

Figure 2. Simulation estimates of reach and frequency of media coverage of pro-Soviet and pro-U.S. reactions during Cuban missile crisis, by media type.

ceived by persons with less than four years of education. For newspapers, the ratio is about 7 to 1; for domestic radio, 1.5 to 1; and for television (where it is available), not distinguishable.

In short, the simulation suggests that the key factor behind the high knowledge of world views about the crisis among educated Russians was the voice of shortwave broadcasting. Simulations show different patterns in the spread of news, depending on the nature of the different crises, and, of course, the simulation output depends on the assumptions used; however, the role of foreign radio as a balancing force comes through clearly.

For important people in the Soviet Union, we can assume by now that major news from the West and the contents of the most important Western news sources are fully available. That has not always been so. What has happened in the past two decades in the Soviet Union can well be described as a communications revolution. As a result of that revolution, what is talked about in the West shapes what will happen in the Socialist world also.

COMMUNICATIONS REVOLUTION: CHINESE STYLE

Probably no regime in history has relied as heavily on mass mobilization to achieve its goals as did Mao's regime in China. The Cultural Revolution was almost an experimental test of how far agitation and propaganda could successfully transform human nature throughout a whole nation.

The Chinese borrowed most of their initial ideas about propaganda technique and mass mobilization from the Russians and then carried them to further extremes.

However, unlike the Russians, the Chinese have not been able to base their communication system on an industrialized economy. Newsprint shortages that characterized Russia in the 1930s no longer existed in the 1960s; in China, newsprint shortages exist and will for long into the future. In Russia in 1935 there was one radio for every seventy-five persons; today, there is one for every six. In China it was about one for every seventy persons in the late 1960s (Liu, 1964b). Therefore, the Chinese have had to invent labor-intensive means such as mass meetings and *tatzepao* (big-character posters) to do what a successfully modernizing country like Russia does by capital investment in modern means of communication.

The Chinese case also differs from that of other poor, preindustrial but non-Communist countries. While developing nations everywhere have been radically changed by the transistor radio and other means of communication, elsewhere that has happened inadvertently. Governments have generally underrated the power and significance of mass media and have relied on them but little. Not so China. China, without the resources for a modern communication system, has nonetheless spent millions on an ingenious, low-cost system designed to reach every citizen while seeking to avoid the disruptive antiregime effects that access to mass media has had in Russia and elsewhere. The Chinese, by reliance on wired loudspeakers, have opened channels to village squares and public places but, up to now, have given their population but little access to foreign broadcasts or a choice of what to hear. The transistor revolution in China is just beginning; it remains to be seen how rapidly it will transform the present unique communication system.

The Chinese Communist communications system has been described by several scholars, most notably Frederick T. C. Yu (1963; 1964), Alan Liu (1971), and Paul Hiniker (1966). In addition, there are several studies of the special phenomenon of brainwashing, i.e., confrontation of opponents in small-group "struggle sessions," in which the victim is brought under intense group pressure (Hunter, 1951; 1956; Bauer, 1957; Chen, 1960; Lifton, 1961; Schein et al., 1961; Bidermann, 1963; Tung & Evans, 1966). Also relevant is the extensive literature on Party organization (MacFarquhar, 1960; Union Research Service, 1963; Goldman, 1966; King, 1966; Yu, 1967; Baum & Teiwes, 1968; Sheridan, 1968; Broman, 1969; Vogel, 1969) and on the great campaigns such as the Cultural Revolution (Asia Research Center, 1967; Baum, 1967; Bridgham, 1967; Commerce Department, 1967; Hsiao, 1967; Grey & Cavendish, 1968; Union Research Institute, 1968; Liu, 1969; Yee Tin Tong Press, 1969; Wilson & Wilson, 1970; Yu, 1970), and a few studies attempting psychocultural analysis of Chinese behavior (Lewis, 1963; Hiniker, 1966; MacFarquhar, 1966; Shurman, 1966; Barnett, 1967; 1969; Neuhauser, 1967; Solomon, 1967; 1971; Townsend, 1967; Vogel, 1967; Pye, 1968; Liu, 1971).

If the Soviet Union is an example of a Communist country that has been opened up to world news by mass media and in particular by shortwave radio, China is a Communist country that has kept itself sealed off from the world, while nevertheless undergoing a mass communication revolution.

Depending upon one's mood and the facts one chooses, one can be struck either by the similarities between the Soviet and Chinese communications systems or by the differences.

If one wishes to stress the similarities, one would look not at the Soviet Union of today, with its highly industrialized society, but rather at the Soviet Union of the 1930s, when living standards had not yet passed those of the peasant society of 1917. One would then have found in Russia many of the prototypes of the present communications system of Communist China. During the 1920s and 1930s, when the present Chinese leadership learned their bolshevism, one would have found in Russia a regime committed to producing a "new Soviet man" by massive propaganda and indoctrination, but forced by an extreme shortage of resources to do so by extraordinary labor-intensive methods in place of modern mass media.

A stringent paper shortage limited newspaper and magazine circulation. To assure that each paper would reach many readers, the regime turned to such devices as wall newspapers, reading rooms in workshops and clubs, and reading newspapers aloud in meetings. Radios were scarce; wired loudspeakers were used in their place. A corps of millions of oral agitators was organized and trained. Almost everyone was made to attend frequent meetings, mostly at places of work, but also in residential neighborhoods. Censorship was strict; the leading Party organ set the line for the other publications. Party factions operated in the media; worker correspondents (*rabsel'kors*) were used to prevent the professionalization of the press. There was a central news agency, and print media were subscribed to at post offices and circulated mostly through the mails.

Every word of that description now applies to Communist China. Russia and China faced the same problem, that of trying to transform a primitive, peasant society rapidly into a modern industrial state by mobilization of the population for heroic effort (Liu, 1971). The Chinese copied solutions from their Soviet mentors.

If one wants to emphasize the differences between the Russian and Chinese communication systems, however, one would look not at the mechanisms adopted but at the intensity of the effort. By Soviet standards, the Chinese are guilty of the deviation of voluntarism, namely, the sin of disregarding objective economic determinants of the possible and attempting to proceed as if willpower could make it so. In this departure from Marxian materialism the Chinese are but carrying a Leninist deviation one step further. Lenin, too, tried to impose his vision on history, but with severe constraints of realism reinforced by his Marxist heritage. Maoism, on the other hand, represented an unmitigated faith in what can be achieved by people purging themselves of their old beliefs and affirming the doctrines of the little red book (Mao Tse-tung, 1966).

Seldom in human history, and never in as primitive a society as China's, has as much agitation reached so many people with as high an intensity as in the Maoist experiment at remolding man by mass persuasion. How far has Mao proven right in his faith in the plasticity of man? How far have his critics proven right in denying the power of will and propaganda to overcome the constraints of the real environment?

A topic of great interest to social scientists is the limit of what communication can do to change human behavior. This question appears in many guises. Historically, an early form—at least as early as the myth of the wolf children—was the issue of nature versus nurture: How far is man at birth frozen into a mold of what he will become, or how far does he take form according to the things he is taught and told? A normative form of the same question is, How should we teach? What can good pedagogy do to develop a student's knowledge or skills? These are some of the matters with which social scientists in the democratic West have concerned themselves as they addressed the central problem of the limits of mass persuasion.

In a different guise, this issue is central to Chinese Communist politics and ideology as well. Hidden behind the Party curtains a bitter debate apparently raged between bureaucratic elements on the one hand and the Maoist left wing on the other about precisely that issue (Lewis, 1963; Hiniker, 1966; MacFarquhar, 1966; Shurman, 1966; Barnett, 1967; 1969; Neuhauser, 1967; Townsend, 1967; Vogel, 1967; Liu, 1971). The bureaucrats, as Dr. Alan Liu tells us, had limited faith in mass persuasion. They believed that the political consciousness of the masses could not be precipitated by agitation. "These leaders believed that a long period of education was needed to cultivate a degree of intellectual sophistication in the people" (Liu, 1971:7). The bureaucratic wing was thus in essential agreement with the Russian Communists, whose past experience in propaganda and mass communication provided both wings with their model of how to organize and mobilize people.

Mao and such disciples as Lin Piao, on the other hand, believed that "sheer political agitation can bring forth a new world outlook in the constricted mind of the peasantry" (Liu, 1971: xi). Maoists seemed to believe that the mass media, coupled with grass-roots oral participation, could transform one-fourth of the human race. They acted on the assumption that incessant meetings, discussion groups, political aphorisms, and blaring loudspeakers can change man and society in fundamental ways.

Over the years since 1948, power in China has oscillated between the bureaucratic right and the Maoist left. 1948–1953 were years of revolution and of leftist attacks on what remained of the past society. 1953–1957, on the other hand, were years of consolidation and growth of a new Communist bureaucratic structure (Liu, 1971).

Mao's first major experiment in voluntarism was the Great Leap Forward in 1958, which sought to reverse China's course toward conventional bureaucratic methods of development. Backyard furnaces were to produce what factories produce elsewhere. For the peasants, communes were to replace millennia-old links of family and village. With the failure of the Leap, Mao's opponents forced, temporarily, acceptance of a policy of economic reconstruction and bureaucratic regularization. But Chairman Mao did not accept defeat for very long. By 1963 his counterattack had begun; in 1966 Mao launched the Cultural Revolution, a second attempt to transform China by exhortation and to replace the routines of the bureaucracy by enthusiasm. By 1970 the Cultural Revolution had receded and the army was largely in control. The Red Guards and the uncensored, one-sheet newspapers vanished. By 1972 the army, too, lost its monopoly of control, and the Party organization was being reconstituted in many provinces. The national communication system is once again dominated by central agencies such as Radio Peking, the *People's Daily*, and the New China News Agency. They have, however, not fully recovered from virtual dissolution during the Cultural Revolution. Nonetheless, it is becoming increasingly clear that the Chinese revolution is no exception to the general rule of revolutions, that ultimately the wave must recede.

How can we understand the Maoist hysteria of the Cultural Revolution? As with any complex social phenomenon, explanations are numerous. Mao's repeated attempts to storm against reality and to deny the limits of politics can be explained at many levels, and validly so.

In the 1950s it was popular to explain Maoism as if it were a startling new discovery in human psychology. One may recall the early literature on brainwashing. In particular, after a certain number of American POWs in the Korean war had accepted the Maoist line, there was widespread belief in the United States that the Chinese had discovered a technique capable of making otherwise rational people believe that two and two make five or whatever else their masters chose to proclaim. The evidence, besides the performance of a few American prisoners, was the massive practice of self-criticism and thought reform carried out in meetings and discussion groups that have been a major part of contemporary Chinese life, particularly during propaganda campaigns.

Several studies have documented what happens in these propaganda campaigns. A decision is made in Peking to organize a mass campaign around some topic such as the Korean war, communes, the exemplary soldier Lei Feng (known as the "rustfree screw"), the sins of the Kremlin, or the thoughts of Mao Tse-tung. Instructions go out to local Party authorities (or, after the virtual decomposition of the Party, to the army or other organization) secretly to prepare for the campaign. The local organizers in the school, office, factory, or committee decide in advance who will be the victims, who will be forced to confess sins, and whether each will be forgiven or punished and in what way. Thus the detailed scenario is secretly settled before the campaign even begins. At the start of the campaign the mass media proclaim the slogans to be featured, generally by describing how some group of workers or peasants somewhere "spontaneously" began raising these slogans and acting in accordance with them. Suddenly from all over the country, as if by magic, response and imitation begin.

The population has learned to recognize the signs of a new campaign and knows how to act. Meetings are called with abnormal frequency—at the height of a campaign sometimes daily—even though it interferes with normal work habits. People write *tatzepao* by the score and post them to provide evidence of their loyalty and conviction. At the meetings, certain individuals will be accused of backsliding and deviation. They know how to respond, realizing well the possible consequences of having been accused but not knowing what exculpation they are to be allowed. The unfortunate ones may be killed or sent to reform camps or to live in the countryside. The more fortunate ones may be allowed to continue their lives after abject self-abasement, parading with dunce caps and claiming to have seen the error of their ways.

The question is whether this brainwashing works. Some earlier observers believed that Mao had found in these struggle movements a way of basically transforming the population of China. More careful studies, however, have found little magic in the brainwashing technique and little reason to identify it as a resounding success. Biderman's (1963) studies of American prisoners of war show that few surrendered psychologically and that those who did came from very demoralizing backgrounds. Edgar Schein's thorough study of the so-called brainwashing process makes the same point (Schein et al., 1961).

A field experiment was conducted by Paul Hiniker (1964; 1965) in Hong Kong to test the hypothesis that Chinese culture makes it easy to conform to the demands of the group and that, correspondingly, public declarations of sentiments not really believed are less efficacious as a psychological device among Chinese than they would be among Westerners. Replicating a Festinger experiment on forced-compliance dissonance (Festinger, 1957), Hiniker established that Chinese subjects did, as expected, behave differently from American subjects. They did not feel the pressure to change their true beliefs after engaging in forced advocacy of other beliefs. The evidence all adds up to a rejection of the notion that Maoism has successfully brainwashed 700 million people.

Reality lies somewhere between two oversimple notions: the notion on the one hand that China is like Hungary or Czechoslovakia, countries with overwhelmingly anti-Communist populations, hostile to their own government and its ideology and only waiting for the moment when they can again say what they really think; and the notion on the other hand that the Chinese sincerely believe all the hysterical slogans of Maoist propaganda. The amount of attitude change and conversion that Maoism has achieved is truly impressive, comparable only to that achieved in other great revolutions or religious crusades. Hundreds of millions of people have abandoned traditional beliefs, religious practices, superstitions and customs.

Observers of the new China comment that, much like members of evangelistic religious sects, the people work harder, are more disciplined and clearly more loyal than before the acceptance of the new faith. Yet just as religion fails to transform most men to its ultimate standards, so too with the Maoist faith. What exists is what has existed under so many revolutionary totalitarian regimes in the past—apparent enthusiasm camouflaging widespread passive acceptance coupled with some covert disbelief and skepticism. There seems little reason to doubt the applicability of the generalization that totalitarian regimes are typically fragile. Maoism may gradually erode in spirit despite the continuing hegemony of the present regime, or it may collapse more dramatically. What seems excluded is triumph of the ideals of the Cultural Revolution as presented in its propaganda.

Hiniker's explanation of Maoism's propagandist extremism uses dissonance theory even though it rejects the applicability of forced-compliance dissonance. Festinger recognizes a number of types of dissonance. Among these is the dissonance created by disproof of a prediction. Festinger, Riecken, and Schachter (1956) reviewed the history of various movements that predicted earth-shaking events such as the coming of the Messiah or the end of the world. They found that characteristically these movements did not start actively the world. They found that characteristically these movements did not start actively proselytizing until their prophecy had been disproven to ordinary men by the course of events. Instead of their being finished off when their prophecy failed, that seemed to be the moment of their takeoff.

This form of dissonance reduction should explain the history of many movements that have snatched justification out of the jaws of failure. It fits the history of Maoism as outlined by Hiniker with substantial precision. In particular, the catastrophic failure of the Great Leap Forward required the launching of the Cultural Revolution if Mao was to continue to be seen as a prophet and not discarded as a failure.

The Great Leap announced in 1958 was intended to replace the family, the village, all of the traditional Chinese institutions, with communes and, simultaneously, to advance the industrialization of the country overnight by such devices as backyard steel furnaces. The net effect of the Great Leap was a catastrophic decline in production, conditions of chaos and famine. Virtually all of the curves of Chinese economic growth that had been moving upward well and steadily since 1948 (due more to the restoration of peace and order on the Chinese mainland than to any other magic) suddenly plunged downward. Aside from fantastic and absurd propaganda claims about overnight expansion (for example, in number of radios or production of steel), statistics disappeared, for the story they would have told was too catastrophic.

By 1960 Mao was virtually overruled; at the Lushan plenum in August of 1959 the moderates in the Party tried to scrap the Great Leap and almost succeeded in removing Mao from power. That was the defeat that Mao strove to overcome in the Cultural Revolution. That was the movement that he later called the road to capitalism and that he attempted to reverse by a new leap as great as the old one. It was designed to prove, if it succeeded, that the radical transformation of society by mobilization that Mao had proclaimed in 1958 was not a fatal error, but a feasible goal.

Another explanation of Maoist fanaticism can be given in terms of Chinese national character and culture. Lucian Pye (1968) and Richard Solomon (1971) have examined the structure of the Chinese family and personality and have noted both the wish-fear of disorder and the prevalence of hatred in the culture, as well as the rebellion of sons against fathers that goes with the traditional notions of filial piety. Maoist storming is the institutionalization of hatred and rebellion. It would be hard to think of any political movement that has so glorified hatred and demanded the expression of it to such a degree as has Maoism. Clearly Maoist activism and Confucian restraint are opposite extremes on a value continuum.

It should not surprise us to find both extremes of the continuum expressed in the same culture. That is usually the case when the psychological mechanism of reaction formation is operative. A reaction formation is extreme behavior in one direction by which a person proves to himself, and to the world, that he is not guilty of reverse impulses that, at a deeper level, are the ones really driving him. Thus, a militant pacifist violently obstructing access to the Pentagon may be trying to deny by his pacifism violent impulses which his behavior reveals. Such frightening impulses, to which the demonstrator fears he might yield, are denied by his proclamation of nonviolence.

Most psychocultural patterns are of that character. A culture is preoccupied with some problems that its social and family structure emphasizes but makes it difficult to resolve. Under such circumstances one may expect to find extreme behavior both denying and expressing that pattern. Pye's and Solomon's work notes such extremes in Chinese culture. Solomon analyzes the Chinese family structure in which overt hostility is tabooed in the deep fear of the chaos that might follow any impairment of ordered, regular relations. But that Confucian order is only the reaction formation against the expression of hatred that is the other side of the cultural coin. Alan Liu (1971) also notes that, in contrast to the elite Confucian tradition, Chinese popular culture (which Mao extolled) has always emphasized conflict.

A fourth explanation of Mao's methods is presented by Alan Liu (1971) in his *Communications and National Integration in Communist China*. Dr. Liu's approach maintains that one need not look entirely into psychopathology; there are also rational reasons, given the realities of China's situation, for proceeding by the communications devices that Mao used to achieve the goals that he had. Dr. Liu finds in both Mao's personality and ideology parts of the explanation, but he also sees in the Maoist reliance on propaganda a partly successful attempt to cope with a real problem under circumstances where other resources were lacking.

The real problem was the national integration of a backward country. The circumstance was the almost total lack of the prerequisite conditions for the creation of a nation: the lack of a common language, the lack of roads and railroads to tie the land surface together, the lack of literate people capable of communicating over distance, the lack of an effectively organized bureaucracy to govern the nation, the lack of radios, newspapers, telephones and telegraph to provide normal modern communication.

To an extent that is truly extraordinary, Chinese efforts surmounted these obstacles by creating a novel and innovative mass-communication system at fantastically low capital costs, although at very high labor costs. During mass campaigns, discussion meetings attended weekly or more often by hundreds of millions of people substituted for scarce newspapers, magazines, and books. A highly economical wired loudspeaker system that reaches most Chinese villages substitutes for radios that even in battery-transistor form would be more expensive (Liu, 1964a; 1964b). Movies are shown in fantastic numbers by mobile projection teams who may move the equipment by bicycle (Liu, 1965; 1966a). Newspapers are rented by the hour at the post office to people too poor to buy them (Liu, 1966b). Confidential information bulletins that tell the cadres what is going on in the world are brought by delivery boy and picked up again after being read. During campaigns the walls are covered by *tatzepao*—posters with short, handwritten large-character slogans—which everyone is asked to write (King, 1966; Broman, 1969; Liu, 1969; Yu, 1970).

Table 3 presents some of the basic estimates of the distribution of the main mass media. These estimates are subject to wide margins of error, but they are the best statistics available. They are based mostly upon published Chinese data in addition to some one hundred interviews with recent refugees organized by Dr. Hiniker in Hong Kong. These estimates indicate both the

TABLE 3

MEDIA IN CHINA

Year	Movies		Radio			Newspapers		
	Theaters	Mobile Projector Teams	Private Wireless Sets (millions)	Loud-speakers	Wired Stations	Number	Total Circula-tion (millions)	Circulation *People's Daily* (thousands)
1949	596	100		500	8	382*	3.0*	
1954	815	2,723		47,500	577	392†	12.0†	710
1958	1,030	6,692		2,987,500	6,772	1,884	30.0	
1959	1,386	8,384	3	4,570,000	11,124	1,455	20.9	
1964	2,000	12,000	5	6,000,000	1,975			1,600

SOURCE: Data from Liu (1966a; 1966b; 1971).

NOTE: In 1959, the literacy rate in China was 37 percent; 8.5 million Chinese were members of drama groups, and 59 percent of the adult population attended political study groups (Hiniker, 1966).

* Year 1950

† Year 1956

very rapid growth of mass media and also the extreme thinness of the coverage by the more conventional capital-intensive communication facilities.

The extraordinary fact is how much has been achieved with those meager physical facilities. We do not necessarily need to believe all the Chinese claims: for example that in the "heart surrender" campaign among workers in commerce and industry 145,000 persons produced 33,000,000 *tatzepoa*, or that motion picture attendance jumped in the year 1958 from 1.3 billion to 3 billion (King, 1966; Liu, 1966a). The reality may not be quite that spectacular; but at its height, a major campaign occupies a substantial portion of the lives of hundreds of millions of people. Nonetheless, there is no evidence that the new Chinese man has abandoned all the old values of Chinese culture and become totally Maoist. There is every evidence in the events of 1972, when China entered the UN, welcomed President Nixon, reopened universities, and restored the Party, that the bureaucratic, conservative elements of China will come out on top, leaving such movements as the Cultural Revolution as an interesting footnote on history.

If the object is nationalist modernization, the evaluation of the degree of success of the communications revolution in China is more ambiguous. In at least one respect relevant to modernization, the effort has been an outstanding success. Today in China there is a communications system reaching into almost every commune and work team, conveying the orders of the day, the slogans, and the demands of the central government to the population. It is a truly extraordinary communications system, capable not only of a high volume of communication but also of a high measure of security.

The communication revolution relies most heavily upon wired loudspeakers. It is claimed that wires reach 95 percent of all counties, and that six million loudspeakers are in operation (Liu, 1964b). This is an efficient, cheap system not easily monitored from abroad. In each county or similar area (among them virtually covering the country) there exists a center with a radio that can pick up the Peking broadcasts and also produce local programming. The broadcasts go via ordinary telephone wire to loudspeakers in public squares, homes, offices, and any other places where people may congregate. Between these loudspeakers and numerous meetings it is possible for the government to get any information widely known and in the briefest compass of time.

The wires for the loudspeakers can also be and are used for point-to-point official communication. The Chinese government was fully aware that it was buying not only a cheaper system than one using transistor radio sets, but also one that in case of invasion or civil war could be the basis of secure military mobilization. We have no data on the use of this system during the fighting on the Sino-Soviet border. It is significant, however, that coincident with the flare-up of this conflict was a renewed drive to expand the radio-diffusion system in the relatively underdeveloped frontier areas. Chinese statements from earlier crises (such as the Quemoy-Matsu confrontation) indicate that their contingency plans for an American invasion, which they unrealistically regarded as fairly probable, relied heavily on use of this network, and on peasant mobilization through it, to resist the invasion.

What the Chinese have established by dint of enormous effort and ingenuity is a mass communication system that does indeed reach every remote corner of the land and that can spread the propaganda line with fearful effectiveness (although not necessarily persuasion). It successfully excludes any significant flow of messages from the outside world. When at the height of the Cultural Revolution the system broke down under conditions of virtual civil war, a kind of freedom of the press returned, with every small group putting up its wall bulletins or publishing its two-page newspaper. That breakdown did not expose the

Chinese to real news of the outside world as the rest of the world sees it, however, since those uncontrolled bulletins and newspapers contained virtually nothing except information about the local disputes and supposed deviations of various "bad" people (Commerce Department, 1967). They had no access to press services, wire services, or even effective radio broadcasts from abroad beamed and oriented to the needs of the internal Chinese audience.

There are not yet enough radios in China capable of receiving shortwave to make direct transmission to the public the powerful influence that it is in Russia. However, there are enough sets to provide the starting point for retransmission whenever central power breaks down and China becomes the scene of warring communications between different conflicting elements, as happened during the Cultural Revolution and may again during any major crisis.

Nonetheless, very little foreign influence has been felt in recent crises. This is not because key people in the Chinese government and army do not follow foreign broadcasts. We have substantial evidence that they do, both directly and via monitoring reports. The limited influence of foreign communications is due largely to the dearth of communication transmitted from outside addressed specifically to China, with the real interests and problems of contemporary China in the broadcaster's central focus. China is isolated today, but only partly because of the design of her communications system. That has two chinks in its armor: shortwave radio and the breakdown of central controls in crises. More important, however, is the fact that there is but little in the world news media that seems directly relevant to China, and no one on the outside is transmitting substantial material designed to be more relevant.

In most respects, beyond doubt, both the Great Leap and the Cultural Revolution were failures. There is little doubt that the future, after Mao, lies with the bureaucratic wing whose propaganda strategy was far more conventional—professionalized newspapers, a press service (the New China News Agency), a ministry of culture, a propaganda department of the Central Committee with various sections, and a national radio structure based largely on rebroadcasts from Radio Peking. Yet, however transitory may be Mao's efforts to replace these structures with ad hoc mass campaigns, and however much the results of these campaigns must be deemed failures, the fact remains that they did reach virtually the whole Chinese population—not once, but repeatedly.

To the extent that mass persuasion can work, it had the opportunity to do so. Despite the poverty of China, the nation was successfully organized to listen. To Mao's disappointment, the power of repeated chantings of his thoughts proved inadequate. But it would be equally foolish to think that such techniques had no effect. They have served, to some degree at least, to create national consciousness. The new Communist values in China are not merely imposed upon unwilling subjects; but neither has every Chinese become a true believer. As with every new creed, the outcome is both the sincere acceptance of the new belief by converted millions and at the same time the failure of the faith to permanently transform human behavior to conform to its canons. So will it be with Maoism in China. We cannot as yet draw the final balance sheet. History does not yet permit us fixed conclusions. But certainly whatever the power of mass persuasion, it has been tested to its limits.

REFERENCES

Ahlberg, Rene.
1968 Entwicklungs Probleme der Empirischen Socialforschung in der UdSSR (1917–1966). Wiesbaden: Verlag Otto Harrassowitz.

Allport, Gordon W., and Leo J. Postman.
1947 The Psychology of Rumor. New York: Holt.

Aron, Raymond.
1969 Democracy and Totalitarianism. New York: Praeger.
Artemov, V. A., et al.
1967 Statistika byudzhetov vremeni trudyashchikhsya (Statistics of the Toilers' Time Budgets). Moscow: Statistica.
Barghoorn, Frederick C.
1950 The Soviet Image of the United States. New York: Harcourt, Brace.
1960 The Soviet Cultural Offensive. Princeton, New Jersey: Princeton University Press.
1964 Soviet Foreign Propaganda. Princeton, New Jersey: Princeton University Press.
Barnett, A. Doak.
1967 Cadres, Bureaucracy, and Political Power in Communist China. New York: Columbia University Press.
Barnett, A. Doak (ed.).
1969 Chinese Communist Politics in Action. Seattle: University of Washington Press.
Bauer, Raymond A.
1952 The New Man in Soviet Psychology. Cambridge, Massachusetts: Harvard University Press.
1957 "Brainwashing." Journal of Social Issues 13(No. 3):41–47.
Bauer, Raymond A., and David B. Gleicher.
1953 "Word-of-mouth communication in the Soviet Union." Public Opinion Quarterly 17:297–310.
Baum, Richard D.
1967 "The new revolution: Ideology redivivus." Problems of Communism 16(May):1–11.
Baum, Richard D., and Frederick C. Teiwes.
1968 Ssu-Ch'ing: The Socialist Education Movement of 1962–1966. China Research Monograph. Berkeley: Center for Chinese Studies, University of California.
Beliaev, E. V., et al.
1962 "Workers time-budget research: A method of concrete sociological investigation." Soviet Sociology 1:44–57.
Bell, Daniel.
1960 "Ten theories in search of reality: The prediction of Soviet behavior in the social sciences," in Alexander Dallin (ed.), Soviet Conduct in World Affairs. New York: Columbia University Press.
Berger, Peter.
1969 Marxism and Sociology: Views from Eastern Europe. New York: Appleton-Century-Crofts.
Biderman, Albert.
1963 March to Calumny: The Story of American POW's in the Korean War. New York: Macmillan.
Blake, Patricia, and Max Hayward.
1962 Dissonant Voices in Soviet Literature. New York: Pantheon Books.
Blücher, Graf Viggo.
1959 "Content analysis of the press of the East German Republic." Gazette 5:89–107.
Boglovskiy, T., and Z. L'vov.
1963 Posledniye Izvestiya Po Radio (The Latest News on Radio). Moscow: Scientific-Methodological Department of the State Committee on Radio and Television.
Bramsted, Ernest Kohn.
1965 Goebbels and National Socialist Propaganda: 1925–1945. East Lansing: Michigan State University Press.
Bridgham, Philip.
1967 "Mao's cultural revolution: Origin and development." China Quarterly 29:1–35.
Broman, Barry M.
1969 "Tatzepao: Medium of conflict in China's cultural revolution." Journalism Quarterly 46:100–104, 127.
Bronfenbrenner, Urie.
1970 Two Worlds of Childhood: U.S. and U.S.S.R. New York: Russell Sage.
Brzezinski, Zbigniew.
1956 The Permanent Purge: Politics in Soviet Totalitarianism. Cambridge, Massachusetts: Harvard University Press.
Buckner, H. T.
1965 "A theory of rumor transmission." Public Opinion Quarterly 24:54–70.
Bukhalov, Yu. F., and E. A. Yakuba (eds.).
1968 Rol' Obshchestvennosti v upravlenii proizvodstvom (The Role of the Citizenry in Economic Management). Kharkov: Kharkov University Press.
Center for Study of Media, University of Novosibirsk.
1970 "Literaturnaya gazeta i yeye chitatel" ("Literary Gazette and its reader").

Problemy sotsiologii pechati 2:92–136.

Chen, Theodore H. E.
1960 Thought Reform of the Chinese Intellectuals. Hong Kong: University Press.

Clews, John C.
1964 Communist Propaganda Techniques. New York: Praeger.

Commerce Department.
1967 Information from Red Guard Press. Washington, D.C.: U.S. Department of Commerce, Joint Publication Research Service No. 41898.

Conquest, Robert.
1968 The Great Terror. New York: Macmillan.

Dasbach, Anita Mallinckrodt.
1966 "U.S.-Soviet magazine propaganda: America Illustrated and USSR." Journalism Quarterly 43:73–84.

Duma, Andrzej.
1965 "Research on TV viewers in Poland." Gazette 11:261–273.

Dunn, Stephen P. (ed.).
1969 Sociology in the USSR: A Collection of Readings from Soviet Sources. White Plains, New York: International Arts and Sciences Press.

Durham (Hollander), Gayle F.
1965a Radio and Television in the Soviet Union. Center for International Studies Monograph C/64-10. Cambridge: Massachusetts Institute of Technology.
1965b Amateur Radio Operation in the Soviet Union. Center for International Studies Monograph C/64-10A. Cambridge: Massachusetts Institute of Technology.
1965c News Broadcasting on Soviet Radio and Television. Center for International Studies Monograph C/64-10B. Cambridge: Massachusetts Institute of Technology.
1966 The Use of Free Time by Young People in Soviet Society. Center for International Studies Monograph C/66-3. Cambridge: Massachusetts Institute of Technology.

Eisenstadt, S. N.
1963 The Political Systems of Empires. New York: Free Press of Glencoe.

Engels, Friedrich.
n.d. Herr Eugen Duhring's Revolution in Science. New York: International Publishers.

Fesenko, A., and T. Fesenko.
1955 Russki iazyk pri Sovetakh (The Russian Language Under the Soviets). New York: Rausen Publishers.

Festinger, Leon A.
1957 A Theory of Cognitive Dissonance. Evanston, Illinois: Row, Peterson.

Festinger, Leon A.; Henry W. Riecken, Jr.; and Stanley S. Schachter.
1956 When Prophecy Fails. Minneapolis: University of Minnesota Press.

Festinger, Leon A.; Stanley S. Schachter; and Kurt W. Back.
1950 Social Pressures in Informal Groups: A Study of Human Factors in Housing. New York: Harper.

Firsov, Boris.
1967 "'Srednevo sritelya' nyet" ("There is no 'average viewer'"). Zhurnalist 12: 42–45.
1968 "Leningrad's TV Audience." The Soviet Press 6(No. 3).
1971 Televideniye glazami sotsiologa (Television as Seen by a Sociologist). Moscow: Iskusstvo.

Fischer, George.
1964 Science and Politics: The New Sociology in the Soviet Union. Ithaca, New York: Cornell University Press.
1967 Science and Ideology in Soviet Society. New York: Atherton Press.

Friedberg, Maurice.
1968 "What price censorship?" Problems of Communism 17 (September): 18–23.

Friedrich, Carl J. (ed.).
1964 Totalitarianism. New York: Grosset and Dunlop.

Friedrich, Carl J., and Zbigniew K. Brzezinski.
1956 Totalitarian Dictatorship and Autocracy. Cambridge, Massachusetts: Harvard University Press.

Gazette.
1962 "Czechoslovak television." Gazette 8:318–321.

George, Alex.
1959 Propaganda Analysis. Evanston, Illinois: Row, Peterson.

Gerasimov, N.
1967 "Shtoty skazhesh, chitatel?" ("What do you say, reader?") Pravda, June 15.

Goldman, Merle.
1966 "The fall of Chou Yang." China Quarterly 27:132–148.

Goncharenko, M. P., et al.
1963 Metodika i Nekotoryye Rezultaty Konkretnogo Sotsialnogo Issledovaniya. Byudzhet Vremeni Trudyashchikhsya. Nauchniye Doklady Vysshei Shkoly, Filosofskiye Nauki, No. 1.

Gorer, Geoffrey.
1962 The People of Great Russia. New York: Norton.

Gosnell, Harold F.
1937 Machine Politics: Chicago Model. Chicago: University of Chicago Press.

Grey, Jack, and Patrick Cavendish.
1968 Chinese Communism in Crisis. New York: Praeger.

Grushin, B. A.
1967 Suobodnoye Vremya—Actualniye Problemy. Moscow: Mysl'.

Grushin, B. A., et al.
1969 "47 pyatnits" ("47 Fridays"). Informatsionnyi byulletin, Sovetskoi Sotsiologicheskoi Assotsiatsii, No. 25.

Guevara, Ernesto.
1968 Che Guevara Speaks. New York: Grove Press.
1969a "Che" Guevara on Revolution: A Documentary Overview. Coral Gables, Florida: University of Miami Press.
1969b Selected Works of Ernesto Guevara. Cambridge, Massachusetts: M.I.T. Press.

Harper, Samuel N.
1929 Civic Training in Soviet Russia. Chicago: University of Chicago Press.

Hayward, Max, and Leopold Labedz.
1963 Literature and Revolution in Soviet Russia, 1917–1962. London: Oxford University Press.

Hayward, Max, and E. L. Crowley (ed.).
1964 Soviet Literature in the Sixties. New York: Praeger.

Higher Party School and Academy of Social Science of CPSU.
1963 The Moral Code of the Builders of Communism. Moscow: Publishing House of the Higher Party School and Academy of Social Science, CPSU.

Hiniker, Paul J.
1964 "Chinese reactions to forced compliance: Dissonance reduction or national character?" Journal of Social Psychology 77:157–176.
1965 Chinese Attitudinal Reactions to Forced Compliance. Center for International Studies Monograph C/65-18. Cambridge: Massachusetts Institute of Technology.
1966 "The effects of mass communications in communist China." Ph.D. Dissertation, Massachusetts Institute of Technology (unpublished).

Hitler, Adolph.
1939 Mein Kampf. New York: Reynal and Hitchcock. First published 1925.

Hollander, Gayle F. Durham.
1967 Soviet Newspapers and Magazines. Center for International Studies Monograph C/67-5. Cambridge: Massachusetts Institute of Technology.
1968 "Communication and social modernization in Soviet society." Ph.D. Dissertation, Massachusetts Institute of Technology (unpublished).
1972 Soviet Political Indoctrination. New York: Praeger.

Hollander, Paul.
1965 "The dilemma of Soviet sociology." Problems of Communism 14 (November): 34–46.
1966 "Models of behavior in Stalinist literature. American Sociological Review 31:352–364.

Hollander, Paul (ed.).
1969 American and Soviet Society. Englewood Cliffs, New Jersey: Prentice-Hall.

Hopkins, Mark W.
1970 "The meaning of censorship and libel in the Soviet Union." Journalism Quarterly 47:118–125.

Hsiao, Gene T.
1967 "The background and development of the proletarian cultural revolution." Asian Survey 7:389–404.

Hungarian Radio and Television Mass Communication Research Center.
1970 Radio and Television Review. A special issue prepared for the Seventh World Congress of Sociology, Varna, Bulgaria, September 14–19. Buda-

pest: Hungarian Radio and Television Mass Communications Research Center.

Hunter, Edward.
1951 Brainwashing in Red China. New York: Vanguard.
1956 Brainwashing. New York: Farrar, Straus and Cudahey.

Ikonnikova, S. N., and V. T. Lisovsky.
1969 Molodezh o sebe, o voikh severstnikakh (Young People About Themselves and Their Age Group). Leningrad: Lenizdat.

Inkeles, Alex.
1958 Public Opinion in Soviet Russia: A Study in Mass Persuasion. Cambridge, Massachusetts: Harvard University Press.
1966 "Models and issues in the analysis of Soviet Society." Survey 60(July):3–17.

Inkeles, Alex, and Raymond A. Bauer.
1959 The Soviet Citizen: Daily Life in a Totalitarian Society. Cambridge, Massachusetts: Harvard University Press.

Johnson, Priscilla.
1965 Krushchev and the Arts: The Politics of Soviet Culture, 1962–1964. Cambridge, Massachusetts: M.I.T. Press.

Jones, Nancy C.
1966 "U.S. news in the Soviet press." Journalism Quarterly 43:687–696.

Karemyaye, Ruth.
1967 "Kak tyazholiye pushki v boiu" ("Like heavy guns into battle"). Sovietskoye Radio I Televideniye 7: 30–33.

Kassof, Allen.
1965 The Soviet Youth Program: Regimentation and Rebellion. Cambridge, Massachusetts: Harvard University Press.

Katz, Zev.
1971 "Sociology in the Soviet Union." Problems of Communism 20(May): 22–40.
1972 Soviet Dissenters and Social Structure in the USSR. Cambridge: Center for International Studies, Massachusetts Institute of Technology.

Kecskemeti, Paul.
1950 "Totalitarian communication as a means of control." Public Opinion Quarterly 14:224–234.
1961 The Unexpected Revolution: Social Forces in the Hungarian Uprising. Stanford, California: Stanford University Press.

Keesing, Felix, and Marie Keesing.
1956 Elite Communication in Samoa. Stanford, California: Stanford University Press.

Kempers, F.
1968 "Communist information policy in practice: Reporting of events in Czechoslovakia and Poland by the party press of friendly nations." Gazette 14:271–292.

Khmara, G. I.
1971 Mesto televidenia v sisteme massovykh kommunikatsii (Television's Place in the Mass Media System). Moscow.

King, Vincent U. S.
1966 Propaganda Campaigns in Communist China. Center for International Studies Monograph C/66-1. Cambridge: Massachusetts Institute of Technology.

Kiss, Gabor.
1967 "History of the development of sociology in Hungary from 1945." American Sociologist 2(August): 141–144.

Koestler, Arthur.
1941 Darkness at Noon. New York: Macmillan.

Kogan, L.
1969 "My i sovremennoye TV" ("Contemporary TV and Us"). Sovetskoye radio i televideniye 1:22–25.

Kogan, V. Z., and V. S. Tapilina.
1970 "K voprosu ob obespechenii nadezhnosti pervichnoi sotsiologicheskoi informatsi" ("On the issue of ensuring the reliability of primary sociological information"). Problemy sotsiologii pechati 2:137–146.

Kris, Ernst, and Hans Speier.
1944 German Radio Propaganda. London: Oxford University Press.

Kruglak, Theodore E.
1962 The Two Faces of Tass. Minneapolis: University of Minnesota Press.

Lasswell, Harold D., and Dorothy Blumenstock.
1939 World Revolutionary Propaganda: A Chicago Study. New York: Knopf.

Lasswell, Harold D., et al.
1949 The Language of Politics: Studies in Quantitative Semantics. Cambridge, Massachusetts: M.I.T. Press.

Leites, Nathan.
1953 A Study of Bolshevism. Glencoe, Illinois: Free Press.

Leites, Nathan, and Elsa Bernaut.
1954 Ritual of Liquidation. Glencoe, Illinois: Free Press.

Lenin, V. I.
1929a "Where to begin." Pp. 109–116 in V. I. Lenin, Collected Works. Book 1, Volume 4. New York: International Publishers. First published in 1901.
1929b "What is to be done? Burning questions of our movement." Pp. 89–258 in V. I. Lenin, Collected Works. Book 2, Volume 4. New York: International Publishers. First published in 1902.
1940 Left-wing Communism, An Infantile Disorder. New York: International Publishers (reprint). First published in 1920.

Levikov, A.
1970 "Puteshestviye v srednii gorod" ("Visit to an average city"). Literaturnaya gazeta (June 10): 12–13.

Lewis, John Wilson.
1963 Leadership in Communist China. Ithaca, New York: Cornell University Press.

Lifton, Robert J.
1961 Thought Reform and the Psychology of Totalism: A Study of "Brainwashing" in China. New York: Norton.

Liu, Alan P. L.
1964a "Growth and modernization function of rural radio in communist China." Journalism Quarterly 41: 573–577.
1964b Radio Broadcasting in Communist China. Center for International Studies Monograph C/64-8. Cambridge: Massachusetts Institute of Technology.
1965 The Film Industry in Communist China. Center for International Studies Monograph C/65-5. Cambridge: Massachusetts Institute of Technology.
1966a "Movies and modernization in communist China." Journalism Quarterly 43: 319–324.
1966b The Press and Journals in Communist China. Center for International Studies Monograph C/66-9. Cambridge: Massachusetts Institute of Technology.
1969 "Mass communication and media in China's cultural revolution." Journalism Quarterly 46: 314–319.
1971 Communication and National Integration in Communist China. Berkeley: University of California Press.

MacFarquhar, Roderick.
1960 The Hundred Flowers Campaign and the Chinese Intellectuals. New York: Praeger.
1966 China Under Mao: Politics Takes Command. Cambridge, Massachusetts: M.I.T. Press.

Mao Tse-tung.
1965 Selected Words. 4 volumes. Peking: Foreign Language Press.
1966 Quotations from Chairman Mao Tse-tung. Peking: The Little Red Book.

Markham, James.
1967 Voices of the Red Giants: Communications in Russia and China. Ames: Iowa State University Press.

Marx, Karl, and Friedrich Engels.
1954 Communist Manifesto. Chicago: Regnery. First published in 1848.

Mead, Margaret.
1951 Soviet Attitudes Toward Authority. New York: McGraw-Hill.

Mickiewicz, Ellen Propper.
1967 Soviet Political Schools. New Haven, Connecticut: Yale University Press.

Milosz, Czeslaw.
1953 The Captive Mind. Translation by Jane Zielonko. New York: Knopf.

Morozov, M. A. (ed.).
1966 Spravochnik propagandista i agitatora (Handbook for the Propagandist and Agitator). Moscow: Political Literature Publishing House.

Neuhauser, Charles.
1967 "The Chinese communist party in the 1960s: Prelude to the cultural revolution." China Quarterly 32: 3–36.

Nowak, S.
1962 "Social attitudes of Warsaw students." Polish Sociological Bulletin 2: 91–104.

O'Keefe, M. Timothy.
1967 "A study of advertising in the Mos-

cow News." Journalism Quarterly 44:724–726.

Orientation Center of Publishers and Distributors.
1965 Kőnyvolvasás és Kőnyvvásárlas Magyarorszagon (Reading and Buying of Books in Hungary: The Results of a Representative Public Opinion Poll). Budapest: Orientation Center of Publishers and Distributors.

Orwell, George.
1949 1984. New York: Harcourt, Brace.

Ostrogorski, Moisei.
1902 Democracy and the Organization of Political Parites. New York: Macmillan.

Parsons, Talcott.
1965 "An American impression of sociology in the Soviet Union." American Sociological Review 30:121–125.

Partenov, G. S.
1968 "Nekotoryye itogi issledovania pechati Novosibirskoi oblasti" ("Some results from researching the press of Novosibirsk oblast"). Vestnik MGV, Zhurnalistika, No. 4.

Petrosyan, G. S.
1965 Vnerabocheye vremya trudyashchikhsya vo SSSR (Non-Working Time of Workers in the USSR). Moscow: Izdatyel'stvo "Ekonomika."

Pool, Ithiel de Sola.
1966 "The changing Soviet Union: The mass media as catalyst." Current (January): 12–17.
1970a The Prestige Press: A Comparative Study of Political Symbols. Cambridge, Massachusetts: M.I.T. Press.
1970b "Public opinion in Czechoslovakia." Public Opinion Quarterly 34:10–25.
1971 Report: Research Program on Problems of International Communications and Security. Center for International Studies Monograph C/69-26. Cambridge: Massachusetts Institute of Technology.

Pospielovsky, Dimitri.
1970 "Two years of the 'Chronicle of current events.'" Radio Liberty Research Paper No. 37. New York: Radio Liberty Committee.

Powell, David.
1967 "The effectiveness of Soviet anti-religious propaganda." Public Opinion Quarterly 31:366–380.

Powell, David E., and P. Shoup.
1969 "The emergence of political science in communist countries." American Political Science Review 64:572–588.

Prudenskiy, G. A. (ed.).
1961 Unerabocheye vremya trudyashchikhsya (Non-Working Time of Workers). Novosibirsk: Izdatyel'stvo Sibirskovo Otdyelyeniya AN SSSR.

Pye, Lucian W.
1968 The Spirit of Chinese Politics: Authority Crisis in Political Development. Cambridge, Massachusetts: M.I.T. Press.

Radio Free Europe.
1969a Attitudes Toward Key Political Concepts in East Europe: An Exercise in the Measurement of Meaning. Munich: Audience and Public Opinion Research Department, Radio Free Europe.
1969b Central Europeans and Communications Appeal. Munich: Audience and Public Opinion Research Department, Radio Free Europe.
1970a The Czech and Slovak Self-Image and the Czech and Slovak Image of the Americans, Germans, Russians, and Chinese. Munich: Audience and Public Opinion Research Department, Radio Free Europe.
1970b The Hungarian Self-Image and the Hungarian Image of Americans, Russians, Germans, Rumanians, and Chinese. Munich: Audience and Public Opinion Research Department, Radio Free Europe.

Radio Liberty Committee.
1968 To the Soviet Troops: A Selection of Czechoslovak Radio Appeals to Soviet Citizens, Broadcast in Russian, August 21–26, 1968. New York: Radio Liberty Committee.

Reddaway, Peter (ed.).
1970 Russia's Underground Intellectuals. New York: Praeger.
1972 Uncensored Russia: Protest and Dissent in the Soviet Union. New York: American Heritage Press.

Reisky-Dubnic, Vladimir.
1961 Communist Propaganda Methods: A Case Study on Czechoslovakia. New York: Praeger.

Remington, Robin.
1969 Winter in Prague: Documents on

Czechoslovak Communism in Crisis. Cambridge, Massachusetts: M.I.T. Press.

Reve, Karel van Het.
1969 Dear Comrade: Pavel Litvinov and the Voices of Soviet Citizens in Dissent. New York: Pitman.

Robinson, Gertrude J.
1970 "Foreign news selection is non-linear in Yugoslovia's Tanjug agency." Journalism Quarterly 47:340–351.

Rogers, Rosemarie.
1967 "The Soviet audience: How it uses the mass media," Ph.D. Dissertation, Massachusetts Institute of Technology (unpublished).
1968 How Russians Read Their Press: Patterns of Selection in Pravda and Izvestia. Center for International Studies Monograph B/68-6. Cambridge: Massachusetts Institute of Technology.
1969 "The Soviet audience expects and gets more from its media." Journalism Quarterly 46:767–776.
1970 "Education and political involvement in U.S.S.R. elite newspaper reading." Journalism Quarterly 47: 735–745.
1971 "The Soviet mass media in the sixties: Patterns of access and consumption." Journal of Broadcasting 15: 127–146.

Rosenberg, Arthur.
1939 Democracy and Socialism. New York: Knopf.

Rossi, Peter H., and Raymond A. Bauer.
1952 "Some patterns of Soviet communication behavior." Public Opinion Quarterly 16:653–670.

Rubin, B., and Yu. Kolesnikov.
1968 Student Glazami Sotsiologo (Students as Seen by Sociology). Rostov: Rostov University Press.

Rzhevskii, Leonid D.
1951 Iazyk i totalitarizm (Language and Totalitarianism). Munich: Institut po Izucheniiu SSR.

Schein, Edgar H., et al.
1961 Coercive Persuasion: A Sociopsychological Analysis of the "Brainwashing" of American Civilian Prisoners by the Chinese Communists. New York: Norton.

Schramm, Wilbur.
1959 One Day in the World's Press: Fourteen Great Newspapers on a Day of Crisis. Stanford, California: Stanford University Press.

Schramm, Wilbur; Jack Lyle; and Ithiel de Sola Pool.
1963 The People Look at Educational Television. Stanford, California: Stanford University Press.

Schwartz, Harry.
1969 Prague's 200 Days. New York: Praeger.

Selesnick, Herbert.
1970 "The diffusion of crisis information: A computer simulation of Soviet mass media exposure during the Cuban missile crisis and the aftermath of President Kennedy's assassination." Ph.D. Dissertation, Massachusetts Institute of Technology (unpublished).

Selznick, Philip.
1952 The Organizational Weapon. New York: McGraw-Hill.

Serrays, Paul L. M.
1962 Survey of the Chinese Language Reform and the Anti-Illiteracy Movement in Communist China. Berkeley: Center for Chinese Studies, Institute of International Studies, University of California.

Sheridan, Mary.
1968 "The emulation of heros." China Quarterly 33:47–72.

Shippee, John S.
1969 "Empirical sociology in the eastern European communist party-states," in Jan F. Triska (ed.), Communist Party States. Indianapolis: Bobbs-Merrill.

Shurman, Franz.
1966 Ideology and Organization in Communist China. Berkeley: University of California.

Sicinski, Andrzej.
1963a "Public opinion survey in Poland." International Social Science Journal 15(No. 1):91–110.
1963b "Surveys on media of mass communication of the Polish Public Opinion Research Centre." Gazette 9:237–241.
1966 "Television and radio in the structure of material and cultural needs of the

Polish society." Polish Sociological Bulletin. 2:124–134.
1967 "Developments in eastern European public-opinion research." Polls 3: 1–10.

Sicinski, Andrzej (ed.).
1966 Spoleczenstwo polskie w badaniach ankietowych (Polish Society in the Light of Opinion Research). Warsaw: Polish Academy of Science.

Simirenko, Alex (ed.).
1966 Soviet Sociology. London: Routledge and Kegan Paul.
1969 Social Thought in the Soviet Union. Chicago: Quadrangle Books.

Siniavskii, Andrei D.
1966 On Trial: The Soviet State Versus "Abram Tertz" and "Nikolai Arzhak." New York: Harper and Row.

Smith, Don D.
1969 "America's short wave audience. Public Opinion Quarterly 33:537–545.

Solomon, Richard H.
1967 "Communication patterns and the Chinese Revolution." China Quarterly 32:88–110.
1971 Mao's Revolution and the Chinese Political Culture. Berkeley: University of California Press.

Sorenson, Robert C., and Leszek L. Meyer.
1955 "Local use of wired radio in communist-ruled Poland." Journalism Quarterly 32:343–348.

Soviet Sociological Association.
1969 "Chitatel i gazeta" ("The reader and the newspaper"). Informatsionny byulleten Sovetskoi Sotsiologicheskoi Assotsiatsii, No. 35.

Steffens, Joseph Lincoln.
1931 The Autobiography of Lincoln Steffens. New York: Harcourt, Brace.

Szalai, Alexander (ed.).
1966 Multinational Comparative Time Budget Social Research Project: A Venture in International Research Cooperation. American Behavioral Scientist 10(No. 4):1–30.

Tarsis, Valerii.
1965 Ward 7: An Autobiographical Novel. London: Collins and Harwell.

Tatu, Michel.
1968 L'heresie impossible: chronique due drame tchechoslovaque. Paris: Bernard Grosset.

Tigrid, Pavel.
1969 La chute irresistible d'Alexander Dubcek. Paris: Colmann Levy.

Townsend, James R.
1967 Political Participation in Communist China. Berkeley: University of California Press.

Trotsky, Leon.
1961 Terrorism and Communism: A Reply to Karl Kautsky. Second Edition. Ann Arbor: University of Michigan Press. Published in England in 1922 under the title, The Defense of Terrorism.

Tung, Chi-ping, and Humphrey Evans.
1966 The Thought Revolution. New York: Coward McCann.

Uledov, A. K.
1963 Obshchestuyennoye mnyeniye sovietskogo obshchestva (Public Opinion in Soviet Society). Moscow: Mysl'.
1968 Struktura obshchestvennogo soznania (Structure of Social Consciousness). Moscow: Mysl'.

UNESCO.
1963– Statistical Yearbook. New York: UNESCO Publications Center. Annual.
1964 World Communications: Press, Radio, Television, Film. Fourth Edition. New York: UNESCO Publications Center.

Union Research Institute.
1968 CCP Documents of the Great Proletarian Cultural Revolution, 1966–1967. Hong Kong: Union Research Institute.

Union Research Service.
1963 "Learn from Lei Feng movement—A new campaign of class education among young people." Union Research Service (January 21):31.

United Nations.
1949– Statistical Yearbook, 1948–. New York: United Nations. Annual.

Vakar, Nicholas.
1956a "Communism and language." Slavic East European Journal 14:13–19.
1956b "Mass communication index: Some observations on communist Russian discourse." Symposium 10:42–59.

Vogel, Ezra F.
1967 "From revolutionary to semi-bureaucrat: The regularization of cadres." China Quarterly 29:36–60.

1969 Canton Under Communism. Cambridge, Massachusetts: Harvard University Press.

Weber, Max.
1958 "Politics as a vocation," in From Max Weber: Essays in Sociology. Translated and edited by H. H. Gerth and C. Wright Mills. New York: Oxford University Press. First published in 1919.

Wechsberg, Joseph.
1969 The Voices. Garden City, New York: Doubleday.

Weinberg, Elizabeth Ann.
1964 Soviet Sociology: 1960–1963. Center for International Studies Monograph C/64-30. Cambridge: Massachusetts Institute of Technology.

Whaley, Barton.
1962 Sources of News in America for Soviet Mass Media Gate Keepers. Center for International Studies Mimeo D/62-2. Cambridge: Massachusetts Institute of Technology.
1964 Daily Monitoring of the Western Press in the Soviet Union and Communist States. Center for International Studies Mimeo D/64-13. Cambridge: Massachusetts Institute of Technology.
1969 Soviet Clandestine Communication Nets. Center for International Studies Monograph C/67-10. Cambridge: Massachusetts Institute of Technology.

Whaley, Barton; George Schueller; and John Scott.
1961 PROPIN—China: A Study of Word-of-Mouth Communications in Communist China. Washington, D.C.: Special Operations Research Office, American University.

Wilson, Richard W., and Amy A. Wilson.
1970 "The red guards and the world student movement." China Quarterly 42:88–104.

Wittfogel, Karl August.
1957 Oriental Despotism: A Comparative Study of Total Power. New Haven, Connecticut: Yale University Press.

Yakobson, Sergius, and Harold D. Lasswell.
1949 "May day slogans in Soviet Russia, 1918–1943," in Harold D. Lasswell et al., The Language of Politics. Cambridge, Massachusetts: M.I.T. Press.

Yaroshenko, V. N.
1966 "Izucheniye radioauditorii" ("Study of a radio audience"). Vestnik MGV, Zhurnalistika, No. 1.

Yee Tin Tong Press.
1969 The Great Power Struggle in China. Hong Kong: Yee Tin Tong Press.

Yevladov, B., et al.
1969 "Chetyre tysyachi i odno interv'uy" (Four thousand and one interviews"). Zhurnalist 10:34–37.

Yu, Frederick T. C.
1963 "Communications and politics in communist China," in Lucian W. Pye (ed.), Communications and Political Development. Princeton, New Jersey: Princeton University Press.
1964 Mass Persuasion in Communist China. New York: Praeger.
1967 "Campaigns, communications, and development in communist China," in Daniel Lerner and Wilbur Schramm (eds.), Communication and Change in the Developing Nations. Honolulu: East-West Press.
1970 "Persuasive communications during the cultural revolution." Gazette 13:73–87, 137–148.

Zeman, A. A. B.
1969 Prague Spring: A Report on Czechoslovakia, 1968. Middlesex, England: Penguin.

Zhurnalist.
1970 "Problemy obratnoi svyazi" ("Feedback problems"). Zhurnalist 6:42–45.

ADDITIONAL READING

Almond, Gabriel A. *The Appeals of Communism.* Princeton, N. J.: Princeton University Press, 1954.

Babitsky, P., and Rimberg, J. *The Soviet Film Industry*. New York: Praeger, 1955.

Bauer, Raymond A., ed. *Some Views on Soviet Psychology*. New York: Timely Press, 1962.

Bereday, George Z. F. "Education: Organization and Values Since 1917." In *The Transformation of Russian Society*, edited by Cyril E. Black. Cambridge, Mass.: Harvard University Press, 1960.

Bogdanov, N., and Vyazemskiy, B. *Spravochnik zhurnalista* [The Journalists Handbook]. rev. ed. Leningrad: Lenizdat, 1965.

Buzek, Anthony. *How the Communist Press Works*. London: Pall Mall Press, 1964.

Cantril, Hadley. *The Politics of Despair*. New York: Basic Books, 1958.

———. *Soviet Leaders and Mastery Over Man.* New Brunswick, N. J.: Rutgers University Press, 1960.

Cendrowsky, Henry. "Sound Broadcasting in Poland." *Gazette* 6(1960):273–280.

Cheng, J. Chester, ed. *The Politics of the Chinese Red Army: A Translation of the Bulletin of Activities of the People's Liberation Army*. Stanford, Calif.: Hoover Institution on War, Revolution and Peace, Stanford University, 1966.

Childs, Harwood L., and Whitton, John B. *Propaganda by Short Wave*. Princeton, N. J.: Princeton University Press, 1942.

Chin, Tak-kai. *A Study on Chinese Communist Propaganda, Its Police and Operations* (in Chinese). Hong Kong, 1954.

Chuvikov, P. A., ed. *Pechat SSR za 50 Lyet* [The Press of the USSR Through 50 Years]. Moscow: Izdatel'stvo Kniga, 1967.

Crozier, Ralph C. *China's Cultural Legacy and Communism*. New York: Praeger, 1970.

Current Scene. "A Day with Radio Peking." 2(July 15, 1964):1–13.

Davison, W. Phillips. *International Political Communication*. New York: Praeger, 1965, esp. chap. 5, 6, 9.

Dizard, Wilson P. "Television in the USSR." *Problems of Communism* 12(1963).

Ebermayer, Erich, and Meissner, H. O. *Evil Genius: The Story of Josef Goebbels*. London: Wingate, 1963.

Fein, L., and Bonnell, J. "Press and Radio in Roumania: Some Recent Developments." *Journalism Quarterly* 42(1965):443–449.

Fisher, Ralph Talcott, Jr. *Pattern for Soviet Youth: A Study of the Congresses of the Komsomol, 1918–1954*. New York: Columbia University Press, 1959.

Gorokhoff, Boris I. *Publishing in the U.S.S.R.* Russian and East European Series, no. 19. Bloomington, Ind.: Indiana University Russian and East European Institute, 1959.

Great Cultural Revolution in China. Hong Kong: Asia Research Center, 1967.

Holt, Robert T. *Radio Free Europe*. Minneapolis: University of Minnesota Press, 1958.

Houn, Franklin W. *To Change a Nation*. New York: Crowell-Collier, 1961.

Huang, Ling-ling. "Yang Chen Wan Pao: A Newspaper in Communist China." *Current Scene* 2(1963).

Kaftanov, S. V., et al., eds. *Radio and Television in the USSR*. Washington, D.C.: Joint Publication Research Service: 4838, CSO: 1908-S, 1961. (Translation of *Radio: televideniye v SSSR*. Moscow: State Committee on Radio Broadcasting and Television of the Council of Ministers, USSR, 1960.)

Kermish, Joseph. "On the Underground Press in the Warsaw Ghetto." *Gazette* 8(1962):1–21.

King, Vincent U. S. *A General Study of the Channels of Communication Between Communist China and the Western World*. Cambridge, Mass.: Center of International Studies Monograph C/64-9, Massachusetts Institute of Technology, 1964.

Kloskowska, A. "Mass Culture in Poland." *Polish Sociological Bulletin* 2(1964):106–115.

Kolaja, Jiri. "Sociology in Romania." *The American Sociologist* 3 (August 1968):241–243.

Lasswell, Harold D. "Strategy of Soviet Propaganda." *Proceedings of the Academy of Political Science* 24(1951):214–226.

Leites, Nathan, and Pool, Ithiel de Sola. "The Response of Communist Propaganda to Frustration." In *The Language of Politics: Studies in Quantitative Semantics* by Harold D. Lasswell et al. Cambridge, Mass.: M.I.T. Press, 1949.

Leyda, Jay. *Kino: A History of Russian and Soviet Film*. New York: Macmillan, 1960.

Liao, Kai-lung. "The Press in the People's Republic of China." *Current Background* June 9, 1965, p. 333.

Lion, Jill A. *Long Distance Passenger Travel in the Soviet Union*. Cambridge, Mass.: Center for International Studies Monograph C/67-13, Massachusetts Institute of Technology, 1967.

Littell, Robert, ed. *The Czech Black Book*. New York: Praeger, 1969.

Liu, Alan P. L. *Adaption of Traditional Story Telling to Political Propaganda in Communist China*. Cambridge, Mass.: Center for International Studies Monograph C/65-22, Massachusetts Institute of Technology, 1965.

———. *Book Publishing in Communist China*. Cambridge, Mass.: Center for International Studies Monograph C/65-25, Massachusetts Institute of Technology, 1965.

Ludz, Peter-Christian, ed. *Soziologie der DDR*. Cologne: Opladen, 1964.

Mass Communications in Eastern Europe. Washington, D.C.: Bureau of Social Science Research, 1958.

Matejko, A. "Newspaper Staff as a Social System." *Polish Sociological Bulletin* 1 (1967):58–68.

Mond, George, and Richer, R. "Writers and Journalists: A Pressure Group in East European Politics." *Journalism Quarterly* 43 (1966):95–106.

Nők Helyzete a Munkahelyen És Otthon [The Position of Women at the Place of Work and in the Home]. Budapest: Central Bureau of Statistics, 1962.

Nunn, Raymond. *Publishing in Mainland China.* Cambridge, Mass.: M.I.T. Press, 1966.

O masterstvye agitatora—metodicheskiye Sovyety [On the Agitators Art—Methodological Counsel]. Moscow: State Publishing House for Political Literature, 1960.

Olsen, K. "The Press in Albania, Europe's Least Known Land." *Journalism Quarterly* 42(1965):639–642.

Pike, Douglas. *Viet Cong: The Organization and Techniques of the National Liberation Front of South Vietnam.* Cambridge, Mass.: M.I.T. Press, 1966.

Press in Authoritarian Countries. Zurich: International Press Institute, 1959.

Radio Free Europe. *Poland's New Generation: An Attempt at a Sociological Description and Analysis.* Munich: Audience Research Department, 1963.

———. *The Polish Self-Image and the Polish Image of Americans, Russians, Chinese, Germans, and Czechs.* Munich: Audience and Public Opinion Research Department, 1968.

———. *The Arab-Israeli Conflict and Public Opinion in Eastern Europe: Including a Comparison with West European Opinion.* Munich: Audience and Public Opinion Research Department, 1968.

Romanovskiy, S. K. *Mezhdunarodniye kulturniye i nauchiye svyaozi SSSR* [International Cultural and Scientific Connections of the USSR]. Moscow: International Relations Publishing House, 1966.

Rossbacher, Peter. "The Soviet Journalistic Style." *Gazette* 12(1966):201–211.

Schneider, Maarten. "Bacteria as Propaganda Weapon." *Gazette* 4(1958):47–62.

Schramm, Wilbur, and Riley, John W., Jr. "Communication in the Sovietized State as Represented in Korea." *American Sociological Review* 16(1951):757–766.

Semmler, Rudolf. *Goebbels, the Man Next to Hitler.* London: Westhouse, 1947.

Sicinski, Andrzej. "A Two-Step Flow of Communication." *Polish Sociological Bulletin* 1(1963):33–40.

Stepakov, B. P. *Rasprostranneniye, ekspedirovaniye, i dostavka gazet i zhurnalov v SSSR* [Distribution, Dispatching, and Obtaining Newspapers and Journals in the USSR]. Moscow: Moscow University Press, 1955.

Sylla, J. "The Periodical Press in the People's Democratic Republics" *Gazette* 6(1960): 181–197.

Taylor, Edmund. *The Strategy of Terror: Europe's Inner Front.* Boston: Houghton Mifflin, 1940.

Todorov, D. "Press and Broadcasting in Present Day Bulgaria." *Journalism Quarterly* 39(1962):212–214.

———. "The Press in Bulgaria." *Gazette* 8(1962):246–250.

Twenty-four Hours of the Day: Analysis of 12,000 Time Budgets. Budapest: Central Statistical Office, 1965.

U.S. Information Service. *A Statistical Sketch of the Press in Communist China.* Hong Kong: USIS Research Report, May 1961.

USSR Ministry of Culture. *Pechat' SSSR za sorok lyet: 1917–1957* [The Press in the USSR Through Forty Years: 1917–1957]. Moscow: Glavizdat, 1957.

———. *Pechat' SSSR [19–] godakh* [The Press of the USSR in (year)]. Moscow: Izdatyel'stvo vsyesoyuznoy knizhnoy palaty (various years).

———. *Latopis periodischeskikh izdaniy SSSR: 1955–1960* [Yearbook of Periodical Publications in the USSR: 1955–1960)]. Moscow: Izdatyel'stvo vsyesoyuznoy knizhnoy palaty, 1962.

Whaley, Barton. *Guerrilla Communications.* Cambridge, Mass.: Center for International Studies Monograph C/67-4, Massachusetts Institute of Technology, 1967.

———. *Operation Barbarossa: A Case Study of Soviet Strategic Information Processing Before the German Invasion.* Cambridge, Mass.: M.I.T. Press, forthcoming.

———. *Stratagem: Deception and Surprise in War.* New York: Praeger, forthcoming.

Wilson, Richard W. *Learning to be Chinese: The Political Socialization of Children in Taiwan.* Cambridge, Mass.: M.I.T. Press, 1970.

Yao, Ignatius Peng. "The New China News Agency: How It Serves the Party." *Journalism Quarterly* 40(1963):83–86.

CHAPTER 15 Communist Esoteric Communications: Explication de Texte

WILLIAM E. GRIFFITH
Massachusetts Institute of Technology

This chapter describes a particular aspect of communication in Communist countries, namely, the extensive use of Aesopian communications. Actually, there is nothing uniquely Communist about this practice. In any civilization where there are taboos against open expression of opinion on major issues, people will find ways to discuss those issues by means of circumlocutions. These circumlocutions may take the form of parables or fables (hence the name Aesopian). *They may be historical analogies (e.g., before the French Revolution, criticisms of the French court were sometimes couched as discussions of China).*

American communication research, evolving in a free-speaking, democratic society, has paid little attention to the phenomena of esoteric communications. It has, however, been studied by students of Communist politics, such as Professor Griffith, by students of Fascist propaganda (George, 1959), and by some students of the history of political theory, particularly Leo Strauss (1952; 1959; 1963; 1970) and his disciples. Strauss has persuasively shown how classical texts in the corpus of political theory were often tracts on behalf of a particular political position that could not effectively or safely be advocated openly.

In recent years the analysis of Communist communications has progressed considerably as a result of the international and internal Communist fissures growing out of the Sino-Soviet dispute. This chapter attempts to sum up and comment upon the growing discussion about its methodology—what Myron Rush (1958:88–94) has christened the "decipherment of esoteric communications."[1]

First, as the title indicates, this type of analysis is nothing new in history. Esoteric communication—ostensibly ideological or theological communications but actually policy directions by ruling elites to subelites—have been characteristic of all authoritarian, theologically or ideologically oriented societies. To give a few examples: in Byzantium, doctrinal disputes between Homoousians and Homoiousians over the

[1] In addition to Rush (1958), writings I have found particularly useful are Leonhard (1962:17–30), Dallin and Brzezinski (1963:xxxvii–xliv), and Zagoria (1964:24–35). See also Leites and Bernaut (1954), George (1959), Conquest (1961: chaps. 1–3), and the man who first taught me the method and whose intuition in these matters was unsurpassed, Franz Borkenau (1954).

relationship between the divine and human natures of Christ, and the iconoclastic controversies over the propriety of statues, as opposed to icons, in churches involved, in fact, major, specific policy issues.[2] In Tudor and Stuart England, theological controversies about proper church doctrine reflected much more specific power interests. Lacking completeness of sources, classical and medieval scholarship has always employed what the Paris school of diplomatics, the Ecole des Chartes, made famous as *explication de texte* to analyze these controversies.

Nor has the advent of modern media of elite and mass communication changed to any decisive extent the phenomena or the problems of deciphering their meaning. It has only increased the number and length of communications. With respect to Communist communications the situation is even worse since, unfortunately, Marx—and to a lesser extent Lenin—had little else to do in exile other than write at interminable length. The tradition of these two Communist patriarchs, to the misfortune of Western students of their outpourings, has been maintained by contemporary Communist ideologists.

Second, there are some characteristics common to all such elite authoritarian societies that affect the content of their esoteric communications and, consequently, are relevant to methods of deciphering them.

A theologically or ideologically oriented society, which depends upon commonly held doctrine for its legitimacy, requires a myth of unanimity. This myth can rest either on the divine inspiration of the ruler or, as it did with Calvin and Marx, upon the assumption that no rational person can come to any other conclusion—i.e., that the ideology or theology is "scientific" or "rational," and that no other one is or can be.

Conflict among the controlling elite is incompatible with the need to protect this myth, which is a fundamental prop for maintaining itself in power. Yet an authoritarian, theologically or ideologically oriented elite is prone to internal conflict, either to gain the leadership or to curry favor of an already existing leader. As in ancient Rome, the leaders of this elite have their own *clientes*, for the advancement of whose careers they have been responsible, upon whose support they rely for their own success, and with whom they must be able to communicate in order to mobilize and direct their efforts.

Obviously this cannot be done directly. In such societies, however, the pursuit of heretics is considered necessary and is both widespread and fierce, for heretics represent a threat to power as well as to ideological interests. Thus, while ostensibly carrying on public controversy in theocratic or ideological terms (otherwise the myth of unanimity would be lost), actual power conflicts are also presented in these terms—thus further polarizing and instrumentalizing the theology or ideology.

Normally these societies have sacred texts, authoritative (because prophetic) inspirations, and sets of angels, prophets, and devils, other-worldly or secular. Moreover, history, and its constant revisions for ostensibly rational (i.e., ideological) but actually political purposes, plays a large role. Ritual and protocol are also very important, particularly in such secular ideocratic societies as Russia and China, in which the ruling elite has increasingly tried to strengthen its legitimacy by rituals analogous to, and therefore deriving additional strength from, traditional ruling patterns (Stalin's military uniform, Mao's classical poetry, etc.).

In such a situation, when ideology becomes primarily an instrument of manipulation by elites, its interpretation may be most fruitfully studied within Karl Mannheim's definition of it: ex post facto justification of policy steps.

[2] I know of no better training for analysis of Communist esoteric communications; I learned something of it with respect to French medieval history from Prof. Charles H. Taylor at Harvard before the Second World War.

KEY TO ELITE COMMUNICATION

Let us, therefore, attempt to list some principles for deciphering Communist ideological communications. These principles are by now generally accepted by the great majority of practitioners in this field, and all of them are receiving empirical confirmation (Rogers, 1968; 1970).

1. Normally, esoteric elite communication is the major routine means of transmitting guidance to subelites, and its ideological language is sufficient to conceal its true meaning both from the masses and from most of the West.

   In the overwhelming majority of cases, however, the esoteric communication of ruling elites is decipherable, at least to a large degree, by Western students of it. True, this is more difficult when deliberate deception toward subelites has been practiced, occasions where crucial issues, usually of international Communist relations, have deliberately been concealed. For example, the November 1960 meeting of eighty-one Communist parties was publicly presented as a success when actually it was a failure (Griffith, 1962:38–57).[3] But such instances are rare. In such cases, subelites are usually informed by secret communications. Such communications have increasingly been "leaked" in recent years, probably deliberately, by Western governments whose interest in so doing must be taken into account in determining the authenticity of the communications.
2. Overt ideological conflict almost always reflects policy, and usually personal conflict as well. Moreover, conflict within such an authoritarian society, particularly a Communist one, where power and ideology rather than tradition or charisma legitimatize the leadership, becomes more personal as the level of conflict rises.
3. Analysis of changes in ideological line in esoteric communications can be checked against three varieties of simultaneous developments: (*a*) personnel changes—appointments, dismissals, changes in rank order, frequency of citation or praise; (*b*) reports of Westerners on the scene—newsmen, travelers, diplomats— although these are often subject to deliberate distortion by means of rumors planted by regime elites; (*c*) the rarest and often the most reliable and illuminating, defectors from the elite itself; (*d*) judgment of Western experts, rated according to their past interpretative "batting average."

Indicators of Internal Change

We turn now to the more detailed significant indicators of internal change; first, those involving change in ideological line. Our analysis is primarily with respect to the Soviet Union, since deciphering of Soviet esoteric communications has been going on longer and has been therefore more reliably tested against subsequent empirical evidence. However, with some exceptions, which are listed below, it may be considered generally valid for other Communist states and parties as well.

Changes in Ideological Line

Changes in ideological line are important in direct proportion to the collective or individual authority of their proponents, which range roughly as follows, in descending order of importance:

1. Personal statements of a universally recognized absolute ruler; the importance of the statements varies according to their form
2. Major reports at and resolutions of Party congresses
3. Major reports at and resolutions of Central Committee plena

[3] Additional subsequent bibliography is cited in Griffith (1964:19, fn. 14).

4. Major articles in the Party press, particularly Party dailies (e.g., *Pravda*) and ideological journals (e.g., *Kommunist*). Of these, articles embodying the "general line" on a specific subject are the most important. Anonymous articles (i.e., those representing the collective opinion of the leadership) are more important than those signed by a staff member or ideological official, and ones signed by pseudonyms which, experience has shown, indicate particular authoritativeness (e.g., "Observer" in *Pravda* or *Jenmin Jih-pao*) are more authoritative still.
5. Government statements
6. Articles indicating a change of line in elite academic or literary journals of small circulation (e.g., *Mirovaya Ekonomika i Mezhdunarodnaya Otnosheniya*), or the beginning or progress of a "thaw" against the will of the leadership (e.g., *Novy Mir*), or a factional struggle within the leadership (e.g., recently, Peking *Liberation Daily*).

Certain other factors must be taken into account. Frequently a forthcoming change in line is first signaled by apparently spontaneous proposals for it "from the base"—i.e., from subelites; the authoritativeness of these as an indicator varies directly with the extent to which they are repeated and inversely with the extent to which they are contradicted. Another important indicator is the relative frequency, order, and degree of emphasis on labels, epithets, and past historical events that have meanwhile acquired symbolic policy significance. For example, attacks on "dogmatism" or the "cult of the personality," or favorable references to the Twentieth CPSU Congress indicate a more moderate line; no references to these three, and/or attacks on "revisionism," "reformism," or "liberalism" indicate the contrary. The same is often true, *mutatis mutandis*, with respect to the attitude taken toward the United States and West Germany.

Then there is the whole area of history, Party and otherwise. The constant rewriting of history, particularly national and Party history, is a characteristic Communist method of indicating and implementing changes in line. In recent Soviet historiography, the focus has been on the role and significance of Stalin; in more recent Chinese developments, on the Yenan and guerrilla-war periods of Chinese communism. There are many more subtle indicators of changes in line, however. For example, in the USSR or among pro-Soviet Parties, a more favorable view toward Bukharin indicates a more moderate line, even as a favorable view of Stalin means a more extreme one.

Finally, there is the area of citations from the canonical texts. If living members of the elite are cited, this indicates their power and influence, if dead ones (e.g., Stalin), it indicates the direction of the Party line; reference to certain phrases (e.g., "course on the middle peasant"—a Bukharinist line) means a change in course as well. Changes in regularly recurring lists of slogans (i.e., May Day or October Revolution) are also significant indicators (Yakobson & Lasswell, 1949).

Changes in Personnel

Turning to changes in personnel, the significance of appointments and removals can best be understood by detailed career analyses of the persons involved. Usually the *shefsto* to which they belong (i.e., the *clientes* of their leader) can be determined by their past associations. Primacy of equivalent Party over government posts must always be taken into consideration. Sometimes (e.g., under Stalin and, recently, after the Twenty-third CPSU Congress) names of the leadership—i.e., Politburo and Secretariat—are given in nonalphabetical order; this can safely be assumed to be order of rank. Conversely, alphabetical order of names means at least some degree of collective leadership. Order in photographs is also important, notably on such important occasions as the October Revolution parade. Distorted photographs (i.e., removal of some figures, such as was done in 1953 to make Malenkov appear to have been closer to Stalin) is a rare but always important indicator.

Criticism or self-criticism of leaders always indicates their weakness. Length and frequency of references to or quotations of a leader is also significant (e.g., in the *Great Soviet Encyclopedia*), as is the number of constituencies to which he is nominated for the Supreme Soviet or other governmental organizations. Deletions made in reprinted speeches indicate quantitatively the person's stature and, if of qualitative significance—i.e., if they refer to some current issue of importance—may indicate the way the wind is blowing on the subject.

Indicators of External Change

We turn now to the deciphering of esoteric communications among Communist parties rather than within them and, specifically, to the Sino-Soviet dispute and its ramifications. In general, the above rules, *mutatis mutandis*, apply. However, some additional elements are naturally involved.

In general, the Sino-Soviet dispute has led to an increasingly severe, complex, and factionalized struggle within the international Communist world; to the rising importance of nationalistic as opposed to ideological Communist elements; to an increasing distortion, cynical manipulation, and emptying of ideological content and, thereby, to its discrediting throughout the Communist world. In power terms, the dispute has led not to polycentrism but to pluralism; i.e., to increasing national independence of all Communist states and parties.

These developments in turn are reflected in ideological pronouncements, which become increasingly differentiated and within which national history and objectives play increasing roles. It therefore becomes necessary to keep in mind the history, personalities, and lines of all the parties concerned. Moreover, the volume of polemics has become much greater. All these factors have rendered analysis of international Communist developments much more complex, requiring much more documentation and knowledge of history and of the areas concerned.

Perhaps the most important task involved is to fix as accurately as possible the position, past and present, of each Communist state and party toward (1) each of the two major states involved, the Soviet Union and China, and (2) because of increasing flexibility in the Communist world, toward its neighbors and other significant parties in the dispute.

Intraparty Clues

How does the analyst of Communist politics go about determining the position of Communist parties toward Moscow and Peking on the limited basis of such simultaneously published declarations? The technique is fairly simple. First he makes a list of what he hypothesizes to be the main ideological issues that are currently at stake between Moscow and Peking. Then he assembles, to the extent possible in the original complete text, the declarations of the various Communist parties and, after a careful reading, revises and expands his categories to correspond as closely as possible to what seem to be the actual subjects of ideological differences.

He then goes through all the speeches again, evaluating them according to a rough gradation of intensity—strong, medium, minor (or formal)—and scores each speech, vis-à-vis each issue, on this gradation.

This having been done, he is now in a position to judge the position of the various Communist parties in relation to those of the Soviet Union and Communist China. The degree of similarity, or lack thereof, will give a rough indicator of the position of each party with regard to the Sino-Soviet dispute. Naturally, the more ideological points at issue one can isolate, and the more this method is carried on over time, the more accurate the classification of parties will be.[4]

One caveat, based on historical experience, must be made: the line-up on ideological issues may sometimes, although not normally, be misleading. A good example is the *prises de position* of the various Communist parties at the beginning of the 1960s vis-à-vis the issue of whether or not the international Communist movement is, or should be, "headed by the Soviet Union." One reason why many Western analysts at the time regarded the November 1960 international conference of eighty-one Communist parties in Moscow as having restored some degree of unity was that the Chinese and Albanians, who had been regarded (correctly) before the meeting as moving toward an anti-Soviet position (Griffith, 1963:44), placed particular emphasis on the necessity of accepting the formula of the Moscow Declaration while the Soviets and their allies almost ostentatiously avoided it (Griffith, 1963:102–105).[5]

This practice of acknowledging CPSU primacy continued for some months after the Moscow conference, but was later replaced by the Chinese view that the "Soviet revisionists" had forfeited the leadership of the international Communist movement, which had therefore passed to Mao Tse-tung. We know, from subsequent disclosures, that the Soviets were quite aware in 1960 why the Chinese had insisted in 1957 and again in 1960 that the USSR must be the head of the international Communist movement, and that this Chinese position was merely an intermediate and essentially anti-Soviet position.

If one looks back at the ideological position taken at the time by the various Communist parties, one can clearly see that the position of the Chinese and their allies in favor of "the international Communist movement headed by the CPSU" was in conflict with all their other ideological positions, which were essentially anti-Soviet. This further demonstrates the effectiveness of a multi-factoral analysis of ideological *prises de position*, since it enables the analyst not to be misled by an apparent contradiction in only one of the ideological issues (Khrushchev, 1961:24–25; Flynn, 1963).

It is also possible to make a rough scale of escalation in Sino-Soviet polemics or in the differences of Moscow or Peking with any other Communist state or party. Based on experience to date, the scale (in ascending order of worsening relations) may be sketched out as follows:

1. Divergent ideological lines, each without reference to the other (e.g., Chinese and Soviet declarations in 1958–1959)
2. Polemics against historical surrogates easily identifiable as the opponent—(the best example is the 1962 Chinese polemics against Bernstein, Kautsky, and the Economists (Griffith, 1966: 38–41)
3. Camouflaged proxy polemics, with only anonymous identification of proponents of ideologically condemned positions (e.g., "some comrades" or "modern revisionists"—Chinese symbols for Moscow, 1957–1959—or, conversely, "dogmatists" or "revisionists"—Soviet symbols for China and Yugoslavia respectively, same period)
4. Individual contemporary proxies (for the Soviets, Albania or Hoxha; for the Chinese, Yugoslavia or Tito, 1961–1962)
5. Reprinting, without comment, of explicit polemics by other, allied parties against one's main rival (e.g., Soviet reprinting of French Communist attacks on China; Chinese reprinting of Albanian attacks on the Soviet Union, 1962)
6. Completely explicit polemics (Soviet

[4] This technique was first developed by Zbigniew Brzezinski (cf. 1967:416).

[5] The Moscow Declaration acknowledged the Communist Party of the Soviet Union (CPSU) as the "vanguard of the international Communist movement" (Griffith, 1963:190).

and Chinese, July 1963 and thereafter); this stage has seen many variations in addresses of the attacks, in severity of epithets, etc.

Moreover, there are many other indicators of Sino-Soviet relations now that they have reached so largely an unesoteric —i.e., overtly polemical—state: Soviet agreements with the United States; changes in tourist and cultural agreements and in recipients of economic aid and specialists; in attendance at or departure from national or international meetings; in applause or boos during these meetings; in level of attendance at, attitude in, and conduct of international Communist-front forums such as the World Federation of Trade Unions and the World Peace Council.

There has also occurred, at various stages and for various reasons, the development of what might be called a neutralist-nationalist position within the dispute—held notably by Rumania, Cuba, North Korea, and North Vietnam (Griffith, 1964; 1966). There are also clearly differentiated degrees of support by allies of each of the major powers, degrees that can usually be determined by a close analysis of their communications.

Symbols of the Sino-Soviet Dispute

In addition to all the verbal symbols mentioned above for intraparty discourse, the Sino-Soviet dispute and its ramifications have given rise to a whole new set of symbols, many of them with changing meanings. Since space precludes any detailed discussion of these symbols (and their changing meaning would soon make such a discussion largely obsolescent in any case), suffice it to list some of them and to point out that the analyst must have the current important indicators in his head at any one moment so that he can judge and note the significance of changes from them.

We have already mentioned revisionism and dogmatism; *modern revisionism* is a pro-Chinese term. Each side has tried, as any Communist leadership always does, to take the centrist position or, as a minimum, a position to the left (but never to the right) of center. The Russians, therefore, accuse the Chinese of "left-wing revisionism"; the Chinese accuse the Russians of "nationalist dogmatism." The attitude toward Yugoslavia and Albania has remained a key indicator; such previously pro-Chinese neutrals as Pyongyang and Hanoi indicate by attacks on Yugoslavia that they have not become totally pro-Soviet. Similarly, Rumania indicates its relatively pro-Soviet neutrality by its omission of attacks on the Albanians and Chinese, as well as by its overt support of such pro-Soviet slogans as "peaceful coexistence." Both the Soviets and the Chinese profess their allegiance to the concept of peaceful coexistence, but since the Twenty-third CPSU Congress, the Soviets have referred to peaceful coexistence as the "general line of the international Communist movement" (i.e., it has priority over the national liberation struggle, something which the Chinese reject).

Finally, one should note the basic importance of the organizational issue, i.e., the desire of the Soviets to maintain their leadership and influence, of the Chinese to diminish it and eventually replace it by their own, and of the neutrals to replace it by pluralism. The ideological expressions of the Soviet view are "collective mobilization" against the "main danger" (China) and the "struggle against factionalism" (Chinese); the Chinese use "unanimity through consultation" (i.e., a Chinese veto).

To compound the reader's confusion, we need only add that symbols can occasionally reverse their meaning. Originally the phrase "the leading role of the Soviet Union" was a pro-Soviet (Stalinist) phrase. The fact that China and Albania continued to use it after the Soviets and their allies had adopted the "vanguard" role of Moscow proved that the phrase had become an anti-Soviet symbol, both because it was anti-Yugoslav (Belgrade having always refused to accept Moscow's "leading role") and because Peking later declared Moscow deposed from that role (implying that Mao had taken it over).

PROBLEMS OF COMPUTERIZATION

It would be, to say the least, unfashionable if we did not raise the question of whether or not this deciphering could be better and more easily done by an electronic computer. In theory, perhaps it could; but it would require constant reprogramming of the changing symbols (the time and extent of whose change would have to be determined by the analyst). Also, it would be necessary to program the whole history of the countries and parties concerned—which by now includes all of them—adjusted for the changing significance of deliberate historical distortion, plus adjustment for the graded importance of personalities, forums, and length and intensity of conflict. Finally, there would always be one element missing: the intuition, the "feel" of the analyst derived from long experience and practice.

The study of history and politics is primarily an art, not a science. Nowhere is this more true than in Communist studies, where the evidence is always only partially available and in a sample that is at best unrepresentative, but we do not know to what extent or why. Although the deciphering of esoteric communications requires the most rigid standards and the most careful *explication de texte*—and the texts available are increasing geometrically—the skill remains, like the reconstruction of the text of a fragment of Sappho, an art.

REFERENCES

Borkenau, Franz.
1954 "Getting at the facts behind the Soviet facade." Commentary 17(April): 393–400.

Brzezinski, Zbigniew.
1967 The Soviet Bloc. Third Edition. Cambridge, Massachusetts: Harvard University Press.

Conquest, Robert.
1961 Power and Policy in the USSR. New York: St. Martin's Press.

Dallin, Alexander, and Zbigniew Brzezinski.
1963 "Introduction," in Alexander Dallin et al., Diversity in International Communism. New York: Columbia University Press.

Flynn, Elizabeth Gurley.
1963 "Recollection of the 1960 conference." Political Affairs 42 (November): 22–38.

George, Alexander.
1959 Propaganda Analysis: A Study of Inferences Made from Nazi Propaganda in World War II. Evanston, Illinois: Row, Peterson.

Griffith, William E.
1962 "The November 1960 Moscow meeting: A preliminary reconstruction." China Quarterly No. 11:38–57.
1963 Albania and the Sino-Soviet Rift. Cambridge, Massachusetts: M.I.T. Press.
1964 The Sino-Soviet Rift. Cambridge, Massachusetts: M.I.T. Press.
1966 Sino-Soviet Relations 1964–1965. Cambridge, Massachusetts: M.I.T. Press.

Khrushchev, N. S.
1961 "For new victories for the world communist movement." World Marxist Review 4(January): 3–28.

Leites, Nathan, and Elsa Bernaut.
1954 Ritual of Liquidation. Glencoe, Illinois: Free Press.

Leonhard, Wolfgang.
1962 The Kremlin Since Stalin. New York: Praeger.

Rogers, Rosemarie.
1968 How Russians Read Their Press: Patterns of Selection in Pravda and Izvestiia. Center for International Studies Monograph B/68-6. Cambridge: Massachusetts Institute of Technology.
1970 "Education and political involvement in USSR elite newspaper reading." Journalism Quarterly 47: 735–745.

Rush, Myron.
1958 The Rise of Khrushchev. Washington, D.C.: Public Affairs Press.

Strauss, Leo.
1952 Persecution and the Art of Writing. Glencoe, Illinois: Free Press.
1959 What Is Political Philosophy? Glencoe, Illinois: Free Press.
1963 On Tyranny. New York: Free Press of Glencoe.
1970 The Political Philosophy of Hobbes. Chicago: University of Chicago Press.

Yakobson, Sergius, and Harold D. Lasswell.
1949 "Trend: May Day slogans in Soviet Russia," in Harold D. Lasswell et al., Language of Politics: Studies in Quantitative Semantics. Cambridge, Massachusetts: M.I.T. Press.

Zagoria, Donald S.
1964 The Sino-Soviet Conflict. New York: Atheneum.

CHAPTER 16 The Press as a Communication System

WILLIAM L. RIVERS
Stanford University

The next three chapters take up the three great mass media which dominate the present communication scene. This chapter considers newspapers and magazines. It sketches the development of periodicals, describes how different kinds of newspapers and magazines operate, and considers at some length the performance of the press. Finally it presents some criteria for measuring the freedom of the press. In a short appendix, Frank A. Philpot of Kaiser Broadcasting discusses television news, its strengths, its weaknesses, and its differences compared with print media.

A stark view of the press as a communication system was offered by Lyndon Johnson shortly before he was to leave the White House. It was contained in a thirty-thousand-word article, written for the *Encyclopaedia Britannica*, in which he summarized the major trials and goals of his presidency. He termed it "the musings of a man who has seen the press in recent years only from the open end of the gun barrel—an angle from which the press rarely has occasion to see itself."

Much of the article was in that petulant tone. Mr. Johnson began by paying a mild tribute to the press as the principal conduit from government to citizen, then the complaints began:

> Yet what happens to [the officials'] explanations of policy in print, or on the television screen, may be something far different from what they intended. Policy may be distorted. Rumors of dark motives, or of unspecified dissent, may be given equal prominence with the expressed purposes of the administration. Failure and conflict will certainly be emphasized wherever they can be found or presumed.
>
> The theory on which much of the press seems to operate is that expressed by an old friend of mine one day in the Oval Office. When I asked him why the press seldom reported success and seemed to concentrate on mistakes and controversy, this man—a distinguished and experienced publisher—said, "Mr. President, good news is no news. Bad news is news" (Johnson, 1969:45).

Mr. Johnson offered two prescriptions for the press:

> First, journalism is one of the professions. Yet it is the only profession that has no entrance examinations or requirements. Since these would probably be impractical, the task of maintaining high personnel standards re-

mains a continuing and urgent one for the press itself.

I think that a good journalist should know American and world history as intimately as does a competent historian. He should have a substantial and specific understanding of economics and politics and foreign affairs; especially under the most recent five or six Presidents. He should be able to find the meaningful material in the welter of data that is thrown at him—and not simply rely on someone's cynical evaluation for a sensational lead sentence.

Second, I suggest that it may be time to change the basic attitude of journalism. Too little attention is devoted to the common everyday problems that plague society and to the efforts that succeed and therefore contain lessons we need to know (Johnson, 1969:46).

The president's reflections on the state of government-press relationships ended:

I do not think our government should or can do a thing about this situation. It is a matter purely for the free press itself. I have offered a suggestion for improving the competence and the professionalism of the press; the further task of imposing a degree of moderation on itself—lest in the search for the scandalous it neglects the real and the enduring—is a matter for the conscience of editors and writers everywhere (Johnson, 1969:46).

If these were the thoughts of Lyndon Johnson alone, they might be dismissed as merely the reaction of one wounded president. But the statement was much more than that. It epitomized the reactions of many public officials who have had to contend with a significant fact of American public life: The press is a broker of official information, gathering it from the halls of government and disseminating it among the people—then carrying their reactions and hopes back to government. No function of the press as a communication system is more important.

This is not, of course, the only function of the press as a communication system. In various writings, Wilbur Schramm has explored several—all of them functions that the press shares with the other media. One of the chief functions is to help us watch the horizon, much as the ancient messenger once did. Another is to help us correlate our response to the challenges and opportunities that appear on the horizon and to reach consensus on social actions. Still another is to help us transmit the culture of our society to new members. Looming larger since the advent of television is the function of entertainment. In fact, television and its companion medium, film, are so heavily devoted to entertainment that the print media are becoming more informative, less entertaining. Finally, mass communication helps us to sell goods and services.

The individual's perspective may suggest that one or another of these functions is the most important. For example, an audience study commissioned by *Life* magazine carried this sentence: "The delivery of an audience for the advertiser is the fundamental function of any medium." Many an advertiser would agree. But we shall focus here on the function of the press as a broker of information because this function subsumes large parts of the others. To understand this function, it is necessary to consider the beginnings of the American experience, and the weaving of the press into the fabric of the American system of government.

DEVELOPMENT OF THE PRESS IN THE UNITED STATES

The press had proved during the Revolution that it was a significant force in America. As the founders pondered the form of the new government, James Madison suggested the central role for the press:

Knowledge will forever govern ignorance. And a people who mean to be their own governors must arm themselves with the power knowledge gives. A popular government without popular information or the means of acquiring it, is but a prologue to a farce, or a tragedy, or perhaps both (Hunt, 1910:398).

Thomas Jefferson made much the same point in a different way. Referring to Shay's Rebellion, which seemed to him to be a consequence of ignorance, he wrote:

> The way to prevent these irregular interpositions of the people, is to give them full information of their affairs through the channels of the public papers, and to contrive that these papers penetrate the whole mass of the people. The basis of our government being the opinion of the people, the very first object should be to keep that right; and were it left to me to decide whether we should have a government without newspapers or newspapers without a government, I should not hesitate a moment to prefer the latter (Ford, 1899:69).

Similar quotations from other framers of the American system can be multiplied, but it should suffice to add one from the addresses of Patrick Henry. On other matters Henry was often in disagreement with Madison and Jefferson, but his thoughts on the necessity for an informed public opinion strike the same chord:

> The liberties of the people never were, or never will be, secure, when the transactions of their rulers may be concealed from them .... I am not an advocate of divulging indiscriminately all the operations of government, though the practices of our ancestors, in some degree, justified it. Such transactions as relate to military operations or affairs of great consequence, the immediate promulgation of which might defeat the interests of the community, I would not wish to be published, till the end which required their secrecy should have been effected. But to cover with the veil of secrecy the common routine of business, is an abomination in the eyes of every intelligent man (Henry, 1891:496).

Clearly, the founders considered informing the people to be central in a democracy, but they carefully refrained from setting up an official information system. Instead, the informing function was turned over to the press. In effect, the press—privately owned, beyond official control—was incorporated into the machinery of government.

Surely, some of the genius of the American idea flows from the fact that the apparatus of information was involved in governing in a way that insured its freedom from any particular administration. Instead of employing controls of censorship, the founders left to the press a significant responsibility of governance.

Officials from the first have had to adapt to the anomaly of an information system that is *of*, but not *in*, the government. This established a natural struggle between the men of the press and the men of the official government. It is no accident that the "strong" presidents revered by many historians and political scientists—Washington, Jefferson, Jackson, Lincoln, Theodore Roosevelt, and Franklin Roosevelt—are also the presidents who have most adroitly used the press. Much of the history of American government pivots on the use of the press as an instrument of political power.

Those who established the firm footing of the United States in its earliest years were eminently practical in their use of the press. The stern figure of George Washington becomes much less austere viewed through the prism of his worried statement to Alexander Hamilton regarding the Farewell Address:

> The doubt that occurs at first view is the length of it for a News Paper publication.... All the columns of a large Gazette would scarcely, I conceive, contain the present draught (Pollard, 1947:23).

Earlier, both Jefferson and Washington had revealed their essential practicality while Jefferson was serving in Washington's cabinet. Alexander Hamilton, Washington's chief lieutenant, had established *The Gazette of the United States* to trumpet the cause of Washington's Federalists. Eager to develop an editorial voice for Anti-Federalism, Jefferson tried to enlist Philip Freneau, a talented poet-journalist who had become famous as the "Poet of the Revolution."

Freneau declined Jefferson's first offer. Lamenting the rejection, Jefferson revealed in a letter to Madison how much favoritism he was willing to bestow on a right-thinking editor:

> I should have given him the perusal of all my letters of foreign intelligence and all foreign newspapers; the publication of all proclamations & other public notices within my department & the printing of all laws... (Pollard, 1947:23).

Later, the itch for a newspaper that would speak for him led Jefferson to woo Freneau again by letter:

> The clerkship for foreign languages in my office is vacant; the salary, indeed, is very low, being but two hundred and fifty dollars a year; but it also gives so little to do as not to interfere with any other office one may choose... (Pollard, 1947:23).

The sinecure lured him. Freneau moved to Philadelphia and established *The National Gazette*, which soon became the loudest Anti-Federalist voice. It was also the leading critic of President Washington. The attacks were "outrages on common decency," the president protested. He questioned Jefferson closely regarding Freneau's reason for coming to Philadelphia. Jefferson replied that he had simply lost his translating clerk and had hired Freneau to replace him. "I cannot recollect," Jefferson told Washington, "whether it was at that time, or afterwards, that I was told he had thought of setting up a newspaper." In any case, Jefferson pointed out, he could control his employee only in the clerkship; Freneau was a free agent while he was editing *The National Gazette*.

Washington did not ask that Freneau be fired, but he could not control his anger. Jefferson described one scene that took place at a cabinet meeting held shortly after Freneau had published a scalding satire on Washington:

> The President was much inflamed, got into one of those passions when he cannot command himself, ran on much on the personal abuse which had been bestowed on him, defied any man on earth to produce one single act of his since he had been in the government which was not done on the purest motives, that he had not repented but once the having slipped the moment of resigning his office, and that was every moment since.... That *that* rascal *Freneau* sent him three of his papers every day as if he thought he would become the distributor of his papers (Pollard, 1947:15).

When Jefferson himself was elected president, he found that none of the Washington and New York newspapers had sent reporters to chronicle the movement of the capital from Philadelphia to Washington. He persuaded a young printer named Samuel Harrison Smith to set up shop on the mudflats of the Potomac, luring him with printing-contract patronage. Smith's *National Intelligencer* was the preeminent newspaper for more than a decade, and it served Jefferson well (Cater, 1959:76–77).

When Andrew Jackson became president, he established the *Washington Globe*. Its editor, Amos Kendall, was so significant a member of the famed Kitchen Cabinet that a congressman of the time declared: "He was the President's thinking machine, his writing machine—aye, and his lying machine." Jackson was not content, however, to have only a single organ grinding his tune. At one point, fifty-seven journalists were reported to have been on the government payroll (Cater, 1959).

The party press began to wane after Jackson, but the period was far from tranquil. This was the time when American newspapers, which had always been aimed at the most literate, began to appeal to the masses. Other editors had tried to establish "penny papers," but none was successful until Benjamin H. Day brought out his *New York Sun* in 1833. Before the *Sun*, editors had been charging six to ten dollars a year in advance for subscriptions—more than many a skilled worker could earn in a week. Day's *Sun* was not only inexpensive, it emphasized local news, especially human interest, crime, and violence. The *Sun* soon had a circulation of 8,000.

The *Sun* and the other penny papers were certainly sensational, but they achieved what the sober journals failed utterly to do: They appealed to the common man and helped to make him literate. More important, they made him believe that he, too, had a voice in the leading affairs of his time, for they mixed in with the sensationalism readable reports on domestic and foreign governments.

The Civil War and Reconstruction periods brought on a marked change in the American press. Slowly, the press was working itself free of predictable partisanship. Although most newspapers continued to align themselves with one party or another ideologically, hardly any were dependent upon party allegiance.

The party press was all but dead in 1860, when the Government Printing Office was established, thus cutting off many of the lucrative printing contracts that Washington papers had enjoyed. The party press declined, too, because of the establishment and growth of Washington bureaus of the strong New York newspapers. A president or a congressional leader could benefit only moderately from establishing a party organ when alert reporters for James Gorden Bennett's *New York Herald* or Horace Greeley's *New York Tribune* were covering Washington more ably than any Washington newspaper could. And by this time, the Associated Press was distributing dispassionate reports to a variety of papers, ushering in the period of "objective reporting."

Thus began the era of independence that was to shape a concept of self that the press has never relinquished.

From the end of the Civil War to the end of the nineteenth century, power was atomized in the world of the American press. Editors discovered that their influence was not dependent on party affiliation. Instead of seeking support from party leaders, they sought to build their own centers of strength among readers.

The result was a series of experiments somewhat like the "penny press" era of the early nineteenth century. The difference was that America itself was changing radically during the latter part of the century. In *Rise of the City, 1878–1898*, Arthur M. Schlesinger (1932) analyzes the exploding urbanization of the period. During the decade from 1880 to 1890, more than five million immigrants came to the United States. Nearly four million arrived in the following decade.

The press was changing to meet the new conditions of American life. The number of newspapers increased from 850 in 1880 to 1,967 in 1900. More important, whereas 10 percent of all adults were subscribers in 1880, 26 percent subscribed in 1900. This came about not only because of increased educational opportunities and a revolution in printing technology, but especially because of the promotion of a new journalism of the common man. Led by Joseph Pulitzer and William Randolph Hearst (whose contests with Pulitzer brought on yellow journalism), metropolitan newspapers invited the immigrants into the American community with splashy crusades and stunts. Himself an immigrant, Pulitzer set forth his essential aims in a signed statement in the first issue of his *New York World*:

> There is room in this great and growing city for a journal that is not only cheap but bright, not only bright but large, not only large but truly Democratic—dedicated to the cause of the people rather than that of the purse-potentates—devoted more to the news of the New than the Old World—that will expose all fraud and sham, fight all public evils and abuses—that will serve and battle for the people with earnest sincerity (*New York World*, May 11, 1883).

Pulitzer allowed Hearst to push him into sensationalism, and Hearst carried journalism into outrageous fiction. Other editors were similarly extravagant. For good or ill, these were the people's universities and a universal sideshow as the nineteenth century ended. That they were also deeply involved in affairs of great moment is generally agreed by historians of the period. There is no questioning the fact that Hearst promoted the Spanish-American War with relentless propaganda. He sent a famous illustrator, Frederic Remington, to Cuba. Remington cabled: "Everything is quiet. There is no trouble here. There will be no war. Wish to return." Hearst responded: "Please remain. You furnish the pictures and I'll furnish the war" (Mott, 1962:529).

Similar arrogance—and power—appeared in the pronunciamentos of other lords of the press at the end of the nineteenth century. Much of it grew from the fact that newspapers, most of which had long been shoestring enterprises, had suddenly become established institutions of the industrial order.

Lincoln Steffens, that keen analyst of American institutions, took a long look at newspaper journalism across the United States in 1897 and shared with the readers of *Scribner's Magazine* just what he had found. Talking shop the previous spring, the executive heads of two-score great newspapers had spoken of their properties as factories, he reported, and had likened the management of their editorial departments to that of department stores. "Journalism today is a business," he wrote with a little of the awe of discovery.

And with the beginning of the new century, journalism had become a very big business. It had left far behind the personal journalism of colonial days and the party organs of the first half of the nineteenth century. Education, industrialization, mass production of newspapers—all had combined with shrewd editorial judgment to turn the craft of journalism into an industry. Pulitzer's *World*, which he had bought for $346,000 in 1883, was deemed to be worth $10 million little more than a decade later. It employed 1,300 (Emery, 1962:386). Many other papers, especially those that promoted themselves as "people's champions," were similarly large. Circulations in the hundreds of thousands were becoming common.

The business of journalism gave rise to allied businesses, especially the press associations. They began with the great European financial houses, the Fuggers and the Rothschilds, and flowered with the ideas of a German named Reuter and a Frenchman named Havas. In the middle of the nineteenth century, the Reuter Agency in England, the Havas Agency in France, and the Wolff Agency in Germany divided up the world with a news cartel. The United States was part of Reuter's territory, but he found that a number of American publishers had in 1848 organized a cooperative agency called the Associated Press. Because the British government did not relish diplomatic difficulty with the United States over a relatively small matter, British officials persuaded Reuter that he should cooperate rather than compete with AP. He persuaded Havas to let AP into the cartel, although formal membership had to wait until 1887.[1]

So it was that the AP was able to grow during its early years with little competition. Although the cooperative arrangement with the cartel restricted AP largely to the United States until the end of the nineteenth century, it had by then become the chief source of national news. Its arrangement with the cartel also made AP the chief distributor of international news.

In 1907, the Scripps family, owners of several newspapers that could not buy AP service because of AP's exclusive-franchise agreements with competing papers, organized the United Press Associations. Then Hearst formed his International News Service. By 1920, UP had made contracts with a number of Latin American papers. AP followed UP into Latin America. Then UP began to cooperate with several

[1] The best summary of the beginnings of the world press associations is White and Leigh (1960). Much of this material comes from this source.

British newspapers, which formed the British United Press. The tight cartel was broken, in part because of the growth of UP, in part because Germany's defeat in 1918 had removed the Wolff Agency from contention. AP and UP grew rapidly then, and in 1958 UP took over INS and became United Press International. Although newspapers like the *New York Times* and the *Chicago Daily News* and broadcasting networks like NBC and CBS began to set up their own large and able news-gathering organizations, AP and UPI remained the basic services.

Growing also were the syndicates that supply features on a contract basis. Syndication began in 1861 when Ansel Kellogg, the publisher of a small Wisconsin newspaper, began to supply other small papers with "insides"—entire pages or inside-page filler material. Irving Bacheller began a similar service for metropolitan papers in 1884. By the first quarter of the twentieth century, syndicates were an integral part of American journalism, with Hearst's King Features, which had been established in 1896, well on its way to domination.

Magazines, too, were becoming giants as the twentieth century began. Although Andrew Bradford had published the first American magazine in 1741 (a few days before Benjamin Franklin had founded the second), for more than a century the magazines were enfeebled by small circulations, too little advertising, and limited editorial vision. Not until the 1890s were S. S. McClure, Frank Munsey, and Cyrus Curtis able to bring magazine content into harmony with the tastes and interests of the great middle class. Munsey put *Munsey's Magazine* on sale at ten cents in 1893, Curtis began to sell his *Saturday Evening Post* at five cents a short time later. Both began to teach other magazine publishers what they had learned from newspapers: that with reading material for the masses they could sell their publications at less than cost, draw huge lists of readers, and lure advertising dollars with high readership. Shortly after the turn of the century, the *Ladies Home Journal* became the first magazine to reach a circulation of one million. Edward W. Bok, the editor, achieved that level by giving women readers practical advice on running a home and rearing a family, by trying to elevate their standards in art and architecture, and by crusading against public drinking cups and patent medicines.

This was the period, too, when the muckrakers—Steffens, Ida Tarbell, Ray Stannard Baker, and others—were exerting a stunning impact on government with their exposés. The second of Steffens' "Shame of the Cities" articles began:

> Whenever anything extraordinary is done in American municipal politics, whether for good or evil, you can trace it almost invariably to one man. The people do not do it. Neither do the "gangs," "combines," or political parties. These are but instruments by which bosses (not leaders; we Americans are not led, but driven) rule the people and commonly sell them out. But there are at least two forms of the autocracy which has supplanted the democracy here as it has everywhere it has been tried. One is that of the organized majority by which, as in Tammany Hall in New York and the Republican machine in Philadelphia, the boss has normal control of more than half the voters. The other is that of the adroitly managed minority. The "good people" are herded into parties and stupefied with convictions and a name, Republican or Democrat; while the "bad people" are so organized or interested by the boss that he can wield their votes to enforce terms and decide elections. St. Louis is a conspicuous example of this form. Minneapolis is another. Colonel Ed. Butler is the unscrupulous opportunist who handled the non-partisan minority which turned St. Louis into a "boodle town." In Minneapolis "Doc" Ames was the man (Steffens, 1903:1).

The influence of the work of Steffens and the other muckrakers helped usher in the age of the reporter in American journalism. By-lines, which were used sparingly or not at all in many newspapers in the nineteenth century, also helped reporters. So, too, did the practices of the press associations. At first AP was a combine of like-minded publishers, and a reporter who slanted his stories to please one publisher pleased them all. Then AP expanded, taking in publishers with other prejudices. Soon, it served many papers of varying political persuasions, and slowly developed a style of "objective reporting" so that any paper could safely use any story.

Reporters for newspapers helped the press-association men develop the form. So it was that even as newspaper proprietors gained strength financially, they lost some of their control over their product. When the correspondent in a state capital, Washington, or a foreign capital could routinely file to his home office "straight" stories that bowed not at all to the partisanship or the whims of the proprietor, naturally he felt a large degree of independence. Not many newspaper proprietors surrendered their coutrol easily or happily—and a few have not yet surrendered it—but most relinquished it slowly as the twentieth century began.

Events since then have enhanced the independence of most reporters. The coming of the Newspaper Guild and such journalistic societies as Sigma Delta Chi and Theta Sigma Phi have helped reporters develop a sense of professionalism that has strengthened their independence. The result during this century has been significant. Officialdom, which once dealt and jousted primarily with editors and publishers, has increasingly had to deal and joust with reporters instead. Republicans, who had once been secure in the knowledge that most newspaper proprietors were Republican, began to complain while Franklin Roosevelt was president that the liberalism and Democratic orientation of the reporters more than made up for the conservatism of the proprietors. In 1962, the day after Richard Nixon lost his race for governor of California, he made it clear in his celebrated "last press conference" just how bitter he was.

He attacked President Kennedy for cutting off White House subscriptions to the hostile *New York Herald Tribune*: "Unlike some people, I've never canceled a subscription to a paper and also I never will" (forgetting that on two occasions of high anger he had canceled subscriptions to the *Washington Post*. A few days later, he canceled the *Los Angeles Times*. For Nixon, this was an acquired distaste. The paper had supported him editorially in every campaign, including the contest for the governorship. But while the *Times* had been lopsidedly for him before, it was scrupulous about giving the Democrats an even break in the news columns this time).

But Nixon's most savage criticism was aimed at the reporters. He was harsh about the coverage of the gubernatorial race, beginning with, "Now that all the members of the press are so delighted that I have lost," and ending with a plea that the mass media "put one lonely reporter on the campaign who will report what the candidate says now and then." Nixon attacked the *Los Angeles Times* by name. Carl Greenberg was the only reporter "who wrote every word I said," Nixon charged.[2]

The press as a communication system for government information, then, has over the decades developed these characteristics:

It is, as it has been from the beginning, a broker of information, gathering news from the halls of government and dissem-

---

[2] Greenberg was embarrassed by the accolade, but he need not have feared that he would be suspected of slanting his reporting in Nixon's direction. On at least one occasion, the Republican candidate was quoted as calling President Kennedy a "carpetbagger" for invading California to help Governor Brown. When Nixon denied later that he had ever used the term *carpetbagger*, Greenberg quietly pointed out in print that he had used the word three times.

Several reporters were incensed by Nixon's self-appreciative estimate of his own attitudes toward the press: "Never in my sixteen years of campaigning have I complained to a publisher, to an editor, about the coverage of a reporter." Actually, Nixon had complained only a few weeks earlier about Richard Bergholz of the *Los Angeles Times*.

inating it among the people. The new communication media have reduced the effectiveness of this role to some degree because it is possible for a president who does not fear overexposure to go directly to the people through radio and television. But other officials (even U.S. senators) cannot command such attention. Moreover, as the print media become less important as purveyors of news events, they become more important as interpreters. With radio and television telling what happened—and telling it first—the press must emphasize why it happened—exact the meaning of the words and place them in a substantial context. This is seldom pleasing to officials, most of whom would prefer to have their own views go unchallenged and uninterpreted.

When Nixon became president, he tried to reduce the role of the press as interpreter by limiting the Washington correspondents' opportunities to question and challenge his programs and policies. His immediate predecessor, Lyndon Johnson, had held fifty press conferences during his first two years in office. In their first two years, John F. Kennedy had held forty-six conferences, and Dwight Eisenhower had held fifty-eight. But in *his* first two years, Nixon held only eighteen press conferences, fewer than one a month.

Rather than submitting to questions, Nixon seemed to prefer to report directly to the American people through radio and television. At first, the networks broadcast analyses of the president's statements immediately after they were made, with newscasters and commentators exploring the meaning and probable consequences of presidential pronouncements, and sometimes pointing up misleading statements. Then Vice President Spiro Agnew attacked, and the "instant analyses," as they had come to be called, began to fade away.

Moreover, the reponsible press is an adversary to government. The stance of many a journalist as he confronts a public official is a mixture of tact and antagonism, cooperation and conflict. This does not mean that there is a natural enmity between the press and the government, nor does it mean that reporters and public officials are enemies. It means that the American press takes as a duty the seeking out of abuses of power.

If all this presents a picture of journalist and public official forever circling each other warily, the official protecting his jugular, it is misleading. They are adversaries much as lawyers in a courtroom are adversaries; the system decrees it. In fact, like the lawyers, the journalist and the public official may be the best of friends during social hours (and some journalists are guilty of letting social-hour friendships erode the adversary stance).

One of the best commentaries on the adversary role came, curiously, from a former public official, Pat Brown. He wrote to his successor as governor of California, Ronald Reagan:

> There's a passage in *War and Peace* that every new Governor with a big majority should tack on his office wall. In it young Count Rostov, after weeks as the toast of elegant farewell parties, gallops off on his first cavalry charge and then finds real bullets snapping at his ears.
>
> "Why, they're shooting at me," he says. "Me, whom everybody loves."
>
> Nothing worse will happen to you in the next four years. Learn to live with that; the rest is easy.
>
> As you must have noticed by now, the press fires the first real bullets at new governors. And the hardest lesson to learn is that it is futile to fire back. Never get into an argument with a newspaper unless you own it. A newspaper fails to get in the last word only if it goes broke in mid-debate.
>
> Publishers in California generally will be more tolerant of a governor before he raises taxes, much as a young man will take more nonsense from a fiancee whose father is rich. But you will be amazed at how easily even a friendly publisher's tolerance is strained by trivial matters—a freeway route through his backyard; a rollback in government construction in his city; failure to follow his advice on the appointment of a judge.
>
> There is also not much I can tell you about

the weekly news conference that you haven't already learned. You will find that while both surgeons and reporters operate with professional detachment there is only one real difference between them. Surgeons make more money for cutting you up.

But their motives are the same—to make sure everything is running properly. And in the case of the press, they operate with a proxy from the voters. For the voters, news conferences are as close to a first-hand accounting of what happened to their money as they ever get....

Invest as much time preparing for these inquisitions as you can spare, but don't feel bad if you are caught off-guard. I can still hear a voice from the back of the room asking: "Governor, do you think lobbyists should be required to wear little green buttons on their lapels?" Maybe you would have a ready answer for that. I didn't.

Harrowing as they are, news conferences do provide a chance for correspondents to bore in, a practice that philosophers find a healthy thing for the democratic process. Few governors take any comfort in that.

One last word about dealing with reporters. If you don't want it in the papers, don't do it (*San Francisco Chronicle*, February 27, 1967:1).

It should be pointed out hastily that some officials deserve sympathy because they may be faced with brilliant reporters—or with mediocre reporters, and reporters who are often in error but seldom in doubt. Several thoughtful journalists who served one year as the Freedom of Information Committee of Sigma Delta Chi asked these questions about the attitudes of journalists toward the secret sessions of government bodies which so inflame the press:

1. Is the star chamber session actually one in which public officials are discussing things which belong in the public prints? For example: Premature publicity on a city council's plan to condemn private property for a street or parks project might artificially inflate the price of property under consideration. The council members feel an obligation to the taxpayers and hope to arrange a good deal for them. If the proposition they are considering is actually on the up-and-up, they would not hesitate to tell the newspaper about it for background purposes. But do they have the assurance that the newspaper is as interested in acting with patience and restraint in the public interest as it is in obtaining a story and printing it—regardless of its implications?
2. Are public officials given enough protection against inaccurate, adolescent, or outright malicious treatment of "sensitive" information. Do competitive pressures by two or more newspapers force reporters to betray confidence after they have been admitted to executive sessions of public officials? Are the stories the reporter writes published as written? Or are they jazzed up to his embarrassment and to the humiliation of his news sources?
3. When news and information are withheld or suppressed, does the newspaper enter its complaint on sound ground and with clean hands?
   (*a*) Does the paper have a consistent and generally unimpeachable record of having tried to cover the area of news in contention with intelligent, knowledgeable, and trustworthy reporters? Or is it asserting its traditional rights to information through personnel who are demonstrably unfit to treat it with perspective, balance, and comprehension?
   (*b*) Does the paper burden the source of information by spasmodic attention which demands time-consuming explanations of the obvious, the only alternative being a distorted and possibly damaging report?
   (c) Is the information sought and published in an objective manner, or is it treated as an instrument of editorial policy preconceived by the front office?
4. Are objections to the suppression and withholding of information asserted and argued personally by responsible people in a manner that is considerate, logical, and convincing? Or do the objections take the form of personal recrimination, arbitrary criticism, or reckless insinuation?
5. Are newspapers alert enough and consistent enough in their insistence upon "all the news that's fit to print"? Or do some of them invite indifference to release of news through neglect of offices upon which they are supposed to keep a sharp eye? Are not some

newspapers guilty of encouraging news suppression that they may promote a certain candidacy, a pet project, or protect a special set of friends? (*Quill*, January 1953:7).

Working together, journalists and officials have developed policies on attributing news that allow officials to disclose more information than they could if the simple system of "Senator John Jones said today" were always used. The policies are not foolproof.

Misunderstandings arise fairly often because even the most basic conventions of political reporting are so varied. A few inexperienced correspondents, and many public officials, simply do not understand the most widely used terminology. *Off the record* means that the information is for the correspondent's general understanding and is not to be reported in any form. *Background only* means that the information may be reported, but not attributed to its source. *Not for direct quotation* means that information may be reported and the source named, but the correspondent must paraphrase, using neither quotation marks nor the official's exact words. (An ancient convention, this was devised to enable presidents and secretaries of state to speak without fear that slips of the tongue would bring serious consequences.)

Too often, officials who actually intend to offer information for background only will say, "This is off the record," or, "Don't quote me directly." Some who want to speak off the record say, "This is for background only," thinking that the correspondents will not report the information but will use it only for their background understanding of issues. On Capitol Hill, some congressmen who have been around nearly forever occasionally use phrases unfamiliar to the younger correspondent. "This is neither *from* me nor *for* me" is intended to mean that the information may be reported but should not be attributed to the source or his friends. To many correspondents, it means nothing.

Alfred Friendly, the former managing editor of the *Washington Post*, once wrote a long memorandum to clarify the most common terms for his staff. Widely read throughout the press corps, the memo gives reporters considerable latitude in applying the off-the-record convention. A correspondent may seek the same information from another source, Friendly wrote, provided that he does not indicate that he has heard the news.

> If he accepts the off-the-record convention as to information itself, he usually may use it upon its public disclosure somewhere else.... In a public meeting or gathering, open to all without specific invitation, any attempt by a speaker to put all or part of his remarks off the record may be firmly and blandly ignored as an absurdity.

During the 1960 presidential campaign, the Protestant preachers who were dubbed "the Peale Group" (after Norman Vincent Peale, one of their spokesmen) held a press conference in Washington to explain their opposition to a Catholic president. Nearly a hundred correspondents were on hand. When one speaker prefaced his remarks with, "Now this is off the record," the reporters ignored the injunction.

Friendly's memo warned against the sometimes slippery practice of disclosing off-the-record and background-only information to other correspondents. Such disclosures are not uncommon, in many cases because the correspondents simply enjoy talking politics and are proud of their inside information; at times because one who is bound to secrecy feels that the news he has is too important to be hidden and should be given to a correspondent who has not been tied up by a promise. Shortly after taking office, Defense Secretary Robert McNamara held an off-the-record briefing to announce that the "missile gap" about which Kennedy had made such an issue during his presidential campaign actually did not exist. Correspondents who had not attended the briefing learned of it from those who had, and promptly published it.

THE U.S. PRESS TODAY

In the 1970s it is still true that as long as the proprietor of a newspaper or magazine shows decent respect for a few laws, he may do what he likes with his publication. If he opposes the Democratic candidate for president—and he probably does—the candidate's name can be eliminated from the paper. If he hates golf, he can instruct his sports editor to forget that the game exists. If he visualizes thousands of little circles of family readers being offended by photos revealing the sex of naked animals, he can have his art department use an airbrush appropriately. The Democrats, the golfers, and the artists on his staff may rebel, readers may protest, a rival publication may thrive as a result, but the publisher's power in such cases is unmistakable.

His freedom springs from the libertarian philosophy on which this country was founded: that every man should speak and write his own thoughts. The clash of conflicting ideas, the founding fathers believed, would produce something called the Truth. That may have been useful philosophy when any literate man could start his own newspaper or magazine with little more than a shirttail full of type—although some of the things we have since learned about the way men develop and hold to their attitudes despite all the information available to them suggest that our forebears were probably stunningly uninformed.

Fortunately, publishers do not take full advantage of their freedom. Whether this is because they fear the financial consequences of indulging their whims and idiosyncracies, because they want to avoid the professional condemnation of their papers and their employees, or because they feel a sense of social responsibility, most publishers give space to the Democrats and the golfers and allow pictures of dogs and cows to run au naturel.

This does not mean that they are ultimately free and fair. In the beginning, publishing was controlled by the church, then by government, and now it is firmly embedded in the structure of business. Publishers maintain, usually correctly, that they are controlled neither by their business friends nor by their advertisers. They do not need to be. The businessman who runs a newspaper or magazine will nearly always understand the sanctity of the business ideology. His business is different from all the others—it is the only one guaranteed protection by the Constitution—and the color of the public interest is upon it. But even though his editorials may question the morality of individuals—sometimes those in business, more often those in government—they are not likely to question the basic structure of either the capitalist system or the governmental status quo.

All this is true even though the growth of a professional spirit among journalists has reduced the real power of the proprietors of newspapers and magazines. It is especially the case that publishers of small and relatively small newspapers are active in news decision-making, as is shown in a notable study by David R. Bowers (1967: 43). Very few employers will *order* a reporter to write a story that lies—rarely is it even suggested that a story be slanted—but the proprietor's policy fairly often is filtered into the news.

One of the best studies of this process was done by Warren Breed (1955). Breed found that many staff members assimilated policy almost by osmosis. The staff was affected by rewards and punishments, discussions and staff meetings, esteem for superiors, an "in-group" posture—all the subtle actions and attitudes that make up the atmosphere. Donohew (1967) made a similarly valuable study. He found that the attitude of the publisher toward Medicare was the chief factor in determining how newspapers handled Medicare news. It should be emphasized that neither of these studies showed or charged that the publishers *ordered* any particular policy. In fact, the whole point of both studies is that the publisher's attitudes need not be translated into orders; they are a heavy overlay on the atmosphere of the newsroom.

One factor that combats social control is the increasing difficulty in discerning company policy. The effort to appeal to masses of readers causes many publications to express fewer editorial attitudes or none at all for fear of offending readers; many others editorialize far less sternly than did the stentorian editors and publishers of an earlier day. Then, too, when newspapers and magazines were small, the publisher might work in the same room with his employees, or in the next room, and it was difficult to escape his opinions. Today, in sharp contrast, many reporters never even meet the publisher. And as newspaper and magazine chains grow larger, policy and the sense of a proprietor are often distant and indistinct.

Newspapers

Chains—newspaper executives prefer *groups*, which they consider a less pejorative term—have increased in size and number, among other reasons because creating mass markets that only large and costly units could service efficiently has led to concentration. Chains have also grown because, as *Business Week* made clear in "Why Newspapers Are Making Money Again" (August 29, 1970), newspapers are a growth industry.

Contrary to popular belief, the number of dailies has not declined significantly in recent years, even though many metropolitan dailies have died and less than 4 percent of all U.S. cities now have competing newspapers. It is also true that there are nearly 300 fewer dailies than there were in 1920. But there are only a dozen fewer dailies than there were in 1950 (1,772 to 1,760) and total circulation, about 62 million, has kept pace with population growth despite the coming of the electronic media.

Newspaper employment has grown by more than a third in the last twenty years, making the industry the fifth largest employer in the United States. Obviously, suburban and small-city papers have become much larger and stronger, as have the remaining metropolitan dailies, more than offsetting the loss of many metropolitan papers. *Editor & Publisher*, the trade weekly, which reports annually on the revenues and profits of three anonymous dailies that seem fairly typical, reported in 1970 that the 250,000-circulation paper recorded a profit rate of 23 percent of revenue before taxes, which is almost three times the rate for all U.S. manufacturing industries. The 55,000-circulation paper had a before-tax profit rate of 32.6 percent. The 96,000-circulation daily had before-tax profits of 20.3 percent. It is perhaps no wonder that newspapers are attractive and chains are growing.

But great size and monopoly characteristics bring problems, and one of the most important is indicated by the success of some of the underground papers. Among other reasons, the underground press flourishes because of the vast distance that now stretches between conventional newspapers and large segments of their potential audience. Decades ago, when many newspapers served many small publics in a single city, an editor could speak directly and somewhat personally to the central interests of most of his readers. But as newspapers grew larger, in part by swallowing their rivals, the editors tried to corral even larger audiences, which usually meant that they could neither appeal very strongly to one group nor offend another. The marketplace of ideas began to look more and more like a common denominator, and unorthodox thoughts gave way to the safe conventional wisdom.

The larger media have to some degree withdrawn from the people and have become parallel to and associated with other power centers such as business and government. In such circumstances, it is not surprising that many underground papers have been able to build close and enduring relationships with their readers by speaking directly to relatively homogenous groups. Nor is it surprising that conventional dailies have become aware that they do not reach the subcultures of society and have begun to move cautiously toward establishing lines of communication, perhaps primarily by using the printable language of youth.

There are, of course, other problems. Distribution in the increasingly crowded and dangerous metropolitan centers is a vexing one. A more important problem may be that the subscriber has become accustomed to paying far less for his newspaper than it costs; circulation income is only 20 to 25 percent of the average newspaper's total revenues, with advertising bringing in 75 to 80 percent. Circulation revenues do not even pay for the paper used by most newspapers (and many magazines), which readers could take to mean that the publication is not worth the paper it is printed on. Like magazines, however, newspapers have begun to move toward a more reasonable revenue balance. The fifteen-cent weekday issue had become fairly common in large cities by 1972.

Many foreign observers applaud the effort to achieve a more reasonable balance, but they believe the chief problem of the American newspaper is more basic. They admire American fact-gathering techniques (but think little of the writing that relates the facts), and they credit American publishing with technological innovations. But they deplore the sheer bulk of American newspapers, and they consider such size a wounding flaw.

In a 1967 speech reprinted by *Editor & Publisher*, Cecil King, publisher of the London *Daily Mirror*, echoed the thoughts of many foreigners. He argued that large publications are not essential for either communication or economic well-being. His own *Daily Mirror* had averaged twenty-six pages in 1966, only 36 percent was devoted to advertising—which produced only 32 percent of total revenues—and yet profits were $15 million in "a bad year." He said to American news executives:

> I regret that you have allowed advertising to dominate over editorial contents and by its bulk to create technical problems which destroy your impact and the possibility of good make-up, good photographic reproduction, and good printing.
>
> ... The American newspaper has achieved prosperity by turning itself into a bargain basement, a fate made possible by the unique willingness of your retailers to spend 2½% to 6% of turnover on advertising. The advertisers have been allowed to run riot, to occupy four-fifths of your space, to contribute four-fifths of your revenue. After the first page or two, in the typical American paper, all you get is a rivulet of news flowing sluggishly by a wide meadow which has been leased to some department store or supermarket (King, 1967: 19, 98).

King overstated the case somewhat. Relatively few American papers allow four-fifths of their revenue to come from advertising, and the typical American paper gives 55 to 65 percent of its space to advertising rather than four-fifths. But the economics and critical success of the *Wall Street Journal*, which is slender and far from dominated by advertising, may suggest that the principles King espoused can be made to work in the United States.

During recent years, many American editors and publishers have become concerned, if not actually nervous, about the monopoly power inherent in single-newspaper cities. Accordingly, even their editorial pages have become less partisan. Some of those with liberal leanings are now careful to publish at least one or two syndicated columnists who lean the other way. Some with conservative leanings seek liberal columnists. And, of course, some of those with strong political passions of one kind or the other publish a columnist of the opposite persuasion for window dressing only.

Despite the gradual drift away from fierce partisanship, a notable study by Ben Bagdikian (1964) shows that only one American newspaper in six has columnists balanced against its own opinion, only one in five strikes a real balance between liberal and conservative columns, and seven papers out of ten exhibit an imbalance heavily on the conservative side.

A later study persuaded Bagdikian (1966) that editorial pages were becoming less partisan. Assessing the power of the syndicated columnists in that study, Bagdikian traced their chief influence to the fact that decision-makers read them. The White House and the State Department are concerned because foreign embassies in Washington try to gauge American opinion from the work of the columnists. Significantly, many columns deal with the losing side of an argument over policy because the loser gives information to columnists to try to justify his position or to attempt to reverse the decision. This performs the important role of moving issues from the closed halls of government to the public arena.

Local news, which is by far the most expensive news to produce, makes up far less than half of the newshole of the average American daily. News from world capitals is provided, for most newspapers, by the Associated Press or United Press International, each of which serves more than one thousand newspapers and more than three thousand radio and television stations. Other news services—such as those provided by the *New York Times*, the *Chicago Daily News*, and the *Los Angeles Times-Washington Post*—serve scores or hundreds of papers, often with penetrating reportage that the huge wire services cannot match. But of the American-based services, only AP and UPI, each of which has about two thousand reporters, try to cover all the major news events every day. How their stories reach readers is worth examination. The detailed activities in the three reports which follow were produced by Daniel E. Garvey and John Mayo for a study (as yet unpublished) sponsored by The Rand Corporation. These reports represent several weeks of closely observing the operations of many newspapers.

A Suburban Afternoon Daily

Virtually all of this daily's state, national, and international news is received from an Associated Press wire and two United Press International wires. This news is processed by a news editor and his two assistants. In addition to making decisions on more than 100,000 words that come over these wires every day, these three men also edit and place all local news, which may run as high as 10,000 words a day, and select a dozen or so news pictures from approximately 100 provided by a wirephoto machine every day. Except for the society, sports, business, editorial, and comic pages, the three editors fill all the news columns.

The news editor does much of the work himself, discarding large quantities of wire copy and dividing the remaining stories among his assistants' desks and his own. Because all wire copy is received on punched tapes as well as on paper, editing consists largely of choosing between the AP and UPI versions of a story, checking for accuracy and typographical errors, and finding suitable cutting points for stories. The punched tapes can be set into type rapidly and inexpensively if few changes are made. These are strong arguments against thoughtful editing.

There is little rewriting, and little time for it. When the news editor arrived at 6:00 A.M. on one of the mornings when his work was being observed, he found approximately 50,000 words of wire copy. (The wire-service cycle for supplying news to afternoon papers begins shortly after midnight. Thus, most news editors who start work during the dawn hours find many stories waiting for them.) He swiftly discarded all but about 8,000 words. During the next seven hours, as the wires continued to spew stories, the news editor and his assistants used more than 20,000 words of wire copy (of a total of about 110,000 available—much of it useless because AP and UPI report many of the same events). They edited lightly, wrote headlines, placed stories on each page, and then sent the selected stories to the composing room to be put into type.

They also edited and placed about 6,000 words of local news, and selected and placed sixteen pictures. During the last hour of their working day, they prepared some material for the next day's edition—just as, the day before, they had devoted the final hour to preparing material for today's paper. During a single working day, then, they edited the rough equivalent of a small book. (In contrast, after a book manuscript is in hand, a publishing house customarily devotes at least six months, and often a year or more, to its editing and production.)

This thumbnail description ignores some of the underlying doubts that afflict the news editor. He knows that many of his readers will have already read elsewhere some of the stories he plays up, and that other readers will have been satisfied with the top-of-the-news sketches of the same stories heard on their car radios or seen on television. But he is concerned to provide for those readers who want more than they are able to get elsewhere.

Other questions and doubts arise. How much serious news can his readers take? How many of them will read yet another report on Vietnam, another story on the indecisive Paris peace talks, and still another report on the interminable battle between president and Congress? On the other hand, is the editor adequately serving those who follow such matters intently—they may be few but important people—if he publishes five-inch stories rather than twenty-inch stories?

Is the editor furthering the causes of rioters if he emphasizes their actions? Can a community really be informed if an editor decides to play down all news of conflict? If he answers the clamors of local critics and tries to balance stories of conflict with stories of cooperation, how many subscribers will actually read all the reports on the good works? If he boldly headlines a story of conflict, his paper will be accused of sensationalism. Reports on the "new morality"—and especially using the language that is its hallmark—will offend some older readers. Failing to give adequate attention to it will persuade many younger readers that they were right all along in thinking that the Establishment press was stodgy.

These are the demands imposed by the effort to inform and entertain a heterogeneous audience.

Thanks to court decisions made years ago, the suburban dailies now receive the same basic wire services (AP and UPI) that are available to the metropolitan papers. But they cannot obtain all the special services that most metropolitans purchase. Some of the special news services and some of the syndicates that supply news and features draw contracts—or have "understandings"—with metropolitan papers that close out the suburban papers. The metropolitans argue that their survival depends upon their ability to provide features that are unavailable to their competitors.

This explains, for example, the dreary comic strips that appear in some suburban papers. They are not offered because the editors believe that many of their readers will be enthralled by "Priscilla's Pop," and "Fred Bassett," but because the metropolitan papers publish "Peanuts" and "Bobby Sox" and "Dennis the Menace." Few metropolitan papers will permit their strips to appear in the suburban papers.

All metropolitan editors treasure the attractive comic strips, and some who discovered quite late which ones are attractive have used cash to wrest "Peanuts" and "Dennis the Menace" from the smaller papers that accurately forecast the popularity of the strips when they were first offered by the syndicates. Small-town papers may be able to assert territorial rights in some cases, but their contracts with syndicates have a way of running out, whereupon syndicate salesmen draw up more profitable contracts with metropolitan dailies.

There are other hazards in the jungle of comic-strip syndication. The editor who tries to jettison "Orphan Annie" because he and his staff are sickened by it soon has forty irate readers calling him regularly at 3:00 A.M. to protest.

Such are the problems of publishing suburban and small-town dailies. Like the metropolitans, these papers serve such a variety of readers—the leading banker in town and the janitor who cleans the bank, the college professor and the high school dropout—that this variety would seem to be problem enough. But the small daily editor must cope with the appeal of the metropolitan paper that looms next door, and with the local weekly that nibbles away in his own backyard.

A City Daily

In every newspaper observed, the pace in an office producing a morning paper was somewhat more relaxed than in offices producing evening papers. This does not mean that editors laze through their working hours. In fact, the editor who was by far the fastest worker observed processed world news for a morning paper. In general, deskmen for morning papers are able to work steadily rather than frenetically.

The pace is suggested by the operation of a city morning daily with a somewhat larger circulation than the suburban daily described above. Wire news is processed by the telegraph editor, who arrives shortly after 2:30 P.M. to begin work on the mass that has already accumulated. A copy girl who arrived earlier has stripped the copy from the wire machines and distributed it among the various desks (sports, society, etc.). Most of it goes to the telegraph editor, who had long before instructed the girl as to how he wants the news stacked and arranged.

Disciplined and orderly, the editor becomes absorbed. He is seemingly unhurried, but he works almost mechanically, pausing only now and then for a cup of coffee. His copyreader comes in at 5:00 P.M., but the telegraph editor delegates relatively little of the work. He has developed his system, and he is pleased with it. He discards story after story with only a glance. Some of the stories he selects are pencil-edited and passed to the copy girl to send to the composing room by pneumatic tube. Others are set aside in neat piles, later to be discarded or pieced into another story with pencil, scissors, and paste. This paper does not use punched tape, and thus the telegraph editor has the freedom really to edit a story rather than merely print what the wire services provide.

The managing editor had arrived at 2:00 P.M. By 3:00 P.M., the news editor and the county editor are on hand. The paper tries to cover a far-flung county. During the next hour, all of them confer briefly with the telegraph editor. Then they go to their desks. It becomes clear that, unlike the suburban daily described earlier, this is decentralized operation. The managing editor is chiefly a supervisor who advises the subeditors on important matters and devotes much of his remaining time to mail, syndicated columns, and administrative decision. Nonetheless, on the evening his work was observed, the managing editor processed more than 6,000 words of syndicated material and press releases.

The tempo does not seem to vary greatly during the evening. Everyone works steadily until about 9:00 P.M., then in a more relaxed fashion until 10:00 P.M., when the first edition must be locked up, printed, and transported nearly a hundred miles. At this time, only the county editor and his copyreader, who are still receiving stories from reporters in outlying cities and who must prepare pages for four regional editions, are still hard at work. The hours from 10:00 P.M. to midnight are relaxed for most of the others. Night baseball scores and a few other late items complete the day.

And yet the lack of frenzy is deceptive. For not only are there more editors and copyreaders at work here than work on the suburban afternoon paper described above—twice as many, in fact—their duties are spread across more hours. The effective hours of work for most of those who produce afternoon papers are 6:00 A.M. to noon, with the noon hours devoted to late-breaking items. The effective hours for the paper described, and for most other morning newspapers, are 2:00 or 3:00 P.M. to midnight, and sometimes later.

The production of the editors of this morning paper suggests the degree of deception. Consider only the material used by the telegraph editor and the news editor. In all, the telegraph editor and his copyreader processed nearly 18,000 words. From 3:00 to 10:00 P.M., the news editor and his copyreader (whose task was somewhat simpler because much of the material they considered was preselected by the telegraph editor) processed 23,600 words (about ninety stories). In addition, the news desk prepared 3,200 words for the Sunday edition. Thus, together the telegraph editor and the news editor edited and placed nearly 45,000 words and fourteen photos.

A Metropolitan Daily

Although "the larger the paper, the larger the staff" is a satisfactory rule of thumb, it is not necessarily true that a huge staff reduces the pressures on deskmen. A metropolitan daily not only subscribes to many more services than does a suburban newspaper or a small-city daily; it is likely to do much more with what comes in.

The editors of a metropolitan paper of nearly half a million circulation who were interviewed for this study scoffed at the papers that publish wire copy from punched tape (like the suburban paper described above) and had little more to say for those that piece together two or more wire reports (like the city daily). The metropolitan city editor, an acid man, said of wire reports: "They're like the symphonies you hear on recordings, with one movement coming from this performance, another from that one. The whole thing never really happened." He cited examples of wire reports that he had found to be lacking in details, riddled with minor errors, or wrong. (This editor is probably unduly negative in his total condemnation of the wire services. It is true, though, that many editors complain that they find wire-service reports on events in their areas misleading.)

Some wire stories do find their way into this metropolitan daily without change, but most of these are reports from locales the fifty-man city staff or the small staff of state capital, Washington, and foreign correspondents cannot reach. The editors make a manful effort to check out everything. Trips to the sites of important stories are fairly frequent. Calls to California, Texas, and Cuba are common. At the very least, subeditors will check the reports of one service against another, and piecing together a story from several submitted by AP, UPI, and special-report services is routine.

Not only is there thorough checking and rewriting of wire-service reports as well as the stories provided by special services—most of it by the city editor's staff—there is a constant and mind-rattling spewing of reports from twenty-two machines. The staff hold that all these services are essential to produce the five major editions and the three replates (editions with minor changes) that come out every day. The staff opposes producing so many different papers—the city editor holds that the hastily produced first edition is "the worst newspaper in the world"—but management believes that all of them are necessary to retain the slender circulation edge over the competing daily.

Tensions are produced by the processes of multiple editing. Stories are stripped from the machines by copy boys in the wire room and most of them are handed via a pass-through to the wire editor in the newsroom. Appropriate stories are carried directly from the wire room to the sports and business editors; those that originated in the state go directly to the city editor. From the wire editor's desk, much of the copy goes to the foreign-national desk and to the city desk. Because the foreign-national editor is aided only by one rewrite man, while the city editor may command as many as twenty reporters and rewrite men during peak periods, some of the foreign and national stories go to the city desk for checking and rewriting.

From the various desks, rewritten copy goes to the news editor. He makes final decisions about publishing it, then passes the stories he has selected to the makeup editor, who assigns each a place in the paper. The stories then go to the copy editor, who parcels them out to the copyreaders on the rim of the universal desk for final editing and headlines. The stories are returned to the copy editor, who sends them to the composing room via pneumatic tube. The complexity of the operation promotes jurisdictional disputes and ragged nerves.

Although there are slack periods, editing this metropolitan daily—which is an afternoon paper even though one of its many editions is available at almost any time—is virtually a twenty-four-hour operation. Observation began at 6:00 P.M., when the work was relaxed. During the next seven hours until 1:00 A.M., fewer than fifty stories were sent to the composing room. From 1:00 A.M. to 11:00 A.M. was the high point: twenty to thirty stories an hour moved for nine hours, with forty-one moving between 10:00 and 11:00 A.M. The pace slowed during the afternoon and dropped off sharply at the beginning of the new publishing cycle at 6:00 P.M.

Because the city desk and the foreign-national desk handle wire copy and the rewritten stories that spring from it, they process substantially more copy than does the wire desk, which does little more with most stories than pass them along to the appropriate desk. On the day the operation was observed, the city desk handled more than 150,000 words (almost 900 items), about 12 percent of which was used. The foreign-national desk handled nearly 90,000 words (more than 400 stories), and used less than 10 percent.

In all, the metropolitan daily handled nearly 2,500 wire items made up of more than 400,000 words. (This figure, like the figure for the other papers, does not include sports, society, business, and editorial pages.) The staff used more than 40,000 words (approximately 300 stories). Although the quantity of the smaller operations described earlier compares favorably with this, the quality is not at all similar. The editing of the metropolitan paper was much less productive per man-hour—and much more skeptical, vigorous, and intense.

Magazines

Pasted on the wall at eye level above a typewriter in the office of a movie-fan magazine editor is a small picture of a young girl who works as a sales clerk in a Woolworth store. The editor has never met her; he keeps the picture in view to remind him of his primary readership. When he chooses and edits stories and photographs, he thinks of the tastes of the young girl.

This is a pointed illustration of a basic fact about magazines: most are written and edited for particular audiences. The illustration may be too pointed; few editors restrict their view of the audience so severely, and many would deny that anything more graphic than a vague, out-of-focus picture of any special audience is possible. Nothing is more obvious, however, than the fact that most magazines, unlike newspapers, do not attempt to appeal simultaneously to the bank president and the janitor who sweeps up, the teller and his eleven-year-old son.

Better than most of the others who work in mass communication, magazine journalists understand that thinking of one great mass as the "public" is our favorite folly. The world, a nation, a city, a small town—each by the fact of its existence represents a single community of interest, but each also embraces a multitude of varying interests and concerns. A small township is actually a patchwork of groups that may be considered "publics." There are as many publics as there are groups with varying levels of income, education, taste, and civic awareness, as many as there are groups with varying political allegiances, different religious loyalties, and so on. What concerns and convinces one public may be trivia to another.

All this helps to explain what has been happening in the magazine world. During the first half of the twentieth century, the big general magazines—*Collier's*, *Saturday Evening Post*, *Coronet*, and the like—were able to lure several million subscribers by shrewdly appealing to literate people in several different publics. They were able to do so because, as Theodore White (1960: 80–81) has observed, for the first time

> the whole country is one market, you can make one brand image for the nation and deliver—but only if you can find a way of talking to the whole country at once. They need a big horn—a horn that will reach everybody.

Speaking of the editors who ran the mass-circulation magazines, White wrote,

> It was the first time anybody except the President of the United States had to sit in an office and think about this whole damned country all at once. Some editor had to think not just what the local people in Chicago, or New York, or Charleston, or San Francisco might want to read, but what would hold an audience together across the whole land, from coast to coast.

The big general magazines were successful also because advertising paid most of their costs. This became painfully clear when television became the chief medium for general information and entertainment and lured advertising away from the general magazine. Lewis Gillenson, the last editor of *Coronet*, one of the many mass magazines that died, pointed out:

> Contemplate the cost of a subscription. A giant weekly publisher begs you to sign up for a year with an enticing "9 cents a copy" offer. The magazine sells weekly on the newsstand for 25 cents. The following are, roughly, average costs to the publisher: production, 40 cents; mailing, 4 cents; fulfillment, billing, delinquency, 3 cents. Total, 47 cents. In all, the magazine is behind 38 cents an issue on subscriptions, or about $20 for the year. Multiply this figure by three million, a reasonable estimate of the number of cut-rate subscribers a big magazine might carry, and you begin to get an idea of the deficit that must be made up by advertising (Gillenson, 1962: 36).

Before midcentury, there were a dozen weekly magazines of general appeal. Now there is none. *Life* was the last to go. After several years of operating in the red, it finally ceased publication with the December 29, 1972 issue.

This is not to say that magazines are moribund, only that general magazines are. There is evidence, in fact, that the magazine world as a whole is stronger than ever. As the general magazines have weakened and disappeared, the magazines of special interest—which seek out the individual publics—have become far stronger. It is noteworthy that some of the greatest new successes in publishing during the last twenty years are special-interest magazines: *Sports Illustrated*, *American Heritage*, *TV Guide*, and *Scientific American*. The Crowell Collier Company, which gave up on the mass-circulation *Collier's* nearly twenty years ago, is back in magazine publishing with no fewer than six magazines, all of them special interest.

A related change is described by a veteran magazine editor, Robert Stein:

> It used to be that we could cover almost any subject in a popular magazine by assigning a very good writer to go to a number of obvious sources, get the necessary facts and figures and dramatize them with a few anecdotes or individual experiences, then put it all together in a neat, well-rounded way. The result would be that the reader would be superficially informed, would quite possibly be entertained, but would be left with very little of real value to him.
>
> Now, on some of the most serious subjects, we find that we are investing as much as two years of time; that we're using not only writers, but (often) teams of researchers to help them. In some cases we're working with research organizations to do basic research which goes far beyond reporting, simply to find out what the reality of the situation is before we can figure out what we're going to say about it, how we're going to treat it in a magazine. This

is a growing trend because readers can discern the difference between an exploitation of their interest on the part of the magazine and the magazine's desire to serve their interest by clarifying confusion about issues that are important to them.

When I first started writing magazine articles on almost any subject of direct concern to the reader, I finished with ten rules on how to handle the subject. Well, the ten-easy-rules days are over, because any issue that can be treated with ten easy rules isn't worth considering in the first place (Newquist, 1967: 392–393).

To produce articles that will involve readers and to tailor publications to the special interests of audiences, many editors now rely less upon free-lance writers than upon staff writers. Many who were once free lancers have joined magazine staffs.

READER RESPONSE TO THE PRESS

The superficial evidences of response to the print media can be summarized easily. According to a 1969 study by W. R. Simmons Associates, 78 percent of all Americans eighteen years old and older read a daily newspaper on the average weekday. (A *Time*-Louis Harris survey of the same period showed nearly 90 percent adult readership.) Thirty-three percent read two or more papers every day. Readership of one or more papers is about the same among men and women, but men are more likely to read two or more papers (35 percent of men, 30 percent of women). As people grow older, they give more attention to newspapers. Among those from thirty-five to sixty-four years of age, newspaper readership is 82 percent. Least readership is at the young end of the scale—73 percent among eighteen- to twenty-four-year-olds.

As all readership studies indicate, the better educated are the most likely to read newspapers. Eighty-seven percent of those who have attended college for a year or more read a daily newspaper. The figure is 83 percent for high school graduates—and only 64 percent for those who did not attend high school. Predictably, readership is higher among upper-income groups (Editor & Publisher, 1970:16).

Magazine readership follows similar lines in that the better educated read significantly more, and women are attracted to magazines to a greater degree than are men. In analyzing magazine readership, Rees and Paisley (1967) found a differentiation by education and sex in the number of magazines read (Table 1).

TABLE 1

PERCENTAGE READING TWO OR MORE MAGAZINES, BY EDUCATION AND SEX

Extent of Education	Men	Women
Less than high school graduate	42%	50%
High school graduate	63	65
Some college	70	77
College graduate	80	90

These are important figures, but there is much more to report about response to the press than readership studies. What do all these readers think of what they read? Do they trust the press? We have little evidence from early times about what the generality of readers thought, but public men in every period have been eager to make known their discontent. Thus, Cotton Mather in writing about the *New England Courant* during a controversy over smallpox inoculations railed:

> . . .we find a Notorious, Scandalous paper, called the *Courant*, full freighted with Nonsense, Unmannerliness, Railery, Prophaness, Immorality, Arrogancy, Calumnies, Lyes, Contradictions, and whatnot, all tending to Quarrels and Divisions, and to Debauch and Corrupt the Minds and Manners of New-England (Gallagher, 1969:6).

Viewing the press in 1842, Charles Dickens wrote ". . .that Press has its evil eye in every house, and its black hand in every appointment in the state from a

President to a postman, while with ribald slander for its only stock in trade, is the standard literature—in a newspaper" (Gallagher, 1969:6).

Although the first American book extensively attacking the press was published in 1859, the wave really began with the publication of a remarkable series of articles by Will Irwin in *Collier's* in 1911. The scatter-shot criticisms of earlier times became obsolete with Irwin's closely reasoned articles. He argued that the influence of the newspaper had shifted almost unnoticed from the editorials to the news columns, that the commercial nature of the newspaper was responsible for many of its faults, and that the press had become so distinctively big business that it was inextricably linked to all the other big businesses. Upton Sinclair's savage *Brass Check* followed in 1919. In 1935 George Seldes bitterly attacked the press in *Freedom of the Press*, then in a newsletter, *In Fact*, which was published during the 1940s. During the 1930s, newspapers were targets in the general attacks on business, especially in such books as *America's House of the Lords* by Harold Ickes, and Ferdinand Lundberg's *Imperial Hearst*.

In recent years, although criticism has varied, as always, in degree of responsibility, critics have become more knowing as well as more responsible. The late A. J. Liebling's articles in the "Wayward Press" department of *The New Yorker* (collected in a paperback entitled *The Press*) are shrill at some points, but Liebling was a shrewd and witty critic. Ben Bagdikian's articles in the *Columbia Journalism Review*, which is the only continuingly valuable critical organ that journalism has ever had, have from the first demonstrated that Bagdikian realizes the limits of perfectibility in human affairs and yet demands of the press what it should be able to give.

The most cogent single body of criticism was formed in the late 1940s by the Commission on Freedom of the Press. Supported by private philanthropy, staffed by scholars, the commission couched its assessment in words of attack:

> It becomes an imperative question whether the performance of the press can any longer be left to the unregulated initiative of the few who manage it. . . . Those who direct the machinery of the press have engaged from time to time in practices which the society condemns and which, if continued, it will inevitably undertake to regulate or control (Commission on Freedom of the Press, 1947).

Considering the sensitivity of journalists to criticism, and especially the fact that *regulate* has always been a red-flag word, it is not surprising that the commission's critique was harshly received.

Ironically, most of the commission's ideas about responsible performance were much like those of the leading journalists: It is the duty of the press (and the commission meant broadcast as well as print journalism) to provide "a truthful, comprehensive, and intelligent account of the day's events in a context which gives them meaning." The press should serve as "a forum for the exchange of comment and criticism," give a "representative picture of the constituent groups in society," help in the "presentation and clarification of the goals and values of the society," and "provide full access to the day's intelligence." The major mission of mass communication, the commission argued, is to raise social conflict "from the plane of violence to the plane of discussion" (Commission on Freedom of the Press, 1947).

The general themes of the criticisms of all the media have been summarized by Theodore Peterson:

1. The mass media have wielded enormous power for their own ends. The owners have propagated their own opinions, especially in politics and economics, at the expense of opposing views.
2. The mass media have been subservient to big business and at times have let advertisers control editorial policy and editorial content.

3. The mass media have resisted social change.
4. The mass media have often given more attention to the superficial and the sensational in their coverage of human happenings than to the significant, and their entertainment has often lacked substance.
5. The mass media have endangered public morals.
6. The mass media have invaded the privacy of individuals without just cause.
7. The mass media are controlled by one socio-economic class—loosely, "the business class," and access to the media is difficult for the newcomer; therefore the free and open market of ideas is endangered (Siebert, Peterson, & Schramm, 1957: 78–79).

Criticism is likely to become more intense. Certainly, its intensity has traced a rising curve in recent years. The roar of approval from conservatives when General Eisenhower attacked "the columnists and commentators" in a speech at the Republican National Convention in 1964 was only more concentrated—not more vehement—than the wrath of the radicals at "the Establishment press" during the 1968 Democratic National Convention in Chicago. Right and left seem equally convinced that the mass media are slanted against them.

All of the major critical themes listed above *and* the criticisms of the political right and left can be supported with examples from one newspaper or magazine or another. The question is whether the *generality* of newspapers and magazines is being criticized accurately. Many of the charges, of course, can be traced to the fact that readers are subject to selective exposure, selective perception, and selective retention (phenomena that are explained in detail elsewhere in this volume). The irrationality of much of the criticism is revealed by an incident related by Robert Donovan, associate editor of the *Los Angeles Times*:

> Last month, a man I do not know telephoned me from California to deplore a story I had written about the Nov. 15 peace march on Washington. He felt that my article deliberately lent encouragement to demonstrators. When, in the course of questioning me, however, he learned that I am 57, was an infantryman in World War II and have a son who will be commissioned in the Army in June through ROTC, his whole attitude toward me and the article changed.
>
> If only, he said, readers knew that I was not young and not unpatriotic, they would read my stories in a very different light. In other words the facts and the writer's interpretation of them, as in this case, were not enough. The reader's confidence was undermined by suspicion about the writer and the writer's motive (Donovan, 1970: 10).

And yet there is ample reason, it seems, for the criticisms of the press from the right, the left, and the center. For it is certain that individuals change much more rapidly than institutions change. Many individuals, especially among the young, are supporting change. The overwhelming majority of newspapers and magazines are linked inextricably to the other powerful institutions of society, and even as they publicize the violent activities of those who would revolutionize society, they deplore the revolutionary effort. This is enough to invite the condemnation of the radical left.

And even as the print media support the status quo editorially, many of the news and feature columns are given over to radical left activities. This excites the radical right and invites the condemnation of the center as well.

The basic question that springs from this consideration is whether the print media should stress the negative to the extent that they do. A continuing refrain is that the media should report many more positive actions. Among the statements of those who dealt with this problem in reporting to the National Commission on the Causes and Prevention of Violence, Ben Bagdikian's thoughts are instructive:

> I do not agree with those who say that the news is required to include more happy information than unhappy, or, by reflex, balance

violence with nonviolence. I find fallacious the complaint that one thousand children may reach school safely but the news tells only of the one killed crossing the street. Society has a more urgent need to know about the one child killed, than it does of the remainder. It needs to know causes and cures, too, and the mass media not concerned with breaking news must see the whole panorama of life. But first it needs to know its ills.

Neither do I agree that dramatizing conflict situations is necessarily arbitrary. Few of our social institutions are devoted to placid and satisfactory conditions, including most of government, this Commission, the League of Women Voters, the United States Chamber of Commerce, public libraries, and, alas, my favorite baseball team, the Washington Senators. All are concerned with problems, conflict, change, and the distinctive.

The press especially cannot be expected to be responsible for the spreading of happiness if things are not happy. One of its most important functions, though not the only one, is to act like the eye in the medical laboratory that concentrates in the diseased tissues.

For one thing, reporting of violence is one way to discover resolutions of violence. In 1960 there was a wave of swastika paintings and other desecrations on synagogues and Jewish temples in the United States. Some local news organizations decided to suppress this news for fear it would stimulate imitations. Others reported the incidents. Afterward the Anit-Defamation League sponsored a study by David Caplovitz and Candace Rogers of the effects of publicity versus nonpublicity. They found that news coverage did tend to increase the incidents. But they found something else. Where there was coverage of the incidents there was mobilization of community opinion to condemn such activities, and where there was no publicity there was no community reaction. Caplovitz and Rogers concluded that the publicity and the reaction to it instructed a generation of citizens in that community on the true meaning and danger of anti-Semitism, forcing a great many people to consider the consequences and the social judgment of what had been for them, up to then, thoughtless practice and toleration of group hatred.

So we cannot expect a realistic and intelligent response to violence unless we know about the violence, and we must know about it while it is a live issue.

Having said that, it is necessary to say that there is some violence in the news for purely commercial, self-serving reasons with no redeeming benefit to society. Where newspapers and television compete they tend to emphasize sex and violence more than where they do not. Where newspapers have different editions for home delivery and for street sales, the editions for street sales, which depend on eye-catching, are noticeably more devoted to violent news in big headlines.

Furthermore, though all publishers say they are responsible in reporting violence, it is obvious that publishers differ on where to draw the line. In the Winter 1963 issue of *Journalism Quarterly*, Herbert Otto of the University of Utah reported on a study of sex and violence displayed on newsstands. Among his findings was that of the ten largest papers studied, the sexiest one had seven times more sex than the next highest, and the same paper had four times more violence in it—34 percent of total news content—than the second most violent paper. They cannot all be equally justified.

Between the socially justified reporting of violence and its commercial exploitation there is a large grey area where it is difficult to tell when significance stops and cynicism begins. One reason is that the decision often includes a mixture of both good and mean motives. Another is that the most venal use is usually cloaked with high purpose. I suspect that this Commission has not been deluged with requests by news, periodical and broadcasting operators who want to testify that they use sex and violence solely bcause it makes money for them but it is obvious that many do exactly that (Bagdikian, 1968).

All this leaves unanswered the question of how much violence appears in the print media. Dr. Jack Haskins (1969:12) of Syracuse University surveyed many research studies and found:

In 1913–15, all U.S. dailies, a study by Garth showed that "violence" as a proportion of *total news* was 23%

In 1929, New York City dailies, a study by Kingsbury indicated that violence as a proportion of *front page headlines* amounted to 43%

In 1939–50, over 100 small and medium-sized dailies, a study by Charles Swanson indicated that violence as a proportion of total news amounted to. 11%

From 1900 to 1960, Sunday comic strips in U.S. dailies, a study by Barcus showed that "crime and detective" strips comprised (*a*) zero % in 1900, up to (*b*) in 1955–59. . 26%

In 1950, in syndicated Sunday comic strips of U.S. a study by Steigleman showed the violence proportion of all activity depicted was 9% (female characters), 18% for males. In 1950, on the Wisconsin state wire of AP, a study by Van Horn showed that violence news as a proportion of the total amounted to. . . 9%

In 1959, using crime-accident-disaster news as a proportion of the total, Deutschman found in the seven New York City dailies an average of 22%
in five metropolitan Ohio dailies an average of 15%

In 1961, four large Michigan dailies, Stempel used same categories as above, the violence proportion was. 9%

In 1961–62, in the ten largest U.S. dailies, Otto found the violence proportion of total news to be. 5%
(varying from 2% in one newspaper to 34% in another)

In 1939–51, in 97 medium-to-large dailies studied by Nixon and Jones, the violence proportion amounted to. 4%
In 1955, the same newspapers measured 7%

In 1967, four metropolitan Ohio dailies studied by Stott showed the violence proportion to be. 13%

These are percentages of the total newspaper, including the advertising. Nonetheless, the more recent figures above—13 percent, 7 percent, 4 percent, 5 percent, 9 percent, 15 percent, 22 percent, and 9 percent—are probably surprising to anyone who had assumed that newspapers were much more devoted to violence than these figures indicate. An oversimplified explanation is that readers tend to read and to *remember* stories of violence more than they do tranquil stories and stories of cooperation.

For example, if one can imagine two stories, side-by-side on the front page of a newspaper, one relating that a city councilman praised the police chief for his excellent work, the other relating that another city councilman charged the police chief with torturing prisoners, it is no feat to guess which story is most likely to be read and remembered by most subscribers. This is borne out by a readership survey that classified news items according to the degree of violence portrayed. The results shown in Table 2 indicate that the more violence an item contains, the more interested readers will be.

TABLE 2

RELATIONSHIP OF READER INTEREST TO NEWS OF VIOLENCE

Degree of Violence Shown	Number of Items	Avg. Interest Index
High violence	38	52.2
Some violence	10	49.9
No violence	72	37.4

SOURCE: Haskins (1968:38).

After considering these and other studies, Haskins offered as reasonable hypotheses:

1. Small dailies probably carry about equal amounts of negative and positive news.
2. Big-city dailies probably carry more negative than positive items.
3. Negative items probably get more preferential display treatment than positive items, except in the case of teen-age news.
4. Teen-age boys are more likely to be depicted negatively than positively on front pages; girls, on the other hand, are more likely to be shown in a favorable light (Haskins, 1968:38).

If these studies and hypotheses seem too kind to the press, they are misleading. For although it is true that much less violence appears than we imagine, and although it is true that readers and their interests are at least implicated in the violence that does appear, it is also true that, quite beyond violence per se, the press promotes conflict. That is, many reports that appear in the press would not be classifiable as stories of "violence," but they are evident examples of efforts to build conflict situations. Indeed, part of the folklore of journalism is the fact that a fight—even if only verbal—between a citizen and his neighbor, a mayor and a councilman, or a president and a senator is automatically a "good story."

The journalist's first defense of such an ethic is that the conflict situations are real and his reports are true. Even if accurate, this fails to account for the possibility that too many of these "good stories" cause a serious overbalance in news presentation to the point of distortion. It may sometimes seem to readers that all is conflict. As Irwin Edman once remarked, "The mind of the newspaper reader, if it could be photographed after ten minutes of reading, would not be a map, but an explosion."

The journalist's second defense of conflict is that dramatic presentations—and conflict is central to drama—capture the reader's attention. This is certainly true. And yet it leaves us to wonder whether the great unexplored territory in journalism may be how to write stories of cooperation in a way that will lure readers.

Criticism of magazines is much less voluminous and intense than criticism of the other media, although it is certainly true that charges directed at mass communication in general embrace magazines as well. No doubt many critics intended their indictments of newspapers and "the press" to include magazines. Certainly, Upton Sinclair lumped magazines with newspapers and charged all with being parties to the conspiracy with big business to keep the public uninformed or misinformed on important issues. Advertising pressure has killed off the magazines that dared to tell the truth, Sinclair stated, and it has even corrupted the authors of magazine fiction, who tend to treat themes favorable to big business and the status quo.

For the most part, though, criticism of magazines has meant criticism of individual publications—especially *Time*, *The Reader's Digest*, and the little magazines of politics and opinion. Critics of newspapers who often seem incapable of distinguishing between newspapers as a whole on the one hand and responsible newspapers on the other are much more selective when they indict magazines.

The Print Media and Their Rivals

It is apparent that the coming of the electronic media did not doom print. With newer media looming on the horizon of mass communication, it is important to make clear exactly how the printed and the electronic media have accommodated themselves to one another—and thus suggest how they may accommodate themselves to the coming changes.

As *information* media, radio and television are primarily useful in signalizing events, making the immediate—and usually sketchy—reports that announce a happening. When broadcasters give full attention to an important subject or a momentous event, as in the case of documentaries and special-events reports, they must scan other news. This leaves an important role for the newspaper, which supplies many more details than the newscast and covers many more stories than the broadcast documentary or special report.

In turn, newspaper reports leave a role for magazines, which are chiefly devoted to fleshing out the information that has been shown only in silhouette through broadcasting and newspapers, and to reporting matters that the faster media have missed in the rush of meeting deadlines. Magazine writers also take advantage of their wide-spaced deadlines to fashion articles more graceful and unified than most writers for TV, radio, or newspapers have time to achieve. As a consequence, the interpretive writing used to explore the meaning of events is more advanced in magazine journalism.

The media do not always work within the boundaries of these roles, and it must be obvious that they seldom take full advantage of their best qualities. Broadcasting is swift, but it sometimes misses important aspects of quick-breaking events. Newspapers are large, but they sometimes ignore significant stories. The long periods that go into the writing of magazine articles do not prevent the worst of them from exuding a helter-skelter, thrown-together quality. All in all, though, each medium has a clear and substantive role in supplying information and interpretation.

POLITICAL AND LEGAL CONTROLS: THE U.S. AND THE WORLD

Whatever its constitution states, every society restricts expression. Those who believe that the U.S. press enjoys untrammeled freedom because the First Amendment to the U.S. Constitution states that the press must be free, may obtain a different perspective by considering that the late Justice Hugo Black and Justice William O. Douglas of the United States Supreme Court consistently argued that the First Amendment means literally what it says—and they argued in vain. Justice Black held in *Ginsburg* v. *United States*: "I believe the Federal Government is without power whatever under the Constitution to put any type of burden on speech and expression of ideas of any kind." Justice William Douglas has written:

> The first Amendment does not say that there is freedom of expression provided the talk is not dangerous. It does not say that there is freedom of expression provided the utterance has not tendency to subvert. . . . All notions of regulation or restraint by government are absent from the First Amendment. For it says in words that are unambiguous, "Congress shall make no law . . ." (Douglas, 1958:21).

Because few members of the U.S. Supreme Court have believed as Black and Douglas do that the First Amendment should be taken literally, political and legal controls have been applied to the press from its beginnings. Zechariah Chafee (1947) has listed most of them: Licensing in advance; censorship before publication; seizure; injunctions against publication; requirement of surety bonds against libel and other offenses; compulsory disclosure of ownership and authority; postpublication criminal penalties for objectionable matter; postpublication collection of damages in civil action; postpublication correction of libels and other misstatements; discriminations in access to news sources and facilities; discrimination and denial in using communications facilities; taxes; discriminatory subsidies; and interference with buying, reading, and listening.

As Schramm has pointed out in a number of writings, almost any mass media system is subject to basic statutory controls, among them a law to protect individuals or groups against defamation, a copyright law to protect authors and publishers, a statute to preserve the common standard of decency and morality, and another basic statute to protect the state against treasonable and seditious utterances. To gauge whether a mass media system is truly subordinate to political authorities and the extent to which the controls go far beyond these basic statutes requires that one judge the degree to which the system is authoritarian or libertarian. In Spain, Portugal, the Eastern European countries, and the USSR, for example, the media are clearly subordinate. In the United States, Great Britain, and most of the countries of Western Europe, the printed media are clearly not subordinate (although broadcasting is subordinate in varying degrees—quite strongly in some).

In an effort to refine the judgments of whether mass media systems are free, Ralph Lowenstein (1967) and his colleagues at the University of Missouri School of Journalism have developed a measure

TABLE 3

Measurement of Press Freedom Throughout the World (1966), Using Press Independence and Critical Ability Criteria

		Free—High Degree		
Australia	Denmark	The Netherlands	Philippines	United States
Belgium	Finland	Norway	Sweden	Uruguay
Canada	Guatemala	Peru	Switzerland	Venezuela
Costa Rica				
		Free—Moderate Controls		
Austria	Ecuador	Honduras	Jamaica	Panama
Bolivia	El Salvador	Ireland (Eire)	Japan	Singapore
Colombia	France	Israel	Malaysia	Turkey
Cyprus	West Germany	Italy	New Zealand	United Kingdom
		Free—Many Controls		
Argentina	China (Taiwan)	India	Mexico	Tanzania
Brazil	Dominican Republic	Kenya	Morocco	Thailand
Ceylon		Lebanon	Rhodesia	Uganda
Chile	Greece	Malawi	South Africa	Zambia
		Transitional		
Burma	Ghana	South Korea	Nigeria	South Vietnam
Congo, The	Indonesia	Laos	Pakistan	Yugoslavia
		Controlled—Low Degree		
Afghanistan	Iran	Jordan	Portugal	Tunisia
Cambodia	Iraq	Nepal	Spain	
		Controlled—Medium Degree		
	Cameroon	Hungary	Syria	
	Haiti	Senegal	U.A.R.	
		Controlled—High Degree		
Albania	Chad	Cuba	East Germany	Rumania
Algeria	China (Mainland)	Czechoslovakia	North Korea	USSR
Bulgaria		Ethiopia	Poland	Upper Volta
		Unranked (Insufficient Information)		
Burundi	Ivory Coast	Mali	Rwanda	Sudan
Central African Republic	Liberia	Mongolia	Saudi Arabia	Togo
	Libya	Nicaragua	Sierra Leone	North Vietnam
Dahomey	Malagasy Republic	Niger	Somalia	Yemen
Guinea		Paraguay		

Source: Lowenstein (1967:4).

of Press Independence and Critical Ability (PICA). Recognizing that all constitutional systems affirm the principle of free expression and that one cannot estimate degrees of freedom merely by considering such affirmations, the Missouri group set forth twenty-three criteria for judging press freedom:

1. Legal controls on the press, not including libel and obscenity laws (but including laws involving official censorship, contempt, forced corrections and retractions, suspensions, privacy, security, incitement to riot, etc.).
2. Extralegal controls (threats, violence, imprisonment, confiscation, etc.).
3. Libel laws.
4. Organized self-regulation (press councils, courts of honor).
5. News and editorial personnel (all media) subject to government licensing, certification, and appointment.
6. Favoritism in release of government news.
7. Media allowed to utilize services of foreign news agencies.
8. Government control over domestic news agencies.
9. Print media subject to government licensing.
10. Government control of circulation and distribution, not including postal service.
11. Degree of press criticism of local and regional governments and officials within country.
12. Degree of press criticism of national government and national officials within country.
13. Government or "government party" ownership of media (including radio, television, and domestic news agencies).
14. Publications of opposition political parties banned.
15. Broadcasting and press units owned by networks and chains (concentrated ownership).
16. Government control of newsprint.
17. Government control of foreign exchange and/or purchase of equipment.
18. Government subsidies and/or bribes to press and newsmen.
19. Government loans to media.
20. Media dependency on government advertising.
21. Tax rate on press (either higher or lower) compared with other businesses.
22. Pressure from labor unions (to influence editorial policy, to suspend publication).
23. Number of marginal (economically insecure) press units.

Using these criteria, Lowenstein and his colleagues attempted to measure press freedom around the world in 1966. The results made it clear that press freedom in the Communist countries could not be measured properly using the PICA criteria. There were difficulties, too, with measuring the degree of freedom in India, South Africa, and Rhodesia. Emphasizing these qualifications, the Missouri researchers announced that PICA is probably a good indicator whose sensitivity needs further refining. Their findings are shown in Table 3.

REFERENCES

Bagdikian, Ben H.
1964 "How newspapers use columnists." Columbia Journalism Review 3(Fall): 20–24.
1966–67 "Oracles and their audiences." Columbia Journalism Review 5(Winter): 22–29.
1968 Testimony prepared for delivery to the National Commission on the Causes and Prevention of Violence (December 18).

Bowers, David R.
1967 "A report on activity by publishers in directing newsroom decisions." Journalism Quarterly 44(Spring):43.

Breed, Warren.
1955 "Social control in the newsroom: A functional analysis." Social Forces 33:326–335. (Also pp. 178–194 in Wilbur Schramm [ed.], Mass Communication. Second Edition. Urbana: University of Illinois Press, 1960.)

Cater, Douglass.
1959 The Fourth Branch of Government. Boston: Houghton Mifflin.

Chafee, Zechariah, Jr.
1947 Government and Mass Communica-

tion. Chicago: University of Chicago Press.
Commission on Freedom of the Press.
1947 A Free and Responsible Press. Chicago: University of Chicago Press.
Donohew, Lewis.
1967 "Newspaper gatekeepers and forces in the news channel." Public Opinion Quarterly 31:61–68.
Donovan, R. J.
1970 "The rules have changed." Nieman Reports 24(No. 1):7–10.
Douglas, William O.
1958 The Right of the People. Garden City, New York: Doubleday.
Editor & Publisher.
1970 "Newspaper reading habit holds steady in cities." 103(March 14):16.
Emery, Edwin.
1962 The Press and America. Second Edition. Englewood Cliffs, New Jersey: Prentice-Hall.
Ford, P. L. (ed.).
1893 The Writings of Thomas Jefferson. Volume 2. New York: Putnam.
Gallagher, W.
1969 "What halo? We never had one." Seminar 4(September):5–8.
Gillenson, L. W.
1962 "The struggle for survival." Columbia Journalism Review 1(Spring):36.
Haskins, J. B.
1968 "Stories of violence get high readership." Editor & Publisher 101(October 19):38.
1969 "Too much crime and violence in the press?" Editor & Publisher 102(February 8):12.
Henry, W. W. (ed.).
1891 Patrick Henry: Life, Correspondence and Speeches. Volume 3. New York: Scribner's.
Hunt, Gaillard (ed.).
1907 The Writings of James Madison. Volume 6. New York: Putnam.
Irwin, Will.
1911 "The American newspaper." (15-article series.) Colliers January 21–July 29.
Johnson, Lyndon B.
1969 "Agenda for the future: A presidential perspective." Pp. 16–48 in The Britannica Book of the Year, 1969. Chicago: Encyclopedia Britannica.
King, Cecil H.
1967 "An English view of American newspapers conceived without sin; conceived without joy." Editor & Publisher 100(April 29):19, 98–100.
Liebling, A. J.
n.d. The Press. New York: Ballantine Books.
Lowenstein, R. L.
1967 World Press Freedom, 1966. Columbia, Missouri: Freedom of Information Center Publication No. 181 (May).
Mott, F. L.
1962 American Journalism, 1690–1960. Third Edition. New York: Macmillan.
Newquist, Roy (ed.).
1967 Conversations. Chicago: Rand McNally.
Pollard, J. E.
1947 The Presidents and the Press. New York: Macmillan.
Rees, Matilda, and William J. Paisley.
1967 Social and Psychological Predictors of Information Seeking and Media Use. Stanford, California: Institute for Communication Research.
Schlesinger, Arthur M.
1932 The Rise of the City, 1878–1898. New York: Macmillan.
Siebert, F. S.; Theodore Peterson; and Wilbur Schramm.
1957 Four Theories of the Press. Urbana: University of Illinois Press.
Steffens, Lincoln.
1903 "The shame of Minneapolis." McClure's Magazine 20(No. 3):1.
White, Llewellyn, and Robert D. Leigh.
1960 "The growth of international communications." Pp. 70–94 in Wilbur Schramm (ed.), Mass Communications. Second Edition. Urbana: University of Illinois Press.
White, Theodore.
1960 The View from the Fortieth Floor. New York: New American Library-Signet Books.

APPENDIX

A Note on Television News and Newspaper News

FRANK ALLEN PHILPOT
Kaiser Broadcasting Corporation

It is fairly obvious that there is a qualitative difference between the news we receive from newspapers and the news we receive from television. All too often that difference is attributed simply to the fact that "television is a visual medium"—as though newspapers were printed only in braille. The reasons for the difference are much more subtle and complex.

The preceding pages have treated news as it is presented by the print media. At least four kinds of factors interact to make television news the institution it is: technical, legal, economic, and—for lack of a better name—traditional assumptions. The differences show up most clearly when we draw comparisons with newspaper news, but this does not imply that newspapers represent the perfect model of a news channel.

True Technical Differences

Newspaper readers can scan the headlines in two minutes or devote an hour and a half to scouring the entire paper. They can reread difficult stories. But television news must be viewed at a single sitting; it cannot be repeated for the benefit of those who did not understand the significance the first time. At least one result of the transient nature of television news is that it is much more difficult to analyze and study.

Newspapers regularly print far more news than any single reader is likely to want to read. Headlines, lengths of stories, and page positions index the material. But television is not indexable—at least in our present technology. This means that the longer the program, the more material a viewer must sit through to get to the items that interest him. The practical effect is that, with very few exceptions, even the longest newscasts are limited to an hour.

Another result is that television newscasts are forced to seek the widest—if not the lowest—common denominator. All stories must be prepared for nearly all viewers.

Television news transmits less verbal information per unit of the consumer's time than does the newspaper. Or to put it another way, most people read silently much faster than Walter Cronkite reads aloud. Combined with the length limitation caused by our inability to index television, this factor means that television news is inherently less complete than newspaper news.

A front-page story in the *New York Times* frequently runs to 1,000 words, but a typical television news story seldom uses more than 200 to 350 words. One study concluded that "the *most* detailed of television stories roughly compares to the *least* detailed of newspaper stories" (Lyle & Wilcox, 1963:163). David Brinkley (1965) once observed, "When it comes to covering news in any thorough and detailed way, we are just not in the ball game and we know it."

The public, however, does not perceive TV news to be inadequate or incomplete. In fact, viewers ranking newspapers and TV news on a seven-point scale of "complete-incomplete" rated TV as significantly more complete than newspapers (Jacobson, 1969:25). This may result from television's ability to convey more nonverbal information, i.e., motion, color, detail, etc.

Television news is transmitted instantly. There is no distribution delay comparable to the three or four hours required for newspapers to be printed and trucked to newsstands or delivered to individual homes. Thus, much of the evening newscast is not competing with the afternoon paper but the one that will arrive the following morning. Television has an inherent advantage in covering late-breaking stories.

Television performs a function in covering events such as moon landings, national conventions, presidential funerals, and the like for which there is simply no equivalent in the newspaper world. Because television can be live, and because it involves pictures, the public may assume that it is less mediated by human judgment. In any event, 49 percent of the public say that, faced with conflicting reports of the same news from radio, television, magazines, and newspapers, they would believe the television version, while only 20 percent would choose the newspaper version (Roper, 1971:3). In this respect, newspapers may suffer from their historical partisan editorial tradition.

The limiting dimension of a newspaper is space; the limiting dimension of television news is time. A publisher can fairly easily expand the space in his paper by adding pages if he feels the news requires it. But the minutes in a broadcast day are finite, and expanding broadcast news requires subtracting from something else—usually more profitable entertainment programs.

One need not be able to read to use television. One survey indicates that as many as half of the adults in the United States lack the necessary literacy to cope with a driving manual, a job application form, or a newspaper (Rosenthal, 1970:1). A number of studies support a conclusion of Serena Wade and Wilbur Schramm:

> Television is more likely to be the major source of public affairs information for people with little education, for females, nonwhites, and farm and blue-collar workers than for others; whereas the print media are more likely to be the major source for the highly educated groups, whites, males, professional, managerial and white-collar workers, and high-income groups than for others (Wade & Schramm, 1968:200–201).

Because television can transmit a large amount of nonverbal information, it is capable of communicating with an intensity that is unmatched by the print medium. There seem to have been no vigorous studies of this factor, but a number of authorities have reached the same conclusion based on casual evidence. Dr. Louis H. Masotti, author of the report on the Cleveland shoot-out for the National Commission on the Causes and Prevention of Violence, argues that coverage of riots on television has helped spread riots to other cities.

> People see people like themselves involved in riots. Electronic proximity accomplishes the purpose [of physical proximity] by allowing Negroes of Hough to sympathize with Negroes of the black ghetto of Detroit or Newark.

Television has that kind of effect (Barrett, 1969:18).

Reuven Frank, president of NBC News, says: "The highest power of television journalism is not in the transmission of information but in the transmission of experience" (Whitworth, 1968:56). Robert E. Kintner (1965b), formerly president of NBC, has suggested that television was instrumental in the civil rights revolution of the 1960s—not because it promoted a particular cause, but because it communicated instances of injustice and inequality with an intensity that the newspaper had never achieved.

Given our present technology, television equipment is very bulky and obvious. People are more aware of the presence of a television news team—consisting in some instances of four people with cameras, bright lights, and recorders—than they are of a newspaper reporter with a pad and pencil and a photographer with a 35-mm. camera shooting with natural light. The implication is that television is more likely to influence the events it is reporting than are other news media.

No one has ever developed an efficient way to file newsfilm or video tape the way news clippings can be filed. Perhaps that seems trivial, but the result is that even long-established TV stations do not have the complete files or morgues that many newspapers have. Therefore television reporters have less background information to work with when preparing a story.

Legal and Political Differences

Publishing a newspaper is a right guaranteed by the First Amendment to the Constitution. Broadcasting is a privilege granted by the federal government, and a license to broadcast does not carry with it the same First Amendment rights—even on a news program.*

* *Red Lion Broadcasting Co.* v. *FCC*, 395 U.S. 367 (1969)—reply time.

There are a limited number of television licenses available in each community. Theoretically there can be an unlimited number of newspapers operating in any community. Economic factors, of course, counteract this and, in fact, there are more television stations in most communities than there are newspapers. But the limited number of licenses provides the foundation of our regulatory system and that system works subtly to shape television journalism.

Simply put, the Federal Communications Commission regulates the operation of a television station in a way that would be simply unthinkable if applied to newspapers. Technically, the equal opportunities provisions of the Communications Act (often incorrectly referred to as the "equal-time" law) do not apply to newscasts, and the most burdensome provisions of the commission's "fairness doctrine" (the personal attack rules) also exempt newscasts. Nevertheless, the general provisions of the fairness doctrine do apply to newscasts and television station managers are very much aware of the FCC's power. In several instances the FCC has required stations or networks to publicly justify some aspect of their news coverage. And although the commission has yet to take any action against a station for this reason, the possibility of action has led to a system which one network president refers to as "regulation by lifted eyebrow" (Kintner, 1965a: 128).

Not only is FCC censure a threat, but every three years when a station's license comes up for renewal the public—at least theoretically—may present evidence to show why the license should not be renewed. Compare this to the situation of a newspaper publisher who knows that as long as he pays his taxes, avoids libel, pays his employees minimum wages, and obeys a few minor laws *no one* can stop him from publishing his newspaper, no matter how distorted the news coverage or inadequate the reporting. Implication: television journalism is certain to be timid in comparison with newspapers.

Newspapers developed during a period when the libertarian theory of the mass media was commonly accepted, when the free clash of conflicting views was seen by political philosophers as the proper way to determine truth. Television, in contrast, has grown up in a period when the social responsibility theory is widely accepted—when the owners and managers of the mass media are expected to present a balanced and impartial account of the events of the day. The result is that newspapers have a well-developed editorial tradition and broadcasters have an extremely weak editorial tradition. In fact, until 1949 the FCC held that a broadcasting station could not editorialize.

A sizable urban area may have one or two metropolitan newspapers and more than a dozen suburban dailies serving specific geographic areas. But almost all the stations for that area will be assigned to the central city and their signals will cover more than 10,000 square miles. Within that coverage pattern there may be dozens of communities with separate economic and political problems. Thus a news director of a station in a metropolitan area is reluctant to cover more than the major news items from the central city because residents of other cities are watching his program. Nor can he cover even moderately important events in the satellite communities. One result is that suburban communities receive very little coverage from television news.

This limitation is reflected in a national poll by The Roper Organization, Inc. Asked where they got their information about political candidates for local offices, 37 percent of the respondents named newspapers and 32 percent named television. For state offices the percentages were quite different, with 50 percent saying they got most of their information from television compared with 30 percent for newspapers. Asked about candidates for national offices, 62 percent said they got most of their information from television while only 24 percent identified newspapers as their principal information source (Roper, 1971:8).

Economic Differences

Reporting the news is so vital to a newspaper that no publisher would ever consider abolishing his news department. But television—at least as we use it commercially in this country—is primarily in the entertainment business. Although many stations do make a profit on their news, most could make *more* money by substituting a program that costs less. Station managers schedule news programs because they think it helps their station's image, because it keeps them on good terms with the FCC and, in some cases, because the management has a sense of obligation to the community. The result is that when financial problems become serious, the budget of the news department is one of the first to be cut and the department itself may be eliminated. This can create tremendous pressure on the news director to keep his ratings up and his costs down regardless of conflicts with his news judgment.

All but a handful of the nation's daily newspapers are cozily established in monopoly or semimonopoly positions, alone either in the morning or evening. The vast majority of the country's television stations are in multiple markets competing with two or three stations for the same audience and usually at the same hour.

Thus, in most communities people subscribe to the local newspaper whether or not they are particularly pleased with its news content. Only in the newspaper can they find the grocery ads, the movie listings, the classified ads, the obituaries, etc. But they have a choice of TV news programs. Publishers are therefore to a limited extent immune to the pressures of public taste. A television station is not.

At some stations reporters are paid according to the number of film stories they produce per week, a situation which discourages reporters from spending extra time on complex stories. In small markets, a newsman may deliver commercials—on the newscast or during other parts of the day—and his salary may fluctuate depending on the number of commercials he announces. Even if the newscaster does not actually deliver the commercial, he may provide an anchor for it with phrases such as, "And we'll be back with more news after this word from Brand X." In this situation television reporters are likely to be more sensitive to the impact of their stories on advertisers and more subject to pressure from sponsors.

If we assume that most television sets are purchased for their entertainment value—a safe general assumption—then television news is free while newspapers cost money, perhaps a significant amount for a person with a marginal income. This is another reason television news is particularly important to the poor.

Newspapers collect as much as 30 percent of their revenues directly from their readers in subscriptions. Television has no comparable source of income. Newspapers also derive a significant portion of their income from classified advertising—a source so fragmented that no single advertiser can exert any pressure on editorial policy. Even if we compare only display advertising with all local television advertising, a newspaper still has a larger number of advertisers. All these factors combine to make newspapers less subject to pressure from any single important advertiser.

The structure of the news business is different for the two media. A newspaper editor takes a number of inputs—wire services, syndicated features, local reports, etc.—and chooses among them to make up his newspaper. He has absolute control; if he wants to eliminate all stories about a particular politician or all stories with a liberal or conservative viewpoint, he can. Most television stations prepare only local newscasts. The network prepares the national newscast. Thus, even though the local station holds the license and is technically responsible for everything it puts on the air, the local station manager has no practical control over the national news he broadcasts. During the late 1960s many local station managers complained that the national news programs of some networks were too liberal—too opposed to the war in Vietnam.

Perhaps it is only an aesthetic consideration, but newspaper advertising is much easier to avoid than television advertising. If one wants to look at a department store ad or to search the classified section for a used car, he may; but these ads do not intrude upon those who are not interested in them. Unfortunately, the same cannot be said for TV commercials. It may be that this is another factor that works to make television executives and journalists more conscious of the advertising that supports their medium.

Differences Based on Traditional Assumptions

In our present technology, differences in the news media resulting from technical factors are fixed. Economic and political factors are almost as difficult to modify. But the differences that arise from preconceived ideas about how the media "should" operate are much easier to modify. Thus, if we are unhappy with some aspect of broadcast journalism, it should be examined first because the potential for change is greatest here.

Television news managers seem to have developed a belief that viewers will turn off their sets if a piece of film is not shown every two minutes. Because film is superior for some stories (e.g., the damage from a hurricane, or a coronation), news directors seem to assume that all stories ought to be covered on film if humanly possible. In a national survey of television news directors, 75 percent agreed with the statement that newsfilm is "the chief reportorial tool of television news" (Schuneman, 1966: 283).

Because they consider motion picture

film so important, television news directors spend a great deal of effort and money getting it. A newspaper can send a reporter to cover an event and he can then telephone in his story. A TV assignment editor may frequently dispatch a reporter, cameraman, soundman and, sometimes, a field producer, electrician (lights), and driver. Then after shooting the film, the TV crew must return it to the station in time for processing and editing before the next newscast. Richard Salant, president of CBS News, once observed, "We spend more money just getting the story from one place to another than other media spend covering it" (Zalaznick, 1969:94).

This preoccupation with film introduces at least two kinds of distortion into the TV news process. First, so much effort is frequently required to get film that a news director may assume that merely shooting film covers a story, even though the coverage may be very superficial. Second, the station is likely to allot more time to those stories with a strong visual element (fires, parades, ribbon cuttings, etc.) regardless of their importance.

A study of news on Los Angeles television stations by the UCLA Department of Journalism supported the conclusion that the selection of stories on a TV newscast is influenced by the availability of visual material (Lyle & Wilcox, 1963). This makes TV news highly susceptible to the lure of what Daniel Boorstin has called pseudo events—happenings that are created specifically to be covered by the media. Or, as NBC board chairman Walter Scott observed, "Because television is a visual medium, it may scant the background and significance of events to focus on the outward appearance—the comings and goings of statesmen instead of the issue that confronts them" (MacNeil, 1968:75).

Ironically, there appears to be no experimental support for this preoccupation with motion picture film. A dissertation by Erling S. Jorgenson at the University of Wisconsin compared the effectiveness of a newscaster alone, a newscaster using still pictures, and a newscaster using motion pictures. The study showed no difference in information retention among the three methods and the test audiences preferred the newscaster-alone format with the newscaster plus still pictures ranking second in popularity (see RTNDA, 1955:2).

A San Francisco educational television station, KQED-TV, has produced a highly acclaimed news program using very little motion picture film. Instead, reporters sit around a table discussing informally the stories they covered. Still pictures are used perhaps more frequently than 16-mm. film. The Ford Foundation has provided funds for several other educational stations to develop similar programs, but commercial stations have so far been unenthusiastic about the concept.

Television news operates under the star system, with one or two newsmen on each station or network delivering most of the news. They become celebrities. The problem is acute on the network level. For example, in 1960 David Brinkley attempted to report personally on the West Virginia presidential primary but had to give up when he discovered that more people were interested in meeting a TV star than a presidential candidate. The implications of the star system are not easy to assess, but it probably increases the credibility of TV news and the likelihood that TV will influence the events it covers.

At many stations the news story is actually written by a writer, a writer-producer, or the newscaster rather than by the reporter who covered the story. The reporter's principal function at these stations is to be visible on the film clip asking questions. The writer-producer or the star bases his stories on the reporter's notes, the newspaper account, or the wire-service report. The problem is obvious. The longer the chain between the observer of an event and the person who prepares the written account, the greater the chance for distortion and inaccuracy. Of course, the rewrite desk of a large newspaper can create the same problem.

By tradition—or perhaps out of necessity because of their small staffs—most television stations depend on the newspapers and wire services to cover the day-in and day-out events of the world—the police department, city hall, the state legislature, the zoning board, etc. TV newscasters thus spend most of their time responding to events, covering stories that print reporters identified initially.

Regularly scheduled news programs draw substantial audiences, but news documentaries—the equivalent of newspaper special sections or full-page features—are not very popular. Documentaries are also extremely expensive to produce. A single newspaper reporter freed from his regular duties for a week or two can usually develop a substantial feature. A half-hour television documentary on the same subject may require two dozen people and cost thousands of dollars just for film and editing. Not surprisingly, the number of documentaries produced by individual stations is declining.

The majority of newspaper reporters are assigned to cover a regular beat. They become specialists—in crime reporting, city politics, science, art culture—and develop a considerable body of information and expertise. Television reporters, in contrast, are almost all general assignment reporters. They come to a story with much less background. Television news directors are aware of this problem and there is a slow but perceptible trend toward the appointment of special beat reporters in television newsrooms. This trend is most pronounced at the networks and at the large stations in New York, Los Angeles, and Chicago.

Some differences are difficult to attribute to any one factor but result from several factors. One of the most important is the tendency of television news to be less an adversary toward government than are newspapers. This is hard to quantify, but it is strongly supported by several impressionistic studies. For example Neil Hickey, New York bureau chief for *TV Guide*, wrote:

> . . . a sampling of TV news-reporting techniques around the U.S. leaves one with the impression that, much too frequently, the reporters hand over their medium to public figures and special pleaders who are "on the make"; that interviewees frequently are given a platform for the unchallenged dissemination of half-baked opinions; that reporters are either not sufficiently prepared or not competent to ask the sort of digging, probing question that will produce the real truth of the matter; and that TV news is all too frequently a conduit for, and not a processor of, the events which take place before its cameras and microphones (Hickey, 1968:12).

The 1968–1969 Survey of Broadcast Journalism sponsored by the Alfred I. duPont Foundation and Columbia University concluded:

> . . . it seems clear that television, although increasing its probing, could often be accused of reluctance to undertake hard hitting exposés, particularly where these might be expected to arouse major controversy. Only rarely during the year studied by the Survey did a television station attempt to expose wrongdoing by a public official, or to challenge the actions of powerful forces in the community. Most investigations were aimed instead at what might be considered relatively safe targets, such as the abuse of drugs by teenagers, pollution, conditions in urban ghettos, and the inadequacy of hospitals, schools, and other public facilities. Despite the impact and unquestioned value of such programs, they in many instances made less effort than might have been expected to assess responsibility for the conditions they exposed, or to recommend specific remedies (Barrett, 1969:70).

We have already considered some of the factors that undoubtedly contribute to this weakness in television news: the lack of First Amendment protection, the lack of an advocacy or editorial tradition, the scrutiny of the FCC, the weaker position of TV news vis-à-vis advertisers, etc. Whether this should be considered explanation or excuse is not entirely clear.

Nonetheless, it may be misleading to compare. The proper comparison may well be with television today and newspapers in the prebroadcast era. Indeed, it may be that many of the commendable aspects of newspapers are possible because of television.

In the prebroadcast days a large metropolitan newspaper might put out a dozen editions during the day. The emphasis was likely to be on reporting the news as quickly as possible. Interpretation was not nearly as important as speed. Now television and radio report the news as it happens. Newspapers—which are usually available after one has learned the sketchy outlines of a story—must do more than report the facts. To justify their existence—and to stay in business—they must offer more details, more background, and more interpretation.

Properly evaluating the performance of television news requires considering the total mix of news available to the average citizen. Measured against this standard, the citizen seems much better off today than he was twenty-five or fifty years ago. He gets more news faster and he has access to more explanation and interpretation than ever before. Admittedly, he cannot get all of this from a single source, but then he never could.

One does not expect to get yesterday's news from a monthly magazine or the quotations from a specific stock on the radio. Why, then, should one expect to get a newspaper at 6:00 P.M. on television? Perhaps television news could be much better than it is, but it is a waste of time to complain because an apple is not an orange.

REFERENCES

Barrett, Marvin (ed.).
1969 The Alfred I. DuPont-Columbia University Survey of Broadcast Journalism, 1968–1969. New York: Grosset and Dunlap.

Brinkley, David.
1965 Speech to the American Society of Newspaper Editors, Washington, D.C. (April).

Hickey, Neil.
1968 "Do we really know what's going on?" TV Guide March 9.

Jacobson, H. K.
1969 "Mass media believability: Study of receiver judgments." Journalism Quarterly 46:20–28.

Kintner, R. E.
1965a "Television and the world of politics." Harper's Magazine 230 (May): 121–123+.
1965b "Televising the real world." Harper's Magazine 230(June):94–96+.

Lyle, Jack, and Walter Wilcox.
1963 "Television news—an interim report." Journal of Broadcasting 7 (Spring): 157–166.

MacNeil, Robert.
1968 "The news on TV and how it is unmade." Harper's 237(October): 72–80.

Roper, Burns W.
1969 An Extended View of Public Attitudes Toward Television and Other Mass Media, 1959–1971. New York: Roper Organization.

Rosenthal, J.
1970 "Functional illiteracy found high in U.S. study at Harvard." New York Times May 20.

RTNDA.
1955 "Film presentation not the best." RTNDA (Radio and Television News Directors Association) Bulletin 9 (December):2.

Schuneman, R. S.
1966 "Visual aspects of television news: Communicator, message, equipment." Journalism Quarterly 43: 281–286.

Wade, Serena, and Wilbur Schramm.
1969 "The mass media as sources of public affairs, science and health knowledge." Public Opinion Quarterly 33:197–209.

Whitworth, William.
1968 "An accident of casting." New Yorker 44 (August 3):34–60.

Zalaznick, Sheldon.
1969 "The rich, risky business of TV news." Fortune 79 (May 1):92–97+.

CHAPTER 17 Film as Communication

HENRY S. BREITROSE
Stanford University

The history of the film industry in America, like the history of radio, has been profoundly influenced by television. After a rapid growth to astonishing heights of prestige and prosperity, the industry lost perhaps three-fourths of its audience after television became easily available. The film industry has been experimenting with different kinds of products and different systems for producing and marketing them in order to find its unique place among the media. This chapter focuses on film as communication rather than as art or business. It deals with the nature of film, different kinds of films, strengths and weaknesses of the medium, and its relation to its audiences.

PLAN OF THE CHAPTER

This chapter is primarily concerned with how film works as a communication device. Previous film literature has ranged from the "grand theory" level of speculation (primarily in Europe), through precise and controlled laboratory experimentation dealing with a single variable of film communication (generally in the learning or attitude area), to studies of audience preferences. Whether film can in fact communicate information seems to have been clearly settled by a number of positive verdicts rendered by researchers, beginning with Lashley and Watson (see Hoban & Van Ormer, 1950). The issue of attitude change as a result of film communication, however, although dating back at least to the Lashley and Watson studies, seems to be considerably more moot. There appears to be no question that films can effect shifts in attitudes, but the psychological mechanisms underlying such shifts have become an important area for recent and current research. This chapter will be concerned with what have been termed *media variables*, and with the demographic and economic determinants that affect them.

THE NATURE OF THE MEDIUM

Film, as generally defined, is a series of images alone or with sounds, existing in a predetermined interrelationship, and stored on some sort of flexible plastic base that can be displayed using standardized equipment. For the purposes of this discussion, the purposeful organization of relationships among visual and auditory components differentiates *films* from unstructured *film recordings*, in which the medium is utilized to perform the sole function of continuously recording an ongoing event, generally from an unvarying point of view. The process of manipulating images and attempting to derive meaning from the interrelationship of images and sounds is basic to the nature of the medium. Kracauer (1960) attempts to deal with this difference functionally by using the paradoxical constructs of the film as record and as revelation.

Physically, the information-storage characteristics of film are similar to those of still photography. Since both motion picture and still photography depend for image storage on the oxidation of grains of silver halide when struck by light, the major limiting factor on the amount of storable information is the number of grains of silver halide available. Larger silver halide grains are more easily affected by light than are smaller ones. Consequently, films more sensitive to light tend to store less information than those less sensitive to light.

The physical measurement of the amount of storable information is termed *resolution* and is based on the number of lines per millimeter of light-sensitive material that can be photographed. The subjective measure of image sharpness, which is related to but not contiguous with resolution, is *acutance*. Thus, films designed for theatrical projection in 35-mm. width will have better information storage capability and better image sharpness than films in 16 mm.; similarly, films in 16 mm. will store more information and give better sharpness than those in 8 mm. Generally, color films tend to have a higher capacity for information storage and better sharpness than black-and-white films (Spottiswoode, 1951).

Since moving pictures are a series of still pictures photographed with a constant time interval between them and placed in consecutive position along a strip of film, each new photograph must be in precise position relative to previous and subsequent ones. This positioning, or *registration*, is accomplished in the camera by a device that engages the perforations along the edge of the film and holds the film in position while the photograph is being made. Similarly, in the projector each consecutive photograph, or *frame*, must be precisely registered during the time it is being projected. Small errors in frame registration are evidenced in lack of image sharpness. Thus, despite high information-storage capability, considerably less than the maximum acutance may result.

In the most general terms, then, the process of film production consists of recording images photographically, selecting and reordering these images, and relating the images to a series of sounds. When the relationship of images and sounds is optimal, a number of prints of the reordered original materials may be struck.

Because the recording properties of film are essentially photographic, what can be photographed is limited to what reflects light. Although some experimenters such as Len Lye and Norman McLaren have endeavored to paint or etch material directly on clear film, the overwhelming proportion of films is made using photographic processes. The subject matter can be either the extant environment, which is most common in newsreel, instructional, and documentary films, or material especially prepared for photography, most commonly live-action fictional story films, and animated films (Rotha, 1949; Spottiswoode, 1950).

Strategies of Film Mediation

One common definition of communication has to do with the transmission of meaning, cognitive and affective, which ultimately is derived from direct experience. In modes of communication that rely on verbal signs and symbols there is little problem in recognizing that the encoding and transmission processes inexorably distort what the on-the-scene observer might perceive as experimental data. In essence, then, not only does the individual observer not necessarily perceive all that he has witnessed, but the very act of translating his perceptions into forms intelligible to others further removes those others from veridical perception of what was directly observed. The essential and obvious character of film as a photographic medium has, apparently, made people believe that, because photography bypasses verbal encoding, it is in some way more direct and less confounding than traditional verbal description.

I would argue to the contrary; mediation by the camera confounds in different but no less confusing ways. The camera is an instrument generally operated by a human intelligence and, therefore, prone to problems of selective perception. Deciding which portion of exposed film to use and which to discard in assembling the final product, while more conscious than selective retention and more obviously involving intent, still has much in common with the psychological phenomenon.

More important, however, and somewhat different from the problems encountered in written or spoken communication, is the problem of distortion. Not only are modes of distortion inherent in the photographic process, but deliberate distortions are introduced in the construction process through the use of grammatical, syntactical, or rhetorical devices that are generally deemed necessary for transforming the material that emerges from the camera and sound recorder into film. The term *editing* signifies the strategies of intentional distortion for purposes of construction.

A Taxonomy of Distortion

What are the ways in which the discrepancy between film and reality occurs? Generally, one may posit two stages of distortion: (1) in the original photography and (2) in the editing process.

Distortions of Photography

Photographic mediation—The human eye has a field of view of about 120 degrees, including most peripheral vision (Spottiswoode, 1951). Depending on the nature of the scene viewed, only a portion of this arc may be said to be subjectively perceived. The widest angle lenses normally used in film production give a horizontal angle of about 84 degrees (5.7-mm. lens with 16-mm. full aperture or 37-mm. lens in combination with 1:2.5 anamorphic lens and 65-mm. Ultra-Panavision). Lenses capable of photographing this great an angle of view tend to distort perspective so much that they are used quite sparingly. The most commonly used lenses tend to view an angle of about 23 degrees (Carlson & Carlson, 1970). These are "normal" lenses, so called not because of their field of view, but because their distortion of perspective tends to resemble most closely the perspective perceived by the human eye.

Given that the lens itself distorts, the filmmaker may use the distortion characteristics of various lenses intentionally in order to achieve certain effects. An example is the use of the so-called telephoto lens which, in addition to its powers of magnification, also has the attribute of reducing the perceived distance between objects in its field of view (Carlson & Carlson, 1970). For instance, this lens tends to reduce the distance between people in a crowd and renders the group considerably more compact than it might be in reality. Another attribute of the telephoto lens is its relatively discriminating field of focus. When a telephoto lens is focused on an object, the field of focus in front of and behind the object will tend to be much shallower and the foreground and background will tend to be out of focus, compared with wider angle lenses used under the same conditions. Thus background and foreground cues may be eliminated by the particular characteristics of the telephoto lens (Clarke, 1964).

Camera placement and size distortion—The size of objects may be visually manipulated by the placement of the camera in relation to the subject being photographed. Placing the camera higher than, say, a man, with the lens looking down at him, will tend to diminish his height. Conversely, placing the camera at a low angle with the lens looking up at the subject will tend to exaggerate the height. These techniques, which are basic to camera operation, are found in most films, although Orson Welles's film *Citizen Kane* is generally recognized as the classic example of this technique (Kael, 1971).

Temporal distortion—A camera actually records samples of an event over time, with the frequency of the sample being held constant. Each frame of a film represents such a sample. Generally speaking, the projection rate of a motion picture projector is 24 frames per second (fps). When the camera speed (or sampling frequency) is also 24 fps, the film, when projected at a rate of 24 fps, will give the illusion of real time. By decreasing the camera speed—called *undercranking*—to, for example, 8 fps and keeping the projection speed constant at 24 fps, the speed of the action perceived will be condensed to one-third of its real time. Similarly, if the camera speed is increased to, say, 48 fps, with the projector speed constant at 24 fps, the perceived action will take twice as long as it did in reality. These techniques of *fast motion* and *slow motion* are convenient ways of distorting the time frame and may be used for purposes as varied as the hectic chases of the Keystone Cops, the slow-motion study of an Olympic diver, or the speeding up of phenomena for investigation as in time-lapse photography (Spottiswoode, 1951).

Temporal reversal—Some cameras may be used to reverse normal action. In this technique the film is run through the camera backwards, and the camera is inverted. When the film is projected normally, the end of the action photographed appears at the beginning of the sequence, which progresses in reverse order to the beginning of the action as seen in reality. This effect may also be generated from normally shot film in the laboratory, using an optical printer (Spottiswoode, 1951).

Until now we have been concerned with the modes of distortion available in the motion picture camera. What differentiates a *film* from a *film recording*, however, is the manipulation of time, space, and relationships inherent in the film-editing process (Reisz, 1953). The observer-stimulus interactions in editing are enormously complex. Although a considerable amount of observation and anecdotal material has been generated about the psychology of film editing, there has been relatively little rigorous behavioral investigation. Gregory (1960) used a psycholinguistic model to investigate the nature of cognitive interaction among shots placed in succession.

Distortion in Editing

Most discussions of film editing deal with the constructs of filmic space and filmic time. These constructs relate to the perceived distance in space and time between objects or events communicated in film. Inherent in the constructs is the notion of discrepancy between time and space in the real world and time and space as perceived from films (Reisz, 1953; Eisenstein, 1957; Pudovkin, 1960).

Filmic space—Functionally, there are two major approaches to the construction of filmic space: *holistic* and *associative*.

Holistic space relationships are created by the statement of a field of action within which objects and events occur. The statement of the field of action generally is made by a shot that shows the entire field of action, that is, an *establishing* shot. Once the topography is established, objects and events within the field are viewed in closer detail, but their relationships to one another in space are perceived within the frame of reference originally created by the establishing shot.

Associative space is organized in terms of the assumptions about organization that are carried into the viewing situation by the observer. Locations are organized spatially in terms of their inherent cues within the context of associations learned by the viewer outside the frame of reference of the film itself. Thus, for example, although the topography of a house has not been specified, it is quite reasonable to see someone stepping from a kitchen directly into a living room, even though a hallway which might connect them would not be shown.

Filmic time—The editing process enables the filmmaker to abstract from any complex set of actions those actions that are significant to the statement intended. For example, it is not necessary to show someone walking from outside a room into the room and across the room to a table to pick something up. In filmic time what is significant is that the person enters the room and picks something up from a table; these two actions may be abstracted and shown sequentially either by accounting for the missing time by a syntactic device such as *matched action* or by simply making a *jump cut* (Reisz, 1953).

Similarly, one may signal that time is passing rather than actually show time passing. Significant aspects of an object or an event can be abstracted and concentrated in a series of relatively brief shots that show these aspects in progressive stages of transformation. Rather than showing events in real time, the film medium is able to deal with discrete time samples—i.e., shots—as units of utterance. Likewise, real time may be lengthened on the screen by using a number of shots of the same event and overlapping them, using the beginning of each subsequent shot to repeat the action at the end of the previous shot. This technique was best shown in the bridge-raising sequence in Sergei Eisenstein's 1928 film classic *October* (distributed outside of the Soviet Union as *Ten Days That Shook the World*).

MUSIC AND PICTURES

Since film is an audiovisual medium, the occurrence of dialogue, narration, sound effects, and music simultaneously with the pictures generates another order of interactions: the meaning of sound and picture when each is taken separately is modified by their coexistence in time. In addition, the observer's memory of their previous use, either within the context of the film or, for that matter, from some other and seemingly unrelated previous experience, provides further complexity. The conscious manipulation of the relationship between sound and picture is inescapable in the production of films. Yet aside from a manifesto by Eisenstein, V. I. Pudovkin, and G. V. Alexandrov (1957), some early works by Spottiswoode (1950) and Cameron (1947), and a long discussion by Kracauer (1960), there are surprisingly few discussions in the literature on sound and picture interaction. On the whole, works devoted to film music tend to define the notion of film music rather narrowly, thereby simplifying the issue of visual and aural interaction (Eisler, 1947; Manvell & Huntley, 1967).

THEORIES AND GRAMMARS

The film medium has been subjected to several *a posteriori* analyses by filmmakers turned theoreticians as well as by bona fide theoreticians. Like most analyses of this kind, these are primarily concerned with accounting for what seems right versus what seem wrong in terms of a set of assumptions having to do with so-called intrinsic properties of the medium.

In *Film Forum*, Eisenstein (1957:45–63) offers a series of sophisticated analyses of successful films, mostly his own, in an attempt to relate the structure of film statement to dialectic argument. The interaction of shot with shot, or idea with idea, where the shots represent antithetical statements which, as a result of their conflict, generate a synthesis of meaning in the mind of the audience, is for Eisenstein a natural extension of the dialectical materialist framework in which he operated. The sophistication of his ideas, notwithstanding their contextual dogma, derives from a wide variety of sources, most notably from the early experiments of his fellow Russian, Lev Kuleshov. Eisenstein's transformation of Kuleshov's initial experiments into a cohesive theory is amply and clearly traced by Leyda (1960). A former student of Eisenstein and a scholar of the Russian and Soviet film industries, Leyda is able to deal with the historical and political aspects of Eisenstein's situation as film director and theoretician.

Vsevold Pudovkin, Eisenstein's rival in the Soviet film industry of the 1920s, disagreed strongly with Eisenstein's philosophical position. In a series of statements on the nature of the film medium, Pudovkin viewed editing as an accretion of meaning and the shot as a kind of building block. In his *Film Technique* (1960), Pudovkin implied a much greater commonality between film and theater than Eisenstein was to acknowledge. At the root of their disagreement lay the conflict between Eisenstein's position that the technology of the medium and, above all, the editing principle could transform nonactors into credible screen characters so long as their external physical attributes were appropriate (*typage*), and Pudovkin's insistence on professionalism in front of as well as behind the cameras. It should be noted that, in practice, both men differed from their stated theoretical positions.

While the Eisenstein-Pudovkin argument was largely concerned with different theories of editing, the Hungarian film theoretician and screenwriter Béla Balázs (1953) constructed a theory that dealt with some of the attributes of film as a photographic medium. For Balázs, film was a way of getting at an assumed cross-cultural nonverbal language. Basically his position was that verbal culture consisted of a set of linguistic symbols for objects, events, and states of being. Being abstractions, these linguistic symbols were, perforce, not accessible to those persons who were not trained in the decoding of the symbol system. Thus, for Balázs, the universal nonverbal language was made to "fall into desuetude," and its symbolic representations became reified. The solution, as Balázs saw it, was in the cinema, which by virtue of its photographic nature could bypass symbols and relate directly the world of objects and events, and of nonverbal statements of being. Most important for Balázs was what he termed "the rediscovery of the human face" as a direct and universally understandable indicator of inner states of being.

In *Theory of Film: The Redemption of Physical Reality*, Siegfried Kracauer (1960) presents a somewhat more sophisticated theory of film based on its photographic attributes. While Kracauer's position on the efficacy of the photographic image in universalizing human understanding is similar to Balázs's, he proceeds through a somewhat different, if no less torturous, route. Kracauer begins with the statement that the inherent attributes of film are essentially those of photography. All photographed images are formed by the interaction of reflected light with image-forming chemicals, hence only physical reality—i.e., that which reflects light—can be photographed. He specifies a set of affinities on the basis of what photography can do "best" and then makes a series of extensions from these affinities to styles of content that are cinematic.

At its basis, Kracauer's position argues for the primacy of the neorealistic style and, to a large measure, insists that heavily structured stories, historical reconstructions, and filmed plays are not the true province of the cinema essentially because they do not take advantage of the inherent affinities of the medium. In his conclusion, Kracauer maintains that the postindustrial revolution malaise of Western culture is largely a result of excessive reliance on symbols, abstractions, and reifications, and that the true role of film is to serve as a device for the redemption of physical reality and, although not explicitly stated, of man.

In general, the problem with so-called film theory is that its stance has been largely proscriptive; its practitioners have been concerned with defining fitness and correctness on the basis of *a posteriori* statements derived from the analysis of a set of films that seem to fit some standard. The problem here, quite obviously, is that the limits and possibilities of the medium are expanding faster than can be accounted for by the theoreticians. The inherent attributes propounded by theoreticians seem too often to resemble the "humors" of medieval alchemists, and the theoretical positions in general suggest what the chemical sciences must have been like before Priestley and Lavoisier.

Kinds of Film

For purposes of description it is useful to delineate various kinds of films. When Raymond Spottiswoode (1950) wrote *A Grammar of the Film* as his A.B. thesis some thirty-odd years ago, it was a somewhat easier and more apparently fruitful task than it seems today. Just as in the biological sciences, taxonomy has been superseded by the study of internal structure. For purposes of description, however, one must begin with some notion of function.

The Feature Film

Erwin Panofsky (1959) and Rudolf Arnheim (1957) both point out that the defining characteristics of movies is that they move. Attempts to confer status on the film produced for entertainment purposes by describing it as a photoplay or, for that matter, a motion picture have been doomed from the beginning by the public's seemingly tenacious desire to call a movie a movie. The term *movie* is explicit in its reference to the fact that something on the screen moves, but it also implies a relationship of informality between audience and object. When a movie is perceived as being of extraordinary cultural or intellectual importance it is invariably referred to as a film, thus implying a quality of uplift and reverence quite inconsistent with the phrase "going to the movies."

Panofsky speculates that the easy and informal rapport of audience with movies is a function of the type or style of content that tends to restate a relatively limited number of themes, made familiar through mass publications, dime novels, and popular songs, that initially derived from folk art. He views these themes as gratifying a set of essential human concerns: a sense of justice and decorum, a propensity for sentimentality, "a primordial instinct for bloodshed and cruelty," and a taste for mild pornography and for slapstick humor (Panofsky, 1947:7). According to Panofsky, the movies represent an adaptation of folkloristic themes to the demands of a new, inexpensive, easily accessible mass medium. Many, if not all, of the genres of film content can, even today, be derived from these archetypes.

The economic function of the feature film is to provide a reason for people to pay admission fees to theaters in which such films are exhibited, since the economics of the film industry in America and, indeed, in most of the world evolved from the individual patron buying his admission ticket at the local theater. Film producers were quick to note that, in addition to story and theme, other attributes seemed helpful in attracting people to movie theaters. "Production values" such as scale, scope, and the inclusion of exotic or foreign locations were all important.

More than any other attribute of the industry, however, the "star system" was looked upon as the major way to lure customers into theaters (Jacobs, 1939). The star system functioned as a means of attaching identifiable attributes to an otherwise unknown film, and merchandising the star became an important part of making and distributing films. The rise and decline of the star system is amply documented in a number of volumes, but at its core was the creation of a synthetic public personality designed to appeal to audience phantasies, presumed by the producers to be both unspoken and unspeakable (Morin, 1960).

The production of feature films, especially in the age of television, has become considerably more risky than other areas of the industry. The probability of any feature film earning back its initial investment is said to be on the order of one in seven. Sale of television rights makes the investment somewhat less precarious, but the financing of feature films is an expensive proposition not only because of the actual cost of production but also because of the cost of borrowing the high-risk capital inherent in feature production.

From the financier's point of view, the task is obviously to minimize risk and maximize at least the probability of return. This is normally done by relying on actors, directors, and producers whose past performances are known and, more often than not, on a story that has gained currency, notoriety, or visibility in another medium. This is the so-called presold property. Most novels published in the U.S. are read in galley proof or in a prepublication edition by representatives of the major film producers. It is not unknown for an original film script to be novelized, published, promoted to a position on the bestseller list, all before it is publicly announced that the work will be made into a film. While the audience talks about "movies," the producers tend to talk about "product" and "properties." Few, if any, people talk about "art."

Documentary

According to John Grierson (1966:13), documentary is "the creative treatment of actuality." Grierson believed that the film medium could operate as an educational force on a grand scale by making its audience aware of people and events that were unknown to most of them. For Grierson, education meant uplift; implicit in his writing is the idea that man is perfectible by education and that educated man will make the right decisions in a democracy. The documentary film was a way of providing education and uplift in a relatively painless, informal, and enjoyable manner through the use of a medium that had the power of sight and sound and did not rely on literacy. That the documentary film was designed to change attitudes was also implicit in Grierson's ideas, and the mechanism was simple: documentary film imparts new information, and new information naturally changes existing attitudes.

Relatively few documentaries are distributed through the channel of the commercial theater. With notable exceptions, such as Robert Flaherty's *Nanook of the North* and Merian C. Cooper and Ernest Schoedsack's *Grass*, the documentary form was in practice incompatible with theatrical exhibition until the late 1960s when there emerged a spate of films dealing with various manifestations of the youth and music scene, such as *Woodstock*. For the most part, the documentary film found its audience in schools, church halls, clubs, and on television (Starr, 1951).

The advent of television and the contemporaneous development of portable sound and camera equipment brought a new renascence in the documentary, and an informal style of exposition that dispensed with the traditional omniscient narrator in favor of letting the event speak for itself. This style, generally known as *cinéma vérité*, readily sacrificed technical polish for informality and intimacy. It attained a certain measure of cultic following among those who felt that compressing and structuring film content in the editing room was "truer" than preproduction planning and preconception.

The rise of cinéma vérité was a boon to the television documentarian who, bound by the restrictions of the FCC's fairness doctrine, could deal with controversial material in a relatively noncontroversial way by letting the story tell itself without obvious comment in the narration. The more socially engaged filmmakers seem to have taken up the style as a reaction to the overtly propagandistic and sometimes bravura attempts at social influence such as Pare Lorentz's classic *The River* and Willard Van Dyke's seminal film *The City* (whose panaceas, advocated loudly and eloquently, failed to materialize). Cinéma vérité was an opportunity to document factually an aspect of the human condition and, by implication, the need for improvement without taking the dangerous step of offering possible solutions (Breitrose, 1964).

The documentary form has been used for other kinds of advocacy also. A major type of factual film is the so-called business film (Starr, 1951). Such films are designed either to detail the advantages of the sponsor's product or to enhance the image of the sponsor by showing a problem or phenomenon of interest and then indicating either directly or indirectly how the sponsor or his product relates to the solution of such a problem. Business films or "sponsored" films are made available without charge to television stations, schools, and organizations through agencies specializing in this kind of distribution. In return, the agency solicits a report on how many times the film was shown and an estimate of its audience. As the number of television channels increase through the use of cable television installations, it is probable that the demand for and the audience available to the sponsored film among the general public will increase.

Educational Films

All films are educational whether by accident or design. An industry of considerable size has developed that is concerned with the production of films specifically for instructional purposes. Although educational films date back almost to the beginning of the medium, they did not become important until the development of relatively portable projection equipment and increased use of 16-mm. safety film rather than the 35-mm. highly flammable nitrate-based film that was for many years the standard for theatrical production. This meant that films could be brought into any classroom and shown by teachers and students rather than remaining the province of specially trained and licensed motion-picture projectionists.

Educational films are distributed in various ways. The most common means of dissemination is sale to educational film libraries maintained by local school systems, county and state educational agencies, state universities, and public libraries. Often producers or distributors of educational films maintain private rental libraries from which, for a fee, educational films may be rented. Many of these libraries also rent 16-mm. versions of theatrical films that may have curricular or extracurricular interest to schools and colleges.

Usually educational films are designed to complement the more widely adopted texts. Among publishers of educational materials, McGraw-Hill has been a leader in producing what they call "text-films" that are correlated with standard texts in various fields. The underlying philosophy for these text-films is the presentation of curricular materials by means of film in addition to presentations by text and teacher. A somewhat different philosophy lies behind the efforts of those educational film producers whose films, while not specifically correlated with commonly used texts, offer supplemental information. These films are generally treated under the general heading of enrichment materials.

The usual way in which films were introduced into a school system was by means of a salesman who solicited requests for previews from the audiovisual coordinator. The coordinator then viewed the film, either alone or with a consultative committee of teachers or administrators, and a decision was made to purchase or not to purchase the film. During the years 1958 to 1968, the National Defense Education Act gave U.S. school systems virtually a blank check for the subsidized purchase of educational films. As a result, the industry prospered.

The primary criticism of these teaching aids came when educational films were compared with newly developed means of instruction such as programmed teaching and computer-assisted instruction. Because of pretesting, programmed instruction could be introduced with the assurance that specified criteria of instruction would be met. Very few serious efforts had ever been made to test whether educational films were really educational in the ways intended.

Another serious criticism of educational films was that, unlike programmed or computer-assisted instruction, they did not provide for individualization of instruction. These criticisms of educational films, together with the expiration of the National Defense Education Act, have led to a reexamination of the issue of validation of effectiveness and to the development of new technology that will enable students to view educational films at their own rate of speed. It will soon be possible for film producers to make films that can be controlled by the learner to allow for variation in rate of presentation, that will include response items, and that can be incorporated into a somewhat more complex learning system that will take advantage of the strengths of every kind of instructional methodology. Development of sophisticated computer-assisted instruction, its integration with two-way cable television, and the development of inexpensive and easily used presentation and response systems would seem to be in the middle-range future. In the short-range future, super-8-mm. cartridge films, electronic videorecorders (EVR), and video-cassette presentation systems that can easily be cued to stop, reverse, and present single frames, may very well supplant the 16-mm. classroom film.

AUDIENCES

The relationship of audience to the film industry is somewhat different from that of readership to newspapers. In newspaper publishing, income is basically a function of advertising sales, and the cost of advertising is only indirectly a function of circulation. In the motion picture industry, the admission price paid by the audience to the theater is quite directly the basis for the economic success or failure of a production company. The situation of profit being tied to admission has been altered slightly by the possibilities of sale to television, but even the potential sale price of a film to television is a function of how successful the film was in its original theatrical run.

The insoluble dilemma of the film industry is that audience tastes change at a far more rapid rate than can be responded to by the industry. Whereas the television industry can make programming adjustments with a view toward maximizing audiences two or three times within the nine-month "season," the film industry typically is characterized by an eighteen-month to two-year lag between the inception of an idea for a film and the actual theatrical release. What occurs, in effect, is a situation in which the audience's taste may shift radically within the two-year period and the film producer is incapable of reacting to such changes except superficially by making minor alterations to work already in progress. Most often these alterations consist of increasing the prominence of an actor whose popularity has grown or adding some gratuitous nudity or violence. Once the basic design for any film is set, however, its progress is almost inexorable.

The relationship between producer and audience has been explored in several studies. Handel (1950), Mayer (1946) and, more recently, a study by Daniel Yankelovitch, Inc. (1967) for the Motion Picture Association of America use a kind of need and gratification formulation to explain the relationship of producer and audience as seen from the producer's point of view. This formulation is based upon the assumption that it is the role of the film producer to cater to the desires of the audience and that these desires are, in fact, the manifestation of certain needs. The successful film will gratify whatever needs exist. Although this formulation is not too different from Erwin Panofsky's (1947) notions of the role of film as folk art, it has tended to be expressed in somewhat different ways.

STRUCTURE OF THE FEATURE FILM INDUSTRY

The theatrical film industry can be characterized by three major functions: production, distribution, and exhibition. Although this is a convenient means for delineating the major functions within the industry, the categories are not necessarily mutually exclusive despite the efforts of the Department of Justice, which over the years has sought to promote the divestiture of exhibition from production and distribution.

PRODUCTION

Historically, production of motion pictures for theatrical exhibition began because of the necessity of providing material for those who rented or purchased machinery. It is not accidental that the first American production firm was started by Edison who even before projected films were a reality—when films were still being viewed by individual patrons as peep shows—was faced with the problem of supplying a "product." The French firm of Lumière began in precisely the same manner. Thus during the earliest years of the medium, equipment manufacturers were the major sources of films (Sadoul, 1949). More often than not, production of films was the province of technicians with some artistic avocations who functioned as producers, directors, cameramen, and editors, and who also operated the processing machines.

As the industry grew, changes took place. When equipment could be purchased outright rather than rented, and when pictures could be projected and seen by a relatively large audience rather than having to be viewed individually, the importation of films from abroad began, and various entrepreneurs with no connection to equipment manufacturers began to make films. The heyday of the individual or small entrepreneur was in the earliest years of the century, and niceties such as patent rights and licensing agreements were largely ignored in the pursuit of quick gain (Jacobs, 1939).

Few if any people connected with the older forms of dramatic art were involved in the production of these earliest films, a pattern which, like many others of the period, persevered in the film industry until the present day. Rather, the organizers of the early motion picture studios were drawn from groups concerned more with mercantile than artistic effects. What resulted from this unbridled and enthusiastic competition was the formation of an industrial agreement among patent holders, those few film studios that had negotiated licensing agreements, the equipment manufacturers, and the major producer of raw film stock, Eastman Kodak. This agreement was formalized as the Motion Picture Patents Company or, somewhat less formally, "the trust."

The trust was, in full measure, a conspiracy in restraint of trade. Its activities consisted of controlling all phases of the film industry, including exhibition and distribution. More strikingly, however, the trust exerted enormous legal and illegal pressures against nonmember producers. To avoid the threat of prosecution, such producers fled from New York, the headquarters of the Motion Picture Patents Company, to Hollywood, a suburb of Los Angeles, where land was cheap, climate benign, and the Mexican border reassuringly close. Thus, it is said, Hollywood became the production center of the American film industry while New York remained its managerial nexus. Through a combination of tenacity, the implementation of the Sherman Antitrust Act, and the legal efforts of William Fox, an entrepreneur who did not join the trust, the Motion Picture Patents Company was destroyed, and the film industry for the first time took on some of the attributes of a free market (Jacobs, 1939).

What the trust did not accomplish, the free market did. For historical reasons, among which were the increased film audience and such novel merchandising techniques as endowing hitherto anonymous film actors with highly visible "star" status, the cost of filmmaking soared. Actors, who had previously been relatively interchangeable, became the primary means of identifying the films that were to be patronized. Thus, in constructing a star system in which films were merchandised by attributes largely extrinsic to what actually appeared on the screen, the stars were in a position to command salaries far in excess of those that had been previously paid. The pattern for salaries in the film industry became set as a function not of skill or labor but of contribution to the probable profit. The greater the potential profit, the higher the salary, since all other things such as skill and talent were usually equal.

As costs and potential profit soared, production became a high-risk–high-gain undertaking. The nature of the risk led small producers to merge into ever diminishing numbers of studios; the nature of the profit led outside financial organizations, such as the larger banks, into film financing (Ramsaye, 1926; Jacobs, 1939).

Consolidation of small producers into large studios created other pressures. The demand for films increased as motion picture theaters multiplied and audiences began to regard the movies no longer as a novelty but as a habit. The response of the large studios was to supply a standardized product produced by a division of labor that fulfilled Durkheim's model and resembled more closely Henry Ford's notions of automobile manufacture than Ibsen's ideas of dramaturgy.

The chairman of the board was inevitably headquartered in New York while the director of production ran the Hollywood facility of any major studio. Under him were usually several executive producers, each of whom took responsibility for a number of productions. Productions were usually characterized as "important pictures," which were generally high-budget productions with well-known stars, and so-called "B" pictures or "program films," which had minimal budgets, little-known actors, and extremely short production schedules. These B pictures were used to fill out the second half of double-feature programs and were often forced on unwilling exhibitors as part of the price of getting the more desirable important pictures.

Under the executive producer—whose word was law—were the producers who took responsibility for the individual films. Under the producer was the team of writers, the director, cameraman, editors, carpenters, grips, electricians, and other production personnel, each performing his function as needed. It was the norm for only the producer to be involved with the entire production; the writers and director went on to other assignments when their functions on a production were finished (Crowther, 1957).

With a high volume of product being turned out (see Table 1), it was possible for the studios to justify the exceedingly large investments in capital equipment, especially after the coming of sound and the necessity for new technology that it created, and the large amounts of money committed to stars' contracts. The situation made a great deal of sense since the studio could predict the demand for its product in advance and could be virtually guaranteed distribution and exhibition. To ensure predictability, studios established distribution facilities and engaged in the wholesale acquisition of theaters. Thus, as long as the audiences remained large, producers who had control over the distribution and exhibition of their films could look forward to a financially prosperous future (see Table 2).

The divestiture of the production function from distribution and exhibition, accompanied by a decline in the number of people who would pay at the box office to see films, created the current crisis in feature-film production. Simply stated, without guaranteed distribution and exhibition, with little predictability of audience size, and with the competition of

TABLE 1
MOTION PICTURE FEATURES RELEASED BY NATIONAL DISTRIBUTORS

Year	Number	Year	Number
1930	355	1951	399
1931	331	1952	353
1932	330	1953	376
1933	351	1954	296
1934	357	1955	283
1935	372	1956	314
1936	413	1957	359
1937	487	1958	332
1938	448	1959	235
1939	469		
		1960	229
1940	473	1961	223
1941	497	1962	214
1942	485	1963	203
1943	427	1964	219
1944	409	1965	249
1945	367	1966	229
1946	382	1967	218
1947	381	1968	235
1948	406	1969	236
1949	411		
		1970	258
1950	425	1971	255

SOURCE: Motion Picture Association of America.
NOTE: Figures do not include re-releases.

television, the traditional studio system was no longer economically possible.

In its place has emerged a situation in which the studio takes some part in the financing of films and enters into coproduction and distribution agreements with small production firms, some of which have been especially organized for the production of a single film. These independent producers rent studio space, take advantage of the studio's financing, but generally are self-contained except for reliance on technical facilities. In return, the studios receive payment for their facilities, a financial return on their investment and, generally, distribution rights for the film.

In the new configuration of the industry, the studio's functions are financial, technical, and distributive. The independent producer is responsible for the so-called creative functions, such as scriptwriter, producer, director, actors, and often for the acquisition of additional financing. From another point of view, it is more utilitarian for directors, stars, and even scriptwriters to incorporate themselves as independent production companies and partake of the tax advantages than for them to be salaried employees of the studios.

INTERNATIONAL OPERATIONS

Historically, the American film industry has been characterized by a growing dependence on international distribution. Although the silent film could easily be translated into many foreign languages simply by altering titles, the attitude of the industry toward foreign distribution was largely that of a welcomed but extra benefit (Guback, 1969). Sound films presented somewhat more difficult problems, but advances in techniques of postsynchronizing various foreign languages to the lip movements on the screen (*dubbing*) provided a way of adapting sound films for world wide distribution. A somewhat smaller number of films was adapted by simply superimposing titles across the bottom of the screen. In Thailand, the showing of foreign-language films is accompanied by a live interlocutor who relates his impression of what the people on the screen might be saying.

At present, approximately half the revenue from American films is earned abroad (see Table 3). In addition to profits derived from foreign distribution of American films, most large American film-production firms have substantial foreign investment in production, distribution, and exhibition. The implications of international operations by the American film industry are quite complex but tend to fall into three categories: (1) film content, (2) international trade agreements, and (3) operations of foreign subsidiaries.

There seems to be little doubt (as well as little documentation) that numerous deci-

TABLE 2

THIRTY FILMS EARNING HIGHEST BOX OFFICE RETURNS IN U.S. AND CANADA

Title	Director/ Producer	Distributor	Year of Release	Total Rentals
Gone With the Wind	V. Fleming D. Selznick	MGM	1939	$ 74,200,000
The Sound of Music	R. Wise	20th-Fox	1965	72,000,000
Love Story	A. Hiller H. Minsky	Paramount	1970	50,000,000
Airport	G. Seaton R. Hunter	Universal	1970	44,500,000
The Graduate	M. Nichols L. Turman	Avco Embassy	1968	43,100,000
Doctor Zhivago	D. Lean C. Ponti	MGM	1965	43,000,000
Ben-Hur	W. Wyler S. Zimbalist	MGM	1959	40,690,000
Ten Commandments	C. B. DeMille	Paramount	1957	40,000,000
My Fair Lady	G. Cukor J. L. Warner	Warner Brothers	1964	32,000,000
Mary Poppins	R. Stevenson W. Disney	Buena Vista	1964	31,000,000
M.A.S.H.	R. Altman I. Preminger	20th-Fox	1970	30,000,000
Butch Cassidy and the Sundance Kid	G. R. Hill C. Foreman	20th-Fox	1969	29,200,000
West Side Story	R. Wise J. Robbins	Mirisch/7 Arts United Artists	1961	28,100,000
Thunderball	T. Young	Eon United Artists	1965	27,000,000
Patton	F. Schaffner F. McCarthy	20th-Fox	1970	27,000,000
Cleopatra	J. Mankiewicz W. Wanger	20th-Fox	1963	26,000,000
Guess Who's Coming to Dinner	S. Kramer	Columbia	1968	25,500,000
Funny Girl	W. Wyler R. Stark	Columbia	1968	24,900,000
How the West Was Won	J. Ford H. Hathaway G. Marshall	Smith-Cinerama Cinerama-MGM	1962	24,268,000
It's a Mad, Mad, Mad, Mad World	S. Kramer	United Artists	1963	23,800,000

TABLE 2—*Continued*

Title	Director/ Producer	Distributor	Year of Release	Total Rentals
Around the World in 80 Days	M. Anderson M. Todd	United Artists	1956	$23,000,000
Goldfinger	G. Hamilton	Eon United Artists	1964	22,500,000
Bonnie and Clyde	A. Penn W. Beatty	Warner Brothers	1967	22,000,000
2001: Space Odyssey	S. Kubrick	MGM	1968	21,500,000
Love Bug	R. Stevenson W. Walsh	Buena Vista	1969	21,000,000
The Dirty Dozen	R. Aldrich K. Hyman	MGM	1967	20,067,000
Valley of the Dolls	M. Robson D. Weisbart	20th-Fox	1967	20,000,000
The Odd Couple	G. Saks H. Koch	Paramount	1968	20,000,000
To Sir, with Love	J. Clavell	Columbia	1967	19,100,000
Bullitt	P. Yates P. D'Antoni	Warner Brothers	1969	19,000,000

SOURCE: Variety (1972:11).

TABLE 3

THE ECONOMICS OF THE AMERICAN FILM INDUSTRY: SELECTED DATA

Year	Number of Releases	Box Office Receipts (millions)	Number of Theaters	Admission Price Index (1957–59 = 100)
1958	332	$ 992	16,354	100.2
1959	235	958	—	—
1960	229	951	—	110.0
1961	223	921	—	115.7
1962	214	903	—	120.7
1963	203	904	12,652	125.4
1964	219	913	12,879*	135.5
1965	249	927	13,155*	146.4
1966	229	964	13,441*	157.3
1967	218	989	13,531*	169.2
1968	235	1,045	13,822*	185.3
1969	236	1,099	13,939*	200.6
1970	258	1,162	14,350	219.9

SOURCE: Number of releases and number of theaters, Motion Picture Association of America, Inc. Other figures from Commerce Department (1968:309–311; 1969:437–440).

* estimated

sions affecting casting and content of American films are made because of the international nature of film distribution. This is an area about which little has been written, but conversations with film-production and management personnel make clear that, for example, the higher the projected budget of a film and the greater the reliance on foreign distribution for the film's potential earnings, the more important will be the "international" considerations. These considerations may range from including nationals of several countries in the cast to choosing locations and adapting script and action to fit the mores of the nations in which they are to be distributed. The Scandinavian countries, for example, tend to be considerably more strict on the censorship of violence than of sex, and it is not unknown for alternative sequences to be photographed so that the film may be emended in various versions, depending on where the film is released. A more frequent accusation, however, is that American feature films and television films impose upon another culture the values and mores of America.

The complexity and scope of foreign-trade agreements affecting the distribution of American films abroad defies description. The industry is represented abroad by the Motion Picture Export Association (MPEA), which maintains offices and representatives in Europe, Asia, Africa, and South America. The functions of the MPEA are, quite simply, to make American films as freely available as possible for showing on foreign screens and to maximize financial return to the American producer. This becomes a delicate and complicated task because foreign nations do not necessarily have the same interests as American producers. Some nations have taken the position that the motion picture is an important cultural product and have been unwilling to sacrifice the indigenous film industry for the benefit of the American distributor, even though importing American films might be much less costly than supporting a native film industry. Other nations have attempted to protect local production personnel from being displaced by imported films from America. Another attitude on the part of foreign nations is that film import and export demands a *quid pro quo* relationship, i.e., the import of American films should be tied in some way either to export of their films to the U.S. or to American investment in the local film industry (Guback, 1969).

The American film industry, largely through the work of the MPEA, has been quite effective in dealing with foreign protectionist attempts to reduce or limit the number of American films available to the international public. Most often the protectionism has been manifested by an attempt to tie the number of American films that can be imported to the number of films produced locally. In principle, at least, this method would seem to allow for national cinematic expression as well as provide jobs for film-production personnel locally. Not unconnected with this is the underlying assumption that if a necessary condition for the importation of American films is a quantity of local production, then American companies, eager to distribute their films, would provide capital for local production. A variant on this theme is the establishment of low-interest loan funds which are made available locally for the production of films that have a predominantly local production staff. Thus, in principle, with low-interest loans available, American producers would invest in foreign production and hire local crews. Moreover, in quota situations, the American companies would further be eager to support local production in order to earn import certificates that are dispensed as some function of the number of locally produced films.

What, in fact, has occurred has been the colonization of many film industries—most notably the British, and to a lesser extent the French—because of an overdependence on American capital. The American-financed production was either of the "quota-quickie" variety, begun in the late 1920s as an artifact of the financing of the German studio UFA by Paramount and MGM, or it was local production in name only. The Paramount-MGM-UFA negotiations, known as the PARUFAMET agreement, provided financing for UFA in return for the assignment of import certificates resulting from German production to Paramount and MGM for the importation of American films. This resulted in the production of a number of films whose only distinction was that they earned import licenses. Similar post-World War II films produced in England earned the title "quota quickies."

Local production in name only tended to use either American scripts or scripts supervised by American producers, with American or "international" stars, but employing local production crews. Thus the films could qualify for low-interest loans from the government film-financing corporation while operating with reduced labor costs because of the discrepancy between foreign and U.S. wage scales for film technicians. A number of films were made as "international coproductions" by combining subsidiaries in various countries and taking advantage of the definition of a locally produced film and the film-subsidy scheme in each nation (Guback, 1969).

REFERENCES

Arnheim, Rudolf.
1957 Film as Art. Berkeley: University of California Press.

Balázs, Béla.
1953 Theory of the Film. Translation by Edith Bone. New York: Roy.

Breitrose, Henry S.
1964 "On the search for the real nitty-gritty: Problems and possibilities in cinema-verite." Film Quarterly (Summer): 36–40.

Cameron, Ken.
1947 Sound and the Documentary Film. London: Pitman.

Carlson, Verne, and Sylvia Carlson.
1970 Professional 16/35 mm Cameraman's Handbook. New York: American Photographic Book Publishing Company.

Clarke, Charles.
1964 Professional Cinematography. Hollywood: American Society of Cinematographers.

Commerce Department.
1968 "Selected services," in U.S. Industrial Outlook, 1969. Washington, D.C.: U.S. Government Printing Office (December).
1969 "Selected services," in U.S. Industrial Outlook, 1970. Washington, D.C.: U.S. Government Printing Office (December).

Crowther, Bosley.
1957 The Lion's Share. New York: Dutton.

Daniel Yankelovich, Inc.
1967 "Report for the Motion Picture Association of America." Unpublished paper.

Eisenstein, S. M.
1957 Film Forum [and] The Film Sense. Edited and translated by Jay Leyda. New York: Meredian Books (reprint).

Eisenstein, S. M., V. I. Pudovkin, and G. V. Alexandrov.
1957 "A statement on sound-film," in S. M. Eisenstein, Film Forum [and] The Film Sense. Edited and translated by Jay Leyda. New York: Meredian Books (reprint). The statement was first published in the Leningrad magazine Zhizn Iskusstva, August 5, 1928.

Eisler, Hanns.
1947 Composing for the Films. New York: Oxford University Press.

Gregory, John Robert.
1960 "Some psychological aspects of motion picture montage." Ph.D. Dissertation, University of Illinois (unpublished).

Grierson, John.
1966 Grierson on Documentary. Revised Edition. Edited by Forsyth Hardy. Berkeley: University of California Press.

Guback, Thomas H.
1969 The International Films Industry: Western Europe and America Since 1945. Bloomington: Indiana University Press.

Handel, Leo A.
1950 Hollywood Looks at Its Audience; A Report of Film Audience Research. Urbana: University of Illinois Press.

Hoban, Charles F., Jr., and Edward B. Van Ormer.
1950 Instructional Film Research 1918–1950 (Rapid Mass Learning). New York: Arno Press (reprint).

Jacobs, Lewis
1939 Rise of the American Film; A Critical History. New York: Harcourt, Brace.

Kael, Pauline.
1971 Citizen Kane Book. Boston: Little, Brown.

Kracauer, Siegfried.
1960 Theory of Film: The Redemption of Physical Reality. New York: Oxford University Press.

Leyda, Jay.
1960 Kino: A History of the Russian and Soviet Film. New York: Macmillan.

Manvell, Roger, and John Huntley.
1967 Technique of Film Music. Second Edition. New York: Hastings House.

Mayer, Jacob Peter.
1946 Sociology of Film: Studies and Documents. London: Faber and Faber.

Morin, Edgar.
1960 The Stars. Translation by Richard Howard. New York: Grove Press.

Panofsky, Erwin.
1947 "Style and medium in the motion picture." Critique 1 (No. 3): 7.

Pudovkin, V. I.
1960 Film Technique; and Film Acting. Edited and translated by Ivor Montagu. New York: Grove Press.

Ramsaye, Terry.
1926 A Million and One Nights; A History of the Motion Picture. New York: Simon and Schuster. (Reissued in 1964.)

Reisz, Karel.
1953 Technique of Film Editing. New York: Farrar, Straus, and Cudahy.

Rotha, Paul.
1949 The Film Till Now: A Survey of World Cinema. Revised and Enlarged Edition. New York: Funk and Wagnalls.

Sadoul, Georges.
1949 Histoire de l'art du cinéma. Paris: Flammarion.

Spottiswoode, Raymond.
1950 A Grammar of the Film: An Analysis of Film Technique. Berkeley: University of California Press.
1951 Film and Its Technique. Berkeley: University of California Press.

Starr, Cecile (ed.).
1951 Ideas on Film. New York: Funk and Wagnalls.

Variety.
1972 "All-time boxoffice champs." Variety (January 5): 11+.

CHAPTER 18 Broadcasting

WILBUR SCHRAMM and JANET ALEXANDER
Stanford University

The two electronic media that have grown up in our own century are the subjects of this chapter. The way in which radio and television developed, the structure of the broadcasting industry, the dimensions of its support and the mechanisms for its control, the content of the broadcast media (including a typical day on the airwaves), the audiences for different kinds of programs and for different hours of the day—all are described. The chapter then turns to some of the industry's problems of policy and responsibility: the relation of ownership to performance; the problem of how to insure appropriate access to the media; the "fairness doctrine"; and present concerns about such matters as television's effects on children, political "packaging," and possible harmful effects of some broadcast advertising.

DEVELOPMENT OF BROADCASTING

Seeing, hearing, communicating over great distances have always been part of man's dream. During the Renaissance, when the study of magnetism led to the first primitive understanding of electronics, these dreams took a new form.

As early as 1558, Giovanni Battista della Porta described a "sympathetic telegraph" which could send messages through magnetism (see Barnouw, 1956). Joseph Glanvil predicted in London in 1661 that "the time will come, and that presently, when by making use of the magnetic waves that permeate the ether which surrounds the world, we shall communicate with the Antipodes." There were many such predictions in the seventeenth and eighteenth centuries, and in the nineteenth century they began to come true.

In 1844 Samuel F. B. Morse sent from Washington to Baltimore the first official message by wired telegraph, said to have been "What hath God wrought!" (What *un*official messages preceded that, we do not know, but anyone who has tried to get a

---

This chapter will focus on broadcasting in the United States. It is regrettable that it must be so limited, because broadcasting is not essentially an ethnocentric topic. Radio and television developed in several countries at about the same time, and drew on science and engineering from many countries. International radio has long been an important activity, and satellites and cables are now carrying television worldwide. The problems of developing, regulating, programming, supporting, and evaluating broadcasting are much the same everywhere. Indeed, the different ways in which these problems have been solved—for example the different relationships to government and to private enterprise that have been worked out—serve to illuminate the problems and practices of any one

new communication link to work will suspect that "What hath God wrought!" came fairly late in the process of trial.) Marconi demonstrated in 1897 that dots and dashes could be sent through space without wires, and in 1899 he sent Morse code across the English channel; in 1901, across the Atlantic.

Meanwhile work was under way in transmitting the human voice itself. Alexander Graham Bell demonstrated in 1876 that understandable speech could be sent over a wire. Edison was working on the phonograph by 1877. Just before the turn of the century experiments in sending the human voice by "wireless" were in progress. Stubblefield claimed to have sent and received a voice one mile without wires in 1899.

A key development at this time was the invention of the Alexanderson alternator, which produced a smooth continuous set of high frequency waves, suitable for voice modulation. Using this method, Fessenden, a former Westinghouse engineer who had gone to teach at the University of Pittsburgh, began to experiment with sending both music and voice through the air. Ham operators and ship radio officers began to report as early as 1905 that they occasionally received voice programs from Fessenden's laboratory.

DeForest's triode tube, patented in 1907, made voice broadcasting easier, and DeForest himself entered voice radio experimentation. He did a voice broadcast from the Tour Eiffel in 1909, and in 1910 put Caruso on the air, to be heard by ships at sea. In 1916 he broadcast election returns from New York City; like most other newsmen on that election day, he announced that Charles Evans Hughes was the next president of the United States.

One of the first official uses of voice radio was a broadcast made by President Wilson (who *had* won the 1916 election) from his ship returning from the Paris Peace Conference in 1919. Unfortunately, he seems to have been heard only by ships at sea.

Marconi and other European innovators had been very active with radio-broadcast experiments during the first two decades of the century, and experimental stations were springing up in both Europe and America. One of the first of these was KQW, San Jose, California, which was on the air in 1909. It was a short step from "ham" and experimental stations to stations designed to serve homes. The present KCBS in San Francisco is a lineal descendant of KQW.

In 1888, Edward Bellamy's book *Looking Backward* had contained a passage that drew more attention thirty years later than when it was first published. He described a scene in the year 2000, in which a hostess asked a guest whether he wanted to hear some music. She handed him a list of titles and let him make a selection, then "crossed the room and as far as I could see merely touched one or two screws and at once the room was filled with the music of a great organ anthem."

Probably Bellamy's imagination was stimulated by Edison's new phonograph, but thirty years later a telegrapher for the American Marconi Company (who later became president of the Radio Corporation

---

nation. It would be useful, therefore, if this chapter could provide something that does not really exist in an adequate form anywhere in the literature: a broad, comparative study of broadcasting, worldwide.

Given the pages and time available, however, that is infeasible. We shall try to set some comparative background, but must necessarily concentrate on data from one country only; and the United States system of broadcasting is so large and so complex that even this kind of treatment will be lacking in many details and many respects. Readers who want to fill in the international background more fully will find a number of single-country studies of broadcasting, and a few useful essays in comparison, for example, UNESCO (1964), Paulu (1967), St. John (1967), Schramm, Coombs, Kahnert, and Lyle (1967), Emery (1969), and such reference books as the *World Radio TV Handbook*.

of America) believed that he saw a way to make the scene come true long before the year 2000. This was David Sarnoff, who wrote a memorandum to his superiors, as follows:

> I have in mind a plan of development which would make radio a household utility.... The idea is to bring music into the home by wireless. The receiver can be designed in the form of a simple "Radio Music Box" and arranged for several different wavelengths, which can be changeable with the throwing of a single switch or the pressing of a single button.... The same principle can be extended to numerous other fields, as for example receiving lectures at home, which could be perfectly audible; and events of national importance which can be simultaneously announced and received. Baseball scores can be transmitted in the air.... This proposition would be especially interesting to farmers and others living in outlying districts... (entire letter is reproduced in St. John, 1967:33).

The same vision came to others. Radio station 8MK, Detroit, became station WWJ. Out of the Westinghouse experimental station, in 1920, came station KDKA. There were 30 licensed stations on the air in the United States by the end of 1921, and 500 by the end of 1922. At that time approximately three million receivers were in use.

The Growing Pains of Radio

With the development of home radio in this country and elsewhere, problems swiftly developed: how to support it, how to regulate it, how to guide its use. It was thought at first that stations could be maintained by the sale of receivers and by the tangible or intangible returns from the prestige of broadcasting. Sarnoff himself did not conceive of radio as a vehicle for direct profit-making. He spoke of it as something that will "be regarded as a public institution of great value in the same sense that a library, for example, is regarded today" (Archer, 1939:30). In 1922, however, the American Society of Composers, Authors, and Publishers demanded payment for music that was played on the air. This pointed to even greater program expenses in the future, and forced the new stations to look for an additional source of substantial income. They found it in advertising.

The first recorded radio commercial was sold in 1922 by station WEAF, New York, to promote the sale of real estate lots on Long Island. Thereafter, advertising was to be the chief method of support for broadcasting in the United States.

There were vigorous protests against a commercial system. Secretary of Commerce Hoover said in 1922, "It is inconceivable that we should allow so great a possibility for service, for news, for entertainment, for education, and for vital commercial purposes, to be drowned in advertising chatter" (Chester, Garrison & Willis, 1963). He predicted that "the American people will never stand for" advertising on the radio. It was a celebrated miscalculation. By 1930, radio advertising had risen to $60 million a year, and there were 14,750,000 receivers in use. Presently, the bill for radio advertising is over a billion dollars a year, and for television more than two billion.

One of the chief reasons for the formation of networks (NBC in 1926, CBS in 1927) was the need to make it easier for advertisers and their agencies to deal quickly and efficiently with a group of stations. The first network show on American radio, at the inaugural of NBC on 15 November, 1926, illustrated the quality of talent that was on radio at that time, and also indicated what kind of display window radio was prepared to provide for the commercials on which it subsisted. The program originated at the Waldorf-Astoria in New York, and included the New York Symphony Orchestra under Walter Damrosch, the humorist Will Rogers, opera singers Mary Garden and Tito Ruffo, and the dance bands of Vincent Lopez and Ben Bernie, among others.

It is interesting to speculate what might have happened to radio in the United States if in 1922 it had chosen the way that most European countries took: government-owned radio supported wholly or in part by a tax on receiving sets. This was a fundamental decision for the United States communication system. It built commercial competition for audiences (and consequently for advertising dollars) into the system for as long as can be foreseen. It created property values for frequency assigments so that, in practice, they came to be treated as the broadcasters', rather than the public's, channels. It transferred the responsibility for programming to the broadcasters rather than to the government, and government regulatory agencies ever since have had the greatest difficulty doing anything about it. It tended to substitute audience size and resultant profit for other measures of public service. And, most obviously, it determined that American broadcasting thereafter would be a showcase for sales messages that were permitted to intrude into entertainment and informational programming.

Before radio could realize the financial and entertainment success it was destined to attain, however, it was necessary to regulate the assignment of frequencies to stations. American radio began with one frequency, then two, and finally the whole band of 550 to 1600 kilohertz (kHz). As more stations came on the air, and as power was increased, stations began to interfere with each other.

Secretary Hoover called a conference on standards and allocations as early as 1922, and most of the 1920s was taken up in sorting out frequency assignments and providing a way to make and enforce them. Finally the chaos on the air became so intolerable that the broadcasters themselves petitioned for regulation. The result was passage of the Federal Radio Act of 1927, which established the Federal Radio Commission. Seven years later the Federal Communications Act of 1934 replaced the 1927 law and established the Federal Communications Commission. We shall have more to say later about the FCC and the problems of broadcast regulation.

Once these basic decisions had been made and order established on the airwaves, radio became a thriving industry. Despite the depression, more than 50 million sets were in use and 700 stations operative by the end of the 1930s. Income from the sale of time was appròaching $200 million. Radio won a historic victory over the newspapers in gaining the right to buy wire news services.

The new medium came to absorb somewhere near three hours of the average American's day. It contributed to everyday American life and experience familiar voices like those of Ed Murrow, William L. Shirer, H. V. Kaltenborn, and Lowell Thomas; the Philharmonic with Toscanini and the Saturday afternoon Metropolitan opera broadcast; quality drama such as CBS Playhouse; family serial drama, some of it as memorable as "One Man's Family"; satiric comedy like that of Fred Allen.

On Halloween, 1938, Orson Welles scared substantial numbers of listeners out of their lounge slippers with a program that demonstrated what radio had come to mean to Americans. It was outwardly innocuous—a dramatization of H. G. Wells's novel, *War of the Worlds*, which tells the story of an imagined invasion from Mars. It was well labeled as fiction and radio drama—but it was in the form of news broadcasts. In less than twenty years radio had come to be so deeply trusted, so much depended on for news, that in several parts of the country uncritical listeners literally ran for the hills.

The Coming of Television

Even as early as 1938, a shadow was beginning to fall over the prosperity and popularity of radio. The shadow came from a new medium, still in an experimental stage, called television.

The development of television traces back at least as far as the invention of the daguerreotype, about 1839. Within a little over forty years, people found out how to make the picture move. Senator Leland Stanford of California bet that at one point in its stride a horse has all four feet off the ground. The photographer Eadweard Muybridge took a series of consecutive still pictures and mounted them on a rotating disc so that only one picture could be seen at a time through an aperture; the result was the illusion of a running horse. Stanford won his bet; there *was* one point at which all four of the horse's hooves were off the ground.

When Eastman's films became available in the late 1880s, Edison used them to develop the Kinetoscope, which was long used in penny arcades. In France, Auguste and Louis Lumière invented the Cinématographe which projected these consecutive exposures in a large room. Films began to be shown in nickelodeons, theaters where the admission was as low as five cents, and where a piano thumped out mood music for whatever action was being shown.

Barnouw (1956) notes wryly that as early as 1907 the *Chicago Tribune* was charging that films were ministering to the "lowest passions of children." A judge wrote that "nickelodeons indirectly or directly caused more juvenile crimes coming into this court than all other causes combined" (Barnouw, 1956:18). Many of the same things were said in the 1950s and 1970s of television. But motion pictures gained more respectability with the coming of great stars such as Mary Pickford who by 1914 was being signed to annual contracts of more than $100,000 a year. And when a standard film width of 16 mm., and a fire-resistant film substance were agreed upon, teaching and training films began to come into use. The first sound films were shown in theaters in 1926, and sound took over most of the field from silent films during the early thirties.

Dizard (1966:22) feels that the marriage of films and radio, resulting in television, is most appropriately dated at 2 November 1936 when the British Broadcasting Corporation inaugurated the first continuing public television broadcasting service in the world, from an experimental studio at Alexandra Palace on the north edge of London. But there were many developments before that. The scientific sources were international.

Jakob Berzelius, a Swedish chemist, discovered the element selenium that became the basic component of photoelectric cells. In 1875 Carey, an English scientist, designed a plan for "television" using selenium cells. Caselli, an Italian, claimed to have transmitted a picture by wire in 1862. Paul Nipkow, a Russian living in Germany, developed a scanning disc in 1884 for transmitting pictures by wireless, an idea developed into working systems in the 1920s by Jenkins in the United States and Baird in England. Vladimir Zworykin, a Russian employed by Westinghouse in the United States, patented an electron-beam pickup that led to an all-electronic system and to the iconoscope or electronic camera tube, and the kinescope or electronic receiver system.

Development and testing went forward, on a variety of systems, throughout the late twenties and thirties. Television transmission over a wired circuit between New York and Washington was demonstrated by Bell Laboratories in 1927. On 11 May 1927, Station WGY, Schenectady, started experimental telecasts three afternoons a week. By 1932, twenty-five experimental television stations were operating in the United States; thirty-six were operating on 2 November 1936, which Dizard proclaimed the birthday of television. In 1938 David Sarnoff, echoing his famous memorandum about radio, wrote that he felt television was now feasible for use in the home.

The Federal Communications Commission approved a plan for commercial telecasting in 1940. Both CBS and NBC began television operations in July 1941, in New York, fifteen hours a week. Within a year, eight other commercial television stations came on the air, and six of them continued to broadcast throughout World War II.

The war, however, held up the development of television throughout the world. The United Kingdom, France, and the Soviet Union all stopped their television services in 1939. The British had 20,000 receivers when they ceased broadcasting at the start of the war. They resumed in 1946. France stopped in 1939 and resumed on a very limited scale after liberation in 1944. The Soviet Union had begun television in 1938, using equipment purchased from RCA. They also resumed on a limited scale in 1946. No other country except the United States had a regular television service before 1950.

In the United States only a small amount of television was available during the war, but the service and the industry grew rapidly when the war ended. In one year alone, 1948, the number of TV sets in this country increased from about 100,000 to about one million.

The Federal Communications Commission had to make two fundamental decisions before television in the United States could develop as it was destined to do. One of these concerned frequency allocation. It became apparent that there was not enough room in the frequency spectrum for all the stations that would be needed to bring three networks, as well as independent programming, to the whole country. For nearly four years (1948–1952), therefore, the commission maintained a freeze on new station authorizations until a satisfactory allocation plan could be developed for the country.

One result of this freeze and the new allocations was that American educators were able to secure 242 channel assignments, both very high frequency (VHF) and ultra high frequency (UHF)—12 percent of all those available at that time—for educational noncommercial use, making it possible for a second system to grow beside the commercial one. The first ETV station, KUHT at Houston, went on the air 8 June 1953. Thanks in no small degree to strong and continuing support from the Ford Foundation and later to the Educational Facilities Act of 1962 and the Public Broadcasting Act of 1967, there are now 191 of these noncommercial stations owned by citizens' groups or by educational institutions.

The second decision had to do with color television. The introduction of color was delayed for several years while the networks and their engineers battled over whether the approved color system should be "compatible" with black-and-white television—that is, whether color and black-and-white broadcasts should be receivable on the same set. The noncompatible system, built around a rotating color disc, was ready earlier. But the compatible system, based on the electronic system of Zworykin, ultimately won out; when color sets appeared in the stores they could receive either black-and-white or color programs.

Once these decisions were taken, television swept over the country. Less than twenty years had elapsed between the time television receivers were in 5 percent of American homes and the time they were in 90 percent. Radio had grown at nearly the same rate twenty-five years earlier. But when the Old Champion faced the New Challenger in the 1950s, it was a clear victory for the challenger. Television took from radio its position as the home entertainment center, its huge audiences, and its fat national advertising contracts. At the same time it kept a substantial part of movie audiences at home looking at the picture tube rather than at theaters watching the silver screen.

Radio and films were both badly hurt by

the impact of the new medium. The 1950s and early 1960s were a period of re-adjustment. Radio gave up its prestigious entertainment programs, but found certain services it could perform uniquely well: news and music, sports broadcasts, background music for people who were reading or studying, broadcasts for automobile receivers. Now radio's advertising income is twice what it was when television came in. Film attendance is still down from its high during the 1930s and 1940s, but films have found a place for themselves on television. So the older media are still flourishing, but Americans now devote approximately as much time to television as to the other mass media combined.

Certain new developments promise to introduce changes of some considerable importance in television. One of these—cable television (CATV), with its probable extension into the "wired city" and the possibility of developing a home communication center that will combine the services of several media—may have an impact comparable almost to the introduction of television itself. Another of these is the home television recorder-player that may have great effect both on home entertainment and on instructional uses of television. And finally the new generations of communication satellites make it increasingly easier to distribute television programs without the limit of national boundaries. We shall have more to say about these new developments.

Some Characteristics of the U.S. System

Before leaving the development of broadcasting, let us note several characteristics of the system that emerged in the United States.

For one thing, it emerged ad hoc. Regulation and direction came after technology. In the past decade, certain Asian and African nations have been able to plan and introduce their media systems in a way that integrates them smoothly into their existing sociopolitical systems and their goal patterns. In the United States, however, the technology was in use before there were appropriate governmental structures to regulate and control its development. Therefore, the broadcast system reflects many of the conflicts prevailing at the time of its growth.

Nevertheless, the ideology that shaped the system was based consistently on the First Amendment and the idea of free enterprise. For example:

The airwaves are recognized as belonging to the public. Private interests are merely franchised to use a portion of the spectrum, for a three-year period, "in the public interest, convenience, and necessity." The franchise granted by the FCC does not in any way constitute legal ownership, but rather public trusteeship whose renewal is dependent on the licensee's performance.

The profits belong to the licensee. Broadcasting requires the investment of risk capital by the private sector, with little or no regulation of rates, profits, or services.

Broadcast frequencies are allocated to local communities. The FCC assumes that the best frequency allocation is one that assures each local community a voice of its own. The licensee is charged with fulfilling this public service for the community. This is one reason why stations, rather than networks, are licensed, and why the licensee is required to return to the FCC every three years for the renewal of his license.

Consequently, the proper working of the system requires a balance between private and public interest. In return for the use of a public resource, the broadcaster is responsible for serving the public. What this "service" consists of is necessarily worked out in a balance of power and authority between the public and private sectors. The broadcasters are charged with providing a "free market-place of ideas," and yet the government is loath to do anything about the programming of the stations. The private licensees operate franchises that acquire fabulous property values (for example, in a large city a television station may represent a capital investment of less than $5 million, but a property value of $50 million), and yet the broadcaster feels himself in jeopardy every three years when he faces the possibility (a very small possibility, it must be admitted) that the license may be taken from him.

STRUCTURE OF THE INDUSTRY

Perhaps the best way to approach the complex structure of the United States broadcasting industry is by means of a simple chart (Figure 1).

In essence, that is the way it works. With the aid of outside program sources, stations and cable services produce and transmit programs for audiences. Because it is a private enterprise system, it necessarily has a double goal—not only to please and serve audiences but also to attract the kind and size of audiences that in turn will attract advertisers to buy time on the system and, consequently, to make a profit for the owners. The system therefore serves two masters, and operates within limits set by government regulatory agencies that have rigorously maintained a policy of keeping hands off programs.

This is simple enough, but the picture is complicated when we start to fill in some of the details. For example, the mere matter of size—much larger than any other broadcasting system in the world—itself adds an element of complexity. Suppose we fill in some numbers for the circles in the previous chart (see Figure 2).

The figures are for about the beginning of 1972; true totals will doubtless be larger by the time this is in print.

Because of the many different types of stations, their interrelationships in networks and chains of ownership, and their relationships to cable transmission of signals, most of which originate with stations; because of the great variety in programming; and because of the number of different audiences to be served—for these reasons it is impossible to describe American television and radio in any

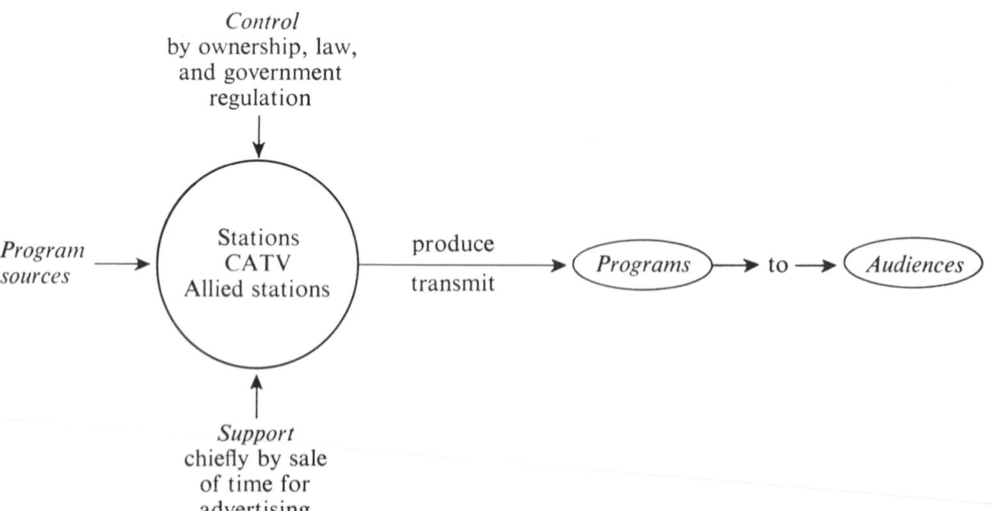

Figure 1. Structure of the U.S. broadcasting industry.

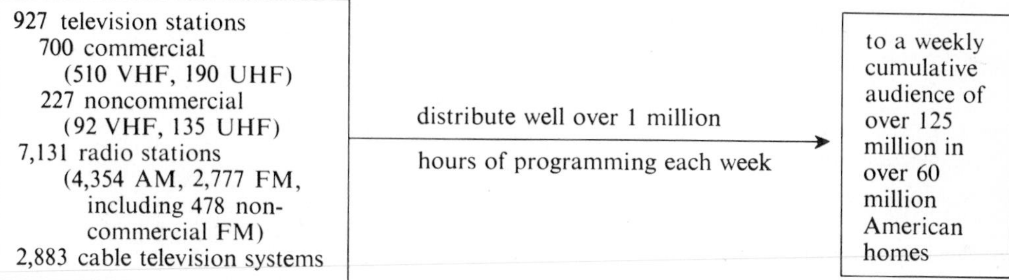

Figure 2. Size of the U.S. broadcasting industry.

such simple way as one can describe, for example, the broadcasting system of a country that has a state-owned network or a single public corporation responsible for broadcasting. For the majority of American stations, their programming and their policies are their own; they are responsible to their owners rather than to a government agency or public corporation. They all come together under the umbrella of benevolent government regulation for, as indicated, the Federal Communications Commission since its founding in 1934 has been considerably more interested in allocating frequencies than in concerning itself over what a broadcaster does with his frequency.

The system is complex also because it includes a number of organizations and agencies that have become essential to the operation of broadcasting but are separate from the act of broadcasting. In Figure 3 we have inserted some numbers, where they are readily available, in order to provide some idea of the magnitude of these related services.

This is the kind of structure that broadcasting has evolved in the United States. In later sections of this chapter we shall talk about the support of the system, the pattern of control, and the programs and audiences. In the remaining pages of this section we shall add some notes about the comparable size and complexity of the system we are dealing with.

Some Notes on Size

It may be useful to look at the gigantic U.S. broadcasting system in international perspective. Almost every national state and large territory in the world has radio, and more than half of them have television—as Table 1 illustrates.

In 1969 there were estimated to be a little over 600 million radios in the world, distributed about as follows: 192 million in Europe, 43 million in North and South America outside the United States, 9 million in Africa, 62 million in Asia (of which 22.5 million were in Japan), and 4 million in Oceania. At the same time there were estimated to be about 236 million television receivers in the world; 97 million in Europe, 20 million in North and South

TABLE 1
Number of States and Territories with Radio and Television Systems

	Radio	Television
Africa	52	22
North and Central America	26	16
South America	15	10
Asia (and Asian Middle East)	40	24
Europe (and USSR)	35	29
Oceania	17	4
Totals	185	105

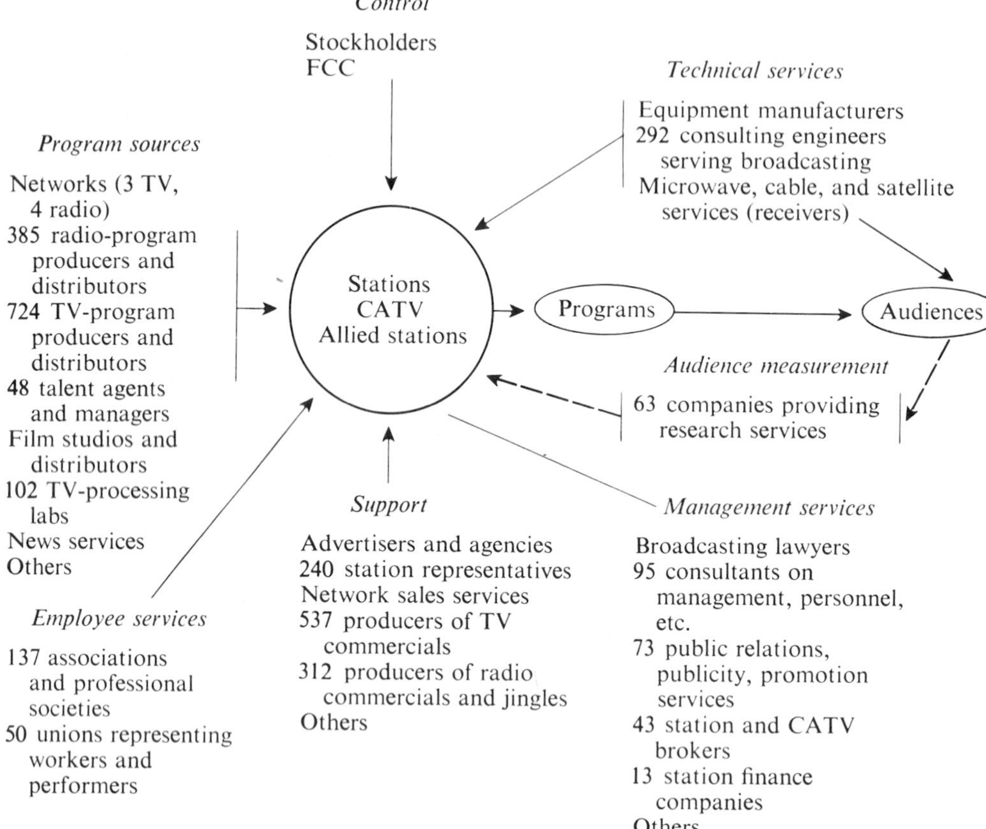

Figure 3. Related agencies and services essential to U.S. broadcasting industry.

America outside the United States, 24 million in Asia (of which 20.6 million were in Japan), 1 million in Africa, and less than 1 million in Oceania. These figures are from the 1971 *Dimensions of Radio* and *Dimensions of Television*, which are published by the National Association of Broadcasters, and which depend considerably on the *World Radio TV Handbook* for the same year. By the time this is read these figures can safely be raised by at least 10 percent.

The striking fact about this inventory of radio and television receivers is that approximately *half* of all the radios in the world, and over *one-third* of all the television receivers are in the United States. The estimated U.S. totals are 331 million radios and 93 million television receivers.

What does this mean in practical terms? For one thing, over 95 percent of American homes have radio and television. Thus, broadcasting has become a universal medium in the United States, reaching more homes and absorbing far more time than newspapers and considerably more time than magazines. There are about 63 million homes in the United States; therefore, many of them have more than one television set to cater to different tastes and different viewing patterns in the family. Many offices, clubs, schools, and places of entertainment also have television.

But what exactly does it mean to have an average of nearly five radios for every dwelling unit in the United States? We must assume that the estimate may include a certain number of radios that are lying unused or in disrepair. Even if one reduces the total to account for these, however, still it is a striking figure and signifies that Americans have become accustomed to having radio available wherever they are. For example, about 75 million automobiles in this country have radio receivers in them, for listening while driving to and from work or during motor trips. Children are more and more coming to have their own radios, for use in their own rooms or for background music while they study. There are radios in different rooms of the home; radios in offices, entertainment places, and summer cottages; portable radios for use on picnics or on dates, or even for listening to the radio announcer while watching a football game. In other words, broadcasting is nearly omnipresent in the United States, and this has resulted in a system of phenomenal size and extent.

A word about the different kinds of stations. Broadcasting in the United States, as elsewhere, began with amplitude modulation (AM) and with the 550–1600 kHz band, which is relatively low in the frequency spectrum. The majority of American stations stili operate in this band. In the last two decades, however, there has been a rapid growth of stations that operate on frequency modulation (FM), meaning that they modulate the carrier wave by changing the frequency rather than by changing the size of the wave. FM occupies bands higher in the spectrum, around 100 millihertz (mHz).

Television began with VHF frequencies, which now provide twelve channels in two bands (2–6, 7–13) near the FM band in the spectrum. After 1952, however, channels 14 to 83 were also assigned to television in the so-called UHF band, which reaches up to about 1,000 mHz. In 1964 legislation was passed requiring all receivers sold in interstate commerce to be able to get both VHF and UHF. Table 2 shows the rate at which the number of stations has grown.

The great growth in number of radio stations after 1945 reflects the new role forced on radio by the advent of television—from network radio providing the basic home entertainment service, to local, usually independently owned, radio stations providing local and specialized services and low-cost programming. The great jump in number of television stations after 1950 reflects the end of the freeze and the opening of the UHF bands. Both FM and UHF stations have had a hard time financially and therefore have had more failures, hence their numbers have increased more slowly. About two out of every three television outlets are still in the more crowded but more profitable VHF band; more than two-thirds of the radio stations are in the more crowded but more profitable AM band.

TABLE 2

NUMBER OF COMMERCIAL BROADCASTING STATIONS IN THE U.S., BY FIVE-YEAR PERIODS, 1922–1972

	AM	FM	TV
January 1, 1922	30*		
June 20, 1925	571*		
July 1, 1930	612*		
January 1, 1935	685		
January 1, 1940	765		
July 20, 1945	933	56*	6
January 1, 1950	2,086	733	97
January 1, 1955	2,669	552	439
January 1, 1960	3,398	688	573
January 1, 1965	4,009	1,270	586
January 1, 1969	4,237	1,938	672
December 1, 1971	4,354	2,777	904

SOURCE: Data from *Broadcasting Yearbook*, 1922–1972 (which depends on FCC records).

* Stations authorized to broadcast; number actually on the air not available from these sources for those particular years.

Both commercial and noncommercial stations use VHF and UHF, AM and FM.

About one out of every five television stations is now noncommercial, supported by gifts or by public or educational funds. The proportion of noncommercial radio stations is much lower.

Another kind of television service in the United States is cable television, which delivers television to homes, offices, and schools by coaxial cable. This kind of service began in an effort to provide clear reception for viewers who had difficulty with direct reception because of distance, or because buildings or terrain were in the way. Recently these systems have begun to originate some of their own programs and thus, in effect, are becoming broadcasting rather than merely delivery services. The possibility of greatly increasing the amount and variety of local and specialized programming is what excites observers about the future potential of CATV. Recently the FCC has ruled that all cable systems with more than 3,500 subscribers must originate programs (see Table 3).

TABLE 3

ESTIMATED NUMBER OF CABLE TELEVISION SYSTEMS, 1959–1972

	CATV Systems	CATV Homes	Approximate % of TV Homes
1959	560	550,000	1.1
1961	700	725,000	1.5
1963	1,000	950,000	1.9
1965	1,400	1,600,000	3.0
1967	1,781	3,000,000	5.4
1969	2,385	4,500,000	7.8
1972	2,883	6,000,000	10.4

SOURCE: Data from National Cable Television Association, and *Cable TV Sourcebook*, No. 42, 1972.

The activities we are describing represent only a small part of total activity in the U.S. radio spectrum. They do not represent, for example, point-to-point or mobile radio, such as taxicab radios and telephones in private automobiles. They do not include public security radio—fire, police, highway, or communication-maintenance radio. They do not include the very large systems of military radio and television. They do not include many closed-circuit systems, air and sea navigation and communication systems, international broadcasting stations, satellites or microwave systems, radio astronomy, space telemetry, facsimile. Extensive as it is, radio and television broadcasting is still only the visible part of the iceberg.

OPERATIONAL COMPLEXITY

The basic operation of the system is, thus, simple; however, the very size of the structure complicates it.

The appetite of the American broadcasting system for programs is gargantuan. Over one million hours per week must be programmed. This is a quantum jump from the programming needs of a system like that of France or Britain, where independent stations are almost nonexistent and most programming comes from a few networks. That is why such a large number of programming-production services are needed by the American broadcasting structure.

Relatively little of a station's programming actually originates within the station itself. A network station signs a contract that commits the network to furnish a certain number of hours of programming in return for which the station promises to take a certain number of these programs and to permit the network to sell a certain amount of the station's time to national advertisers. The station thus receives programs of broad audience interest and also a substantial share of the time charges collected by the network.

The network makes some of the programs it distributes and contracts for the making of others. Behind the network, as behind the individual station, stand the program producers and distributors, the film studios and distributors, feature services, wire news services, and many other program sources. Where possible, the network covers live events of wide interest. For some of these (e.g., football games), the network must pay for the privilege of broadcasting; for others (e.g., a presidential press conference, a moon shot, or a public meeting or demonstration), it pays no fee but must meet the very considerable expense of coverage.

A network station receives by no means all of its programs from the network. The station provides some if its own programs and buys others, which means that it, too, deals with wire services, film distributors, program producers, and the like. Stations that are not affiliated with networks make even more use of these programming services, and often buy network shows that are available for reshowing after a season or two. Independent radio stations in particular build as much of their program as possible around low-cost programming, such as disc jockeys playing phonograph records or tapes, or talk shows relying upon telephone calls to the station.

Approximately one-tenth of broadcasting time can be filled by commercials. Some of these are read by station announcers from scripts written in the station or provided by advertisers. A national television commercial or a radio jingle, however, usually originates in an advertising agency or in the studio of a producer hired by the agency. In the case of television, particularly, loving care is usually lavished on the commercial, and the process of planning, studying, pretesting, making, and remaking usually costs considerably more per minute than does the program that the commercial accompanies. It comes to a station usually on film or magnetic tape, or embedded in a network program.

Noncommercial stations do not have quite the same relationship to their network, if they belong to one. The noncommercial network does not act as a national advertising salesman, and the station's promise of how much programming it will take is somewhat less strict, but the network does provide a certain number of programs. Like the programs of a commercial network (NBC, CBS, or ABC), the programs circulated by the Public Broadcasting System may be made by the affiliated national program center NET (as, for example, was "Sesame Street") or purchased from other sources (as were "The Forsyte Saga" and "Civilisation," which were purchased from BBC). Noncommercial stations also exchange a certain number of their own best programs.

Because of the need to transmit so many programs promptly, a nationwide microwave system and cables have become necessary, and numerous proposals have been made to supplement these with domestic satellites. Because of the number of individual outlets that must be maintained and the great number of programs that must be paid for, a very large system of advertising sales has become necessary. We shall say something in the next section about the size of this support structure. Here we should merely note that it includes, in addition to the network sales departments, many hundreds of advertising agencies handling radio or television advertising, many hundreds of sales representatives who solicit and sell spot announcements for local stations and, of course, many thousands of local station sales departments which deal directly with local and regional advertisers. The stations and networks themselves employ over 100,000 persons.

The number of local units in the system and the intensely competitive nature of the industry place rather heavy responsibility on management for the economic survival of the station, and for dealings with unions and national professional organizations as well as with government regulatory agencies and local pressure and power groups. Whether the responsibilities are any less in a less-fragmented industry is debatable, but observers have continually noted the intensely competitive nature of American broadcasting in comparison, for example, with European broadcasting systems built around national networks.

TABLE 4

PROPORTIONS OF DIFFERENT PATTERNS OF OWNERSHIP—RADIO

	Government or Public Corporation	Private	Mixed
Africa	88%	4%	8%
North and Central America	31	38	31
South America	13	20	67
Asia and Middle East	74	5	21
Europe and USSR	77	14	9
Oceania	94	0	6
Overall proportion	69%	13%	17%

THE SUPPORT OF BROADCASTING

Some international setting may be useful at this point.

Let us hasten to make clear that tables 4 through 7 do not reflect the different sizes of the system nor the different amount of support. If these were taken into account, the enormous size and amount of advertising support in the U.S. system would weight the results toward private ownership and commercial support. The percentages in the tables are the relative proportions of national *systems* in a particular region which fall into one pattern or another.

Tables 4 and 5 show the distribution of privately owned and governmentally owned systems throughout the world. In both radio and television, the United States has a "mixed" system of ownership, although it is predominantly privately owned: about one out of five television stations and one out of ten radio stations are operated by nonprofit organizations. The American system is thus in a minority among the systems of the world. Except in the Americas, the majority of governments prefer to keep ownership out of private hands, and control either within an agency of government or a public corporation established by and responsible in some degree to an agency of government.

The international pattern of support, however, is not quite parallel to what we have described because many government systems, particularly in television, are authorized to carry advertising in order to help meet expenses (see Tables 6 and 7).

Thus more countries find it necessary to accept advertising support for television (which is relatively more expensive) than do for radio, and more of them are willing to accept commercial support than are willing to accept private ownership.

TABLE 5

PROPORTIONS OF DIFFERENT PATTERNS OF OWNERSHIP—TELEVISION

	Government or Public Corporation	Private	Mixed
Africa	100%	0%	0%
North and Central America	7	77	16
South America	22	22	56
Asia and Middle East	58	25	17
Europe and USSR	68	23	9
Oceania	75	0	22
Overall proportion	59%	23%	18%

TABLE 6

PATTERNS OF SUPPORT—RADIO

	Some or All Commercial	Non-Commercial
Africa	44%	66%
North and Central America	73	27
South America	85	15
Asia and Middle East	41	59
Europe and USSR	34	66
Oceania	24	76
Overall proportion	49%	51%

TABLE 7

PATTERNS OF SUPPORT—TELEVISION

	Some or All Commercial	Non-Commercial
Africa	87%	13%
North and Central America	92	8
South America	67	33
Asia and Middle East	77	23
Europe and USSR	52	48
Oceania	12	88
Overall proportion	63%	37%

SUPPORT OF U.S. BROADCASTING

The advertising support of commercial broadcasting in the United States amounts to more than $4.5 billion per year, of which almost two-thirds goes to television. It is interesting to observe how this support has grown (Tables 8 and 9).

These tables show what the swift rise of television, after the freeze ended in 1952, did to radio revenues, and also where radio was hardest hit—in network advertising income. The first year in which the total income of television exceeded that of radio was 1955, and 1956 was the first year since before World War II when radio's total sales fell below the level of the preceding year. After 1956, radio's national nonnetwork and local advertising began to rise again, but the rate of total growth in support was only about half that of television.

How does a station spend its money? That is answered in Table 10. The radio station spends relatively more on sales because a greater part of its support has to come from selling local advertising. The television station has higher technical costs because it is technically more complex, and it spends more on programs because television material costs more than sound broadcast material.

How profitable is broadcasting? The

TABLE 8

TELEVISION TIME SALES, 1948–1970

	National Network	National Nonnetwork	Local	Total
		(in $ millions)		
1948*	$ 2.5		$ 6.2	$ 8.7
1950	35.2	25.0	30.4	90.6
1955	308.9	222.4	149.8	681.1
1960	471.6	459.2	215.8	1,146.6
1965	585.1	785.7	302.9	1,673.7
1968	637.1	998.0	452.5	2,087.6
1970	1,551.1	1,102.6	589.1	3,242.8

SOURCE: Data from FCC compilations reported in 1972 *Broadcasting Yearbook*.

* FCC figures for 1948 included revenue of all kinds; time sales comparable with other years would therefore be less than $2.5 million. The figures for 1970 are reported on a different formula which somewhat inflates them in comparison to previous years.

TABLE 9

RADIO TIME SALES, 1935–1970

	Network	National Nonnetwork	Local	Total
	(in $ millions)			
1935	$ 39.7	$ 13.8	$ 26.1	$ 79.6
1940	73.8	37.1	44.8	155.7
1945	134.0	76.7	99.8	310.5
1950	131.5	118.8	203.2	453.5
1955	64.1	120.4	272.0	456.1
1960	35.0	202.1	385.3	622.4
1965	44.6	247.9	535.2	827.7
1968	46.8	332.4	697.1	1,076.3
1970	48.8	355.3	852.7	1,256.8

SOURCE: Data from FCC compilations reported in 1972 *Broadcasting Yearbook*. The figures for 1970 are reported on a different formula which somewhat inflates them in comparison to previous years.

TABLE 10

EXPENDITURES OF A "TYPICAL" STATION, 1967

	Radio Station	TV Station
Program	30.4%	36.7%
Technical	9.5	16.2
Sales	18.9	12.4
General administration	41.2	34.7

SOURCE: Data from *Dimensions of Radio, 1968–1969*, and *Dimensions of Television, 1968–1969*.

question cannot be answered simply because there is a great variation among types of stations. VHF stations, carrying network service in metropolitan markets, may be immensely profitable whereas many UHF stations have been in severe financial difficulty. *Broadcasting Yearbook*'s 1970 "typical TV station," which was supposedly a VHF station, reported a profit of 18.1 percent on gross before federal income taxes. The "typical radio station" for the same year made 8.7 percent before federal income taxes. These compare favorably with profits from other industries. For example, the steel industry has been making about 7 percent before federal income taxes, and printing and publishing has reported something over 9 percent.

Illustrating how unevenly the returns from broadcasting are divided, however, are the FCC financial reports for 1970, which show that almost 40 percent of the total income of television went to the three networks and their fifteen owned and operated stations.

Fifteen advertisers provided about one-third of television income in 1970. These were Procter and Gamble, General Foods, Colgate-Palmolive, Bristol-Myers, American Home Products, R. J. Reynolds, Lever Brothers, General Motors, Warner-Lambert, Sterling Drug, Phillip Morris, Gillette, General Mills, Ford Motor, and Miles Laboratories. All of these corporations deal in products with very wide appeal over economic, age, and social groups. That is, they sell goods like soaps, toothpastes, cigarettes, automobiles, and the contents of the home medicine cabinet. The top twenty advertisers—dealing almost wholly with the same kind of products—provided more than 40 percent of television income.

It might be predicted that this concentration of income in products of general, rather than specific, interest would encourage television programming of a kind that would also have the widest possible audience appeal; and this is precisely what we find. Programs of broad interest = large audiences = large product sales = large time sales and high advertising rates.

There is a corresponding concentration of this flow of advertising in a few large agencies. One advertising agency alone (J. Walter Thompson) was responsible for nearly 15 percent of all television time sales in 1969. The top ten agencies together were responsible for nearly two-thirds of total television time sales.

What does it cost to make a sales pitch to a large television audience? More than one-third of all the television homes in the United States are in the ten largest markets: New York, Los Angeles, Chicago, Philadelphia, Boston, San Francisco, Detroit, Cleveland, Washington, and Pittsburgh. To buy 1 percent of these television homes (one rating point) costs on the average $850 during prime time. This is for a brief spot announcement during prime time, 7:30 to 11:00 P.M. In the daytime it costs less, but the maximum audience is much less and does not include many adult males.

In the smaller markets of the country, an audience of the same size would cost more. The individual station time rates are lower, but the audiences are smaller, too. This is one reason why stations in large cities have a market value far above the investment that has been made in them: With the same program and corresponding facilities, they can reach a vast audience; consequently, they charge very high rates and still offer an attractive buy to national advertisers.

The heavy flow of advertising support and the need for programs of wide interest have had effects far beyond the broadcasting industry itself. For example, much of the entertainment of the country is dependent in no small part on television and radio. Exposure on the air is almost a requirement for successfully building an entertainer's career. Most professional sports would be much less popular and less prosperous without broadcasting. For example, the networks alone pay professional football about $50 million a year—$2.5 million of it for one game, the Super Bowl. Professional football schedules and times (e.g., whether the game is played on Saturday, Sunday, or Monday, and at what hour) will often depend more on the needs of television than the convenience of the local audience. And in order that commercials may get enough attention during a game, special time-outs for advertising are called a number of times during the game.

THE PATTERN OF CONTROL

No broadcasting system is completely free from control. There are countless degrees of political control between the extremes that Terrou and Solal (1951) describe as "subordination to political authorities" and "nonsubordination."

Toward one end of that spectrum would be a country like Spain, in which broadcasting is actually a part of the government and its content is carefully watched; or a country like the Soviet Union, in which broadcasting operates under the minister of culture and under the careful surveillance of the Party. Toward the other end would be a country like Sweden, in which television operates as a private company under the direction of a board of eleven members, the chairman and five other members being appointed by the government; or the United States, where most stations are privately owned and subject to very light government regulation.

Between those extremes lie a variety of patterns. For example, the British Broadcasting Corporation operates under a nonprofit, corporate body set up by a royal charter with a board of governors appointed by the queen; BBC is given almost complete freedom in its programming policies and is expected to exercise responsibility. NHK in Japan is a public juridical person, free in large part from government control although regulated by a governmental agency much like the Federal Communications Commission in the United States. Both Britain and Japan have a parallel system of commercial stations, but neither BBC nor NHK takes advertising.

German broadcasting is conducted by chartered corporations in the several Länder (states); they are neither government agencies nor private companies, and are designed to be as free as possible of government control. Radiodiffusion-Télévision Française (RTF) in France is a public establishment under the joint supervision of the minister of information and the minister of finance and economic affairs, who have in the past exercised rather close control over the news policies of the organization.

There are thus many patterns of relationship to government, subtly different from each other (for descriptions of a number of these, see Emery, 1969), but even the systems that seem to be most free are not completely free. Any nation feels the obligation to allocate frequencies for its stations to prevent interference or chaos on the air. Any nation is almost certain to have a law protecting copyright owners from unauthorized broadcast, protecting audiences against obscenity or libel, and protecting the state against treason or sedition. Additional political and legal controls vary in their strictness. But governmental control is not the only kind of control exerted upon broadcasting.

When a Western broadcaster says that Soviet broadcasting is not "free" he means that it is not *politically* free. When a Soviet broadcaster says that American broadcasting is not "free" he probably means that it is not *economically* free. That is, he would argue that it is owned by wealthy people and financial organizations, and is likely therefore to be in the control of owners who represent a class interest. The interests of ownership are likely to be reflected in the content (see Rosten, 1937; Vyshinskii, 1948; Breed, 1955; Rivers & Schramm, 1969). There are differences of opinion as to how much control is exerted by ownership in different privately owned systems, but at least one can hardly contend that the need to make a profit from advertising does not affect the content of commercial broadcasting.

There is also the kind of social control that is expressed in the United States by the act of viewing or not viewing, listening or not listening, in letters and messages to stations and networks, in criticisms and rewards.

All broadcasting systems are to some degree subject to each of these kinds of control. It happens that the United States system is uncommonly free from control by government, and ownership is (except for noncommercial stations) private rather than public or governmental. The owner has a great amount of freedom to set policy for the same public service concerning which many governments are so concerned that they own and operate it themselves or control it tightly.

The agency by which the United States government chiefly exercises its regulatory control over broadcasting is the FCC—the Federal Communications Commission. This was actually the third pattern by which the United States tried to regulate broadcasting. The first such attempt to control general broadcasting was the Radio Act of 1912. It made the secretary of commerce and labor (these were then combined in one department) responsible for licensing radio stations and operators.

When stations multiplied rapidly in the 1920s, however, the courts decided that the secretary did not have the authority, under this act, to limit broadcast time and power, enforce frequency allocations, and cure the growing chaos on the air waves. President Coolidge asked Congress for new legislation, and the result was the Dill-White Radio Act of 1927, which established a five-member Federal Radio Commission with regulatory powers over licensing, allocating frequency bands to different services, assigning frequencies to stations, and controlling power. The Radio Commission went to work to straighten out the mess in frequency use, and its new rules forced about 150 of the more than 700 existing stations to surrender their licenses.

In 1933 President Roosevelt appointed an interdepartmental committee to restudy the needs of broadcast regulation in the context of national and international electronic communication as a whole. This committee recommended that "the communication service, as far as congressional action is involved, should be regulated by a single body. It recommended that a new agency be created with responsibility for regulating all interstate and foreign communication by wire or by radio, including telephone, telegraph, broadcast, and other uses of the radio spectrum'" (See Gillingham, 1970).

This agency, the Federal Communications Commission, was created by the Communications Act of 1934 which, with its subsequent amendments, is the main body of U.S. communication law. The FCC was to carry out the law as written by Congress, and to promulgate new rules and regulations not contained in the law but necessary to carry out the law's intent. Thus, at the outset, the FCC became administrator, legislator, and judge.

The FCC is an independent regulatory commission. It consists of seven commissioners, appointed by the president with the advice and consent of Congress. Appointments are for seven years, and no more than four members may belong to a single political party. The commission has a staff numbering about fifteen hundred, a large number of whom are assigned to engineering work, such as monitoring the use of frequencies and power, and tracing interference.

The responsibilities of the FCC are far wider than broadcasting. They include the management, in the public interest, of the entire radio spectrum, the allocation of frequencies to different services, and the coordination of the United States' position regarding new spectrum allocations for the meetings of the International Radio Consultative Committee (CCIR—Comité Consultatif International des Radio-Communications), which is the international frequency-allocation board. The commission also regulates common carriers engaged in interstate and foreign communication by telephone and telegraph, and in so doing decides upon rates and charges. It examines and licenses radio operators of many kinds. These and others. But the best known of its activities, and the ones that chiefly concern us here, are those that relate to broadcasting, where it is responsible, among other things, for licensing every radio and television station.

In carrying out its responsibilities for broadcasting, the commission has made decisions of far-reaching importance. Among these are the frequency allocation plan for television that came into effect in 1952, opening up the UHF band, and providing much more complete coverage for the country. Another influential decision was the so-called chain regulations concerning monopoly of ownership: No individual or group may own more than one network, or more than seven AM, seven FM, or seven TV commercial stations anywhere in the United States, and no more than five of the seven TV stations may be in the VHF band.

Still another important decision had to do with adoption of a television system that would provide for "compatible" color—the reception of both black-and-white and color television on the same receiver. The FCC also reacted firmly to the "payola" and "quiz" scandals of the 1950s; as a result, the Communications Act was amended in 1960 to prohibit the plugging of phonograph discs or other commercial items without making clear when money had been received for doing so; and also to prohibit the broadcasting of quiz shows that were "fixed." (For these regulations, see Kahn, 1972.)

A great deal of the argument generated around the commission, however, has arisen from the responsibility for licensing stations, and in particular from the possible relation of that responsibility to station programming.

Let us make clear that the commission has no direct authority over programs. It can neither put a program on nor take it off the air. The Communications Act says:

> Nothing in this Act shall be understood or construed to give the commission the power of censorship over the radio communications or signals transmitted by any radio station, and no regulation or condition shall be promulgated or fixed by the commission which shall interfere with the right of free speech by means of radio communication.

The act stipulates certain requirements that must be met by applicants for a broadcast license. They must be legally, technically, and financially qualified to operate a station. They must be citizens of the United States. No officer or director of a corporation applying for a license may be an alien, nor may more than one-fifth of the capital stock of such a corporation be held by foreign owners. And an applicant must show that the proposed operation will be in the public interest.

That is where programming enters into the act of licensing. When a broadcaster endeavors to show that his operation will be in the public interest, he has to talk about what kind of programming he proposes to provide.

In this respect, the commission has not been dogmatic. In a 1960 report they suggested the kind of programming they considered to be in the public interest:

> In the fulfillment of his obligation the broadcaster should consider the tastes, needs and desires of the public he is licensed to serve in developing his programming and should exercise conscientious efforts not only to ascertain them but also to carry them out as well as he reasonably can. He should reasonably attempt to meet all such needs and interests on an equitable basis. Particular areas of interest and types of appropriate service may, of course, differ from community to community, and from time to time. However, the commission does expect its broadcast licensees to take the necessary steps to inform themselves of the real needs and interests of the areas they serve and to provide programming which in fact constitutes a diligent effort, in good faith, to provide for those needs and interests.
>
> The major elements usually necessary to meet the public interest, needs and desires of the community in which the station is located as developed by the industry, and recognized by the commission, have included: (1) Opportunity for local self-expression, (2) the development and use of local talent, (3) programs for children, (4) religious programs, (5) educational programs, (6) public affairs programs, (7) editorialization by licensees, (8) political broadcasts, (9) agricultural programs, (10) news programs, (11) weather and market reports, (12) sports programs, (13) service to minority groups, (14) entertainment programming.
>
> The elements set out above are neither all-embracing nor constant. We re-emphasize that they do not serve and have never been intended as a rigid mold or fixed formula for station operation. The ascertainment of the needed elements of the broadcast matter to be provided by a particular licensee for the audience he is obligated to serve remains primarily the function of the licensee. His honest and prudent judgments will be accorded great weight by the commission. Indeed, any other course would tend to substitute the judgment of the commission for that of the licensee (Federal Communications Commission, 1960).

This is not a very threatening statement, and in practice the commission has paid relatively little attention to an applicant's programming except in two circumstances—when there is competition for the frequency, and (recently) when an applicant returns for a renewal of his license after three years (and there are complaints on file regarding his services). In the former circumstance, when the commission has before it more than one applicant for the same channel, all of whom are apparently adequately qualified legally, financially, and technically, then it has seemed necessary to examine the kind of programming they propose. And in the latter circumstance, when an applicant has received a license because he promised to provide certain kinds of programming, the commission has come to think that perhaps before it renews the license it should examine the program records he submits to see whether he has kept his promises.

The commission has been most loath to take any action based on programming. It does little more than pass on to a station any complaints that come to the commission concerning the station's programming. It has almost never revoked a license at the time of renewal, although it has sometimes renewed the license for less than three years.

In the last few years, however, the commission has taken a few actions of this kind. Certain commissioners have spoken very frankly about the level of broadcast programming (former chairman Newton Minow's "Vast Wasteland" speech still echoes through the stations and the networks), a "fairness doctrine" providing the right of reply to a political nonnews broadcast has been promulgated (see Kahn, 1972) and, in general, the matter of program quality and station responsibility for programs has been brought to public attention more vividly than in the past. This has frightened many broadcasters and raised the specter of the First Amendment and government control. We shall return to this and related problems of policy in the next section. Here it need merely be said that the degree of government control over broadcasting represented by the FCC is very mild indeed in comparison with many other systems in the world.

THE PRODUCT AND ITS USERS

What do the weekly million hours of programming consist of? Here is what flickers on the screen during a typical day in a West Coast city.

The television day gets under way about 6:00 A.M. Programs for a few dedicated viewers are likely to come at this hour—for example, the college lecture series on "Sunrise Semester." Newscasts come on, too, for the early viewers. By seven o'clock the local NBC outlet is launched on its "Today" show—interviews and news. The other networks are presenting news. From 8:00 to 9:00 A.M. the children get some special attention. Captain Kangaroo hops in from CBS, and an independent station shows a cartoon and a children's program.

9:00 A.M. The children are at school, the men at work. Women's day begins on television. Two of the networks are showing Lucy and Dinah. The third network tries to pre-empt some of their audience by starting, half an hour earlier, a 1951 movie suited to over-the-coffee viewing. "Beverly Hillbillies" appears on an independent channel at 9:30. Another independent cranks up a 1955 movie. One network has a game show; another presents a discussion of Pearl Harbor. By 10:00 "I Love Lucy" has already appeared on a second station, a UHF; many of the UFH stations start a little later.

Meanwhile the local public television station is showing instructional programs for the schools, beginning at 9:00 and continuing until 11:30, when "Sesame Street" comes on for an hour, followed by "Misterogers Neighborhood" for the children at home. The diet of women's programs is interrupted at noon by a half hour of news on two of the networks, and a "Noony Cartoony" for children on one of the independents. Then back to the women's programs on the commercial stations and the school programs on the public station.

The networks bring on serials. More independents and UHF stations are now on the air. One of them is showing a 1954 movie, another a 1948 movie. Others have reruns. Still another offers instruction in Yoga. "Have Gun Will Travel" appears on another. One station is showing a Deanna Durbin movie from 1943, and a second reaches back to 1941 for Abbott and Costello. A second noncommercial station is showing "Sesame Street" again.

4:00 P.M. The public television station

is through with its school programs and repeats "Sesame Street" and "Misterogers Neighborhood." By late afternoon women have less time to view. Children are home from school. The programming is changing from women's shows to children's programs, adventures, reruns—a transition to the news and evening entertainment. Popeye cartoons are on one station; Bugs Bunny on another. David Frost comes on with interviews for the generation who are no longer attracted to Bugs Bunny or Popeye. Adventure programs and comedies begin to appear.

By 5:30 P.M. the transition time is over. One station begins to show professional basketball: the home team is playing three time zones east. One of the networks comes on with its news from New York. At six o'clock the other two networks show a half hour of local news, followed by a half hour from the network, and then another half hour local. Meanwhile the public station is teaching viewers how to play the guitar. The dial is very full now; the UHF stations have been broadcasting throughout the afternoon. One of them starts up another movie. Others are showing network reruns and programs from special producers. When one of the networks has finished its 5:30 news it turns to a special night professional football game. At seven o'clock the public station starts its own hour of local news.

7:30 P.M. The networks (except for the station showing football) launch their prime-time programs. These are the entertainment hours for the whole family, the programs that, week in and week out, get the highest ratings: comedy, adventure, whodunits, variety, and popular music. These are the backbone of network programming: the Archie Bunkers, the Laugh-Ins, the Gunsmokes, the Carol Burnetts, the Disneys, Lucys, Doris Days, and so forth.

It is interesting to see what a few noncommercial and independent stations offer as an alternative. The public television station has a chamber music program, then some serious talk, and finally William Buckley at 11:00. There are a few adventure and Western programs. "Great Fights" appears for the second time. At 7:30 one of the UHFs begins to show a film of the Billy Graham crusade, opposite Red Skelton, Gunsmoke, a Richard Widmark movie, and the football game. As the evening goes on, the commercial alternatives become for the most part movies. Four of them, three from the 1950s, one from the 1940s, are under way at nine o'clock.

At 11 P.M., one of the networks is showing a movie; the other two have a half hour of news from their own studios. Then the NBC outlet turns to its "Tonight" show, and ABC to the "Dick Cavett Show." More and more movies begin to light up the screens for late viewers. Six of them are available just before midnight. And the television night moves on toward sign-off time, with Dorothy Lamour, Tyrone Power, Victor Mature, James Booth, and Brigitte Bardot as we saw them a decade or two ago.

During the eighteen-plus hours of the television day, receiving sets in this area had access to something in the order of 150 hours of programming of an almost unbelievable variety. True, most of the variety is in light entertainment, including a football game, a basketball game, and no fewer than twenty-one old movies. Most of the public-affairs programming, with the exception of news, is likely to have come from noncommercial stations. Some of the programming is repetitious, which is convenient because it gives a viewer a second opportunity to see what he wants. For example, "Sesame Street" is on three times during the day. But the point is that there is a choice, within a limited variety, for anyone who cares to exercise it.

Meanwhile the people in the area we have been describing have been able to tune in from twenty-five to fifty radio stations, according to the time of day and how carefully they wanted to tune. It is much more difficult to describe the radio day because the radio stations tend to specialize, rather than offer general services. One of the stations in the area broadcasts news twenty-four hours a day (with pauses for commercials, Arthur Godfrey, Dear Abby, and a few other features). Others concentrate on hard rock, and still others on the "top ten" or some other selection of current favorites. Some of the FM stations and a few of the AM stations specialize in classical music; typical of their "prime time" offerings is a tape of the Boston Symphony or a recorded opera.

In radio, as in television, there are two publicly owned stations concentrating on public affairs and BBC Third-Programme types of offerings. Radio stations carry professional and college sports for persons unable to see the game or to view it on television. There are religious stations, foreign-language stations. There are still some light variety programs available on radio as there used to be twenty-five years ago. But for the most part, if one casually turns the radio dial, he hears music and news.

The question is, then, Where *do* they turn the dial?

The Broadcasting Audience

According to the Nielsen Television Index, during the measurement period ending in March of 1972 the average American home used its television receiver forty-two hours and fourteen minutes a week, or just over six hours a day. Over one-third of this was in the "prime time" hours—7:30 to 11 P.M. This pattern varies by day of the week, time of the year, and individual homes. For the kind of day we have described, however, it comes close to being the average for a supposedly representative sample of American homes.

There are no precisely comparable figures for radio because radio receivers are so widely distributed and, consequently, more difficult to survey. The common estimate of time devoted by a family to radio is about half the time for television. Yet radio in one day or one week reaches more people than does television, if we can depend upon an NBC audience study of 1965 that was reported in *Broadcasting Yearbook* for 1972 beside the 1972 Nielsen figures. The cumulative audiences of people eighteen years of age and over reached by the two broadcast media are shown in Table 11.

These figures are highly approximate, and may or may not be comparable. NBC says that it regards the radio estimates as "approximate" but "conservative" benchmarks, and that the comparison "does not imply that television and radio are equal in impact or effectiveness" but "does suggest that radio's broad reach makes the medium an ideal choice for backing up television advertising" (Broadcasting Yearbook, 1970: A-125).

One other note of interest is that radio reaches a higher proportion of teen-agers (twelve to seventeen) than of adults. The difference is only a few percentage points, but suggests the attractiveness of radio's popular music programs.

Another set of old survey figures, compiled by Sindlinger and Company in 1964 for the Radio Advertising Bureau, provides a chance to compare the use of radio with that of television at different times of the day (see Table 12). The television figures are those of Nielsen for 1971.

TABLE 11

Cumulative Audiences of Radio and Television

	In One Day	In Seven Days
Radio	92,100,000 (75.1%)	111,000,000 (90.5%)
Television	80,900,000 (65.9%)	106,500,000 (86.8%)

TABLE 12

HOURLY PATTERNS IN USE OF RADIO AND TELEVISION

	Television (% of TV homes)	Radio (% of all adults)
6:00– 7:00 A.M.	1.8	25.4
7:00– 8:00	7.7	31.6
8:00– 9:00	15.3	25.9
9:00–10:00	19.3	21.7
10:00–11:00	20.8	19.5
11:00–12:00 noon	22.5	19.0
12:00– 1:00 P.M.	25.8	18.0
1:00– 2:00	27.3	15.5
2:00– 3:00	28.7	15.3
3:00– 4:00	29.9	15.8
4:00– 5:00	32.9	18.4
5:00– 6:00	39.9	18.7
6:00– 7:00	48.3	16.3
7:00– 8:00	58.1	14.4
8:00– 9:00	64.0	12.1
9:00–10:00	63.7	10.5
10:00–11:00	55.8	9.7
11:00–12:00	34.4	7.2

SOURCE: Data from *Broadcasting Yearbook* (1972:73).

Both because of the time difference and the differences in method, the comparison must be considered suggestive rather than conclusive.

The pattern of a high level of radio listening in the early morning and of television viewing in midevening is almost too neat, and yet it calls attention to one of the qualities that kept radio alive when television arrived: it can be listened to while the listener is doing something else. In the early morning a man can hear the news while he is shaving, a woman while she is preparing breakfast. They can listen while they ride in the car. The housewife can keep an ear cocked on the broadcast while she does the housework; the teenager can take in a little hard rock without distracting his major attention from the textbook he is studying.

Who is viewing, and how many? Latest answers to these questions come from Nielsen, for February 1971, and are presented in Table 13.

TABLE 13

COMPOSITION OF THE TV AUDIENCE

	Homes Using TV	Viewers per Home	% of Viewing Audience Made Up of			
			Men	Women	Teens	Children
Monday-Friday						
10:00 A.M.–1:00 P.M	25.3%	1.33	17	57	5	21
1:00–5:00 P.M.	32.8	1.42	16	56	8	20
All Nights						
7:30–11:00 P.M.	65.1	2.07	32	41	11	16

These figures indicate that television is largely a women's and children's medium through the working hours of the day, an all-family medium in the evening. About three out of five homes, on the average, will have the TV receiver turned on in prime time. In ten representative homes, we should expect in prime evening time to find about six sets in use, about thirteen people viewing, of whom four would be men, five women, one or two teen-agers, and perhaps two or three children. Of course, audience composition would vary greatly by program and by family.

The average network prime-time evening program will go into 15 to 20 percent of television homes. Daytime programs will get a much lower rating. Top network news programs will draw an audience nearly comparable to that of prime-time entertainment. Reruns of popular comedies like "I Love Lucy," in good time slots, will draw very well. Evening programs on public television, in competition with the top commercial entertainment, will draw at the most 5 to 10 percent of homes, and on the average 2 or 3 percent. The most popular of the independent stations will average higher ratings than the public stations; some of the independents, particularly those on UHF, will average less.

In Table 14 are some average program ratings for different kinds of network prime-time programs.

When these program ratings (percentages of television homes) are translated into people, they mean that the average evening network situation comedy is viewed in about 13 million homes by perhaps 28 million people. A fair guess (without the benefit of a national survey) of how many people in how many homes view a public television program like Kenneth Clark's "Civilisation" in a single showing would be 3 million homes and perhaps 6.5 million people. This program is repeated once on most public stations; that would probably add 3 million viewers. But it is clear that there is still a considerable difference between the size of audience for a situation comedy and for even a very fine noncommercial program on the history of art.

Television gathers its largest audiences for coverage of great events. One of the largest audiences ever in front of television in this country was for the first moonwalk, covered by all three networks, and viewed in American homes by perhaps 125 million people. When President John F. Kennedy was killed, it is estimated that 166 million Americans viewed the ensuing events on television at some time during that weekend.

TABLE 14

NIELSEN AUDIENCE RATINGS FOR DIFFERENT KINDS OF PRIME-TIME NETWORK PROGRAMS (MARCH-APRIL, 1971)

	Number of Programs	Percentage of Evening Hours	Average Rating
General drama	8	10%	16.6
Variety	16	21	17.4
Western drama	5	7	20.8
Situation comedy	27	35	20.8
Quiz and audience participation	3	4	15.6
Mystery and suspense drama	9	12	19.9
Feature films	8	10	19.9
All programs	*77*	*100*	*18.2*

PROBLEMS OF POLICY AND PERFORMANCE

Any industry that serves as many people with information and entertainment, and commands as many of the waking hours of a nation as does American broadcasting is bound to raise problems of public policy.

In many countries these problems are internalized within the government. In the United States, however, the private enterprise nature of the system and the historic relations of mass media to government give matters of this kind a high public visibility.

Most of these problems are twofold: Does some aspect of the industry or its performance involve the public interest? What, if anything, should the government do about it?

Needless to say, American tradition has been that the government should do as little as possible, and the media should be as free as possible to operate within a freely competitive situation. Therefore the public problems of broadcasting, as they have grown more urgent, have raised over and over again long-standing and still sensitive issues of private versus public interest, licensing and censorship, freedom and control, and the degree of public responsibility to be expected of a broadcaster. These are familiar issues but the impact of electronic technology has modernized them.

While we cannot discuss these problems in adequate detail in these pages, we can at least suggest their nature, dividing them into four headings: the problems of ownership and performance, of fairness and access, of social effects, and of new technology.

Ownership and Performance

The electromagnetic spectrum has been recognized by the broadcasters, by the courts, and by the critics as public property, a public resource to be allocated by the FCC for the public good. The distinctive nature of this resource was pointed out in a 1964 report of the Joint Technical Advisory Committee, which noted:

1. This resource is used, not consumed. Therefore, it is wasted both when it is used inefficiently and when it is not used.
2. This resource has dimensions of space, time, and frequency. All three are interrelated. Time and frequency are interchangeable in the same geographic area and can be used over again in different areas.
3. It is an international resource. Local plans for its use can be adopted only within an overall framework of international agreement. That is why the nations of the world have created organizations like the International Consultative Committee on Radio (CCIR) and the International Frequency Registration Board (IFRB).
4. The resource is wasted when assigned to do tasks that can be done as easily in other ways. In many cases radio is called upon to perform tasks that can be done as easily and economically and perhaps better by cable or wire, and this is one reason why some observers think that cable television may replace much open-circuit broadcasting in the future. On the other hand some tasks, like communicating with moving vehicles, could hardly be accomplished without radio.
5. This resource is wasted when not correctly applied to a task. For example, there is a real question whether the AM frequencies of 550 to 1600 kHz are efficiently applied to local radio, because these frequencies provide a powerful skywave at night, and therefore create interference at a distance.
6. This resource is subject to pollution. Radio noise resulting from the other instruments of an electronic civilization is a kind of pollution, and so is the interference from an over-

crowded spectrum (Joint Technical Advisory Committee, 1964:4-6).

These are engineering considerations that must enter into spectrum management by the FCC. In addition, there is the problem of allocating parts of the spectrum for a public service to private enterprises that must make a profit in order to provide this service. The regulatory agency must therefore consider both public and private interests.

In assigning channels and frequencies, the FCC has traditionally tried to keep its hands off programming. If a frequency is available, if the applicant is qualified legally, financially, and technically to operate a broadcast service, and if there is no competing application, then ordinarily the allocation is made. If there is a contest for the frequency, then the agency would first consider whether more than one applicant is legally, financially, and technically qualified. Only if there is a contest between otherwise well-qualified applicants would the commission have to consider in detail the proposals of the applicants for meeting the needs and serving the interests of their audiences. Once the license is awarded, renewals usually come fairly automatically at the end of three years; the past record seldom shows a contest for the frequency once it has been assigned and the successful applicant has begun to broadcast on it. At least that is the way it *has* been. Lately there have been signs of change.

Most controversy during the last few years has arisen from renewal applications. In more and more cases these are being challenged by other groups who want to use the frequency. Increasingly the argument of these competing groups has been that they can furnish a broadcast service more in the public interest than the licensee has been furnishing. This challenges the FCC to examine *performance*. The original application has to specify what kinds of program services, and approximately how much of each, the applicant promises to perform. In contested cases, licenses have often been awarded initially to applicants who made better promises than other applicants. Therefore, members of the commission have asked, Are we not obligated at least to see whether the successful applicant has lived up to his promises?

Understandably, this has shocked the owners of broadcasting stations. The First Amendment has been held up to prove that FCC attention to a station's programming constituted infringement of "freedom of speech and of the press." But the real concern is not that the commission is tanpering with free speech—rather that it is tampering with frequency assignments which, in the case of metropolitan television especially, have acquired enormous value. It has been estimated that the total market value of existing television licenses in the United States may be $3 billion. These valuable property rights are being challenged.

When the present chief justice of the U.S. Supreme Court, Warren Burger, was on the bench of the U.S. Court of Appeals for the District of Columbia, he wrote: "After nearly five decades of operation the broadcast industry does not seem to have grasped the simple fact that a broadcast license is a public trust subject to termination for breach of duty" (*Office of Communication of the United Church of Christ* v. *FCC* 359 F.2d 994, 1003 [1966]). Yet the FCC has repeatedly declined to pay much attention to "breach of duty."

Nicholas Johnson, one of the most outspoken of the commissioners and a continual burr under the saddle of the industry, has cited some examples when the FCC has been, to say the least, permissive about station performance in granting licenses or renewals. Commissioner Johnson (1969–70:29) noted that:

—The FCC once decided that a radio station proposing thirty-three minutes of commercials per hour would be serving the public interest (*Accomack-North Hampton Broadcasting Co., 1967*).

—It permitted the wholesale transfer of construction permits from one licensee to another, prompting the Special Investigations Subcommittee of the House Interstate and Foreign Commerce Committee to conclude in 1969: "The Commission apparently confused its role as guardian of the public interest with that of guardian of the private interest."

—The FCC approved a license transfer application for a station that quite candidly conceded it proposed to program no news and no public affairs programs at all (*Herman C. Hall, 1968*).

Despite this amount of restraint on the part of the FCC, three cases of license renewal have, within the last few years, been decided at some level against the incumbent licensees (see Barnett, 1970:222 ff.). Two of these were decided on the argument of overlapping ownership, one on programming policy. This last was the case of station WLBT in Mississippi. The FCC, when presented with evidence of racist policies in the station's programming, at first decided that the complainants should not be permitted to participate in the case, then ruled that the station's performance entitled it to a renewal. The courts reversed this decision, in an appeal brought by the Office of Communication of the United Church of Christ.[1]

Needless to say, these decisions have stirred up the owners of broadcasting stations as few other developments in broadcasting history have done. The broadcasters, always very influential in Congress, have encouraged the introduction of a bill (the so-called Pastore Bill) that would have forbidden the FCC to consider a competing application for a licensee unless it first determined that the present holder was not qualified. Senator Pastore withdrew his bill when the FCC undertook on its own to adopt that procedure.

It is very doubtful that the definition of qualification could be based entirely on legal, financial, and technical grounds. For example, when Commissioners Johnson and Cox sponsored a survey of the performance of a number of stations in Oklahoma, on the occasion of the renewal of Oklahoma licenses, here is their own summary of what they found:

> Of the ten commercial television stations which submitted renewal applications in the instant proceedings (which take in a total of more than $16 million in gross revenues annually), only one station devotes as much as two hours a week to programs which can be classified as "local public affairs" (out of 105 to 134 hours per week of programming). Two stations devote between one and two hours to local public affairs. Six stations carry less than one hour. Two stations carry none at all.
>
> Three of the TV stations carry less than eight hours of news per week.
>
> There is not in the entire state a single regularly scheduled prime-time program devoted to presentation, analysis, or discussion of controversial issues of public importance in the state or the community.
>
> There is not in the state a single station which carries as much as one hour per week of locally originated programming in the prime viewing hours, other than news, weather, and sports. Radio, although a fairly significant source of news, and not infrequently of local news, provides almost literally no public affairs service at all other than news. With but a handful of exceptions, Oklahoma radio stations do not offer even a token effort to serve as a forum for discussion of local issues of public importance.
>
> . . . Our principal conclusion is this: As far as Oklahoma broadcasting is concerned, the concept of local service is largely a myth. With a few exceptions, Oklahoma stations provide almost literally no programming that can meaningfully be described as "local expression." They provide very little that can be considered tailored to specific needs of their individual communities (Cox & Johnson, 1968).

In these cases, the licenses were renewed. Yet these two commissioners, and many critics outside the commission, feel that the FCC must consider performances like those mentioned in granting renewals.

---

[1] *Office of Communication of the United Church of Christ* v. *FCC*, 359 F.2d 994, 1003 (1966). Also, *Office of Communication of the United Church of Christ* v. *FCC*, 425 F.2d 543, 548 (1969).

The U.S. Court of Appeals has spoken sympathetically of the FCC's problem in handling license renewals and applications:

> . . . It is appropriate to note the extreme difficulty and delicacy of the tasks which the First Amendment imposes on the Federal Communications Commission. The Commission is charged with administering a scarce communications resource, the broadcast spectrum, in such a manner that the great objectives incorporated into the First Amendment are realized and debate on public issues is "uninhibited, robust, and wide-open" (*New York Times Co.* v. *Sullivan*, 376 U.S. 254, 270 [1964]). Thus the Commission must seek to assure that the listening and viewing public will be exposed to a wide variety of "social, political, esthetic, moral, and other ideas and experiences" (*Red Lion Broadcasting Co.* v. *FCC*, 395 U.S. 367, 390 [1969]). In seeking to provide the broadcasting media with the diversity demanded by the First Amendment, however, the commission must avoid the peril of both inaction and overzealousness—of abdication which would allow those possessing the most economic power to dictate what may be heard, and of censorship which would allow the government to control the ideas communicated to the public. The need to make choices of this kind requires the Commission to take some cognizance of the kind and content of programs being offered to the public . . . (*National Association of Theatre Owners* v. *FCC*, 17 P and F Radio Reg., F.2d 2010 [D. C. Sept. 30, 1969]).

But what degree of cognizance? What is the desirable middle road between inaction and overzealousness, between abdication and censorship?

The FCC is thus caught between the First Amendment and responsibility to the public interest. It is faced by a long history of regulated industries acquiring a large degree of control over the agency that regulates them. It is under constant oversight by Congress, which is strongly influenced by the broadcasters. And even if there were no other difficulties in the way, the commission's work load alone would keep it from any very extensive attention to programming. The commission grants and renews licenses for about 5 million transmitters. Each year it handles some 800,000 license and renewal applications. About 2,500 commercial television and radio licenses come up for renewal each year. For these tasks it is understaffed, and Congress is not about to give it more staff to examine station programming.

Access and Fairness

Students of the American mass media system have often been concerned lest the concentration of ownership in the hands of a wealthy and powerful group of persons might limit the access of the American people to a "free marketplace of ideas"—that the media might come to carry only one set of viewpoints, and information might be filtered through the lens of one social class or group. One of the more significant statements in the opinion quoted from *National Association of Theatre Owners* v. *FCC* is that diversity is "demanded" by the First Amendment.

Vice President Agnew, no matter what his motives, was in a solid tradition when he spoke, during the 1970 congressional campaign, of broadcasters holding "a concentration of power over American public opinion unknown in history," and of the networks having "a virtual monopoly of a whole medium of communication." Over 80 percent of all the commercial television stations on the air are served by the three networks. These networks, together with their fifteen owned stations, take in 40 percent of the annual income of broadcasting.

In some ways, multiple ownership of stations is more impressive than the concentration of power in networks. Rucker (1968: 193) calculates that multiple ownership now accounts for 73.6 percent of all commercial stations. Fourteen group broadcasters, in addition to three networks, own chains of five television stations each. Seven others own chains of six stations each. In addition to the networks, four other multiple owners have five VHF stations in the top fifty markets, and others such as RKO and Metromedia have combinations that may reach even larger audiences than those mentioned (see the summary in Barnett, 1970:276 ff.).

In 1968, 37 of the 40 VHF stations in the top ten markets (which contain nearly 40 percent of the nation's television homes) were licensed to multiple owners. In the top fifty markets (containing 75 percent of American television homes) 127 of 156 VHF stations were licensed to multiple owners. One hundred eighty-nine commercial television stations (out of 682 at the time) were licensed to newspapers and/or magazines. Newspapers and/or magazines also owned 394 AM stations and 245 FM stations.

Concentration of ownership in all the media has been encouraged by rising costs and the need to take advantage of economies of scale. Yet it becomes more worrisome in view of the recognized influence of television in electoral campaigns, and the growing proportion of people who say that they get most of their news from television and are more willing to believe television than other media. For a number of years, Roper Associates have made sample surveys on public attitudes toward television. Tables 15 and 16 show the trends on two questions they have asked repeatedly.

TABLE 15

ROPER POLLS ON SOURCE OF MOST NEWS

"First, I'd like to ask you where you usually get most of your news about what's going on in the world today—from newspapers, radio, television, magazines, talking to people, or where?"

Source of most news	12/59	11/61	11/63	11/64	1/67	11/68
Television	51%	52%	55%	58%	64%	59%
Newspapers	57	57	53	56	55	49
Radio	34	34	29	26	28	25
Magazines	8	9	6	8	7	7
People	4	5	4	5	4	5
Don't know or no answer	1	3	3	3	2	3
Total mentions	154	157	147	153	158	145

SOURCE: Roper Organization (1971:2).

NOTE: Columns total more than 100 percent because some people mentioned more than one source, e.g., "television and newspapers."

TABLE 16

ROPER POLLS ON MOST BELIEVABLE SOURCES OF NEWS

"If you got conflicting or different reports of the same news story from radio, television, the magazines and the newspapers, which of the four versions would you be most inclined to believe—the one on radio or television or magazines or newspapers?"

Most believable	12/59	11/61	11/63	11/64	1/67	11/68
Television	29%	39%	36%	41%	41%	44%
Newspapers	32	24	24	23	24	21
Magazines	10	10	10	10	8	11
Radio	12	12	12	8	7	8
Don't know or no answer	17	17	18	18	20	16

SOURCE: Roper Organization (1971:3).

Quoting the courts on the First Amendment's requirement of promoting "diversity," the commission voted unanimously in 1968 to prohibit new acquisitions of more than one full-time broadcasting station of any type in the same market (33 Federal Register, p. 5315). The Department of Justice then made two additional suggestions to the FCC: that it consider applying the proposed policy to license renewals as well as to new acquisitions, and also to newspaper-broadcasting combinations (comments of the United States Department of Justice, FCC Docket No. 18, 110, Aug. 1, 1968). The commission has not yet taken action on these suggestions, but it has been active, with the strong encouragement of the Department of Justice and the courts, in trying to reduce concentration.

In the WHDH case in Boston, in 1969, the commission denied renewal of a valuable Boston VHF license to a company that already owned two daily newspapers and two radio stations in the city, and gave the channel to a competing applicant who had almost no association with other media. This decision was subsequently upheld by the courts. Later in 1969, an FCC hearing examiner recommended that one of the most valuable VHF licenses in the country, KHJ in Los Angeles, be taken from RKO and given to a competing local group. RKO is one of the chief multiple owners of broadcasting franchises.

In a number of other cases in 1968 and 1969 the commission exercised its influence to reduce or limit concentration of ownership, often by inducing multiple owners to withdraw applications. The courts and the Department of Justice have usually been out in front of the commission. For example, the FCC approved the acquisition of a Chicago FM station by the Chicago Tribune Company, which already owned two daily newspapers, a VHF station, and an AM station in the city. However, the courts, acting on a challenge, sent the case back to the commission; ultimately the FM station went to the Chicago public television organization.

The policy of limiting or reducing multiple ownership is now somewhat in doubt. The Pastore Bill, if passed, would seem to reduce the likelihood of considering concentration in renewal hearings, and it may be that the new members of the commission appointed by the Nixon administration may be less in favor of activity along this line. Indeed, in early 1970 the commission seemed to abandon the policy of considering media concentration as a key element in license renewals (Federal Communications Commission, 1970). It may well be that cross-media ownership—for example, newspapers and broadcasting stations—will come under more active scrutiny in the near future than will multiple ownership of broadcasting outlets.

The justification for concern over multiple ownership, as we have noted, is simply that Americans will not be presented a free marketplace of ideas because spokesmen for opinions other than those held by media owners will have more difficulty in gaining access to the media. The commission can more easily approach the problem in this way, which it can do without touching program content, than to deal with the other side of the problem—whether station *policy* and *practice* permit a fair statement of contrary viewpoints. The ownership aspect of the problem is more often referred to as the problem of "access"; the station-policy aspect, as "fairness." But it is obvious that they are parts of the same concern.

The commission has for a number of years supported a "fairness doctrine," which requires that when "a person's honesty, character, or integrity is attacked on the air, the station must notify the person attacked, submit a tape or transcript of the offending program, and offer him free time for a reply" (see Thomas, 1970:866; Houser, 1972; also *Times-Mirror Broadcasting Co.*, 24 P and F Radio Reg. 404, FCC 1962; 32 Fed. Reg. 11,531, 1967; 33 Fed. Reg. 5362, 1968). Furthermore, the doctrine requires radio and television stations to "balance the broadcast opportunities given different viewpoints on controversial issues," including political campaigns. The "equal time" principle was recognized in a congressional amendment to Section 315 of the Communications Act, in 1959 (Kahn, 1972).

Several well-known cases have challenged this doctrine in recent years. In one such instance the Red Lion Broadcasting Corporation had aired over Pennsylvania radio station WLBT a program called "Christian Crusade" in which the Reverend Billy James Hargis personally attacked a political writer named Fred Cook. The station denied Cook's request for free time to reply. Cook brought suit, and the case ultimately reached the Supreme Court, where a unanimous court upheld the fairness doctrine and the personal attack rules.[2] (For comment on this Supreme Court decision, see Thomas, 1970:866 ff.)

It seems that the right of reply is established in American broadcasting, but the interpretation of fairness and balance, and the kind of attacks that deserve free time for a reply, are not yet entirely clear. The WLBT case seemed flagrant enough to persuade the court. However, a circuit court of appeals decided in 1969 that the personal attack rules were "unconstitutionally burdensome and vague."[3] Justice White, in the Red Lion decision, did not accept that circuit court opinion, but the shadow of this uncertainty still hangs over broadcast practice.

Some of the most difficult problems arise during political campaigns. *How many* viewpoints have a right to be represented in the reply? If there were only one opposition party, the answer would be easy; but there is more than one, especially in local elections. Moreover, in the opposition party there may be several shades and groupings of opinion which claim the right to be represented. When one party or candidate has a great deal more money than another, have broadcasters any obligation to "balance" the exposure of these competitors on the airways? (In 1970 a bill to limit the total expenditure of any one candidate on radio and television was passed by Congress but was vetoed by the president. A much milder bill was passed in 1972.) When the president speaks on the air, with the advantage of his position and his ability to commandeer the networks at a time of his choosing, is any right of reply justified? (During 1970 a group of congressional opponents to the U.S. policy in Vietnam asked and received time to reply to a nationwide broadcast address by the President defending that policy.)

Thus, at present, the principles of "fairness," "balance," and "access" seem to be established. There is general agreement that the right of reply does not apply to news reports per se. There is general agreement that the right of reply extends both to personal attack and political opinions. But there is a host of interpretive rules that remain to be worked out in practice.

Problems of Social Effects

No one doubts that broadcasting, and television especially, may be exerting a profound social effect on American culture and life. The amount of time commanded by the two media, the vividness of their presentation, and the growing proportion of public information delivered through broadcasting—all raise the question of what the social effects of this new concentration of information may be, and whether any of the effects may be sufficiently harmful to warrant doing something about them.

This is a hot topic, because it requires examination of particular programs and kinds of programming. The FCC has therefore been understandably loath to do anything about it, saying that it is a matter for Congress. Critics of the media, however, have been far from unwilling to discuss it,

[2] *Red Lion Broadcasting Co.* v. *FCC*, 381 F.2d 908 (D.C. 1968); affirmed in *Red Lion Broadcasting Co.* v. *FCC*, 395 U.S. 367 (1969).

[3] *Radio Television News Directors Association* v. *FCC*, 400 F.2d (7th Cir. 1968); reviewed in *Radio Television News Directors Association* v. *FCC*, 395 U.S. 367 (1969).

and a considerable amount of debate has been generated, in and out of government. Let us take a few examples of the kinds of content that have come under fire.

Commercials

The FCC has spoken out against overcommercialization on radio and television, but the *content* of the ads has been considered the province of the Federal Trade Commission, and the FCC has ordinarily taken no more active part in regulating the content of commercials than to pass on to stations the warnings or objections of the FTC. In the last few years, however, there has been a great increase in public monitoring of ads.

Much of this increased public awareness can be traced to the efforts of Ralph Nader, but some of it can also be traced to the example of government agencies. The tobacco companies have fought a losing fight for a decade against the growing evidence in the U.S. Public Health Service that cigarette smoking was related to the incidence of cancer and heart disease. The American Cancer Society served as spearhead of a public campaign, in the course of which the right of reply was interpreted even to require stations to carry anticigarette commercials to balance the substantial advertising of tobacco companies. Broadcasters carried this rule to the Supreme Court, without success. Finally, as of 1 January 1971, broadcast advertising of cigarettes came to an end, at a cost to broadcasters of somewhere in the neighborhood of $200 million per year in income, and with an effect as yet unpredictable on the incidence of smoking. This ban on certain kinds of advertisement represents a precedent of considerable importance for consideration of the social effects of other broadcast content.

Effect on Children

There is a long social science literature on the effect of television on the ideas and behavior of young children. Much of it is summarized in Chapter 8. It may be said in general, however, that a number of psychologists, psychiatrists, and experts in child development have found evidence that concerns them about the extent to which children learn and imitate the violence they see on television.

In one sense, this concern is exactly the same kind as that voiced against advertisements for cigarettes and for potentially harmful drugs: television may be encouraging the use of poisons. In two other senses, however, it is very different. For one thing, the effect of television programs on children is much more subtle and harder to measure than the incidence of lung cancer in smoking and in nonsmoking groups, or the incidence of death or damage from proprietary drugs. In the second place, whereas in the case of cigarettes and drugs the objection is merely to the *advertising* of a presumably dangerous product, in the case of violence the objection is to television's *own* product and is, therefore, both more awkward to regulate and more directly an attack on the stewardship of broadcasters.

Predictably, the concern over children and television has not gotten very far. In Congress it has been diffused into hearings that have resulted in no legislation. The president's Commission on the Causes and Prevention of Violence included a task force on mass media whose report was particularly critical of television violence and its effect on children's actions in real-life situations (Baker & Ball, 1969). Approximately one million dollars was provided for additional research on the effect of television on children under a committee appointed by the National Institute of Mental Health, with all the members approved by the industry. Despite disagreement among members of the commission, the general conclusion was that there is a proved connection between the watching of large amounts of violence on television and greater probability of violent behavior in real life (see National Institute of Mental Health, 1972; Senate Commerce Committee, 1972).

The broadcasters have taken some of the more violent Saturday morning programs for children off the air, and have apparently taken steps toward reducing the amount and kind of violence in Westerns, whodunits, and adventure programs in the evening. Money from foundations and from the government made possible in 1969 an "alternative" kind of children's program, "Sesame Street," which proved once and for all that good programming without violence could be as attractive to very young children as televised violence or crime. An easier solution to the problem of suitable programming for children would be for the broadcasters to take the initiative in trying to create programs that would attract large audiences of children without depending on the proved attractions of violence or lawbreaking. If there is any hope for this, then "Sesame Street" may indeed turn out to be a landmark.

Political Packaging for Television

Television has assumed a degree of importance in electoral campaigns that could hardly have been predicted twenty years ago. A candidate's television image is one of his most important assets, and if his image is not satisfactory, then any of a number of political public relations agencies is ready to try to build a new one for him.

The television budget is the most important item in a candidate's campaign chest, and enormous sums are now spent on spot political announcements and televised addresses or interviews. The television requirements for a presidential campaign cost hundreds of millions of dollars; for a close gubernatorial or senatorial race in a large state, they run into the millions; and even in a campaign for city office, they may well be in the thousands or tens of thousands.

Social and political critics have expressed two concerns over this situation. One is that the cost of television may price less-affluent candidates and parties out of the race. The second is that the showmanship of television, the ability to create an attractive candidate in the same way that an entertainer or a commercial product is made attractive on television, may result in voting for the best production agency or the best television performance rather than the candidate's stand on the issues.

There have been no very good suggestions for combatting this latter problem, and it may be that a solution will have to await the development of a more sophisticated viewing public. On the other hand, a strong movement is under way to limit the amount of money that may be spent for political advertising or political appearances on television, and to provide for all candidates a certain amount of TV time at reduced rates.

Some advocates have suggested a system like that of the British Broadcasting Corporation, or of public television stations in this country, where fixed amounts of time are made available to candidates, free of charge, and no other time can be bought by them. As we have noted, a bill to limit expenses in national elections went to the president's desk in 1970 and was vetoed. The Federal Election Campaign Act, a milder campaign-spending bill, passed two years later and went into effect 7 April 1972. Basically, the law (1) requires candidates for federal elective office as well as their campaign committees to report and publicly disclose all campaign contributions and expenditures, and (2) limits the amount of money that can be spent by candidates or political parties for political advertising on radio, television, newspapers, magazines, and billboards.

The New Technology

As we noted earlier, technology of great power and potentiality is about to come into use in electronic communication. Chief among the new instruments are communication satellites, cable television, and electronic video recorders (EVR).

The EVRs, of which no fewer than four

types, each incompatible with the others, are now being developed for market, are essentially television phonographs that will play tape cassettes or some type of film or disks through a television receiver. These may well become as popular as the phonograph in the home, and a great deal more useful than the phonograph in the schoolroom, where they will give a teacher a degree of control over televised instruction that has never been possible with either closed- or open-circuit broadcasting. But the other two new technologies are likely to have more direct influence on broadcasting itself.

Communication satellites have developed very swiftly. From the feeble signals of Sputnik in 1957 and Early Bird in 1968, the industry has increased the capacity of satellites by two orders of magnitude. Telstar already had 240 telephone channels, and could transmit one television program. The new Intelsat satellites have 1,200 channels, and could theoretically handle at least four television programs at a time. The next generation of satellites will be much larger still. This quantum jump in capacity has a consequence in making new uses possible. Furthermore, as the number of channels increases, the cost of using a channel goes down. So communication satellites present a quite different picture from ten years ago.

The International Telecommunication Satellite Corporation (Intelsat) now has satellites over the Atlantic, Pacific, and Indian Oceans, giving them an ability to transmit around the world. Seventy-five nations belong to Intelsat, and operate forty-one stations. The policy problems concerning Intelsat have to do mostly with the dissatisfaction of many of these member nations over the majority control of the operation by the U.S. agency Comsat, and by the cost required of small nations to share in the system.

For some years now, there has been consideration of domestic satellites for the United States. Such satellites would greatly supplement the capacity of existing land lines and microwave to move the telephone, television, telegraph, and other data that already overtax the ground facilities. The networks feel that domestic satellites could considerably reduce the cost of serving affiliated stations. The Ford Foundation has suggested that the profit from a domestic satellite (chiefly delivering commercial television) would pay for a high-class programming service for public television. The cable television association has suggested a domestic satellite to serve the scattered cable systems.

The problem with domestic satellites is chiefly one of how best to absorb them into the existing commercial system. The American Telephone and Telegraph Company has had a virtual monopoly on long-range distribution in this country, and understandably is not anxious to share that with a new common carrier. On the other hand, if A.T.&T. were permitted to put up its own satellites, then its resources are so large that competing groups would probably be loath to enter the field. Does the public good call for an extension of the present near-monopoly, or an increase in competitive services? It is not an easy question.

It is further complicated by the advent of cable television, which, many people think, will ultimately replace open-circuit television except in sparsely settled areas. Cable television may make possible the dream of the wired city, providing for the home a type and variety of media service hardly dreamed of when the FCC struggled with a channel allocation plan in the early 1950s.

Even at the present time, a home that subscribes to a cable TV system, at five dollars a month, in upper Manhattan has available three full network channels, three local independent stations, one public broadcasting channel, one channel for the New York City station, one for the Associated Press news wire twenty-four hours a day, one channel split between the Board of Education station and the ticker tapes of the main stock exchanges, one channel that gives the program schedules of all the others, and one channel that intersperses background music with weather and time reports and public announcements, and originates its own programming between noon and 8:00 P.M. daily.

That is twelve channels. Forty or more channels are entirely possible with new cables and converters. This opens a great variety of possibilities: home instruction, a facsimile news service, shopping by television, picture phones made easier, meetings and conferences by television, and possibly a kind of control by means of computerized services that would permit the user to search libraries and data banks for needed information or to order up news, films, or recorded entertainment to meet his individual interests—in other words, something close to a complete home medium. The existing capacities of open-circuit broadcast would permit no such variety and breadth of service.

After some initial reluctance, the FCC has asserted jurisdiction over cable television systems. It has liberalized its rules over their right to come into the top markets (at first, cables were thought of chiefly as ways to get good reception into areas with few stations or poor reception). It has permitted cable stations to carry advertising, and has ruled that any cable system with 3,500 or more subscribers *must*—not *may*—also originate programs.

This is a period of trial and experimentation with cable television, and many of the most awkward and disturbing questions are not yet answered with any finality. Some of these questions are:

Should cable systems operate as common carriers, leasing their channels to the originators of programs or services? (For an example of the arguments in favor of this, see Barnett, 1970; 1972.)

If cable television is to be treated as a common carrier, should it be separate from and competitive with, or merely an extension of, A.T.&T.? If the former, what will happen to the rather delicate relationship of cable systems to the telephone companies, some of whose facilities the cable systems often lease?

If cable television is to be more than a common carrier, to what extent is it to become, as was said in the FCC hearings, "a fully competitive communication medium"? Are cable operators to become a new group of broadcasters, originating many of their own programs and selling advertising separate and distinct from broadcast advertising? What effect will the cables have on open-circuit broadcasting? (The FCC said that it did not think cable advertising would hurt television advertising at present, but might affect the volume of radio advertising; if the latter happened, said the commission, it would take appropriate action.)

What about the copyright problem? If cable television lives, and profits, on programs made and originally broadcast by television stations, should not some of the income be paid back to the original broadcasters? The new copyright law will doubtless have to face this question (see Rothenberg, 1971).

Then what about the long-range view? If cable television becomes popular by furnishing a broader service and better reception than even the total of open-circuit stations available to subscribers could possibly furnish, will not the audiences for open-circuit television greatly decline and, if so, what effect will that have on the income of open-circuit stations? An FCC spokesman has noted that nothing in present rules keeps cables from charging for a service they themselves have originated: does not this hold up the possibility of pay television, via cables, providing still more competition for open-circuit television?

In other words, is the encouragement of cable television the first step in replacing open-circuit television? Will the present open-circuit broadcasting fade away while networks and program centers feed the cables? This is a vision that understandably disturbs the broadcasters. The policy question that must be answered is whether this is the way that broadcasting should develop, in the public interest, and if it is, how can the development be managed to cause the least damage to existing investment and facilities and to a skilled labor force?

Thus the bright vision of broadband service to the home must be balanced against a set of public-policy questions that admit of no very facile answer. It is the classic question of public interest and private interest which, in the American system, are intended to be allies rather than opponents.

IN CONCLUSION

All discussions of broadcasting ultimately come back to programming and, consequently, to the public interest.

In any country where people can speak out, there are complaints about broadcast programs. It is too dull, or too violent, or too full of commercials, or too highbrow, or too lowbrow, or too much controlled by government, or not enough controlled by government, or too serious, or not seriously enough concerned with public affairs. These complaints take different forms in different countries, and the fact that they are heard in the United States, where criticism is widely articulated, is in no sense extraordinary.

Yet the democratic orientation of U.S. broadcasting provides an easy answer from the industry to such criticisms: that the competitive nature of the industry insures that the people will be given the programming they want. When 75 million people are watching television every evening, when a prime-time program goes into 15 to 20 percent of all the television homes in the country, when more than 100 million people use radio and television each week, when they have a number of stations to choose from, then it is hard to say that people do not want the programming they are getting.

The critics' answer is that audiences are not being offered a real choice. The competition for rating points requires stations to program always for the largest possible audience, and to imitate each other when one of them finds a formula for reaching that audience. The public television stations, which endeavor to provide an intellectual alternative to commercial television, are underfinanced. Many of the independent stations are themselves struggling for support, and their programming alternatives are limited. Critics contend, therefore, that broadcasting is not serving the tastes and needs of the audience so much as it is *creating* those tastes. People learn to like what they get and, so it is said, they would learn to like a wider range of programming if they had full access to it.

It is a complex question. We are not saying that broadcasters are irresponsible or that they have not, on many occasions, provided public service broadcasting at the cost of considerable income to them. The obvious answer of the broadcasting industry to its critics is that *you* want the people to be given what you think *they ought to have*; *we* give them *what they want.* Carrying this argument to its logical conclusion, some stations turned aside from the advertisingless homage the networks and most stations were paying John F. Kennedy, during the days after his assassination in 1963, to broadcast light entertainment—because, they said, people wanted it.

This question of responsibility will be continually with a broadcasting system that is expected to pay in responsibility for its freedom. There is no easy answer or simple rule to define programming responsibility, but it may be instructive to quote what the Pilkington Committee in Britain said in 1962 about the same problem as it impinged on British broadcasting:

> The choice is not between *either* giving the public what it wants, *or* giving the public "what someone thinks is good for it," and nothing else. There is an area of possibility between the two; and it is within this area that the choice lies. The broadcasting authorities have certainly a duty to keep sensitively aware

of the public's tastes and attitudes as they now are and in all their variety; and to care about them. But if they do more than that, this is not to give the public "what someone thinks is good for it." It is to respect the public's right to choose from the widest possible range of subject matter and so to enlarge worthwhile experience. Because, in principle, the possible range of subject matter is inexhaustible, all of it can never be presented, nor can the public know what the range is. So, the broadcaster must explore it, and choose from it first. This might be called "giving a lead": but it is not the lead of the autocratic or arrogant. It is the proper exercise of responsibility by public authorities duly constituted as trustees for the public interest (Committee on Broadcasting, 1962).

REFERENCES

Archer, G. L.
1938 History of Radio to 1926. New York: American Historical Society.

Baker, Robert K., and Sandra J. Ball.
1969 Violence and the Media. Staff report to National Commission on Causes and Prevention of Violence (November). Washington, D.C.: U.S. Government Printing Office.

Barnett, S. R.
1970 "Cable television and media concentration. Part I: Control of cable systems by local broadcasters." Stanford Law Review 22(January:) 221–329.
1972 "State, federal, and local regulation of cable television." Notre Dame Lawyer 47(April): 685–697.

Barnouw, Erik.
1956 Mass Communication, Television, Radio, Film, Press; The Media and Their Practice in the United States of America. New York: Rinehart.

Breed, Warren.
1955 "Social control in the news room." Social Forces 33: 326–335.

Broadcasting Yearbook.
1970 "Radio and television audiences." Washington, D.C.: Broadcasting Yearbook, Inc.

Chester, Giraud; G. R. Garrison; and E. E. Willis.
1963 Television and Radio. New York: Appleton-Century-Crofts.

Committee on Broadcasting.
1962 Report of Committee on Broadcasting, 1960. Sir Harry Pilkington, chairman. Command Paper No. 1753. London: H.M. Stationery Office.

Cox, K. A., and N. B. Johnson.
1968 "Broadcasting in America and the FCC's license renewal process: An Oklahoma case study." A statement... on the occasion of the FCC's renewal of the licences of Oklahoma broadcasters for a three-year term, June 1, 1968. Washington, D.C.: Federal Communications Commission.

Dizard, W. P.
1966 Television: A World View, Syracuse, New York: Syracuse University Press.

Emery, W. B.
1961 Broadcasting and Government: Responsibilities and Regulations. East Lansing: Michigan State University Press.
1969 National and International Systems of Broadcasting: Their History, Operation and Control. East Lansing: Michigan State University Press.

Federal Communications Commission.
1960 Report and Statement of Policy re: Commission en banc Programming Inquiry, July 29. (Reprinted in F. J. Kahn, ed., Documents in American Broadcasting. Revised Edition. New York: Appleton-Century-Crofts, 1972.)
1970 Policy Statement on Comparative Hearings Involving Regular Renewal Applicants. FCC Public Notice No. 70–62 (January 15). Washington, D.C.: Federal Communications Commission.

Gillingham, George.
1970 "Primer of broadcasting." P. C-44 in Broadcasting Yearbook. Washington, D.C.: Broadcasting Yearbook, Inc.

Houser, T. J.
1972 "Fairness doctrine—an historical perspective." Notre Dame Lawyer 47(Fall): 550–564.

Johnson, N. B.
1969 "What the FCC must do." Columbia Journalism Review 8(Winter): 28–33.

Joint Technical Advisory Committee.
1964 Radio Spectrum Utilization: A Program for the Administration of the Radio Spectrum. New York: Joint Technical Advisory Committee of the Institute of Electrical and Electronics Engineers and the Electronic Industries Association.

Kahn, Frank J. (ed.).
1972 Documents of American Broadcasting. Revised Edition. New York: Appleton-Century-Crofts. National Institute of Mental Health.
1972 Television and Social Behavior: The Impact of Televised Violence, a Report to the Surgeon General, United States Public Health Service, from the Surgeon General's Scientific Advisory Committee on Television and Social Behavior. Washington, D.C.: U.S. Government Printing Office.

Paulu, Burton.
1967 Radio and Television Broadcasting on the European Continent. Minneapolis: University of Minnesota Press.

Rivers, W. L., and Wilbur Schramm.
1968 Responsibility in Mass Communication. New York: Harper and Row.

Roper Organization.
1971 An Extended View of Public Attitudes Toward Television and Other Mass Media. New York: Television Information Office.

Rosten, Leo C.
1937 The Washington Correspondents. New York: Harcourt, Brace.

Rothenberg, S.
1971 "Current United States Practices in Copyright Law." Bulletin of the Copyright Society of the U.S.A. 18(August):422–456.

Rucker, Bryce W.
1968 The First Freedom. Carbondale: Southern Illinois University Press.

St. John, R.
1967 Encyclopedia of Radio and TV Broadcasting. Milwaukee: Cathedral Square Publishing Company.

Schramm, Wilbur; P. H. Coombs; Friedrich Kahnert; and Jack Lyle.
1967 New Educational Media in Action: Case Studies for Planners. Three Volumes. Paris: UNESCO.

Senate Commerce Committee.
1972 Surgeon General's Report by Scientific Advisory Committee on Television and Social Behavior, hearings before Subcommittee on Communication, 92d Congress, 2d Sess., March 21–24, 1972.

Terrou, Fernand, and Lucien Solal.
1951 Legislation for Press, Film, and Radio. New York: Columbia University Press.

Thomas, G. L.
1970 "The listener's right to hear in broadcasting." Stanford Law Review 22(April):863–902.

UNESCO.
1964 World Communications: Press, Radio, Television, Film. Fourth Edition. New York: UNESCO Publications Center.

Vyshinskii, Andreii.
1948 The Law of the Soviet State. New York: Macmillan.

World Radio TV Handbook.
1947– World Radio TV Handbook. Hellerup, Denmark: World Radio-Television Handbook Company, Ltd. Annual.

ADDITIONAL READINGS

General Titles

Bailyn, Lotte. "Mass Media and Children: A Study of Exposure Habits and Cognitive Effects." *Psychological Monographs* 73 (1959):1–48.

Berkowitz, Leonard. *Aggression: A Social Psychological Analysis.* New York: McGraw-Hill, 1962.

Cantril, Hadley. *Invasion from Mars: A Study in the Psychology of Panic.* Princeton: Princeton University Press, 1940.

Cassirer, H. *Television Teaching Today.* Paris: UNESCO, 1960.

Codding, G. A., Jr. *The International Telecommunication Union: An Experiment in International Cooperation.* Leiden: E. J. Brill, 1952.

———. *Broadcasting Without Barriers.* Paris: UNESCO, 1959.

Dieuzeide, H. *Teaching Through Television.* Paris: Organisation for Economic Cooperation and Development, 1953.

Glanvill, Joseph. *The Vanity of Dogmatizing.*

London (1661). New York: Columbia University Press, Facsimile Text Society, 1931.

Himmelweit, Hilde; Oppenheim, A. N.; and Vince, Pamela. *Television and the Child: An Empirical Study of the Effect of Television on the Young*. New York: Oxford University Press, 1958.

Hocking, W. E. *Freedom of the Press: A Framework of Principle*. A report from the Commission on Freedom of the Press. Chicago: University of Chicago Press, 1947.

International Telecommunications Union. *From Semaphore to Satellite*. Geneva: International Telecommunications Union, 1965.

Katz, Elihu, and Lazarsfeld, P. F. *Personal Influence: The Part Played by People in the Flow of Mass Communications*. Glencoe, Ill.: Free Press, 1955. (A paperback edition was published in 1964.)

Klapper, J. T. *The Effects of Mass Communication*. Glencoe, Ill.: Free Press, 1960.

Lang, Kurt, and Lang, Gladys E. "The Unique Perspective of Television and Its Effect: A Pilot Study." *American Sociological Review* 18(February 1953):3–12.

Lazarsfeld, P. F. *Radio and the Printed Page: An Introduction to the Study of Radio and its Role in the Communication of Ideas*. New York: Duell, 1940.

McLuhan, Marshall. *Understanding Media: The Extensions of Man*. New York: McGraw-Hill, 1964. (A paperback edition was published in 1965.)

Namurois, A. *Problems of Structure and Organization of Broadcasting in the Framework of Radiocommunications*. Geneva: European Broadcasting Union, 1964.

Packard, V. O. *The Hidden Persuaders*. New York: McKay, 1957. (A paperback edition was published in 1958 by Pocket Books.)

Pons, E. *License Fees for Radio and Television Sets*. Geneva: European Broadcasting Union, 1964.

Riley, J. W., Jr., and Riley, Matilda W. "Mass Communication and the Social System." In *Sociology Today: Problems and Prospects*; under the auspices of the American Sociological Society, edited by Robert K. Merton et al., pp. 537–578. New York: Basic Books, 1959.

Rivers, W. L., and Schramm, Wilbur. *Responsibility in Mass Communication*. 2d ed. New York: Harper, 1969.

Schramm, Wilbur; Lyle, Jack; and Parker, E. B. *Television in the Lives of Our Children*. Stanford, Cal.: Stanford University Press, 1961.

Vasari, B. *Financial Aspects of Broadcasting*. Geneva: European Broadcasting Union, 1965.

Broadcasting in the United States

Barnouw, Erik. *To 1933, A Tower in Babel: A History of Broadcasting in the United States*, vol. 1, 1966; *1933–1953, The Golden Web*, vol. 2, 1968; *1953–1970, The Image Empire*, vol. 3, 1970. New York: Oxford University Press.

Bogart, Leo. *The Age of Television: A Study of Viewing Habits and the Impact of Television on American Life*. 2d ed. New York: Ungar, 1958.

Chafee, Zechariah, Jr. *Free Speech in the United States*. Cambridge, Mass.: Harvard University Press, 1941. (Supersedes Chafee's *Freedom of Speech*, 1920.)

Columbia University, Bureau of Applied Social Research. *The People Look at Radio: Report on a Survey Conducted by the National Opinion Research Center*. Chapel Hill: University of North Carolina Press, 1946.

Commission on Freedom of the Press. *The American Radio: A Report on the Broadcasting Industry in the United States*. Chicago: University of Chicago Press, 1947.

Coons, J. E., ed. *Freedom and Responsibility in Broadcasting*. Evanston, Ill.: Northwestern University Press, 1961.

Federal Communications Commission. *Public Service Responsibility of Broadcast Licensees*. Washington, D.C: Government Printing Office, 1946.

Gillmor, D. M., and Barron, J. A. *Mass Communication Law, Cases and Comments*. St. Paul, Minnesota: West Publishing, 1969.

Interstate and Foreign Commerce Committee. *Regulation of Broadcasting, Half a Century of Government Regulation of Broadcasting and the Need for Further Legislative Action*. Study for the Committee on Interstate and Foreign Commerce, House of Representatives. Washington, D. C.: Government Printing Office, 1958.

Johnson, N. B. *How to Talk Back to Your Television Set*. Boston: Little, Brown, 1967.

Katz, Elihu, and Feldman, J. J. "The Debates in the Light of Research: A Survey of Surveys." In *The Great Debates: Background,*

Perspective, Effects, edited by Sidney Karus, pp. 173–223. Bloomington: Indiana University Press, 1962.

Krasnow, E. G., and Longley, E. D. *The Politics of Broadcast Regulation.* New York: St. Martin's Press, 1972.

Minow, Newton. *Equal Time.* New York: Atheneum, 1964.

Rosten, Leo C. *Hollywood: The Movie Colony, the Movie Makers.* New York: Harcourt, Brace, 1941.

Schiller, H. I. *Mass Communications and American Empire.* New York: Augustus M. Kelly, 1970.

Schramm, Wilbur; Lyle, Jack; and Pool, Ithiel de Sola. *The People Look at Educational Television: A Report of Nine Representative ETV Stations.* Stanford, Cal.: Stanford University Press, 1963.

Skornia, H. J. *Television and Society: An Inquest and Agenda for Improvement.* New York: McGraw-Hill, 1965.

———, and Kitson, J. W. *Problems and Controversies in Television and Radio* (readings). Palo Alto: Pacific Books, 1968.

Sopkin, Charles. *Seven Glorious Days, Seven Fun-filled Nights.* New York: Simon and Schuster, 1968.

Steiner, G. A. *The People Look at Television: A Study of Audience Attitudes.* New York: Knopf, 1963.

Thomas, G. L. "Regulating the Use of the Radio Spectrum." *Stanford Journal of International Studies* 5(June 1970):23+.

Wilensky, H. L. "Mass Society and Mass Culture: Interdependence or Independence?" *American Sociological Review* 29(April 1964):173–197.

Broadcasting in Other Countries

Awasthy, G. C. *Broadcasting in India.* Bombay: Allied Publishers Private Limited, 1965.

Briggs, Asa, *The Birth of Broadcasting.* The History of Broadcasting in the United Kingdom, vol. 1. London: Oxford University Press, 1961.

Butt, A. "Radio Pakistan Today." *EBU Review* 81B(September 1963):28–31.

Canada. *Report of the Committee on Broadcasting.* Ottawa: Queen's Printer, 1965.

Canadian Broadcasting Corporation. *Broadcasting in Canada: History and Development of the National System.* Ottawa: Canadian Broadcasting Corporation, 1960.

Ching, J. C. "Mass communications in the Republic of the Congo (Leopoldville)." *Journalism Quarterly* 41(Spring 1964): 237–244.

Cohen, N. The broadcasting authority in Israel. *EBU Review,* 94B(November 1965): 73–74.

Council of Europe. *European Agreement for the Prevention of Broadcasts Transmitted from Stations Outside National Territories.* European Treaty Series No. 53. Strasbourg: Author, 1965.

Crawford, R. P. "Comparative Aspects of British and American Commercial Television." *Journal of Broadcasting* 10(Spring 1966):103–110.

DaPiedade, H. "Radio-Dahomey: The First Ten Years." *EBU Review* 78B(March 1963):6–7.

Dumazedier, J. *Television and Rural Adult Education: The Tele-Clubs in France.* Paris: UNESCO, 1956.

Durham, F. G. *News Broadcasting on Soviet Radio and Television.* Cambridge, Mass.: Center for International Studies, Massachusetts Institute of Technology, 1965.

Eisler, G. "Twenty Years of the German Democratic Radio." *Radio and Television (OIRT)* 6(March 1965):6–10.

Emery, W. B. "A Comparative Study of Broadcasting Law and Regulations in Mexico and the United States." *Journal of Broadcasting* 8(Spring 1964):185–202.

European Broadcasting Union. "Broadcasting in the Ivory Coast." *EBU Review* 81B(September 1963):28–31.

Hahr, H. "The Code of Broadcasting Practice in Sweden." *EBU Review* 76B(November 1962):41–43.

Independent Television Authority. *ITV 1967: A Guide to Independent Television.* London: Author, 1967.

Instituto de la Opinión Pública. *Estudio sobre los medios de comunicación de masas en España.* Second Part. Madrid: Instituto de la Opinión Pública, 1964.

Liu, A. P. L. *Radio Broadcasting in Communist China.* Cambridge: Center for International Studies, Massachusetts Institute of Technology, 1964.

Mackay, I. K. *Broadcasting in Australia.* Melbourne: Melbourne University Press, 1957.

Moreira, Mária da S. "The Legal Position of

Broadcasting in Portugal." *EBU Review* 82B(November 1963):53–61.
Namurois, A. "The New Charter for Broadcasting in Belgium." *EBU Review* 63B(September 1960):2–10.
NHK. *The History of Broadcasting in Japan.* Tokyo: NHK Press, 1967.
Norgaard, P. "Radio and Television in Denmark." *EBU Review* 67B(September 1961):2.
Paulu, Burton. *British Broadcasting: Radio and Television in the United Kingdom.* Minneapolis: University of Minnesota Press, 1956.
———. *British Broadcasting in Transition.* Minneapolis: University of Minnesota Press, 1961.
Pigé, F. *La télévision dans le monde—organisation administrative et financière.* Paris: Société Nationale des Entreprises de Presse, 1962.
Reich, D. R. "Accident and Design: The Reshaping of German Broadcasting Under Military Government." *Journal of Broadcasting* 7(Summer 1963):191–208.
Ruiz, A. A. *La radiodifusión Española.* Madrid: Publicaciones Españolas, No. 453, 1964.
Rydbeck, O. "Broadcasting in Sweden." *EBU Review* 80B(July 1963):6–10.
Sakontikov, N. "The Experience of the Central Television of the USSR in the Field of Political Broadcasts." *Radio and Television (OIRT)* 3(November 1962):3–6.
Sandor, G. "The Experience of the Hungarian Television." *Radio and Television (OIRT)* 5(July 1964):6–9.
Shea, A. A. *Broadcasting: The Canadian Way.* Montreal: Harvest House, 1963.
Tavares, R. "What Is the ABERT?" (*Broadcasting in Brazil*) *EBU Review* 92B(July 1965):29–31.
Tolga, S. "Legislation Setting Up the Radio-Television Association of Turkey (TRT)." *EBU Review* 88B(November 1964):48–52.
UNESCO. *New Educational Media in Action.* 3 vols. Paris: UNESCO, 1967.
Wedell, E. G. *Broadcasting and Public Policy.* London: Michael Joseph Ltd., 1968.
Williams, R. "The Soviet Philosophy of Broadcasting." *Journal of Broadcasting* 6(Winter 1961):3–10.
Wilson, H. H. *Pressure Group: The Campaign for Commercial Television in England.* New Brunswick, N. J.: Rutgers University Press, 1961.

Periodicals

Broadcasting. Washington, D. C.: Broadcasting Publications, Inc. Weekly.
EBU Review (Part B: General and Legal). Geneva: European Broadcasting Union. Bimonthly.
Educational Broadcasting Review. Washington, D. C.: National Association of Educational Broadcasters. Bimonthly.
Federal Communications Commission Reports (2d Series). Washington, D. C.: Government Printing Office. Weekly. (For decisions, reports, public notices, and other documents of the FCC.)
Television Age. New York: Television Editorial Corporation. Biweekly.
Television Quarterly. New York: National Academy of Television Arts and Sciences. Quarterly.
U.S. Federal Register. Washington, D. C.: Government Printing Office. Daily, except Sunday and Monday. (For official FCC documents.)

Annuals

Broadcasting Yearbook. Washington, D. C.: Broadcasting Publications, Inc., 1931–.
Dimensions of Radio. Washington, D. C.: Research Department, National Association of Broadcasters, 1961–. (A compilation of data on radio broadcasting.)
Dimensions of Television. Washington, D. C.: Research Department, National Association of Broadcasters, 1961–. (A compilation of data on television broadcasting.)
World Radio TV Handbook. Hellerup, Denmark: World Radio-Television Handbook Co., Ltd., 1947–.

CHAPTER 19 Technological Change and the Mass Media

EDWIN B. PARKER
Stanford University

Considering the great development of computer technology, the advent of cable television, and the trend toward giving the receiver greater power to order what he wants from the mass media when he wants it, what will the next medium be? This chapter describes a new kind of media service that might bring into the home television, radio, printed news, and information and educational services according to the tastes and needs of the home audience. This kind of service is expected to be well within the state of the art during the next decade. The author suggests some of the effects such a development might have on other media and on society in general.

INTRODUCTION

Communication and technology have played a dominant role in both the biological evolution of man and the development of social structure. The utilization of tools by our biological ancestors apparently was a major factor in shaping the biological nature of man (Washburn, 1960). Similarly, primitive vocal communication was a major factor that helped shape the human species into its present form (Hockett, 1960). Man did not evolve to his present form and then learn speech and adopt tools. Speech was a necessary component in the complex of attributes that allowed small groups of humans (or prehumans) to cooperate and hence to survive and evolve. The development and maintenance of large social structures depends on a communication technology that permits communication through space and time in addition to face-to-face oral communication.

The communication system of any society, and the technology that makes that system possible, should not be thought of as either a cause or an effect of other aspects of the society. Rather, it should be thought of as an integral component of that social structure, without which the society itself would be quite different in a large number of respects.

Canadian economic historian Harold

This chapter is based in part on two earlier papers (Parker, 1970b; 1970c). Much of the writing was done with the support of a fellowship at the Center for Advanced Study in the Behavioral Sciences.

Innis, in two now classic works, *Empire and Communication* (1950) and *The Bias of Communication* (1951), was perhaps the first to present that argument in a systematic, scholarly way. He argued, for example, that in the context of ancient Egyptian culture, writing on stone tablets permitted the maintenance of social structures in small areas, but that the invention of papyrus plus transportation of people in boats was essential for the maintenance of integrated society extending along the Nile Valley. He argues that the Romans could not have long maintained a large land empire without both written communications and a road system. The development and maintenance in both Canada and the United States of democratic political systems that span the entire continent depended in part on the railroad and the telegraph.

The transportation and communication system used by the elite in a society may increase their span of control. Transportation and communication systems used by the mass of people, such as automobiles and television in our society, may increase their geographic and psychic mobility. The communication of models of social behavior not found in an individual's face-to-face group makes possible more rapid social change.

Without providing credible alternate models, it is virtually impossible, as many developing countries have found, to change local social structures. With a wider range of models to choose from, both the rate of social change and the diversity of social behavior are likely to increase. Changes in the communication system that permit more people to have access to a wider selection of information and entertainment may thus have more impact on social change than does the particular content at any one point in time. Changes in communication technology that permit easy electronic access to information without requiring transportation may well be the most significant technological and social change in the twentieth century.

Even though Marshall McLuhan's style is derived from James Joyce (of whom McLuhan is a long-time scholar), we should recognize the significance of his slogan: "The medium is the message" (McLuhan, 1964). Major intellectual influences on McLuhan were Harold Innis, and his anthropologist friend and colleague, Edmund Carpenter, from whom he apparently learned to think like an anthropologist about the broad relationship between the technology of a society and the total culture. Viewed from the perspective of a social historian or an anthropologist, the effects of changes in communication technology may be more significant than the transmission of particular messages.

The utilization of papyrus, the printing press, and the computer may have more influence on the nature of human society than the particular messages sent down the Nile, the content of printed books and papers, or the specific problems programmed for computers. Kranzberg and Pursell (1967) provide a more extended general discussion of technology and social change. Lynn White (1962), in his book *Medieval Technology and Social Change*, makes a convincing case for the dominant role of medieval technology in the rise of feudalism. Eisenstein (1969a; 1969b) provides an excellent analysis of the effects of printing technology on Western society.

We are now entering a period during which computer technology is likely to bring about major changes in our communication system that are possibly as far-reaching as the effects of printing technology were. Communication technology influences the basic structure and the decision-making process in society by determining who can communicate with whom, and who can obtain what information. Just as we do not like the air pollution that has resulted from internal combustion engines in automobiles, so we may not like some of the changes in political power that may result from changes in communication technology. Major changes in our mass communication system will result from the introduction of computer technology and, therefore, we should plan and control the direction of that technological change. Control of communication technology may be the best place to start a social chain reaction with wide implications for other sectors of society (Platt, 1966).

Future social historians are likely to agree that the dominant technological change in the last half of the twentieth century was the significant increase in the society's information-processing capacity. It is already evident that the primary social significance of the computer is not as a calculator, or even as a basis for factory automation, but as a versatile device for storing, manipulating, and transmitting information—in other words, as a medium of communication.

The next section gives an overview of the information utility that is now a likely outcome of the application of computer technology to mass communication. Later sections describe in more detail the technology that is making this possible, the current systems in which this technology is being used, and a possible transition from present mass communication systems. Some optimistic social predictions are presented as well as a more pessimistic view of how this technology will be used. The final section discusses the significance of communication technology problems in the context of problems of our times.

AN OVERVIEW OF INFORMATION UTILITIES

This new communication medium, which is coming to be called an *information utility*, will have one radical new property that previous mass media lack: what is transmitted over the communication channel can be controlled more directly by the receiver than by the sender of the message. It may look like a combination of a television set and a typewriter, function like a combination of a newspaper and a library, and permit a communication network that is something like a combination of a telephone and telegraph system.

We can think of all present media as being predominantly either storage media (books, newspapers, films, recordings) or transmission media (radio, television, telephone). Typically, storage media have required that the message be duplicated and then transported by traditional means. Many copies of books and newspapers are printed and then delivered by mail, trucks, or carrier boys. Sometimes it is cheaper for people to transport themselves to the medium, as in going to the movies.

Transmission media, such as broadcasts on radio and television, leave both the selection and the time of transmission controlled at the sending end. Broadcast television is like the passenger railroad: people are taken to scheduled places at scheduled times. The information utility is to communication what the automobile is to transportation: a means for people to choose their own routes and schedules. The main transmission medium that has permitted receivers to have some direct control over the transmission is the telephone, which has no storage properties. Receiver control over transmission from storage media has been limited to direct physical manipulation of the storage medium itself, as in selecting a book from a library or bookstore.

An information utility combines an electronic (or electronically controlled) storage medium and an electronic transmission medium. It permits a single copy of a large number of communications to be stored on a storage medium (typically computer magnetic-disk storage or microphotographic storage). Duplication of the message in storage is not required to transmit electronically on demand the information contained in storage. Receivers may thus select any particular communications (book, newspaper article, etc.) from a large storage medium for transmission at a time and place of the receiver's choosing. A discussion of the information-utility concept, including discussion of technical, economic, legal, and social considerations, is provided by Parkhill (1966). More recent discussion of potential consequences is provided by Sackman and Nie (1970), Parker and Dunn (1972), and Sackman and Boehm (1972).

An Imaginary Trip

A fantasy trip into the future may give a feeling for such a communication medium. Sitting at the breakfast table, you might cause the latest headlines to appear on a small display screen simply by touching a key. These headlines might have been rewritten five minutes before. Pointing at a headline might get the story displayed. If it is a continuing story about, say, the Middle East or an election campaign, you might want to get either a report of the latest incident or background information or interpretation. For someone with a special interest—for example, in some legislation pending in Congress—it could be possible to retrieve the latest story whether or not it received a headline, or even appeared in the latest edition.

With a slightly more expensive computer terminal, your news summary can be printed out for you while you are shaving or getting dressed. A wide variety of background information might be made available by an information utility, on demand by the receiver. Suppose you encounter a name of a person you would like to know more about: ask for a biographical sketch. Suppose you do not completely understand the economic reasoning behind an action by the International Monetary Fund: there might be available a short tutorial program on some aspect of international economics, or you may just seek a brief explanation of some technical term.

Suppose you do not see any sense in the actions of the local campus radicals and are genuinely curious about their motivation. You might request their own original statement. Suppose you want to have their actions interpreted in the framework of a viewpoint you already understand and appreciate: ask for the latest analysis by your favorite columnist. Suppose you want to search the wants ads or the supermarket ads. Instead of shuffling pages, you may just ask to have displayed ads in a particular category.

A child, home from school, may wish to have the computer display what the *Children's Encyclopedia* says in answer to a question. Suppose a high school student wishes to search the equivalent of the local public library for information needed to write a term paper. He can quickly search the equivalent of the card catalog and soon be browsing in relevant material.

A frequent use of home communication terminals by both children and adults may turn out to be game playing. Present computer chess programs can win in Class D tournaments (Greenblat, Eastlake, & Crocker, 1967). A screen with colorful moving images that shift in response to the touches of a two-year-old's fingertips may hold more fascination for such a child than passive viewing of television. Use of such a finger-pointing input system by preschool children has been demonstrated in one project in Pittsburgh (Glaser & Ramage, 1967; Fitzhugh & Katsuki, 1970). The habit of active participation and a constant rewarding of curiosity (by providing interesting answers at an appropriate level) could lead to lifelong habits of information seeking that blur the distinctions between game playing and instruction. This assumes a large set of computer-aided instruction programs that children approach voluntarily because it is fun to learn.

One other feature of such a communication medium derives from its capability for receiving and storing information for subscribers as well as retrieving it. Thus, the medium could operate like a combination of a letters-to-the-editor column and a radio talk show in which everyone could participate. Time-shared computer systems are now frequently and routinely used for sending messages back and forth between users. If the recipient is not at home, or does not want to be disturbed, the messages can be held in storage until he returns. If some subscribers are willing to be contacted by others with similar interests to theirs, they could store an interest profile that could be searched. This would permit all those interested in a particular civic action project or even a rock group to get together.

THE TECHNOLOGY

Computer Time-Sharing

The key technology that makes possible this new communication medium is time-shared computing. The computer can be simply described as a machine for storing, manipulating, and transmitting symbols. Time in the computer is measured in milliseconds (thousandths of a second), microseconds (millionths of a second) and nanoseconds (billionths of a second). One nanosecond is to one second as one second is to thirty years. In one nanosecond, light travels one foot. Computer designers restricted by that theoretical limit, the speed of light, are making computer parts smaller and arranging them so they can fit closer together.

Time-sharing is possible because of the mismatch between the speed of the computer and the speed of the human mind. Suppose, as is common these days, 100 people, each with their own computer console, are connected by telephone lines to the same computer. Now suppose the computer is operating in a time scale of nanoseconds, and suppose that it gives ten milliseconds of its attention to one user, then ten milliseconds to the next, and so on. By the time the computer has served all 100 users with perhaps thousands of operations each, it can return to the first user less than one second after it left him to serve the request of others. Even if the task of a particular user requires more than one "time-slice" to complete, the response can still appear to be instantaneous.

The great potential of time-sharing lies not in the fact that the computing power of large computers can be economically provided on demand to many users at remote locations, although that major accomplishment is why time-sharing was developed. Rather the primary economic, social, and political potential of this technology lies in its use for multiple access to large shared files of information in a way that permits each user rapid selection of desired information. The computing power also permits additional processing of that information.

Five Components

The time-shared computer system that will provide the switching capability to connect each user to a storage medium is one of five components into which the major features of an information utility can be classified.

A second major component is a storage medium that permits rapid access to any part of a very large store of information. Devices are now becoming available that can store in excess of one hundred billion characters of information (more than one hundred thousand densely packed four-hundred-page books) with access times short enough to retrieve any given group of characters in a time-scale suitable for use in a time-sharing system. These and other improved storage devices are expected to become widespread in the next few years. It seems likely that frequently accessed material and indexing to less frequently needed material will be stored in digital form (i.e., in computer manipulatable form), while large quantities of less frequently used information will be stored in analog form on some microphotographic medium. Analog information, such as that in a photograph, is not directly manipulatable by computer, although the selection and transmission could be under computer control.

A third major component is the "console" or "terminal" device that permits the user to interact with the system. The most common terminals in the early days of time-shared computing were typewriter or teletype terminals. Some computer systems use touch-tone telephone pads as the input medium with voice recordings stored by the computer to provide voice answers back to the users. Many other systems use cathode ray tube (CRT) display devices for rapid electronic display of information. A television picture tube or a standard television set is often used in a CRT display terminal.

The fourth major component is the communication link connecting the terminal with the system. Telephone lines are most frequently used, although coaxial cable is increasing in use. The latter type of cable is preferred for rapid display on television or other CRT screens because of its greater capacity. Because of the greater capacity, cable television channels may provide the needed transmission links for this new medium. Telephone lines may provide the links for those without cable connections, and they may provide the return communication from subscribers to the computers at the transmitting end of one-directional cable systems. Many cable TV companies are likely to develop their own two-way communication capability.

The techniques involved are those of selecting appropriate information from the storage medium to meet the requests of subscribers. This is quite different from the telephone company's switched network connecting people without an intervening storage medium. The techniques are currently used by time-shared computer companies and are likely to be extended and improved to provide the kind of reliable service required.

Whether there is two-way communication on the same cable that is used for transmission to the home or whether parallel lines will be provided for return communication is primarily an economic matter having to do with the cost of repeater devices in the cable. Several cable television companies have laid parallel communication lines for return communication to a computer at the "head-end" (transmitting end) of the cable as a currently cheaper solution than using two-way repeaters. Providing line capacity to handle the quantity of messages directed at individual terminals is not a difficult technical problem. A simple, although potentially expensive, solution would be to lay additional cable to handle the capacity. More complex switching and multiplexing (sharing the same channel for different subscribers just as the computer is shared) will most likely prove to be cheaper. A more detailed discussion of telecommunication technology is provided by Martin (1969).

The fifth main component is the set of computer programs required to translate the user's request into instructions the computer can understand. They carry out the information-retrieval and content-analysis tasks necessary to obtain the appropriate content for the user in the rapid time-scale required. Computer programs that perform this kind of task are now in operation, but present programs should be viewed as crude first approximations. Major intellectual effort is needed in automatic indexing, content analysis, and query language-processing techniques. The problems are not ordinary programming problems but intellectual problems of how to specify explicitly and unambiguously the instructions for performing such tasks. Only when the tasks themselves are well understood is it possible to write good computer programs to perform them.

CURRENT SYSTEMS

It is easy to discuss computer-information systems in the future tense. The ideas are relatively novel, and we are accustomed to a substantial lag between the time new ideas are proposed and when they become practical economic realities. Thus, we could overlook the fact that a wide variety of time-shared computer systems permitting shared access to storage media are already in existence and that the number is now growing rapidly (Licklider, 1968).

Such systems were first developed on university campuses. Massachusetts Institute of Technology and Stanford University are two among several examples of university communities with a time-shared computing environment. A wide variety of noncomputing uses have been made of such campus time-sharing systems. The on-line text-editing system at Stanford receives considerable use for secretarial and clerical chores. It is used for mailing list maintenance, for information retrieval, and for editing of research reports and Ph.D. dissertations. Drafts of this manuscript were edited via this system. The system permits authors of papers to obtain a clean copy of the current draft incorporating the latest changes without secretarial retyping. The Project MAC time-sharing system at MIT is being used for a bibliographic information retrieval service and experimentation by at least two major projects (Overhage & Harmon, 1965; Project INTREX staff, 1966–1970; Kessler, 1967).

In such environments it is not unusual to find hundreds of remote computer terminals in a variety of places, including private homes. Various computer-aided instruction projects, ranging from first-grade reading to college Russian, can be observed. The educational results of such time-shared individualized instruction are impressive (Suppes, 1967; Silberman & Filep, 1968; Alpert & Bitzer, 1970). These examples have led to the rapid development of several new computer time-sharing companies that offer this kind of service commercially, as well as to the providing of such service by older computer companies. It is a growing market, although still concentrated primarily on computing, on storage and retrieval of private files, and on shared libraries of computer programs.

More visible to the general public are the airline reservation systems and the stock market information systems. Both are special purpose time-shared information storage and retrieval systems that have received the high level of public acceptability necessary for long-term economic success. The airline reservation systems now used by airline company ticket agents are being extended to include travel agents and large corporate users of airline services. The stock market information systems permitting brokers and others to retrieve the latest information on specific stocks or general market trends are now commonplace in stock brokers' offices (Overhage, 1969). The sale of tickets for theatrical, musical, and athletic events is another example of this type of special purpose system that appears to be gaining public acceptance in several communities.

A variety of government systems at local, state, and federal levels are in operation. Police information systems permit rapid searches by name or by automobile license number as an aid to law enforcement (Carter, 1967). Some state employment agency records can be searched on demand either to find people for jobs or jobs for people. In some cities, other records, such as welfare case records, are maintained in central computer files for direct access from remote computer terminals. Some computerized hospital information systems are under development (Levy & Cammarn, 1968).

Much of the initial research and development was performed in connection with military command and control systems and intelligence agencies' information-retrieval systems. However, the initiative and the large volume of effort has apparently shifted to the business community. Inventory control applications were among the first to be put onto time-shared systems. The advantages of being able to obtain immediate information out of centralized inventory records from decentralized locations has obvious advantages in a variety of business settings. Some of the systems developed by National Aeronautics and Space Administration (NASA) contractors in connection with the Apollo space program perform this function particularly well, with inquiry from terminals widely scattered across the United States. More generalized management-information systems, including budget, personnel, and other records, are coming into fairly common use (Senko, 1969).

These special markets may eventually evolve into a mass market with shared terminals and communication lines permitting the user to switch into any of several special systems. This is particularly true if cable television channels provide economical communication links into homes, schools, and offices, and if general multipurpose terminals are developed to permit either television or computer reception. The marginal costs of providing additional special systems, including educational systems, will then be considerably less. Present systems do not benefit from the economies of scale that will be possible later.

Mass Media Systems

Time-shared information systems have been extended into mass communication applications far enough to produce both operational systems and research and development projects with promising long-run implications. Libraries are the first communication institutions to use such systems. The Bell Telephone Laboratories' library has activated an on-line circulation system (Kennedy, 1968). That system includes the catalogs of three libraries several miles distant from each other. It permits on-line inquiry concerning the status of any volume. Changes in the status of a volume can be recorded so rapidly that a remote inquiry made a few seconds after an item has been charged out will be answered by reporting that new status. This is a system capability not possible for large libraries using a manual system.

Project INTREX (INformation TRansfer EXperiments), using the MIT engineering library for its "augmented catalog experiment" and for its "text access experiment," is developing and demonstrating both on-line reference retrieval and on-line display of full text of documents stored in a random-access microfiche device (Overhage & Harmon, 1965; Project INTREX Staff, 1966–1970).

The Public Systems Division of the System Development Corporation in Santa Monica is developing an on-line library system based on common access by many libraries to a single computer file of bibliographic information obtained in machine-readable form from the Library of Congress' MARC tapes. In addition, a common set of computer programs for performing a variety of technical processing functions is being developed. Their system was successfully demonstrated at the annual meeting of the American Society for Information Science in San Francisco in October 1969.

The Stanford Public Information REtrieval System (SPIRES) has been used for on-line searches of physics preprint files at the Stanford Linear Accelerator Center since the spring in 1969, and is being expanded in conjunction with the Stanford library's Project BALLOTS (Bibliographic Automation of Large Library Operations using a Time-sharing System) to provide on-line technical processing service for the Stanford libraries. An on-line, local, in-process file forms the heart of that system. Additional computer programs permit computer production of purchase orders, claims and cancellation notices, requestor notices, and acquisition lists (Parker, 1969; SPIRES Project, 1968; 1970; 1971a; 1971b; 1971c).

The NASA bibliographic retrieval system now in operation permits users in different parts of the United States to search interactively in the file of some 270,000 references to reports of interest to NASA and its contractors (Summit, 1968).

Projects like these appear to be pointing the way toward a future library system through which large numbers of people may retrieve information from libraries at the time and place they want it without much of the inconvenience now associated with library use, and with confidence that the material they want will be accessible. More advanced visions of the future incorporate features that are beginning to be called "augmented intellect" facilities (Engelbart & English, 1968). Such facilities include many computer facilities for manipulation and communication of information as well as storage and retrieval.

In computer-aided conferences held by Engelbart at Stanford Research Institute, participants were able to share a common set of documents and diagrams, and have any part displayed on their screen. Participants used the terminals to edit drafts of documents, to transmit suggested revisions to the display screens of other participants, or to draw attention to interesting features. When this technique becomes more available, there can be rapid sharing of "scratch pad" information, whether verbal or pictorial, as communicators share both current messages and a common storage medium. Visions of possible future technology of this type are provided in the book *Libraries of the Future* (Licklider, 1966), and in two stimulating essays by Vannevar Bush (1945; 1967).

No similar systems for newspapers or magazines yet exist, although planning and development projects have begun. Many daily newspapers in the United States are using computers for typesetting or other aspects of newspaper production. The first step of newspapers toward use of time-shared computer systems for information distribution is likely to come as a result of applying the time-shared computer library systems to newspaper libraries. In the mid-1960s, a group of newspaper publishers commissioned a study by Diebold & Associates to inform them of the status and prospects of computer technology for newspaper information production and distribution systems.

Diebold predicts that by the mid-1970s this new information medium will "change totally the ways in which much business and professional work is conducted." He further predicts, "By the late 1970s and the early 1980s the decreasing costs and improved capabilities of this technology will allow the communications center of the home to be a reality" (Diebold, 1969: 12). The American Newspaper Publishers Association has awarded a grant to Project INTREX at MIT for research into such systems (Reintjes, 1969). An interesting projection of the techniques for newspaper distribution is provided by Thomas Billings (1966). A recent questionnaire and interview study by Ben Bagdikian (1971) for the Rand Corporation has probed into a variety of possible technological changes in newspaper production and distribution techniques.

A significant recent development was the signing of two contracts by the *New York Times* in 1969, one with IBM to provide an on-line information system for the New York Times library, starting with the *New York Times* index, which is already computer produced; the other with the Arthur D. Little company to study the market potential and marketing strategy for time-shared computer information. The system was scheduled to be completed in 1972.

CABLE TELEVISION: A POSSIBLE TRANSITION?

Predicting possible avenues of transition from our present communication media to future information utilities is a risky business. The purpose in engaging in such a form of science fiction writing at all is to indicate that there is at least one plausible path by which our present media system could evolve into the kind of public information utility system indicated above. At present, the most plausible path for development of information utilities appears to be by way of cable television.

The provision of more television channels, easier tuning of UHF stations, and better quality reception (particularly color reception) without rooftop antennas is likely to provide sufficient incentive for many households to subscribe to cable TV services. Early cable (or CATV for Community Antenna Television) systems had only five channels and were introduced as a way of importing distant signals into communities without local television or with only a limited number of local channels. Current systems now permit in excess of forty channels (the Akron, Ohio, cable system permits eighty channels).

In addition to broadcast services, "narrowcasting" is anticipated on some channels (e.g., for doctors, or for pay TV audiences). Some sets would be able to receive information on such channels and others would not. For example, different political broadcasts might be transmitted to different precincts. Some channels can be dedicated to municipal information services, such as broadcasting local council proceedings or other public meetings. Time on some channels could be made available to the public. Such "common carrier" broadcasting would be likely to attract additional subscribers, particularly from minority groups. The broad bandwidth communication capability that cable TV will bring into homes, schools, and offices throughout the country can provide the basic communication channels needed for the kinds of public information systems we have been predicting.

The tempo of change has picked up as a result of the new FCC cable television rules that went into effect at the end of March 1972. Distant television signals can now be imported into the top 100 television markets, although copyright rules will make that option less attractive in the top 50 markets than in the second 50 (Federal Communications Commission, 1972). The new cable ruling requires a minimum of twenty channels, with channels reserved for free public access, education, and government services. It also requires program origination by cable operators and the provision of channels available for lease by others. The new ruling requires two-way communication capability (at least permitting digital response from subscribers) in new construction and requires that capacity be expanded when the available channels are becoming full.

Excellent earlier discussions of cable television policy issues were provided in a Rand Corporation report (L. Johnson, 1970) and in a special issue of *The Nation* (Smith, 1970). More recent discussion is provided in the report of the Sloan Commission on Cable Communications (Sloan Commission, 1971) and in the report of a cable television policy analysis conducted at Stanford (Barton et al., 1972).

Looking farther into the future, we can expect mergers and joint agreements between cable TV operators and computer time-sharing companies to offer computer-based services to their customers via cable TV. At first these services are likely to be those presently available—computing services, stock market and financial information services, computer games, and computer-aided instruction—making it a novelty market for the rich.

The expanding market of the time-shared computer companies is an indication of the direction of the future. As more users purchase such services and as the variety of the services is extended, their offerings will begin to look more like an information utility service than a computer utility service. As more information services are added (including access to library services), this market can be expected to expand. As the number of users expands, we can expect that there will be much greater total demand for information than for traditional computing services. The computing market, large though it is, is small compared to a public information market reaching every home.

The next step beyond the connection of computer terminals to cable TV systems will almost certainly be the development and marketing of devices that permit existing standard television sets to be used as CRT display terminals. New, all-purpose, home communication terminals designed initially for both television and computer services and also to play video recordings like the Columbia Broadcasting System's

EVR (Electronic Video Recording) device will be developed and marketed. The technological problem is to develop a home communications terminal that can economically store a single picture or page of text transmitted from a computer or from a photographic storage medium, as well as display television pictures.

A device apparently meeting many of these requirements is the Digivue terminal developed by Donald Bitzer at the University of Illinois (Alpert & Bitzer, 1970). This device does not need to be "refreshed" thirty times a second (as a television set does). Each small segment continues showing the previous signal until it is replaced by a new signal. A terminal based on similar principles could be designed to receive television also.

In the meantime, however, the large number of existing television sets may provide a sufficient market for an adapter that will permit present sets to be used for this purpose. The Mitre Corporation has demonstrated the feasibility of this technique in the Reston, Virginia, cable system (Volk, 1971). Such adapters may be built for connection to telephone systems as well as to cable TV systems for use in areas not yet served by cable TV or in areas where the cable TV companies are not offering a generalized computer service.

By the time such home communication terminals are ready for marketing, a variety of potential services may be available. Either the cable TV companies or the associated computer companies, or both, are likely to be aggressively seeking out a variety of new services to offer, including computer-aided instruction and computerized library information services. Development of computer-based information systems for Congress and for state legislatures, permitting on-line inquiry into the status of pending legislation, could lead to the marketing of such service to the public (House Administration Committee, 1969).

Since additional storage capacity is likely to be low in cost, and can be added as funds are available to pay for it, it should be possible to guarantee to every citizen the right of access to the sending as well as the receiving end of this medium of public communication. Instead of a space limitation restricting the number of letters to the editor that can be printed, the space could be open at least to all who chose to pay the cost of storage. This is somewhat like the present advertising function in media, although advertisers in the present media sometimes have to compete for a limited amount of space or time available and must pay for the duplication and transmission costs as well as (or instead of) the storage costs.

So far, this argument has assumed that the development of the medium will be on a local basis, which is the way cable TV operations (and, for that matter, broadcast radio and television operations) are now franchised. Just as a small number of networks developed in the broadcasting industry and a single network in the telephone industry, it is likely that an interconnected network will develop in this new medium.

One local operation may choose to duplicate some or all of the information stored in a different location (e.g., New York or Los Angeles), or it may choose to switch a subscriber to a more distant service when comparable service is not available locally. Depending on the volume of requests for such service, it is a straightforward matter of economic calculation to determine whether the transmission costs associated with such distant service are greater than the cost of duplicating the storage locally. Satellite communication may be expected to sharply reduce the costs of long-distance transmission and indeed to make these costs almost independent of distance. The Hughes Aircraft Company has applied to the FCC for authority to launch a domestic communication satellite to interconnect cable systems.

Some of the costs of information services are likely to be recovered through advertising. Present CATV regulations permit sponsorship of programs and advertising at the beginning and end of each "program" and at natural intermissions provided no interruptions are created for the purpose of inserting advertising. Although more FCC regulations are likely to be forthcoming with respect to advertising support of computer services, both the form and intent of the present regulations appear consistent with such advertising. The FCC is encouraging CATV operators to obtain such revenue as may increase the variety of services available.

Advertising in conjunction with computer services offered via CATV could be of two types: either involuntary on the part of the subscriber (as in present television advertising), or voluntary, as in the use of newspaper classified advertising and directory advertising (e.g., telephone directory yellow pages). Both types of advertisers will presumably provide revenue for the service to permit subsidy of the subscriber's access to other information in the system. CATV revenue is estimated to reach $1.8 billion per year by 1975. Sales of CATV equipment by 1975 are estimated to be $500 million per year (Dunlop, 1970).

In the initial stages of development of such a medium, it is likely that the content will consist primarily of content prepared for another medium (just as much of television was initially film, or radio with pictures, or broadcasting of stagelike presentations with or without a studio audience). It is conceivable that a large amount of material will represent secondary distribution of material prepared for print media, including both newspapers and magazines.

In the later stages, it is likely that a large amount of material will be prepared directly for the new medium. Presumably, new uses of such a medium, not possible in existing media, will develop. For example, some subscribers may be willing to have the system store information about themselves and their interests, so that other people with similar interests may find out who they are. This would facilitate the task of local civic action groups. The medium could also permit subscribers to use the medium for communication with other subscribers via the intermediary of the computer storage.

SOME OPTIMISTIC SOCIAL PREDICTIONS

It is possible to be optimistic about the social consequences of information utilities for those who have access to it, provided that inequitable distribution through the society does not create worse social problems that counterbalance the beneficial effects. In the present section, I shall discuss first the positive consequences for individuals using such a system and, second, the positive consequences for the society under a highly unrealistic set of distribution assumptions. For the purpose of the argument, I shall assume that all members of the society have the financial resources, the skill, and the motivation to utilize a computer-based information utility.

Many individuals in our society value information highly. For some, information is its own reward. For many, information is significant because of its instrumental value. It may facilitate specific problem-solving. It may mean economic or occupational advancement. It may mean an increase in social status. It is likely to give an individual increased power in manipulating his environment, both physical and social.

Most of the increased power that often results from improved information is absolute in the sense that information useful in managing one person's environment is still an advantage if other people also have that information. Some of it may be relative in the sense that the increased power comes from having information that others do not have, or from having it earlier. The plight of the disadvantaged in our society stems in large part from the fact that much of the society's information and its information-processing capability are not easily accessible. Equalized access to information could serve the disadvantaged well.

Seven characteristics of the new information technology may serve individuals who positively value information:

1. The amount of information available will increase. The amount of news in the daily newspaper can be greater when all of it does not have to be distributed to everyone at great cost in duplication and distribution (primarily in newsprint costs). For some people, already suffering from too much information rather than too little, this may not appear to be an advantage. It certainly would not be an advantage unless some of the additional information were relevant to their needs and interests. The extra information potentially available should not make things worse, provided that the criteria for selection of relevant information are known. For many people, however, an increase in the availability of information would be helpful if they have efficient access to that information. This will be particularly true if there is open access to the sending as well as the receiving end of the system, thus permitting users to seek out sources they trust.

2. Greater variety can be offered in the packaging of information. The trend of the magazine business away from general magazines toward specialized magazines for specialized audiences would be observed in much accelerated fashion in a computer-based communication medium. Since the effective "unit" of information in such a system can be specific stories or items rather than an entire newspaper or an entire magazine, it should prove economical to tailor specific packages for specific audiences. The equivalent of one's daily newspaper or weekly magazine can be constructed out of those stories or sections that are of interest. To take only a single example, there would no longer be any need to send all female subscribers the sports section and all male subscribers the women's section, whether they wanted it or not. The potential of special audience-packaging techniques is likely to more than counterbalance any difficulties resulting from increased quantities of information available.

The logical extension of specialized packaging of information is individualized information, where the size of audience for each particular package is one. This individualized information service is made technically possible by such a medium, although it will be more expensive than packages prepared for groups of people. Scientists now have commercially available to them information-alerting services that inform them of the availability of articles matching their "interest profiles" in any of several thousand technical journals.

3. The power of selection is in the hands of the individual receiver. In most present mass media, including newspapers, radio, and television, what information is transmitted is under the control of the sender. Transferring control of both the selection of content and the timing of transmission to the receiver permits him to select from a wider variety of sender-prepared information packages and to select and prepackage in ways tailored to his individual interests. This power to select information is likely to be viewed by the individuals involved as increased efficiency of information access. Individuals who become skilled in the use of such media will value that power.

4. The user's information-processing capacity is improved. Computer-aided browsing or scanning of large numbers of documents could permit the user to obtain excerpts of relevant passages or to obtain counts of frequencies of occurrence of different words or phrases and an examination of the variety of different contexts in which they are found. The numerical manipulation capability of computers could be used to tabulate statistical or numerical information in ways other than that in which it is stored. Automated abstracting or extracting techniques could

be utilized to prepare shorter summaries of longer items of potential interest. The power of the computer can be used to scan large amounts of text to select particular passages, provided that the process of scanning can be specified (e.g., to find all paragraphs containing the phrase *information utility* or *information utilities*).

5. More effective feedback is possible in such information systems. In present media, publishers and broadcasters often do not know in any useful detail what part of their product is attracting their audience. The newspaper publisher may know whether his sales are going up or down, but he usually does not know whether it is the sex-and-sensationalism stories or the *New York Times* news service that is contributing to the trend. Consequently, he does not have clear information on which to base changes in his product. With detailed information on how many people of what kind are reading each item through the information utility, it will be possible to determine subscriber interest in detail never before possible. Thus, those in the business of packaging information will be able to readjust their information service continuously to make it more responsive to the interests of their subscribers.

6. Communication can increasingly be substituted for transportation. The time of travel to information sources can be saved in many cases. Remote access may be of special value to those who are physically isolated, whether by job requirements, economics, or physical disability. Alleviation of some mass transportation problems may be possible through use of improved communication as a substitute for some transportation of people.

7. Social barriers to accessibility of information are removed. The most frequent source of information for most people, including scientists and engineers seeking technical information, is other people. A major advantage of interpersonal sources is that they are conveniently accessible. We may often ask a neighbor or family member for information, not because he is the best information source but because he is the closest information source. An information medium that is available at home or at work may be more accessible than are other people, who may be busy or uninterested in either the questioner or his question. Also, answers to questions may be of better quality through such a medium than are answers one typically gets from a friend or neighbor. Often people hesitate to ask questions of other people for fear of being rebuffed, or for fear of demonstrating their ignorance, or through reluctance to pay the subtle social price of admitting a kind of status inferiority through the implicit assumption that the questioner has less information on the topic in question than the person being asked. Many working-class or unemployed persons are reluctant to attend evening classes or other adult education classes because these are perceived as middle-class institutions in which they would feel uncomfortable. None of these social inhibiters to information seeking is present in the computer-information utility.

Social Advantages

It is possible to paint a very rosy picture of the advantages for society if every member of the society has the economic resources to obtain access to such an information utility from earliest childhood. One can make an economic argument that investment in information for individuals in the society will provide a large economic and social return for the society. Having a large segment of U.S. society poor in information resources and, consequently, poor in skills relevant for the society (e.g., the unemployed and underemployed) may constitute a major drag on the growth of the U.S. economy relative to what would otherwise be possible.

What appears to be needed most in a rapidly changing society is not a single set of skills or body of information but a more generalized information-processing capacity. If we can bring up a new generation of people who have had access to both information and electronic aids to information processing from earliest childhood, then we may no longer have serious training and retraining problems throughout the lifespan of such generations. If information-seeking habits are rewarded from earliest childhood, rather than being punished or ignored as they are now for many children (particularly the disadvantaged), we may have a more productive society. The particular content individuals choose to learn may be much less important than learning information-selection and processing skills and having curiosity rewarded.

The traditional concept of formal education may be pushed somewhat out of shape when individualized instruction and information are available on demand. Even if students choose to learn something different from what their formal classroom teachers are trying to teach them at a particular time, they will learn information-seeking skills that prepare them for lifelong learning. The basic curiosity that we all seem to be born with could be enhanced rather than stifled, as it is now, by attempts to force people to learn things other than what they are curious about. This difference in motivation resulting from rewarding of information-seeking behavior as such may stimulate people to continue learning far longer than is presently the case in the underprivileged segments of our society.

This redistribution of information would permit more informed participation in establishing and choosing the goals of the society—in other words, in the political process generally. An obvious example is the proposed congressional information system. Some recent developments in Congress are indicative of an inching toward improved congressional information systems. One can foresee a computer-based information system that permits congressmen to determine the text, the status, the legislative history, and relevant background information for each piece of legislation pending in Congress (Saloma, 1969).

Congressman John Brademas of Indiana, in a film presentation at the Fall Joint Computer Conference (held in Las Vegas, November 1969), said that such information systems were being resisted by present congressional leadership because it would tend to distribute information more widely within the Congress itself, and hence dilute the information advantage (and the power) of those presently in control by reason of seniority. He was quite explicit in saying that the senior members recognized that knowledge was power and that improved information systems would give more power to junior congressmen. The resistance appears to be weakening, however. In 1970, the U.S. House of Representatives awarded a $450,000 contract to Stanford Research Institute to develop plans and concepts for a computerized information system.

Meanwhile, much information on the status of pending legislation is being compiled commercially by information services that sell the information to lobbyists and others interested in following the course of legislation. Robert Chartrand (1970) of the Legislative Reference Service of the Library of Congress, in the same session at the Fall Joint Computer Conference, suggested that since Congress did not have the technical capability to develop such information systems, they might well be developed commercially and sold back to the Congress. If such a computer information system containing status information on pending legislation could be as accessible to the discontented as it is likely to be to lobbyists, protestors might have more motivation to participate in the political process nonviolently.

Another social advantage that could result from a shift in emphasis from print to electronic media is a reduction in problems of waste disposal and deforestation. Since paper constitutes a large proportion of the waste that contributes to pollution and requires expensive collection and disposal techniques, the information utility may be welcomed by conservationists and ecologists.

A MORE PESSIMISTIC VIEW

It would be naive to think that the potential individual and social advantages outlined in the previous section will naturally follow from the development of the technology that makes such a system possible. It would also be naive to think that the changes likely to take place are without potentially dangerous side-effects that should be guarded against. Modification of the system for distributing education, information, and entertainment in a society is a basic structural change that has ramifications throughout the entire social and political structure. In the case of the technologically based changes now upon us, we no longer have the option of inaction as a means of protection. Whether we like it or not, the technological changes are developing momentum. Positive action is needed soon to avoid side-effects of uncontrolled technological change in the communication industry.

The greatest danger would be for a single corporation (or small number of corporations) to obtain monopoly control over the mass communication system of the society. It appears that the communication channels for the information utilities will be a "natural monopoly" just as the telephone system is a "natural monopoly"; consequently, we will not have competing distribution systems to choose from. The cable television industry is predicting that 85 percent of U.S. homes will have access to cable television (and, consequently, to the information utility) by 1985 (Dunlop, 1970). That 1985 prediction may come perilously close to George Orwell's (1949) predictions for 1984 if control of the content of the information utilities is in the wrong hands.

Although information-utility users will be able to select what they want from the utility and choose the time at which they wish to receive it, their selection will necessarily be limited to what is available within the system. If a commercial monopoly controls what goes into such a communication system, the dangers could be even worse than the dangers of government monopoly caricatured by Big Brother's two-way communication system in *Nineteen Eighty-Four*.

Economies of scale in the communications industry are serving to reduce further the amount of competition in the mass media. The dangers of monopolistic or oligopolistic control of communication media are already present, as the steady decline of competing daily newspapers and the increasing dominance of the broadcast industry by a small number of "media barons" indicates (N. Johnson, 1968). This tendency toward monopoly in the communication industry has long been under attack from the left and more recently from the political right (Agnew, 1969). An excellent discussion of regulatory alternatives for cable television in the context of media-concentration problems is given by Barnett (1970). For a more recent discussion of the institutional structure of media, see Parker (1972a).

The dangers of monopolistic control of communication content, whether by business or government, can be avoided by regulations to guarantee all citizens freedom of access to both the sending and receiving ends of the communication system. In this respect the model of telephone regulation seems appropriate. The telephone company has a monopoly of communication channels but does not control the communication going over those channels. A cable-based system of mass communication with message-storage capacity can be operated in comparable fashion. Additional cable channels and storage capacity could be added as needed to permit every citizen access to the communication system. Such a system would give new meaning to the protection of freedom of speech intended by the First Amendment to the U.S. Constitution. Legal scholars are now debating the merits of such an interpretation guaranteeing a right of access to the media or a listener's right to hear (Barron, 1967; 1969; Thomas, 1970).

Two major dangers in the development of information utilities are inequitable distribution and shortage of educational content. In the absence of an aggressive national policy backed with public funds, the information utilities will be developed by private industry with profit motivation. Without federal regulation or federal subsidy, it is unlikely that the economically and geographically disadvantaged will have access to the information utilities. In the short run it is likely that the gap will widen between the information rich and the information poor. It will be much easier to make profits from homes geographically easiest to connect to cable systems and from those with sufficient income to be able to pay for such services.

Without federal subsidy of educational and public information content, it is likely that the content will be primarily entertainment and advertising. Considering the way television has developed, it would be hard to predict otherwise. Education has traditionally been paid for out of public funds, both for formal schooling and for continuing education services such as those offered by public libraries. Without adequate funding, those public sectors of the economy could be deprived of access to the information utility and would be forced to rely on traditional communication techniques, such as face-to-face classroom instruction and manual distribution of books.

If the only way to get information into the information utility is for someone with an economic incentive to put it there, we may have "information pollution" on a grand scale. Public education and information, like public parks and clean air and water, may not be well suited to the private marketplace unless government subsidy provides incentives. Fred Friendly (1970) describes this problem of financing in an article aptly titled, "Asleep at the Switch of the Wired City."

Without such government action, it appears inevitable that the information utilities will serve primarily that segment of the population that already has both the financial resources and the information-seeking and information-processing skills needed for efficient utilization. Only two kinds of information are likely to be available. One is information for which there is already a large market of subscribers. The other is information that individuals and corporations are willing to pay to have others see (for example, advertising). Thus, the needs of large corporations and the middle and upper classes generally are more likely to be served than the interests of less privileged segments of society. This could lead to increased disaffection and alienation of the less privileged.

Another problem worth serious consideration can be labeled "death of the melting-pot ethic" or "the end of consensus" (Pool, 1968). One of the purposes of public education in the United States has been the development of a measure of cultural homogeneity. The public school system was the major "melting pot" for achieving cultural homogeneity out of the cultural pluralism of the varied immigrant groups that made up much of the population.

The system of mass media also served to facilitate the achievement of consensus in society by providing the same information to large numbers of people. Information utilities will permit and foster both greater diversity of content and greater consumer control over selection of that content. Those who now reach for the sports page, ignoring front-page news, will find it even easier to do so in future systems. Those who are interested in local problems but not international problems (or vice versa) will find it easier to pursue their interests in greater depth and to ignore issues and problems that do not concern them. This tendency is already present and is evident in the shift of readership from general to specialized magazines. The new media technology is likely to continue those trends towards pluralism and diversity, with both its social values and social dangers.

A danger that is more frequently discussed in the context of the information-utility technology is the question of invasion of privacy. This is a serious question most appropriately directed toward the "data bank" components of an information utility rather than to the more obviously "mass media" components. There are two aspects to the privacy question. One is the distinction between private and public information. The other is the question of selective access to information that is nominally public.

It is now generally accepted in the field of computer technology that there is no completely technological solution to the maintenance of privacy of data in computer data banks any more than there is a completely technological solution to the maintenance of privacy in written records (Hoffman, 1969). Increasingly sophisticated hardware and software devices to protect privacy can be developed and implemented. Generally speaking, the more expensive the lock the harder it will be to pick, although there is always the possibility of an inside job where someone who knows the "combination" will obtain information for illicit purposes or sell the combination for someone else's use. To the extent that data banks are developed that contain private rather than public information, a sophisticated combination of technological and legal techniques will be required to maintain privacy.

Sometimes the concept of privacy is invoked to keep information out of public files as a protection against its inequitable distribution. This could be the case when a government agency or a privileged elite (such as bankers or credit bureaus) has easier access to public information than do other members of the public. If individuals feel that unequal access to public information can work to their disadvantage, they may attempt to keep information "private." An alternate solution to this kind of abuse is to make "public" information as easily accessible to individual citizens as, say, to police administrators or lobbyists.

There will still be need for strong legal and technical safeguards against invasion of privacy, just as we need legal safeguards against wire tapping of private telephone conversations. The danger is great in the case of data banks because of the need to store individual records as a basis for computing aggregate statistics, e.g., census returns for cross tabulation of census data. A general discussion of the legal problems associated with protection of privacy is provided by Westin (1967).

Increased availability and more equitable distribution of information may lead to political and social side effects that can be viewed as either beneficial or dangerous, depending on one's political perspective. To the extent that information is a source of power, widespread availability of public information will help to bring "power to the people." This is the reverse side of the arguments concerning the undesirable consequences of inequitable distribution of information. Unless strongly perverted from its natural tendency, the information utility, like the printing press, seems destined to distribute power more widely in society. The issue appears to be drawn between those who value that distribution of power, and hence want to speed up the process, and those who fear that distribution of power, and hence want to slow down the process.

COMMUNICATION AND THE PROBLEMS OF OUR TIMES

At a time when social problems are approaching crisis proportions, it is necessary to order the priorities carefully. We need to ask ourselves how much of our attention, our energies, and our resources should be devoted to problems of education and communication.

In a recent article in *Science*, John Platt (1969) developed a classification of problems and crises by estimated time to crisis and by estimated intensity. The classification of intensity was based on a subjective judgment of the number of persons affected and the degree of effect. The eight grades of intensity ranged from total annihilation to noncrisis problems being overstudied. The eight grades of intensity were:

1. Total annihilation
2. Great destruction or change (physical, biological, or political)
3. Widespread, almost unbearable tension
4. Large-scale distress
5. Tension-producing responsive change
6. Other problems—important, but adequately researched
7. Exaggerated dangers and hopes
8. Noncrisis problems being "overstudied"

Platt rated a variety of social problems by this classification scheme, indicating also that in each succeeding time period problems are likely to escalate to a higher level of intensity if not solved. For example, racial conflict in the United States was classified as being of grade-three intensity in the one-to-five-year period, with the indication that it could become a grade-two crisis ("great destruction or change") in the five-to-twenty-year period, if not solved or mitigated.

In this scale of crises for the next five years, Platt classified participatory democracy as a grade-three crisis, privacy on computers as grade five, and new educational methods as grade six. He did indicate that at grade-five level of intensity there were opportunities as well as dangers. He cited as an example the positive opportunity for invention of new channels of personal communication. Within the five-to-twenty-year period, participatory democracy may have escalated to a grade-two crisis, the communications gap to grade four, and educational inadequacy to grade five, according to Platt. By the twenty-to-fifty-year period both education and communications may, he believes, escalate to grade-two crises.

Because of subjective factors entering into such a classification, it is easy to suggest minor shifts in this general pattern. For example, a case can be made for shifting new educational methods from grade six to grade five on the basis of both the positive opportunities presented and the dangers to the political process if there is not improvement in the educational system. Platt's claim that new educational methods are adequately researched neglects the fact that the relatively inexpensive research to date has brought the level of understanding and the technology to the point where expensive field studies and pilot programs are needed. If we do not increase our attention to the educational opportunities in the next five years, educational inadequacy may become a grade-four rather than grade-five crisis within five to twenty years.

During the next five years the structure of control of the new communication technology will be determined. The best opportunity to direct it in socially useful ways will occur in this period.

Participatory Democracy

An improved communication system may provide help in what Platt calls the crisis of participatory democracy. Changes in communication technology may have the potential for bringing more power to the people in a nonviolent way. It may be possible to maintain the present system in which political decisions are made largely on the basis of the pressures of competing interest groups, but still to redress the balance by providing information resources to consumer groups or "people's lobbies" so that they can compete on a more equal basis with interest groups that have the backing of corporations (or unions) whose financial interests are at stake. In a highly educated society that is already committed in principle to broad-based democratic participation in decision-making, the power of information may help to combat a privileged elite using their economic resources to maintain or improve their position in society.

The possibility of instant electronic two-way communication connecting every home in the country has raised in some minds the potential of electronic town meetings with instant referenda (or at least public opinion polls) on all manner of complex issues, many of which may be of little real interest to the people expressing opinions. There are three basic points to be made concerning the possibility of a nation-wide town meeting. First, in its more simplistic form, it is probably unworkable and undesirable. Second, despite some disadvantages and dangers, it could possibly be made to work. Third, it may not be necessary: the same goal of broader political participation may be accomplished by other means. Discussion of these issues is provided in a recent paper on on-line polling and voting (Parker, 1927b).

Arguments against participatory democracy are more likely to be made by those whose interest are served by the status quo. Nevertheless, some of the dangers are real and should be taken seriously. One criticism is that most people are not sufficiently interested or informed on most issues, therefore the complexity of problems in modern society requires full-time representatives to study and decide rather than to have the issues decided on simplistic grounds by the uninformed. The danger of "tyranny of the majority" is real but may be overrated, provided there are adequate guarantees of protection of the rights of minorities.

Another criticism is that "he who calls for power to the people is really calling for power to himself"; in other words, there are dangers of demagoguery in populist politics. In most forms of direct popular decision-making, the real power may lie not with the people but with those who can control the form in which questions are put to the people. This is a more serious criticism which reflects that in such systems the flow of information is from the people to the elite. From the viewpoint of those interested in broader participation, the more important features would be those that facilitate the people's access to information rather than the elite's access to information about the people.

Despite the danger and disadvantages, it is possible that a modified version of an electronic town meeting could be made to work. It would require a greater trust in the ability of people to calculate their own self-interest than many elitists are willing to grant. Nevertheless, the higher the level of the people's education and information, the more likely it is that such a system will work.

Since the earliest date at which such a system could interconnect all homes in the United States is 1985 (based on estimates of growth of cable television), the level of education may be sufficient to make such a system possible. That optimistic conclusion assumes that the system would be primarily designed for getting relevant information to each individual who wanted it at the time he is considering each issue in question. It assumes that the elected representatives and appropriate technical staff would structure the issues in such a way that detailed plans for each of the social alternatives would be spelled out, perhaps along lines similar to the program-planning and budgeting concepts now coming into more general use. It assumes that people would learn to vote only when they had an interest in the issue in question.

The third point is that the goal of broadening political participation sufficiently to maintain political stability may not require electronic referenda. The present system of political decision-making appears to work as a complex balancing of the interests of a large number and variety of organized groups. In theory, political decisions are made in the public interest. In practice, the "public interest" is usually decided on the basis of the countervailing arguments and proposals of those groups with enough interest to participate more intensely than merely voting in elections. These include labor as well as management, consumer groups as well as producer groups, left-wing as well as right-wing interests.

The difficulty is that in order to participate effectively in this process a large amount of energy and expense must be devoted to gathering information, preparing arguments, and getting them to the right people at the right time. When large financial interests are at stake, much money and time is spent in protecting those interests. A consumer group interested in lower fuel oil prices in one segment of the country is not likely to have the time or the financial resources to compete with the oil lobby, for example. Citizens groups for better television are fighting unequally with the combined economic power of the television industry. The point is not that the consumer is always right and the producer always wrong. Rather, the point is that two sides of an argument are unequally heard when one side has volunteer help and a low budget and the other has a large well-financed staff.

The main commodity that the additional financial resources buys is information (*intelligence* is an appropriate word for it in this context). The more blatant uses of financial resources, both legal and illegal, can be combatted when information about the transactions and about the financial interests of the parties involved is made public. Since the ultimate base of power lies within the electorate in a democratic system, the battle is largely one of who has the best information and who controls which communication channels.

Appropriately structured computer information utilities would facilitate the formation of interest groups by making it easier to locate and communicate with others having common interests. It would make the operation of such groups easier if a member of the group could get access to any information that is in the public domain. Making it cheaper to send and retrieve messages through the mass communication channels can equalize the power of well-financed and underfinanced interest groups. It may be that such changes in communication policy could go a long way toward averting what Platt refers to as the crisis of participatory democracy. The implications and opportunities of new communication and educational technology deserve much higher social priority than they are now being given.

Implications for Communication Research

Much research needs to be done to bring to fruition the social potential of the new communication technology and to determine the possible social benefits and dangers before the technology has been widely adopted. The major studies of the effects of television (Himmelweit, Oppenheim, & Vince, 1958; Schramm, Lyle, & Parker, 1961) were completed after television had been widely diffused through the society. This was some twenty years after television became publicly available. By the time the studies were completed, it was too late to change the technology and, at least in the United States, too late to change the economic and regulatory structure of the television industry in anything except very minor ways.

The challenge for communication research in connection with the information utility is to develop the potential in ways that serve positive social goals with a minimum of undesirable or unanticipated side effects. This implies not only research leading to more effective techniques for using computer technology for communication, but also studies of social effects and studies of policy alternatives for implementing and regulating the new technology.

Traditionally, communication research has been an interdisciplinary behavioral science research area that has been more oriented to social problems than to disci-

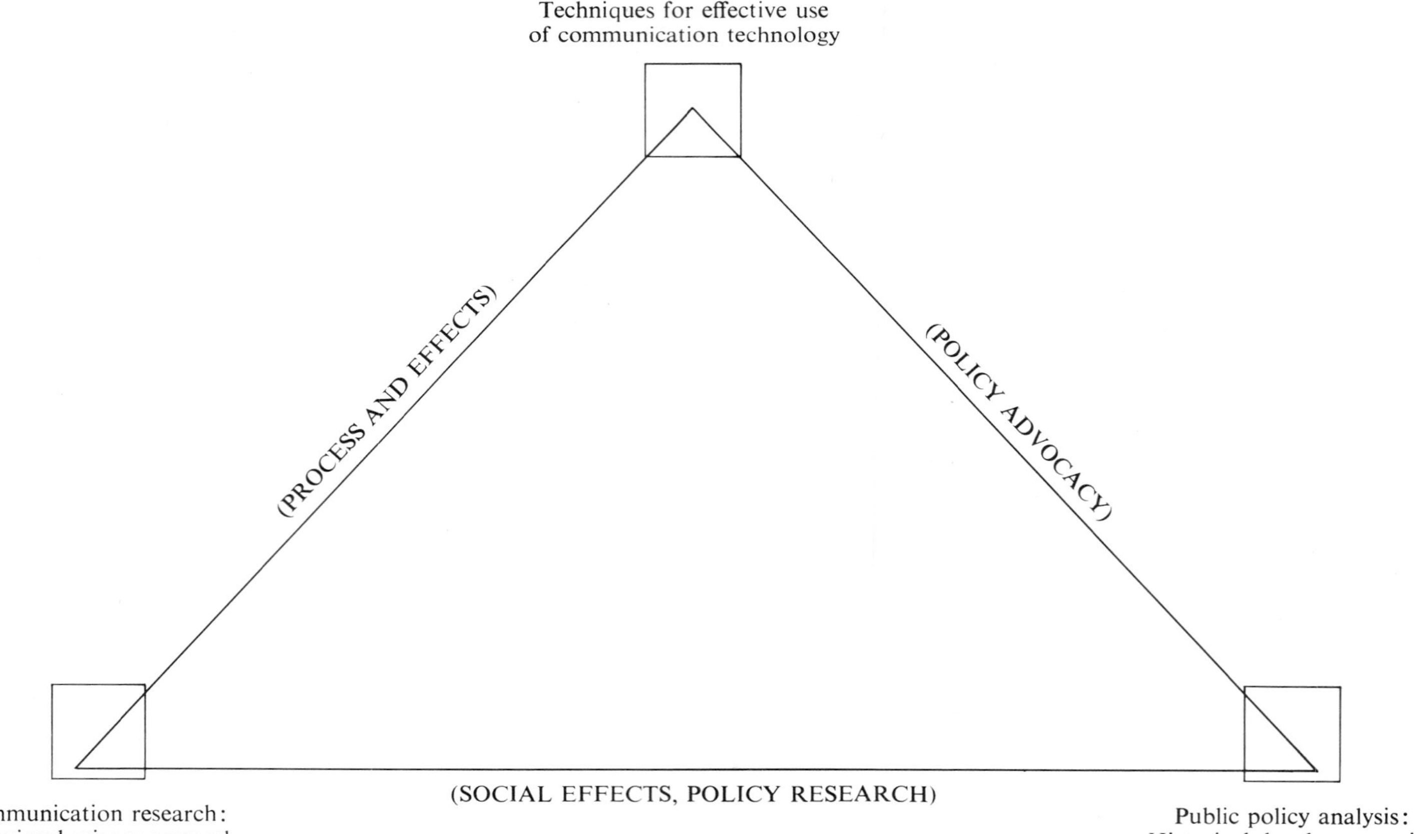

Figure 1. Three facets of the study of communication, applicable to both traditional and new communication media.

pline-based science. It has had the advantage of close involvement in schools of journalism and communication with the technology and practice of journalism, broadcasting, and filmmaking. When we view computers as a technology to be used for communication, just as we use the technology of filmmaking, radio and television broadcasting, and the printing press, then the similarities and differences with current communication research become clearer.

Figure 1 shows three facets of the study of communication as it has typically developed in schools of communication. All three facets—communication media, communication research, and public policy analysis—have been strong in the schools with the best reputations. All three apply to all communication media, not just to the traditional ones. Development of computer software for more effective communication (including information storage and retrieval) has a direct analog in the development of film, broadcasting, or writing techniques.

The link between communication media and communication research, labeled "process and effects" in the figure, is intended to represent a two-way exchange. Not only can the process and effects of independently developed techniques be studied, behavioral research can also be useful in the development of useful techniques for mediated communication, particularly if the problems are posed in terms of the communication requirements without prejudging which medium is appropriate. The agenda of research needed to improve communication among scientists outlined by Parker and Paisley (1966) can be applied to the general public as well as specialized audiences. Behavioral research techniques used in the development of one computer-based information retrieval system are outlined by Parker (1970a). Nevertheless, the primary skills needed for effective development of computer-based media are computer science skills of system analysis, system programming, and application programming.

The link between communication research and public policy analysis labeled "social effects, policy research" in the figure is also a two-way exchange. Research on social effects of communication media can be expected to raise policy questions, either to avoid undesirable effects or enhance desirable ones. Behavioral research can also be helpful to study or predict the consequences of real or proposed policy alternatives. Nevertheless, the core of policy analysis is in the explication of values and in the historical, legal, economic, and political analysis necessary to explicate goals and policy proposals. Behavioral communication research is necessary, but not sufficient, for these tasks.

The significance of policy analysis is much greater when the communication technology is changing than when it is static. Policy questions with respect to a stable technology are likely to be questions of minor deviations from the status quo. When a new and radically different technology is involved, the policy options can shape, in major rather than minor ways, the direction of the new communication medium and its social effects.

The situation with respect to regulatory policy toward the information utility at the present time is comparable to that of broadcasting policy in the early decades of the twentieth century, before the Federal Communications Commission was established and legislation governing its activities was passed. Just as the economic and legal structure of the broadcasting industry has changed little in the past thirty-five years, so policies established in the next five years may determine the structure of the communications industry for the next thirty-five years.

The link between communication media and public policy analysis, labeled "policy advocacy" in the figure, is two-way, like the other two links in the triangle. Changes in the technology or techniques of communication (such as computers and cable television) often raise policy questions; many of these questions stem from the fact that new communication technologies may have a significant economic impact on institutions dependent on earlier technologies. The broadcast television industry is resisting FCC regulations and legislation that would facilitate the growth of cable television and hence lead eventually to fractionation of the television audience. Newspaper publishers should perhaps be advocating more vigorously cable television policies that will protect the access of publishers to the cable system in the event that cable becomes a more economical means of distribution of newspapers.

The sometimes conflicting interests and recommendations of the different institutions with vested interests in communication policy should constitute one of the major inputs to scholarly analyses of public policy. But the process should work in the other direction also: the results of policy analysis should lead to policy advocacy if the results of that policy analysis are to be of maximum use to society. Different federal government policies concerning communication technologies and institutions in turn affect the rate of development and the economic viability of different technologies and institutions.

All three components (and the three links connecting them) are essential to a research and development program intended to maximize the social benefits of the new technology. The intersection of behavioral science and computer science research is necessary to develop the kind of man-machine symbiosis in which man can have the power of the computer technology readily available to help meet his information needs, as he (not the machine) defines them. Policy research and policy advocacy will also be required to maximize the potential benefits and minimize the potential dangers of the new technology. The maximum social impact would be obtained from a "mission-oriented" research and development program. The mission could be the goal of creating equal opportunity for all citizens to obtain on-demand access to all publicly available information in the society.

As this chapter has attempted to indicate, that goal is technically feasible. Achievement of that goal could go a long way toward solving some of the crises of our times.

REFERENCES

Agnew, Spiro T.
1969 "Television news coverage." Speech delivered at Des Moines, Iowa, November 13. Reprinted in The New York Times November 14:24.

Alpert, D., and D. L. Bitzer.
1970 "Advances in computer-based education." Science 167(March 20): 1582–1590.

Bagdikian, Ben H.
1971 The Information Machines. New York: Harper and Row.

Barnett, S. R.
1970 "Cable television and media concentration, Part I: Control of cable systems by local broadcasters." Stanford Law Review 22:221–329.

Barron, J. A.
1967 "Access to the press—a new first amendment right." Harvard Law Review 80:1641+. (Reprinted in D. M. Gillmor and J. A. Barron, Mass Communication Law: Cases and Comment. St. Paul: West Publishing Company, 1969, pp. 117–130.)
1969 "An emerging first amendment right of access to the media." George Washington Law Review 37:487+. (Reprinted in D. M. Gillmor and J. A. Barron, Mass Communication Law: Cases and Comment. St. Paul: West Publishing Company, 1969, pp. 178–186.)

Barton, J. H.; D. A. Dunn; E. B. Parker; and J. N. Rosse.
1972 Nondiscriminatory Access to Cable Television Channels. Discussion Paper No. 11. Stanford, California: Institute for Public Policy Research, Stanford University.

Billings, T. N.
1966 "The information business 1985." Seminar (No. 1): 15–19.

Bush, Vannevar.
1945 "As we may think." Atlantic Monthly 176(July): 101–108. (Reprinted in Manfred Kochen, ed., The Growth of Knowledge. New York: Wiley, 1967, pp. 23–35.)
1967 "Memex revisited." In Vannevar Bush, Science Is Not Enough. New York: Morrow.

Carter, L. F., et al. (eds.).
1967 National Document-Handling Systems for Science and Technology. New York: Wiley.

Chartrand, Robert L.
1970 "Computer technology and the Congress." Information Storage and Retrieval 6: 229–240.

Diebold, John.
1969 Man and the Computer. New York: Praeger.

Dunlop, R. A.
1970 "The emerging technology of information utilities." In Harold Sackman and Norman Nie (eds.), Information Utility and Social Choice. Montvale, New Jersey: AFIPS Press.

Eisenstein, E. L.
1969a "Advent of printing and the problem of the Renaissance." Past and Present 45: 19–88.
1969b "Some conjectures about the impact of printing on western society and thought: A preliminary report." Journal of Modern History 40 (March): 1–56.

Engelbart, D. C., and W. K. English.
1969 "Research center for augmenting human intellect." Pp. 395–410 in Proceedings of the Fall Joint Computer Conference, San Francisco, Volume 37. Montvale; New Jersey: American Federation of Information Processing Societies.

Federal Communications Commission.
1972 Rules and Regulations, Cable Television Service, Cable Television Relay Service. Federal Register 37(February 12): 3252–3341.

Fitzhugh, R. J., and D. Katsuki.
1970 The Touch-Sensitive Screen as a Flexible Response Device in CAI and Behavioral Research. Technical Report. Pittsburgh: Learning Research and Development Center, University of Pittsburgh.

Friendly, Fred W.
1970 "Asleep at the switch of the wired city." Saturday Review 53(October 10): 58–60.

Glaser, Robert, and W. W. Ramage.
1967 "The student-machine interface in instruction." Pp. 52–59 in IEEE International Convention Record, Part 10. New York: Institute of Electrical and Electronics Engineers.

Greenblatt, R. D. ; D. E. Eastlake; and S. D. Crocker.
1967 "The Greenblatt chess program." Proceedings of the American Federation of Information Processing Societies 31: 801–810.

Himmelweit, H. T.; A. N. Oppenheim; and Pamela Vince.
1958 Television and the Child. New York: Oxford University Press.

Hockett, C. F.
1960 "Origin of speech." Scientific American 203(September): 48, 88–96.

Hoffman, Lance.
1969 "Computers and privacy: A survey." Computing Surveys 1:2, 85–103.

House Administration Committee.
1969 First Progress Report of Special Subcommittee on Electrical and Mechanical Office Equipment. Prepared by working group on automatic data processing for the House of Representatives (October). Washington, D. C.: Committee on House Administration, House of Representatives.

Innis, Harold.
1950 Empire and Communication. London: Clarendon Press.
1951 The Bias of Communication. Toronto: University of Toronto Press.

Johnson, Leland.
1970 The Future of Cable Television: Some Problems of Federal Regulation. RM-6199-FF (January). Santa Monica: The Rand Corporation.

Johnson, Nicholas.
1968 "The media barons and the public interest." Atlantic Monthly 221 (June): 43–51. (Reprinted in Nicholas Johnson, How to Talk Back to Your

Television Set. New York: Little, Brown, 1970.)

Kennedy, R. A.
1968 "Bell Laboratories' library real-time system (BELLREL)." Journal of Library Automation 1:2, 128–146.

Kessler, M. M.
1967 "The 'online' technical information system at MIT: Project TIP in 1967." Pp. 40–47 in IEEE International Convention Record, Part 10. New York: Institute of Electrical and Electronics Engineers.

Kranzberg, Melvin, and C. W. Pursell (eds.).
1967 Technology in Western Civilization. 2 volumes. New York: Oxford University Press.

Levy, R. P., and M. R. Cammarn.
1968 "Information systems applications in medicine." Pp. 397–428 in C. A. Cuadra (ed.), Annual Review of Information Science and Technology. Chicago: Encyclopedia Britannica.

Licklider, J. C. R.
1966 Libraries of the Future. Cambridge, Massachusetts: M.I.T. Press.
1968 "Man-computer communication." Pp. 201–240 in C. A. Cuadra (ed.), Annual Review of Information Science and Technology. Chicago: Encyclopaedia Britannica.

McLuhan, Marshall.
1964 Understanding Media. New York: McGraw-Hill.

Martin, James T.
1969 Telecommunications and the Computer. Englewood Cliffs, New Jersey: Prentice-Hall.

Orwell, George.
1949 Nineteen Eighty-Four. New York: Harcourt Brace.

Overhage, C. F. J.
1969 "Information networks." Pp. 339–377 in C. A. Cuadra and A. W. Luke (eds.), Annual Review of Information Science and Technology. Chicago: Encyclopaedia Britannica.

Overhage, C. F. J., and R. J. Harman (eds.).
1965 INTREX. Cambridge, Massachusetts: M.I.T. Press.

Parker, E. B.
1969 "Developing a campus based information retrieval system." Pp. 213–230 in Proceedings of Stanford Conference on Collaborative Library Systems Development. Stanford, California: Stanford University.
1970a "Behavioral research in the development of a computer-based information system." Pp. 281–292 in Carnot E. Nelson and Donald K. Pollock (eds.), Communication Among Scientists and Engineers. Lexington, Massachusetts: Heath.
1970b "Information utility and mass communication," in Harold Sackman and Norman Nie (eds.), Information Utility and Social Choice. Montvale, New Jersey: AFIPS Press.
1970c "The new communication media," in C. S. Wallia (ed.), Toward Century 21: Technology, Society, and Human Values. New York: Basic Books.
1972a "Assessment and control of communication technology." Paper prepared for the International Symposium on Communication Technology, Impact and Policy, Philadelphia, Annenberg School of Communication, March 23–25.
1972b "On-line polling and voting." Chapter 4 in Harold Sackman and Barry Boehm (eds.), Planning Community Information Utilities. Montvale, New Jersey: AFIPS Press.

Parker, E. B., and Donald A. Dunn.
1972 "Information Technology: Its Social Potential." Science 176(June 30): 1392–1399.

Parker, E. B., and W. J. Paisley.
1966 "Research for psychologists at the interface of the scientist and his information system." American Psychologist 21:1061–1071.

Parkhill, D. F.
1966 The Challenge of the Computer Utility. Reading, Massachusetts: Addison-Wesley.

Platt, John R.
1966 The Step to Man. New York: Wiley.
1969 "What we must do." Science 166 (November 28):1115–1121.

Pool, Ithiel de Sola.
1968 "Social trends." Science and Technology for the Technical Man in Management 76(April):87–101.

Project INTREX Staff.
1966– Semiannual Activity Report. Cam-

bridge: Massachusetts Institute of Technology. Semiannual (March 15; September 15).

Reintzjes, J. F.
1969 Computer-Aided Processing of the News. Research Institute Bulletin No. 993. New York: American Newspaper Publishers Association.

Sackman, Harold, and Barry Boehm.
1972 Planning Community Information Utilities. Montvale, New Jersey: AFIPS Press.

Sackman, Harold, and Norman Nie (eds.).
1970 The Information Utility and Social Choice. Montvale, New Jersey: AFIPS Press.

Saloma, J. S.
1969 Congress and the New Politics. Boston: Little, Brown.

Schramm, Wilbur; Jack Lyle; and E. B. Parker.
1961 Television in the Lives of Our Children. Stanford, California: Stanford University Press.

Senko, M. E.
1969 "File organization and management information systems." Pp. 111–143 in C. A. Cuadra and A. W. Luke (eds.), Annual Review of Information Science and Technology. Chicago: Encyclopaedia Britannica.

Silberman, H. F., and R. T. Filep.
1968 "Information systems application in education." Pp. 357–395 in C. A. Cuadra (ed.), Annual Review of Information Science and Technology. Chicago: Encyclopaedia Britannica.

Sloan Commission on Cable Communications.
1971 On the Cable: The Television of Abundance. New York: McGraw-Hill.

Smith, Ralph L.
1970 "The wired nation." The Nation 210(May 18):582–606.

SPIRES Project.
1968 SPIRES 1968 Annual Report. Stanford, California: SPIRES/BALLOTS Project, Stanford University (January).
1970 SPIRES 1969–70 Annual Report. Stanford, California: SPIRES/BALLOTS Project, Stanford University (June).
1971a Requirements for SPIRES II. Stanford, California: SPIRES/BALLOTS Project, Stanford University (April).
1971b Design of the Stanford Public Information Retrieval System (SPIRES II). Volume 1. Stanford, California: SPIRES/BALLOTS Project, Stanford University (July).
1971c SPIRES 1970–71 Annual Report. Stanford, California: SPIRES/BALLOTS Project, Stanford University (December).

Summit, R. K.
1968 Remote Information Retrieval Facility, Ames Research Center and NASA Headquarters. Palo Alto, California: Lockheed Missiles and Space Company (June).

Suppes, Patrick.
1967 "On using computers to individualize instruction." In D. D. Bushnell and D. W. Allen (eds.), The Computer in American Education. New York: Wiley.

Thomas, G. L.
1970 "The listener's right to hear in broadcasting." Stanford Law Review 22:863–902.

Volk, John L.
1971 The Reston, Virginia, test of the Mitre Corporation Interactive Television System. Report, MTP, 352. McLean, Virginia: The Mitre Corporation (May).

Washburn, S. L.
1960 "Tools and human evolution: With biographical sketch." Scientific American 203(September):48, 62–75.

Westin, Alan F.
1967 Privacy and Freedom. New York: Atheneum.

White, Lynn.
1962 Medieval Technology and Social Change. London: Clarendon Press.

CHAPTER 20 Communication in Small Groups

FRED L. STRODTBECK
University of Chicago

Over the past twenty years there have been thousands of investigations of behavior in face-to-face settings. To organize these findings, this chapter identifies schools of thought by the type of group studied. In evaluating contributions, attention is directed to the necessary relationship between the range of behavior of the particular groups observed and the resultant theory. While the review is positive in tone, the deeper message is a call for new theory that will relate more certainly the accumulated knowledge about group process to the distinctions in interaction settings.

If a person, wholly unfamiliar with small-group studies, were to encounter the literature as it might be produced through citations from a massive computer, he would most surely be confused by the large number of studies reported in irritatingly inconsistent ways. When one attempts to search the literature in the field, the titles of papers are clear guides neither to the techniques used, nor to the characteristics of the subjects, nor indeed, in many cases, to the findings themselves. Yet the loose way in which the field is internally organized has not prevented substantial consensus about the boundaries.

To be considered a small-group study, two or more people must have interacted with one another. The central term *interaction* implies that the consensus about symbolic acts is sufficient to enable participants to adopt roles and, through time, evolve norms about both their behavior toward one another and the topic at hand (Bales, 1951:33).[1]

This widely used definition of a small group takes on additional meaning when it is contrasted with Cooley's earlier description of a primary group:

> By primary groups, I mean those characterized by intimate face-to-face association and cooperation. They are primary in several senses but chiefly in that they are fundamental in forming the social nature and ideals of the individual. The result of intimate association, psychologically, is a certain fusion of individualities in a common whole, so that one's very self, for many purposes at least, is the common life and purpose of the group. Perhaps the simplest way of describing this wholeness is by

[1] Bales stresses, in addition, that this interaction must proceed until each of the participants has, to some degree, evolved "awareness of each other as an individual."

saying that it is a "we"; it involves the sort of sympathy and mutual identification for which "we" is the natural expression. One lives in the feeling of the whole and finds the chief aim of his will in that feeling.

It is not to be supposed that the unity of the primary group is one of mere harmony and love. It is always a differentiated and usually a competitive unity, admitting of self-assertion and various appropriative passions; but these passions are socialized by sympathy, and come, or tend to come, under the discipline of a common spirit. The individual will be ambitious, but the chief object of his ambition will be some desired place in the thought of the others, and he will feel allegiance to common standards of service and fair play. So the boy will dispute with his fellows a place on the team, but above such disputes will place the common glory of his class and school.

The most important spheres of this intimate association and cooperation—though by no means the only ones—are the family, the play-group of children, and the neighborhood or community group of elders. These are practically universal, belonging to all times and all stages of development and are accordingly a chief basis of what is universal in human nature and human ideals (Cooley, 1909: 23).

Cooley reasoned that the early and complete experience of social unity in highly permanent small groups creates categories for an individual that are used in the interpretation of later experiences. Cooley tended to consider simultaneously the development of personality and the institutional source of the stimulation and support that makes it possible. The modern position is to start from a restricted conception of a small group as a set of persons talking together, then treat the emergence of conflicts, norms, and transformations of character of the type described by Cooley as matters to be demonstrated, rather than assumed.

While Cooley was effective in establishing the primacy of small groups for sociological consideration, sociologists in the mid-1950s were still inclined to believe that only the most limited of social experiences could be revealed in the laboratory. Becker (1954) was particularly biting in his criticism of "cage" studies. "The sociological theorist," he wrote,

will learn how students, in the "laboratory" for an hour or so ... can be entirely immunized not only with regard to the attitudes they have acquired during the eighteen or twenty years of their previous existence, but also with regard to their other curricular and extracurricular activities ... (Becker, 1954: 383).

Becker's disparagement was not meant to extend to the subject matter of small groups themselves. The subject matter of sociology encompasses all cases of social interaction and, as such, Becker directed the sociological theorist to pay particular attention to what was being studied in the laboratory. If he does so, he will almost certainly discover that small groups are far too important for general sociological theory to be disdainfully relinquished to the ultraspecialized, psychologically restricted cage keepers (Becker, 1954:384).

The small-group field now understands that experiments cannot prove theories, only probe them (Campbell, 1969:377). Since theories can be probed by other means—further formalization, field observation, and the like—the experiment per se has decreased in importance while the role of theory has increased. The jury research described below illustrates Becker's point in showing how macrosocial regularities penetrate small-group process. And, by its substantive nature, a jury reminds one that ad hoc groups, like primary groups, are inventions of society imitated in research, not the reverse.

JURY STUDIES

The courts may be viewed as an instance in which a social institution has for several hundred years operated much like the typical small-group experimenter. They summon an ad hoc set of potential jurors and select a subset to serve. They control the information the jury receives, and they require it to render a verdict. This service ordinarily does not affect the personal lives of the jurors beyond the time required to give the service—this, too, parallels the typical experiment.

A great limitation on the ability of courts to analyze their own process arises because they must take cases in which material bearing on essential legal doctrines is embedded in the unique fact situation of a given case. While some cases are retried, this is done to correct errors, not to explore replicated instances or to present experimentally controlled variations. By using recorded trials and jurors from the jury pool as subjects, social psychologists have made a number of discoveries that would otherwise have remained outside the reach of jurisprudential cognizance. For example, it has been demonstrated that the alternation of testimony by one side and the interrogation by the other, along with the alternation of closing arguments, avoids either *primacy* or *recency* effects that would otherwise bias the case of one of the parties (Miller & Campbell, 1959).

On another more technical matter (the question of whether a mother's use of a commercial product which causes injury to her child can be considered negligent), the legal doctrine has shifted from "yes" to "no" in the last sixty years. Experiments show that the thinking of juries is guided by a criterion which falls between the earlier and later form of the law, one subtly contingent upon the degree of negligence of the mother (Strodtbeck, 1962). Such findings suggest that, by use of sets of carefully designed experimental trials, creative new jurisprudential insights could be attained. Real juries and experimental juries are so close, that to an unusual degree the research to discover the nature of the decision-making of the institution produces information that officers of the court can use directly, without recourse to social psychological theory.

Beyond the practical and scientific interchange, the jury situation is one in which a set of subjects with wide and representative background differences participate as equals, and this presumption of equality is reinforced by the requirement that the verdict be unanimous. While this situation provides wide latitude for a loosening of usual status differentiations, the data in Table 1 show the relative participation of the jurors to be in exact conformity with what one would have expected from their respective social statuses (Strodtbeck, James, & Hawkins, 1957).

TABLE 1

RELATIVE PARTICIPATION IN 49 JURY DELIBERATIONS

Sex	Percent, by Occupation			
	Proprietor	Clerical	Skilled	Labor
Male	12.9	10.8	7.9	7.5
Female	9.1	7.8	4.8	4.6
Combined	11.8	9.2	7.1	6.4

NOTE: Pro rata equals one-twelfth, 8.3 percent.

Other investigators have also demonstrated that macrosocial indicators of power are predictive of relative participation in face-to-face situations. Caudill (1957) observed the daily exchange of information at administrative conferences among the staff of a small psychiatric hospital and found that the relative participation by the director of the service, the residents, the head nurse, the nurses, and the occupational therapist was ordered by their statuses in the hospital, even though the lower status persons ordinarily spend more time with the patients. Torrance (1954: 130–140), although using nonmilitary problems, found that pilots, navigators, and gunners recognized a power hierarchy in the contrived situation that paralleled the situation usually in effect in airship operation. Strodtbeck (1951) demonstrated that the greater economic and religious power of Navaho women in contrast with Mormon women was reflected in their greater power in husband-wife decision-making.

These findings do not in themselves

prove the legitimacy of the small-group approach in such natural settings. But as demonstrations of process continuity between the small group and society have accumulated, the question of legitimacy is asked less frequently.

SYMBOLIC INTERACTION

For those who have been touched by some variety of the encounter-group movement, the small group is no longer an academic oddity. In their eyes, the salient fact about groups is found in their power, when appropriately led, to motivate participants to lay aside nonfunctional defenses, admit their affective feelings, and live more spontaneously. The role expectations in the behavior setting (Barker, 1968:18-26) where such therapeutic interaction is held enable sets of total strangers to interact with one another with what, by comparison with the intimacy of primary groups, might well be called "superintimacy." This has led to the recognition that, if the effect of relaxation of defensiveness is so great, there may be an even deeper insight to be won by understanding the functions—both good and bad—of the elaboration of defenses in general social process. In this sense, one again looks to small groups not only for the knowledge about their functioning, but for deeper understanding of society in general.

It should come as no surprise that the investigator most influential in probing this question is one whose own work style is highly atypical, hence difficult to evaluate. Erving Goffman's first statement of his highly original perspective appeared under the title *The Presentation of Self in Everyday Life*, in 1956.[2] While this work was stimulated by discussions with teachers at the University of Chicago who themselves had been students of George Herbert Mead, it was a highly innovative approach within the symbolic interactionist framework. This became apparent in a series of later books in which the concerns of this early study have been reworked and elaborated in a way that has attracted wide readership.

Goffman has noted the existence of a special set of rules called "situational properties" that govern the individual's allocation of attention between the "main involvement"—the one that concerns all participants—and the less inclusive "side involvements" (see Goffman, 1963). The existence of situational properties, these constraints on involvement, is used as evidence that the "situation" is a real entity or, as Goffman calls it, a "social reality" which can vary from being loose to being tight: roughly, the informal-formal distinction. From the standpoint of mental health, it is an actor's inability to read and react in accordance with these situational realities that defines illness. It follows from Goffman's analysis that the normal way of acting is never "natural"; properly understood, behavior in public places is regulated to effect social functions.

In a 1967 collection of papers, Goffman stresses the purposive nature of social behavior in still another way; the term *face* is defined as "the positive social value a person claims for himself by the *line* he presents in social encounters" (Goffman, 1967: 5). This beginning is the base for a set of definitions through which everyday words are related to one another, not as in a system but as in an ever-differentiating tree of specifications. For example, the motivation to carry out the actions to protect or defend threats to one's face is "pride"; when face work is done because of duty to a wider social unit, the motivation is "honor"; and when the response compunctions have to do with postural or expressive events, one speaks of "dignity."

"Tact," "savoir faire," and "diplomacy" are social skills prescriptively or proscriptively mobilized by a consideration of face.

[2] The 1956 version was published by the Social Science Research Center at the University of Edinburgh. This was purportedly revised and expanded for the Doubleday edition (see Goffman, 1959).

"Discretion" is leaving unstated facts that might contradict the positive claims of others. The combined tendency to use "snubs" (points relating to class) and "digs" (points relating to moral responsibility) is "bitchiness."

More seriously, the sequence of acts initiated by a threat and terminated by the reestablishment of ritual equilibrium is Goffman's natural empirical unit for studying interactions of all kinds, the *interchange*. Interchanges ideally go through phases of challenge, offering, acceptance, and thanks. The ideal pattern is not necessarily a prediction, for when the phases are not clearly present, the author suggests that certain "classic" alternative moves have probably been taken. For example, the challenged person can elect not to "give in" (i.e., make an offering); he might just withdraw in a righteous huff, etc.

In places Goffman (1967:25) writes as if he were using exchange theory, but in his distinction between ritual and social order it becomes clear that Goffman is a fundamental critic of the rationalistic premises of exchange theory. He suggests that there is a schoolboy conception of the world as a place in which those who work hard are rewarded and those who cut corners are caught and punished. But the ritual order is different, for in the social order society and the individual play an easier game. Through half-truths, rationalizations, and the tactful support of an intimate circle, a person can be what he wants to be and forego doing what others have done to advance. He can construct an ordered social life by staying away from topics and times when he is not wanted; he can cooperate with others to save face by not raising questions. One learns that there is much to be gained by venturing nothing.

Goffman also treats gambling, race-car driving, boxing, and the like from the standpoint of the rate at which threats to one's well-being arise or, more accurately, are sought. This enables one to appreciate that the capacity of "total institutions" to disable—as Goffman (1961) points out in earlier essays—arises expressly from the degree to which one's opportunity to earn undeserved status by face work or risk-taking is restricted.

One may be reluctant to accept Goffman's naming of classes of social interchanges as a serious scientific enterprise. When he lists possible responses to a challenge of one's presentation of self, he should probably concern himself with how to predict which route will be followed. He does not cite the writings of others so that similarities and differences between his work and theirs can be easily identified. He is justifiably admired for going it alone in terms of style of expression and sense of problem, but he stops short of being sufficiently specific to be disconfirmed by stubborn facts. In this sense, Goffman appears to have read Goffman; he defends his *line* too well.

Goffman's objective is the description of man as an interactant in shifting gatherings. Whether he selected this emphasis as a conscious differentiation from Cooley is not known, but his concern emerges as relating to the real-life opposite of the primary group. Goffman's conception of man is Machiavellian. It is as if man roots in a bag of many faces to pick out one to maximize his rank on a short-run basis. For this reason, Goffman is necessarily silent on the possible benefits of better communication (or reduced pretensions) in work, family, or related enduring and structured situations. Goffman would most surely manifest an urbane pessimism about the value of candor in the more secondary, shifting gatherings of everyday life. He would probably view encounter groups as based on little more than a process of infinite regress in the selection of defenses.

SELF-ANALYTIC GROUPS

Some have held that Freudian therapy is for Jews and Rogerian therapy is for WASPs. If so, one could hold that client differences define the distinction between midtown America's encounter group and the highly cognitive, curriculum-oriented, self-analytic groups conducted during the past ten years at Harvard by R. F. Bales and his associates. A review of their procedures as described in Bales's 1970 volume, *Personality and Interpersonal Behavior*, suggests that Social Relations 120 is the thinking-man's primary group.

For readers familiar with Bales's *Interaction Process Analysis* (1950) and the various editions of Hare, Borgatta, and Bales (1965), the shift from research on laboratory groups to something that seems like therapy groups might be unexpected. But during the interim, three books by Bales's associates—Theodore M. Mills (1964), Philip E. Slater (1966), and Richard D. Mann (Mann, Gibbard, & Hartman, 1967)—have publicized the fact that the self-analytic groups they describe are best understood as a kind of engaged research setting in which the investigator moves out from behind the one-way screen. Bales's agenda requires short-range attention to the development of his group for the given year (the seminar runs a whole year with the same students), and a continuing, deeper commitment to the operationalization and the development of a dimensionalized model of group process. Only the second of these concerns is salient to this review, but a brief discussion of the "method" as it emerges in the course is needed to introduce the substantive criticism.

To get into the course the student must virtually sign a contract. He must not drop or change sections after one semester, his roommate (or girl friend) cannot be in the same section, he must not have been in a similar group, he must be prepared to improve his understanding of himself and work in the group to create the conditions for effective analysis. He must accept an instructor who, a good deal of the time, will remain silent. Although the instructor will be willing to meet with the student privately any time, the student should understand that the aim of the instructor and the purpose of the course is educational—not therapeutic.

The student is advised to keep a diary of subjective as well as objective observations. At least three times a semester the student is to absent himself from the group and watch through the oneway glass to see what the group is like in his absence. He may watch only his section, not any other. He must not take anyone else into the observation room to observe with him. He may be given didactic training on techniques for observing groups if he is interested.

The student is warned that although there is no requirement to disclose more than one chooses, he may both intentionally and unintentionally give material that is considered appropriate for discussion. He is told that fear of self-disclosure (and the immediate consequences that follow) may prevent a person from having the freedom to think things through for himself and *develop in his own unique way*. The emotions of boredom, elation, excitement, or affection which may arise in the groups are to be understood, discussed, interpreted—not acted upon. He must not try to extend the time of the meeting, have outside meetings, or employ any special pressures in trying to break down the natural reluctance of other individuals.

There are self-analytic course papers and extensive readings in the writings of Bales, his colleagues, and psychoanalytic writers including Freud. All of this so humane, so carefully engineered, it is almost as if the student-subjects were being taught the roles of a play and left free to do no more than improvise in compliance with the ideology set forth in the contract.

One need not assume that Bales and his associates were oblivious to the degree to which they were shaping the behavior of their subjects. During the principal period of their work, confidence in small-group and other experimental findings was thoroughly shaken by their colleague Robert

Rosenthal's (1966) examination of experimenter bias. They did not share Rosenthal's implicit premise that research thrives or falters on the precision with which a given parameter is estimated.

Probably to show that their conception of the scientific enterprise was not so simple, they moved further from traditionally positivistic procedures. This was a wholly amiable difference, one which would have left both parties unchanged if the principals had been at different locations. But during the late Emerson Hall stage of the social relations department at Harvard, ideologies to differentiate research cultures were never lacking.

This particular controversy began with Riecken's suggestion that laboratory subjects came to experiments wanting rewards (i.e., course credit, money, and psychological insight). To get these, they feel they must "penetrate the experimenter's inscrutability." However, as they work to discover the rationale of the experiment, they must be alert to represent themselves in a favorable light. The experimenter's efforts to be "scientific" about masking his intentions has a wholly unintended motivational consequence. It tends to create a situation in which the subject can avoid evaluation anxiety by ingratiating himself. Theory predicts that he does this by going along with what he believes to be the experimenter's covert request. If the experimenter were more explicit, he would induce resistance (Riecken, 1962).

Rosenthal's empirical approach to the demonstration of the effect postulated by Riecken is quite straightforward. Fifty-seven faces of about postage-stamp size are clipped from a weekly news magazine and mounted on three-by-five-inch cards. In the case in question seventy male and thirty-four female introductory psychology students from the University of North Dakota rated the faces in terms of how patently these represented "extreme failure" (-10 on the scale) to "extreme success" ($+10$). Ten photos judged within one scale point of zero and averaging zero—a veritable distillation of incommensurability—were used in subsequent experiments. The experiments utilized the ingratiating twist of asking subjects to serve not as subjects, but as experimenters. They were told that they would be paid and, in addition, they were to receive an extra dollar if their group of subjects came close to the "average" judgment for the ten pictures. Half of the naive experimenters were told that the average was -5; half, $+5$. Despite the fact that experimenters were to say nothing to the subjects, a significant bias in favor of the hypothesis was obtained in an original experiment and two replications.

In later research, additional parameters suggested by this demonstration have been investigated. For example, experimenters who were told that they had maze-bright rats would, in fact, run the rats and report performance in ways that confirm expectations. Marked and hitherto unanticipated interactions arise when boy experimenters are used with girl subjects and vice versa. Experimenter bias becomes more demonstrable in later replications of experiments than in earlier ones. Students arbitrarily designated for teachers as "late bloomers" have been demonstrated to show significant gains on I.Q. tests.

Rosenthal's work meant many things to many people. To the director of a survey organization, it was the deserved misfortune of a competitor, for the lore of surveys does have a developed candor about errors of estimation that small-group experiments had lacked. But a subtle and unanticipated consequence came from another source. It had been demonstrated that a person who was paid one dollar to do a boring task described it more favorably than one who had been paid twenty dollars (Festinger & Carlsmith, 1959). Even in the Rosenthal paradigm, if one pays a very high reward to an experimenter who obtains a biased result, the bias in the performance of such an experimenter's subjects is *reduced*—not increased, as one might expect. The explanation of this counterintuitive finding in terms of cognitive dissonance involved consideration of the actor's restructuring of his own attitudes to legitimate to himself his participation. Rosenberg (1965; 1966; 1968; 1969) designed a demonstration involving counter-attitudinal shift which showed that counter-intuitive effect was not present when the postexperimental attitude was collected by a person other than the experimenter.

Rosenberg's explanatory construct, "evaluation apprehension," focuses on the disposition of the subject-actor to expect that the experimenter has an unrevealed purpose in the high-reward situation. The experimental situation is like an everyday life situation where the experimenter, or boss, has some degree of control over the subject. After a brief orientation of the subject by the experimenter, a task is intruded which prevents the subject from coping with his evaluation anxiety by means of gossip, references to common identities, and the relaxed interaction that ordinarily attends the growth of norms and feelings of trust. In short, the original dissonance effect could probably not have been produced if the experimenter and subject were members of the same family.

By breaking the experimenter role into "order-giver" and "reaction-taker," Rosenberg delineates the role of evaluation anxiety and removes the "surprise" from the earlier experiments. He shows that these experiments depended upon a very narrow spectrum of conditions. For the purpose of this review, it would have been helpful if Rosenberg had treated the conditions for inducing "evaluation apprehension" more explicitly as an effect of group structure—one that arises because of the relative position of experimenter and subject. Taken together, the work of Rosenthal and Rosenberg removed the experimenter from behind the glass in theory as Bales has done in practice.

Returning to the tight confines of Social Relations 120—now in William James Hall—there was for a time in the sixties still another experimental tradition, one brought by Stanley Milgram from Yale. Milgram (1965) had demonstrated that if subjects think they are following orders, they will operate equipment that they have every reason to believe is giving a painful shock to a victim. To rule out the possibility that the effect was due to the prestige of a great university, Milgram tried his experiment with nondescript research associates in a sheet metal building in Bridgeport—it worked there just as it had at Yale.

Milgram included in his reports indications that subjects would shock their victims less if they were very close to them. Since bomber pilots are insulated from opportunities to empathize with their victims, it was almost plausible to assume that Milgram's research was, in fact, an applied program designed to discover ways in which *executants* can resist *authority* on behalf of *victims*. One says "almost plausible" because Milgram's paradigm itself had, to an unparalleled degree, caused subjects to reveal a capacity for evil. Many viewed the research as the embodiment of the fault it proposed to cure. So, in the mid-sixties at Harvard, when Milgram's compliance studies and Leary and Alpert's enthusiasm for LSD were dramatically expanding the potency of the social investigator, the conservative, humanistic tradition of the self-analytic course emerged. One assumes that decisions of this period will be marked as milestones in the development of professional responsibility in social psychology.

INTERACTION PROCESS ANALYSIS

One might have guessed that during the intervening twenty years between Bales's *Interaction Process Analysis* (1950) and his *Personality and Interpersonal Behavior* (1970) the system would have been radically changed. This is not so. The original interaction process categories—now slightly redefined—remain. But they have been removed from association with the Parsons-Weber pattern variables and embedded in a new three-dimensional system of empirically correlated variables. The objectives of the new system are very ambitious. They seek to relate act-by-act interaction, interpersonal attitudes, personality traits, and value statements—particularly as these actually appear during group interaction. In total, this is all quite overwhelming, but when approached in terms of familiar concepts, it becomes more plausible.

Consider first the question of *rank*. In Bales's rephrasing it becomes a direction of movement, one that is upward (the value name of that direction is Toward Material Success and Power). The key operationalization that he relies upon to relate ongoing interaction to the new dimensions is the rate of interaction process category usage of a given actor. In Table 2 we show the relations between categories and dimensional movement: U (upward), D (downward); P (positive), N (negative); and F (forward), B (backward). For example, in looking for U in Table 2, we see that one who *gives suggestions, dramatizes*, and *requests information* at a high rate, while *giving information, asking for suggestions*, and *showing tension* at a low rate, is accorded higher rank. When one thinks of the very large number of papers that have been devoted to the discovery of rank and the documentation of why it is important, the fundamental nature of Bales's work becomes apparent. He quite serenely describes not only the kinds of acts that generate and indicate rank, he also associates these acts with personality and values.

The member located in the upward part of the group space by his fellow members seems active, talkative, and powerful, but not clearly either friendly or unfriendly. He is neither clearly value- or task-oriented, nor is he expressively oriented against the task. In the realization of his own values he seems to be trying to move toward material success and power. "Our modern industrial and scientific developments are signs of a greater degree of success than that attained by any previous society." "There are no limits to what science may eventually discover." "Let no one say that money is of secondary value—it is the measuring stick of scientific, artistic, moral, and all other values in a society" (Bales, 1970: 193).

In general, the description of a given type in Bales's paradigm links kinds of behavior and other elements which, out of

TABLE 2

THE RELATION OF BALES'S DIMENSIONS TO INTERACTION PROCESS CATEGORIES

Category of Acts	Acts Initiated		Acts Received	
	Low	High	Low	High
1. Seems Friendly	N	P	N	P
2. Dramatizes	DF	UB	NF	PB
3. Agrees	NB	PF	B	F
4. Gives Suggestion	DB	UF	DN	UP
5. Gives Opinion	B	F	NB	PF
6. Gives Information	U	D	N	P
7. Asks for Information	DN	UP	UF	DB
8. Asks for Opinion	N	P	UP	DN
9. Asks for Suggestions	UB	DF	B	F
10. Disagrees	P	N	DPB	UNF
11. Shows Tension	UF	DB	DPF	UNB
12. Seems Unfriendly	P	N	DPB	UNF

NOTE: Norms for magnitudes that are neither high nor low are given in Bales (1970: 96, 97).

caution, most would regard as only loosely dependent. Indeed, Bales urges the same caution. Nevertheless, the descriptions engender resistance. One immediately asks, Do the components that Bales identifies really hang together as he says? But even before digging at the empirical foundations of the descriptions, one must grant that there is something new here—the interaction process analysis *persona*, the actor as he appears to others from his interpersonal behavior (Mills, 1971:117). The "face-to-face behavior" of an actor and the "personality of an actor" are separable, though described as correlated in the types. They are depicted on a single facet of the dimensional system Bales proposes.

For example, if one takes three men—A (fluent in Hebrew, poor in English), B (good, not fluent, in both languages), C (poor in Hebrew, fluent in English)—one can demonstrate that they rank A>B>C on the Upward-Downward dimension when talking Hebrew and C>B>A, when talking English.[3] In other words, Bales invites you to see that the persona of A and of C does change, despite your disposition to hold onto a construct of their *real* personality. Bales does not require that you relinquish your old construct so long as it does not interfere with your understanding his.

The dimensions Upward-Downward relate to rank; Forward-Backward relate to task; and Positive-Negative relate to interpersonal liking. Established investigators will probably see the configuration as a mnemonic device to be used to order previously established categories, while newcomers may be freer to understand the functional continuity which is implied.

The paradigm is remarkably dynamic. Each successive interaction lays down structure and creates the situational motive for the expression of values. One can see how discrete concepts like affection, conation, stubbornness, etc. take their place on one of the twenty-six facets (plus an average position, AVE, with an internal locus). To illustrate combined facets, note DNB; i.e., the Downward-Negative-Backward facet designated as Toward Failure and Withdrawal. Bales described it as follows:

> The member located in the downward-negative-backward part of the group space by his fellow members seems passively alienated and unfriendly toward persons, cynical toward values. He rejects both the persons in the group and the conventional value- and task-orientation of the group. He seems discouraged and dejected, ready to resign and quit, to leave if possible. He wishes to withdraw from the group and all its concerns. In the realization of his own values he seems to be trying to confirm his own failure, perhaps that of the group as well, and to move toward a definitive withdrawal from it, or perhaps more generally from life or from active effort. "The real substance of life consists of a process of disillusionment, with few goals that are worth the effort spent in reaching them" (Bales, 1970: 354).

To attain such a location in the paradigm, one *speaks very little, disagrees, shows tension*, and *seems unfriendly* while avoiding *seeming friendly* or *agreeing*. Taking 200 pages in the book, Bales describes each facet in a similar way.

The new structure, despite its seminal suggestions and aesthetic appeal, rests on a very shaky foundation. Although many sets of data underlie the various pieces of the model, the crucial rotations contain data on only sixty students in twelve groups—and these were Harvard students. Since the number of assessments made greatly outnumbered the number of subjects involved, specious correlations are probably present in the translation of act frequencies and attitude statements to the dimensions. But the very candor with which the underlying data are presented makes the point that the data are used as a guide to theory-building, rather than as the basis for parametric estimates.

The style has been consistent. In the 1951 paper on phases (Bales & Strodtbeck, 1951), only twenty-one groups were used; the basic distinction between task and

[3] This idea was suggested and tested by Gideon Aran.

socioemotional leader required twenty groups (Bales & Slater, 1955); and the "channels" paper (Bales, Strodtbeck, et al., 1951), which established the regularities in the who-to-whom matrix and the near harmonic distribution of ranked participation, used twenty-two groups. When first published, none of these papers had fully adequate empirical support, but all have taken their place as widely understood organizing perspectives in the analysis of small-group data.

Bales does not exert harsh experimental control on the interaction he observes; he lets it vary. He measures, then treats a large amount of data from a few subjects to heavy analysis and theorizing. By culminating the twenty-year period of research and theory with a volume filled with painstaking, how-to-do-it routines, the author invites others to join in the process of still further revision and discovery.

SMALL GROUPS IN THE FIELD

It is clear that it was firsthand empirical observations, not experiments in a narrow sense of the word, that were used by Bales to stimulate his theory. For George Homans, the careful reanalysis of ethnographies carried out by other investigators played a similar role. In 1950, the same year that Bales's somewhat ungainly *Interaction Process Analysis* appeared, Homans (1950) produced a literate, deceptively simple book based on the lectures he had been giving to Harvard undergraduates. Books like *Family and Community in Ireland* (Arensberg & Kimball, 1940), the industrial studies stimulated by Elton Mayo (1933; Whitehead, 1938; Roethlisberger & Dickson, 1939; Homans et al., 1941), *Street Corner Society* (Whyte, 1943), *We, the Tikopia* (Firth, 1936), and related materials had been carefully evaluated both for their intrinsic interest and for their amenability to organization into a set of lectures.

As a result, when the book was produced, the writing was clear, the sections were factually rich, and the propositions concerning group regularities were unobtrusively woven through the book. One reads it with genuine enjoyment and recognizes that there is a structure, despite an awareness that one is not fully mastering it the first time through. The great message of Homans' book is that group process, from Hilltown to Tikopia, in North Boston and Hawthorn, is everywhere the same. Using the words of the original observers—persons who neither knew nor shared Homans' biases—the argument of the book took form.

The impact was immediate. Herbert Simon was favorably enough impressed in 1952 to work out a formal model of the propositions as a function of time (t) using

I (t)—the intensity of *interaction* among the members

F (t)—the level of *friendliness* among the members

A (t)—the amount of *activity* carried on by members within the group

E (t)—the amount of activity imposed on the group by the external environment, i.e., the *external system* (Simon, 1952:203).

These definitions contained no reference to *norms*; it was not clear how *sentiments* or *friendliness* might be operationalized for continuous measurement, but it was clear that Homans' thinking had been well enough organized to permit the construction of a mathematical model.

From the sidelines, most of the methodologically inclined observers started reading the Simon article with the expectation that Homans' theory would be picked to pieces. But this did not occur. Using a system of differential equations, Simon's analysis concluded that the conditions under analysis concluded that there is a basis toward gregariousness in society even though there are limits beyond which external pressures reduce, rather than promote, group cohesion. The bridge from ethnography to mathematical model was viewed in two ways: as a proof that Homans was right, and as an indication that the small group was an intellectually rich discipline. There was even a third result. It was as if sociologists reasoned: if Simon can so dignify Homans, perhaps a new subdiscipline of mathematical sociology should be created; and it was.

Simon was ahead of his time in the sense that, showpiece though it was, little would be done with or about his model. But the topic was picked up again in 1964 by Coleman, and as recently as March 1970 by White. White's formulation, made in terms of marginals of a two-by-two table, is much closer in form to what would be needed to work with the effects of change in activity and friendliness of group participants over a short period of time. Thus, the prospects are for more, rather than less, use of the formalization of Homans' theory in the near future.

In a totally independent approach, Davis and Leinhardt (1973) extracted the following propositions from Homans:

1) In any group the external system (loosely, the group's environment) makes it inevitable that frequencies of interaction will be unevenly distributed among the member pairs (Homans, 1950: 86).
2) Because differential frequencies of interaction, interpersonal liking, and similarity in other sentiments and activities go together, pairs and larger subsets with initially higher rates of interaction come to be increasingly differentiated from the rest of the group, forming subgroups (cliques) characterized by high rates of voluntary interaction, positive interpersonal sentiments, and normative consensus (Homans, 1950:112, 118, 120).
3) Nevertheless, the members are more nearly alike in the norms they hold than in their conformity to these norms (Homans, 1950: 126) and since the closer a person's activities come to the norm, the higher his rank will be (Homans, 1950: 141), all groups develop systems of ranking.

Davis and Leinhardt use these propositions to legitimate a most ingenious project. Collecting more than 900 sociomatrices from different investigators, they created a program to examine each of the triads in a given set. This is laborious; twenty persons make 1,140 distinct triads.

From consideration of Homans, and as an extension of balance theory, one can predict that there will be, in normal groups, a deficit of cycle triads—those in which A likes B, B likes C, and C likes A. This prediction is confirmed; these occur less often than chance prediction in 90 percent of 400 groups (Davis, 1970). There are many other subtleties in the model. For example, when C asymmetrically likes the mutually positive pair, A and B, chances are that A and B will have higher status.

This line of work is recent and will possibly expand. But it is to be noted in passing that the introduction of a parametric value, 90 percent, marks something of a turning point. While the empirical value is ten points from the expectation of 100 percent predicted by the descriptive sentences of the theory, this does not essentially challenge Homans. It does suggest further hypotheses for the examination of deviant cases, and in this way motivates further growth.

Homans' *Social Behavior, Its Elementary Forms* (1961) was far less interesting than his first volume, in part because experiments are not as much fun as cultures, but also because of the author's belief that the addition of a sovereign psychological theory, *operant conditioning*, would advance the integration of his theory. In place of the ethnographic richness of his earlier work there is now the ubiquitous language of rewards and costs. For example, distributive justice is seen as an equilibrium between the proportion of the members' profits (rewards minus costs) and investments (expectations of profit level). Thus, in a dyad, distributive justice for the participants, P (Person) and O (Other), would be:

$$\frac{\text{P's profit}}{\text{P's investments}} = \frac{\text{O's profit}}{\text{O's investments}}.$$

Using this premise, Homans derived three propositions about the consequences of perceived injustices: (*a*) If an inequality exists in favor of O, P will feel dissatisfied (or, in Homans' terms, *anger*). (*b*) If P perceives an inequality in his own favor, then he will feel guilty. (*c*) P will be more apt to act to reduce his dissatisfaction than to reduce his guilt.

In this form, Homans inspired some psychologists to go into their laboratories and other behavioral scientists to take their pens and write with surprising anger. Abrahamsson (1970; see also Maris, 1970) has recently codified the criticism of the reemergence of hedonism in Homans' formulation. The question of whether reductionism speeds the unification of social science is viewed as an open one. While it seems to be attractive to deal with propositions that "explain" both psychological and economic behavior, one may be better advised to seek greater prediction from given situations than to seek a theory that subsumes so many particular hypotheses.

A problem is introduced when the formulation is used in a doubly psychological way. For example, when two men work an hour each and have the same need for money, one would guess that they would divide a common payoff equally. But if one man needs to be leader and the other needs to be follower, an even more equitable payoff would be asymmetric. The separation of givens (such as the time worked) from *utilities* (in this case, role preferences) is very difficult in practice. But, despite the difficulty in practice, the exchange-theory formulation gives exactly the structure and aura of relevance that appeals to social psychologists in the laboratory.

For example, a bargaining board has been devised with ascending payoffs for party A and descending payoffs for party B. The subject's choice determines both his own and the other's payment. Possible patterns include maximizing one's own reward, maximizing the other's reward, being concerned with a principle of allocation, and choosing the alternative that yields the greater sum of payments. In one experiment, role-symmetry, as predicted by Homans, characterized 64.4 percent of the decisions. The interesting finding was the allocation between self-interest and altruistic outcomes. This came out to 34.5 percent for self-interest and only 1.1 percent for altruism (Messé, 1967). One investigator has suggested that the experimental setting itself motivates such competition (Nemeth, 1970).

J. Stacy Adams (1965), who pioneered the experimental investigation of inequity in social exchange in industrial settings, concludes a survey of the work with three quite interesting points. First, he expresses a need for more information on whether overpaid persons will drop back in the work they do and develop unfavorable attitudes toward their employer, their working conditions, pay rate, etc. Next, as in all social comparison theories, it is unclear whom the worker will select for comparison. Finally, since Person and Other might conceivably have different relations with the third party (the employer), a three-body problem arises that promises to be as difficult to solve in social psychology as it has been in physics.

One cannot prejudge where such studies will lead, but there have been fads in social psychology. The experiments on level of aspiration, cognitive dissonance, and risky shift are relatively recent instances. It would be anomalous if, two decades after the impact of Homans' fine synthesis, his concerns were transmuted into laboratory exercises that recreate the network of contingencies from which he departed. It will require broad scholarship, in addition to careful experimentation, to break the particularly seductive set of reward-cost formulations.

GROUP DYNAMICS

In Goffman, Bales, and Homans we have living, breathing superstars of today. At Michigan, the group dynamics movement, which had lost Kurt Lewin in 1947, has passed from the charismatic to the institutionalized stage as a movement. In the introduction to their very widely used reader,

Group Dynamics, Cartwright and Zander (1968) have included a solid history of their group, the society in which it worked, and the change in the use of group insights that their group brought about in both the developed professions and the behavioral sciences.

Less attention is required by group dynamics in this review because much of their contribution was essentially secure by, or shortly after, 1950. Their third, fourth, and fifth scientific generations have taken leadership roles throughout America and, while it is important to know and recognize the historic group dynamic themes, it is equally important to see these investigators in terms of their current contributions. Harary, Norman, and Cartwright's (1965) contribution is a science-for-the-beauty-of-it work on graph theory written for the technical ingroup of social psychologists. It is the kind of product of mind that demonstrates that well-organized applied research can support sustained, pure-science formalizations.

Thibaut and Kelley's *The Social Psychology of Groups* (1959) breaks with the group dynamics tradition. It is a serious effort to use the theory of exchange and the paradigm of a two-person game to unify the field. They were so persuasive that they may now feel some guilt for overstimulating some investigators who uncritically became involved in what appears to be wheelspinning. A recent review of the research literature on experimental games by Vinacke (1969) has described the many permutations of task, situational, and personality variables that influence the level of cooperation in dyadic games, only to complain that so little of what has been demonstrated in one situation has been shown to apply to the same subjects in another situation.

The problem of what to control and what to vary is a fundamental one. Orne (1962), by showing that a personal request in the waking state was as effective as hypnosis in producing conforming behavior, gave a dramatic definition to what is now known as "demand characteristics." In gaming behavior, an area where the investigator seeks to specify most clearly the external situation to which the subject is responding, it is the question of situational demand characteristics—rather than explicitly interpersonal ones—that has been troublesome. The restriction of interaction between players that clarifies the analytic situation also suppresses a great deal of normal interpersonal behavior, hence it is difficult to understand the implications of experimental results for everyday life.

The principal paradigm for research in this area is called the "prisoner's dilemma." This description is a colorful reference to an imagined criminal's state of mind when he considers convicting his accomplice to get off himself. If both remained silent, it is assumed that they would jointly receive a lighter punishment. In social psychological experiments, the subjects discover during successive trials that if both cooperate, both receive a small gain; but if one member cooperates when his partner does not, he loses while the other gains. Since joint aggressive acts result in joint loss the dilemma arises. Simple as it seems, this game has intriguing depth.

Pruitt (1968) found a much higher frequency of reciprocity in a form of the prisoner's dilemma game that reduced uncertainty in the relationship between one person's behavior and the other's outcome. A study by Greenberg, Block, and Silverman (1971), which was explicitly noncompetitive but which necessitated the subject's incurring definite reductions in his financial outcome for reciprocating, likewise found a considerably higher degree of reciprocity than was found within the context of the narrowly structured prisoner's game. Somewhat earlier it had been shown (Kelley, 1968; Kelley et al., 1970) that the type of payoff (real money or points) and the nature of the incentive (positive of negative) used can also affect competitiveness. From such studies it became clear that all participants are not aware of, nor do they seek, all relevant information concerning the situation and, even if they have the information, they do not respond solely on the basis of it.

It was only after defining a purely rational theory of bargaining behavior that one could detect departures from it. Once the departures were at hand, then one could ask what aspects of personality, used in connection with the bargaining paradigm, could broaden its explanatory power. Kelly and Stahleski (1970), for example, found that predominantly competitive players tend to project their own motives onto others, thereby assuming that the other person in the game, whether actually competitive or cooperative, is competitively motivated. The cooperators, in contrast, can differentiate between cooperative and competitive opponents and respond accordingly. Highly authoritarian subjects tend to be competitively oriented while low authoritarian types are generally cooperators. Of such materials are self-fulfilling philosophies created.

Vinacke feels that experimental research on bargaining would benefit considerably if additional games were developed and researchers used more than one type of game in generating their findings. He also suggests that this area of research would be improved if some of the games were less constraining and if broader social interaction were allowed between participants. With this we strongly agree.

LEADERSHIP

It is a great pleasure to describe Fred E. Fiedler's (1967) work on the contingency theory of leadership as the outstanding example of an investigator who found an interesting relationship, faced the complication of replication in a number of different situations, and was finally rewarded by an insight which conferred order on information that had been won with such exemplary personal dedication. It is particularly satisfying to contrast Fiedler's energy in the field with the any-subject-will-do style of others. He managed to study basketball teams, antiaircraft gunners, and business executives in a highly parallel way. Goffman simply observes at cocktail parties, in asylums, on remote islands, and in the presence of people without noses. Homans essentially reads and listens to his colleagues in the business school. Bales talks with identity-seeking Ivy Leaguers in a room conveniently adjacent to his office. The science of small groups which each has developed reflects his method, ergo, Fiedler is needed.

To have a method that would work in so many contexts, it had to be simple. Fiedler asked leaders to consider questions like those posed in Figure 1. He then checked the state of leader-member relations, the clarity of the task structure, and the leader's position power. He found that relationship-oriented leaders (those who had not been so harsh on their least-preferred coworker) had done better in good unstructured or poor structured situations, while the task-oriented leader had done better in the extremes of good structured or poor unstructured situations.

Unfortunately, because the habit of industry was so deeply ingrained, Fiedler

Think of the person with whom you can work least well. He may be someone you work with now, or he may be someone you knew in the past. Use an X *to describe this person as he appears to you.*

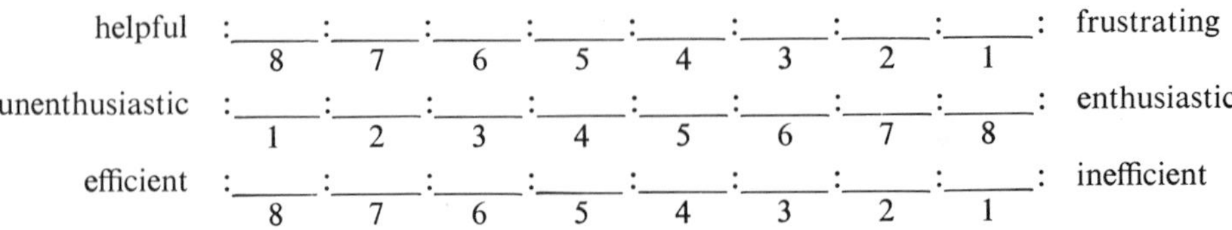

Figure 1. Fielder's scale for describing the least-preferred coworker (LPC).

kept working; while he was grouping his new data with his old, some former colleagues at Urbana (Graen, Alvares, Orris, & Martella, 1970) had the fiendish idea of contrasting the fit of the new data with the contingent prediction from the old. In response to this criticism, Fiedler acknowledged the disparity but limited it to laboratory studies in which, despite clear task structure and positive leader-to-member relations, the leader's position power was weak (Fiedler, 1971). But even this slight adjustment, contrasting laboratory applicability to that in field situations, seemed to break the spell. Others in the field are being forced to conclude that what "designation of a least-preferred coworker" means is not becoming clearer. A radically new approach may be required.

The research of Maier, Hoffman, and their colleagues at the University of Michigan deserves slightly more optimistic comment. It has generally been focused on the method of evaluation, presence of group conflict, leadership behavior, and the quality of solution of a group problem. In assessing quality of solution, they use not only acceptability to members, and the implication for instrumental criteria, but also the improved problem-solving ability of the group.

Hoffman and Maier's (1964) valence observation technique has shown that groups tend to evaluate solutions as they are presented and that the first solution to reach the threshold of support becomes the adopted one. Heterogeneous groups, in terms of personality, are significantly more effective by their criteria (Hoffman, 1959; Hoffman & Maier, 1961). Hoffman's explanation for this phenomenon is that diversity of viewpoints in heterogeneous groups creates the conflict which precipitates a critical evaluation of the problem. To reach consensus wisely, groups must be protected from the tendency to accept the first solution that amasses critical support. There is a danger of talking past a good thing, but these authors feel that in the long run this is not too serious.

Should the reader wish to follow the advice of this team in increasing his own group's effectiveness, he should separate the idea-generation and idea-evaluation stages of discussion—so that a number of ideas are given fair consideration (Maier & Solem, 1952). Require your group to resolve their problem a second time using something other than the first solution (Maier & Hoffman, 1960b). Train yourself in "developmental discussion" technique—that is, learn to emphasize a facilitative leadership style and increase your sensitivity to the stages of group problem-solving (Maier & Hoffman, 1960a).

While this all sounds pragmatic and cheery enough, cold reality is permitted to intrude. Maier and Hoffman differentiate member satisfaction from the quality of the solution. The quality of a decision reflects the group's ability to produce and utilize information effectively. The acceptance of the solution reflects the member's feelings about the solution *and* the way it was reached (Hoffman, Burke, & Maier, 1965). Acceptance—and here is the catch—uncorrelated with quality though it is, is primarily determined by the amount of influence the subject has had over the final decision (Maier & Hoffman, 1965). So, sit there and listen, Mr. Leader!

COALITIONS

It should not be assumed that all face-to-face gatherings are made up of persons who can jointly maximize their utilities—it sometimes makes a difference if you win. "A coalition is the joint use of resources to determine the outcome of a decision in a mixed motive situation involving more than two units" (Gamson, 1964:85). Coalitions can persist, be episodic—or terminal (Caplow, 1968). Investigators have concentrated on the episodic, winner-take-all situations, the ones most applicable to politics, although one investigator has studied coalition formation in families (Strodtbeck, 1954). The family studies suggest that the need to gain support and confirm identity from one's coactors mitigates the harshness of the process that one would predict from simple coalition theory.

The variable that has received the greatest attention has been the effect of the initial distribution of power, or resources, upon the subsequent decision of which players will join forces to beat the remaining ones. Gamson (1961), elaborating upon the previous research of Caplow (1956) and of Vinacke and Arkoff (1957), has found that the coalition that generally forms is the "cheapest" winning coalition, the combination that just surpasses the threshold necessary to win. As Gamson (1961: 566) explains, "Any participant will expect others to demand from a coalition a share of the payoff proportional to the amount of resources that they contribute to a coalition." The cheapest winning combination is the arrangement that maximizes the payoff for the winning players.

Vinacke and his students have investigated the influence of player characteristics upon coalition formation using a modified game of parchisi. Females operate differently from males: they form two-person coalitions to a lesser extent and they tend to distribute rewards equally rather than on the basis of resources contributed (Uesugi & Vinacke, 1963). Despite this, the game strategies of achievant and nurturant male players did not differ much (Chaney & Vinacke, 1960; Amidjaja & Vinacke, 1965).

Theodore Caplow's, *Two Against One* (1968) captures this period of research in trophylike form. There is little interest now being shown in this area.

OVERVIEW

In various ways, the past twenty years have revised such dichotomies as primary group versus small group and real life versus the laboratory. Some nonprimary groups are superintimate; courts in their use of jurors act like social psychologists; and the reality of demand characteristics and, to some degree, experimenter bias has robbed us of the illusions that we can ever be *pure* scientists in our work with people. What was "intangible" concerning groups twenty years ago is generally accepted today. Too much of what is published stops short of making clear the implication of the research for the state of the field, but this may be as much a fault of poor planning in advance of research as it is of the shortage of journal space. Each behavioral science discipline is developing small-group specialists; within the decade to come, when each behavioral scientist has a more deeply integrated component of small-group sophistication in his thinking, broad-range theory that touches on microsocial process may well be freed of some of the simplistic assumptions now present.

REFERENCES

Abrahamsson, Bengt.
1970 "Homans on exchange: Hedonism revived." American Journal of Sociology 76 (September):273–285.

Adams, J. Stacy.
1965 "Inequity in social exchange." Pp. 267–299 in Leonard Berkowitz (ed.), Advances in Experimental Social Psychology. Volume 1. New York: Academic Press.

Amidjaja, Imat R., and W. Edgar Vinacke.
1965 "Achievement, nurturance, and competition in male and female triads." Journal of Personality and Social Psychology 2:447–451.

Arensberg, C. M., and Solon T. Kimball.
1940 Family and Community in Ireland. Cambridge, Massachusetts: Harvard University Press.

Bales, Robert F.
1950 Interaction Process Analysis. Cambridge, Massachusetts: Addison Wesley.
1970 Personality and Interpersonal Behavior. New York: Holt, Rinehart and Winston.

Bales, Robert F., and Philip E. Slater.
1955 "Role differentiation in small decision-making groups." Pp. 253–306 in Talcott Parsons and Robert F. Bales (eds.), Family, Socialization and Interaction Process. Glencoe, Illinois: Free Press.

Bales, Robert F., and Fred L. Strodtbeck.
1951 "Phases in group problem-solving." Journal of Abnormal and Social Psychology 46:485–495.

Bales, Robert F.; Fred L. Strodtbeck; et al.
1951 "Channels of communication in small groups." American Sociological Review 16 (August):461–468.

Barker, Roger G.
1968 Ecological Psychology. Stanford, California: Stanford University Press.

Becker, Howard.
1954 "Vitalizing sociological theory." American Sociological Review 19 (August):383–384.

Campbell, D. T.
1969 "Prospective: Artifact and control," in Robert Rosenthal and R. L. Rosnow, Artifact in Behavioral Research. New York: Academic Press.

Caplow, Theodore.
1956 "A theory of coalitions in a triad." American Sociological Review 21:489–493.
1968 Two Against One: Coalitions in Triads. Englewood Cliffs, New Jersey: Prentice-Hall.

Cartwright, Dorwin, and Alvin Zander.
1968 Group Dynamics, Research and Theory. Third Edition. New York: Harper and Row. (First edition published in 1953.)

Caudill, William.
1957 The Psychiatric Hospital as a Small Society. Cambridge, Massachusetts: Harvard University Press.

Chaney, Marilyn V., and W. Edgar Vinacke.
1960 "Achievement and nurturance in triads varying in power distribution." Journal of Abnormal and Social Psychology 6:175–181.

Coleman, James S.
1964 Introduction to Mathematical Sociology. New York: Free Press of Glencoe.

Cooley, Charles H.
1909 Social Organization. New York: Scribner's.

Davis, James A.
1970 "Clustering and hierarchy in interpersonal relations: Testing two graph theoretical models on 742 sociomatrices." American Sociological Review 35:843–851.

Davis, James C., and Samuel Leinhardt.
1973 "The structure of positive interpersonal relations in small groups," in Joseph Berger et al. (eds.), Sociological Theories in Progress. Volume 2. Boston: Houghton Mifflin (forthcoming).

Festinger, Leon, and J. M. Carlsmith.
1959 "Cognitive consequences of forced compliance." Journal of Abnormal and Social Psychology 58:203–210.

Fiedler, Fred E.
1967 A Theory of Leadership Effectiveness. New York: McGraw-Hill.
1971 "Validation and extension of the contingency model of leadership effectiveness: A review of empirical findings." Psychological Bulletin 76: 128–148.

Firth, Raymond.
1936 We, the Tikopia. London: George Allen and Unwin.

Gamson, William A.
1961 "An experimental test of a theory of coalition formation." American Sociological Review 26:565–573.
1964 "Experimental studies of coalition formation." Pp. 82–110 in Leonard Berkowitz (ed.), Advances in Experimental Social Psychology. Volume 1. New York: Academic Press.

Goffman, Erving.
1959 The Presentation of Self in Everyday Life. Garden City, New York: Doubleday.
1961 Asylums. Garden City, New York: Doubleday.
1963 Behavior in Public Places. New York: Free Press of Glencoe.
1967 Interaction Ritual: Essays on Face-to-Face Behavior. Chicago: Aldine.

Graen, George; Kenneth Alvares; James Burdeane Orris; and Joseph A. Martella.
1970 "Contingency model of leadership effectiveness: Antecedent and evidential results." Psychological Bulletin 74:285–296.

Greenberg, Martin S.; Myron W. Block; and Michael A. Silverman.
1971 "Determinants of helping behavior: Person's rewards versus other's costs." Journal of Personality 39 (No. 1):79–93.

Harary, Frank; Robert Z. Norman; and Dorwin Cartwright.
1965 Structural Models, An Introduction to the Theory of Directed Graphs. New York: Wiley.

Hare, A. Paul; Edgar F. Borgatta; and Robert F. Bales.
1965 Small Groups: Studies in Social Interaction. Second Edition. New York: Knopf. (First edition published in 1955.)

Hoffman, L. R.
1959 "Homogeneity of member personality and its effect on group problem-solving." Journal of Abnormal and Social Psychology 58:27–32.

Hoffman, L. R.; R. J. Burke; and N. R. F. Maier.
1965 "Participation, influence, and satisfaction among members of problem-solving groups." Psychological Reports 16:661–667.

Hoffman, L. R., and N. R. F. Maier.
1961 "Quality and acceptance of problem solutions by members of homogeneous and heterogeneous groups." Journal of Abnormal and Social Psychology 62:401–407.
1964 "Valence in the adoption of solutions by problem-solving groups: Concept, method and results." Journal of Abnormal and Social Psychology 69:264–271.

Homans, George C.
1950 The Human Group. New York: Harcourt, Brace and World.
1961 Social Behavior: Its Elementary Forms. New York: Harcourt, Brace and World.

Homans, George C., and others.
1941 Fatigue of Workers. New York: Reinhold.

Kelley, H. H.
1968 "Interpersonal accommodation." American Psychologist 23 (No. 6):408.

Kelley, H. H., and Anthony J. Stahleski.
1970 "Social interaction basis of cooperator's and competitor's beliefs about others." Journal of Personality and Social Psychology 16(No. 1):66–91.

Kelley, H. H., and others.
1970 "A comparative experimental study of negotiation behavior." Journal of Personality and Social Psychology 16(No. 3):411–417.

Maier, N. R. F., and L. R. Hoffman.
1960a "Using trained 'developmental' discussion leaders to improve further the quality of group decisions." Journal of Applied Psychology 44: 247–251.
1960b "Quality of first and second solutions in group problem solving." Journal of Applied Psychology 44: 278–283.
1965 "Acceptance and quality of solutions as related to leaders' attitudes toward disagreement in group problem solving." Journal of Applied Behavioral Science 1:373–386.

Maier, N. R. F., and A. R. Solem.
1952 "The contribution of a discussion leader to the quality of group thinking: The effective use of minority opinions." Human Relations 5:277–288.

Mann, Richard D.; Graham S. Gibbard; and John J. Hartman.
1967 Interpersonal Styles and Group Development. New York: Wiley.

Maris, Ronald.
1970 "The logical adequacy of Homans' social theory." American Sociological Review 35(December):1069–1081.

Mayo, Elton.
1933 Human Problems of Industrial Civilization. New York: Macmillan.

Messé, Lawrence A.
1967 "Parameters of air play: An investigation of differences in the just distribution of rewards." Ph. D. Dissertation, University of Chicago.

Milgram, Stanley.
1965 "Some conditions of obedience and disobedience to authority." Pp. 243–262 in Ivan D. Steiner and Martin Fishbein, Current Studies in Social Psychology. New York: Holt, Rinehart and Winston.

Miller, Norman, and Donald T. Campbell.
1959 "Recency and primacy in persuasion as a function of the timing of speeches and measurements." Journal of Abnormal and Social Psychology 59:1–9.

Mills, Theodore M.
1964 Group Transformation: An Analysis of a Learning Group. Englewood Cliffs, New Jersey: Prentice-Hall.
1971 "Review of Personality and Interpersonal Behavior by Robert Freed

Bales." American Sociological Review 36:115–119.

Nemeth, Charlan.
1970 "Bargaining and reciprocity." Psychological Bulletin 74(No. 5):297–308.

Orne, Martin T.
1962 "On the social psychological experiment." American Psychologist 17(No. 11):776–783.

Pruitt, Dean.
1968 "Reciprocity and credit building in a laboratory dyad." Journal of Personality and Social Psychology 8(No. 2, Part 1):143–147.

Riecken, H. W.
1962 "A program for research on experiments in social psychology," Pp. 22–36 in N. F. Washburne (ed.), Decisions, Values, and Groups. Volume 2. New York: Pergamon Press.

Roethlisberger, F. J., and W. J. Dickson.
1939 Management and the Worker. Cambridge, Massachusetts: Harvard University Press.

Rosenberg, M. J.
1965 "When dissonance fails: On eliminating evaluation apprehension from attitude measurement." Journal of Personality and Social Psychology 1:18–42.
1966 "Some limits of dissonance: Toward a differentiated view of counterattitudinal performance," in Shel Feldman (ed.), Cognitive Consistency. New York: Academic Press.
1968 "Hedonism, inauthenticity, and other goads toward expansion of a consistency theory." Pp. 73–111 in R. P. Abelson, Elliot Aronson, W. J. McGuire, T. M. Newcomb, M. J. Rosenberg, and P. H. Tannenbaum (eds.), Theories of Cognitive Consistency: A Sourcebook. Chicago: Rand McNally.
1969 "Conditions and consequences of evaluation apprehension." Pp. 279–349 in Robert Rosenthal and R. L. Rosnow, Artifact in Behavioral Research. New York: Academic Press.

Rosenthal, Robert.
1966 Experimenter Effects in Behavioral Research. New York: Appleton-Century-Crofts.

Simon, Herbert A.
1952 "A formal theory of interaction in social groups." American Sociological Review 17:202–211.

Slater, Philip E.
1966 Microcosm, Structural, Psychological, and Religious Evolution in Groups. New York: Wiley.

Strodtbeck, Fred L.
1951 "Husband-wife interaction over revealed differences." American Sociological Review 16(August):468–474.
1954 "The family as three-person group." American Sociological Review 19:23–29.
1962 "Social process, the law and jury functioning." Pp. 144–164 in William T. Evan, Law and Sociology: Exploratory Essays. New York: Free Press of Glencoe.

Strodtbeck, Fred L.; Rita M. James; and Charles Hawkins.
1957 "Social status in jury deliberations." American Sociological Review 22 (December):713–719.

Thibaut, J. W., and H. H. Kelley.
1959 The Social Psychology of Groups. New York: Wiley.

Torrance, E. P.
1954 Some Consequences of Power Differences on Decision-Making in Permanent and Temporary Three-Man Groups. (Research Studies No. 22). Pullman: State College of Washington.

Uesugi, Thomas K., and W. Edgar Vinacke.
1963 "Strategy in a feminine game." Sociometry 26:75–88.

Vinacke, W. Edgar.
1969 "Variables in experimental games: Toward a field theory." Psychological Bulletin 71(No. 4):293–318.

Vinacke, W. Edgar, and Abe Arkoff.
1957 "An experimental study of coalitions in the triad." American Sociological Review 22:406–415.

White, Harrison C.
1970 "Simon out of Homans by Coleman." American Journal of Sociology 75:852–862.

Whitehead, T. N.
1938 The Industrial Worker. Cambridge: Harvard University Press.

Whyte, William Foote.
1943 Street Corner Society. Chicago: University of Chicago Press.

CHAPTER 21 Communication Between Bureaucracy and the Public: A Review of the Literature

ELIHU KATZ and BRENDA DANET
Hebrew University and
Israel Institute for Applied Social Research

Bureaucracies, it is said, depersonalize relationships; their function is, after all, to routinize behavior. How, then, are communications within bureaucracies and, more particularly, between a bureaucracy and its clients handled? Do bureaucracies retain the capacity to deal with idiosyncratic cases, or do they become trapped by their own routine? Can relationships be personalized without threatening the organization? And, if they are not personalized, can the client receive his just due? What are the variables that determine the degree of routinization in the relationship?

Studies of the consequences for clients of bureaucratic behaviors have usually been conducted in the tradition of macrosociological inquiry. Katz and Danet approach these issues in a rather different way, focusing their attention on the microrelationships that characterize the communications process. Because their approach is quite different from that which has been conventionally employed, they rely heavily on inferences derived from an unusually wide range of studies, including a number originally undertaken for rather different purposes. Accordingly, the chapter may be read not only for its substantive contribution, but also as an illustration of the creative application and integration of disparate scholarly traditions.

INTRODUCTION

We live in an age which is characterized by the growth of bureaucratic organizations, both in size and in number. Increased specialization of function, both within and among organizations, appears to be a concomitant of these trends. There are two major consequences of these developments.

This chapter was written as a by-product of a series of studies of communication between bureaucracy and the public in Israel. The project was financed by the National Science Foundation (Grants NSF-GS-41 and NSF-1385). Many discussions with our colleagues on this project, Dr. Michael Gurevitch and Mrs. Tsiyona Peled, have shaped this chapter either directly or indirectly. We are particularly indebted to Dr. Gurevitch for his suggestions and comments.

One is the rise of large concentrations of power, in opposition to which the man in the street may well feel quite helpless. The other is the transformation of interpersonal relations.

Normatively at least, bureaucratic organizations require a style of interpersonal relations that is universalistic, highly specific, and affectively neutral. Organizational roles, whether of officials or clients, are explicitly defined, and ascribed characteristics are officially irrelevant. A related aspect of the transformation of interpersonal relations is that face-to-face communication is frequently subordinated to communication in writing. Written records, noted by Weber as a defining characteristic of bureaucracy, are functional for organizations because they insulate officials from illegitimate influences, or indeed from any direct influence of individuals and groups. But the depersonalization of communication may be dysfunctional for individuals.

These two consequences of bureaucratization frequently serve as grist for the mills of critics of the mass society, who see the forces of depersonalization and the loss of individual autonomy as working against the very grain of human nature. Pessimism about the consequences of bureaucratization is not, however, a new phenomenon. Weber, the articulator of the "ideal model" of bureaucracy, himself was extremely discouraged about the chances for survival of humanist values of individual autonomy and creativity in the modern world (Weber, 1943).

It is surprising to note, therefore, that students of formal organizations have not focused in depth either on general problems of the relation between organizations and their environments or, more specifically, on the social psychology of official-client relations. In general, the object of analysis has been what goes on within the organization, and the relation among variables that characterize it, such as size and complexity. In recent years the field has expanded to incorporate certain aspects of organization-environment relations (Eisenstadt, 1959; Blau & Scott, 1962; Peabody & Rourke, 1965; Stinchcombe, 1965; Udy, 1965; Litwak & Meyer, 1966; Downs, 1967). But the approach used is typically macrosociological.

Neither of the two most comprehensive overviews of the field of formal organizations treats problems of communication with clients in any detail. Each contains a chapter on communication, but deals only with communication *within* organizations. Blau and Scott devote a pioneering but rather sketchy chapter to the relations between bureaucratic officials and the public with whom they have direct contact. They examine the significance of orientations of both the organization and its clientele for the nature of interaction between them, and speculate on some of the sources of conflict with clients (Blau & Scott, 1962: chap. 3). In all, they review perhaps fifty titles that are relevant to the problem of communication between bureaucracy and its public. And though March's *Handbook of Organizations* (1965) contains quite a few articles which touch on aspects of official-client relations, there is no explicit treatment of this topic per se.

Dynamics of Official-Client Communication: A Working Model

The subject of this chapter is officials and clients and the relationships between them. An official will usually be any individual who, in the employ of a bureaucratic organization, has contact with individual nonmembers of the organization. Bureaucratic organizations are social units with explicitly defined goals, hierarchical structure, and a set of rules governing procedures for the allocation of goods and services. A client will be any individual who has contact with a bureaucratic organization in connection with his own personal interests and obligations. In view of the rising trend toward bureaucratization of professional services, we will sometimes use the terms *official* and *client*

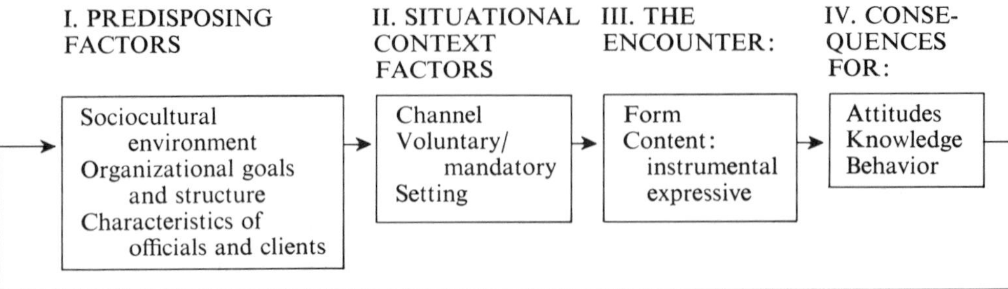

Figure 1. The dynamics of official-client communication.

loosely to include professional practitioners and their clienteles. Communication will be said to take place whenever official and client influence each other's behavior. We will assume that *interaction* and *communication* are synonymous.

The body of literature reviewed here has been drawn from the fields of sociology and social psychology, psychiatry, public administration, political science, and social work. We do not claim to have covered all the relevant literature, although we hope that we have sampled a representative group of articles and books. Our analysis and review are organized in terms of four clusters of variables: (*a*) those that characterize behavior during a bureaucratic encounter; (*b*) predisposing factors that may impinge on the encounter; (*c*) situational variables characterizing the immediate context of interaction; and (*d*) variables dealing with the consequences of any given encounter. The relations among these four clusters are shown in Figure 1.

The heart of the diagram is the set of interaction variables labeled III. We divide all behavioral events into two aspects, those of *form* and *content*.[1] Form refers to such aspects of the messages sent or exchanged as the amount and frequency of "talk" in a given encounter. As for content, the principal distinction made by social psychologists is that between its *instrumental*, or task-oriented, aspects and its *expressive*, or socioemotional, aspects (Hare, 1962). Weber's "ideal model" of bureaucracy stipulates that interaction is universalistic, achievement oriented, specific (hence primarily task oriented), and emotionally neutral (hence expressive aspects ideally never become an end in themselves).

While it is important to keep in mind these criteria or norms of "bureaucratic behavior," our goal is to develop a behavioristic orientation to account for *variation* in role performance. We distinguish between the allocation of goods and services per se (the question of "who gets what") and the *procedures* by which resources are distributed. Together, these two constitute the instrumental aspect of interaction. The socioemotional aspect refers to the "manner" of both official and client. For example, an official may request a client to fill out a form in either a pleasant or a rude tone of voice. In brief, bureaucratic transactions may vary in three ways: in the type and amount of resources transferred, in the procedures the client must follow in order to obtain his rights or fulfill his obligations, and in the handling of interpersonal relations by the official and client.

In turn, in each of these three areas

[1] This is a widely used distinction in social psychological models of interaction; see, for example, Hare (1962).

there are three possible outcomes: legitimate bureaucratic behavior, illegitimate behavior in the client's *favor*, and illegitimate discrimination *against* the client. Theoretically, there are thus twenty-seven possible combinations of these elements, although obviously some are empirically more frequent than others and, indeed, some may be totally absent empirically. The "pure" bureaucratic profile may be rare; that in which only the manner is personalized may be more frequent than we realize.

The three types of positive favoritism vary in the degree of their illegitimacy. Clearly, personalization of the relationship while preserving the bureaucratic quality of instrumental aspects is almost, or perhaps completely, legitimate. Next is the case where the procedure is simplified or speeded up, as for example the receipt of a passport in less than the usual time that normal procedure requires. Finally, granting the clients goods or services to which they have no right, or demanding less than a client is supposed to pay (e.g., lowering the price of a service or the amount of tax due), are obviously the most illegitimate types of deviation in the client's favor.

We must distinguish, of course, between the *pressures* on the official, and his *response* to them. Whatever the pressures, the official may ignore them and follow normal bureaucratic procedure. Or he may yield in a direction quite opposite to the felt pressure. If there is pressure to grant a favor, he may be more rigid than usual, whether in interpreting the law strictly so as to deny a resource, or in making procedure unnecessarily wieldy. Or, again, if there is pressure to discriminate negatively, he may bend over backward to show that he discounts it. Alternatively, the official may simply yield to the pressure, whether to grant or deprive someone a procedural or substantive favor. The various possibilities are summed up in Figure 2.

Figure 1 suggests that there are three major groups of "predisposing" factors (labeled I) which may impinge on official-client encounters. The most general of these is what we have designated the

PRESSURE ON OFFICIAL

HIS RESPONSE	None	Pressure to Grant Favor	Pressure to Discriminate Negatively
Neutral	conforms to rules—"pure" bureaucratic encounter	resists—adheres to the rules	resists—adheres to the rules
Positive	dispenses favors at own initiative	acquiesces to pressures—corruption, "pull"	overcompensates—reaction in opposite direction to "prove" resistance to pressure
Negative	overconforms to rules—"bureaucratic personality"	reacts in opposite direction to "prove" resistance to pressure	acquiesces to pressure; discrimination

Figure 2. Outcomes of official-client contact: pressure to deviate from the rules and possible responses.

"sociocultural environment," i.e., the wider culture and social structure in which organizations are embedded. Then there are effects of organizations themselves, of their goals and structure, on official-client communication. Finally, social and psychological characteristics of officials and clients have important effects of their own; in particular, the literature has a great deal to say about the ways in which social class impinges on official-client interaction.

Group II of Figure 1 refers to effects of the immediate context of interaction. Such variables as whether contact is voluntary or mandatory, and the locus of contact in space and time, may intervene between the actual outcomes of bureaucratic encounters and the set of predisposing factors listed above.

Characteristics of the encounter constitute the major set of dependent variables. Perhaps equally important are the *consequences* of interaction (IV in Figure 1). Officials and clients come away from any given encounter with certain responses. Experience may modify or reinforce attitudes toward bureaucracy in general, as well as toward particular organizations or individuals. Similarly contact may affect role-relevant knowledge; through contact clients learn more about their rights and obligations and how to behave in bureaucratic situations. Thus we introduce the possibility of feedback—any given encounter may lead to changes in any or all of the variables in I, II, and III of Figure 1.

We may now define the term *communication* more broadly to include the complex interaction between the attitudes and expectations that officials and clients bring to contact, behavior in the encounter itself, as well as the changes or additions, if any, in the attitudes and expectations of both parties as a result of contact.

Plan of the Chapter

The remainder of this chapter is divided into five sections. In the first three, we review the effects on the official-client encounter of the sociocultural environment, organizational characteristics, and characteristics of officials and clients respectively. Then we devote a brief section to the effects of situational variables. Finally, in the last section we return to the theme presented in the beginning of the chapter, that of bureaucracy as a social problem. We present a brief overview of some of the institutional innovations that have been suggested or introduced in recent years in order to strengthen the role of the client vis-à-vis bureaucracy.

EXTRAORGANIZATIONAL FACTORS: SOCIOCULTURAL ENVIRONMENT

General Theoretical Approaches

There have been a number of efforts to conceptualize organization-environment relations in very general macrosociological terms. While most have not dealt directly with problems of communication with clients-in-contact, they provide potentially useful frameworks within which to approach such problems.

In their comprehensive review of the field of formal organizations, Blau and Scott (1962) include a chapter on "The Social Context of Organizational Life." The three major topics reviewed are (*a*) the social environment of organizations, including both interorganizational relations and influences of the community on organizations; (*b*) analysis of organizational characteristics, including a reevaluation of the validity of the Weberian model of bureaucracy in the light of cross-cultural comparisons; and (*c*) interorganizational processes of ecological adaptation, competition, and exchange.

Eisenstadt's (1959) elaboration of the concepts of bureaucracy, bureaucratization, and debureaucratization provides a helpful framework within which to analyze variations in official-client relations in different societies, particularly in modernizing ones. Especially noteworthy is his specification of the conditions under which bureaucracy maintains or fails to maintain a "healthy" balance with its environment.

A quite different approach is that of Thompson and McEwen (1958), who focus on relations with other organizations as the significant aspect of a particular organization's environment. In a programmatic article, Stinchcombe (1965) recommends for study five aspects of the relation between organizations and the wider social structure, among which two may provide useful background for the study of official-client communication: the impact of organizational structure on relations between the social classes, and the effects of ethnic and communal organizations on feelings of identity and solidarity.

Litwak and Meyer (1966) have been working on a balance theory of coordination between bureaucratic organizations and community primary groups. Downs (1967) has developed a theory of organizational decision-making that places heavy emphasis on the interrelations of organizations and their environment. Interesting typologies of organizations based explicitly on aspects of relations with clients have been suggested by Bidwell and Vreeland (1964) and by Lefton and Rosengren (1966).

Cultural Setting, Bureaucracy, and Modernization

We are beginning to learn about non-Western bureaucracy, thanks to the efforts of sociologists and students of comparative public administration. The most striking characteristic of bureaucracy in non-Western societies, and particularly in developing countries, appears to be the continuing dominance of particularism and diffuseness of orientation in the Parsonian sense. While particularism refers to the phenomenon of relating to an individual on the basis of "who" he is, diffuseness refers to the breadth or scope of one's orientation to another, to the number of areas of life included in the relationship. Most commonly these two phenomena appear together.

Blau and Scott (1962) have reviewed a number of the relevant sociological studies. Presthus (1959) has provided a general discussion of particularism in bureaucracy, with special reference to the Middle East. The volume edited by LaPalombara (1963) presents several approaches to the study of bureaucratization in developing societies. Riggs (1967) develops a "sala" model of bureaucracy in transitional societies. The word *sala* means both "office" and "drawing room," thus epitomizing the lack of differentiation between the two in these societies.

There are a number of case studies of bureaucracy in Asia, the Middle East, Africa, and Latin America. We have found five studies of bureaucracy in Asia. In his report on a study of the civil service in Pakistan, Ahmad (1964) devotes a chapter to the attitudes of civil servants toward the public. They tended to stress their own social superiority and social distance, rather than an orientation of service to the public. In a survey of contacts of the public with government bureaucracy in India, Eldersveld (1965) found major differences between urban and rural populations in the amount of contact and in the attitudes toward the quality of service. For rurals, the amount of contact was positively related to favorableness of attitude, while urbanities were uniformly more critical than rurals, regardless of contact.

According to Kearney and Harris (1967), caste and family memberships influence recruitment and promotion to civil service posts in Ceylon. In particular, officials dealing with the public must belong to relatively high-status castes, since the public is unwilling to deal with public servants of low caste. In Japan, Abegglen (1958) found a diffuse, neofeudalistic relation between factory managers and their workers. Caudill's (1961) study of the "tsukisoi," the around-the-clock servant-companion of Japanese mental patients, provides another example of a more diffuse role relationship than is customary for the nurse in the West.

Moving from Asia to the Middle East, we note first a study by Berger (1957) of the Egyptian civil service. His chief finding was that the bureaucratic and professional components of the role of civil servant did not relate to each other in the same way that they did in Western culture. In general, the ethic of public service was not highly developed. Second, Bradburn (1963) studied interpersonal relations in factories and businesses in Turkey. He reports the dominance of a paternalistic pattern much like that found by Abegglen. Businesses are perceived as families, with their managers as authoritarian figures deserving loyalty; the employees are evaluated more in terms of their relation to the manager than according to their performance. Friedl's (1958) study of hospital care in provincial Greece presents still another way in which the wider culture may impinge on bureaucratic organization in a developing country. Here the lack of differentiation between the hospital and the family is reflected in the fact that relatives of patients all sleep together with a number of patients in the same room.

Africa is represented by Fallers' (1965) investigation of the Soga, a Bantu-speaking people in Uganda. He, too, reports a conflict between particularistic and universalistic norms in the civil service. While the conflict occurred at several levels, it was sharpest for the civil servant–chief. At the same time certain aspects of the traditional social structure made the Soga state receptive to bureaucratization.

As for bureaucracy in Latin America, a study of custodial versus therapeutic orientations in a Peruvian mental hospital showed that doctors and nurses stressed custodial goals to about the same low extent as did comparable staff in hospitals in Boston and London; aides, on the other hand, were much more custodial in orientation than aides in the other two hospitals (Stein & Oetting, 1964). In a Chilean health center, doctor-patient relations broke down when nurses were removed from clinic work and sent on home visits only (Simmons, 1955). The conclusion was that the nurses served an important mediating function, bridging the cultural gap between patients and doctors.[2]

Not much is known about cultural variations in bureaucratic role relations in North America or Europe. Banton's (1964) study of relations between police and the public in Great Britain and the United States is full of insights of all kinds. Generally, he notes, police morality can be expected to be no better than that of the wider society. The extent to which a society respects the law may be expected to influence police activities. Banton suggests that there may be greater respect for the law in Great Britain than in the United States.

Another influence is the relative cultural gap between police and the public. In developing countries with a colonial background, the police may be perceived as belonging to the elite, with consequent tensions in public-police relations. Finally, there may be genuine cross-cultural differences in the communication "styles" of the police. Banton found that in the United States the police were more personal both among themselves and with the public. For example, unlike British police, they remove their hats when entering a house. American police are less deferential, more friendly, and are more likely to use a joking relationship as a means of persuasion.[3]

In addition to the above influences of cultural context on official-client relations, there are two very basic but unresearched factors which may play a role. These are a society's orientation to time, and its beliefs about man's relation to the physical environment (Kluckhohn & Strodtbeck, 1961). It is well known that in the West, particularly in the United States, time itself

---

[2] This finding has implications for bureaucracy even in modern Western societies—see the section on class and subcultural variations in bureaucratic attitudes and behaviors.

[3] For a study of differences in role relations between British and American ships, see Richardson (1956).

is considered a valuable resource—"time is money." This belief tends to correlate with an emphasis on doing, or achieving. In contrast, many countries of the Middle East, Southern Europe, and Latin America are more present oriented, and put less emphasis on goal achievement. Unfortunately, there is little or no research on such cross-cultural comparisons or on conflicts in intercultural official-client interaction arising from such differences in attitudes toward time.[4]

Closely related to a society's orientation to time is its orientation to the physical world. In the language of Kluckhohn and Strodtbeck (1961), man can see himself as "in nature" (living in harmony with it), or "over nature" (ruling nature), or "under nature" (subjugated to it). In modern Western society, especially the United States, man is believed capable of controlling and transforming his environment. This stands in contrast to the passive *fatalism* of traditional societies. We hypothesize that a consequence of this difference for bureaucracy is that Western officials and clients are more likely, other things being equal, to see bureaucracy as a means to an end; the rules may be questioned. Moreover, in societies with an active orientation toward the environment, the public is more likely to reserve to itself the right to complain, to question, and even to counterorganize. In contrast, the passivity of the public in non-Western societies (in particular, that of the public without personal connections) reinforces the monolithic authoritarian quality of bureaucracy.

Technological Developments

There are no studies of the direct effects of technology or technological complexity on official-client relations. In part this may be because this variable leads to others that in turn affect official-client relations. For example, many studies in the literature on formal organizations report a relationship between technological complexity and size. Size of organization in turn may affect relations with clients (see the discussion on size in the section on intraorganizational factors). The one study we know of which touches on the influence of technology is that of Strodtbeck and Sussman (1956). In a study of relations between watch owners and repairers, they report that the status of watch repairmen as skilled craftsmen has declined, and their relations with customers have become depersonalized as a result of increasing mechanization of watch manufacture and "spare parts" technology.

Interorganizational Relations

The influence of the relations among organizations on official-client relations has not been extensively examined. Banton (1964) notes that the police tend to arrest offenders less often in the United States than in Great Britain because American courts frequently fail to provide the necessary backing. Consequently, the police know there is often no point in arresting someone who will not be convicted. In a quite different context, Cumming and Harrington (1963) suggest that tensions in the role of clergyman are partially due to the fact that they refer members of their congregation to other organizations or persons more often than these others refer individuals to them.

Finally, Lipset, Trow, and Coleman (1956) identify a number of interorganizational factors that influence the extent of democracy in unions. First, the greater the autonomy of member locals, the greater the chances for democracy in the locals. Second, unions that come into existence through the federation of existing independent locals are more likely to be democratic in structure than those organized from

[4] These differences may in part explain the frustrations of American tourists when encountering the inefficiencies of bureaucracy abroad. For speculations and anecdotes on orientations to time in intercultural contacts of American businessmen abroad, see Edward Hall's *The Silent Language* (1966).

"the top down." Third, the more decentralized the ownership in the industry associated with a particular union, the less the union in turn feels obliged to create a centralized bureaucratic structure of its own.

INTRAORGANIZATIONAL FACTORS

Bureaucratization of Professional Services

One expression of the increased bureaucratization of modern society is the general trend toward providing professional services of various kinds in bureaucratic settings. Medicine, law, social welfare, scientific activity—all formerly stressed the autonomy of the individual practitioner; today, in contrast, practitioners are part of bureaucratic hierarchies, subject to bureaucratic rules and receiving salaries.[5]

Blau and Scott (1962) have summarized the similarities and differences between professional and bureaucratic orientations among practitioners. A more recent treatment is that of Wilensky (1964), who distinguishes among *three* orientations which may come into conflict—professional, organizational, and client-centered. While some have argued that bureaucratic hierarchy is incompatible with the collegial authority characteristic of the free professions, Wilensky argues that bureaucracy may enfeeble the service ideal more than it threatens autonomy.

Medical Care

There is a lot of discussion about the effects of type of practice on the quality of medical care and on patient satisfaction. "Third-party" (or bureaucratically organized) care supposedly increases collegial supervision, pools resources, and hence improves the quality of care, but the evidence suggests that the technical aspects of care are improved at the expense of personal interest in patients and their satisfaction (Ferguson, 1958; Freidson, 1961; 1963).

Both Blum (1960) and Bloom (1965) discuss the effects of organizational aspects of hospitalization on patient care. Blum notes the findings of two studies which showed that two-thirds of the hospitalized patients interviewed had been dissatisfied with their hospital experiences; yet other studies show that most patients do not complain. Seventy percent of malpractice suits are based on hospital incidents; nonpayment of bills, another indication of patient dissatisfaction, is greatest after hospitalization. Blum summarizes an earlier review of the literature, showing that bureaucratization of hospital procedures is related to psychological, medical, and social adjustment difficulties of patients. Wilson (1963) adds that often the hospital setting is foreign to the doctor *as well as* to the patient, with deleterious consequences for the doctor-patient relationship.

As for the job satisfaction of doctors in solo versus third-party practice, it is difficult to compare them since doctors of differing personality may be attracted to the two types of practice. Freidson (1961) concludes that although the data are not good, it seems that doctors are better able than other professionals to resist bureaucratic authority. Goss's (1961) study of the authority structure among physicians in an outpatient clinic of a teaching hospital seems to support this view. She found that physicians adhered to professional norms, and were free to make their own decisions in purely professional matters as opposed to administrative concerns. Supervision was provided in the form of "advice" from superiors who were themselves physicians, thus minimizing the status gap. A less optimistic picture is presented by Ben-David (1958) who studied doctors in National Health Service clinics in Israel. There he found that most physicians were dissatisfied and felt a loss of professional indepen-

[5] See Mills (1956) for a representative exposition of the spread of bureaucracy in many fields.

dence as well as of the respect and trust of their patients.

Evidence of negative effects of bureaucratization on attitudes of nurses is provided by Corwin (1961). Among graduate and student nurses there were inherent conflicts between professional and bureaucratic principles. Moreover, the degree program in nursing was more professional in orientation while the diploma program stressed bureaucratic principles.

Mental Illness

Workers in the field of mental illness are concerned with the effects of bureaucratic structure of mental hospitals on patient progress. Detailed treatments of this problem in the context of particular institutions are found in Stanton and Schwartz (1954) and Levinson and Gallagher (1964). Generally, these authors see a contradiction between the needs of bureaucratic structure and modern treatment goals. In a theoretical exposition of the problem, Kahne (1959) also takes a negative position. Longabaugh, Eldred, Bell, and Sherman (1966) describe a situation of "social bankruptcy" among schizophrenic patients in a mental hospital because of institutionalization in a bureaucratic framework. Patients are unable to provide socially valued companionship for each other, and their dependency on the staff reinforces their failure to establish rewarding interpersonal relationships. Since the hospital setting makes it difficult for patients to maintain or achieve feelings of self-esteem, it is difficult to conclude to what extent this state of social bankruptcy leads to psychopathology or vice versa.

Other types of rehabilitative organizations encounter the same dilemma. Mitchell (1966) argues that the basic structure of treatment-oriented prisons runs counter to their explicit goal. Much energy is spent on adaptation to the power structure, rather than on development of consensus among inmates and staff on rehabilitation goals. In a halfway house for chronic alcoholics, workers who are themselves alcoholics similarly encounter conflicts between the treatment culture and the requirements of bureaucratic structure and efficiency (Rubington, 1965).[6]

Professionals in Other Organizations

Bidwell (1965), in a review of theory and research on schools as formal organizations, analyzes the conflict between two functional problems or tasks of the schools: (*a*) to coordinate the activities of individual teachers and schools in order to insure minimum uniformity of outcomes; and (*b*) to maintain sufficient latitude vis-à-vis the public (including parents of pupils) and the board of education for the exercise of professional judgment of teachers and supervisors. W. H. Whyte (1956) has argued that the bureaucratization of scientific activity has diminished creativity and initiative.

Organizational Typologies

Two very basic characteristics of organizations which may influence official-client communication are their *goals* and their *structure*. These two factors are so closely linked that it is not always possible to separate them. Goals often dictate or imply a certain kind of structure. For example, if the goal of a prison is to protect society from convicted criminals, then the structure of the prison will have certain characteristics, among them involuntary entrance of inmates and use of physical coercion to control them.

Several students of formal organizations have developed typologies of organizations that have explicit or implicit implications for relations with clients. Blau and Scott (1962) classify organizations by the identity of their prime beneficiary—whether

[6] For other aspects of this problem see the sections below on the special problems and characteristics of total institutions and on the effects of bureaucratization on personality.

the public-at-large, the clients-in-contact, the members, or the owners (examples are the Bureau of Internal Revenue, a social welfare agency, a union, a department store). These authors analyze the "dilemmas" of each type of organization, in each of which relations with clients are quite different.

Etzioni's (1961; 1965) approach to what he calls organizational "control structure" is in some respects quite similar. He suggests a three-part typology of organizations based on (*a*) utilitarian power (material inducements), (*b*) identitive power (using symbolic means that make people identify with the organization), (*c*) coercive power (use of physical means to control "lower members").[7] Etzioni devotes much attention to different types of socialization of lower members (read *clients*) in each of the three types. In the 1961 volume he includes an explicit analysis of the kinds of communication in the three organizational types as well. But there is no empirical testing of hypotheses about relations with clients derived from his theory.

Thompson (1962) classifies organizations according to (*a*) whether the treatment of the client is preprogrammed or tailored to individual needs, and (*b*) whether the client's participation is mandatory or voluntary. Bidwell and Vreeland (1964) dichotomize client-serving organizations into client-inducting and noninducting types, each of which has different implications for the authority structure of the organization. This approach has been extended by Lefton and Rosengren (1966), who see organizations as varying along a "lateral" dimension—the breadth of interest in the client's current life-space—and a "longitudinal" dimension, or extent of interest in the client's future.

Litwak and Meyer (1966) suggest that organizations can be described in terms of three models: the Weberian model, dealing with uniform wants; the human relations model, dealing with nonuniform events; and the professional model, in which uniform bureaucratic aspects are combined with aspects involving professional judgment. Naegle's (1956) analysis of the division of labor among clergymen, teachers, and psychiatrists in the job of socialization is also relevant here. Each type of role differs in its relations with clients in four ways: in the nature of recruitment and acceptance of a client; in the degree of permissiveness in the regulation of the client's behavior; in the regulation of reciprocity; and in the provision of rewards.

Despite the suggestiveness of the various typologies reviewed above, virtually no empirical research has been done on the effects of type of organization on relations with clients. The only comparative study of which we know is our own (Katz & Danet, 1966). In a pilot study of a research project on communication between bureaucracy and the public, we were able to show that the strategies of persuasion which clients use in order to receive favors from organizations are in part determined by the type of organization.

Consequences of "Mixed" Goals

Few organizations have but one clear-cut goal. More frequent is the case of duality or multiplicity of goals. In particular, organizations may subscribe to several goals which under certain circumstances may come into conflict.

The police are an excellent example of this. Ostensibly, they serve the general public, with prime emphasis on their function of *social control*; but the public is often unaware of the *helping* or *service function* of the police. Banton (1964) has made explicit this dilemma of the built-in tension between the helping and control functions. For example, a citizen is reluctant to ask a policeman for help, because the policeman may note that the citizen is in some way suspicious and arrest him. Because of this potential discomfort of the public, and be-

[7] Etzioni deliberately categorizes lower staff and clients or inmates together.

cause the police have a virtual monopoly on the use of violence in society, questionable uses of it are readily attacked. Police brutality is a frequent theme in today's newspapers. Wilson (1963), himself a chief of police, pleads for greater police authority, pointing out the public's ambivalence toward the use of force: on the one hand, the public expects them to prevent crime and keep order; on the other, they should not use force.

Cumming, Cumming & Edelle (1965) analyzed the incoming telephone calls to a police station, observed prowl cars, and interviewed detectives concerned with special assignments. Their observations led to the conclusion that the public is almost totally unaware that the greater part of the policeman's duties is "social work" in which he gives advice, or support, in personal problems.[8]

A particularly pessimistic analysis of the problems of the police in relation to the public is that of Westley (1964), although his conclusions are based on observation of the police in one particular place (Chicago) and time (1949). He tries to elucidate factors leading to the genesis and function of the illegal use of violence by the police. In his view, because the public distrusts the police, individuals recruited to the occupation must develop professional norms as defenses; when the rookie experiences hostility on the part of the public, he undergoes "reality shock" and develops a need for norms that can protect him from threats to his dignity, occupational goals, and self-esteem.

Two other types of commonweal organizations whose secondary beneficiary is the individual client are government employment and social welfare agencies. An early, simplistic study (Francis & Stone, 1956) pointed out the basic conflict between service and procedure (i.e., bureaucratic efficiency) in a state employment security agency. This agency has two goals, to give unemployment compensation, and to place the unemployed in jobs. The investigators concluded, from interviews, observation, and content analyses of agency manuals, that procedure was emphasized at the expense of service to clients.

A more recent study of this conflict is that of Catrice-Lorey (1966), this time of the French social security system. She emphasizes the preoccupation with administrative procedure on the part of staff, while the public expects officials to be personal and accessible. In Blau's (1955) study of a state employment agency, there was structured conflict with clients because of the duality of the agency's goals. On the one hand, the agency's job was to place clients, to serve their interests; on the other, they had to check their eligibility for unemployment compensation. Workers could resolve the conflict either by joking about clients among themselves and thus displacing their aggression while maintaining the service orientation, or they could develop anticlient norms. In a later study of orientations toward clients in a public welfare agency, Blau (1960) found a similar conflict between service to clients and the need to check their eligibility for service.

Two interesting cases of conflict between loyalties to prime and secondary beneficiaries of organizations are the dilemmas of physicians and chaplains in the armed services. The armed forces, of course, exists to protect society as a whole; attention to the men's medical or spiritual needs is, from the viewpoint of the organization, designed to keep them functioning well on the job. Burchard (1954) examined the problems of military chaplains in the San Francisco Bay area in 1952. Their role conflict is especially acute, since war may be explicitly incompatible with their religious beliefs. Little (1956) provides a similar analysis of the role of medical war officer in the armed services. Medical officers must be suspicious of the "sick" soldier's motives and symptoms. In this respect, they face a situation quite similar to Soviet

[8] Of course the work of policemen depends in part on the area and population to which they are assigned.

physicians, whose first responsibility is to the state (see Field, 1953).

Although organizations have overall definitions of their goals, there is much variation *within* organizations in goal implementation; different departments handle different goals, with consequences for clients. Blau and Scott (1962), in a study of two departments of a county agency, showed that clients of the public assistance division were dependent and had to accept aid on the agency's terms. On the other hand, in the child welfare division, although the clients were technically children, workers had to deal with foster-parents and adoptive parents, on whom the agency was dependent for cooperation. Interestingly, caseloads in the child welfare division were lower, and the work assigned on somewhat different bases. In the public assistance division, professional principles were more often sacrificed; workers in this division enjoyed lower prestige; and there was a higher proportion of black workers.

A study by Coser (1963) of two departments of a hospital produced parallel results. In one department patients were chronically ill, while in the other, patients could be rehabilitated. In the latter ward, "good" patients were those who were active and socialized with others; in the chronic ward, "good" patients were those who were merely physically neat. Nurses in the chronic ward were less emotionally involved in their work, interacted with patients less and among themselves more.

Custodial vs. Therapeutic Orientations

An important theme of the literature on organizational goals is that of the so-called custodial versus therapeutic orientations in mental hospitals and prisons. Changes in emphasis from the one to the other may be defined in Blau and Scott's terms as a reversal of primary and secondary beneficiaries. Custodial institutions are designed primarily to protect society from their inmates (i.e., they are commonweal organizations), while therapeutic or treatment milieu institutions make public welfare subordinate to rehabilitation of inmates (i.e., they are service organizations).

Comprehensive reviews of theories, practices, and research on this topic, as well as extensive bibliographies, are provided by Perrow (1965) on hospitals and by D. R. Cressey (1965) on prisons. Each type of orientation has direct implications for organizational structure, patterns of communication and decision-making, and particularly for relations with inmates. Central to the factors which led to the change in orientation in the direction of rehabilitation and treatment was the discovery that institutionalization can make inmates "worse." Two key studies of mental hospitals—Stanton and Schwartz (1954) and Caudill (1958)—pioneered in elucidating the consequences for inmates, and for institutional structure generally, of the two types of orientations.

Basic work on this problem in prisons was carried out by Grusky (1959a; 1959b) who, like Stanton and Schwartz and Caudill, employed a case study method. More recent recognition of the limitations of case studies has led to the development of comparative studies (Street, 1965; Berk, 1966). Generally, these studies find that informal leaders are more supportive of the institutions when a treatment orientation prevails. In custodial institutions, the informal organization among inmates seems to work against the status quo; in therapeutic institutions it supports it. While the change from the more traditional custodial orientation to a newer one may be viewed as a positive step forward, specific changes within an institution may create problems that never existed before. McCleery (1961) analyzed the temporary chaos in a maximum-security prison when a new warden introduced a therapeutic orientation.

Characteristics of Total Institutions

Total institutions, according to Goffman (1961:1–124), are those in which a group of inmates live together in an enforced, bureaucratically managed round of life. Their "total" character derives from their isolation from the outside world.[9] Included are prisons, hospitals, and other institutions which exist, at least in part, in order to keep their inmates away from society. A second major type of total institution is that with some specific instrumental goal requiring isolation: ships, boarding schools, the armed services, and monasteries are examples. While there are some differences between the two types of total institutions, from the viewpoint of official-client communication, they have significant characteristics in common.

Because work, play, and sleep take place in the same setting, there must be constant supervision of inmates (subordinates). In fact, it may be argued that the central problem of these institutions is that of control of inmates. Since virtually all activities must be bureaucratically managed, and since entrance to, and/or exit from, these institutions is frequently involuntary, there arises a natural opposition of interests between staff and inmates, with many implications for their relations. These include the emergence of mutually hostile stereotypes, a redefinition of the nature of "work," the elaboration of a complex socialization ritual which stresses the mortification of the self among inmates, and the development of a system of "privileges" for good behavior.

As Etzioni (1965) has pointed out, in modern society differentiation of various types of activities typically means compartmentalization; individuals and groups are able to reduce tensions from one area of life in another. But in total institutions this is impossible; hence the constant potential for all-pervading conflict. Mechanisms of tension release, such as the annual staff-inmates party, are only partially successful. The dilemma of the staff is heightened by the fact that, even in organizations which legitimately use physical coercion to keep inmates in line, there are serious limits on the use of such means. The isolation and role dependence of the staff make them, especially lower-ranking staff who have the most contact with inmates, vulnerable to the establishment of informal exchanges with inmates, in order to gain compliance.

Perhaps the most interesting aspect of total institutions, at least from the viewpoint of the present chapter, is their *informal* organization. Blau and Scott (1962) review Goffman and others on this topic, citing several functions and dysfunctions of informal organization among inmate-subordinates in prisons, mental hospitals, and schools.[10] In another essay, Goffman (1961:171–320) himself further explores the informal organization of life in a mental hospital, expanding the concept of "secondary adjustment" or "habitual arrangements by which a member of an organization employs unauthorized means, or obtains unauthorized ends, or both" (Goffman, 1961:189). Goffman tends to view the activities of inmates as undermining the institutional order. Papers by Anselm Strauss and his colleagues (1963) and Roth (1963) present a more neutral view of informal organization, in which the social structure of total institutions is seen as a "negotiated order."

The problem of control in total institutions and its interrelations with the informal organization constitutes one major aspect of interest for students of official-client communication. A second major aspect is the effects of bureaucratic regimen on goal attainment. This aspect has already been discussed in the more general sections on the effects of bureaucratization on professional goal attainment and on custodial versus therapeutic orientations, although there we did not make a distinc-

---

[9] This section is heavily indebted to Goffman (1961:1–124).

[10] Even nonresidential schools are nearly total institutions, with implications for teacher-pupil relations; see Bidwell (1965).

tion between total and nontotal institutions. Here we add the hypothesis that, other things being equal, the negative consequences of bureaucratization for goal attainment are probably greater in total than in nontotal institutions. This seems reasonable since, in addition to the effects of bureaucratization on relations within the organization, there are the additional effects of *isolation from the community*. The adherents of the "social psychiatric" approach to mental illness, whose theories, practices, and research have been expounded in a series of volumes beginning with Stanton and Schwartz (1954), have been increasingly aware of the negative effects of isolation from the community. In a recent book, for example, Schwartz, Schwartz et al. (1964) include a chapter on ways of "breaking down the barriers between the hospital and the community."

Although Goffman distinguishes between the incarcerating and the instrumental goal types of total institutions, his analysis perhaps overemphasizes the first type. Private schools, the armed services, ships—all differ in their staff-subordinate relations from those in the first type (the word *inmate* is less appropriate here). In part, the difference is between voluntary and compulsory entrance of inmates-subordinates, although this does not apply to the armed services, where service is largely compulsory, or to voluntary self-incarceration in a mental institution. But, generally, subordinates in the second type of institution are not negatively stereotyped by society. Also, the staff-subordinate hierarchy is probably perceived as less sharply dichotomous. And though many aspects of the socialization of subordinates in schools, the army, or on a fishing ship may resemble the socialization process in prisons and mental hospitals, staff and subordinates presumably are united by common goals.[11]

[11] For discussions of ships as total institutions, see Aubert and Arner (1958) and Berkman (1946). On the military, see Dornbusch (1955).

Size of Organization

There are few studies of the size of an organization as a variable affecting official-client relations. Bidwell (1965) reviewed two studies in the sociology of education that focus on the effects of size. Gross, Mason, and McEachern (1957) found that size of school board, as well as size of school system, were highly related to the degree of consensus within school boards, and between school boards and superintendents. In Bowman's (1963) replication of this study, size affected both the school boards' and the superintendents' definitions of their own roles. Both studies agreed that, in the bigger systems, the superintendent is the chief decision-maker, while in the smaller systems both saw him as an agent for carrying out decisions of the board. Bowman notes, however, that these findings may be the result of differential recruitment of the superintendents; larger school systems may recruit men with more progressive, professional orientations.

Thomas (1966) studied the role conceptions, degree of role consensus, and quality of work among welfare workers in different-sized units of a state welfare department. Generally, the smaller the office, the greater the role consensus between workers and supervisors. Second, there was less specialization in the worker's role in the smaller offices. Third, workers in the smaller offices showed higher commitment to professional ethics. Finally, quality of performance was also higher in the smaller offices. Thomas qualifies his findings with the view that effects of size of organization may really be the product of differences in size of community. Impressions from talks with workers suggested that in the smaller rural offices there was more contact with clients, and contact was more personal.

Thomas and Fink (1963) have summarized thirty-one empirical studies of effects of size in small groups; several of these have consistently found that smaller groups, especially two-person groups, must inhibit the expression of tension. The authors review findings on the relation between size of voluntary organization and member participation. On the whole, size of organization is negatively related to the amount of communication among members, although the relation is qualified by a number of intervening variables.

Data on effects of size of a clinic on doctor-patient relations are provided by Shuval (1962) in a study of Israeli medical clinics. She found that amount of negative stereotyping of patients of North African origin increased with clinic size. Apparently, when the strains of the bureaucratic system increased, i.e., when size of practice or proportion of North African patients increased, it became more difficult to maintain a universalistic norm.

Staff Relations: Status and Solidarity

It is reasonable to suppose that relations among the members of an organization's staff may have important consequences for relations with clients. Much more has been written on effects of status considerations than on effects of staff solidarity or the lack of it. In his review of interpersonal relations in medical settings, Croog (1963) summarizes a number of relevant studies. Seeman and Evans (1961) demonstrated that the stratification system of a hospital makes a difference for medical care, in particular for the performance of interns. Where status differences were less stressed, interns were more likely to receive favorable evaluations; and interns themselves reported greater psychological support of the patient. In addition, where the head physician did not emphasize the status differences, and where there was low communication among the staff, interns communicated more with patients and spent more time explaining their problems and treatment to them.

In a study of nurse-patient relations in a mental hospital, Pearlin and Rosenberg (1962) found a complex interaction between organizational status relations of staff and patients and their wider social statuses. Distinguishing between status distance (subordination of mental patients to staff) and personal distance (emotional indifference to patients), they found that factors regulating the former had little influence on those regulating the latter. Personal distance was most common among personnel assigned to wards of their own sex and of differing age. Status distance, on the other hand, occurred most often when relatively high-status staff were deferential toward superiors, had blocked mobility aspirations, and worked with patients of low social status.

The official's status in the organization can also make a difference for the type of control he uses over client-inmates. Bidwell (1965) quotes a finding that the less secure a teacher's *tenure*, the more likely he or she is to resort to affective means of control of pupils.

Rosenberg and Pearlin (1962) also report status differences in preferences for strategies of persuasion in managing patients. Lowest-status attendants were most likely to prefer appeals to their organizational authority. Highest-status nurses—supervisors—were more likely to prefer "benevolent manipulation" of patients.

Several authors have found that persons of differing status in organizations may perceive or define organizational goals differently. Croog (1963) has summarized the findings of three separate studies with regard to medical staff. Generally, they all find that doctors and nurses vary in perception of goals, and in perception of patients and patients' use of a clinic. Levinson and Gallagher (1964) review work by Gilbert and Levinson on variations among mental hospital staff by status in custodial versus therapeutic orientations. In three different mental hospitals, attendants were more custodial than nurses who, in turn, were more custodial than doctors. These findings were confirmed by Stein and Oetting (1964) in a study of four mental hospitals in Peru.

Catrice-Lorey (1966) has noted the consequences of the low status of officials in French social security offices. The fact that employees at counters have too low qualifications, low salaries, and low esteem by the public leads to absenteeism and negative attitudes toward both job and clients. This variable of the status of officials having contact with clients, particularly in commonweal organizations which are potentially "against" clients (e.g., the income tax or customs authorities, or officials in a registry of motor vehicles), clearly needs more research.

Several other effects related to status of officials might be mentioned. One is W. F. Whyte's (1948) analysis of the conflict in the role of waitress resulting from the reversal of the flow of demand: where orders typically flow down the chain of command in organizations, waitresses relay orders for food to higher status chefs. Another effect is that hypothesized by Janowitz and Delany (1957): The higher the status of the official, the less information he seems to have about clients. Higher status is seen to be associated with increased knowledge of the organization's goals as a whole at the expense of knowledge of clients and their problems.

There are some very interesting findings on effects of staff disagreement in mental hospitals on patients' behavior. Both Caudill (1958) and Stanton and Schwartz (1954) devote chapters to this theme. Caudill reports that when there was conflict among the staff, *all* role groups restricted participation and withdrew from each other, relations among patients broke down, and collective disturbance was the result. Stanton and Schwartz found that patients who were the subject of secret staff disagreement became pathologically excited; when the disagreement was resolved, their excitement subsided.

As for the effects of solidarity (or the lack of it), Banton (1964), in his comprehensive analysis of relations of the police with the community in Britain and the United States, notes that particularly because of the genuine danger of some police work, staff solidarity is crucial for job satisfaction and for confidence and skill in dealing with the public. Blau (1955) analyzes the complex interaction between staff relations and cohesiveness on the one hand, and relations with clients on the other. Cohesiveness among staff may, under certain conditions, foster good relations with clients. In a later study of a public welfare agency, Blau (1960) found an interesting structural effect. Officials could attempt to resolve the conflict between service and checking of clients by discussing it among themselves. For individuals, talking about clients was not related to their orientation toward clients as manifested in work. But for groups, the more they talked negatively about clients, the more negative their orientation in practice.

A quite different aspect of staff relations deals with effects of different numbers of officials, in this case nurses, on interaction patterns. Croog (1963) found that the total amount of interaction between patients and nurses increases when more nurses are added to hospital wards. However, when more than five nurses are placed together, interaction among themselves increases at the expense of interaction with patients.

CHARACTERISTICS OF OFFICIALS AND CLIENTS

Bureaucracy and Personality

A major theme of the humanists, from Weber (1943) himself to the more contemporary critics of "organizational society" and "organization man" (Merton, 1952; Mills, 1956; W. H. Whyte, 1956; Bensman & Rosenberg, 1960; Erich Strauss, 1961; Presthus, 1965) is the deleterious effects of bureaucratization on personality. Stuart-Bunning (1931), an early student of public administration, recognized that civil servants were often unpleasant, or otherwise made life difficult for their clients, but tended to justify the status quo. Strauss devotes an entire chapter of his aptly titled book, *The Ruling Servants*, to an analysis of the defects of bureaucracy. Focusing on the characteristics of the "bureaucratic mind," he lists overdevotion to precedent, remoteness from the community, inaccessibility, lack of initiative, buck-passing, and overemphasis on procedure. Strauss's position is wholly pessimistic—bureaucracy is an ineradicable and uncontrollable evil that is constantly growing.

Merton (1952) takes a more dispassionate position. In his view, bureaucracy fosters a "trained incapacity" or inflexibility of mind on the part of officials which in turn leads to displacement of goals, such that procedure becomes an end in itself. Merton analyzes the structural sources of overconformity of officials to the requirements of procedure.

Whyte, Presthus, and Mills all develop book-length treatments of the consequences of bureaucratization in both the public and private sectors of the economy. Presthus' book, the most recent of the three, sums up the arguments of the others, and describes two dysfunctions of "big organization" for the personalities of their members: (*a*) loss of initiative, autonomy, and creativity; and (*b*) depersonalization and loss of interest in work—in short, alienation. Presthus argues that organizations look for and encourage personalities with a low tolerance for ambiguity, with conventional ways, and with high acceptance of authority. He develops a typology of modes of adaptation to the stresses involved in working in big organizations. Whyte similarly talks of a "bureaucratic ethic" which stresses conformity, loyalty, belief in the group rather than the individual as the source of creativity, and the ultimate need of the individual for belongingness. The alienation theme is especially strong in the article by Bensman and Rosenberg (1960) and in the work of their intellectual predecessor, C. Wright Mills (1956).

The great weakness of all these authors is that although they deal with very important aspects of the phenomenon we call bureaucracy, they do so in an unsystematic way which does not lead to the empirical testing of hypotheses. A few empirical studies are beginning to appear, however. D. R. Miller and Swanson (1958) found significant differences between the child-rearing practices of parents of the entrepreneurial versus the bureaucratic middle classes. Bureaucratic parents, like entrepreneurial parents, emphasize the need for their children to be active and independent, but they put less stress on risk-taking and competitiveness, and more on interpersonal skills, being cooperative and easy to get along with.

Surprisingly, Miller and Swanson arrive at conclusions quite opposite to those of the pessimists just reviewed. They argue that bureaucracy brings about a lessening of psychological pressures on the individual; that he has less need to repress impulses or feel guilt, and hence is psychologically healthier than the more traditional entrepreneurial personality. Further evidence that entrepreneurial versus bureaucratic family background does make a difference comes from an interesting study by Crowne (1966). In an experiment on two-person bargaining in a non-zero-sum game, he found that, controlling for level of aspiration, subjects whose fathers had a bureaucratic occupation were more cooperative; moreover, competitive bargaining was strongest when two subjects of entrepreneurial background were paired.

Another line of empirical work is that on attitudes toward bureaucratic authority. Experiments by Block and Block (1952), and more recently by Milgram (1965), seem to suggest that individuals can be easily influenced to perform tasks that they dislike or even oppose on moral grounds when legitimate authority orders them to do so. It should be noted, however, that the applicability of these experiments to the real world remains controversial.

While there has been much discussion in the literature about consequences of bureaucratization for *workers*, very little has been said by the humanists about effects of bureaucratization on *clients-in-contact*, and on the public generally. A few empirical studies have been reviewed in the section on the bureaucratization of professional services. Studies of attitudes toward bureaucracy of both officials and the public will shortly be reviewed, but it should be remembered that since these studies do not hold degree of bureaucratization of the organization constant, they cannot be true tests of the effects of this variable-cluster.

Direct Effects of Personality

Almost nothing is known of the relation between personality characteristics of officials and/or clients and what happens in interaction in bureaucratic settings. An early study by Almond and Lasswell (1934) of aggressiveness among recipients of unemployment insurance during the depression in the 1930s examined the correlates of aggressiveness. These were: longer contact with the agency; a higher proportion than among nonaggressives had been employed in government jobs; a higher proportion of them had broken the law and had contacts with prisons; surprisingly, more came from higher income and educational groups. The authors' interpretation of their findings is that familiarity with government agencies fosters assertive behavior.

Stark (1959) discusses the communication problems that may arise in social casework when the client's problems arouse anxiety in the worker. Bidwell (1965) reviews several studies of the relation between teacher style and pupil achievement. There is some evidence that a combination of neutrality and affectivity is most effective. One study found that an autocratic style produced higher achievement among high school students than a democratic style.

Attitudes, Expectations, and Role-Relevant Knowledge

In a programmatic article, Barton and Mendlowitz (1960) have stressed the need to study the experience of injustice as a general research problem. In a very simple exploratory pilot study they asked a sample of college students to mention situations in which they had experienced injustice. About 50 percent of the cases mentioned were of perceived injustice at the hands of bureaucratic officials. Gouldner (1952) analyzes the characteristics of red tape, and speculates on why the problem arises. In a study of attitudes toward government bureaucracy in Israel, Guttman and Foa (1951) found that amount of contact per se was related not to direction of attitudes—positive or negative—but to the *intensity* of the attitude held.

There are a few studies of attitudes and knowledge of the public in specific areas. In that of medical care, Koos (1958) and Freidson (1961) found that patients approved the quality of medical care but said that the doctor was typically too impersonal or lacked warmth. A more recent study (Feldman, 1966) with a more comprehensive sample examined both attitudes and health information of the public. It found that most members of the sample had a high opinion of the medical profession and were very satisfied with the care they received. Seeking an explanation for underutilization of medical services, Feldman was forced to discredit negative attitudes toward medical care as an explanation. As for health information, he found evidence that information campaigns had over time increased the amount of knowledge, and that amount of knowledge varied with a number of demographic variables.

Two studies of attitudes toward social welfare services are those of Janowitz et al. (1958) and Catrice-Lorey (1966) in the United States and France, respectively. Janowitz and his colleagues found a generally low level of knowledge of social security rights among the public. They asked respondents to rate the prestige of civil servants, and the morality and efficiency of social security services. In the French study, Catrice-Lorey demonstrated the existence of a gap between public expectations for service and the excessively procedure-oriented approach of officials.

An article by Falk (1964) analyzes the reasons for the public's prejudice against the police. Kiani (1962) reports on a study of the public's image of bureaucracy in Pakistan; while his sample was so small that findings do not merit mention here, his questionnaire is suggestive.

In our opinion, the most significant research on the problem of the powerlessness of the public vis-à-vis bureaucracy is that of Seeman (1966). In a series of studies in the United States he has demonstrated several important relationships: (*a*) union members feel less powerless than nonunion members; (*b*) tuberculosis patients high on powerlessness knew less about health matters than those who felt less powerless; (*c*) prison inmates high on powerlessness learned less when exposed to parole-relevant information than the less powerless. These findings were replicated and extended in a companion study in Sweden.[12]

In general, there is even less research on official's attitudes toward clients than vice versa. One study by Borgatta, Fanshel, and Meyer (1960) analyzed social workers' perceptions of clients. A factor analysis of data on clients' background and personality and social workers' judgments of the problem involved and treatment potential, as well as outcomes of treatment, showed that the strongest factor was a "personality assessment component," an estimate of the client's ability to assume responsibility for his problem. Pratt, Seligmann, and Reader (1958) found that physicians overestimated the level of medical information among patients.

More profound are studies of the degree of consensus in expectations among various members of role sets. In the sociology of education, studies by Gross, Mason, and McEachern (1957) and by Biddle, Rosencranz, Tomich, and Twyman (1966) have focused on the degree of consensus in expectations of various members of the role sets of superintendents and teachers, respectively. Both these groups of investigators develop ingenious methods of investigating mutual perceptions and expectations empirically.

Papers by Kutner (1958) and Mechanic (1961) are theoretical discussions of the need for compatibility of expectations of surgeon and patient, and psychotherapist and patient, respectively. In Wheeler's (1961) study of role conflict between inmates and staff in a state reformatory, the *perceived* amount of conflict was greater than the actual amount. Finally, Wilkening (1958) found a lack of consensus between county extension agents and county agency committee members in the definition of the role of the former.

Another type of study looks at the relation between expectations for behavior in bureaucratic or professional encounters, and the behavior itself. Interestingly, this important problem has been of concern primarily to practitioners in the field of psychotherapy. Lennard and Bernstein (1960) have shown that the therapist's definition of his own role is consistent with his behavior, and that the more dissimilar the expectations of therapist and patient for therapy, the more socializing behavior the therapist introduces in order to teach the patient his role.

In a pilot study of former clients of ministers, physicians, and psychotherapists then applying to a religiopsychiatric clinic, Kadushin (1962) analyzed the factors associated with stability of interaction. He stresses that stable interaction is most likely when norms and expectations of practitioner and patient are similar. Heine and Trosman (1960) have demonstrated that initial expectations of therapy patients

---

[12] Note, however, that Seeman does not ascribe causal connections to these relationships. The fact that the relatively more powerless actually learn less when exposed to relevant information has important implications for the problems of the poor. It suggests that simply making information available to the poor will not automatically lead them to claim their rights.

are a major factor in determining whether they continue or drop out of therapy.[13] Dinitz, Angrist, Lefton, and Pasamanick (1966) have found that former mental patients' own expectations for successful adaptation after leaving the hospital, as well as the expectations of staff for their success, were in fact related to this success.

The gap between clients' expectations and what they actually find to characterize bureaucratic or professional encounters may have an effect on future behavior outside the encounter itself. Thus Cobb (1958) has argued that cancer patients who turn to quacks usually do so because of physicians' lack of attention to patients' need for emotional support and explanations. And M. S. Davis (1968) found that while demographic characteristics of patients are *not* associated with their compliance with doctors' orders, communication difficulties in the doctor-patient relationship *are* so related. Patients who became increasingly active with repeated visits, and vied with their doctor for control of the relationship, tended not to comply with his orders.

Still another type of study of the relation between attitudes and expectations on the one hand, and role performance on the other, examines the way in which officials or practitioners "manage" their roles. Thus Daniels (1960) has analyzed how medical interns learn to control affect when dealing with patients. A classic study of the management of role conflict is that of Gross, Mason, and McEachern (1957). They list the following strategies used by school superintendents: (*a*) passing the buck to the school committee; (*b*) compromise; (*c*) modification of the expectations of one party only; (*d*) development of an independent plan of action. The authors go on to develop impressively accurate predictions of the conditions under which a given superintendent will choose one type of strategy rather than another.

Bar-Yosef and Schild (1966) have developed a similar typology of defense mechanisms used by line-bureaucrats caught between conflicting pressures and demands of superiors and clients. Officials either overconformed to the organization, yielded to clients' pressures, developed their own independent policy, organized "joint" organizational defenses, or used third parties to serve as buffers between themselves and the clients.

Social Networks of Clients Outside the Organization

A few studies have analyzed the effects of the social networks of clients on their relations with organizations. More specifically, the focus has been on what Freidson (1961) has dubbed "lay referral systems." In an analysis of the channels by which patients reach medical services, Freidson proposes a fourfold typology of such lay referral systems, based on two dimensions: (*a*) the degree of congruence between the lay and professional culture; (*b*) the relative number and cohesiveness of lay consultants who interpose between doctor and patient.

A different approach has been developed by Liberman (1965), who studied relations between "influentials" and "influencees" in the use of mental health resources. The former are older, more gregarious, of higher socioeconomic status, and have had more experience with mentally ill relatives or friends. Pairs of influentials-influencees are most likely to be similar on religion, socioeconomic status, sex, and attitudes toward mental health resources. In the sphere of psychiatric social work, Mayer and Rosenblatt (1964) examined the effect of the client's social context on continuance in treatment. They, too, propose a typology based on two dimensions: (*a*) the availability of alternatives to institutional help, and (*b*) the attitude that prevails toward getting help in the social context of the patient.

[13] Continuation in therapy or a good therapist-patient relationship is, however, by no means a guarantee of the outcome of therapy; see Eaton (1959).

Class and Subcultural Variations

We turn now to a review of the evidence for variations in bureaucratic attitudes and behavior of clients according to their class or subcultural memberships. As was suggested earlier, even in modern, relatively stable and homogeneous societies, individuals may display considerable variation by occupation, education, and income in attitudes and in role performance. The special problems of the lower class and the culturally deprived in dealing with bureaucracy are just beginning to be recognized.

Sjoberg, Brymer, and Farris (1966) made a comprehensive theoretical analysis of the special set of conditions characterizing the interrelations between bureaucracy and the lower class. Their main argument is that bureaucratic organizations implicitly sustain the stratification system. The lower class is unable to negotiate for its fair share of the resources and services available.

Unlike the middle class, the poor know neither the rules of the game nor the techniques for getting around them. The staffs of organizations—physically middle-class in origin—reinforce the gap because they implicitly or explicitly discriminate against the lower classes. The latter, whose style of interpersonal relations emphasizes the local, the personal, and the concrete, feel strange in impersonal bureaucratic settings. S. M. Miller (1964) has written on the problems of the poor in dealing with bureaucracy and calls for reforms.

While Sjoberg et al. offer a general description of this problem, it is evident that they have the United States primarily in mind. Hoggart (1961) provides a similar, though more descriptive, picture for the working class in contemporary England. The world is divided into Them and Us. "Them" are the people who run the institutions of society, the police, the civil services, the schools, etc. In short, the lower classes, it is argued, feel powerless and confused before this vast and complex world of Them.

If within stable modernized societies certain groups have problems contending with bureaucracy, these problems are at least as acute in immigrant and/or modernizing societies, where large proportions of the population may be unfamiliar with bureaucratic ways. Katz and Eisenstadt (1960) have described some of the consequences for bureaucracy of the rapid absorption of large numbers of immigrants of traditional backgrounds in Israel. One such consequence was that officials broadened their roles in order to "teach" clients what was expected of them. In some cases officials came to overidentify with the immigrants and to represent their interests to the parent organization, rather than vice versa. In a later study in Israel, Katz and Danet (1966) found that clients of non-Western origin were more likely than Westerners to appeal to officials' altruism when requesting services. Westerners, on the other hand, were higher on normative appeals, apparently reflecting their greater socialization to bureaucratic role relations.

Medical Care

In the area of medical care, a number of studies have focused on attitudes and knowledge about health and illness, diagnosis, and treatment. Blum (1960), Rosenblatt and Suchman (1946; 1964a), Freidson (1961), and Feldman (1966) find that members of the lower class typically know less about illness and define being ill differently. In part, these differences reflect more basic differences in general value orientation. Rosenblatt and Suchman (1964b) report that "blue-collars" show little interest in preventive medicine, in part because of a general fatalism. In addition they are slower to accept the role of a "sick" person, although once defined as sick, they are more dependent than "white-collars" (Rosenblatt & Suchman, 1964a). Middle-class individuals have, on the other hand, a rational orientation to illness (Freidson, 1961) and a more critical attitude toward the services they receive.

As for subcultural or ethnic differences in the use of medical care, Saunders (1954) compared the attitudes and behavior of the Anglo-Saxon and Spanish-speaking populations of the American southwest. One of the reasons why Spanish-speakers failed to take advantage of medical services was their different definition of illness; another was lack of knowledge of "Anglo" medical ways. And once defined as sick, they find it more comfortable to be dependent. Bloom (1965: chap. 2) suggests that differences among ethnic groups in utilization of services are likewise partly due to differing value orientations. Blum (1960) summed up much of this literature on cultural and class differences and shows how superstition, etiology, and religious beliefs all influence patient behavior and attitudes.

Another set of attitudes which influences patients' behavior in relation to organized medical services is their response to the purely bureaucratic aspects. Rosenblatt and Suchman (1964b) cite still another factor accounting for underutilization by blue-collarites of medical services, namely their discomfort with the impersonality, achievement-orientation, and bureaucratization that dominate interpersonal relations. Saunders comes to much the same conclusion regarding the Spanish-speakers in the American southwest.[14] To isolate the effects of bureaucratization in greater detail, comparative studies of private or solo parctice versus organized practice are needed.

Most of the studies cited above also provide information on class and subcultural variation in actual behavior related to medical care. A basic question is, Through what channels does the patient arrive in the doctor's office? The most thorough study of this, perhaps, is that of Freidson (1960). In his New York City study, he found differences in the "lay referral systems" of members of the lower and middle classes. The lower-class system was "parochial"—individuals had only limited familiarity with available medical resources, and consulted a good deal with family and friends—while the middle-class patient was involved in a "cosmopolitan" system—he was more prone to make a decision regarding medical care himself without the help of lay consultants outside the home. Rosenblatt and Suchman (1964b) also stress the importance of lay referral systems, and note that blue-collar individuals are slower to go to the doctor.

Blum (1960) reviews evidence that members of the lower classes go to chiropractors and to quacks more often, that they more often use the druggist as a source of advice, that they are less likely to have a regular doctor, etc. Zola (1964) specifies five factors that affect the timing of decisions to see a doctor, and then shows that the different factors affect various ethnic groups differently. Italians were especially likely to see a doctor when they experienced an interpersonal crisis or their illness interfered with other social activities. The Irish more often went when "told" to go by someone else, rather than making their own decision; they also saw a doctor when they perceived their condition as a threat to their occupation or some other activity; Anglo-Saxons were influenced more than the other two groups studied by the nature and/or quality of symptoms themselves.

Bloom (1965) cites several studies which found that the lower the socioeconomic class, the smaller the proportion who either consulted a doctor or were hospitalized (this in spite of the fact that it is known that the highest proportion of "sick" persons, defined clinically, is found in the lower socioeconomic groups). Cartwright (1967), in a survey of citizens and doctors connected with the British National Health Service, found, on the contrary, that consultation rates were higher among the working than among the middle class,

[14] Of course, impersonality of orientation on the part of the doctor is a professional as well as a bureaucratic characteristic.

and among unskilled workers than among skilled. One American study (Graham, 1958) found no differences among the social classes in use of medical services. A last finding which we may note is that upper-middle-class individuals are more likely to use services outside the organized practice to which they belong (Freidson, 1960). Of course, this is in part because they can afford it financially. But this phenomenon is also related to their more critical attitude toward medical care.

Many of the factors cited above are also related to the way in which the patient presents himself to the doctor. A comprehensive treatment of ethnic differences of responses to pain and in presenting symptomatology can be found in Zola (1964). Even when patients were matched for diagnosis, there were still significant differences in the way members of the different ethnic groups presented themselves to the doctor. Presentation of self may actually affect diagnosis and treatment. In a later article, Zola (1966) reports that patients of Italian origin were disproportionately diagnosed as psychiatric cases, although there was no evidence of a higher frequency of psychosocial problems among them. Apparently Italians tended more than others to act out and to dramatize their symptoms.

Mental Illness

It appears that subcultural and class variations in clients' behavior in other areas are, relatively, much less researched. There are some findings on class differences in the handling of the patient role in psychotherapy and in mental hospitals. Two chapters in the volume *Mental Health of the Poor* are probably representative of current findings with regard to therapy: In a study of expectations of psychotherapy of lower-class patients, Overall and Aronson (1965) found that, generally, these patients expect the therapist to behave in an active medical way; more specifically, the less accurate the patients' expectations, the less likely they were to return for further treatment.

With regard to the response of lower-class members to psychological tests, Riessman and Miller (1965) report that their responses to projective tests—TATs, for example—may be a reaction to the stress of the unfamiliar test situation; also, they may lack interest or involvement in the situation because it is foreign to their culture. The authors conclude that TATs may not be a good measure of lower-class personality.

In Levinson and Gallagher's study *Patienthood in a Mental Hospital* (1964), they devote a full chapter to "The Relevance of Social Class." The authors review the literature on class differences in patients' expectations of the therapist, in attitudes toward mental illness, and in the career of hospitalized patients.

Social Welfare

In the field of social welfare we have sampled only a few of the probably relevant studies. In a study of the public's knowledge of, and attitudes toward, social security, Janowitz et al. (1958) found that though the general level of knowledge of rights was quite low, it was particularly low among the lower socioeconomic groups and among blacks (i.e., those most in need of that knowledge). These groups were also least satisfied with government services and had less confidence in the morality of public administration. At the same time, these same groups, ironically, most admired public officials.

In an analysis of nonuse of social welfare services (similar to that of Rosenblatt and Suchman for medical services above), Rosenfeld (1964) concludes that nonusers are typically of lower general social status, and that services are probably not attuned to the expectations and patterns of the social relations that characterize these individuals. In an attempt to clarify the legal issues involved in problems of welfare recipients, Reich (1965) concludes that clients of welfare are seldom in a position to know if they are wrongly treated, and lack both adequate representation and the resources to fight public agencies when necessary. While counterorganization of citizens to fight for their rights vis-à-vis bureaucracy has often been proposed as a partial remedy to such problems (see the section on counterorganization below), there is ample evidence in the literature on voluntary organizations that members of the working class do not join such organizations in any great numbers.[15]

Officials' Response to Clients' Background Characteristics

In the preceding section we showed how social characteristics of clients may influence their own attitudes and behavior in contacts with officials. Here we review evidence that social characteristics of clients may influence officials' response to them (and vice versa). Such latent or role-irrelevant characteristics include friendship, kinship, sex, age, race, class, ethnicity, and religion. Examples of the consequences of the impingement of such characteristics are: (*a*) an official favors a client because they have been friends for twenty years; (*b*) an elderly man is allowed to cash a check without waiting in line; (*c*) a postal clerk is especially friendly to a pretty girl, (*d*) a white waitress refuses to serve a black.

It seems reasonable to argue that whenever client and official are "equals" in one of these latent characteristics, there may be implicit pressure on the official to deviate from organizational norms in the client's favor. Common minority-group membership, for example, may lead to nonbureaucratic behavior.[16] A discrepancy in latent characteristics may, on the other hand, lead to negative discrimination against the client, as in the case of the waitress above.

There are several general discussions of the impingement of latent social identities on official-client relations. Banton (1964) analyzes the need for segregation of the police officer's role in Britain; thus, in Scotland, policemen are forbidden to be politically active in order to prevent the impingement of political influences on their role performance. In an analysis of the dynamics of salesman-customer communication, Evans (1963) notes a case in which the impingement of latent identities may have desirable effects. Similarity of attributes, whether physical build, income, religion, education, personality, politics, or even smoking habits, appears to increase the likelihood of a sale. In the field of social work, Martin (1957) argues that differences of class, race, ethnicity, or religion between caseworker and client constitute barriers to successful casework with delinquents.

Socioeconomic Status

The impingement of the latent social status of both official and client on their role relations is particularly interesting. There are, of course, three possibilities: they are equals; the client enjoys superior general social status; the official is the superior. When the pair are status equals, there is some chance of solidarity and deviation from bureaucratic norms, although, more likely, previous acquaintance or having a mutual friend would also be

[15] See the review article by Hausknecht (1964) on this topic.

[16] A timely example at the writing of this chapter is the anecdote of the Russian soldier who took part in his country's invasion of Czechoslovakia. A fleeing Czech of Jewish origin appealed to let him cross the border; the soldier, admitting that he too was Jewish, allowed the man to cross "illegitimately." An especially noteworthy kind of pressure is what we ordinarily call "pull." This is the conscious manipulation by the client of such role impingement (see Katz & Danet, 1966). Note, however, that even if clients do not consciously attempt to take advantage of these impingements, they may still influence the official in various ways.

necessary. More direct are the effects of a disparity in status. If the official enjoys superior status, the pressure may be to discriminate negatively; on the other hand, if the client is the superior, the pressure may be to grant him favors out of deference.[17]

Merton (1952) notes that tension between officials and clients may be aggravated by ambiguities of status of official and client, particularly when the latter is superior in status. Both Banton (1964) and Falk (1964) discuss the generally low social status of the police as a factor causing tension in public-police relations. Either the status of the organization as a whole (e.g., civil servants) or of particular ranks of officials dealing with specific tasks may be relevant here.

Another way in which status impinges on the official-client dyad is illustrated by relations between police and the working class in Britain. Since the police are more familiar with the life style of the British working class, who typically are more violent in their behavior, they show greater tolerance of certain kinds of misdemeanors among them than when members of the middle class are involved. For example, the police would be less likely to arrest a lower-class husband who beat his wife than a middle-class one (Banton, 1964).

In the field of mental health, a client's class impinges on officials in several ways. First of all, there are several studies showing that members of the lower class are *less often accepted* for therapy (Myers & Schaffer, 1954; Hollingshead & Redlich, 1958; Levinson & Gallagher, 1964; Brill & Storrow, 1965). Second, Myers and Schaffer found that lower-class patients were disproportionately assigned relatively low-status therapists (i.e., younger, those with less training, experience); however, no such relation was found in a similar study by Brill and Storrow.

Haase (1965) reports that the socio-economic status of a patient also affects diagnosis. Levinson and Gallagher review the ways in which class affects the patient's course of progress, although it does not necessarily directly influence staff response; rather, in part, the channels by which members of the various classes arrive at the hospital differ. These same authors also note that private mental hospitals typically have staff and patients of the same social status; some patients may manipulate their equal status with the psychiatrist to develop a friendship and use him as a provider of special services.

We have found only a few studies of the impingement of a client's class in other areas. In social work, Rein (1965) suggests that public welfare agencies ironically seek to avoid lower-class clients because the middle-class values of workers lead them to see dependency as a morally undesirable state. In the sphere of religion, Cumming and Harrington (1963) analyze the role of the clergyman as counselor. Among other things, they conclude that conflicts in the role of clergyman may be the product of differences in educational level or social-class identification of the clergyman and his congregation.

In yet another area, Gold (1951) studied janitors whose income was higher than that of their middle-class tenants. One "solution" to the dilemma caused by this situation was to emphasize the professional aspects of janitorial work. Kearney and Harris (1967) found, in their study of the civil service in Ceylon, that the latent caste of the official influenced clients' response to him. An unusual impingement of status is seen in the dilemma of the navy disbursing officer who is caught between pressure to conform to regulations on the one hand, and pressure to grant superior officers favors on the other (Turner, 1952).

[17] An example of the first case is the middle-class social worker who must avoid being patronizing toward his lower-class client. And a classic example of the second is the dilemma of the policeman who must give a traffic ticket to a distinguished public figure, such as a politician or a famous author.

Ethnicity

There appear to be fewer studies of the impingement of client's ethnicity or subcultural memberships on communication with officials. Lieberson (1958) analyzed the factors that determine the choice of a physician in Chicago. Among them was ethnicity—physicians of given ethnic groups tended to distribute themselves spatially where members of their own ethnic group lived. In a study of doctor-patient relations in national health service clinics in Israel, Shuval (1962) found that physicians, accepting a norm held in the wider society, discriminated against patients of North African origin. As reported in the section on size of organization, the larger the clinic, the greater the amount of discrimination, thus suggesting that under certain conditions bureaucratization may actually decrease universalism.

Race

Most discussions of the effects of race on contacts are in the field of social work. Brown (1950), Curry (1964), Fibush (1965), and Gochros (1966) all call for greater awareness of the significance of the racial factor in establishing a successful relationship. The articles are, on the whole, purely theoretical. Bradley (1966), on the other hand, presents research findings from a very specific setting, adoption agencies. In a study of caseworkers' perceptions of adoptive applicants in eight agencies in New York City, she found that among couples applying to adopt a child, the percentage of black couples accepted was lower than among the whites, and that the proportion of blacks who withdrew their application, although judged good prospects for adoptive parenthood, outweighed the proportion of acceptable white couples who withdrew. These agencies were *not* aware that they were discriminating against blacks. As for the withdrawal rate, it might be explained by the discomfort of the black couples in the bureaucratized middle-class setting.

In his study of public-police relations, Banton (1964) noted that in the southern United States a black might be let off for attacking another man, although a similar offense by a white would lead to an arrest. In part this is, as mentioned above, tolerance for the culture of particular groups. Banton cites the opposite possibility also: typically it is the case of police brutality where white policemen are excessively cruel to blacks.

Sex

Two examples of the impingement of a person's sex are those of Whyte (1948) and Williams (1950). Whyte analyzed the reasons for conflict in the role of waitress in the restaurant industry. There was a structured conflict to begin with, since waitresses gave orders to higher-status cooks, a reversal of the usual flow of demand in organizations. But the tension was exacerbated by the fact that a woman was giving the orders. Williams' article is an analysis of the special problems of the woman physician.

SITUATIONAL FACTORS

Intervening between the actual outcomes of bureaucratic contact and the three sets of predisposing factors outlined above is a series of variables characterizing the immediate context in which contact takes place. This aspect of official-client communication appears, unfortunately, to be the least researched, consequently our discussion in this brief section will be more programmatic than in preceding ones.

One key variable is whether contact is voluntary or mandatory. A citizen *must* pay his income tax but he may choose his insurance agent or his doctor. We may hypothesize that, other things being equal, the more compulsory the contact, the more potential there is for hostility and lack of cooperation on the part of the client.[18]

Another situational variable is the channel or medium of contact—is it face-to-face or is it indirect, that is, through the mail or by telephone? The channel may have implications for consequences of interaction, particularly for clients' and workers' satisfaction or feelings of alienation or powerlessness.

When contact is face-to-face, the cluster of variables called "setting" comes into play. The "props" of interaction, and the intricacies of impression management, are a favorite topic of Goffman (1959), although these speculations have not led to much systematic research. Lombard (1955), for one, has noted the function of counters between salespeople and their customers—they make it easier for the former to control the relationship.

Other questions that might be asked are: Does the official come to the client's home, where he is "king," or must the client go to the organization, where the official feels the stronger? Is contact private? And if it takes place on the official's territory, are there partitions or walls which guarantee privacy, or do officials receive several clients at a time?

Still another situational variable is the accessibility of officials—how far must clients travel to see them? Are office hours convenient? Are there long lines, or is business done by appointment?

Stinchcombe (1963) has made a theoretical analysis of the differences in police practices according to whether crimes are committed in public or private places. Also in the realm of the police, Banton (1964) has described the special characteristics of police work owing to the presence of physical danger. Another situational factor in police work is the fact that the policeman on the street often makes decisions without the supervision of superiors: he is literally alone on the job.

Isolation from the normal web of social life introduces special conditions of its own, in which "latent social identities" may influence interpersonal relationships (Gouldner, 1957; 1958). It is a strong force toward increased diffuseness of role relations, since officials and clients are dependent upon each other for human contact above and beyond the requirements of their respective roles. Katz and Eisenstadt (1960) have reviewed a number of studies which show how these factors lead to debureaucratization of role relations. Lipset, Trow, and Coleman (1956), for example, have described how the isolation and unusual hours that characterize the working conditions of printers foster unusual solidarity among them. The effects of isolation aboard ship on its crew are still more complex. Isolation is functional for instrumental purposes; there are no distractions from normal routine. At the same time, crew members are dependent on one another for friendship. Thus Berkman (1946) has shown how the crew of an armed-guard ship, strictly organized when at sea, disintegrates as a social unit when the ship comes into port.

As for the effects of timing, particularly the variables of frequency and duration of contact between officials and clients, we have come across a few relevant studies. Fred Davis (1959) analyzed the unique characteristics of the relationship between cabdrivers and their fares; the fact that such relationships are fleeting, one-time affairs causes tensions which the passenger tries to resolve by tipping. Paul Cressey (1932), in an early descriptive study of taxi-dance halls, showed somewhat similar tensions in a fragmentary contractual relationship. Lennard and Bernstein (1960) have shown that with repeated contact over time, psychotherapists and their patients become increasingly more alike in verbal behavior.

---

[18] The mandatory-voluntary distinction is one of the dimensions on which Thompson (1962) bases his typology of organizations.

IMPROVING OFFICIAL-CLIENT COMMUNICATION

Need for Control of Bureaucracy

The theme of bureaucracy as a social problem, a problem for the public in particular, is threaded throughout this chapter. As was noted above, organizations are growing both in size and number, and they are constantly becoming more specialized. Downs (1967) cites evidence that the proportion of the labor force employed in bureaucracies has risen steadily since 1900. The two major consequences of these trends are the rise of concentrations of power, and the transformation of interpersonal relations. Aspects of the latter of these two consequences have been reviewed above in the discussion of bureaucratization and personality, in the sections on attitudes and knowledge of clients, and on class and subcultural variations. We turn now to the problem of concentrations of power, which raises issues beyond that of the alienation of the individual citizen.

Many writers have seen an inherent contradiction between the principles of bureaucracy and of democracy. Nisbet (1966: chap. 4) shows that Tocqueville, Weber, and Michels saw the problem although each approached it differently. Among more contemporary authors, Bendix (1952), Blau (1955), and Goodman (1965) all discuss the problem in general terms. A collection of papers on this theme edited by Charlesworth (1954) pays surprisingly little attention to the problems of the individual client. Blau notes the existence of a paradox: On the one hand, bureaucracy is a mechanism for goal attainment that stresses hierarchy in order to maximize efficiency. On the other hand, democracy requires the participation of all, primarily in the determination of the goals to be pursued but also in the supervision or *control* of the activities of bureaucracy. The question becomes, *Who* shall control bureaucracy and *how*?

The problem cuts across both the public and private sectors of modern or modernizing societies. In the private sector, despite the presence of competition, there is a felt need to protect the consumer against big business. Etzioni (1958) discusses this problem. The need for mechanisms of control by clients is much greater in the public sector, however. Indeed, most of the literature on the problem deals explicitly with government bureaucracy. Among students of public administration we find eloquent critiques of government bureaucracy (Finer, 1931; E. Strauss, 1961; Peabody & Rourke, 1965; Rourke, 1965: chap. 5).

Not every student of bureaucracy thinks bureaucracy is necessarily "bad" for society and/or for individuals. Gouldner (1955) has taken a more skeptical position. And most recently Downs (1967) has suggested that freedom of the individual has two meanings: (*a*) power of choice; (*b*) absence of restraint. Thus, while bureaucratization has brought increased restraints in the form of rules, taxes, forms, etc., it is also associated with a greater power of choice—the individual has more alternatives from which to choose.

This is not the place to resolve these issues. Suffice it to say that, although the psychological and social consequences of bureaucratization have not yet been specified adequately, the need is often felt for mechanisms to strengthen the position of the individual vis-à-vis bureaucracy. This is particularly evident in the problem of the lower classes in dealing with bureaucracy. We formulate the tentative hypothesis that strengthening the power position of the client may have the positive side effect of diminishing the negative effects of the bureaucratization of interpersonal relations. That is, a client who feels strong in the knowledge of his rights and obligations and the procedures involved in obtaining them will not be so disturbed by the need to be impersonal in contacts with officials. We turn now to a brief review of some of the innovations that have been introduced in recent years to meet this need.

Institutional Innovations

Better Socialization

One way to strengthen clients is by means of more adequate bureaucratic socialization—to improve the client's knowledge of his rights and obligations. This is more difficult than it sounds, since in many cases—as is known from the study of information campaigns—those sectors of the population most in need of information are either least exposed to it or least capable of learning or understanding it. Moreover, it can be argued that in many cases it is probably the organizations that require change, not their clients.

Another approach, then, is to improve the socialization of officials. Ahmad (1964) describes such an effort by the government of Pakistan to change the attitudes of civil servants toward the public to a more democratic service orientation. Rubin (1958) has described information campaigns of the State of New York that were designed to strengthen the citizen. Gellhorn (1966b) reviews a number of information-spreading devices, including the establishment of Citizens' Advice Bureaus in England. Research is badly needed to study the effectiveness of such information campaigns. More studies along the lines of those by Seeman (1966) are needed, as well as before-and-after studies of effects of exposure to information.

Counterorganization

One remedy for the weakness of the individual in mass society is for individuals to counterorganize. This, of course, is the raison d'être of unions and other types of professional associations. We reviewed Seeman's work above, which demonstrates that union members feel less powerless about work-related matters than do nonmembers. Tannenbaum (1965) describes the grievance procedures instituted by unions for the benefit of their members, and summarizes research findings on other positive effects of union membership on workers.

There is little or no research on counterorganization among clients of nonmember-beneficiary organizations. The idea is not altogether new. There are users' organizations and consumers' cooperatives designed to protect the interests of consumers vis-à-vis producers and marketers. A newer phenomenon is the rise of block clubs in the large cities of the United States. Neighbors band together to strengthen their bargaining position vis-à-vis landlords and municipalities in preserving and improving the physical and social character of their neighborhood (Cousens, 1964; S. M. Miller, 1964).

Structural Changes within the Organization

It is interesting to note that certain students of bureaucracy suggest that the ills of bureaucracy are better corrected by more, not less, bureaucracy. For those whose major concern is the inefficiency, red tape, and dissatisfaction and conflict resulting from bureaucratic contacts, the answer given is often increased centralization within the organization, or more formality and greater specificity in relations with clients. In contrast, the humanists concerned with the alienating effects of life in mass society want less bureaucracy. For them the need to "correct" the structure of interpersonal relations in bureaucracy is paramount. Thus they argue for *decentralization* in order to restore autonomy and initiative in the instrumental aspects of bureaucratic activities, and the personal touch in the expressive aspects. While Erich Strauss (1961) calls for decentralization as one of a series of remedies of government bureaucracy, the most outspoken crusader on this topic is perhaps Paul Goodman (1965).

Mediating Mechanisms Between Clients and Organizations

Some of the studies cited above have shown how there may be a need for a mediator or go-between between official and client wherever there is a cultural gap between the two. Simmons (1955) showed that when nurses in a Chilean health clinic stopped mediating between patients and their doctors, the relationship broke down. Rosenblatt and Suchman (1964b), concerned with the underutilization of medical services by the lower class and other ethnic groups, describe the use of "health visitors" among the Navaho Indians—these are Navahos with limited training in Western medicine who serve as translators, advance contacts, and cultural bridges. Another trend is what Cloward and Elman (1966) have called "advocacy in the ghetto." Social workers in a youth rehabilitation project became representatives of their clients in their dealings with relevant bureaucracies and at the same time tried to teach their clients their rights. Eventually the informal arrangements were institutionalized.

Note that while in most instances the need is to bring the client closer to the organization, in the case of total institutions it may be to break down the isolation between the organization and the community. The isolation of mental hospitals from the community is dysfunctional for patients' recovery as was suggested earlier in this chapter (see Schwartz, Schwartz, et al., 1964). Another illustration of bridging the gap between an organization and the public is the use of volunteers in the Soviet Union to fulfill some functions of the police (Wesson, 1964).

The letters-to-the-editor columns in newspapers serve an important mediating function, offering citizens the opportunity to air their complaints against organizations that have maltreated them. Inkeles and Geiger (1952) did a content analysis of letters to the editor in Russian newspapers. In other countries, too, such letters seem to serve as a means of social control. Of course, it is difficult to know whether newspapers are biased in the selection of letters chosen to be published; nevertheless, it would be interesting to follow up on the response of the institutions involved. An exception to this is the more active role played by the newspapers in investigating citizens' complaints in Poland (see Gellhorn, 1966b). Certain radio stations have assumed this role in the United States and Israel.

Of course letter writing to political officeholders is an established channel of complaint. An analysis of letters to Franklin Roosevelt during the 1930s was done by Leila Sussman (1963). Letters to congressmen in Washington are numerous, and congressmen frequently become mediators for the interests of individual constituents (Gellhorn, 1966b).

Generally, there is a need to improve and expand the channels of complaint available to clients. Gellhorn (1966b) provides a comprehensive review of the various grievance procedures and channels of complaints available in the United States today. Roth (1965) has analyzed why dissatisfied consumers hesitate to complain and calls for improvements.

The most dramatic and attention-catching innovation of all is probably that of the *ombudsman*. Originating in Scandinavian countries, this is a state-appointed role charged with investigating the complaints of citizens about treatment in public bureaucracy. Typically, the ombudsman is a respected citizen, perhaps a retired lawyer or judge, and is independent of both the bureaucratic hierarchy and of the political machinery of government. Rowat (1965) and Gellhorn (1966a) offer book-length treatments of the topic. Rowat's book is a collection of articles on the ombudsman in various countries, while Gellhorn's is a systematic comparison of the institution in nine countries. In a companion volume, Gellhorn (1966b) calls for the institutionalization of an ombudsman in the United States. This institution may prove to be one of the most effective of a growing number of procedures for strengthening the position of the individual citizen in a heavily bureaucratized society. For a more up-to-date overview of our thinking on problems of communication between bureaucracy and the public, see Katz and Danet (1972).

REFERENCES

Abegglen, J. G.
1958 The Japanese Factory. Glencoe, Illinois: Free Press.

Ahmad, Mushtag.
1964 The Civil Servant in Pakistan. London: Oxford University Press.

Almond, Gabriel A., and Harold D. Lasswell.
1934 "Aggressive behavior by clients toward public relief administrators." American Political Science Review 28:643–655.

Aubert, Vilhelm, and Oddvar Arner.
1958 "On the social structure of the ship." Acta Sociologica 3:200–219.

Banton, Michael.
1964 The Policeman in the Community. London: Tavistock.

Barton, Allen H., and S. Mendlovitz.
1960 "The experience of injustice as a research problem." Journal of Legal Education 13:24–30.

Bar-Yosef, Rivka, and E. O. Schild.
1966 "Pressures and defenses in bureaucratic roles." American Journal of Sociology 71:665–673.

Ben-David, Joseph.
1958 "The professional role of the physician in bureaucratized medicine." Human Relations 11:255–274.

Bendix, Reinhard.
1952 "Bureaucracy and the problem of power." Pp. 114–134 in Robert K. Merton et al. (eds.), Reader in Bureaucracy. Glencoe, Illinois: Free Press.

Bensman, Joseph, and Bernard Rosenberg.
1960 "The meaning of work in bureaucratic society." Pp. 181–197 in Maurice R. Stein et al. (eds.), Identity and Anxiety: Survival of the Person in Mass Society. New York: Free Press of Glencoe.

Berger, Morroe.
1957 Bureaucracy and Society in Modern Egypt: A Study of the Higher Civil Service. Princeton, New Jersey: Princeton University Press.

Berk, Bernard B.
1966 "Organizational goals and inmate organization." American Journal of Sociology 71:522–534.

Berkman, Paul L.
1946 "Life aboard an armed-guard ship." American Journal of Sociology 51: 380–387.

Biddle, B. J.; H. A. Rosencranz; E. Tomich; and J. P. Twyman.
1966 "Shared inaccuracies in the role of the teacher." Pp. 302–310 in B. J. Biddle and E. J. Thomas (eds.), Role Theory: Concepts and Research. New York: Wiley.

Bidwell, C. E.
1965 "The school as a formal organization." Pp. 972–1022 in J. G. March (ed.), Handbook of Organizations. Chicago: Rand McNally.

Bidwell, C. E., and Rebecca Vreeland.
1964 "Authority and control in client-serving organizations." Sociological Quarterly 4:231–242.

Blau, Peter M.
1955 Dynamics of Bureaucracy. Chicago: University of Chicago Press.
1960 "Orientation toward clients in a public welfare agency." Administrative Science Quarterly 5:341–361.

Blau, Peter M., and W. R. Scott.
1962 Formal Organizations. San Francisco: Chandler.

Block, Jeanne, and Jack Block.
1952 "An interpersonal experiment on reactions to authority." Human Relations 5:91–98.

Bloom, S. W.
1965 The Doctor and His Patient. New York: Free Press.

Blum, R. H.
1960 The Management of the Doctor-Patient Relationship. New York: McGraw-Hill.

Borgatta, E. F.; David Fanshel; and H. J. Meyer.
1960 Social Workers' Perceptions of Clients: A Study of the Caseload of a Social Agency. New York: Russell Sage.

Bowman, T. R.
1963 "Participation of superintendents in school board decision-making." Administrator's Notebook 11:1–4.

Bradburn, N. F.
1963 "Interpersonal relations within formal organizations in Turkey." Journal of Social Issues 19:61–67.

Bradley, Trudy.
1966 "An exploration of caseworkers' perceptions of adoptive applicants." Child Welfare 45:433–443.

Brill, N. Q., and H. A. Storrow.
1965 "Social class and psychiatric treatment." Pp. 68–75 in Frank Riessman et al. (eds.), Mental Health of the Poor. New York: Free Press.

Brown, Luna B.
1950 "Race as a factor in establishing a casework relationship." Social Casework 31:91–97.

Burchard, W. W.
1954 "Role conflicts of military chaplains." American Sociological Review 19:528–535.

Cartwright, Ann.
1967 Patients and Their Doctors: A Study of General Practice. New York: Atherton Press.

Catrice-Lorey, Antoinette.
1966 "Social security and its relations with beneficiaries: The problem of bureaucracy in social administration." Bulletin of International Social Security Association 19:286–297.

Caudill, William.
1958 The Psychiatric Hospital as a Small Society. Cambridge, Massachusetts: Harvard University Press.
1961 "Around-the-clock patient care in Japanese psychiatric hospitals—the role of the Tsukisoi." American Sociological Review 26:643–655.

Charlesworth, James C. (ed.).
1954 Bureaucracy and Democratic Government. Annals of the American Academy of Political and Social Science 292(March).

Cloward, R. A., and R. M. Elman.
1966 "Advocacy in the ghetto." Transaction 4(December):27–35.

Cobb, Beatrix.
1958 "Why do people detour to quacks?" Pp. 283–287 in E. G. Jaco (ed.), Patients, Physicians and Illness. Glencoe, Illinois: Free Press.

Corwin, R. G.
1961 "The professional employee: A study of conflict in nursing roles." American Journal of Sociology 66:604–615.

Coser, Rose L.
1963 "Alienation and the social structure: Case analysis of a hospital." Pp. 231–265 in Eliot Freidson (ed.), The Hospital in Modern Society. New York: Free Press of Glencoe.

Cousens, F. R.
1964 "Indigenous leadership in two lower-class neighborhood organizations." Pp. 225–234 in Arthur B. Shostak and William Gomberg (eds.), Blue-Collar World: Studies of the American Worker. Englewood Cliffs, New Jersey: Prentice-Hall.

Cressey, D. R.
1965 "Prison organizations." Pp. 1023–1070 in J. G. March (ed.), Handbook of Organizations. Chicago: Rand McNally.

Cressey, Paul G.
1932 Taxi-Dance Hall. Chicago: University of Chicago Press.

Croog, Sidney H.
1963 "Interpersonal relations in medical settings." Pp. 241–271 in H. E. Freeman, Sol Levine, and L. G. Reeder (eds.), Handbook of Medical Sociology. Englewood Cliffs, New Jersey: Prentice-Hall.

Crowne, D. B.
1966 "Family orientation, level of aspiration, and interpersonal bargaining." Journal of Personality and Social Psychology 36:641–645.

Cumming, Elaine; I. M. Cumming; and L. Edelle.
1965 "The policeman as philosopher, guide and friend." Social Problems 12(Winter):276-286.

Cumming, Elaine, and Charles Harrington.
1963 "Clergyman as counselor." American Journal of Sociology 69:234–243.

Curry, A. E.
1964 "The negro worker and the white client: A commentary on the treatment relationship." Social Casework 45:131–136.

Daniels, M. J.
1960 "Affect and its control in the medical intern." American Journal of Sociology 66:259–267.

Davis, Fred.
1959 "The cabdriver and his fare: Facets of a fleeting relationship." American Journal of Sociology 65:158–165.

Davis, Milton S.
1968 "Variations in patients' compliance with doctor's advice: An empirical analysis of patterns of communication." American Journal of Public Health 58:274–288.

Dinitz, Simon; Shirley Angrist; Mark Lefton; and Benjamin Pasamanick.
1966 "Instrumental role expectations and posthospital performance of female mental patients." Pp. 338–343 in B. J. Biddle and E. J. Thomas (eds.), Role Theory: Concepts and Research. New York: Wiley.

Dornbusch, Sanford M.
1955 "The military academy as an assimilating institution." Social Forces 33:316–321.

Downs, Anthony.
1967 Inside Bureaucracy. Boston: Little, Brown.

Eaton, Joseph W.
1959 "The client-practitioner relationship as a variable in the evaluation of treatment outcome." Psychiatry 22: 189–195.

Eisenstadt, S. N.
1959 "Bureaucracy, bureaucratization and debureaucratization." Administrative Science Quarterly 4:302–320.

Eldersveld, S. J.
1965 "Bureaucratic contact with the public in India." Indian Journal of Public Administration 12:216–235.

Etzioni, Amitai.
1958 "Administration and the consumer." Administrative Science Quarterly 3:251–264.
1961 A Comparative Analysis of Complex Organizations. New York: Free Press of Glencoe.
1965 "Organizational control structure." Pp. 650–677 in J. G. March (ed.), Handbook of Organizations. Chicago: Rand McNally.

Evans, Frank B.
1963 "Selling as a dyadic relationship—a new approach." American Behavioral Scientist 5:76–79.

Falk, G. J.
1964 "The public's prejudice against the police." American Bar Association Journal 50:754–757.

Fallers, Lloyd A.
1965 Bantu Bureaucracy. Chicago: University of Chicago Press.

Feldman, Jacob. J
1966 The Dissemination of Health Information. Chicago: Aldine.

Ferguson, R. S.
1958 "The doctor-patient relationship and 'functional' illness." Pp. 433–439 in E. G. Jaco (ed.), Patients, Physicians, and Illness. Glencoe, Illinois: Free Press.

Fibush, Esther W.
1965 "The white worker and the Negro client." Social Casework 46:271–277.

Field, Mark G.
1953 "Structured strain in the role of the Soviet physician." American Journal of Sociology 58:493–502.

Finer, Herman.
1931 "Officials and the public." Public Administration 9:23–36.

Francis, R. G., and R. C. Stone.
1956 Service and Procedure in Bureaucracy. Minneapolis: University of Minnesota Press.

Freidson, Eliot.
1960 "Client control and medical practice." American Journal of Sociology 65: 374–382.
1961 Patients' Views of Medical Practice. New York: Russell Sage.
1963 "The organization of medical practice." Pp. 299–320 in H. E. Freeman, Sol Levine, and L. G. Reeder (eds.), Handbook of Medical Sociology. Englewood Cliffs, New Jersey: Prentice-Hall.

Friedl, Ernestine.
1958 "Hospital care in provincial Greece." Human Organization 16:24–27.

Gellhorn, Walter.
1966a Ombudsmen and Others: Citizens' Protectors in Nine Countries. Cambridge, Massachusetts: Harvard University Press.
1966b When Americans Complain: Governmental Grievance Procedures. Cambridge, Massachusetts: Harvard University Press.

Gochros, J. S.
1966 "Recognition and use of anger in

Negro clients." Social Work 11: 28–34.

Goffman, Erving.
1959 Presentation of Self in Everyday Life. Garden City, New York: Doubleday Anchor.
1961 Asylums: Essays on the Social Situation of Mental Patients and Other Inmates. Garden City, New York: Doubleday Anchor.

Gold, Ray.
1951 "Janitors vs. tenants: A status-income dilemma." American Journal of Sociology 57:486–493.

Goodman, Paul.
1965 People or Personnel: Decentralizing and the Mixed System. New York: Random House.

Goss, Mary E. W.
1961 "Influence and authority among physicians in an out-patient clinic." American Sociological Review 26: 39–50.

Gouldner, Alvin.
1952 "Red tape as a social problem." Pp. 410–419 in Robert Merton et al. (eds.), Reader in Bureaucracy. Glencoe, Illinois: Free Press.
1955 "Metaphysical pathos and the theory of bureaucracy." American Political Science Review 49:496–507.
1957 "Cosmopolitans and locals: Toward an analysis of latent social roles—I." Administrative Science Quarterly 2(December):281–306.
1958 "Cosmopolitans and locals: Toward an analysis of latent social roles—II." Administrative Science Quarterly 2(March):444–480.

Graham, Saxon.
1958 "Socio-economic status, illness, and the use of medical services." Pp. 129–134 in E. G. Jaco (ed.), Patients, Physicians and Illness. Glencoe, Illinois: Free Press.

Gross, Neal C.; W. S. Mason; and A. W. McEachern.
1957 Explorations in Role Analysis. New York: Wiley.

Grusky, Oscar.
1959a "Role conflict in organization: A study of prison camp officials." Administrative Science Quarterly 3(March):452–472.
1959b "Organizational goals and the behavior of informal leaders." American Journal of Sociology 65:59–67.

Guttman, Louis, and Uriel Foa.
1951 "Social contact and an interpersonal attitude." Public Opinion Quarterly 15(No. 1):43–53.

Haase, William.
1965 "The role of socio-economic class in examiner bias." Pp. 241–247 in Frank Riessman et al. (eds.), Mental Health of the Poor. New York: Free Press.

Hall, Edward T.
1959 The Silent Language. Garden City, New York: Doubleday.

Hare, A. P.
1962 Handbook of Small Groups Research. New York: Free Press of Glencoe.

Hausknecht, Murray.
1964 "The blue-collar joiner." Pp. 207–215 in A. B. Shostak and William Gomberg (eds.), Blue-Collar World: Studies of the American Worker. Englewood Cliffs, New Jersey: Prentice-Hall.

Heine, Ralph W., and Harry Trosman, M.D.
1960 "Initial expectations of the doctor-patient interaction as a factor in continuance in psychotherapy." Psychiatry 23:275–278.

Hoggart, Richard.
1961 The Uses of Literacy. Boston: Beacon Press.

Hollingshead, A. B., and F. C. Redlich.
1958 Social Class and Mental Illness. New York: Wiley.

Inkeles, Alex, and H. Kent Geiger.
1952 "Critical letters to the editor of the Soviet press: Areas and modes of complaint." American Sociological Review 17:694–703.

Janowitz, Morris, and William Delany.
1957 "The bureaucrat and the public: A study of informational perspectives." Administrative Science Quarterly 2:141–162.

Janowitz, Morris, et al.
1958 Public Administration and the Public. Ann Arbor: University of Michigan Institute of Public Administration.

Kadushin, Charles.
1962 "Social distance between client and

professional." American Journal of Sociology 67:517–531.

Kahne, M. J.
1959 "Bureaucratic structure and impersonal experience in mental hospitals." Psychiatry 22:363–375.

Katz, Elihu, and Brenda Danet.
1966 "Petitions and persuasive appeals: A study of official-client relations." American Sociological Review 31:811–822.

Katz, Elihu, and Brenda Danet (eds.).
1972 Bureaucracy and the Public: A Reader in Official-Client Relations. New York: Basic Books.

Katz, Elihu, and S. N. Eisenstadt.
1960 "Some sociological observations on the response of Israeli organizations to new immigrants." Administrative Science Quarterly 5:113–133.

Kearney, R. N., and R. L. Harris.
1967 "Bureaucracy and environment in Ceylon." Pp. 306–324 in Nimrod Raphaeli (ed.), Readings in Comparative Public Administration. Boston: Allyn and Bacon.

Kiani, Acquilla.
1962 "People's image of bureaucracy." Pp. 377–398 in Inayatullah (ed.), Bureaucracy and Development in Pakistan. Peshawar, Academy Town: Pakistan Academy for Rural Development.

Kluckhohn, Florence R., and Fred L. Strodtbeck.
1961 Variations in Value Orientations. Evanston, Illinois: Row Peterson.

Koos, Earl.
1958 "Metropolis—what city people think of their medical services." Pp. 113–119 in E. G. Jaco (ed.), Patients, Physicians and Illness. Glencoe, Illinois: Free Press.

Kutner, Bernard.
1958 "Surgeons and their patients: A study in social perceptions." Pp. 384–397 in E. G. Jaco (ed.), Patients, Physicians and Illness. Glencoe, Illinois: Free Press.

LaPalombara, Joseph G. (ed.).
1963 Bureaucracy and Political Development. Princeton, New Jersey: Princeton University Press.

Lefton, Mark, and William R. Rosengren.
1966 "Organizations and clients: Lateral and longitudinal dimensions." American Sociological Review 31:802–810.

Lennard, Henry L., and Arnold Bernstein.
1960 The Anatomy of Psychotherapy. New York: Columbia University Press.

Levinson, Daniel J., and Eugene B. Gallagher.
1964 Patienthood in the Mental Hospital. Boston: Houghton Mifflin.

Liberman, Robert.
1965 "Personal influence in the use of mental health resources." Human Organization 24:231–235.

Lieberson, Stanley.
1958 "Ethnic groups and the practice of medicine." American Sociological Review 23:542–549.

Lipset, Seymour; Martin A. Trow; and James S. Coleman.
1956 Union Democracy. Glencoe, Illinois: Free Press.

Little, Roger W.
1956 "The 'sick' soldier and the medical ward officer." Human Organization 15:22–24.

Litwak, Eugene, and Henry J. Meyer.
1966 "A balance theory of coordination between bureaucratic organizations and community primary groups." Administrative Science Quarterly 11(June):31–58.

Lombard, George F.
1955 Behavior in a Selling Group. Cambridge, Massachusetts: Harvard University Press.

Longabaugh, Richard; S. Eldred; Norman Bell; and L. Sherman.
1966 "The interactional world of the chronic schizophrenic patient." Psychiatry 29:78–99.

McCleery, Richard H.
1961 "The governmental process and informal social control." Pp. 149–188 in D. R. Cressey (ed.), The Prison: Studies in Institutional Organization and Change. New York: Holt, Rinehart and Winston.

March, James G. (ed.).
1965 Handbook of Organizations. Chicago: Rand McNally.

Martin, J. M.
1957 "Socio-cultural differences: Barriers in casework with delinquents." Social Work 2:22–25.

Mayer, J. E., and Aaron Rosenblatt.
1964 "The client's social context: Its effect on continuance in treatment." Social Casework 45:511–518.

Mechanic, David.
1961 "Role expectations and communication in the therapist-patient relationship." Journal of Health and Human Behavior 2:190–198.

Merton, Robert K.
1952 "Bureaucratic structure and personality." Pp. 361–371 in Robert K. Merton et al. (eds.), Reader in Bureaucracy. Glencoe, Illinois: Free Press.

Milgram, Stanley.
1965 "Some conditions of obedience and disobedience to authority." Human Relations 18:57–76.

Miller, D. R., and G. E. Swanson.
1958 The Changing American Parent. New York: Wiley.

Miller, S. M.
1964 "Some thought on reform." Pp. 298–306 in A. B. Shostak and William Gomberg (eds.), Blue-Collar World: Studies of the American Worker. Englewood Cliffs, New Jersey: Prentice-Hall.

Mills, C. Wright.
1956 White Collar. New York: Oxford University Press.

Mitchell, Jack N.
1966 "Cons, square-johns, and rehabilitation." Pp. 207–212 in B. J. Biddle and E. J. Thomas(eds.), Role Theory: Concepts and Problems. New York: Wiley.

Myers, J. K., and Leslie Schaffer.
1954 "Social stratification and psychiatric practice: A study of an out-patient clinic." American Sociological Review 19:307–310.

Naegle, K. D.
1956 "Clergymen, teachers and psychiatrists: A study in roles and socialization." Canadian Journal of Economics and Political Science 22:46–62.

Nisbet, R. A.
1966 The Sociological Tradition. New York: Basic Books.

Overall, Betty, and H. Aronson.
1965 "Expectations of psychotherapy in patients of lower socio-economic class." Pp. 76–87 in Frank Riessman et al. (eds.), Mental Health of the Poor. New York: Free Press.

Peabody, R. L., and F. E. Rourke.
1965 "Public bureaucracies." Pp. 802–837 in J. G. March (ed.), Handbook of Organizations. Chicago: Rand McNally.

Pearlin, Leonard, and Morris Rosenberg.
1962 "Nurse-patient social distance and the structural context of a mental hospital." American Sociological Review 27:56–65.

Perrow, Charles.
1965 "Hospitals: Technology, structure, and goals." Pp. 910–971 in J. G. March (ed.), Handbook of Organizations. Chicago: Rand McNally.

Pratt, Lois; Arthur Seligmann; and George Reader.
1958 "Physicians' views on the level of medical information among patients." Pp. 222–229 in E. G. Jaco (ed.), Patients, Physicians, and Illness. Glencoe, Illinois: Free Press.

Presthus, Robert V.
1959 "Social bases of bureaucratic organizations." Social Forces 38:103–109.
1965 The Organizational Society. New York: Vintage Books.

Reich, Charles A.
1965 "Individual rights and social welfare: The emerging legal issues." Yale Law Journal 74:1245–1257.

Rein, Martin.
1965 "The strange case of public dependency." Trans-action 2(No. 3):16–23.

Richardson, Stephen A.
1956 "Organizational contrasts on British and American ships." Administrative Science Quarterly 1:189–207.

Riessman, Frank, and S. M. Miller.
1965 "Social class and projective tests." Pp. 248–258 in Frank Riessman et al. (eds.), Mental Health of the Poor. New York: Free Press.

Riggs, Fred W.
1967 "The 'sala' model: An ecological approach to the study of comparative administration." Pp. 412–432 in Nimrod Raphaeli (ed.), Readings in Comparative Public Administration. Boston: Allyn and Bacon.

Rosenberg, Morris, and Leonard I. Pearlin.
1962 "Power orientations in the mental

hospital." Human Relations 15:335–350.

Rosenblatt, Daniel, and Edward A. Suchman.
1964a "Blue-collar attitudes and information toward health and illness." Pp. 324–333 in A. B. Shostak and William Gomberg (eds.), Blue-Collar World: Studies of the American Worker. Englewood Cliffs, New Jersey: Prentice-Hall.
1964b "The underutilization of medical care services by blue-collarites." Pp. 341–349 in A. B. Shostak and William Gomberg (eds.), Blue-Collar World: Studies of the American Worker. Englewood Cliffs, New Jersey: Prentice-Hall.

Rosenfeld, Jonah M.
1964 "Strangeness between helper and client: A possible explanation of non-use of available professional help." Social Service Review 38:17–25.

Roth, Julius.
1963 "Information and the control of treatment in tuberculosis hospitals." Pp. 293–318 in Eliot Freidson (ed.), The Hospital in Modern Society. New York: Free Press of Glencoe.
1965 "Who's complaining: The inhibitions of the dissatisfied consumer." Trans-action 2(No. 5):12–16.

Rourke, Francis E. (ed.).
1965 Bureaucratic Power in National Politics. Boston: Little, Brown.

Rowat, Donald C. (ed.).
1965 The Ombudsman: Citizen and Defender. London: Allen and Unwin.

Rubin, Bernard.
1958 Public Relations and the Empire State: A Case Study of New York State Administration, 1943–1954. New Brunswick, New Jersey: Rutgers University Press.

Rubington, Earl.
1965 "Organizational strains and key roles." Administrative Science Quarterly 9:350–369.

Saunders, Lyle.
1954 Cultural Difference and Medical Care: The Case of the Spanish-Speaking People of the Southwest. New York: Russell Sage.

Schwartz, Morris S.; Charlotte R. Schwartz; and others.
1964 Social Approaches to Mental Patient Care. New York: Columbia University Press.

Seeman, Melvin.
1966 "Alienation, membership and political knowledge: A comparative study." Public Opinion Quarterly 30(Fall):353–367.

Seeman, Melvin, and John W. Evans.
1961 "Stratification and hospital care: Part I. The performance of the medical intern." American Sociological Review 26:67–79.

Shuval, Judith.
1962 "Ethnic stereotyping in Israeli medical bureaucracies." Sociology and Social Research 47:455–465.

Simmons, Ozzie G.
1955 "The clinical team in a Chilean health center." Pp. 325–348 in Benjamin Paul and W. B. Miller (eds.), Health, Culture and Community. New York; Russell Sage.

Sjoberg, Gideon; R. A. Brymer; and B. Farris.
1966 "Bureaucracy and the lower class." Sociology and Social Research 50:325–337.

Stanton, Alfred H., and Morris S. Schwartz.
1954 The Mental Hospital. New York: Basic Books.

Stark, Francis B.
1959 "Barriers to client-worker communication and intake." Social Casework 40:177–183.

Stein, William W., and E. R. Oetting.
1964 "Humanism and custodialism in a Peruvian mental hospital." Human Organization 24:278–282.

Stinchcombe, Arthur L.
1963 "Institutions of privacy in the determination of police administrative practices." American Journal of Sociology 69:150–160.
1965 "Social structure and organization." Pp. 142–193 in J. G. March (ed.), Handbook of Organizations. Chicago: Rand McNally.

Strauss, Anselm; Leonard Schatzmann; Danuta Ehrlich; Rue Bucher; and M. Sabshin.
1963 "The hospital and its negotiated order." Pp. 147–169 in Eliot Freidson (ed.), The Hospital in Modern

Society. New York: Free Press of Glencoe.

Strauss, Erich.
1961 The Ruling Servants: Bureaucracy in Russia, France and Britain. New York: Praeger.

Street, David P.
1965 "The inmate group in custodial and treatment settings." American Sociological Review 30:40–54.

Strodtbeck, Fred L., and Marvin B. Sussman.
1956 "Of time, the city and the 'one-year guarantee': The relations between watch owners and repairers." American Journal of Sociology 61:602–609.

Stuart-Bunning, G. H.
1931 "The personal relations of officials with the public." Public Administration 9:36–40.

Sussman, Leila A.
1963 Dear FDR: A Study of Political Letter-Writing. Totowa, New Jersey: Bedminster Press.

Tannenbaum, Arnold S.
1965 "Unions." Pp. 710–763 in J. G. March (ed.), Handbook of Organizations. Chicago: Rand McNally.

Thomas, E. J.
1966 "Role conceptions, organizational size and community context." Pp. 164–171 in B. J. Biddle and E. J. Thomas (eds.), Role Theory: Concepts and Research. New York: Wiley.

Thomas, E. J., and C. F. Fink.
1963 "Effects of group size." Psychological Bulletin 60:371–384.

Thompson, J. D.
1962 "Organizations and output transactions." American Journal of Sociology 68:309–324.

Thompson, J. D., and W. J. McEwen.
1958 "Organizational goals and environment: Goal setting as an interaction process." American Sociological Review 23:23–31.

Turner, R. H.
1952 "The navy disbursing officer as a bureaucrat." Pp. 60–68 in in Robert K. Merton et al. (eds.), Reader in Bureaucracy. Glencoe, Illinois: Free Press.

Udy, S. H., Jr.
1965 "The comparative analysis of organizations." Pp. 678–709 in J. G. March (ed.), Handbook of Organizations. Chicago: Rand McNally.

Weber, Max.
1943 "Bureaucratization." Appendix I, pp. 95–99, in J. P. Mayer, Max Weber and German Politics: A Study in Political Sociology. London: Faber and Faber.

Wesson, R. G.
1964 "Volunteers and soviets." Soviet Studies 15:231–249.

Westley, W. A.
1964 "The police: A sociological study of law, custom and morality." Pp. 304–313 in E. W. Burgess and Donald Bogue (eds.), Contributions to Urban Sociology. Chicago: University of Chicago Press.

Wheeler, Stanton.
1961 "Role conflicts in correctional communities." Pp. 229–259 in D. R. Cressey (ed.), The Prison. New York: Holt, Rinehart and Winston.

Whyte, William F.
1948 Human Relations in the Restaurant Industry. New York: McGraw-Hill.

Whyte, William H., Jr.
1956 The Organization Man. New York: Simon and Schuster.

Wilensky, H. L.
1964 "The professionalization of everyone?" American Journal of Sociology 70:137–158.

Wilkening, E. A.
1958 "Consensus in role definition of county extension agents." Rural Sociology 23:184–197.

Williams, J. J.
1950 "The woman physician's dilemma." Journal of Social Issues 6:38–44.

Wilson, O. W.
1963 "Police authority in a free society." Journal of Criminal Law and Criminology 54:175–177.

Wilson, R. N.
1963 "Patient-practitioner relationships." Pp. 273–295 in H. E. Freeman, Sol Levine, and L. G. Reeder (eds.), Handbook of Medical Sociology. Englewood Cliffs, New Jersey: Prentice-Hall.

Zola, I. K.
1964 "Illness behavior of the working-

class: Implications and recommendations." Pp. 350–361 in Arthur B. Shostak and William Gomberg (eds.), Blue-Collar World: Studies of the American Worker. Englewood Cliffs, New Jersey: Prentice-Hall.

1966 "Culture and symptoms: An analysis of patients' presenting complaints." American Sociological Review 31; 615–630.

CHAPTER 22 Consumer and Advertising Research

LEO BOGART
Bureau of Advertising,
American Newspaper Publishers Association

From the earliest beginnings of communication research as an area of investigation, there has been an interplay between basic behavioral research into the processes of human communication and the application of findings and research techniques to consumer and advertising research problems. Many people—perhaps the best known is Paul Lazarsfeld—have worked in both areas, providing benefits of cross-stimulation for both scientific understanding and practical application. This chapter describes some of the history of that interplay between basic research and commercial applications, and summarizes the current state of communication theory and methodology as applied to advertising research problems.

Consumer and advertising research are essentially fields of business practice rather than scholarly disciplines. They are eclectic in nature and bring together practitioners whose original academic training is less likely to be in one of the behavioral sciences than in economics, statistics, or engineering. In fact, many practitioners have learned their skills on the job and lack formal specialized training of any kind. The execution of consumer and advertising research requires the efforts of many people who operate at a clerical or subprofessional level, and who are totally oriented to the immediate tasks they perform rather than to more sweeping social or scholarly objectives.

Commercial research is a commodity that is bought, sold, and used for totally selfish and idiosyncratic purposes. This puts a premium on the skills of the entrepreneur and salesman rather than on those of the scholar. In fact, the wisdom ascribed to the practitioner of commercial research more commonly reflects his substantive knowledge of the industry in which he works than his expertness as a social scientist.

Yet in spite of the fact that most commercial research is conducted for business reasons by semiskilled hired hands working for businessmen, it is difficult to draw a line between it and the traditional research on communication that is carried out by university professors and their graduate students. One reason for this is that commercial research persistently confronts the same unanswered questions which stand at the frontiers of academic communication research. Another reason is that the large scale and resources of commercial research have always attracted the interest of academically trained scholars, and many continue their scholarly pursuits after they move into the business world. Finally, marketing, as an interdisciplinary department of academic instruction, has reared a generation of university scholars of its own, for many of whom communication research represents a central or highly relevant field of study.

Much of the theoretical speculation and scholarly research in marketing and advertising is conducted by the academic members of the profession. They constitute 10 percent of the membership of the American Marketing Association but account for nearly 75 percent of the journal articles published within the field in the past three years. Since not only research results but also methodologies are often considered proprietary by the client or sponsor, a good deal of potentially significant commercial research is published belatedly or not at all.

Viewed from the standpoint of communication theory, many significant contributions of marketing and advertising research have been made by marketing professors or by practitioners whose original training was as psychologists or sociologists. These scholarly contributions tend to reflect their original interests as social scientists who happen to be using as subject matter the data most conveniently and richly accessible to them. Thus, while the literature in marketing research abounds in numerous interesting studies in such fields as attitude formation and change, decision-making, learning theory and perception, it is not possible to abstract these contributions from the texture of continuing scholarship and experimentation in the general field of social psychology. In fact, many of the contributors to this literature consider their work as an integral part of this broader field.

Consumer research and advertising research are both subsumed by marketing research, along with such other specialties as the analysis of sales, pricing, and distribution. The latter fields of study are as remote from communications as any other technical areas in economics, and yet they are extremely germane to the study of consumer behavior and advertising performance.

SCOPE OF COMMERCIAL RESEARCH

Consumer and advertising research are both concerned with the processes of information and persuasion by which people's tastes are created and modified, by which they acquire economic values and express them in the marketplace in the form of effective demand. Vast resources and efforts are applied to marketing research: an estimated half-billion dollars a year in the United States alone. A substantial part of this expenditure is represented by consumer surveys and the secondary analysis of survey data. The machinery which has been developed to conduct these surveys is indistinguishable from that employed in public opinion research. The two areas overlap substantially in personnel, technique, and theory.

Commercial research has introduced a number of mechanical techniques into the study of communication. In broadcast-audience measurement, the standard tool used to measure the number of sets tuned to a program has been the audimeter, an electromechanical device developed by the A. C. Nielsen Company. Arbitron, an instantaneous monitoring system, has served a similar function for a competing rating service, the American Research Bureau. The Lazarsfeld-Stanton program analyzer and other switching or rheostat devices have been used to gauge the direction and intensity of audience response to programs and commercials from moment to moment.

Questioning, in person, on the telephone,

in groups, and by mail, is the basic source of data for most commercial research. Because of the vast scale and continuity with which it is conducted, commercial research has contributed to the study of communication through many minor innovations and improvements in the technology and methodology of field surveys. Planning and management of sampling design and execution, supervision of field work, processing of research data—the practical lore in all these matters reflects the experience of many anonymous practitioners, as well as of those who have contributed to the literature.

Large-scale survey research has encountered new problems of validity as a result of increasing pressures on the interviewers (Manfield, 1969) and respondents whose privacy and patience are sometimes abused (Baxter, 1969; Carlson, 1969; Sheatsley, 1969). The empirical evidence on this point is not conclusive. Research organizations report some increases in the interview refusal rate, but this may reflect urban insecurity rather than excessive interviewing. A survey of interviewers found that 37 percent reported some refusals when respondents confused them with salesmen (Schwartz, 1963). Survey respondents who had prior experience with intensive interviews did not become more suspicious of sales attempts or change their attitudes toward legitimate surveys (Allen & Colfax, 1968).

The use of survey methods would appear to place much of marketing research squarely within the purview of communication, but the number of trained social scientists within the field of marketing research is actually very small. The American Psychological Association has some four hundred members in its consumer psychology division out of a total membership of thirty thousand, and the number of sociologists and anthropologists in marketing research is smaller still. However, the importance of social science as a source of marketing and advertising theory cannot be measured entirely by the proportion of social scientists employed in the field.

Since scientific studies of marketing and advertising first began in the early years of the twentieth century, they have furnished little inspiration for theory-oriented psychological research, but the marketing studies have themselves drawn heavily on the literature of psychology as a source of ideas, usually after a time lag. For instance, some ten years after the publication of Leon Festinger's *A Theory of Cognitive Dissonance* (1957), Robert Holloway (1967) applied cognitive dissonance theory to the study of automobile battery purchases. He reported that consumers who buy when they have strong inducements experience less dissonance than those buying without inducement. Dissonance was increased when "competing" products had very similar attributes; it was reduced by a strong inducement to buy and also by adequate information.

Osgood's semantic differential (Osgood, Suci, & Tannenbaum, 1957) similarly became incorporated into the body of marketing research tools only after a period of time in which it had been widely adopted and investigated by academic psychologists. A decade earlier, the California F-scale (Adorno, Frenkel-Brunswik, Levinson, & Sanford, 1950) underwent the same process of adaptation. Harold Kassarjian (1965) used Riesman's dichotomy of inner-directedness and other-directedness (Riesman, Denny & Glazer, 1950) to classify respondents and found this typology to be related to a choice of visual appeals in advertisements.

These instances not only indicate that some marketing professors and commercial research practitioners are followers of the psychological journals, but they also reflect the voracious appetite of marketing, as a field of endeavor, for new concepts, methods, and gimmicks that promise to give someone an edge over his competition. Social scientists, especially psychologists, have been prominent figures in commercial research since its inception.

The father of American behaviorism, John B. Watson, left academia to become an advertising agency account executive (*not* a researcher). As business schools have expanded their curricular and research interests into the social sciences, they have attracted such psychologists as Raymond Bauer at Harvard and the late Gary Steiner and William Wells at Chicago.

THE STUDY OF ADVERTISEMENTS

The contribution of social science to marketing has undergone important shifts in subject matter and direction over the years. In the early decades of the twentieth century, when advertising was confined largely to newspapers and magazines, much of the research emphasis was on the learning and forgetting of advertising messages. This research dealt with the practical problems of how big an ad should be and how often it should be repeated to serve the advertiser's purpose. (These practical problems still remain, since with advertising as with other forms of communication there is a vast array of complex variables which interact uniquely in each case.)

In 1903 Walter Dill Scott, a psychologist at Northwestern University, checked the recollection of streetcar cards among people riding the trolleys between Chicago and Evanston (Scott, 1912:215–225). In 1912 another psychologist, Edward K. Strong of Columbia, was retained by the Association of National Advertisers to conduct experiments on the recall of advertisements of different size and repeated with varying frequency (Strong, 1912; 1914; 1916). The first advertising researchers studied the Ebbinghaus (1885) research on memory and applied the laboratory techniques of the psychological experiment to the reading of actual advertisements.

Concurrent with this kind of experimentation there came into being techniques for evaluating specific advertisements, either by forced artificial exposure at the idea stage before they had actually run (pretesting) or after they had appeared in print in their normal context and had been read under normal circumstances (posttesting). A pioneer in this type of research was a president of the American Psychological Association, Daniel Starch, who established in 1932 one of the first successful syndicated research services, using a measurement of "noting" or reported recognition of newspaper and magazine ads by readers of the publications as a gauge of their performance.

Since vast bodies of recognition data have been collected on a comparable basis, it has been possible to analyze the characteristics of ads that perform unusually well or badly in many fields and to make generalizations about ad size, color, shape, and the ratio of space devoted to illustrations, headlines, and text. These generalizations have not undergone significant change over a period of some thirty years. Troldahl and Jones (1965) found that three-fifths of the variability in readership of newspaper ads could be explained by the size of the ad and the product advertised. Increasing the size of an ad does not produce additional memorability for the message in proportion to the increase. (Studies on television commercials of different lengths have produced parallel results.)

The recognition interview technique employed by Starch (1946), Carl Nelson (1955–), and others has been criticized as a projective measure of the product's familiarity or interest to the reader rather than an accurate register of his perceptions at the original time of exposure. Recognition scores can be obtained from people who have not been exposed to the ads before (Appel & Blum, 1961; Marder & David, 1961; Davenport, Parker, & Smith, 1962). However, a large-scale, comparative Study of Printed Advertising Rating Methods (PARM) under the auspices of the Advertising Research Foundation showed that recognition and recall produced parallel rank-ordering for the readership of individual advertisements (Lucas, 1960).

A reexamination of the PARM data by William Wells (1964) concluded that recognition scores represent not so much real memory as the respondent's subjective estimate of the probability that he originally saw the ad, while recall scores are more objective and trustworthy. On the other hand, consumers' ratings of advertisements were significantly related to subsequent sales. Since only a small proportion of advertising messages are expected or sought for by the consumer, spontaneous recall is low (Foote, Cone, & Belding, 1964). Within two minutes after a commercial appears, two-thirds of a telephone sample watching the program on which it appeared were unable to recall it spontaneously (Bogart, 1967).

Abruzzini (1967), reviewing systems for evaluating the comprehensibility of advertising copy, concluded that comprehension and interest are more important for long texts than for slogans and headlines designed to capture the reader's initial attention.

Research on shopping activity for advertised products suggests that when the consumer has a positive interest in an advertised item he is often engaged in a search for specific factual information (Bogart, 1967). The selectivity with which people look at and remember advertising of interest to them was first noted by Starch and has been repeatedly documented with observational as well as memory measures. The amount of time spent on an ad as measured by an eye-camera record is related to the memorability of the same ad as determined by the recognition technique (Starch, 1966).

Wolf, Newman, and Winters (1969) took operant behavior measures of the amount of time experimental subjects spent "working" a foot treadle that permitted them to read fourteen articles. They compared these measures with the results of telephone readership interviews obtained from a separate and larger sample. Interest (measured by time and the rate of working the treadle) was related to the rank order of ad lib readership.

Another eye-camera experiment suggests that while recognition of an ad is sometimes claimed by people who had not looked at it, such overstatement is very small compared with the underreporting of recognition by people who had actually looked at an ad. The same study indicates that selectivity operates not only at the level of conscious recognition but also at the unconscious level of eye movement; women tended to move their eyes in the direction of ads featuring products of interest to women but not to those of interest to men (Bogart, 1962).

The eye movements of better educated persons show the greatest tendency to search wide areas of an advertisement rather than merely to concentrate on the most dominant focal point. The simplest ad designs produce the greatest focus of eye movements among readers in general (Payne, 1967).

A few experimental attempts have been made to telemeter autonomous physiological functions while subjects are exposed to advertising communications. In at least one instance, hypnosis was used to probe (unsuccessfully) for responses to advertising that are not articulated at the level of consciousness (Bauer & Greyser, 1968). (People are consciously aware of only a small proportion of the advertising messages to which they are exposed each day.) Tachistoscopes have been used as an aid in evaluating the comparative attention value of different print advertising layouts. Hess has used an eye camera not to measure eye movement (as in the studies mentioned earlier) but to photograph pupil dilation, which he offers as a measure of emotional arousal in response to television commercials (Hess & Polt, 1960). Krugman (1971) has compared the EEG pattern of a subject reading and watching television and found greater evidence of brain wave activity while reading.

To study the effects of varying the size

and context of the advertising unit, it has been necessary to develop ways of actually manipulating the content and context of mass media. This is done in print media through the technique of the split printing run, which permits matched samples of readers to receive what is essentially the same publication with changes only on the experimental pages. In broadcasting, an electronic device has been used to suppress or mute selected television input in a sample of homes specially equipped. Cable television facilities also have been used to send different signals into matched samples of households.

The evidence from isolated experiments corroborates the well-established conclusion from psychological laboratory evidence that the content of a specific communication is always perceived in relation to its total environment in the medium. In print, if surrounding messages attract the reader's eye, they enhance the possibility that he will stop long enough to pay attention to other messages on the page; however, a particularly powerful message may overwhelm his attention to the disadvantage of others in the immediate area. Bogart and Tolley (1964) eliminated ads of different size from a page of an experimental newspaper and found that even a blank space was perceived by the reader in the context of the entire page or spread rather than in isolation. They concluded that an ad received an additional opportunity to win attention from its proximity to other items on the same page that arrested the reader.

A number of other studies have focused on the contextual setting for advertising messages. People who give high ratings to the editorial content of a publication or program are also most responsive to the advertising. Charles Winick (1962) compared the results of the same advertisements presented in different contexts in magazine and television programs and found that the environment significantly affected the results.

Gary Steiner (1966) had observers record the behavior of people watching TV commercials. The proportion of viewers paying full attention dropped from 70 percent for the preceding programming to 47 percent when the commercial came on, with a further attrition of attention after the next commercial in a series.

Although copy research has taught the makers of ads and commercials a good deal about the principles of winning attention, this research has also established the fact that attention attracted by sheer technical virtuosity is not necessarily translated into effective persuasion for the advertiser's product or service. The measurement of advertising effects—as opposed to advertising attention or interest—has remained the main preoccupation of the field.

COMMUNICATION AND ACTION

The design of a great deal of advertising research starts from the premise that there is a hierarchy of response to persuasive communication, from information to favorable attitude to actual purchase behavior. Lavidge and Steiner (1961), for example, use a "stair-step" model that ranges from awareness through knowledge, liking, preference, conviction, and purchase. This represents a plausible model for field studies that seek to measure effects, since opinions and information about a product may be found among substantial numbers of people who have not actually bought it. Comparative data may therefore be gathered from larger subsamples of the public, and statistically significant results are easier to obtain than from a sample of actual purchasers.

Consumer surveys of buying mood and intentions, pioneered by George Katona (1951; 1960; 1964) and Eva Mueller (1963), have attained importance and authority as forecasts of general business and economic activity. Verbal indications of buying intentions (Stapel, 1968) and brand attitudes (DuBois, 1959; Achenbaum, 1966) provide good predictors of actual buying behavior, but the relationships of purchase, attitude, and advertising response are more uncertain and therefore apparently more specific to the product and the message (Adler & Crespi, 1968).

Studies that relate the memorability of advertising to interest in the product inevitably find a correlation, although it is sometimes argued that consumer preference is reflected in selective response to advertising rather than the other way around. Haskins (1964) concluded from an examination of seven advertising studies and twenty-one published nonadvertising studies that measures of recall and retention are irrelevant to the changing of attitudes and behavior. One study found that interest in the advertised product significantly affects the recall of magazine advertisements but not of television commercials (Buchanan, 1964).

A large-scale experimental study in six cities related newspaper advertising exposure to actual purchases of twenty-four advertised brands on the day after the paper appeared. Although individuals who recalled an ad were far more likely than others to purchase the advertised brand, a rank-order correlation showed no relationship between the memorability of an ad compared with other ads and its comparative sales effect (Bogart, Tolley, & Orenstein, 1970).

SAMPLE SURVEYS AND CONSUMER MOTIVATION

In the period between the two world wars, survey research in marketing moved from the crudest type of compilation of a manufacturer's own sales and inventory information to more complex and subtle assessments of consumer purchase and usage patterns and attitudes toward the product and its competitors. The vast expansion of commercial research coincided with a growing insistence by its clients on accuracy and projectibility, and this in turn led to considerable innovation and to growing experience in the technology of large-scale sample surveys and their analytical techniques. Probability sampling methods, although pioneered by the U.S. government, were quickly adopted by commercial research, and such government statisticians as W. Edwards Deming, J. Stevens Stock, and Lester Frankel joined the ranks of men like Alfred Politz and Willard Simmons, who pioneered in demonstrating the merits of the more expensive but more exact methodology.

One of the first major areas of application for probability sampling emerged during the late 1930s, as the growth of radio spurred the study of mass media audiences. The new competition of broadcasting and print advertising spurred a new wave of research on the nature of mass communications as well as a vast outpouring of repetitive measurements of the size and characteristics of specific media audiences. This new field of interest coincided with the political developments of the time—the growth of fascism, the threat and reality of war—and the growth of public opinion and propaganda research. Paul Lazarsfeld (1969), whose work in consumer behavior and in applied social research began in his Vienna days, brought to Princeton and then to Columbia a far-ranging set of interests that encompassed the growing social effects of the mass media in both the commercial and the political realms.

The Second World War had brought a new and urgent interest in the subject of mass media persuasion. Marketing had its modest counterparts of Harold Lasswell's studies of propaganda symbolism (Smith, Lasswell, & Casey, 1946) and Carl Hovland's investigations of army troop indoctrination techniques (Hovland, Lumsdaine, & Sheffield, 1949).

Media organizations such as Time, Inc., and the Columbia Broadcasting System (whose research director, Frank Stanton, a psychologist, became its president) sponsored notable studies in which their commercial self-interest was married to useful secondary analyses of high academic interest (see, for instance, Havemann & West, 1952; Steiner, 1963). The Katz and Lazarsfeld (1955) two-step flow theory of communications effects (which holds that mass media content is mediated and retransmitted in conversation) derives from a field study in Decatur, Illinois, conducted under the auspices of MacFadden Publications, with a direct commercial objective. The role of conversation in communicating product information was subsequently investigated by Arndt (1967), who suggested that word-of-mouth advertising could be used deliberately to supplement the mass media.

Studies of radio audience motivation, such as Robert Merton's (1946) study of Kate Smith's war bond sales marathon, the soap opera studies of Herta Herzog (1944a; 1944b) and of W. Lloyd Warner and William Henry (1948), and Rudolf Arnheim's (1944) study of the "Professor Quiz" format, became the prototypes of the school of "motivation research" that flourished in the 1950s. Applied to the realms of packaging, product design, copy themes, and brand differentiation, motivation research represented the first real attempt to apply clinical psychology for commercial purposes.

The primary objective of motivation research was to uncover areas of susceptibility to persuasion by revealing the unconscious components of consumer attitudes toward commonly used products, many of them of low interest. Motivation research stressed the importance of the brand and corporate "image"—the composite symbolism created by name, packaging, and promotion that gave a product an identity distinct from its competition. The idea was that this aroused an automatic emotional response from the consumer without the need of any factual rationale.[1]

[1] For further illustrations of this approach, see Dichter (1957), Martineau (1957), and Henry (1958).

Motivation research was often presented by both its supporters and enemies as a "rape" of the vulnerable and gullible consumer; a sensational journalist's view was given by Vance Packard (1957). Although its more colorful practitioners sought and attained some notoriety, their specific insights for the most part defy codification, and do not appear to represent enduring contributions to the study of communication.

The subject of subliminal advertising achieved a great deal of public attention at this time as the result of one well-publicized (though inconclusive) experiment in a drive-in movie theater (Henderson, 1957). While subliminal advertising became widely cited as sinister evidence of "hidden persuasion," it represented more of a preoccupation of laymen than of either advertising practitioners or researchers. A review of the relevant psychological literature on subliminal perception discouraged pursuit of this avenue of research (Klass, 1958; Parker, 1960).

ADVERTISING EXPERIMENTS

In the ten-year period following World War II, advertising billings in the United States tripled. They reached $20.5 billion in 1971. Advertisers and agencies became increasingly concerned with the efficient utilization of these growing expenditures. Marketers sharpened their interest in research that promised to help plan introductions of the new products that account for a growing proportion of consumer goods sold. They expanded the demand for research on the effects of variation in pricing, packaging, or product ingredients, and on different approaches to advertising themes, layouts, and media strategies.

The character of marketing research took a new turn in the direction of communication as a result of the advent of the computer, with its promise of sifting vast quantities of data on consumers and on media audiences to make wiser advertising media decisions (Langhoff, 1964). The development of decision-making models in marketing and advertising has demanded a searching examination of existing knowledge regarding the same fundamentals of communication technique to which the pioneers of advertising research addressed themselves: length of message unit, the effects of repetition, the comparative persuasiveness of different media, the effect of the communication context, etc.

The answers to such questions could not come from conventional consumer surveys. Nor would they emerge from an examination of the existing scholarly literature in social psychology, which has largely ignored such mundane matters. It could only come from the painstaking and expensive application of the methods of laboratory experimentation to the persistent queries of the marketer.

In one of the largest field experiments of this kind, Stewart (1964) compared the effect of repeating the same newspaper ads for two products, a frozen food and a bleach. While the results were different in each case, it was apparent that repetition of the identical advertisement produced no further return after an optimum point had been reached, but did maintain the effect at a level from which it might have dropped without reinforcement.

Wells and Chinsky (1965) used numbers as "messages" in a series of experiments. They found that choice of "message" increased in proportion to its share of "messages" up to a point, beyond which repetition became inefficient. The perceived salience of a message could be increased by raising its share of the message stream, by moving it toward the end of the message stream, or by issuing it in "flights" or "bursts."

Grass and Wallace (1969) compared laboratory experiments with field research on television commercials. They found that repetition and cumulative exposure to repeated messages increased attention and information up to a point of maximum effect, beyond which further repetition was followed by a decline in attention and learning. However, the commercials continued to generate favorable attitudes after the satiation point for attention and information. Commercials that resembled each other superficially in content differed sharply in the rate of their "wear-out." The use of a number of different messages on behalf of the same product postponed "wear-out." By permitting some time to elapse after a message reached the point of satiation, it was possible to revive the viewer's attention and interest when it was reintroduced.

PERSONALITY AND CONSUMPTION

Advertisers try to use media whose audience profiles best match the characteristics of their most valuable customers. Research on the consumer market has focused heavily on describing what kinds of people use different brands of the same product with differing degrees of frequency, volume, and repetitiveness. Similarly, media research has placed a high premium on accurate descriptive comparisons of the audiences for different magazines, newspapers, and television or radio programs.[2]

In both consumer and media research, the descriptions are conventionally expressed in terms of demographic variables: sex, age, income, city size, and education. (Systematic study of the symbolic content of media in relation to their audience characteristics has been largely a matter for the academic researchers.) Periodically, attempts have been made to move away from the stock demographic descriptions to a differentiation of product usage and media habits in terms of personality types.

For a period of time, the social-class

[2] Claycamp and Massy (1968) have developed a mathematical theory of defining mutually exclusive market segments in relation to the possibility of reaching them via different advertising media.

analyses of W. Lloyd Warner (1963) and his associates played an influential role among commercial researchers in relating psychological traits to social background. Burleigh Gardner (Gardner & Levy, 1955) and Lee Rainwater (Rainwater, Coleman, & Handel, 1959) depicted the basic personality structure and personal values of the "middle-majority housewife" as inseparable from her cultural milieu, consumption style, and media exposure habits. The market may be segmented not merely by demographic variables but by various types of benefits that consumers look for from the same products (Haley, 1968; Foote, 1969).

Periodically, attempts have been made to apply personality inventory measures adapted from classical, self-administered pencil and paper tests to large-scale field surveys of the general population. One notable piece of research conducted by Arthur Koponen (1960) at the J. Walter Thompson Company and based on a large, nationwide mail panel, produced evidence of how personality traits relate to brand preferences and other variations in consumption behavior. However, in this study, as in other similar research, the psychological differentiation among product users within any demographic group seems modest compared with the sharper differences that are found using the standard indicators of age, income, or social class.

In making a choice between brands, some consumers behave rationally and others require either more or less information than they actually need to make a decision (Green, Halbert, & Minas, 1964). Brand loyalty varies widely among different products and among different types of consumers (Kuehn, 1962a; 1962b).

Studies sponsored by specific media (usually consumer magazines) have concentrated attention on readiness to accept innovation as an attribute linked to early purchase of new products (and, inevitably, to preference for the sponsor of the research). "Innovators" are more likely than other people to have been presold by advertising on a new product and less likely to shop around (Lazer & Bell, 1966).

Some of these studies linking personality to marketing behavior have never entered the published literature because of their ambiguous results. Individual psychological traits, as defined by the measuring instruments commonly employed in this type of study, are difficult to isolate from the cultural reflections of social class. Frank, Massy, and Lodahl (1969) used household purchase records for three frequently purchased household beverages (beer, coffee, and tea) to see whether brand loyalty and store loyalty related significantly to personality data from the Edwards Personal Preference Schedule above and beyond what might be expected from socioeconomic classifications. They concluded that the additional sensitivity and predictive power did not justify the added expense and difficulty of getting the psychological data, and that personality variables made an "extremely small contribution."

ADVERTISING INVOLVEMENT AND EFFECTS

Krugman (1965) postulates a difference between consumer reactions to high-involvement and to low-involvement advertising messages. He theorizes that a message for a low-involvement product may make it seem more familiar without changing conscious attitudes toward it. Familiarity means that the product is perceived in a new and more acceptable light when it is encountered in the store and, if it is actually purchased, a change in conscious attitude might follow. Krugman (1966a; 1966b) suggests that TV lends itself to the "incidental learning" appropriate to low-involvement messages, while print requires more active participation; the reader must be distracted from his primary interest (in the editorial matter) in order to get the advertising message, thereby producing a direct change of attitude at the moment of exposure.

There is evidence that interest and involvement for different products may be arrayed in a continuum. At the point where an individual is ready to make a purchase, a low-interest product may achieve a measure of salience which it otherwise lacks (Bogart, 1967).

Since most commercial research deals with low-interest subjects and with extremely low-key stimuli, its stock in trade is in dimensions of communication that are generally beyond the province or concerns of the university scholar. The commercial researcher is typically concerned with describing specifics. He wants to measure accurately the dimensions of change attributable to advertising communication so that these may be translated into the monetary terms that represent the usual criteria of business judgment.

The academic student of communication effects has been interested primarily in isolating variables that relate the form and content of the message to those predispositions of the audience (either in its earlier level of information and opinion or in its social or personality characteristics) that make it more or less receptive to new communications and that may or may not be congruent with its earlier ideas.

The commercial researcher, by contrast, is generally content to accept the characteristics of the target audience as immutable, and to concentrate his field experiments on such variables as the total amount of communications pressure, the comparative efficiency of different media or different strategies of scheduling or distributing messages through a given medium.

In such field experiments, commercial researchers invariably encounter the problem of disengaging the specific effects of the communication campaign (which can be experimentally controlled) from the effects of other forces at work in the marketplace. These include the design of the product and its package, its brand name, distribution, and pricing, as well as competitive countermeasures.

Britt (1969), reviewing proofs of success offered by forty advertising agencies for a sample of 135 ad campaigns, found that 99 percent did not state their objectives in quantifiable terms; 69 percent did not relate "proofs of success" to the stated objectives. He concluded that "most of the advertising agencies do *not* know whether their campaigns are successful or not."

Palda's (1964) review of the literature on the sales effects of advertising concluded that while a substantial number of studies deal with limited advertising objectives, only a handful of attempts have been made to appraise the total effect of advertising.

The presence of many uncontrollable variables in marketing communication field experiments makes it extremely difficult to obtain significant and practical results at a level of research investment in proper proportion to the investment in the communications campaign itself. The results tend to be highly specific to the particular products and campaign tactics under investigation. This means that the findings are usually kept confidential and that the comparative data available thus far have not built up to a level from which substantial theoretical implications can be drawn. However, a few generalizations may be made from major surveys reported in the published literature:

1. The boomerang effect of self-defeating communications, which was identified under laboratory conditions by Carl Hovland and his associates (Hovland, Lumsdaine, & Sheffield, 1949; Hovland & Weiss, 1951), also is manifested in large-scale advertising campaigns. Millions of dollars may be expended to convey messages that because of their ineptitude or inappropriateness produce results unfavorable to the advertiser's interests (Ule, 1966; 1969; Gibson, 1968).
2. The behavioral or action consequences of advertising campaigns are not necessarily a direct reflection

of their ability to convey information or change ideas. For instance, one test made for DuPont found that TV advertising best communicated knowledge about the product but did not significantly affect sales while newspaper ads in the test increased sales significantly, although they were less successful in adding to the consumer's knowledge (McNiven, 1963). Another DuPont sales test of cookware coated with Teflon found evidence of the effectiveness of advertising at a high level of expenditure but none at a low level of expenditure (Becknell & McIsaac, 1963).

3. In spite of the rapid decay of memory, awareness, information, and other indicators of what an advertisement communicates, some effects of advertising persist long after the messages stop. Tull (1965) examined the reasons for a decline in sales of Packer's Tar Soap between 1919 and 1929 and concluded that advertising impressions accumulated over time create sales in a subsequent purchase period. Repeated purchases made by a loyal consumer to a particular brand may be attributed to earlier advertising exposures. Palda (1964a), in a similar sales analysis of Lydia Pinkham's Vegetable Compound, also found a lag between advertising pressure and results. Carry-over effects lasting well after the advertising ran were also reported by Jessen (1961) and by Becknell and McIsaac (1963).
4. With the vast expansion of mass communication, messages that appear to be delivered with compelling force on the printed page or the television screen may still register little or no effect when they are perceived in the stream of distracting and contradictory messages. It has been plausibly argued that in highly competitive product fields, the functions of advertising may not be persuasion, but achieving an accepted position in the normal communication environment. A company may have to maintain a certain minimal level of advertising and promotional pressure merely to maintain a franchise of visibility, familiarity, and acceptability to the mass consumer (Weinberg, 1960).

The agenda of unanswered questions in advertising and consumer research continues to remain almost identical with those that face the academic student of communication and persuasion.

REFERENCES

Abruzzini, Pompeo.
1967 "Measuring language difficulty in advertising copy." Journal of Marketing 31(April):22–26.

Achenbaum, Alvin A.
1966 "An answer to one of the unanswered questions about the measurement of advertising effectiveness." Pp.24–32 in Proceedings: 12th Annual Conference, Advertising Research Foundation. New York: Advertising Research Foundation.

Adler, Lee, and Irving Crespi (eds.).
1968 Attitude Research on the Rocks. New York: American Marketing Association.

Adorno, T. W.; Else Frenkel-Brunswik; Daniel J. Levinson; and R. Nevitt Sanford.
1950 The Authoritarian Personality. New York: Harper and Row.

Allen, Irving L., and J. David Colfax.
1968 "Respondents' attitudes toward legitimate surveys in four cities." Journal of Marketing Research 5(November):431–433.

Appel, Valentine, and Milton L. Blum.
1961 "Ad recognition and respondent set." Journal of Advertising Research 1(June):13–21.

Arndt, Johan.
1967 Word-of-Mouth Advertising: A Review of the Literature. New York: Advertising Research Foundation.

Arnheim, Rudolf.
1944 "The world of the day-time serial," in Frank Stanton and Paul Lazarsfeld (eds.), Radio Research 1942–43. New York: Duell, Sloan and Pearce.

Bauer, Raymond A., and Stephen Greyser.
1968 Advertising in America: The Consumer View. Boston: Harvard University Division of Research.

Baxter, Richard.
1969 "The harassed respondent: I. Sales solicitation in the guise of consumer research," in Leo Bogart (ed.), Current Controversies in Marketing Research. Chicago: Markham.

Becknell, James C., Jr., and Robert W. McIsaac.
1963 "Test marketing cookware coated with Teflon." Journal of Advertising Research 3(September): 2–8.

Bogart, Leo.
1962 "How do people read newspapers?" Media/Scope 6(January): 53–60.
1967 Strategy in Advertising. New York: Harcourt, Brace and World.

Bogart, Leo, and B. Stuart Tolley.
1964 "Impact of blank space: An experiment in advertising readership." Journal of Advertising Research 4(June): 21–27.

Bogart, Leo; B. Stuart Tolley; and Frank Orenstein.
1970 "What one little ad can do." Journal of Advertising Research 10(August): 3–13.

Britt, S. H.
1969 "Are so-called successful advertising campaigns really successful?" Journal of Advertising Research 9(June): 3–9.

Buchanan, Dodds I.
1964 "How interest in the product affects recall: Print ads vs. commercials." Journal of Advertising Research 4(March): 9–14.

Carlson, Robert.
1969 "The issue of privacy in public opinion research," in Leo Bogart (ed.), Current Controversies in Marketing Research. Chicago: Markham.

Claycamp, Henry J., and William F. Massy.
1968 "A theory of market segmentation." Journal of Marketing Research 5(November): 388–394.

Davenport, John Scott; Edwin B. Parker; and Stewart A. Smith.
1962 "Measuring readership of newspaper advertisements." Journal of Advertising Research 2(December): 2–9.

Dichter, Ernest.
1957 Handbook of Consumer Motivations. New York: McGraw-Hill.

DuBois, Cornelius.
1959 The Story of Brand XL: How Consumer Attitudes Affected Its Market Position. New York: Foote, Cone and Belding.

Ebbinghaus, Hermann.
1885 Das Gedächtnis. Berlin: Duncker und Humbolt.

Festinger, Leon.
1957 A Theory of Cognitive Dissonance. Stanford, California: Stanford University Press.

Foote, Cone and Belding.
1964 How Many Packages of Breakfast Cereal Will Television Buy. New York: Foote, Cone & Belding, Inc.

Foote, Nelson N.
1969 "Market segmentation as a competitive strategy," in Leo Bogart (ed.), Current Controversies in Marketing Research. Chicago: Markham.

Frank, Ronald E.; William F. Massy; and Thomas M. Lodahl.
1969 "Purchasing behavior and personal attributes." Journal of Advertising Research 9(December): 15–24.

Gardner, Burleigh B., and Sidney J. Levy.
1955 "The product and the brand: Qualitative research into consumer motives." Harvard Business Review 33(March-April): 33–39.

Gibson, Lawrence D.
1968 "If I don't want to loan you the plow . . . ." Pp. 37–43 in Proceedings: 14th Annual Conference, Advertising Research Foundation. New York: Advertising Research Foundation.

Grass, Robert C., and Wallace H. Wallace.
1969 "Satiation effects of TV commercials." Journal of Advertising Research 9(September): 3–8.

Green, Paul F.; Michael H. Halbert; and J. Sayer Minas.
1964 "An experiment in information buying." Journal of Advertising Research 4(September): 17–23.

Haley, Russell I.
1968 "Benefit segmentation: A decision-oriented research tool." Journal of Marketing 32(July): 30–35.

Haskins, Jack B.
1964 "Factual recall as a measure of advertising effectiveness." Journal of Advertising Research 4(March):2–8.
Havemann, Ernest, and Patricia S. West.
1952 They Went To College. New York: Harcourt, Brace and World.
Henderson, Carter.
1957 "A blessing or a bane? TV ads you'd see without knowing it." Wall Street Journal September 13:1.
Henry, Harry.
1958 Motivation Research. New York: Ungar.
Herzog, Herta.
1944a "Motivations and gratifications of daily serial listeners," in Paul Lazarsfeld and Frank Stanton (eds.), Radio Research, 1942–43. New York: Duell, Sloan and Pearce.
1944b "What do we really know about daytime serial listeners," in Paul Lazarsfeld and Frank Stanton (eds.), Radio Research, 1942–43. New York: Duell, Sloan and Pearce.
Hess, Eckhard H., and James M. Polt.
1960 "Pupil size as related to interest value of visual stimuli." Science 132:349–350.
Holloway, Robert J.
1967 "An experiment on consumer dissonance." Journal of Marketing 31(January):39–43.
Hovland, Carl I.; A. A. Lumsdaine; and Fred D. Sheffield.
1949 Experiments in Mass Communication. Princeton, New Jersey: Princeton University Press.
Hovland, Carl I., and Walter Weiss.
1951 "The influence of source credibility on communication effectiveness." Public Opinion Quarterly 15(Winter):635–650.
Jessen, Raymond J.
1961 "A switch-over experimental design to measure advertising effect." Journal of Advertising Research 1(March):15–22.
Kassarjian, Harold H.
1965 "Social character and differential preference for mass communication." Journal of Marketing Research 2(May):146–153.
Katona, George.
1951 Psychological Analysis of Economic Behavior. New York: McGraw-Hill.
1960 The Powerful Consumer. New York: McGraw-Hill.
1964 The Mass Consumption Society. New York: McGraw-Hill.
Katz, Elihu, and Paul F. Lazarsfeld.
1955 Personal Influence. Glencoe, Illinois: Free Press.
Klass, Bertrand.
1958 "The ghost of subliminal advertising." Journal of Marketing 23(October):146–150.
Koponen, Arthur.
1960 "Personality characteristics of purchasers." Journal of Advertising Research 1(September):6–12.
Krugman, Herbert.
1956 "The impact of television advertising: Learning without involvement." Public Opinion Quarterly 39(Fall):349–356.
1966a "The learning of consumer likes, preferences, and choices." Paper delivered at Purdue University, Lafayette, Indiana, July (unpublished).
1966b "The measurement of advertising involvement." Public Opinion Quarterly 30(Winter):383–396.
1971 "Brain wave measures of media involvement." Journal of Advertising Research 10(April):3–9.
Kuehn, Alfred A.
1962a "How advertising performance depends on other factors." Journal of Advertising Research 2(March): 2–10.
1962b "Consumer brand choice as a learning process." Journal of Advertising Research 2(December):10–17.
Langhoff, Peter (ed.).
1964 Models, Measurements and Marketing. Englewood Cliffs, New Jersey: Prentice-Hall.
Lavidge, Robert J., and Gary A. Steiner.
1961 "A model for predictive measurements of advertising effectiveness." Journal of Marketing 25(October): 59–62.
Lazarsfeld, Paul F.
1969 "Perspectives—an episode in the history of social research—a memoir," in Donald Fleming and Bernard Bailyn (eds.), The Intellectual Mi-

gration: Europe and America, 1930–1960. Cambridge, Massachusetts: Harvard University Press.

Lazer, William, and William E. Bell.
1966 "The communications process and innovation." Journal of Advertising Research 6(September): 2–7.

Lucas, Darrell B.
1960 "The ABC's of ARF's PARM." Journal of Marketing 25(July): 9–20.

McNiven, Malcolm.
1963 Speech before the National Industrial Conference Board, New York City, September.

Manfield, Manuel N.
1969 "The status of validation in survey research," in Leo Bogart (ed.), Current Controversies in Marketing Research. Chicago: Markham.

Marder, Eric, and Mort David.
1961 "Recognition of ad elements: Recall or projection?" Journal of Advertising Research 1(December): 23–25.

Martineau, Pierre.
1957 Motivation in Advertising. New York: McGraw-Hill.

Merton, Robert K.
1946 Mass Persuasion: The Social Psychology of a War Bond Drive. New York: Harper.

Meuller, Eva.
1963 "Ten years of consumer attitude surveys: Their forecasting record." Journal of American Statistical Association 53(December): 899+.

Nelson, Carl J.
1955– Survey of the Month. Chicago: Publication Research Service.

Osgood, Charles; George Suci; and Percy Tannenbaum.
1957 The Measurement of Meaning. Urbana: University of Illinois Press.

Packard, Vance.
1957 The Hidden Persuaders. New York: McKay.

Palda, Kristian S.
1964a The Measurement of Cumulative Advertising Effects. Englewood Cliffs, New Jersey: Prentice-Hall.
1964b "Sales effects on advertising: A review of the literature." Journal of Advertising Research 4(September): 12–16.

Parker, Edwin B.
1960 "Subliminal stimulation and voting behavior." Journalism Quarterly 37(Fall): 588–590.

Payne, Donald.
1967 "Looking without learning: Eye movements when viewing print advertisements." pp. 78–81 in 1967 June Conference Proceedings. Chicago: American Marketing Association.

Rainwater, Lee; Richard P. Coleman; and Gerald Handel.
1959 Workingman's Wife. Dobbs Ferry, New York: Oceana Publications.

Riesman, David; Reuel Denny; and Nathan Glazer.
1950 The Lonely Crowd. New Haven, Connecticut: Yale University Press.

Schwartz, Alvin.
1963 "The public relations of interviewing." Journal of Marketing 27(July): 34–37.

Scott, Walter Dill.
1912 The Psychology of Advertising. Boston: Small, Maynard.

Sheatsley, Paul B.
1969 "The harassed respondent: II. Interviewing practices," in Leo Bogart (ed.), Current Controversies in Marketing Research. Chicago: Markham.

Smith, B. L.; Harold D. Lasswell; and R. D. Casey (eds.).
1946 Propaganda, Communication, and Public Opinion. Princeton, New Jersey: Princeton University Press.

Stapel, Jan.
1968 "Predictive attitudes," in Lee Adler and Irving Crespi (eds.), Attitude Research on the Rocks. Chicago: American Marketing Association.

Starch, Daniel.
1946 Factors in Readership Measurement. New York: Daniel Starch and Staff.
1966 Measuring Advertising Readership and Results. New York: McGraw-Hill.

Steiner, Gary.
1963 The People Look at Television. New York: Knopf.
1966 "The people look at commercials: A study of audience behavior." Journal of Business 39(April): 272–304.

Stewart, John P.
1964 Repetitive Advertising in Newspapers. Boston: Harvard University Division of Research.

Strong, Edward K.
1912 "The effect of length of series upon recognition." Psychological Review 19(November): 421–447.
1914 "The effect of size of advertisements and frequency of their presentation." Psychological Review 21(March): 136–152.
1916 "The factors affecting a permanent impression developed through repetition." Journal of Experimental Psychology 1(August): 319.

Troldahl, Verling C., and Robert L. Jones.
1965 "Predictors of newspaper advertisement readership." Journal of Advertising Research 5(March): 23–27.

Tull, Donald S.
1965 "The carry-over effect of advertising." Journal of Marketing 29(April): 46–53.

Ule, G. Maxwell.
1966 "Two years of the Milwaukee ad lab: First report." Pp. 58–65 in Proceedings: 12th Annual Conference, Advertising Research Foundation. New York: Advertising Research Foundation.
1969 "The Milwaukee advertising laboratory—a continuing source of advertising serendipity." Pp. 71–76 in Proceedings: 15th Annual Conference, Advertising Research Foundation. New York: Advertising Research Foundation.

Warner, W. Lloyd (ed.).
1963 Yankee City. New Haven, Connecticut: Yale University Press.

Warner, W. Lloyd, and William E. Henry.
1948 "The radio daytime serial: A symbolic analysis." Genetic Psychology Monographs 37: 3–71.

Weinberg, Robert S.
1960 "An analytical approach to advertising expenditure strategy." Paper prepared for the Association of National Advertisers, New York.

Wells, William D.
1964 "Recognition, recall, and rating scales." Journal of Advertising Research 4(September): 2–8.

Wells, William D., and Jack M. Chinsky.
1965 "Effects of competing messages: A laboratory simulation." Journal of Marketing Research 2(May): 141–145.

Winick, Charles.
1962 "Three measures of the advertising value of media context." Journal of Advertising Research 2(June): 28–33.

Wolf, Abraham; Dianne Z. Newman; and Lewis C. Winters.
1969 "Operant measures of interest as related to ad lib readership." Journal of Advertising Research 9(June): 40–45.

CHAPTER 23 Communication in Political Parties

DWAINE MARVICK
University of California, Los Angeles

In most countries—democratic or totalitarian—political parties play a critical role. Foremost among their functions are (1) to integrate the many diverse agencies of government, and (2) to link that government with the people. A political party, moreover, like any other complex organization, is internally laced together by various strands of communication. Communication is therefore vital to the major functions of political parties and essential to their structure. These two aspects of communications in political parties are provocatively examined in the following chapter, which offers a broad perspective on many important but little studied aspects of political parties regarded as organized, goal-seeking structures of power, communication, and activity.

INTRODUCTION

In a useful compendium on communications and political development, editor Lucian Pye (1963) emphasized the diversity of functions which, in any political system, one expects its communications processes to perform: to create mutual awareness and system comprehension; to amplify or ignore certain acts by public figures or bodies; to furnish a common factual basis for rationality and for sustaining confidence in the rationality resources available to others; to maintain standards for evaluating the motives and intentions of other political actors and for judging their insightfulness and vision, and for understanding their behavior and hence for holding them accountable or free.

In a nation-state, communication mechanisms will either produce and sustain these and related system effects or else there will be no political system. Pye puts it succinctly: "Without a network capable of enlarging and magnifying the words and choices of individuals there could be no politics capable of spanning a nation" (Pye, 1963:6).

Professor Pye goes on to observe that "a peculiar advantage of the communications approach is that it provides a common basis for analyzing both the most manifest structural problems and the most subtle questions of attitudes and values in the total process of political change and nation building" (Pye, 1963:10). Yet his contributors focus attention almost exclusively on *mass communication* media and the audiences and publics reached by them.

So it is also with most other communications work about political systems (Allardt & Littunen, 1964). *Organizational* channels of communication—including party channels—are *not* often examined in ways that deliberately parallel the study of mass communication phenomena.

Perhaps this is understandable. In the twentieth century the political communication system of the nation-state has changed more dramatically than any other aspect of the processes of governance. Electronic devices—telephones and computers as well as television and radio—link together publics and elites in new ways, both along selective channels and in broad streams of contact. Senders and receivers share the immediacy and the dramatic impact of mass media messages. In ways unparalleled by earlier modes, these media seem to foster mutual awareness and alert people to their reciprocal dependence and vulnerability (McLuhan, 1962; Waltzer, 1966).

Work on the significance of communication processes to political life has focused on two extremes: the mass media apparatuses that are available in varying degree to political leaders and party functionaries, and the informal fabric of contacts and comparison that typifies the social communication processes at the grass-roots level (Katz & Lazarsfeld, 1955). In the past, a political campaign—its themes, agenda, itinerary—was largely planned by the candidate and his party colleagues; for some years now, specialists in mass communications have been active also in shaping the issues, imagery, tempo, and schedule of most electoral campaigns for significant office in America and Western Europe (Kelley, 1960). Commercial opinion surveys and computer routines to analyze them proliferate also as both the interested public and the political elites in modern democracies try to gauge electoral moods and trace shifts in popular support for the men and issues to be judged (Harris, 1963; Pool, 1964; King & Schnitzer, 1968).

Yet it is a mistake to see the political communication system as mainly the work of journalists, commentators, pollsters, opinion analysts, and public relations men. Those who participate in key decisional processes, the political and governmental elites, initiate the bulk of the newsworthy developments conveyed to the public. At the same time, they communicate less conspicuously with associates and affiliates via nonpublic modes (Hunter, 1959; Watts, 1968). Nor is it realistic to view the audience side as an amorphous tangle of informal exchanges. Publics are not atomistic masses; rather they are intricately linked social audiences (Kornhauser, 1953; Katz & Lazarsfeld, 1955; Pye, 1963).

Research attention is now shifting to interstitial processes: to the organizational channels within which communications flow out and down, up and in; to institutionalized message-flows that have neither the diffuse randomness of mass media communications nor the ad hoc casualness of personal conversations (Bauer, Pool, & Dexter, 1963). Political parties are important examples of the secondary associations to which people belong, to whose norms and standards they are socialized, to whose articulated interests they are responsive in special measure. To be a partisan is to be part of a distinctive communication apparatus.

In other ways, of course, the significance of politically relevant structures has received much attention: how different associational forms function to facilitate interest aggregation and articulation (Almond & Coleman, 1960; Weiner, 1967); how avenues of apprenticeship equip those whose careers come to have political weight (Ranney, 1965; D. Marvick, 1968); how barriers to cooperation curb factions and isolate pockets of group disaffection (Barnlund & Harland, 1963; Golembiewski, 1965; Wallerstein, 1967); how state bureaucracies are watched and controlled by a "steel frame" of party *apparatchiki*

(Selznick, 1960; Brzezinski & Huntington, 1964; Lodge, 1968b).

But looked at in these ways, organizational channels—whether of political parties, trade associations, unions, professional societies, community groups, religious organizations, caste or tribal associations—are not systematically viewed as the blood vessels that sustain and nourish a polity's infrastructure. One concentrates instead on considerations of power, efficiency, morale, ideology, or allegiance. Only in a generalized fashion has attention been given to what Professor Karl Deutsch (1963) calls "the nerves of government" or what Professor V. O. Key (1961) viewed as "linkage mechanisms" between governments and publics.

A definitional problem exists. It is not easy to delimit the field of "party phenomena." Many formulations give primary attention to parties as corporate structures. In work on political development processes, "party" is largely seen as an associational form by which interest articulation and aggregation are achieved. This usage is not too different from the treatment by those who study monolithic regimes and view "party" as an organizational weapon to monitor bureaucratic performances. Nor is it really dissimilar to the notion of "party" as an electoral or legislative coordinating apparatus, fashioned to conform to the institutional arrangements it exists to serve or to exploit (Campbell, Converse, Miller, & Stokes, 1960; 1966).

It is difficult, however, to keep an essentially corporate notion of party in mind when one turns to work on modern electoral behavior, where "party" becomes a psychological perspective that largely determines voter conduct (Coleman & Rosberg, 1964; Key, 1964; Dahl, 1966). Or when one considers the growing body of research on political socialization, in which "party" is a key component in the culturally derived frame of reference toward political life to which one is socialized from an early age (Almond & Verba, 1963). Or, again, in work by historians or political sociologists aiming to trace through time the partisan alignments that typify a nation or region—work in which "party" refers to basic attitudinal faultlines discernible as persistent patterns in a changing electoral scene (Chambers & Burnham, 1967; Lipset & Rokkan, 1967).

In modern social science, recognition of the importance of communications has led to a basic reassessment of organizational theory (Simon, 1957). In contrast to the power and solidarity formulations of those who follow Max Weber's lead, a counteremphasis stemming from the work of Chester Barnard has been placed on communication patterns (Scott, 1965; Etzioni, 1961). Organized role relationships have been viewed not so much in terms of legitimacy as in terms of exchanges. The emphasis has been placed on how to secure consciously coordinated efforts from differently oriented participants, rather than how to obtain routinized contributions from personnel sharing a commitment to collective goals (Barnes, 1967; 1968).

Political parties have heretofore mainly been studied in ways that reflect the strong influence of Weber (1946; Lipset, 1964). The focus has been on authority and loyalty rather than on communication extents and barriers. An awkward disjunction has persisted. Starting with the notion of party as an organization in the older sense—that is, as a human association pursuing relatively specific shared goals—it has been uncomfortably necessary to treat the "party-in-public" as somehow a less integral component of the partisan association than party leaders, functionaries, or activists. Thus, when impressive research discloses the significance of partisanship as a perspective acquired in early youth that persistently guides the political behavior of modern citizens, it has not been easy to relate these findings to a theory of party that starts by thinking of a corporate structure acting freely on its environment (Easton & Hess, 1962; Almond & Verba, 1963; Hess & Torney, 1968).

Political parties are complex structures—attitudinal as well as corporate—for coordinating political efforts across extended domains (Eldersveld, 1964; Marvick, 1970). They may not be the only kind of extended political apparatuses. They may not be the only means for coordinating political effort. Exclusiveness is not critical to the specification of meaning given here. It is important to emphasize that the notion of "party" regularly conveys the idea of some organizational scaffold that operates in more than a single institutional arena, that has footing in more than one geographic locality, that entails coordinated effort at more than one organizational level. It is equally important to emphasize that the operative "structures" are attitudinal in the last analysis, and are nourished by message flows that, as Professor Pye noted, should work to enhance mutual awareness, politicize certain men and events, foster a common basis for looking at political facts, and permit more continuous evaluations than otherwise of the competence and performance of political actors (Key, 1961; Pye, 1963; Luttbeg, 1968).

It does not seem desirable in approaching the subject of communication processes in political parties to specify with too much particularity the institutional context in which a party apparatus implements political interests. In some polities, parties are mainly geared to electoral processes, and they may also have an imperfect penetration into governmental decision-making processes. Sometimes parties are the vehicles for revolutionary effort—grooming a disciplined cadre, conducting clandestine activities, mobilizing a paramilitary force (Wallerstein, 1967). Those same party structures in the subsequent stages of modernizing dictatorship have often been specialized to the tasks of a bureaucratic control apparatus (Selznick, 1960; Unger, 1965).

It is meaningful in conventional terms to call this congeries of disparate entities by the same generic term—*political party*. Those who report the news as well as those who make it and those who receive it are quite matter-of-fact in the ease with which they treat Republicans in America, Tories in Britain, or Communists in Russia as generically belonging to the same kind of entity although analytically distinguishable. Whether systematic research will yield more meaningful constructs for identifying different kinds of structures for coordinating political efforts extensively is an empirical question (Riggs, 1968; Sorauf, 1967).

There is need for a conception of "party phenomena" that, in the same paradigm of inquiry, will facilitate systematic study not only of tightly disciplined party structures but also of loosely knit party apparatuses, and that will encourage attention to the attitude structures of partisanship as well as the corporate structures of party effort (McDonald, 1955; Scarrow, 1967; Anderson, 1968). A communications approach seems promising.

What are the hallmarks of a communications approach to party phenomena? Three salient features are highlighted that are otherwise hard to keep in focus. Structurally, since parties are extended apparatuses, they face problems of penetration and receptivity: not only how easy is it to send messages but how easy is it to hear what is communicated. Research needs to be sensitive to the *acoustics* of the various sectors and grids making up the extended party structure (Luttbeg, 1968).

Developmentally, since parties make political efforts, they face problems of timing and volume: not only what is the tempo of a political buildup but what is its impact on the larger political system (Nettl, 1967). One needs to measure the fluctuating *loads* of political communication handled by party channels—or flooding them—in order to gauge their system effects (Hyman, 1963; LaPalombara & Weiner, 1966).

Behaviorally, since parties seek to coordinate conduct, they face problems of human recalcitrance and inflexibility. Not only do people create unforeseen difficulties for one another, but they also reveal unexpected capacities to improvise and work together. Key questions arise: From the various action fronts of party effort, what *feedback* mechanisms are working (Heard, 1960; Rosenthal & Weiss, 1967)? At what level of coordination, if any, is the information available that is needed to recognize and correct a faulty course of action?

Neither in design nor content can it be said that the literature on political parties is very scientific. Much of the early work was reformist. Duverger's (1967) lengthy discussion in 1950 was largely speculative. Those who have studied party phenomena in postwar developing areas have either been preoccupied with current events and rumors or they have struggled rather vainly to locate each party along "dimensions" characterized by words like *competition*, *ideology*, *pluralism*, and *democracy*. Perhaps the most incisive work has been analytical history, which charts the emergence of party apparatuses and rivalries as specific responses to crises of legitimacy, identity, participation, and so forth, and seeks to demonstrate changes through time in the "functions" performed by parties—sometimes noncommitally, sometimes with interesting speculations (Namier 1957; Jennings, 1961; Chambers & Burnham, 1967).

Nevertheless, this historical, comparative, speculative work has raised many of the conceptual and methodological problems that plague this field. "They supply a research orientation, indicate the type of questions that should be asked, provide criteria for limiting and comparing phenomena and for interrelating findings in a generally meaningful, although still loose, manner" (Crotty, 1968a:7). Since we are concerned with taking stock of how communication aspects of party life have been handled, it seems appropriate in the next section to examine this literature selectively but in some detail. After doing so, an attempt will be made in the final section to review in orderly fashion the small but growing body of research that seeks to be systematic, empirical, and rigorous about party phenomena. What has been alluded to by such phrases as structural extent and network acoustics, developmental impact and message loads, behavioral adaptation and feedback mechanisms should be somewhat clearer, and at least the silhouette of a systematic approach geared to these considerations can be sketched.

COMMUNICATION, PARTY, AND SOCIETY

The interdependence of structure and purpose in the functioning of political parties has preoccupied many investigators. Looked at in this way, communication problems per se are not often explicitly discussed. However, the emphasis on instrumental action and joint effort is strong, and this draws critical attention to the extent and complexity of what is called a party, its unwieldiness for some missions, its sluggishness for certain functions, the desirability of some internal barriers and insulating arrangements, the need to maintain certain contacts with other groups, etc.

It is not too much to say that the political communication system which permits a society's transition from a traditional mold to modernity has largely been built around the scaffolding provided by political party structures (LaPalombara & Weiner, 1966). As Hans Daalder (1966) shows, in nonautocratic circumstances, whenever parliaments began to be influential, the paraphernalia of extraparliamentary party structures proliferated in response to pressures from new social groupings that wanted representation.

> The process of party formation tended to spread therefore from existing competing elites downwards, but this very process also facilitated a reciprocal movement. Party organization itself created many new elite-posts even if only at subparliamentary levels.... Party competition for various groups in the electorate made some existing parties more responsive to new demands, while new social

groupings came to imitate and expand forms of party organization (Daalder, 1966:51).

On the other hand, where autocratic regimes persisted, there was no such competitive nourishment of an infrastructure catering to the political demands of emerging social claimants, parochial elites, or economic parvenus. Rather, the new political communication structures that emerged took the form of "intellectual protest movements or outright conspiratorial activity... often secret societies" (Daalder, 1966:51).

Daalder is especially concerned with the "reach" or "permeation" of the party system. His analysis of European parties proceeds on three lines: conditions affecting the involvement of traditional political elites, those determining the absorption of new claimants seeking political representation, and those facilitating the integration of national and local elites. Throughout his inquiries he tries to evaluate the significance of attitudes and style. Thus traditions of oligarchic aloofness tended to undermine the full acceptance by right-wing parties of the substance of democratic ideals and practices. Feeling coerced into electoral processes, they remained basically antidemocratic in spirit; this, in turn, narrowed the base of democratic rule, disillusioned other groups, and eroded support for democratic regimes.

Especially in studies of developing areas and modernizing regimes, much effort has been spent seeking to appraise the consequences of party activities and partisan attitudes—in terms of whether they are "functional" or "bad," according to an analytical model (Coleman & Rosberg, 1964; Zolberg, 1966). Evidence is not of high quality and conclusions are often hedged, but the thrust is toward clarifying communication barriers, both within parties and when publics are in view. How effectively does the party get its program across to adherents and critics alike, in remote villages as well as centers of government? What distortions and misunderstandings result across cultural barriers? Are they especially noticeable in the vernacular press? On radio? Which subgroup rivalries within the party's support coalition create persistent publicity problems? Within the party apparatus, what tensions and demands from below are those at higher echelons alert to or indifferent about?

Change and *development* are key terms. Party structures can lose their appeal when they seem to lack social utility (Rudolph & Rudolph, 1960; Geertz, 1963; Coleman & Rosberg, 1964). Analyzing party participation in Morocco, Douglas Ashford (1961a; 1961b) reported party cadre responses in 1961 from localities that were backward, midway, or advanced toward modernity. In backward areas, party structures were central and attractive organizational forms; in those localities they flourished before and instead of more general-purpose social organizations. However, in areas where more social progress had been made, party organizations tended to lack this distinctive appeal. Participation in secondary group life centered instead on "more useful" formulations.

Consider the strong emphasis given to communication aspects of party effort by the editors of *Political Parties and Political Development*. According to LaPalombara and Weiner, the political party is a distinctively modern piece of machinery. It emerges whenever "the notion of political power comes to include the idea that the mass public must participate or be controlled" (LaPalombara & Weiner, 1966:3). Whether in emergent African states, sluggish Latin American republics, European democracies, or militant totalitarian regimes, entities called party have emerged. Moreover, despite differences in social, political, and economic development, a wide range of political systems feature parties that are clearly performing similar broad functions.

Political parties, they say, are expected to "organize public opinion and to communicate demands to the center of governmental power and decision" (LaPalombara & Weiner, 1966:3). Party-borne messages go the other way also. "Somehow, too, the party must articulate to its followers the concept and meaning of the broader community even if the aim of the party leadership is to modify profoundly or even to destroy the broader community and replace it with something else" (LaPalombara & Weiner, 1966:3). In short, the political party is a communication structure that is indispensable when those who seek to win or maintain political power "are required to seek support from the larger public" (LaPalombara, & Weiner, 1966:19).

LaPalombara and Weiner are quite insistent, however, that pseudoparties must be kept distinct from modern parties. In seventeenth- and eighteenth-century Europe, cliques and clubs and groups of notables gave one another limited and intermittent cooperation for purposes of parliamentary maneuver or court intrigue. This cooperation occasionally extended to counterpart groupings in the outlying localities and constituencies affected. At most, however, these were makeshift arrangements. Similar flimsy paraphernalia for facilitating oligarchic rule are to be found, they argue, in some countries of Latin America, Africa, and Asia.

The hallmarks of a genuine political party are fourfold: basic expectations of organizational continuity in the minds of participants, regular linkage between locality outposts and central party units, decisional office-holding as the prime goal, and popular support-seeking as the persistent concern. It is clear that they see parties mainly as translocal communication structures used to maintain political power under modernizing circumstances.

They do not, however, equate modern society with mass-media-serviced society. Publics are basic new ingredients in the processes of governance. But publics are to be managed and even allowed to participate through the good offices of "party." In their formulation, publics are neither viewed as audiences to be entertained nor as human aggregates to be vicariously involved in public affairs via television, radio, or the mass press. The distinctive communication features of twentieth-century political life in Europe and America are *not*, to them, features that critically affect the emergence of the truly "modern party" apparatus. Nor do they consider how modern parties are affected by the novel implications of the "communications industry" to campaigning, decision-making, and nation-building, or the nourishment of spontaneous informal nets of opinion leaders and solidary groups which give "mass" audiences some insulation against elite efforts to manipulate them.

The political communication systems of even late nineteenth-century European and American societies were still *pre*-mass-society systems. Perhaps they were sensitive to publics in new ways, although Daalder's probings of earlier party growth patterns suggest not. They were still largely confined to organizational channels or to informal exchanges among the notables of scattered localities and the political agents found near the effective decisional centers. The pamphlets and handbills, the personal correspondence nets, the messages carried by interest spokesmen and constituency agents solicitous of their sponsors and mindful of their own personal advancement, even the newspapers that circulated mainly among the party faithful—this was the party-framed communication pattern whose flimsy structure led Maurice Duverger to speak of "cadre parties" (apparatuses whose base of operations in each locality was little more than a semipermanent electoral committee):

> At the end of the nineteenth century in Europe, schematically one can distinguish two types of committees: one, corresponding to those in conservative parties, composed of aristocrats, industrialists, bankers, even influential churchmen; the other, corresponding to those of liberal or (in the French sense) radical parties, composed of lesser industrialists, merchants,

functionaries, professors, lawyers, journalists and writers (Duverger, 1967:38).

Duverger noted that a structure whose basic units made no efforts to enlarge their membership and which relied heavily on social channels of communication to keep its members informed was tailored to serve those conservative and moderate political forces that sought to maintain their advantages and to fight essentially a holding action in politics. Only the communication necessary to maintain a minimal coherence and a modest level of mutual awareness among "like-minded" men was undertaken. In each community the flimsy organizational superstructure merged with the established infrastructure—the village notables, country squires, and the activists of politicized gentry families (Namier, 1957; Daalder, 1966).

By contrast, when it was felt necessary to find and sponsor a counterelite, what Duverger called "externally created" parties emerged. In the twentieth century, these have taken the form of "mass parties," committed to militant programs of political change, aimed at organizing the masses, educating them, grooming leaders from among them. Typically, these parties have enrolled their membership directly, but often they have been supported by the organizational resources of trade unions, cooperatives, student associations, and religious groups. Liaison with these auxiliaries was sometimes casual. In other cases, schemes for formal group representation were elaborated. Intellectuals often gave to such mass parties a militant and doctrinaire ideological tone.

For students of political development in modernizing countries, these European cases of externally created parties have seemed more relevant than those instances of parties that grew through the initiative of colonial legislators (Rudolph & Rudolph, 1960). As LaPalombara and Weiner, 1966:10) note,

Most of the political parties now functioning in Africa and Asia were formerly nationalist movements, messianic and chiliastic movements, and caste, religious, or tribal associations that developed outside, and in some instances hostile to, whatever parliamentary framework has been created by colonial governments.

One key question about a mass party was what kind of *basic unit* it employed. Sections, cells, and squads—each was a significant political invention, made respectively by the Socialists, Communists, and Fascists. In Duverger's view, the party option was chosen to fit the ideological and strategic purposes that gave vitality to its plans. Thus, the "section" was a Socialist invention, open to all, geared not only to elections but to a continuous program of political education and member participation, but forced by its very permanence to install the rudiments of bureaucracy—paid, full-time, specialized functionaries, hence prone to oligarchic tendencies, as Michels (1949) warned. More radically intended, the cell was a Communist invention, the militia squad was a Fascist one. These organizational building blocks—small, solidary, zealous, action-oriented, continuous, disciplined entities—were ideally suited to clandestine operations, efforts at infiltration, and manipulation of other groups (Almond, 1954; Degras, 1960).

In each case, prime tasks—crucial to the party leadership's purposes—were carried out by the basic units. As a task group, each unit would develop some status structure and an internal communication net. The more sustained and intensive the effort to communicate with each other up and down within the party and out to the local environment, the more might one expect cumulative effects to appear. Some goals would at least be approximated, some obstacles successfully bypassed, some opportunities seized.

From the memoirs and polemics of "mass party" participants it seems clear that communicating with one another affected both senders and receivers. It gave them experience, self-confidence, know-how; at the same time they acquired a certain dependence on those with whom an interchange had occurred. Those who had responded, even with hostility, came to seem more important than those who were silent (Amann, 1963; Duverger, 1967).

Duverger identified a second key question. Within the party apparatus, what kind of *decentralization* was to be found, and what kind of power distribution was thus indexed? Four different modes of decentralizing power were distinguished: along *geographic* lines, as when regional or local matters were settled without central clearance; in *ideological* terms, as when time is allotted at party conclaves and on conference agendas to spokesmen for different tendances or factions; among *social groupings*, as when the party structure provides for separate membership categories—for farmers, salaried workers, middle class, students, and so on; and in *federal* form, as when provision is made for separate nationality groups to function semiautonomously within the party despite the ostensible continuance of a unitary structure. Here it is the decisional process that is in focus; the lines of decentralization reflect both historical facts and socioeconomic conditions.

In discussing the real location of power within parties, Duverger went on to note the persistent influence of organized pressure groups on American party life—e.g., the CIO's influence at all levels of the Democratic party (Calkins, 1952)—and of intellectual groups in many other countries, such as the Fabian society within the British Labour party (McKenzie, 1955; Rose, 1966). Especially in crisis periods, control of the party press could be a critical asset, as was true for Lenin's power base in 1917.

> In almost all Socialist parties, statutory provisions contemplate a position for the party journal subordinate to the official party directors. However, the editorial team always retains a certain independence which permits it to influence in some degree party adherents, cadres and leaders alike (Duverger, 1967:177).

This line of analysis was not pursued by Duverger, nor has it yet been brought to bear in the kind of discussion of electoral alignments which asks how a stable coalition of socioeconomic forces comes to support a particular partisan configuration in a given country (Alford, 1963; Janowitz & Segal, 1967). Yet the internal decisional process is probably a prime determinant of the persistent image projected by a party.

Consider a conceptual contribution by Lipset and Rokkan, in which they sketch a developmental model for understanding the linkage between a nation-state's specific sequence of basic social cleavages and the imprint of those cleavage patterns on the structure of the resulting party system. To them, parties are "alliances in conflicts over policies and value commitments within the larger body politic" (Lipset & Rokkan, 1967:5). Parties both play up conflicts and promote coalitions to bridge cleavage lines.

Lipset and Rokkan are concerned with the historical development of the party systems found in today's mass democracies. They hold that the crystallization stage occurred before the post-World War I acceptance of universal adult suffrage in Western polities. Thus party systems reflect the cleavage lines of past generations. Cleavages arise over (*a*) dominant versus subject-culture conflicts, including elite-folk differences; (*b*) church versus state interests, including control over the nation's educational system; (*c*) agricultural versus industrial priorities, including rural-urban and central-periphery overtones; and (*d*) worker versus employer disagreements, including various Marxist formulations of class struggle. In a given country, the timing and sequence of these electoral cleavages structure the party system for generations thereafter.

It is not possible here to examine their

stimulating approach in detail. One point is relevant now. They do *not* attempt to examine the internal decisional processes that each party historically developed, while striving to survive organizationally and/or succeed in its mission when confronted with the sequence of these electoral cleavages. Yet their model rests on tacit assumptions that those decisional processes were roughly adequate—that is, able to gauge reality correctly and to respond realistically.

It is possible to infer the party's decisional process by looking at the socioeconomic electoral support it persistently receives, or by examining its liaison lines with other ancillary groups and affiliates, or by tracing what Duverger saw as various kinds of "decentralization" embedded in the party's formal structure.

Perhaps it is true that each country's party system indelibly reflects the historical accidents that led to its idiosyncratic sequence of crises and cleavages. It must surely *also* be true that another formative factor was the quality of controversy and dialogue within each party, between its several power centers, across its various tiers and levels, out to its farthest removes, and out also to the responsive ears of party adherents in the electorate. To understand the workings of a party's decisional system, it is important to consider its *acoustics*—how well participants can hear and be heard—as well as the power position and socioeconomic interests of those who take part (Wilson, 1960; 1966; Watts, 1968).

Duverger's third key question went directly to the communication-channels problem: How did a party's basic units *articulate* to form an effective apparatus? What limitations on lateral (horizontal) communication between units at the same level were maintained? Looking at the "inner democracy" practiced by Social Democratic and Social Christian parties, few formal barriers could be identified. The Communist party provided a more distinctive lesson.

> A disagreement born in one cell is not able directly to contaminate neighboring cells. It is only able to reach the section level through the medium of the cell's delegate, but there one is already in a safer and more exclusive setting. At each of the higher levels, the same inhibiting factors are found, each time more powerfully present because the framework is more formal and more demanding. Liberty of discussion is great within the cells (all witnesses agree on this point) but it diminishes in proportion as one rises in the hierarchy (Duverger, 1961:68).

The rules governing communication in Communist and Fascist parties were ideally suited to subversive work. Higher echelons could send messages selectively, could learn unobtrusively about individuals or cells guilty of backsliding or disloyalty, could mute and isolate intramural factionalism. Moreover, lateral penetration and infiltration of auxiliary groups could readily be accomplished.

Even so, factory cells could become parochial and stale. The steady increase in locality cells in the French Communist party intrigued Duverger. Some measure of lateral communication, perhaps even more than vertical, is needed to sustain a sense of mutual awareness, to show that similar efforts are simultaneously going on elsewhere, and to provide periodically something like political intelligence bulletins to give those in isolated settings a sense of what else is happening within party walls (Shoup, 1968).

Duverger stressed that a party's structural character is not dependent on whether it stands in democratic competition with others. The same cellular apparatus that serves the Communist party in its electoral, agitational, infiltrational efforts in Western Europe can perform rather different functions in a one-party state. The function of a monopoly party, however, is distinctive: ". . . not so much to administer as to ensure that administration will be dynamic and to verify its fidelity" to the party's leadership (Duverger, 1967:288). To this end, party representatives are deployed to all levels of government; they participate in local and central decisional processes; they work not only in the administrative milieus but also in unions, cooperatives, cultural associations, and other auxiliary bodies.

The monopoly party, he argued, is essentially a two-way communication structure.

> The same pyramidal structure which enables the summit to know the reactions at the base in all their diversity, permits the base to respond to directives from the top with commentaries adapted to each milieu. The party gives to government the opinion of the people; it makes understandable to people the decisions of government (Duverger, 1967:288).

Duverger was, of course, aware that such an idealized picture could conceal the reality of a tyrant's weapon—a Praetorian guard. He conceded that the distinctive feature of the monopoly party is as a conduit for downward communication. Where possible, the party relies on propaganda; where necessary, it uses police methods, even terror:

> The monopoly party cannot be separated from modern techniques of crowd control. It constitutes an organ of propaganda most perfectly of all. It is an admirable tool for molding opinion, for shaping it, giving it a framework, canalizing it, and guiding it (Duverger, 1967:290).

Listen to the masses: that is the classic "party line." Duverger added that the masses repeat more and more what one tells them, so the leaders progressively tend to hear only the echo of their own voices. "It is less the contents of its doctrine than the technique of indoctrination that secures the genuine image of a discipline freely accepted" (Duverger, 1967: 290).

Using content analysis, Milton Lodge (1968a; 1968b) has been able to show empirical trends in the growth of more pluralist configurations of strategic elites in the Soviet system. The economic elite, legal elite, military elite, and literary elite as well as the party *apparat* have long maintained specialist journals which emphasize their instrumental functions, shortcomings, and needs. By using selected years from 1952 to 1965, Lodge readily demonstrated that, for each strategic elite, what he calls group self-consciousness (indexed by references to themselves) and mutual awareness (indexed by references to another elite category) have risen sharply. Moreover, through time, radically changing conceptions have been emerging of the Party's central role in indoctrinating and socializing those who enter Soviet decisional processes. In later years as well as earlier ones, the Party journal assigns greater weight to the Party's educative role than do the specialist elite journals. For economic and legal elites, the perceived influence of the Party as a socializing agent had more than halved; for the military and literary elites, the decline in emphasis was from a quarter to a third.

Consider the rationale for this analysis. Resource allocation—whether public policy should emphasize military and heavy-industry requirements or education, light industry, and agricultural priorities—of course reflects the regime's budgeted response to the historical conditions and emerging problems confronting it. In a Party-dominated Communist state, however, only Party members would possess the "historical consciousness" to grasp with socialist realism what priorities were needed. Specialist elites would be used, but only as transmission belts, carrying the messages of a revamped allocation of manpower or materials to those affected, whipping up enthusiasm for the Party line, spelling out the new directives. Content analysis discloses, however, that the Party's shift in emphasis over the years studied (a shift from stressing the needs of heavy industry and the military to asserting the requirements called for in agriculture, education, and light industry) had lagged behind the orientation found in the economic, literary, and legal journals. Through their house organs, "the three specialist elites all manifested these values earlier and with more emphasis than did the Party" (Lodge, 1968a:22).

Thus, within the formal ranks of the Soviet Communist party—comprising all the elites—one finds a continuous tension between strategic elites whose knowledge and skills are technical and the *apparatchiki* whose knowledge and skills are doctrinal. One sees also the extent to which the growth of task-specialized information networks (a feature of any complex organization) fosters a sense of group identity and differentiation in the group's view of other groups and their proper roles.

There have been other "mass parties" also, and again the particular structural forms they took were reflections of their purposes: the democratic variants of European socialism, seeking to capture parliamentary machinery for the proletariat by educational and electoral means; the Social Christian parties, seeking through education and leadership recruitment to imbue political life with higher moral standards. When a party seeks mass membership—as continental Socialist and Social Christian parties in this century have systematically done—its organizational forms are plausibly judged by whether they serve or frustrate inner-party democracy. Since Michels' warnings, this issue has been much debated by participants as well as observers. Some recent complications are worth noting.

In West Germany, for example, the SPD (Social Democratic party) has come to dominate a number of urban centers; local government takes energy and attention away from the party's classic mission. The electoral scheme by which *Bundestag* representation is allocated includes not only voting for party lists but also voting for district representatives; campaign problems peculiar to specific geographic constituencies intrude in planning the party's electoral strategy. After its Bad Godesberg Conference in 1959, the party ceased to characterize itself officially as a class-oriented party; instead, it has sought for itself a *volkspartei* image as one more acceptable to the electorate. Its party congresses, once occasions for heated dispute among contending factions with different views on party policy issues, have now taken on a mainly demonstrative character; with television and radio permitting a mass audience to watch and listen, the "mass party" congress becomes too public an arena for serious inner-party discussion (Allardt & Littunen, 1964; Ebbighausen, 1966; Lipset & Rokkan, 1967).

Simultaneously the character of modern electoral campaigns has been radically altered. Leaders at various party levels and in different locales are seeking better and more sustained methods of communicating with their partisans—known and potential—in the electorate. Commercial organizations offer to handle the whole range of advertising problems and public relations confronting them. Party organizational channels seem too sluggish; they echo too much with irrelevant doctrines. Moreover, communication with the partisan electorate can be two-way communication. The commercialization of electoral propaganda facilities has been paralleled in West Germany by the commercial availability of a systematic feedback procedure—use of mass opinion surveys.

The same processes have been taking place in Britain, France, Italy—and the smaller democracies of Western Europe—as "mass parties" have tried to adjust to a mass-media-serviced political system (Rose, 1966). The mass parties of Europe for nearly two-thirds of this century sought to sustain inner-party democracy in what amounted to complex corporate structures better known to their functionaries and permanent cadres than to their dues-paying members. At the constituent level—among members, affiliate groups, auxiliary forces—disenchantment with the corporate party's agenda seems to be widespread and persistent (McKenzie, 1965).

Ironically, it is the mass communications media that permit a "dialogue" of sorts on substantive questions—on the merits of leaders and the priorities set for public actions—between those at the top and bottom of the party, between partisans-in-government and partisans-in-publics (Converse & Dupeux, 1962). Thus it is the mass media that in some ways seem to be transforming mass parties into cadre parties—that is, into skeletal apparatuses that provide only a framework for party effort (Hartenstein & Liepelt, 1962; Sartori, 1966).

The nineteenth-century cadre party in Europe was designed to defend and exploit the status quo and to create as little political disturbance as possible; the twentieth-century mass parties of Europe were vehicles for creating counterelites and for effectuating radical social changes. In America, where mass parties never emerged, recent historical work suggests a more dynamic process.

At the start of national life, the mere size of a legislative district disrupted the older style of "deference politics" in which "established notables could count on habits of political allegiance from men who held lesser status in the community" (Chambers, 1967).

> The larger and more diverse an electoral unit was in population and social structure, and the greater the number of different social groups it contained, the harder it was for a few to control things through informal arrangements (Goodman, 1967:71).

Nor could the emergence of a common political arena be discounted. By the early 1790s Congress had become, in Goodman's words, "a dramatic arena within which rival groups quarreled over policy questions" (Goodman, 1961:71). The federal system permitted diversity and political experimentation. Its national component gave a focus to public attention and cast state and local struggles in a different light for some.

In the urban centers, where vocational cadres manned the party machines, the socialization and assistance given to immigrant citizens helped to mobilize ethnocultural sentiments in periodic defense of party prerogatives. On the frontier, local notables were more likely to run the party show; picnics, parades, and patriotic occasions made political events an important form of popular entertainment, one that muted bitterness and fostered new community identities (Hays, 1967). By the twentieth century, America's major parties were largely interest-accommodation structures and electioneering apparatuses. Neither the educational intricacies of ideology nor the policy-making complexities of public programming were matters on which party orthodoxy was expected (Ranney & Kendall, 1956; Key, 1964; Sorauf, 1968).

A fresh look at nineteenth-century American party history leads Samuel P. Hays to argue that party communication processes involved the mobilization of local impulses for national, cosmopolitan objectives, while in the twentieth century the administrative mentality of men schooled to corporate methods of accomplishment has engendered a more coercive and manipulative attitude, impatient toward the pace and pattern of local communities—including the party outposts fitted to them.

From the beginning, the party press was a cosmopolitan force (Blumberg, 1954).

> The partisan newspaper editor had the task of defining a common ground within the party and a ground of distinction from other parties.... To do this he called upon ideas relatively divorced from community concerns and more relevant to the cosmopolitan world (Hays, 1967:161).

This seeming inconsistency in the basis of American party appeals to the electorate is explored by noting the simultaneous emphasis on emotional and rational considerations of partisanship:

The party mobilized voters on the community level by stressing ethno-cultural issues which sustained local party loyalties and party differences, and at the same time emphasized altogether different issues, such as tariff and trusts, on the national level of debate (Hays, 1967:161).

Meanwhile, the growth of corporate forms of organization in America began to reverse the flow of messages between center and periphery. Increasingly, in modern industrial and business life, these new corporate lines of communication had an administrative character, and were designed to translate central decisions into peripheral action rather than to register grass-roots sentiments in central decisional arenas, as political parties had largely been thought to do.

This same evangelical certainty concerning their diagnoses characterized most reform movements from the late nineteenth century onward—whether municipal merit systems, federal regulation of business, or state provisions for ensuring electoral democracy in nominating processes was the panacea in question. Initiative and understanding came from the top, not from the middle layers, not from the grass roots.

In the twentieth century, America's major parties have exhibited a kind of arrested development, confining their roles to office-contesting and interest-accommodating processes. They have largely foregone the political education and policy-making functions that increasingly have preoccupied party personnel in Europe, in developing societies, and in monolithic regimes. Historical evidence suggests this had *not* been so in the nineteenth century:

There is evidence that during the nineteenth century the parties were engaged in propaganda and political socialization activities on a scale which knows no parallel today. This intense activity seems to have been closely related to the quasi-monopoly which election campaigns and the partisan press of that period had on entertainment prior to the development of other mass media, and also to the relatively extreme frequency of elections and variability in election dates which existed prior to about 1880 (Burnham, 1967:279).

Continuing this interpretation by Walter Burnham, the twentieth century saw the party press disappear and the political campaign dislodged from its central place as a species of entertainment:

American parties during the twentieth century have not been organized to provide political education or indoctrination for their clienteles on a month-in-month-out basis. Such an effort would require, in all probability, stable dues-paying memberships and the development of permanent ancillary party agencies for reaching a mass clientele whether or not an election was pending (Burnham, 1967:279).

Confronted by the intricacies of contemporary formulations of public policy, the relevance of "party politics" as a mode for sustaining public control over men and issues seems strained and unrealistic to many investigators (Verba & Nie, 1972). This is not to deny the central role of party mechanisms in knitting together the political community, in reconciling classes, ethnic groupings, and parochial interests to accept the political formula for achieving legitimate acts of government even while encouraging electoral cleavages over a limited range of men and issues.

Theodore Lowi argues that the basic function performed *within* each major party (even while the office-seeking function is shared between them) is to choose among contending interests and issues those which become the agenda of formal public discourse; this process of selection is not quiet and placid:

On an agenda, broadly defined, interests have reached a relatively late stage of development .... Party leaders find themselves in the uncomfortable position of leading a party comprised of *both* sides of each issue. The leaders inevitably become brokers .... More clear debates on the issues, and more mass decisions on candidates that are clearly associated with specific policies alternatives, have been made *within* parties between candidates for nomination rather than between two candidates for election (Lowi, 1967:264).

Lowi argues that this "constituent" function of parties has been the persistent function performed by them in American history. Each major party has been a channel making possible a popularly based policy-making process "without very much directing the policy outcomes themselves" (Lowi, 1967:264). Not the "inner-party democracy" of European socialism, but a complex communication network for alerting those in government to the concerns and grievances of different sorts of ordinary citizens: such is each major American party, kept so in large part by the presence of its rival (Wahlke, 1967; Gatlin, 1968).

In a sense, the American party system was "modern" from its inception, as LaPalombara and Weiner use that term—sensitivity to public support being the distinguishing mark. By contrast, although the European socialist movement produced democratic as well as totalitarian varieties of "mass parties," none of them was genuinely "public conscious" until after the Second World War, while its cadre parties gradually became more so (Lipset & Rokkan, 1967).

In America, as in the new states of the twentieth century, parties from the beginning were vehicles for achieving national integration by getting general agreement on a working agenda of "urgent" business, and leaving to legislatures and public officials the task of finding solutions or palliatives if possible (Lipset, 1963). By contrast, however, coercive and tutorial attitudes toward the unpoliticized masses are characteristic among the activists of the single monopoly party that controls political development in many of these new states (Geertz, 1963; Pye, 1965; Zolberg, 1966; Wallerstein, 1967).

Again, in substantial measure, what Hays calls "corporately organized" solutions to health, housing, and welfare needs were forthcoming by "cosmopolitan" efforts in the private sector of American life. But the modernizing demands in today's new nations and the weakness of the private sectors there have made parties assume the functions of policy formation and bureaucratic supervision as government programs proliferate.

Preoccupied with these various and changing functions, students of party phenomena have nevertheless come to see the structural silhouettes of different kinds of party apparatuses in comparative terms (see Epstein, 1968). They have speculated about the properties of alternative "basic units": which encouraged participation and discussion, and which fostered discipline and missionary zeal? They have considered the significance of different rules to govern lateral and vertical communication lines within party structures: what barriers ought to keep cadres in line, and what barriers should curb factional alliances? Many have been fascinated with the way party apparatuses seem to be shaped by the exoskeleton of governmental and electoral forms. But faced by so many militant mass parties bent on radical, social, and political change, the most consistent thesis seems to be that a party's structure is shaped by its ideological and strategic purposes (Ostrogorski, 1902; Michels, 1915).

THE PARTY AS A COMMUNICATION STRUCTURE

In the discursive work we have been examining, the notion that political parties are complex communication structures has never been far below the surface. Rarely sustained by empirical evidence, this work consists of insightful commentaries, suggestive leads for future inquiries, and provocative essays (Crotty, 1968a; Hennessy, 1968). The concept of structural articulation recurrently injects awareness of communication barriers. Sketches of historical transformations in party functions highlight half a dozen distinctive communication processes: electioneering, interest accommodation, socialization, indoctrination, mutual awareness, legitimation. What impact on modern parties will be had by the electronic media and the public relations firm is recognized as an open question (Crotty, 1971; Agranoff, 1972).

We turn to a body of research that seeks to be systematic, empirical, and rigorous in examining contemporary party phenomena. To focus attention on communications more systematically, we will use a simple analytical scheme. Some of its key terms are first discussed, after which its analytical utility is briefly illustrated. Thereafter a number of parallel and converging lines of inquiry by those working in this research area are discussed.

Party is understood to refer to *extended structures* for coordinating political efforts. Attention first centers on structures—both organizational and attitudinal. From *any* partisan perspective (and not only from the leadership positions), a prime question is what help the apparatus provides—what grasp it improves, what penetration it facilitates, what reach it affords. A concept of "effective structural extent" is useful; it calls for explicit delineation of that segment of a party apparatus relevant to a given political effort. To decide what is relevant, the "acoustical properties" of each possible component need to be estimated empirically.

Next the phenomenon of *developmental impact* is broached. Distinctions are useful among "constituent interests" represented in the decisional net at the planning, implementation, and result stages of any political effort. Integral to this aspect is the problem of measuring fluctuations in "message loads" in the relevant channels of the party apparatus.

Finally, examination is made of the *behavioral adjustment* patterns of those making the partisan effort. The concept of feedback, through which higher level control and direction in corporate structures are sustained, becomes of problematic value in actual performance of party apparatuses. Two somewhat related concepts—those of "spontaneous field correction" in face-to-face situations and "default corrections" which require a repertoire of stopgap routines—are discussed.

Wherever political parties assume tasks—contesting elections, organizing legislative bodies, reconciling group interests, distributing patronage, articulating group grievances, facilitating bureaucratic access—that affect the normal functioning of political and governmental institutions in ways that become controversial, it is likely that the weight of governmental authority will be invoked to impose a statutory grid of structural constraints on the previously free party organizations. Electoral history provides countless examples. Thus in earlier times with respect to the nominating process, American party leaders could proceed largely as they pleased: e.g., establish time, place, method, eligibility, and control arrangements. Later, of course, statutory specification of these details has become quite common (Hennessy, 1968).

To illustrate our analytical scheme, consider two American rival party units in a constituency where a special election has been called to fill a vacancy. Part of what is meant by "effective extent" is immediately apparent. The specific electoral circumstances have eliminated the problems of intercontest coordination, slate support, and similar complications present when a general election takes place. On the other hand, special statutory requirements concerning nomination procedures, campaign finance, etc., probably are invoked.

It seems probable that during the campaign weeks ahead, the local press and broadcast media will cover only sketchily the events: who are contending, what issues and interests are involved, what significant campaign episodes occur, what drives and rallies are carried out by the rival apparatuses. In such campaigns, coverage is typically not thorough enough to be picked up by partisans who make only ordinary efforts to keep informed (Converse, 1966a). Yet the volume of information flow provided by the public media is a basic determinant of the campaign's penetration to the electorate's peripheral segments.

Perhaps, if a two-step communication process were traced, the local mass media might be found to have reached enough opinion leaders so that the relevant messages did percolate down to most would-be activists (McClosky, 1959). But even this is problematic. In the more crowded and hectic weeks of a general election campaign, many of the most elementary facts—who and what the contest is about—fail to reach significant fractions of the partisan electorate, even of the party activists (Dennis, 1966). Miller and Stokes (1966) suggest that only about half the 1958 electorate knew anything about their local congressional candidates.

In the one-contest circumstance of a special election, each party's task at first seems straightforward: get enough votes to win. But how? By mobilizing the party faithful? Recruiting people new to the electorate? Converting followers of the rival party? Clearly, if there is any one-sidedness in party strength among the voters, different combinations of these strategies would be appropriate for the dominant and minority party, respectively.

Who will plan the campaign? Somehow the nomination of a candidate must be arranged, if a free-for-all is to be avoided. Until that is settled—or can be presumed with confidence—it is hard to estimate how much campaign money, auxiliary group support, local party-activist effort, and presumptive voter support will be *needed* to make victory a distinct and serious possibility. Hung up with these questions is a shadow set: how much of each critical resource will probably be *forthcoming*.

The mere recitation of these considerations clarifies what the "effective structural extent" of each party apparatus is. To make the impending contest feasible—that is, to have a serious chance of winning—how far up and in, how far out and down in the extended party apparatus does one have to go to mobilize the needed resources?

Suppose that each party's campaign planners had a complete "partisan status roster" for the constituency in question, classifying citizens as leaders, functionaries, backers, activists, militants, sympathizers, supporters, gloaters, and so forth. Even a rough facsimile of such a roster would help to specify the upper limits possible by a total coordination of partisan effort, involving an optimal number of each party-status type.

To be sure, in a hopeless district, not even outside resources could produce a respectable effort. Short of that, however, such a roster would suggest alternative plurality-building strategies. It would also help to clarify what kinds of campaign communication media were needed. Some types could only be reached by mass media, some through organized party rallies or parades, others by organized personal contact drives, still others only through informal contact patterns, and a few—the activists—by membership communication channels and occasions (Wood, 1959).

The communication media mix presumably should be optimized by using some marginal payoff criteria, not only in terms of monetary costs but also in terms of the possible boomerang effect of overcommunicating with some people in order to reach others via the same medium in a short time span. To nail it down, at least the elementary *acoustical* properties of each channel in the available communications apparatus need to be estimated:

Who can hear and who can be heard? What receptivities or resistances do receivers have? What skills and sensitivities do senders possess? No doubt several media mixes for the same set of target groups might prove equally efficacious. No doubt, too, several alternative sets of target groups might be equally likely to yield enough votes to win (Riker, 1962; M. Leiserson, 1968).

Friendship nets provide one of the best gauges of the penetration into the ethnocultural and socioeconomic subcommunities of a locality that potentially is available to the party as part of the effective extent to which a serious political effort could reach (Crotty, 1967). Evidence from a 1956 survey of Los Angeles party activists by Marvick and Nixon suggests some ironical features. In each kind of political locale—sure, doubtful, or lost—more than half the party activists reported that they had met most of their friends through political activities. Furthermore, in the most competitive area, there was a distinct rise in the proportion who said that most of their house guests were party activists. And in all areas, it was the less-reliable fringe activist who was more likely to entertain ordinary nonpoliticized guests in his home. The very motives that make core cadremen find friends among their fellow activists cause them to be exposed to less typical samples of district opinion. And it is ironical that the party apparatus that occupied the most competitive ground found its intelligence network less farflung because of the very politicization engendered by the tense rivalry (Marvick and Nixon, 1961; D. Marvick, 1968).

Eldersveld (1964) developed a communication-style typology based on the amount and levels of organizational liaison work done. *Cosmopolitans* had wide contacts throughout the party structure, including the precinct level. *Elite associates* had little interaction at lower echelon levels, while *localists* interacted exclusively within narrow geographic orbits. *Isolates* sustained virtually no significant communication links. Not surprisingly, the different styles reflect differences in motivation and time given to party work. The style adopted was also a reflection of the socioeconomic subcoalitions represented within party ranks and in the lines it maintained to auxiliary groups—unions, business associations, ethnic and nationality clubs, etc.

The markedly individualized nature of liaison efforts by active partisans was related to their noncoercive character, he noted. "There was a certain 'anarchy' in communicative interaction in the party. Personal relationship patterns developed. Contacts might be haphazard and unplanned. And the individual leader was free to develop his own communication lines according to his own drive, whim, and time determinations" (Eldersveld, 1964:359). Seeking to measure the prevalence of "broken" patterns between party levels from precinct up, Eldersveld found about one in every four precinct leaders sustained only a selective and eccentric circuit of intramural contacts with higher echelons.

In 1965 Marvick and Eldersveld made a survey of 365 party cadres in Munich following the national election. Both city-executive personnel and cadremen in every segment of each party's district apparatus were interviewed. In both SPD (Social Democratic party) and CSU (Christian Social Union) ranks, the city-level liaison men overwhelmingly relied on informal conversation with other party activists to keep up with Munich political developments. At the opposite extreme, the dominant tendency among district outpost "basemen" was to rely entirely on mass media for Munich news. District-based "linkmen"—those who regularly kept in contact with city-level party leaders—considered the more formal party conferences and briefing procedures to be their appropriate way of learning about party politics in Munich (D. Marvick, 1966).

In organizations held together loosely by the versatile performance of liaison figures—and party apparatuses must rely especially on such men because sporadic and unusual patterns of coordinated effort are called for in electoral, agitational, and legislative arenas, and timing considerations are often crucial to success—feedback barriers arise from their personalities and preoccupations: ambition, spitefulness, embarrassment, garrulity are terms that suggest the range (Marvick & Eldersveld, 1961). If key liaison figures adopt rigid ideological positions, or espouse policies antipathetic to basic support groups, the kinds of impedances they introduce into the larger feedback network become systematic sources of distortion and sabotage.

The classic political response to this threat has been to try to co-opt dissident elements into the party's decisional structure. Any dissident element is easier to cope with if it *seeks* to be heard. But subunit cadres—loyal as they see it, stubborn in their methods, proud of their records—often do not seek a voice in higher councils. They are veto elements in a dual sense: failing to cooperate with new tactics or use new methods; delaying, distorting, even suppressing feedback information about how well the new and old approaches are working (Salisbury, 1965; Bowman & Boynton, 1966; D. Marvick, 1968).

The crucial point that is brought out by emphasizing a communications approach is that the *effective reach* of each segment in the party apparatus depends on various types of partisans (including potentials) who are at different removes from the politicized center of party direction and control for the political effort in question. As Crotty has suggested, party needs to be viewed as "a set of interdependent actors operating within a given group context and performing acts calculated to realize instrumental and adaptive objectives" (Crotty, 1968b:10). There is nothing basically different about applying the concepts of effective structural extents and acoustical properties of apparatus channels to any political effort for which an extended coordinating apparatus—i.e., a political party—is appropriate.

Some useful research along the lines thus far sketched has been done. In Gary, Indiana, Rossi and Cutright sent mail questionnaires to a sample of Democratic and Republican precinct captains inquiring how active they were in trying to influence voters. What was the volume of each precinct leader's politically relevant daily contacts? What was the amount of time he gave to his role? Estimates were also obtained about how many workers were active and how many house meetings were held in behalf of the party's legislative candidate. A multiple-regression analysis of demographic and electoral statistics established what the precinct vote would have been if it had depended only on socioeconomic variables. Party activity was then demonstrated to be a plausible explanation for why some precincts were poorly predicted by socioeconomic variables (Cutright & Rossi, 1958a; 1958b; Rossi & Cutright, 1961; Perry, 1968).

A more elaborate inquiry has been reported by Katz and Eldersveld, (1961; Eldersveld, 1964). Using systematic interviews with 142 precinct leaders and a sample of 596 voters drawn at random from the eighty-seven Detroit precincts in which the precinct leaders worked, they, too, found that party organizational efforts seemed to modify the vote that could be expected on the basis of socioeconomic composition of the precinct. When the rival parties matched each other's campaign efforts, they cancelled each other out. Socioeconomic predictors then came very close to predicting the actual presidential vote in that kind of precinct. In localities where one-sided efforts occurred, however, a modification of as much as 10 percentage points was attributable to organized party activities.

Harold Guetzkow (1965) has suggested that a number of "task-specialized" information nets are likely to emerge in any complex organization. These nets tend to generate rather specialized jargon, often evade official prescriptions in order to get the work done, and tend to involve more lateral message flow and more two-way patterns of communication than most nets do. In a series of case studies of electoral campaigns, the encroachment of public relations men as specialists in mass-communications campaign problems into the campaign-planning circles of American party leadership at all levels has been effectively traced (Kelley, 1956; 1960; 1962; Leuthold, 1968; MacNeil, 1968).

To a large firm like Whitaker and Baxter in California, the commercial advertising campaign is a model with significant modifications. First, in politics you have to win, not come in a close second. Next, in politics the whole campaign is telescoped into a few short weeks. Moreover, in politics the skilled party propagandist is forced to meet vigorous and direct attacks on his "merchandise" by equally skilled men in the rival camp. None of these constraints is found in most commercial advertising work.

To blueprint a campaign means three things: issues have to be developed, a time sequence of campaign actions has to be planned, and the desired media mix has to be chosen. Little wonder that emphasis is heavy on headquarters' keeping close control over which issues to play up and which to ignore, on molding a candidate's image to fit the constituency "market," and on continuing to steer the campaign vehicle as the few short weeks unfold. Grass-roots feedback findings—especially those of competent commercial polls—may suggest changes in style or theme; if so, only a centralized decisional structure plus a disciplined task force can hope to revise matters appropriately (Kelley, 1956; White, 1960; 1965; Levin & Blackwood, 1962).

Once the campaign has been blueprinted, the task of securing its implementation begins. Perhaps some parts can be farmed out to a commercial advertising firm and tailored to whatever market research indicates will sell. This is mainly plausible for the mass media portions of the plan. When the organizational side of the campaign effort is considered, however, it is soon evident that important effects will only become known as the campaign unfolds. Like any other political effort mounted by a party, the campaign moves from a beginning through a buildup to a climax.

After the campaign effort by both sides has been made, the actual vote will reflect the constituent interests that *did* guide voting behavior. In the campaign-planning stage, however, there is no guarantee that the pattern of constituent interests taken into account will prove to be a winning formula. There are many technical and strategic calculations on which error is always possible: how to reach young voters is a technical problem; what appeal will succeed in winning their support is a strategic one.

The process of making a campaign plan may well involve preliminary talks with knowledgeable people, long sessions with a small group of party strategists, and subsequent spot clearances on controversial points with influential figures. Those participating in the planning process will, of course, spontaneously represent some constituent interests because of their own backgrounds; more calculatedly, they will take into account other constituent interests because of information received from available backlogs and current sources—e.g., they will read voting analysis papers, opinion-polling reports, local editorials, private correspondence, and so forth. Each political activist holds ethical, ideological, and communal attitudes that represent cumulative overlays of social and political education; no matter how professionally detached he may feel from his social origins, presumably his basic attitude structure will affect the way he approaches the complex task of campaign planning (Eldersveld, 1964; Lamb & Smith, 1968).

During the campaign period itself, distinctive problems will result because rival campaigns are being mounted in the same area. Depending on how ambitious the mass media plans of each side are, and what kind of tempo for the buildup has been scheduled, the political rhetoric heard and read will be correspondingly distorted, incoherent, or drowned out. Corrections can still be made on some points, depending on what is learned through feedback processes, and depending also on whether there are built-in default corrections—stopgap routines—previously made available to be invoked whenever feedback "readings" disclose messageflow troubles of specific kinds.

In mass media political communication, it can be argued that there is almost no spontaneous correction, since the audience is not physically present as a sounding board. So far as audience response goes, once a blooper occurs, the damage is done. After the fact, a situation can be patched up. Unless it was a canned release or a delayed broadcast, it cannot easily be suppressed or retrieved.

In the same campaign, there are also message flows carried by activists and enthusiasts who take partisan appeals to lukewarm and even hostile quarters. These human exponents give a personalized version to the standardized campaign appeals. Whether they make speeches, contact voters systematically, or talk politics casually with acquaintances, they not only convey the basic message (so far as they understand the desired emphasis) but they also contribute their own ideological and/or ethical comments by word or gesture, and they reflect the social and political backgrounds to which they have been socialized (Forthal, 1946; Hirschfield, Swanson, & Blank, 1962; Wolfinger, 1963; Bowman & Boynton, 1966; D. Marvick, 1968).

It is possible, of course, to act in light of feedback information about truly flagrant examples of issue distortion; campaign managers sometimes can shunt aside public speakers whose views or style make their contributions more damaging than helpful. It is also true that much can be learned (although it is more doubtful if "corrections" are so easily achieved) by paying attention to the volunteered feedback messages coming from party workers about the audience reactions and neighborhood responses they have found while electioneering (D. Marvick, 1968).

The most important point about these human exponents—these party activists—is that they are able, in a face-to-face situation, to make spontaneous corrections in their performances. They are on the scene, aware of a political error made or a false note sounded, and they have some ability to correct it or compensate for it before it is too late to retrieve the situation. The remaining consideration is whether they *want* to correct the "error" (Forthal, 1946; Flinn & Wirt, 1965). They are not neutral instruments. Like other ordinary adults, they have moral reservations about some political tactics, even when used by their own side. They have views—strong or mild—on the issues played up and the issues ignored, and on the group interests catered to and brushed aside. In their own persons, moreover, they possess (or lack) the social credentials needed for easy interchanges in face-to-face or group discussion (Hirschfield, Swanson, & Blank, 1962; Wolfinger, 1963; Althoff & Patterson, 1966).

Some other features of feedback mechanisms in politics are suggested by this example. At most, higher level party personnel can be alerted to lost chances and to bad guesses. When the feedback message goes beyond the "effective extent" of the task-specific party apparatus, it probably should only be considered background information, cumulatively enlightening but *not* a basis for corrective action now (Rosenthal & Weiss, 1967).

On some points, directives might be sent down from some distance to the basic party unit, insisting on attention to a forgotten or unappreciated issue. Consider the difficulties. Suppose that public opinion research has disclosed a remarkably high level of concern about the care of mental patients, and a desire for public action, among specific target groups in the electorate. An unknown but widespread level of ineptitude and recalcitrance probably exists among grassroots party workers about how to handle this new issue. The party activists are thus a kind of semipermeable barrier to achieving any campaign publicity focused on the candidate's concern for this problem.

A candidate shifting his thematic emphasis, articulating the new line he wants to follow, and using radio and television as the media for doing so probably has a better chance of reaching his supporters in time and with meaningful detail embodied in his message to them than by using the older intramural party channels to communicate downward and outward to the boundary personnel of the party apparatus. If so, this is one basis for suggesting that the modern "activist party" is not so clearly about to lose its electioneering function to mass media specialists and commercial services—and it may well do a better job *in tandem* than it did before (C. Thompson, 1956; Nexon, 1971).

As Raymond Bauer has noted, "even with respect to a formally organized feedback system, there is a minimum of one or two organizational layers between the relevant decision points and the entrance of the information into the organization" (Bauer, 1966:63). Feedback information is channeled—and edited, distorted, annotated in the process—along circuitous paths inside organizations like political parties. It comes largely from persons in "boundary roles"—these roles that bring party activists into contact with the task-specific environment. Many whose party work gives them some grasp of environmental forces lack authoritative status within the party, but they can and do control the flow of information and disseminate it selectively. What Easton has called "withinputs" often consist of editorial feedbacks commenting on messages from outside in ways that reflect the variety of perspectives, criteria for judgment, and status preoccupations of activists at different points in the party apparatus (Verba, 1961; Salisbury, 1965; Rosenthal & Weiss, 1967).

Parties, if one charts their natural history, seem typically to start as conscious efforts at practical measures of cooperation. "Like-minded men"—however subversive or complacent their outlook—find it easy to work together, especially if the association is transitory and sporadic. Institutionalized occasions often set the pace and determine the focus of party work. Even agitation for ideological causes tends to proceed by fits and starts, and activists are busy in some locales, quiescent in others.

Gradually, from an accretion of events and in ways as yet poorly understood, the symbols of a party serve to establish attitude structures in the minds of those who identify themselves as party adherents. Whatever kind of political activity the party activists undertake, so long as a minimum amount of publicity results and unactivated, often distant adherents are encouraged to believe in the reality of an organization for coordinating political efforts, some of the lukewarm nonactivists will probably be mobilized, some will consciously defect, others simply drop out (Wolfinger, 1963).

The turnover of partisan affiliations is a dynamic aspect of political socialization now beginning to receive systematic attention by investigators. It stands at the edge of our present concern. The impetus for this work was the empirical comparative inquiry into attitudes sustaining *The Civic Culture* in five Western countries by Almond and Verba (1963). Four types of partisans—open, apathetic, intense, and parochial—were identified in seeking to measure the extent to which the connotations of partisanship applied to relationships in what was conventionally considered the political sphere, or to private and communal worlds as well (Almond & Verba, 1963; E. W. Marvick, 1968).

Once partisanship has crystallized, it

shows considerable persistence as a presumptive guide for the lukewarm as well as the fervid partisan to follow. It helps him to sort out issues and men without too much effort. It stirs up a temporary intensity of feeling in him, which is vented during the campaign weeks (when a certain partisan license is acceptable) and which is put aside in an "adult" manner once the time for partisan politics has passed (Berelson, Lazarsfeld, & McPhee, 1954).

Converse (1966b) has interpreted party loyalty as an inertia or momentum force, reflected in the consistency of one's voting behavior but temporarily subject to disruption by sufficiently powerful short-term forces. Thus in a system where party loyalties are well crystallized, party fortunes are responsive to the sheer volume of information flow, he argues. The more backlog knowledge of politics a person has, the more stable his partisanship, once established.

When a lukewarm partisan is not upset by any flow of current information, he is likely to persist in his habitual voting pattern. If new and disturbing interpretations of the current political scene do reach him, however, he is likely to be highly suggestible, at least temporarily. As for participation, "prior political involvement clearly predisposes both to a more vigorous information search *and* to an increased tendency to form and give opinions" (Converse, 1966:155).

In another study by Stokes and Miller, also using the extensive interview files of the Survey Research Center at the University of Michigan, some implications about the constituency "accountability" of a legislator and his willingness to break with party discipline in casting legislative votes are traced to the *lack* of information back home about what congressmen do in Washington. Nor does the public see individual candidates for Congress in terms of party programs: "Our constituent interviews indicate that the popular image of the Congressman is almost barren of policy content" (Miller & Stokes, 1966:206).

In a tentative way, their analysis suggests that quite a different set of considerations affects a legislator's visibility to his constituents. Except in metropolitan districts, a great deal depends on whether candidate and voter live in the same community. "Candidates will be joined by formal and informal communication networks to many of the voters living in the same community, and they may also be objects of considerable community pride" (Miller & Stokes, 1966:208).

Neither of these lines of inquiry is concerned with how the party apparatus by its coordinated effort affects the psychological reality of his party to an ordinary citizen. Other work that is similarly impressive in its use of survey materials also stands at one margin of our concern here. For example, Stokes (1966) has proposed what he calls a "spatial model" of voters' attitudes toward parties as a way of learning more about what rival parties in the same system stand for. How close one party is to another, how distant in ideological terms, how available as a vehicle for championing one's class or ethnic interests—these are some of the complexities that can be explored in terms of such models. Efforts to clarify the commonalities of policy concern, neighborhood residence, or the social characteristics that link party members will similarly contribute to our understanding of the complexities of partisanship as an attitude structure which adults in most modern countries use, one is tempted to feel, as much to avoid the intrusion of organized party business into their private lives as to encourage it (McPhee & Glaser, 1962; Converse, 1964; 1966b; Stokes, 1966; D. F. Thompson, 1970).

CORPORATE PARTISAN STRUCTURES

Eldersveld, whose work contains the most extended treatment of intraparty communication processes yet made, began with the assumption that the nexus between structure and purpose was complex, obscure, and probably tailor-made to each locale. "Parties are merely a particular structural response to the needs of a social and political system in a particular milieu" (Eldersveld, 1964:2). Nevertheless, in democratic societies, parties are specialized systems of action. Their primary goal is to occupy some public leadership posts; they stand in electoral competition with one another, and pursue distinctive strategies to secure public support and to adapt to a changing environment.

To study political parties thus understood, Eldersveld argued the importance of three basic conceptions of a party's structure: as a task group, as a decisional system, and as an informational network. The same structural relationships need to be considered in three analytically different ways in order to build up contrasting models of party structure. Hence the old "boss-ridden machine" in American politics featured a communication pattern "emphasizing low reciprocity, instrumentalist content, and bureaucratic conformity" (Eldersveld, 1964:338). At the same time, high efficiency in task performance was expected, and only limited involvement by lower cadres in party decision-making.

Quite a different type is the "ideological party association." Here the flow of communications is open in all directions, but decisions tend also to involve everyone and task performance is likely to be inefficient. Another variant, the "status-oriented structure," is nearly moribund in all three respects: few tasks are undertaken, few decisions are made, and barely enough communication takes place to sustain the expectation among relevant partisans that it continues to be a meaningful structural entity. The model at the opposite extreme from this—an "economic team" as proposed by Anthony Downs—is quite artificial: a coalition whose members agree on all goals and formulate policies in order to win elections. As Eldersveld notes, "Implicit in his model is the expectation of effective communicative relationships, high efficiency, and high decisional involvement" (Eldersveld, 1964:339).

System constraints may impose functions on them, but party structures are basically shaped by their environment and by their intramural dynamics also. Eldersveld, after looking at the empirical evidence from his Detroit study, highlights features of the kind of party structures that fit the modern American scene:

1. "Organizational slack" is present because central control is weak, indoctrination is poor, competition is worrisome only in some arenas and locales, and party cadre motivations are highly diverse.
2. "Partial communication" patterns are common because of "the presence of large numbers of social deviants recruited for party work, the unequal status of the subcoalitions in the structure, the isolation of the individual activists within the organization, and the differential mobility aspirations of the careerists" (Eldersveld, 1964:340).
3. "Autonomization of decision-making" therefore tends to characterize the extended party structure: at each geographic outpost, a preoccupation with how to win votes locally; at the coordinating center, persistent concern with substantive matters of organizational policy and status.

In Eldersveld's picture, screening and discussion of conflicts that threaten party vitality or success begin mainly in the middle layers of structure—layers that exist partly as buffers to protect the top party elite from lower level demands, and partly as transmission belts to carry out the tasks of coordinating the activities of the organization's base personnel.

Schlesinger started his stimulating discussion of party organization by eschewing interest in the tightly knit parties with their oligarchic tendencies which so often dominate nondemocratic settings now as in the past. Analysis of the "office-seeking parties" found in electoral democracies has been neglected. These are loosely structured organizations—the kind that observers find hard to distinguish from their environment (Schlesinger, 1965; 1966). The number of elective offices at various levels plus the statutory bases of eligibility and nomination by parties combine to create an externally imposed grid. The political opportunity structure narrows to the number of vacancies likely to occur in a given time span, either because incumbents voluntarily leave, or because they can be ousted electorally (Schlesinger, 1967).

To Schlesinger there is little point in looking at the formal organizational chart of an American election-oriented party. He is convinced that we must avoid fostering an "illusion of organization" by the uncritical belief that an organizational scaffolding does exist, that its officials have minimal control of the situation in every constituency, and that they are minimally informed of developments in each locality. None of this, he suggests, may necessarily be the case. Instead, he radically confines his attention to "election-winning machinery." He proposes a model that focuses on the truly meaningful nuclear unit: a candidate and enough votes to win. All else is secondary, if not superfluous.

In his formula, those who achieve contact with voters are the people making the primary contribution to the nuclear unit's task—to get and keep a given public office. There are "connective" contributions that also serve party interests. Leadership, recruitment practices, issue formulation, money, campaign services, communications, and intelligence are the main headings he uses to discuss them. They are all useful but they are not vital in furthering the basic goal: winning elections.

The nuclear unit is virtually autonomous, an organization to itself. So loosely knit is the coalition of such units that one wonders what forces sustain any trans-local effort. Of course, a sporadically available opportunity will occur to capture statewide or national office, and hence "nuclear units" keyed to the office-seeking tasks dictated by those larger constituencies will also appear. He concedes the place of multi-nuclear relationships, and is at pains to distinguish the interlocking and overlapping character of constituency boundaries. Congruent, enclaved, and disjointed constituencies are his main types. The prime question is always who needs whom in each political phase: nominations, election campaigns, or governing processes. Clusters and factions form almost entirely on opportunistic terms.

If power must be won through competition, electoral sensitivity is the basic quality needed by office seekers. How to win becomes a key consideration, especially for those seeking to build a career in political life. It is also important for those limiting their ambitions to holding a specific office, term after term, or even those who aim only to spend a single term in public life. It is the ambition of the office-seeking politician—especially the progressively ambitious one—plus his skill in fitting his appeal to the character of his constituency that determine electoral success, and hence the vitality of party organization. Understandably, the kind of communication and intelligence most significant in Schlesinger's model is that which informs the candidate about his voters—the press, polls, his own files kept for personal use.

Unlike Eldersveld's case, in Schlesinger's model little or no place is given to ideological goals, to social considerations motivating participants, or the bureaucratic outlook that long participation in organizational politics can sometimes produce. Schlesinger sees slight danger from activists bent upon endowing the party with a purposive mission; key decisional circles should merely be insulated against them and they should be discouraged by a truly success-minded candidate. Schlesinger is skeptical of prophecies holding that organizational cadres will turn into a party bureaucratic class. In the kind of success-minded political subculture he envisages, when a party unit is truly bent on winning, this is not likely. In brief, Schlesinger's model is meant to provide an explicit and deliberately unsentimental set of criteria for making comparative judgments about the functionality of contributions large and small to the single objective for which electoral parties exist—to win elections.

An analytical scheme for highlighting communication factors in party work was introduced earlier in this chapter. It differs from Schlesinger's model in three ways. First, it would treat winning an election as *one* kind of political effort mounted by a party apparatus. Only to the candidate is it directly significant as a career step furthering his ambition, however. To others, winning is a group achievement for those "constituent" interests taken into account when the campaign plan was devised, further embellished and modified during the campaign period, and implicit in the plurality coalition that prevailed on election day.

Second, it would ask how large and complex a party apparatus is probally needed to do the job—in this case, win an election. How far up and in, how far out and down does the party apparatus need to be extended to be large enough in resources to accomplish the coordinated task ahead?

Finally, it treats behavioral phenomena like ideology, sociability, bureaucratic unimaginativeness, and other kinds of sluggishness and cleavage within a given party unit as factors that have to be taken into account by those seeking to fashion a workable plan. In fact, those factors enter on the ground floor, since the personal stamp of active participants is an inescapable element in the "constituent interest" configuration that de facto emerges and for which the campaign is waged (Lindblom, 1965).

CONCLUSION

Political parties are complex structures—attitudinal as well as corporate—for coordinating political efforts across extended domains. This definition does not neatly exclude pressure groups, or newspaper syndicates, or secret subversive armies. On the contrary, it includes them. If investigation shows party apparatuses to have distinctive characteristics, more precise specifications can be added. Nor does this definition stipulate that any specific set of purposes or functions are essential. Parties can aim at capturing public offices; educating a mass following; recruiting a political elite imbued with higher ethics or superior analytical skills; engaging in revolutionary agitation, clandestine subversion, or bureaucratic policing work. Whatever its functions or purposes, as investigators have explored the complexities entailed by any of these tasks, they have recognized that each party was an *extensive* coordinating apparatus (A. Leiserson, 1958; Crotty, 1968b).

Comparatively speaking, each variant has exhibited distinctive constraints and options when observed in historical perspective. We have tried to trace the differences between elite-sensitive and public-sensitive parties, and especially the ways in which European mass parties were attempts to *avoid* becoming public-sensitive structures. What impact on modern parties the advent of mass media, especially television, and commercial coordinating services will have has been briefly examined; the prognosis seems reasonably good that the kind of activist-enrolled, public-sensitive parties America has always had will continue to perform their "constituent" function, and may even do it better. The mass-enrolled, non-public-sensitive parties of Western Europe are structures gradually transforming their support coalitions away from dominance by workers and intellectuals. Inner-party democracy is no longer a pattern of doctrinal polemics; as party functionaries become increasingly committed to electoral democracy, their success-mindedness prompts them to become brokerage politicians, building support by interest accommodation strategies (Epstein, 1968).

Examination of the behavioral research relevant to communication processes in parties has meant giving attention to work on how partisan attitude structures are formed, how volume of political information affects their expression, and what commonalities of group interests, shared likes and dislikes, or ideological judgment those who identify with the same party symbols have. Findings about partisan attitudes by many scholars have contributed forcefully to the widely felt need to reformulate the recalcitrant notion of "party" itself.

Eldersveld's insistence on the use of three analytical approaches to the same structural relationships has produced our most subtle formulation to date of what are the distinctive features of parties as organizations functioning in modern democracies. He examines party life in all its diversity with contemplative calm. Schlesinger, more impatient to fashion a tool for comparative analysis and for normative evaluation of what is "functional" or "bad" in terms of his model, has proposed a special model of the "multinuclear" party organization that singlemindedly is bent upon winning elections. How useful it will be in anticipating and analyzing patterns of behavioral evidence of the kind that Eldersveld's more eclectic approach subsumes remains to be demonstrated.

Finally, an "extended coordination apparatus" scheme has been outlined here to highlight communication features. Its main points are three: (*a*) the effective *structural extent* of a party is task specific, and involves estimating the *acoustical properties* of various channels in the available party apparatus; (*b*) the *constituent interests* embodied in a plan and implemented by a campaign are only imperfectly reflected in the formal results, the interpretation of which requires analysis of the *message flows* that have nourished the political effort from start to finish; and (*c*) the main adjustments to a campaign plan during its execution time result from spontaneous field corrections and simple default strategies rather than from intramural direction and control.

REFERENCES

Agranoff, Robert.
1972 The New Style in Election Campaigns. Boston: Holbrook Press.

Alford, Robert.
1963 Party and Society: The Anglo-American Democracies. Chicago: Rand McNally.

Allardt, Erik, and Y. Littunen (eds.).
1964 Cleavages, Ideologies and Party Systems. Helsinki: Westermarck Society.

Almond, Gabriel.
1954 Appeals of Communism. Princeton, New Jersey: Princeton University Press.

Almond, Gabriel, and James Coleman (eds.).
1960 The Politics of the Developing Areas. Princeton, New Jersey: Princeton University Press.

Almond, Gabriel, and Sidney Verba.
1963 The Civic Culture: Political Attitudes and Democracy in Five Nations. Princeton, New Jersey: Princeton University Press.

Althoff, Phillip, and Samuel Patterson.
1966 "Political activism in a rural county." Midwestern Journal of Political Science 10(No. 1):39–57.

Amann, Peter H.
1963 "The changing outlines of 1848." American Historical Review 68 (July):938–953.

Anderson, Lee.
1968 "Organizational theory and the study of state and local parties." Pp. 375–403 in William L. Crotty (ed.), Approaches to the Study of Party Organization. Boston: Allyn and Bacon.

Ashford, Douglas E.
1961a "A case study in the diplomacy of social revolution." World Politics 13(April):423–434.

1961b "Patterns of group development in a new nation: Morocco." American Political Science Review 55(June): 321–332.

Barnlund, Dean C., and Carroll Harland.
1963 "Propinquity and prestige as determinants of communication networks." Sociometry 26(December): 467–479.

Barnes, Samuel H
1967 "Leadership style and political competence." Pp. 59–83 in Lewis J. Edinger (ed.), Political Leadership in Industrialized Societies. New York: Wiley.
1968 "Party democracy and the logic of collective action." Pp. 105–138 in William J. Crotty (ed.), Approaches to the Study of Party Organization. Boston: Allyn and Bacon.

Bauer, Raymond A.
1966 "Detection and anticipation of impact: The nature of the task," in Raymond A. Bauer (ed.), Social Indicators. Cambridge, Massachusetts: M.I.T. Press.

Bauer, Raymond A.; Ithiel deSola Pool; and Lewis A. Dexter.
1963 American Business and Public Policy. New York: Atherton Press.

Berelson, Bernard R.; Paul Lazarsfeld; and William N. McPhee.
1954 Voting: A Study of Opinion Formation in a Presidential Campaign. Chicago: University of Chicago Press.

Blumberg, Nathan B.
1954 One Party Press. Lincoln: University of Nebraska Press.

Bowman, Lewis, and G. R. Boynton.
1966 "Activities and role definitions of grass-roots party officials." Journal of Politics 28(No. 1): 121–143.

Brzezinski, Zbigniew K., and S. P. Huntington.
1964 Political Power: USA/USSR. New York: Viking Press.

Burnham, Walter Dean.
1967 "Party systems and the political process." Pp. 211–307 in W. N. Chambers and W. D. Burnham (eds.), The American Party System. New York: Oxford University Press.

Calkins, Fay.
1952 The CIO and the Democratic Party. Chicago: University of Chicago Press.

Campbell, Angus; P. E. Converse; W. E. Miller; and D. E. Stokes.
1960 The American Voter. New York: Wiley.
1966 Elections and the Political Order. New York: Wiley.

Chambers, William N.
1967 "Party development and the American mainstream." Pp. 3–32 in W. N. Chambers and W. D. Burnham (eds.), The American Party System. New York: Oxford University Press.

Chambers, William N., and Walter Dean Burnham (eds.).
1967 The American Party System: Stages of Political Development. New York: Oxford University Press.

Coleman, James, and Carl G. Rosberg (eds.).
1964 Political Parties and National Integration in Africa. Berkeley: University of California Press.

Converse, Philip E.
1964 "The nature of belief systems in mass politics." Pp. 206–261 in David Apter (ed.), Ideology and Discontent. New York: Free Press of Glencoe.
1966a "Information flow and the stability of partisan attitudes." Pp. 136–158 in Angus Campbell et al., Elections and the Political Order. New York: Wiley.
1966b "The problem of party distances in models of voting change." Pp. 175–207 in M. Kent Jennings and L. Harmon Zeigler (eds.), The Electoral Process. Englewood Cliffs, New Jersey: Prentice-Hall.

Converse, Philip E., and Georges Dupeux.
1962 "Politicization of the electorate in France and the United States." Public Opinion Quarterly 26(Spring): 1–24.

Crotty, William J.
1967 "The social attributes of party organizational activists in a transitional political system." Western Political Quarterly 20(September): 669–681.
1968a Conceptual Developments in Political Parties' Research. International Comparative Political Parties Report No. 3. Evanston, Illinois: Inter-

national Comparative Political Parties Project.
1968b "The party organization and its activities." Pp. 247–306 in William J. Crotty (ed.), Approaches to the Study of Party Organization. Boston: Allyn and Bacon.
1971 "Party effort and its impact on the vote." American Political Science Review 65(June):439–450.

Cutright, Phillips, and Peter Rossi.
1958a "Grass roots politicians and the vote." American Sociological Review 23(April):171–179.
1958b "Party organization in primary elections." American Journal of Sociology 64(November):262–269.

Daalder, Hans.
1966 "Parties, elites and political developments in western Europe." Pp. 43–78 in J. L. LaPalombara and Myron Weiner (eds.), Political Parties and Political Development. Princeton, New Jersey: Princeton University Press.

Dahl, Robert (ed.).
1966 Political Oppositions in Western Democracies. New Haven, Connecticut: Yale University Press.

Degras, June.
1960 "United front tactics in the comintern, 1921–28." Pp. 9–22 in David Footman (ed.), International Communism. St. Antony's Papers No. 9. London: Chatto and Windus.

Dennis, Jack.
1966 "Support for the party system by the mass public." American Political Science Review 60(September):600–615.

Deutsch, Karl.
1963 The Nerves of Government. New York: Free Press of Glencoe.

Duverger, Maurice.
1967 Les Partis Politiques. Sixth Edition. Paris: Colin.

Easton, David, and Robert D. Hess.
1962 "The child's political world." Midwest Journal of Political Science 6(August):229–246.

Ebbighausen, Rolf.
1966 "Inner-party democracy as a research topic: The conception of a 'public opinion' within political parties." Paper presented at the Sixth World Congress of Sociology, Évian, France, September.

Eldersveld, Samuel J.
1964 Political Parties: A Behavioral Analysis. Chicago: Rand McNally.

Epstein, Leon D.
1968 Political Parties in Western Democracies. New York: Praeger.

Etzioni, Amitai (ed.).
1961 Complex Organizations. New York: Holt, Rinehart and Winston.

Flinn, Thomas A., and Frederick W. Wirt.
1965 "Local party leaders: Groups of like-minded men." Midwest Journal of Political Science 9(February):77–98.

Forthal, Sonya.
1946 Cogwheels of Democracy: A Study of the Precinct Captain. New York: William-Frederick Press.

Gatlin, Douglas S.
1968 "Toward a functionalist theory of political parties: Interparty competition in North Carolina." Pp. 217–246 in William J. Crotty (ed.), Approaches to the Study of Party Organization. Boston: Allyn and Bacon.

Geertz, Clifford (ed.).
1963 Old Societies and New States. New York: Free Press of Glencoe.

Golembiewski, Robert T.
1965 "Small groups and large organizations." Pp. 87–141 in James G. March (ed.), Handbook of Organizations. Chicago: Rand McNally.

Goodman, Paul.
1967 "The first American party system." Pp. 56–89 in W. N. Chambers and W. D. Burnham (eds.), The American Party System. New York: Oxford University Press.

Guetzkow, Harold.
1965 "Communications in organizations." Pp. 534–573 in James G. March (ed.), Handbook of Organizations. Chicago: Rand McNally.

Harris, Louis.
1963 "Polls and politics in the United States." Public Opinion Quarterly 27(Spring):3–8.

Hartenstein, Wolfgang, and Klaus Liepelt.
1962 "Party members and party voters in West Germany." Pp. 43–52 in Stein Rokkan (ed.), Approaches to the

Study of Political Participation. Bergen, Norway: C. Michelsen Institute.

Hays, Samuel P.
1967 "Political parties and the community-society continuum." Pp. 152–181 in W. N. Chambers and W. D. Burnham (eds.), The American Party System. New York: Oxford University Press.

Heard, Alexander.
1960 The Costs of Democracy: Financing American Political Campaigns. Chapel Hill: University of North Carolina Press.

Hennessy, Bernard.
1968 "On the study of party organization." Pp. 1–44 in William J. Crotty (ed.), Approaches to the Study of Party Organization. Boston: Allyn and Bacon.

Hess, Robert D., and Judith V. Torney.
1968 Development of Political Attitudes in Children. Chicago: Aldine.

Hirschfield, Robert S.; Bert E. Swanson; and Blanche D. Blank.
1962 "A profile of political activists in Manhattan." Western Political Quarterly 15(September): 489–506.

Hunter, Floyd.
1959 Top Leadership, USA. Chapel Hill: University of North Carolina Press.

Hyman, Herbert.
1963 "Mass media and political socialization: Role of patterns of communication." Pp. 128–148 in Lucian Pye (ed.), Communications and Political Development. Princeton, New Jersey: Princeton University Press.

Janowitz, Morris, and David R. Segal.
1967 "Social cleavage and party affiliation: Germany, Great Britain, and the United States." American Journal of Sociology 72(May): 601–608.

Jennings, W. Ivon.
1961 Party Politics. Volume 2: The Growth of Parties. Cambridge, England: Cambridge University Press.

Katz, Daniel, and Samuel J. Eldersveld.
1961 "The impact of local party activity upon the electorate." Public Opinion Quarterly 25(Spring): 1–24.

Katz, Elihu, and Paul Lazarsfeld.
1955 Personal Influence. Glencoe, Illinois: Free Press.

Kelley, Stanley.
1956 Professional Public Relations and Political Power. Baltimore: The Johns Hopkins Press.
1960 Political Campaigning. Washington, D. C.: Brookings Institution.
1962 "Campaign debates: Some facts and issues." Public Opinion Quarterly 26(Fall): 351–366.

Key, V. O.
1961 Public Opinion and American Democracy. New York: Knopf.
1964 Politics, Parties, and Pressures Groups. Fifth Edition. New York: Crowell.

King, Robert, and Martin Schnitzer.
1968 "Contemporary use of private political polling." Public Opinion Quarterly 32(Fall): 431–436.

Kingdon, John W.
1966 Candidates for Office: Beliefs and Strategies. New York: Random House.

Kornhauser, William.
1953 The Politics of Mass Society. Glencoe, Illinois: Free Press.

Lamb, Karl A., and Paul A. Smith.
1968 Campaign Decision-making: The Presidential Election of 1964. Belmont, California: Wadsworth.

LaPalombara, Joseph, and Myron Weiner (eds.).
1966 Political Parties and Political Development. Princeton, New Jersey: Princeton University Press.

Leiserson, Avery.
1958 Parties and Politics: An Institutional and Behavioral Approach. New York: Knopf.

Leiserson, Michael.
1968 "Factions and coalitions in one-party Japan: An explanation based on the theory of games." American Political Science Review 62(September): 770–787.

Leuthold, David A.
1968 Electioneering in a Democracy: Campaigns for Congress. New York: Wiley.

Levin, Murray B., with George Blackwood.
1962 The Compleat Politician: Political Strategy in Massachusetts. Indianapolis: Bobbs-Merrill.

Lindblom, Charles.
1965 The Intelligence of Democracy:

Decision-Making Through Mutual Adjustment. New York: Free Press.

Lipset, S. M.
1963 The First Nation. New York: Basic Books.
1964 "Ostrogorski and the analytical approach to the comparative study of political parties," in Moisei Ostrogorski, Democracy and the Organization of Political Parties. Volume 1. Edited and abridged by S. M. Lipset. Translated by Frederick Clarke. New York: Doubleday.

Lipset, S. M., and Stein Rokkan (eds.).
1967 Party Systems and Voter Alignments: Cross-National Perspectives. New York: Free Press.

Lodge, Milton.
1968a Gruppovshchina in the Post-Stalin Period. Laboratory for Political Research Report No. 14. Iowa City: Laboratory for Political Research (March). Mimeographed.
1968b "Soviet elite participatory attitudes in the post-Stalin period." American Political Science Review 68(September):827–839.

Lowi, Theodore.
1967 "Party, policy and constitution in America." Pp. 238–276 in W. N. Chambers and W. D. Burnham (eds.), The American Party System. New York: Oxford University Press.

Luttbeg, Norman K. (ed.).
1968 Public Opinion and Public Policy: Models of Political Linkage. Homewood, Illinois: Dorsey Press.

McClosky, Herbert, and Harold E. Dahlgren.
1959 "Primary group influence on party loyalty." American Political Science Review 53(September):757–776.

McDonald, Neal A.
1955 The Study of Political Parties. New York: Doubleday.

McKenzie, R. T.
1955 British Political Parties. London: Heinemann.

McLuhan, Marshall.
1962 The Gutenberg Galaxy. Toronto: University of Toronto Press.

MacNeil, Robert.
1968 The People Machine: The Influence of Television on American Politics. New York: Harper and Row.

McPhee, William N., and William A. Glaser (eds.).
1962 Public Opinion and Congressional Elections. New York: Free Press of Glencoe.

Marvick, Dwaine.
1966 "Les cadres des partis politiques en Allemagne." Pp. 619–635 in Mattei Dogan (ed.), Le Comportement Politique. Paris: Revue Française de Sociologie, Numéro Spécial.
1968 "The middlemen of politics." Pp. 341–374 in William J. Crotty (ed.), Approaches to the Study of Party Organization. Boston: Allyn and Bacon.
1970 "Party cadres and receptive partisan voters in the 1967 Indian national elections." Asian Survey 10(November):949–966.

Marvick, Dwaine, and Samuel J. Eldersveld.
1961 "National convention leadership: 1952 and 1956." Western Political Quarterly 14(March, Part 1):176–194.

Marvick, Dwaine, and Charles Nixon.
1961 "Recruitment contrasts in rival campaign groups." Pp. 193–217 in Dwaine Marvick (ed.), Political Decision-Makers. New York: Free Press of Glencoe.

Marvick, Elizabeth W.
1968 "Democratic partisan perspectives." Ph.D. Dissertation, Columbia University (unpublished).

Michels, Robert.
1949 Political Parties: A Sociological Study of the Oligarchical Tendencies of Modern Democracy. Translated by Eden and Cedar Paul. Glencoe, Illinois: Free Press.

Milbrath, Lester W.
1965 Political Participation. Chicago: Rand McNally.

Miller, Warren, and Donald Stokes.
1966 "Constituency influence in congress." Pp. 351–372 in Angus Campbell et al., Elections and the Political Order. New York: Wiley.

Namier, Lewis.
1957 The Structure of Politics at the Accession of George III. Second Edition. New York: St. Martins Press.

Nettl, J. P.
1967 Political Mobilization: A Sociological Analysis of Methods and Concepts. New York: Basic Books.

Nexon, David.
1971 "Asymmetry in the political system: Occasional activists in the Republican and Democratic parties, 1954–1964." American Political Science Review 65(September):716–730.

Ostrogorski, Moisei.
1902 Democracy and the Organization of Political Parties. 2 volumes. Translated by Frederick Clarke. New York: Macmillan.

Perry, James M.
1968 The New Politics: The Expanding Technology of Political Manipulation. New York: Clarkson N. Potter.

Pool, Ithiel deSola; Robert Abelson; and Samuel Popkin.
1964 Candidates, Issues, and Strategies: A Computer Simulation of the 1960 Presidential Election. Cambridge, Massachusetts: M.I.T. Press.

Pye, Lucian.
1965 Aspects of Political Development. Boston: Little, Brown.

Pye, Lucian (ed.).
1963 Communications and Political Development. Princeton, New Jersey: Princeton University Press.

Ranney, Austin.
1965 Pathways to Parliament: Candidate Selection in Britain. Madison: University of Wisconsin Press.

Ranney, Austin, and Willmoore, Kendall.
1956 Democracy and the American Party System. New York: Harcourt, Brace and World.

Riggs, Fred.
1968 "Comparative politics and the study of political parties: A structural approach." Pp. 45–104 in William J. Crotty (ed.), Approaches to the Study of Party Organization. Boston: Allyn and Bacon.

Riker, William H.
1962 The Theory of Political Coalitions. New Haven, Connecticut: Yale University Press.

Rose, Richard (ed.).
1966 Studies in British Politics. New York: St. Martins Press.

Rosenthal, Robert A., and Robert S. Weiss.
1967 "Problems of organizational feedback processes." Pp. 302–340 in Raymond A. Bauer (ed.), Social Indicators. Cambridge, Massachusetts: M.I.T. Press.

Rossi, Peter, and Philips Cutright.
1961 "The impact of party organization in an industrial setting." Pp. 81–116 in Morris Janowitz (ed.), Community Political Systems. New York: Free Press of Glencoe.

Rudolph, Lloyd I., and Susan H. Rudolph.
1960 "The political role of India's caste associations." Pacific Affairs 33 (March): 5–22.

Salisbury, Robert H.
1965 "The urban party organization member." Public Opinion Quarterly 29(Winter): 550–564.

Sartori, Giovanni.
1966 "European political parties: The case of polarized pluralism." Pp. 137–176 in Joseph LaPalombara and Myron Weiner (eds.), Political Parties and Political Development. Princeton, New Jersey: Princeton University Press.

Scarrow, Howard A.
1967 "The function of political parties: A critique of the literature and the approach." Journal of Politics 29 (November): 770–790.

Schlesinger, Joseph A.
1965 "Political party organization." Pp. 764–801 in James March (ed)., Handbook of Organizations. Chicago: Rand McNally.
1966 Ambition in Politics: Political Careers in the United States. Chicago: Rand McNally.
1967 "Political careers and party leadership." Pp. 266–293 in Lewis Edinger (ed.), Political Leadership in Industrialized Societies. New York: Wiley.

Scott, W. Richard.
1965 "Theory of organizations." Pp. 485–529 in Robert Faris (ed.), Handbook of Modern Sociology. Chicago: Rand McNally.

Selznick, Philip.
1960 The Organizational Weapon. New York: Free Press of Glencoe.

Shoup, Paul.
1968 "Comparing communist nations:

Prospects for an empirical approach." American Political Science Review 62(March): 185–204.

Simon, Herbert.
1957 Models of Man: Social and Rational. New York: Wiley.

Sorauf, Frank.
1967 "Political parties and political analysis." Pp. 33–55 in W. N. Chambers and W. D. Burnham (eds.), The American Party System. New York: Oxford University Press.
1968 Party Politics in America. Boston: Little, Brown.

Stokes, Donald.
1966 "Spatial models of party competition." Pp. 161–179 in Angust Campbell et al., Elections and the Political Order. New York: Wiley.

Thompson, Charles.
1956 Television and Presidential Politics. Washington, D. C.: Brookings Institution.

Thompson, Dennis F.
1970 The Democratic Citizen. London: Cambridge University Press.

Unger, Aryeh L.
1965 "Public opinion reports of the nazi party." Public Opinion Quarterly 29(Winter): 565–582.

Verba, Sidney.
1961 Small Groups and Political Behavior. Princeton, New Jersey: Princeton University Press.

Verba, Sidney, and Norman H. Nie.
1972 Participation in America: Political Democracy and Social Equality. New York: Harper and Row.

Wahlke, John C.
1967 Public Policy and Representative Government. Laboratory for Political Research Report No. 9. Iowa City: Laboratory for Political Research (September).

Wallerstein, Immanuel.
1967 "Class, tribe, and party in West African politics. Pp. 497–518 in S. M. Lipset and Stein Rokkan (eds.), Party Systems and Voter Alignments. New York: Free Press.

Waltzer, Herbert.
1966 "In the magic lantern: Television coverage of the 1964 national conventions." Public Opinion Quarterly 30(Spring): 33–53.

Watts, Thomas M.
1968 "Application of the attribution model to the study of political recruitment: County elective offices." Pp. 307–340 in William J. Crotty (ed.), Approaches to the Study of Party Organization: Allyn and Bacon.

Weber, Max
1946 Essays in Sociology. Edited by H. H. Gerth and C. Wright Mills. New York: Oxford University Press.

Weiner, Myron.
1967 Party Building in a New Nation: The Indian National Congress. Chicago: University of Chicago Press.

White, Theodore H.
1961 The Making of the President, 1960. New York: Atheneum.
1965 The Making of the President, 1964. New York: Atheneum.

Wilson, James Q.
1960 Negro Politics. New York: Free Press of Glencoe.
1966 The Amateur Democrat: Club Politics in Three Cities. Second Edition. Chicago: University of Chicago Press.

Wolfinger, Raymond E.
1963 "The influence of precinct work on voting behavior." Public Opinion Quarterly 27(Fall): 387–398.

Wood, Robert C.
1959 Suburbia, Its People and Politics. Boston: Houghton Mifflin.

Zolberg, Aristede R.
1966 Creating Political Order: The Party States of West Africa. Chicago: Rand McNally.

CHAPTER 24 Scientific Communication

BERTITA E. COMPTON
National Academy of Sciences

Communication of scientific and technical information is an integral part of the process of research and development. Studies of scientific communication may be motivated by basic curiosity about social communication processes, but they are often motivated by the goal of increased research productivity through improved communication. A wide range of research techniques has been employed in the study of both formal and informal communication of scientific information. This chapter reviews the methodology and the findings of such studies.

Science has distinctive traditions and a set of social norms and values that are not readily modified and that tend to be much the same wherever scientists are found. Since scientific communication is shaped by the characteristics and goals of science, it is a distinct form of communication. It is also one of our greatest national assets and one of our most challenging national problems.

Scientific communication is highly motivated. A scientist's primary goal is to produce knowledge, and he is aware of the premium placed on originality and priority. He must communicate his findings to establish himself and to add to the cumulative structure of science. Not only is he strongly oriented to produce and communicate scientific information, he is determined to persevere in seeking and using such information. Menzel (1966a) has emphasized the strongly motivated information seeking of the scientist and his persistent information-search patterns. Garvey and Griffith (1964) also have described the active researcher as bending every effort to discover all possible means of obtaining information, especially on recent work relevant to his own. Scientific communication, therefore, represents both major input to and ultimate objective of scientific productivity; commonality of knowledge is means and end.

Scientific communication is a major concern not only of individual scientists and the professional societies and employing institutions to which they adhere but also of both the legislative and executive branches of the federal government. More effective scientific communication has been the subject of a number of congressional studies and hearings and of numerous special panel and task-group

The author is Secretary to the Council of the National Academy of Sciences.

reports sponsored by the President's Science Advisory Committee and the Federal Council for Science and Technology's Committee on Scientific and Technical Information (COSATI).[1] The reasons for this widespread and top-level concern are indicated in the answers to two questions.

First, what is scientific information? Very simply, it is the principal product of research and development, the major return on an annual investment by the U.S. government of some $16 billion (in 1968), and more than half again as much by U.S. industry. Research yields knowledge, typically embodied in published papers and reports; technology produces both hardware and knowledge, the latter presented in various specialized media. As our national investment in research and development expanded following World War II, both the need for and the volume of scientific information increased rapidly. Current pressures to maximize the return on our substantial investment in research and development and to speed the application of scientific knowledge to the solution of such problems as pollution, transportation, and urban renewal are intensifying this need.

This brings us to the second question: What is the nature of the scientific communication problem? It has three dimensions. One is the growing volume of scientific information. Because science has grown exponentially for the last three centuries (Price, 1961), most scientists now cannot be aware of all relevant information, or cannot find specific information that they need when they need it.

Bernal (1959) once used the analogy of an irrigation system to depict the communication problem in science. He described a system fed from many sources, with individual plants (the users) depending on what reached them at a given time. Ideally, each would receive the right amount at the right time; in fact, much evaporated, ran off in the wrong direction, or arrived too late. At other times, the flow was so abundant that the user could not absorb what he needed.

A second dimension of the problem is that scientific and technical disciplines, and the specialties within disciplines, are becoming increasingly interrelated. As knowledge grows, new links emerge, and formerly distinct subject areas become closely related. Recently, Herring (1968) compared the situation in the 1930s, when in most instances a conscientious scientist could keep abreast of most of the information in his own research area, with that in the 1960s, when new links between previously unrelated areas were continually appearing, the quantity of relevant information was far greater, and the production of information was more rapid. In some fields, reportedly, it may be less time-consuming to rediscover previous knowledge than to exhaust all avenues of search for an existing answer.

A third dimension of the information problem is that emerging fields and subfields and new multi-disciplinary problem areas produce new and diverse user groups with varying information needs. Information must be readily accessible and intelligible to disparate groups of users who often are far removed in orientation and background from the producers of the information. The need to apply research findings in a variety of task-related contexts requires increasingly specialized information.

In view of these trends, it is not surprising that scientific comunication has been described as a frustrating and burdensome unsolved problem (Ackerman, 1967:1), and that the federal government and the

[1] For a brief summary of some of the major governmental studies and reports, see chapter 8 of the report of the Committee on Scientific and Technical Communication, National Academy of Sciences-National Academy of Engineering (1969).

scientific community have been increasingly concerned with it.

To cope effectively with the scientific communication problem, we must learn more about it. We must understand the information-acquisition and information-dissemination patterns in various disciplines and areas of application, the usefulness of existing communication systems and services, the nature of needed modifications, and the best ways of introducing them. Comprehensive analyses of the functioning and use of both formal and informal components of scientific communication systems are greatly needed, as well as measures of the value and effectiveness of scientific communication procedures and services.

Such studies can provide the required foundation for (*a*) realistic funding and pricing policies and an economic rationale for scientific communication, and (*b*) more efficient management and coordination of scientific communication services. Further, such studies can speed the development of feasible innovations, guide educational and marketing efforts so essential in overcoming resistance to new services, and enhance the effectiveness of science in meeting the new and growing demands posed by social, environmental, and technological problems.

This chapter deals with studies of scientific information-exchange behavior—of the ways that scientists shape and use their communication media and systems. Its principal objective is to provide a background from which new approaches and better focused research on scientific communication will follow. The first section indicates some of the types of data collected and the methods employed in their collection. The second describes some of the main trends and findings of scientific communication studies. Two comprehensive programs of research and their implications form the subject matter of the third section; the final section looks briefly at probable trends in future work.

RESEARCH ON SCIENTIFIC COMMUNICATION

The need to develop better ways of coping with the increasing output of science has resulted in research in a number of disciplines on the nature of scientists' information needs, the functioning of scientific communication media, and the ways in which scientific information is applied. The development of this research effort was neither orderly nor coordinated. Discrete, disconnected studies occurred in a variety of disciplines, and a number of methods, sampling techniques, classifications, and analyses were employed.

A recent review (Herner & Herner, 1967) of research on information needs and uses pointed to the following shortcomings: (*a*) the relatively few techniques used; (*b*) the diverse groups to which they were applied; (*c*) the ambiguity of the language used to describe techniques and results; (*d*) the lack of innovation; (*e*) the failure to relate to or build on past gains or to profit from past mistakes; and (*f*) the frequent lack of rigorous experimental designs. A subsequent reviewer (Paisley, 1968) found evidence of increasing methodological sophistication but noted the absence of a sound conceptual framework that would aid in interpreting results and guiding future efforts. In short, research on these aspects of scientific communication, although emerging from infancy, still has far to go.

In surveying earlier communication studies, Menzel (1960) identified three general types dealing, respectively, with (*a*) the operation, coverage, and cost of scientific information-exchange media, (*b*) classification procedures, search and retrieval systems, and languages, and (*c*) scientific communication behavior. The latter included the needs and experiences of research scientists in their search for and dissemination of information, the media they employed, the effectiveness of such media in fulfilling their needs, and the flow of scientific information among producers and users.

Two studies reported by Bernal (1948) and Urquhart (1948) were among the earliest examples of this type, marking what is generally regarded as the beginning of research on the behavioral aspects of scientific communication. Bernal stressed the value of research on information-exchange behavior at the International Conference on Scientific Information ten years later when he stated:

> There is . . . a danger, and necessarily a growing one, that the service of scientific information will develop as an activity entirely in its own right, ever more and more competent to take in, store, and hand out information regardless as to whether this information is superfluous, inaccurate, or unwanted . . . . It is legitimate to ask not only *how* the information is to be dealt with but also *what* that information is, *who* it is intended for, and *to what degree* does the process of transmission of information help in the advancement and use of science (Bernal,1959:77).

Data and Objectives

Research on information-exchange behavior has produced data on four main aspects of scientific communication: (*a*) use or nonuse of information sources; (*b*) time spent in use of one or more sources; (*c*) instances of use (communication acts), their nature and frequency; and (*d*) attributes of the information sought or received in relation to the reasons that it was sought, its sources, and its effectiveness in application. Of these four, the simplest is use or nonuse of particular information sources, typically coupled with a specific time interval and some indication of frequency.

Somewhat more useful are data on the time spent on various communication activities. Such data, when recorded by an observer, tend to be accurate, although they may be biased by the interval and location selected for observation. For example, records based solely on hours spent in a work setting obviously do not give an adequate overall picture of scientific communication activities. Self-reported estimates of the time spent in communication, say, in a diary record, are particularly subject to vagueness and errors.

A more productive approach is to divide communication behavior into acts, such as the reading of a journal article, an informal conversation in which information was given or received, or use of an index or abstract. But here, too, there are procedural problems. In addition to the same drawbacks that affect estimates of time, the investigator must define clearly what constitutes an act and equate such acts or place them on a meaningful scale. A widely employed unit, and one that has proved useful, is the message itself—the information received or the so-called *critical incident*. This unit was employed effectively in a communication study by Herner (1959). Research since that time has focused increasingly on critical incidents, particularly in relation to the ways in which information is received, the auxiliary sources that lead to or supplement the principal delivering source, and the impact of the information on scientific work.

Among the recent studies dealing with critical incidents in scientific communication are those of Rosenbloom and his colleagues (McLaughlin, Rosenbloom, & Wolek, 1965; Rosenbloom & Wolek, 1967). The questionnaire that they developed produced data on (*a*) the most recent instance of receiving useful information, (*b*) the most useful piece of information received in a six-month interval, and (*c*) the most recent instance of receiving useful information from a written source. These instances were analyzed in relation to the specific task of the seeker, the type of information needed (e.g., procedural or theoretical), and the effect of the information on work activities. In addition, the influence of personal and organizational factors on information seeking was emphasized.

Allen (1966a) also studied the message received to determine the sources of ideas that influenced the progress of research and development. He found that several sources typically played a part in the delivery of each message. Menzel's (1966b) analysis of 1,036 information-receiving episodes to discover the main channel delivering the information, the supplementary channels involved when the information is conveyed by more than one, and the lead channels that direct a scientist to those supplying needed information provided further support of Allen's findings.

Menzel also examined the nature of the information sought (procedures, findings, or theory) and the manner of acquisition (deliberate search, brushing up, or accidental communication) in relation to the use of particular channels. The Auerbach Corporation (1965), in a study of user needs of the Department of Defense, reduced the critical incident to an information chunk—the smallest unit of information required to answer a task-related question. They studied certain characteristics of the chunk, such as the scientific or technical field from which it came, in relation to the time and behavior involved in its acquisition, the way it was used, and some of the characteristics of the user.

The kinds of data collected depend, of course, on the kinds of questions asked. Studies of scientific communication behavior have dealt principally with the following:

1. Patterns of exposure to information sources
2. Preferences for and evaluations of information sources
3. Prevalence of certain information skills and practices
4. Functions of information
5. Impact of information on performance
6. Flow of information from generator to user.

Studies of exposure to information sources and preferences for and evaluations of such sources have been initiated chiefly to guide in the management of particular services and to facilitate the solution of local information problems. Data on exposure frequently do not relate contact with a source to the motives for use, the nature of the information received, or its effect on work; therefore, these data contribute little to the understanding of information-exchange behavior.

Preferences and evaluations usually result from opinion polls. These expressions of satisfaction and dissatisfaction, descriptions of difficulties in the use of sources, ratings of services, and the like are highly subjective and frequently unreliable. Consequently they, too, are of limited value, although they may provide some useful insights in comparing different disciplines or different groups within a discipline, e.g., teachers and practitioners.

Information skills and practices include facility in languages, maintenance and organization of personal files, the delegation of information-gathering activities to assistants, library use, and requests made to information centers for documents and other task-related information. Such data often reveal many of the folkways and idiosyncracies that characterize a scientist's use of information-exchange media and services. Additionally, they sometimes supply clues to the amount of indifference or resistance that must be overcome in effecting modifications or introducing new services.

Rubenstein and his colleagues suggest that information-search behavior is highly stable and resistant to change, and that a clear understanding of existing information practices must precede the design of new media and services (Rubenstein, Trueswell, Rath, & Werner, 1966). Such understanding is not always sufficient to assure utilization, however; reeducation and selling are often required, as indicated in several studies.

Lipetz (1964), for example, when examining the impact of a citation index in physics, found that only a small fraction of the recipients made use of it. Herner and Johanningsmeier (1965) found widespread lack of interest in and awareness of a newly published thesaurus in chemical engineering; they concluded that this low use and interest resulted not so much from shortcomings of the tool itself as from the way in which it was presented and publicized.

The Infosearch Project at Northwestern University (Werner, 1965; Rubenstein et al., 1966), which introduced a new service in eleven medical research organizations, elicited only sixty-one requests for service in approximately seven weeks of pilot operation. And in seventeen weeks of experimental operation, an information clearinghouse for biological scientists, studied by Van Cott and Kincade (1967), received somewhat less than 400 requests, generated by approximately one-third that number of calls. In fact, 5 percent of the participating scientists accounted for roughly 25 percent of the requests. Wooster's (1969) very readable description of users' reactions to microfiche provides additional insight into the apathy and resistance of scientists faced with new information tools and services.

A productive line of investigation is defining the roles and functions of scientific communication. Herner (1962) advocated careful study of communication procedures to discover information functions that are not adequately performed, as well as those that are effectively handled and thus can be excluded when planning systems innovations. He found useful six categories of information functions developed by Hertz and Rubenstein (1953)—conceptual, empirical, procedural, stimulatory, policy, and directive. Certain of these functions were associated with particular sources; for example, stimulatory information—encouragement and ideas—came rarely from written or published sources but typically from supervisors' or colleagues' suggestions and observations.

Menzel (1958), using an interview study of the information practices of chemists, biologists, and zoologists in an academic setting, developed the following list of functions: (*a*) answering specific questions; (*b*) maintaining awareness of current developments in a special area of interest; (*c*) brushing up on or acquiring general information in subjects related to an area of specialization; (*d*) certifying the reliability of information (i.e., getting a value judgment or standard to guide in screening and sifting information); (*e*) redirecting attention; (*f*) obtaining critical or reinforcing feedback; and (*g*) placing work in context (i.e., relating it to other research efforts and potential applications). Subsequently, he further refined these categories and distinguished between the communication channels best serving each of them (Menzel, 1966c; 1966d). Apparent throughout Menzel's studies is the importance of informal, interpersonal communication in fulfilling such functions as certifying reliability, providing feedback, and redirecting attention.

Rosenbloom conceives research and development as a problem-solving process to which the acquisition, dissemination, and use of information are essential. He and his colleagues developed a series of studies to examine such factors as the stage of work at which various inputs are most effective (Rosenbloom, 1965; Rosenbloom & Wolek, 1967).

Since "... steps taken to enhance the performance of some communication functions may work to the detriment of the performance of others" (Menzel, 1960: 26), studies of the functions of scientific information are necessary for effective modification of communication media. Recognizing this, the American Psychological Association instituted studies to distinguish the functions performed by various informal and formal media in that field (Project on Scientific Information Exchange in Psychology, 1963; 1965). On the basis of the results, they experimented with the modification of certain media so that they would complement one another in the more effective performance of specific functions (Garvey & Griffith, 1966; 1967). Recently, Menzel (1966d) described a number of ways in which new operating procedures and new technologies might be used to extend the scope of formal media to include the peculiar advantages (for example, speed of response and highly user-oriented information) of informal communication.

Efforts to define the impact of information on performance have been relatively few compared to studies of the functions of scientific information. Urquhart (1948) mentioned "information misses" in one of the earliest studies of user behavior, and Menzel (1958) also described a number of instances in which information was received too late to prevent losses of time or money in needless duplication. Some years later, Bernard and Shilling gathered data on "failures" and "near misses" in information seeking and made an effort to relate information-exchange behavior to productivity, one measure of which was the number of publications (Bernard, Shilling, & Tyson, 1963; Shilling & Bernard, 1964).

Currently, some of the greatest advances in the area of performance appear in the work of Marquis, Allen, and their colleagues (Allen, 1964; 1966a; Marquis & Allen, 1966), For example, they have studied the information inputs to groups involved in the same task—solution of a design problem and submission of proposals to a government agency that monitors and evaluates each group's performance. However, the development of effective ways of measuring and evaluating the impact of scientific information remains one of the challenging problems of communication research.

In the early 1960s, the accumulation of data on the flow of information from generator to user began to receive increasing attention. For example, a chief goal of the APA Project on Scientific Information Exchange in Psychology was to trace the dissemination of information on research from the time work first became reportable (Garvey & Compton, 1967). Included in the study were the various informal occasions and nonarchival media chosen by a scientist for early announcement of his findings, journal and other archival publication, secondary coverage in abstracts and, finally, incorporation of the work in a review or state-of-the-art survey.

The time intervals associated with the dissemination process, and the audience for and nature of the various types of dissemination were established for psychology. With the creation of the Johns Hopkins Center for Research in Scientific Communication in 1966, this type of research was extended to ten other disciplines, including social sciences, physical and earth sciences, and three fields of engineering (Compton, 1968).

In the biomedical field, Orr (1961; Orr & Crouse, 1962) has reported on the metabolism of information—defined as digestion, absorption, and assimilation into the scientific community. He used papers presented at scientific meetings as "tracers," and followed these papers through the primary or journal stage of publication to their secondary coverage in several of the abstracting and indexing services used by the biomedical profession, noting the time intervals involved, the degree of dispersion through primary outlets, and overlaps in secondary coverage. He also compared his findings with data obtained by Liebesny (1959) in studies of physicists, and by Gray and Rosenborg (1957) in their study of the publication fate of material issued in technical-report format. Studies of the APA project (Compton, 1965; Project on Scientific Information Exchange, 1965: Report 13) reflected the same general trends.

The preceding discussion of data and

research objectives indicates some of the main emphases of studies of communication behavior. Menzel's (1960; 1966e) reviews offer a more detailed analysis.

METHODS OF DATA COLLECTION

One of the methods most frequently used in studying scientific communication is the questionnaire. In his description and critique of methodology, Paisley (1965) speaks of the questionnaire as a compromise technique, expedient to use when a sample is widely scattered but subject to such shortcomings as low response rates, respondents' set (annoyed, disinterested, joking), respondents' understanding or interpretation of the questions, and the inability to clarify incomplete responses. In spite of these drawbacks and the occasions on which findings have not been qualified by response rate or have been generalized to an extent not justified by a low response rate, the method has been used effectively in a number of studies—for example, those of Wuest (1965), Rosenbloom and Wolek (1967), Tornüdd (1959), and the APA's Project on Scientific Information Exchange (1964; 1965).

Rosenbloom and Wolek (1967) followed up their questonnaires, to which they had exceedingly high response rates, with special interviews to be sure that they were correctly interpreting responses. Herner and Johanningsmeier (1965), faced with a low response rate in a questionnaire study, did a follow-up on nonrespondents, found no statistical difference between their replies and those of respondents, and were able to proceed on the basis of their initial results. A questionnaire, when pretested to eliminate any items that are confusing, qualified by response rate, and combined with other methods, can be a useful tool.

A second technique is a diary. Although productive of background information and a broad overview of a respondent's information-exchange activities and problems, a diary can seldom be kept up-to-date by active researchers and is particularly subject to incomplete or exaggerated recall. Shaw (1956), for example, discovered substantial discrepancies between the materials known to have been in scientists' hands and those reported in their diary records. He repeated his study a year later with the same group to check the reliability of his findings and concluded that the diary record was not the best way to study information-exchange behavior, particularly over long periods of time. Additional support for this view is found in a study by Hogg and Smith (1959), who also encountered inaccuracies and inconsistencies in the data they obtained from diary records of participants in their study.

One of the most fruitful techniques employed is the interview. Herner's (1954) interview study of basic and applied researchers in an academic setting was an especially rewarding one and was among the first to suggest differences in the communication patterns associated with these research orientations. Menzel's (1958) interview study of three groups of scientists in an academic setting, and the interview study described in Report No. 11 of the Project on Scientific Information Exchange (1965) showed many similar trends and emphasized the ubiquitous role of informal communication.

The Auerbach Corporation (1965) and North American Aviation (1966) conducted two of the most extensive interview studies. The objective of these studies was to define information needs and the acquisition of information by contractual and in-house researchers of the Department of Defense. Both studies were comprehensive and yielded a wealth of data on many aspects of scientific communication behavior. The interview, when conducted by carefully trained persons and based on specific, pretested questions, constitutes one of the most effective techniques employed in scientific communication research.

A fourth and little used method employs a participant observer who provides data on communication activities in a particular setting. This method is exemplified in a study by Halbert and Ackoff (1959) in which trained observers recorded on a previously prepared checklist the activities of industrial and academic chemists at two random moments each day for nine consecutive work days. They found that scientific communication was the most frequently reported activity for the groups studied.

Another method is analysis of library withdrawal records or requests made to an information center. Paisley (1965:3) has pointed out that: "At best we cannot relate these demands to scientists' other information-seeking efforts. At worst, in some cases, there is no evidence that the users were even scientists." Such studies typically are directed toward problems of operation of particular services and for this purpose can afford useful information. A variation on these so-called demand studies is that of Atherton (1965), in which research physicists requested current and past references relevant to their work from an hypothesized ideal reference retrieval system. The findings provided data on the need for current and retrospective literature searches, the degree of retrospection usually required, and the feasibility of a planned indexing terminology.

The study of citations is a widely employed method that Menzel excluded from his 1960 review and Paisley also omitted, since "references listed at the end of a journal article tell us little about the information inputs that actually shaped the research being reported" (Paisley, 1965:2). Perhaps the best known proponent of this method is Price (1961), who has used it to trace the orderly and exponential growth of science—in both output and manpower. This method also has proved useful in studies like those of Kessler (1963) and Xhignesse and Osgood (1967), in which an investigator is interested in bibliographic coupling, reciprocal citation, or characteristics of networks of citation. The technique was applied to communication research by Parker, Paisley, and Garrett (1967).

Recent Methodological Refinements and Emphases

A method used by Allen (1966b; Allen & Gerstberger, 1967) is the solution-development record, which he describes as a record over time of the progress of an individual or a group toward the solution of a problem. Alternative approaches are identified and new approaches that emerge during the course of work also can be added. At various stages of work the probability of acceptance of possible solutions is indicated and a time plot of probability estimates developed. The respondent is then interviewed to determine the information inputs leading to rejection or adoption of solutions, or to the development of new alternatives. The message received, the critical incident leading to a decision at each step in the solution of a design problem, is the focus of research when this method is employed. Parker and Paisley (1966) consider the record a kind of specialized diary that Allen supplements with interview data.

Another technique emphasized in a number of recent communication studies is sociometric analysis. Allen and Cohen (1966) found a closely knit, highly interactive Ph.D. group and a considerably less well organized and less interactive non-Ph.D. group in a research and development laboratory that they studied. Between these two groups there was little or no interaction or information exchange. Maurice, Menzel, and Meyersohn (1966) studied social relationships and interaction in communities of physicians and found that information levels were related to the amount and nature of social interaction in these groups.

Current research on the invisible colleges of science—groups of scientists involved in closely related work who communicate their research results to one another informally prior to publication (see Price & Beaver, 1966)—attempts to show ways in which their scope is delimited and defined, the links among them, and the underlying social dynamics. Mullins (1966) studied social networks among biological scientists and discovered that communication clusters and links were more often based on like orientation to research or use of similar methodological approaches than on commonality of discipline or specialty. He further found that such social networks of communication often conveyed many of the newest ideas and unpublished findings.

Quasi-experimental methods occur with increasing frequency. Allen's (1966a) study on research and development teams competing to reach the best solution of the same task exemplifies this approach. Another example is the APA project's study of the institution of a preconvention publication of papers (Garvey & Griffith, 1966). The trial of this innovation by APA followed studies of paper-reading sessions at a previous annual convention to provide baseline data on the amount and effects of interaction related to presentations. When the innovation was introduced, only half the convention papers were included in the preconvention publication, which was distributed some two months prior to the meeting. As a result, there was a control group of papers not prepublished as well as data from a previous year with which to compare and measure the effect of the new procedure.

One of the most challenging avenues of investigation is the application of computer technology to information problems. Kessler (1965), for example, is using the computer effectively as a research tool in his experimental work on system design, evaluation of search strategies, and approaches to information processing. Another outstanding project in this area is the Stanford Physics Information Retrieval System (SPIRES), the principal objectives of which are to study the information needs and information-seeking behavior of a group of some 100 high-energy physicists, and to develop an on-line interactive reference retrieval system that is maximally responsive to user needs and easily modified in the light of user experience with the system (Parker, 1967). The project is planned so that

> much of the necessary information about users will be obtained "on-line" as part of the computer retrieval system. This will include frequency-of-use statistics for various features of the computer system, on-line "questionnaires" asking users about the relevance of various documents and the success or failure of various searches, and provision of a "commenting" feature making it easy for users to communicate any difficulties they encounter in the course of their interaction with the system (Parker, 1967:2).

Such an approach is potentially among the most effective thus far applied to the study of communication behavior.

TRENDS AND FINDINGS

Because of the diverse populations studied, the various methods employed, and the tendency to focus efforts on highly specific objectives, with little or no attempt to relate results to those of other investigators, twenty years of research on scientific communication behavior have produced relatively few findings that can be regarded as well established or generally accepted. However, a few recurrent trends and patterns have emerged, although their implications often are not clear and suggest many questions that only additional research can answer.

One recent trend is toward comprehensive descriptions of all facets of scientific communication in particular disciplines. In the biomedical field, Orr and his associates made an intensive study of scientific communication; their efforts were confined largely to analyses of interlibrary loan records, of the number of biomedical meetings and the growth in attendance and amount of program material, and of the increase in biomedical literature (Division of Medical Sciences, 1964). The APA Project on Scientific Information Exchange in Psychology, which began in the early

1960s, employed a variety of methods and approaches to develop a comprehensive picture of the flow of information in psychology and of the characteristics of all the major media used to acquire and disseminate information in that field. Currently, the Johns Hopkins Center for Research in Scientific Communication has in progress a series of studies in various scientific and engineering disciplines; these should produce comprehensive data comparable to those amassed in psychology and in several major disciplines, such as physics (Koch, 1968), in connection with their efforts to develop information services and systems of national and international scope.

Closely related to the comprehensive study of scientific communication in a discipline is the tendency to regard scientific communication—including all the publications, occasions for reporting work, facilities, and services that it entails—as a system. Halbert and Ackoff (1959) adopted a systems approach to the study of communication and, in research reported in 1958, stressed system organization rather than isolated components as the most profitable approach to the study of communication. Since that time, Herner (1962), Orr, Abdian, et al. (1964), Menzel (1966f), and Garvey and Griffith (1965; 1967) are among those who have found this orientation especially productive.

Garvey describes scientific communication as a social system—based on social institutions, governed by social norms, and best measured through the behavior of individuals. Since the generators of the information conveyed in this system are also among the principal users, the system continually feeds back into itself; however, information in it impinges on elements other than those comprising it, just as other inputs are received than those generated in the system. Further, discipline-oriented systems must interface with each other as well as with the mission-oriented systems of government agencies. These links and overlaps are becoming increasingly important, particularly in the context of network development (Becker & Olsen, 1968) and more effective management and coordination of scientific communication services (Committee on Scientific and Technical Communication, 1969).

Consistent with the adoption of a systems approach to the study of scientific communication, the interrelationship and interdependence of the various media comprising communication systems are receiving increased attention. This interrelationship is such that modification of the functioning of one component directly or indirectly affects all others in a system (Garvey & Griffith, 1967). Communication media tend to supplement and complement one another in conveying information. Some, particularly informal interpersonal ones, often function as leads to those actually delivering needed information. Additionally, informal media may supplement formal ones by transmitting information that does not lend itself to formal publication. On the other hand, when informal written media make available, at least as widely and much more rapidly, the same information subsequently appearing in formal media, they compete with and can detract from the effectiveness of the latter. Research on such interrelationships is prerequisite for effective systems design and modification.

Three aspects of the interrelationship of communication media considered in recent research are: (*a*) identifying the roles of various media—those serving principally as leads, as auxiliary sources, and as main sources (see, for example, Menzel, 1966b); (*b*) establishing the functions of various media and introducing innovations that result in a more appropriate distribution or coordination (e.g., Garvey & Griffith, 1966); and (*c*) applying new technologies and procedures to the fulfillment of multiple information-handling functions and the production of numerous special services and media (e.g., Koch, 1968).

Another major trend is the growing awareness of the social character and social organization of scientific communication, as reflected in studies of invisible colleges or highly interactive groups (Mullins, 1966; Price & Beaver, 1966; Parker, 1967); the accumulation of data on the role and influence of certain key individuals, sometimes referred to as "information men" or "gatekeepers" (Project on Scientific Information Exchange, 1963: Report No. 1; Allen & Cohen, 1966); and preprint exchange group experiments, such as those sponsored by the National Institutes of Health (see Abelson, 1966; Green, 1967) and the one considered by the American Institute of Physics (Libbey & Zaltman, 1967).

Price depicts the nature and functioning of an invisible college as follows:

> . . . the group of everybody who is anybody in the field at that segment of the research front; an unofficial establishment based on fiercely competitive scientific excellence. They send each other duplicated preprints of papers yet to be published and for big things they telephone and telegraph in advance. They collaborate in teams of joint authorship, almost as a mode of close communication, even in cases where there is no big machine that needs a team for its operation. By substituting the technology of transportation for that of publication they keep warm the seats of jet planes and commune with each other at small select conferences and seminars throughout the world. The institution that is lucky enough to own such an eminent character does not have him around this year, for he is working with a colleague in another place, perhaps in another country (Price, 1965:236).

This description leads us to the information man encountered in the initial report of the APA series "who attends a large number of . . . meetings, spending a good part of his time in travel and then in imparting the information gained from such sources to his research staff, his colleagues, and the students whose research he directs." He becomes ". . . a kind of walking encyclopedia of methodology and current findings . . . who can refer his associates to those with relevant research currently under way" (Project on Scientific Information Exchange, 1963:12).

There are further indications in the Project on Scientific Information Exchange in Psychology (1965: Report No. 11) and in recent studies by Menzel and his colleagues (Coleman, Katz, & Menzel, 1966; Maurice, Menzel, & Meyersohn, 1966) that the information man has his own small-scale local cluster that builds up about him. He appears to be Menzel's "advisor colleague" and possibly, also, Allen and Cohen's (1966) "gatekeeper," who keeps abreast of relevant information and translates it into terms that are meaningful to the user.

Libbey and Zaltman (1967) studied patterns of communication among theoretical high-energy physicists throughout the world as part of an effort to determine the feasibility of establishing an experimental, centrally operated preprint-exchange mechanism for this subfield. Subsequently, Zaltman (1968) analyzed the communication patterns and characteristics of those named as research leaders and as local or nonlocal advisers and developed useful data on the relationship of social factors to communication patterns.

Among the other investigators who recently have been especially concerned with defining the effects of personal and social attributes on communication patterns and performance are Pelz and Andrews (1966) and Rosenbloom and Wolek (1967).

Current data on invisible colleges, information men, work teams, and interpersonal communication networks show that informal person-to-person interaction plays a vital part in scientific communication, although the destination of most reports of research, in conformity with the norms of science, is archival publication in a scientific journal. Informal communication appears to be particularly effective in conveying procedural information, supplying reinforcement and feedback, providing leads to archival sources, and facilitating the application of scientific knowledge. A major concern of recent research efforts is to improve the efficiency and effectiveness of informal media and to demonstrate that informal, unplanned communication is an orderly rather than a random or accidental process (e.g., Menzel, 1958).

Another trend in communication research is defining the role of the scientific meeting and enhancing its effectiveness as a means of information exchange. Some years ago, Orr, noting the increasing amounts of time and funds allocated by scientists to meeting attendance and the prevalent feeling that such gatherings were decreasing in effectiveness, suggested that thorough study was needed (Orr, Coyl, & Leeds, 1964).

One intensive effort in this direction was the APA Project on Scientific Information Exchange in Psychology; eight of its first sixteen technical reports dealt with this topic, and a summary of the findings and implications of several of these reports has been issued (Compton, 1966). These studies dealt primarily with the percentages of meeting attendants who were seeking specific information through their attendance, their success in obtaining it, the nature of the information they sought and/or received, and the factors influencing the value of meetings. For example, a high concentration of active researchers in attendance resulted in a greater yield of information for all attendants—not just for the researchers themselves.

A broad-scale effort to compare and contrast the effectiveness of annual meetings in a number of disciplines was that of the Johns Hopkins Center for Research in Scientific Communication (Compton, 1968). The annual meeting studies involved surveys of at least three groups in each of the disciplines cooperating with the center: authors of program material, attendants of meeting sessions, and requestors of copies of presentations. Authors provided data on the date of inception of reported work, the frequency and types of premeeting reports of this work, the distribution of copies of the paper, and plans for publication or further dissemination subsequent to the meeting. Session attendants supplied data on their reasons for attending the presentation of particular papers, their prior knowledge, if any, of the content of these papers, their professional involvement in the areas of work represented by such papers, any effect on their work resulting from information received, and any continuing interaction planned with authors. Requesters of copies of papers very frequently were not present at the meeting at which these papers were presented. This group provided information on their sources of information about program material, their work involvement in the area of the requested paper, their use of the information it contained, and their interaction with the author.

The center's series of meeting studies fulfilled a twofold purpose: It provided specific data to each participating scientific or engineering group on the functions and effectiveness of its meetings, and it produced a comprehensive picture of the dissemination process from initial reporting through publication of work in each discipline.

The inclusion of engineering groups in the series of studies just described represents another trend in communication research. For many years, research on scientific communication focused largely on the needs and search-and-acquisition patterns of the active researcher. However, the information needs of engineers and practitioners, the use of scientific information in technological development, and pressure to accelerate the widespread application of science and technology to a variety of national problems are offering new challenges to communication research. Papers by Marquis and Allen (1966) and Gordon and Shef (1968) present some of the research emphases and findings in these areas. The Technology Utilization Programs of the National Aeronautics and Space Administration and the Atomic Energy Commission, which involve both interpersonal and formal media as well as various types of specialized services, should provide needed data on and examples of ways to surmount the knowledge-application interface.

Carlson (1967) summarized some of the implications of Department of Defense-sponsored studies of the use of scientific and technical information in design and development work. He emphasized that effective communication results when the information is keyed to the audience. For example, an engineer seeking the answer to a specific problem encountered in work will not be helped by a lenghty list of references or a research report, the format and terminology of which are not meaningful to him. He is more likely to need data sheets, parts catalogs, drawings, or specifications. Management personnel also need a different kind of information and a different method of presentation than meet the requirements of of researchers.

In addition, Carlson reported findings indicating that 70 percent of an engineer's information seeking begins with an informal source, that formal sources tend to be less effective for the engineer than informal ones, and that approximately three-fourths of the most productive technical communication that takes place in the design, development, and manufacturing process occurs through personal interaction.

The nature of the engineer's information problem and the pressing need to develop special services that cut across disciplines to give him intelligible information rapidly has been discussed by Cairns and Compton (1970). They summarized some of the implications of the findings and recommendations of the Committee on Scientific and Technical Communication (1969) for the training of engineers.

Goodman and Jones (1968) also provide useful data and guidelines for improving scientific and technical information systems in industrial settings. One objective of the Goodman study was to introduce an awareness of internal expertise and consultation capability into the formal information system of a company. The Capability Profile and Roster that were developed were incorporated into the company's Literature Search Subsystem and also circulated to selected management personnel. The number of requests for assistance and the effectiveness of the aid provided by those participating in the Capability Profile Pilot Program are being studied and evaluated.

In addition to a clearer understanding of the different needs for and uses of scientific information that characterize the researcher and the engineer or practitioner, we require an understanding of the information needs and uses associated with teaching, graduate and undergraduate study, administration, marketing, and other such areas. Thus far there has been little or no systematic effort to study communication patterns among those engaged in these activities.

TWO RESEARCH PROJECTS

The APA Project on Scientific Information Exchange in Psychology and the Johns Hopkins Center for Research in Scientific Communication are selected for detailed discussion since the author is more familiar with these projects than with others, having been associated with each from its inception.

When proposing a series of studies for future research during the International Conference on Scientific Communication in 1958, Bernal suggested that: "The whole subject of transmission of scientific information needs analysis of a descriptive or natural historical kind before we can hope to find the right . . . questions to ask" (Bernal, 1959:78). He considered such an approach necessary to ensure that the findings obtained would be relevant and applicable to the actual problems of scientific communication.

Such a viewpoint characterized the early development of the APA project. The program of research was threefold and included:

1. Studies of producers and users of scientific information to provide

data on dissemination patterns and user practices;
2. Studies of information-exchange media—journals, books, abstracting and indexing services, technical reports, and scientific meetings (at the state, regional, national, and international levels)—to establish the types of content conveyed, the extent and purposes of use, and the role and interrelationship of these media in the scientific communication system;
3. The institution of innovations on an experimental trial basis and the testing and follow-up of such efforts.

The first two sets of studies made possible a map of the communication system for psychology, showed how elements in the system complemented one another, and established the time intervals involved in the dissemination process. This map of system operation also revealed the points at which innovations might best be introduced and would be least likely to encounter resistance, thus paving the way for the third phase of the program.

A description of the purposes, methods, and results of each of the main project studies appears in Garvey and Compton (1967). Briefly, research on producers and users began with a diary study of active researchers in various work settings, principally academic, and produced a general picture of information problems and practices as well as showing the high percentage of time devoted to maintaining awareness and seeking specific information. A subsequent interview study of researchers in a large university and a government laboratory added further details to the emerging picture of information exchange by indicating the different patterns and objectives of communication associated with various phases of research and the influence of personal, social, and environmental factors in shaping communication.

Studies of authors of journal articles and of papers presented at scientific meetings clarified trends in the dissemination of information, including the time intervals involved, the nature and extensiveness of the audiences for the various early, informal modes of dissemination, and the degree of redundancy existing in the system. A study of scientists preparing review articles for the *Annual Review of Psychology* dealt with the difficulties of covering adequately the increasing output of most subfields and some of the criteria used by reviewers to reduce their subject matter to workable proportions.

The series on information-exchange media included an investigation of the immediate readership of a sample of current issues of core journals in psychology. A study of books showed a large and diverse number that were of use and importance to the work of psychologists but exceedingly few that were of particular use to more than 1 percent of the APA membership. Technical reports exemplified the redundancy common among informal elements of the system in that 88 percent of the material included in a sample of these reports had been reported orally and 85 percent had been reported in a written form other than the technical report. Journal publication was planned for one-third of these.

Of those reports intended for journal use, about one-fourth showed no difference in comprehensiveness of content or treatment of data from technical report to journal version. When such differences did occur, they tended toward the technical report's being a more lengthy and detailed presentation. Studies of the use and operation of *Psychological Abstracts* laid the groundwork for subsequent procedural and operational modifications of this service. The findings relative to scientific meetings depicted the objectives, functions, and effectiveness of different levels—from state to international—and orientations—from small research gathering to large general meeting.

Combining the data derived from these various studies yielded a detailed picture of the dissemination process for the "average" research report appearing in a core psychological journal in the early 1960s; the outstanding characteristics of this picture were: (*a*) the small number of widely accessible media carrying relatively "old" information, and (*b*) the multiplicity of media serving restricted and typically small audiences and carrying up-to-date information on recently completed or ongoing work.

In addition, several breakdowns in communication were evident. The APA project instituted experimental innovations at some of these points and studied their effectiveness. One such trouble spot was the fifteen-month or more lag between publication in a journal and coverage by psychology's main secondary service, *Psychological Abstracts*. Changes in the handling and processing of material and in the production process (see Siegmann & Griffith, 1966) reduced the median time lag for core literature from two years in the early 1960s to eight months by 1964, and to about three months by 1966.

A second obstacle to effective communication was the long lag between submission of a manuscript and journal acceptance and publication. By listing accepted manuscripts by title, author's name, and address in the current issues of certain APA journals with a particularly long publication lag, the journals made information on current work available nearly a year prior to its actual publication and permitted interested persons to communicate with authors (Garvey & Griffith, 1966). Follow-up studies showed that about 90 percent of the authors received requests for information and that the requestors were generally young researchers, new to the field, little known, and not likely to be part of the invisible colleges by means of which information so often circulates.

A third innovation, the institution of a preconvention proceedings, reduced the volume of material submitted for journal publication during the year following the convention and enhanced the effectiveness of paper-presentation sessions.

The program of the Johns Hopkins Center for Research in Scientific Communication is interdisciplinary in approach, personnel, and subject matter. A goal in staffing the center was to obtain representatives from sociology, psychology, library science, history of science, and computer technology, whose different areas of expertise and perspectives would foster a broad, flexible, and innovative approach to the study of problems of scientific communication. A major objective of the center was to develop comprehensive studies of all facets of the dissemination process in a wide range of scientific and engineering disciplines. Cooperating in the program at its inception were societies representing the following disciplines: sociology, geography, geophysics, meteorology, optical science, aeronautical engineering and aerospace sciences, metallurgical engineering, and heating, refrigerating, and air-conditioning engineering (Johns Hopkins Center for Research in Scientific Communication, 1967a–g; 1968a–b).

The initial series of studies dealt with the annual meetings of each of the participating societies. Such a starting point was optimum for tracing the dissemination of information, since annual meeting presentations tend to occur fairly early in the dissemination process and to mark a turning point from more restricted media serving limited audiences to generally accessible archival media. Results of the initial set of studies traced dissemination from the time work first became reportable to the time of the meeting; follow-up studies conducted a year later added further details on subsequent dissemination.

The main findings of the initial studies of the first seven groups taking part in the center's program were as follows: In physical science and engineering groups, the research or design and development work reported at annual meetings tended on the average to be of relatively recent inception, beginning about twelve to eighteen months before the meetings, and first becoming reportable three to six months prior to the meetings. Among sociologists and geographers (chiefly those in economic and urban geography), the median date of inception of reported work was some two to two-and-one-half years before the meetings, and the work first became reportable some eight to nine months in advance—time intervals comparable to those obtained in psychology.

A majority of the work in all groups had been reported orally and/or in written form prior to the annual meetings; colloquia in an employing institution and technical reports were the most frequently indicated oral and written types in most of the groups. Definite plans for publication in a scientific or technical journal, typically in one of those published by the society sponsoring the meeting, characterized three-fourths to nine-tenths of the authors in all but one of the groups; the lowest percentage so indicating (53 percent) occurred among aeronautical and astronautical engineers.

Manuscript preparation began on the average during the same quarter in which meetings took place, with submission of manuscripts planned for some four to six months thereafter. Data from the follow-up studies showed that most of the authors who planned subsequent dissemination did, in fact, submit their work during the year following the meetings, although not always so promptly as they initially indicated, and substantial percentages also planned additional postmeeting dissemination in other formats such as books, technical reports, and oral presentations. More than three-fourths of the authors in all groups received requests for copies of their papers at about the time of the meetings (immediately before, during, or shortly thereafter), and roughly a third made some automatic or routine distribution of their papers to a personal or institutional mailing list.

The most striking characteristic of the data on the initial phase of the center's work was the marked similarity in the dissemination patterns for the various groups studied. Although there were quantitative differences, and some groups, such as the engineers, placed considerably greater emphasis on the production of technical reports and much less emphasis on journal and book publication than did, for example, the sociologists, the overall trends were much the same from social science to physical and earth sciences to engineering. Most authors who planned publication submitted their work rather promptly, and in most groups (with the exception of the sociologists), rejections by the chosen journals were few and revisions chiefly minor and stylistic.[2]

The second phase of the center's work deals with the preparation of articles appearing in 1968 issues of the core journals in each discipline. Data were collected on preprint and reprint distribution, the effect of feedback from presentations or preprint distribution on the subsequently published work, the types of editorial revisions required and their effect on the time intervals involved in dissemination, and the status and early reporting of any new work undertaken by authors in the same areas in which they had published. Such data will add further details to the picture of the dissemination process and would indicate some of the inputs that affect published work.

A future phase of the center's work would examine the use of current journal articles by scientists and engineers either as sources of specific needed information or for purposes of general awareness and background information.

LOOKING AHEAD

In the past twenty years, scientific communication has excited increasing research interest and activity. First came a series of unrelated efforts to arrive at a few facts and implications; next came a stage of

[2] For a detailed description of the Center's preliminary findings, see Compton (1968).

review and self-scrutiny; and recently well-planned, multifaceted, continuing programs of research have developed, the yield of which is just beginning to have some impact.

Among the developments that undoubtedly will do much to shape future efforts is a growing awareness that, for maximum effectiveness, the study of scientific communication requires the cooperation and collaboration of representatives of a number of disciplines and technologies. Merging the contributions and efforts of documentalists, social scientists, historians of science, information scientists, librarians, and others results in a productive approach to problems of scientific communication and helps point the way toward developments that are technologically possible, behaviorally feasible, and maximally beneficial from the systems point of view.

In a recent review, Paisley (1968) states that information science and behavioral science need one another. He foresees continuing productive cooperation between these fields in the study of information needs and uses: "When information scientists see reliable, valid, and nontrivial data on users' behavior, they begin to use behavioral criteria in evaluating information system performance. When behavioral scientists glimpse the full complexity of dissemination, documentation, storage, and retrieval processes, they offer fewer naive solutions . . ." (Paisley, 1968:1).

One of the most stimulating and promising trends is the exploration of the applications of new technologies to scientific communication. An excerpt from an article by Licklider on this subject depicts in part the nature of such efforts:

> Problems of information flood control are beginning to come within the grasp of on-line, interactive communities. M. M. Kessler's . . . Technical Information Project has demonstrated the capability and convenience of a multiple-access computer system as a medium of interaction between physicists and bibliographic information pertaining to journals of physics. Project INTREX is undertaking a program of experiments in information transfer that will exploit the Massachusetts Institute of Technology's advanced facilities for interactive information processing. . . . EDUCOM's Summer Study '66 formulated plans for a network of computer, facsimile, television, and other channels to foster coherent interaction among the people . . . of universities and related organizations. And several Government agencies . . . are seeking to develop new syntheses of brains, computers, and telecommunications for more effective accomplishment of their missions (Licklider, 1966: 1059).

Another probable focus of future effort will be evaluation of the various new systems and services that are emerging as a result of both mission-oriented government agency programs and scientific and technical society discipline-oriented programs. A recent study that well illustrates the scope, dimensions, and implications of such efforts and the need for more of them is Lancaster's (1968) evaluation of the demand search service of the Medical Literature Analysis and Retrieval System (MEDLARS).

One conclusion of this comprehensive and detailed study was "that the greatest potential for improvement in MEDLARS exists at the interface between user and system" (Lancaster, 1968:19[illegible]). About one-fourth of the recall failures and about one-seventh of the precision failures resulted from defective user-system interaction. Further analysis of these failures showed that the request statements most clearly reflecting the requestors' information needs were those prepared without any interaction with either librarians or information searchers. Another finding suggested a shift away from use of an external advisory committee as the principal means of establishing indexing language and terminology and toward terms based on analysis of the demands placed on the system, thus reflecting more closely the actual language of the users.

There are still many more unknowns than concrete findings in the study of scientific information-exchange behavior. More cross-disciplinary studies providing data for comparison are needed as well as more data on the information needs of different professional groups within disciplines. Also, as emphasis on communication across national boundaries increases, there is need for assessment of the problems and practices of international communication. For example, one of the APA studies revealed greater dependence on certain U.S. journals and abstracting services in this particular field among a group of foreign authors than was true of a comparable group of U.S. authors; the former often depended on such sources for knowledge of current work occurring in their own respective countries (Project on Scientific Information Exchange, 1963: Report No. 10).

In planning innovations in such media, a broader audience than the national one obviously must be considered. More recently, the effectiveness of international congresses has been the subject of studies conducted by the Johns Hopkins Center for Research in Scientific Communication (1968b).

These trends and requirements are but a few of those that will determine the direction in which research on scientific communication will move. Both government and the private sector are concerned with increasing the effectiveness and efficiency of scientific communication systems and services. This concern is stimulating research efforts and will foster their extension.

REFERENCES

Abelson, P. H.
1966 "Information exchange groups." Science 154:727.

Ackerman, W. C.
1967 "The AGU and scientific communication." Transactions of the American Geophysical Union 48:1–2.

Allen, T. J.
1964 The Utilization of Information Sources During R & D Proposal Preparation. Report No. 97-64. Cambridge, Massachusetts: Sloan School of Management, Massachusetts Institute of Technology.
1966a "Performance of information channels in the transfer of technology." Industrial Management Review 8: 87–98.
1966b "The problem-solving process in engineering design." IEEE Transactions on Engineering Management 13:72–83.

Allen, T. J., and S. I. Cohen.
1966 Information Flow in an R & D Laboratory. Report No. 217. Cambridge, Massachusetts: Sloan School of Management, Massachusetts Institute of Technology.

Allen, T. J., and P. G. Gerstberger.
1967 Criteria for Selection of an Information Source. Report No. 284–67. Cambridge, Massachusetts: Sloan School of Management, Massachusetts Institute of Technology.

Atherton, P. A.
1965 American Institute of Physics Documentation Research Project: A Review of Work Completed and in Progress, 1961–1965. AIP/DRP 65-3. New York: American Institute of Physics.

Auerbach Corporation.
1965 DOD User Needs Study. Phase I. Report 1151-TR-3. Philadelphia: Auerbach. (Available from the National Technical Information Service, Springfield, Virginia, AD 615 501, AD 615 502.)

Becker, Joseph, and W. C. Olsen.
1968 "Information networks," in Carlos A. Cuadra (ed.), Annual Review of Information Science and Technology. Volume 3. Chicago: Encyclopedia Britannica.

Bernal, J. D.
1948 "Preliminary analysis of pilot questionnaire on the use of scientific literature," in Report and Papers Submitted to the Royal Society Scientific Information Conference. London: Royal Society.
1959 "The transmission of information: A user's analysis," in Proceedings of the International Conference on Scientific Information. Washington,

D.C.: National Academy of Sciences-National Research Council.

Bernard, J. D.; C. W. Shilling; and J. W. Tyson.
1963 Informal Communication Among Bioscientists. Washington, D.C.: George Washington University, Biological Sciences Communication Project.

Cairns, R. W., and B. E. Compton.
1970 "The SATCOM report and the engineer's information problem." Engineering Education 60:375–376.

Carlson, W. M.
1967 "Engineering information for national defense," in Engineering Societies and their Literature Programs. New York: Engineers Joint Council.

Coleman, J. S.; Elihu Katz; and Herbert Menzel.
1966 Doctors and New Drugs. Indianapolis: Bobbs-Merrill.

Committee on Scientific and Technical Communication, National Academy of Sciences-National Academy of Engineering.
1969 Scientific and Technical Communication. A Pressing National Problem and Recommendations for Its Solution. NAS Publication 1707. Washington, D.C.: National Academy of Sciences.

Compton, B. E.
1965 "Convention presentation: Interim or ultimate type of dissemination?" American Psychologist 20:300–302.
1966 "A look at conventions and what they accomplish." American Psychologist 21:176–183.
1968 "Communication and the scientific conference." Technology and Society 4(No. 3):39–42.

Division of Medical Sciences, NAS-NRC.
1964 "Communication problems in biomedical research: Report of a study." Federation Proceedings 23:1119–1331.

Garvey, W. D., and B. E. Compton.
1967 "A program of research in scientific information exchange: Orientation, objectives, and results." Social Science Information 6(No, 2/3):213–237.

Garvey, W. D., and B. C. Griffith.
1964 "The structure, objectives, and findings of a study of scientific information exchange in psychology." American Documentation 15:258–267.
1965 "Scientific communication: Dissemination system in psychology and a theoretical framework for planning innovations." American Psychologist 20:157–164.
1966 "Studies of social innovations in scientific communication in psychology." American Psychologist 21: 1019–1036.
1967 "Communication in science: The System and its modification," in Anthony De Reuck and Julie Knight (eds.), Communication in Science: Documentation and Automation; a Ciba Foundation volume. Boston: Little, Brown.

Goodman, A. F., and S. O. Jones.
1968 User Information Needs: The Challenge and a Response. Doublas Paper 10,008. Huntington Beach, California: McDonnell Douglas Corporation.

Gordon, T. J., and A. L. Shef.
1968 National Programs and the Progress of Technological Societies. Douglas Paper 4964. Huntington Beach, California: McDonnell Douglas Corporation.

Gray, D. W., and S. Rosenborg.
1957 "Do technical reports become published papers?" Physics Today 10 (June):18–21.

Green, David.
1967 "Death of an experiment." International Science and Technology 65:82–88.

Halbert, M. H., and R. L. Ackoff.
1959 "An operations research study of the dissemination of information," in Proceedings of the International Conference on Scientific Information. Washington, D.C.: National Academy of Sciences-National Research Council.

Herner, Saul.
1954 "Information-gathering habits of workers in pure and applied science." Industrial and Engineering Chemistry 46:228–236.
1959 "Information-gathering habits of American medical scientists," in

Proceedings of the International Conference on Scientific Information. Washington, D.C.: National Academy of Sciences-National Research Council.

1962 "Determination of user needs for the design of information systems," in Information Systems Workshop: The Designer's Responsibility and his Methodology. Washington, D.C.: Spartan Books.

Herner, Saul, and Mary Herner.

1967 "Information needs and uses in science and technology," in Carlos A. Cuadra (ed.), Annual Review of Information Science and Technology. Volume 2. New York: Interscience Publishers.

Herner, Saul, and W. F. Johanningsmeier.

1965 "Information storage/retrieval: Is it working?" Chemical Engineering Progress 61:23–29.

Herring, Conyers.

1968 "Distill or drown: The need for reviews." Physics Today 21(September): 27–33.

Hertz, D. B., and A. H. Rubenstein.

1953 Team Research. New York: Columbia University, Department of Industrial Engineering.

Hogg, I. H., and J. R. Smith.

1959 "Information and literature use in a research and development organization," in Proceedings of the International Conference on Scientific Information. Washington, D.C.: National Academy of Sciences-National Research Council.

Johns Hopkins Center for Research in Scientific Communication.

1967a A Comparison of the Dissemination of Scientific and Technical Information, Informal Interaction, and the Impact of Information Associated with Two Meetings of the American Institute of Aeronautics and Astronautics. Report No. 1. Baltimore: Johns Hopkins Center for Research in Scientific Communication.

1967b A Study of Scientific Information Exchange at the Ninety-sixth Annual Meeting of the American Institute of Mining, Metallurgical, and Petroleum Engineers. Report No. 2. Baltimore: Johns Hopkins Center for Research in Scientific Communication.

1967c The Dissemination of Scientific Information, Informal Interaction, and the Impact of Information Received from Two Meetings of the Optical Society of America. Report No. 3. Baltimore: Johns Hopkins Center for Research in Scientific Communication.

1967d Scientific Information-Exchange Behavior at the 1966 Annual Meeting of the American Sociological Association. Report No. 4. Baltimore: Johns Hopkins Center for Research in Scientific Communication.

1967e The Dissemination of Scientific Information, Informal Interaction, and the Impact of Information Associated with the 48th Annual Meeting of the American Geophysical Union. Report No. 5. Baltimore: Johns Hopkins Center for Research in Scientific Communication.

1967f A Comparison of the Dissemination of Scientific Information, Informal Interaction, and the Impact of Information Received from Two Meetings of the American Meteorological Society. Report No. 6. Baltimore: Johns Hopkins Center for Research in Scientific Communication.

1967g A Study of Information Exchange at the Sixty-third Annual Meeting of the Association of American Geographers. Report No. 7. Baltimore: Johns Hopkins Center for Research in Scientific Communication.

1968a The Nature of Program Material and the Results of Interaction at the February 1968 Semiannual Meeting of the American Society of Heating, Refrigerating, and Air-conditioning Engineers. Report No. 8. Baltimore: Johns Hopkins Center for Research in Scientific Communication.

1968b The 1966 International Congresses of Psychology and Sociology: A Study of Information Exchange and Meeting Effectiveness. Series 2, Report No. 1. Baltimore: Johns Hopkins Center for Research in Scientific Communication.

Kessler, M. M.
1963 "Bibliographic coupling between technical papers." American Documentation 14:10–25.
1965 "The MIT technical information project." Physics Today 18 (March): 25–36.

Koch, H. W.
1968 "A national information system for physics." Physics Today 21 (April): 41–49.

Lancaster, F. W.
1968 "Evaluation of the MEDLARS [Medical Literature Analysis and Retrieval System] Demand Search Service." Washington, D.C.: National Library of Medicine, Health, Education and Welfare Department.

Libbey, M. A., and Gerald Zaltman.
1967 The Role and Distribution of Written Information Communication in Theoretical High Energy Physics. AIP/SDD-1. New York: American Institute of Physics.

Licklider, J. C. R.
1966 "A crux in scientific and technical communication." American Psychologist 21:1044–1051.

Liebesny, Felix.
1959 "Lost information: Unpublished conference papers," in Proceedings of the International Conference on Scientific Information. Washington, D.C.: National Academy of Sciences-National Research Council.

Lipetz, B. A.
1964 Evaluation of the Impact of a Citation Index in Physics. AIP/DRP Cl-3 (1964). New York: American Institute of Physics.

McLaughlin, C. P.; R. S. Rosenbloom; and F. W. Wolek.
1965 Technology Transfer and Flow of Technical Information in a Large Industrial Corporation. Boston: Harvard University Graduate School of Business Administration.

Marquis, D. G., and T. J. Allen.
1966 "Communication patterns in applied technology." American Psychologist 21:1052–1060.

Maurice, R. H.; Herbert Menzel; and Rolf Meyersohn.
1966 Physicians' Information Levels as Affected by Milieu, Contact with Colleagues, and Current Awareness Activities: Preliminary Report of a Study. Paper presented to the Subcommittee on Medical Sociology, Sixth World Congress of Sociology, Évian, France, September.

Menzel, Herbert.
1958 The Flow of Information Among Scientists—Problems, Opportunities, and Research Questions. New York: Columbia University Bureau of Applied Social Research. (Available from National Technical Information Service, Springfield, Virginia, PB 144 390.)
1960 Review of Studies in the Flow of Information Among Scientists. New York: Columbia University Bureau of Applied Social Research. (National Technical Information Service, PB 156 941.)
1966a "Sociological perspectives in the information-gathering practices of the scientific investigator and the medical practitioner," in D. McCord (ed.), Bibliotheca Medica: Physician for Tomorrow, Dedication of the Countway Library of Medicine. Boston: Harvard University Medical School.
1966b Formal and Informal Satisfaction of the Information Requirements of Chemists. Interim Report. New York: Columbia University Bureau of Applied Social Research.
1966c "Can science information needs be ascertained empirically?" in Lee O. Thayer (ed.), Communication: Concepts and Perspectives. (Proceedings of the Second International Symposium on Communication Theory and Research, Excelsior Springs, Missouri, 1965.) New York: Spartan Books.
1966d "Informal communication in science: Its advantages and its formal analogues," in Dan Bergen (ed.), The Foundations of Access to Knowledge. Syracuse, New York: Syracuse University Press.
1966e "Information needs and uses in science and technology," in Carlos A. Cuadra (ed.), Annual Review of Information Science and Technology. New York: Interscience Publishers.

1966f "Five themes from social science research." American Psychologist 21:99–104.

Mullins, N. C.
1966 Social Networks Among Biological Scientists. Ph.D. Dissertation, Harvard University (unpublished).

North American Aviation.
1966 DOD User Needs Study. Phase II. 3 volumes. Final Technical Report. Anaheim, California: North American Aviation, Autonetics Division. (Available from National Technical Information Service, Springfield, Virginia, AD 647 111, AD 647 112, and AD 649 284.)

Orr, R. H.
1961 "The metabolism of new scientific information: A preliminary report." American Documentation 12:15–19.

Orr, R. H.; G. Abdian; C. P. Bourne; E. B. Coyl; A. A. Leeds; and V. M. Pings.
1964 "The biomedical information complex viewed as a system." Federation Proceedings 23:1133–1145.

Orr, R. H.; E. B. Coyl; and A. A. Leeds.
1964 "Trends in oral communication among biomedical scientists: Meetings and travel." Federation Proceedings 23:1146–1154.

Orr, R. H., and E. M. Crouse.
1962 "Secondary publication in cardiovascular, endocrine, and psychopharmacologic research." American Documentation 13:197–203.

Paisley, W. J.
1965 The Flow of (Behavioral) Science Information: A Review of the Research Literature. Stanford, California: Institute for Communication Research, Stanford University.
1968 "Information needs and uses," in Carlos A. Cuadra (ed.), Annual Review of Information Science and Technology. Volume 3. Chicago: Encyclopedia Britannica.

Parker, E. B.
1967 SPIRES [Stanford Physics Information Retrieval System] 1967 Annual Report. Stanford, California: Institute for Communication Research, Stanford University.

Parker, E. B., and W. J. Paisley.
1966 "Research for psychologists at the interface of the scientist and his information system." American Psychologist 21:1061–1071.

Parker, E. B.; W. J. Paisley; and R. Garrett.
1967 Bibliographic Citations as Unobtrusive Measures of Scientific Communication. Stanford, California: Institute for Communication Research, Stanford University.

Pelz, D. C., and F. M. Andrews.
1966 Scientists in Organizations: Productive Climates for Research and Development. New York: Wiley.

Price, D. J. de S.
1961 Science Since Babylon. New Haven, Connecticut: Yale University Press.
1965 "The scientific foundations of science policy." Nature 206:233–238.

Price, D. J. de S., and D. de B. Beaver.
1966 "Collaboration in an invisible college." American Psychologist 21: 1011–1018.

Project on Scientific Information Exchange in Psychology.
1963 Reports of the American Psychological Association's Project on Scientific Information Exchange in Psychology. Volume 1. Washington, D.C.: American Psychological Association.
1965 Reports of the American Psychological Association's Project on Scientific Information Exchange in Psychology. Volume 2. Washington, D.C.: American Psychological Association.

Rosenbloom, R. S.
1965 "Information requirements for development decisions" Pp. 391–401 in Joseph Spiegel and Donald E. Walker (eds.), Information System Science, Proceedings of the Second Congress, 1964. Washington, D.C.: Spartan Books.

Rosenbloom, R. S., and F. W. Wolek.
1967 Technology, Information, and Organization: Information Transfer in Industrial R & D. Boston: Harvard University Graduate School of Business Administration.

Rubenstein, A. H.; R. W. Trueswell; G. J. Rath; and D. J. Werner.
1966 "Some preliminary experiments and a model of information-seeking style of researchers." Paper presented to

the 20th National Conference on the Administration of Research, Miami, October.

Shaw, R. R.
1956 Pilot Study on the Use of Scientific Literature by Scientists. Washington, D.C.: National Science Foundation.

Shilling, C. W., and J. D. Bernard.
1964 Informal Communication Among Bioscientists. Part II. Washington, D.C.: George Washington University Biological Sciences Communication Project.

Siegmann, P. J., and B. C. Griffith.
1966 "The changing role of Psychological Abstracts in scientific communication." American Psychologist 21: 1037–1043.

Tornüdd, Elin.
1959 "Study on the use of scientific literature and reference services by Scandinavian scientists and engineers engaged in research and development," in Proceedings of the International Conference on Scientific Information. Washington, D.C.: National Academy of Sciences-National Research Council.

Urquhart, D. J.
1948 "The distribution and use of scientific and technical information," in Report and Papers Submitted to the Royal Society Scientific Information Conference. London: Royal Society.

Van Cott, H. P., and R. G. Kincade.
1967 A Feasibility Study for Determining Requirements of Biological Information Services and Systems. Final Report AIR F-57-11/67-TR-7. Washington, D.C.: American Institute for Research.

Werner, D. J.
1965 A Study of the Information-Seeking Behavior of Medical Researchers. Master's Thesis, Northwestern University Graduate School of Industrial Engineering and Management Sciences (unpublished).

Wooster, Harold.
1969 Microfiche 1969—A User Study. AFOSR-69-1847TR. Washington, D.C.: Air Force Office of Scientific Research.

Wuest, F. L.
1965 Studies in the Methodology of Measuring Information Requirements and Use Patterns. Bethlehem, Pennsylvania: Lehigh University Center for Information Sciences.

Xhignesse, L. V., and C. E. Osgood.
1967 "Bibliographic citation characteristics of the psychological journal network in 1950 and 1960." American Psychologist 22:778–791.

Zaltman, Gerald.
1968 "Professional recognition and communication in theoretical high energy physics." Ph.D. Dissertation, Johns Hopkins University (unpublished).

CHAPTER 25 Public Opinion

ITHIEL DE SOLA POOL
Massachusetts Institute of Technology

More than two centuries ago a shrewd Scot named David Hume wrote: "Nothing appears more surprising to those who consider human affairs with a philosophical eye, than the easiness with which the many are governed by the few; and the implicit submission, with which men resign their own sentiments and passions to those of their ruler. When we inquire by what means this wonder is effected, we shall find, that, as Force is always on the side of the governed, the governors have nothing to support them but opinion. It is, therefore, on opinion only that government is founded; and this maxim extends to the most despotic and most military governments, as well as to the most free and most popular" (from "Essay IV: Of the First Principles of Government," in Essays: Moral, Political and Literary *by David Hume; first published in 1741).*

In the following chapter Ithiel Pool considers the role of public opinion in democracies, where it is presumably most emphasized. Is it really a crucial political force or merely a deceptive facade? How does it help shape the system or fail to alter the established patterns of control? What functions do opinions perform for the individual psyche? Such topics penetrate to the very heart of democratic theory, contemporary political conflict, and personal psychology. In the present chapter, they are analyzed as issues and confronted by the available empirical evidence.

PUBLIC OPINION: WHERE AND WHEN

This chapter is about how public opinion operates in the processes of democratic or responsible government. Public opinion can exist in other situations too. It may lift its head against a feudal oligarchy or a military junta, or in a theocracy it may demand the burning of witches. However, the role of public opinion in such situations is not the subject of this chapter; rather, we are concerned here with how public opinion functions in a participant system of government and how the existence of such a system in turn affects the character of public opinion.

The view just stated, that public opinion is not unique to participant societies, is controversial. A number of writers have argued that the rise of public opinion is a hallmark of the modern world. Its rise is said to be associated with the rise of democracy.

To some extent the issue is a semantic one, but important nonetheless. To understand the discussion of where and when public opinion holds sway, we must know what each writer means by the term.

The author wishes to thank Dr. Leonard Fein for extensive suggestions.

The concept, public opinion, has a long history (F. G. Wilson, 1962). *Vox populi, vox Dei* has been a familiar cliché since medieval political theory (Boas, 1969). Like all venerable concepts, public opinion has been defined in changing ways. The variations depend upon the meaning of each of the two terms *public* and *opinion*.

In referring to *public* opinion, instead of just opinion, public may imply any one of three things: (1) that the opinions referred to are publicly expressed, or (2) that the opinions referred to are about public affairs, or (3) that the opinion is held by the general public instead of by some small group.

If by public opinion one means opinions expressed publicly, then covert dissent in a dictatorship is not public opinion. In that sense, public opinion comprises those issues discussed in the press, parliament, and other public forums.

If, on the other hand, by public opinion one means opinions about public affairs, then the popularity of the Beatles, although widely expressed in mass demonstrations, was not part of public opinion. The term *public opinion* in this usage is analogous to the Roman term for the government, namely, *res publica* or public things. In this usage, public opinion is defined by the subject matter with which it deals. It would, therefore, be perfectly appropriate to talk about secret and unavowed public opinion of dissidents under a dictatorship, insofar as the views they hold are about the policies of their rulers.

Another sense in which the word *public* may be used is to refer to the mass of the people in contrast to an elite or minority group. In talking about public opinion in this sense, one is referring to those opinions widely held in a society. Minority views, which in the first two senses are an important aspect of public opinion, can in this sense be said to be opposed by public opinion.

Just as the modifier *public* is subject to different interpretations, so, too, is the word *opinion*. Opinion is sometimes contrasted with solid knowledge. In that usage, it is not a matter of public opinion that it takes a great deal of money to get men onto the moon. That is clearly true. It is, however, a matter of public opinion that the effort to place a man there has advanced human progress. The first statement is uncontrovertible, while the second is widely debated.

In a different usage, the term *opinion* is contrasted with attitude: an opinion is cognitive; an attitude is evaluative. An opinion is a proposition, while an attitude is a proclivity to be pro or anti something. It is an opinion that proceedings in the U.S. Senate are time consuming; it is an attitude that they are *too* time consuming. That distinction, however, is relatively rare in the literature on public opinion. Typically that literature is just as concerned with attitudes as with cognitions.

More usually the word *opinion* is used as a catchall to designate symbolic expressions of any kind as contrasted with the physical, material, or organizational aspects of society. Thus a writer might say that in order to win, a candidate needs money, competent staff, and a favorable public opinion. In this sense, public opinion encompasses any verbal expression that is public in any one of the three senses noted above. It may be certain or uncertain, factual or normative. But as a *symbolic expression* it is contrasted with property or institutions.

Definitions are arbitrary, and it is not necessary for us to choose among them. It suffices to be clear as to the sense in which a term is used in any given discussion. Propositions and findings that may be true of public opinion in one sense may well be false when the word is used in another sense.

Let us look at an example of a debate in which the outcome depends upon the choice of definition of the term *public opinion*. The discussion of whether public opinion is a cultural universal or a phenomenon specific to certain societies is a case in point. If by public opinion we mean beliefs held by most of a people, then clearly there is a public opinion in every society. Every society has some widely held convictions. It cannot be in that sense, then, that the term is used in the large and significant literature that deals with the historical development of the phenomenon, public opinion.

Hans Speier (1950), in a classic essay, argued that public opinion is a modern phenomenon; he traced its evolution to the era of the French Revolution. When Necker, the minister of finance in the French court, needed fiscal support from the commercial estates, public opinion became a significant factor in European government. Gradually, during the French Revolution and after, the role of public opinion grew. The sphere in which public opinion assumed its ascendency last, according to Speier, was that of foreign affairs.

In the United States, in contrast to Europe, the distinction between domestic politics, as the appropriate sphere of public opinion, and foreign policy, as a realm for experts, has seldom been strongly made, although one can recall frequent use of the cliché "politics stops at the water's edge." In Europe, however, only in the decades between the wars did foreign policy come to be generally considered a legitimate object of partisan debate (cf. Claude, 1965). The Communist and Fascist mass revolutions brought ideology heavily into foreign relations, thereby contributing to the demise of the notion that foreign affairs were the closed reserve of government technicians.[1]

Clearly Speier's thesis, like Dicey's (1905) hypothesis that public opinion became the dominant basis of English law in the nineteenth century, implies a definition of public opinion as the widespread expression of views about public affairs. That phenomenon has not existed in all societies. It is something that has been growing in modern societies (Pool, 1970), accelerated by the development of mass media and of political organization.

The same process of increased expression of views on public affairs that Dicey and Speier describe historically in the West can be seen contemporaneously (and growing much more rapidly) in the developing nations. In *The Passing of Traditional Society*, Lerner (1958) distinguishes among what he calls "traditional," "transitional," and "modern" men, very largely in terms of the extent to which they are capable of empathy with the role of the ruler.

Questions about public affairs asked of traditional peasants are, he found, typically answered by such statements as "I am a common man, I can't think about such things" or "Why do you ask me what the government should do? I could never be president of Turkey." What Lerner calls transitional types—typically, recent migrants from the country to the city or peasants who have been touched by roads and radios—do begin to give answers to questions about public affairs, but their answers are naive and in a sense unpolitical. They cannot conceive what it means to make policy regarding broad issues like NATO or GNP. They tend to answer policy questions in terms of their own immediate environment. Asked what the government should do, a transitional person is likely to reply that it should fill the holes in the road that he travels or dig a well in his village. Modern men, on the other hand, having experienced public affairs through the mass media, are able to role play at being head of state and do so frequently and with exhilaration. They can formulate general political issues.

In a modern society, one may be ashamed if one cannot answer questions such as what the government should do about Vietnam, unilateral disarmament, social welfare, or any one of a myriad of public issues. Public opinion pollers in the

[1] For discussions of public opinion on foreign policy in the United States, see Cohen (1957: 1967), Hero (1959; 1965), Almond (1960), Rosenau (1961), and Caspary (1970).

United States find many people unwilling to admit that they do not know about an issue. In one test in California, people were asked their opinion of the Metallic Metals Act, a pure fabrication; two out of three respondents offered an opinion.

Subsequent studies have supported Lerner's overall thesis about the relationship of communication and modernization (Cutright, 1963; McCrone & Cnudde 1967; Winham, 1970; cf. Neubauer, 1967), and more specifically his thesis about the propensity of people in traditional societies to decline to express opinions about public affairs (Frey, 1966). A survey covering over 400 villages in Turkey by Frederick Frey replicated some of Lerner's earlier work and confirmed the pattern.

A dramatic illustration is provided by Felix and Marie Keesing (1956) in a study of communication in Samoa. In traditional Samoan society, not only were ordinary people not allowed to debate public affairs, but they were not allowed even to utter the words that alluded to matters of state power. Those words were reserved to the chiefs. There were two levels of chiefs, full chiefs and talking chiefs. The top chiefs were too important to expose themselves to the buffets of advocacy, since in the final community decision the advocate might be overruled. Public statements of advocacy were made by the talking chiefs after much quiet consultation as to the popular consensus. The talking chiefs may be considered as functionally equivalent to lawyers or advocates in our own society. Ordinary people, although quietly consulted, did not speak up publicly; it was considered obscene for an ordinary person publicly to use words alluding to power and decision. In Samoa such words are the equivalent of our four-letter words referring to sexual and excretory functions in that there are times and places for their use, but certainly not in public by an ordinary person.

Clearly, public opinion (if one may talk of it at all) among Lerner's traditional peasants or the Keesings' Samoan villagers is a very different thing from public opinion in the West today. One may, therefore, in a very real sense talk of the emergence and growth of public opinion in modern society.

There have been some small earlier societies with a lively public opinion—for example, the democracy of ancient Athens. What is extraordinary and distinctive in modern society is the scope of populations and range of issues over which public opinion operates and with social approval for its expression.

FUNCTIONS OF PUBLIC OPINION FOR THE INDIVIDUAL

The fact that in a modern democratic society people talk politics means that politics must have some personal function that makes talking about it rewarding. There are circles in society about which one may jokingly say that whenever a group of them gets together the talk will be about either sex or politics. For other groups there are other icebreakers: athletics, TV programs, or the lives of entertainment stars. What many of these topics have in common is an element of gossip about a set of people with whose lives the gossipers are quite familiar. The subjects of the conversation may be actors, athletes, or politicians. Whoever they are, as we shall see, they have become part of a pseudo-primary community created by the mass media.

In certain circles, talking politics has this character. Politics is a domain of shared experience about which people in those circles are knowledgeable. Persons who do not share that knowledge are not "with it." Those who do have the knowledge have the ingredients for easy chitchat with other politically minded persons.

But why politics when baseball scores, movie stars, and the latest phonograph records serve these conversational purposes just as well? Having an opinion about *res publica* must have certain additional and special functions for the individual apart from the general pleasure of all forms of gossip; else why would people assume the high costs in time and effort of being informed about public affairs? (On costs of political information, see Downs, 1957.) The special psychological functions of public opinions for those who hold them may be classified into three types, which we will here label the cognitive function, the identification function, and the resolving of internal tensions (M. B. Smith, Bruner, & White, 1956).[2]

Cognitive Functions of Public Opinion

Having opinions helps one handle new pieces of incoming information. For example, on reading a news story some years ago headed "West German Hematologist Flies to Moscow," I made an immediate inference that some top Soviet leader was ill. This inference, which turned out to be partly right and partly wrong, stemmed from a series of opinions about both the Soviet political system and Western news reporting. Implicit in this inference were opinions that the Soviet political system is highly stratified, that the top elite get privileged medical attention and that Soviet medicine has less expertise in some respects than does Western medicine.

The issue is not whether these opinions were right or wrong; the point is that having them led me to jump to one among the many alternative hypotheses available. Perhaps the hematologist was taking a vacation; perhaps he was on his way to a medical congress to read a paper; perhaps he was going to the Soviet Union to learn about a new and more advanced technique in his specialty; perhaps he was defecting to the Communist world. None of these alternatives came to mind, partly because of my opinion that newspapers do not run stories about vacations of private individuals, and that when they report meetings they name the meeting explicitly, and that German medicine does not generally learn from Soviet medicine. Once again, the issue is not whether these opinions were right or wrong, the point is that they were there.

It turned out that the sick person was not in the Soviet political leadership, but was a general. Prior opinions had helped me reach a partially correct conclusion from a limited new piece of information. In some sense I had used my prejudices, i.e., my prejudgments. The literature on public opinion has focused quite extensively on prejudice, with only partial clarification of the relationship between other aspects of prejudice and the processes of inference formation from limited clues.[3]

It is obviously impossible to have complete information for action. We always act on probable inferences from limited clues. When we hear a distinctive ring we go to the telephone, disregarding the conceivable but implausible alternative hypothesis that we are hearing a recording of a telephone ring. So with all actions, we act on presumptions. In popular parlance, we call such a presumption a prejudice to suggest either that it is not subject to change in the face of evidence or that it is used to impose penalties on individuals based on the group or class to which they belong (for literature on prejudice, see Adorno, Frenkel-Brunswik, Levinson, & Sanford, 1950; Allport, 1954; Rokeach, 1960; Klineberg & Yinger, 1968). The prejudice that the "natives" are lazy is condemnable as a prejudice if it continues to be asserted in the face of contrary evidence that it is

[2] See also Daniel Katz (1960), Froman (1962: 20–21), Kelman (1965), and Himmelstrand (1970).

[3] Compare studies of conceptualization (Bruner, Goodnow, & Austin, 1956; Perlmutter & Bruner, 1957; R. W. Brown, 1958; Carter, 1962; Lane, 1962; Barber, 1969: chap. 3); of person perception (Bruner & Tagiuri, 1954; Tagiuri & Petrullo, 1958; Tagiuri, 1968); of accuracy, inaccuracy, and selectivity in these (Rommetveit, 1960; Sarbin, Taft, & Bailey, 1960: chap. 9; Freedman & Sears, 1965; Harding, 1968); of complexity and structure in conceptualization (Coelho, 1958; Scott, 1965); and the functions of vagueness (Moore & Tumin, 1949).

an illusion, or (even if it were statistically arguable) if individuals were denied jobs or promotions on their own merit on the grounds of such statistical generalizations. Aversion to that kind of prejudice should not blind us to the fact that we all think in stereotypes, and that given the finiteness of decision time and of the mind we cannot do otherwise.

The concept of stereotype as applied to public opinion was first popularized by Walter Lippmann in 1922 in his classic book, *Public Opinion*. Lippmann's book is part of a large and important literature in modern social science, by authors who may be called empirical critics of democratic theory. Ostrogorski (1902), Michels (1915), Weber (1919), Pareto (1935), Mosca (1939), Carl Becker (1941), Schumpeter (1942), James Burnham (1943), Berelson, Lazarsfeld, and McPhee, (1954), and Key (1961) have all documented the discrepancy between the norms of classical democratic ideology about how citizens should make up their minds, and the way in which they actually do.

To some degree all of these books attack a straw man in their description of the democratic ideal as it was formulated by eighteenth-century rationalist political philosophers such as Rousseau (1962), Locke (1690), and Jefferson; the formulators of democratic theory were not totally unrealistic about human nature. To some degree, however, their critics are justified. Rousseau, for example, maintains that a society is free to the degree that there is direct participation of the citizens in the making of laws, and insofar as in acting on laws each citizen considers not his own interests but what the general will would be. The image of a public, each member of which objectively studies each issue so as to arrive at a judgment of the public good and then votes accordingly, quickly falls before any empirical study of how actual parties or citizens behave. People in real politics do not behave that way. They are often lazy, ill-informed, uninterested in becoming more informed, prejudiced about issues, and more concerned with what government will do for them than what they can do for the government.

In contrast to the classic image of an atomized public, each member of which is seen as acting as an independent individual rationally assessing the public interest, Ostrogorski and Weber documented by historical examples the crucial role that leadership plays in a democracy. Charismatic leaders, Weber pointed out, are more important in a democracy than in any other political system. Michels, in a case study of German social democracy, documented how these leaders acquire vested interests of their own. Lippmann argued further that people need leadership. Ordinary people think mainly about things outside of politics, and reach political conclusions by the quick, off-hand, and oversimplified device that he called stereotyping. Lippmann, as did most of these critics, disapproved of such simplified decision-making devices, and addressed himself to the problem of how to provide the masses with the facts needed for rational decision by means of educational and directive activities by a rational elite.

Berelson, Lazarsfeld, and McPhee (1954: chap. 14) carried the critique of democratic theory one step further by reaffirming the empirical statements of Lippmann and other critics on the basis of a careful study of voter behavior in presidential elections, but departing from the earlier literature in identifying positive functional values of citizens behaving the way they do.[4] Berelson and his colleagues argue that a measure of apathy and indifference is what keeps society from tearing itself apart in bitter ideological conflict. Election campaign data demonstrate that the most informed citizens are the most partisan and the least capable of being converted by argument. A society consist-

---

[4] See also Dahl (1961; 1963), Almond and Verba (1963), and Froman (1963) for similar views.

ing entirely of such knowledgeable, opinionated individuals would consume itself in partisan conflict. The fact that on each particular issue a substantial proportion of citizens care little about it places restraints upon the committed ideologues, who in a democracy act to win the support of that majority of uncommitted persons in the middle.

The critique of the rationalism of naive democratic theory was further advanced by Bauer, Pool, and Dexter (1963) and by Milbrath (1963) in their descriptions of the behavior of lobbyists, congressmen, and other political elites (cf. also Dexter, 1963a; 1963b). Observation revealed the same oversimplified, rapid-decision processes and the same stereotyping among political elites as among the uninformed citizens whose behavior Lippmann had deplored. No one in a busy world full of problems can handle political decisions other than by a certain amount of jumping to stereotypic conclusions. Busy congressmen, who must act on thousands of bills a year, inevitably develop shorthand means for deciding how to vote. They align themselves with an ideological bloc; they learn which fellow congressmen generally feel as they do and follow their lead; they discover all sorts of semireliable, time-saving devices. Like other citizens, they cannot decide each issue *de novo*, but must use opinions arrived at earlier in order to categorize and reach a decision on new items of information.

The cognitive function of public opinion is to provide a context for new judgments. If, for example, a person (whether congressman or citizen) has an opinion in favor of civil rights, this will help him reach a decision when faced with the new issue of school bussing. If earlier he concluded that communism is oppressive, that will help him decide whether to believe a man who has fled from the Soviet Union. If he has previously judged all politicians to be crooks, that will help him decide later whether he favors higher taxes to give the government more money with which to work. Without a wide-ranging variety of opinions, which detractors might call stereotypes, no one could operate effectively in the fast-flowing world of current events.

Nonetheless, stereotypes are often wrong; their oversimplicity can lead to error. Inadequacy is their characteristic as much as inevitability.

Stereotypes, like proverbs, have another characteristic: they tend to come in contradictory pairs, each member of which is sufficiently vague to cohabit in the human mind without obvious contradiction. The stereotype of Germans includes the images "hard," "authoritarian," and "strict," but there is also the stereotype of German Gemütlichkeit. Among the stereotypes of the Chinese is the wily, cruel, inscrutable Fu Manchu and the wise Confusian sage (Isaacs, 1958; Stephenson, 1967), the wild, fanatic Red Guard and the hard-working, thrifty, ambitious peasant or entrepreneur. The presence of such opposite stereotypes permits any new fact to be accepted as understandable and "natural," because each fact fits in with one or another of the opposed available images. People are seldom sufficiently self-critical to force themselves to think about the disconfirmed part of the stereotype and worry about reconciling it.

To illustrate these patterns we need only think about any country or group toward which attitudes have changed sharply in the gyrations of politics. Consider, for example, American images of China and Japan (Isaacs, 1958). In the 1930s Japan was generally viewed as a ruthless aggressor against whom the heroic Chinese people were putting up a brave, partiotic resistance. These images were accentuated during World War II, when the American image of Japan focused on the insane, suicidal fanaticism of Japanese kamikase pilots or the human waves of troops who threw away their lives in mass attacks. The Chinese, on the other hand, were seen as patient, long-suffering, hard-working people of high moral character. Then came the peace and China's fall to communism; simultaneously, Japan developed into a prosperous, friendly, peaceful, and democratic nation. The images reversed. The Japanese became the epitome of hard-working sobriety. The Chinese became the inscrutable, suicidal, human-wave attackers, fanatical and insane in their politics.

Between the time the above paragraphs were written and the time this book went to press, another swing of the pendulum has begun. President Nixon went to Peking and suddenly once again Americans see the Chinese as a remarkably self-disciplined, hard-working, idealistic people who have cleaned up their country and eliminated hunger. At the same moment the honeymoon with Japan suddenly ended. Instead of admiration for Japan's economic performance there is now fear of its economic drive. The image of charming, decorous Japanese landscapes gives way to the image of polluted, auto-clogged Tokyo.

At all times the American public had available a pair of images of Asia, on the one hand justifying fears of the yellow hoard, and on the other providing an admiring image of an extraordinarily patient, hard-working, creative people; only the nations to which the specific images attached were transposed.

Such pairs of images are similar to the so-called splits to which psychiatrists refer when discussing the analyses of dreams and other fantasies. In a dream there may be a witch and a good fairy, both of whom are associated to the dreamer's mother—the good mother and the bad mother (Fenichal, 1945; Freud, 1955). So, too, in political stereotypes. The good and bad are placed in psychological balance (Heider, 1958; Abelson, Aronson, McGuire, Newcomb, & Tannenbaum, 1968) by being split into paired but separated images.

Thus in these various ways a person's stock of established opinions serves him in interpreting the new bits of information that come his way.

Identification Functions of Public Opinions

Many opinions are what Harold Lasswell (1935; 1936) called "symbols of identification." That is to say, holding such an opinion serves to identify an indivudial with some group.

"There is another reason, besides economy of effort, why we so often hold to our stereotypes when we might pursue a more disinterested vision. The systems of stereotypes may be the core of our personal tradition, the defenses of our position in society" (Lippmann, 1922:95).

"Many voters vote not for principle in the usual sense but 'for' a group to which they are attached—their group" (Berelson et al., 1954:309).

"Opinions can play another role: that of facilitating, disrupting, or simply maintaining an individual's relations with other individuals.... It is by holding certain views that one identifies with, or indeed differentiates oneself from various reference groups within the population" (Smith, Bruner, & White, 1956:41f.).[5]

The role of social identification in public opinion is illustrated by what is called motivation research (Advertising Research Foundation, 1953). While one may question the reliability and soundness of most of the work in this field, the basic idea is an interesting one. Motivation research is the examination for advertising and marketing purposes of the images that people have of a product and its users. Cigarette brands, for example, are hardly distinguishable from each other; yet one cigarette company will portray its product as rugged and he-manish, another as distin-

[5] For basic discussions of group identification, see Freud (1922), Redl (1942), and Erikson (1959; 1966). For discussions of national identity, see Buchanan and Cantril (1953), Grodzins (1956), Isaacs (1958; 1968), Doob (1964), Klineberg (1964), LeVine (1965) and DeRivera (1968). For discussions of ethnic identity in American politics, see Glazer and Moynihan (1963), Wolfinger (1965), and Parenti (1967).

guished and sophisticated, and yet another as feminine and delicate. The consumer's choice of brand is partly motivated by how he sees himself and wants to be seen by others. Similar kinds of motivations enter into choices of clothing, cars, foods, and beverages. Purchase is an act of identification that helps the individual establish for himself who he is (Dichter, 1964).

Every group has its identifying symbols. They take the form of an emblem, or flag, or catechism, or platform, or simply a set of telltale characteristics that go with being a certain kind of person. For a person to hold the wrong views for his role or affiliation may be more disturbing and shocking to others than the same views held by a member of an appropriate group. For an Hindu peasant to believe in astrology bothers no one, but for an American scientist to express the same beliefs would cause heads to turn. For a North Vietnamese to mourn Ho Chi Minh's death is normal; for an American student to chant Ho's rhythmic name causes shock.

There are many completely logical positions that practically never occur because group identifications have made them seem utterly incongruous. Consider an SDS member who favors strict parietals in the dormitories. There is no inherent reason why a person who agreed with the SDS on war, peace, economic reform, and socialism should not favor strict regulation of social relations between the sexes (the Chinese Communists have that view). However, an American student who took such a view would generate shock and disdain. He would cut himself off from the respect of his radical colleagues and he would have a hard time defining himself as a true radical, either to himself or to the world. Thus, beliefs are symbols of identification just as much as flags, slogans, or anthems.[6] Accepted ideological structures make some beliefs consonant with or balanced with others. People avoid beliefs that create a sense of dissonance from their group identification (Heider, 1958; Froman, 1962: chap. 2; Abelson et al., 1968).

[6] For discussions of identity and ideology, see Pye (1961), Lane (1962), Edelman (1964), and S. R. Brown and Ellithorp (1970).

Resolving Internal Tensions

One of the more important insights of political psychology is that people use the political arena to act out psychic dramas that are important to them in their private fantasy lives. If private fantasies in the unconscious break through in dreams, slips of the tongue, literature, mythology, and religion, then political ideologies and behavior can hardly be exempt. The pioneer in applying Freudian theories to political behavior was Harold Lasswell (1930), who in *Psychopathology and Politics* published case histories of a dozen or more politicians who happened to end up in psychotherapy. More recently Erik Erikson has explored the psychobiography of Adolph Hitler (Erikson, 1964), George Bernard Shaw (Erikson, 1959), Martin Luther (Erikson, 1962), and Mahatma Gandhi (Erikson, 1969; see also Lasswell, 1948; McConaughy, 1950; George & George, 1956; Rogow, 1963). An extensive literature has developed on the psychodynamics of politics (e.g., Devereux, 1955; M. B. Smith, Bruner, & White, 1956; Browning & Jacob, 1964; Coles, 1965; M. Wolfenstein & Kliman, 1965; DiRenzo, 1967; Slote, 1967; E. V. Wolfenstein, 1967; Mitscherlich, 1969).

Psychodynamic analysis may be used to help explain both the political roles that people choose to play and the ideological symbols to which they attach themselves. Lasswell (1930; 1936), in his early work on the unconscious motivations for political roles, distinguishes first between those who choose to become involved in politics and those who do not; of those who choose to become involved, he distinguishes between those who play the role of the agitator and those who play the role of the organizer. The terms *agitator* and *organizer* are not used in a pejorative sense. By agitator we mean someone who stirs up public interest and attention. Using devices of rhetoric, the agitator mobilizes popular support and generates enthusiasm. The organizer, on the other hand, is someone who works in small groups to achieve results by administrative processes.

In Lasswell's case studies, it emerges that individuals who were highly inhibited over a large range of interpersonal relations during their formative years were more likely to play agitational roles, while persons whose inhibitions were narrower and more specific in range tended to play more organizational roles. Interpersonal relations in the agitational roles are mediated by remote political relationships. The agitator on a platform enjoys the cheers of the crowd as a substitute for a close personal relationship that would confront his inhibitions. He escapes to abstract political symbols rather than dealing directly with problems of individuals. The organizer, on the other hand, tends to deal face-to-face with individual human beings and their conflicts and desires.

The distinction between agitator and organizer may be extended to a continuum as is done in Figure 1. There we add the category of political theorist. The theorist's political activity withdraws him most completely from interpersonal relations. The historical examination of the biographies of political theorists shows a very high incidence of wide-ranging inhibition. Further along the scale, lying between the agitator and the routine administrator, is the promoter-organizer. At the extremes of the scale, in some respects, the ends meet. The most routine administrator and the most abstract theorist tend to withdraw somewhat from the clash of human relations in the political amphitheatre.

Leaving aside the question of whether the scale should be thought of as a line or as a circle, let us address ourselves rather to the question of whether it is a scale at all. If it is a scale, then any individual politician should function best in some continuous sector of it rather than at scattered points along it. That seems to be the case. Able politicians may function well along a broad segment of the scale; others may be more specialized and function well only over a short sector. But it does usually seem possible to characterize

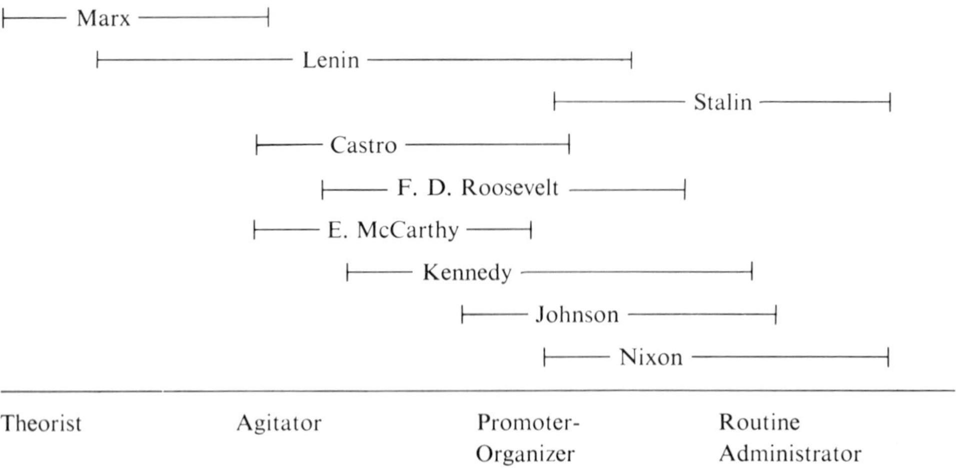

Figure 1. Speculative distribution of politicans along a function scale.

some continuous segment of the scale as the sphere of competence of any particular politician. A purely speculative set of characterizations is attached in Figure 1 for illustration. These speculations are no more than one man's opinion, but they seem to justify the notion of a scale or pattern.

Thus the argument is made that the role that political leaders choose to play in politics and in the mobilization and formation of public opinion is at least in part shaped by unconscious psychic needs. In the same way, joining a political movement, or such activities as demonstrating, picketing, canvassing from door to door, or proselytizing one's friends may fill psychic needs for less prominent political participants.

Lane (1959), M. B. Smith, Bruner, and White (1956), and others (e.g., Hoffer, 1951; Almond, 1954; McClosky, 1959; D. H. Smith, 1966; Kenniston, 1968; Feuer, 1969; Allardt, 1970; S. R. Brown & Ellithorp, 1970) have done research on what it is that makes people join movements. A major factor is the need for a sense of belonging. Joining a crowd that shares the same passions, the same values, the same discontents and perspectives on life relieves loneliness. Contact exhilarates and makes the movement meaningful. Young people, in particular, in that stage of their lives when they seek to establish their identity in society, will often comment about a demonstration or similar mass activity to the effect that: "The vibrations were great. We found ourselves with strangers who felt exactly as we did. We realized that there were thousands of us feeling the same anger about how things are."

Some years ago Almond (1954) did a comparative international study of why people join Communist parties. In the United States particularly, and also in England, he found that kind of "neurotic" need for belonging to be dominant. People joined the Communist party or its youth movement in search of a warm and cohesive home. To a considerable degree they did not find what they were looking for; the Communist party turned out to be a rather strict and cold home. Nonetheless, the dominant motive for joining in those years and in those countries was clearly a craving to belong.

In France and Italy, where the Communist party was a mass party, the motives for joining were entirely different. There young workers joined because their families, friends, and neighbors were in the Party. Joining was more a matter of identification than a way of working out individual psychic problems. By joining the mass party of his folks, the new recruit integrated himself further into the subcommunity of which he was a part. What Almond calls the "neurotic" motives for joining, or what we are calling the resolution of internal tensions, played a much smaller role there.

Not only is the choice of political roles psychologically motivated, but so, too, is the choice of symbols or ideologies (Lane, 1969; but cf. Schoenberger, 1968). Generally there is a high measure of consistency in the themes that any particular person emphasizes in politics. One person may be concerned with morality and corruption; another may be preoccupied with violence; another with power and oppression; another with discrimination against his group.

Consistency of preoccupation, we should emphasize, does not imply logical consistency or even consistency of tendency. Consider, for example, a militant pacifist; he may become so incensed by war that he demonstrates violently against it. Or consider the cynic who argues that politicians are all crooks and grafters, out for themselves; he may well conclude that that being how it is, he might as well take care of himself when the opportunity arises because no one else will. Indeed, we may offer the hypothesis that an individual or group that is preoccupied with any particular theme will tend to manifest behaviors or views that represent opposite extremes of that theme. It is predictable, not anomalous, that a Goebbels or a Göring would be solicitous of animal pets, or that Lenin would rage against Czarist repression but establish his own as the only way he could see to "free" the proletariat. Each was preoccupied with some central theme about violence or oppression while his behavior ranged between opposite extremes in regard to it.

Such ambivalent and extreme expressions on the topic of a person's preoccupation are characteristic of what in psychoanalytic literature is called "reaction formation" (Fenichal, 1945). The person who is reacting defends himself against his own unconscious impulses by extreme behavior that is designed to prove to himself and to others that he does not have such impulses at all. Lasswell (1930) presents a case study of one man preoccupied by his own illicit sexual desires who became an antismut campaigner and of another man preoccupied by his illicit violent impulses who became an antiwar crusader. Such overreactive behavior serves to provide apparent evidence to the world and, more important, to the person himself that he could not possibly be guilty of the particular sins that bother him. Else why would he express such views as he does? The person who so overreacts, however, seldom carries through the reaction altogether successfully. Typically, the strong illicit impulse breaks through from time to time. That is why ambivalent or contradictory patterns of extreme behavior emerge, as in the violent pacifist or the dictatorial rebel.

The reactive pattern of opinions that has received most attention in the literature on political behavior is that of authoritarianism. This concept was formulated and popularized in the book *The Authoritarian Personality* by Adorno, Frenkel-Brunswik, and others (1950). Authoritarianism is a pattern of behavior attributed by the authors to persons who have an unconscious desire to rebel against a strict and rigid father figure, but who defend themselves against this impulse by adopting highly conventional and stereotyped views in favor of traditional morality and the exercise of strict authority, and against deviance, outgroups, and radical challenges to existing authority.

The research on the authoritarian personality arose from an interest of the authors in the psychology of anti-Semitism. They developed a scale for measuring hostility toward Jews and other ethnic minorities which they called the E scale. They also developed a scale (the F scale) for measuring the extent of authoritarian attitudes such as ingroup/outgroup polarization, rigid polar judgments of moral issues, and support for strict authority. It was found that these two scales were highly correlated. The F scale, easily administered and frequently highly correlated with other variables, became one of the most widely used attitude measures in modern social science. (For reviews of the literature, see Titus & Holland, 1957; Christie & Cook, 1958, Kirscht & Dillehay, 1967.)

Much of the subsequent literature on authoritarianism revised the interpretation of the F scale (Christie & Jahoda, 1954; Rokeach, 1960). Some studies which measured the incidence of authoritarianism in different cultures and social classes (Simpson & Yinger, 1958; Diab, 1959; Lipset, 1960) generally demonstrated that scale items were sufficiently culturally specific so that score comparisons were more meaningful within cultures than between them. Successor studies showed that the scale would be improved by having items verbally formulated against, as well as for, authority since some people show more tendency than others to answer any question affirmatively; some people like to say "yes" and some people like to say "no" (Christie & Jahoda, 1954; Couch & Kenniston, 1960; Rokeach, 1960; Wells, 1961; 1963; B. W. Becker & Myers, 1970). Other studies showed that rigidity and polar moral judgments were not limited to prejudiced reactionaries on the right, but in some cultural milieus would be found among doctrinaires of the left; it is possible to be authoritarian about socialism or reform as much as about fascism or reaction (Shils, 1954; Lipset, 1960).

Authoritarianism is generally characteristic of extreme nationalists or chauvinists. However, it has been found that authoritarianism is also high among xenophiles, i.e., persons who prefer other countries to their own, who describe other countries as more moral, more cultured, more desirable in various ways (Perlmutter, 1956; 1957). These xenophiles have the same sort of ambivalence about authority as do the chauvinists, but allow their deep hostility to the authority of their own state to become explicit. But being authoritarians, they do not simply reject state authority in general. They resolve their ambivalence by imagining that some other state authority represents the good authority for which they are looking and which they do not find at home. They may idealize the Soviet Union, or Cuba, or India, or Israel, or Samoa as the place where values, priorities, and way of life are better; hence even if they rebel against authority at home, they reconcile themselves to some kind of authority (cf. Isaacs, 1958; 1963; Pool, 1965).

Reaction formation is only one of the ways in which inner needs may find outlet. Sublimation, its opposite, consists of the socially approved expression of an otherwise illicit impulse. For example, instead of controlling himself by pacifism, a man of violent impulses may express his impulses in a socially approved way, such as being a war hero. Sublimation is generally a less conflictful way of handling an impulse than is repressing it by reacting against it. It is, therefore, less apt to be accompanied by extremes than is the kind of reactive behavior described above.

It is easy to exaggerate psychological determination, as indeed any determinism, and by exaggeration to debunk it. Political opinions and ideologies are not merely the expression of neurotic psychic impulses. To assert that psychological factors operate is not to say that they always dominate. Such writers as Erikson, Lasswell, Almond, Lane, Smith, and Bruner, White, and Adorno are not suggesting that political views are adopted solely for psychological reasons. We noted before Almond's (1954) comments on the difference between countries in the weight of neurotic versus social factors in recruitment to the Communist party (cf. Krugman, 1967). Clearly, some people engage in politics mostly for psychic satisfaction, others to make money, others to get the street in front of their house repaved, others because they are in professions (such as the law) which make it easy and professionally advantageous to do so.

Second, it must be emphasized that there is no contradiction between noting that psychological factors shape public opinion and noting that other factors operate simultaneously. Of the myriad political views available to an individual, he adopts those that satisfy many functions for him at once. Consider, for example, a man in the South who joins a White Citizens' Council. He is likely to be an authoritarian personality expressing his prejudices. Even more likely he will also be a workman worried about loss of his job advantages if racial customs change. He will also find that his friends share similar views. Perhaps he has aspirations for low-level public office and is looking for organized support. If any one factor were reversed, he might not join a White Citizens' Council, but might look for some other activity that better met the total set of his particular needs. Any one factor—be it psychological, social, economic, or other—is only a partial determinant. It is appropriate to examine the social research findings about each factor, but not to assume that when doing so one is denying the other factors (Greenstein, 1968; 1969).

Other than the psychological, the most prominent determinative theories about why people hold the opinions they do are economic. The theories go back to Marx and, in fact, further. Since Aristotle, it has been common wisdom that democratic political views serve the interests of the masses of the poor while the rich and well-born prefer more elitist doctrines. James Madison (1788) noted in the tenth *Federalist* paper that "The most common and durable source of factions has been the various and unequal distribution of property."

There is little reason to doubt that most opinions about *res publica* tend to serve the interests of those who hold them. The term *ideology* is often used to denote political views that are adhered to not because of their truth-value, but because of the group advantages to be gained from having people hold them (Mannheim, 1940). Any ideology of a ruling class will include justifications of the authority of the rulers, consisting perhaps of allegations of divine selection, or of the ruler's magical powers, or of sanction by free election by the ruled.

The ideology of revolutionaries, on the other hand, will contain denials of the legitimacy of the rulers; allegations of wrongdoing on their part; claims of popular support for the rebels; and assertions about their moral, intellectual, or physical superiority. To label these assertions ideology is to say that one is not considering whether the assertions are true or false but only how they serve to bolster the advantage of some group.

Needless to say, an ideological statement may also be true. The government of South Vietnam, for instance, claims that it has the support of most of the people. The Viet Cong makes the same claim. Some neutralists and non-Communist opposition groups deny both these statements and assert that most South Vietnamese support neither side. Presumably at any given date at least one of these statements was true, although possibly different ones at different times. In any case, for each of the three contending groups, the assertion it makes is clearly ideological, although at any given moment one of the ideological statements is presumably true and the other two are not. The truth or falsity of an opinion and the social function of an opinion are two quite separate matters, not to be confused. As social scientists, we are apt to be interested in the functions of opinions. Citizens, one hopes, may be concerned more with their truth.

COMMUNICATION AND THE SCOPE OF THE PUBLIC

Up to this point we have been considering the satisfactions that individuals find in political action; why, at least in modernized societies, they play the game of saying what they would do if they were the ruler.

To play that game they must to some extent be informed. There must be a communication system that tells the public about the state of the world and identifies the issues that must be resolved. Without shared information of those kinds, there would be only private experiences, not a public forum.

The scope of the shared communication system may determine to a large extent the scope of public concerns and of the resulting political community. It may extend over a city, a nation, or the whole world. Lerner (1958), as noted earlier, attributes the differences among traditional, transitional, and modern men to differences in the scope of the communication systems of which each is a part. He considered illiteracy the definitive limitation on the communication system of the traditional peasant whose scope of empathy was restricted to the range of word-of-mouth communication. When Lerner's study was being made, the transistor revolution had not yet hit the Middle East, although radio, and particularly international radio, was already providing modernized men with the information base that gave them a cosmopolitan perspective. World news heard on the radio enabled them to empathize with the role and problems not only of a village chief or district chief, but also with the role of a head of state in the world of nations.

Karl Deutsch (1957; 1966) and a number of other scholars following him (e.g., Russett, 1963) have written persuasively about the relation of communication networks and community formation (see chapter 1 in this book). They plot statistics on origin and destination of trade, mails, telephone calls, and travel, in a network representation; the discontinuities in the network tend to become the boundaries of social groupings. Deutsch's thesis, developed by him with special reference to nation formation, is that the boundaries of political communities tend to evolve along these social boundaries, and that these two sets of boundaries then reinforce each other. A trend toward growth of a world community—or away from it, which Deutsch (1956) has also found—can be indexed by changes in the foreign/domestic ratio in scientific citations, mails, travel, trade, or other communications.

Similar analysis can be done intranationally. Urban sprawl, resulting from migration from the central city to the suburbs, tends to produce a diffuse megalopolis extending, for example, from Boston to Washington, or over much of Southern California, with possible consequences for people's sense of their community identification. The structure of public opinion in a traditional concentric-type large city, with its own city center, its own newspapers, its own broadcasting stations, and its own mayor, might change significantly when people come to live in a residential suburban community within driving distance of a number of scattered shopping and working centers in a number of different political units, without any single downtown.

Such changes in sense of community may be mediated and reinforced by the mass media, which also have to decide in what range of locations to seek their audience and what local news to cover. In a traditional concentric city, what happened in city hall was news for everyone. But in a megalopolis the audience may, while interested in neighborhood community news, have only a limited interest in any one other center. The editors and reporters for large-circulation media which cannot provide neighborhood coverage may increasingly find it profitable to focus on national or nonlocalized leadership figures such as the president or entertainment stars.

These are but examples that illustrate the general point that the scope and structure of the political community, of the economic community, and of the communication net mutually shape and set the bounds on each other.

COMMUNITY AND THE SENSE OF COMMUNITY

It has long been noted by sociologists that the mass media in the modern world create a surrogate community to serve some of the psychological functions that in earlier times were served by close relations in the village community (Simmel, 1950; cf. also Cooley, 1922; Schramm, 1949; Duncan, 1962; McLuhan, 1964; Stephenson, 1964; 1967). In a small rural community, where everyone knows everyone else, gossip is one of the main themes of human communication. The foibles, idiosyncracies, peccadillos, and scandals of each person are known to all. In a modern urban society, on the other hand, many people hardly know their next-door neighbors.

The media, however, provide isolated city dwellers with a population of culture heroes whose crimes, accomplishments, marriages, divorces, affairs, personal joys, and personal tragedies are known to all, and are available for the pleasure of shared gossip. These favorite stars in entertainment or politics become like friends. They provide an easy topic for conversation. People at work who otherwise hardly know each other can find a conversational bond in discussing the latest fling of John Lennon and his wife or the latest tour de force of a sports hero. And in politics, as we have already noted, people can establish a common bond of identification by discovering that they share the same enthusiasm or revulsion about a particular political figure.

Human interest stories thus help to integrate a community, a function not unlike that of folk tales in a traditional society (Hughes, 1939). Family situation comedies and soap operas perform a similar function (Herzog, 1944; Warner & Henry, 1948). They not only entertain; they convey information about appropriate ways to act. They provide what we earlier called behavioral models. Herzog found that women who were avid followers of soap operas felt that they learned a lot from them about how to handle their problems of daily life.

In nondemocratic societies, and to a limited degree in democratic societies, political organizations may perform some of the same functions of providing a surrogate community. In totalitarian societies, as described in chapter 14, the Party and its adjunct youth, sports, welfare, cultural, and recreational organizations are supposed to encompass totally the individual's extra-familial social life and to provide him with a sense of belonging and with behavioral guidance.

Political clubs in democratic societies are weaker, but they exist and often operate in a similar way. Some labor movements try to provide comprehensive life services, including welfare, education, sports clubs, and youth movements. The Histadruth in Israel is a particularly comprehensive example (Fein, 1968). The old-fashioned political machine in American cities used to provide a club and clubhouse, give uniforms to ball teams, and coal and Christmas baskets to its followers (Peel, 1935; Gosnell, 1937). It served as a significant institution for assimilation and guidance of immigrants to this country.

Thus political organizations, and now, to an even greater extent, the mass media, serve to cement a community in which public opinion operates. They serve to establish a consensus on underlying conceptions and on the definition of issues. They also serve to define the identity of the community to which the person belongs.

The mass media serve many other functions besides those we have so far considered. The functions of the media are best studied by observing changes in audience behavior when there are changes in media availability. For example, twenty-five years ago Berelson (1949) studied newspaper strikes to discover what missing the newspaper means. Interviews with people deprived of their newspapers revealed only a moderate amount of substitution of other news sources. People listened more to broadcast news or read more news magazines, but not to the degree one might expect. On the other hand, to a greater degree than expected, they sought equivalent activities to fill the time slots ordinarily devoted to newspaper reading. The tired father of the family, home from work and waiting for dinner, might even pick up last week's newspaper and re-read it.

Studies somewhat similar in conception have examined what media use was replaced or changed when TV first came in. A pioneer study by Hilda Himmelweit in Great Britain examined the effect of TV on children (Himmelweit, Oppenheim, & Vince, 1958). TV cuts into radio listening but not into outside sports. When a child wants to run and exercise, even sporting events on TV are no substitute. TV cuts into casual movie going but not into movie going on dates. For those who want to be with friends away from home, TV movies will not serve. The important thing is the activity rather than the message.

The information the media convey is thus often only a by-product of the activity of using the media (McLuhan, 1964). Information about public affairs may be acquired more because of enjoyment of reading or viewing than because of interest in public affairs as such. On the other hand, it is also true that Americans generally do attach considerable value to being well-informed on public affairs. When asked to make suggestions about TV programming, a large proportion of interview respondents suggest an increase in news and public affairs material.

When such programs are offered, however, few watch. Top ratings for such programs are generally half what they are for top entertainment shows (Jaffe, 1968). Public television stations get even lower ratings, only rarely breaking above 2 percent of the sets in use (Schramm, Lyle, & Pool, 1963). The obvious interpretation is that people say what they think they should say about their program preferences, not what they really prefer.

That explanation is offered by Steiner (1963). He conducted an experiment in New York City, which then had seven television channels and therefore substantial choice. He had viewers keep TV logs. He found that people who had advocated having serious programs on the air generally chose something lighter at those times when they actually had the option to view serious programs. Steiner took this to be a denial of the significance of their verbal commitment to public affairs programming.

This interpretation may be challenged, however. The verbal commitment is highly significant for it tells us that the norms of this society value public opinion and public involvement in public affairs. People feel some pressure of conscience to be involved, even if they do not live up to their standards. Furthermore, one really should not equate the number of minutes spent doing something with how much a person values it. Economists have long recognized that marginal returns of a good diminish with increased amounts of it. Certainly we do not say people are not interested in food because they stop eating after the first hour. So, too, with news and public information; the amount of time a person spends with it is not a measure of his desire for it. The fact that a person's appetite for news flags after half an hour cannot be taken as evidence of indifference if he earnestly sought the news during the first half hour.

Serious public affairs viewing is relatively hard work. It takes attention. Beyond doubt most people are ready to give more of their total evening hours to easy, relaxing entertainment material than they are to serious concentrated viewing, and that is true also of highly intelligent and informed viewers. It would be a rare avid lecture goer who spent more hours at lectures than in casual broadcast listening and viewing, yet one would not deny his interest in lectures. The test of a person's interest is not what he does at any random moment, but what he does at appropriate times and places.

At some level of volume the public really does want public affairs information in its media. Attempts to publish newspapers with features, columns, and comics only, and without the costly up-to-the-minute news services, have failed. Conscientious citizens may be dissatisfied with the amount of interest in public affairs shown by the mass of their fellow citizens, but it is clear from many studies such as Herzog's (1944) and Berelson's (1949) that, for a large majority of the public, one of the gratifications that they get out of the media is the sense that they are learning something.

PARTICIPATION

Levels of Participation

Various writers on public opinion have found it useful to classify the public into layers by degree of their political participation. At one extreme are the apathetic know-nothings. They are not interested in public affairs and are uninformed. Next to them are the passive majority who are casually exposed to a certain amount of news, but under most circumstances engage in no special information-seeking activities and do not do anything about what they hear. During a campaign or world crisis they may turn to the media more actively for extra information, but only then. A step more active are what Gabriel Almond (1960) has called the "attentive" minority. They do not engage in organized public affairs activities, but satisfy their impulse to be heard by talking to friends and by voting. They read news magazines as well as daily papers, and do watch news specials on TV. They prize being informed, but treat politics largely as a spectator sport. A much smaller group are the active citizens who join organizations, go to meetings, sign petitions, and write their congressmen. Fewest of all but most influential are the small numbers who are officers of public affairs organizations, who write article for publication, and who know congressmen and high members of the executive branch to the point where they see them socially or can phone them (Adler & Bobrow, 1956; Bauer, Pool, & Dexter, 1963).

Various attempts have been made to estimate the sizes of these various publics (DeGrazia, 1951; James Robinson, 1967; Rosenau, 1968; John Robinson, Rusk & Head, 1968). Hyman (1971) finds that less than one-half of the adult population belong to any organization except a trade union. Hero (1959: vol. 5) shows that only 10 percent belong to any organization where foreign affairs are discussed. Those who do belong to organizations often belong to several so that 3 percent of the adult population account for one-fourth of all the organizational memberships (cf. Wright & Hyman, 1958; Hausknecht, 1962; Nie, Powell, & Prewitt, 1969). If one measures active membership, the numbers are even lower and the concentration even greater. Studies of unions, for example, generally show that meetings draw from 1 percent to 20 percent of the members.

There have been several attempts at fairly comprehensive measurement of citizen activity in its various forms. A pioneering American effort was by Woodward and Roper (1950). They asked a national cross-section sample seven questions about participation in politics (organization memberships, amount of discussion of politics, writing congressmen, campaign activity, campaign contributions, attending meetings, frequency of voting). From these items they constructed an index of political activity. Table 1 shows the distribution of replies on a new run of the raw cards. More recent comprehensive data on the distribution of political activity in its various forms will be found in an important book by Verba and Nie, *Participation in America* (1972), which appeared while this chapter was already in press.

Cross-national comparisons of political participation based on national surveys with questions covering a variety of types of participation have been reported by Converse and Dupeux (1962), Almond and Verba, (1963), and Inkeles (1969). They show that participation in the "civic culture" grows with the modernity of the political system. Nonetheless, there is much debate as to whether public participation in politics is increasing or decreasing. Organizational membership, for example, is increasing (Hyman & Wright, 1971).

One line of argument supported by the Almond and Verba and Inkeles data stresses the nonparticipatory character of traditional society. That picture emerges in studies discussed earlier (Speier, 1950; Lerner, 1958) and also in *The Moral Basis of a Backward Society* (Banfield, 1958), which compares an impoverished South Italian mountain village with the modern society of North Italy. In the more primitive area lack of trust undercuts the possibility of civic participation. In more advanced societies, the presence of an economic surplus not only makes possible the growth of more generous interpersonal relations, but also allows for the extension of literacy and leisure, the prime prerequisites of political participation. No earlier society has had as much of these as we do. The argument that modern democratic societies are more participant than the feudal, or colonial, or autocratic societies that preceded them may seem so obvious as to be thought banal.

TABLE 1
POLITICAL ACTIVITY INDEX

Occupation	Low →					High	Total No.
Professional or executive	7%	24%	25%	21%	13%	10%	251
Farm proprietor	29	28	30	7	4	2	165
Small store owner	24	29	25	12	8	2	206
White collar	23	30	30	12	3	2	412
Personal service and protective	40	27	21	9	3	–	269
Farm labor	51	25	15	6	2	1	122
Factory labor	36	29	26	6	2	1	604
Nonfactory labor	37	33	24	5	1	–	257
Homemaker	39	29	21	8	2	1	1,385
Other	31	26	30	8	3	2	253
Total No.							3,924

SOURCE: Data from Woodward and Roper (1950).

Yet there is a large literature to the contrary, which argues that modern industrial society is marked by reduced political participation, that there is growing alienation and helplessness of man before the impersonal forces of industrial society. Preindustrial society, it is argued, was based upon primary communities that had a high degree of consensus and communion. The individual met his needs in close interaction with the same few people who formed his community. Modern society, on the other hand, is characterized as increasingly fragmented and lonely. The individual does not live among people he knows, but moves frequently among strange, cold, urban agglomerations. He is the object of forces far beyond his comprehension. The air he breathes, the prices he pays, the availability of jobs, even war and peace are resultants of the actions of strangers manipulating an advanced technology with consequences that no one can anticipate. In reaction to the meaninglessness of his environment and his impotence in controlling it, modern man, it is said, withdraws into alienation (Greer, 1958; Levin, 1960; Kariel, 1961; Walker, 1966; Goodman, 1968; Klein, 1971).

Some current political movements seek to counter this trend by recreating meaningful communities. Hippie communities, basic encounter groups, attempts to establish community decision-making and "maximum feasible participation" through neighborhood organizations are all efforts to overcome what is felt to be the isolation of man in modern society (Nisbet, 1953; Davies, 1966; Fried, 1966; Marris & Rein, 1967; Gamson, 1968; Kotler, 1969; Ralph Kramer, 1969; Altshuler 1970; Lipsky, 1970; Peterson, 1970).

It is conceivable that both contradictory sets of assertions could be true. It is conceivable that at an early stage the transition from authoritarian feudal to modern representative government did increase political participation by the masses, but that at a later stage of industrial development a reversal took place,

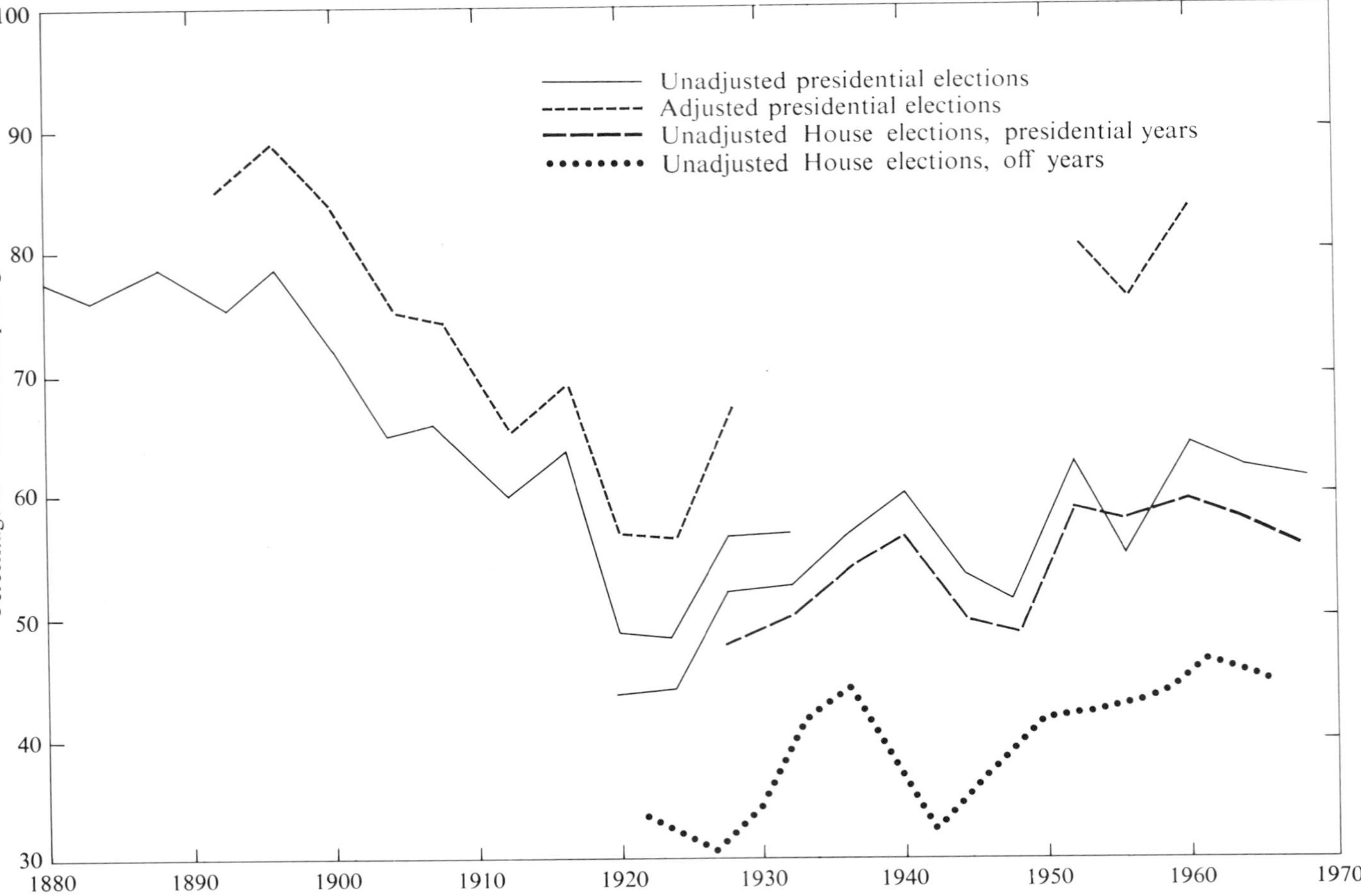

Figure 2. Election turnout trends since 1880. Presidential election for 1880–1932 from Titus (1935); for 1892—1928 from Gosnell (1930: 196); for 1920–1968 from Congressional Quarterly Service (1945–); for 1952–1960 from Andrews (1966) and Associated Press (various years). House election data from Census Bureau (1960; 1965a).

with technological progress undercutting the very freedom that it had created. That is conceivable, but it is neither evident nor is it *a priori* very plausible. Certainly nothing like that has been demonstrated by the essayistic, undocumented polemics that this subject has generally elicited.

Voting Turnout

One set of hard data exists covering political participation over a long time period. That is the data on voting.

Thanks to the ready availability of such data, the literature on participation by voting is extensive indeed. The primary source data, the voting statistics, are published by most national governments, but in the United States are reported by different jurisdictions for different levels of elections.[7]

Numerous studies have compiled turnout statistics over time (Gosnell, 1930; Titus, 1935; Key, 1961; 1963; Flanigan, 1968; Congressional Quarterly Service, 1969: 439). Others have examined demographic and psychological correlates (Merriam & Gosnell, 1924; Rosenberg, 1954; Levinson, 1958; Tigsten, 1963; Census Bureau, 1960; 1965a; Kessel, 1965; Milbrath, 1965; Alford & Lee, 1968; Lang & Lang, 1968a; Olsen, 1970). Others have compared turnout rates between political systems (Tingsten, 1963) and, in particular, examined why American voting levels are so much lower than European levels (Gosnell, 1930; Roper, 1961; President of the United States, 1963; Milbrath, 1965; Andrews, 1966; Kelley, Ayers, & Bowen, 1967). Other studies have examined the form of representation provided by various political systems and the incentives which they provide for political participation (Duverger, 1954; Ross, 1955; T. E. Smith, 1960; Nettl, 1967; Rose, 1967; Gordon, 1970; Peterson, 1970).

In the United States in particular, voter registration laws in the past have been a major restriction on voting (Merriam, 1924; Roper, 1961; President of the United States, 1963; Kelley, Ayers, & Bowen, 1967). However, a great expansion of the eligible electorate is now taking place thanks to the Twenty-fourth Amendment, which in 1964 eliminated the poll tax as a condition for voting in federal elections; the Voting Rights Act of 1965, which suspended literacy requirements for federal voting; and the Voting Rights Act of 1970, which banned literacy tests in all elections, barred residence requirements of over thirty days in presidential elections, and gave the federal vote to eighteen-year-olds. The new eligibles in 1972 are predicted to be 11.5 million eighteen- to twenty-year-olds, 10 million previously barred by residence requirements, and 1 million barred by literacy tests (Congressional Quarterly Service, 1970:729).

Figure 2 plots some turnout trends since 1880. Comparisons of turnout figures are complex. First of all, one must distinguish among types of elections: presidential, congressional, state, local, final, and primary. Popular interest and turnout peak in presidential campaigns. At the other extreme, local primaries draw only a small, unrepresentative minority to the polls. Congressional elections, although bienniel, have a different dynamic in presidential years, when voters are stirred by the big contest, than they do in off years (Miller, 1955; McPhee & Glaser, 1962). Furthermore, even compiling such turnout figures is not altogether simple. There are a certain number of ineligibles: resident aliens, illiterates, convicts, unregistered persons, recent movers. Figures measuring political apathy should exclude involuntarily unregistered persons. However, good estimates of the varying number of eligibles over the entire time span are hard to come by. The usual procedure in calculating turnout is simply to sum the vote and divide by the census

[7] For comprehensive guidance on sources, see Rokkan and Meyriat (1969); for major U.S. returns, see Scammon (1956–68; 1965); Census Bureau (1960; 1965a; 1965b); Congressional Quarterly service (1945–).

figure for the citizenry over the legal voting age. However, more serious estimates try to take account of some of the varying kinds of ineligibility such as sex, race, or legal restrictions.

In Figure 2 we cite some estimates made at different periods by different scholars using different methods, so the absolute levels vary from series to series, depending on how far ineligibles are taken into account. Nonetheless, the basic trend is clear. At the end of the nineteenth century, American voter participation in elections was high and steady. Then from the turn of the century until 1924, there was a steady decline in turnout. At that point a reversal set in, and from 1928 to 1940 electoral participation grew to about 60 percent. Since 1940 it would be harder to assert a trend. One could say that the basic turnout level has been roughly constant since then, with a temporary drop in 1944 and 1948. A closer look at some of the specific years and the factors at work would add some further insight.

The decline in participation during the first quarter of the twentieth century was due to at least three structural factors. The first was immigration. That was the period of massive arrivals of non-English-speaking migrants from southern and western Europe. For the first few years after arriving, most immigrants could not legally vote, but even when they had been here long enough to vote legally, it still took them a while to become assimilated enough into American political life to acquire the voting habit firmly (cf. Handlin, 1951; Glazer & Moynihan, 1963).

A second factor was the introduction of registration laws. In an attempt to curb voting fraud on the one hand and to restrict black and immigrant voters on the other, laws were passed requiring the citizen to enroll himself on the voter list in advance of election day. This requirement of foresight discouraged the more apathetic citizens, whose involvement might reach a level for action only by election day. It has been argued that the registration requirement largely accounts for the difference in turnout between contemporary America and either nineteenth-century America or contemporary Europe, where police lists are used as voter lists (Kelley, Ayers, & Bowen, 1967).

The third factor was the enfranchisement of women. Gradually in different states women were acquiring the vote. In 1920 all women were enfranchised by the Nineteenth Amendment. Women, like immigrants, did not all accept the responsibility and the habit of voting as soon as they won the right (Merriam & Gosnell, 1924). Nonvoting among women remained (and remains) higher than among men, although gradually the women's vote built up.

In addition, it can be argued—and has been argued persuasively by Walter Dean Burnham (1972)—that the decline in turnout after 1890 represented basic attitudinal changes in American society in addition to all of these structural facts. In the nineteenth century, Burnham argues, politics was the sporting passion of most American males, who saw it as also having a direct significance for the development of their communities. With the rise of industrial capitalism, much of this direct sense of the immediacy of politics in their lives and the sense of political efficacy may have been lost. There is currently active debate over how much of the decline in turnout cannot be accounted for by structural facts and remains to be explained as an attitudinal shift of this kind (Converse, 1972).

The habituation of women to the vote along with the end of mass immigration about 1920 would account for the rise in turnout after 1924. The continued rise until 1940 may also reflect the success of Franklin D. Roosevelt and the New Deal in mobilizing some popular enthusiasm among those poor and poorly educated strata who are the main contributors to nonvoting.

The rising trend was sharply reversed in 1944, a year when millions of men were abroad in the armed forces and other millions of people lost their votes by moving across state lines to take war jobs.

That predictable anomaly in the trend would hardly deserve comment were it not for the further decline in voting in 1948, when World War II was over. Any assumption that the low turnouts in those two elections were related is probably wrong, however. The 1948 election was one in which millions of voters were dissatisfied with both candidates; consequently many stayed away from the polls. The biggest walkout was among rural Republicans, costing Dewey the election. This unique election shows that it is possible for groups of voters to become alienated enough seriously to affect turnout (see Table 2).

TABLE 2

PERCENTAGE OF NONVOTERS

	1940	1948	1952
Metropolitan	25%	17%	21%
Towns	32–35	37	27
Rural	39	59	32

SOURCE: Lane (1959:48).

By 1952 when two attractive candidates, Eisenhower and Stevenson, were running, the turnout trend returned to its prewar value. By 1956 the same two candidates' running once more had lost some glamour, but in 1960 voting again reached a new high.

The decline since 1960 is too short-run at the time of writing to permit any assertions about a trend. Perhaps the 1924–1952 recovery in voter turnout led to a stable plateau at about the 60 percent turnout level for presidential elections. On the other hand, the plateau may be temporary. In 1964, 1968, and 1972, many voters were disenchanted with their party's candidate. At press time, accurate 1972 figures are not yet available, but turnout did fall sharply to about 55 percent, the lowest level since 1948. There is good reason to believe, however, that a new turnout high since 1908 would be scored in any future election in which both parties offered attractive candidates.

There are several reasons for believing this. The most important is the enfranchisement of blacks in the South. The national percentage shown in Figure 2 and Table 3 is actually a consequence of two very different figures. In Table 3, there is a Southern turnout figure and a non-Southern turnout figure. The non-Southern turnout figure is reasonably high. When adjusted figures are calculated allowing for ineligibles, the non-Southern figure comes close to Titus' figures for the end of the nineteenth century, and is also in line with European voting figures. The familiar comparison of poor American election turnouts with good European turnouts loses much of its validity when the comparison excludes the South.

Voting turnouts in the South have typically been much lower. Until recent years, blacks were de facto disenfranchised. A realistic adjusted figure of turnout, such as Titus calculated, had to treat Southern blacks as disqualified, whatever the Constitution might say. In recent years, however, there has been a surge of black voting in the South, and with that, an equal countersurge among white voters who had not bothered to vote when the blacks were disenfranchised but have recently gone to the polls in concern about the black vote (Price, 1957; Matthews & Prothro, 1966; Keech, 1968; Pomper, 1968:229; President of the United States, 1963; on Negro participation in the North, see J. O. Wilson, 1960; Orum, 1966; Olsen, 1970).

In 1968 there was an increase of more than 1 million votes over 1964 in the four states of Texas, Alabama, Mississippi, and Louisiana. Conversely, it follows that the drop-off in voting outside the South was greater than appears on the chart. One may assume that the Southern trend in both black and white voting is permanent. That is one reason to expect new records in turnout whenever the presidential candidates are sufficiently attractive to bring turnouts outside the South back to the 1952 and 1960 levels.

On the other hand, the enfranchisement of eighteen-year-olds in 1972, along with

TABLE 3

PERCENTAGE WHO VOTED IN 1964 ELECTION

Age	U.S. Total	Black	White	South	Non-South	College		High School		Grade School	
						Completed	Some	Completed	Some	8 years	0–7 years
21–24	52.2	45.7	53.3	37.0	57.6	78.9	69.9	55.4	33.7	24.9	17.6
25–44	69.5	62.2	68.8	57.1	73.9	86.9	83.2	75.8	60.9	55.3	38.4
45–64	76.6	64.9	77.9	63.2	81.1	92.3	87.3	85.8	77.3	74.0	57.2
Over 65	66.9	45.4	68.7	53.8	71.0	90.2	84.5	80.2	75.0	70.5	55.8
Over 21	70.0	59.2	71.3	56.8	74.6	88.2	82.6	76.5	65.9	67.4	51.6

SOURCE: Data from Census Bureau (1965b).

some illiterates and many frequent migrants, caused a drop in the percentage of eligibles who vote. Voting is a habit that must be learned. Young voters just over twenty-one are often nonvoters (see Table 3); in 1968 only 33 percent of them voted (Congressional Quarterly Service, 1970: 720). It takes them a while to firm up the voting habit. We may expect young voters from eighteen to twenty to continue to show a pattern of extensive nonparticipation during their first years as eligibles.

In summary, if voting turnout is an index of what people have in mind when they talk about political participation or alienation, then there is indecisive evidence of a serious decline in participation in the recent past, and solid evidence of a rather drastic decline just after the turn of the century.

Voting, however, is far from an adequate index of all that we have in mind when we talk of political participation (Riesman & Glazer, 1950; Himmelstrand, 1970). Unfortunately, we simply do not have adequate long-run data for other indicators of political participation. (But cf. Verba & Nie, 1972.)

Factors Affecting Involvement

If we know too little about the real *trends* in political participation, we do, however, have rather good information about factors that affect the involvement in politics of different strata of the population (Himmelstrand, 1960; 1970). In recent years the subject of political participation and involvement has been one of the most and best researched topics in the study of public opinion (Verba & Nie, 1972).

One can list a whole series of factors that induce a person either to get into politics or stay out.

Some authors, like Lipset (1960) in his comprehensive review of the literature on political life, have stressed situational, sociological, and organization factors. Others, such as Almond and Verba (1963), have stressed psychological factors. Still others, like Morris Rosenberg (1954), have reviewed both types of gratifications to the individual. Among these treatments there are a number of well-documented and systematic catalogues of the factors affecting participation (Merriam & Gosnell, 1924; Lipset, Lazarsfeld, Barton, & Linz, 1954; Milbrath, 1965; Dawson, 1966:63; Alford & Scoble, 1968; Flanigan, 1968; Barber, 1969). We know, for example, that:

People in jobs or businesses affected by political decisions (e.g., civil servants) are more active in politics (Lipset, 1960; Bauer et al., 1963; Lindenfeld, 1964).

People in "free professions," i.e., professions where the person makes his own schedule and plan of activity (e.g., the law), are more apt to engage in politics.

People of higher income, status, and education are more apt to engage in politics.

Where the balance of political forces is relatively even and elections tend to swing on a few votes, people are more likely to bother to cast a vote (Lipset, 1960).

In most countries city dwellers vote more regularly than rural residents (Lane, 1959; Milbrath, 1965:128–130). (This is a nonobvious finding, for it contradicts the theory that urban anonymity depoliticizes and that the cohesive rural community encourages participation.)

Turnout is much lower in congressional, state, and local elections than in presidential elections, and still lower in primaries and referenda (Alford & Lee, 1968).

Turnout is higher for unambivalent partisans and among people under cross-pressure between attractive alternatives than it is for people under cross-pressure between unattractive alternatives (Berelson et al., 1954; Campbell, Converse, Miller, & Stokes, 1960:chap. 5; Pool, Abelson, & Popkin, 1965). Political participation is a habit, remaining consistently high once the habit has been acquired. Political socialization into this habit usually takes place in the early adult years (Campbell et al., 1960:153–156; Dawson, 1966; Sears, 1969:370–372, 382–383; Sigel, 1970).

Organization increases activity. Campaign efforts may change few people's opinions, but they can get the faithful out to vote (Gosnell, 1927; Berelson et al., 1954; President of the United States, 1963; G. H. Kramer, 1965; 1966).

Members of cohesive groups are more apt to be mobilized to activity than members of less cohesive ones (Lipset, 1960). That is why some labor union organizations, as we noted above, have tried to become comprehensive whole-life services.

Political activity will be greater when it is socially approved and less when it is socially disapproved. For example, women will be less active to the extent that political participation is not viewed as ladylike. Conversely, a large proportion of young radicals come from families that view their political involvement with some favor (Kenniston, 1968; Lane, 1969).

People who may be endangered by participation in politics will avoid it. The dangers are many, and often much milder than violence by armed policemen or terrorists. Storekeepers who deal with a cross-section of the public try to avoid a partisan image for fear of loss of trade. Those with employers, friends, or relatives on the other side may stay quiet. People aware of their own ignorance may avoid situations where it will be exposed (Morris Rosenberg, 1954).

Political activity is greater when it seems likely to make a difference. A rational expectation of achieving something by political activity may in turn be affected by a variety of circumstances of which a few important examples are:

1. Voting is higher when the structure of constituency lines facilitates representation by meaningful groups. Redistricting is sometimes used to give a district to a black or other ethnic community, sometimes to split it among several districts so they will go unrepresented. Occupational representation, instead of geographic representation, has been popular with radical labor movements because such movements are often organized along occupational lines; geographic representation unites people on issues common to their areas of residence only, which may not be the biggest issues (Duverger, 1954; Ross, 1955; T. E. Smith, 1960; Rae, 1967; Gordon, 1970; Peterson, 1970).
2. Political participation is reduced when an entrenched oligarchy seems unmovable. People "cop out" on the system when they believe that it is controlled by a power elite over which they can exercise but little influence.
3. Political participation is enhanced when authorities respond to communication from citizens, e.g., when they show up at meetings, weddings, and funerals, when they answer letters, or appear to be interested in poll results (Wyant & Herzog, 1941; Dexter, 1956; Sussman, 1963; Gellhorn, 1966).

A corrolary restating the last point from a psychological viewpoint is the proposition that political activity depends upon a sense of political efficacy (Morris Rosenberg, 1954; Campbell et al., 1960: 105; Almond & Verba, 1963). Hensler (1971), summarizing various studies, has shown that a sense of inefficacy (or powerlessness) actually involves two independent dimensions: (1) a lack of confidence in oneself, which spreads from the individual's overall personality to the political arena, and (2) the person's judgment as to the responsiveness or nonresponsiveness of a particular political institution, which judgment may be quite different for local and central government. If a person feels efficacious he has reason to be active. But people are not blind; if in fact the system is unresponsive, people will feel powerless.

The sense of efficacy (unlike some other aspects of political alienation) correlates highly with a number of social variables such as income and occupation. Education, the culture's view of the relation of the individual to fate, or individual differences in self-confidence may affect how far a person believes that his actions can change the world (Levinson, 1958; Morris Rosenberg, 1962).

Almond and Verba, in one of the most influential recent studies of political participation, *The Civic Culture*, have compared samples of citizens in the U.S.A., Great Britain, Germany, Italy, and Mexico on their sense of civic competence. That feeling was measured by answers to such questions as:

> Suppose a law were being considered . . . that you considered to be unjust or harmful, what do you think you could do? If you made an effort to change this law, how likely is it that you would succeed? How likely is it that you *would actually* try? (Almond & Verba, 1963: 184).

Their findings support the notion that modernization is associated with an increased sense of efficacy and thus with growing participation. At one extreme, the Mexicans had little belief that their elite would be affected by anything they might say. At the other extreme were the Americans and British. However conscious we may be of political cynicism in this country and of the "you can't fight city hall" syndrome, it is less strong than in most other countries.

Mobilizing Citizen Participation

Ernst Kris and Nathan Leites (1950) have argued that *in some respects* there is a secular increase in political disenchantment but this need not result in depolitization provided the approach used to encourage political participation is an appropriate one. The argument is related to the one more recently developed by Daniel Bell (1962) in *The End of Ideology*. Kris and Leites' argument is that people have become more skeptical of propaganda and of ideologies. They are less willing to believe on faith what leaders tell them. They are, therefore, less responsive to appeals to act that are based on doctrine or moralizing. If that is so, then to appeal to the public, the democratic leader must be more sober, less moralistic, and more factual than in the past. He has a double task. He must provide the public with information so that it can understand the situation realistically, and he must by his acts offer himself as a model of how to behave in the situation. He must (and this is a point that Bell also develops) offer realistic pragmatic goals and opportunities rather than quixotic ideals.

Whether there is in fact a trend away from ideology and doctrinaire moralism toward more pragmatic politics is much argued, and mostly without hard evidence. Some support for the notion of such a trend may be found by examining the way that television has changed the kind of candidate who appeals to the public (Pool, 1959; Kraus, 1962; Rubin, 1967; Lang & Lang, 1968b; Whale, 1969). It is widely believed now that the kind of rabble-rouser who was effective on a platform before a mass meeting of ardent followers in the days of barnstorming campaigns does not do well in the family's living room on the television screen. What fares well on television seems to be the affable, friendly man who speaks quietly and reassuringly. Indeed in this respect, television has simply accelerated a trend that began on radio when Franklin Roosevelt recognized the power of the "fireside chat." This direct approach to the people in their homes gave him a chance to do what Kris and Leites had described as providing the public quietly with the facts as he saw them, plus providing the behavioral model of his own reaction to the facts. Television was to give Richard Nixon a similar platform for his Vietnam policy.

From the many factors which affect participation, various lessons can be drawn about how to mobilize public involvement. One important set of devices for mobilization are those that give people a sense of being listened to as well as of listening (Wyant & Herzog, 1941; Dexter, 1956; Sussman, 1963; Gellhorn, 1966). Congressmen often mail questionnaires to their constituents. Organizations get people to write letters to their congressmen, and the congressmen in turn try to respond with attentive, albeit noncommittal, replies. One of the main themes of comment by the discontented who have petitioned and demonstrated is whether or not the authorities "are getting the message"; the participants want to know.

Another set of mobilization devices of great importance link small cohesive groups (that are able to mobilize their members readily) to larger, comprehensive, national movements. Political parties patronize or affiliate with local clubs and ethnic associations (Peel, 1935; Gosnell, 1937; Handlin, 1951: chap. 8; Greenstein, 1963: chap. 4; Wilson, 1966). Urban redevelopment and antipoverty programs create neighborhood councils. Needless to say, such multiplication and devolution of authority can create problems for those at the top. They must weigh the advantages of unified, centralized control against the potentially divisive, but also mobilizing, effect of grass-roots organization (Janowitz, 1961; Marris & Rein, 1967; Kotler, 1969; R. Kramer, 1969; Altshuler, 1970; Bachrach & Baratz, 1970; Lipsky, 1970; Peterson, 1970).

Much of political theory from Rousseau (1762), through Tocqueville (1835–40), Ostrogorski (1902), Weber (1919), to the present has been concerned with the net effect of the formation of intermediary groups on the creation of a national consensus (Pool, 1967: chap. 2). Increasingly, modern sociology has brought awareness that there is no other way to get consensus. The nation is too far away from most people to be able to mobilize them directly. Nonetheless, the more complex process of integrating small groups into a larger whole presents many problems, to which we now turn.

ISSUE FORMULATION

Before a democratic process of decision-making can take place, the infinity of possible actions must be reduced to a limited number of alternatives among which a choice can be made. One classic study of how a vague problem was turned into a bipolar issue and then decided is Steven K. Bailey's (1950) *Congress Makes A Law*, a book which has been described as the starting point for the contemporary study of the Congress (Huitt & Peabody, 1969).

The employment bill of 1948 was supported in Congress by a liberal-labor alliance. The sponsors of the bill wished to enact an unenforceable legislative declaration that the federal government would guarantee jobs to all. Their expectation was that in an economic depression, which they expected shortly, such a declaration of policy would provide the rationale for Congress to vote deficit financing to create jobs. The conservative coalition in Congress, which was certainly not in favor of unemployment, opposed the strategy of deficit spending which, while not explicitly in the bill before Congress, might in the future be promoted by adopting the declaration. Their problem was to so amend the bill that it would not have the feared effect of increasing the probability that future Congresses would vote deficit budgets.

The amendment that the conservatives offered to achieve their goal established a council of economic advisors who would report to the Congress on what actions to take to counteract unemployment. If that amendment had passed, any budgetary proposal from the executive branch for deficit spending would have come under the potentially unsympathetic scrutiny of a group of Congress's own experts. Thus with this amendment, the original liberal-labor bill might have served as a conservative barrier to the growth of executive power. The liberal-labor congressmen countered by amending the amendment to make the council of economic advisors responsible to the president rather than to Congress, and succeeded in passing the bill in that form, thus guaranteeing that the council would not oppose any presidential proposal.

What the country saw, and what made action possible, was a two-sided conflict between liberals, labor, and the president, on the one hand, and conservatives and supporters of congressional power, on the other, about the right to jobs. The various issues concerning the structure of an economic-planning staff never entered public attention. The general public saw only an employment bill, unaware that the crucial fight was actually on the amendment to an amendment concerning the lines of reporting by an advisory commission. Yet on the outcome regarding that procedural detail turned the real effect of the bill. It was quite misleading to describe the bill as either a liberal or a conservative one. Which it would end up being depended entirely on a subordinate vote on an inconspicuous detail.

A more recent example of the multidimensionality of issues was the congressional debate on federal support for education. The manysidedness of that issue, and the difficulty of reducing the debate to a two-sided pair of coalitions, kept the bill from being passed for many years. There were divisions between those who thought education was a legitimate object of federal support and those who wished it left to state and local governments; between those who wanted support for parochial schools and those who opposed government support for any religious activities; between persons who were willing to see unrestricted grants and those who would put federal money into bricks and mortar and school buses, but not into payrolls (helping thereby to restrict federal control).

There was also the issue of nonreligious private schools: Should aid go to all schools, excepting only religious ones? There was the issue of segregation: Should aid be denied to segregated schools? There was the division between those, on the one hand, who were willing to see federal aid go to colleges and high schools but not to primary schools, the bulwark of community power in education, and those, on the other hand, who wanted to support all schools.

Of the many permutations and combinations that were possible, a few appeared with fairly high frequency: the liberal secularist position for federal aid exclusively to public schools, and only desegregated ones; the common Catholic position for federal aid for bricks and mortar to all schools without discrimination; and the pure conservative position of no federal aid whatsoever. On the other hand, many perfectly rational positions did not appear at all. No one was heard to advocate the view that because religion is a vital part of man's proper life there should be aid for parochial schools only. No one was heard to argue the view that buildings do not make an education, but teachers do, so there should be federal aid for salaries only and not for bricks and mortar.

Occasionally an unusual combination of views emerges and is greeted with the old saw that "politics makes strange bedfellows." A few years ago, when Chinese troops invaded India in a border dispute, the Formosa-based Republic of China, exhibiting more Chinese nationalism than anticommunism, gave moral support to the Chinese Communist border claims. Even more ironically, some John Birch Society spokesmen, reflecting their historical sympathy for Nationalist China and their dislike for Nehru's India, echoed these views, as did the conservative dictatorship of Portugal, which also had territorial conflicts with India.

There is an infinity of perfectly logical positions. If some of them seem surprising, or shocking, or oddball, it is not because they are inherently illogical, but because they are not politically viable. World government, for example, is a goal believed in by a small number of people. Ordinarily, its supporters do not even discuss it in the course of American national politics because it is not now a viable issue. In day-to-day politics, advocates of world government join instead in movements for more popular goals such as international cooperation, for which they have allies. As a result, the idea of world government does not even get introduced to the majority of voters, who think only about the issues that have been publicized in wide public debates. Issues are nonviable when it is predicable that they cannot become the focal point for a sufficiently extensive coalition; as a result, they disappear from public view.

The way in which the infinite variety of extant feelings and attitudes gets reduced to a two-sided issue around which people coalesce varies from political system to political system (Almond & Powell, 1966: 100). The locus where issues get formulated depends upon the particular structure of the government. The president (Cornwell, 1965), interest groups, professional experts, associations, and media all play a role. Much normative literature exists arguing the merits or demerits of pluralistic versus centralized issue formulation. Some of the literature on interest groups and lobbies dwells upon their contribution to issue clarification (Herring, 1929; Truman, 1951; Bauer, 1963; Milbrath, 1963; Dexter, 1969a) and some deplores the lack of a synthetic perspective on public policy where pluralism rather than central leadership prevails (McConnell, 1966; Lowi, 1969).

In any parliamentary system, the parliament is one of the major arenas for the definition of issues. It is an illusion to think that issues are somehow sitting out there in the real world and that congressmen line up to vote on the two sides of preexistent issues. Until the Congress gets into the act, there is likely to be nothing but an inchoate mass of ill-defined reactions among the citizenry.

While most of the literature on the Congress focuses on its authoritative decision-making role (for example, by roll-call votes), in reality the largest activity of the Congress is in issue formulation (Bauer, 1963) or, as it is commonly called in current political science discussion, interest aggregation (Almond & Powell, 1966:98). Congressmen need issues that they can stand on. Fighting for causes is their stock in trade. They make themselves prominent by being the advocates of popular demand, hence they must invent causes that have a wide appeal.

For example, the Employment Bill of 1948, to which we referred above as a liberal-labor bill, started out without labor support and little liberal support. It was invented on Capitol Hill by some congressmen who were looking for an issue to galvanize their liberal support. Contrary to the usually assumed process by which lobbyists write congressmen, Senator Wagner sent out one thousand letters to prominent citizens soliciting their views, with an eye to generating public pressure behind him (Bailey, 1950). This procedure is not unusual. If one wishes to create a political issue, there is no better place to get it to public attention than on the floor of the Congress. It is common and normal for congressmen to take the lead and for lobbyists to follow them (Bauer, 1963). Congress is better thought of as the arena in which issues are formulated than as just a voting body to which issues are referred for final action.

The process of issue formulation in a legislative body tends (as the discussion of the issue proceeds) to produce a simplification of the alternatives or dimensions of the problem (Sears, Freedman, & O'Connor, 1964). The extent to which unidimensionality is achieved in the thinking of legislative bodies has been the subject of considerable recent study. Scale analysis applied to roll call votes generally shows a fairly strong unidimensional patterning within what is regarded as a single issue (McCrae, 1958; 1965; Patterson, 1962; Alker, 1964; Anderson, 1964; Rieselbach, 1964; Munger & Blackhurst, 1965; Wood, 1968).

Thus, for example, on any one issue such as civil rights or foreign trade, one can rank congressmen from those who will vote "aye" on even extreme motions, through those who come on board on less extreme ones, through those who will vote consistently against it. The extent to which the scaling is perfect—or, in other words, the extent to which unidimensionality exists—is a function of various factors in the environment. For example, scalarity increases with the controversiality of the issue, and on many issues is greater for the majority party in the Congress than for the minority (Anderson, 1964).

The domain of such unidimensionality constitutes a single issue. Normally that is what we imply when we call something *an* issue; if people scatter over two dimensions, we are likely to call it two issues. What kind of thing turns out to be isolatable from the infinity of events as an issue is a revealing fact about a political system. The more eclectic and pragmatic the system, the more often decisions will be conceived of as defined by small discrete issues, each standing on its own feet. The more ideological the system, the more all issues will be felt to hang together.

The most ideological situation is one in which all issues are conceived of as representing a single scale, such as left-right. In some political systems, one can predict all of a politician's votes, whether on economics or culture, labor relations or sex, from knowing where he stands on a single left-right scale. For political life to be characterized by such unidimensionality, the discussion of issues must be highly organized and subjected to fairly strict discipline, for it is clear that no inherent logic requires all attitudes to hang together. Political parties are the most common enforcers of that discipline.

Party discipline plays a varying though important role in the formulation of issues in different political systems. In Great Britain, for example, parties in the Parliament are highly disciplined. Important bills are introduced from the cabinet rather than by individual M.P.'s. It is in the government or in the opposition-party hierarchy that issues are formulated, rather than on the floor of Parliament. The opposition party's annual congresses are, therefore, of considerable substantive significance, as is the cabinet on the government side. The Parliament is much more of a ratificatory body.

In other countries, with disciplined multi-party systems, the parties themselves can sometimes be scaled along an ideological continuum. In countries with coalition governments, the cabinet may be the place where issues get formulated. Wherever it may be, it is clear that issues are made and not born. An issue gets formulated only when it seems possible that that formulation may become a viable focus for widespread support.

In any modern democracy one of the places where issues are formulated is in nongovernmental private political associations and pressure groups. These organizations are so characteristic of modern democracy that one must be reminded that until this century it was a controversial question whether such organizations should have a role in representative government. The U.S. Constitution contains no references to political parties, and most of the founders hoped they would not be significant. The prevailing attitude was expressed in the tenth *Federalist* paper, which called them factions and addressed itself to the problems of "curing the mischiefs of faction." (For the extensive recent discussion among political scientists of *Federalist* paper no. 10, see Dahl, 1963; Dye & Brett, 1967; Lowi, 1968.)

In Great Britain, the origin of organized pressure groups can be traced back to about 1768, the date of the Wilkes riots. This history is well described in Ostrogorski (1902). John Wilkes was a radical journalist who was elected to Parliament. The Parliament expelled him. His constituents reelected him several times, and each time Parliament declared his election null and void. His followers filed organized petitions and formed a Society of the Supporters of the Bill of Rights, which Ostrogorski calls the first political association. The same type of organization appeared again in 1780 when, according to Horace Walpole, the "Committees of Association... voted themselves a right of considering and deciding on questions pending in Parliament, and of censuring or approving the part taken by particular members" (Ostrogorski, 1902: 121f.).

The parliamentary reaction to these new movements was one of alarm. Such public policy organizations were viewed as an unconstitutional attempt to preempt the prerogatives of Parliament. Parliament, since Magna Charta, had been established as the place where the representatives of the British people assembled to discuss issues and to debate what actions the government should take on them. For a private association to arrogate to itself the right to conduct a similar forum where there would be discussion and votes on what national policy ought to be seemed to constitute what Lenin later called a "dual power."

In 1795 Parliament responded to these challenges by adopting an act barring "all societies... which were composed of distinct sections or branches." In 1831 a royal proclamation declared illegal and unconstitutional "political associations composed of separate bodies with various divisions and subdivisions under leaders with gradation of rank and authority and subject to the general control and direction of a superior committee council" (Ostrogorski, 1902: 126f.). Not until 1871–75 was complete freedom of association established in Great Britain with the final legalization of labor unions (Fellman, 1963: chap. 6).

Thus the admission of voluntary associations and mass political parties into the constitutional process is a modern thing in both Great Britain and the United States, and certainly elsewhere. From our contemporary perspective it may be hard to see what the authors of the *Federalist* papers or Walpole and his colleagues in England were so worried about. But that is because, in the meantime, certain conventions have been established that confine pressure groups and parties to a limited preliminary role in the discussion and decision process. In the stable democracies, though voluntary associations have claimed for themselves the right to formulate policy positions just as Parliament does, they have conceded that their conclusions have no authoritative right to be implemented. That is not a self-evident conclusion about the rights of a party. Indeed, we need only look at the role that Communist parties have claimed for themselves in those countries where they are in control to recognize that the fears expressed by Walpole and others were not ridiculous.

The formation of associations to discuss and decide upon public policies could easily have become elsewhere, as it has in the Communist world, the establishment of a new layer of government. Even in the United States, occasionally, protest movements that have turned to direct compulsive action, like sit-ins, will justify themselves by saying that those to whom their demands were addressed seemed to pay no attention or "did not get the message." These activist groups are implicitly claiming the right to be obeyed, not merely the right to be heard. Yet, for the most part, private groupings have been willing to accept certain self-restraining constitutional limitations on their power. The result has been a structure, now taken for granted, of layers of institutions that formulate public opinion, each with certain accepted rights, and each with certain confining limits to its authority.

Among these institutions we must list not only the political party and the pressure group, but also the media. Examples of the kind of media practices that have come to be accepted as more or less constitutional are the division of the newspaper into editorial and news columns, the right of access for reporters to public officials and to meetings, the acceptance by the media of the privileged status of off-the-record and background briefings, and the establishment of channels for expressing a variety of opinions in the letters to the editor and columnists' columns. On radio and television, other conventions have been established for sharing time. In one way or another, a structured set of institutions has grown up in which the infinite variety of individual attitudes gets reduced to a manageable set of simplified issues, with a recognized set of procedures for bringing them to public attention.

It follows that not all issues have an equal chance of getting admitted to the arena of public debate, nor all positions to the honor of a vote. Not all positions are equally viable. Which ones are viable depends upon the structure of the public opinion forum (Allardt & Littunen, 1964). A Congress with geographic representation will give voice to spokesmen of regions. Movements that are photogenic get covered on TV, while abstract ideas do not. It would be naive not to recognize that the structure of the arena of discussion determines to a large extent what issues ever get talked about. And by a feedback process people become interested only in those issues that have some chance of getting into wider attention. Issues are not all created equal.

LEADERS AND FOLLOWERS

Issues are formulated by political activists not by common men. They are of interest in this chapter on public opinion because they are used by leaders to mobilize ordinary people. In the last section we looked at the activists and at how they formulate and choose issues in order to gain political support. Now we look at common men and how they behave in respect to political issues.

Much of what we have just said about how issues get structured in high politics could be repeated here, as applied to the man on the street. For him, too, the infinity of desires get structured into issues, which, as we noted above in comparing traditional and modern men, may be more or less abstracted from his immediate experience (Lerner, 1958). The issues may be pragmatically isolated into discrete practical questions or welded together into an ideology.

The views of the ordinary citizen, however, tend to be far less logically structured than those of politicists. Axelrod (1967) demonstrated the absence of any liberal-conservative or internationalist-isolationist structure in American public attitudes; the only structure that emerged from an empirical analysis of public opinion poll replies was a weak syndrome that could be described as populism (see also Becknell & Maher, 1962; Converse, Clausen, & Miller, 1965; Robinson, Rusk, & Head, 1968; Ladd, 1969). Hensler's (1971) factor-analytic review of the structure of the American political belief system does isolate certain patterns among a number of rather abstract political concepts.

The structure of beliefs that Hensler discovers may be represented as a linear chain among (1) involvement in politics, (2) sense of personal efficacy, (3) belief in the responsiveness of political institutions, and (4) evaluation of political behavior and institutions. Each adjacent pair of terms on the chain correlates at the level of 0.6 or 0.7. The correlations between more remote terms attenuate until one finds no correlation at all between involvement in politics at one end and evaluation of the system at the other. To state the same thing slightly differently, the American lay political belief system separates, like most semantic structures, into first an evaluative factor and, second, an efficaciousness factor.

People may be politically active and critical of government, active and favorable to government, inactive and critical, or inactive and favorable. Perceptions of the responsiveness of government share in both main factors. Political involvement, on the other hand, depends solely upon a sense of efficaciousness, not upon approval or disapproval of the political scene.

On specific political issues there is very little ideological consistency in the views of ordinary citizens. Various interview studies have shown no systematic affirmation of the basic tenets of American democratic doctrine by average citizens who consider themselves to have conventional American beliefs. The elites do better in affirming, for example, the various principles of the Bill of Rights (Stouffer, 1955; Prothro & Gregg, 1960; McClosky, 1964), i.e., in adhering to a unified American ideology. Regarding Vietnam, too, most Americans were neither consistent hawks nor doves. They have been increasingly discontented, but a discontented person may equally support an immediate pull-out and bombing of the North in response to two successive questions (Verba, Brody, et al., 1967; John Robinson & Shaver, 1969; A. H. Cantril, 1970; Milton Rosenberg, Verba, & Converse, 1970; on class differences, see Hahn, 1970). On complex issues of public policy, lay public opinion is often a mood rather than a doctrine.

Many things can affect this mood. It can be affected by the tone and posture of a leader, whether he is confident or not. Indeed, a recent study has shown that, in a debate, expressions of certainty are sometimes the strongest factor in producing persuasion (London, Meldman & Lanckton, 1970). Public moods are affected by events such as war, peace, riots, or price rises (Deutsch & Merritt, 1965), and what is affected are not just moods about these particular matters; political events affect citizen moods in general (Maisel, 1970).

The mood thesis can be overstated. Ordinary people as well as more politically minded ones are affected by the logical force of propositions in an argument—or, more accurately, by their psycho-logic, as Abelson and Rosenberg (1958) call it, or their enthymemes, to use Aristotle's (1926) term. That is to say, people bring their beliefs into plausible relations. The world seems to be in balance when good people do good things and bad people do bad things. Consistency theory in psychology in its various forms is devoted to the proposition that attitude change occurs when a person becomes aware of affectual inconsistencies (i.e., imbalance) in his beliefs (Brown, 1962; Abelson et al., 1968).

One way of getting rid of uncomfortable consciousness of inconsistency, such as, for example, the awareness that your party's candidate favors a policy you oppose, is to misperceive the situation. A considerable literature deals with the extent to which people use selective perception and distortion to create for themselves a world in which all the people whom they respect feel as they do and all the enemies are bad (Berelson et al., 1954; Froman & Skipper, 1962; McGrath & McGrath, 1962; Sigel, 1964; Jervis, 1968). Many voters are convinced that their candidate agrees with them although he may be vigorously advocating the other side.

Ironically, it is the most committed citizens who are also the most informed, most partisan, thus the most selective in their perceptions, and the hardest to persuade. It is the least informed citizens who are least interested, least partisan, hardest to reach because they are paying no attention, but easiest to persuade if reached (Hovland, Janis & Kelley, 1953; Berelson et al., 1954). These facts have significant, albeit depressing, political implications. People who are alert in politics are largely talking to themselves and reinforcing their previous beliefs.[8]

The people who do change their minds as a result of an election campaign are largely the uninformed and uninterested, and they are better described as being unstable rather than being converted, for they are likely to change back again if influenced once more. Since it is so much easier to

[8] Berelson, Lazarsfeld, and McPhee (1954) found that 65 percent of strong Republicans, 35 percent of weak Republicans, 54 percent of strong Democrats, and 46 percent of weak Democrats had all three of their best friends in their party.

make an uninformed person flip than to convert an informed one, there is a strong temptation to pitch a campaign at the lowest level of difficulty. The 30-second spot commercial, for example, reaches those who have no interest in a political broadcast and perhaps are the easiest marks for the campaigner.

One implication of these facts might be (and sometimes is taken to be) that issues are ineffective in politics and that one should "sell" one's candidate or cause by personality. The common contrast of an "image" campaign versus an "issue" campaign is misleading, however. Issues are the rhetoric of politics. The way a man conveys the image that he has fiscal integrity may be to raise the issue of financial malpractice by his opponents. The way a man may convey the image of being humanitarian may be by opposing a war. The way a man may convey the image of being patriotic may be by exposing Communists. Image and issue are not polarities; they are intertwined.

Just as stands on issues help leaders build images of themselves, so the image of the leaders' behavior helps the citizen come to a position on issues (Kris & Leites, 1950). When Churchill stood firmly before Britain after Dunkirk and offered nothing but "blood, toil, tears, and sweat," he was showing by his behavioral model what policy Englishmen could take regarding the further conduct of the war. The conduct of a political leader towards minorities provides a model for his followers and thus powerful support for a policy.

The relation of elite to mass in public opinion is a complex one indeed. We have already discounted the usual image that there is a preexisting public opinion on issues, which politicians can simply follow. Equally rare is the situation of a public so devoted to any leader that he can tell them what to think and they will do so. While leaders do lead in ways we have been describing, such as behavioral modeling and formulation of issues, they do it by skillfully anticipating which formulations out of the vast array of possible ones will gain public support. Politicians are far less often influenced by overt expressions of public opinion than by the need to take anticipatory maneuvers to avoid the consequences of future public opinion. The Employment Bill of 1948 was introduced not because any public opinion existed in its favor but because congressmen anticipated that there would be a mood of public anger if unemployment rose, and they wanted to be able to say they had done something about it (Bailey, 1950).

Numerous studies of the relation of constituency attitudes to stands of congressmen have shown only a weak relationship in which the congressman needs to conform to his constituents current views on just a few overriding issues of that area (and those generally ones where he agrees with his community anyhow) and for the rest he is free (Bauer et al., 1963; Froman, 1963; Miller & Stokes, 1963; Eulau & Hinkley, 1966; Miller, 1970; but cf., McCrae, 1952; Crane, 1960). In any case his constituents typically do not know his stands; he is a man of their kind and so shares most of their views; and in the few situations where there is an opposition of views, there are many parliamentary tricks for obscuring just what he is working for (Bauer et al., 1963).[9]

In sum, the public opinion to which the representative has to listen is usually not the public opinion that is already there, but feared reactions to what might occur in future circumstances. Any politician who read the polls and simply did what the majority favored at any time would soon be in trouble, for when untoward consequences make present policies unpopular, the public will not forgive the politician for having shared their mistakes. He should have been in favor of what they then decide

[9] We are considering here the way it works empirically, not the large normative literature on what the relationship of representative to constituent ought to be, for which consult Burke (1837), Pitkin (1967), Pennock and Chapman (1968).

is wise. In the words of the old joke, leaders try to anticipate where their followers are going so they can get there first.

TWEEDLEDUM AND TWEEDLEDEE

To some extent, parties and other public organizations dampen down issues as well as promote them. People who would like to see issues more hotly debated often describe the two major American political parties as Tweedledum and Tweedledee.

Organizations realize the limits of their capabilities. They realize that their power to mobilize people is very limited and that often the best they can do is to follow their constituency in what it already believes. All research on propaganda and advertising shows the limited capability of the propagandist to convert people (Star & Hughes, 1950; J. F. Kramer, 1969); most of the time all he can do is to stimulate his audience to actions to which they are already predisposed (Klapper, 1960). Studies of elections illustrate the point that few people are converted by any campaign. The net effect of the campaign, Berelson and Lazarsfeld argue, is to draw people back to their basic political affiliation, by restimulating their interest and involvement in politics (Lazarsfeld et al., 1948; Berelson et al., 1954).

The implication is that the effect of propaganda on public opinion is often best thought of as a trigger rather than as a force (Bauer et al., 1963). Instead of pushing the audience in the direction of the propaganda message itself, propaganda serves often simply to stimulate action; however, the direction of that action is determined much more by the predispositional mass of the person triggered than by the contents of the propaganda itself. That is what we mean by a trigger; if you want to know where a gun will shoot, look at the gun barrel, not at the trigger.

The relative stability of the underlying structure of public opinion under the impact of propaganda certainly does not deny the observation that public opinion is volatile. It can be that, too. The effective opinions operating upon the government can change even when the structure of personal attitudes is highly stable. That is possible either because of differential activation of different parts of the public or because of changes in the context and the terms of reference in which people see an issue. By changing the terms of reference, their conclusion may change even while their attitudes remain constant.

Earlier, when we talked of stereotypes, we noted how they come in contradictory pairs. As a result, people may change their mind about a tax bill, say, depending entirely upon whether they think of it as (1) an antiinflation device, (2) a way of raising more money for the politicians, or (3) a way of soaking the rich. Without changing any of his basic attitudes, an individual may thus reverse himself on the specific bill by changing the way in which he categorizes it. If he is both against higher budgets and against inflation, his attitude toward the bill may be a function of which goal he has in mind. The point is well illustrated by the studies of how people make up their minds on how to vote. Campaigns largely affect which issues are salient rather than changing people's minds about them (Berelson et al., 1954).

The relation of particular public policy outcomes to a rather stable underlying structure of public opinion is not unlike the relation of weather to climate. The climate is stable; spring will come in May and cold weather in January with high reliability, yet the weather is volatile. So, too, election outcomes are highly volatile despite very small changes in basic public attitudes. One can well simulate what the election outcome is likely to be under different circumstances from data referring to underlying public attitudes (Pool, 1965). Yet without any changes in those underlying attitudes the impact of circumstances can easily produce drastic changes in the outcome.

One subject that has been receiving

increasing attention among political scientists is the attempt to understand what accounts for the particular patterns of distribution of opinions that are found. It is clearly not by chance that for decades the two major political parties have split the vote just about fifty-fifty (Stokes & Iversen, 1962). Once more, it would be a mistake to assume that parties and other groups just follow some natural distribution of opinions and that the distribution is fifty-fifty by chance. The causal process is much more the other way around. In a two-party system, parties tend to move their positions until they reach the 50 percent point. The reasons why have been analyzed in econometric and game theoretic terms.

One analysis is offered by Downs (1957). He applies and summarizes the literature that arises from the application of economic location theory to politics (see also Campbell et al., 1966). At the same time Downs does tend to argue to some extent that the distribution of parties (as between two-party and multi-party systems) may be a reflection of the way in which political opinions distribute themselves as two-peaked or multi-peaked. That seems dubious. A rather important analysis of the party distribution in the United States, which applies game theory as well as considerable historical analysis, is William Riker's (1962) *Theory of Political Coalitions.*

Riker presents reasons why in a democracy the fifty-fifty division between two parties is so likely. To spend resources to win more then the needed majority does not pay. On the other hand, a political party that is much below that point had better change its policies and programs to bring within its own orbit a larger proportion of the population (see Riker, 1962; Riker & Ordeshook, 1968; O. A. Davis, Hinich & Ordeshook, 1970). If both parties act in that way, a division at the fifty-fifty line is most likely. It is therefore not surprising that to such a large extent American political parties tend to have a Tweedledum-Tweedledee character (Riker, 1962; 1965).[10]

The characterization of Tweedledum-Tweedledee is usually made in criticism of the parties. It is argued that they cannot thus represent public opinion, for they do not give the people a choice. In fact, it may be the other way around. The parties have done such a good job in locating the center of gravity of public opinion, that the two parties enter the lists with much the same position. This does not prove their imperviousness to public opinon; on the contrary, it shows how skillfully the parties have located the center of gravity of public opinion and have been submissive to it.

THE PYRAMID OF THE PUBLIC

We have just been looking at some of the institutions that provide forums for the crystallization of public opinion. But as we noted earlier, only a very small part of the public ever becomes involved in a high level of political activity. Most people are in either the attentive minority or the apathetic majority.

One question about the active minority that has interested many political scientists and sociologists in recent years is whether there is a single political leadership group, or whether in a democratic system the activists are a floating, rotating population, with persons sometimes playing the leader role and sometimes more passive roles. In some ways the literature on this subject is rather unsatisfying because the answer is obviously a quantitative one, and no writer has provided a metric to make his conclusions rigorous.

One branch of the debate started with Floyd Hunter (1953), who showed that in the city studied there was an elite generally recognized as the community leaders. A number of other studies followed Hunter in using reputational measures of influence or

---

[10] See Torgersen (1970) for a similar trend in Norway.

in showing that society is hierarchical with well-identifiable leaders (Agger, Goldrich, & Swanson, 1964). If there were any doubt about this fact, one might have gone back a little way to look at the community study literature in sociology, such as Lloyd Warner's Yankee City series (Warner & Lunt, 1941), for example.

Nonetheless, the thesis of centralized community power structure in the U.S.A. has been effectively challenged, most notably in Robert Dahl's (1961) *Who Governs*, which, like Katz and Lazarsfeld's (1955) *Personal Influence*, demonstrates fairly conclusively that the same individuals do not exercise influence in all fields of activity (Polsby, 1963). That is clearly true in some places for some issues. But until such time as we have a quantitative measure of the degree of concentration and dispersion of influence over various fields by an elite, this discussion has probably reached a dead end.

The vehemence and volume of the debate has been extensive (for a review of the literature, see Dye, 1970). However, most of the critiques of Dahl and others (whom their critics have labeled neoelitist) have been purely normative, saying nothing more than that from their point of view pluralism of power is not democratic enough (Bottomore, 1964; Bay, 1965; Walker, 1966; by far the best statement is by Lane Davis, 1964). Empirically all that one can say is that the existence proof has been provided both for the presence of opinion and power elites and for the fluidity of their composition. Little else can be added.

On any one issue there is always a large majority who are relatively apathetic and a minority who are passionate. It is rare to find the apathetic majority and the passionate minority distributing themselves in the same way in their attitudes on an issue. Snce it is the passionate minority that gets heiard, it may, by its vociferousness, give a very distorted view of the statistical distribution of opinion in the public as a whole. Letters to the editor, for example, rarely represent mass public opinion. It was Nixon's contention that the silent majority was more sympathetic to government policy on Vietnam than the vocal minority.

One of the merits of public opinion polls is that they are likely to correct the misleading impression given by vocal advocates. For example, the polls generally do show clear age differences in attitudes on race, war, the draft, drugs, sex, and various other matters—often called the generation gap—but the differences are far from sensational and much less than one might believe from the exponents of the gap (see Murphy & Likert, 1967; Lubell, 1968; Sears, 1969). So polls tell us what the apathetic majority thinks, not just what the passionate advocates would like us to believe that the majority thinks.

On the other hand, it may be misleading to report the majority views, since for some purposes it is the passionate minority, or at least some combination of passionate minorities, that really counts. Anthony Downs (1957) presents an ingenious analysis of the circumstances under which combinations of passionate minorities will negate majority preferences. Where the majority of persons is each in the minority on the issue that is of supreme importance to him, this will happen. Passionate minorities are therefore worth some attention. If there is a large number of relatively quiet, conventional people among the young, perhaps that is less important for some purposes than the fact that the more vocal young tend to be the ones who deviate more from the national norms of opinion. Pollers, of course, are aware of this, and they frequently report separate results for persons with high levels of knowledge or opinion and those without.

As we have already noted, it is often the case that involvement and passion, degree of knowledge and degree of partisanship, all tend to go together. The so-called independents in politics are generally the uninformed and uninterested (Berelson et al., 1954; Campbell et al., 1960); the most knowledgeable people are most partisan.

The same result appeared in Bauer's study of American businessmen's behavior on foreign-trade matters (Bauer et al., 1963). Activist protectionists were most informed about where their congressmen stood and what the legislative issues were. As one moved down the pyramid to the level where less-involved, less-informed businessmen were found, one found also a much higher proportion of supporters of liberal trade policies. They, however, were less likely to write their congressmen. Interestingly enough, as one moved still further down the pyramid there was a second reversal. At the bottom of the pyramid, among the least-informed elements of the population, one found many instinctive protectionists who were worried about foreign competition.

A schematized picture of the situation is given in Figure 3. In the figure, a change in the saliency of the issue is represented by moving the horizontal "participation cutoff" line up (*a*) or down (*b*). What is below the line is the part of the opinion iceberg that does not show in the public debate. By stimulating attention through agitation and propaganda, one can move that line down (*b*). More of the public then expresses itself. But as that happens, the proportion of liberal traders and protectionists may change. Indeed in the study cited, it was found that the net effect of the League of Women Voter's proliberal trade drive between 1954 and 1955 was probably to increase the expression of protectionist views, because it activated a larger stratum of the population, a stratum, so it happened, with more protectionist leanings.

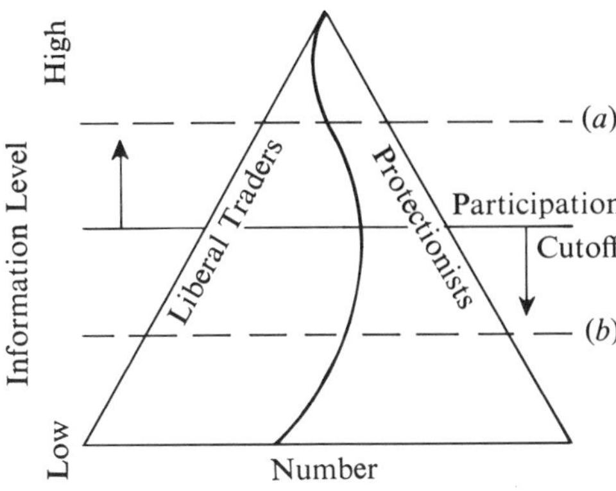

Figure 3. Public opinion pyramid on U.S. foreign-trade policies.

A similar phenomenon is noted by Gerald Kramer (1965; 1966; 1970–71) in his analysis of the cost-effectiveness of election canvassing. It is very easy by canvassing in areas where the opposition is strong to stir up more votes againts than for one's candidate.

POLLS

Perhaps the most important development in the past forty years in the study of public opinion is the fact that for the first time in history we have a relatively reliable way of measuring what public opinion is and how it is changing, namely, the sample survey. Until roughly 1935, most research on public opinion relied on the analysis of newspaper and other editorial statements. Scholars, such as Dicey (1905), had to assume that what agitated the editors was also what agitated the general public. That is a highly unsatisfactory assumption.

Since 1935, a growing archive of national opinion surveys on many topics has been available. Polling got its start when George Gallup and Elmo Roper did rather well in predicting the 1936 election with small samples, while the mammoth postcard straw vote conducted by the *Literary Digest* failed. The secret of the polling pioneer's success was the application of the principles of scientific sampling. Since that time, every year hundreds of poll questions have been asked, many of them repeatedly, thus making trend measurements possible.

Recognizing the social value of the historical record that they owned, the main polling organizations have agreed to deposit their old cards in archives, mostly at the Roper Public Opinion Research Center at Williams College, from which the data are available to scholars. The result has been a slowly increasing (although still small) set of historical studies about trends in modern public opinion.

In 1951 Hadley Cantril and Mildred Strunk published an extensive selection of poll results from the first ten years, 1936–1946. The results to that date could still fit into a single mammoth hard-cover book. Today that would be impossible; there is a library of results, not one volume. Nonetheless, published reference sources are available which cover some of the results, most notably the section of *Public Opinion Quarterly* called "The Polls." During its early years, *Public Opinion Quarterly* aimed at full, current coverage, but eventually had to give up on that. More recently, it has published topical roundups of poll results on many issues. For a period in the 1960s, there was also a magazine published in Holland called *Polls*. Since 1965, the Gallup organization has published its own magazine called *The Gallup Opinion Index*, which reports all their main results. The explosion in the volume of data is not limited to the United States; polling has become worldwide. The amount of data is such that while the publications of results are useful, the serious scholar must increasingly work in an organized data archive.

There are by now a few important studies that have followed trends in opinion on some topic through a period of time. The earliest effort was by Hadley Cantril (1940), and traced the gradual erosion of American isolationism before this country entered World War II. More recently Lloyd Free and Hadley Cantril (1967) have summarized much data on *The Political Beliefs of Americans*. The present author, with Robert Abelson and Samuel Popkin, used American political polls from 1950 to 1964 to establish a model of changing voting behavior as a function of issue attitudes (Pool et al., 1965). Daniel Lerner and Morton Gorden (1969) followed the evolution of European elite attitudes toward European integration over a ten-year period. Alfred Hero (1965a; 1956b) has examined the trends in American attitudes toward foreign aid.

Several authors have reviewed the trends in American public opinion toward the Vietnam war (Robinson & Jacobson, 1969; Hadley Cantril, 1970; Milton Rosenberg, Verba, & Converse, 1970); Robinson and Jacobson have also shown that there is an almost exact parallelism between the trend of growing discontent with the Vietnam war and the trend of discontent generated by the Korean conflict, although the trend of disenchantment over Vietnam has continued longer than the three years of the Korean war. Mueller (1970) has similarly found a pattern in the trend of declining presidential popularity in the course of an administration. The studies by Mueller, Robinson, and Pool are efforts to identify climatic regularities in the changing weather of opinion.

TRENDS IN PUBLIC OPINION

Clearly, in the confined space of this review we cannot attempt to summarize substantively what the polls have shown about the mass of changing attitudes over recent decades. We might, however, review briefly some current literature that deals with asserted major changes in what we have called above the climate of public opinion.

One form of "climatic" change in opinions is that which occurs in so-called critical elections. V. O. Key (1955) introduced this concept. Walter Dean Burnham (1970) has developed it most fully in his historical-statistical studies of American voting. The swings that occur from election to election seldom produce any fundamental change in the American political lineup. The basic number of Republicans, Democrats, and Independents changes glacially, mostly by the process of recruitment of the young and dying off of the old. The Gallup

Public Opinion Index reported 42 percent Democratic self-identifiers in 1950, 44 percent in 1970; 33 percent Republicans in 1950, 29 percent in 1970; and 22 percent Independents in 1950, 27 percent in 1970. In each election, circumstances cause some of them to switch their votes, but their basic affiliation remains.

Every so often, however, an election comes along that shakes up the whole line-up (Chambers & Burnham, 1967). The last such national election in the United States was in 1932, when what had been a national Republican majority became a Democratic majority. After each recent election, the Survey Research Center team has published an analysis of the election results (Converse, 1961; Converse, Clausen, & Miller, 1965; Campbell et al., 1966; Converse, Miller, Rusk, & Wolfe, 1969). There have been no fundamental realignments of the voters in recent years, although there has been a steady trend toward increase in voter independence. Partisan theses have appeared asserting that basic realignments have been taking place, such as the emergence of a new conservative Republican majority. The data, however, does not support notions of any massive change up to the moment of writing on the morn of the 1972 elections (Polsby, 1969; Scammon & Wattenberg, 1970). I will not indulge here in predictions of the future.

To date surprisingly little use has been made for historical writing of the rich public opinion poll data that now exist. There has been relatively little analysis of any basic climatic changes in public opinion. The transient changes from day to day are easy to document in the polls, but are of little scientific interest. What we would really like to know is whether there have been basic changes in political commitment that are not explainable by changes in current circumstances.

The studies that have come closest to establishing such changes are those that have sought to separate cohort changes from sequential changes (Cutler, 1968; Carlson & Karlson, 1970). Younger people are more liberal on sex and civil rights. Will they still be more liberal when they become older?

The answer varies with the topic; usually, part of the difference is age specific and part is cohort specific (Eisenstadt, 1956). To separate out the effects of aging and generation requires that one have survey data with the same questions repeated over many years (Evan, 1959). A study of that kind covering 1946–1966 shows the younger cohorts to have been more interventionist than the older ones. There is a debate among analysts as to whether there is a tendency for voters to become Republican as they get older (Crittenden, 1962; Cutler, 1969–70).

Even when there are clear longitudinal changes taking place, as for example in the increase in internationalism, one wishes to know if those changes occur across the board or merely as by-products of changes in social structure. For example, better educated people are more internationalist, and the number of better educated people is rising. Does that fully account for any rise in internationalism? Clearly both by-product changes and independent changes occur. What is required, but is relatively rare, are historical studies that partial out the two processes (Dogan & Rokkan, 1969; Stephens & Long, 1970).

Complicated processes of change occur whenever a particular pattern of behavior gets learned and once learned tends to be maintained conservatively. Electoral partisanship has that character. Most people become socialized into their particular political affiliation in the seventeen to twenty-two age period. People who went through that stage in years of strong Democratic surges tend to become Democrats; and vice versa in years of Republican surge. As they pass out of the youthful years of extensive nonvoting into their late twenties and thirties, they reinforce their party; three decades later that wave begins to recede. All the time, of course, some people are changing their affiliation, but most do not.

Consensus and Dissent

The opinions of the powerful and of the majority of the public have always been of interest to students of public opinion. Most poll results are reported with a focus on what the bulk of the public thinks and on what influences those who will vote. They deal with either the prevailing opinion or that of the elite. Less attention has been paid in the past to the attitudes of those who opt out of the political system or those whose attitudes represent minority deviant views.

During the late 1960s, however, there was a marked increase in social science attention to dissent, to alienated elements of the population, and to the culture of poverty. Two factors stimulated this interest. The first was President Johnson's Great Society program, starting in 1964. Concern with civil rights and with the conditions of life of the poor that had been shared all along by most American social scientists were officially proclaimed prime national priorities. The government set up programs addressed to solving these problems. That activity created opportunities for social scientists to be heard on what would work and what would not work, thus creating attractive professional opportunities for social researchers backed by substantial research funds.

The shift of social science interest to the alienated and the poor was reinforced by the emergence of the so-called New Left among students and intellectuals throughout the world. Because the growth of dissent in the 1960s was largely a phenomenon of the intelligentsia, it had its resonance also in the social scientists among them.

As a result of these shifts in attention, we now have a number of valuable studies of the political and social culture of the ghetto, of attempts to create new political forums for the disadvantaged (such as the Model Cities Program), and of movements of protest and dissent (e.g., Donovan, 1967; Marris & Rein, 1967; Gamson, 1968; Greenstone & Peterson, 1968; Skolnick, 1969; Sundquist, 1969; Aberbach & Walker, 1970a; 1970b; Lipsky, 1970; Moynihan, 1970; Peterson, 1970).

One main theme in the literature on the politics of the disadvantaged is that established bureaucratic structures such as city administrations and welfare bureaucracies resist transfer of power to their clients. The other main theme is the incapacity of the disadvantaged because they are disadvantaged to assert their own claims. Repeated case studies show the extreme difficulty of modifying adult behavior in the direction of initiative, responsibility, achievement orientation, trust, and autonomy among those to whom early socialization conveyed a sense of worthlessness, distrust, or futility. Little is accomplished in these directions by secondary institutions such as schools unless they are reinforced by the home and community culture. The studies tend to show the ineffectuality of partial measures and the importance of working on all aspects of the environment at once (jobs, homes, schools, etc.) if the debilitating effects of a culture of poverty are to be overcome.

In the meantime, the main political manifestation of the culture of poverty is not protest but alienation. Alienation is a vague concept that means many things.[11] However it may be defined, it is associated with nonparticipation, withdrawal, and cynicism about the political system (McLeod, Ward, & Tancill, 1965; Templeton, 1966; Aberbach, 1969). The most interesting question, however, is whether it is increasing.

Alienation, and also protest and dissent, are, in the journalistic literature, all said to be increasing in what is asserted to be a period of unprecedented malaise. It is alleged that a growing sense of powerlessness and alienation is affecting large

[11] On the dimensions of alienation, see Struening and Richardson (1965); Neal and Rettig (1967); Finifter (1970); Hensler (1971).

sectors of society resulting in increased radicalization of minorities and youth (Goodman, 1968).

At least in the short run and in the United States, solid evidence reveals an alarming current trend. In June 1972, the Harris poll released comparative figures for six years on agreement with several statements indexing alienation (Table 4).

The gross disenchantment is unmistakable. But is it a systemic trend or is it a passing wave? Is it the nature of modern society or is it a lack of charisma of a couple of particular national administrations? Is it a worldwide phenomenon of industrial societies or is it a problem of one country unable to extricate itself from an unpopular prolonged war?

Until better evidence is in, one must question easy answers. The decay of morale and confidence in contemporary society is a historical phenomenon concerning which substantial disturbing data now exist, but the evidence has not been adequately probed. *A priori* it is not clear that there is any fundamental trend toward alienation or dissent in modern industrial society, although it is perfectly clear that there have been such short-run trends at particular times and places and among specific population groups such as students (Yankelovich, 1971). The numerous statements that appear in popular writing asserting, on the one hand, that society's values are being challenged as they never have been before or, on the other hand, that a right-wing swing is under way by the silent majority in defense of its prejudices and comforts must both be relegated to the status of largely untested hypotheses (but see Lipset & Raab, 1970).

Most nearly relevant to these issues were three surveys of youth conducted in 1969 by major American survey organizations. One area in which several serious attempts have been made to discover how much change there has been is sexual behavior. On the whole, the surveys of actual sexual behavior show more constancy than change in the United States since the 1920s, but they do show a growing frankness in regard to the facts.

Even if we found on inspection of poll results, as we certainly would, that there were many changes concerning such matters as trust in the government or how to treat dissenters, we would still be faced with the problem of separating short-run changes in the public opinion weather from long-run changes in the climate. The genuineness of a change cannot be easily established by a quick reading of a few poll results. It takes serious research to separate the cohort from the age differences, and the situationally determined variations from those that rise above situational changes. Such studies unfortunately are rare. There may well be fundamental changes taking place in the operation of public opinion in our society; many astute observers believe so, but the hard evidence of social research does not yet exist.

TABLE 4

TREND TOWARD ALIENATION

Statements of Alienation	Percentage in Agreement			
	1966	1968	1971	1972
The rich get rich and the poor get poorer.	48	54	62	68
What you think doesn't count.	39	42	44	53
The people running the country don't really care what happens to people like yourself.	28	36	44	50
You feel left out of things around you.	9	12	20	25

REFERENCES

Abelson, Robert P.; Elliot Aronson; William J. McGuire; Theodore M. Newcomb; and Percy H. Tannenbaum.
1968 Theories of Cognitive Consistency: A Sourcebook. Chicago: Rand McNally.

Abelson, Robert P., and M. J. Rosenberg.
1958 "Symbolic psycho-logic." Behavioral Science 3:1–13.

Aberbach, Joel D.
1969 "Alienation and political behavior." American Political Science Review 63:86–99.

Aberbach, Joel D., and Jack L. Walker.
1970a "Meanings of black power: A comparison of white and black interpretation of a political slogan." American Political Science Review 64:367–388.
1970b "Political trust and racial ideology." American Political Science Review 64:1199–1219.

Adler, Kenneth P., and Davis Bobrow.
1956 "Interest and influence on foreign affairs." Public Opinion Quarterly 20:89–101.

Adorno, Theodor W.; Else Frenkel-Brunswik; Daniel Levinson; and R. Nevitt Sanford.
1950 The Authoritarian Personality. New York: Harper.

Advertising Research Foundation.
1953 An Introductory Bibliography to Motivation Research. New York: Advertising Research Foundation.

Agger, Robert E.; Daniel Goldrich; and Bert Swanson.
1964 The Rulers and the Ruled: Political Power and Impotence in American Communities. New York: Wiley.

Alford, Robert R., and Eugene Lee.
1968 "Voter turnout in American cities." American Political Science Review 62:796–813.

Alford, Robert R., and Harry M. Scoble.
1968 "Sources of local political involvement." American Political Science Review 62:1192–1206.

Alker, Hayward R., Jr.
1964 "Dimensions of conflict in the general assembly." American Political Science Review 58:642–657.

Allardt, Erik.
1970 "Types of protests and alienation," in Erik Allardt and Stein Rokkan (eds.), Mass Politics: Studies in Political Sociology. New York: Free Press.

Allardt, Erik, and Yrjo Littunen.
1964 Cleavages, Ideologies and Party Systems. Helsinki: Westermark Society.

Allport, Gordon.
1954 The Nature of Prejudice. Reading, Massachusetts: Addison-Wesley.

Almond, Gabriel A.
1954 The Appeals of Communism. Princeton, New Jersey: Princeton University Press.
1960 The American People and Foreign Policy. New York: Praeger.

Almond, Gabriel, and G. Bingham Powell, Jr.
1966 Comparative Politics: A Developmental Approach. Boston: Little, Brown.

Almond, Gabriel A., and Sidney Verba.
1963 Civic Culture. Princeton, New Jersey: Princeton University Press.

Altshuler, Alan.
1970 Community Control: The Black Demand for Participation in Large American Cities. New York: Pegagus.

Anderson, Lee F.
1964 "Variability in the unidimensionality of legislative voting." Journal of Politics 26:568–585.

Andrews, William G.
1966 "American voting participation." Western Political Quarterly 19:639–652.

Aristotle.
1926 The Art of Rhetoric. English translation by John Henry Freese. (Loeb Classical Library No. 193.) Cambridge, Massachusetts: Harvard University Press.

Axelrod, Robert.
1967 "Structure of public opinion on policy issues." Public Opinion Quarterly 31:51–60.

Bachrach, Peter, and Morton S. Baratz.
1970 Power and Poverty. New York: Oxford University Press.

Bailey, Steven K.
1950 Congress Makes a Law. New York: Columbia University Press.

Banfield, Edward C.
1958 Moral Basis of a Backward Society.

Glencoe, Illinois: Free Press.

Barber, James D.
1969 Citizen Politics: An Introduction to Political Behavior. Chicago: Markham.

Bauer, Raymond A.; Ithiel de Sola Pool; and Lewis A. Dexter.
1963 American Business and Public Policy. New York: Atherton Press.

Bay, Christian.
1965 "Politics and pseudopolitics." American Political Science Review 59: 39–51.

Becker, Boris W., and John G. Myers.
1970 "Yeasaying response style." Journal of Advertising Research 10(December): 31–37.

Becker, Carl L.
1941 Modern Democracy. New Haven, Connecticut: Yale University Press.

Becknell, J. C., Jr., and Howard Maher.
1962 "Utilization of factor analysis for image clarification and analysis." Public Opinion Quarterly 26:658–663.

Bell, Daniel.
1962 The End of Ideology, New York: Collier.

Berelson, Bernard.
1949 "What missing the newspaper means, in Paul F. Lazarsfeld and Frank Stanton, Communications Research, 1948–1949. New York: Harper.

Berelson, Bernard; Paul F. Lazarsfeld; and William McPhee.
1954 Voting. Chicago: University of Chicago Press.

Boas, George.
1969 Vox Populi: Essays in the History of an Idea. Baltimore: Johns Hopkins Press.

Bottomore, T. B.
1964 Elites and Society. London: C. A. Watts.

Brown, Roger W.
1958 Words and Things. Glencoe, Illinois: Free Press.
1962 "Models of attitude change," in Roger Brown, Eugene Galanter, Eckhard H. Hess, and George Mandler, New Directions in Psychology. New York: Holt, Rinehart and Winston.

Brown, Steven, R., and John D. Ellithorp.
1970 "Emotional experiences in political groups: The case of the McCarthy phenomenon." American Political Science Review 64:349–366.

Browning, Rufus P., and Herbert Jacob.
1964 "Power motivation and the political personality." Public Opinion Quarterly 28:75–90.

Bruner, Jerome S.; Jacqueline Goodnow; and George Austin.
1956 A Study of Thinking. New York: Wiley.

Bruner, Jerome S., and Renato Tagiuri.
1954 "The perception of people," in Gardner Lindzey (ed.), Handbook of Social Psychology. Reading, Massachusetts: Addison-Wesley.

Buchanan, William, and Hadley Cantril.
1953 How Nations See Each Other. Urbana: University of Illinois Press.

Burke, Edmund.
1837 "Speech at the Guildhall in Bristol (1780)." Pp. 256–272 in Edmund Burke, Works. Volume 1. London: Samuel Holdsworth.

Burnham, James.
1943 The Machiavellians: Defenders of Freedom. New York: John Day.

Burnham, Walter Dean.
1970 Critical Elections: The Mainsprings of American Politics. New York: Norton.
1972 "Theory and voting research: Some reflections on [Philip] Converse's 'Change in the American electorate.'" Mimeograph (unpublished).

Campbell, Angus; Philip E. Converse; Warren Miller; and Donald E. Stokes.
1960 The American Voter. New York: Wiley.
1966 Elections and the Political Order. New York: Wiley.

Cantril, Albert H.
1970 The American People, Viet-Nam, and the Presidency. Princeton, New Jersey: Institute for International Social Research.

Cantril, Hadley.
1940 "America faces the war." Public Opinion Quarterly 4(No. 3):387–407; 4(No. 4):651–656.

Cantril, Hadley, and Mildred B. Strunk (eds.).
1951 Public Opinion 1935–1946. Princeton, New Jersey: Princeton University Press.

Carlson, Costa, and Katarina Karlson.
1970 "Age cohorts and generation of generations." American Sociological Review 35:710–718.

Carter, Roy F.
1962 "Stereotyping as a process." Public Opinion Quarterly 26:77–91.

Caspary, William R.
1970 "The 'mood theory': A study of public opinion and foreign policy." American Political Science Review 64:536–547.

Census Bureau.
1960 Historical Statistics of the United States: Colonial Times to 1957. Washington, D.C.: U.S. Government Printing Office.
1965a Continuation to 1962 and Revisions. Washington, D.C:. U.S. Government Printing Office.
1965b Voter Participation in the National Election, November 1964. Current Population Reports: Population Characteristics. Series P-20, No. 143 (October 25).

Chambers, William Nisbet, and Walter Dean Burnham (eds.).
1967 The American Party System: Stages of Development. New York: Oxford University Press.

Christie, Richard, and Peggy Cook.
1958 "A guide to published literature relating to 'The Authoritarian Personality' through 1956." Journal of Psychology 45:171–199.

Christie, Richard, and Maria Jahoda (eds.).
1954 Studies in the Scope and Method of the Authoritarian Personality. Glencoe, Illinois: Free Press.

Claude, Inis L.
1965 The Impact of Public Opinion Upon Foreign Policy. The Hague: Mouton.

Coelho, George V.
1958 Changing Images of America: A Study of Indian Students' Perceptions. Glencoe, Illinois: Free Press.

Cohen, Bernard C.
1957 The Political Process and Foreign Policy. Princeton, New Jersey: Princeton University Press.
1963 The Press and Foreign Policy. Princeton, New Jersey: Princeton University Press.

Coles, Robert.
1965 "Public evil and private problems: Segregation and psychiatry." Yale Review 54:516–530.

Congressional Quarterly Service.
1945– Congressional Quarterly Almanac. Washington, D.C.: Congressional Quarterly, Inc. Annual.
1969 Congress and the Nation. Volume 2. Washington, D.C.: Congressional Quarterly, Inc.
1970 Congressional Quarterly Weekly Report. Volume 28. Washington, D.C.: Congressional Quarterly, Inc.

Converse, Philip E.
1961 "Stability and change in 1960: A reinstating election." American Political Science Review 55:269–280.
1972 "Change in the American electorate," in A. Campbell and P. E. Converse (eds.), Human Meaning of Social Change. New York: Russell Sage.

Converse, Philip E.; A. Clausen; and Warren E. Miller.
1965 "Electoral myth and reality." American Political Science Review 59: 321–336.

Converse, Philip E., and Georges Dupeux.
1962 "Politicization of the electorate in France and the United States." Public Opinion Quarterly 26:1–23.

Converse, Philip E.; Warren E. Miller; Jerrold G. Rusk; and Arthur C. Wolfe.
1969 "Continuity and change in American politics: Parties and issues in the 1968 election." American Political Science Review 63:1083–1105.

Cooley, Charles Horton.
1922 Human Nature and the Social Order. New York: Scribners.

Cornwell, Elmer R., Jr.
1965 Presidential Leadership of Public Opinion. Bloomington: Indiana University Press.

Couch, Arthur, and Kenneth Kenniston.
1960 "Yeasayers and naysayers: Agreeing response set as a personality variable." Journal of Abnormal and Social Psychology 60:151–174.

Crane, Wilder, Jr.
1960 "Do representatives represent?" Journal of Politics 22:295–299.

Crittenden, John.
1962 "Aging and party affiliation." Public Opinion Quarterly 26:648–657.

Cutler, Neal E.
1968 Alternative Effects of Generations

and Aging Upon Political Behavior: A Cohort Analysis of American Attitudes Toward Foreign Policy, 1946–1966. Oak Ridge, Tennessee: Oak Ridge National Laboratory.
1969 "Generation, maturation and party
–70 affiliation: A cohort analysis." Public Opinion Quarterly 33:583–591.

Cutright, Phillips.
1963 "National political development," in Nelson Polsby et al. (eds.), Politics and Social Life. Boston: Houghton Mifflin.

Dahl, Robert A.
1961 Who Governs. New Haven, Connecticut: Yale University Press.
1963 Preface to Democratic Theory. Chicago: University of Chicago Press.

Davies, J. Clarence.
1966 Neighborhood Groups and Urban Renewal. New York: Columbia University Press.

Davis, Lane.
1964 "The cost of the new realism." World Political Quarterly 17:37–46.

Davis, Otto A.; Melvin J. Hinich; and Peter C. Ordenshook.
1970 "An expository development of a mathematical model of the electoral process." American Political Science Review 64:426–448.

Dawson, Richard E.
1966 "Political socialization," in James A. Robinson (ed.), Political Science Annual: An International Review. Volume 1, 1966. Indianapolis: Bobbs-Merrill.

DeGrazia, Alfred.
1951 Public and Republic. New York: Knopf.

DeRivera, Joseph.
1968 Psychological Dimensions of Foreign Policy. Columbus, Ohio: Merrill.

Deutsch, Karl W.
1956 "Shifts in the balance of communication flows." Public Opinion Quarterly 20:143–160.
1957 Political Community and the North Atlantic Area. Princeton, New Jersey: Princeton University Press.
1966 Nationalism and Social Communication. Second Edition. Cambridge, Massachussetts: M.I.T. Press.

Deutsch, Karl W., and Richard L. Merritt.
1965 "Effects of events on national and international images," in Herbert C. Kelman (ed.), International Behavior: A Social-Psychological Analysis. New York: Holt, Rinehart and Winston.

Devereux, George.
1955 "Charismatic leadership and crisis." Psychoanalysis and the Social Sciences 4:150–151.

Dexter, Lewis A.
1954 "What do congressmen hear: The mail." Public Opinion Quarterly 20:16–27.
1969a How Organizations Are Represented in Washington. Indianapolis: Bobbs-Merrill.
1969b The Sociology and Politics of Congress. Chicago: Rand McNally.

Diab, L. N.
1959 "Authoritarianism and prejudice in near-eastern students attending American universities." Journal of Social Psychology 50:175–187.

Dicey, Albert.
1905 Lectures on the Relation Between Law and Opinion in England in the 19th Century. London: Macmillan.

Dichter, Ernest.
1964 Handbook of Consumer Motivations. New York: McGraw-Hill.

DiRenzo, Gordon J.
1967 Personality, Power, and Politics. Notre Dame, Indiana: University of Notre Dame Press.

Dogan, Mattei, and Stein Rokkan (eds.)
1969 Quantitative Ecological Analysis in the Social Sciences. Cambridge, Massachusetts: M.I.T. Press.

Donovan, John C.
1967 The Politics of Poverty. New York: Pegasus.

Doob, Leonard.
1964 Patriotism and Nationalism: Their Psychological Foundations. New Haven, Connecticut: Yale University Press.

Downs, Anthony.
1957 An Economic Theory of Democracy. New York: Harper and Row.

Duncan, Hugh D.
1962 Communication and the Social Order. London: Oxford University Press.

Duverger, Maurice.
1954 Political Parties. New York: Wiley.

Dye, Thomas R.
1970 "Community power studies," in James A. Robinson (ed.), Political Science Annual: An International Review. Volume 2:1969–70. Indianapolis: Bobbs-Merrill.

Dye, Thomas R., and W. Hawkins Brett (eds.).
1967 Politics in the Metropolis. Columbus, Ohio: Merrill.

Edelman, Murray.
1964 The Symbolic Uses of Politics. Urbana: University of Illinois Press.

Eisenstadt, Shmuel Noah.
1956 From Generation to Generation; Age Groups and Social Structure. Glencoe, Illinois: Free Press.

Erikson, Erik H.
1959 "The problem of ego identity," in Identity and the Life Cycle. Psychological Issues Monograph. Volume 1, Number 1. New York: International Universities Press.
1962 Young Man Luther. New York: Norton.
1964 Childhood and Society. Second Edition. New York: Norton.
1966 "The concept of identity in race relations." Daedalus 95(Winter): 145–171.
1969 Gandhi's Truth. New York: Norton.

Eulau, Heinz, and Katherine Hinkley.
1966 "Legislative institutions and processes," in James A. Robinson (ed.), Political Science Annual: An International Review. Volume 1, 1966. Indianapolis: Bobbs-Merrill.

Evans, William M.
1959 "Cohort analysis of survey data: A procedure for studying long-term opinion change." Public Opinion Quarterly 23:62–72.

Fein, Leonard.
1968 Israel: Politics and People. Boston: Little, Brown.

Fellman, David.
1963 The Constitutional Right of Association. Chicago: University of Chicago Press.

Fenichal, Otto.
1945 The Psychoanalytic Theory of Neurosis. New York: Norton.

Feuer, Lewis S.
1969 The Conflict of Generations: The Character and Significance of Student Movements. New York: Basic Books.

Finifter, Ada W.
1970 "Dimensions of political alienation." American Political Science Review 64:389–410.

Flanigan, William.
1968 Political Behavior of the American Electorate. Boston: Allyn and Bacon.

Free, Loyd A., and Hadley Cantril.
1967 The Political Beliefs of Americans. New Brunswick, New Jersey: Rutgers University Press.

Freedman, J. L., and David O. Sears.
1965 "Selective exposure," in Leonard Berkowitz (ed.), Advances in Experimental Social Psychology. Volume 1. New York: Academic Press.

Freud, Sigmund.
1922 Group Psychology and the Analysis of the Ego. Translated by James Strachey. New York: Boni and Liveright.
1955 The Interpretation of Dreams. Translated by James Strachey. New York: Basic Books.

Frey, Frederick.
1966 The Mass Media and Rural Development in Turkey. Cambridge: Center for International Studies, Massachusetts Institute of Technology.

Fried, Marc.
1966 "Grieving for a lost home," in James Q. Wilson (ed.), Urban Renewal. Cambridge, Massachusetts: M.I.T. Press.

Froman, Lewis A.
1962 People and Politics. Englewood Cliffs, New Jersey: Prentice-Hall.
1963 Congressmen and Their Constituencies. Chicago: Rand McNally.

Froman, Lewis A., and J. K. Skipper.
1962 "Factors related to misperceiving party stands on issues." Public Opinion Quarterly 26:265–272.

Gamson, William.
1968 Power and Discontent. Homewood, Illinois: Dorsey Press.

Gellhorn, Walter.
1966 When Americans Complain: Governmental Grievance Procedures. Cambridge, Massachusetts: Harvard University Press.

George, Alex, and Juliette L. George.
1956 Woodrow Wilson and Colonel House:

A Personality Study. New York: Day.

Glazer, Nathan, and Daniel P. Moynihan.
1963 Beyond the Melting Pot. Cambridge, Massachusetts: M.I.T. Press.

Goodman, Paul.
1968 People or Personnel: Decentralizing and the Mixed Systems; and Like a Conquered Province: the Moral Ambiguity of America. 2 volumes in 1. New York: Vintage Books.

Gordon, Daniel N.
1970 "Immigrants and municipal voting turnout: Implication for the changing ethnic impact on urban politics." American Sociological Review 35: 665–681.

Gosnell, Harold Foote.
1927 Getting Out the Vote. Chicago: University of Chicago Press.
1930 Why Europe Votes. Chicago: University of Chicago Press.
1937 Machine Politics, Chicago Model. Second Edition. Chicago: University of Chicago Press.

Greenstein, Fred I.
1963 The American Party System and the American People. Englewood Cliffs, New Jersey: Prentice-Hall.
1969 Personality and Politics. Chicago: Markham.

Greenstein, Fred I. (ed.).
1968 Personality and Politics: Theoretical and Methodological Issues. Journal of Social Issues (special issue). Volume 24.

Greenstone, David, and Paul Peterson.
1968 "Reformers, machines, and the war on poverty," in James Q. Wilson (ed.), City Politics and Public Policy. New York: Wiley.

Greer, Scott.
1958 "Individual participation in mass society," in Roland Young (ed.), Approaches to the Study of Politics. Evanston, Illinois: Northwestern University Press.

Grodzins, Morton.
1965 The Loyal and the Disloyal. Chicago: University of Chicago Press.

Hahn, Harlan.
1970 "Correlates of public sentiments about war: Local referenda on the Vietnam issue." American Political Science Review 64:1186–1198.

Handlin, Oscar.
1951 The Uprooted. Boston: Little, Brown.

Harding, John.
1968 "Stereotypes," in David L. Sills (ed.), International Encyclopedia of the Social Sciences. Volume 15. New York: Macmillian.

Hausknecht, Murray.
1962 The Joiners. Englewood Cliffs, New Jersey: Bedminister Press.

Heider, Fritz.
1958 The Psychology of Interpersonal Relations. New York: Wiley.

Hensler, Carl P.
1971 "The structure of 'Orientations Toward Government.'" Ph.D. Dissertation, Massachusetts Institute of Technology (unpublished).

Hero, Alfred O.
1965a "Foreign aid and the American public." Public Policy 14:71–116.
1965b The Southerner and World Affairs. Baton Rouge: Louisiana State University Press.

Hero, Alfred O. (ed.).
1959 Studies in Citizen Participation in World Affairs. 7 volumes. Boston: World Peace Foundation.

Herring, E. Pendleton.
1929 Group Representation Before Congress. Washington, D.C.: The Brookings Institution.

Herzog, Herta.
1944 "What do we really know about daytime serial listeners," in Paul F. Lazarsfeld and Frank Stanton (eds.), Radio Research, 1942–1943. New York: Duell, Sloan and Pearce.

Himmelstrand, Ulf.
1960 Social Pressures, Attitudes and Democratic Processes. Stockholm: Almqvist and Wiksell.
1970 "Depolitization and political involvement: A theoretical and empirical approach," in Erik Allardt and Stein Rokkan (eds.), Mass Politics: Studies in Political Sociology. New York: Free Press.

Himmelweit, Hilda; A. N. Oppenheim; and Pamela Vince.
1958 Television and the Child. London: Oxford University Press.

Hoffer, Eric.
1951 The True Believer. New York: Harper.

Hovland, Carl I.; Irving Janis; and Harold H. Kelley.
1953 Communication and Persuasion. New Haven, Connecticut: Yale University Press.

Hughes, Helen MacGill.
1939 News and the Human Interest Story. Chicago: University of Chicago Press.

Huitt, Ralph K., and Robert L. Peabody.
1969 Congress: Two Decades of Analysis. New York: Harper and Row.

Hunter, Floyd.
1953 Community Power Structure. Chapel Hill: University of North Carolina Press.

Hyman, Herbert, and Charles C. Wright.
1971 "Trends in voluntary association memberships of American adults." American Sociological Review 36: 191–206.

Inkeles, Alex.
1969 "Participant citizenship in six developing countries." American Political Science Review 63:1120–1141.

Isaacs, Harold.
1958 Scratches on Our Minds: American Images of China and India. New York: Day.
1963 The New World of Negro Americans. New York: Day.
1968 "Group identity and political change: Nationalism revisited." Survey 69 (October): 75–98.

Jaffe, Gerald M.
1968 "Emerging nations: What the public watches." Television Quarterly 2:85.

Janowitz, Morris (ed.).
1961 Community Political Systems. New York: Free Press of Glencoe.

Jervis, Robert.
1968 "Hypothesis on misperception." World Politics 20:454–479.

Kariel, Henry S.
1961 The Decline of American Pluralism. Stanford, California: Stanford University Press.

Katz, Daniel.
1960 "The functional approach to the study of attitudes." Public Opinion Quarterly 24:163–205.

Katz, Elihu, and Paul F. Lazarsfeld.
1955 Personal Influence. Glencoe, Illinois: Free Press.

Keech, William R.
1968 The Impact of Negro Voting: The Role of the Vote in the Quest for Equality. Chicago: Rand McNally.

Keesing, Felix, and Marie Keesing.
1956 Elite Communication in Samoa. Stanford, California: Stanford University Press.

Kelley, Stanley, Jr.; Richard E. Ayers; and William G. Bowen.
1967 "Registration and voting: Putting first things first." American Political Science Review 61:359–379.

Kelman, Herbert C. (ed.).
1965 International Behavior: A Social-Psychological Analysis. New York: Holt, Rinehart and Winston.

Kenniston, Kenneth.
1968 Young Radicals. New York: Harcourt, Brace and World.

Kessel, J. D.
1965 "Cognitive dimensions of political activity." Public Opinion Quarterly 29:377–389.

Key, V. O., Jr.
1955 "A theory of critical elections." Journal of Politics 17:3–18.
1961 Public Opinion and American Democracy. New York: Knopf.
1963 Politics, Parties and Pressure Groups. New York: Crowell.

Kirscht, John P., and Ronald C. Dillehay.
1967 Dimensions of Authoritarianism. Lexington: University of Kentucky Press.

Klapper, Joseph T.
1960 The Effects of Mass Communication. New York: Free Press of Glencoe.

Klein, Alexander (ed.).
1971 Dissent, Power and Confrontation. New York: McGraw-Hill.

Klineberg, Otto.
1964 The Human Dimension in International Relations. New York: Holt, Rinehart and Winston.

Klineberg, Otto, and J. Milton Yinger.
1968 "Prejudice," in David L. Sills (ed.). International Encyclopedia of the Social Sciences. Volume 12. New York: Macmillan.

Kotler, Milton.
1969 Neighborhood Government: The Local Foundations of Political Life. Indianapolis: Bobbs-Merrill.

Kramer, Gerald H.
1965 "A decision-theoretic analysis of canvassing and other precinct-level activities in political campaigning." Ph.D. Dissertation, Massachusetts Institute of Technology (unpublished).
1966 "A decision-theoretic analysis of a problem in political campaigning," in Joseph L. Bernd (ed.), Mathematical Applications in Political Science. Volume 2. Dallas: The Arnold Foundation.
1970–71 "The effects of precinct level canvassing on voter behavior." Public Opinion Quarterly 34:560–572.

Kramer, John F.
1969 A Computer Simulation of Audience Exposure in a Mass Media System: The United States Information Campaign in Cincinnati, 1947–1948. Cambridge: Center for International Studies, Massachusetts Institute of Technology.

Kramer, Ralph.
1969 Participation of the Poor. Englewood Cliffs, New Jersey: Prentice-Hall.

Kraus, Sidney.
1962 The Great Debates. Bloomington: University of Indiana Press.

Kris, Ernst, and Nathan Leites.
1950 "Trends in 20th century propaganda," in Bernard Berelson and Morris Janowitz (eds.), Reader in Public Opinion and Communication. Glencoe, Illinois: Free Press.

Krugman, Herbert E.
1967 "The role of hostility in the appeal of communism in the United States," in J. K. Zawodny (ed.), Man and International Relations. San Francisco: Chandler.

Ladd, Everett Carl, Jr.
1969 Ideology in America: Change and Response in a City, a Suburb, and a Small Town. Ithaca, New York: Cornell University Press.

Lane, Robert E.
1959 Political Life: Why and How People Get Involved in Politics and Political Ideology. New York: Free Press of Glencoe.
1962 Political Ideology: Why the American's Common Man Believes What He Does. New York: Free Press of Glencoe.
1969 Political Thinking and Consciousness: The Private Life of the Political Mind. Chicago: Markham.

Lang, Kurt, and Gladys Lang.
1968a Voting and Non-Voting. Chicago: Quadrangle Books.
1968b Politics and Television. Chicago: Quadrangle Books.

Lasswell, Harold D.
1930 Psychopathology and Politics. Chicago: University of Chicago Press.
1935 World Politics and Personal Insecurity. New York: McGraw-Hill.
1936 Politics: Who Gets What When and How. New York: McGraw-Hill.
1948 Power and Personality. New York: Viking.

Lazarsfeld, Paul F.; Bernard Berelson; and Hazel Gaudet.
1948 The People's Choice. New York: Columbia University Press.

Lerner, Daniel.
1958 The Passing of Traditional Society. Glencoe, Illinois: Free Press.

Lerner, Daniel, and Morton Gorden.
1969 Euratlantica. Cambridge, Massachusetts: M.I.T. Press.

Levin, Murray.
1960 The Alienated Voter. New York: Holt, Rinehart and Winston.

LeVine, Robert A.
1965 "Socialization, social structure and intersocietal images," in Herbert C. Kelman (ed.), International Behavior: A Social-Psychological Analysis. New York: Holt, Rinehart and Winston.

Levinson, Daniel J.
1958 "The relevance of personality to political participation." Public Opinion Quarterly 22:3–10.

Lindenfeld, Frank.
1964 "Economic interest and political involvement." Public Opinion Quarterly 28:104–111.

Lippmann, Walter.
1922 Public Opinion. New York: Harcourt Brace.

Lipset, Seymour M.
1960 Political Man. Garden City, New York: Doubleday.

Lipset, Seymour M.; Paul F. Lazarsfeld; Allen H. Barton; and Juan Linz.

1954 "The psychology of voting." Chapter 30 in Gardner Lindzey (ed.), Handbook of Social Psychology. Volume 2. Reading, Massachusetts: Addison-Wesley.

Lipset, Seymour M., and Earl Raab.
1970 The Politics of Unreason: Right-Wing Extremism in America, 1790–1970. New York: Harper and Row.

Lipsky, Michael.
1970 Protest in City Politics: Rent Strikes, Housing, and the Power of the Poor. Chicago. Rand McNally.

Locke, John.
1960 An Essay Concerning the True Origin, Extent and End of Civil Government. London. Also New York: Oxford University Press, 1948.

London, Harvey; Philip J. Meldman; and A. Van C. Lanckton.
1970 "The jury method: How the persuader persuades." Public Opinion Quarterly 34:171–183.

Lowi, Theodore.
1969 The End of Liberalism: Ideology, Policy, and the Crisis of Public Authority. New York: Norton.

Lowi, Theodore (ed.).
1968 Private Life and Public Order. New York: Norton.

Lubell, Samuel.
1968 "That 'generation gap,'" in Daniel Bell and Irving Kristol (eds.), Confrontation; the Student Rebellion and the Universities. New York: Basic Books.

McClosky, Herbert.
1959 "Primary group influence on party loyalty." American Political Science Review 53:757–776.
1964 "Consensus and ideology in American politics." American Political Science Review 58:361–382.

McConaughy, John B.
1950 "Certain personality factors in state legislators in South Carolina." American Political Science Review 44:897–903.

McConnell, Grant.
1966 Private Power and American Democracy. New York: Knopf.

McCrae, Duncan, Jr.
1952 "The relation between roll call votes and constitutencies in the Massachusetts house of representatives." American Political Science Review 46:1046–1055.
1958 Dimensions of Congressional Voting. Berkeley: University of California Press.
1965 "A method for identifying issues and factions from legislative votes." American Political Science Review 59:909–926.

McCrone, Donald J., and Charles F. Cnudde.
1967 "Toward a communication theory of democratic political development: A causal model." American Political Science Review 61:72–79.

McGrath, J. E. ,and M. F. McGrath.
1962 "Effects of partisanship on perception of political figures." Public Opinion Quarterly 26:236–248.

McLeod, Jack; Scott Ward; and Karen Tancill.
1965 "Alienation and uses of the mass media." Public Opinion Quarterly 29:583–594.

McLuhan, Marshall.
1964 Understanding Media. New York: McGraw-Hill.

McPhee, William N., and William A. Glaser (eds.).
1962 Public Opinion and American Democracy. New York: Knopf.

Madison, James.
1901 "Paper No. 10," in Alexander Hamilton, James Madison, and John Jay, The Federalist. New York: Wiley.

Maisel, Richard.
1970 Study of the Impact of Public Events on the American Public. Cambridge, Massachusetts: Laboratory of Community Psychiatry, Harvard Medical School.

Mannheim, Karl.
1940 Ideology and Utopia. New York: Harcourt Brace.

Marris, Peter, and Martin Rein.
1967 Dilemmas of Social Reform: Poverty and Community Action in the United States. New York: Atherton Press.

Matthews, Donald R., and James W. Prothro.
1966 Negroes and the New Southern Politics. New York: Harcourt, Brace and World.

Merriam, Charles E., and Harold Foote Gosnell.
1924 Non-Voting. Chicago: University of Chicago Press.

Michels, Roberto.
1915 Political Parties. Translated by Eden and Cedar Paul. New York: Hearst's International Library. Also New York: Free Press, 1966.

Milbrath, Lester.
1963 The Washington Lobbyist. Chicago: Rand McNally.
1965 Political Participation. Chicago: Rand McNally.

Miller, Warren E.
1955 "Presidential coattails: A study in political myth and methodology." Public Opinion Quarterly 19:353–368.
1970 "Majority rule and the representative system of government," in Erik Allardt and Stein Rokkan (eds.), Mass Politics: Studies in Political Sociology. New York: Free Press.

Miller, Warren E., and Donald E. Stokes.
1963 "Constituency influence in congress." American Political Science Review 57:45–56.

Mitscherlich, Alexander.
1969 Society Without the Father. London: Tavistock.

Moore, Wilbert E., and Melvin N. Tumin.
1949 "Some social functions of ignorance." American Sociological Review 14: 787–795.

Mosca, Gaetano.
1939 The Ruling Class. New York: McGraw-Hill.

Moynihan, Daniel P.
1970 Maximum Feasible Misunderstanding: Community Action in the War on Poverty. New York: Free Press.

Mueller, John E.
1970 "Presidential poularity from Truman to Johnson." American Political Science Review 64:18–34.

Munger, Frank, and James Blackhurst.
1965 "Factionalism in the national conventions, 1940–1964: An analysis of ideological consistency in state delegation voting." Journal of Politics 27:375–394.

Murphy, Gardner, and Rensis Likert.
1967 Public Opinion and the Individual: A Psychological Study of Student Attitudes on Public Questions. With a Retest Five Years Later. New York: Russell and Russell.

Neal, Arthur G., and Salomon Rettig.
1967 "On the multidimensionality of alienation." American Sociological Review 32:54–64.

Nettl, J. P.
1967 Political Mobilization. London: Faber and Faber.

Neubauer, Deane E.
1967 "Some conditions of democracy." American Political Science Review 61:1002–1009.

Nie, Norman H.; G. Bingham Powell, Jr.; and Kenneth Prewitt.
1969 "Social structure and political participation." American Political Science Review 63:808–832.

Nisbet, Robert A.
1953 The Quest for Community. New York: Oxford University Press.

Olsen, Marvin E.
1970 "Social and political participation of blacks." American Sociological Review 35:682–697.

Orum, Anthony M.
1966 "A reappraisal of social and political participation of Negroes." American Journal of Sociology 72:32–46.

Ostrogorski, Moisei.
1902 Democracy and the Organization of Political Parties. Translated by Frederick Clarke. New York: Macmillan.

Parenti, Michael.
1967 "Ethnic politics and the persistence of ethnic identification." American Political Science Review 61:717–726.

Pareto, Vilfredo.
1935 Mind and Society. New York: Harcourt Brace.

Patterson, Samuel C.
1962 "Dimensions of voting behavior in a one-party state legislature." Public Opinion Quarterly 26:185–200.

Peel, Roy V.
1935 The Political Clubs of New York City. New York: Putman.

Pennock, J. Roland, and John W. Chapman.
1968 Nomos X: Representation. New York: Atherton Press.

Perlmutter, Howard.
1956 "Correlates of two types of xenophilic orientation." Journal of Abnormal and Social Psychology 52:130–135.
1957 "Some relationships between xenophilic attitudes and authoritarianism

among Americans abroad." Psychological Reports 3:131–137.

Perlmutter, Howard, and Jerome S. Bruner.
1957 "Compatriot and foreigner: A study of impression formation in three countries." Journal of Abnormal and Social Psychology 55:253–260.

Peterson, Paul E.
1970 "Forms of representation: Participation of the poor in the community action program." American Political Science Review 64:491–507.

Pitkin, Hanna F.
1967 The Concept of Representation. Berkeley: University of California Press.

Polsby, Nelson.
1963 Community Power and Political Theory. New Haven, Connecticut: Yale University Press.
1969 "An emerging Republican majority?" The Public Interest No. 17:119–126.

Pomper, Gerald M.
1968 Elections in America: Control and Influence in Democratic Politics. New York: Dodd, Mead.

Pool, Ithiel de Sola.
1959 "TV: A new dimension in politics," in Eugene Burdick and Arthur J. Brodbeck (ed.), American Voting Behavior. Glencoe, Illinois: Free Press.
1965 "Effects of cross-national contact on national and international images," in Herbert C. Kelman (ed.), International Behavior: A Social-Psychological Analysis. New York: Holt, Rinehart and Winston.
1967 Contemporary Political Science. New York: McGraw-Hill.
1970 The Prestige Press: A Comparative Study of Political Symbols. Cambridge, Massachusetts: M.I.T. Press.

Pool, Ithiel de Sola; Robert P. Abelson; and Samuel Popkin.
1965 Candidates, Issues, and Strategies. Second Edition. Cambridge, Massachusetts: M.I.T. Press.

President of the United States.
1963 Report of the President's Commission on Registration and Voting Participation. Washington, D.C.: U.S. Government Printing Office.

Price, H. Douglas.
1957 The Negro and Southern Politics. New York: New York University Press.

Prothro, James W., and Charles M. Gregg.
1960 "Fundamental principles of democracy." Journal of Politics 22:276–294.

Pye, Lucian.
1961 "Personal identity and political ideology." Behavioral Science 6: 205–221.

Rae, Douglas W.
1967 The Political Consequences of Electoral Laws. New Haven, Connecticut: Yale University Press.

Redl, Fritz.
1942 "Group emotion and leadership." Psychiatry 5:571–596.

Rieselbach, Leroy N.
1964 "The demography of the congressional vote on foreign aid, 1939–1958." American Political Science Review 58:577–588.

Riesman, David, and Nathan Glazer.
1950 "Criteria for political apathy," in Alvin W. Gouldner (ed.), Studies in Leadership. New York: Harper.

Riker, William.
1962 The Theory of Political Coalitions. New Haven, Connecticut: Yale University Press.
1956 Democracy in the United States. Second Edition. New York: Macmillan.

Riker, William H., and Peter C. Ordeshook.
1968 "A theory of the calculus of voting." American Political Science Review 62:25–42.

Robinson, James A. (ed.).
1970 Political Science Annual: An International Review. Volume 2:1969–70. Indianapolis: Bobbs-Merrill.

Robinson, John P.
1967 Public Information About World Affairs. Ann Arbor: Survey Research Center.

Robinson, John P., and Solomon G. Jacobson.
1969 "American public opinion about Vietnam," in Walter Isard (ed.), Vietnam: Some basic Issues and Alternatives. Cambridge, Massachusetts: Schenkman.

Robinson, John P.; Jerrold G. Rusk; and Kendra B. Head.
1968 Measures of Political Attitudes. Ann Arbor, Michigan: Survey Research Center.

Robinson, John P., and Philip R. Shaver.
1969 Measures of Social Psychological Attitudes. Ann Arbor, Michigan: Survey Research Center.

Rogow, Arnold.
1963 James Forrestal. New York: Macmillan.

Rokeach, Milton.
1960 The Open and Closed Mind. New York: Basic Books.

Rokkan, Stein, and Jean Meyriat (eds.).
1969 International Guide to Electoral Statistics. Volume 1: Western Europe. The Hague: Mouton.

Rommetveit, Ragnar.
1960 Selectivity, Intuition, and Halo Effects in Social Perception. Oslo: Oslo University Press.

Roper, Elmo.
1961 "How to lose your vote." Saturday Review (March 18): 14–15.

Rose, Richard.
1967 Influencing Voters: A Study of Campaign Rationality. New York: St. Martin's Press.

Rosenau, James N.
1961 Public Opinion and Foreign Policy. New York: Random House.
1968 The Attentive Public and Foreign Policy: A Theory of Growth and Some New Evidence. Princeton: Center of International Studies.

Rosenberg, Milton J.; Sidney Verba; and Philip E. Converse.
1970 Vietnam and the Silent Majority. New York: Harper and Row.

Rosenberg, Morris.
1954 "Some determinants of political apathy." Public Opinion Quarterly 18:349–366.
1962 "Self-esteem and concern with public affairs." Public Opinion Quarterly 26:201–211.

Ross, J. F. S.
1955 Elections and Electors: Studies in Democratic Representation. London: Eyre and Spottiswoode.

Rousseau, Jean Jacques.
1762 The Social Contract. Amsterdam.

Rubin, Bernard.
1967 Political Television. Belmont, California: Wadsworth.

Russett, Bruce M.
1963 Community and Contention: Britain and America in the Twentieth Century. Cambridge, Massachusetts: M.I.T. Press.

Sarbin, Theodore R.; Ronald Taft; and Daniel Bailey.
1960 Clinical Inference and Cognitive Theory. New York: Holt, Rinehart and Winston.

Scammon, Richard M.
1956–68 American Votes. Volumes 1–8. New York: Macmillan.
1965 America at the Polls: The Vote for President, 1920–1964. Pittsburgh: University of Pittsburgh Press.

Scammon, Richard M., and Ben J. Wattenberg.
1970 The Real Majority. New York: Coward-McCann.

Schoenberger, Robert A.
1968 "Conservatism, personality and political extremism." American Political Science Review 62:868–877.

Schramm, Wilbur.
1949 "The nature of news." Journalism Quarterly 26:259–269.

Schramm, Wilbur; Jack Lyle; and Ithiel de Sola Pool.
1963 The People Look at Education Television. Stanford, California: Stanford University Press.

Schumpeter, Joseph A.
1942 Capitalism, Socialism, Democracy. New York: Harper.

Scott, William A.
1965 "Psychological and social correlates of international images," in Herbert C. Kelman (ed.), International Behavior: A Social-Psychological Analysis. New York: Holt, Rinehart and Winston.

Sears, David O.
1969 "Political behavior," in Gardner Lindzey and Elliot Aronson (eds.), Handbook of Social Psychology. Volume 5. Second Edition. Reading, Massachusetts: Addison-Wesley.

Sears, David O.; J. L. Freedman; and E. F. O'Connor.
1964 "The effects of anticipated debate and commitment on the polarization of audience opinion." Public Opinion Quarterly 28:615–627.

Shils, Edward A.
1954 "Authoritarianism: 'Right' and 'left.'" Pp. 24–49 in Richard Christie and Marie Jahoda (eds.), Studies in the Scope and Method of the

Authoritarian Personality. Glencoe, Illinois: Free Press.

Sigel, Roberta S.
1964 "Effect of partisanship on the perception of political candidates." Public Opinion Quarterly 28:483–496.
1970 Learning About Politics: A Reader in Political Socialization. New York: Random House.

Simmel, Georg.
1950 The Sociology of Georg Simmel. Glencoe, Illinois : Free Press.

Simpson, G. E., and J. Milton Yinger.
1958 Racial and Cultural Minorities. New York: Harper.

Skolnick, Jerome.
1969 The Politics of Protest. New York: Simon and Schuster.

Slote, Walter.
1967 "Case analysis of a revolutionary," in Frank Bonilla and J. A. Silva-Michelena (eds.), A Strategy for Research on Social Policy. Volume 1: The Politics of Change in Venezuela. Cambridge, Massachusetts: M.I.T. Press.

Smith, David H.
1966 "A psychological model of individual participation in voluntary organizations: Application to some Chilean data." American Journal of Sociology 72:249–266.

Smith, M. Brewster; Jerome M. Bruner; and R. W. White.
1956 Opinions and Personality. New York: Wiley.

Smith, T. E.
1960 Elections in Developing Countries: A Study of Electoral Procedures Used in Tropical Africa, Southeast Asia, and the British Caribbean. New York: St. Martin's Press

Speier, Hans.
1950 "The historical development of public opinion." American Journal of Sociology 55:376–388.

Star, Shirley, and Helen MacGill Hughes.
1950 "Report on an educational campaign: The Cincinnati plan for the United Nations." American Journal of Sociology 55:389–400.

Steiner, Gary.
1963 The People Look at Television. New York: Knopf.

Stephens, William N., and Stephen C. Long.
1970 "Education and political behavior," in James A. Robinson (ed.), Political Science Annual: An International Review Volume 2: 1969–70. Indianapolis: Bobbs-Merrill.

Stephenson, William.
1964 "The Ludenic theory of newsreading." Journalism Quarterly 41:367–374.
1967 The Play Theory of Mass Communication. Chicago: University of Chicago Press.

Stokes, Donald E., and G. R. Iversen.
1962 "On the existence of forces restoring party competition." Public Opinion Quarterly 26:159–171.

Stouffer, Samuel.
1955 Communism, Conformity, and Civil Liberties. Garden City, New York: Doubleday.

Struening, E. L., and A. H. Richardson.
1965 "A factor analytic exploration of the alienation, anomie, and authoritarianism domain." American Sociological Review 30:768–776.

Sundquist, James L. (ed.).
1969 On Fighting Poverty: Perspectives from Experience. New York: Basic Books.

Sussman, Leila.
1963 Dear FDR: A Study of Political Letter Writing. Englewood Cliffs, New Jersey: Bedminster Press.

Tagiuri, Renato.
1968 "Person perception." Pp. 560–567 in David L. Sills (ed.), International Encyclopedia of the Social Sciences. Volume 11. New York: Macmillan.

Tagiuri, Renato, and Lugi Petrullo (eds.).
1958 Person Perception and Interpersonal Behavior. Stanford, California: Stanford University Press.

Templeton, Fredr ic.
1966 "Alienation and political participation." Public Opinion Quarterly 30:249–261.

Tingsten, Herbert.
1963 Political Behavior: Studies in Election Statistics. Translated by Vilgot Mammerling. Englewood Cliffs, New Jersey: Bedminster Press.

Titus, C. N.
1935 Voting Behavior in the United States.

Berkeley: University of California Press.

Titus, H. E., and E. P. Holland.
1957 "The California F-scale in psychological research: 1950–1955." Psychological Bulletin 54:47–64.

Tocqueville, Alexis de.
1835–40 Democracy in America. 4 volumes. Paris. Translated by Henry Reeve; edited by Phillips Bradley. 2 volumes. New York: Knopf, 1945.

Torgersen, V. I. F.
1970 "The trend toward political consensus: The case of Norway," in Erik Allardt and Stein Rokkan (eds.), Mass Politics: Studies in Political Sociology. New York: Free Press.

Truman, David.
1951 The Governmental Process. New York: Knopf.

Verba, Sidney; Richard A. Brody; et al.
1967 "Public opinion and the war in Vietnam." American Political Science Review 61:317–333.

Verba, Sidney, and Norman H. Nie.
1972 Participation in America: Political Democracy and Social Equality. New York: Harper and Row.

Walker, Jack L.
1966 "A critique of the elitist theory of democracy." American Political Science Review 60:258–295.

Warner, W. Lloyd, and William E. Henry.
1948 "The radio daytime serial: A symbolic analysis." Genetic Psychology Monographs 37:3–71.

Warner, W. Lloyd, and Paul S. Lunt.
1941 The Social Life of a Modern Community. New Haven: Yale University Press.

Weber, Max.
1919 Politics as a Vocation. Munich: Duncker and Humboldt. Reprinted in H. H. Gerth and C. Wright Mills (eds.), From Max Weber: Essays in Sociology. New York: Oxford University Press, 1958.

Wells, William D.
1961 "The influence of yeasaying response style." Journal of Advertising Research 1(No. 4):1–12.
1963 "How chronic overclaimers distort survey findings." Journal of Advertising Research 3(No. 2):8–18.

Whale, John.
1969 The Half-Shut Eye: Television and Politics in Britain and America. New York: St. Martin's Press.

Wilson, Francis G.
1962 A Theory of Public Opinion. Chicago: Regnery.

Wilson, James O.
1960 Negro Politics: The Search for Identity. New York: Free Press of Glencoe.
1966 The Amateur Democrat. Chicago: University of Chicago Press.

Winham, Gilbert.
1970 "Political development and Lerner's theory: Further test of a causal model." American Political Science Review 64:810–818.

Wolfenstein, E. Victor.
1967 The Revolutionary Personality: Lenin, Trotsky, and Gandhi. Princeton, New Jersey: Princeton University Press.

Wolfenstein, Martha, and Gilbert Kliman (eds.).
1965 Children and the Death of a President. Garden City, New York: Doubleday.

Wolfinger, Raymond.
1965 "The development and persistence of ethnic voting." American Political Science Review 59:896–908.

Wood, David M.
1968 "Majority vs. opposition in the French national assembly, 1956–1965: A Guttman scale analysis." American Political Science Review 62:88–109.

Woodward, Julian L., and Elmo Roper.
1950 "Political activity of American citizens." American Political Science Review 44:872–885.

Wright, Charles R., and Herbert H. Hyman.
1958 "Voluntary association memberships of American adults: Evidence from national sample surveys." American Sociological Review 23:284–294.

Wyant, Rowena, and Herta Herzog.
1941 "Voting via the Senate's mailbag." Public Opinion Quarterly 5 (Fall): 359–382; 5 (Winter):590–624.

Yankelovich, Daniel.
1971 Youth and the Establishment. New York: JDR 3d Fund.

CHAPTER 26 Bargaining and Communication

FRED CHARLES IKLE
The Rand Corporation

Among the most important communications are those that take place when parties with partially opposed objectives sit down to negotiate with each other. Whether the opponents be nations, management and union, buyer and seller, or legislators on a committee, the principles of bargaining they use are much the same.

The literature on bargaining stems largely from economics and from the mathematical theory of games. Most of it deals with the equilibrium points that would be reached in bargaining between fully rational opponents. Much less of it tries, as Dr. Iklé does, to describe the process of diplomatic exchanges between opponents.

One merit of Dr. Iklé's analysis is that it helps us correct the inevitable tendency of any compendium on communication to focus primarily on communications that persuade. Indeed, in a large class of communication situations people do talk to each other, hoping that the listener will come to accept the content of the speaker's message as something that he, too, believes in. That is not the usual purpose of communication in bargaining, however. In real-life bargaining the communication is between recognized opponents who can rarely be expected to convert each other. In the conflict situations analyzed in this chapter, communication serves such purposes as signaling intent of action, redirecting the opponent's attention, filling time, confusing the opponent, informing the opponent of crucial facts, and affecting the support offered by allies and backers who overhear what the opponents say to each other.

All bargaining requires communication. In fact, almost all the action in bargaining consists of communication if the term *communication* is defined broadly enough to include everything that a party does to make its opponent aware of its wishes, intentions, and interpretations of the adversary relationship. In everyday interpersonal bargaining, opponents communicate with words, signals, or gestures. In international negotiations, the parties may also communicate through their military postures, economic measures, and other policy changes. Even such moves as personnel changes can be used to communicate in a bargaining situation: for instance, the replacement of a "dove" by a "hawk" in a key government position can convey a threat.

THE ESSENCE OF BARGAINING

Bargaining can be defined as a process of interaction between two or more parties for the purpose of reaching an agreement on an exchange, or an agreement to satisfy a common interest where conflicting interests are present. The agreement may be explicit (for instance, expressed in a contract) or tacit (that is, an unspoken mutual understanding). Agreement, by definition, is the coincidence of offer and acceptance, both of which are acts of communication. Three conditions are necessary for bargaining to occur:

1. The parties must have some common interests, which means that they jointly prefer certain outcomes over other possible outcomes (e.g., the joint preference that war not break out, or that a sale take place).
2. The parties must have conflicting interests, which means that some of the jointly preferred outcomes are better for one party whereas others are better for the other party (e.g., divergent preferences regarding the conditions under which a conflict is settled short of war, or regarding the price of a sale).
3. The parties must be able to communicate somehow.

It is useful to distinguish between *negotiation* as a form of bargaining where explicit proposals are being put forward, and *tacit bargaining* where the parties do not explicitly propose terms or explicitly consent to a settlement. Note, however, that in negotiation the explicit exchanges are only part of the bargaining process. In international negotiation, especiably, the most important moves are often tacit, while the verbal exchange is secondary.

Bargaining can also be examined in terms of economic variables alone. Indeed, for many real-life bargaining situations, the essentials are explainable with the concepts and language of economics (Cross, 1969). Yet, the role of communications in bargaining tends to be oversimplified in such approaches, and other social and psychological aspects, of course, fall outside an economic analysis.

The basic moves in bargaining and negotiation are commitments and threats. A *commitment* can be defined as an action whereby one party changes his *own* incentives in order to alter the opponent's expectations about his future conduct. That is, one party seeks to convince his opponent that he will carry out some prediction (such as holding firm or implementing a threat) by making it more difficult for himself not to do so—in other words, by committing himself.

A *threat* can be defined as a special kind of conditional prediction that a party addresses to his opponent. To threaten is to let one's opponent know that, should he fail to comply with your position, you will make a special effort to inflict a certain damage on him (Ikle, 1964; 1968).

Since the nuclear era, the concept of the threat has been extensively analyzed in writings on military strategy and disarmament. Nuclear deterrence, of course, is based on a threat. A key question about threats is their credibility: Will they be carried out if the opponent fails to comply, or will the first party be "caught bluffing"? To make threats more credible, they are usually buttressed by commitments.

THE FUNCTION OF LYING AND TRUTHFULNESS

As seen by the opponents in a bargaining situation, communication ordinarily serves to convey some truthful information as well as to give false information (or at least to conceal the truth). If one or both parties conveyed either only false or only truthful information, bargaining would tend to atrophy. Thus, if a party became known to give information that is almost invariably false, its threats and commitments would lose credibility, while its offers to agree would lose all value. If, on the other hand, a party consistently conveyed truthful information, its explicit commitments and threats would become highly rigid. With complete truthfulness, every explicit threat would be carried out whenever the opponent failed to comply, and every explicit commitment would be upheld. For instance, if a completely truthful seller argued that he would not accept a lower price, he would in fact be predicting with certainty that a sale at a lower price will never take place.

If the definition of truthfulness is extended to mean that the parties not only abstain from knowingly making false statements but also fully reveal their intended moves and their own (cardinal) preferences, the process of bargaining atrophies to a "game with complete information" (in the mathematical game-theory sense of the term). The outcome is then given by the parties' payoff structure. Stated in this form, the fact that bargaining is incompatible with completely truthful communication sounds like a truism. However, in many proposed "rules" for negotiators, the requirement for and complexity of *partial* truthfulness is lost sight of.

To exploit the common interests in a bargaining situation, the parties can often benefit from mutual frankness. Of course, the more they are like partners engaged in common enterprises—rather than like hostile antagonists—the better can they jointly search for common interests. This search takes the form of discovering, or inventing, outcomes that leave both parties better off—a process that will be facilitated if the parties reveal their true preferences. Thus, bargaining can become partly common problem solving (Walton & McKersie, 1965: 356–357; Shure & Meeker, 1969).

MISUNDERSTANDINGS AND LONG-TERM CONDITIONS

The possibility for exploring common interests is related to the notion that conflict frequently stems from misunderstandings. The valid core of this notion must be separated from unwarranted extensions. Of course, the proposition that conflict would be eliminated if people (or nations) understood each other better can become tautologically true, depending on the definition of "understanding." But the view that people and nations would overcome their conflicts if only they could better communicate their objectives and intentions to each other is based on too rosy a picture of the world. Indeed, one can easily find illustrations where a full communication of antagonistic objectives would only have deepened existing conflicts. Also, evidence from experiments in interpersonal bargaining indicate that the opponents would have been unable to converge on certain mutually advantageous outcomes had they had more complete information about each other's payoffs (Shure & Meeker, 1969).

One of the interesting features of the "prisoner's dilemma" game is the very fact that the parties' knowledge of the opponent's payoff matrix does not help in resolving the conflict. Indeed, one can invent "prisoner's dilemma" games where misinformation between the parties would help both sides to achieve a better outcome. If communication between the parties cannot be blocked or used for misinformation, the mutually deleterious outcomes of a "prisoner's dilemma" will be avoided only if the parties remain concerned about a long-term "super game," that is to say, if they expect and plan for recurrent conflicts of the "prisoner's dilemma" type.

The valid core of the notion that conflict can be reduced through better communication has several elements:

First, there is the before-mentioned possibility that through frank discussion the parties can discover new outcomes that are to their mutual advantage.

Second, if the actual differences between parties have been exaggerated, better communication will help to reduce antagonistic feelings.

Third, clear communication of a commitment or threat can help to deter the opponent from an initiative that would exacerbate the conflict. That is to say, if a party really means to carry out its threat or to stick with a commitment, and if the opponent will yield if he learns of this determination, communicating firmness obviously helps to prevent a clash. Since World War II, this thought has found wide expression in the literature on international relations and nuclear deterrence. For instance, it has often been argued that the Communist attack on South Korea would not have taken place had the United States made it clear that it would come to South Korea's help.

Fourth, communication in bargaining serves what might be called a "systemic" purpose, that is, the purpose of altering the long-term relationship with the opponent rather than the outcome of a particular negotiation. Indeed, the full implications of threats and commitments cannot be ascertained realistically without reference to long-term expectations among the parties. In simulation experiments in bargaining, where subjects (say, college students) take the role of parties, it is most difficult, if not impossible, to introduce realistically these long-term expectations and the processes by which they change. This is one reason why the results of simulation studies of threats are difficult to apply to real-life situations.

Another reason for the limited applicability of game experiments is the richness and importance of the context of bargaining situations, which modifies the nature and functioning of threats and commitments. As one reviewer of the extensive literature on such games observed:

> Game experiments on "threat" have shown most clearly the futility of posing psychological hypotheses containing terms like "threat" in a way that suggests the existence of a "theory of behavior under threat." Hypotheses so formulated cannot be tested, because the "threat conditions" set up by different investigators may have little in common except a designation as such (Journal of Conflict Resolution, 1970:65).

Even if the researcher is prepared to disregard the long-term context (or "super game") in his gaming experiments, he will find it difficult to operationalize the concept of threat. Several otherwise interesting experiments have been criticized on this score (Kelley, 1962).

Since full communication of a threat or commitment is required to make it effective, the opponent, whose bargaining position is supposed to be softened by such moves, may have an interest in not receiving this communication. The efficacy of this "burning of communications bridges" has been observed in the way children bargain with parents, in day-to-day bargaining among adults, and even in labor-management negotiations (Schelling, 1960: 17–18, 146–150; Walton & McKersie, 1965:113–115). It has much less application in international negotiations for the simple reason that modern governments cannot convincingly pretend that they do not hear messages that the opponent broadcasts to them. (Sometimes governments refuse to accept a diplomatic note that a messenger from a foreign embassy attempts to deliver. This occasional practice has symbolic meaning only: it conveys strong disapproval or disdain regarding the content of the note, or underlines the lack of diplomatic relations with the sender country; but it cannot mean that the message has not been heard.)

AMBIGUITY vs. SPECIFICITY

Ambiguity has several important effects in negotiation. On the one hand, ambiguous agreements can lead to a reopening of the conflict later on. On the other hand, an attempt to introduce specificity might prolong negotiation or even prevent agreement altogether. Hence, parties often tolerate ambiguous agreement deliberately, thereby postponing the residual points of disagreement—perhaps in the hope that these would never lead to conflict. Ambiguity in an agreement can also be unintended, resulting from inadequate communication between the parties regarding each other's understanding of the terms on which they converge.

In international negotiation, particularly in East-West conferences, a great deal of time is sometimes spent in disputes about how specific an agreement should be made. These disputes are essentially a symptom of disagreement about the substance of the settlement, not about its form. If there were agreement on the substance of the settlement, there should, on the one hand, be no objection to spelling it out in detail and, on the other, little interest in recording the details. If a party objects to giving an agreement greater specificity, this is usually a concealed way of communicating that there is continuing disagreement. Sometimes, disputes about how specific an agreement should be can stem from different preferences as to how much latitude future mediators should have (Ikle, 1964:8–15).

Ambiguity in conveying commitments or threats serves to soften these moves. Thus, an ambiguous threat is unspecific concerning either the occasion when the threatened action would occur or the content of that action. From the point of view of the threatening party, an ambiguous threat has the disadvantage of being less credible, but the advantage of allowing more freedom to react mildly without proving oneself a bluffer. Moreover, the opponent might give in (or stay deterred) regardless, since he, too, faces uncertainty.

PROPAGANDA AND RHETORICAL DEBATE

If the bargaining parties are not private individuals, but organizations or institutions (such as governments or labor unions), the communication flow affects third parties as well as the internal bureaucracy of each party. Consequently, much of what is said in negotiations may be addressed to (1) outsiders, in the hope that they in turn would influence the opponent (for instance, through propaganda to affect "world opinion"); or (2) one's own internal bureaucracy. Representatives of labor unions have to make statements for the benefit of rank-and-file membership; government delegates at international conferences may have to address themselves to interagency conflicts back home or to domestic public opinion. Indeed, such internal audiences are often the only justification for the negotiator's rhetoric.

The exchange of words across the conference table thus is only partly relevant to the outcome and, even when relevant to the outcome, is often effective indirectly through third parties. This limited relevance can be analyzed in more detail:

1. Weak rhetoric at the conference table may lead to weak delegation reports to the home government. The delegate at the conference site, as a result of his ineffectiveness in debating tactics, may get the impression that his government's position is difficult to defend and that the opponent is unlikely to budge. Hence, he will report to his government that the opponent's position is firm and advise making a concession. (This hypothesis might be tested by correlating weak defenses at the conference table with the recommendations that the delegation sends back home afterwards.) The same applies to the conference talk between delegates of nongovernmental organizations, such as labor unions and business corporations.

2. Weak rhetoric at the conference makes it easier for "soft" allies to maneuver a party into concessions. If the opposing sides are strong adversaries, the rhetorical aspects of the debate will have little direct effect on their positions, since the relationship between such opponents cannot be affected much by words alone. However, *within* a team of close allies (such as the United States and the United Kingdom in the nuclear test ban negotiations), where words *are* used to settle differences, the "rhetorical loss" of a point with the common opponent might lead to the "forensic loss" of the same point in the private debate with an ally who prefers to soften the com-

mon allied position. Thus, while the rhetoric in long-winded negotiations may have little effect on "world opinion" because the news media will have long ceased to pay attention to it, debating defeats might, nonetheless, be exploited by allies (the ever-present witnesses at the green table) in the private forum where the interallied policy is hammered out.

3. In a protracted conference where little real bargaining occurs, the formal debates may nonetheless generate major themes that become part of the agenda or the negotiating position for subsequent bargaining. This may be a deliberate tactic of one or the other party, or it may be inadvertent. In the 1957 London Disarmament Conference, principal aspects of the nuclear test ban—such as the moratorium and the isolation from other arms controls—were already raised to such a status during the prolonged debates that it would have been hard to reject them out of hand when the real negotiations started a year later (Zoppo, 1961).

4. Sometimes negotiators at the conference table—like human beings in other situations—talk without really knowing what they wish to accomplish with their words. That is, communication during bargaining situations may serve no bargaining purpose at all—or, at the most, may serve merely to fill the time until new conditions lead to a change in the position of one or the other side.

One of the advantages of mediation is that it tends to do away with the largely dysfunctional rhetoric so common in direct negotiations. Part of the function of a mediator is to facilitate, as well as to filter, communication between opponents. Proposals and counterproposals conveyed through a mediator are more tentative, since the mediator can be more easily disavowed than an official delegate. Also, a mediator, not being part of the bureaucracies of either side, does not have to insert statements addressed to these home constituencies.

SUMMARY

The many functions of communication in bargaining situations can be grouped as follows:

1. Communication, especially of the explicit, verbal type, serves to convey or to accept offers. When an offer is made very precisely and explicitly, or when an acceptance is final, the statements of the negotiator become, in part, "performative sentences" (in J. L. Austin's meaning of this term). That is, the very saying of the sentence is also the act described in this sentence: e.g., "my government offers, . . ." "I accept" (Austin, 1965).
2. Communication, explicit as well as tacit, is used to change the opponent's expectations as to the probable outcome from the time bargaining begins until agreement is reached or contact is broken off.
   a) Expectations are changed through the terms of offers and counteroffers (they convey the range of the outcome), as well as through commitments (they indicate the probability that a position will be maintained) and through threats (they alter the expected loss in the event no agreement is reached).
   b) In addition, the way in which offers are conveyed and the language used to describe the issues can highlight one particular outcome within a range. The communications signal a "focal point" toward which the opponent's (and perhaps one's own) expectations regarding the outcome are being guided (Schelling, 1960: 111–113).
3. Communications between the opponents can also accomplish changes in the way in which they *evaluate* alternative outcomes. In interpersonal bargaining, this may take the form of direct persuasion. In international negotiations, direct persuasion be-

tween opposing governments occurs rarely. Nonetheless, in prolonged international negotiations, a similar, although somewhat more indirect, process can be of prime importance. The ways in which the parties evaluate their own payoffs and those of their opponent can be changed gradually, not because diplomats are such persuasive people, but because these evaluations are highly complex, often result from intricate intragovernmental compromises, and involve a great deal of uncertainty. Hence, the gain and loss calculations regarding specific outcomes tend to be uncertain and can be modified by the casualness or reluctance with which a concession is given, the way in which a certain outcome is labeled, the boundaries that are drawn around the bargaining issues, and other ways of defining or describing the situation (Ikle, 1964: chap. 10).

This change in the evaluation of a specific outcome should not be confused with a change in expectations as to the characteristics of possible outcomes. (The former, for instance, would be the view that a certain territorial settlement means a loss or a gain. The latter would be the expectation that agreement can be reached that the eighteenth or nineteenth parallel will become the new boundary.) Incidentally, diplomatic histories tend to neglect the fact that such a change in evaluations often results from the communications flow in prolonged negotiations.

4. Finally, communication between negotiators serves to reveal new outcomes. The parties, by exchanging information about their preferences and about various constraints and opportunities regarding the issues under negotiation, might help each other to discover or to invent outcomes that would leave both sides better off than with the outcomes initially sought.

REFERENCES

Austin, J. L.
1965 How To Do Things With Words. New York: Oxford University Press.

Cross, John G.
1969 The Economics of Bargaining. New York: Basic Books.

Ikle, Fred C.
1964 How Nations Negotiate. New York: Harper and Row.
1968 "Negotiation." Pp. 117–120 in David L. Sills (ed.), International Encyclopedia of the Social Sciences. Volume 11. New York: Macmillan.

Journal of Confiict Resolution.
1970 "Editorial comments." Journal of Conflict Resolution 14:65.

Kelley, Harold H.
1965 "Experimental studies of threats in interpersonal negotiations." Journal of Conflict Resolution 9:79–105.

Schelling, Thomas C.
1960 The Strategy of Conflict. Cambridge, Massachusetts: Harvard University Press.

Shure, Gerald H., and Robert J. Meeker.
1969 "Bargaining processes in experimental territorial conflict situations." Pp. 109–122 in Walter Isard and Julian Wolpert (eds.), Peace Research Society (International) Papers. Volume 11. Philadelphia: Peace Research Society.

Walton, Richard E., and Robert B. McKersie.
1965 A Behavioral Theory of Labor Negotiations. New York: McGraw-Hill.

Zoppo, Ciro E.
1961 The Issue of Nuclear Test Cessation at the London Disarmament Conference of 1957: A Study in East-West Negotiation. RM-2821-ARPA. Santa Monica, California: Rand Corporation (September).

ADDITIONAL READINGS

Borah, Lee A., Jr. "The Effects of Threat in Bargaining: Critical and Experimental Analysis." *Journal of Abnormal and Social Psychology* 66(1963):37–44.

Hermann, Margaret, and Kogan, Nathan. "Negotiation in Leader and Delegate

Groups." *Journal of Conflict Resolution* 12 (1968): 332–344.

Rapoport, Anatol, and Chammah, A. M. *Prisoner's Dilemma: A Study in Conflict and Cooperation.* Ann Arbor: University of Michigan Press, 1965.

Shubick, Martin. "Some Reflections on the Design of Game Theoretic Models for the Study of Negotiation and Threats." *Journal of Conflict Resolution* 7(1963): 1–12.

———. *Games of Status.* Santa Monica, Calif.: The Rand Corporation, August, 1968.

CHAPTER 27 Propaganda

PAUL KECSKEMETI
Brandeis University

The treatment in this chapter makes use of Max Weber's concept of the "ideal type"; that is, a prototype of the essential form of a concept, not to be confused with a normative ideal of what should be. In the literature on propaganda, one finds a number of ideal types of propaganda. One paradigm uses truth and falsehood to distinguish propaganda from other forms of communication, treating propaganda as a form of lying. A related paradigm distinguishes propaganda from education. The chapter author provides a more useful conceptualization, identifying propaganda as streams of instrumentally manipulated communications from a remote source that seek to establish resonance with an audience's predispositions for the purpose of persuading it to a new view that the propagandist prefers. Among the devices used by the propagandist is "channel sharing": introducing his message into channels that already carry attractive material to which the audience voluntarily turns.

Independently of those who formulate such conceptualizations of what is meant when a communication is called propaganda, empirical researchers in recent years have done extensive content analyses of propaganda output as well as studies of propaganda effects on audiences. Among the models of the means by which propaganda achieves its effects is one derived from conditioned reflex theory. In general, laboratory studies tend to show some effect by the propaganda stimulus on the subject, but sociological studies in the field tend more often to show communications reinforcing or canalizing previous predispositions of the audience rather than effecting conversion.

DEFINITION

The term *propaganda* is taken from the name of the Congregatio de Propaganda Fide, a central organ of the Catholic church established by Pope Gregory XV in 1622 to direct and coordinate the church's missionary activities among non-Christian populations. In modern usage, however, the term is mainly employed in secular contexts. It refers to a variety of disparate promotional activities falling under two main categories, the commercial and political, plus a few less important ones.

Commercial propaganda includes advertising, salesmanship, and public relations operations. In the field of political propaganda, we encounter, to begin with, the activities of political parties and movements aimed at securing acceptance of their doctrines, recruiting adherents, winning votes, and the like. Other types of political propaganda embrace promotional techniques used by governments and regimes to enhance their prestige at home and abroad, maintain domestic morale, and undermine the opponent's morale in hot and cold war.

Propagandistic activities outside the commercial and political field include caritative and public-interest campaigns, efforts to gain popular recognition for scientific theories or artistic styles, the promotion of hygienic principles or fads, and the like.

In order to define propaganda one has to specify those properties that commonly characterize all these activities while differentiating them from all others that are comparable in certain respects. This is a difficult task, and it is not surprising that the definitions put forward in the literature diverge widely.

A plausible common generic trait is that all propaganda uses communications disseminated through various media in order to shape the recipients' beliefs, attitudes, or behavior in accordance with the communicator's intentions. Thus one of the definitions of propaganda in *Webster's Third New International Dictionary* refers to "doctrines, ideas, arguments, facts, or allegations spread by deliberate effort through any medium of communication in order to further one's cause or to damage an opposing cause." The definition given by Qualter (1962:27) refers to the deliberate modification of attitudes by means of communications as the distinctive objective of propaganda:

> Propaganda is the deliberate attempt by some individual or group to form, control or alter the attitudes of other groups by the use of the instruments of communication with the intention that in any given situation the reaction of those so influenced will be that desired by the propagandist.

This type of definition treats propaganda as purely symbolic interaction. But this leaves out the "propaganda of the deed," an important variant of political propaganda (Lasswell, 1934:522). Some definitions of propaganda accordingly dispense with any reference to communications as the specific vehicle of propaganda. Lasswell (1934:521) defines "propaganda in the broadest sense" as "the technique of influencing human action by the manipulation of representations." According to Bernays (1928:25),

> Modern propaganda is a consistent, enduring effort to create or shape events to influence the relations of the public to an enterprise, idea or group.

In order to do justice to "the propaganda of the deed," *Webster's Third* gives, as an additional definition, "a public action or display having the purpose or the effect of furthering or hindering a cause."

The most difficult as well as theoretically most important definitional problems, however, have to do not with what is common to all propagandistic communications, but with what differentiates them from other types that are also meant to shape the recipients' attitudes and behavior yet are not commonly referred to as propagandistic. Examples of such communications are not difficult to find; legal enactments, medical and expert advice, schoolbooks, etc., clearly belong in the second group. Some definitions of propaganda, however, fail to draw this distinction. Thus the Lasswell formula is clearly too broad: not only propagandistic but also nonpropagandistic communications designed to produce behavior effects are "techniques of influencing human action by the manipulation of representations." The same applies to the Qualter definition. Once the distinction is made, however, the proper criteria to set off propagandistic from nonpropagandistic communications raise considerable conceptual problems.

As we shall see, many theorists base the distinction on value criteria (truth versus falsehood, good faith versus manipulation, and so on). Most frequently, education serves as the paradigm of "truthful," nonpropagandistic communications. The employment of value criteria, however, has its pitfalls: it is only too apt to give the theoretical discussion of propaganda a propagandistic tinge.

Among the definitions cited, the most satisfactory ones seem to be those given by the dictionary. They relate the propagandist's intent to a partisan or competitive "cause." A specific difference between propagandistic and nonpropagandistic discourse is set forth in this way without introducing value criteria.

In the following section a number of theoretical views dealing with propaganda as a cultural, social, and political phenomenon will be examined mostly from an evaluative point of view. Next the behavioral effects of propagandistic and other mass communications will be investigated. In conclusion, an approach toward propaganda based upon certain sociological aspects of propagandistic as distinct from nonpropagandistic discourse will be outlined.

CONCEPTUAL APPROACH

Propaganda and Education

The early scholarly literature of propaganda, showing the impact of the propaganda phenomenon as a menace (Lumley, 1933), was primarily concerned with clarifying the conceptual difference between propagandistic (manipulative) and nonpropagandistic (straightforward) communications. A salient theme of the conceptual, ideal-typical treatment of the problem of propaganda was the dichotomy between education and propaganda (Martin, 1932; Lasswell, 1934; Doob, 1948; Bartlett, 1954; Albig, 1956).

Lasswell and Doob sought to characterize the propaganda-education dichotomy in empirical, nonevaluative terms. Lasswell would prefer to restrict the term *education* to the transmission of "techniques such as spelling, letter forming, piano playing, lathe handling and dialectic," and to designate as *propaganda* those techniques by which "value dispositions (hatred or respect toward a person, group or policy) are organized." He adds, however, that in actual usage the "inculcation of traditional value attitudes is generally called education while the term *propaganda* is reserved for the spreading of subversive, debatable or merely novel attitudes" (Lasswell, 1934: 552).

According to Doob (1948:237), education is "the imparting of knowledge or skill considered to be scientific or to have survival value in a society at a particular time." Propaganda, by contrast, is "the attempt to affect the personalities and to control the behavior of individuals toward ends considered unscientific or of doubtful value in a society at a particular time" (Doob, 1948:240).

For both authors, the decisive conceptual criterion differentiating education from propaganda is the existence or nonexistence of consensus in the society concerning the factual truth or normative validity of whatever thesis is being promoted. Agreement on matters on which no consensus prevails can be solicited only in the propagandistic mode. Thus the propagandistic character of any given stream of communications reflects the objective situation with respect to the availability of information, rather than subjective factors such as the communicator's mischievousness. As Doob (1948:244) put it, propaganda, being imposed by the uncertainty of scientific knowledge and survival values, "is absolutely inevitable and cannot be exorcised by calling it evil-sounding names."

The other authors referred to, however, treat the education-propaganda dichotomy as a value contrast. Propaganda "strives for the closed mind rather than the open mind"; the propagandist "merely wishes you to think as he does," while the educator "is so delighted if you think at all that he is willing to let you do it in your own way" (Martin, 1932:29). Propaganda seeks to influence opinion and conduct "in such a manner that the persons who adopt the opinion and behavior indicated do so without themselves making any definite search for reasons"; education influences thinking and conduct in such a manner that those influenced "are stimulated to seek to understand for themselves why they do what they do" (Barlett, 1954:464, 465). "Education endeavors to show people why they think and act as they do.... The objective of the propagandist is to achieve public acceptance of conclusions, not to stimulate the logical analysis of the merits of the case. In this he differs from the avowed objective of the educator under democracy" (Albig, 1956:276, 292).

Contrasting with the ideal type of the democratic educator, the undemocratic propagandist is described as looking down upon his audience, viewing it as a "poor lot [who] are, and should stay, at a low level of intellectual development" (Barlett, 1956:464). Such elitist contempt for the common people is widely considered as a hallmark of Fascist and Nazi propaganda.

Propaganda and Falsehood

Falsehood as an inherent trait of propaganda runs through many conceptual discussions of the subject. It appears in many variations, beginning with Tönnies (1922), who describes propaganda as an endeavor to spread ideas without regard to truth or accuracy. Deliberate distortion of facts appears as a defining characteristic of propaganda in Lumley (1933:122f.), Albig (1956:292), and Choukas (1965:33f.). Sophistry in reasoning, too, has been treated as a defining mark of propaganda. In Lee and Lee (1939), the propagandist's art is broken down into a number of rhetorical tricks that create an illusion of evidence and proof: name calling, glittering generalization, card stacking, the bandwagon phenomenon, and so on.

Merton (1957:509), on the other hand, sees no necessary connection between propaganda and falsehood. Ellul (1965:53, 113) goes even further:

> The idea that propaganda consists of lies (which makes it harmless and even a little ridiculous in the eyes of the public) is still maintained by some specialists.... But it is certainly not so. For a long time propagandists have recognized that lying must be avoided. "In propaganda, truth pays off"—this formula has been increasingly accepted.... Propaganda does not base itself on errors, but on exact facts. It even seems that the more informed public or private opinion is (notice I say "more," not "better"), the more susceptible it is to propaganda.

Elsewhere, however, Ellul (1965:61) asserts the essentially lying character of propaganda with even greater vigor:

> Propaganda feeds, develops, and spreads the system of false claims—lies aimed at the complete transformation of minds, judgments, values and actions (and constituting a frame of reference for systematic falsification).

In an empirical investigation of wartime propaganda to the enemy, *credibility* was found to represent a strong constraint. According to Lerner (1949:195), avoiding *detectable* lies was one of the cardinal rules guiding Allied psychological warfare operations in World War II. Psychological warfare practitioners even refrained from making propagandistic use of true statements when there was reason to believe that the audience would find them incredible (Lerner, 1949:138).

The credibility constraint has to do with expected audience responses, rather than truth and falsehood as such. In the context of psychological warfare studies, it represents an independent strategic variable. In conceptual analyses based upon the essentially untruthful character of propaganda, however, credibility sometimes appears as a basic *dependent* variable: the propagandistic mode of communication is said to be so contrived as to *induce* belief, to render the propagandist's statements credible regardless of their truth or falsehood. The audience is seen as helpless in the face of the techniques of suggestion applied by the propagandist.

Ellul (1965:11) describes propaganda as a "total" communication technique that surrounds the propagandee on all sides,

> reaching and encircling the whole man and all men.... We are here in the presence of an organized myth that tries to take hold of the entire person. Through the myth it creates, propaganda imposes a complete range of intuitive knowledge, susceptible of only one interpretation, unique and one-sided, and precluding any divergence.

By creating and imposing myths, propaganda isolates its audience from the world of real facts and ensnares it in a web of illusions. In this vein, propaganda has often been described as operating on the Big Lie principle attributed to Hitler (1936: 203); while small inaccuracies are likely to be detected, the audience can be induced by constant repetition to accept enormous untruths.

A less extreme concept of myth has a psychological content: it refers to deeply ingrained beliefs about social reality which are essential to the maintenance of the subject's self-esteem and sense of identity. Such myths are likely to be strongly defended against contrary factual evidence (Bettelheim and Janowitz, 1950:178; Saenger, 1953:chap. 11); hence they furnish highly effective propaganda themes.

The New Propaganda

The conceptual analyses of the propaganda phenomenon frequently stress its novel, unprecedented character. Propaganda is viewed as a new social, cultural, and political force, sharply differentiated from the promotional (instrumental) types of communications current in earlier historical periods. Propaganda in the specific, modern sense is said to be characterized by distinctive features such as detachment, concealment, and scientific sophistication—traits absent from earlier types of promotional discourse.

Lasswell and Blumenstock (1939:5) contrast the missionaries of old—propagators of beliefs to which they themselves were attached—with the new breed of propagandist; "the modern propagandist does not necessarily believe what he says." Ellul (1965:196, 241) puts the contrast far more sharply:

> Propaganda no longer obeys an ideology. The propagandist is not, and cannot be, a believer. ...
>
> The true propagandist must be as cold, lucid and rigorous as a surgeon. There are subjects and objects. A propagandist who believes in what he says and lets himself become the victim of his own game will have the same weakness as a surgeon who operates on a loved one or a judge who presides at a trial of a member of his own family.

Another modern trait of propaganda frequently referred to in the literature is its devious character: in modern propaganda, the originators of the message as well as the goals actually promoted are hidden from the audience. Lumley (1933:44) defines propaganda in these terms. According to Albig (1956:302), propaganda is the "dissemination of conclusions from concealed sources or with concealed objectives."

Bernays (1928:9) calls the propagandist "the invisible government which is the true ruling power of our country. We are governed, our minds are molded, our tastes formed, our ideas suggested, largely by men we never heard of."

Finally, some theorists have attributed to contemporary propaganda a specifically modern scientific character. This is essential to both Choukas' and Ellul's conceptual definition of propaganda.

Choukas (1965:93) describes the modern propagandist as "a social engineer attempting to construct behavior patterns as the physical engineer builds bridges, roads, steamboats"; he must have "an accurate understanding of how the individual human behaves." Ellul (1965:4) maintains that "modern propaganda is based on scientific analysis of psychology and sociology"; he constructs a typology of national styles of propaganda, relating Stalinist propaganda to Pavlovian reflexology, Nazi propaganda to Freudian psychoanalysis, and American propaganda to Dewey's theory of teaching.

The Soviet Marxist Concept of Propaganda

In Soviet revolutionary Marxism (Leninism, Stalinism), instrumental communications in general and propaganda in particular are envisaged in a conceptual framework radically different from that of contemporary Western thought. To begin with, revolutionary Marxism makes no sharp conceptual distinction between instrumental (promotional, propagandistic) and informative (factual, theoretical) communications: theory is not separated from practice; all thought systems, traced to their basic presuppositions, will reveal themselves as designed to promote one or another cause, either that of the exploiters or that of the exploited. Furthermore, theory and practice being inseparably blended together, the distinction between truth and falsehood applies, not to factual-theoretical discourse as such, but to thought-action complexes identified with one or the other cause. The distinction between truth and falsehood is put forward as an objectively grounded one; the Leninist doctrine rejects relativism and upholds the concept of absolute truth (Lenin, 1962: 123ff.).

The major dividing line is drawn, then, not between propaganda and nonpropaganda (e.g., education), but between the revolutionary propaganda of the working class and the reactionary propaganda of the exploiters, standing for truth and falsehood, respectively. The question whether propaganda *as such* is tainted with falsehood makes no sense in this context. Nor is Lenin's conceptualization of propaganda compatible with the image of the propagandist as a detached operator, uncommitted to the truth of the message he disseminates. Since thought is inseparable from action, disbelief in the "true" theory goes together with pursuit of the "wrong" practical goals.

It also follows from the principle of the unity of thought and action, however, that belief in the "true" theory in the abstract is not enough. One must also be able to apply the theory correctly in dealing with concrete issues—but how can one tell in each particular case which solution is correct? The basic Soviet Marxist conceptual approach toward the Party's propaganda as truth suggests two different answers to this question. One is that the Party will always find the correct solution; the other is that the Party will make mistakes but will learn from them and correct them. Depending on circumstances, the Party's claim to be the sole possessor and embodiment of truth can be presented in terms of either infallibility or flexibility. In either case, the truth in the Party's possession is characterized as "scientific" truth.

In this context, however, science and scientific truth are understood in a sense different from the current Western terms *science* and *scientific*. The Soviet Marxist thesis about the scientific nature of the Party's propaganda has nothing to do with Western views ascribing to modern propaganda an applied-science character. According to these views, science is a body of information that can be utilized for whatever practical end one has in mind, whereas science in the Soviet Marxist sense means true knowledge of the totality of physical as well as human (cultural, social) reality, culminating in the specification of *one* set of collective goals as the "scientifically" warranted one.

Propaganda-as-science in the Soviet sense has encyclopedic scope: it covers basic theory as well as correct assessment of all contingent facts bearing upon the Party's revolutionary struggle. Mastering this material in its entirety, however, is considered beyond the capacity of ordinary people. Hence the need for "agitation" as distinct from propaganda proper. Agitation consists of stimulating mass action by hammering home one salient (i.e., outrageous, iniquitous, threatening) feature of the situation, whereas propaganda is designed to provide the audience with a comprehensive conceptual framework for dealing with social and political reality "scientifically" in all its aspects. (On this distinction, see Inkeles, 1950:39.)

Discussion

Most of the conceptual analyses of the propaganda phenomenon surveyed above reflect the value perspective, the ethos of the academic liberal for whom communication, ideally speaking, serves to resolve disagreements and work out generally acceptable, fair solutions of intellectual and practical problems based upon the impartial weighing of the relevant empirical, observational evidence. Propaganda in all its forms, commercial as well as political, jarred upon this ethos. Accordingly, much of the theoretical literature written after World War I was concerned with constructing an ideal-typical portrait of the propagandist as the polar opposite of the bona fide communicator, i.e., the educator and scientist.

Within a normative perspective, this critique of propagandistic discourse certainly had merit. It is, however, a different question what such normatively oriented conceptualizations could contribute to the objective, scientific study of propagandistic communications and their effects. The ethos—the norm system—of the empirical scientist in the name of which propaganda was condemned makes a sharp distinction between subjective value judgments and objective obsrevational statements. The value contrast drawn between propaganda and education could not itself be presented as a scientific finding satisfying the empirical canon. Realizing this, such scholars as Doob and Lasswell recast the dichotomy in value-neutral, empirical terms; thus the propaganda phenomenon itself emerged not as a cultural anomaly and a threat to all democratic values, but as a "normal" response to an objectively existing condition (the nonavailability of sufficient information). Hence the dichotomy still retained a normative aspect: it involved more than value-free, factual observation. But this did not necessarily disqualify it as irrelevant to scientific research.

The work of science, in fact, does not consist solely in developing and correlating empirical, observational findings. The construction of scientific models and theories also calls for idealizing concepts. These are needed to provide a framework for organizing the empirical data; we encounter various types of them in all scientific theories.

Idealizing or ideal-typical concepts of a *normative* character are indispensable for constructing theoretical models of human behavior in its cultural setting, i.e., behavior mediated by symbolic communication. These idealizing components of behavior theories cannot be verified or falsified: they are not factual statements (or, for that matter, logical inferences subject to proof or disproof). Yet adopting or discarding them is not a matter of arbitrary choice. The question is how well they organize the empirical data material to which they refer. Idealizations must be assessed from this point of view: being empirically open, do they lend themselves to satisfactory empirical closure? In other words, when the ideal concepts entering into our theoretical model are replaced by their observational counterparts, will the relationships observed among the data form a pattern corresponding adequately to the model?

Let us, then, take a look at the various conceptualizations before us as the ideal-typical components of a theory of propaganda, and see whether they provide for good closure. Clearly, only tentative suggestions can be offered on this subject.

The normative version of the education-propaganda dichotomy does not appear to have good closure potentialities. It implies, to begin with, a nondirective ideal model of the educational process that is seriously at variance with reality; by eliminating every element of normative guidance from education, it extends the boundaries of propagandistic discourse beyond all reason.

It would also be hard to substantiate the

idealizing concept of modern propaganda as a kind of scientific technique of controlling the audience's behavior. There is no reason to ascribe to successful propagandists a thorough scientific knowledge of human behavior and all its laws; the key to their success must be sought elsewhere.

Contempt for the low intellectual level and gullibility of the audience, on the other hand, does seem to characterize certain types of propaganda operators, but it should not be taken as an ideal-typical attribute of the propagandist as such. The theoretical model we seek ought to allow for both this cynical variant of propaganda and a wholly different one, incompatible with any sense of duping the audience. Hitler, to be sure, laid it down as a cardinal principle of propaganda that the language used should correspond to the level of comprehension of the unschooled mass. But for him this implied no contempt: he despised, rather, the intellectuals who did not respond to his propaganda. Hitler (1936:200f.) believed that the unschooled mass had a better grasp of the essential truths of life than the overeducated intellectuals. As for the Bolsheviks, they found that their ideological propaganda made no impact upon the rural mass and concentrated their efforts on urban audiences, including the highly educated. In fact, it takes a high level of formal education to understand Marxist-Leninist theory, the crowning piece of Communist propaganda.

Similar considerations apply to such idealizing concepts as concealment and detachment. They provide for partial closure. The success of certain propaganda operations is in fact predicated upon their being perceived by the audience not as propaganda at all, but as straight information. The covert, ironical, Aesopian use of conformist themes for driving home subversive conclusions is another empirically observable example of concealment. Detachment is shown by propagandists who knowingly use untrue statements to stir up their audiences as much as possible, but such practitioners may well be totally involved in the cause they are promoting. Detachment in the sense of noninvolvement, exemplified by propagandists offering their services to promote any cause whatever, is a different matter.

Neither concealment nor detachment, however, can be taken as a necessary ideal-typical attribute of propaganda as such. There is overt as well as covert propaganda; propagandists may be detached or involved. Propaganda theory must accommodate the whole range of values of these variables. (It may be added that a detached kind of propaganda cannot be viewed as a specifically modern, contemporary phenomenon: many early historical examples can be found.)

The empirically oriented variant of the education-propaganda dichotomy (Lasswell, 1934; Doob, 1948) gives good closure in relation to propaganda (commercial as well as political) promoting novel, unprecedented, or nonconformist choices and behavior patterns. This conceptualization, however, still leaves the important phenomenon of conformist propaganda unaccounted for.

To conclude: the conceptual analyses we encountered in our survey furnished a number of ideal-typical concepts suitable for organizing certain groups of observational data falling within the field of promotional (propagandistic) discourse, but no model covering the entire field seemed to emerge. Nothing more could be achieved, because our theorists looked at the propaganda phenomenon, as it were, from the outside, applying extraneous normative standards to it. In building theoretical models of distinct fields of symbolically mediated human behavior, however, we need ideal-typical concepts *intrinsic* to any given field. Such concepts have to be derived from the specific characteristics of the various symbol systems (or languages) by which interaction within the field is mediated. A conceptual scheme of this nature will be presented in the concluding part of this chapter.

THE EMPIRICAL APPROACH

Independently of the conceptual analyses dealing with the propaganda phenomenon, certain specific categories of propaganda operations, notably psychological warfare during World War II and cold war propaganda during the postwar period, stimulated a considerable body of systematic policy-oriented empirical research. We shall now consider some types of this research activity.

OUTPUT STUDIES

During World War II the monitoring services of the United States and Great Britain kept a running record of the Axis powers' propaganda output, which then was scrutinized by advisory staffs with various policy ends in view. One sought to find effective counters to the enemy's propaganda line, discover his political and psychological vulnerabilities, and the like. The data, however, also were available for scholarly studies of more general theoretical scope. During the war, Kris and Speier (1944) made a comprehensive analysis of Nazi radio propaganda from the psychological and sociological points of view. After the war, when attention shifted to Soviet propaganda activities, a comprehensive study dealing with the ideological presuppositions, organizational framework, and sociological background of the Soviet regime's political handling of the mass media was presented by Inkeles (1950).

The Communist seizure of power in China and the Korean war stimulated officially sponsored research into Chinese Communist propaganda organization and output (Chen, 1955; Yu, 1955a; 1955b). Here, too, sociological background factors are taken into account.

The Sino-Soviet controversy of the late 1950s and early 1960s produced a novel phenomenon: public ideological polemics within the Communist party system. This was explored from the historian's point of view in Hudson et al. (1961), Zagoria (1962), and Griffith (1964). Subsequently, the Chinese "cultural revolution" of 1965 and after generated voluminous propaganda material of an intraparty polemical character. This has been discussed by Mehnert (1966), with reference to highly revealing documentary evidence.

An important research technique developed in connection with Soviet mass communication studies consists of administering interviews to persons previously exposed to official propaganda, and scrutinizing the answers obtained for cues regarding propaganda effects and related problems. Bauer (1952) pioneered in this type of study. His small sample consisted of defectors and hence was not treated as representative, but the psychological variables found are of considerable interest in themselves.

More recently, a small interview project of this type was carried out with Czechoslovak respondents who had not left their homeland (Pethybridge, 1967). While this sample also was not representative, the interviews did suggest an interesting generalization about the strength of nationalism (in the sense of attachment to the goal value of national independence) in Czechoslovakia. (The study antedated the 1968 events by one year.)

CONTENT ANALYSIS

The empirical research technique of content analysis was developed during World War II. The original objective, as formulated by Lasswell in February 1942, was to draw from certain objectively ascertainable, quantifiable features of the German propaganda output inferences concerning decisions made or contemplated by German policy-makers, as well as concerning the material or psychological conditions prevailing in Germany (George, 1959:30). Thus content analysis was conceived as a scientific technique related to general intelligence.

The fundamental hypothesis underlying the Lasswellian content analysis technique is that the relative frequency of symbols of various categories occurring in the propaganda output of a source reveals considerable information that the source does not intend to communicate; for example, its actual as against purported intentions or assessments of the situation. This analytical research design raises a number of methodoligical problems, notably that of the coding of symbols in order to group them under appropriate, numerically comparable categories (Pool, 1959; Berelson, 1952; George, 1959; North et al., 1963).

Content analysis as a special technique or discipline, however, did not remain confined either to its original frequency model or to its pragmatic intelligence orientation.

Without denying the appropriateness of the frequency approach to certain research problems, Pool (1959) called attention to the importance of developing analytical and interpretive techniques of a nonfrequency character, making it possible to base inferences, for example, upon the *single* occurrence of a symbol (or its nonoccurrence), rather than upon variations in the number of times the symbol (or its cognates) occurs in various segments of the output.

> The conscious selection of content categories and sample size with an eye to satisfying technical requirements of statistical analysis may be justified when the research objective is to make general inferences. But such a criticism is inappropriate when, as in propaganda analysis, the object is to make specific inferences about events at particular times and places. In the latter case valuable opportunities for making inferences are lost if the investigator ignores or minimizes the value of nonfrequency and low frequency indicators (Pool, 1959: 24).

The analytical approach introduced here transcends the specific frame of reference of propaganda analysis, and even that of instrumental communications in general. It is applicable to all kinds of symbol activity. The volume introduced by Pool's essay consists of seven papers presented at a conference on content analysis held under the auspices of the Social Science Research Council at Monticello, Illinois, in 1955; the papers range over a number of disciplines, including, besides propaganda analysis itself, folkloristics, biography, history, and psychology. Considerable attention was paid to the nonrepresentational (nonconnotative) aspects of verbal symbols as a source of diagnostic information. Thus the original Lasswellian idea of extracting from symbolic communications information they are not intended to convey was extended from propaganda to symbol-using behavior in general.

Discussion

In the empirical studies referred to, propaganda is treated not as a cultural and social phenomenon in its own right, but as an adjunct of political forces or source of supply of unintended information.

Most of the studies considered in this section confine themselves to the treatment of data taken from the output of a single propaganda machine covering a limited period. The theoretical generalizations aimed at are, accordingly, middle-level ones, or else the analysis is cast in historical terms. The highest level of theoretical generalization is reached by propaganda analysis, especially at the later stages of its development. Here the empirical study of propaganda materials transcends its original frame of reference, merging into a general theory of expressive (verbal as well as nonverbal) symbolic communication.

Thus here again, as in the case of the conceptual analyses considered, no theoretical model dealing specifically with propagandistic communication has emerged: the empirical studies referred to either cover only a circumscribed segment of propaganda activity or encompass a wider field than propaganda.

COMMUNICATION EFFECTS

In this section we shall consider causal theories purporting to account for the persuasive effects produced by propaganda. We shall distinguish two main theoretical lines, one tending to magnify the propagandist's power over the audience and the other tending to downgrade it.

The first type, cognate with some of the dichotomous conceptualizations dealing with the propaganda phenomenon, will be referred to as conditioning theory. Here the propagandist appears as the source of stimuli that determines the recipient's responses; these theories postulate a unilateral relationship of dominance between the propagandist and the propagandee. The second type of theory, which will be called sociological, implies no such one-sided dominance; instead of attributing a specific control potential to propaganda, it subsumes propaganda under the general category of instrumental communications (communications designed to influence or shape the recipient's beliefs, attitudes, or overt conduct).

Conditioning Theories

It is characteristic of the conditioning view that it attributes any persuasive effect achieved by propaganda mainly to the stimuli administered by the propagandist (their nature, frequency, volume, and so on), minimizing the role played by intervening variables such as the propagandee's preexistent beliefs and attitudes, the perceived role and status of the source, and contingent situational factors. The stimuli are supposed to produce *automatic* effects: the recipient does not act as an autonomous system. Conditioning theorists may grant at most that preexistent attitudes, and so on, can have some limiting or facilitating effect (e.g., Ellul, 1965:33), but to them the main thing is that appropriately chosen stimuli persistently applied will overcome audience resistance or indifference. The hallmark of effective propaganda is that it will make people go where they do not want to go (Ellul, 1965:35). This supreme achievement of propaganda conceived as a potentially limitless technique of conditioning is sometimes accounted for in terms of Pavlovian conditioned reflex theory.

According to Chakotin (1940:44), "collective action, especially of the masses, is the result of political acts within the governmental machines of the present day," acts that build "conditioned reflexes and systems of conditioned reflexes" upon some "fundamental instinct." Chakotin (1940:98) distinguishes four "fundamental instincts"–hostility, nutrition, sexuality, and maternity—one or the other of which will predominate during any given historical period. Mass conditioning will be achieved by that propaganda which appeals to the prevalent instinct of the day; for Chakotin's own period, that was the instinct of struggle or hostility. This is how Chakotin explains the relative weakness of "nutritionally" oriented democratic propaganda, and the total suggestive effect achieved by Hitler with his appeal to combative instincts.

The central thesis of Ellul's theory of propaganda effects is that propagandistic persuasion consists in the stimulation of overt acts; it has nothing to do with implanting or changing ideas or opinions (Ellul, 1965:25). The technique by which propagandists shape the audience's overt behavior is that of reflex conditioning:

> Propaganda tries first of all to create conditioned reflexes in the individual by training him so that certain words, signs or symbols, even certain persons or facts, provoke unfailing reactions. Despite many protests from psychologists, creating such conditioned reflexes, collectively as well as individually, is definitely possible (Ellul, 1965:31).

Some theorists attribute to propaganda a conditioning effect (control of attitudes, beliefs, and so on by administration of appropriate stimuli regardless of intervening variables) without referring to Pavlovian conditioning mechanisms. According to Choukas (1965), the suggestive effect of propaganda is due to the fact that the stimuli administered by the propagandist become associated with the recipient's stored memories of emotional states (fear, pleasure, hatred, love). A stimulus so enriched becomes a "symbol"; that is, an active principle organizing the subject's behavior. "With each symbol the individual acquires, he accepts automatically and unreflectingly an image of the thing he is directed to love or hate, cherish or despise" (Choukas, 1965:95).

Sarnoff, Katz, and McClintock (1954: 310–311) refer to "authoritarian suggestion" as distinct from "nonauthoritarian information." The former is based upon the communicator's perceived power position, which is seen as leading to a conditioning effect in the sense here defined. This variant of the conditioning view, however, does not attribute determining efficacy to the stimulus per se, but only to the stimulus in connection with an intervening "source" variable, the preexistent power position of the communicator as perceived by the audience. Chakotin's theory, too, places a constraint upon the propaganda stimulus: to be effective, it must appeal to the dominant instinct of the age. Given this, however, audience response will be automatic and nonautonomous.

Discussion

Conditioning theories of propaganda effects are intuitively plausible. Successful mass propaganda, whether of the commercial or political type, produces the impression of automatic, mechanically released cial of the political type, produces the impression of automatic, mechanically released responses generated on a mass scale. The enraptured audiences of spellbinding demagogues, the people flocking *en masse* to buy products advertised in the mass media do not show autonomous behavior. One is easily led to conclude that propagandists do to their audiences what scientists performing Pavlovian experiments do to laboratory animals: they build conditioned reflexes into the propagandees' behavior. Yet the analogy is of doubtful value in accounting for audience responses to propagandistic stimuli.

Conditioning experiments of the Pavlovian and post-Pavlovian type (Pavlov, 1928: chap. 22; Spence, 1956:37ff., 46ff.) indeed generate automatic (or rather automatized) responses by administering appropriately designed mixtures of stimuli to the experimental animals. Here, however, the control achieved by one organism over others by means of stimulation is not the object of study; it is just a part of the investigating procedure. What is being studied is the development and microstructure of biologically adaptive habits. The point is to make the animals behave in such a way as to render the microstructure of their adaptive habits visible; it is not to train the animals to perform specific acts desired by the experimenter. Conditioning experiments conducted with such ends in view would be methodologically faulty. But apart from this, it is also questionable whether propagandistic persuasion itself may be viewed as a training process, designed to establish a fixed pattern of automatized overt acts performed upon presentation of standard verbal or nonverbal stimuli.

Such training for automatized responses does occur in certain institutionalized, hierarchical settings; the drilling of recruits in military units is an example. Neither advertisements nor political slogans, however, act like military commands; it is not the point of advertising to make people jump and buy a product every time they see or hear it advertised, nor are citizens supposed to vote for candidate X every time they are exhorted to do so.

It cannot be denied that propaganda messages often call forth automatized responses. All symbolic communications do this; the decoding of symbols, for example, is an involuntary, automatic, reflex-like response, once the code has been learned. Some propaganda effects indeed seem related to the involuntary decoding and memorizing of brand names and the like. But conditioning effects of this type cannot provide a theoretical model accounting for the entire range of responses for which propagandistic communications are designed. What we need is a model doing justice to the major role played by autonomous, nonautomatic responses called forth by propaganda.

A theoretical approach oriented toward *autonomous* responses to symbolic communications of various kinds was in fact developed on an empirical basis in recent communications research. This will be discussed in the next section.

Sociological Research

In his survey of post–World War II research in mass communications, Klapper (1960:5) notes

> a shift away from the tendency to regard mass communication as a necessary and sufficient cause of audience effects, toward a view of the media as influences, working amid other influences, in a total situation. The old guess of specific effects stemming from the communication has given way to the observation of existing conditions or changes, followed by an inquiry into the factors, *including* mass communication, which produced those conditions and changes, and the roles which these factors played relative to each other. In short, attempts to assess a stimulus which was presumed to work alone have given way to an assessment of the role of that stimulus in a total observed phenomenon.

In a similar vein, Riley and Riley (1959: 542f.) speak of

> the need for certain extensions of the traditional approach which, in its more extreme versions, has focused exclusively on the simple act of communication, from source to audience. Often implicit in it are notions of a communicator concerned only with sending his message and making it as persuasive as possible and a recipient, alone in his ivory tower, coming to a decision—often purely rational—about how to act upon the message. The very simplicity of such a scheme makes it an effective framework for both survey research and laboratory experiment. . . . Yet the traditional view does not take fully into account ongoing processes of social interaction of which the single communicative act is merely one component. Nor does it take into full account those psychological processes which, although they may be going on within the individual recipient quite apart from a particular communication, may nevertheless markedly affect his reaction to it. Extensions of this view in both the sociological and the psychological direction seem necessary if the mass-communication process is to be explained more adequately or its outcome predicted more accurately.

The extensive empirical research work dealing with the impact of mass media upon people's attitudes (e.g., voting decisions) since World War II has produced a much lower estimate of the power of propaganda than had been current earlier. Thus, panel studies by Lazarsfeld, Berelson, and Gaudet (1948) dealing with attitude changes during the 1940 electoral campaign in Erie County, Ohio, and by Berelson, Lazarsfeld, and McPhee (1954) on such changes during the 1948 campaign in Elmira, New York, indicate that only a relatively small percentage of voters (5 percent and 8 percent, respectively) changed their allegiance during the campaign. This is interpreted as implying that voting behavior depends more on audience variables such as preexistent attitudes and reference group memberships than on persuasive mass communication stimuli. At the same time, certain source variables, notably personal influence and opinion leadership in person-to-person groups, also emerge as potentially significant (Hovland, 1954; 1959; Katz & Lazarsfeld, 1955).

It has long been known that in industrially developed democracies the majority vote tends to be out of line with the editorialconsensus of the mass-circulation press (Hovland, 1954). This consensus, it seems, has not been effective in swaying the readers' political attitudes. In other words, the mass circulation press does not act as a potent instrument of propagandistic persuasion.

The informational role of the mass media, however, is a different matter. In this capacity, they do contribute to the formation of political attitudes in the mass. As Lang and Lang (1959:226) point out, they "provide perspective, shape images of candidates and parties, help highlight issues around which a campaign will develop, and define the unique atmosphere and areas of sensitivity which mark any particular campaign." The opinion leaders, in fact, mainly exercise a transmission function between the mass media and the mass audience. According to these authors, the information conveyed by the mass media is used in the majority of cases to reinforce and crystallize preexistent attitudes, but it also enters, in ways that are difficult to specify, into attitude changes that occur between elections.

In any case, the panel and survey studies dealing with political behavior fail to reveal extensive opinion changes produced by communications. The impact of communications upon the attitudes and opinions of the recipients has also been studied by means of laboratory experiments, however, and the amount of change observed under experimental conditions has been considerably larger than that revealed by surveys. Hovland (1959:655) refers to experimental studies in which the opinions of a third to a half or more of the audience are changed.

How can one explain this discrepancy between experimental and survey results? Lipset argues that "the controlled experiment always greatly overrates effects, as compared with those that normally occur, because of the self-selection of audiences" (Lipset et al., 1954:1158). Hovland (1959) suggests a more detailed explanation of the discrepancy; according to him, the experimental studies do not deal with realistic communication situations at all, but with situations so arranged that measurable opinion effects can be expected to occur.

In fact, it is difficult to introduce the intervening variables involved in responses to propagandistic political communications into the laboratory setting. To be sure, in a number of experimental studies the independent variables are audience variables such as reference group membership, or source variables such as the credibility or attractiveness of the communicator. Experiments like this occasionally reveal degrees of resistance to persuasion traceable to sociological factors (e.g., Kelley & Volkart, 1952). Other investigations suggest that opinion changes are less likely to be due to the impact of mass communications than to personal influence (Katz & Lazarsfeld, 1955; see also Klapper, 1960:70); here we have to do with a source variable. But the experiments in question do not bring into play the full range of audience, source, and situational variables related to communication effects in real life, and so they do not provide a basis for assessing the limitations of political and other propaganda operations.

A central theme of experimental studies dealing with communication effects is change in beliefs or attitudes brought about by communications. A study by Hovland, Lumsdaine, and Sheffield (1949), dealing with opinion changes caused by exposure to documentary war films shown to military personnel in World War II, belongs in this category.

The extent of the cognitive or attitudinal changes induced by propaganda has been treated as a measure of the instrumental effectiveness of communications under the general heading of "conversion" (Klapper, 1960:chap. 4). The adoption of this criterion raises certain methodological questions. Thus, it was found that persuasion was "particularly successful among persons who, prior to exposure, either professed to have no opinion on the issue at hand, or who scored in the 'neutral' zone in pertinent attitude tests" (Klapper, 1960:54). But then it appears doubtful whether the distance between a neutral or uncommitted position and a definite belief adopted without resistance is in any way commensurate with the distance between a strongly held initial position and a contrasting final position that a person is induced to adopt after a struggle leading to "conversion."

In any case, experimental studies have

not produced much evidence of conversion in this strong sense; the experimentally observed effects of instrumental communication are more likely to fall into the category of reinforcement of existing attitudes (Klapper, 1960:15) or of canalization of existing behavior tendencies (Klapper, 1960:120ff.).

An important intervening variable mediating communication effects is reference group affiliation (Riley & Riley, 1959: 547ff.). Reference groups may be visualized as forming concentric circles ranging from the primary group to more and more inclusive groupings with their more and more widely ramified communication circuits. The communication effects generated within these interlocking circuits enter into the individual recipient's response to communications of whatever origin.

Discussion

While the sociological communication studies just discussed show a considerable variety of methods and research designs, they all represent a type of research that may be designated as empirical analysis. Empirical-analytical research is concerned with discovering and substantiating functional relationships among empirical, observational variables defined with reference to a limited particular universe of data. This type of research does not produce comprehensive theories (e.g., a theory of communication), or even theories of major subcategories of a general field (e.g., a theory of propaganda); it generates only functional models of narrow scope. Characteristically, however, empirical-analytical research is oriented toward the eventual emergence of more and more comprehensive theoretical models. The researchers expect that the narrow-scope, particularized functional regularities established by them will in due course be synthesized into a general theory.

Using the terminology applied above, we may say that empirical-analytical research starts with empirical closure and seeks to develop open, idealizing model structures of comprehensive range. This perspective is the reverse of that of the conceptual approach. At the early stages, no use is made of ideal-typical organizing concepts; empirical analysis does not articulate its field in terms of distinct interactive roles. Hence it does not lend itself to the construction of a theory dealing specifically with propaganda as a distinct mode of instrumental communication.

The problem of constructing such a theory with the help of idealizing concepts based upon the normative structure of promotional languages, and the interactive roles associated with their use, will be considered in the next, concluding part of this chapter.

TOWARD A THEORY OF PROPAGANDA

Instrumental Languages

The term *language* is used in this discussion to designate various distinct modes of symbolization having a normative structure of their own, defining the necessary and sufficient conditions under which, ideally speaking, the type of communication effect specific to the language in question will be achieved. This concept of language does not refer to basic linguistic codes such as the French language, the English language, and so on, but rather to distinct, contextually differentiated ways in which French, English, and so on will be used, depending on the type of communication effect intended.

Considered from this point of view, languages fall into two main groups, the instrumental and the expressive. Instrumental languages consist of message types designed to inculcate beliefs and attitudes in the recipient corresponding to the communicator's intent, or to stimulate some overt behavioral response. The message types making up expressive languages are not oriented toward circumscribed effects of these kinds, but serve to make the communicator's personal feelings and states of mind manifest so that the recipient may participate in them in a personal, existential sense.

"What a beautiful day!" or "Life is hard" are expressive messages, and so are works of poetry and imaginative literature; factual, informative statements, requests, commands, exhortations, and the like are instrumental ones. But although the two kinds of message types are formally distinct, the line dividing expressive from instrumental communication is not a sharp one: a personal community of feeling, established by expressive intercommunication, may provide the starting point for some instrumental communication. Propagandistic messages, for example, are instrumental in themselves, but they may be conveyed by expressive messages—poems, for example—which serve as vehicles. Such combinations of codes are frequently observed in the field of symbolic communication. We shall, however, deal with the languages of propagandistic persuasion in its primary, instrumental context.

The normative structure of any language correlates a distinct mode of symbolization with an ideal pattern of reciprocal roles played by the communicators and the recipients. The instrumental language of commands, for example, presupposes, for its meaningful use, a hierarchical role pattern in which the communicator is perceived as the recipient's superior. We may distinguish, from the point of view of the underlying role pattern, four main classes of instrumental languages, each having several distinct subclasses: the languages of authority, power, influence, and persuasion. We are specifically concerned with the language of persuasion.

Before going into the specific role patterns associated with the use of propagandistic languages, let us briefly consider some message types representative of the other three classes, and see what role relationships, are presupposed by them. This will provide a useful foil for the very different role constellations associated with persuasion.

In the category of authoritative message types, let us take legal enactments and hierarchical commands on the one hand, and expert advice on the other to stand for the two main subtypes of authority: prescriptive and informational. In all three cases, the messages are supposed to have binding force by virtue of the role played by the communicator as legislator, or hierarchical superior, or expert, which entitles him to expect deference from the recipients, subject to certain limiting conditions and qualifications.

The normative structure of prescriptive authoritative communications reflects ideal role requirements based on the prevailing institutional order and norm system of the society—requirements imposing role obligations both upon the authority-wielders and upon those subject to their authority. This generates a role pattern of considerable ambiguity. Noncompliance with hierarchical commands, for example, may be condemned as counternorm, deviant behavior, or justified on the ground that the communicator has overstepped the bounds of his authority (or usurped authority altogether). The actual (empirical) working of prescriptive authority systems will reflect these ambiguities.

The interactive role pattern underlying informational authority is based upon the authority-wielders' perceived exclusive or differential access to various stores of societally significant information. Such stores of information may deal with production techniques, laws of nature, institutionalized rules regulating conduct, health problems, and so on. Essential to this role pattern is the confidence of the recipients in the communicator's knowledge as well as in his helpfulness. This ideal role pattern, too, involves ambiguities of various kinds.

Power roles are related to one interacting

party's ability to affect the other's well-being in a positive or negative sense. The effectiveness of message types of this category is predicated upon the communicator's command of positive or negative incentives that work with the recipient.

Incentive-related instrumental communications include market bids, negotiatory offers and counteroffers, threats and counterthreats. For example, consider a message type conveying an extortionate threat: "You will transfer to me such-and-such an asset (or render such-and-such a service), or I shall inflict such-and-such a penalty on you." For the threat to be effective, the threatened party must perceive the threatener as actually possessing the coercive or destructive potential he claims to possess; otherwise the threat will be considered empty. If the threat is not dismissed as empty, the threatened party will have to decide whether to comply (yield to the threat) or expose himself to the threatened penalty, threatening resistance in his turn.

In this case, the parties rely mainly on negative incentives to obtain compliance; the negative incentives, however, are coupled with positive ones (a threat also implies a promise of impunity in case the threatened party yields). This gives rise to complex, ambiguous role relationships, involving both incompatible and shared interests (Schelling, 1960).

To add to the complexity, we must bear in mind that authoritative roles, although ideally calling for *voluntary* deference, often are combined with coercive power roles: laws stipulate penalties for violation, and so on. Messages backed by prescriptive authority may carry weight with the recipients not only by virtue of the communicator's claim to deference, freely recognized by the recipient, but also by virtue of the coercive power at the communicator's command.

Influence in the specific sense in which the term is used here is a largely unexplored area of social interaction. The term is often employed in a very broad sense, covering *all* effects achieved by instrumental communications. We use it, however, with reference to a specific role pattern, such that a communicator's pleas, requests, suggestions, recommendations, and the like carry decisive (or at least differential) weight with the recipient because of the heightened, unique (or at least differential) value position the communicator occupies in the recipient's eyes as a source of strength, security, or gratification.

This relationship is apt to be the reverse of the authority or power relationships prevailing between the parties: it is not the hierarchical superior who is influential with his subordinate in the sense here defined, but the other way around. In any case, the normative structure of the message types of this category (pleas, requests, recommendations) presupposes a mutual role pattern characterized by strong personal bonds of solidarity and loyalty. Actual influence relationships, however, have their ambiguities: many influence-wielders manipulate an influenced party for their own benefit, while the influenced party may become jealous of the influence-wielder. Thus, here too it is a critical question whether the interacting parties live up to their ideal role attributes.

The reciprocal role relationships between persuaders and persuaded, however, have an entirely different character from that of the other three instrumental languages, and the normative structure of the languages of propagandistic persuasion accordingly has to be set forth along different lines.

The main point is that propagandists, unlike the users of instrumental languages of the other classes, do not have to show their credentials, as it were, in order to get a hearing for their messages. Propagandists are not required to provide symbolic or nonsymbolic evidence that they are entitled to use the language by which they seek to achieve an instrumental effect. On the contrary, it is better from the propagadist's point of view if his role or effectiveness as persuader does not become too conspicuous. The critical normative requirements of persuasive propagandistic communication lie in a different dimension.

One critical problem facing propagandists is whether and how they can establish communication links that lend themselves to achieving a "persuasive" effect on an audience. The language of propaganda is one that can be used only in communication settings satisfying certain requirements as to the configuration, capacity, and flow pattern of the available communication channels. This type of setting is needed so that the specific role relationships involved in the use of the languages of persuasion may develop. Accordingly, we shall start our discussion of the normative structure of the instrumental languages of propaganda by considering the relevant channel characteristics.

The Language of Propaganda

Propaganda as Distant Communication

The instrumental objective of propagandistic communications has been designated as persuasion, but it should be understood that we are dealing here with only one variant of the persuasive use of language. The users of all instrumental languages may be said to practice persuasion of one sort or another, using arguments of authority, of force, of common sense, of scientific truth, and so on. The threatener, for example, can achieve a rough sort of persuasion by pointing a pistol at the threatened party. This is the argument of force, which the propagandist as propagandist cannot use in his own behalf, just as he cannot invoke his own authority to achieve a persuasive effect. The propagandist can, at most, make use of arguments of force, authority, scientific truth, and the like at one remove, pointing to the might, authority, scientific competence, and so on of others.

Such an indirect use of arguments of force, authority, and truth, however, does not put at the propagandist's disposal the persuasive potentials of threateners, authority-wielders, experts, and the rest. The direct use of persuasive potentials of these types calls for two-way communication, developing interaction governed by a reciprocal role pattern. Propaganda messages, however, do not, as a rule, flow in two-way channels. Advertising, for example, is a type of communication reaching an indefinitely large number of recipients through typographical or electronic mass media. There is no significant communication back from the recipients to the source; the instrumental effect for which this type of communication is designed consists of acts performed by the recipients (purchases of goods, etc.) which presuppose no symbolic or nonsymbolic interaction between the source and the audience. The interactive roles involved in the acts that the advertiser seeks to stimulate are those of buyer and seller; the persuader's role as such is limited to unilateral, one-way, one-to-many communication. Political propaganda, too, operates in a similar communication setting, though the media utilized are more varied than those used for advertising.

Political propagandists disseminate their message in part through mass media, but in addition they often address crowds face to face at mass meetings, which provide a setting particularly adapted to the purposes of political persuasion. Meetings, of course, allow for more reciprocal communication than mass media; the crowd's response (cheering and the like) makes an important contribution to the persuasive effect that the speaker seeks to achieve. Orators, however, are typically in a position to preserve the monopoly of articulate communication. This may be challenged by hecklers, but meetings will be run in such a way as to keep disturbances of this sort under control (or else the meeting will dissolve). In view of the speaker's monopoly of articulate communication, the mass meeting, too, may be regarded as a one-to-many medium.

Political propaganda messages are designed for a wider range of instrumental effects than commercial ones. One class of intended effect is attitudinal; the party's or movement's symbols, slogans, goal concepts, and the like are presented in such a way as to reinforce the audience's sense of forming a cohesive opinion and action group. Another kind of intended effect is the stimulation of overt acts, such as voting for the party's candidate or participating in demonstrations or street combat. The organization and conduct of such mass activities, however, transcend the field of propaganda as such; they involve the creation of hierarchical structures with their own communication circuits. Here, too, reciprocal role patterns distinct from the persuader's role come into play. The propagandist's own role is that of the "distant" communicator reaching a collective audience through one-to-many channels.

Here, then, propaganda is *defined* as distant one-to-many communication. But is this definition not unduly restrictive? Commercial and political propaganda operations are, after all, regularly associated with close person-to-person contacts between salesmen or canvassers on the one hand and individual members of the public on the other. Can we construct an adequate model of the use of the propagandistic language if we exclude these close communication types from the general category of propaganda?

Canvassing, individual solicitation, and the like must indeed be classified as propaganda activities, but by the same token they should be understood as particular forms of one-to-many communication: the canvasser presents an appeal to the members of a group successively rather than simultaneously, but this is just an alternative way of disseminating the center's message without the development of any significant dialogue between the source and the collective audience. As for salesmen, they do make propaganda for their wares, but their role as salesmen goes beyond this: their objective is to conclude deals. This calls for a real dialogue, two-way communication; the language employed in concluding deals, however, is no longer that of propaganda.

It is characteristic of the distant communication pattern of propaganda that the burden of producing instrumental effects is borne not by individual messages and the exchanges to which they give rise, but by *streams* of unilateral messages adding up to a continuous process. While commands, pieces of expert advice, threats, and so on are significant in and by themselves, the impact of an individual propaganda message, taken by itself, may well be negligible, a major effect being built up only by a campaign that drives home its point by endlessly repeating the same motif, or else by marshaling a variety of arguments leading to the same conclusion. Sometimes, to be sure, audiences experience a single propaganda event (e.g., a speech delivered by a charismatic leader) as highly significant in itself, but responses of this type, too, presuppose a continuing campaign of which they mark the climax.

Propagandistic persuasion as an objective thus reflects the opportunities as well as the limitations inherent in its distant communication setting. The number of recipients reached, and possibly persuaded, is large, but a massive persuasion effect is unlikely to be produced at one stroke. It takes many messages carrying a uniform emotional charge to achieve persuasion. In this sense we may say that propagandistic persuasion as an instrumental objective is predicated upon input homogeneity. This means that all the successive messages that reach the audience express the same positive or negative value judgment, or convey the same positive or negative emotional attitude, when referring to one and the same object. Homogeneous streams of communication thus divide the objects referred to into a positively and a negatively valued class (disregarding objects referred to in value-neutral terms that are external to the theme of propaganda campaigns as such).

An extreme form of input homogeneity

is achieved by the propaganda activities of totalitarian systems. Here a central authority controls all of the mass communication networks that exist in the society and permits only messages reflecting the regime's evaluation of good and bad objects to reach the mass audience. This, at least, is the principle on which totalitarian input control policy operates. In practice, the ideal of homogeneity can only be approximated.

In any case, the propaganda operations with which we are directly concerned are those carried on in nontotalitarian societies. Under nontotalitarian conditions, input homogeneity can be imposed only upon individual channels existing alongside many others. In advertising as well as political propaganda, a number of homogeneous message streams will compete for the audience's attention. Each of these separate campaigns can produce a persuasive effect only within that segment of the public that constitutes itself as a steady audience—a group that, to the extent that it is persuaded, will provide a clientele for a product or a following for a cause or movement, as the case may be.

There are various ways in which propaganda operators ensure input homogeneity in the channels they control. One method, widely used in commercial advertising, consists of avoiding any reference to rivals, opponents, and the products they promote: advertisers seldom mention their competitors and their wares. This type of homogeneous message stream treats the opposition as nonexistent rather than as a force to be combatted. Calls to combat, in fact, would make little sense when the rival persuaders appeal to the same needs and the same tastes, and when the communicators' aim is not to stimulate coordinated collective activities.

The method of ignoring the opponent is occasionally employed in political propaganda too, but not often. Political propaganda thrives on polemics conveying a negative image of the opponent. The homogeneous message streams produced by political propagandists make explicit, affectively charged references to the "good" as well as the "bad" forces active on the political scene. Political issues are defined and presented, as a rule, as choices between alternative courses proposed by "well-intentioned" and "evil" actors, respectively. Thus a real dialogue is cut off.

Political propagandists do not put the opponent's case in his own terms when they polemicize against it. Rather, they translate the opponent's program into their own homogeneous symbolism, so that it will carry a thoroughly negative value connotation. Of course, no issue can be examined from different points of view on this basis; political propaganda provides room for presenting only one side of any argument.

Presenting only one side of an issue is, of course, not necessarily the most effective persuasive strategy; there are experiments to show that debaters who present arguments on both sides may score better with the audience than those who ignore possible objections. The persuasion achieved by this method, however, presupposes a communication setting like that of a dialogue, with two-way channels available. Effective or not, this mode of persuasion is beyond reach for the *propagandistic* persuader, who, restricted to one-way channels, practices persuasion based not on the close communication pattern of the dialogue, but on input homogeneity.

One may cite as counterinstances certain propaganda events in which homogeneity is deliberately abandoned, such as the public debates between contenders for office featured in some electoral campaigns. This device, however, is seldom used because it goes against the grain. Also, the debates in question do not serve to argue out issues; their main purpose is to build up the public image of candidates. Image-building (a more and more prominent concern of contemporary mass propaganda) is closely related to the objective of achieving input homogeneity: a favorable image consists of a variety of traits, all of which are supposed to elicit the audience's approval.

The Persuader's Role

The nature of the ideal-typical role relationship between propagandists and audiences responsive to persuasion is indicated by the homogeneity characterizing propagandistic message streams. That role relationship may be schematically represented as follows:

The communicator diffuses through one-to-many channels a homogeneous stream of emotionally and affectively charged discourse referring to threatening, destructive, or frustrating objects and conditions, on the one hand, and to unfailingly working objects or agencies overcoming the threats and frustrations, on the other. It is essential to the achievement of a collective persuasive effect, to begin with, that the members of the audience should experience the states of tension (anxiety, frustration, deprivation) evoked by the message stream as their own. Likewise, the classes of objects that the homogeneous message stream endows with unvarying positive or negative value characteristics must also appear in the same light from the recipients' point of view; persuasion is hindered if the propagandist's division of the universe into "good" and "bad" objects runs counter to the recipients' feelings and attitudes. In other words, persuasion requires, ideally speaking, complete emotional and affective resonance between the persuader and the audience. As the propagandist develops his master theme, "There are the sources of your deprivations, and here are the means for removing them," he must not encounter any emotional or affective resistance.

"Resonance" implies that the recipient does not experience the master theme or propaganda myth as a belief imposed upon him by an outside authority to which he is required or committed to defer. To be persuasive, the propaganda theme has to be perceived as coming from within. The propagandist's ideal role in relation to the propagandee is that of alter ego, someone giving expression to the recipient's own concerns, tensions, aspirations, and hopes. Thus propaganda, a distant form of communication in that it precludes significant two-way communication, by the same token also denies all distance between the source and the audience: the propagandist voices the propagandees' own feelings.

The two-way types of persuasion associated with the use of other persuasive languages have a different character: they presuppose tension rather than resonance. The Socratic type of persuasion, for example, is based upon demonstrating an inconsistency between certain beliefs, goals, or attitudes entertained by the interlocutor on the one hand and his own most fundamental commitments on the other. Here the persuader adopts a dual attitude toward the interlocutor—partly antagonistic, partly concurring and solicitous. We may call this type of persuasion, combining antagonism with solidarity, dialectical persuasion. All dialogues involving the use of instrumental languages other than those of propagandistic persuasion have a dialectical character, and therefore preclude homogeneity and resonance. Propagandistic persuasion, then, may be described as nondialectical persuasion.

Merely specifying emotional-affective resonance and the alter ego function as the basic role attributes of the propagandistic persuader does not, however, suffice to clarify the normative structure of persuasion. That the propagandist can achieve persuasion only by a nondialectical approach represents only a *negative* condition; it leaves open the question of what *positive* conditions are required to achieve the necessary degree of resonance.

Merely echoing the feelings, aspirations, and so on of the audience would guarantee resonance of a sort, but this has nothing to do with persuasion; the propagandistic themes, driving home a specific approach toward resolving anxieties and removing threats, necessarily go beyond the collective action patterns, profiles of motivation, and so on that already exist in the audience at which the campaign is directed. The propagandist is mainly concerned with achieving resonance with regard to those elements of his theme that transcend the audience's existing action and attitude patterns.

This may be simply a matter of obtaining mass acceptance for a novel way to satisfy existing needs, as is the case with advertising campaigns promoting a new drug or automobile model. Another type of propaganda objective, however, is the stimulation of novel needs or previously unexpressed aspirations; this problem looms large in both commercial and political propaganda. The question in either case is the degree of novelty that can be introduced under constraint of emotional-affective resonance.

This question can be treated in terms of various ideal-typical models of the process of generating resonance. Ascertaining which of these models fits reality best, or rather, which can account best for one or another aspect of propagandistic persuasion processes, is an empirical operation.

Models of Persuasion

The ideal role played by the successful propagandistic (nondialectical) persuader may be visualized either as a weak or a strong one. The distinction refers not to persuasive strength or effectiveness as such, but to the nature of the interaction between the successful persuader and those he persuades.

According to the weak model, homogeneous message streams produce collective persuasion by a gradual process in which a subgroup of audience members who find the propagandist's theme emotionally appealing selects itself out from the rest. Preexistent attitudes that differentiate one subgroup of the audience from another are important variables in this type of model: novel attitude and behavior patterns promoted by the propagandists will take root in those subgroups where favorable predispositions for adopting the novelty already exist. The weak model portrays persuasion processes as something like fishing expeditions in which baits are used to attract the fish. To have a large catch, the fisherman must sense which fish will like what bait, where they abound, and so on.

The strong model depicts the working of homogeneous message streams in a different fashion: according to it, the cumulative effect produced by such streams has no selective character. Rather, the homogeneity of the propagandist's theme is directly reflected in the favorable collective response evoked by it. This model metaphorically likens the persuasion process to the working of a stamping apparatus imprinting an identical pattern upon the objects put into it, regardless of their material composition.

To be sure, the strong model does not exclude the possibility that some elements of the audience will respond to the message with particular eagerness while others will reject it altogether; to continue the metaphor, some objects will accept the stamp particularly well, while others will remain unmarked. The point is, however, that for those who apply the model, either as practitioners or as theorists, there variations have no strategic significance.

One may design empirical tests to determine whether the weak or the strong model best accounts for the working of a particular propaganda operation. If it is found that the distribution of favorable responses shows marked changes at the boundaries of social categories differing as to income, occupation, education, religion, and so on, this can be taken as *prima facie* evidence for the relevance of the weak model. The same conclusion is suggested when propaganda operators vary the symbols they employ according to the social category or stratum they are addressing. Conversely, the absence of changes in the distribution of responses at the boundaries of social categories, or the use of a uniform symbolism in addressing socially differentiated groups, would argue for the applicability of the strong model.

Abrupt temporal changes in the response pattern provide another empirical test. Examples of this are the fluctuations in the voting appeal of extremist parties depending on the sharpening or subsidence of economic crises; the rapidly swelling Nazi vote in Germany from 1930 on represents a particularly spectacular instance. It appears, in general, that political propaganda operations of certain types fall under the weak model of persuasion. This applies both to ideologically oriented propaganda and to propaganda appealing to traditional party loyalties.

Image-building and related propaganda techniques frequently employed in both the political and the commercial fields, on the other hand, are designed for strong effects in the sense here defined. Image-building as a political propaganda device serves to overcome traditional party loyalties as well as ideological commitments. Propaganda operators who chafe under the constraints of the weak model are particularly attracted to the image-building approach. What success along such lines they can achieve, and under what conditions, is an empirical question.

Commercial propaganda effects are also likely to show a mixture of weak and strong features. The markets commanded by certain products mirror the division of a society into various categories (income, educational, ethnic, and so on); advertisers by and large have to accept this market configuration as given. Strong propaganda techniques, designed to dictate rather than follow tastes, can be applied only within the various categories—and then it is problematic to what extent audience tastes will be influenced by advertising as against the example set by fashion leaders. This question has to be explored by empirical research. The strong model of persuasion seems to be relevant, in any case, to mass advertising promoting products with a clientele stretching over the entire social spectrum.

All propaganda activities utilizing mass channels have a strong aspect—key symbols, brand names, and the like can be made familiar throughout the public by homogeneous streams of messages of sufficient volume.

This introduction of new symbols into the current vocabulary is an imposed effect, independent of preexistent audience attitudes. It occurs by an automatic process in the nature of conditioning; no autonomous responses are involved. The conditioning effect, however, is confined within the realm of symbolization (encoding and decoding). It has no direct attitudinal or behavioral significance. It may, however, have important *indirect* consequences of an attitudinal or behavioral nature. In many choice situations where the choosing subject cannot follow established value criteria, his decision is governed by the greater or lesser familiarity of the symbols designating the available alternatives. Hence, gaining currency for new symbolic labels or images is a prime objective of commercial as well as political propaganda.

Conditioning for new symbols as a collective effect depends, however, on the volume and length of audience exposure achieved by the communicator, and this condition is not under the propagandist's control. The audiences actually reached by messages conveyed through mass communication channels mainly constitute themselves by self-selection: newspapers must be bought, channels must be tuned in on. This is a weak feature of the persuasion process. Except for arrangements resulting in captive audiences, readers and listeners must be attracted toward the channels through which persuasive streams of messages flow.

It is a crucial question in this connection what categories of communications are most likely to attract very large self-selected audiences, corresponding in volume to the full capacity of mass channels.

The decisive variable is the audience's preexistent "need" for one or another type of communication. The strongest mass need seems to exist for communications falling in the category of entertainment—in itself an expressive, not an instrumental, type of communication. The need for news, authentic information about impressive, dramatic happenings taking place in the near or distant environment, also is universally felt. Political propaganda appeals may attract limited, self-selected audiences such as the adherents already gained by a movement, but the problem facing persuaders is how to reach the entire mass audience. Commercial propaganda as such, on the other hand, satisfies no audience need of any sort and hence is unlikely to attract self-selected audiences by itself.

To solve the problem of securing sufficiently large self-selected audiences, propagandists using mass media must resort to the expedient of channel sharing; they must find means to introduce their message streams into channels carrying contents that satisfy audience needs. A typical instance of this is provided by advertising that flows through media shared with purveyors of news or entertainment. This type of sharing presupposes formal arrangements. Space or time available in the mass networks must be bought, and the propagandistic and nonpropagandistic inputs have to be symbolically differentiated. There are, however, other informal or covert types of channel sharing, such as the systematic, tendentious selection and slanting of the news material; this plays a significant part in political propaganda. Propaganda messages embedded in entertainment material (e.g., imaginative works) also may be viewed as a form of channel sharing. In any case, it is the nonpropagandistic channel content that is primarily responsible for audience self-selection on a mass basis.

What makes for audience self-selection is not what is required for achieving persuasion. There is a tension between these two sets of requirements that may work to the detriment of persuasive strategies based on channel sharing. For example, news operations slanted so as to produce input homogeneity may achieve persuasion, but if the audience becomes aware of the slanting, this is likely to interfere with audience self-selection. The same may also happen in the case of entertainment materials rendered homogeneous in relation to official propaganda objectives. Thus, the effectiveness of channel-sharing strategies, intended to obtain wide currency for propaganda themes by coupling them with nonpropagandistic material attracting self-selected mass audiences, is subject to definite limitations.

This variant of the channel-sharing strategy can be empirically studied, for example, in the totalitarian setting, where the authorities who control all mass communication channels impose a homogeneous propagandistic tendency upon entertainment as well as news materials. The objective is to superimpose emotional-affective resonance upon other role patterns—the expressive role of the purveyor of entertainment as well as the authoritative informational role of the news source. Our model of the normative structure of the languages involved implies, however, that these disparate role relationships are bound to interfere with each other. Entertainment loses some of its attractiveness, and news (as well as other informational material) loses some of its credibility, when these inputs are pressed into a propagandistic mold.

The magnitude of these effects can be determined only empirically. One has to ascertain, for example, what concessions one or another totalitarian or near-totalitarian regime was induced to make to popular demands for pure entertainment or authentic information in order not to lose contact with its public. A future theory of propaganda will have to deal with these and many other empirical problems. This discussion has been intended not to outline a theory, but only to contribute certain elements of it, related to the role pattern underlying the use of persuasive languages.

REFERENCES

Albig, William.
1956 Modern Public Opinion. New York: McGraw-Hill.

Bartlett, F. C.
1954 "The aims of political propaganda." Pp. 463–470 in Daniel Katz et al. (eds.), Public Opinion and Propaganda. New York: Dryden Press.

Bauer, Raymond A.
1952 The Developmental History of the Political Attitudes of Individuals Toward the Soviet Regime. H.R.R.I. Research Memorandum No. 6, Maxwell Air Force Base, Alabama.

Berelson, Bernard.
1952 Content Analysis in Communications Research. Glencoe, Illinois: Free Press.

Berelson, Bernard; Paul Lazarsfeld; and William N. McPhee (eds.).
1954 Voting: A Study of Opinion Formulation in a Presidential Campaign. Chicago: University of Chicago Press.

Bernays, Edward L.
1928 Propaganda. New York: H. Liveright.

Bettelheim, Bruno and Morris Janowitz.
1950 Dynamics of Prejudice. New York: Harper.

Chakotin, Sergei.
1940 The Rape of the Masses. London: Labour Book Service.

Chen, Wenn-hui C.
1955 Wartime "Mass" Campaign in Communist China. H.R.R.I. Research Memorandum, Maxwell Air Force Base, Alabama (October).

Choukas, Michael.
1965 Propaganda Comes of Age. Washington, D.C.: Public Affairs Press.

Doob, Leonard W.
1948 Public Opinion and Propaganda. New York: Henry Holt.

Ellul, Jacques.
1965 Propaganda—the Formation of Men's Attitudes. Translated by Konrad Kellen and Jean Lerner. New York: Knopf.

George, Alexander L.
1959 Propaganda Analysis. Evanston, Illinois: Row Peterson.

Griffith, William E.
1964 The Sino-Soviet Rift. Cambridge, Massachusetts: M.I.T. Press.

Hitler, Adolf.
1936 Mein Kampf. 183rd-184th Edition. Munich: Fritz Eher Verlag.

Hovland, Carl I.
1954 "Effects of the mass media of communication." Pp. 1062–1103 in Gardner Lindzey (ed.), Handbook of Social Psychology. Reading, Massachusetts: Addison-Wesley.
1959 "Reconciling conflicting results derived from experimental and survey studies of attitude change." American Psychologist 14:8–17.

Hovland, Carl I.; A. A. Lumsdaine; and F. D. Sheffield.
1949 Experiments in Mass Communication, Princeton, New Jersey: Princeton University Press.

Hudson, G. F.; Richard Lowenthal; and Roderick MacFarquhar.
1961 The Sino-Soviet Dispute. Praeger Publications in Russian History No. 95. New York: Praeger. (Originally published as special issue of China Quarterly.)

Inkeles, Alex.
1950 Public Opinion in the Soviet Union: A Study in Mass Persuasion. Cambridge, Massachusetts: Harvard University Press.

Katz, Elihu.
1957 "The two-step flow of communication." Public Opinion Quarterly 21:61–78.

Katz, Elihu, and Paul Lazarsfeld.
1955 Personal Influence: The Part Played by People in the Flow of Communication. Glencoe, Illinois: Free Press.

Kelley, H. H., and E. H. Volkart.
1952 "The resistance to change of group-anchored attitudes." American Sociological Review 17:453–465.

Klapper, Joseph T.
1960 The Effects of Mass Communication. New York: Free Press of Glencoe.

Kris, Ernst; Hans Speier; et al.
1944 German Radio Propaganda. Ithaca,

New York: Cornell University Press.

Lang, Gladys E., and Kurt Lang.
1959 "The mass media and voting," in Eugene Burdick and A. S. Brodbeck (eds.), American Voting Behavior. Glencoe, Illinois: Free Press.

Lasswell, Harold D.
1934 "Propaganda." Pp. 521–528 in The Encyclopedia of the Social Sciences. Volume 12. New York: Macmillan.

Lasswell, Harold D., and Dorothy Blumenstock.
1939 World Revolutionary Propaganda. New York: Knopf.

Lazarsfeld, Paul G.; Bernard Berelson; and Hazel Gaudet.
1948 The People's Choice. Second Edition. New York: Columbia University Press.

Lee, Alfred McClung, and Elizabeth B. Lee (eds.).
1939 The Fine Art of Propaganda. New York: Harcourt, Brace.

Lenin, V. I.
1962 Collected Works. Volume 8. Moscow. (English translation published by Universal Distributors, New York, 1962.)
1965 Collected Works. Volume 29. Moscow. (English translation published by Lawrence & Wishart, London, 1965.)

Lerner, Daniel.
1949 Sykewar. New York: Steward.

Lipset, Seymour M.; Paul F. Lazarsfeld; H. F. Barton; and Juan Linz.
1954 "The psychology of voting: An analysis of political behavior." Pp. 1124–1177 in Gardner Lindzey (ed.), Handbook of Social Psychology. Reading, Massachusetts: Addison-Wesley.

Lumley, Frederick E.
1933 The Propaganda Menace. New York: Century.

Martin, Everett D.
1932 The Conflict of the Individual and the Mass in the Modern World. New York: Henry Holt.

Mehnert, Klaus.
1966 "Maos zweite Revolution." Osteuropa 16 (No. 11/12): 741.

Merton, Robert K.
1957 Social Theory and Social Structure. Revised Edition. Glencoe, Illinois: Free Press.

North, R. C., et al. (eds.).
1963 Content Analysis. Evanston, Illinois: Northwestern University Press.

Pavlov, Ivan P.
1928 Lectures on Conditioned Reflexes. New York: Liveright.

Pethybridge, Roger.
1967 "The assessment of ideological influences on East Europeans." Public Opinion Quarterly 31: 38–50.

Pool, Ithiel de Sola (ed.).
1959 Trends in Content Analysis. Urbana: University of Illinois Press.

Qualter, T. H.
1962 Propaganda and Psychological Warfare. New York: Random House.

Riley, John W., Jr., and Matilda W. Riley.
1959 "Mass communication and the social system," in R. K. Merton, Leonard Broom, and L. S. Cottrell (eds.), Sociology Today. New York: Basic Books.

Sarnoff, Irving; Daniel Katz; and Charles McClintock.
1954 "Attitude-change procedures and motivating patterns." Pp. 305–312 in Daniel Katz et al. (eds.), Public Opinion and Propaganda. New York: Dryden Press.

Schelling, T. C.
1960 The Strategy of Conflict. Cambridge, Massachusetts: Harvard University Press.

Spence, Kenneth W.
1956 Behavior Theory and Conditioning. New Haven, Connecticut: Yale University Press.

Tönnies, Ferdinand.
1922 Kritik der Öffentlichen Meinung. Berlin: Springer.

Yu, Frederick T. C.
1955a The Propaganda Machine in Communist China. H.R.R.I. Research Memorandum, Maxwell Air Force Base, Alabama (May).
1955b The Strategy and Tactics of Chinese Communist Propaganda as of 1952. H.R.R.I. Research Memorandum, Maxwell Air Force Base, Alabama (June).

Zagoria, Donald.
1962 The Sino-Soviet Conflict, 1956–1961. Princeton, New Jersey: Princeton University Press.

ADDITIONAL READINGS

Berelson, Bernard, and Janowitz, Morris, eds. *Reader in Public Opinion and Communication*. 2d ed. New York: Free Press, 1966.

Bruntz, George G. *Allied Propaganda and the Collapse of German Morale in 1918*. Stanford, Calif.: Stanford University Press,1938.

Dallin, Alex, ed. *Diversity in International Communism*. New York: Columbia University Press.

Dewey, John. *Interest and Effort in Education*. Boston: Houghton Mifflin, 1913.

———. *Experience and Education*. New York: Macmillan, 1938.

Doob, Leonard W. "Goebbels' Principles of Propaganda." In *Public Opinion and Propaganda*, edited by Daniel Katz et al., pp. 510–522. New York: Dryden Press, 1964.

Freud, Sigmund. *Group Psychology and the Analysis of the Ego*. New York: Liveright, 1951.

Katz, Daniel; Cartwright, Dorwin; Eldersveld, Samuel J.; and Lee Alfred McClung, eds. *Public Opinion and Propaganda*. New York: Dryden Press, 1954.

Lasswell, Harold D. *Propaganda Techniques in the World War*. London: Kegan Paul, 1927.

———; Casey, Ralph D.; and Smith, Bruce L. *Propaganda and Promotional Techniques, An Annotated Bibliography*. 2d ed. Chicago: University of Chicago Press, 1969.

Linebarger, P. M. A. *Psychological Warfare*. Washington, D.C.: Infantry Journal Press, 1948.

Merton, Robert K. *Mass Persuasion: The Social Psychology of a War Bond Drive*. New York: Harper, 1946.

———. "Patterns of Influence: A Study of Interpersonal Influence and Communications Behavior in a Local Community." In *Communications Research, 1948–1949*, edited by Paul F. Lazarsfeld and F. N. Stanton. New York: Harper, 1949.

Ponsonby, Arthur. *Falsehood in War-Time*. London: Allen & Unwin, 1928.

Read, James M. *Atrocity Propaganda, 1914–1918*. New Haven, Conn.: Yale University Press, 1941.

Saenger, Gerhart. *The Social Psychology of Prejudice*. New York: Harper, 1953.

Schramm, Wilbur, ed. *Communications in Modern Society*. Urbana: University of Illinois Press, 1948.

———, ed. *Mass Communications*. Urbana: University of Illinois Press, 1949.

———, ed. *The Science of Human Communication*. New York: Basic Books, 1963.

Shils, Edward A., and Janowitz, Morris. "Cohesion and Disintegration in the Wehrmacht in World War II." *Public Opinion Quarterly* 12(1948):289–315.

Speier, Hans. *Social Order and the Risk of War*. New York: Stewart, 1952.

Thimme, Hans. *Weltkrieg ohne Waffen*. Stuttgart: Cotta, 1962.

Weber, Max. *Gesammelte Aufsätze zur Wissenschaftslehre*. Tübingen: S. B. C. Mohr,1922.

CHAPTER 28 International and World Public Opinion

W. PHILLIPS DAVISON
Columbia University

Is there such a thing as world public opinion? How does it develop? And what difference does it make? Those are central questions toward which this chapter is addressed. To answer these broad questions, the author marshals evidence concerning four somewhat more empirical matters, namely: (1) How much parallelism is there from country to country in the topics on which public opinion focuses? (2) What is the volume of communication of ideas between publics in different countries, and through what channels does it occur? (3) How much impact does world opinion have on the behavior of governments? (4) How will new communications technology affect the growth of world opinion?

The expectation of the author is that international opinion may grow sooner and more fully among scientific, technical, and professional communities than in the arena of politics.

There is a conspicuous lack of agreement among scholars as to what public opinion is, but they generally concede that within various countries it exists.[1] World public opinion not only lacks an agreed definition; even its existence is frequently questioned.[2]

One view of public opinion is that it is a distribution of individual opinions on a public issue, as discovered by public polls or other means. If this definition is adopted, the current frequency of multi-national surveys, which often produce similar results between countries, suggests that international opinion does indeed exist. But, as Bogart (1966) has observed, "Does multinational polling prove any more than that parallel research exercises may be carried out in many places at once, like the spring maneuvers of armies not allied?" Similar opinion distributions may be found among various national publics, but the opinions themselves may have quite different origins and significance and cannot necessarily be

---

The writer wishes to acknowledge the helpful criticisms of Dr. Ithiel de Sola Pool, who read a preliminary version of this chapter, as well as the encouragement and advice of Dr. Wilbur Schramm.

[1] For a discussion of various definitions of public opinion, see Key (1961), Childs (1965), Davison (1968).

[2] Several articles express this doubt in their titles; for example, "Is World Public Opinion a Myth?" (Morgenthau, 1962), and "Is There a World Public Opinion?" (Bogart, 1966).

considered as parts of a single phenomenon.

Another definition of public opinion is that it is an opinion on a public issue, shared by a segment of a population, that comes to the attention of higher authorities. This approach recognizes that a relatively small number of people can dominate opinion in a specific area, since their voices may be the only ones heard, and it links public opinion intimately to the political process. Nevertheless, by implication, it suggests that public opinion does not exist when it is not noted by the authorities, or when there are no appropriate authorities who might be influenced—as is true of many questions that go beyond the competence of individual national governments.

In this discussion, public opinion will be treated as a consensus on a particular issue that is produced by a process of communication and reciprocal influence.[3] It can be considered a form of organization because it is able to coordinate the thought and action of a large number of people and can also lead to a differentiation of roles among those participating in the consensus. Thus, within a public sharing an opinion, one can usually distinguish among leaders, disseminators, spokesmen, and followers. Under this definition a public may embrace relatively few persons, or it may involve millions, but in either case those participating are related to each other by communication networks. An international public opinion relates nationals of two or more countries; world public opinion binds together at least some citizens of all, or nearly all, countries.

If this definition is adopted, the presumption is strong that international and world public opinion do indeed exist. One needs only consider the difficulty of defending the opposing proposition, namely, that public opinion can form only within national boundaries. To do this one would have to maintain that people in two or more countries cannot participate in a common body of opinion, and that factors associated with nationality are always of overriding importance in the formation of views on public issues. Nationality is certainly an extremely important determinant of opinion, especially with regard to political matters, but cases where other factors seem to have played an important role can be found throughout modern history. Dissent within the United States regarding the war in Vietnam is one recent example; the aspiration of many Soviet intellectuals for greater freedom of expression is another.

Rather than to debate whether or not international and world opinions exist, this discussion will examine the conditions favoring or inhibiting their growth, attempt to evaluate their strengths and weaknesses, try to define the areas in which they play a role, and speculate about their development in the future. Definitive observations on any of these subjects are difficult to make; reliable data are sparse. Nevertheless, one can at least arrive at some possibly viable approximations.

PUBLIC OPINION AND THE DESIRE FOR WORLD PEACE

When Woodrow Wilson presented his design for a League of Nations to the Versailles Peace Conference, he stressed that the proposal rested on the assumption that the main force sustaining the League would be the moral influence of world public opinion. This idea occurred repeatedly in later speeches where he stressed his belief in the power of world opinion. Similarly, when defending the League concept in the British Parliament, Lord Cecil observed: "What we rely on is public opinion, and if we are wrong about it then the whole thing is wrong" (Fraenkel, 1962:35–36).[4]

In invoking public opinion as a pillar of the League of Nations, Wilson and Cecil were following in the tradition of a number

[3] This is substantially the view adopted by Charles Horton Cooley (1956).

[4] The following historical discussion is based largely on material presented by Fraenkel (1962) and Herberichs (1969).

of distinguished thinkers of the preceding two centuries. At the end of the eighteenth century, several peace plans were advanced, perhaps the best known being Bentham's (1939) *Plan for a Universal and Perpetual Peace*, first published in 1789, and Kant's (1963) proposals in his essay *Zum ewigen Frieden*, first published in 1795. Both plans were based on the belief that public opinion is peace loving, and that international peace-keeping organizations can be sustained by it.

Similarly, the nineteenth-century optimists believed that if the rule of public opinion could be extended around the world it would force nations to adhere to peaceful policies. James Mill, recommending a "code of international law," wrote that: "A moral sentiment would grow up, which would, in time, act as a powerful restraining force upon the injustice of nations, and give a wonderful efficacy to the international jurisdiction" (Herberichs, 1966–67:628).

Nor were such ideas confined to prominent European thinkers. The American Peace Society, founded by William Ladd in 1828, sponsored an essay contest on the subject of a congress of nations. All the prize winners made use of the public opinion concept. One maintained that the international body would have to be upheld by public opinion, or it would not function effectively. Another wrote: "... the law of nations is placed, in the first place, under the protection of public opinion. It is enforced by the censures of the press, and by the moral influence of those great masters of public law who are consulted by all nations..." (Herberichs, 1966–67:629).

In view of this widespread reliance on public opinion as a force for peace, it is important to inquire just how its authority would be exercised. Several answers to this question were proposed. The eighteenth-century philosopher John Locke formulated a "law of opinion and reputation," according to which opposition to public opinion led to an unbearable loss of reputation and even to social condemnation and boycott. Socialist thinkers later suggested that, if war threatened to break out, the universal desire for peace could be given expression through a universal general strike. This recourse was debated at the World Congress of Socialist Parties in Copenhagen in 1910, but the idea did not receive general endorsement and was never tried (Fraenkel, 1962:10, 28–29).

Most of those who looked upon world public opinion as a guarantor of peace did not, however, inquire closely into the exact processes through which war was to be outlawed; they invoked public opinion as a mystical force that could be effective without being understood. When William Ladd proposed that a world court and a permanent international organization of envoys be established, he was content to leave to public opinion, "the queen of the world," the functions of enforcing the decisions of those bodies (Fraenkel, 1962:25).

The belief that world public opinion was somehow the key to an enduring peace survived even the disillusionment following the Second World War. It was apparently in the minds of the framers of the UNESCO charter, who wrote that because the origin of wars was to be found in the minds of masses of men, it was in the minds of men that the defenses of peace should be constructed.[5]

Today's academicians are still interested in the part that world or international public opinion can play in the preservation of peace, but they tend to formulate their ideas much more cautiously and modestly than did their predecessors. Pool (1959:7) expresses the belief that research will establish the importance of public opinion as a factor in international politics and observes that one task of research is "to establish the facts of world opinion regarding matters such as the probability of war, the images of foreign peoples, fear of nuclear weapons, belief in international organizations, and national goals and aspirations." Raser (1966:300), surveying

[5] For an extensive criticism, see Dunn (1950).

research on deterrence, noted, "The academic community was increasingly aware that effective deterrence is as much a matter of minds and emotions as of hardware." Deutsch (1966), reporting on an extensive investigation of European willingness to accept arms-control measures, focused on the extent to which a common public opinion had grown up in France, Germany, and Great Britain.

In short, a substantial body of scholars would conclude with Fraenkel that international public opinion as a force in world politics is not a myth, but that we simply have not understood it well enough heretofore. Since nonviolent international control mechanisms are more necessary than ever, we should concentrate on devising ways of strengthening world public opinion and harnessing it to the cause of peace (Fraenkel, 1962:39).

REQUIREMENTS FOR INTERNATIONAL PUBLIC OPINION

For international or world public opinion to develop as a political force, three requirements must be satisfied. People in several countries must give their attention to a given issue; they must have sufficient means of interacting so that common and mutually reinforcing attitudes can form; and there must be some mechanism through which shared attitudes can be translated into action. All of these requirements are partially met at the present time; none is completely satisfied.

As far as common attention is concerned, various studies emphasize the degree to which people in different countries are concerned with different issues. If one compares survey questions asked by public opinion research organizations throughout the world, it is striking how few subjects are dealt with by more than one organization.[6] Opinion researchers naturally explore subjects that are of current interest within their own societies, and their questions therefore deal most frequently with political or cultural matters that are of primary relevance to their fellow nationals.

Multi-country surveys of news coverage have shown the extent to which editors differ in their definition of "top" stories. A 1953 UNESCO study attempted to define the nineteen principal stories of the week, and then checked to see how many of these were covered in seventeen leading newspapers throughout the world. *O Estado* of Sao Paulo included all but one of the stories, the best record of any paper examined. New York's *Daily News* missed five, Moscow's *Pravda* missed nine, and several other papers included even fewer (Kayser, 1953). It is possible that if this study were replicated at the present time a greater convergence of attention would be found, but even an unsystematic inspection of newspapers and news broadcasts from various countries shows that divergence of attention is still more impressive than convergence, even insofar as major stories of international interest are concerned.[7]

The degree to which attention is likely to be given to the same issue by people in different countries is limited by the rather low interest in international affairs found among most populations. Recent studies in the United States and other countries tend to confirm a picture established during the past twenty years: an uninterested majority and an attentive minority.[8] Robinson (1967) concluded that about one-third of the American public was almost completely insulated from information about world events, while at the other end of the spectrum there was a relatively small group of "hard-core know-it-alls." In India, Bose (1964) found that 80 percent of

[6] Poll results from more than twenty nations were printed in *Polls*, a quarterly journal published in Amsterdam from 1965 to 1969.

[7] Divergent national interests are recognized by wire services, which provide different news files to clients in different countries (Kruglak, 1957).

[8] Earlier surveys are summarized in Davison (1965:51–53).

the newspaper readers in his sample were primarily interested in domestic news and only 8 percent in foreign news, although among those readers with a higher education, interest in foreign news climbed to 23 percent.

In spite of the extent to which the attention of most people is focused on national or even parochial affairs, a few subjects can be found on which there is considerable convergence. In *Polls* magazine one can find topics on which survey organizations in several countries have asked similar questions—the United Nations, the European Common Market, the Indochina war, or leading personalities such as Chairman Mao, President DeGaulle, President Johnson, or the principal Soviet leaders.

When cross-sections in France, Norway, and Poland were asked during the winter of 1964–1965 to name the most important recent event in world affairs, the replies showed convergence of interest on a few subjects, as well as striking differences in attention with respect to many more. Political changes in the Kremlin were mentioned by about a quarter of the respondents in each country; other subjects that were regarded as very important by appreciable numbers in all three countries concerned troubles in the Congo, the death of President Kennedy, and elections in the United States. On the other hand, the Vatican Council was mentioned by 17 percent in France and by 4 percent in Poland, but was not included at all among the Norwegian responses. The conflict in Vietnam was mentioned by 49 percent in Poland and by 5 percent in France, but apparently was mentioned by very few Norwegians. Of the twenty-one subjects volunteered as the most important event by an appreciable number of respondents in any country, five were raised by people in all three countries, and nine were referred to by people in only one country.[9]

In other words, there appears to be a rather limited number of subjects to which appreciable numbers of people in many countries simultaneously give their attention. A very few subjects, such as the assassination of President Kennedy, gain the attention of large numbers in practically all countries. Smaller numbers of people in nearly all countries, including the better educated and politically interested, are aware of broader ranges of political events. The attention of this group converges on a few additional subjects. International or world public opinion is therefore more likely to reflect the views of relatively small groups of people in several countries than it is to find a mass basis, although the latter is occasionally possible.

A subject is not, of course, the same thing as an issue, and public opinion forms around issues. Even when a given subject receives worldwide attention, it may be presented as a very different issue to people in different countries. For example, when Schramm (1959) compared the content of fourteen newspapers from fourteen different countries for November 2, 1956, the day the Anglo-French invasion of Suez and Soviet intervention in Hungary were reported, he found striking differences in the news handling of the two stories.

When the Committee for Non-Violent Action, an American pacifist organization, conducted a San Francisco-Moscow Peace Walk, the event was reported in a number of ways by media in countries through which the walkers passed. Only in Belgium did the press emphasize the policy proposals that the demonstrators sought to publicize; media in other countries tended to interpret the walk in a way that supported national positions (Gwyn, 1966). Differing interpretations of those relatively few events on which appreciable interna-

[9] From *Polls* 1(Spring 1966):89. The survey was directed by Jean Stoezel under the auspices of the European Coordination Center for Research and Documentation in the Social Sciences. Results for the three countries are not strictly comparable, since respondents were permitted to give multiple responses in France and Poland, but not in Norway.

tional attention converges thus limit still further the range of issues on which multinational public opinion can form.

DEVELOPMENT OF INTERNATIONAL MEDIA

The present state of the international communication network is such that, in theory, almost any person can obtain information about almost any major event or issue if he is willing to make the necessary effort, and if he is not effectively barred from access to the media by illiteracy, poverty, or political restraints. Frequently, however, the effort required is a major one, especially in the case of persons living in developing countries.

Although advocates of worldwide broadcasting via satellites hold high hopes that this channel will make it possible for people everywhere to enjoy a communality of experience, satellite broadcasting has as yet provided no marked stimulus to the formation of international public opinion. One reason for this is technological. The state of the art now permits only for relaying programs over long distances for retransmission by local stations in receiving countries; it does not allow international programs to be picked up directly by listeners and viewers (UNESCO, 1963; 1967).[10] Factors that influence the content of national media thus continue to operate.

A more important reason for the limited impact of international television on world public opinion is that the ground rules for this kind of programming require the avoidance of controversial issues. Thus, when millions of viewers in twenty-six nations witnessed a live global telecast entitled "Our World" in June 1967, they saw newborn babies in Japan, Denmark, Mexico, and Canada; agricultural experiments in various countries; sports events; and the activities of artists. The most controversial material in the program dealt with the relatively placid meeting between Soviet Premier Kosygin and President Johnson at Glassboro, New Jersey. Even so, Jack Gould, television critic of the *New York Times*, regarded "Our World" as "a compelling reaffirmation of the potential of the home screen to help unify the peoples of the world."[11]

More systematic and vigorous international radio and television programming is likely in the near future. In 1968, the International Broadcast Institute, backed mainly by American foundations as well as by some foreign foundations and governments, opened an office in Rome. The institute, headquarters of which were moved to London in 1971, conducts international symposia on the expanding communication technology and explores ways of stimulating international broadcasting in general.[12]

Simultaneous exposure of relatively small numbers of people in many countries to material on public issues is currently achieved by shortwave broadcasting, conducted primarily by information and propaganda organizations of many governments. A survey conducted in 1966, for instance, showed that approximately one million people in the United States were then listening to shortwave broadcasts from abroad at least once a week (Smith, 1969–70).

Some printed media, including both propaganda materials and nonofficial publications, also reach audiences outside the country of original publication. Thus, all

---

10 However, Indian communication satellite plans for 1972 are reported to provide for direct transmission of TV from satellite to village receiver, aided only by a special dish antenna costing about one hundred dollars per set.

11 *New York Times*, June 26, 1967. Viewers would have been even more numerous if the Soviet Union and four East European countries had not dropped out of the consortium arranging the telecast a few days before it was aired, charging Western broadcasters with conducting anti-Arab propaganda in connection with the Middle East crisis.

12 *New York Times*, August 5, 1968. See also the *Newsletter* published twice yearly by the International Broadcast Institute in London.

newspapers belonging to the so-called world press circulate widely across national boundaries (Fischer, 1966) and numerous magazines either print special foreign editions or circulate internationally in their original format. These include, among many others, the London *Economist*, *Réalités*, the *Swiss Review of World Affairs*, *Time*, *Life*,[13] the *National Geographic Magazine*, and the *Reader's Digest*. The last-named is by far the largest, with international editions totaling well over ten million copies a month (Davison, 1965: 332–333).

Government information and propaganda organizations print a number of magazines that are aimed at a multi-national readership. One fairly recent addition to the growing list of international periodicals is *Sputnik*, a pocket-sized magazine published by the Soviet Novosti Press Agency, which started circulating in fifty-nine countries in 1967. Another is *Dialogue*, a quarterly journal sponsored by the U.S. Information Agency and intended to appeal to intellectuals in all countries. *Dialogue* started publication in 1968 in English and Spanish, with plans for a French edition.

FACILITIES FOR DIALOGUES AMONG PEOPLES

While a necessary precondition for international public opinion is that at least some people in two or more countries give their attention to the same issue, public opinion in the sense that we are speaking of it here cannot grow until these people form opinions about the issue and discuss it with each other. At the present time, facilities for the international exchange of opinions are considerably less developed than those for the one-way dissemination of information and views.

The mass media make some effort to promote an international dialogue. Newspapers frequently report editorial opinion from other countries, print letters from foreign readers, and occasionally carry the results of cross-national opinion polls. Major radio and television networks, either on national broadcasts or on international hookups, carry a limited number of discussions among people from different countries, and program exchanges are increasingly common—especially within Eastern and Western Europe. Nevertheless, these efforts are clearly peripheral in most cases.

In connection with a study of West European integration, Deutsch (1966) notes that the press in the United States, Great Britain, and France each tends to pay the most attention to the proposals of its own government and less attention to the proposals or moves by other countries. He concludes that "the evidence confirms the familiar picture of the national press of each country conducting often a kind of national monologue rather than genuine cross-national communication within the Western alliance" (Deutsch, 1966:362). Bogart (1966:5) observes that the growing global unity of information and culture is accounted for largely by national mass media systems rather than through international mass media.

An international dialogue is promoted by a number of more specialized media, even though these have relatively small audiences when compared with the principal mass media systems. In the United States, *Atlas* magazine, which in 1970 had a circulation of more than 125,000, reprints articles from some 600 publications around the world. A similar journal in Russia, *Za Rubizhom* ("From Abroad"), has a circulation of 1.5 million. It is one of the most successful Russian magazines, and a similar Czech journal was equally successful there. In 1967 another magazine, *Interplay*, started publication in an effort to provide a stronger communication link between Europe and North America. Although

---

[13] In 1970, *Life* announced the suspension of its international edition, despite record circulation, due to rising costs. *Life* ceased publication entirely in December 1972.

based in the United States, its editorial advisory board included leading figures from eight countries. It ceased to appear in 1971.

International political and religious organizations, business and labor groups, scientific associations, and many other kinds of bodies play an increasingly important role in exposing their members to ideas originating in various countries. The *Annuaire des Organisations Internationales* for 1962–1963 listed more than 1,500 nongovernmental groups, the overwhelming majority of which sponsored publications or information services of some kind. It also listed over 150 international organizations in which governments were members, and these were likewise prolific publishers. The rapid proliferation of international organizations is suggested by the fact that the 1970–1971 edition of the *Annuaire* includes 2,296 private bodies and 242 intergovernmental associations. The UN itself, besides publishing a wide variety of reports and documents, produces radio and television programs that are aired through the facilities of cooperating nations.

Even the specialized mass media and the publications or broadcasts of international organizations have serious limitations when it comes to promoting a multi-nation dialogue on current issues. They do, it is true, advance the process by one step in that they carry views of country B back to country A. The publishers of *Atlas*, for instance, see their role as letting the rest of the world tell its story to the American people—a sort of Voice of America in reverse. But it is still difficult for the readers in the United States to pick up the conversation from there. For international public opinion to grow, a more extended dialogue is generally necessary, a process in which participants in the consensus are influenced to some degree by other participants.

It is for this reason that face-to-face communication is such an important mechanism in building international public opinion. In spite of the miracles of modern technology, the encounter where two or more individuals from different nations are present is still the most efficient way of arriving at a meaningful exchange of ideas. Only a limited number of people can effectively take part in each such encounter, but the total number that could be involved if they wanted to be is appreciable, even when compared with the total world population. Moreover, the volume of personal international contacts appears to be growing fairly rapidly each year. Angell (1967: 129), who excluded tourists from his analysis, found that the growth rate of "transnational participation" by business men, national and international civil servants, and some other groups, appeared to be between 5 and 10 percent a year.

As of 1965, it was estimated that there were about thirty-four hundred private programs bringing foreign nationals to the United States for educational purposes (see Sargeant, 1965:101). If government-sponsored educational exchanges, programs not involving education, and those that sponsor foreign travel by Americans were included, the total for this country would be much higher. Student exchange is at least as lively among the countries of Western Europe, even though more of it may take place on an informal rather than a program basis, and student exchange is also very active in Arab and Eastern European nations.

When one adds travel and foreign residence for government and business purposes, the number of persons involved may approximate 1 percent of the world's population each year. This total is, of course, unevenly distributed. The mobility of people from industrialized nations is far greater than the mobility of those from developing countries, and members of the higher educational and economic groups are more likely than others to be exposed to foreign societies.

The degree to which a meaningful dialogue takes place in the course of foreign contacts differs greatly according to the nature of the contact. International political and professional meetings often involve extended exchange of ideas about current issues. The annual meetings of the Inter-Parliamentary Union, for instance, usually touch upon major international issues; its 1967 meeting in Palma, Spain, was dominated by discussions of Vietnam.

Perhaps the most intensive interchange about current issues comes, however, in the context of international educational ventures. A few international schools and institutions of higher education already exist in various parts of the world, and it is probable that their number will grow fairly rapidly during the coming decades. The East-West Center of the University of Hawaii is one of the most fully developed of these. The idea of a world university has captured many imaginations; during the last fifty years, more than 1,000 proposals for establishing a world university have been made (Zweig, 1967).

International contacts, together with international media, compose a matrix within which there can be a continuing exchange of opinions. The two channels of communication stimulate and complement each other. Contacts with persons from other countries tend to promote attention to media bringing information from abroad; attention to international media is likely to encourage international contacts. For instance, Russett (1962:304) found that legislators with economic or personal ties with another country were more likely to pay attention to information from that country than were other legislators. And 25 percent of the subscribers to *Atlas* expected to take one or more international trips during 1967.

INTERNATIONAL INSTITUTIONS

Even if multi-nation exchanges of opinions allow international or world public opinion to form, it will have few avenues of expression in the absence of international institutions that are responsive to it. Some observers have regarded the United Nations as such an institution, but this view can be questioned (Fraenkel, 1962: 6). The United Nations is an organization of governments, and could even be regarded as inhibiting the expression of international public opinion rather than favoring it. There are no elections through which individuals can participate in the selection of delegations to the United Nations, and while the UN Secretariat and constituent agencies are receptive to public advice and petitions, and accept the advice of nongovernmental organizations, major policy decisions are arrived at by representatives of national governments. The Office of the Secretary General could develop as an institution expressive of world opinion, but thus far successive Secretaries General have been extremely cautious not even to give the appearance of appealing to a world public over the heads of member governments. Bogart (1966:2) notes that there are no responsible political mechanisms of world public opinion analogous to those in national states.

Nevertheless, there are signs that truly international political institutions may be not far in the future. Herberichs observes that the Council of Europe owes its existence to the pressure of public opinion, even though its members are not popularly elected. "In other words, the Strassbourg institution appears to confirm that it *can* happen, in exceptional circumstances, that public opinion plays an active and constructive role in the process of international organization" (Herberichs, 1966–67:633). Private international associations, whether of an economic, scientific, religious, or political nature, all have to take account of the shared opinions of their international membership, although frequently they are concerned with balancing varicus national viewpoints and avoiding issues that might prove divisive.

Some efforts have been made to use international opinion to exert pressure on individual governments. The degree to which these have been successful is, however, impossible to demonstrate. Literary circles in many countries combined in an effort to prevent the Soviet government from taking measures against Boris Pasternak and again to protest the prosecution of Soviet writers Sinyavsky and Daniel. Similarly, the Moscow radio canceled regular programs on nineteen overseas channels in April 1967 to appeal to international opinion to help prevent the execution by the Greek military junta of Manolis Glezos, a World War II partisan hero.

Nevertheless, national governments continue to be more responsive to domestic than to foreign opinion. China and France continued to develop nuclear weapons in the face of very substantial foreign opposition. The United States government did not seem to be appreciably influenced by European protests regarding the war in Vietnam. Soviet military suppression of Czechoslovak liberalization in 1968 was almost universally condemned by foreign public opinion even in many Socialist states, but Moscow proceeded nonetheless. Israel stirred a storm of protest when it raided the Beirut airport later in the same year, but was clearly more interested in putting an end to Arab attacks on Israeli planes than in courting world favor.

Given present institutional arrangements, this is not surprising. National governments are not set up to register and give effect to international opinion. If they did, they would soon fall. Appeals to world public opinion are frequent. They may succeed, or partially succeed, when no vital national interest opposes them, but they do not appear to exert appreciable influence on governments that believe a matter of national security to be at stake.

THE PRESENT STATE OF INTEGRATION

Even in Western Europe—an area where more than in any other region of the world there are common foci of attention, many channels for exchanging opinions, and a number of regional institutions—the level of integration of international opinion seems to be fairly low. Two separate investigations by Gorden and Lerner (1965) and by Deutsch (1966:360–361, 364) have established certain areas in which one can speak of an international European opinion, but they also emphasize the extent to which national divergencies prevail.

Lerner, polling leadership panels in France, West Germany, and Great Britain, found nearly unanimous affirmation of the idea of the European Community, and a strong trend in the direction of further international association. But there were deep differences among the panel members in the three countries as to the favored arena for cooperation, the degree of cooperation to be sought with the United States, and other questions.

Deutsch, questioning a sample of leaders in France and Germany, found substantial agreement that Great Britain ought to be included in a United Europe, that both European and Atlantic integration should be supported, and that Europe was still dependent on the deterrent power of the United States, but the national panels differed in regard to the saliency they attached to various issues and perhaps in their underlying expectations as well. A provisional factor analysis of his survey data suggested that nationality was between two and ten times as powerful in determining opinions on these questions as any one cross-national factor, such as religion, occupation, or Socialist party affiliation.

In Western Europe there thus appears to be a substantial consensus, at least among leadership elements, on general issues affecting regional cooperation, but a much lower degree of consensus about what should be done about these issues, and according to what time schedule. To emphasize the degree to which a Western European public opinion has not yet been completely developed is, however, to ignore the immense change in the direction of consensus on important issues that has taken place during the past generation. In an earlier study, Deutsch (1962) noted that European publics found the idea of a war among Western European nations simply unthinkable in the world of the 1960s. This idea, unthinkable to contemporary Europeans, had for their fathers and grandfathers been an almost universally accepted fact of life.

On another level of investigation, Cantril (1965:159–161, 171–173) studied the concerns of populations of fourteen nations that had different forms of government and were at different stages of development. He found it possible to group all personal concerns (hopes and fears) in seventy-five code items, and all national concerns in ninety items. The extent to which people in all countries shared personal hopes and fears, and expressed similar national hopes and fears, suggests that the basis for many shared opinions exists. Thus, substantial numbers in nearly every country mentioned economic, health, and family worries. Those mentioning economic worries, for example, range from 30 percent of the sample in Brazil to 65 percent in Nigeria. Similarly, substantial numbers everywhere mentioned their hope for social gains within their nations, ranging from 13 percent in the Philippines to 70 percent in Israel.

At the same time, Cantril found large differences among the nations he studied, not only in the incidence of certain concerns, but in their patterning. Small proportions (4 percent or less) in the Dominican Republic, Panama, Brazil, and the United States were concerned about the independence of their countries, but this concern was mentioned by 44 percent in Egypt, 37 percent in Israel, and 24 percent in Nigeria. Some populations mentioned many more different hopes, or many more fears, than others. Cantril concluded that the concerns of people are patterned largely according to the phases of development within their own societies.

Much more important than the political ideology to which a nation subscribes is the way in which people regard the stage of economic development in which they find themselves: whether they simply acquiesce to their current circumstances, whether they are awakening to the potentialities of themselves and their nations and are aware of the means to realize their goals, whether they are experiencing gratifications they have achieved through their own action, or whether they are already enjoying the satisfactions afforded by an affluent society (Cantril, 1965:301–310).

Cantril's analysis suggests that the raw material for convergence of world attention and intersociety discussion is present, even though many and long intermediate stages may well be necessary before it becomes world opinion. People everywhere want much the same things and share many of the same fears, even if these have a different salience for the populations of different countries. There is a common language of aspiration and apprehension. At the same time, those populations that are at roughly the same psychological phase of development share somewhat the same pattern of concerns, and therefore may find it simpler to enter into communication with each other than with populations that are at different phases. On a very long-range basis, the data hold out the prospect that international opinions will develop first among people in groups of states sharing common characteristics, and that these opinions will gradually coalesce into world opinions.

Most of us have a strong tendency to emphasize areas of conflict or contrast at the expense of areas of agreement and similarity. As Cantril (1965:315) observes: "In describing the differences found among people in any study of wide scope, it is all too easy to neglect basic uniformities which take diverse forms in different cultural settings."

In the realm of personal and national aspirations it is clear that definition of the good life is in terms of Western industrialized society, and this provides a unifying force for people everywhere. Cantril (1965: 313) concludes that no developing people will choose to go in a different direction, no matter how critical they may be of some Western values. This growing consensus is in part a result of the world communications explosion. The proliferation of the mass media has allowed people everywhere to window-shop for the qualities they would like to have in their own lives, and they seem to have made up their minds what they want to buy.[14]

PROSPECTS FOR THE FUTURE

International and world opinion, presently weak in most areas, may be expected to grow stronger in the years ahead if current trends continue, although this cannot be taken for granted. Forces favoring further development of world opinion include continuing technological progress in international communication, the emergence of more and more problems for which there are no national solutions, and the proliferation of international associations. Whether the development of world opinion will be rapid, slow, or inhibited will depend in large part on the role played by nationalism in the coming decades, on the policies of national governments, and on the degree to which increasing numbers of politically conscious people throughout the world can be included in international dialogues. Initially, at least, it is likely that an international consensus will grow more rapidly in regard to issues that are not defined as primarily political.

Recent technological developments in communication make it increasingly possible for people everywhere to focus their attention on the same issues and to engage in an exchange of ideas about them. Satellite broadcasting, in particular, has led to the expectation of closer international contacts. Following the successful launching of the first communications satellite, the General Assembly of the United Nations, in December 1962, adopted a resolution recording the view that "communication by satellite offers great benefits to mankind, as it will permit the expansion of radio, telephone and television transmissions, thus facilitating contact among the peoples of the world."

A UNESCO report, issued in the following year, noted that artificial satellites do not actually provide a new medium of communication, but rather make possible the extension of existing media. Thus they can be used to relay every type of information commonly transmitted by telegraph or telephone, radio or television, and offer to these channels a potential extension of range and scope that will permit them to play a greater role than before (UNESCO, 1963:6). For example, the advent of space communication is expected to accelerate the trend toward newspaper expansion, and to make possible the simultaneous publication of newspaper editions or features in several countries or throughout whole regions (UNESCO, 1963:18–19).

Of particular significance for the development of international opinion is the probability that satellite broadcasting will stimulate person-to-person communication across national boundaries. As reported by UNESCO (1963:22):

> Space communication is likely to have unpredictable and ultimately astonishing effects on person-to-person communication generally. For example, it may accelerate the growing tendency of our time to develop contact between people from different countries for the discussion and solution of common problems and the exchange of information. Thus, when adequate facilities have become available and costs are sufficiently low, satellites could be used for international conferences and seminars in which the participants would confer with each other by means of closed-circuit television.

Of greater immediate significance than the possibilities offered by new techniques of communication is the continuing spread of existing technologies to new areas. More and more people everywhere have access to films, radio, and television. The growth of the press in developing areas is more gradual, since its expansion depends in

[14] Graphic illustrations of the role of communications in molding values are given in Lerner (1958).

part on literacy, but nevertheless a steady extension of newspapers and other print media seems to be taking place.[15]

At the same time that the mass media are permeating to all corners of the world, problem areas are emerging that increasingly defy national solutions. Some of the most obvious of these are economic. For example, provision of adequate food supplies to many areas of the world requires international cooperation; national markets cannot provide an adequate basis for efficient industries. Other problems are in the realm of communication and transportation. Still others concern scientific development or moral issues.

Weather control is often mentioned as one scientific area where international cooperation is necessary; others include space exploration, population and disease control, and oceanographic research. Some scientific research undertakings are now so expensive that they strain the resources of even the most wealthy nations and eventually will have to be sponsored internationally if they are to be carried on. Among international moral issues are those that concern religious doctrine directly, and those implicit in efforts to outlaw slavery and the narcotics traffic and to control crime in general.

In the political realm the greatest problem requiring international cooperation is, of course, the establishment of enduring peace. Others include arms control, the future of former colonial territories, and the assurance of universal human rights. Population control is also coming to be seen as an international political problem.

International discussion of issues in all these areas has increased markedly in the course of the past generation. Many such discussions take place among governments, whether through diplomatic channels or in the context of the United Nations or one of its subsidiary organizations. The World Health Organization, the International Telecommunications Union, and the World Food Organization are examples of international bodies in which governments discuss specialized questions.

In addition, international private organizations deal with many of the same problems. They provide a forum and a focus for discussions among individuals in many nations, and also the institutional means through which international public opinion can find at least some expression. A Vatican Council, or a meeting of the World Council of Churches, for instance, may lead to efforts to influence national governments, but may additionally lead to action taken directly through international religious institutions. The same is true of international business groups, which also have their own institutional means for acting, and, to a lesser degree, of international scientific and educational groups. All these are dependent on national governments to some extent, but not completely.

It is for this reason that international public opinion as an organized force is likely to develop more rapidly on economic, scientific, and moral issues than on political matters. The groups primarily concerned with these issues are relatively small and homogeneous, at least when compared with those that are concerned with broader political issues. Furthermore, the economic, scientific, and religious communities already have achieved a more common focus of attention and more adequate means for exchanging opinions than is the case with groups that are primarily concerned with political questions. Scientists and clergymen may not always agree, but at least they know what they want to talk about and they exchange ideas with considerable intensity.

Some young people (a rather small minority, to be sure) in countries with very different political systems all around the world seem to have already formed a kind of international community based on com-

[15] The growth of media throughout the world is documented in the UNESCO publication, *World Communications* (UNESCO, 1950; 1951; 1956; 1964).

mon opinions on such issues as individual freedom, and characterized by certain styles of dress and tastes in music. Their means of intercommunication have included personal encounters, magazines and recordings (often smuggled), and short-wave radio.

Public opinion and communication researchers themselves comprise an international group among which opinions on various questions are forming. Their attention is focused on many of the same problems. Professional publications and meetings, as well as cross-national research projects, bring them together and provide opportunities to exchange ideas. Galtung (1967) suggests the way that comparative research can help to form international opinion, even if among a rather select group, when he notes that "in personal terms, it [comparative research] is a great experience in international cooperation—especially if it bridges some of the cleavages found between the nations in the world today" (Galtung, 1967: 18).

It is probable that during the next decades world opinion will develop more rapidly among fairly limited groups and on fairly specialized questions than it will within a broader public on major political issues. The former development will, however, set the stage for the latter, especially as major political questions are nibbled at within the context of scientific, philosophical, or other discussions, and various institutional mechanisms for expressing world opinions are experimented with. Although it is unlikely that we shall see the emergence of powerful political institutions responsive to world opinion within the present generation, the seeds for such institutions are already in evidence, including some organizations that are currently dominated by national governments and some that are of a private nature, such as the Atlantic Council and various international political party groups.

Incorporation of increasingly large numbers of politically conscious citizens into international opinion networks is likely to be a slow process. Deutsch (1967) estimates that as of 1815 the thoughts and reactions of only a few million people had to be taken into account in international politics. During the period prior to the First World War, there were on the order of 200 million such people, but by now there are about 1 billion "whose mass attitudes and actions have at least a potential effect on world politics and international peace today" (Deutsch, 1967: 104). For world opinion to grow relative to national opinion, communication and coordination mechanisms at the international level must expand their capabilities at a rate that will more than keep pace with the growth of politically attentive publics (Boulding, 1967: 156).

The policies of national authorities will play an important role in determining the rate at which world opinion will grow. If they loosen the restrictions now surrounding international travel and the exchange of information, the growth will be more rapid. If they reinforce the present barriers, or if they encourage a spirit of narrow nationalism, growth will be slowed and the process might even be reversed. If governments were willing and able to redesign their national information and propaganda programs so as to make these into vehicles for international exchanges of opinion rather than mainly a means of expounding national viewpoints, this would speed up the process considerably.

One certainly cannot assume that world opinion grows automatically with the passage of time. Indeed, insofar as Europe is concerned, international opinion was probably more influential in the nineteenth century than in the first half of the twentieth. A relatively small and homogeneous group of opinion leaders in the nations of the area maintained a network of communication that enabled them to interact and exert reciprocal influence on each other, so that the major cultural and political trends of the time were usually given expression by developments in several countries. Examples may be found in the wave of revolutions in 1848 and in the Socialist movements that developed in Europe on a roughly parallel timetable.

During the first half of the twentieth century, however, the influence of international opinion was overshadowed by increasing preoccupation with national problems and the growth of political participation by those who had not been incorporated into international communication networks. Following the end of World War II, the trend in Europe as well as in most other regions of the world appears to have been again in the direction of stronger international consensus.

Since world opinion is usually thought about by idealists, it is generally seen as a beneficent force, and especially as a force for peace. This is not necessarily the case. One can envisage situations where a powerful world opinion would lead to a condition of tyranny, stifling individual freedom on a global scale as efficiently as national governments have been able to do in their own countries. Or one can anticipate that, just as in one country there are likely to be several bodies of opinion on any major issue, so there are likely to be several bodies of world opinion on such issues. If two strong but conflicting international opinions grew up on a given issue, this would make conflicts between states less likely but, in extreme cases, might promote civil war within all countries.

Nevertheless, whatever the potential risks of world opinion, it also seems to offer one of the most attractive, albeit distant, mechanisms for the reduction of international conflict.

REFERENCES

Angell, Robert C.
1967 "The growth rate of transnational participation." Journal of Social Issues 23(January): 108–129.

Bentham, Jeremy.
1939 A Plan for a Universal and Perpetual Peace. Edited by C. J. Colombos. London: Peace Book Company.

Bogart, Leo.
1966 "Is there a world public opinion?" Polls (1(No. 3): 1–9.

Bose, A. B.
1964 "The newspaper reader in India." Indian Journal of Social Research 5(No. 1): 34–40.

Boulding, Elise.
1967 "The study of conflict and community in the international system." Journal of Social Issues 23(January): 144–158.

Cantril, Hadley.
1965 The Pattern of Human Concerns. New Brunswick, New Jersey: Rutgers University Press.

Childs, Harwood.
1965 Public Opinion. Princeton, New Jersey: Van Nostrand.

Cooley, Charles Horton.
1956 Social Organization. Glencoe, Illinois: Free Press.

Davison, W. Phillips.
1965 International Political Communication. New York: Praeger.
1968 "Public opinion," in David L. Sills (ed.), International Encyclopedia of the Social Sciences. Volume 13. New York: Macmillan.

Deutsch, Karl W.
1962 "Towards western European integration: An interim assessment." Journal of International Affairs 16(No. 1): 89–101.
1966 "Integration and arms control in the European political environment." American Political Science Review 60(June): 354–365.
1967 "Changing images of international conflict." Journal of Social Issues 23(January): 91–107.

Dunn, Frederick S.
1950 War and the Minds of Men. New York: Harper.

Fischer, Heinz-Dietrich.
1966 Die Grossen Zeitungen. Munich: Deutscher Taschenbuch Verlag.

Fraenkel, Ernst.
1962 Oeffentliche Meinung und Internationale Politik. Tübingen: Mohr.

Galtung, Johan.
1967 "Some aspects of comparative research." Polls 2(No. 3): 1–19.

Gorden, Morton, and Daniel Lerner.
1965 "The setting for European arms con-

trols: Political and strategic choices of European elites." Journal of Conflict Resolution 9(December):419–433.

Gwyn, Robert J.
1966 "Political dissent and the free market of ideas: An eight-nation study." Gazette 12(No. 2/3):187–200.

Herberichs, Gerard.
1966–67 "On theories of public opinion and international organization." Public Opinion Quarterly 30(Winter):624–636.

Kant, Immanuel.
1963 Perpetual Peace, a Philosophical Essay. Translated by Lewis W. Beck. Indianapolis: Bobbs-Merrill.

Kayser, Jacques.
1953 One Week's News: Comparative Study of Seventeen Major Dailies for Seven-Day Period. Paris: UNESCO.

Key, V. O., Jr.
1961 Public Opinion and American Democracy. New York: Knopf.

Kruglak, Theodore E.
1957 "The foreign correspondents." Nieman Reports 11(January):15–18.

Lerner, Daniel.
1958 The Passing of Traditional Society. Glencoe, Illinois: Free Press.

Morgenthau, Hans J.
1962 "Is world public opinion a myth?" New York Times Magazine March 25:23+.

Pool, Ithiel de Sola.
1959 Communication and Values in Relation to War and Peace. New York: Institute for International Order.

Raser, John R.
1966 "Deterrence research." Journal of Peace Research 4:297–327.

Robinson, John P.
1967 "World affairs information and mass media exposure." Journalism Quarterly 44(Spring):23–31.

Russett, Bruce M.
1962 "International communication and legislative behavior: The Senate and the House of Commons." Journal of Conflict Resolution 6(December): 291–307.

Sargeant, Howland H.
1965 "Information and cultural representation overseas," in The Representation of the United States Abroad, edited by Vincent M. Barnett, Jr., for the American Assembly. New York: Praeger.

Schramm, Wilbur.
1959 One Day in the World's Press. Stanford, California: Stanford University Press.

Smith, Don D.
1969–70 "America's short-wave audience: Twenty-five years later." Public Opinion Quarterly 33(Winter):537–545.

UNESCO.
1950 World Communications: Press, Radio, Television, Film. First Edition. New York: Columbia University Press.
1951 World Communications: Press, Radio, Television, Film. Revised Edition. New York: Columbia University Press.
1956 World Communications: Press, Radio, Television, Film. Third Edition. New York: Columbia University Press.
1963 "Space communication and the mass media," in Reports and Papers on Mass Communication. Paris: UNESCO.
1964 World Communications: Press, Radio, Television, Film. Fourth Edition. New York: UNESCO Publications Center.
1967 Communication in the Space Age. Paris: UNESCO.

Zweig, Michael.
1967 The Idea of a World University. Carbondale: Southern Illinois University Press.

CHAPTER 29 Freedom and Control of Communication

MARC A. FRANKLIN
Stanford Law School

This chapter, by a professor of law, analyzes the balance that the American tradition requires courts and regulatory agencies to maintain between the individual's freedom of expression and society's right to be protected from certain exercises of that freedom. It traces the developing legal relationship between communication freedom and control, and suggests some emerging themes that will bear watching as the relationship is further defined in the coming years.

WHY FREEDOM?

The American political tradition requires that government justify any decision to restrict private activity. This general presumption in favor of individual choice is especially appropriate in the realm of communication, the process by which members of a society exchange messages with one another.

Freedom of communication is a fundamental concept of Western political thought needing no elaborate restatement here (cf. Emerson, 1970). It benefits the individual and the society. Man as an individual is distinguished from the lower animals, and functions in his world, by his capacity to communicate his thoughts to others. For society as a whole, the gains may be stated in terms of the "attainment of truth" in such varied areas as scientific knowledge, social conduct, and political judgment, as we develop and refine the ideas of others.

Since our government is defined as deriving its powers from the governed, citizens must be heard, individually and collectively, on the important issues of the time. Giving each citizen a role in the decision-making process maximizes the potential soundness and acceptability of the eventual decision by introducing the fullest range of positions. Through rational discussion and free interchange of ideas a society is more likely to be dynamic:

This study was completed in the course of a Fellowship at the Center for Advanced Study in the Behavioral Sciences. The author wishes to thank the Center, his colleague Gerald Gunther, who read and commented upon an earlier draft, and Donald E. Brown, Jack Owens, and Edward Steinman who, while students at the Stanford School of Law, assisted in the preparation of this paper.

changes occur more gradually and are more acceptable.

Even the most passionate advocate of freedom to communicate would concede, however, that certain circumstances may justify governmental restraint of this freedom.[1] The problem is to define with precision those conditions that justify such regulation (Freund, 1961:74–87). We shall turn first to general noncontent arguments for limiting communication and then consider those primarily based on the content of the message.

WHOSE FREEDOM OF WHAT?

Freedom from What?

We will discuss solely controls or regulations invoked by government—whether federal, state, or local. Unless there is significance for government regulation, we shall not explore such substantial private inhibitions as the motion-picture industry's self-regulation (see Emerson, Haber, & Dorsen, 1967:831–868), or the responsiveness of television programming to the demands of prospective advertisers. These are part of the give-and-take of the private sector, and few would involve the government in insulating private individuals from efforts of other private individuals to affect the substance of their communication.

We also exclude government inhibitions that apply to communication media along with other enterprises, such as our general antitrust,[2] labor-relations,[3] or tax laws.[4] In brief, the communication industries may generally be regulated like other industries but not singled out for special regulation.

The regulation with which we are concerned may have various sources and forms. We may first distinguish between politically motivated regulation, framed in the heat of legislative battle, and judicial decisions that validate or set aside on constitutional grounds regulations initiated elsewhere. To overlook this difference would be to ignore the fact that our judiciary has freer rein when it is creating or developing common law than when it is assessing constitutionality.

For many, the finality and drama of constitutional adjudication have caused the question of whether a particular restraint is "constitutional" to overshadow the primary political question of the wisdom of imposing the restraint in the first place. While this imbalance may occur in any field of government action, the dependence of unpopular minorities upon majoritarian tolerance makes it especially important that, in the realm of communication, the focus be kept at the political level and not put solely on "law."

The political-legal dichotomy is an important one whether "activist" or "modest" judicial review otherwise be thought preferable. At the legal level, most of the issues are constitutional and arise from legislative efforts to restrain some form of communication in the face of the First Amendment:

> Congress shall make no law respecting an establishment of religion, or prohibiting the free exercise thereof; or abridging the freedom of speech, or of the press; or the right of the people peaceably to assemble, and to petition the government for a redress of grievances.

Originally directed solely against the federal government, the First Amendment has now been extended to state and local governments through the Fourteenth Amendment.[5] Concurrently, however, a

---

1 See Louis D. Brandeis' concurring opinion in *Whitney* v. *California*, 274 U.S. 357 (1927).

2 *Associated Press* v. *United States*, 326 U.S. 1 (1945).

3 *Associated Press* v. *National Labor Relations Board*, 301 U.S. 103 (1937).

4 *Grosjean* v. *American Press Co.*, 297 U.S. 233 (1966)—state effort to tax only large publications.

5 *New York Times Co.* v. *Sullivan*, 376 U.S. 254 (1964)—discussion of the role of the Fourteenth Amendment and an example of holding a common law rule unconstitutional.

significant number of other inhibitions on communication, such as right of privacy, have been developed on a state-by-state basis by the courts acting on their common law initiative.

The protection against government control was once thought to extend only to the denial of "prior restraint," i.e., suppression of a communication before it would reach its proposed recipients. This view, closely associated with Blackstone, made it entirely proper for the government to punish afterward those whose communications violated existing bans (see Chafee, 1941). Such protection was obviously inadequate and it is now established that, where First Amendment protection from government interference does exist, it extends both to the initial circulation and to subsequent responsibility for the substance of that communication.[6] On the other hand, as the case involving the Pentagon papers suggests, it may often be possible to punish publications criminally after their appearance even though prior restraint would have been impermissible.

Prior restraint, the classic form of censorship, while generally impermissible for newspapers, books, and most electronic media (except, perhaps, for reasons of national security), has survived for motion pictures.[7] Although a series of Supreme Court decisions has brought movies within the protection of the First Amendment, requiring government censors to act expeditiously and to justify their rejections at a judicial proceeding,[8] and although a recent decision has reiterated the "heavy presumption" against any system of prior restraints,[9] the Court has so far been unwilling to prohibit all prescreening censorship of films on the grounds that one medium is not "necessarily subject to the precise rules governing any other method of expression."[10] The evocative and explicit nature of the medium, particularly when it entails depiction of allegedly obscene or shocking content, has been asserted to justify the different treatment in the past, and advance licensing still exists in the motion picture area in a few states and cities.

Concern for prior restraints led also to attacks on such statutes as those requiring notice to the police and application for permits to parade and to use loudspeakers. Although such permits are, indeed, "prior restraints," the government may constitutionally require that they be sought if the regulations are administered in accordance with "narrow objective and definite standards."[11] Although civic authorities have a substantial, valid interest in "maintaining public order"[12] and flow of commerce and in preserving the privacy and property rights of the majority of citizens, there has been concern that the frequent justification of "undue disturbance of public convenience" may become a grant of discretionary authority rather than a meaningful guideline unless the ground rules are uniformly applied (Blasi, 1970).

Freedom for Whom?

Although no individual can be wholly excluded from the First Amendment's protection, the degree of permissible government restriction may vary with status. States have been permitted to circumscribe the conduct of young children, for example, with respect to distributing literature in the streets[13] or buying material that may be ad-

[6] *Near* v. *Minnesota*, 283 U.S. 697 (1931)—newspaper prior restraint held unconstitutional.

[7] *Times Film Corp.* v. *Chicago*, 365 U.S. 43 (1961)—refusal to outlaw all forms of film censorship.

[8] *Joseph Burstyn, Inc.* v. *Wilson*, 343 U.S. 495 (1952).

[9] *Freedman* v. *Maryland*, 380 U.S. 51 (1965)—film case in which "heavy presumption" was stated.

[10] *Bantam Books, Inc.* v. *Sullivan*, 372 U.S. 58 (1963)—book case.

[11] *Shuttlesworth* v. *Birmingham*, 394 U.S. 147 (1969).

[12] *Cox* v. *Louisiana*, 379 U.S. 536 (1965).

[13] *Prince* v. *Massachusetts*, 321 U.S. 158 (1944).

judged obscene only for minors.[14] When the regulation is applicable by virtue of one's locus, such as being in a school, prison, or military establishment, there must be an attempt to reconcile individual rights of communicative expression with institutional demands of order and of discipline.[15]

The Supreme Court has upheld the right of high school students to protest the Vietnam war by wearing black armbands, but has distinguished such silent expression of opinion unaccompanied by threats or acts of disturbance on school grounds from student conduct that materially disrupts class work or involves invasion of the rights of others and is "not immunized by the constitutional guarantee of freedom of speech."[16] Generally, public universities may reasonably restrict demonstrations in order to "protect safety and property, maintain normal operations, facilitate traffic and the like" (Harvard Law Review, 1968), but may not fire faculty for publicly criticizing the school administration, absent proof of deliberately or recklessly false statements.[17]

Freedom of communicative expression is necessarily limited in institutions of incarceration, and courts have been reluctant to interfere with prison regulations, security, or discipline. Recent decisions, however, have sustained prisoners' First Amendment rights to complain about conditions to state officials or to news media (Turner, 1971).

The military presents a difficult and changing area of communication control (Kester, 1968); restrictions on freedom of expression must consider both the need to maintain discipline and good order in the organization, and the principle of maintaining civilian supremacy over the military establishment.[18] The military judicial system has been, inevitably, somewhat inattentive to the serviceman's First Amendment rights, and direct review of military judgments by civilian courts has been largely restricted to narrow jurisdictional questions (Georgetown Law Journal, 1970). Several lower federal courts, however, have begun to consider the related constitutional issues.[19]

There are also situations in which their status may subject certain individuals to restraints because of the purpose of their communication. Thus, Congress and several state legislatures have required that lobbyists register and identify their clients to make their biases and activities discernible (Walter, 1961). While not directly affecting the substance of lobbyists' communications, such regulations, which have been sustained, do set lobbyists apart and presumably reduce the impact of their communication. In other areas, such as political pamphleteering, state efforts to ban anonymous pamphlets have been invalidated because of their inhibitory effect (Yale Law Journal, 1961).

An additional problem concerns the relationship between the general public and those who operate the mass media. The issue has been raised sharply by Professor Barron (1967), who argues that traditional First Amendment theory is unrealistic in assuming a freely accessible marketplace of ideas because the concentration of mass media control actually operates to repress unorthodox ideas. He contends that the First Amendment should be interpreted not only to protect words that have found a medium but also to assure members of the public access to the media to present their views.

---

[14] *Ginsberg* v. *New York*, 390 U.S. 629 (1968).

[15] *Engel* v. *Vitale*, 370 U.S. 421 (1962)—prayer; *Abington School District* v. *Schempp*, 374 U.S. 203 (1963)—Bible reading; *Epperson* v. *Arkansas*, 393 U.S. 97 (1968)—evolution.

[16] *Tinker* v. *Des Moines School District*, 393 U.S. 503 (1969).

[17] *Pickering* v. *Board of Education*, 391 U.S. 563 (1968).

[18] *United States* v. *Howe*, 17 U.S.C.M.A. 165 (1967)—dual interests of military.

[19] *Cortwright* v. *Resor*, 325 F. Supp. 797 (E.D.N.Y. 1971)—soldiers' petition.

First the media sought to invoke the Constitution to prevent coercion of publishing; now the Constitution is being invoked by the other side to justify that very coercion in the name of the public's freedom to communicate.

Supreme Court opinions have noted the problem on occasion and have sought to ensure availability of other modes of communication for those who do not have access to mass media. This concern is implicit in cases dealing with door-to-door canvassers, use of the mail, use of loudspeakers, distribution of leaflets on public streets, and sit-ins and other large-scale protests by civil rights or antiwar groups (Kalven, 1965).

Freedom of What?

We have so far spoken generally of freedom of communication without defining it. *Communication* will refer to any form of conduct whereby a message is expressed; *speech* will be used more narrowly to denote the verbal mode of communication rather than in its constitutional sense. Since the Supreme Court distinguishes verbal from nonverbal forms of communication, we phrase the legal question to determine whether the communication is "protected conduct" or "protected speech."

When the Supreme Court was recently confronted with nonverbal communication, it "emphatically rejected" the view that "the First and Fourteenth Amendments afford the same kind of freedom to those who would communicate ideas by conduct such as patrolling, marching, and picketing on streets and highways, as these amendments afford to those who communicate ideas by pure speech."[20] In a case involving draft-card burning, the majority refused to "accept the view that an apparently limitless variety of conduct can be labeled 'speech' whenever the person engaging in the conduct intends thereby to express an idea."[21]

At the same time, however, the Court has not limited the First Amendment's protection to verbal conduct alone; it is now grappling with forms of communication that either combine verbal and nonverbal elements or are entirely nonverbal. The Court may well come to view any conduct with a substantial communication element as being "speech" for purposes of the First Amendment, although this will not necessarily mean that the conduct will be protected from restraint. Whether specific conduct will be shielded depends upon whether the argument for limiting communication is addressed to the substance of the communication or toward some aspect of the conduct apart from its substantive component. We shall consider the latter situation in the remainder of this section: we shall examine the former in the next section.

At this point, for the sake of clarity, it will be helpful to discuss briefly the modes of judicial protection. Federal courts may review a particular law on its face without regard to the constitutional status of a particular claimant's conduct—based on the principle that "a governmental purpose to control or prevent activities constitutionally subject to state regulation may not be achieved by means which sweep unnecessarily broadly and thereby invade the area of unprotected freedoms."[22]

An overly broad statute acts as a disincentive to action and imposes a "chilling effect" on conduct or speech within the protection of the First Amendment (Harvard Law Review, 1970). Invalidation through the vagueness doctrine reflects this concern: lack of fair warning to actors or lack of adequate standards to guide enforcers also may inhibit privileged activity by creating fear or uncertainty of punishment. Thus, courts may invalidate a statute as overly broad or vague on its face, rather

[20] *Cox* v. *Louisiana*, 379 U.S. 536 (1965).

[21] *United States* v. *O'Brien*, 391 U.S. 367 (1968).

[22] *Zwickler* v. *Koota*, 389 U.S. 241 (1967).

than go through a case-by-case adjudication of its application to particular conduct. Depending on the specific facts of a case, however, the court may instead reverse a conviction on the ground that an ordinance is unconstitutional only as applied to the particular facts before the court.[23]

Government restraints not based on content have traditionally been upheld where they have sought to regulate, with administrative safeguards for fairness, the "time, place, and manner" of the communicative conduct in the interest of public convenience (O'Neil, 1966:48–65). The general rule with regard to public property allows regulation of the exercise of First-Amendment rights "so as to prevent interference with the use to which the property is ordinarily put by the public."[24] Thus, parades may be barred in the center of a city at rush hour, loud speakers mounted on trucks may be either forbidden entirely or limited to certain hours in residential neighborhoods, mass meetings may be permitted in public parks but not on busy streets, the number of pickets may be limited, and billboards may be banned along scenic highways. In all of these situations, the asserted basis of government regulation goes not to the substance of the message (although it may affect the size and nature of the audience), but to the ground rules for all communication.

Much regulation addressed ostensibly to time, place, and manner, however, has been overturned because the restraint seemed to deal more with the content of the proposed message, or because it was to be enforced arbitrarily or gave too wide a margin for official discretion. The Court has developed guidelines in this area: the criteria must be formulated quite specifically, the procedures for obtaining permission must be administered fairly, and the administrative process must be subject to prompt judicial review. It has therefore held to be unconstitutionally vague an ordinance that simply forbids three or more persons to assemble on public streets and act in an "annoying" manner,[25] and an ordinance that granted a city commission absolute discretion to issue parade permits with unreviewable judgment as to the effect of the parade on public health and morals.[26]

When the communicative conduct is completely nonverbal, as with draft-card burning, flag burning, or other methods of politically oriented protest, the content of the message and the mode of its communication are, in a sense, inseparable. The conventional way to approach this difficult situation has been to recognize two distinct governmental interests: an interest in regulating the conduct involved without regard to the message being communicated, and a possible interest in regulating the content of the message (Columbia Law Review, 1968).

Although unwilling to assert flatly that any legislative restraint on any communicative interest—speech or conduct—carries with it a high burden of justification, the majority of the Court have generally focused on speech aspects of given conduct, thus affording a defendant's action maximum First Amendment protection. The wearing of black armbands to high school in a peaceful antiwar protest was described as constitutionally protected action "akin to pure speech,"[27] and silently wearing a jacket labeled "Fuck the Draft" in a courthouse was considered verbal expression protected against the state's charge of "offensive conduct."[28] In a flag-burning decision, the Court scrutinized the defendant's

[23] *Palmer* v. *City of Euclid*, 402 U.S. 544 (1971) —an instance of "vague as applied."

[24] *Amalgamated Food Employees Union Local 590* v. *Logan Valley Plaza*, 391 U.S. 308 (1968). But see *Lloyd Corp., Inc.* v. *Tanner*, 407 U.S. 551 (1972).

[25] *Coates* v. *Cincinnati*, 402 U.S. 611 (1971).

[26] *Shuttlesworth* v. *Birmingham*, 394 U.S. 147 (1969).

[27] *Tinker* v. *Des Moines School District*, 393 U.S. 503 (1969).

[28] *Cohen* v. *California*, 403 U.S. 15 (1971).

speech rather than his conduct, and decided that angry rhetoric that did not approach incitement to violence could not justify a conviction under a state statute making it a crime to "publicly . . . deface . . . or cast contempt upon" the flag by "words or act."[29] Nevertheless, the Court has yet to develop a coherent approach to the speech-conduct area.

REGULATION OF CONTENT

As we turn to government efforts to limit communication because of the substance of the communicative element, we must realize that communication never occurs in the abstract—there is no "pure speech." In each of the following situations, the argument for limiting communication is based on the substance of the message and the circumstances in which it is communicated, providing the classic confrontation between the individuals' desire to communicate and the considerations that motivate government officials to seek to prevent or punish certain speech.

Since a decision against speech in these cases often means that the message in question cannot be conveyed in alternative ways, such restraint has led to the most difficult constitutional questions. Here, again, as when they seek to reconcile governmental interests with individual rights in noncontent (time, place, manner) situations, courts generally utilize a balancing process. The main thrust of recent analysis of the First Amendment by the Supreme Court has been to balance the governmental interests asserted to justify restraining speech against the effect of the restraints on freedom of expression. The Court will generally accept at face value the state's justifications for its restriction and not explore the motives of the officials who initiated it, but whether the Court will defer to their assessment of the importance of the perceived danger or will make its own evaluation is less predictable.

[29] *Street* v. *New York*, 394 U.S. 576 (1969).

The Court tends to defer in its judgment in areas, such as foreign affairs, in which it claims little experience or expertise. In recent years, however, the Court has formulated the doctrine that statutory classifications that are based upon certain "suspect" criteria (e.g., race or wealth) or affect "fundamental rights" (such as free expression) will be held to deny Fourteenth Amendment equal protection of the laws unless justified or outweighed by a "compelling" governmental interest. Thus, the Court independently assessed and invalidated a state's demands for lists of all resident NAACP members for an investigation of subversive activities,[30] and invalidated another state's denial of admission to the bar to an applicant who refused to answer a question concerning her previous political associations.[31]

Protecting the Individual and Society from Domestic Violence

In seeking to avoid domestic violence, the state has necessarily emphasized nonverbal conduct rather than the speech element. Government has traditionally punished those whose actions threatened harm to others; it has also regarded speech content as sufficient to provoke public annoyance, breach of peace, or incitement to riot. In addition, it has upheld prohibitions on face-to-face insults and curses. Indeed, vituperative "fighting" words,[32] lewd and obscene language,[33] and intentional defamation[34] are considered to be of such insignificant substantive value as to be beyond First Amendment protection.

In the street-corner orator situation, governmental regulation must balance the substance of the message itself against the

[30] *NAACP* v. *Alabama*, 357 U.S. 449 (1958).

[31] *Baird* v. *State Bar of Arizona*, 401 U.S. 1 (1971).

[32] *Chaplinsky* v. *New Hampshire*, 315 U.S. 568 (1942).

[33] *Roth* v. *United States*, 354 U.S. 476 (1957).

[34] *Garrison* v. *Louisiana*, 379 U.S. 64 (1964).

probability of imminent disturbance. One must distinguish between the threats of violence caused by the crowd's hostile reaction to the speaker and those caused by the crowd's enthusiastic response to his exhortations.

In the former case, police have tended to seize upon the danger to the speaker as justification for forcibly interrupting him or prosecuting him for failure to obey a police order or for inciting a riot. Here some justices have emphasized the need for police action to prevent violence, while others have suggested that the more vociferous hecklers and antagonists in the crowd should have been the ones arrested.[35] That may be an impractical alternative, with large crowds and small police forces, and there is presumably some limit to the size of police force a government must maintain to protect this form of unpopular speech. In recent civil rights cases, however, the Supreme Court has closely scrutinized a state's claim that demonstrations had to be stopped because of a menacing crowd and, where the defendants were not specifically convicted for obstructing traffic or overstaying their time limit, the Court has demanded proof of real or imminent violent conduct on the part of either demonstrators or onlookers.[36]

The speaker who exhorts his listeners to violence presents a different problem. The state must satisfy the courts that the speaker's conduct, if protected, carries with it the strong likelihood of an imminent invasion of a serious governmental interest.[37] Whereas "advocacy" of violent means to effect political and economic change was sufficient justification for invoking national security to restrain such speech through criminal sanctions, a state may not proscribe advocacy of the use of force or the violation of law unless that advocacy is "directed to inciting or producing imminent lawless action and is likely to produce such action."[38] In that case, the Court reversed the conviction of a Ku Klux Klan leader who was charged with advocating criminal syndicalism when he denigrated blacks and Jews and threatened "revengence." And in Communist party membership cases, the Court stressed the need for careful examination of the evidence, distinguishing protected advocacy and teaching of abstract doctrine from advocacy of forbidden action, and requiring of the defendant both knowledge of a revolutionary organization's illegal advocacy and specific intent to violently accomplish the organization's illegal aims.[39]

Protecting Individuals from Nonphysical Harm

Defamation

As with legal systems throughout the world, the English common law has long protected an individual's reputation from false attack (cf. Prosser, 1971). Basically, one who makes false statements that subject another to hatred, ridicule, or contempt, or cause him to be shunned in the community, must compensate that person for damages thus inflicted. Traditionally, the interest in reputation was valued so highly and the interest in speech—especially false speech—was thought so minimal that defendants were held liable even for defamatory statements they reasonably but erroneously believed to be true.

In the past two centuries, however, the law has become increasingly protective of speech regardless of its truth or falsity. Legislators, judges, and high executive officers have received an absolute privilege to express themselves within the scope of their official duties without being subjected to defamation suits. Our society values the process of informing the electorate of actions taken by the government and there-

35 *Feiner* v. *New York*, 340 U.S. 315 (1951).

36 *Gregory* v. *Chicago*, 394 U.S. 111 (1969).

37 *Edwards* v. *South Carolina*, 372 U.S. 229 (1963).

38 *Brandenburg* v. *Ohio*, 395 U.S. 444 (1969).

39 *Scales* v. *United States*, 367 U.S. 203 (1961).

fore protects fair and accurate reports of the proceedings of legislatures, courts, administrative bodies, and elected officials, even when those proceedings include defamations. This privilege of "record libel" also counteracts the general rule holding those who repeat defamations to be as liable as those who originated them.

The value of community discussion was also recognized when courts granted qualified privileges for "fair comment" criticism of publicly accessible literary and artistic works. No matter how devastating the critic's opinion, so long as it was sincere he was not liable for harm to the artist's reputation. Qualified privileges were developed through common law because defamatory speech was considered outside the protection of the First Amendment.

Within the last several years, however, the Supreme Court has brought nonintentional defamation within the First Amendment.[40] The Court reversed a state court decision that criticism of public officials would be privileged only if the supporting facts were entirely accurate, deciding that this ruling unduly restricted the right to criticize government officials. The balance articulated by the majority was that in such a case speech, although false, must be protected unless the speaker either deliberately misstated the facts or recklessly disregarded the possibility of falsity. In subsequent cases, the Court maintained its refusal to protect deliberately false defamatory speech, contending that such speech does not further rational discussion and is not a legitimate political weapon in our society.[41]

The constitutional protection of nondeliberate and nonreckless defamatory comment has gone beyond public officials.[42] Most recently, the Court extended "constitutional protection to all discussion and communication involving matters of public and general concern, without regard to whether the persons involved are famous or infamous."[43] The rationale was that protection of discussions of public events, rather than the reputation of public officials or figures, was the paramount basis of general community interest—even though it may be difficult to delineate the boundaries of "matters of public or general concern."

Personal Attack Doctrine

The Federal Communications Commission oversees all radio and television broadcasting and is empowered to grant licenses "if public convenience, interest, or necessity will be served thereby" (O'Neil, 1965). The public-interest standard would justify nonrenewals of licenses when the FCC considers performance inadequate. The FCC has established affirmative obligations on licensees to meet certain standards such as balanced programming, diversity of ownership holdings, and local programming and, in addition, has imposed on all broadcasters the requirement that discussion of public issues be presented and that each side of the issue be given fair coverage ("the fairness doctrine"). The Federal Communications Act, moreover, requires that equal time be allotted all qualified candidates for public office.

The Supreme Court has upheld regulations obligating broadcast licensees to immediately notify and allow reply time to individuals or groups whose personal integrity or character had been attacked during a presentation of controversial issues, and also requiring broadcasters to allot reply time to political editorials. The Court noted that the First Amendment was designed to preserve an open forum, not to further either governmental or private interests: "It is the right of the viewers

[40] *New York Times Co.* v. *Sullivan*, 376 U.S. 254 (1964).

[41] *Garrison* v. *Louisiana*, 379 U.S. 64 (1964).

[42] *Curtis Publishing Co.* v. *Butts*, 388 U.S. 130 (1967).

[43] *Rosenbloom* v. *Metromedia, Inc.*, 403 U.S. 29 (1971).

and listeners, not the right of the broadcasters, which is paramount."[44]

On what basis can the Federal Communications Commission tell its licensees that if they air views on a particular issue they must also air opposing views? Although no government agency now makes such rulings for print media, the government on behalf of the American people owns the airwaves and is empowered by the people through Congress to issue licenses to licensees as community proxies or fiduciaries. This ownership, then, is asserted to entitle the government to impose certain conditions on the licensees. The available broadcasting spectrum is limited, and some criteria must be developed to decide which applicants should be given access to these limited facilities: balanced treatment of major issues is one permissible criterion (see Kalven, 1967).

This traditional limited-access rationale may have to be reevaluated in the future, however, with the advent of cable television systems (CATV) (Columbia Law Review, 1971). CATV operates via coaxial cables rather than airwaves, and the number of channels (one or even two-way) is virtually unlimited.

Privacy

One interest that continues to conflict with freedom of communication is the personal interest in privacy. Basically, the assertion is that an individual should be permitted to protect his life and affairs from exposure to, and intrusion by, others. In terms of communication, the individual claiming the privacy interest may object to being made an unwilling source, an unwilling subject, or an unwilling recipient.

The plight of the unwilling source may be seen in interceptions that range from peeping toms to eavesdropping and wiretapping, intrusions upon communications meant only for a particular audience.

The Supreme Court recently included electronic surveillance within the Fourth Amendment's prohibition against unwarranted search or seizure where the communication was uttered under a reasonable expectation of privacy, without regard to physical trespass.[45] An appropriate judicial order, however, may authorize limited electronic surveillance.

The primary effects of privacy have been in the other two categories, subject and object. In 1890, a radical argument proposed that mass media be barred from communicating true information about events in the personal lives of ordinary citizens (Warren & Brandeis, 1890). A decade or two later that argument provided a basis for holding the media liable for such stories (cf. Franklin, 1963). In nonstatutory rulings, however, the courts have subsequently tended to elevate the public's interest in learning about fellow citizens, at least where the subject is independently "newsworthy" (e.g., politician, artist, sports figure, or movie star) or where the subject is voluntarily or involuntarily involved in some "newsworthy" event (Kalven, 1966). The Supreme Court expanded this notion further by deciding that an ordinary individual's stake in personal privacy must, on balance, yield to reports on "matters of public interest" in consideration of constitutional protection of free speech and the fact that "exposure of the self to others . . . is a concomitant of life in a civilized community."[46] If the report is otherwise protected, its falsity will not bar protection unless it was published with deliberate or reckless disregard of the truth.

Some limits continue to exist, however: the most intimate details of a person's life would probably be beyond the defense of public interest (Prosser, 1960). In addition, a recent California case[47] has insisted that

---

[44] *Red Lion Broadcasting Co.* v. *FCC*, 395 U.S. 367 (1969).

[45] *Katz* v. *United States*, 389 U.S. 347 (1967).

[46] *Time, Inc.* v. *Hill*, 385 U.S. 374 (1967).

[47] *Briscoe* v. *Reader's Digest Association*, 4 Cal. 3d 529, 483 P. 2d 34 (1971).

in determining "newsworthiness" the court must carefully consider the social value of facts published, and the degree of the intrusion into ostensibly private affairs, as well as the extent to which the complaining party voluntarily acceded to a position of public notoriety and thereby waived his right of privacy.

The final aspect of privacy, implicit in the earlier discussion of time, place, and manner regulation of loudspeakers and door-to-door canvassers, involves the individual as unwilling recipient of communication. The Supreme Court has upheld a federal law allowing the addressee to request the post office to require the mailer to cease future mailings of advertisements that he alone believes to be erotically arousing or sexually provocative. The decision emphasized that no one was constitutionally compelled to receive "any unwanted communication, whatever its merit," and that "no one has a right to press even 'good' ideas on an unwilling recipient."[48]

Earlier, the Court had rejected a government requirement that addressees of Communist propaganda from abroad state affirmatively their wish to receive this mail, since the inhibitory effect outweighed the asserted interest in protecting the privacy of those who did not want to do so.[49] Given the Court's usually restrictive approach where alleged obscenity is concerned, the propaganda case is consistent with a recent decision[50] in which a real estate broker tried to stop distribution in his neighborhood of a leaflet criticizing his business practices as racially prejudiced. Striking down an injunction against the leafletting, the Court noted that the distribution was peaceful and that no individual could enjoin communication to the general public.

[48] *Rowan* v. *Post Office Department*, 397 U.S. 728 (1970).

[49] *Lamont* v. *Postmaster General*, 381 U.S. 301 (1965).

[50] *Organization for a Better Austin* v. *Keefe*, 402 U.S. 415 (1971).

Emotional Distress

The law has explicitly recognized the individual's interest in avoiding intentional infliction of emotional distress; the words at issue are not likely to provoke breaches of the peace nor be defamatory, and have not yet been brought within the "unwilling recipient" category of privacy. No constitutional problems have been seen in imposing liability on those who make indecent or harassing telephone calls or on creditors who use outrageous language or conduct to collect debts (Prosser, 1971: 49–62).

Deceptive Advertising

An essentially economic interest, honest business dealing is a less conspicuous facet of freedom to communicate. The common law deterred deliberate misrepresentation of goods offered for sale, but was reluctant to handle failure to disclose unfavorable aspects of the product. Today, the Federal Trade Commission has the major role in preventing deceptive advertising, and acts both by punishing false claims and by requiring sellers to provide extensive information about their products; intent to deceive and knowledge of falsity on the part of advertisers may be irrelevant (cf. Kintner, 1971).

Speech aimed at inducing individuals to breach contracts with third parties may also lead to liability. Here, the law treats an interest in the security of contract relationships as superior to the competitor's interest in resort to speech—even true speech—to convey a message that would disrupt contract relations. The commercial area as a whole has given rise to virtually no First Amendment problems (Harvard Law Review, 1965).

Fair Trial

The continuing fair trial–free press controversy involves the apparent conflict between freedom of the press and the individual's right to fair trial (guaranteed by the Sixth Amendment's requirement of an "impartial jury") and the fair administration of justice (cf. Franklin, 1968: 708–748). The principal dispute concerns the use of pretrial stories that report whether the suspect has confessed or has taken a lie-detector test or, perhaps most crucial, whether he has a prior criminal record. Courts used to resort to holding the press in contempt, but the focus is now on restraining communication by lawyers and, when necessary, by law-enforcement officials.[51] Contempt citations will be constitutionally invalidated unless clear and present danger to the administration of justice can be proven by the state.[52]

Advocates of restraint argue that the advance publication of such material creates an atmosphere that undermines chances of a fair trial for the defendant.[53] They assert that the public's right to know would be unhampered because the ban on such stories would be lifted after the trial. The press has countered by asserting that judicial techniques such as change of venue can, if necessary, assure the defendant a fair trial even after such stories have been published; that there is no empirical proof that newspaper reports prejudice jurors; and that the public interest in knowing about crime in the community requires immediacy.

The press rarely objects to judicial restraints on attorneys, but a proposed restraint on statements by law-enforcement officials seems less acceptable. The problem of coverage during trial is less serious because jurors may be ordered not to discuss or read about the case or, if necessary, may be sequestered for fuller insulation from possibly prejudicial publicity. Inherent institutional antagonisms between the press and the bar and the absence of firm data exacerbate this controversy.

The question of television in the courtroom raises a further problem. The Supreme Court's current view is that, given the present state of television technology and public reaction to the medium, a defendant's right to a fair trial—at least in notorious cases—is violated by televising his trial over his objections.[54] If the provocative impact and obtrusive physical presence of the medium change, so may the law, but meanwhile the public can learn about the trial in other media; what is at stake is the narrower question of the right of a particular medium to cover a particular event, and this is restrained in terms of the impact of the coverage on the actual event.

Finally, it should be noted that no constitutional guarantee is an absolute, and that an accused may lose his constitutional right to be present during a trial if, after repeated warnings, he conducts himself in a manner "disorderly, disruptive, and disrespectful" of the court so that the trial cannot proceed in his presence.[55]

National Security

Limits on Free Speech

Efforts to protect the government from violent overthrow have produced some of the most famous and bitter discussions of the permissible limits on free speech. The Alien and Sedition Acts of 1798 aside, this concern did not really emerge until during and after World War I, with the federal Espionage Act and related state statutes banning "criminal anarchy" and "criminal syndicalism." It was then that Justices Holmes and Brandeis formulated their "clear and present danger" test,[56] which soon gained majority acceptance.

After World War II, however, in Com-

[51] *Bridges* v. *California*, 314 U.S. 252 (1941)—limitations on contempt-of-court citations.

[52] *Wood* v. *Georgia*, 370 U.S. 375 (1962)—clear-and-present danger test in press contempt cases.

[53] *Irvin* v. *Dowd*, 336 U.S. 717 (1961)—first state conviction set aside by Supreme Court for prejudicial publicity.

[54] *Estes* v. *Texas*, 381 U.S. 532 (1965).

[55] *Allen* v. *Illinois*, 397 U.S. 337 (1970).

[56] *Whitney* v. *California*, 274 U.S. 357 (1927).

munist subversion cases, the Court discarded the Holmes-Brandeis approach as having been formulated in cases involving relatively isolated events that did not seriously threaten the safety of the community. In the Court's view, the Cold War involved "the development of an apparatus designed and dedicated to the overthrow of the Government, in the context of world crisis after crisis."[57] Acting on this perception, the Supreme Court adopted the balancing approach first espoused by Judge Learned Hand when he reviewed the *Dennis* case in the court of appeals.[58] This approach meant that, in each case, courts "must ask whether the gravity of the 'evil', discounted by its improbability, justifies such invasion of free speech as is necessary to avoid the danger."[59] In this area, then, a balance must be struck; when confronted with national security cases, the Court is more receptive than in other areas to the legislature's perception and evaluation of the dangers and of the need for limitations on communication.

Yet even here, the governmental interest must be proven substantial to withstand the presumption of the protection of fundamental rights such as freedom of expression. Thus, although the Court has held constitutional a statute making it a felony to knowingly threaten to kill the president of the United States,[60] it has been careful to distinguish true threats from constitutionally protected expressions of political hyperbole. Likewise, the Court determined that a state legislature's resolution excluding a representative from membership for allegedly unpatriotic remarks critical of Vietnam-war policy violated the representative's First Amendment rights.[61]

The Court has also scrutinized employment restrictions based on national security, both on the campus and in defense plants. A state proposal to prevent the appointment or retention of subversives in academic posts was invalidated:[62] its vagueness prevented a teacher from knowing the extent to which his statements might go beyond protected comments on abstract doctrine and protected forms of advocacy. Similarly, the Court struck down as unconstitutionally overbroad a statute barring any member of a Communist organization from engaging "in any employment in any defense facility."[63] In barring proscribable associations the statute might also bar associations protected by the First Amendment, because the defendant could have been an inactive member, or have lacked knowledge of the organization's aims, or have disagreed with those aims, or he might have occupied a nonsensitive position of employment.

Access to Information

Although many discussions of communication have treated freedom to learn or to acquire information as integral to the broader freedom of communication, the law has tended to separate these notions. For example, a limitation on permissible travel has not been viewed as a First Amendment problem. While recognizing that any restrictions on movement could inhibit the flow of information, the Court has treated this problem as one of "liberty" under the due process clause. This permits greater leeway for the government than might a First Amendment analysis.

The issue of access to information has led to serious political controversy compelling the legislative and executive branches to seek appropriate balances. Under wartime censorship, for example, a court is unlikely to direct a military official to reveal information that the military has classified; however, the media, through

[57] *Dennis* v. *United States*, 341 U.S. 494 (1951).

[58] *United States* v. *Dennis*, 183 F. 2d 201 (U.S. Ct. of Appeals 1950).

[59] *Dennis* v. *United States*, 341 U.S. 494 (1951).

[60] *Watts* v. *United States*, 394 U.S. 705 (1969).

[61] *Bond* v. *Floyd*, 385 U.S. 116 (1966).

[62] *Keyishian* v. *Board of Regents of New York*, 385 U.S. 589 (1967).

[63] *United States* v. *Robel*, 389 U.S. 258 (1967).

their persistence, might effect voluntary reconsideration by the military that could lead to some declassification.

A broader question is government suppression, or prior restraint, of further publication of secret documents concerning current wartime strategy that were obtained illegally and transmitted to leading newspapers for serial publication. The Supreme Court faced this issue recently and ruled[64] that the prior restraint imposed a heavy burden of showing justification for enforcement against the rights of free speech and press—a burden that the government failed to sustain. Dissenting opinions, however, deplored judicial interference with executive assessments of peril to national security, and criticized the failure to consider such issues as whether the publisher knew how the documents had been obtained.

The problem of unauthorized declassification of documents via publication remains; although the Court has encouraged "open and robust debate" on public issues,[65] the citizen has not yet been given the right to view whatever government record might interest him for discussion or voting purposes. When access has been afforded, it has been through the political process.

In the 1966 Freedom of Information Act, Congress attempted to set out categories of documents to be made generally accessible. In some areas the traditional administrative claim of "executive privilege" was rejected in favor of the public's interest in having the information. In others, the balance favored ensuring the candor of intragovernmental communications by preserving their confidentiality. Finally, in many sections, Congress has in effect called upon the courts to resolve the question (cf. Davis, 1967).

[64] *New York Times Co.* v. *United States*, 403 U.S. 713 (1971).

[65] *New York Times Co.* v. *Sullivan*, 376 U.S. 254 (1964).

GOVERNMENTAL NEED FOR INFORMATION

Not only the citizen, but also the government claims a right of access to information. Whether it is a court seeking to resolve a dispute or a legislature investigating situations that may need attention, governmental bodies need to gather information. Sometimes this means coercion by use of the legal instrument known as the subpoena, which requires a citizen having information on the subject under inquiry to appear and divulge that information. To ensure the accuracy of the information, the government further regulates the citizen's speech by subjecting him to the threat of prosecution for perjury.

In general, these coercions have not been thought to raise First Amendment problems. The subpoena addressed personally to an individual should be distinguished from standard loyalty oaths, which may present First Amendment issues because they force the citizen to make a declaration in an area from which the state is usually barred, and they interfere with his interests in speech and association.

In the civil rights area, the Supreme Court has defined a constitutional privilege allowing voluntary associations to resist government demands for their membership lists when such disclosure is likely to affect adversely the group's freedom to associate, and to frighten others from associating or speaking in the future.[66] The Court recognized the right of the state to inform itself and protect its legitimate interests, but held that it must first show a substantial connection "between the information sought and a subject of overriding and compelling state interest."[67] This is an "essential prerequisite to the validity of an investigation which intrudes into the area of constitutional rights."

A further restraint on the power of the state deals with persons on trial, and trial-

[66] *NAACP* v. *Alabama*, 357 U.S. 449 (1958).

[67] *Gibson* v. *Florida Legislative Investigation Committee*, 372 U.S. 539 (1963).

court witnesses. The Fifth Amendment protection against self-incrimination is not addressed to freedom of speech, but rather reflects the determination that the prosecution in a criminal case may not rely on the coercive power of the state to obtain confessions (Griswold, 1955; Hook, 1957). This becomes even clearer when courts hold that if an individual who refuses to testify for fear of self-incrimination is offered complete immunity from prosecution in return for his testimony, the witness may constitutionally be required to testify.[68]

Other privileges not to communicate information have been recognized at common law: priests, attorneys, and physicians need not testify to matters learned in professional confidence from a penitent, a client, or a patient. The long history of this type of privilege implies that confidentiality is accepted as essential to the initial communication and that the benefit to the individual of thus expressing himself outweighs the possibility that important evidence may be lost. Scholars in the law of evidence dispute the wisdom of these privileges (McCormick, 1954: 166, 183).

The newsman's interest in keeping some of his sources confidential has raised a recent problem (Yale Law Journal, 1970). Several states have passed statutes recognizing this privilege, but in other states courts have found no common law basis for it. Efforts to give the privilege constitutional status or federal statutory protection, making it binding on all states, have failed. Despite the claim that this privilege would enhance freedom of the press by giving newsmen broader access, the courts demand identification of sources even where this discourages persons from giving stories to newsmen or, more likely, forces newsmen to accept imprisonment for contempt of court in order to keep sources confidential.[69]

A more sweeping contention, that the reporter need not even appear before a grand jury if that appearance would destroy access to sources, has also been rejected.[70]

Encouraging Creative Thought

As authorized in Article I, Section 8, of the Constitution, the first Congress enacted patent and copyright laws to protect inventors and authors from having their creations duplicated. From the standpoint of communication, the government, by promising protection and opportunity for financial gain, was seeking to encourage both creation and dissemination. In patent law, the emphasis is on disclosure, for even without patent laws it would be advantageous for a person to develop a machine or production technique that he himself could use in his factory and preserve as a trade secret.

The patent law seeks to encourage that inventor to share his innovation with others. In the copyright area, the emphasis is presumably on creation, for artists and writers might be deterred from communicating an initial act of creativity that could be stolen and marketed immediately by others. The price for such encouragement is inevitably some inhibition on communication by others.

In general, copyright and patent laws permit the owner of the patent or copyright to establish the terms for reproduction of his creation (Nimmer, 1963; Kaplan, 1966). Those who copy passages or products without permission are infringers. Although there is some economic argument to the contrary (Hurt, 1966), Congress has decided that the restraint on copying is justified by the social value of the initial inducement to create and disclose.

Because of the impact on speech, some exceptions to the creator's copyright claims have been permitted (O'Neil, 1966: 98–115). Courts have decided that copyright protects

[68] *Ullmann* v. *United States*, 350 U.S. 422 (1956) – immunity statutes.

[69] *Branzburg* v. *Hayes*, 408 U.S. 665 (1972).

[70] *United States* v. *Caldwell*, 408 U.S. 665 (1972).

the concrete expression of ideas and facts and not the ideas or facts themselves. They have also developed a "fair use" exception under which critics and scholars may, without permission, take limited excerpts from copyrighted works for discussion and illustration. In a related vein, courts now value the interest of one who would parody an existing work as greater than the interest in protecting the antecedent work.

Potential First Amendment problems may arise if a copyright owner refuses to permit particular uses of his work beyond the limits of "fair use" (Nimmer, 1970). A recent federal court decision[71] involved an infringement action by the holder of the copyrighted Kennedy assassination movie film against publishers who employed an artist to make charcoal sketch copies of several film frames, to illustrate a book covering the event. Although not specifically addressing the First Amendment, the court upheld the defendants' right to copy the frames on the grounds of the substantial public interest in the photographs. One proposal endeavoring to accommodate the conflicting interests of the Copyright Act and the First Amendment is that copyright infringement be excused if the subject matter of the infringed material is relevant to the public interest and the appropriator's use of the material independently advances the public interest (Goldstein, 1970).

Regulation of Elections

The crucial role of the election process in our society has led to numerous regulations designed to ensure its fairness. Inevitably, some impinge on freedom of communication. Perhaps the most obvious is the prohibition of electioneering at or near the polls—a time, place, and manner regulation designed to keep the polls orderly and the voters free from undue harassment.

Yet recently the Supreme Court upset the conviction of a newspaper editor whose publication of an editorial on election day had violated a statute prohibiting electioneering or solicitation of votes on the day of the election.[72] The state said the statute was aimed at charges and countercharges that could not be answered until after the election. The Court noted unsympathetically that under the statute such charges could appear on the day before election day and still could not be answered before the election. Because the publication caused no greater disturbance at the polls than elsewhere, this case was distinguished from bans on personal electioneering at the polls.

In an effort to prevent broadcast media from favoring any one candidate, Congress in 1927 enacted an "equal opportunities" law. This survives today as the famous Section 315, and provides that if a station permits one legally qualified candidate for office to speak, it must extend the same opportunity to all other candidates for the same office. Sometimes this provision is awkward in practice (e.g., when there is a long list of candidates, some serious and some frivolous), but it is increasingly important in light of the impact on public opinion of television exposure of political candidates (E. Katz & Feldman, 1971). Some broadcasters have sought repeal of this provision contending that it distorts journalistic assessments of newsworthiness: the broadcaster must either underplay the whole campaign or give equal coverage to every candidate for the office. This has not yet appeared as a constitutional problem, but the statute has led to much debate and legislators keep trying to develop a formula that would permit broadcasters to cover political campaigns more realistically. When a political issue is at stake, such as a bond authorization or a constitutional amendment, the FCC has acted through the fairness doctrine to prescribe balanced coverage (Commerce Committee, 1968).

[71] *Time, Inc.* v. *Bernard Geis Associates*, 293 F. Supp. 130 (S.D.N.Y. 1968).

[72] *Mills* v. *Alabama*, 384 U.S. 214 (1966).

Another possible need for restraint on communication in presidential elections may be necessitated by the practice of making nationwide projections on the basis of returns from the Atlantic seaboard before the polls have closed in states further west. There is disagreement about the nature of the impact of these projections, but Congress is sufficiently concerned about it to explore constitutionally valid alternatives, such as nationwide uniform voting hours (Commerce Committee, 1967). All polls would close at the same moment—and perhaps no votes would be counted until then. Retaining the present poll closings but prohibiting reports of voting totals or projections of winners until the last poll in the country closed would be more debatable. The former might limit access less and leave speech untouched, while in the latter case available information would be barred from further dissemination.

Obscenity: A Prohibition in Search of a Rationale

A particularly acute clash between freedom and control, highly perplexing to the Supreme Court, occurs in the area of obscenity. Although whatever is found to be obscene loses constitutional protection—courts will not attempt a balancing approach since they regard obscenity as beyond the scope of the First Amendment—the governmental interests justifying such exclusion have not been easy to identify. The state of the law remains, as one scholar has observed, a *sui generis* category of censorship (Emerson, 1970:467–515).

Although the most persuasive argument against obscenity would be that pornographic material induces criminal and antisocial conduct, thus linking obscenity with our earlier concern about violence and protection of individual security, the federal Commission on Obscenity and Pornography (1970:26–32), after exhaustive research, could discover no adequate empirical support for this assertion.

Unfortunately, vagueness—a fatal flaw in other areas of the law—pervades the obscenity area. The Supreme Court attempted to define obscenity as "whether to the average person, applying contemporary community standards, the dominant theme of the material taken as a whole appeals to prurient interest."[73] The decision of a subsequent case refined this and demanded that three elements coalesce under the definition: "It must be established that (*a*) the dominant theme of the material taken as a whole appeals to a prurient interest in sex; (*b*) the material is patently offensive because it affronts contemporary community standards relating to the description or representation of sexual matters; and (*c*) the material is utterly without redeeming social value."[74] Thus, even though a book is found to possess the requisite prurient appeal and to be patently offensive, it cannot be proscribed unless it is found to be "utterly without redeeming social value."

Certainly the notion of obscenity censorship rests upon some fundamental concern for the moral fabric of the community, but it raises troublesome questions. Can any group constitutionally impose on others its moral standards of sexual behavior? Is an analogy to religious freedom appropriate? Who has the last word as to "dominant theme," "community standards" and "social value"? Can an author reasonably determine whether his work will meet these standards or do they, in effect, operate as a prior restraint by inhibiting the permissible range of expression?

Cognizant of the presumption against prior restraint, the Supreme Court has required rigorous procedural safeguards when permitting obscenity restraints on media from motion pictures to the mail. In a recent instance, the Postmaster General, acting on his own initiative rather than on request from an addressee, sought to halt the use of the mails for allegedly obscene

---

[73] *Roth* v. *United States*, 354 U.S. 476 (1957).

[74] *Memoirs* v. *Massachusetts*, 383 U.S. 413 (1966).

materials. The Court held[75] that such a prior restraint was unconstitutional where the following administrative safeguards were absent: (1) the censor bears the burden of initiating judicial review and proving that the material is unprotected expression; (2) "prompt judicial review" on the merits must be available, and (3) any restraint imposed in advance of the final judicial determination must be limited to the briefest fixed period possible.

Perhaps because the last decade has witnessed a more flexible and less moralistic approach to the arts, community standards on obscenity have changed dramatically. The obscenity commission report, for example, questions "whether any material whatsoever may any longer be deemed obscene for adults under general prohibitions, and it appears that only certain highly explicit pictorial material may be so deemed (Commission on Obscenity and Pornography, 1970:425). Similarly, recent Supreme Court opinions have avoided moralistic distinctions and admonitions and attempted instead to measure alleged violations with reference to the practical evils sought to be prevented—evils more attached to the sale and distribution of allegedly obscene material than inherent in the quality of the material itself.[76] Thus, the Court reversed several obscenity convictions in one decision[77] by holding that in none of the cases was there: (1) a claim that the obscenity statutes reflected a specific and limited concern for juveniles; (2) any suggestion of an assault on individual privacy "by publication in a manner so obtrusive as to make it impossible for an unwilling individual to avoid exposure to it"; or (3) evidence of blatant pandering. Granting the government's concern with keeping pornography from juveniles,[78] which may be as legitimate as limiting access to liquor, the most acceptable attack is addressed not to the material itself, but to offensive promotion that threatens to affront private sensibilities.[79] (See also Krislov, 1968.)

This approach, logically extended, would put voluntary private sexual practices and discreetly circulated written matter beyond the reach of the law, and permit regulation only along the lines of the time, place, and manner statutes. If the "moral fabric" justification is finally declared unacceptable, a focus on privacy would make irrelevant the impact on the public of mere awareness of the existence of disconcerting ideas unless that impact were linked directly to antisocial behavior. It might also imply an assumption of risk approach, or voluntary waiver of privacy rights, as defenses to objections of obscenity where an individual knowingly accepts or views allegedly obscene material.

The privacy approach enables one observer to spotlight the interest of the recipient and to reject all claims of the seller to freedom of communication; he concludes that obscenity is really proscribed because it is viewed as "sin," an echo of the "moral fabric" argument (Henkin, 1963). He then asserts that the punishment of sin is beyond the scope of our temporal law and is an invasion of the expanding interest in the privacy of the individual—at least so long as one keeps these matters to oneself.

The Supreme Court took a cautious step in this direction when it attempted to distinguish a state's power to control public morality (constitutional) from its power to control private morality (unconstitutional) (A. Katz, 1969). The Court overthrew a conviction for possession of obscene films found during a warranted search of an individual's room, holding that statutes regulating obscenity should not reach into the privacy of one's home:

---

[75] *Blount* v. *Rizzi*, 400 U.S. 410 (1971).

[76] *Lee Art Theatre, Inc.* v. *Virginia*, 392 U.S. 636 (1968)—motion picture administrative safeguards.

[77] *Redrup* v. *New York*, 386 U.S. 767 (1967).

[78] *Ginsberg* v. *New York*, 390 U.S. 629 (1968)—material may be banned from sale to juveniles although not obscene for adults.

[79] *Ginzburg* v. *United States*, 383 U.S. 463 (1966)—pandering: unsolicited mail advertisements may be assault on privacy.

"If the First Amendment means anything, it means that a State has no business telling a man, sitting alone in his own house, what books he may read or what films he may watch."[80]

Subsequent decisions upholding the constitutionality of federal statutes prohibiting importation of obscene material and providing for its seizure by customs officials,[81] and prohibiting knowing use of the mails for the delivery of obscene materials even to willing adults,[82] have circumscribed rather than expanded this privacy analysis.

OTHER CONSTITUTIONAL APPROACHES

As indicated earlier, the balancing approach has not been accepted universally. Apart from the specific clear-and-present danger test—which is still used occasionally, as in contempt-of-court cases—two major constitutional approaches have been suggested as alternatives to the conventional balancing analysis.

In 1948, Professor Alexander Meiklejohn urged a division of speech into two categories. The first, political speech, related to governance of the society and would be categorically protected by the First Amendment, which would be applied to the states via the Fourteenth Amendment. Here, the public's right to know and be informed of political issues would be paramount. The second category covered other speech, such as ideas about science, literature, and entertainment, which the state could more readily regulate. Professor Meiklejohn explicitly recognized the role of time, place, and manner restrictions in ensuring maximum benefit from political discussion, and was willing to curtail the private right to speak if it were substantially contrary to the common good (Meiklejohn, 1948). For objections to the theory, see Chafee (1949).

[80] *Stanley* v. *Georgia*, 394 U.S. 557 (1969).

[81] *United States* v. *Thirty-Seven Photographs*, 402 U.S. 363 (1971).

[82] *United States* v. *Reidel*, 402 U.S. 351 (1971).

The Supreme Court initially applied the Meiklejohn theory in the defamation area, yet eventually found it too confining. Professor Meiklejohn's emphasis on absolute protection of political debate was expressly followed by the Court in the first libel decision[83] bringing nonintentionally defamatory statements against public officials and candidates within the protection of the First Amendment (Brennan, 1965). The Court later moved from this special attention to political issues, however, to extend constitutional protection to all discussions of public interest.

A "literal" or "absolute" view of the First Amendment was espoused by Supreme Court Justice Hugo Black (Cahn, 1962). His approach involved a somewhat narrow view of the scope of the word *speech* as used in the First Amendment and tended to demean nonverbal activity. His initial question was whether to characterize the particular conduct as "speech"; if so, he would give that conduct absolute protection. In ascertaining whether to bring the conduct in question within the First Amendment, he considered such questions as whether the conduct was verbal, and the relation between verbal conduct and action that the legislature could legitimately prohibit (Emerson, 1970).

In the areas of privacy and defamation, Justice Black disagreed with the majority by contending that once the speech was found to be within the First Amendment it should have absolute protection even if deliberately false. In the national security cases, Justice Black would have declared all speech completely protected under the First Amendment unless it was the virtual equivalent of a command to action that could itself be proscribed.[84]

[83] *New York Times Co.* v. *Sullivan*, 376 U.S. 254 (1964).

[84] See Justice Black's opinions in the following exemplary cases: *Dennis* v. *United States*, 341 U.S. 494 (1951); *Barenblatt* v. *United States*, 360 U.S. 109 (1959); *Konigsberg* v. *State Bar of California*, 366 U.S. 36 (1961); *New York Times Co.* v. *Sulli-*

THE FUTURE

Several themes developed in this chapter bear watching in the coming years. The first and most pervasive is our tendency to stress the law and the Constitution and to avoid the political issue of the wisdom of a proposed restraint on communication. Although the courts can tackle these difficult questions, that is rarely an adequate substitute for legislative attention to the tension between freedom and control of communication.

A second recurrent theme is the need for empirical data on the relationship between speech and induced action. Such data would aid greatly in approaching such areas as obscenity, fair trial vs. free press, mass media and violence, and the early announcement of election returns.

We may ask, also, who is entitled to the full extent of freedom of communication, and how far does freedom extend. Will distinctions continue to be drawn between speech and conduct or will all communicative expression be considered initially protected by the First Amendment, subject to showing that, on balance, it causes impermissible harm to the rights of others? Will the concept of public interest become sufficiently clear to enable some equilibrium between free press and defamation, copyright, or privacy claims? Will greater freedom be extended to those constrained by virtue of their status, such as servicemen, prisoners, or students? So far as intramedia tensions and ambiguities exist, will the broadcast media acquire the fuller freedom now enjoyed by the press or might the print media be brought under greater restriction by analogy to current broadcasting regulation?

---

van, 376 U.S. 254 (1964); *Ginzburg* v. *United States*, 383 U.S. 463 (1966); *Time, Inc.* v. *Hill*, 385 U.S. 374 (1967); *Rosenbloom v. Metromedia, Inc.*, 403 U.S. 29 (1971); *New York Times Co.* v. *United States*, 403 U.S. 713 (1971).

REFERENCES

Barron, Jerome A.
1967 "Access to the press—a new first amendment right." Harvard Law Review 80:1641–1678.

Blasi, Vince.
1970 "Prior restraints on demonstrations." Michigan Law Review 68:1481–1574.

Brennan, William J., Jr.
1965 "The Supreme Court and the Meiklejohn interpretation of the first amendment." Harvard Law Review 79:1–20.

Cahn, Edmond.
1962 "Justice Black and first amendment 'absolutes': A public interview." New York University Law Review 37:549–563.

Chafee, Zachariah, Jr.
1941 Free Speech in the United States. Cambridge, Massachusetts: Harvard University Press.
1949 "Book review" [of Meiklejohn's Free Speech and Its Relation to Self-Government]. Harvard Law Review 62:891.

Columbia Law Review.
1968 "Symbolic conduct." 68:1091–1126.
1971 "Cable television and the first amendment." 71:1008–1038.

Commerce Committee.
1967 Projections, Predictions of Election Results and Political Broadcasting. Hearings before Subcommittee on Communications, 90th Congress, 1st Session, held July 18–20. Washington, D.C.: U.S. Senate, Committee on Commerce.
1968 Staff Report on FCC's Actions and the Broadcasters' Operations in Connection with the Commission's Fairness Doctrine. Prepared for Subcommittee on Communications, 90th Congress, 2d Session. Washington, D.C.: U.S. Senate, Committee on Commerce.

Commission on Obscenity and Pornography.
1970 Report of the Commission on Obscenity and Pornography. Washington, D.C.: U.S. Government Printing Office (September).

Davis, Kenneth C.
1967 "The information act: A preliminary

analysis." University of Chicago Law Review 34:761–816.

Emerson, Thomas I.
1970 The System of Freedom of Expression. New York: Random House.

Emerson, Thomas I.; David Haber; and Norman Dorsen.
1967 Political and Civil Rights in the United States. Volume 1. Third Edition. Boston: Little, Brown.

Franklin, Marc A.
1963 "A constitutional problem in privacy protection: Legal inhibitions on reporting a fact." Stanford Law Review 16:107–148.

Franklin, Marc A. (ed.).
1968 Dynamics of American Law: Courts, the Legal Process and Freedom of Expression. Mineola, New York: Foundation Press.

Freund, Paul A.
1961 The Supreme Court of the United States. New York: Meridian Books.

Georgetown Law Journal.
1970 "Dissenting servicemen and the first amendment." 58:534–568.

Goldstein, Paul.
1970 "Copyright and the first amendment." Columbia Law Review 70: 983–1055.

Griswold, Erwin.
1955 The Fifth Amendment Today. Cambridge, Massachusetts: Harvard University Press.

Harvard Law Review.
1965 "Freedom of expression in a commercial context." 78:1191–1211.
1968 "Developments in the law: Academic freedom." 81:1045–1159.
1970 "The first amendment overbreadth doctrine." 83:844–927.

Henkin, Louis.
1963 "Morals and the constitution: The sin of obscenity." Columbia Law Review 63:391–414.

Hook, Sidney.
1957 Common Sense and the Fifth Amendment. New York: Criterion Books.

Hurt, Robert.
1966 "Economic rationale of copyright." Edited by Robert Schuchman. American Economic Review Papers and Proceedings 56(May):421–432.

Kalven, Harry, Jr.
1965 "The concept of the public forum." Pp. 1–32 in Philip B. Kurland (ed.), 1965 Supreme Court Review. Chicago: University of Chicago Press. Annual.
1966 "Privacy in tort law—were Warren and Brandeis wrong?" Law and Contemporary Problems 31(Spring):326–341.
1967 "Broadcasting, public policy and the first amendment." Journal of Law and Economics 10:15–49.

Kaplan, Benjamin J.
1966 An Unhurried View of Copyright. New York: Columbia University Press.

Katz, Al.
1969 "Privacy and pornography: Stanley v. Georgia." Pp. 203–217 in Philip B. Kurland (ed.), 1969 Supreme Court Review. Chicago: University of Chicago Press. Annual.

Katz, Elihu, and Jacob J. Feldman.
1971 "The debates in the light of research: A survey of surveys." Pp. 701–753 in Wilbur Schramm and Donald F. Roberts (eds.), The Process and Effects of Mass Communications. Urbana: University of Illinois Press.

Kester, John.
1968 "Soldiers who insult the president." Harvard Law Review 81:1697–1769.

Kintner, Earl W.
1971 A Primer on the Law of Deceptive Practices: A Guide for the Businessman. New York: Macmillan.

Krislov, Samuel.
1968 "From Ginzburg to Ginsberg: Unhurried children's hour in obscenity litigation." Pp. 153–197 in Philip B. Kurland (ed.), 1968 Supreme Court Review. Chicago: University of Chicago Press. Annual.

McCormick, Charles (ed.).
1954 Handbook of the Law of Evidence. St. Paul: West.

Meiklejohn, Alexander.
1948 Free Speech and Its Relation to Self-Government. New York: Harper.

Nimmer, Melville B.
1963 Copyrights. Albany, New York: Bender.
1970 "Does copyright abridge the first amendment guarantees of free speech and press?" UCLA Law Review 17: 1180–1204.

O'Neil, Robert M.
1965 "Television, tort law and federalism." California Law Review 53:421–485.
1966 Free Speech: Responsible Communication Under Law. Indianapolis: Bobbs-Merrill.

Prosser, William L.
1960 "Privacy." California Law Review 48:383–423.
1971 Handbook of the Law of Torts. Fourth Edition. St. Paul: West.

Turner, William B.
1971 "Establishing the rule of law in prisoners' rights litigation." Stanford Law Review 23:473–518.

Walter, Francis.
1961 "Federal regulation and lobbying." Southern California Law Review 34: 111–129.

Warren, Samuel D., and Louis D. Brandeis.
1890 "The right to privacy." Harvard Law Review 4:193–220.

Yale Law Journal.
1961 "The constitutional right to anonymity: Free speech, disclosure and the devil." 70:1084–1128.
1970 "Reporters and their sources: Constitutional rights to a confidential relationship." 80:317–371.

PART III Communication Research

Notes on Communication Research Methods

NATHAN MACCOBY
Stanford University

There are a few developments in communications research that need citing at this point. There have been important developments in the use of content analysis of communications and the role of the interview and questionnaire—the use of survey research methods has increased greatly.

Computers can reduce the enormous amount of coding detail that normally has to take place in dealing with lengthy verbal messages. Holsti (1968) reports, for example, on an automatic computer program for the measurement of attitudes. In this instance, the text must still be coded manually before computer processing. There are, however, information storage and retrieval systems that do not require manual coding, such as Rochester's SMART system reported by Salton (Gerbner et al., 1969). The use of computers for content analysis as reported by J. Zvi Namenwirth (Gerbner et al., 1969), for example, demonstrates that the Democratic party platforms are more sensitive to economic changes than are the Republican platforms. This is done by comparing party platforms over long periods of time and relating these to major economic events.

One of the more interesting applications of content analysis in nonverbal material is in the area of authorship and aesthetics. Mosteller and Wallace (1964) were able to do historical detective work on the disputed authorship of some of the Federalist papers by the use of content-analysis methods. Paisley (1964), employing what he calls minor encoding habits, has been able to identify disputed painters and composers. A musicologist, Barry S. Brook, describes the development of what he calls "A Plaine and Easie code" of musical analysis (Gerbner et al., 1969).

Another unusual and ingenious application of content-analysis method is Paul Ekman, Wallace Friesen, and Thomas Taussig's technique of coding film and videotape onto computers in such a way that retrieval is readily possible (see Chapter 4). Ekman and his colleagues have developed a system called VID-R (Visual Information Display and Retrieval). They can either take their primary information on 16-mm. film and transfer it to videotape or take it directly on videotape. If it is taken with a 16-mm. camera, they are able by use of a computer-controlled camera chain to transfer the film images to videotape. A high speed search and retrieval system called SCAN (Systematic Classification of Analysis of Nonverbal Behavior) has been developed to code the stop and start motion of given body areas and for studying the change of visual configurations in continuous movement. This system has been applied separately to each of six body regions.

This editor has seen the Ekman retrieval system in operation and is impressed with the speed with which given sequences can be located via the computer. Anyone who has worked with the use of film recordings is aware of the tremendous contribution that Ekman and his colleagues have made in developing this system.

A number of computer applications have grown out of Stone's general inquirer system, in which a sort of detective system is employed by the computer to achieve the right text by successive approximations (Stone, Bales, Namenwirth, & Ogilvie, 1962). Probably the potential of the computer in coding varieties of communications and information has only begun to be realized. More success thus far appears to have been obtained in developing retrieval systems than in the automation of storage systems.

The field of content analysis is concerned with attempting to quantify like-characteristics of communications of all sorts. In the early days, verbal material was the only subject matter treated in this way. The changes that have occurred in the field within the last decade are clearly represented by the headings of the four parts of the volume entitled *The Analysis of Communication Content* (Gerbner et al., 1969). The material that has been subjected to analysis ranges from music to visual behavior, and even to the measurement of vocal information of a nonlinguistic sort. However, in some ways, the most important developments in the field are in the computer techniques that have been developed for content analysis, particularly the close relationship that has been emerging between content analysis and computational linguistics. Stone et al. (1962), Holsti (1968), and others have made important advances in the use of computers for content-analysis work.

Krippendorff (Gerbner et al., 1969) offers three prototype models of analytical constructs that for him appear to be basic for current research involving content analysis. These are: association models, which realize content in statistical correlations between variables; discourse models of messages, which consider content as linguistic meanings; and communication models of messages, which manifest themselves in processes of control in interaction systems. This classification of models would seem to have some utility in analyzing the varieties of uses of content analysis and as a way of relating content analysis to information theory.

Historically, content analysis has been essentially an atheoretical approach to data analysis in much the same way that factor analysis has been represented as a fishing expedition designed to discover some generalities in the data. Verbal copy of almost any sort, be it open-interview data or protocols of discussions, meetings, printed matter, or what have you, has been subjected to analysis to see what regularities occur. This coding can range all the way from length of sentences—something completely quantifiable—to highly judgmental categorizations, such as the intent of the communicator. In our judgment—notwithstanding the technical advances that have been developed—content analysis is still basically a way of approaching a mass of data to make some sense out of it. Such is by no means a modest achievement. On the contrary, its applications are enormously varied and highly useful; however, it should not be a substitute for theory development and hypothesis testing.

It would seem to be evident that while content analysis has important uses and wide applicability in the testing of all sorts of hypotheses about communication contents, as well as in fishing for potential hypotheses to be tested in other ways, the method is not a substitute for deductive thinking and deductive theorizing and experimentation. However, when used in its appropriate place and in conjunction with other research methods, it can be a highly important and useful tool in behavioral communication research.

The interview continues to be a basic research tool in studying the communication process behaviorly. It may or may not have a place in any particular piece of research. It is not in itself a complete research design or method. For example, if the object of the research is to test some hypotheses concerning the effects of communications on attitudes, a paper and pencil test or a set of behavioral observations or even some unobtrusive measures of behavior may well be preferable to the use of an interview. Even if it were proved to be the case that the interview were a desirable device to use in such a study, its application would not in itself constitute the method by which the hypotheses under consideration could be tested. It would still be essential to formulate a specific research design in which specified interview measures might play an important part in the assessment of dependent variables of attitude change.

Too often the interview or the questionnaire is used as though it were a fully self-sufficient method of inquiry. Certainly in many studies in which true experimental designs are not feasible, estimations of cause and effect relationships may be made via matching on certain independent variables or other means of "holding things constant." But it must not be forgotten that these are at best substitutes for true manipulation of independent variables under controlled conditions. In fact, it must be stated that in studies of communication effects, researchers have frequently made the mistake of assuming too early that true experimental designs were not practicable and resorted too soon to correlational designs.

The interview may have other roles in the collection of primary information for testing hypotheses. There are many communication studies in which the primary purpose is to gather data descriptive of a population—e.g., how much what kinds of people know, what the attitudes of various kinds of people are on various issues. Clearly no hypotheses are being tested; it is just that certain population parameters are being sought.

The interview may also be useful in developing more objective measures. The situation may be studied in a preliminary fashion intensively through use of the interview, and other measures may be devised on the basis of the interview data for the main investigation.

Sometimes also the interview can help to make clear data that have been obtained in other ways. Responses measured automatically by instruments or responses made verbally to communications may be best understood if the subject is interviewed in order to find out what he had in mind.

Interviews may be informal, or they may be highly structured. There are circumstances under which one or the other would be preferable. For example, in attempting to get at the dimensions of a problem in pretesting, unstandardized interviews in which the interviewer knows what his objectives are but does not use a set of fixed-worded questions may be more useful than starting out with fully standardized questions. On the other hand, when the study has been fully pretested and the need is to obtain standard information from all respondents, then perhaps the structured interview is to be preferred. One of the major problems in the use of interviews or questionnaires is the need to begin the study with a clear-cut list or statement of objectives. The value or appropriateness of interview questions can only be assessed in the light of these study objectives.

One of the more serious problems in the use of the personal interview is the role relationship of the interviewer to the respondent. In most field interviews in the U.S., it has been the custom for whites to interview white respondents and for blacks to interview black respondents. Moreover, almost all interviewing agencies employ middle-class housewives as the people most likely to get cooperation from respondents.

Since the data have consistently indicated that the way the interviewer is perceived by the respondent makes some difference in the way he answers attitudinal questions, the selection of the interviewer can make an important difference.

The use of portable recorders has increased considerably as a means of obtaining more accurate data in the interview. Along with this development has been that of rapidly rising costs of carrying out personal interview surveys. The increasing use of probability samples which are necessary in descriptive studies designed to study population parameters has also contributed to the inflationary situation. Locating or obtaining interviews from predetermined respondents who are becoming increasingly difficult to find in these days of fear for personal safety is another important cost factor.

REFERENCES

Gerbner, George, et al. (eds.).
1969 The Analysis of Communication Content; Development in Scientific Theories and Computer Techniques. New York: Wiley.

Holsti, O. R.
1968 "Content analysis," in Gardner Lindzey and Elliot Aronson (eds.), Handbook of Social Psychology. Second Edition. Reading, Massachusetts: Addison-Wesley.

Mosteller, Frederick, and D. L. Wallace (eds.).
1964 Inference and Disputed Authorship: The Federalist. Reading, Massachusetts: Addison-Wesley.

Paisley, W. J.
1964 "Identifying the unknown communicator in painting, literature and music: The significance of minor encoding habits." Journal of Communication 14:219–237.

Stone, P. J.; R. F. Bales; J. Z. Namenwirth; and D. M. Ogilvie.
1962 "The general inquirer: A computer system for content analysis and retrieval based on the sentence as a unit of information." Behavioral Science 7(No. 4):484–498.

CHAPTER 30 Aggregate Data

HOWARD ROSENTHAL
Carnegie-Mellon University

Much data analysis in behavioral science research involves units of analysis that are identical with the units of interest. We may use questionnaire data from individuals to make inferences about individual behavior. We may use characteristics of groups, such as group size or structure, to make inferences about group behavior. However, communication researchers often find themselves in the position of having data aggregated into units larger than the units of interest. For example, we may wish to make inferences about individual voting behavior, but find that we can obtain only precinct level summaries of voting totals. There are many pitfalls in the process of making statistically reliable inferences about individuals from aggregate data (or about smaller aggregates from data in larger aggregates). This chapter explains the details of model formulation and statistical estimation when individual or small aggregates are the units of interest but when data is aggregated into a larger unit of analysis. Illustrative examples from communication research problems are provided.

INTRODUCTION

An aggregate unit of analysis is any unit that can be further divided into meaningful subsets. Thus, states are aggregates with respect to either counties or households or individuals; firms are aggregates with respect to their operating divisions; years are aggregates with respect to days or months.

Frequently, researchers have no choice but to work with aggregate data. The usual illustration of this point is voting, where the secrecy of the ballot prohibits obtaining individual information. Another instance is historical studies, where data may be available only in aggregated form. Even in studies where "individual" data can be collected, cost considerations may force reliance on aggregate data. Dogan and Rokkan (1969) contains several varied examples of the use of aggregate data.

From the standpoint of theory rather than data, aggregation is also often a part of the simplification of reality inherent in model building in the social sciences. For instance, one may be able to formulate a model that would explain the total com-

This work was supported mainly by a grant from the National Science Foundation. Computational support was also provided by the Communications Institute, Hebrew University, Jerusalem.

munications between firms while finding it much more difficult to build a model that would explain interpersonal communications among all the personnel of the firms. Similarly, aggregate measures can be used to summarize the "environment" for an individual. While an individual is influenced by specific contact with other individuals of varying educational achievement, we often summarize the whole contact pattern by a measure of the average level of education in the community.[1]

In general, aggregate measures can be thought of as summaries or reductions of more complex bodies of data. Consequently, there is always a loss of information when one passes from a less aggregated to a more aggregated level. The consequences of this loss of information were explored in considerable depth by economists who have a critical concern for understanding the conditions where macroeconomic models will apply at the micro level and vice versa (Ando, Fisher, & Simon, 1963; Green, 1964; Theil, 1964; Christ, 1968; Nataf, 1968). This chapter, however, will be devoted to topics of more direct concern to current communications research where model building has not attained the sophistication that is found in economics.

Let us first briefly describe some of the types of literature where aggregate communications data are employed. At virtually the highest level of aggregates—nations—a growing number of studies employ communications variables (literacy, television ownership, number of cinema seats, etc.). These studies were in large part stimulated by the work of Lerner (1957), who was concerned with the causal connections between urbanization and communications. Many of the later studies do not represent attempts to estimate a specified model of the relationships between independent and dependent variables. Largely blind attempts at applying statistical analysis procedures made feasible by electronic computing, these studies were apparently conducted with the expectation that statistical procedures such as factor analysis would suggest meaningful patterns in the data. Among the literature one can list Banks and Textor (1963), Russett et al. (1964), Fagen (1964a; 1964b), Farace and Donohew (1965), Gregg and Banks (1965), Donohew and Thorp (1966), Farace (1966a; 1966b), and Sawyer (1967).

At a less exploratory and less macroscopic level, there are studies like Parker's investigation of effects of one communications medium on another (Parker, 1963). Similar studies, such as Simon and Stern (1955) and Rosenthal and Sen (1970), consider communication effects upon voting and other behavioral variables influenced by communications.

The studies above have been concerned with relationships among aggregates. Can the aggregate data also be useful when the units of interest are individuals? In general, *no*, as we learned from the classic demonstration of Robinson (1950) with regard to the relationship between illiteracy and race in the United States. Despite the validity of the argument, the Robinson essay has to some extent been harmful in that a number of researchers rejected aggregate data as irrelevant for the study of individuals and chose to rely primarily on survey data and other direct observations on individuals. Such a rejection ignores the existence of metholdology—the key piece of which is the essay by Goodman (1959)—that enables one to use aggregate data to study individual units in specific circumstances.

Exposition of this methodology will occupy most of this chapter, for it seems uniquely specific to aggregate data problems. If the investigator is concerned solely with relationships among aggregates rather than using aggregates to study individuals, he can find his methodology covered by standard texts in statistics and economet-

[1] See Lazarsfeld and Menzel (1961) for a much more detailed discussion on the conceptual relationships between aggregate and individual measures.

rics. However, this chapter also covers a number of topics that are particularly salient in aggregate communications studies regardless of the unit of interest. These include (1) the correlation of errors in models as a result of the geographic contiguity of aggregate units; (2) the usefulness of transformations of variables and products of variables; (3) the question of weighting observations; and (4) the question of raw versus per capita measures.

A noneconometric problem somewhat akin to the aggregate-to-individual inference problem has been treated by Mosteller (1968). Suppose one has two sets of survey results from different populations. In both sets one has the marginal distribution of a number of items (e.g., readership, sex, race, income). One set has the complete cross-classification of these items (e.g., the number of male, white, upper-income readers, etc.); the other set does not have this classification. The investigator may want to create this classification in the second set, assuming that certain statistical relationships found in the first population will hold in the second, regardless of any differences in the marginals. Mosteller has developed a methodology for computing the cross-classification.

This related area, as well as several other aggregate methodologies such as use of aggregate data in simulation or flow models (e.g., Hagerstrand, 1965; Wolpert, 1967), will not be covered in detail. We also omit possible application of Bayesian approaches, which utilize partial, subjective information regarding individual properties, to the aggregate-to-individual inference problem. In brief, the focus of this chapter is the application of econometric techniques to the analysis of aggregate communications data.

Since reading this chapter requires a higher level of mathematical training than that required by most other chapters in this volume, most sections have been prefaced with italicized introductions. The reader may find it useful to skim these portions before reading the detailed text.

AGGREGATE-TO-INDIVIDUAL INFERENCE

In this section, we discuss the problem of the inference of individual correlations from aggregate correlations. To place the problem in the framework of an example, suppose we know for each of a set of geographic units the proportion of the population that reads newspaper A and the proportion that reads newspaper B. What can we say about the proportion that reads both A and B? First, we will show that, in general, it is impossible to make any estimate of the proportion reading both A and B.

If aggregate data are used strictly for the purpose of making inferences at the aggregate level—for example, in a study of the relationship between communications infrastructure measured on a per capita basis and the per capita GNP—the problems met are those commonly found in statistical analysis. Problems specific to aggregate analysis are encountered, however, when aggregate data are to be used to draw inferences about more detailed units. If the aggregate units are states, for example, "more detailed units" would be counties, individuals, etc. While a geographic example will be used here, the same problems can arise in other orientations, such as between more and less detailed classifications of the labor force. Each of the more detailed units is assumed to be wholly included in one of the aggregate units; we will not consider the more difficult problem of overlapping units such as counties and congressional districts.

The aggregate-to-individual (or smaller aggregate) inference problem can be illustrated by exploring a case involving two dichotomous variables. This case is representative of the major methodological problems encountered.[2] It might be convenient to think of one variable as representing readership versus nonreader-

[2] For generalizations about multivariate models and continuous variables, see the literature, particularly Goodman (1959).

ship of newspaper A and the second as representing the same dichotomy for newspaper B.

For each aggregate unit, we are interested in the fourfold table (Table 1). Our aggregate data will give us, in addition to N, the total population of the unit, the marginal values, p_i and p_j, which represent the proportions who read newspapers A and B, respectively. What is not available in the aggregate data is the additional item of information, p_{ij}, the proportion who read both A and B, that would permit a specification of the cells of the table. Equivalently, to anticipate our interest in regression analysis, aggregate data does not contain the *component-specific* rate (Duncan, Cuzzort, & Duncan, 1961), denoted by $p=p_{ij}/p_j$, the proportion of newspaper B readers who read newspaper A; p is, of course, also the conditional probability of reading newspaper A given that newspaper B was read. Without the component-specific rate, we cannot calculate the Pearson correlation coefficient, ϕ, Yule's Q coefficient, or any other bivariate measure one would usually make for individual data.

TABLE 1

GIVEN AGGREGATE UNIT: READERSHIP OF A AND B

	B*	B†	
A*	p_{ij}	$p_{i\bar{j}}$	p_i
A†	$p_{\bar{i}j}$	$p_{\bar{i}j}$	$p_{\bar{i}}$
	p_j	$p_{\bar{j}}$	

* readers; † nonreaders.

TABLE 2

CALCULATION OF A CORRELATION COEFFICIENT: ECOLOGICAL AND INDIVIDUAL POPULATIONS

Unit 1			Unit 2			Unit 3			Unit 4		
0.0	0.2	0.2	0.0	0.4	0.4	0.2	0.4	0.6	0.6	0.2	0.8
0.2	0.6	0.8	0.4	0.2	0.6	0.4	0.0	0.4	0.2	0.0	0.2
0.2	0.8		0.4	0.6		0.6	0.4		0.8	0.2	
$N=100$			$N=100$			$N=100$			$N=100$		

NOTE: The ecological correlation is 1.0; the individual correlation is negative (-0.2).

Data for computing ecological correlation:

	Unit 1	2	3	4
p_i	0.2	0.4	0.6	0.8
p_j	0.2	0.4	0.6	0.8

$r=1.0.$

Computation of individual correlation:

$p_{ij}=(0.0+0.0+0.2+0.6)/4=0.2$

$p_i=p_j=(0.2+0.4+0.6+0.8)/4=0.5$

$\phi=(p_{ij}-p_ip_j)/\sqrt{p_ip_jp_{\bar{i}}p_{\bar{j}}}=-0.2.$

SOURCE: Adapted from Boudon (1963).

TABLE 3

EFFECT OF CHANGING THE CELL VALUES FOR CONSTANT MARGINALS

Unit 1			Unit 2			Unit 3			Unit 4		
0.2	0.0	0.2	0.4	0.0	0.4	0.6	0.0	0.6	0.8	0.0	0.8
0.0	0.8	0.8	0.0	0.6	0.6	0.0	0.4	0.4	0.0	0.2	0.2
0.2	0.8		0.4	0.6		0.6	0.4		0.8	0.2	

NOTE: Both the ecological correlation and the individual correlation are 1.0.

Now, if we redirect our attention from a given aggregate unit as specified in Table 1 to a population or sample of aggregate units as illustrated in Table 2, we find that we can calculate a correlation coefficient, known as the ecological correlation, by calculating the correlation of p_i and p_j over the population of aggregates.[3] But this is not the individual population correlation coefficient that is computed after summing the cells of the four aggregate units shown in Table 2. (Expressions giving the exact relationship between ecological and individual correlations are found in Robinson, 1950; Duncan, Cuzzort, & Duncan, 1961; Boudon, 1963.) The difference between the two coefficients can be seen readily by comparing Table 2 with Table 3. By changing the values of the cells while holding the marginals constant, we are able to change the value of the individual correlation while the ecological correlation remains constant.

This example suffices to demonstrate the following conclusions: *In general, aggregate data cannot be used to estimate component-specific information. In particular, the ecological correlation cannot be used to estimate the individual correlation.* In the sociological literature, Robinson (1950) first drew attention to this conclusion with an example involving race and a communications variable, literacy. Alker (1969) provides a more extensive discussion of problems of fallacious estimation and inference.

[3] An exact definition is given in equation (34).

BOUNDS ON COMPONENT-SPECIFIC RATES

One way of partially escaping the preceding pessimistic conclusion is to place bounds on the individual correlation. Let us

TABLE 4

TELEVISION-VIEWING EXAMPLE

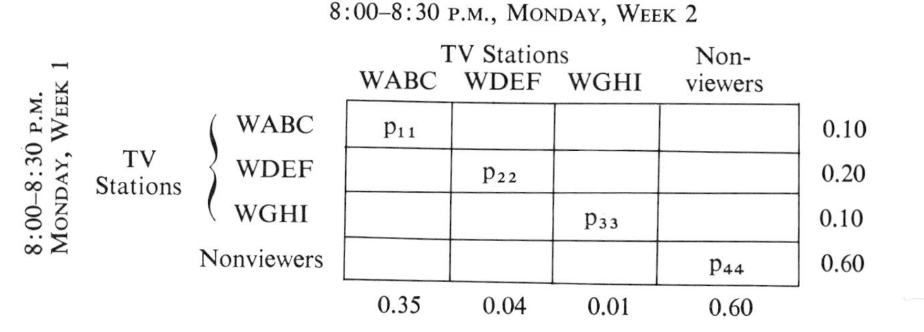

8:00–8:30 P.M., MONDAY, WEEK 1	8:00–8:30 P.M., MONDAY, WEEK 2: TV Stations WABC	WDEF	WGHI	Nonviewers	
TV Stations: WABC	p_{11}				0.10
WDEF		p_{22}			0.20
WGHI			p_{33}		0.10
Nonviewers				p_{44}	0.60
	0.35	0.04	0.01	0.60	

return to our example of the readership of newspapers A and B. Given the aggregate data, we can always calculate for each geographic unit a minimum possible amount of joint readership and a maximum amount of joint readership.

Knowledge of only the p_i and p_j can thus be used to give upper and lower bounds for component-specific rates. In Table 2, we have filled in the cells so as to minimize p_{ij} for each table. In Table 3, the cells show the maximum value of p_{ij}. After calculating minimum and maximum values of p_{ij} in this manner, we can use these values to calculate minimum and maximum values for the individual correlation coefficient. The true value *must* lie within these bounds. Consequently, the bounds are one of the partial checks that can be used with the estimation models below.

Duncan and Davis (1953) give a systematic discussion of the calculation of bounds for the case of 2×2 tables.

Their approach is also valid for more complex cases. Assume, for example, that we had data on television channel viewing in a geographic locale for the same day and half-hour slot on each of two successive weeks, as portrayed in Table 4. The proportion of the population that were nonviewers in both weeks, p_{44} in the table, is at least 0.20 and at most 0.60. The total proportion who made the same choice in both weeks, $p_{11}+p_{22}+p_{33}+p_{44}$, is at least 0.20 and at most 0.75. If one is dealing with a set of geographic units, one can similarly compute the upper and lower bounds for each unit and then average over the units to obtain upper and lower bounds for the entire population.

In all cases where bounds are calculated, the bounds from more detailed aggregate units will always be at least as good as those calculated from higher levels of aggregation. If the bounds have the disadvantage of frequently giving a very imprecise range for the parameter of interest, they have the advantage of requiring no special assumptions about the nature of the component-specific rate.

Methods for Estimation of Component-Specific Rates

The discussion now turns to methods of actually estimating the individual correlation. In order to carry out the estimation, one has to make a restrictive model of the geographic variation of the parameters to be estimated—that is, the amount of joint readership in our model. The estimation technique—linear regression—serves the important purpose of providing a means for rejecting the model. That is, even though one can never confirm the validity of his model assumptions concerning geographic variation, certain sets of data will indicate reasonable grounds for rejection.

Besides achieving bounds, the p_i and p_j can be used to obtain direct point estimates of the component-specific rates if an appropriate statistical model is applied. By *appropriate*, one means a correctly specified hypothesis concerning the component-specific rates. Consequently, all the estimation models should be used with great caution unless one has strong reasons for selecting the underlying hypothesis. On the other hand, application of these models can be useful as a means of rejecting certain hypotheses.

For example, one's model might be that p, the proportion of newspaper B's readers who also read newspaper A, is constant for all aggregate units. Given this model, one can then proceed to estimate the value of p. If this estimate were *significantly* greater than one or less than zero, one would reject the model since the true value of p must lie between zero and one. Some alternate model, one that allows for geographic variation in the value of p, must be adopted.

Most of the literature and the ensuing treatment here focuses on models that use regression techniques to estimate component-specific rates in cases where the dependent variable is dichotomous at the individual level. We shall distinguish three classes of models:

1. Those using a *linear regression* as the

estimation procedure, where the component-specific rates are *linear* combinations of the regression coefficient
2. Those using *linear regression*, where at least some component-specific rates are *nonlinear* functions of the regression coefficient
3. *Nonlinear regression.*[4]

While component-specific estimates can be calculated for the population as a whole, in all of these cases they can also be calculated for each aggregate unit. This information can be extremely important to practical applications where budgetary allocations, sampling, etc. are to be made on a geographic basis. The availability of this information has been insufficiently stressed in the sociological literature, which has remained focused in terms of Robinson's original interest in overall individual correlation coefficients.

Models Linear in the Regression Estimates

There are various ways in which regression models can be related to the parameters (e.g., the proportion of newspaper B readers who also read newspaper A) needed to estimate the individual level correlation. One particular form of relationship is the linear relationship. One advantage of linear relationships is that these lead to a simple procedure for estimating the standard errors of the parameter estimates.

The class of linear relationships, although restricted, is quite broad. It encompasses a wide variety of models where the parameters can depend upon features of the environment. For example, the readership proportions might be a function of education level. Furthermore, even within this linear class, there is no unique model of individual behavior that corresponds to a given regression equation. On the contrary, a variety of interpretations are possible. There are also statistical problems connected with the interpretation of the regression results. Consequently, we provide an extensive methodological survey of the linear case.

In all estimation procedures, the central problem is correct specification of a model. Not only can a variety of linear regression models be used, but each linear regression can be associated with several underlying models concerning the component-specific rates. We will illustrate this latter point before setting forth some of the regression models that have been proposed.

For this discussion, we replace p_i by Y, the usual regression symbol for the dependent variable, and p_j by X. To take the simplest case:

$$Y = b_0 + b_1 X + u, \tag{1}$$

where b_0 and b_1 are constants and u is a stochastic disturbance. After applying least-squares procedures, one obtains an estimated equation:

$$\hat{Y} = \hat{b}_0 + \hat{b}_1 X. \tag{2}$$

The simplest underlying component-specific model, proposed first by Goodman (1959) and reviewed by Mosteller (1968), assumes that the component-specific rates $p(p = p_{ij}/p_j)$ and $q(q = p_{i\bar{j}}/p_{\bar{j}})$ are constant for all aggregate units subject to a stochastic disturbance. Formally,

$$p = \bar{p} + v \quad \text{and} \quad q = \bar{q} + w, \tag{3}$$

where $\bar{p}$ and $\bar{q}$ indicate the "average" values of p and q, and where v and w are stochastic disturbances.

Given (3), and using the identity,

$$Y \equiv pX + q(1 - X), \tag{4}$$

we find that

$$\begin{aligned} Y &= (p + v)X + (q + w)(1 - X) \\ &= (\bar{p} - \bar{q})X + q + vX + w(1 - X). \end{aligned} \tag{5}$$

Comparing (1) and (5) shows that

$$\begin{aligned} b_0 &= q \\ b_1 &= p - q \\ u &= vX + w(1 - X). \end{aligned} \tag{6}$$

[4] Econometric texts such as Johnston (1963) and Malinvaud (1966) should be consulted for introductory discussions and bibliographic references regarding statistical techniques covered in this chapter.

Now, letting E express expected value, ordinary least-squares procedures require that $E(u)=0$ and $E(u^2)=\sigma^2$, a constant, for all aggregate units. This is achieved if we assume that $E(v)=E(w)=0$ and that

$$X^2[E(v^2)]+(1-X)^2[E(w^2)] + 2X(1-X)[E(vw)]$$

is constant. (Note that this condition holds if $v=w$.) In addition, assume that the disturbances are uncorrelated for all pairs of units. Of course, we also must require that our variables show some variation over the geographic units; that is, X and Y have nonzero variances. With these assumptions, we can estimate p and q by

$$\hat{p}=\hat{b}_1+\hat{b}_0 \quad \text{and} \quad \hat{q}=\hat{b}_0. \qquad (7)$$

Hereafter, to facilitate presentation, we will drop the error terms and expected value and estimator symbols; hence,

$$p=b_1+b_0 \quad \text{and} \quad q=b_0. \qquad (8)$$

Methods for carrying out partial checks on these estimates are given by Goodman (1959).

By no means, however, can we equate the linear-regression model (1) with the constant-proportion (component-specific rate) models (3). Consider a television program that exactly doubles its audience in each aggregate unit from one week to the next. Assume that all of the first week's viewers tuned in during week two. Letting X denote the proportion of the population that was viewing during the first week, we find that $p=1.0$ and $q=X/(1.0—X)$. The second week's viewing is given by $Y=1.0X+[X/(1.0—X)](1.0—X)=2X$. A regression will show $Y=2X$ and model (8) gives $p=2$ and $q=0$. Of course, instead of using the constant-proportion model, we should be using a model of the form:

Given

$$p=c_1, \quad q=d_1+d_2X/(1-X), \qquad (9)$$

and applying the identity (4), then

$$Y=(c_1+d_2-d_1)X+d_1. \qquad (10)$$

The difficulty with this equation is that not all of its parameters can be identified since there are three parameters but only two regression coefficients. However, if one is willing to introduce an additional assumption, estimates can be calculated; for example, if $c_1=1.0$, $d_1=b_0$ and $d_2=b_1+b_0-1.0$. This model illustrates the point that one should keep in mind alternative uses of given regression models. Goodman (1959) and Stokes (1968) indicate that the values of p and q which lead one to reject the null hypothesis that $0\leqslant p\leqslant 1$ *and* $0\leqslant q\leqslant 1$ should lead one to reject the constant proportion model; however, they did not emphasize that such a rejection was not a reason for rejecting the simple linear regression. This regression might indeed be associated to an alternative model.

Alternative multivariate models, where p and q are variable proportions, have been proposed in the literature (Goodman, 1959; Duncan, Cuzzort, & Duncan, 1961; Boudon, 1963). These models become particularly important when p and q are viewed as depending upon environmental influences. To return to our initial example, the proportions of both the readers and the nonreaders of newspaper B who read newspaper A could depend directly upon the proportion reading newspaper B (models 11 and 13) or they could depend upon per capita income levels, etc.

The use of more complex, environmental and, hence, multivariate models raises problems of econometric estimation that have not been considered in the sociological literature. In particular, one can suggest that high intercorrelations between the independent variables are built into the environmental models. These intercorrelations will often result in multicollinearities that make estimates imprecise. When collinearities occur, the standard errors of the estimated regression coefficients become very large. Consequently, we cannot obtain precise estimates of the coefficients of the models.

The models found in the literature fall into two classes. In the first class, the regression of Y depends only upon various functions of X. Within this class, for cases involving more than simple constant proportion, this writer's empirical experience suggests that collinearity will usually be severe. In the second class, Y depends also upon external variables. Occupation and age would be examples of external variables for the newspaper A, newspaper B case. When we use variables of this type, collinearity problems exist but are attenuated. These statements can be illustrated by reviewing the models and giving an example with estimates.

Models using a single independent measure. In addition to the constant-proportion model (3), one can look upon p and q as variables. Specifically, one can view p and q as being functions of the independent variable X. To return to the newspaper reading case, the simplest manner for the general level of readership of newspaper A to influence readership of newspaper B would be through linear variation:

Given

$$p = c_1 + c_2 X, \quad q = d_1 + d_2 X \tag{11}$$

then

$$Y = (c_2 - d_2) X^2 + (c_1 - d_1 + d_2) X + d_1. \tag{12}$$

Since the regression equation (12) will yield only three coefficients, either c_1, c_2, or d_2 must be arbitrarily given. (A solution for d_1 is always available since d_1 equals the regression intercept.) If, for example, $d_2 = 0$, then we can solve for the remaining coefficients. Likewise, we can solve given $c_1 = 2c_2$, etc.

In the foregoing linear function, if p and q are not constants, their *rate of change* with respect to X is a constant. In some applications, it might be more reasonable for this rate of change to be a decreasing, inverse function of X. For example, in comparing units where the total readership of newspaper A varies from 90 to 95 percent, one might expect to find less variation in the readership of newspaper B than one would find if one compared units where newspaper A readership varies from 5 to 10 percent. The following logarithmic function model contains a decreasing rate of change:

Given

$$p = c_1 + c_2 \ln(X), \quad q = d_1 + d_2 \ln(X) \tag{13}$$

then

$$Y = (c_2 - d_2) X \cdot \ln(X) + (c_1 - d_1) X + d_2 \ln(X) + d_1. \tag{14}$$

All four parameters can be estimated in this model.

To illustrate the estimation techniques and the problems of collinearity, models (3), (11), and (13) were used in connection with a problem in voting analysis. The substantive interest was in estimating the percentage of registered voters in Jerusalem who, having voted for the rightist Gahal party in the 1965 Knesset (legislative) election, also voted for the Gahal party in the municipal elections. Since voting for the Knesset and the municipality took place simultaneously, dependent and independent aggregate measures are based upon *exactly the same* population. These measures were computed for sixty-four census tracts.

To begin with the simplest case, it is easy enough to reject the basic constant-proportionality model. Replacing Y by GL_M, the Gahal municipal proportion, and X by GL_K, the Gahal Knesset proportion, we obtain estimates for equation (3) as shown in Table 5.

Although very precise estimates are obtained, we find a negative value for q. This is clearly inadmissible, since the proportion of non-Gahal Knesset voters who switched to Gahal in the municipal elections cannot be less than zero. Furthermore, since Gahal support fell from 28 percent of the Knesset vote to 17 percent of the municipality vote, it is impossible that the party retained 78 percent (p) of its Knesset support.

If one must thus reject the constant pro-

TABLE 5

ESTIMATES OF THE CONSTANT-PROPORTION MODEL

Parameter	Estimate	Standard Error	t-Statistic	Significance Level
p	0.777	0.0342	22.655	0.0005
q	−0.041	0.0097	−4.246	0.0005
		$R^2=0.850$		

portion model in this case, one can seek an alternative model for the regression. In the context of the election, it would be reasonable to assume $q=0$. If one then assumes $p=c_1+c_2(1-X)/X$, it follows that

$$Y=(c_1-c_2)X+c_2. \tag{15}$$

The estimates then show that $p=0.777-0.041(1-X)/X$. The difficulty with this expression is that it also gives unreasonable estimates. In some tracts, the Gahal party received as little as 5 percent of the Knesset vote; for such tracts, p is estimated to be roughly zero. As this seems far too small, we are lead to consider alternative regressions.

Coefficients for the linear-function model (11) are given in Table 6. The high standard errors of the parameter estimates reflect the fact that the standard errors of the coefficient estimates from the basic regression increased substantially over those for the constant-proportion model, the error of the constant term increasing by a factor of two, while the GL_K term increased by a factor of five. These high standard errors indicate the collinearity of the GL_K and $GL_K{}^2$ terms.

Not only are the standard errors high, but also the estimates appear unreasonable. We have reported the model setting $d_2=0$, since setting $c_1=0$ or $c_2=0$ leads to very wild estimates. With $d_2=0$, p becomes very small for low values of GL_K. At $GL_K=0.1$, p is only 0.36. Even in neighborhoods where Gahal was not particularly strong, it seems unreasonable that 64 percent of its Knesset voters would switch on the same day.

For the logarithmic-proportion model (13) whose estimates appear in Table 7, collinearity is even more severe than in the linear-proportion case. The standard errors are extremely large. Thus the complete logarithmic model is not very useful for this data.

There is little improvement if we reduce the number of variables in the regression by setting $d_2=0$ and thereby eliminate the term corresponding to $\ln(X)$ in equation (14). For example, in census tracts where the Gahal party received 14 percent of the Knesset vote, this reduced model would

TABLE 6

ESTIMATES OF THE LINEAR-PROPORTION MODEL

Parameter	Estimate	Standard Error	t-Statistic	Significance Level
c_2	1.419	0.4979	2.850	0.005
c_1	0.219	0.1616	1.355	0.100
d_1	0.021	0.0237	0.896	0.250
d_2	0.0*	–	–	–
$R^2=0.868$		$p=0.219+1.419\mathrm{GL}_K$	$q=0.021$	

* Assumed.

TABLE 7

ESTIMATES OF THE LOGARITHMIC-PROPORTION MODEL

Parameter	Estimate	Standard Error	t-Statistic	Significance Level
c_2	1.868	1.2224	1.526	0.10
d_2	0.201	0.2171	0.926	0.25
c_1	1.577	1.4752	1.066	0.25
d_1	0.828	0.8224	1.007	0.25
$R^2 = 0.868$	$p = 1.577 + 1.868 \ln(GL_K)$		$q = 0.828 + 0.201 \ln(GL_K)$	

indicate that Gahal retained 11 percent of its voters for the municipality elections. In addition, this model estimates q at 0.067. This value seems far too large, considering that all the known appeals in the municipal election were away from Gahal candidates and toward the Rafi list headed by the popular Teddy Kollek, who subsequently became mayor of Jerusalem. We can also conclude that collinearity is present even in this reduced version of the logarithmic-proportion model.

Both the logarithmic and the linear-proportion models seem to have failed because all of the independent variables are monotonic functions of GL_K. Unless GL_K shows very great variation, the intercorrelations of the various functions of GL_K will be very high. Yet GL_K, which has a mean of 0.21 and a standard deviation of 0.062, seems to be a very typical aggregate variable. The problems met in applying the first class of models to GL_K ought to arise widely in empirical communications research.

Models with environmental variables. If the models that rely solely on functions of X do not seem to have much empirical promise, the same is not true for models where the environment's influence on p and q is indicated by additional variables. Such models were proposed in Goodman's (1959) original paper. For exposition, we consider the case where p and q are linear functions of a single independent variable, Z.

Given

$$p = c_1 + c_2 Z, \qquad q = d_1 + d_2 Z \qquad (16)$$

then

$$Y = (c_2 - d_2)\,XZ + (c_1 - d_1)\,X + d_2 Z + d_1. \qquad (17)$$

To return to our empirical example, the proportion of voters who remained loyal to Gahal was influenced by the energetic and exceptional campaign of the Rafi candidate, Kollek. A man of national reputation and a former assistant to David Ben-Gurion, Kollek appeared to have a particular appeal to higher-status groups. Thus, the Gahal party ought to have retained more of the vote in neighborhoods with a high proportion of low-status individuals.

Two items from the 1961 census were used to index low-status characteristics. One is the proportion of the adult population with less than two years of schooling, denoted by E (mean, 0.173; std. dev., 0.157). The other is the proportion of the total population made up of pre-1948 immigrants of Afro-Asian ethnicity, denoted by S (mean, 0.040; std. dev., 0.137).

If these variables can be looked upon as affecting the proportion p, there is less reason to see them or any other variables as influencing q, for the Gahal municipal list had no particular appeal distinct from that of the Knesset list. In any event, estimating various equations showed that collinearity resulted whenever we attempted to have both p and q become linear or logarithmic functions of the control variables E and S. Consequently, we settled on the reduced model.

Given

$$p = c_1 + c_2 E + c_3 S, \qquad q = d_1, \qquad (18)$$

then

$$GL_M = c_2 GL_K \cdot E + c_3 GL_K \cdot S + (c_1 - d_1)\, GL_K + d_1. \quad (19)$$

This led to the estimates shown in Table 8. Among the indications of this model's superiority to the others is the increase to 0.932 of the squared multiple correlation. At the same time, the standard errors for the intercept and GL_K terms are roughly the same as in the constant-proportion model. Even if both E and S were simultaneously equal to zero, which never actually occurs, the Gahal party would retain 47 percent of its Knesset supporters. At the other end of the range, we find that p always remains less than 1.0 for all census-tract districts. Finally, the fact that q is not significantly greater than zero is in keeping with the tenor of the actual election campaign. Of all the models, only the environmental variable variant shown in Table 8 maintains low standard errors and gives reasonable coefficient estimates.

To illustrate the calculation of standard errors for cases like (18), where the parameters are all linear combinations of the regression coefficients, let us rewrite (19) as

$$\widehat{GL_M} = \hat{b}_0 + \hat{b}_1 GL_K + \hat{b}_2 GL_K \cdot E + \hat{b}_3 GL_K \cdot S. \quad (20)$$

Now any linear combination of the regression coefficients can be expressed in matrix notation as $\mathbf{k}'\hat{\mathbf{b}}$, where $\mathbf{k}$ is a column of constants and $\hat{\mathbf{b}}$ is the column vector of estimated regression coefficients. A well-known result gives the estimated variance of $\mathbf{k}'\hat{\mathbf{B}}$:

$$\widehat{\mathrm{var}\,(\mathbf{k}'\hat{\mathbf{b}})} = \mathbf{k}'\,\widehat{\mathrm{var}\,(\hat{\mathbf{b}})}\,\mathbf{k}.$$

$\widehat{\mathrm{Var}\,(\hat{\mathbf{B}})}$ in turn is simply the estimated variance-covariance matrix of the regression coefficients, an output option available on many regression programs. As an example, let us calculate the estimated variance for p given E and S. Since $p = b_0 + b_1 + b_2 E + b_3 S$, $\mathbf{k}' = [1\ 1\ E\ S]$ and

$$\begin{aligned}\mathrm{var}(p \mid E, S) = \mathrm{var}(b_0) &+ \mathrm{var}(b_1) \\ &+ E^2\,\mathrm{var}(b_2) \\ &+ S^2\,\mathrm{var}(b_3) \\ &+ 2\,\mathrm{cov}(b_0, b_1) \\ &+ 2E\,\mathrm{cov}(b_0, b_2) \\ &+ 2S\,\mathrm{cov}(b_0, b_3) \\ &+ 2E\,\mathrm{cov}(b_1, b_2) \\ &+ 2S\,\mathrm{cov}(b_1, b_3) \\ &+ 2SE\,\mathrm{cov}(b_2, b_3).\end{aligned} \quad (21)$$

Of course, the standard error of p is just the square root of this variance.

Fortunately, the reduced environmental variable model gives a reasonable solution to the collinearity problem for this data set. If, to summarize the purpose of this section, collinearity problems arise in almost all econometric work,[5] they are likely to be especially acute in aggregate-to-individual

[5] See Massy (1965) for the use of principal components as a possible solution to collinearity problems.

TABLE 8

ESTIMATES OF THE REDUCED ENVIRONMENTAL VARIABLE MODEL

Parameter	Estimate	Standard Error	t-Statistic	Significance Level
c_2	0.429	0.0559	7.671	0.0005
c_3	1.197	0.2172	5.512	0.0005
c_1	0.467	0.0408	11.446	0.0005
d_1	0.005	0.0088	0.610	–
$R^2 = 0.932$	$p = 0.467 + 0.429E + 1.197S$		$q = 0.005$	

inference problems because the regression models will repeat the same *measure* in two or more independent *variables*. As examples, in the full logarithmic-proportion model of equation (14), X appears three times—in X, $\ln(X)$, and $X \cdot \ln(X)$—and, in the full environmental variable model of equation (17), both X and Z appear twice. These multiple appearances build in intercorrelations among the independent variables. Even if the first class (function of X) models might apply to cases where the variance of X is large and even if environmental variables may frequently be useful, empirical distributions of data will seriously restrict use of regression models more complex than the simple regression of model (2).

Alternative models using the same regression. Use of linear-regression models is also restricted in cases where we are unable to identify the parameters of the component-specific rates. Duncan, Cuzzort, and Duncan (1961) called attention to this problem for the special case constituted by model (12). We are now able to give a more general result for the case where the component-specific rates are linear combinations of a column vector $\mathbf{z}$ of m linearly independent variables. Specifically, if $\mathbf{c}$ and $\mathbf{d}$ are column vectors, given

$$p = \mathbf{c}'\mathbf{z}, \qquad q = \mathbf{d}'\mathbf{z} \tag{22}$$

then

$$Y = (\mathbf{c} - \mathbf{d})'\mathbf{z}X + \mathbf{d}'\mathbf{z}. \tag{23}$$

For example, if p and q are assumed constant, then $\mathbf{z}$ is the scalar "1." Provided the variables $\mathbf{z}X$ are all distinct from variables $\mathbf{z}$, we will have a regression with $2m$ independent variables, which are sufficient to identify the $2m$ parameters represented by $\mathbf{c}$ and $\mathbf{d}$. However, if $\mathbf{g}$ and $\mathbf{h}$ are also column vectors, given

$$p = \mathbf{c}'\mathbf{z} + \mathbf{g}'\mathbf{z}[(1 - X)/X],$$
$$q = \mathbf{d}'\mathbf{z} + \mathbf{h}'\mathbf{z}[X/(1 - X)], \tag{24}$$

then

$$Y = (\mathbf{c} - \mathbf{g} - \mathbf{d} + \mathbf{h})'\mathbf{z}X + (\mathbf{d} + \mathbf{g})\,\mathbf{z}. \tag{25}$$

So, with regression equation (25), we can always associate a model having $4m$ parameters of which at least $2m$ cannot be identified. All the models represented by equations (3) through (20) essentially assumed $2m$ of the parameters to be zero or otherwise given.

If one of these models is rejected because the parameter estimates are unacceptable, but if, at the same time, the regression leads to a very high value of R^2 (the example of the television program that doubled its audience being an extreme case), we can consider one of the alternative specifications that can be developed from (24). In fact, these specifications must be considered in those instances where the value of R^2 approaches 1 since, in this case, additional variables cannot improve the model. On the other hand, if $4m$ parameters truly govern the underlying process and we have no way of giving at least $2m$ of these a priori, there is no way in which regression analysis can be used to infer the component-specific rates.

Constrained estimating procedures. We have known some researchers to try to overcome the problems arising from use of the constant-proportion model by forcing the estimates of p and q to fall within 0, 1. Unless p and q do not fall "significantly" outside 0, 1, we cannot endorse this approach, since finding that the least-squares estimate falls outside 0, 1 must lead to a rejection of the constant-proportion assumption. We share the emphasis of Boudon (1963) that communication scientists must be prepared to work with models where the proportions are not constant.

Models Nonlinear in the Regression Estimates

Some writers have proposed models where the proportions are not constant and, in addition, the component-specific rates become nonlinear functions of the regression coefficients. A variant for the parabolic regression found in (12) has been given by Goodman (1959). Here, q remains as in (11); p, however, is given as $p = Jq$, where J is a constant to be estimated. Since Goodman's model has but three parameters, d_1, d_2, and J, it has a unique solution in terms of the three regression coefficients. Unfortunately, the parameters of the model become nonlinear functions of the regression coefficients. As a result, we can neither calculate the standard errors of the estimated parameters nor assume that the estimates are unbiased, unless we make restrictive assumptions about the distribution of the regression estimates. Consequently, the linear-function models are to be preferred unless one has strong substantive reasons for using a nonlinear function model.

Nonlinear Regressions

Nonlinear regressions are a still more complex case. The econometric literature can be consulted for estimation procedures. Among the nonlinear forms with potential substantive interest is an example given by Boudon (1963), where the component-specific rates depend upon the rate for the total unit.

Given

$$p = c_1 + c_2 Y, \qquad q = d_1 + d_2 Y, \tag{26}$$

then

$$Y = \frac{(c_2 - d_2)\,X + d_1}{1 - d_2 - (c_2 - d_2)\,X}. \tag{27}$$

Simultaneous Equations Models

The preceding discussion has concerned cases where one could clearly identify a "dependent" variable. Frequently, however, there is feedback between variables. If reading newspaper A influences readership of newspaper B, so does readership of B influence readership of A. This section deals briefly with simultaneous equations problems.

All of the models that have been mentioned previously, both linear and nonlinear, are concerned solely with the estimation of p and q. In these cases, Y is clearly the dependent variable and X is the independent variable. This is true, for example, when p and q depend upon some environmental variable, Z, representing, say, family-income level. In terms of our newspaper-reading example, we recall that p and q denote the respective proportions of readers and nonreaders of newspaper B who read newspaper A.

A more complex case occurs when we allow the proportions of newspaper A readers and nonreaders who read newspaper B to vary as a function of another environmental variable, W, representing, say, sex. Let us denote these proportions by $r = p_{ij}/p_i$ and $s = p_{\bar{i}j}/p_{\bar{i}}$. In this case, given

$$\begin{aligned} p &= c_1 + c_2 Z, \qquad & q &= d_1 + d_2 Z, \\ r &= g_1 + g_2 W, \qquad & s &= h_1 + h_2 W, \end{aligned} \tag{28}$$

then

$$\begin{aligned} Y &= (c_2 - d_2)\,XZ + (c_1 - d_1)\,X \\ &\qquad + d_2 Z + d_1 + u_1, \\ X &= (g_2 - h_2)\,YW + (g_1 - h_1)\,Y \\ &\qquad + h_2 W + h_1 + u_2, \end{aligned} \tag{29}$$

where u_1 and u_2 denote the appropriate disturbance terms. In this case, it is easy enough to show that, when X and Y are used as explanatory variables, they are correlated with the disturbance terms. Consequently, ordinary least-squares estimation is inappropriate and one must consider various techniques for estimating the relationships of simultaneous equations.

Although we know of no examples of the use of models like (28) in the sociology of communications, such models should find applications in situations where simultaneous influences are manifestly evident, such as split-ticket voting (Geisel, Kies, McGuire, & Rosenthal, 1971).

This brief mention of simultaneous-equations models concludes our examination of the different types of models that can be used to infer component-specific rates. The remainder of the chapter covers problems that aggregate-to-individual inference models share with other uses of aggregate data. We begin with a consideration of the effects of interunit communications that have not been explicitly included in a model.

CORRELATION OF DISTURBANCE TERMS

The procedures developed in the previous section will not be wholly appropriate if contiguous or otherwise communicating aggregate units are subject to common influences that are not included in the specification of the models. Such common influences should be of direct concern to communications scientists in that the paradigm of communications analysis must obviously allow for interdependence among the analytical units. This interdependence can safely be ignored if we are studying the communications inputs and outputs of a largely unrelated set of individuals as in a sample of the American adult population.

When we study a population where intensive communications occur within the population, however, as when Bauer, Pool, and Dexter (1963) interviewed most of the heads of American corporations with over ten thousand employees, the interviewees can no longer be treated as independent observations. Similarly, we must account for interdependencies in studying geographic aggregates whenever we have reason to believe that interunit communications are important. This section reviews the methodology that can be applied to this essential problem of interdependency.

Interdependency in time series has long been studied by econometricians. Temporal interdependence is a far too restrictive concept to be useful to the communications scientist. More appropriate is the work in statistical geography (Dacey, 1968; King, 1969; Cliff & Ord, 1970; Berry, 1971).

Our interest in this work lies in the fact that conventional statistical tools are inappropriate when interdependency exists. In particular, the ordinary least-squares procedures we have discussed require that the disturbance terms—u in equation (1)—be, as mentioned previously, uncorrelated for all pairs of observations. If, because of interdependencies or other reasons, this condition is not satisfied, the estimates, although still unbiased, are inefficient in the sense of having needlessly large sampling variances. If correlated disturbances exist, more elaborate methods may be appropriate. Preliminary to applying these methods, one must have a means of detecting the existence of correlated disturbances.

As a means of detecting correlated disturbances, Geary (1954) proposed the contiguity ratio

$$c = \frac{\dfrac{1}{2\sum_i k_i} \sum_i \left[\sum_{i'} (z_i - z_{i'})^2 \right]}{\dfrac{1}{n-1} \sum_i (z_i)^2}, \tag{30}$$

where z_i is the residual from the regression for the ith aggregate unit ($i=1,\ldots,n$), $\sum_{i'}$ denotes summation over contiguous units (denoted by i') only, and k_i is the number of units contiguous to the ith unit. One can readily see that the contiguity ratio is a generalization of the Durbin-Watson statistic used for testing autocorrelation in time series. The Durbin-Watson statistic is given by

$$d = \frac{\sum_{t=2}^{n} (z_t - z_{t-1})^2}{\sum_{t=1}^{n} z_t^2}. \tag{31}$$

If we regard each period of time as being contiguous, we see that $\sum_i k_i$ is $2(n-1)$ and that

$$\sum_i \left[\sum_{i'} (z_i - z_{i'})^2 \right] = 2 \sum_{t=2}^{n} (z_t - z_{t-1})^2. \tag{32}$$

Substituting these expressions in (30), one

sees that $c=d/2$. Dacey (1968) gives an alternative to c.[6]

The use of c, as compared with d, can be criticized insofar as simple geographic contiguity is an imperfect gauge of likely correlations. While the concept of time contiguity employed in the Durbin-Watson d is relatively straightforward, it is clear that the length and type of boundaries, etc., affect the ability of one unit to be like another.

Among the alternatives to c, one possibility is suggested by Hagerstrand's diffusion simulation (Hagerstrand, 1965). Hagerstrand used measures of communications volume between units to predict diffusion patterns. In the context of regression analysis, one might hypothesize that the extent to which units will be like one another will depend upon their communications volume. On the basis of this, we can suggest an interaction measure, I, given by

$$I = \frac{\dfrac{1}{2\sum\limits_{i=1}^{n}\sum\limits_{\substack{j=1\\ j\neq i}}^{n}\Psi_{ji}}\left\{\sum\limits_{i=1}^{n}\left[\sum\limits_{\substack{j=1\\ j\neq i}}^{n}\Psi_{ji}(z_i - z_j)^2\right]\right\}}{\dfrac{1}{n-1}\sum\limits_{i=1}^{n} z_i^2} \tag{33}$$

where ψ_{ji} measures the proportion of the ith units communications (measured by some suitable index) that takes place with unit j. Therefore,

$$0 \leqslant \psi_{ji} \leqslant 1 \quad \text{and} \quad 0 \leqslant \sum_{\substack{j=1\\ j\neq i}} \psi_{ji} \leqslant 1.^{7}$$

Geary's (and Dacey's) measure has a more fundamental weakness, one that cannot be corrected through a weighted measure such as I. This weakness is that it is simply a poor test for interdependence. Lebanon and Rosenthal (1973) have constructed generalized first-order Markov process and first-order spatial averaging models that appear to be reasonable approaches to modeling communication interdependencies. These models are all characterized by a unique correlation parameter. Simulations that Lebanon and Rosenthal have conducted show that the Geary and Dacey tests are of low power in rejecting the null hypothesis of noncorrelation when correlated errors in fact exist; corollary to this result, the Geary and Dacey statistics are typically biased to underestimating the true correlation parameter.

Models can be developed for which the Geary and Dacey statistics can be shown to be consistent estimators of the correlation parameter. These models, however, are substantively unattractive. One case requires, for example, positive feedback between adjacent units, negative feedback between units separated by one other unit, and zero feedback between units separated by more than one unit. In contrast, substantively interesting models should require feedbacks that are always positive, if diminishing with distance or decreases in communications volume. Only where one had a very specific and peculiar model of "boomerang" effects would the Geary model prove attractive.

What, however, can be done if prior knowledge or analysis of ordinary least squares results indicates correlated disturbances? One possibility is to reformulate the model in terms of a more amenable specification. Among the alternatives are coordinate-system variables (longitude and latitude) or regional dummy variables, which can be introduced much as time is introduced in longitudinal studies. One should keep in mind, however, that variables of this type do not "explain" the behavior of the dependent variable but only indicate that a more complex theoretical structure is needed.

When one cannot eliminate correlated

---

[6] For other developments concerning c, see Althauser, Burdick, and Winsborough (1966).

[7] See Lebanon and Rosenthal (1973) for a review of the sampling theory for the Geary and Dacey measures.

disturbances through specification, one can apply generalized least squares if the variance-covariance matrix of the disturbances is known or can be estimated. Ad hoc estimation procedures are available in Lebanon and Rosenthal (1972). Simulation results indicate these procedures are to be preferred to ordinary least squares even for relatively low values of the true correlation parameter. One disadvantage of the procedures is that they are much more expensive computationally than ordinary regression.

TRANSFORMATION AND PRODUCTS

This section discusses two techniques for modifying "raw" measures (e.g., data in census reports, UN documents, etc.) with a view to improving the specification of a model. One of these techniques is transformation (e.g., taking the natural logarithm) of the raw measure. The other involves creating a new variable by forming products (e.g., multiplying proportion urban by automobiles per capita).

In the previous section, we have considered some of the statistical problems connected with the use of aggregate data in communication research. This section treats two topics related to specification of the model. Although researchers are frequently inclined to develop their specification on the basis of the measures found in the data source, transforming these measures and/or considering products of these measures con often improve the specification.

TRANSFORMATIONS

Researchers using aggregate communications variables, particularly those dealing with data collected for a set of nations, have noticed that cross-sectional data distributions were highly skewed. Despite the discussion of Simon (1957) and others, there is no substantial consensus on growth models that would explain these distributions. The reader can, however, consult Bain (1964) for a strong empirical argument for a log-normal model in the case of television in Great Britain. Methods for summarizing the strong "inequalities" implied by the skewness are given in Alker (1965) and Aitchison and Brown (1957).

On a practical basis, skewness can often be eliminated by a variety of transformations (logarithmic, square root, reciprocal, etc.). In a regression analysis, such transformations often appear to help linearize the regression, to reduce heteroscedasticity of error variances, and to make more appropriate the assumption of normality required for significance tests. Sawyer (1967), in a factor analysis of 236 variables for a set of nations, provides an elaborate illustration of the use of transformations.

As used in the Sawyer study, transformations are perhaps a worthwhile exploratory effort. Transformations make even more sense when they can be connected to an underlying model. Thus, in terms of the preceding discussion of aggregate-to-individual inferences, the square and the logarithm of the independent variable can be given definite substantive interpretations. The properties of a model can also indicate that transformations are inappropriate. For example, in all of the models proposed thus far for the aggregate-to-individual inference problem, none calls for a transformation of the dependent variable. Consequently, even if the distribution of the dependent variable is skewed, it makes little sense to apply a transformation if one also wishes to apply any of the given models.

PRODUCTS

Like transformations, products of independent variables are a natural consequence of some aggregate-to-individual inference models. In the example of the Gahal vote, the assumption that p depended on education led to the introduction of a $GL_K \cdot E$ term. Even when the concern is strictly with aggregate relationships, one finds a frequent use of products in the analysis of covariance where a "dummy" variable (qualitative variable) is multiplied by a quantitative variable. Here we are dealing with two quantitative variables. Such product terms often make excellent sense in substantive terms and can lead to substantial improvement in the variance "explained" by the model. It is an unfortunate consequence of factor analysis and other "blind" techniques that many researchers never consider products.

To illustrate the use of product terms, let us first isolate one of the relationships that will be used in a detailed example. One can assume that the willingness to vote for a movement of discontents (Poujadism in France) will be related to the presence of an economic group (winegrowers) where economic discontent is present. One can also assume that communication channels were necessary in order for the economic discontent to have found political expression. If mass media channels are denied to the political movement, per capita automobile registrations can provide an index of communications possibilities in rural areas. If we wish to make use of both the economic and communications variables, however, it is unreasonable to think that their effects will be additive as is the case in the standard regression model. If we take the view that neither variable is a *sufficient* indicator of a tendency to political discontent, then their product will be a good indicator (assuming that both variables are always greater than zero) of instances when both variables are "acting" in common. Equivalently, it is necessary to "weight" the economic variable by the communications variable.

The contrast between simple specifications and product specifications can be effectively illustrated by the following multiple regression estimates for the cross section of French departments.

Let us first examine the simple case by considering the following variates:

Dependent variable: Percentage of votes cast for Poujadist lists, 1956 elections.

Independent variables:

- X_1 Percentage of male labor force in agricultural occupations (1954).
- X_2 Independent nonagricultural proprietors as percentage of male labor force (1954). (Independent proprietors consist almost entirely of the *commerçants* and *artisans*.)
- X_3 Registered winegrowers (1951) as percentage of labor force (1954).
- X_4 Registered home distillers (1951) as percentage of labor force (1954).
- X_5 Percentage of votes cast for Communist list, 1951 election.
- X_6 Automobile registrations per capita (1955). Since the Poujadists did not have access to the mass media, we have taken this variable as an indicator of communications ability.
- X_7 North-South. (South = 1; largest city in department under Vichy control during World War II. North = 1; largest city in department under German control during World War II.)

In a simple multiple regression, the independent variables have an adjusted squared multiple correlation of 0.43 with the dependent variable. This result by itself presents a striking contrast with the much weaker associations found in earlier analyses.[8] It suggests the extent to which it is important to select variables directly related to the spread of Poujadism (alcohol and communications). Further examination of this regression, however, suggests that the underlying equation is a poor model. As Table 9 indicates, t-tests would lead us to reject the null hypothesis that a coefficient is equal to zero at the 0.05 level for only three of the seven variables.

Alternatively, one can consider a specification that emphasizes covariation between the basic variables:

Independent variables:

[8] Cf. MacRae (1967)

TABLE 9

RESULTS OF SIMPLE REGRESSION

Variable	Coefficient	t-Statistic	Significance Level
X_1	0.004	1.15	—
X_2	0.246	0.85	—
X_3	0.481	1.22	—
X_4	0.908	2.54	0.01
X_5	−0.048	0.80	—
X_6	0.892	3.45	0.0005
X_7	1.099	1.99	0.05

$X_2 \cdot X_1$ *Commerçants* more likely to vote Poujadist in agricultural areas.

$X_3 \cdot X_6$, $X_4 \cdot X_6$ The alcohol variates weighted by the communication ability needed to turn discontent into votes.

X_5, $X_5 \cdot X_1$ The Poujadists should succeed in areas predisposed to extremism as witnessed by Communist voting; however, in agricultural areas Communists and Poujadists competed for votes.

$X_6 \cdot X_1$ Communications ability is more important in rural, agricultural areas.

$X_7 \cdot X_1$ Regional differences should be greater in agricultural areas.

Not only is the squared multiple correlation of 0.53 for this regression considerably higher than that observed for the simple regression, but all of the coefficients pass the significance tests (see Table 10). All coefficients have the proper signs; in particular, while communism has a positive simple association with Poujadism, communism weighted by the nonagricultural measure has a negative association.[9]

WEIGHTING OBSERVATIONS

With any set of aggregate variables, be they transformations, products, or other forms, the researcher is still faced with an important problem in computing the basic correlations used in linear models.

For two variables, X and Y, Robinson (1950) defined the ecological correlation, r_e, as the aggregate correlation between X

[9] If, in addition to these two specifications, others might be considered, it should be noted that adding additional covariance terms or original variables causes collinearity problems. Removing a covariance term, say, $X_6 \cdot X_1$, and substituting a simple term, say, X_6, always lowers R^2. In particular, removing $X_5 \cdot X_1$ considerably weakens the regression.

TABLE 10

RESULTS OF REGRESSION WITH PRODUCT TERMS

Variable	Coefficient	t-Statistic	Significance Level
$X_2 \times X_1$	0.016	3.28	0.005
$X_3 \times X_6$	0.053	1.98	0.05
$X_4 \times X_6$	0.089	3.02	0.005
X_5	0.431	4.49	0.0005
$X_5 \times X_1$	−0.012	5.02	0.0005
$X_6 \times X_1$	0.014	2.43	0.01
$X_7 \times X_1$	0.025	2.08	0.05

and Y, each geographic area being weighted by its population. He then found that

$$r_e = \frac{1}{\eta_{XA}\eta_{YA}} \cdot [r - r_w/\sqrt{(1-\eta_{XA}^2)(1-\eta_{YA})^2}] \quad (34)$$

where r is the individual level correlation, r_w is the weighted average of the within-area individual correlations, and η_{XA} and η_{YA} are the ratios of between-area variance to total variance.

However, weighting in the computation of "ecological" correlations should not depend upon the fact that the weighted correlations lead to the foregoing equation (34). Perhaps the most critical issue about weighting is whether weighting leads to approximately constant (homoscedastic) variances for the linear models discussed in the earlier sections. In this case, weighting may lead to more efficient estimates than ordinary least squares.

For example, if one assumes that the disturbance variances are inversely proportional to n_j, one may wish to multiply the values for both the dependent and independent variables by $\sqrt{n_j}$. This procedure yields disturbances with constant variance. Ordinary least squares can be applied to these transformed values. Such a procedure corresponds precisely to that employed in computing the ecological correlation. It would seem to be appropriate in cases where the dependent variable has been measured by sampling techniques where it can be assumed that the precision of the estimate is inversely proportional to the number of interviews. The attitude measurements for people-type aggregates computed from opinion poll data by Pool, Abelson, and Popkin (1964) correspond to this type of aggregated variable.

When sampling is not involved, however, as in election data, and when proportions are the dependent variable, it would seem unreasonable to assume that the disturbance variances are inversely proportional to population. In this case, one should prefer to adhere to simple correlations and ordinary least squares. In other cases, where more unusual hypotheses occur, still different weighting schemes can be used.

The question of weighting is also related to the question of whether one should use "raw" or "per capita" variables, discussed in the following section.

"RAW" VERSUS "PER CAPITA" MEASURES

Research utilizing aggregate data is generally performed either on "raw" measures (number of cinema seats, number of television sets, number of votes) or on "per capita" measures (television sets per capita, percentage of total vote, etc.). The raw measures generally have a number of disadvantages. First, they are typically more skewed than the same variable converted to per capita figures. In turn, the greater the degree of skewness, the less reasonable the assumption of normality for testing.

Another disadvantage is that the error variance for raw figures is likely to be proportional to a monotonic function of the size of the geographic unit, thus heteroscedastic. How one wishes to correct for heteroscedasticity depends upon assumptions about error variances, as indicated in Table 11.

Of the various assumptions, the second might seem most tenable in complete ignorance. The third, however, would also be reasonable if we assume (1) that larger units will be more heterogeneous, and (2) that specification errors will produce larger errors for heterogeneous units. The fourth case would represent a more severe case of error conditions similar to those given for the third case. The first case, simple raw data, would seem the least merited.

The most important disadvantage of raw figures, however, is the possibility of introducing spurious correlation, since raw figures are heavily correlated with the size of the unit. Although, as Kuehn and

TABLE 11

ASSUMPTIONS ABOUT ERROR VARIANCE AND RESULTANT HOMOSCEDASTIC REGRESSION

Assumptions of Error Variance of Proportions or Per Capita Measures for Unit j	Homoscedastic Regression
1. Proportional to $1/n_j^2$	Raw data
2. Proportional to $1/n_j$	Raw data/$\sqrt{n_j}$
3. Common for all units	Proportions
4. Proportional to n_j^2	Proportions/n_j

NOTE: Assumption 2 is equivalent to binomial sampling (see Zellner & Lee, 1965).

Rohloff (1967) point out, even per capita figures contain possibilities of spurious correlation insofar as size enters the denominator of both of two per capita variables, at least direct correlation with size is discounted in per capita measures. Nevertheless, some recent research—see O'Lessker (1968) for an example—continues to use raw figures with no attempt to account for size effects.

CONCLUSION

This chapter has hopefully given some taste of the complexity of the methodological problems facing the proper analysis of aggregate data. Beyond a knowledge of the analytical techniques, it is even more important to have a good substantive understanding of the problem at hand. Only with such understanding, for example, will one be able to devise a plausible aggregate-to-individual inference model rather than blindly applying the Goodman constant-proportion technique. Also, with substantive understanding, one can spot those data characteristics that violate the assumptions of the simpler linear models and subsequently take appropriate action.

In general, one must fit techniques to the analytical problem. The development of "canned" electronic computer programs has in many respects caused an inverse development. Many researchers seem to have fed their data into the factor-analysis and multiple-regression programs in the program library come what may. If we sound a warning, the availability of more sophisticated methodologies shows there is no need for despair.

REFERENCES

Aitchison, J., and J. A. C. Brown.
1957 The Lognormal Distribution. Cambridge University, Department of Applied Economics Monograph No. 5. London: Cambridge University Press.

Alker, H. R., Jr.
1965 Mathematics and Politics. New York: Macmillan.
1969 "A typology of ecological fallacies," in M. Dogan and S. Rokkan (eds.), Quantitative Ecological Analysis in the Social Sciences. Cambridge: M.I.T. Press.

Althauser, R. P.; D. S. Burdick; and H. H. Winsborough.
1966 "The standardized contiguity ratio." Social Forces 45(December):237–245.

Ando, Albert; F. M. Fisher: and H. A. Simon.
1963 Essays on the Structure of Social Science Models. Cambridge: M.I.T. Press.

Bain, A. D.
1964 Growth of Television Ownership in the United Kingdom Since the War: A Lognormal Model. London: Cambridge University Press.

Banks, A. S., and R. B. Textor.
1963 A Cross-Polity Survey. Cambridge: M.I.T. Press.

Bauer, Raymond A.; Ithiel deS. Pool; and Lewis A. Dexter.
1963 Business and Public Policy: The Politics of Foreign Trade. New York: Atherton Press.

Berry, B. J. L.
1971 "Problems of data organization and analytical methods in geography." Journal of the American Statistical Association 66:510–523.

Boudon, Raymond.
1963 "Propriétés individuelles et propriétés collectives: un problème d'analyse écologique." Revue Française de Sociologie 3:275–299.

Christ, C. F.
1968 "Econometric models, aggregate." Pp.344–345 in David Sills (ed.), International Encyclopedia of the Social Sciences. Volume 4. New York: Macmillan.

Cliff, A. D., and K. Ord.
1970 "Spatial autocorrelation; A review of existing and new measures with applications." Economic Geography 26(Supplement):269–292.

Dacey, Michael F.
1968 "A review of measures of contiguity for two and K-color maps," in B. J. L. Berry and D. F. Marble (eds.), Spatial Analysis: A Reader in Statistical Geography. Englewood Cliffs, New Jersey: Prentice-Hall.

Dogan, Mattei, and Stein Rokkan (eds.).
1969 Quantitative Ecological Analysis in the Social Sciences. Cambridge, Massachusetts: M.I.T. Press.

Donohew, L., and R. W. Thorp.
1966 "An approach to the study of mass communications within a state." Journalism Quarterly 43:264–268.

Duncan, Otis D.; R. P. Cuzzort; and Beverly Duncan.
1961 Statistical Geography. New York: Free Press of Glencoe.

Duncan, Otis D., and Beverly Davis.
1953 "An alternative to ecological correlation." American Sociological Review 18(December):665–666.

Fagen, R. R.
1964a "Relation of communication growth to national political systems in the less developed countries." Journalism Quarterly 41:87–94.
1964b "Mass media growth: a comparison of communist and other countries." Journalism Quarterly 41:563–567.

Farace, R. V.
1966a "A study of mass communication and national development." Journalism Quarterly 43:305–313.
1966b "Identifying regional 'systems' in national development research." Journalism Quarterly 43:753–760.

Farace, R. V., and L. Donohew.
1965 "Mass communication in national social systems: A study of 43 variables in 115 countries." Journalism Quarterly 42:253–261.

Geary, R. C.
1954 "The contiguity ratio and statistical mapping." The Incorporated Statistician 5:115–145.

Geisel, M. S.; N. E. Kies; T. W. McGuire; and Howard Rosenthal.
1970 "A simultaneous equations model of split-ticket voting in Israeli elections," in American Statistical Association, Proceedings of the Social Statistics Section, 1970. Washington, D.C.: American Statistical Association.

Goodman, L. A.
1959 "Some alternatives to ecological correlation." American Journal of Sociology 64:610–625.

Green, H. A. J.
1964 Aggregation in Economic Analysis. Princeton, New Jersey: Princeton University Press.

Gregg, P. M., and A. S. Banks.
1965 "Dimensions of political systems: Factor analysis of a cross-polity survey." American Political Science Review 59:602–614.

Hagerstrand, Torsten.
1965 "A Monte Carlo approach to diffusion." European Journal of Sociology 6:43–67.

Johnston, John.
1963 Econometric Methods. New York: McGraw-Hill.

King, L. J.
1969 Statistical Analysis in Geography. Englewood Cliffs, New Jersey: Prentice-Hall.

Kuehn, A. A., and A. C. Rohloff.
1967 "On methods: Fitting models to aggregate data." Journal of Advertising Research 7(No. 1):43–47.

Lazarsfeld, P. F., and H. Menzel.
1961 "Relations between individual and collective properties," in Amitai Etzioni (comp.), Complex Organizations. New York: Holt, Rinehart and Winston.

Lebanon, Alexander, and Howard Rosenthal.
1973 "Least squares estimation for spatially correlated data." G.S.I.A. Working Paper. Pittsburgh: Carnegie-Mellon University.

Lerner, Daniel.
1957 The Passing of Traditional Society. Glencoe, Illinois: Free Press.

MacRae, Duncan, Jr.
1967 Parliament, Parties, and Society in France, 1946–1958. New York: St. Martin's Press.

Malinvaud, Edmond.
1966 Statistical Methods of Econometrics. Amsterdam: North-Holland.

Massy, W. F.
1965 "Principal components regression in exploratory statistical research." Journal of the American Statistical Association 60:234–256.

Mosteller, F. R.
1968 "Association and estimation in conginency tables." Journal of the American Statistical Association 63: 1–28.

Nataf, André.
1968 "Aggregation." Pp. 162–167 in David Sills (ed.), International Encyclopedia of the Social Sciences. Volume 1. New York: Macmillan.

O'Lessker, Karl.
1968 "Who voted for Hitler? A new look at the class basis of Naziism." American Journal of Sociology 74: 63–69.

Parker, E. B.
1963 "Effects of television on library circulation." Public Opinion Quarterly 27:573–589.

Pool, Ithiel de S.; Robert P. Abelson; and Samuel Popkin.
1964 Candidates, Issues, and Strategies: A Computer Simulation of a Presidential Election. Cambridge, Massachusetts: M.I.T. Press.

Robinson, W. S.
1950 "Ecological correlation and the behavior of individuals." American Sociological Review 15:351–357.

Rosenthal, Howard, and S. Sen.
1970 "Le problème de la participation electorale." Revue Française de Science Politique 20:545–556.

Russett, B. M., et al.
1964 World Handbook of Political and Social Indicators. New Haven: Yale University Press.

Sawyer, Jack.
1967 "Dimensions of nations: Size, wealth, and politics." American Journal of Sociology 73:145–173.

Simon, H. A.
1957 Models of Man. New York: Wiley.

Simon, H. A., and F. Stern.
1955 "Effect of television upon voting behavior in Iowa in the 1952 presidential election." American Political Science Review 49:470–478.

Stokes, D. E.
1968 "Ecological regression as a game with nature." Unpublished paper.

Theil, Henri.
1964 Linear Aggregation of Economic Relations. Amsterdam: North-Holland.

Wolpert, Julian.
1967 "A regional simulation model of information diffusion." Public Opinion Quarterly 30:597–608.

Zellner, Arnold, and T. H. Lee.
1965 "Joint estimation of relationships involving discrete random variables." Econometrica 33:382–394.

CHAPTER 31 Experiments on Communication Effects

EUGENE J. WEBB
Stanford University

DONALD T. CAMPBELL
Northwestern University

Experimentation is the primary methodology for testing hypotheses about the effects of communication. Sometimes it is possible to conduct elegant controlled experiments. Other times, quasi-experiments are possible, even though true experiments are not. On still other occasions, correlational analysis without experimental control is all that can be accomplished. In all cases where the effects of communication are of interest, the controlled experiment is the standard against which other research methods are judged. In this chapter Webb and Campbell explicate the logic of experimental design and discuss the various potential threats or alternate explanations for results that purport to demonstrate an effect of communication. The discussion includes quasi-experimental as well as experimental designs in a way that points out the underlying principles of research design and encourages innovative development of new research designs.

An event occurs or does not occur. A new television show fails or succeeds, a debate during a presidential campaign helps or hinders a candidate, a decision-maker under high stress calls for more or less information, the personal vagaries of an individual editor do or do not influence the flow of foreign news to the readers of a metropolitan newspaper. In each case, all are part of the intertwined group of processes and effects pertinent to communication effectiveness, the general public or the scholar may seek to document both the level of an effect by describing it and the forces influencing that effect by experimentation or examination of data.

This chapter focuses on experimental design and the ways in which the systematic student may attempt to structure his observations and reduce the risk of false inference. Our position is that no experiment, or series of experiments, for that matter, will unequivocally demonstrate truth. Instead, we believe that any observed effect of communication may be attributable to a long list of possible influences. These can be brought under control—either by ruling out their entry into the experiment or by developing a means to measure their effect when it does enter—but some equivocality remains.

Put a bit more formally, this position argues that any observed effect (including no effect) may be explained by a series of rival plausible hypotheses. If one is to demonstrate the vigor of a particular hypothesis, the experimental design task is to strip of plausibility the long list of rival hypotheses that might also explain the observed finding. Experimental design is thus the architecture of research, the plan for the structure on which inference will be based.

Just as almost every architect knows how to build better buildings than he builds, so too does almost every communications researcher know how to design more adequate research plans than he can execute. Most experiments are neither marble nor mud, but represent a compromise between available resources and the likelihood that one subset of rival hypotheses is greater than another subset. One is forced into making simplifying assumptions about the elements that can influence a communication's effect. Blalock (1964:8) has noted that "the basic dilemma faced in all science is that of how much to oversimplify reality." Aronson and Carlsmith (1968:12) also talk of "the basic dilemma," this time of the experimental social psychologist:

> On the one hand we want maximal control over the independent variable. We want as few extraneous differences as possible between our treatments. We want to specify as precisely as possible the exact nature of the treatment we have administered and its exact effect on the subject. This leads us to try to develop manipulations which are highly specifiable, in which the differences between treatments are extraordinarily simple and clear, in which all manipulations are standardized—in short, to an approximation of something like a verbal learning experiment. On the other hand, if the experiment is controlled to the point of being sterile, it may fail to involve the subject, have little impact on him, and therefore not affect his behavior to any great extent.

At the center of these decisions on simplicity and complexity, on what one holds constant, what one permits to enter his experiment as an influence, and what one assumes away is an implicit or explicit list of rival hypotheses (sometimes called error sources) which must be evaluated for their plausibility. Some of these hypotheses on effect are common to all behavioral science experimentation while others are more pertinent to the study of communication effects. Some are obvious to all experimenters, such as the effect of small samples on chance outcomes. Others evolve from the sociology of the field, such as the influence of the work of Robert Rosenthal (1966) and his associates on the significance of an experimenter's expectations of outcome for his results.

It is not possible to specify the plausibility of any list of rival hypotheses for research on the effect of communication. The broad sweep of different message attributes, subject characteristics, and situational forces forming the legitimate span of this body of research prevents such precision. But what we can do is provide a list of possibly influential rival hypotheses and then discuss some of the design considerations that may bring control over them. At core, these hypotheses are threats to the validity of the inference drawn from experimentation.

THREATS TO VALIDITY

Fundamental to a consideration of rival hypotheses is a distinction between internal and external validity. What does the rival threaten? The truth value of a hypothesis and its generalization to a larger world of different people or different settings? Or the extent to which an observed difference within the limited frame of an experiment can reasonably be attributed to an experimental treatment? This latter point is defined as *internal* validity, and is the basic minimum without which any experiment is uninterpretable: did the experimental treatment make a difference in a specific experimental instance?

External validity refers to generalizability: to what populations, settings, treatment variables, and measurement variables can this effect be generalized? Both forms of validity are critical, but they form a part of the experimenter's trade-off decisions, since they are frequently in conflict. One may find it essential to maintain the most rigid laboratory controls over the experimental setting, and thus sacrifice something in the way of generalization in any findings he produces. Or, heavily concerned with generalization, the experimenter may go into the field and sacrifice some situational control on the test setting by entering private homes to gather his data. But we must remember that internal validity is the essential characteristic for experimental interpretation and, with all other considerations balanced, the creative task becomes one of selecting designs that first protect internal validity and then cover the threats to external validity.

Internal Validity

A group of nine classes of rival plausible hypotheses may, if not controlled in the design, produce effects that can be mistakenly interpreted as the effect of the experimental treatment.

1. *Instability/Chance*. Most experimenters are so indoctrinated in the significance test mode that they seldom consider precisely what a significance test does. As we understand such tests, they provide a measure of the degree to which one can accept the plausibility of the hypothesis that chance alone produces a difference. Thus, one might interpret a <0.01 result as establishing the implausibility that the instability of a series of test scores can explain a difference. From a sociology of science point of view, this test of the rival plausible hypothesis of chance is the most culturally accepted of all tests. The obvious risk is that the ruling out of the chance hypothesis alone is interpreted as convincing evidence of the viability of the experimental hypothesis. Rejecting chance is but one step in the selective rejection of rival hypotheses (Winch & Campbell, 1969). Other threats are as germane.

2. *History*. In the common pretest-posttest design, other elements are at work besides the experimental treatment. These specific, incremental events occurring between a first and second measurement are called history. A political telethon may effect a shift in voter preference, but one also wants to take into account other influences on choice occurring during the same time frame.

3. *Maturation*. Changes are occurring within the individual subject as well as in the world about him. In a short experiment he may grow tired, hungry, or bored. In a long-term experiment he may grow older or pass some critical threshold point (become twenty-one, say). These changes may be called "state variables" of the subject and are themselves worthy of study. Does, for example, the political-information-seeking behavior of an individual change when he or she acquires the capacity to vote? Does a high state of fatigue significantly change the degree to which one pays attention to messages designed to change one's attitude?

4. *Testing*. The experience of having taken a test may significantly influence the response when the same test is taken a second time or an alternative form of it is administered. Indeed, alternative form testing has developed in response to just this plausible rival hypothesis. This hypothesis is obviously more plausible in experiments that employ paper-and-pencil self-report instruments than in experiments based on observations of behavior by others (Webb, Campbell, Schwartz, & Sechrest, 1966).

5. *Instrumentation*. Just as subjects may change over the course of an experiment, so too may the instruments used to measure an effect. The observer may become more sophisticated as the experiment matures, one's coding categories or assignment cri-

teria may fluctuate and, in general, the calibration of the measuring instrument, human or hardware, may vary.

6. *Statistical regression.* Sir Francis Galton (1886) first noted the regression fallacy, a validity threat particularly significant when groups have been selected on the basis of extreme scores. Over time it is easy to observe pseudoshifts that derive from the fact that a series of values usually fluctuates around its average or trend value. At any one point in time, the value of the extreme group may derive from nonrecurring factors. Subsequent testing may show the group to be less extreme—regressing toward the mean or trend value. Thus, the children of very bright parents, while brighter than average, are usually duller than their parents, and the children of very dull parents, while dull, are usually less dull then their parents. Conversely, the parents of very bright children are less bright than their children, and the parents of very dull children are less dull than their children. The persuasive products of propagandists picked at one point in time as very effective or very ineffective may be more "average" in the future solely because of this regression artifact. The effect often appears in subtly disguised forms, and is a severe problem in quasi-experimental analyses of communication impact (Campbell & Clayton, 1961).

7. *Selection.* A large number of biases may be introduced into an experiment when there are differential bases for recruiting people into experimental and control groups. The particular principle upon which self-selection for exposure to communication rests may vary widely with the nature of the content. Lumsdaine and May (1965:482) have observed that "most studies of broadcast television, conducted in naturalistic field situations with a 'noncaptive' audience that largely selects itself, are hampered by grave methodological difficulties of selection bias."

8. *Experimental mortality.* Panel studies are particularly vulnerable to the threat of experimental mortality. As time goes on, even in an experiment with only two points of measurement, some people may drop out and not be available for the second test. Whether the dropping out is due to actions not associated with the experiment (for example, moving to another area) or to voluntary, experiment-linked reasons (boredom or anxiety, for example), the ability to draw valid inferences from the data is reduced.

These main threats to validity can act in consort to provide another series of interaction threats. A particularly common one is the association between selection and maturation threats.

9. *Selection-maturation interaction.* In some multiple-group experimental designs that do not employ random assignment of subjects to groups, there is the risk of interaction between the principle of self-selection to the experimental or control group and the rate of maturation (fatigue, interest, and so on) shown by each group.

When a change or difference is observed, any of these nine rival hypotheses might be offered to explain away an effect attributed to an experimental treatment. We say *might*, for the job of the researcher is to develop experimental procedures designed to avoid these validity risks. Note our position that an experimenter need not control *all* possible threats to have a worthwhile and valid experiment. What he must control are *plausible* threats. The alternative explanation must not only be possible, but be empirically more dependable or more plausible than the experimenter's finding before it can invalidate that finding.

External Validity

Another body of validity threats is specifically concerned with external validity, the capacity of the result to be generalized to other settings, to other people, to other versions of the treatment, and to other measures of the effect.

1. *Interaction effect of testing.* "Many

times the mere measurement of the dependent variable reacts with the independent variable or other events in the laboratory so that effects are found that would not be seen otherwise" (Aronson & Carlsmith, 1968:60). The effect of a pretest may, for example, significantly increase or decrease the individual's sensitivity or responsiveness to the experimental variable. Thus, a carry-over effect may be observed from the first testing to the subsequent presentation of the experimental treatment. This provides another argument for the use of nonreactive measures (Webb et al., 1966).

2. *Interaction of selection and experimental treatment.* The interaction between the selection process and the content of the experiment is a common source of error in disentangling the relative effects of such a communication as an antismoking advertisement. The members of the audience may well select their own groups by reading or not reading, and that selection process may interact with the antismoking theme. If one were comparing smokers and nonsmokers who voluntarily read the ad, for example, the characteristics of smokers who read and who did not read it would be of special interest.

3. *Reactive effects of experimental arrangements.* The artificiality of an experimental setting may explain away some results. The experimental room is atypical of conditions in the world one is trying to predict, and the subjects may well react differently there than they would elsewhere. They can do this through the mechanism of selecting one role from among many that they might play in everyday life when given the experimental treatment. This "Hawthorne effect" has been convincingly demonstrated by Orne (1962) in his discussion of the "demand chatacteristics of the experimental situation." And this potential bias may be more marked in some segments of the public than in others.

The novelty of a test-taking role may be selectively biasing for subjects of different educational levels. Less familiar and comfortable with testing, those with little formal schooling are more likely to produce nonrepresentative behavior. The act of being tested is "more different." The same sort of distortion risk occurs when subject matter is unusual or novel. Subject matter with which the respondent is unfamiliar may produce uncertainty of which role to select. A role-playing choice is more likely with such new or unexpected material (Webb et al., 1966:17).

4. *Multiple treatment interference.* When multiple treatments are jointly applied, it is possible that the interaction among them will produce effects atypical of the effects that would be produced by the same treatments applied separately. This threat may be a greater risk in experiments that embed the true experimental treatment in a cover story. The subject is told that the experiment is about one thing while in fact the critical experimental data are produced after the experimenter says, "By the way . . ." This procedure may help to reduce the reactive effects of the experiment, but it involves the risk of producing a multiple treatment interference.

5. *Irrelevant responsiveness of measures.* All measures of effect are complex, and all include irrelevant and/or unknown components that may produce apparent effects. To the degree that the investigator relies on one and only one measurement of effect, he remains vulnerable to this effect of irrelevancies.

6. *Irrelevant replicability of treatments.* Similarly, all experimental treatments are complex, and replications of them, as in studies of repeated exposure of communication content, may fail to include those components actually responsible for the effects (Aronson & Carlsmith, 1968; Campbell, 1969).

Each of these fifteen validity threats is a potential rival hypothesis for some study of communication effect. Few, if any, experiments will be plagued with the problem of countering or measuring the plausibility of all of them. In the following section we shall attempt to deal with the major structural devices employed to control these rival plausible hypotheses.

BUILDING AND EVOLVING A DESIGN

The experimenter's planning activity is geared to establishing as many pertinent comparisons as he can. Sometimes that comparison will be permitted because an independent control group is created, one that is exposed to all communication messages except the critical experimental one. At other times the comparison is obtained by taking repeated measures of one individual or group over time and then comparing these measures in a time-series design. Or a comparison may be based on the use of random assignments, so that one may employ the yardstick of chance variability against his data. The choices that make up the experimental strategy will be determined by the plausibility of various types of validity threat and by available resources.

The novice experimenter sometimes feels that all controls should be exercised at one time in one critical experiment. The more bloodied experimenter realizes that the appropriate comparisons necessary to establish a hypothesis firmly are likely to come from a series of linked experiments. The necessity for evolutionary testing comes not only from constraints on resources, but also from the usual condition that one either cannot think of or cannot assess an appropriate list of factors that may be extraneous sources of variation in his data.

In his probing of a hypothesis, the experimenter has four main aspects to consider: groups, treatments, time, and observations. He may, after developing a gross hypothesis from observation or introspection, first consider the core condition of a group of people who are exposed to an experimental treatment and who are measured. For simple notational purposes, we shall consider an experimental treatment as an X and an observation or measurement as an O. The core group then is XO. This has been labeled the "one-shot case study" (Campbell & Stanley, 1963), and is the frequent beginning of more elaborate investigation.[1]

Given this core exposure/measurement, the careful investigator then asks what he should do to make more systematic comparisons that will allow a fairer test of his hypothesis. He may first add observations. Thus, the threat that the phenomenon has already been occurring at the same level is probed by adding a pretest measure. This yields:

$$O_1 X O_2.$$

Although far short of a true experiment, the comparison $O_2 - O_1$ is a good step forward. An example is the reports of active switchboard activity at televison stations when a space shot or other public service program interferes with the usual commercial programming. One may observe a good number of calls into a station after a regular show is preempted (XO), and then check to see what the difference is from a comparable preceding day ($O_2 - O_1$). By itself, an absolute number of telephone calls is uninterpretable.

One may then note that the effect of communication is not necessarily permanent and unchanging once it occurs. The wearout of the effect may be measured by adding still more observations stretched over time. Note that for this problem (for example, is there a long-term boomerang effect?) one moves not only to more observations in his design, but also to a consideration of what the appropriate spacing

[1] We were tempted to run a parallel set of examples of these various designs—jokes and axioms that illustrate the logic of the design. The possibilities are endless, ranging from the central epistemological point of comparison ("How's your wife?" "Compared to who?") to specific structural layouts of designs (Al Capone: "You can get much farther with a kind word and a gun than you can get with a kind word.") The one-shot case method:

1st traveler: Why are you throwing paper over the side?
2nd traveler: It keeps elephants off the track.
1st traveler: Who ever heard of elephants on a train track?
2nd traveler: Works, doesn't it?

of observations should be. In lieu of other information, the spacing is typically even, with one day or one week separating each measurement point. Diagramatically, this gives:

$$O_1 X O_2 \quad O_3 \quad O_i \quad O \quad O_n$$

If there is a significant trend in the post-exposure observations, one might have a significant experimental finding, or an artifact of some trend that is independent of the experimental treatment. For example, if the post-X observations show a continuously rising slope, it may be that X was a unique communication that magnified its effect as time went on. Or it could be that the secular trend was already present in the data series. Since there is only one observation before X, this cannot be known. At least it cannot be known if one is dealing with the usual self-report data from respondents. Should one be working with archival records, however, or if one were willing to trust retrospective self-reports, it would be possible in some cases to add more observations before the introduction of the X.

$$O_1 \quad O_2 \quad O_3 \quad O_4 X O_5 \quad O_6 \quad O_i \quad O_n$$

Mindak and colleagues (1963) hypothesized that one of the effects of a Minneapolis newspaper strike would be a decrease in retail shopping. As an index of this, they studied the level of parking-meter collections and noted change in the time series over the prestrike and strike periods. They found marked decreases during the months of the strike. By adding observations spread over time, one can begin to see that a trend of some type may offer a plausible explanation of a set of observed data. The comparison is across a single population in this case. Moreover, if an apparent effect is present, the multiple observations permit some description of its shape—is there an accelerating effect, a boomerang, a short-run increase or decrease returning to the prior level, or what? But one is still (or should be) uncertain about whether X is truly associated with the levels of the observations. Other hypotheses—maturation, history, selection, for example—could explain a time series trend as well.

To achieve control over other rival hypotheses, the experimenter may go to another component of design and add control groups tailored to take these effects into account. When he added observations, he was gaining some advantage from longitudinal study. When he adds groups, he gets some advantage from cross-sectional study.

A simple and engaging example of this approach is demonstrated by Milgram (Milgram & Toch, 1969). Milgram had noted that people tend to look up when they come upon other people looking up. Here we have a nonverbal communications sign (looking up $= X$) and a measurement (bypassers looking up $= O$). Milgram conducted a field experiment by taking groups composed of one, two, three, five, ten, and fifteen members, and placing them on a New York street with a heavy pedestrian flow. "Members of the group performed a clearly observable action, looking up at the window of a skyscraper, and holding the pose for a period of one minute" (Milgram & Toch, 1969:532). The action was filmed and the proportion of passersby who looked up noted. Each condition was replicated five times. So from the simple XO observation that looking up is a sufficient cue to make others look up, a design evolved by adding experimental groups:

$$\begin{matrix} X_1 & O_1 \\ X_2 & O_2 \\ X_3 & O_3 \\ X_5 & O_4 \\ X_{10} & O_5 \\ X_{15} & O_6 \end{matrix}$$

The subscripts on the X's indicate the size of the group, and Figure 1 indicates the change in percentage of uplookers as the group size changed.

Milgram did not include a "blank control" in his report—an observation of how many looked up when no group was present staring skyward. The addition of a

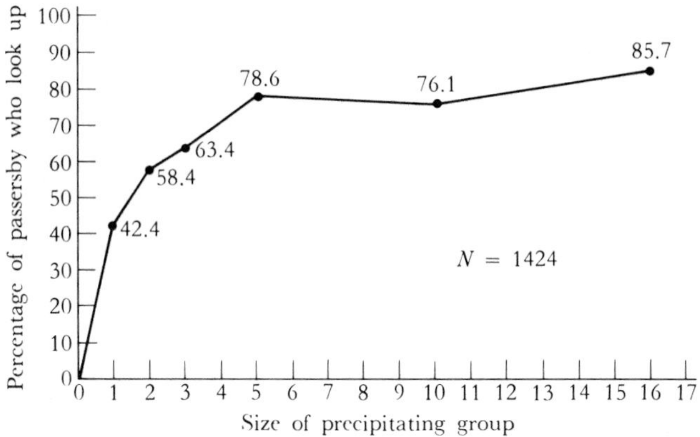

Figure 1. Percentage of passersby who look up as a function of the size of the precipitating group (Milgram & Toch, 1969:532).

blank control is, however, the most common of additional groups and usually is considered because it permits the experimenter to get a reading on the effects of history and maturation. If one starts with a before-after design OXO, this means the addition of a group so that

$$\begin{matrix} O_1 X O_2 \\ O_3 \quad O_4 \end{matrix}$$

This additional group permits a test of the experimental treatment by an examination of the difference $(O_2 - O_1) - (O_4 - O_3)$.

Note that this design may be highly useful for evaluating the effects of instrumentation, history, maturation, testing, and selection. It will be useful to the degree one can assume that these effects follow similar laws in the two groups. This will often be a plausible assumption, but less likely if the experimental group is self-selected.

An example of such a design is a before-after test of attitudes toward the administration's foreign policy of those who voluntarily watched or did not watch a television special on the topic. Those who seek out a particular type of television program, or watch public affairs programming on television in general, may be a very different population from either those who do not look at television at all or those who shun such heavy program content. Thus, we may have a comparison between two different populations with different trends and different responsiveness to testing and other historical events. Any difference between the two groups may be attributable to those distinctions. Adding another group does not by itself correct that problem.

To achieve control over selection biases, ideally the experimenter should randomly assign his respondents to experimental and control treatments. In mass communication research, this is often impossible, but it is and should be standard practice both in laboratory experiments and in those communications studies where random assignment may be possible but less convenient, for example, studies of direct-mail promotion (Campbell, 1969).

Let us introduce the symbol R to indicate random assignment. When this is added to the previous design, by randomly assigning subjects to viewing or not viewing a program, say, and measuring their attitudes both before and after, we have:

$$\begin{matrix} R & O_1 X O_2 \\ R & O_3 \quad O_4 \end{matrix}$$

This is the classic, the standard, research design. It is a "true" experimental design in comparison with the same configuration of O's and X lacking the random assignment.

With the random assignment, we now have a good measure of control over selection biases, statistical regression, selection-maturation interaction, and interaction effects between selection bias and the experimental variable—a very substantial gain for one addition, and the reason random assignment is so valued by scholars. The assignment gives a very high probability that the experimental and control groups will be equivalent on a large group of both known and unknown dimensions that may influence their performance on the measurements employed to observe an effect. This equivalence can be measured by looking at the difference between O_1 and O_3, the two pretest measures. If chance is luckily working, this difference should be relatively minor.

The reasonable person might ask at this point, "If random assignment is likely to give pretest equivalence between groups, why do I need to have pretests at all?" The answer is not unequivocally clear, but there are situations where one might decide *not* to follow the conventional wisdom and use the pretest-posttest design. If one is willing to work with the effects measured in a posttest alone, and further willing to run the risk that the random assignment will give him a particularly bad shake of the dice (that is, show a pretest difference that is statistically significant), then he might consider using another "true" experimental design—the after-only design:

$$
\begin{array}{lll}
R & X & O_1 \\
R & & O_2
\end{array}
$$

Professor E. B. Parker has noted in a personal communication that ". . . increased precision appears to be the main advantage of before-after and that the trade-off [between before-after and after-only] depends on the choice between increased precision or smaller sample size on one hand and the avoidance of testing threats on the other."

In this design, the measure of the effect of X is the difference $(O_1 - O_2)$. Change scores are lost by this design. But note that one does pick up a possibly significant advantage. Since there is no pretest, the risks from the testing artifact are eliminated. So a trade-off decision faces the experimenter: is the gain of controlling for pretest effects and the saving in cost of two observations worth the loss of possible change scores and the direct measurement of initial equivalence of the groups?

In our judgment, the after-only design is a seriously underemployed design. Should one have adequate resources, the most desirable move is to combine the after-only design with the pretest-posttest design. In that way, one achieves a test of initial comparability, controls the pretest effect, guards for maturation, history, and selection effects, and is generally in an excellent position to test the validity of his hypothesis. Diagrammed, this combination design, called the Solomon Four Group Design, looks like this:

$$
\begin{array}{llll}
R & O_1 & X & O_2 \\
R & O_3 & & O_4 \\
R & & X & O_5 \\
R & & & O_6
\end{array}
$$

For a direct test of the effect of X, one has both the difference $(O_5 - O_6)$ and the comparison of the change scores $(O_2 - O_1) - (O_4 - O_3)$.

As a bare-bones type of design, the Solomon Four Group is as satisfactory a structure as is now available. But not all people will necessarily be satisfied with it. With only one measurement after the introduction of the experimental treatment, it cannot fully examine the longer term effects that are of special interest to students of communication effects. For that, one should add observations—preferably both on the front and the back ends of the structure. Thus, in the best of all possible worlds, one might find a design:

$$
\begin{array}{lllllll}
R & O_1 & O_2 & O_3 & X\,O_4 & O_5 & O_6 \\
R & O_7 & O_8 & O_9 & O_{10} & O_{11} & O_{12} \\
R & & O_{13} & O_{14} & & & \\
R & & & O_{15} & & & \\
R & & & & X\,O_{16} & O_{17} & O_{18} \\
R & & & & O_{19} & O_{20} & O_{21} \\
R & & & & & O_{22} & O_{23} \\
R & & & & & & O_{24}
\end{array}
$$

The reader can be assured that he will look a long time before finding such a splendidly elegant design. And when he finds it, he should still ask some questions about external validity—reactive effects from guinea-pigdom feelings, and the overall representativeness of the general sample to begin with. For it will be noted here that the random assignment refers only to the experimental or control group in which a subject finds himself. It says nothing about the random or nonrandom selection of subjects who participate in the experiment.

In another place (Webb et al., 1966), we have outlined at some length alternative response measures that may be used to get around the reactivity problem. These include unobtrusive observation, more extensive use of archival records, and the close study of physical trace and accretion methods. An example of such a nonreactive approach is Frederick Mosteller's (1955) creative study of the degree to which various sections of the *International Encyclopedia of the Social Sciences* were read. He estimated usage by noting the wear and tear on separate sections: dirty edges of pages, frequency of dirt smudges, finger markings, and underlining on pages. He sampled various libraries and even used the *Encyclopaedia Britannica* as a control.

From an experimental point of view, the most useful approach in this genre may be the contrived field experiment in which the experimenter varies some aspect of a natural environment, without the awareness of the subject, and notes an effect. A recent example of this is Schilling's (1968) work on the influence of adding a sign to a door indicating whether the door should be pushed or pulled. While 50 percent of patrons in a restaurant expected unmarked doors to open outward, adding push-pull signs reduced incorrect operations to about 26 percent.

In a similar way, one might evaluate the effectiveness of various types of propaganda messages designed to control speeding by systematically varying a group of themes placed along highways and noting both the short- and long-term effects of the various themes by radar monitoring of speeds. One would randomly assign themes to times and places, note the speeds, and also develop a separate control set of data on speeds when no signs are present. Twedt (1962) has developed just such a design to evaluate the effects of a number of advertising themes. Various versions of ads are displayed prominently at the entry to a supermarket. The ads are rotated through hours and days, and the measurement variable is the amount of sales recorded for the advertised brand.

But full experimental control and "true" experimentation is often impossible when one looks at communication effects. As noted earlier, one might be willing to lose some experimental rigor—if establishing it means that one must artificially force a subject into a situation unrepresentative of his real world. We might be able to make a situation "experimentally realistic" and have it involve the subject in a serious way so that the experimental treatment has an impact on him (Aronson & Carlsmith, 1968). But the situation may be unlikely to occur in the real world and lack "mundane realism."

In their insightful discussion of the difference between experimental and mundane realism, Aronson and Carlsmith cite the experiment of Walster, Aronson, and Abrahams (1966) as high on mundane realism but low on experimental realism, by which they largely mean impact of the treatment on the subject. The subjects read a newspaper article, embedded in a real paper, on the prosecution of criminals in Portugal.

But nothing was happening to the subject. Very few American college students are seriously affected by the reading of a rather pallid article about a remote situation in a foreign country. The procedure does not have a high degree of experimental realism (Aronson & Carlsmith, 1968:23).

For their purpose, the mundane realism was so good that it washed out the experimental realism (impact). But, in the words of a radar expert, one man's signal is another man's noise, and the lack of response of the college students to such an article, in a realistic setting, is a worthwhile datum for students of communication.

SOME QUASI-EXPERIMENTAL DESIGNS

So if one cannot always achieve perfect control, the conclusion is not to stop work or slink around corners because one is not a pure scientist. In studying communication effects, as in anything else, one does the best one can, and if that fails to account for all possible error effects, there is always tomorrow and another experiment ahead. In many cases, we may be able to reach stable findings by a series of imperfect tests that cumulate to a more solid conceptual structure. This is, after all, the thinking behind the approach of multiple methods of stimulus presentation to index a construct and multiple methods of testing to evaluate an effect of some experimental treatment. Any given operationalization of a construct or its effect has unique errors associated with it. A way to approach the problem is to use multiple measures that converge on the effect and multiple operations that define the treatment (Campbell & Fiske, 1959; Cook & Selltiz, 1964; Webb, 1966; Webb et al., 1966).

If one can conduct a series of experiments that overlap a substantive interest, but do not overlap error sources, then an important step toward understanding is reached. The so-called quasi-experimental designs are examples.

We earlier noted the study of Mindak et al. (1963), which evaluated the effect of a newspaper strike on retail sales. Another newspaper strike in another city, the New York strike of 1962–1963, provided the setting for another study of the same subject by Simon and Marks (1965). Theirs was a telephone questionnaire study of consumers in the area affected by the strike. From self-reports, they learned the level of shopping had dropped during the strike.

Diagrammatically, this part of the study is an implicitly OXO design. This might be labeled a "retrospective pretest" (Campbell & Stanley, 1963). But as a check, they went to sales records and made a two-way check on the self-report data. First they looked at sales in the previous year in the area covered by the strike and at comparative sales levels in the general New York/New Jersey area unaffected by the strike. Both comparisons supported the self-reports of lower shopping activity (particularly among bargain shoppers, by the way, replicating the findings of Mindak et al.).

Another example of a weak design approaching an interesting question is the unconfirmed report from Somerset, Kentucky, on the effect of a television blackout (Reuters, 1969). Nine months after a dispute had closed down television in Somerset, the weekly average of births was twenty-three—compared with a maximum of seven in any week of the previous year. Here, as in the case of the effect of the New York power blackout, there are a number of possible alternative explanations, not the least of which is fraud. Nonetheless, this rudimentary

$$O \quad O \quad O \quad O \quad O \quad OXO \quad O$$

design provides a partial test of the effect of the mass media.

An example of a time-series design with both multiple X's and multiple O's is provided by Rarick and Hartman (1966). They were interested in examining the effects of changes in the level of competition on one newspaper's content. They found that increasing competition was associated with more local news and "immediate reward" items. This is a specific case of the more general design often found in econometric analyses: the effect of a series of exogenous variables on a time series:

$$O\ OXO\ \ O\ \ OXO\ \ O\ \ O\ \ OXO\ \ O\ \ OX$$

Star and Hughes (1950) provide another study of a useful quasi-experimental design in their study of the Cincinnati publicity campaign for the United Nations and UNESCO. They were able to exert some control on exposure to messages with a design:

$$\begin{array}{llll} R & O & (X) & \\ R & & X \cdot & O \end{array}$$

Here the rows represent randomly equivalent subgroups, with the parenthetical X standing for a presentation of X irrelevant to the comparison. Brooks (1966) has experimented with this offset before-after design and compared it to the standard before and after. His staggered design was:

$$\begin{array}{lll} O & X & O \\ O & & \\ & X & O \end{array}$$

Such "patched-up" designs are to be applauded and we give a final example of a patch job shrewdly added onto a true experiment. Becknell (1961) studied the effect of different levels of a newspaper tune-in advertising campaign on the viewing of the Du Pont television "Show of the Month." Two different advertising levels (300 and 600 lines) were used, along with no advertising. In each of twenty-one cities assigned an advertising treatment, a coincidental telephone survey was conducted on viewing. The design was:

$$\begin{array}{rl} X_{600}O & \text{(600-line ads)} \\ X_{300}O & \text{(300-line ads)} \\ O & \text{(no adds)} \end{array}$$

The claimed viewing was insignificant across the three conditions. As a patchwork check, Becknell went back to the ratings for the show for the previous four months in the same cities and found the average viewing in that period. Since each of the cities was receiving a standard 300-line ad promoting the show as a regular practice, the design thus became:

$$\begin{array}{l} X_{300}O\,X_{300}O\,X_{300}O\,X_{300}O\,X_{600}O \\ X_{300}O\,X_{300}O\,X_{300}O\,X_{300}O\,X_{300}O \\ X_{300}O\,X_{300}O\,X_{300}O\,X_{300}O \qquad O \end{array}$$

The mean of the four ratings before the experimental period served as a basis of comparison for the ratings after, and even more firmly showed no effect on viewing levels. The high level of previous publicity no doubt carries over, diluting the new treatment level.

In summary, then, we can find quasi-experimental designs that may be created or improved by adding observations; making an OXO design, for example $OOOXOOO$. We can also add groups, such as changing an XO design to

$$\begin{array}{lll} O & X & O \\ O & & O \end{array}$$

and we may change the time of observations at the same time that more observations are added. In certain situations, for example, the availability of subjects or concern with testing effects may move one to go from a time series design,

$$O\ \ O\ \ OXO\ \ O\ \ O$$

to:

$$\begin{array}{lllllll} O & O & O & X & O & & \\ & & & X & O & & \\ & & & & O & O & \end{array}$$

Staggering the placement in time and among groups of the treatments and observations is thus possible and desirable. Conceived of in spatial terms, the standard procedures move a design horizontally out (more observations) or vertically down (more groups). The creative designer will also consider moving diagonally down and across his time/treatment/measurement space.

OUT OF THE ENVIRONMENTAL BLACK BOX

It is our belief that the artificiality constraints of most laboratory settings seriously erode the generalizability of effects studies. The astute use of interlocking quasi-experiments offers strong promise for significant experimental research to be conducted in the field with experimental manipulations provided by nature. Students of communications are in one way blessed because many significant communications events occur at predictable times.

Opportunistic researchers have already exploited these conditions. Kraus (1962) has collected a series of studies on the "great debates" of the 1960 presidential campaign, Schramm and Carter (1959) looked at the effect of a political telethon, and Fuchs (1965; 1966) examined the influence of computer predictions on vote switching in the western United States. Then there is the anecdotal evidence of the large-scale public protest at the time when daytime soap operas are preempted for broadcasting a space shot.

Other events are less predictable, but worthy of investigation. Sawyer (1968) wrote a notable paper, "Communication in a Tragedy," which showed differences between blacks and whites in the degree to which they turned on their car headlights the day of Martin Luther King's funeral. Greenberg and Parker (1965) collected a series of studies pertinent to communication behavior after John Kennedy's assassination, and a large number of studies of natural isolation speak directly to communication issues (Broadbent, 1958; Vernon, 1964; Brownfield, 1965).

The isolation studies are of interest because they reflect an experimental treatment that comes into being by subtraction. Almost always, experimental treatments are additions to the lives or ideas of subjects. In the natural isolation experiences of arctic explorers or of a Truk Islander fisherman, however, the experimental condition is present because something is missing from his usual stimulus state. The same subtractive idea is present in the newspaper strike studies (Berelson, 1949; Cannell & Sharp, 1958; Mindak et al., 1963; Simon & Marks, 1965).

The model for these opportunistic studies of naturally occurring phenomena is the extensive work conducted with disasters. Fritz (1961) has reviewed the rationale for the systematic study of human behavior in disasters and notes some 161 field studies of events ranging from earthquakes and airplane accidents to snowstorms and floods. McGuire (1966) has argued for the establishment of panels of social scientists to move quickly to study student agitations, acute civil rights explosions, and the less frenetic social innovations on narcotics use, sex offenses, and the death penalty.

Investigators of communication effects might with profit establish similar panels, with established procedures, to study critical events that will influence communication behavior and effects. Such studies will almost certainly follow a quasi-experimental form. It is not necessary that the research be purely descriptive or observational, for anticipation of the event by reasonable scholars should lead to an ability to "temper nature" (Weick, 1967) and introduce experimental treatments in a natural setting. In recent years the number of field investigations has increased and the sophistication of experiments beyond the confines of the laboratory has grown. The confluence should have profitable outcomes, although some discomfort must attend the reaching of these outcomes. We could do worse than listen to a non social scientist:

> The more experiments you make the better. What if they are a little coarse, and you get your coat soiled or torn? What if you do fail, and get fairly rolled in the dirt once or twice? Up again you shall never be so afraid of a tumble (Emerson, 1909:302).

REFERENCES

Aronson, Elliot, and J. M. Carlsmith.
1968 "Experimentation in social psychology." Pp. 1–79 in Gardner Lindzey and Elliot Aronson (eds.), Handbook of Social Psychology, Volume 2. Second Edition. Reading, Massachusetts: Addison-Wesley.

Becknell, J. C.
1961 "The influence of newspaper tune-in advertising on the size of a TV show's audience." Journal of Advertising Research 1 (No. 3): 23–26.

Berelson, Bernard.
1949 "What 'missing the newspaper' means." Pp. 111–129 in P. F. Lazarsfeld and F. N. Stanton (eds.), Communications Research, 1948–1949. New York: Harper.

Blalock, H. M.
1964 Causal Inferences in Non-experimental Research. Chapel Hill: University of North Carolina Press.

Broadbent, D. E.
1958 Perception and Communication. New York: Pergamon Press.

Brooks, W. D.
1966 "Effects of a persuasive message upon attitudes." Journal of Communication 16: 180–188.

Brownfield, C. A.
1965 Isolation. New York: Random House.

Campbell, D. T.
1969 "Prospective: Artifact and control." In R. Rosenthal and R. L. Rosnow (eds.), Artifact in Social Research. New York: Academic Press.

Campbell, D. T., and K. N. Clayton.
1961 "Avoiding regression effects in panel studies of communication impact." Studies in Public Communication 3:99–118. (Also a Bobbs-Merrill reprint.)

Campbell, D. T., and D. W. Fiske.
1959 "Convergent and discriminant validation by the multitrait-multimethod matrix." Psychological Bulletin 56: 81–105.

Campbell, D. T. ,and J. C. Stanley.
1963 "Experimental and quasi-experimental designs for research on teaching." Pp. 171–246 in N. L. Gage (ed.), Handbook of Research on Teaching: Chicago: Rand McNally. (Reprinted as Experimental and Quasi-Experimental Design for Research. Chicago: Rand McNally, 1966.)

Cannell, C. F., and H. Sharp.
1958 "The impact of the 1955–56 Detroit newspaper strike." Journalism Quarterly 35: 26–35.

Cook, S. W., and C. A. Selltiz.
1964 "A multiple-indicator approach to attitude measurement." Psychological Bulletin 62: 36–55.

Emerson, R. W.
1909 Journals of Ralph Waldo Emerson. Volume 6. Boston: Houghton Mifflin.

Fritz, C. E.
1961 "Disaster." Pp. 651–694 in R. K. Merton and R. A. Nisbet (eds.), Contemporary Social Problems. New York: Harcourt, Brace & World.

Fuchs, Douglas A.
1965 "Election-day newscasts and their effects on western voter turnout." Journalism Quarterly 42: 22–28.
1966 "Western voting and broadcasts of results on presidential election day: Election-day radio-television and western voting." Public Opinion Quarterly 30: 226–236.

Galton, Francis.
1886 "Regression toward mediocrity stature." Journal of the Anthropological Institute of Great Britain and Ireland 15: 246–268.

Greenberg, B. S., and E. B. Parker (eds.).
1965 The Kennedy Assassination and the American Public: Social Communication in Crisis. Stanford, California: Stanford University Press.

Kraus, Sidney (ed.).
1962 The Great Debates. Bloomington: University of Indiana Press.

Lumsdaine, A. A., and M. A. May.
1965 "Mass communication and educational media." Pp. 475–534 in P. R. Farnsworth (ed.), Annual Review of Psychology. Volume 16. Palo Alto: Annual Reviews, Inc.

McGuire, W. J.
1966 "Attitudes and opinions." Pp. 475–514 in P. R. Farnsworth (ed.), Annual Review of Psychology. Volume 17. Palo Alto, California: Annual Reviews, Inc.

Milgram, Stanley and Hans Toch.
1969 "Collective behavior: Crowds and social movements." Pp. 507–510 in Gardner Lindzey and Elliot Aronson (eds.), Handbook of Social Psychology. Volume 4. Second Edition. Reading, Massachussets: Addison-Wesley

Mindak, W. A., et al.
1963 "Economic effects of the Minnea-

polis newspaper strike on community economic life." Journalism Quarterly 40:312–318.

Mosteller, Frederick.
1955 "Use as evidenced by an examination of wear and tear on selected sets of ESS." Pp. 167–174 in K. Davis et al., A Study of the Need for a New Encyclopedic Treatment of the Social Sciences. Unpublished manuscript.

Orne, M. T.
1962 "On the social psychology of the psychological experiment: With particular reference to demand characteristics and their implications." American Psychologist 17:776–783.

Rarick, G., and B. Hartman.
1966 "The effects of competition on one daily newspaper's content." Journalism Quarterly 43:459–463.

Reuters.
1969 "Births triple in TV-less town." Reprinted in International Herald-Tribune, February 5.

Rosenthal, Robert.
1966 Experimenter Effects in Behavioral Research. New York: Appleton-Century-Crofts.

Sawyer, Jack.
1968 "Communication in a tragedy: Blacks and whites turn on car lights after King's assassination." Evanston, Illinois: Northwestern University (unpublished).

Schramm, Wilbur, and R. F. Carter.
1959 "Effectiveness of a political telethon." Public Opinion Quarterly 23:121–126.

Schilling, T. G.
1968 "Reaction to doors." P. 21 in Richard Seaton (ed.), Miscellaneous Undergraduate Research on Spatial Behavior. Berkeley: University of California Department of Architecture.

Simon, L. S., and M. R. Marks.
1965 "Consumer behavior during the New York newspaper strike." Journal of Advertising Research 5(No. 1):9–17.

Star, Shirley A., and Helen M. Hughes.
1950 "Report on an educational campaign: The Cincinnati play for the United Nations." American Journal of Sociology 55:389–400.

Twedt, D. W.
1962 "A cash register test of sales effectiveness." Journal of Marketing 26 (No. 2):41–43.

Vernon, J. A.
1964 Inside the Black Room. New York: Potter.

Walster, Elaine; Elliot Aronson; and D. Abrahams.
1966 "On increasing the persuasiveness of a low prestige communicator." Journal of Experimental Social Psychology 2:325–342.

Webb, E. J.
1966 "Unconventionality, triangulation and inference." Pp. 34–43 in J. C. Stanley (ed.), Proceedings of the 1966 Invitational Conference on Testing Problems. Princeton, New Jersey: Educational Testing Service.

Webb, E. J.; D. T. Campbell; R. D. Schwartz; and L. B. Sechrest.
1966 Unobtrusive Measures: Nonreactive Research in the Social Sciences. Chicago: Rand McNally.

Weick, Karl.
1967 "Promise and limitations of laboratory experiments in the development of attitude change theory." Pp. 51–75 in Carolyn Sherif and Muzafer Sherif (eds.), Attitude, Ego-involvement, and Change. New York: Wiley.

Winch, L., and Campbell, D. T.
1969 "Proof? No! Evidence? Yes! The significance of tests of significance." American Sociologist 4(No. 2):140–143.

Credits and Acknowledgments

Acknowledgment is made to the following for their kind permission to reprint material from copyrighted sources:

Chapter 2

University of New Mexico Press (*Journeys in Science,* edited by David L. Arm, 1967).

Chapter 5

Academic Press, Inc. (*Advances in Experimental Social Psychology,* Vol. 2, edited by Leonard Berkowitz, 1965); Association for Educational Communications and Technology ("Single and Multiple Channel Communication," by F. R. Hartman, *AV Communication Review,* Vol. 9, No. 6, 1961, pp. 235–262); The Free Press, a Division of The Macmillan Company (*The Effects of Mass Communication,* by Joseph T. Klapper, copyright © 1960); Stanford University Press (*Television in the Lives of Our Children,* by Wilbur Schramm, Jack Lyle, and Edwin B. Parker, 1961); Association for Education in Journalism ("Age, Education, Economic Status: Factors in Newspaper Reading," by Wilbur Schramm and David M. White, *Journalism Quarterly,* Vol. 29, No. 2, 1949, pp. 149–159); Book Manufacturers Institute (*People and Books,* by Henry C. Link and H. A. Hopf, 1946); University of Illinois Press (*Hollywood Looks at Its Audience,* by Leo A. Handel, 1950).

Chapter 7

W. K. Estes ("Reward in Human Learning: Theoretical Issues and Strategic Choice Points," in *The Nature of Reinforcement,* Part I, edited by Robert Glaser, published by the University of Pittsburgh Learning Research and Development Center, 1970).

Chapter 13

University of Chicago Press (*Atlas of Economic Development,* by Norton Ginsburg, © 1961 by The University of Chicago).

Chapter 16

Encyclopaedia Britannica, Inc. ("Agenda for the Future: A Presidential Perspective," by Lyndon B. Johnson, *Britannica Book of the Year, 1969* © 1969); Editor & Publisher Co. ("Too Much Crime and Violence in the Press?" by Jack B. Haskins, *Editor and Publisher,* Vol. 102, Feb. 8, 1969, p. 12); Sigma Delta Chi ("Report of the Freedom of Information Committee of Sigma Delta Chi," *Quill,* January 1953, p. 7); Freedom of Information Center (*World Press Freedom, 1966,* by R. L. Lowenstein, Publication 181, May 1967).

Chapter 17

Variety, Inc. ("All Time Boxoffice Champs," *Variety,* Jan. 5, 1972, p. 11).

Chapter 31

Addison-Wesley Publishing Company, Inc. ("Collective Behavior: Crowds and Social Movements," by Stanley Milgram and Hans Toch, in *Handbook of Social Psychology,* 2nd ed., Vol. 4, edited by Gardner Lindzey and Elliot Aronson, 1969, Addison-Welsey, Reading, Mass.).

Name Index

Subject Index

PRINTED IN U.S.A.